T0335963

Operating Systems

This text demystifies the subject of operating systems by using a simple step-by-step approach, from fundamentals to modern concepts of traditional uniprocessor operating systems, in addition to advanced operating systems on various multiple-processor platforms and also real-time operating systems (RTOSs). While giving insight into the generic operating systems of today, its primary objective is to integrate concepts, techniques, and case studies into cohesive chapters that provide a reasonable balance between theoretical design issues and practical implementation details. It addresses most of the issues that need to be resolved in the design and development of continuously evolving, rich, diversified modern operating systems and describes successful implementation approaches in the form of abstract models and algorithms. This book is primarily intended for use in undergraduate courses in any discipline and also for a substantial portion of postgraduate courses that include the subject of operating systems. It can also be used for self-study.

Key Features

- Exhaustive discussions on traditional uniprocessor-based generic operating systems with figures, tables, and also real-life implementations of Windows, UNIX, Linux, and to some extent Sun Solaris.
- Separate chapter on security and protection: a grand challenge in the domain of today's operating systems, describing many different issues, including implementation in modern operating systems like UNIX, Linux, and Windows.
- Separate chapter on advanced operating systems detailing major design issues and salient features of multiple-processor-based operating systems, including distributed operating systems. Cluster architecture; a low-cost base substitute for true distributed systems is explained including its classification, merits, and drawbacks.
- Separate chapter on real-time operating systems containing fundamental topics, useful concepts, and major issues, as well as a few different types of real-life implementations.
- Online Support Material is provided to negotiate acute page constraint which is exclusively a part and parcel of the text delivered in this book containing the chapter-wise/topic-wise detail explanation with representative figures of many important areas for the completeness of the narratives.

Operating Systems
Evolutionary Concepts and Modern Design Principles

Pranabananda Chakraborty

An Eminent IT Professional and Senior Visiting Professor

CRC Press
Taylor & Francis Group
Boca Raton London New York

CRC Press is an imprint of the
Taylor & Francis Group, an **informa** business

A CHAPMAN & HALL BOOK

First edition published 2024
by CRC Press
2385 NW Executive Center Drive, Suite 320, Boca Raton FL 33431

and by CRC Press
4 Park Square, Milton Park, Abingdon, Oxon, OX14 4RN

CRC Press is an imprint of Taylor & Francis Group, LLC

© 2024 Pranabananda Chakraborty

Library of Congress Cataloging-in-Publication Data
Names: Chakraborty, Pranabananda, author.
Title: Operating systems : evolutionary concepts and modern design principles /
    Pranabananda Chakraborty.
Description: First edition. | Boca Raton : Chapman & Hall/CRC Press, [2024] |
    Includes bibliographical references and index.
Identifiers: LCCN 2023009376 (print) | LCCN 2023009377 (ebook) |
    ISBN 9781032467238 (hbk) | ISBN 9781032467467 (pbk) | ISBN 9781003383055 (ebk)
Subjects: LCSH: Operating systems (Computers)
Classification: LCC QA76.77 .C39 2024 (print) | LCC QA76.77 (ebook) |
    DDC 005.4/3—dc23/eng/20230601
LC record available at https://lccn.loc.gov/2023009376
LC ebook record available at https://lccn.loc.gov/2023009377

ISBN: 978-1-032-46723-8 (hbk)
ISBN: 978-1-032-46746-7 (pbk)
ISBN: 978-1-003-38305-5 (ebk)

DOI: 10.1201/9781003383055

Typeset in Times
by Apex CoVantage, LLC

Access the Support Material: www.routledge.com/9781032467238

Contents

Preface

Operating systems are today an essential core subject of interest both in academic curricula and in the IT industry, as underlined by the IEEE/ACM Computer Curricula, 2005. Computers are now prevalent in every sphere of life. As such, all students/professionals involved in computing culture must have some knowledge about operating systems, not only when designing and structuring applications properly to run most efficiently on a real machine but also to be able to benchmark the various contemporary popular operating systems to select a fitting one for actual use. Although much information about this subject is now available on the internet, but fundamental knowledge is badly lacking in that the internet, only offers a few basic concepts.

The universe of operating systems is relentlessly expanding, spanning a vast area that includes a broad range of concepts and related design issues, and as such it is extremely difficult to entirely explore it within the short space of any book on the subject. Moreover, from its very inception, it has continuously passed through many numerous innovations and improvements to arrive at its present form. In spite of having numerous forms along with a fast pace of continuous changes in the computer field as a whole, the basic philosophy and certain fundamental concepts are consistent throughout. The implementation and application of these concepts, however, depends mostly on the current state of the technology used in the underlying computer hardware systems and also on the existing cost/performance metrics of the system. The primary goal of this book is thus to present a thorough, intuitive discussion of the fundamentals of generic traditional uniprocessor operating systems, not tied to any particular one, as well as to provide the common concepts and most of the important issues associated with advanced operating systems and real-time operating system (RTOSs). In addition, a large number of real-life implementations of relevant topics are cited here as case studies that pertain to the most commercially popular and innovative operating systems, including Microsoft Windows, Linux, UNIX, and Sun Solaris.

As usual, with each publication, there is always a stringent page-count constraint, and as such, there is often a constant struggle with the publisher to maintain a realistic balance between a reasonable page count and the amount of the latest vital materials to be included. To attain this objective and incorporate the minimum amount of the newest innovative, important materials, the needed room is usually created by simply eliminating relatively outdated items and tightening narratives. Yet many currently important materials and vital issues that deserve to be addressed remain untouched, and sometimes not even fully described in the present text for either being out of the scope of the book or being too voluminous. The author deeply expresses his inability to counter this unavoidable situation.

It is important to note that even after squeezing the text as much as possible, the page-count still exceeded the prescribed limit. Accordingly, some of the topics in the text are delivered only with their main theme, and further descriptions and explanations, with figures, have been placed on the book's website hosted by CRC Press. Hence, the text material along with the respective website material (if present) mentioned with any topic within the body of the text is the actual content of the topic for the reader to obtain a clear and complete explanation of the topic or its related aspects. The website hosts downloadable Support Material, visit www.routledge.com/9781032467238. Still, many currently important materials and vital issues that deserve to be addressed are yet remained untouched, and sometimes not even fully described in the present text for either being out of the scope of this book or becoming to be too voluminous. The author deeply expressed his inability to counter such an unavoidable situation.

This book is designed as a text for any course in operating systems at the junior/senior undergraduate level. No topics in this book are original, but there is originality in each of its representations. Here, the objective is essentially to give insight into a generic modern operating system and show how the stepwise evolution of different concepts (both current and historical) is ultimately converted to respective design techniques and subsequently implemented using fitting methods. This approach emphasizes the fact that expertise on operating systems can only be built up if a profound understanding of their concepts can be developed to appreciate the ongoing rapid changes and negotiate the grand challenges of the future. To acquaint readers with the design principles and implementation issues of every relevant aspect, each topic, after a description of the theory, is mapped to various types of contemporary real-world design methodologies wherever applicable, using directions that are exploited in the actual development of almost all widely used representative modern operating systems, including Windows, UNIX, Linux, and Solaris. Placing real-life implementations after a theoretical description of each respective relevant topic is thought to be a much better method for understanding and is thus used throughout the text instead of compiling them separately in a single additional chapter or appendix.

ORGANIZATION OF THE BOOK

The text in this book is organized for gaining knowledge of operating systems following the model suggested by IEEE and ACM curricula. The design of contents presented here is the ultimate outcome of the author's many years of teaching experience on this subject supported by his equal professional experience in the IT industry on systems. Here, the first few chapters, Chapters 1–3, cover fundamental OS principles and designs using traditional approaches, along with the introduction of modern design elements used in the development of advanced operating systems. In the next four chapters, Chapters 4–7, each describes the different constituent resource management modules of OS corresponding to each of the respective computer system resources. Additional emphasis is also placed here on relevant topics to highlight the different derived approaches that are actually implemented in representative modern, widely used commercial operating systems. All these chapters together almost entirely cover the design, principles, and working of a traditional uniprocessor operating system run on a standalone computer system and are considered adequate for an operating system principles course in computer science, IT, and related curricula. Chapter 8 is entirely dedicated to briefly introducing one of the most challenging areas, *security and protection*, which is linked with today's operating systems to safeguard the valuable, sensitive, and confidential information of the user/system as well as the precious assets lying in the computing environment from threats launched from outside/inside the system. Chapter 9 is devoted to describing the basics of advanced operating systems that run on computer systems consisting of multiple CPUs (multiprocessors) and also on computer systems formed by arranging many interconnected computers (networks of computers or multi-computers and computer networks). Chapter 10 describes in brief an increasingly important emerging area, the real-time operating system, which is said to be a very different kind and belongs to a special class distinct from all other traditional/modern operating systems running either on uniprocessor or multiple-processor computing systems.

A number of pedagogic features incorporated in each chapter include numerous figures and tables to clarify and explain the related subjects. Readers are encouraged, as a general rule, to progress sequentially through the chapters, as this approach provides the best way to gain a thorough understanding of operating systems. However, the reader can also select a different ordering of chapters if that is fit for a different situation. However, all topics discussed here cannot be covered in one semester, so a syllabus may be formed only with those chapters which are needed to fulfill the requirements, omitting some of the sections which may be useful for a two-course sequence on operating system principles. The chapters on advanced operating systems (Chapter 9) and real-time operating systems (Chapter 10) may be included at the higher-undergraduate/postgraduate level, and these chapters may then be considered for a substantial portion of that course.

Content of this book

Ten chapters altogether form this book. The logical divisions of the text are as follows:

Part One: The first three chapters deal with basic principles and fundamental issues, detailing the objectives and functions of an operating system in general.

- **Chapter 1** briefly illustrates the evolution of generation-wise operating systems (OSs) from historic to current ones, including distributed and real-time operating systems, along with their salient features that drive the ongoing different generations of uniprocessor/multiple-processor computer architectures.
- **Chapter 2** describes the concepts of the OS, with its ultimate objectives and different functions it provides to offer various supports and related services. It also elaborates on the design factors and related issues involved with the development of generic modern operating systems.
- **Chapter 3** articulates the structures and designs of OSs using layered/level concepts, including the sensational virtual machine and its related OS. The kernel/shell concept, including monolithic and microkernels, and its deployment in the development of operating systems used for networks of computers and computer networks is described. The concept of threads and objects and their use as basic design elements in the development of modern OSs is portrayed.

Part Two: The next four chapters (Chapters 4, 5, 6, and 7) together describe all the operating system modules individually and cover almost all the fundamental OS principles and techniques that are used by generic operating systems of today with additional topic-wise emphasis on how they are actually realized in representative modern widely used commercial operating systems.

- **Chapter 4** depicts the design and development of a processor/process management, a rich constituent of generic operating systems, using the process model as a basic building block. The concept of threads, a smaller basic design element (unit), and subsequently the concept of multithreading and its implementation in the design and development of modern operating systems are shown. Various topics on Oss: process scheduling, interprocess synchronization, interprocess communication, deadlock, and starvation are briefly described with examples.
- **Chapter 5** illustrates the design and development of whole memory management, a vital ingredient of generic operating systems, consisting of primary and different types of secondary memory. Management of virtual memory, paging, and segmented memory are described, along with their actual implementations in UNIX, Linux, Windows, and also in Solaris separately. Although cache is not visible to the OS, yet the objectives, principles, and various design issues related to cache memory are stated in brief.
- **Chapter 6** describes the device management module along with its objectives and functions, including the role of a generic device manager and its constituents: I/O scheduler, interrupt handler, and device driver. The different disk scheduling policies and their individual implementations are explained. The page cache and disk cache, along with their merits and drawbacks, are described. The real-life implementation of the device management realized in UNIX, Linux, and Windows is described individually and separately in brief.
- **Chapter 7** discusses the file management unit, an important part of the general operating system, containing different types of generic file systems, including various types of directory and file organization. Different methods of file allocation in secondary devices and the different techniques used to manage free space in secondary storage are shown. The virtual file system (VFS) and its implementation along with the log-structured file system and pipes are mentioned. The real-life file management systems implemented in UNIX, Linux, and Windows are described in brief.

Part Three: This part includes only Chapter 8, which is entirely dedicated to briefly introducing one of the most challenging areas linked to today's operating systems, security and protection.

- **Chapter 8** gives an overview of the objectives of security and protection needed for an OS to negotiate different types of security threats. Different types of active and passive security attacks and how to counter them; the required security policies, mechanisms, and different proven methods to prevent them are explained. A spectrum of approaches to provide appropriate protections to the system is shown. Different types of malicious programs (malware), worms, and viruses and various schemes and mechanisms to restrict them from entering the system are described. The actual implementation of security and protection carried out in UNIX, Linux, and Windows in real-life situations is explained in brief.

Part Four: This part consists of only Chapter 9 and presents the introductory concepts and fundamental issues of advanced operating systems, describing the different topics involved in these systems.

- **Chapter 9** briefly explains advanced operating systems, including the major issues of multiprocessor operating systems, multicomputer operating systems, and distributed operating systems, and also highlights the differences between them as well as from a conventional uniprocessor operating system. Since the computing resources and controls of these OSs are distributed and geographically separated, it gives rise to many fundamental issues concerning the efficiency, consistency, reliability, and security of the computations as well as of the OS itself. This chapter addresses many of the most common issues and puts less emphasis on their actual implementations, mostly due to page-count constraints. A brief discussion of design issues of distributed shared memory (DSM) and different aspects in the design of distributed file systems (DFSs) is given, with examples of real-life implementation of Windows distributed file system, SUN NFS, and Linux GPFS. The cluster architecture, a modern approach in distributed computing system design to form a base substitute of distributed systems, is explained here, along with its advantages, classifications, and different methods of clustering.

Part Five: Chapter 10 simply describes in brief an increasingly important emerging area, the real-time operating system (RTOS).

- **Chapter 10** attempts to explain the RTOS, indicating why it is said to be a very different kind of system that belongs to a special class, distinct from all the other traditional operating systems running either on uniprocessor or multiple-processor computing systems. The description here mainly provides fundamental topics, useful concepts, and major issues, including kernel structure, signals in the form of software interrupts, the role of clocks and timers, scheduling mechanisms, implementation of required synchronization and communication, memory management, and many other similar distinct aspects. Finally, real-life implementations of RTOS are shown, with a brief description of the Linux real-time extension, KURT system, RT Linux system, Linux OS, pSOSystem, and VxWorks used in Mars Pathfinder.

Despite all-out sincere efforts, many topics still remain untouched, and some are not adequately described. This is mostly due to their being outside the scope of this book or limitations on the text's length.

THE TARGET AUDIENCE

The material presented in this book is intended for use in one- or two-semester undergraduate courses in any relevant discipline that include the subject of operating systems. It also targets professionals who are interested in this field apart from those engaged with academics. It can equally be used as a text book for self-study.

THE PREREQUISITES

The design of this book begins with an introduction to operating systems and gradually steps towards the state of the art of implementation issues and ultimate design of versatile modern operating systems, in addition to the concepts and important criteria of different types of advanced operating systems of today. So, to start with, this book does not assume any specific background. However, today's students know many things related to computers from many different sources but often severely suffer from a lack of fundamental concepts or, more precisely, wrong concepts. Thus, it is suggested to at least go through the basic, familiar material, which is presented here over the first three chapters in a concept-based manner. Also, it is assumed that students and readers have some knowledge of logic design, algorithmic approaches, the fundamentals of computer hardware, and a little bit of C-like programming. It is hoped that users of this book will, after all, find it useful even if they do not have all the prerequisites.

THE PREREQUISITES

Author Bio

Pranabananda Chakraborty has strong, diversified experience in the information technology industry over the last 45 years covering system analysis and design and implementation of system software (like operating system and compiler design) for various types of large mainframe computing systems with the giant multinationals, re-engineering, and project monitoring and management, including banking, insurance, and state-based public examination processing systems; production planning and survey, demographic census (government of India); different areas in postal systems, Ministry of Posts, government of India; staff selection systems, government of India; and many other real-time projects in India and abroad.

As an academician, for the last 45 years, he has also been affiliated with several prominent institutes, including reputed engineering colleges and universities. Recently, he was a senior visiting professor at the Government Engineering Colleges, Kolkata, West Bengal, India, and also guest faculty at Birla Institutes of Technology and Sciences (BITS), Pilani, India, on a regular basis. During this period, he also conducted corporate and institutional training on various academic subjects of core computer science and IT disciplines for large, reputed multinationals, including IBM, and R&D organization using contemporary large systems, as well as seminars and management development programs in India and abroad sponsored by different corporate bodies in information technology-based industry.

Although he has extensive research experience in theoretical computer science and software development, his work is mainly focused on operating systems and real-time operating systems. He has also authored a text book on computer organization and architecture published by CRC Press, USA.

Author Bio

1 Computers and Software

Learning Objectives

- To define different types of generic system software and their relative hierarchical position on a common computer hardware platform.
- To illustrate the evolution of operating systems with their basic functions and role in computer operation.
- To describe the different generations of computers and the salient features of the corresponding generations of operating systems up to modern operating systems.
- To provide an overview of networked operating systems running on computer networks.
- To provide a general idea of distributed operating systems running on multiple-processor machines (multiprocessors and multicomputer systems) separately.
- To explain the cluster architecture of computers, its classification, different methods of clustering, and the role of the operating system in distributed computing.
- To give an overview of real-time operating systems (RTOSs), with a few of their distinct features and characteristics
- To show the genesis of modern operating systems and their grand challenges.

1.1 INTRODUCTION

A brief history of the evolution of operating systems is not only interesting but a journey because it reveals how the concept of operating systems has evolved and subsequently provides a comprehensive overview of operating system principles, design issues, the different forms of their structures, and their functions and activities. It is also observed how the different generations of operating systems, starting from a bare primitive form to today's most modern systems, gradually progressed over a period of the last six-odd decades in order to manage constantly emerging more intelligent and sophisticated computer hardware. A different form of operating system, known as a real-time operating system (RTOS), has been also introduced that evolved to meet certain specific demands of different kinds. Most of the concepts mentioned briefly in this chapter are, however, thoroughly explained in later relevant chapters. This chapter finally comes to an end describing the stage-wise, generation-wise development of operating systems, since their birth in primitive form to the ultimate design and development of the most advanced operating systems: in other words, the genesis of modern operating systems.

1.2 COMPUTER SOFTWARE: SYSTEM SOFTWARE

The architectures of modern computer systems could be realized in numerous ways, but all of them use only four fundamental hardware resources. Those are one or more *processors*, *main memory*, *I/O devices*, and *interconnection buses*. These resources, along with other add-on units, form a very complex system that ultimately provides the necessary computing power the computer system exhibits. This hardware is basically machines and is useless unless it is properly driven to execute very specific and primitive instructions, and that is exactly what particular software does. **Computer software** truly defines and determines the ways in which the hardware resources of a computer

DOI: 10.1201/9781003383055-1

system can be used. The joint effort of the software and hardware of a computer system provides a tool that precisely solves numerous problems, performing logical decisions and various mathematical calculations with astonishing speed.

Software is differentiated according to its purpose and broadly classified into two types, **application software** and **system software**. In the early days, there was only one class of software, application software, which was designed and developed by the user, writing lines of code to solve his or her specific problem and also several additional instructions that were required to keep track of and control the associated machine operations.

In order to release the programmer from this tedious task of writing frequently needed common codes to drive the machine to implement the application software every time, a set of codes in the form of a program could be developed and tested and stored permanently on a storage medium for common use by all users. Any application program could then exploit the service of these common programs by issuing an appropriate call whenever required. These common programs intended for all users of the computer hardware were developed to drive, control, and monitor the operations of computing system resources as and when they were required. These programs together are historically called **system software**, and it essentially hides the details of how the hardware operates, thereby making computer hardware relatively easy and better adapted to the needs of the users. It provides a general programming environment to programmers for the mechanics of preparing their specific applications using the underlying hardware appropriately. This environment, in turn, often provides new functions that are not available at the hardware level and offers facilities for tasks related to the creation and effective use of application software.

Common system software, in particular, is very general and covers a broad spectrum of functionalities. It mainly comprises three major subsystems: **(i) language translators** (*compilers, interpreters, assemblers*) and **runtime systems** (*linkers, loaders*, etc.) for a programming language, **(ii) utility systems**, and **(iii) operating systems** (*OSs*). Numerous input/output (I/O) devices also require device-dependent programs that control and monitor their smooth operation during an I/O operation. These programs are essentially system software known as **device drivers**, sometimes called **input–output control systems** (*IOCSs*). All these programs are mostly written in *low-level languages*, such as *Assembly language, binary language*, and so on, which are very close to the machine's (hardware's) own language or have patterns so that machine resources can be directly accessed from the user level. Nowadays, they are also often developed with the high-level language C.

Some system software, namely *graphic library, artificial intelligence, image processing, expert systems*, and so on, are specific to a particular application area and are not very common in others. The *OS, compiler, assembler, loader*, and to some extent the *utilities* (DBMS) are required to commit physical hardware (machine) resources to bind with the application program for execution. The optimal design of this software, based on the *architecture and organization of the underlying hardware*, its offered facilities, and finally its effectiveness, ultimately determines the efficiency of the hardware and the programmability of the computer system as a whole. Figure 1.1 is a conceptual representation of an overall computing environment when viewed from the user's end with respect to the relative placement of hardware and the different types of software, as already mentioned, including the operating system.

Modern computers use many such system programs as an integral part of them. They are often designed and developed by the manufacturer of the hardware and are supplied along with the machine as inseparable components. The use of third-party–developed system software against additional cost is already a common practice today.

For more details about system software, see the Support Material at www.routledge.com/9781032467238.

1.3 OPERATING SYSTEMS

The operating system (OS) is the most critical and important subset of the system software in a computer system. It has been developed to govern control of the basic hardware resources on behalf of the users, hiding the complexity of the hardware from them. It presents a nice and simple view of the computer system and provides a more modest and user-friendly interface to the users and their programs. Without any exception, almost every computer ranging from small personal computers to supercomputers has an operating system. Other programs in the computer depend on facilities provided by the operating system to gain access to computer–system resources. Operating systems have become so essential to efficient computer operation that they are now considered inseparable from the computer hardware. In fact, the performance of the operating system sets the stage for the concert of all the hardware and the software run on a computer system.

In fact, the operating system consists of various program modules that control the operation of equipment resources such as processor, main memory, secondary storage, I/O devices, and different files. Since the responsibilities of these modules are to operate the computer on behalf of the user, they are historically called **operating systems** or sometimes collectively the **executive, controls**, or **supervisor**. Application-oriented modules, namely language processors, library routines, utilities, debugging aids, and so on, are merely users of the operating system and are not included within the domain of the operating system.

Anything submitted to the computer system is actually handed over to its master, the operating system, which initiates the execution, allocating the needed resources It keeps track of the status of each resource and decides who gets a resource, when, and for how long to resolve conflicting requests to optimize system performance at the time of simultaneous execution of many programs. In fact, the scheduling, the control of traffic, and the entire management of these resources are the responsibilities of the operating system. The operating system here actually acts as a **resource manager**.

The operating system supervises the computer operations and acts as an **interface** between the user, user's program, and physical computer hardware. The user never interacts with the hardware directly, but to get the services of the hardware, the user has to submit the request to the operating system. One component of the operating system module accepts the user's request, acts as the user interface, and arranges everything for the execution of the request. This component of the operating system is called the *command interpreter*, which starts operating as soon as the computer system is booted (login) displaying a prompt, thereby indicating that the computer is ready to interact with the user.

At times, the design of the operating systems was mostly concerned with somehow extracting the highest potential of the underlying hardware, but user convenience and pleasure as well as productivity were of secondary considerations. At the other end of the spectrum, the goal is just the opposite. An operating system for a low-cost single-user personal computer may be designed to increase the productivity and ease of the user as much as possible, with hardware utilization being of much less concern. Since, the operating system initiates the hardware resources, monitoring their operation by way of keeping track of the status of each resource while allocating them during the execution of user programs, it must have a fairly good idea about the resources to be driven as well as the respective actions to be taken by means of executing some of its own programs and other software utilities. Let us now discuss the basic hardware components of a computer system that the operating system drives and the role of the operating system in this regard. The relationship of the operating system to basic computer hardware is depicted in Figure 1.1.

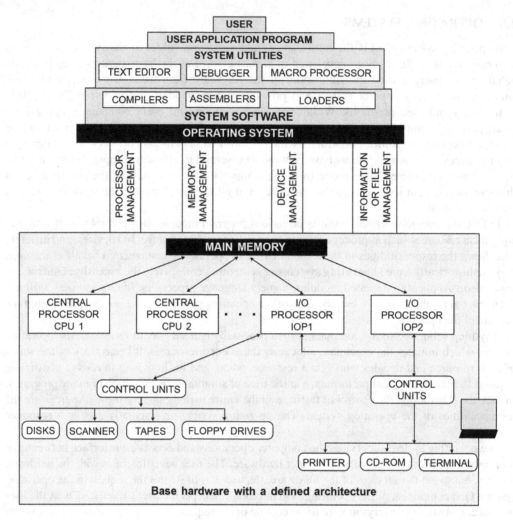

FIGURE 1.1 The level-wise position of operating system, system software and hardware organization in a generic computer system.

1.4   HARDWARE STRUCTURE TERMINOLOGY

A computer comprises two parts, hardware and software. The hardware is physical objects that are driven in an orderly way by the software to achieve the desired goal. In fact, the performance of the computing system is essentially a joint venture of these two parts. The hardware of any computing system (large or small) consists of four fundamental resources: processor, main memory, I/O devices, and interconnection buses. A **processor** is a hardware device capable of interpreting instructions and performing the indicated operations. The **central processing unit** (**CPU**) is the main processor and is a rich resource that manipulates and performs arithmetic and logical operations upon data available in the main memory. It can also control the other processors; for example, the CPU may execute a START I/O (SIO) instruction to initiate an I/O processor. A computer may have more than one CPU. **Main memory**, historically called core memory, is a vital resource operated mostly by the CPU but is also connected to various processors. The **I/O processor** is designed to control various types of I/O devices and handles the movement of data between the main memory and I/O devices. This processor can execute several I/O instructions to simultaneously control many devices. Most I/O devices (e.g. hard disk, CD, tape, printer, etc.) require control circuitry that can also be used to control other devices. That is why, for reasons of economy, the common hardware (i.e. the common control circuitry) is sometimes separated out into a device called a **control unit**.

1.5   PROGRAMMING TERMINOLOGY

System software (compilers, assemblers, loaders, etc.) and application software (user programs) is a collection of programs consisting of a sequence of instructions and/or data that are placed in coded form in main memory and interpreted/executed by a processor to perform certain predefined tasks. These routines are managed and kept track of by the operating system only.

The operating system provides an appropriate *run-time* environment in which particular software packages such as compilers, assemblers, database systems, and user application programs can be executed. The operating system offers the assistance required by the software in regard to memory management as well as to fulfill their other specific needs during run-time. The operating system thus can legitimately be called an **environment creator**.

The operating system really acts as a **mediator** (interface) between the user and the computer. It provides a pleasant and convenient interface, making it easier for the user and the application program to access, control, and use those resources and facilities while the computer system is in operation. An effective operating system optimally manages the allocation and deallocation of resources during the execution of user programs; hence, operating systems can be legitimately called **resource managers**.

1.6   EVOLUTION OF OPERATING SYSTEMS AND THEIR ROLE

In the early days, there was no concept of an operating system. Operating systems started to evolve only from the early 1950s in a primitive form as a *resident monitor program* to today's most advanced **distributed operating system (DOS)** and also RTOS. This process of evolution is still ongoing in search of more advanced and intelligent forms. Since the responsibility of the operating system is to facilitate the use of computer hardware, it has historically been closely associated with the architecture of the computer on which it runs, and as such, there exists a one-to-one, inseparable relationship between the operating system and the underlying computer architecture. As hardware architecture by this time has continuously evolved and progressed generation after generation with numerous innovations, so too have the designs and issues of operating systems been constantly reviewed, redefined, and redesigned, and thus they have also progressed through gradual evolution, generation after generation, for the sake of staying matched with the underlying, continuously evolving advanced hardware technology. However, the mapping of operating system generations to computer generations is not very straightforward, but it at least offers some structure to understand. Language processors, assemblers, loaders, database systems, library routines, debugging aids, and application-oriented modules, though are not included within the domain of the operating system, have equally progressed during this time and are on a par with the continuous advancement of operating system because they are always using the facilities provided by the underlying system (see Figure 1.1).

Starting from the days of Charles Babbage with his *Difference Engine* in 1822 up to World War II, a lot of continuous innovation and subsequent successful implementations of different types of machines to perform numerous types of computational work have constantly been made by scientists and technologists from different countries. Out of those, the most notable one came in 1938 from Konrad Zuse of Germany, who designed a purely mechanical device, Z1, the **first** program-controlled machine, which was then modified to Z2 and further in 1941 to Z3: a binary computer with a 64-word store. Relays were used for circuit elements, punched tape and keyboard for input, and a lamp display for output. A very fast *general-purpose electro-mechanical decimal computer* was proposed by Howard H. Aiken of Harvard University in 1937 which was finally completed later in 1944 as Harvard Mark I by IBM. In 1943, Prof. M. H. Newman and T.H.S. Flowers during

World War II built an electronic computer, COLOSSUS, using 1,500 electronic valves and a fast photo-electric tape reader for input, mainly to crack secret German codes. However, no machine introduced over this period had an operating system, even in concept.

For more details about the evolution of operating system software, see the Support Material at www.routledge.com/9781032467238.

1.6.1 THE FIRST-GENERATION SYSTEM AND ZERO-GENERATION OS (1945–1954)

After World War II, a need for increased speed in computation was observed.

The *first-generation system* ENIAC (Electronic Numerical Integrator And Calculator), a decimal computer, was developed in 1946 by John Mauchley and Presper Eckert at the Moore School, University of Pennsylvania, with Dr. Von Neumann as consultant of the project. This machine, provided a storage facility and could perform arithmetic addition, subtraction, multiplication, division, and also square root operations.

All the computers of the first generation used roughly 15,000–20,000 vacuum tubes, relay memories, and toggle switches interconnected with insulated wires. Each machine was designed, manufactured, programmed, operated, and maintained by a group of experts and precisely was a manually programmed computer with exclusive access to the entire machine. These machines were dedicated to a single program in execution at a time. Absolute machine language was used for writing programs, which again varied from computer to computer. Programming and entering data were done by plugging and unplugging cables on a plugboard as well as with an available set of switches or often by the use of punched paper tape. The output was read by the programmer/operator from a set of display lights on the operator's console. This generation of computers had **no operating system** (**zero-generation OS**) but used a primitive single-user processing *operating environment*, mostly for numerical and scientific computations. Manual programming of the bare machine, however, resulted in low productivity with respect to both users and hardware. It is said that Alan Turing was a master of the particular structure and form that the early Manchester Mark I machine had. Actually, he was the one who first drew the seminal concepts of *operating systems* from ideas used in the Universal Turing Machine.

For more details about this topic, see the Support Material at: www.routledge.com/9781032467238.

1.6.2 THE SECOND-GENERATION SYSTEM AND FIRST-GENERATION OS (1955–1964)

By the mid 1950s, the architecture of the computer had radically changed, with the introduction of semiconductors in the digital logic circuit replacing vacuum tubes, and it became more versatile and enormously simplified, even with the introduction of numerous input/output devices such as magnetic tapes, magnetic drums, and line printers. The cost of the computer as well as the overhead for maintenance proportionately came down, and above all, the functioning of computers became more reliable.

To relieve the programmer, a set of system programs, commonly referred to as **utilities**, were developed mainly to implement frequently used functions needed in program creation, to manage files, and to control the operation of these I/O devices. Various types of I/O routines (IOCS) were developed to automatically control the numerous newly included I/O devices. Higher-level languages were developed to ease program development, and related translators, such as *compilers* and *interpreters*, were developed to convert programs to an executable form. Assemblers were also developed, and a *linking loader* was introduced that automated the process of linking and loading the finally created executable modules into memory to begin the execution. Truly speaking, these system programs gave rise to a primitive form of operating system that offered support and services to the other system programs such as editors, language translators/interpreters, debuggers, and so on which are generally not considered part of the operating system. However, in many situations, the programmer had to operate the machine on his or her own with programs being punched on a deck of cards to carry out serial processing of jobs using all of the machine resources.

For more details about this topic, see the Support Material at www.routledge.com/9781032467238.

1.6.2.1 Second-Generation Operating Systems: Simple Batch Systems

Manual handling of machines and engaging full-machine resources, most of the time with no use, however, ultimately severely affected both user productivity and utilization of system resources. In order to get rid of these negative impacts, the ultimate aim was thus to develop a system to *automate* the operator's job to minimize the amount of idle time spent for manual handling of the machine. This meant that the proposed system would work on behalf of the operator all the time as long as the computer was on. Since its major task is *to operate* the computer system, *masking* (hiding) the details of the hardware from the programmer and providing necessary software support as demanded by the user, this system program was historically called an **operating system**. A small module was thus developed to monitor and supervise the control of all internal activities of the computer system while the users' jobs were under execution. This program, called the **resident monitor**, was kept resident in the computer at all times after the computer was switched on.

Operating systems of this type could handle *one job at a time to completion and one after another* (in sequence) from a number of jobs submitted in the form of *batches* by the operator. Such operating systems were thus legitimately called a **batch systems** or **monitors**, widely used in systems, including the most popular ones, the IBM 1401 and 7090/7094. They summarily relieved the user from *direct access* to the machine to control the hardware and handled the task of *scheduling jobs* queued up in a batch and also *controlling the sequence* of events in a job.

One of the serious drawbacks of batch system approach was that the currently executing job monopolized the entire machine irrespective of actual usage of all the resources. Moreover, it was observed that the response time for most small jobs that arrived at later times was too high when large jobs were already present in the machine waiting for execution.

Buffering: Further enhancements in batch processing were carried out to improve resource utilization by overlapping CPU operations with I/O operations to proportionately increase the throughput. One such technique to realize this is *buffering*, which allowed operation of both the CPU and I/O devices of one job to go on in parallel all the time. With the advancement of technological developments, this buffering technique, however, has been gradually improved and is in use today in various forms in different categories of modern computers.

Offline processing: Another approach was to replace the online involvement of slow card readers and printers with executing jobs by deploying fast magnetic tape units with input data created separately by a satellite computer to be used in the job under execution. Similarly, tape units can also be used to store output data in printable format, replacing the printer online. This mode of operation, called *offline processing*, was very popular and in heavy use until the mid-1980s to handle the bulk of commercial data processing. But due to suffering from several drawbacks, and also with the advent of other coinciding technological developments, particularly in the area of introduction of disk systems, this form of offline processing fell out of favor and ultimately disappeared.

Spooling: The introduction of faster disk systems created a more sophisticated form of I/O buffering. Input data were temporarily created in the disk and then fed to the executing job whenever needed, and the output of this execution could also be stored on the disk. Output of the execution to be printed, if there was any, could be written as line images in another area of the disk instead of sending it directly to the slower printer. Later, this line image output of an already completed job could be sent directly to a printer at a convenient time to get the printed output. Carrying out card-to-disk operations for the subsequent jobs and disk-to-printer operations of the previous jobs is called SPOOLing (simultaneous peripheral operations on line), which could be carried out concurrently with the execution of a program by the CPU.

Spooling operation allowed overlapping the input and output of several *different jobs* kept in queue on disk as necessary with the execution of another job by the CPU in parallel to sustain high rates of processor utilization and also increase effective I/O transfer rates during program-execution time. Buffering, on other hand, overlaps the I/O of one job with the execution of the same job. Since spooling brought significant performance improvements, numerous upgrades of it are present in different types of operating systems used in mini, supermini, and mainframe large systems, even up to today's small microcomputers.

Second-generation computers with single-user batch operating systems in the early 1960s were mostly used for both commercial processing using COBOL or some form of dedicated language and scientific/engineering computations using FORTRAN and Assembly languages. Typical operating systems were developed by different computer manufacturers exclusively for their own systems. Since batch processing with a bulk of information does not require any human interaction while it is executed, hence, all modern operating systems usually incorporate facilities to support batch-style processing.

For more details about second-generation OSes, see the Support Material at: www.routledge.com/9781032467238.

1.6.3   THE THIRD-GENERATION SYSTEM AND THIRD-GENERATION OS (1965–1980)

With the pulsating invention of integrated circuits (ICs) in electronic engineering, computer systems entered a new generation, replacing traditional semiconductor components with faster, tiny ICs that brought about a revolutionary change in the design and architecture of computers. The inclusion of higher-speed CPUs with increased memory size and also pipelining in the design of CPUs along with introduction of speedy cache memory for quick access by CPU reduced the speed gap between main memory and the CPU, thereby substantially increasing the speed of execution. Numerous I/O devices such as high-speed disk drives, high-speed printers, and terminals were also included. In order to fully extract the potential of this enormous and powerful hardware, new ideas in the design and development of operating systems evolved. Software additions, including utilities and libraries of most commonly used functions, were incorporated to support executions of a diverse spectrum of emerging applications. In essence, third-generation computer systems could be considered a renaissance (major breakthrough) because of having advanced computer architecture and design equipped with enhanced, powerful operating systems supported by numerous system software and utilities that ultimately created a vibrant rhythmic orchestra in the computing environment.

Multiprogramming: Simple-batch operating systems failed to negotiate this changed environment, as a single executing user program only in memory could not make use of both the costly CPU and I/O devices properly all the time. In most situations, both user productivity and utilization of potential system resources were severely affected. Even use of offline processing and spooling systems did not make any notable improvement in the effective utilization of all these resources. One way to resolve this issue and maximize machine utilization is to let a different user program in the batch in memory use the processor whenever it is idle with the attached program currently involved in I/O operation. The same approach could also be taken while the I/O devices attached to one executing program are idle. In short, these underutilized resources could be assigned to different programs in the batch available in the memory to allow them to execute their different activities concurrently. This approach leads to a significant performance enhancement that has been realized by overlapping the execution of programs by way of **time-multiplexing** the processor and loading multiple programs into space-multiplexed memory. This mode of operation is usually called **multiprogramming (advanced batch processing)**. It should not be considered as parallel execution of programs, since with a single processor, at most only one program can be attached to the processor at any point in time. But switching of the processor is automatically carried out from one program to another by the OS whenever the former is in the input/output phase of its execution.

Since the distributions of processor-bound activities and I/O phases of the jobs are neither predictable nor normal, to increase resource utilization, an attempt was usually made to accommodate as many programs as possible in the memory and let them compete for system resources at any point in time. Thus, multiprogramming also invites competition for memory space. However, the number of jobs that can be accommodated at one time depends both on the size of the main storage and hardware availability for dividing up that space with proper security against inadvertent or malicious interference or inspection by one another, as well as to guard the resident monitor (operating system) because not one but many jobs will suffer if it is damaged. The maximum number of programs allowed in main memory at any instant, actively competing for resources, is called the **degree of multiprogramming**. Intuitively, the higher the degree, of course, up to a certain extent, the higher the resource utilization. A multiprogrammed operating system supervises and monitors the state of all active programs and system resources, provides resource isolation and sharing with proper scheduling, manages memory with protection, and deals with several other issues related to directly supporting multiple simultaneously active users in the machine. As a result, this operating system became comparatively complex and fairly sophisticated. However, this OS was quite able to handle both sophisticated scientific applications and massive volumes of commercial data processing, which is considered today the central theme of all modern operating systems.

However, the major drawback of this system was that there was no provision for the user to *interact* with the computer system during runtime to study the behavior of the executing program in order to avoid unpleasant situations, if it happened. Consequently, it caused serious inconvenience for professional users, particularly when technological development began to rapidly progress and numerous software designs and development processes started to emerge in more and more new areas as major activities in computer usage. Moreover, for some types of jobs, such as *transaction processing*, user interaction with the system during runtime is mandatory.

Interactive multiprogramming: To resolve all these limitations, time-shared operating systems were further enhanced to empower them to facilitate interactive support to the user, known as *interactive multiprogramming*. By this arrangement, the user could now interact with the system during runtime from an interactive terminal to execute specific types of jobs, such as **online transaction processing** (OLTP). The principal user-oriented I/O devices now changed from cards or tape to the interactive terminal (keyboard and display device CRT), and data were then fed from any input devices, especially from the terminal according to the status and demands of the executing program. This summarily made computer users more productive, since they could directly interact with the computer system on an as-needed basis during runtime. With continuous technological development, the tangible benefits of interactive computing facilities, however, have been extended, and are often extracted today by the use of dedicated microcomputers used as terminals attached to large main systems. Today, the term multiprogramming simply implies multiprogramming together with its other aspects.

Interactive computing resulted in a revolution in the way computers were used. Instead of being treated as number crunchers, systems became information manipulators. Interactive **text editors** allowed users to construct files representing programs, documents, or data online. Instead of speaking of a job composed of steps, **interactive multiprogramming** (also called "timesharing") deals with **sessions** that continue from initial connection (begin/logon) to the point at which that connection is broken (end/logoff).

Machines from IBM, and from other giant manufacturers, like NCR, Burroughs, DEC, and UNIVAC, etc., with almost compatible architecture implemented all these ideas in their designed operating systems. Of all of them, the most notable came from IBM with a series of models in the **System/360 family** running under operating systems like DOS/360, OS/360, etc., and also many others.

Multiuser systems: This form of multiprogramming operating systems in single-processor hardware with some sort of attached *computer terminal* enables multiple users to interact with the system during runtime in a centralized fashion instead of traditional advanced batch processing. Here, the main objective is that the system be responsive to the needs of each user and yet, for cost reasons, able to support many users simultaneously. Precisely, this type of operating system essentially provides facilities for the allocation and maintenance of each individual user environment, requires user identification to authenticate for security and protection, preserves system integrity with good performance, and offers accounting of per-user resource usage. With the advent of the tremendous power of today's 32- or even 64-bit microprocessors, which rival yesterday's mainframes and minicomputers in speed, memory capacity, and hardware sophistication, this multiuser approach with modern hardware facilities gradually became more versatile, opening new dimensions in application areas providing a graphical user interface (GUI).

Multiaccess systems: A multi-access operating system allows simultaneous access to a *single program* by the users (not multi-users) of a computer system with the help of two or more terminals. In general, multi-access operation is limited mainly to one or in some cases a few applications at best and does not necessarily imply multiprogramming. This approach, however, opened an important line of development in the area of online transaction processing (OLTP), such as railway reservation, banking systems, etc. Under a dedicated transaction-processing system, users enter queries or updates against a database through hundreds of active terminals supported under the control of a *single program*. Thus, the key difference between this transaction processing system and the multiprogramming system is that the former is restricted mainly to one application, whereas users of a multiprogramming system can be involved in different types of activities like program development, job execution, and the use of numerous other applications. Of course, the system response time is of paramount interest in both cases.

For more details about third-generation OSes, see the Support Material at: www.routledge.com/9781032467238.

1.6.3.1 Preemptive Multitasking Systems: Time-Sharing

Multiprogramming led to significant performance enhancement, allowing many users to execute their jobs in an overlapping manner, and increased resource utilization by way of providing solutions for resource isolation and sharing. However, if a large job were submitted earlier, it would get control of the CPU and continue until its completion with no interruption, provided no I/O request was issued. Now, if a small job (e.g. a command from the operator's console) were submitted at this time, it would have to wait a long time for its turn to come. As a result, not only would system throughput be substantially decreased, the response for this type of small job would be poor, and the turnaround time would also be appreciably high. Multiprogramming in this form in those days really had no way to restrict programs from monopolizing the processor.

In order to resolve the drawbacks and realize a quick response time for small jobs (like a command given to the OS from terminals using the interactive computing facility), the existing efficient multiprogramming scheme was modified and was referred to as **time sharing**, a variant or enhancement of existing multiprogramming. In this innovative approach, the processor's time is equitably shared among multiple contesting users, although an illusion is created to the users that they individually have exclusive access to all the resources, similar to batch processing.

The basic technique followed in a time-sharing system is to allow multiple users present in main memory to work all together, sometimes also using the system through terminals. Here, the operating system interleaves the execution of each user program, and hence the processor's time is actually shared among multiple user programs present in the machine. Each program, in turn, gets a particular short duration (burst) of CPU time, also called *quantum* or *time-slice*, for its execution and is then forced (preempted) to relinquish the CPU, which now switches to another program.

If an I/O operation is encountered before the expiry of the time slice, control will then go to the next program. Thus, the time slice is the maximum span of time during which a program can get the service of the CPU. Hence, if there are n active users present in the memory requesting service at a time, each user, then, on average, will have $1/n$ of effective computer speed if administrative overhead of the operating system is not taken into account. Since human reaction time at the terminal is relatively slow in comparison to CPU speed, the response time for a properly designed system appears to be closely comparable to that on a single-user dedicated computer. This environment thus could provide fast interactive services on one hand to a number of users and perhaps also work simultaneously on big batch jobs in the background when the CPU is otherwise idle.

While batch-style multiprogramming maximizes processor usage, time-sharing is targeted to minimize response time and provide equitable processor sharing. To initiate a job, while batch-style multiprogramming requires a set of job control instructions (Job Control Language) along with the job at the time of its submission, the time-sharing approach usually needs short commands to be entered at the terminal. However, purely batch-style multiprogramming with no interactive computing can also be implemented with a time-sharing option.

Time-sharing systems demand sophisticated processor scheduling to fulfill certain requirements of the environment ensuring system balance. Numerous approaches in this regard have been thus developed to meet certain goals, which are discussed in the following chapters. Memory management should ensure perfect isolation and protection of co-resident programs. Of course, some form of controlled sharing is offered in order to conserve memory space and possibly to exchange data between active programs. Generally, programs from different users running under time-sharing systems do not usually have much need to communicate with each other. Device management in time-sharing systems should be adequately equipped to handle multiple active users while negotiating their simultaneous requests to access numerous devices. Allocation of devices and later their deallocation must be done keeping in view safeguarding the users' interest, preserving system integrity, and at the same time optimizing device utilization. File management in a time-sharing system should be able to resolve conflicting attempts made by different active users over a shared file and should ensure full protection and access control at the time of concurrent accesses. In many cases, it is desirable for a user to create files that are not to be modified by other users, or even sometimes not read by other users. Protection and security became major issues in the early days of timesharing, even though these issues were equally applied to batch-style multiprogramming. These aspects are still crucial in today's systems in multiuser environments and are continually growing in importance due to the ubiquity of computers. All these issues will be discussed in detail later in respective chapters.

1.6.3.2   Case Study: The Compatible Time Sharing System (CTSS)

The first time-sharing operating system, the compatible time sharing system (CTSS), permitting many users to simultaneously access a computer in interactive mode came in 1963 and was later transferred to a specially modified IBM 7094 in the mid-1960s. Both the computer and the primitive CTSS belong to the last part of second generation, and CTSS became popular when third-generation systems evolved and the timesharing concept became widespread. The system ran on a machine with 32K main memory and 36-bit word size, and its resident portion occupied a space of 5K, thereby leaving only 27K of main memory for a maximum of 32 users' programs and data. The time slice used was 0.2 seconds, and at each clock interrupt, the executing program would be preempted, and then this program or only a *portion* of it with its associated data and other status information were to be written out to disk, only if sufficient space in main memory were not available to accommodate the new incoming program that was either to be loaded into or already available in main memory. The operating system then assigned the processor to this newly loaded program to initiate its execution. CTSS was extremely simple and was a pioneer in the initial research on radical scheduling algorithms. Although it was not aware of exploiting the technique of relocation, but it succeeded in offering adequate protection to multiple jobs and keeping interactive users in memory from interfering with one another. It is thus recognized as a pioneer in the concept of modern memory management techniques.

For more details about CTSS, see the Support Material at www.routledge.com/9781032467238.

1.6.3.3   MULTICS

To simplify CTSS, Bell Labs and General Electric (GE, a major computer manufacturer in those days) developed Multics (MULTiplexed Information and Computing Service) with many sensational, innovative ideas that could support hundreds of timesharing users concurrently. It was not just years but decades ahead of its time. Even up to the mid-1980s, almost 20 years after it became operational, Multics continued and was able to hold its market share in the midst of steep competition with other emerging advanced operating systems enriched with many novel ideas in their design. The design of Multics was realized by organizing it as a series of concentric rings instead of layers (to be discussed in Chapter 3). The inner ring was more privileged than the outer ones, and any attempt to call a procedure in an inner ring required the equivalent of a system call, called a *trap instruction*, with its own valid parameters.

Multics had superior security features and greater sophistication in the user interface and also in other areas than all contemporary comparable mainframe operating systems. But it was gigantic and slow, and it also required complicated and difficult mechanisms to implement. Moreover, it was written in PL/1, and the PL/1 compiler was years late and hardly worked at all when it was finally released.

As a result, Bell Labs withdrew from the project, and General Electric totally closed down its computer activities. Yet Multics ran well enough at a few dozen sites, including MIT. Later, Multics was transferred to Honeywell and went on to modest commercial success. Had Honeywell not had two other mainframe operating systems, one of which was marketed very aggressively, Multics might have had greater success. Nevertheless, Multics remained a Honeywell product with a small but trusted customer base until Honeywell got out of the computer business in the late 1980s. However, Multics ultimately fizzled out, leaving behind enormous influence and an immense impact on the design and development of the following modern systems, especially in the areas of virtual memory, protection and security that were implemented on a number of operating systems developed in the 1970s, including the operating systems developed to drive commercially popular minicomputers.

For more details about Multics, see the Support Material at www.routledge.com/9781032467238.

1.6.3.4 Mainframes

By this time, the steady development of IC technology ultimately led to the emergence of large-scale integration (LSI) circuits containing thousands of transistors on a square centimeter of silicon. Consequently, new machines with compatible architectures belonging to the third generation with these powerful components were launched by different manufacturers. Of these, a notable one, the S/360 series (System/360 series, 3 stands for third generation and 60 for the 1960s) came from IBM, the industry's first planned computers with a family concept, comprising different software-compatible machines that offered time-shared multiprogramming with telecommunication facilities using a video display unit (VDU) for interactive use. To drive this potential hardware, appropriate advanced operating systems were developed by different manufacturers implementing the ideas mostly tested by Multics. Two of the most popular operating systems were ultimately released by IBM, *multiprogramming with fixed tasks* (MFT) and *multiprogramming with variable tasks* (MVT) for their large S/360 and early large S/370 (3 stands for third generation and 70 for the 1970s) systems.

The versatile operating systems DOS/360 and OS/360 were developed later by IBM with the main goal of driving their latest System/360 series but also for their existing small systems like 1401s and large systems like 7094s. As a result, an extraordinarily complex large operating system evolved with thousands of bugs that were ultimately rectified and also modified after several versions. This operating system, however, was the first of this kind that was finally able to operate on all different machines belonging to the S/360 family. The awesome success of DOS/360 and OS/360 provoked the other contemporary leading manufacturers like Burroughs, UNIVAC, NCR, CDC, and ICL to come out with their own operating systems, and those were developed along the same lines as DOS/360 and OS/360.

DOS/360 and OS/360, however, were further enhanced by IBM, primarily to accommodate more users of the machine at a time, and also to include some deserving enhanced features. The main bottleneck in this context was the limited capacity of main memory, which was really not enough to simultaneously accommodate all the executing programs with their whole data sets. It was thus finally planned to allocate memory space only dynamically (during runtime) among different competing executing programs and move or "swap" them back and forth between main and secondary memory as and when needed to mitigate this scarcity of memory space. This strategy, however, was ultimately implemented within the operating system as an additional major primary function to automate memory management.

The ultimate outcome of this idea was the concept of **virtual memory**, an *additional facility* implemented in third-generation computers that offered the user an *illusion* of having essentially unlimited addressable memory for use with unrestricted access. IBM successfully implemented the virtual memory mechanism in its line of 360 series machines, and the existing operating systems were also upgraded accordingly to drive these architecturally modified machines. Consequently, operating systems like OS/VS1 and OS/VS2 (VS stands for virtual storage) came out, and later the operating system OS/SVS (single virtual storage) was introduced in 1972 using a 24-bit addressing scheme, a virtual space of 16 MB (2^{24} = 16 MB) for the older S/370 machine architecture. But this 24-bit address space along with separate virtual memory for each job also quickly became inadequate for some situations and the constantly widening spectrum of the S/370 family. Moreover, as newer different application areas were constantly emerging, and there was an upsurge in the memory requirements from the user end, IBM thus introduced **multiple virtual storage** (**MVS**), the top of the line and one of the most complex operating systems ever developed, for its mainframes to manage such situations. With MVS, the limit was a dedicated 16 MB memory *per job*, where each job actually got something less than half of this assigned virtual memory; the remaining space was for the use of the operating system.

IBM extended the architecture of its underlying processor to handle 31-bit addresses, a facility known as *extended addressing* (XA). To extract the potential of this new hardware, a new version of MVS known as **MVS/XA** was launched in 1983 that summarily increased the per-job address space to a maximum of 2 GB (gigabytes). Still, this was found not at all sufficient for some applications and environments. As a result, IBM introduced the last major extension of the 370 architecture, a new form known as enterprise system architecture (ESA), and the corresponding enhanced version of the operating system, known as **MVS/ESA**, emerged in the late 1980s/early 1990s. Out of many distinguishing features of this OS, one was that there were up to 15 additional 2-GB address spaces for data available only to a specific job, apart from the 2 GB address space per job that was already available in MVS/XA. Consequently, the maximum addressable virtual memory per job was now 32 GB, one step further in the implementation of virtual storage.

With the development of semiconductor IC RAM, memory size and speed notably increased, and the price of the memory dropped drastically. The cost of sizable memory then came down to an affordable range that ultimately inspired designers to have *multiple memory modules* instead of just one. A relatively large high-speed buffer memory is thus provided between the CPU and main memory to act as intermediate storage for quick access to information by the CPU that summarily reduces the impact of the speed gap between the fast CPU and relatively slow main memory, thereby improving overall execution speed. This memory is now called **caches** and is in common use by modern CPUs to access both data and instructions.

As the hardware was relentlessly upgraded with the continuous advancement of electronic technology, computer architecture was also constantly enhanced to make use of modern hardware to fulfill the various needs and continually increasing demands of the users. Consequently, new operating systems were required to drive the changed hardware systems, and these new OSs were naturally realized either by developing new ones or by repeated modification of existing older ones. This, in turn, invited another problem: a user's program, while executable under an old operating system, became unusable under a new operating system (enhanced version) without modification, and this modification sometimes could be quite extensive and also expensive. This situation was faced by IBM in particular, since it introduced many different versions of OSs in quick succession for its 360 and 370 series of machines, and those were very similar but not fully compatible. An IBM installation with different versions of operating systems faced a lot of difficulties while changing or switching the operating system periodically to meet all the user needs and demands. To avoid the operational difficulties arising from frequent switching of operating systems caused by frequent updates in hardware architecture, IBM developed a special form of system architecture for its S/360 and S/370 series, popularly known as **virtual machines** (**VMs**).

So many installations resorted to VM that an operating system was designed to emulate multiple computer systems. The ultimate objective of a virtual machine was to multiplex all system resources between the users in such a way that each user was under the illusion they had undivided access to all machine's resources. In other words, each user believed they had a separate copy of the entire machine of their own. Each such copy was termed a **virtual machine**. Each virtual machine was logically separated from all others; consequently it could be controlled and run by its own separate operating system. This led to innovative system organization (discussed in detail in Chapter 3), where several different OSs were used concurrently over a single piece of hardware. The heart of the system, known as *virtual machine monitor* (VMM), ran on the bare hardware (physical hardware) and created the required virtual machine interface. The operating system accordingly was upgraded to drive these architecturally modified machines. The new operating systems thus released based on the existing ones were called DOS/VM and OS/VM. A VM could even be configured to take advantage of systems with multiple processors, but it was unable to provide all of the controls needed to extract the full strength of modern multiprocessor configurations.

In spite of having several merits, *two major drawbacks* were observed in the design of virtual machines. First of all, the cost of the hardware and hardware interface were very high in those days. Second, any fault or failure in the common hardware interface (VMM) or the single piece of basic hardware on which the different virtual machines with their own operating systems were running concurrently would cause a severe breakdown in the operation of every machine, leading to a total collapse of the entire system. In addition, the VMM-interface is still a complex program and was not that simple to realize to obtain reasonable performance. As a result, virtual machines gradually fizzled out, but the concept and its successful implementation eventually had an immense impact that opened new horizons in the architectural design of computer systems and their organization (especially the innovation of computer networks) in the days to come.

For more details about mainframes, see the Support Material at www.routledge.com/9781032467238.

1.6.3.5 Minicomputers

During the third generation, another major development was the introduction of minicomputers. The Digital Equipment Corporation (DEC) in 1961 launched its PDP-1, which had only 4K memory of 18-bit words but with a drastic reduction in price and size, much less than its contemporary, IBM 7094. The performance of the PDP-1 was up to the level of the IBM 7094, and hence it became very popular. A whole new industry came up, with DEC introducing a series of other PDPs: PDP-7 and PDP-8. The block diagram of the organization of PDP-8 is shown in Figure 1.2. Soon, DEC launched its enhanced version, the 16-bit successor PDP-11, a machine totally compatible with

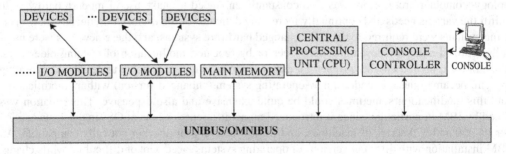

FIGURE 1.2   Operating systems used to drive minicomputers and the hardware structure of such representative minicomputer organization (DEC-PDP–8).

the other members in the family, in the early 1970s. The IBM 360 and PDP-11 had a very close resemblance: both had byte-oriented memory and word-oriented registers. The parameters of the PDP-11, like the cost, performance, size, and overhead expenditure, were so attractive that it became immensely successful both in the commercial and academic arenas, and it was also in wide use until the 2000s for industrial process control applications.

DEC developed many operating systems for its various computer lines, including the simple RT-11 operating system for its 16-bit PDP-11-class machines. For PDP-10–class systems (36-bit), the time-sharing operating systemsTOPS-10 and TOPS-20 were developed. In fact, prior to the widespread use of UNIX, TOPS-10 was a particularly popular system in universities and also in the early ARPANET community.

Technological advancements led to the increasing power of minicomputers' functional operations. The availability of low-cost and larger-capacity main memory attached to the minicomputer allowed a multi-user, shared system to run. Within a short period, the successor to the PDP-11, the first versatile 32-bit minicomputer, VAX, was launched with a powerful VMS operating system that offered a multi-user shared environment.

Minicomputers also came from many other companies with various configurations, but a minicomputer technically consists of a 16-or 32-bit microprocessor or similar type of other processor, a comfortable size of memory and a few input-output-supported chips interconnected with each other or mounted on a single motherboard. DEC with its PDP family soon took a formidable lead over the other manufacturers. The PDP-11 became the computer of choice at nearly all computer science departments. Commercial organizations were also able to afford a computer of this type for their own dedicated applications

For more details about minicomputers, see the Support Material at www.routledge.com/ 9781032467238.

1.6.3.6   UNICS/UNIX

Multics eventually fizzled out. But Ken Thompson, one of computer scientists who worked on the Multics project at Bell Labs, remained under the strong influence of the design approach used by Multics. He wanted to continue with this idea and ultimately decided to write a new, stripped-down, one-user version of Multics using an obsolete and discarded PDP-7 minicomputer. His developed system actually worked and met the predefined goal in spite of the tiny size of the PDP-7 computer. One of the other researchers and his friend, Brian Kernighan, somewhat jokingly called it **UNICS** (UNiplexed Information and Computing Service), although the spelling was eventually changed to **UNIX** after a series of modifications and enhancements. Historically, UNIX appeared at that point as a savior of the popular PDP-11 series, which was in search of a simpler, efficient operating system, since it was running at that time under a dreadful operating system with literally no other alternatives.

Looking at the initial success of UNIX, and after being totally convinced of its bright future, Dennis Ritchie, a renowned computer scientist at Bell Labs and a colleague of Thompson, joined in this project with his whole team. Two major steps were immediately taken in this development process. The first was to migrate the project from the platform of the obsolete PDP-7 to the more modern and larger PDP-11/20, then to the even more advanced PDP-11/45, and finally to the most modern system of those days, thePDP-11/70. The second step was in regard to the language used in writing UNIX. Thompson, at this juncture, decided to rewrite UNIX afresh in a high-level language, leaving its existing line to avoid having to rewrite the entire system whenever the underlying hardware platform was upgraded. He thus used his own designed language, called B, a simplified form of BCPL, which in turn was a form of CPL that never worked. Unfortunately, the structure of this B language was not enough equipped to support his approaches in designing UNIX, and consequently, his strategy for realizing this operating system could not be implemented. At this stage, Ritchie came to the rescue and designed an appropriate successor to the **B** language called **C**, and then wrote a fabulous compiler for it. Later, Ritchie and Thompson jointly rewrote UNIX once again using C. Coincidences sometimes shape history, and the emergence of C at that critical time was precisely the correct approach for that implementation. Since then, the C language has been constantly modified and enhanced, and remains as an important language platform in the area of system program development even today.

UNIX developed using C has been widely accepted in the academic world, and ultimately in 1974, the UNIX system was first described in a technical journal. However, the first commonly available version outside Bell Labs, released in 1976, became the first de facto standard named Version 6, so called because it was described in the *sixth edition* of the UNIX programmer's manual. Soon, it was upgraded to Version 7, introduced in 1978, with a simple file system, pipes, clean user-interface—the shell—and extensible design. Apart from many other contemporary systems, the main non-AT&T UNIX system developed at the University of California, Berkeley was called *UNIX BSD* and ran first on PDP and then on VAX machines. In the meantime, AT&T repetitively refined its own systems, constantly adding many more features, and by 1982, Bell Labs had combined several such variants of AT&T UNIX into a single system that was marketed commercially as *UNIX system III*. Later, this operating system, after several upgrades, incorporated a number of important new features in a commercially viable integrated fashion that was eventually introduced as *UNIX system V*.

By the late 1980s, however, the situation was horrible. Virtually every vendor by this time had started to regularly include many extra nonstandard features as enhancements and part of its own upgrades. As a result, there were no standards for binary program formats, and the world of UNIX was split into many dissimilar ones that greatly inhibited the expected commercial success of UNIX. In fact, two different and quite incompatible versions of UNIX, 4.3 BSD and System V Release 3, were in widespread use. It was then difficult and truly impossible for software vendors to write and package UNIX programs that would run on any UNIX system, as could be done with other contemporary operating systems. The net outcome was that standardization in different versions of UNIX, including the ones from these two different camps, was immediately needed and accordingly demanded. Many attempts in this regard initially failed. For example, AT&T issued its System V Interface Definition (SVID), which defined all the system calls, file formats, and many other components. The ultimate objective of this release was to keep all the System V vendors in line, but it failed to have any impact on the enemy camp (BSD), who just ignored it.

However, the first serious attempt to reconcile the different flavors of UNIX was initiated through a project named POSIX (the first three letters refer to portable operating system, and the last two letters was added to make the name UNIXish) carried out by a collective effort under the auspices of the IEEE standards board, hundreds of people from industry, academia, and the government. After a great deal of debate, with arguments and counterarguments, the POSIX committee finally produced a standard known as **1003.1** that eventually broadened the base of OS implementation beyond that of pure UNIX by standardizing the user–interface to the OS rather than merely organizing its implementation. This standard actually defines a set of library procedures that every conformant UNIX system must provide. Most of these procedures invoke a system call, but a few can be implemented outside the kernel. Typical procedures are *open*, *read*, and *fork, etc.* The 1003.1 document is written in such a way that both operating system implementers and software developers can understand it, another novelty in the world of standards. In fact, all manufacturers are now committed to provide standardized communication software that behaves in conformance with certain predefined rules to provide their customers the ability to communicate with other open systems.

The triumph of UNIX had already begun, and by the mid-1980s, UNIX nearly monopolized the commercial as well as scientific environment, with workstations running on machines ranging from 32-bit microprocessors up to supercomputers. Although UNIX was designed as a time-sharing system, its multiprogramming ability as well as the extensibility function inherent in its design naturally fit into the workstations used in network environments. UNIX gradually became popular in the workstation market and ultimately started to support high-resolution graphics. Today, mainframe environments and even supercomputers are managed by UNIX or a UNIX-like (or a variant of UNIX) operating system.

Another system evolved during this period was the **Pick operating system** that initially started as a database application support program and ultimately graduated to carrying out system works and is still in use as an add-on database system across a wide variety of systems supported on most UNIX systems. Other database packages, such as Oracle, Cybase, and Ingres, etc. came at a later stage and were primarily *middleware* that contained many of the features of operating systems, by which they can support large applications running on many different hardware platforms.

For more details about UNICS/UNIX, see the Support Material at www.routledge.com/ 9781032467238.

1.6.3.7 Multitasking Systems

A task can be defined as a collection of executable statements and data declarations that gives rise to an independent specific activity (process) at runtime. A program can be considered a task or a collection of tasks. With the evolution of time-sharing methodology, processes were sometimes called tasks. A time-sharing system (multitasking system) often allows two or more processes (tasks) to run at any given time. More precisely, a multitasking operating system facilitates concurrent execution of programs on a single processor, setting up appropriate memory protection and regulated file access by means of coupling the available hardware and software tools to safeguard the address spaces of the resident processes and coordinate the file-accesses made by the active processes. This operating system exploits the multitasking operation, which is normally accomplished by scheduling ready-to-execute processes based on their relative importance (priority) and selecting a particular deserving process, which would then be allocated to the processor (CPU or I/O processor) to independently carry out its operation. However, in this system, a single user can run *multiple applications* concurrently, each one competing with the others to gain access to the resources or to run background processes while retaining control of the computer. In fact, more emphasis is put here on *processor management* and *device management*.

In contrast, a multiprogramming operating system is actually a more general concept with well-defined simple policies and strategies to support concurrent execution of programs. Here, the user is represented only by the job they submit, and a batch job would execute only one program at any instant on behalf of the job. The multiprogramming system actually exploits multitasking operation as one of the key mechanisms in managing all the resources available within the computer system. However, in this system, the main target was to put as many jobs as possible in memory, and hence memory management was a major design challenge.

The growth of the *client/server model* of computing using a local/wide area network has once again added further momentum with a different flavor in the increasing motivation for multitasking. With this approach, a client (a personal computer or sometimes a workstation) and a server (a host system or maybe a mainframe) are linked together and used jointly to accomplish a particular application. Each is assigned a portion of the job that is deemed fit for its capabilities. Thus, multiple tasks (portions of the job) are concurrently under execution, even on two different machines, which gives rise to multitasking supported by an operating system capable of driving sophisticated real-time communication hardware and its associated system software while providing ongoing user interaction.

Multitasking operations are even found in **single-user** operating systems of some advanced personal computers and in real-time systems that rely on certain computer hardware features; the notable ones are direct memory access (DMA) and I/O interrupts. In the presence of this type of hardware, when the processor (CPU) issues an I/O command for one job, the I/O operation of the job can be independently carried out by the device controller without the CPU's involvement, and the CPU is released and can then proceed with the execution of another job. After the completion of the I/O operation, the device controller issues an interrupt, the processor is interrupted, and the operating system gains control and takes appropriate actions. For example, a user of a personal computer writes a text using a text editor and at the same time plays music. The writing task (application) is independently carried out by the DMA without any involvement of the CPU, while the task (application) of playing the music is carried out by the CPU at the same time, an ideal example of multitasking in single-user environment. Windows NT was one such operating system that exploited the tremendous power of contemporary 32-bit microprocessors and provided full multitasking with ease-of-use features in a single-user environment. This indicates that a multiprogramming operating system is necessarily a multitasking operating system, but the converse is not always true.

1.6.4 MODERN OPERATING SYSTEMS

Over the years, more advanced hardware organization and architecture constantly evolved, mainly due to the rapid pace of development in electronic technology with the introduction of ICs, primarily large scale integration (LSI), very large scale integration (VLSI), and ultra large scale integration (ULSI). As a result, small, powerful microprocessors as well as tiny, speedier capacious main memory systems have been introduced. The corresponding significant hardware outcomes are powerful microprocessors, multicomputer systems, multiprocessor machines, sophisticated embedded systems, real-time systems, high-speed communication channels used in network attachments, varieties of memory storage devices with increasing speed and capacity, and above all, greatly increased machine speed as a whole. In the application domain, the introduction of related intelligent software, multiuser client–server computing, multimedia applications, Internet and Web-based applications, cloud computing, applications using distributed systems, real-time applications, and many others have had an immense impact on the structure and design of evolving operating systems. To manage these advanced machines and the sophisticated environment, OSs have also constantly progressed, with new ideas and approaches, ultimately incorporating a number of new design elements to organize the OS afresh that eventually culminated in a major change in the existing concept, forms, design issues, and structure, as well as in their nature. These modern OSs (either new OSs or new releases of existing OSs), however, are properly fit to adequately address new developments in hardware to extract its highest potential. They are also found conducive to new applications, and yet able to negotiate increasingly numerous potential security threats.

That is why, beyond the third generation of operating systems, along with continuous releases of enhanced versions, making any sharp demarcation between generations of operating systems is difficult to do, and, in fact, there is less general agreement on defining generations of operating systems as such. Consequently, the classification of operating systems by generation to drive this constantly changing environment becomes less clear and meaningful. It could be summarily said that the scientific, commercial, and special-purpose applications of new developments ultimately resulted in a major change in OSs in the early 1980s and that the outcomes of these changes are still in the process of being worked out. However, some of the notable breakthroughs in approaches that facilitated redefining the concept, structure, design, and development of OSs to realize numerous modern OSs to drive the constantly emerging advanced architecture in the arenas of both scientific and commercial use are mentioned here.

For more details about modern operating systems, see the Support Material at www.routledge.com/9781032467238.

1.6.4.1 Personal Computers

The availability of tiny, low-cost, high computing-powered microprocessors started the regime of microcomputers, with the ultimate emergence of a different class of general-purpose machines called the **personal computer** (PC). These started to be used in a completely different way from large computers and even minicomputers of those days. Text processing, spreadsheet applications, small database handling, and the use of various types of highly interactive applications are only a few of these. One of the most widely used personal computer families is the PC series that came from IBM in 1981 with 8-bit processor chips and has become a de facto standard for this class of machine. The organization of PCs has been gradually improved and enhanced based on the Intel 8088/8086/80286/80386/80486/80586/Pentium family (**Intel X-86 families**) or Motorola 680 10/68020/68030/68040/68050/68060 (**MC 68000 series**) using 16/32/64-bit microprocessors with typical clock rates exceeding a few gigahertz (GHz) today. Other manufacturers started producing PCs in the same line as IBM, and all their machines were compatible with IBM-PCs, but the components used by different manufacturers were obviously different. The most popular single-user highly interactive operating system for early personal computers was **CP/M**, which was then converted to **PC-DOS** by IBM and was finally displaced by **MS-DOS** being developed based on existing PC-DOS by the Microsoft Corporation under license from IBM.

Although single-user MS-DOS was not very intelligent, it was well suited to the organization of the PC machine and had excellent performance. Its design actually put more emphasis on user-friendliness, sacrificing its other vital objectives; one such is resource utilization. All PCs, irrespective of the brand (manufacturer), ultimately used MS-DOS, which eventually became a de facto standard. It has been constantly upgraded on a regular basis, ending every time with a release of a newer version with more advanced features to fulfill most of the users' requirements and, of course, developed in the same line of the existing system, maintaining its family concept. Consequently, MS-DOS on personal computers ultimately dominated other operating system products and finally consolidated its position in the entire personal computer market. MS-DOS is traditionally a single-user system but does provide **multitasking** by way of coupling available hardware facilities (DMA) with existing software support. It was not at all a true multiprogramming system, although it provided a file system similar to the one offered by UNIX.

Due to the constantly decreasing cost of hardware resources, it became feasible to provide graphical user interfaces (GUIs) for many operating systems. The original GUI was developed at **Xerox's Palo Alto Research Center** (**XEROX PARC**) in the early 1970s (the Alto computer system), and then many others were created, including **Apple's Mac OS** and also **IBM's OS/2**. Microsoft finally added this excellent GUI feature in the early 1990s in the form of **Windows** as a platform to the user running on the existing MS-DOS operating system. Windows 3.1/95/98/second version of Windows 98 and even Windows Millennium were this type of platform released by Microsoft running on MS-DOS. Finally, Microsoft launched a **Windows NT-based OS**, a full-fledged standalone operating system providing an extensive graphic user interface.

Hardware technology rapidly advances, offering more tiny, low-cost, sophisticated components for use in all aspects of computers to make the system more powerful and versatile. Side by side, both the system software and third-party–created application software development tools progressed remarkably, yielding lots of different types of useful software for users to fulfill their everyday requirements. As a result, personal computer culture gradually became widespread and matured to ultimately grow into more sophisticated systems, even moving one step forward to almost replace existing larger minicomputer machines.

For more details about personal computers, see the Support Material at www.routledge.com/9781032467238.

1.6.4.2 Computer Networks: Network Operating Systems

The successful implementation of VM370 using advanced operating systems (like IBM's DOS/VM and OS/VM) introduced the idea that with a single piece of hardware exploiting the service of a common hardware interface, different virtual machines could be simultaneously run with their own individual different operating systems, collectively giving rise to a concept of multiple operating systems running independently over a single piece of hardware. This innovative concept, however, addressed many issues and solved many critical problems of those days. In spite of having several merits, two major drawbacks were observed in this design. First of all, the costs of the hardware and hardware interface were very high. The second major drawback of this design was that any fault or failure in the common hardware interface or in the single piece of hardware on which the different virtual machines with their own operating systems were running concurrently would cause every machine to breakdown, leading to a total collapse of the entire system. To alleviate these two major drawbacks, designers desperately searched for a suitable alternative. However, this idea, on other hand, had an immense impact that opened a new horizon in the domain of personal computers and their use.

Both the issues, such as; cost, and fault tolerance of the entire system (or, at least, a part of the entire system) at the time of critical hardware failure have been successfully addressed exploiting a different approach, but keeping preserved the central theme of allowing multiple operating systems to run concurrently.

Now all the costly centralized hardware has been replaced, and the cost was then distributed to realize a collection of low-cost standalone autonomous computer systems, like microcomputers; each one was then run under its own operating system to support its own local users, and all such systems in this domain were then interconnected with one another via their hardware and software tools to enable them to intercommunicate and cooperate. This fulfills the first requirement: cost. Since each such small system in this arrangement can use its own different operating system to support its own local users, this arrangement appeared to have multiple operating system running simultaneously, thus fulfilling the second requirement. In this way, the cost was substantially brought down to an affordable limit, and since the failure of any system or any fault in interconnection hardware in this arrangement will not affect the other systems, the fault-tolerance issue has been solved to a large extent.

The emergence of this design concept of interconnecting a collection of autonomous computer systems capable of communication and cooperation between one another by way of communication links and protocols is popularly known as a **computer network**. Each such autonomous machine running under its own operating system is able to execute its own application programs to support its own local users and also offers computational resources to the networks, usually called a *host*. Computer networks could, however, be considered an immediate predecessor of a true **distributed computing system**, which will be discussed later in detail. Sometimes computer networks are loosely called distributed computer systems, since they carry a flavor of a true distributed computing system comprising hardware composed of loosely bound multiple processors (not multiprocessors).

Apart from the local operating system installed in each machine to drive it, computer networks are managed by a different type of operating system installed additionally in each individual computer to allow the local user to use and access information stored in another computer via high-speed communication facilities. This operating system is known as a **network operating system** (**NOS**) or sometimes **network file system** (**NFS**), a successor of KRONOS, which was developed by Control Data Corporation during the 1970s. In the late 1970s, Control Data Corporation and the University of Illinois jointly developed what was then the innovative **PLATO** operating system that featured real-time chat and multi-user graphical games using long-distance time-sharing networks. In the 1970s, UNIVAC produced the **Real-Time Basic** (**RTB**) system to support a large-scale time-sharing environment.

A NOS enables users to be aware of the presence of other computers, login to a remote computer, and transmit and receive data/files from one computer to another. Since then, a NOS supported multiple users interacting. However, it has crossed a long way with numerous enhancements and modifications in its various forms, and ultimately evolved to *multiuser interactive operating systems*, known as the **client–server model**, a widely used form observed today.

1.6.4.3   Client–Server Model: Multiuser Systems

With relentless progress in hardware technology, a personal computer gradually evolved to a more sophisticated system consisting of a faster and more powerful processor, larger main memory, bigger disk storage, and high-resolution graphic display unit and also connected to many more resources than a personal computer usually has. When this personal computer is connected as a communication terminal to another large computer in a computer network (or, loosely, network of computers), it is called a **workstation**. Almost at the same time, local area networks (LANs) in the form of ethernet and token ring LAN technology came out, enabling the interconnection of small machines/workstations that, in turn, would be connected with a comparatively larger and more powerful machine by relatively high-speed communication links in a network environment in order

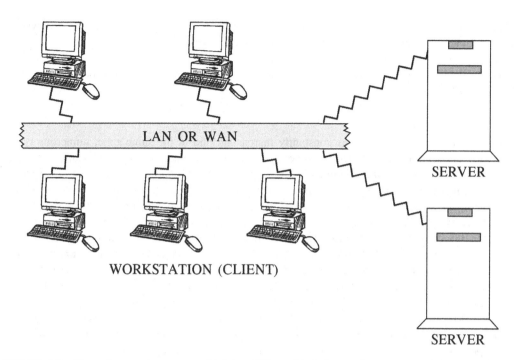

FIGURE 1.3 Network operating system which is a different kind of operating system used in computer networks organized in the form of Workstation-Server (Client-Server) model.

to share both the hardware and software resources available in the entire low-cost arrangement. The environment thus formed is depicted in Figure 1.3. The outcome was a remarkable one in the design of computer hardware configurations that led computing practices to follow a completely different path. To make this approach operative, the entire system naturally requires the service of a different type of more sophisticated and complex operating system to manage all the resources. The resulting operating system developed along the lines of time-sharing technology became well-suited to managing LAN-based computing environments.

The operating system eventually evolved with an innovative concept in the design that structured it as a group of cooperating processes called **servers** that offer services to their users, called **clients**. This client–server model of the operating system was able to manage many cooperating machines with related network communications. It also provided client and server resource management strategies, new forms of memory management and file management strategies, and many other similar aspects. In fact, client and server machines usually all run the same microkernel (the inner level of the operating system), with both the clients and servers running as user processes.

These operating systems running on distributed hardware configurations are well-suited to handle distributed applications offering coarse-grained distribution. Moreover, they provide distributed file systems that facilitate system-wide access to files and I/O devices. Some systems also provide migration of objects such as files and processes for the sake of improved *fault tolerance* and *load distribution*. Another nice feature of this system is its *scalability*, which means that the system configuration can be gradually incremented on demand in size as the workload regularly grows, of course without affecting its high *reliability*. In short, these systems exhibit tremendous strength, offering an excellent cost/performance ratio when benchmarked.

The major drawbacks of this system are in the complex software, weak security, and, above all, potential communication bottlenecks. Since the distributed file system is exposed to the user running commonly as a user process, it is often under potential threat in the form of unauthorized access or snooping by active/passive intruders, casual prying by non-technical users, or determined attempts by unscrupulous users. To protect information from such malicious activities, the system has to provide more elaborate forms of protection mechanisms, including user authentication and, optionally, data encryption for increased security.

For more details about the client–server model, see the Support Material at www.routledge.com/ 9781032467238.

1.6.4.4 Superminis

The power of minicomputers was constantly increasing, and at the same time, numerous types of diverse application areas started to evolve, particularly in the area of large applications. In this situation, the existing 16-bit minicomputers were thus observed to have certain limitations from an architectural point of view. A few of these to mention are: limited addressing capability, a limited number of operation codes due to existing 16-bit instructions, limited scope to use numbers with higher precision, and many others. The solution to all these drawbacks of these machines ultimately led to the introduction of 32-bit minicomputers, following the same line of its predecessor, the 16-bit minicomputer in the late 1970s, and it was popularly known as a **supermini** or **mid-range system**.

The 32-bit supermini computer supported more users working simultaneously, providing more memory and more peripheral devices. These machines were considered far more powerful than the gigantic mainframe of the IBM360/75. DEC launched its most powerful supermini family, popularly known as VAX series. VAX 8842, with the VMS operating system, was one of the most popular and widely used superminis. IBM introduced its supermini AS 400 series of machines with operating system OS 400 is still dominating, and at present, its upgrade version known as P-series is also widely in use in many application areas. A schematic diagram of AS 400 is shown in Figure 1.4. These machines today also provide support to larger computers when hooked up to them. Most superminis, including the AS 400 (P-series) are today commonly used as powerful

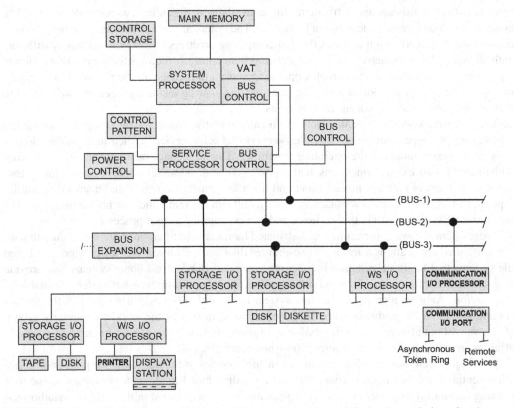

FIGURE 1.4 Operating systems used in supermini computer system and the hardware design of such a representative supermini system (IBM-AS/400).

standalone systems for both scientific and commercial applications as well as servers in a network of computers.

For additional details about superminis, see the Support Material at www.routledge.com/ 9781032467238.

1.6.5 DISTRIBUTED OPERATING SYSTEMS

The successful implementation of networks of computers introduces the concept of distributed computing systems that spread rapidly in the 1990s when the prices of computer hardware sharply dropped, and use of the *open system* standard paved the way for incremental growth of existing systems. An **open system** is identified as having well-defined and non-proprietary interfaces with a universally accepted specific standard that enables a computing system to straightaway add new components and subsystems, thereby facilitating incremental growth. The LAN environment is an appropriate example of an open system. A distributed computing system can then be realized in one way with several individual independent computer systems connected with one another in different fashions by communication links and protocols. Computer systems ranging from expensive supercomputers to cheap PCs can be connected in this way using standard interfaces to build up a distributed computing system. A true distributed computer system, in contrast, is a *multiprocessor system* consisting of tightly coupled multiple processors confined in one system with distributed shared memory organization connected to a pool of I/O devices located in close vicinity or remotely.

A **distributed system** actually comprising multiple computer systems appears to its users essentially a virtual uniprocessor system. Such a system should provide various kinds of transparencies, such as access, control, data, execution, and location and should also be reliable and tolerant to some kind of faults and failures. A rough demarcation between a **distributed system** and a **parallel system** is that the former is designed to allow many users to work together either independently or often with interactions and cooperation, and the latter is targeted to achieve maximum speed in handling a single problem using a set of interconnected multiple processors or computers. This distinction is difficult to maintain because the design spectrum is really a continuum. However, we prefer to use the term "distributed system" to denote any system in which multiple interconnected CPUs or computers work together.

Whatever the form of a distributed computing system, a different type of operating system (not similar to either our known traditional centralized systems or NOSs) is then required to drive this type of computing system, historically known as a distributed operating system (DOS). In fact, it evolved in numerous forms to drive and support many different types of distributed computing systems. A DOS is actually a common operating system shared by a network of computers (not computer networks) or is used to drive a computer system with multiple processors (non-uniform memory access (NUMA) model multiprocessor). Here, we will discuss only the generic DOS that manifests a spectrum of common features.

The ultimate objective of a DOS is something else; to ideally distribute computations, real distributions of the components and resources by completely hiding those from the users and application programs unless explicitly demanded. In this regard, sometimes the difference between a network OS and a distributed OS is somewhat arbitrary, since the network OS will also allow some aspects of the hardware environment to be location transparent, while others will be apparent. For example, in 4.3 BSD UNIX, file servers may be location transparent, although *telnet*, *ftp*, *rlogin*, *rsh*, and other commands make the machine boundaries explicit. In fact, DOSs differ from traditional operating systems or even NOSs in critical ways. However, a generic DOS is committed to addressing a spectrum of common functionalities. A few of them are:

- Resource sharing
- Communication
- Reliability
- Computation speed-up
- Scalability (incremental growth)

Besides, a DOS often requires personal IDs and passwords for users to strengthen security mechanisms to provide guaranteed authenticity of communication and at the same time permit the users to remain mobile within the domain of the distributed system.

However, the advantages of DOSs may be sometimes negated by the presence of certain factors: their ultimate dependence on communication networks; any potential problem in them or their saturation at any time may create havoc. Moreover, easy sharing of resources, including data, though advantageous, may turn out to be a double-edged sword, since remaining exposed may cause a potential threat in security even with the provision of user-ids and passwords in communications. We will now separately discuss in brief the DOS when used in multiprocessor and multicomputer systems.

For more details about common functionalities of DOS, see the Support Material at www.routledge.com/9781032467238.

1.6.5.1 Distributed Operating Systems: In Multiprocessor Machines

A true distributed computing system, in contrast, is a multiprocessor consisting of tightly bound multiple processors. A multiprocessor with shared memory works by centralizing everything, so it is not considered a true distributed system. However, a multiprocessor offers **multiprocessing**, which means simultaneous execution of multiple processes by a computer system with multiple hardware processors rather than a single processor supporting multiple processes to run concurrently. Multiprocessing systems, by definition, are naturally multitasking systems because they provide simultaneous execution of multiple tasks (processes) on different processors. An individual processor in the multiprocessor, in turn, may also offer multitasking depending on the implementation strategy. A representative multiprocessor system with distributed hardware is illustrated in Figure 1.5.

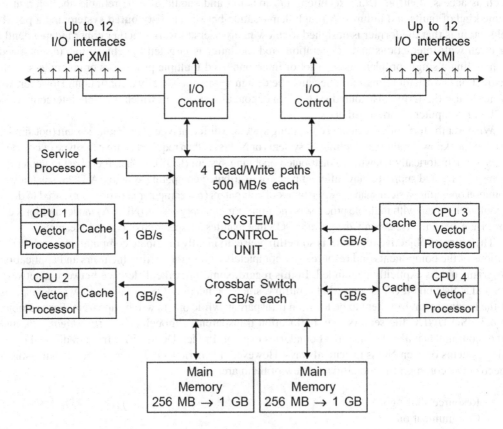

FIGURE 1.5 Operating system used in advanced multiprocessor system and the hardware organization of such a representative multiprocessor system (DEC VAX 9000).

A multiprocessor in the form of true distributed hardware requires different types of operating systems to be designed with an innovative approach using a new set of modules to meet its objectives that ultimately give rise to the concept of a DOS. This system creates an abstract environment in which machine boundaries are not visible to the programmer. A DOS of this type uses a single centralized control system that truly converts the existing collection of hardware and software into a single integrated system.

A multiprocessor when managed by a true *DOS* under which a user while submits a job is not aware of; on which processor the job would be run, where the needed files are physically located, or whether the executing job during execution would be shifted from one processor to another for the sake of balancing load. In fact, the user has no choice and also not informed because everything should be efficiently handled in a transparent way by the operating system in an automated manner. To achieve this, among many options, one is to have more complex processor scheduling mechanisms that would synchronize several coexisting processors' activities in order to realize the highest amount of *parallelism*. Hence, a true DOS should not be considered an extension or addition of code to realize more new features over the existing traditional uniprocessor or NOSs. A DOS though appears to its users very similar to a traditional uniprocessor system offering those system services that may qualify it as time-sharing, real-time, or any combination of them for the benefit of local clients, but it may also facilitate shared access to remote hardware and software resources.

The versatile third-generation OS/360 from IBM gradually evolved to become successively MFT, MVT, and SVS systems and then to higher-generation (fourth-generation) DOSs like MVS, MVS/XA, MVS/ESA, OS/390, and z/OS. Although these operating systems include the essentials of the UNIX kernel, a huge amount of new functions were included. These functions provide numerous supports that are required by modern mission-critical applications running on large distributed computer systems like z-Series mainframes. It is worthwhile to mention that IBM maintained total compatibility with the past releases, giving rise to a full family concept, so that programs developed in the 1960s can still run under the modern DOS z/OS with almost no change. Although z/OS runs UNIX applications, it is a proprietary OS, in opposition to an open system.

1.6.5.2   Distributed Operating Systems: In Multicomputer Machines

Historically, the success of networks of computers gives rise to the evolution of a distributed computing system of another type in which there is a collection of loosely coupled autonomous similar or dissimilar computer systems capable of communication and cooperation via hardware and software interconnections (multicomputers). More specifically, a distributed computing system of this type is a system consisting of two or more complete computers; each is equipped with communication hardware and is capable of performing some of the control functions of an OS.

Managing the operation of this type of distributed computing system requires one kind of DOS which is different from the conventional operating system and also from NOSs in critical ways. A DOS of this type uses a single centralized control system that truly converts the entire existing collection of hardware and software into a single integrated system (single system image). Its main responsibility is to exploit the multiplicity of resources with existing interconnectivity to extract the potential of resource sharing and distribution across computers to accommodate more concurrent applications and to speed-up their computation, with reliability in operation.

A NOS with a multicomputer system in a network environment is simply an adjunct to the local operating system that allows the application machine to interact with a server or other peer systems in a predefined manner. Here, the user is quite aware that there are multiple independent computers and deals with them explicitly. Typically, common communications architecture is employed to support these network applications. In contrast, a multicomputer system in a distributed environment is more than a mere collection of computers forming a network: the functioning of each individual computer must here be integrated by both hardware and software in such a way so as to realize effective utilization of services and the resources in the integrated system in a manner to obtain the needed functionalities of a distributed system, as mentioned before. This is achieved through the participation of all associated computers in the control functions of the distributed OS. However, there always exists a possibility of network failure or even failure of an individual computer system in the collection that may complicate the normal functioning of the operating system. To negotiate such a situation, special techniques must be present in the design of the operating system that will ultimately permit the users to somehow access the resources over the network.

However, the special techniques used in the design of a DOS mostly include **distributed control, transparency**, and **remote procedure calls** (**RPCs**).

Brief details of these special techniques are given on the Support Material at www.routledge. com/9781032467238.

1.6.6 Clusters: A Distributed Computer System Design

A true distributed system is costly to own and equally expensive to scale and subsequently to maintain. But its useful features that provide enormous computational flexibility and versatility cannot be ignored. As an alternative, an arrangement is made interconnecting comparatively low-cost computers that has fully satisfied the user community providing a base substitute of an expensive true distributed system called *clustering*. This approach is a relatively recent development that provides high performance and high availability and is particularly attractive for server applications. A **cluster** can be defined as a group of interconnected homogeneous/heterogeneous self-sufficient computers (multicomputer) working together as a **unified computing system** that can cast a **single-system image** (SSI) as being *one single machine* to the outside world. Each individual computer in a cluster may be a uniprocessor or a multiprocessor and is typically referred to as a *node*, which can run on its own without any assistance from the cluster. The use of a multiprocessor as a node in the cluster, although not necessary, does improve both performance and availability.

Cluster architecture is built on a platform of a computer networks comprising heterogeneous multicomputer systems connected by high-speed LAN or switch hardware and operated by a loosely coupled NOS. This multicomputer system is, however, composed of interconnected nodes (computers) in which each computer in the cluster is a complete, independent, and autonomous system, apart from its operation as a member of the cluster in which it belongs. Now, while the traditional distributed system is run by a DOS, a DOS is not supposed to manage a collection of *independent computers* (as are present in clusters). On the other hand, a network of computers in a computer network being run by a NOS never provides a view of a *single coherent system* (which is what a cluster looks like). So neither DOS nor NOS really qualifies as part of a distributed system in this regard. The obvious question thus arises as to whether it is possible to develop a distributed system that could be run in such a way that it could possess most of the salient features of these two different domains (DOS and NOS environments), such as the transparency and related ease of use provided by DOS and the scalability and openness offered by NOS. One viable solution in this regard was attempted simply by way of enhancement to the services that a NOS provides, such that better support for distribution transparency could be realized. To implement these enhancements, it was then decided to include a layer of software with a NOS in order to improve its distribution transparency and also to more or less hide the heterogeneity in the collection of underlying systems. This additional layer is known as **middleware**, which lies at the heart of cluster-based modern distributed systems currently being built.

The use of a middleware layer of software as included in each computer to build a cluster in a computer network provides a means of realizing **horizontal distribution** by which applications and resources (both software and hardware) are made physically distributed and replicated across multiple machines (computers), thereby providing a distributed nature to the underlying computer networks. In addition, the architecture of underlying computer networks in the form of multi-tiered (client–server) organization inherently offers **vertical distribution** (see multi-tiered architecture, Chakraborty, 2020 and also Chapter 9 of this book). Consequently, cluster architecture when built with server-based hardware supported by fitting middleware and managed by an appropriate operating system (discussed later) can ultimately provide distribution both in the horizontal as well as vertical sense, leading to a feasible implementation of a large-scale distributed system. Middleware-based distributed systems, however, generally adopt a specific model for expressing distribution and communication. Popular models are mainly based on *remote procedure calls*, *distributed files*, *objects*, and *documents*.

Whatever the hardware configuration and arrangement of the cluster, it requires a specific type of operating system and related system software so that this form of distributed computing system can cast a single-system image to the user. An operating system that can project this view (a single-system image) will, of course, be of a special type and will be different for different cluster architectures and is thus essentially required to be fully matched with the underlying respective cluster hardware. Details of cluster architectures and related systems are given in detail in Chapter 9.

1.6.7 REAL-TIME OPERATING SYSTEMS

A real-time operating system (RTOS) is another form of operating system that evolved to meet certain demands. In a class of applications called *real-time applications* it is mandatory that the computer perform certain courses of actions in a time-bound manner so as to control the activities in an external system or even to be involved in them. Real-time applications are often associated with process control applications. In a real-time environment, the course of action to be taken while an application is in execution are not declared before the start of execution; the requirements are not predetermined. In fact, during the execution of such an application, numerous events, mostly external to the computer system, occur very frequently within a short span of time and demand immediate intervention and appropriate actions. All forms of existing operating systems already in use have been developed with a time-sharing design that switches tasks on a clock interrupt as well as on events to attain different targets, either optimal resource utilization or user friendliness and hence are unable to manage a real-time environment.

The proposed operating system should provide necessary support to negotiate the environment while an *event changes* by quickly switching the control from the current event to another targeted event by way of immediately servicing the appropriate interrupt. In doing so, the OS is ready to ignore, and may even sacrifice, its prime responsibilities of resource utilization and user convenience. Indeed, this operating system is essentially an event-driven OS which changes tasks only when an event requires service. It can accept a large number of events and is guaranteed to process them within a short period or within a fixed deadline. Even if it fails to meet the deadline, it continues with its work to provide service rather than simply discarding the service request. The design principle of RTOS is thus entirely different and implements certain specific policies, strategies, and techniques in order to shorten event-response times (not only to speedup execution) and to quickly service bursts of thousands of interrupts without missing a single one. To achieve this target, interrupt servicing required at the time of change in events are sometimes promoted from their natural level (kernel level) as supervisor processes to user level as user processes for the sake of directly managing the events, and thereby permitting the application to have greater control on the operating environment without requiring OS intervention.

The applications being handled by these operating systems are found mostly in embedded applications like programmable thermostats used in the cooling process of nuclear reactors, mobile telephones, industrial robots and scientific research equipment, household appliance controllers, process-controlled industrial systems, guided control of missiles, flight control in aviation, switching systems in telecommunication, interactive graphics, and different forms of real-time simulations. A schematic diagram of a real-time environment and participation of RTOS is shown in Figure 1.6.

Two kinds of real-time systems have essentially evolved depending on the specific policies, strategies, and techniques that are to be realized in OS implementation. A *hard real-time system* is typically *dedicated* to processing real-time applications and perhaps strictly meets the *response requirements* of an application under all possible conditions. A *soft real-time system* does its best

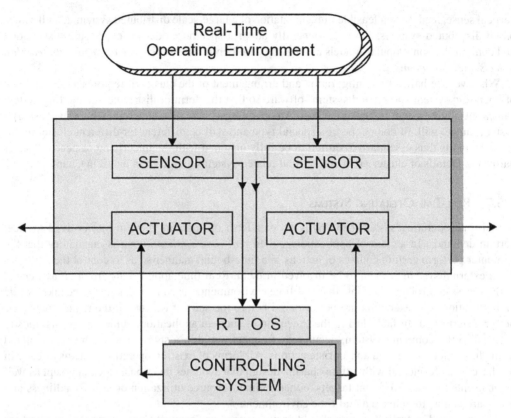

FIGURE 1.6   Hardware model of representative real-time system controlled by Real-Time Operating System (RTOS).

to meet the underlying response requirement of a real-time application but cannot guarantee it will meet it under all conditions. Typically, it meets the response requirements in a probabilistic manner, say, 95% of the time. Control applications like nuclear reactor control, flight control in aviation, and guided control of a missile miserably fail if they cannot meet the response time requirement. Hence, they must be serviced using hard real-time systems. Other types of real-time applications like reservation systems and banking operations do not have any notion of such failure; hence they may be serviced using soft real-time systems. Hard real-time systems should not be used in situations with features whose performance cannot be predicted precisely.

The provision of *domain specific interrupts* and associated interrupt servicing actions facilitates a real-time system to quickly respond to *special conditions* and *events* in the external system within a fixed deadline. When resources are overloaded, hard real-time systems sometimes partition resources and allocate them permanently to competing processes in applications. This reduces OS overhead by way of avoiding repeated execution of the allocation mechanisms done by the OS that summarily allow processes to meet their response time requirements, thereby compromising with the resource utilization target of the system.

A RTOS is thus valued more for efficiency, that is, how quickly and/or predictably it can respond to a particular event, than for the given amount of work it can perform over time. An early example of a large-scale RTOS was the so-called "control program" developed by American Airlines and IBM for the Sabre Airline Reservations System.

The key secret in the success of RTOS lies in the design of its *scheduler*. As every event in the system gives rise to a separate process and to handling a large number of almost-concurrent events, the corresponding processes are arranged in order of priority by the scheduler. The operating system thus emphasizes processor management and scheduling and concentrates less on memory and file management. The RTOS usually allocates the processor to the highest-priority process among those in a ready state. Higher-priority processes are normally allowed to preempt and interrupt the execution of lower-priority processes, if required, that is, to force them to go from an executing state to ready state at any point as per demand of the situation.

Many such processes simultaneously exist, and these must be permanently available in main memory with needed protection, not only for realizing a quick response but also to enable them to closely cooperate with one another at certain times to manage current needs. The processes are, however, seldom swapped to and from main memory.

Another area RTOSs focus on is time-critical device management. For example, a telecommunication system carries out an exchange of information on communication lines by way of transmitting sequence of bits. For error-free message transmission, each and every bit must be received correctly. A bit, while on the line, remains intact only for a very short time known as a *bit period*. The system must respond within this critical time period (bit period) before it gets lost; otherwise erroneous message transmission may happen.

File management is not very important and not even present in most real-time systems. For example, many embedded real-time systems used as controllers, like aviation controllers used in flight control and ballistic missile control have no provision of secondary storage for storing files and their management. However, larger installations with RTOS have this management with almost the same requirements as is found in conventional multiprogramming with time-sharing systems. The main objective of this file management is again to meet time-critical criteria: more emphasis on the *speed of file access* rather than building up an efficient file system for optimal utilization of secondary storage space and user convenience.

RTOS maintains the continuity of its operation even when faults occur. In fact, RTOS usually employs two techniques to negotiate such situations: *fault tolerance* and *graceful degradation*. Fault tolerance is realized by using redundancy of resources (the presence of more resources than the actual requirement) to ensure that the system will keep functioning even if a fault occurs; for example, the system may have two disks even though the application actually requires only one. The other one will actually take charge when a fault occurs in the operating disk. *Graceful degradation* implies that when a fault occurs, the system can fall back to a reduced level of service and subsequently revert when the fault is rectified. In this situation, the user assigns high priorities to critical functions so that those will be performed in a time-bound manner within a specified time even when the system runs in degraded mode.

Designers of RTOSs are quite aware of these and other facts and accordingly developed these systems in order to achieve all these objectives and many others. Different types of RTOSs are thus designed and developed with numerous important features so as to attain their different respective goals. However, some common features, as summarized in the following, must be present in any type of RTOSs. Those are:

- Permits priorities to be assigned to processes.
- Uses priority-driven preemptive scheduling or deadline-oriented scheduling.
- Permits creation of multiple processes within an application.
- Permits a user to define interrupts and related interrupt-servicing routines.
- Provides necessary arrangements to cope with the situation when a fault occurs.

However, more recent RTOSs are found to have almost invariably implemented time-sharing scheduling in addition to priority-driven preemptive scheduling.

1.6.8 GENESIS OF MODERN OPERATING SYSTEMS AND GRAND CHALLENGES

The design and development of modern operating systems have gradually evolved and took a considerable period of the last sixty-odd years to emerge. The first major step was the inclusion of

electronic technology in building the hardware of computer systems, discarding existing mechanical technology, and the concept of the operating system then started to bloom. Computer architecture then progressed through generation after generation, with the sixth generation at present; each
one is, however, distinguished by its own major characteristics. To manage these constantly evolving, more advanced computer systems, different generations of operating systems have continuously
been developed. Sometimes an innovation in design of an operating system awaits the arrival of a
suitable technology for implementation. Market forces also play an important role in encouraging
a particular design feature. Large manufacturers, by their dominance in the market, also promote
certain features. It is interesting to note that despite rapid technological advances, both in hardware
and in software, the design of the logical structure of the operating system as proposed in the 1960s
has progressed rather slowly.

For any change in design of operating system, it demands high cost in related program development and consequently make an impact on the application software run on it. Once the operating
system and related system software of a particular computer become popular and widely accepted,
it is observed that users are very reluctant to switch to other computers requiring radically different
software. Moreover, if the software system comes from a giant manufacturer, a worldwide standard
is enforced by them, and all the newer emerging techniques and methodologies are then implemented by them along the same lines as those of forthcoming members of their family. This has
been observed in operating systems developed by IBM and Microsoft and also in different versions
of Linux/UNIX and Solaris operating systems.

The track of development of operating systems is from single-user operating systems used in
mainframe systems; to batch multiprogramming systems; to timesharing multitasking systems; to
single-user, single-task personal computer-based systems and thereby workstations interconnected
with various forms of networks; and finally DOSs to manage distributed hardware with multiple
processors. An operating system that manages a single computer on its own is popularly known as a
centralized, single-CPU, single-processor, or even *traditional/conventional* operating system. One
of the important aspects in today's computer usage is handling of high volumes of numerous forms
of information generated by individual computer (user) that requires proper sharing and willful
exchange as well as fast simultaneous accesses whenever required by other different computers.
That is why it is observed that essentially all computers in industries, educational institutions, and
government organizations are networked and running under an OS providing adequate protection
from unauthorized access and ensuring free access to all shared resources. This leads us to believe
that the DOS is in coarse-grained form at present, and its fine-grained form is in the future. These
systems also implement multiprogramming techniques inherited from traditional batch and then
timesharing and multitasking systems. The growing complexity of embedded devices has ultimately
led to increasing use of embedded operating systems (RTOS). Figure 1.7 exhibits a schematic evolutionary track in the development of modern operating systems.

Modern operating systems have a GUI using a mouse or stylus for input in addition to using
a command-line interface (or CLI), typically with only the keyboard for input. Both models are
centered around a "shell" that accepts and executes commands from the user (e.g. clicking on a but-
ton or a typed command at a prompt). Choosing an OS mainly depends on the hardware architecture and the associated application environment, but only Linux and BSD run on almost any CPU
and supporting nearly all environments. All Windows versions (both Professional and Server) are
mainly for Intel CPUs, but some of them can be ported to a few other CPUs (DEC Alpha and MIPS
Magnum). Since the early 1990s, the choice for personal computers has largely been limited to the
Microsoft Windows family and the UNIX-like family, of which Linux and Mac OS X are becoming the major alternatives. Mainframe computers and embedded systems use a variety of different
operating systems, many with no direct relation to Windows or UNIX but typically more similar to
UNIX than Windows.

UNIX systems run on a wide variety of machine architectures. They are heavily in use as
server systems in commercial organizations, as well as *workstations* in academic and engineering

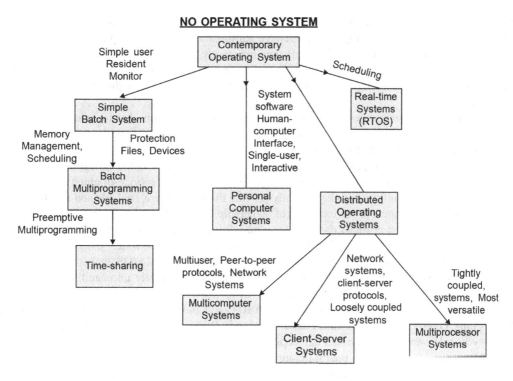

FIGURE 1.7 Graphical presentation of stage-wise evolution of operating systems from its very inception (primitive one) to most modern forms.

environments. Free software UNIX variants, such as Linux and BSD, are increasingly popular and are mostly used in multiuser environments.

The *UNIX-like family*, commonly used to refer to the large set of operating systems that resemble the original UNIX (also an open system), is a diverse group of operating systems, with several major sub-categories, including System V, BSD, and Linux. Some UNIX variants like HP's **HP-UX** and IBM's **AIX** are designed to run only on that vendor's proprietary hardware. Others, such as **Solaris**, can run on both proprietary hardware (SUN systems) and on commodity Intel x86 PCs. Apple's **Mac OS X**, a microkernel BSD variant derived from NeXTSTEP, Mach, and FreeBSD, has replaced Apple's earlier (non-UNIX) Mac OS. Over the past several years, free UNIX systems have supplemented proprietary ones in most instances. For instance, scientific modeling and computer animation were once the province of SGI's IRIX. Today, they are mostly dominated by Linux-based or Plan 9 clusters.

Plan 9 and **Inferno** were designed by Bell Labs for modern distributed environments that later added graphics built-in to their design. Plan 9 did not become popular because it was originally not free. It has since been released under the Free Software and Open Source Lucent Public License and gradually gained an expanding community of developers. Inferno was sold to **Vita Nuova** and has been released under a GPL/MIT license.

The **Microsoft Windows** family of operating systems initially originated as a graphical layer on top of the older MS-DOS environment, mainly for IBM PCs, but also for DEC Alpha, MIPS, and PowerPC, and, as of 2004, it ultimately held a near-monopoly of around 90% of the worldwide desktop market share. Modern standalone Windows versions were based on the newer **Windows NT** core borrowed from **OpenVMS** that first took shape in **OS/2**. They were also found in use on low-end and mid-range servers, supporting applications such as web servers, mail servers, and database servers as well as enterprise applications. The next addition to the Microsoft Windows family was **Microsoft Windows XP**, released on October 25, 2001, and then many others, and finally its next generation of Windows named **Windows Vista** (formerly Windows Longhorn), adding new functionality in security and network administration, and a completely new front-end known as *Windows-Black-Glass*. Microsoft then constantly kept releasing newer and newer versions of Windows, upgrading the latest member of its family with many novel, distinct, important features applicable to both individual computing as well as server-based distributed computing environments.

Older operating systems, however, are also in use in niche markets that include the versatile Windows-like system **OS/2** from IBM; **Mac OS**, the non-UNIX precursor to Apple's **Mac OS X**; **BeOS**; **RISC OS**; **XTS-300**; **Amiga OS**; and many more.

As one of the most open platforms today, the mainframe fosters a tighter integration between diverse applications and provides a strong basis for an organization's service-oriented architecture (SOA) deployment. Mainframes today not only provide the most secure, scalable and reliable platform but also demonstrate a lower total cost of ownership (TCO) when compared to a true distributed system. Today, most business data reside on mainframes. Little wonder that it continues to be the preferred platform for large organizations across the globe. The most widely used notable mainframe operating systems that came from IBM, such as **IBM's S/390 and z/OS**, and other embedded operating systems, such as **VxWorks**, **eCos**, and **Palm OS**, are usually unrelated to UNIX and Windows, except for **Windows CE, Windows NT Embedded 4.0**, and **Windows XP Embedded**, which are descendants of Windows, and several ***BSDs** and **Linux** distributions tailored for embedded systems. **OpenVMS** from Hewlett-Packard (formerly DEC) already contributed a lot and is still in heavy use. However, research and development of new operating systems continue both in the area of large mainframes and in the minicomputer environment, including DOSs.

Although the operating system drives the underlying hardware while residing on it, only a small fraction of the OS code actually depends directly on this hardware. Still, the design of the OS precisely varies across different hardware platforms that, in turn, critically restrict its portability from one system to another. Nevertheless, it will be an added advantage if the same developed code can be used directly or by using an interface to produce a multi-modal operating system, such as general-purpose, real-time, or embedded. Moreover, if the design of the OS could be made so flexible that it would allow the system policy to be modified at will to fulfill its different targeted objectives, then developers could take advantage by varying the compile-time directives and installation-time parameters to make the operating system customized, an important aspect in the development of operating system code. Consequently, it could then fulfill the different operating system requirements of a diverse spectrum of user environments, even those with conflicting needs. For example, an OS developed for a desktop computer could be ported to cell phone by using appropriate installation-time parameters, if provided.

The introduction of cluster/server architecture eventually gave the needed impetus for radical improvement both in hardware architecture and organization as well as in sophisticated OS and related system software development for distributed computing (cloud computing) to users on single-user workstations and personal computers. This architecture, however, provides a blend of distributed decentralized and centralized computing using resources that are shared by all clients and maintained on transparent server systems. Resurgence continues in this domain, maintaining a high pace of enhancements culminating in more refined technological and application developments, and these innovative improvements and upgrades are expected to continue relentlessly in the days to come.

SUMMARY

This chapter explains the need for operating systems in computers and in what ways they can help users handle computers with relative ease. The concept of the operating system and its subsequent continuous evolution through different generations, starting from its bare primitive form to today's most modern versions, to manage different, constantly emerging more powerful and sophisticated hardware platforms gradually progressed over a period of the last six decades. The evolution took place from batch processing (resident monitor) and variants of multiprogramming, multitasking, multiuser, multi-access, virtual machine OSs to ultimately distributed systems of different kinds along with other types: real-time systems and embedded systems. Side by side, system software in its primitive form emerged earlier, and its continuous evolution in different forms has met the rising potential of constantly emerging more advanced hardware and operating systems. In this chapter, an overview of the generational developments of generic operating systems was given chronologically and illustrated with representative systems, mentioning each one's salient features and also drawbacks. With the introduction of tiny powerful microprocessors as well as small speedier capacious main memories, more advanced form of hardware organization and architecture were constantly evolved using multiple processors, the significant hardware outcomes are powerful multiprocessors and multicomputer systems. Due to immense success of networks of computers using sophisticated hardware technology, two different types of models (multicomputers), computer networks, and true distributed system, came out. Each requires the service of a different type of sophisticated and complex operating system to manage resources. This gave rise to two different types of operating systems, NOSs and true DOS, each with its own targets and objectives. In recent years, a third alternative, clustering, built on the premise of low-cost computer networks, emerged, which is essentially a base substitute for an expensive true distributed system that provides enormous computational flexibility and versatility. This system, however, needs a completely different type of operating system to work. Another form of operating system called a RTOS evolved to meet demands of different kinds, known as real-time applications. This chapter concludes by discussing the genesis of modern operating systems and the grand challenges of the days to come. Overall, this chapter is a short journey through the evolution of the operating system that lays the foundation of operating system concepts that will be discussed in the rest of this book.

EXERCISES

1. "In the early days of computers, there was no operating system, but there did exist a form of operating system": Justify this statement.
2. What is meant by generations of an operating system? In what ways have they been classified and defined?
3. State and explain the two main functions that an operating system performs. Discuss the role of the system software in the operation of a computer system.
4. Explain the various functions of the different components of the resident monitor.
5. Why was timesharing not wide spread on second-generation computers?
6. Why is spooling considered a standard feature in almost all modern computer systems?
7. How might a timesharing processor scheduler's policy differ from a policy used in a batch system?
8. State and differentiate between multiprogramming, multitasking, and multiprocessing. Multitasking is possible in a single-user environment; explain with an example.
9. What is meant by degrees of multiprogramming? Discuss some factors that must be considered in determining the degree of multiprogramming for a particular system. You may assume a batch system with same number of processes as jobs.
10. A multiprogramming system uses a degrees of multiprogramming $m \geq 1$. It is proposed to double the throughput of the system by modification/replacement of its hardware components. Give your views on the following three proposals in this context.
    a. Replace the CPU with a CPU with double the speed.
    b. Expand the main memory to double its present size.
    c. Replace the CPU with a CPU with double the speed and expand the main memory to double its present size.
11. Three persons using the same time-sharing system at the same time notice that the response times to their programs differ widely. Discuss the possible reasons for this difference.

12. What is meant by interactive systems? What are the salient features of an interactive multiprogramming system? Write down the differences between multi-user and multi-access systems.

13. Discuss the impact and contributions of MULTICS in the development of UNIX operating systems.

14. "The third-generation mainframe operating system is a milestone in the evolution of modern operating systems"—justify the statement, giving the special characteristics of such systems.

15. What is meant by computer networks? "A network operating system is a popular distributed system": justify the statement with reference to the special characteristics of such a system. Discuss the main features of a client–server model.

16. Discuss in brief the salient features and key advantages of the distributed operating system used in a multiprocessor platform.

17. In order to speed up computation in a distributed system, an application is coded as four parts that can be executed on four computer systems under the control of a distributed operating system. However, the speedup as obtained is < 4. Give all possible reasons that could lead to such drop in speed.

18. What are the main characteristics that differentiate a real-time operating system from a conventional uniprocessor operating system? In a multiprogramming system, an I/O-bound activity is given higher priority than non-I/O-bound activities; however, in real-time applications, an I/O-bound activity will be given a lower priority. Why is this so?

19. A real-time application requires a response time of 3 seconds. Discuss the feasibility of using a time-sharing system for the real-time application if the average response time in the time-sharing system is: (a) 12 seconds, (b) 3 seconds, or (c) 0.5 seconds.

20. An application program is developed to control the operation of an automobile. The program is required to perform the following functions:
    a. Monitor and display the speed of the automobile.
    b. Monitor the fuel level and raise an alarm, if necessary.
    c. Monitor the state of the running car and issue an alarm if an abnormal condition arises.
    d. Periodically record auxiliary information like speed, temperature, and fuel level (similar to a black box in an aircraft).
    Comment on the following questions with reasons in regard to this application:
    i.   Is the application a real-time one? Explain with justifications.
    ii. What are the different processes that must be created in order to reduce the response time of the application? What would be their priorities?
    iii. Is it necessary to include any application-specific interrupts? If so, specify the interrupts, when they would appear, and their priorities.

SUGGESTED REFERENCES AND WEBSITES

Andleigh, P. *UNIX System Architecture*, Englewood Cliffs, NJ, Prentice Hall, 1990.

Chakraborty, P. *Computer Organization and Architecture: Evolutionary Concepts, Principles, and Designs*, Boca Raton, FL, CRC Press, 2020.

Liu, J. W. S. *Real-Time Systems*, London, Pearson Edition, 2008.

Tanenbaum, A. S., Van Renesse, R. "Distributed Operating Systems", *ACM Computing Surveys*, vol. 17, pp. 419–470, 1985.

Weizer, N. "A History of Operating Systems", *Datamation*, 1981.

Wolf, W. "A Decade of Hardware/Software Codesign", *Computer*, vol. 36, no.4, pp. 38–43, 2003.

WEBSITES

www.gnu.org/philosophy/free-software-for-freedom.html

2 Operating Systems
Concepts and Issues

Learning Objectives

- To explain the needs of an operating system and to give an overview of the objectives and functions of generic operating system, including its main role as a resource manager.
- To describe in brief the concepts and the general characteristics of the overall organization of an operating system.
- To give an introductory concept of process and its different types, along with the different views when it is observed from different angles.
- To describe the major issues in the design of generic operating systems, including interrupts and its processing, resource sharing and protection, scheduling, and many others.
- To describe interrupts and their different types, along with their working and servicing and their differences from traps.
- To narrate the different types of schedulers and their level-wise organization.
- To articulate the various supports and services offered by an operating system in making use of hardware resources providing the system calls, procedure calls, signals, message passing, pipes, etc. required for various types of processing that help the user control the working environment.
- To introduce the most important common factors with impact on the design of generic operating systems.

2.1 OPERATING SYSTEMS: OBJECTIVES AND FUNCTIONS

The operating system was introduced mainly to relieve the user from the tedious task of managing the computer system. One of its major responsibilities is thus to *manage* the only three fundamental hardware resources, the *processor, memory*, and *I/O devices*, and the most common software resource, the *files*, on behalf of the user. In the course of managing and supervising these resources while they are in operation, it creates an appropriate working environment for executing programs by way of responding to implicit/explicit resource requests issued by the user's program. In fact, resource management is primarily governed by certain policies, and related strategies are then formed based on design objectives such as optimal utilization of resources, efficiency of operation, and, of course, user convenience.

Based on the policy to be employed in the management of resources, operating systems of various types evolved that are differently defined and individually characterized. For example, a centralized time-sharing system while emphasizes on equitable sharing of resources and responsiveness to interactive requests; distributed operating systems, on the other hand, concentrate mainly on resource migration and obviously on distribution of computations. Real-time operating systems have certain other targets that are more concerned with immediate responsive handling of external events generated by the controlled systems. In addition, several functional requirements were demanded by users to get numerous OS services. Thus, the operating system as a resource manager should ensure that both private and shared resources are readily accessible to all relevant users with adequate protection from any unauthorized access.

DOI: 10.1201/9781003383055-2

2.1.1 OPERATING SYSTEMS: RESOURCE MANAGER

Viewing the operating system as a manager of resources, each resource manager must do the following:

1. Keep track of all the related resources.
2. Enforce policy and impose relevant strategy that determines who gets what, when, and how much.
3. Allocate the particular resource.
4. Reclaim (de-allocate) the resource when it is not needed.

To address all these issues while negotiating such complex requirements, a modular approach in operating system design was initially proposed that resulted in group-wise division of all the programs of the operating system into *four* resource categories along with respective major functions to be carried out as detailed.

Processor Management Functions

1. Keep track of the resources (processors and the status of the process). The program that performs this task is called the *traffic scheduler*.
2. Decide who will have a chance to use the processor. The *job scheduler* first chooses from all the jobs submitted to the system and decides which one will be allowed into the system. If multiprogramming, decide which process gets the processor, when, and for how long. This responsibility is carried out by a module known as *process* (or *processor*) *scheduler*.
3. Allocate the resource (processor) to a process by setting up necessary hardware registers. This is often called the *dispatcher*.
4. Reclaim the resource (processor) when the process relinquishes processor usage, terminates, or exceeds the allowed amount of usage.

It is to be noted that the job scheduler is exclusively a part of process (processor) management, mainly because the record-keeping operations for job scheduling and processor scheduling are very similar (job versus process).

Memory Management Functions

1. Keep track of the resources (memory). What parts are in use and by whom? What parts are not in use (called free)?
2. If multiprogramming, decide which process gets memory, when it gets it, and how much.
3. Allocate the resource (memory) when the processes request it and the policy of item 2 allows it.
4. Reclaim the resource (memory) when the process no longer needs it or has been terminated.

Device Management Functions

1. Keep track of the resources (devices, channels, bus, control units); this program is typically called the *I/O traffic controller*.
2. Decide what an efficient way is to allocate the resource (device). If it is to be shared, then decide who gets it and for how long (duration); this is called *I/O scheduling*.
3. Allocate the resource and initiate the I/O operation.
4. Reclaim resource. In most cases, the I/O terminates automatically.

Information (File) Management Functions

1. Keep track of the resources (information) and their location, use, status, and so on. These collective facilities are often called the *file system*.
2. Decide who gets the resources, enforce protection managements, and provide accessing routines.
3. Allocate the resource (information); for example, open a file.
4. Deallocate the resource; for example, close a file.

This approach is the central theme and was sufficient to derive the conceptual design of an operating system in a multiprogramming environment. Optimal management of available hardware resources with almost no human intervention during runtime is a major function that has been achieved with this operating system design. The introduction of faster hardware technologies and techniques, innovative designs with ever-increasing processor speed, memory and other resources, and finally a sharp drop in the cost of computer hardware paved the way for the emergence of a new concept of parallel architecture in the design and organization of computer systems using many CPUs and larger memories. As a result, additional complexities are imposed in the conceptual design of existing operating systems to properly drive this more powerful hardware organization. Further improvements in different directions in the design of operating systems also have occurred in order to provide a *multi-user* environment that requires sharing and separation of local and global hardware resources. A multiprocessor computer system, on the other hand, demands an altogether different type of operating system, a different concept in the design of the operating system that provides a multiprocessing environment. Since the type of fundamental resources present in modern computers remains unchanged, and only the speed, capacity, and number of resources attached have significantly increased, the central theme of resource management by and large remains the same and has been treated as a backbone for all types of emerging concepts in the design of all modern operating systems.

Since, many different modules are present in the operating system for management of various types of resources, one of the major problems faced by operating system designers is how to manage and resolve the complexity of these numerous management functions at many different levels of detail while offering a product that will be sufficiently efficient, reasonably reliable, easy to maintain, and above all convenient for user. However, operating system design in its early stages was proposed and realized in the form of *monolithic structures*. Later, for larger systems, improved versions of this concept were developed in terms of a *hierarchy of levels* (*layers*) of abstraction with an aim to *hide information* where the details of algorithms and related data structures being used in each manager are confined within respective module. Each module is entrusted to perform a set of specific functions on certain objects of a given type. However, the details of any module's operation and the services it provides are neither visible/available nor of concern to its users. The details of this approach are cited and explained in later sections.

Now, the obvious question raised is how the operating system handles a user's job when it is submitted, and in which way, and at what instant, all these different resource managers will come into action.

2.2 PROCESS: CONCEPTS AND VIEWS

A **job** submitted to the operating system is a predefined sequence of commands, programs, and data that are combined into a single unit performing the activities needed to do the required work. A job may be divided into several steps known as **job steps**. Job steps are units of work that must be done sequentially. For example, if a user submits a job (program) written in a high-level language, the job essentially consists of three steps: *compile, load*, and *execute*.

Once the operating system accepts a user's job, it may create several *processes*. The notion of a process is central to operating systems. A **process** (or **task**) is essentially an *activity* of some kind. Each such activity comprises one or more operations. To realize each operation, one or more instructions must be executed. Thus, process is obtained while a set of such instructions is executed, and these instructions are primitive (machine) instructions and not the user's. In fact, a *process* is a fundamental entity that requires resources (hardware and software) to accomplish its task. Alternatively, a process is actually a piece of computation that can be considered the basis of the execution of a program. In brief, a process is considered the *smallest unit of work* that is individually created, controlled, and scheduled by the operating system.

Thus, a process is precisely an *instance* of a program in execution. For example, the "copy" program is simply a collection of instructions stored in the system. But when this "copy" program runs on a computer, it gives rise to a process, the "copy" process. Multiple processes can be executing the same program. Processes are considered a primary operating-system mechanism for defining, determining, and managing concurrent execution of multiple programs.

A different approach in expressing processes is to consider them *agents* representing the intent of users. For example, when a user wants to compile a program, a process (compilation process) runs a different specific program (compiler) that accepts the user program as data and converts the user program into another form, known as an object program. When the user wants to execute the object program, a process (perhaps a new one) runs a different program (linker) that knows how to convert the object program into a new form to make it runnable (executable). In general, processes run specific appropriate programs that help the user achieve a goal. While performing their task, the processes may also need help from the operating system for such operations as calling specific programs and placing the converted program in long-term storage. They require resources, such as space in the main storage and machine cycles. The resource principle says that the operating system is the owner while allocating such resources.

Another view of a **process** is the locus of points of a processor (CPU or I/O) executing a collection of programs. The operation of the processor on a program is a process. The collection of programs and data that are accessed in a process forms an **address space**. An address space of a job is defined as the area of main memory occupied by the job. Figure 2.1 depicts the relationship between *user, job, process,* and *address space,* with two sample address spaces, one for the CPU process, the other for an I/O process. The operating system must map the *address spaces* of processes into physical memory. This task may be assisted by special hardware (e.g. a paged system), or it may be primarily performed by software (e.g. a swapping system).

However, we now start with the CPU, the most important resource, required by every user, so we need an abstraction of CPU usage. We define a *process* as the OS's representation of an executing program so that we can allocate CPU time to it. Apart from executing user jobs, the CPU is also often engaged in performing many other responsibilities, mainly servicing all types of operating system requests by way of executing related *OS programs* to manage all the existing resources and to create the appropriate environment for the job under execution to continue. All these CPU activities are, by and large, identical and are called *processes* but give rise to different types of processes, namely **user processes** and **OS processes**.

This process abstraction turns out to be convenient for other resource management and usage besides the CPU, such as memory usage, file system usage (disk/tape), network usage, and number of sub-processes (i.e. further CPU utilization), which are all assigned on a per-process basis.

When a particular program code resident in memory is shared by more than one user at the same time, this memory sharing will result in different processes displaced in time and probably in data. Thus processes are truly a *unit of isolation.* Two processes cannot directly affect each other's behavior without making explicit arrangements to do so. This isolation extends itself to more general security concerns. Processes are tied to users, and the credentials of running on a user's behalf determine what resources the process can use.

It should be noted that there exists a *clean and clear distinction* between a program and a process. A program consists of static instructions which can be stored in memory. A program is thus basically a static, inanimate entity that defines process behavior when executed on some set of data.

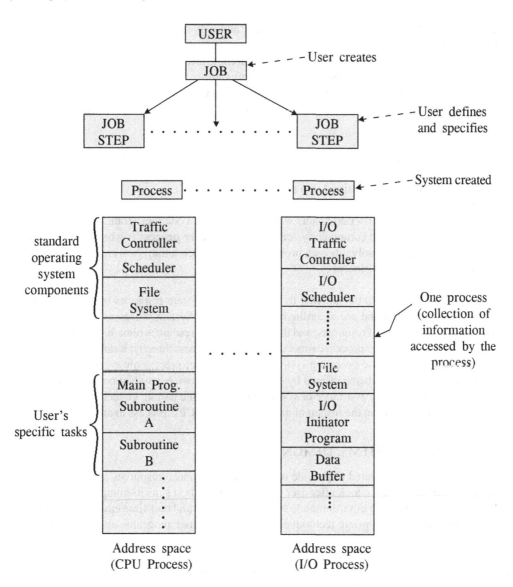

FIGURE 2.1   In a generic operating system, the relationship between User, Job, and Process when mapped by the operating system in two sample address spaces; one for the CPU process, and the other for an I/O process.

A process, on the other hand, is a dynamic entity consisting of a sequence of *events* that result due to execution of the program's instructions. A process has a beginning, undergoing frequent changes in states and attributes during its lifetime, and finally has an end. The same code program can result in many processes. While a program with branch instruction is under execution, the CPU may leave the normal sequential path and traverse different paths in the address space depending on the outcome of the execution of branch instructions present in the program. Each locus of the CPU, while traversing these different paths in address space, is a different process. A single executable program thus may give rise to one or more processes.

Although process is considered the classic unit of computation, some modern operating systems have a specialized concept of one or both of two additional fundamental units of computation: **threads** and **objects**. We will discuss these two units later in this chapter. It is true that there exists no explicit relationship between threads and objects, although some designers have used threads to realize (implement) objects. While most operating systems use the process concept as the basis of threads or objects, a few systems, however, implement these alternatives directly in the design of the operating system as well as in higher-level system software.

A further description of the process when viewed from different angles, such as the user, operating system, and system programmer views, is given on the Support Material at www.routledge.com/9781032467238.

2.2.1 PROCESS TYPES

Processes by nature can be classified into two types:

A **system process** (**OS process**) results when the operating system program is under execution to initiate and manage computer-system resources. *A* **user process** is when a user program is under execution to solve its own problems. A user process may, however, be of two types: CPU process and I/O process.

User processes compete with one another to gain control of system resources by way of requesting operating-system services and are accordingly assigned them. System processes, on other hand, are assigned with an initial set of resources, and these pre-assigned resources remain unaltered during the lifetime of the process. A user process cannot create another process directly; it can only create another process by issuing requests to operating system services. A user process always has a program data block (PDB) for its own use being offered by the operating system, but system process never requires one. User processes need the assistance of system processes while issuing system service requests for many reasons, for example, at the instant of a transition from a CPU process to an I/O process.

2.3 OPERATING SYSTEMS: DESIGN ISSUES

An operating system is targeted to provide mechanisms to manage resources used by the community of processes as well as to look after user convenience that best suits its computing environment.

With different computing environments, such as interactive and real-time environments, an operating system employs appropriate techniques to best handle user programs and system resources. Although there is no universal agreement about the set of functions required for an OS to perform, for this book, the most widely accepted general framework has been chosen for considering more detailed requirements, design issues, architectures, and subsequent implementation. OS functions thus can be broadly classified into four categories:

- Processor/process management
- Memory management
- Device management
- File management

Each management is characterized by principles, or abstractions, developed to handle difficult practical problems. Taken together, these four areas span the key design and implementation issues of modern operating systems. While carrying out these different management functions to monitor and control the operation of computer resources, the operating system is in control of the computer's basic functions, and the control mechanism being employed, unlike other control systems, is internal to the operating system.

The operating system works in the same way as ordinary computer software does. It is, in fact, nothing more than a computer program executed by the processor. The key difference is in the intent and the target of this program. When the computer system is switched on, a portion of the operating system program is loaded and remains resident in main memory that contains the key functions of the operating system and, at a given time, other portions of the operating system currently in use.

The remainder of the main memory contains other user programs and data. The allocation of this memory space (resource) is controlled jointly by the operating system and memory-management hardware located mainly within the processor. When the operating system program is executed by the processor, the result is that it *directs* the processor to use other system resources and controls the timing of the processor's execution with other programs.

Since the processor itself is a rich resource and has to do many different things, it must cease executing the operating system program and execute other programs. Thus, the operating system has to relinquish control for the processor to allow it to do useful and productive work for the user, and then it resumes control once again at the appropriate time to prepare the processor to do the next piece of work. While the user program is under execution, the different management functions of the operating system will come into operation at different times according to the intent of the user program. For example, the normal activity of any job could be halted by the occurrence of a defined event, such as an I/O instruction or an instruction issued by the user seeking a system service. The operating system decides when an I/O device can be allocated to an executing program and controls access to it (device management) and allows use of files (file management). Switching from one management function to another while the user program is under execution by the processor (processor management) or when request is issued from the user program to the processor to execute the operating–system program, and also for such many other similar reasons, the normal processing of the processor with the user program is summarily hindered to a large extent. This event is known as *interrupt* that simply interrupts the ongoing processing, and in this situation, the operating system must have the provision to intervene, to restore normalcy by way of resolving the interrupt to allow ongoing processing to continue. This principal tool was extensively used by system programmers in the early days of developing multiprogramming and multi-user interactive systems.

2.3.1 Event: A Fundamental Concept

An event is any occurrence that requires the attention of the operating system and subsequently its intervention, for example, a resource request issued by a user program or insufficient memory faced by an executing program. When an event occurs, control of the CPU (or other resources) is passed to the operating system, which then analyzes the event and takes appropriate actions to negotiate it. For example, when a program requests a resource, the OS takes appropriate actions to allocate the resource if it is available. Similarly, when an I/O operation ends, the OS informs the program that requested the I/O operation and then makes necessary arrangements to initiate another I/O operation on the device if one is pending. In all situations, whenever an event occurs, it requires the intervention of the OS, and that is why the operating system is sometimes said to be *event-driven*.

Figure 2.2 illustrates the logical view of the functioning of an operating system when it is event-driven. In the corresponding physical view, the end of an I/O operation or a resource request by a program, for example, causes an *event* (*interrupt*) to occur in the computer system. The OS takes

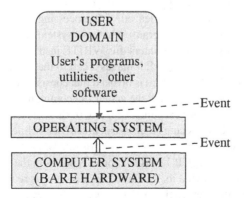

FIGURE 2.2   Location and logical view of functioning of the operating system when it is event-driven in a computing environment.

care of the situation, and does what is needed to service the event. Consequently, an event handler routine (interrupt servicing routine) provided by the OS is executed by the CPU to resolve the event. This physical view is one of the basics for developing a concept about the operating system and its working that will help to formulate the set of functions required in its design.

2.3.2 INTERRUPTS AND TRAPS

All contemporary computers provide a mechanism that gives rise to an interrupt, by which the other resources (I/O modules, memory) may get control, interrupting the normal processing of the processor. The operating system exploits this *interrupt hardware* facility to allow and coordinate multiple simultaneously operations in order to improve processing efficiency.

Interrupts are unusual and exceptional events but quite natural. An interrupt is a mechanism by which a processor is forced to take note of an event. The event forces the CPU to make a temporary transfer of control from its currently executing program to another program (interrupt service routine (ISR)), a part of the operating system program that resolves the event. Interrupt is not a routine called from the user program; rather, the interrupt can occur at any time and at any point in the execution of a user program. Its occurrence is unpredictable. Interrupts are caused by events induced by a variety of sources internal and external to the CPU over which the CPU has no control. The most common **classes of interrupts** are:

- **I/O**: Generated by an I/O module to signal normal completion of an I/O operation or to signal various types of error conditions that occur during I/O execution.
- **Program**: Generated by some condition that occurs as a result of an execution, such as division by zero, arithmetic overflow, violation of protection in memory space, attempt to execute an illegal machine instruction, or many other reasons.
- **Hardware**: Generated by a failure such as memory parity error or even power failure.
- **Clock (Timer)**: One very important interrupt is generated by a device called the **clock** within the processor. Clocks can be designed to interrupt periodically (for example, every 60th part of a second) or to accept an interval from the computer and interrupt when that time has expired. If it were not for clock interrupts, a running process could sit in an accidental infinite loop that may not be in a position to perform any service calls, and the OS would never be able to wrest control from it. The OS, therefore, depends on the clock to enforce and gain access back to its control so that it can make new policy decisions.

User applications always start with the CPU in control. Interrupts are the primary means by which I/O systems obtain the services of the CPU. With an interrupt, the performance of the computer is greatly increased by allowing I/O devices to continue with their own operations while the processor can be engaged in executing other instructions in parallel.

Figure 2.3 shows the interrupt in an application program from the system point of view. Here, the user program has a WRITE instruction interleaved with processing. This WRITE instruction is basically a call to a WRITE program (an I/O program), which is a system utility that will perform the actual I/O operation. When the user program encounters this WRITE instruction during execution, as shown in Figure 2.3, normal execution is interrupted; it makes a call to the operating system in the form of a WRITE call. In this case, the WRITE program is invoked that consists of a set of instructions for preparation (initiation) of the real I/O operation and the actual I/O command which drives the I/O device to perform the requested functions. After execution of a few of these instructions, control returns to the user program, allowing the CPU to execute other instructions. Meanwhile, the I/O device remains busy accepting data from computer memory and printing it. In this way, this I/O operation is carried out simultaneously and overlaps with the CPU's instruction executions in the user program.

When the I/O device has completed its scheduled operation or is ready to accept more data from the CPU, the I/O module for that device then sends an *interrupt-request* signal to the processor. The

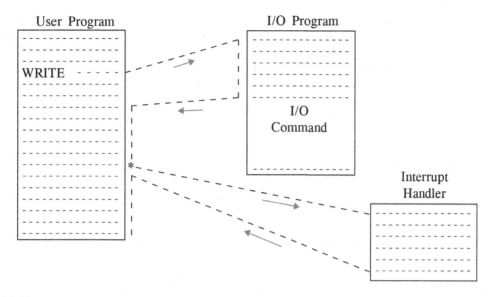

FIGURE 2.3 In an executing program, the program flow of control when an interrupt occurs, indicated by an asterisk (*) in the respective instruction of the program.

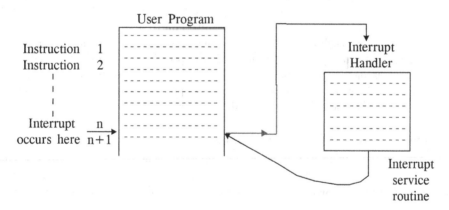

FIGURE 2.4 The mechanism of servicing an interrupt when viewed by a user.

processor immediately responds by suspending its own operation on the current program, branching off to execute the *interrupt handler* program to service that particular I/O device, and then back once again to resume its original execution after the device is serviced. The point at which the interrupt occurs is indicated by an asterisk (*) in Figure 2.3.

From the *user program* point of view, an interrupt is an event that breaks the normal sequence of program execution, and the CPU is then temporarily diverted to execute the corresponding ISR. When the execution of this ISR routine is over, the interrupt processing (servicing) is completed, and control once again comes back to resume the original interrupted program from the point where control was transferred, as illustrated in Figure 2.4. Thus, the user program need not have any special code to accommodate interrupts; the processor and operating system are jointly responsible for suspending the user program and subsequently resuming it from the point it left off. In brief, interrupts are used primarily to request the CPU to *initiate* a new operation, to signal the *completion* of an I/O operation, and to signal the occurrences of hardware and software errors or failures.

A key concept related to interrupt is *transparency*. When an interrupt happens, actions are taken, and a program (ISR) runs, but when everything is finished, the computer should be returned to exactly the same state as it was before the occurrence of the interrupt. An interrupt routine that has this property is said to be **transparent**. Having all interrupts be transparent makes the entire interrupt process a lot easier to understand.

Traps are essentially interrupts but are generated *internally* by a CPU and associated with the execution of the current instruction and result from programming errors or exceptional conditions such as an attempt to:

1. Divide by zero
2. Floating-point overflow
3. Integer overflow
4. Protection violation
5. Undefined op-code
6. Stack overflow
7. Start non-existent I/O device
8. Execute a privileged instruction (system call) when not in a privileged (supervisor mode) state

With a **trap**, the operating system determines whether the error is fatal. If so, the currently running process is abandoned, and switching to a new process occurs. If not, then the action of the operating system will depend on the nature of the error and the design of the operating system. It may go on to attempt a recovery procedure, or it may simply alert the user. It may even carry out a switch of process, or it may resume the currently running process (*see also processor modes*: *mode bit*).

The essential *difference* between *interrupts* and *traps* is that traps are synchronous with the program, and interrupts are asynchronous. If the program is rerun a million times with the same input, traps will reoccur in the same place each time, but interrupts may vary, depending on the run-time environment. The reason for the reproducibility of traps and irreproducibility of interrupts is that traps are caused directly by the program and solved by jumping to a procedure called a *trap handler*, and interrupts are, at best, indirectly caused by the program.

2.3.2.1   Interrupt—How It Works—Processing

An interrupt is a response to an asynchronous or exceptional event that automatically saves the current CPU status to allow a later restart and then causes an automatic transfer to a specified routine called an interrupt handler (ISR). Interrupts should be hidden deep in the bowels of the operating system so that as little of the system as possible knows about them.

2.3.2.2   Interrupt Processing (Servicing)

When the interrupt *begins*, the following steps (in a simplified form) are executed:

Hardware Actions

1. The device controller issues an interrupt signal to tell the processor to start the interrupt sequence.
2. The processor completes its execution on the current instruction before responding to the interrupt. However, an immediate response is sometimes required with no waiting for the completion of the current instruction to service time-critical interrupts. Such an immediate response will result in the loss of the current instruction processing.
3. As soon as the CPU is prepared to handle the interrupt, it asserts an interrupt acknowledge signal on the bus to the device that issued the interrupt. This acknowledgement ensures the device removes its interrupt signal.
4. When the device controller finds that its interrupt signal has been acknowledged, it puts a small integer on the data line to identify itself. This number is called the *interrupt vector*.
5. The CPU takes the interrupt vector from the bus and saves it temporarily.

6. The CPU now prepares to transfer control to the ISR. It needs to save the information needed in the future to resume the current program again after servicing the interrupt. The minimum information required to save is the program status word (PSW) and the address of the next instruction to be executed, which is contained in the program counter (PC). The CPU saves the PC and PSW onto the system control stack (see Figure 2.5a).

7. The CPU then locates a new PC by using the interrupt vector as an index in a table at the bottom of memory. If the PC is 4 bytes, for example, then interrupt vector n corresponds to address $4n$ in the table. This new PC points to the start of the ISRs for the device causing the interrupt. Loading the PC with the starting address of the appropriate interrupt-handling program that will respond to the specified interrupt depends on the architecture of the computer and the design of the operating system, because there may be different programs for different types of interrupts and even for different types of devices.

Once the PC has been loaded, the current content of the PC eventually results in the transfer of control to the beginning of the interrupt-handling program. The start of the execution of this program begins the software actions resulting in the following operations:

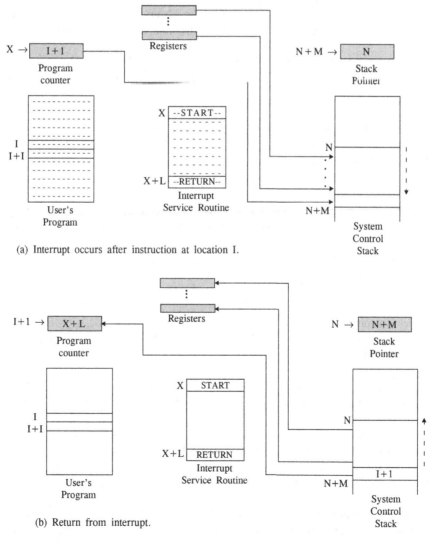

FIGURE 2.5 When an interrupt is serviced, the changes made in memory, registers and stack.

Software Actions

1. The first thing the ISR does is to save all the processor registers on a system control stack or in a system table so that they can be restored later, because these registers may be used by the current program (interrupt handler). Any other "state" information may also need to be saved. For example, as shown in Figure 2.5, assume that a user program is interrupted after the instruction at location I. The contents of all of the registers and the address of the next instruction are now pushed on to the system control stack. The stack pointer is gradually changed due to this pushing and accordingly updated from its initial content to the new top of the stack. The PC is now updated to point to the beginning address of the ISR.

2. Each interrupt vector is generally shared by all devices of a given type (such as a terminal), so it is not yet known which terminal caused the interrupt. The terminal number can be found by reading a device register.

3. Any other information about the interrupt, such as status codes, can now be read in.

4. If an I/O error occurs, it can be handled here. If required, a special code is output to tell the device or the interrupt controller that the interrupt has been processed.

5. Restore all the saved registers (Figure 2.5b).

6. The final step is to restore the PSW and PC values from the stack. This ensures that the next instruction to be executed will be the instruction from the previously interrupted program.

7. Execute the *RETURN FROM INTERRUPT* instruction, putting the CPU back into the mode and state it had just before the interrupt happened. The computer then continues as though nothing had happened.

Like subroutines, interrupts have linkage information, such that a return to the interrupted program can be made, but more information is actually necessary for an interrupt than a subroutine because of the random nature of interrupts.

2.3.2.3 Multiple Interrupts

There are various circumstances in which it is necessary to *prohibit interrupts*. For example, when an I/O interrupt occurs for a device, the current status is stored in the I/O's old PSW location. While processing this interrupt, if another I/O interrupt occurs for another device, the current status is again required to be stored in the I/O's old PSW location, destroying its previous contents. As a result, the original PSW will be lost, and it will then be impossible to restore the original condition. This situation is normally handled by either

1. Completely prohibiting interrupts while processing an interrupt, or

2. Temporarily masking interrupts until the old PSW is safely copied and stacked elsewhere. This is called **interrupt queuing**.

When an ISR completes its execution, the processor checks to see if other interrupts have already occurred. If so, the queued interrupts are then handled in strict sequential order, as shown in Figure 2.6.

This approach is nice and simple, but the drawback is that it does not consider the relative priority or time-critical needs of interrupts waiting in the queue. For example, when an interrupt is issued by a communication line at the time of input arrival, it may need to be serviced immediately to allow the next input to come. If the first set of input has not been processed before the second set arrives, data may be lost.

So another approach in interrupt processing is to accommodate the *priorities* of interrupts. This means that while a lower-priority interrupt processing is under execution, a higher-priority interrupt

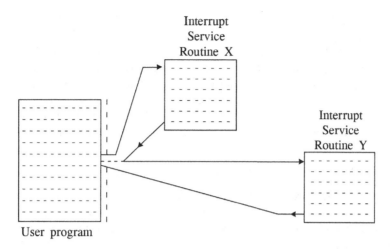

FIGURE 2.6   All the interrupts lying in queue, when the current interrupt is under processing, are then serviced in strict sequential order one after another.

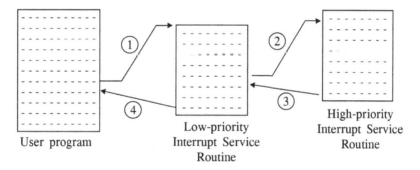

FIGURE 2.7   A higher-priority interrupt interrupts the ongoing lower-priority interrupt processing, and the control is transferred accordingly.

can interrupt the ongoing interrupt processing, and the higher-priority interrupt processing will be started. When this servicing is over, the interrupted lower-priority interrupt processing will once again resume, and when this processing completes, control finally returns to the user program. The flow of control of this approach is shown in Figure 2.7.

2.3.2.4   Interrupt Vectors

When an interrupt occurs, the hardwired interrupt handling system saves everything in regard to current CPU state and loads the PC with the starting address of the required ISR. Now the question arises: How does the interrupt handling system know about the starting address? There are various ways to provide this information. The way the processor chooses the branch address of the service routine varies from unit to unit. In principle, there are *two methods* for accomplishing this branching.

1. **Non-vectored interrupts**: When a branch address is assigned to a *fixed location* in memory.
2. **Vectored interrupt**: Here, the source that interrupts supplies the branch information to the computer, and the PC is modified accordingly for appropriate branching. This information is the starting address of the interrupt-handling program or **transfer vector** and

is also called the **interrupt vector**. This is the fastest and most flexible response to interrupts, since this causes a direct hardware-implemented transition to the correct interrupt-handling routine. This technique, called *vectoring*, can be implemented in a number of ways. In some computers, the interrupt vector is the first address of the I/O service routine. In other computers, the interrupt vector is an address that points to a location in memory where the beginning address of the I/O service routine is stored. This is illustrated in Figure 2.8. In Intel 80386, the interrupt vectors are 8-byte *segment descriptors*, and the table containing the address of the *ISRs* can begin anywhere in memory.

2.3.3 RESOURCE SHARING AND PROTECTION

In principle, computer resources, both abstract and physical, should be shared among a set of concurrently executing programs for optimal utilization in order to increase system performance. This sharing can be broadly classified into two types: **space–multiplexed** and **time–multiplexed**. *Space-multiplexed* sharing indicates that the resource can be physically or logically divided into two or more units. Each different unit can be individually allocated to each of many executing programs, and in this way, different executing programs or *processes* can be given exclusive

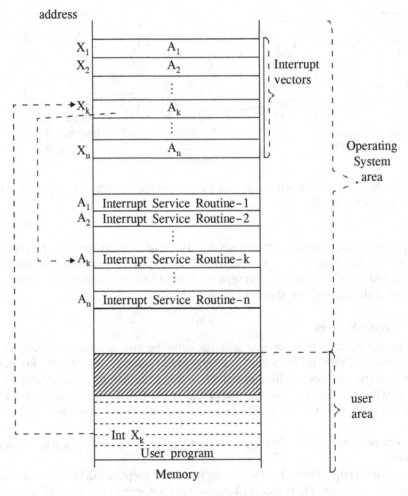

FIGURE 2.8 Interrupt vectors in memory point to locations in memory where the beginning addresses of the respective interrupt service routines are stored.

control of different units of a resource at the same time. Memory and I/O devices are examples of space-multiplexed resources. In the case of *time-multiplexed* sharing, a resource will not be divided into units. Instead a program or a process will be allocated to get exclusive control of the entire resource for a short specified period of time. After this specified time, the resource will be de-allocated from the currently executing process and will then be allocated to another. Time-multiplexing is usually done with the processor resource. Under this scheme, a single processor in the machine is switched among processes which are holding also other resources, like memory space and I/O devices. In this way, it creates an illusion to the user that the concurrently executing processes are really running simultaneously, although the fact is that the execution is strictly sequential. Hence, while referencing concurrent execution, it means that either the execution may actually be simultaneous (in the case of a multiprocessor) or that the single processor is time-multiplexed based on certain pre-defined allocation policy (scheduling) across a set of processes holding space-multiplexed resources.

While encouraging and allowing resource sharing, the operating system should enforce *resource isolation*. This means that the system must be reliable to isolate resource access with sufficient protection based on a certain pre-defined allocation policy (scheduling). The system must also be able to allow resources to share co-operatively when it is required, without creating damage. For example, the operating system must provide a memory isolation and protection mechanism that should ensure loading of two or more programs in different parts of memory at the same time. It should not only provide sufficient protection to prevent any unauthorized access but ensure that neither program will be able to change or reference the memory contents being used by the other program. The operating system must guarantee that the OS codes are kept well protected, allowing *sharing* while in main memory, but are not overwritten by any user program. *Protection hardware* is often used by the operating system to implement such control access to parts of memory.

Similarly, the processor isolation mechanism should insist the processes sequentially share the processor according to a pre-defined allocation policy (scheduling). The processor should also be protected from being indefinitely monopolized by any user program for any unforeseen reason. For example, due to an error in the user program, the CPU enters an infinite loop and gets stuck with no message to the operating system. In this situation, the system must have some mechanism, with the help of a timer, to interrupt the CPU and take control from the CPU to restore operation. The OS software in all such cases really depends on the available hardware support to implement key parts of the mechanism to fully ensure resource isolation with protection. While the operating system implements the abstraction directly from the physical resources, it provides the basic trusted mechanisms to realize and manage resource sharing.

2.3.4 SCHEDULING AND ITS ROLE

Computer resources, both abstract and physical, are always encouraged and allowed to be shared among a set of concurrently executing programs for their optimal utilization in order to increase system performance. To determine how these resources would be shared and managed, a set of policies and mechanisms have been developed in the operating system that govern *the order* in which the work is to be carried out by a computer system. This mechanism refers to *scheduling*, which can also be called *time management*. Scheduling is, however, based on certain defined policies that are implemented in the operating system, thereby producing a good scheduling algorithm to realize optimal system performance. These policies may also be different for different operating systems and are framed using the predefined criteria of an individual operating system to attain its primary objectives. In fact, the goal of scheduling is to provide good service to the execution of multiple processes that are competing for computing resources. It has been found that one of the keys to success in a multiprogramming/multitasking environment is truly proper scheduling. The designers of operating systems, however, believe that the behavior of the scheduler might be critical to the overall behavior of the entire system.

A **scheduler** is an OS module that decides which job is to be selected next and elects the next process to run. The scheduler is concerned with deciding on policy, enforces this policy, and imposes relevant strategy that determines who gets what, when, and how much, but never provides an implementation mechanism.

We can distinguish several classes of scheduling based on how decisions must be made. **Four types of scheduling** are typically involved, as shown in Figure 2.9. One of these is **I/O scheduling** that takes the decision as to which process's pending I/O request shall be handled by an available I/O device. Each device has a device scheduler that selects a process's I/O request from a pool of processes waiting for the availability of that particular device. This issue is discussed in more detail in the following chapter, "Device Management".

The remaining three types of scheduling are types of **processor scheduling** that are concerned with the assignment of processor/processors to processes in such a way as to attain certain system objectives and performance criteria, such as processor utilization, efficiency, throughput, and response time. This scheduling activity is once again broken down into three separate functions: **long-term**, **medium-term**, and **short-term** scheduling, and the corresponding three types of schedulers are long-term, medium-term, and short-term schedulers. All of them may sometimes simultaneously exist in a complex operating system, as depicted in Figure 2.9.

2.3.4.1   The Long-Term Scheduler: Job Scheduler

The long-term scheduler decides which jobs or job steps (programs) are to be added to the system to start processing next. In a spooling system, when a job is submitted, it joins the batch queue and remains there waiting to be processed. When a job finishes and departs the system, this scheduler is invoked, which then makes a decision to select a particular job from the queue and then allows it to enter the system for processing. This selection is carried out based on a number of factors, such as the order of arrival of the jobs, their priorities, and many other important parameters. In batch multiprogramming/multitasking, the decision may be based on the different requirements of the competing jobs and the resources currently available. Interactive multiprogramming often does not have this level of scheduling at all; it is up to the user to decide which job steps to run. An example of this type of scheduler is a **job scheduler**.

In the case of batch jobs, the job scheduler usually obtains certain information either given by the programmer at the time of job submission or system-assigned estimates, such as size of the job

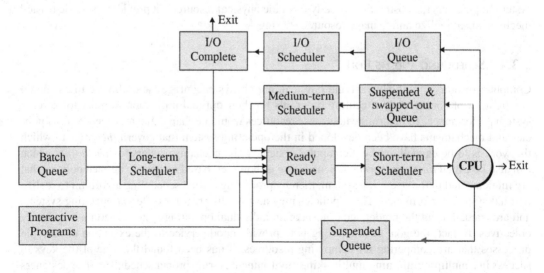

FIGURE 2.9 Four-types of schedulers in a modern uniprocessor operating system and their operational interactions and relationships.

(memory requirement), device requirements, expected execution time, and other related information about the job. Being equipped with such knowledge beforehand, the job scheduler could then select a job from its queue that would ensure system balance, that is, to maintain a proper mix of a desired proportion of processor- and I/O-bound jobs in the system depending on the current environment of the system and availability of resources at that moment.

The long-term scheduler acts here as a first-level regulatory valve in attempting to always keep resource utilization at the desired level. If the scheduler at any point in time detects that processor utilization has fallen below the desired level, it may admit more processor-bound jobs into the system to increase the number of processes to attain system balance. Conversely, when the utilization factor becomes high due to the presence of too many processor-bound jobs in the system, as reflected in the response time, it may opt to reduce the admission rate of batch-jobs accordingly. Since this scheduler is usually invoked whenever a job is completed and departs the system, the frequency of invocation is thus both system- and workload-dependent, but it is generally much lower than that of the other two types of scheduler. The invocation of this scheduler usually occurs after a relatively long time, hence its name.

Since an exact estimate of the workload's characteristics is not regularly available, and the presence of several parameters and their various combinations often create situations in the system, all these together ultimately require the scheduler to incorporate rather complex and computationally intensive algorithms while selecting a job to admit into the system. Once scheduled for execution, a job or user program is admitted into the system with a transition of state from dormant (submit)–to–ready and then spawns processes which finally enter the ready queue awaiting the processor allocation controlled by the short-term scheduler. This issue will be discussed in detail in Chapter 4,"Processor Management".

2.3.4.2 The Medium-Term Scheduler

A running process during execution may become suspended or blocked temporarily due to many reasons, such as resources (e.g. main store) being over-committed or an I/O request that cannot be satisfied at the moment or may be for some other reasons. The suspended process cannot proceed any further until the related condition is removed, but it remains there, occupying costly main memory area. It is thus sometimes felt to be beneficial to remove these processes for the time being from main memory to make room for the other eligible processes. In reality, the capacity of main memory may also impose a limit on the number of processes that can remain resident in the system. As a result, due to the presence of many such suspended processes in main memory, the number of ready processes and also their supply in the system may be reduced to such a level that it prevents the system from working efficiently and also impairs functioning of the short-term scheduler, leaving it few or almost no options for willful selection. The suspended process is hence decided to be temporarily removed from main memory, and its image is saved in secondary storage. This mechanism is called **swapping**, and the corresponding process is said to be **swapped out** or *rolled out*. Swapping is a subject of memory management and will be discussed in detail in Chapter 5.

Processes have been swapped out. All the necessary information in regard to disk addresses and other aspects of the swapped-out processes are added and maintained in a separate queue of swapped-out processes which are under the control of the medium-term scheduler. Not all suspended processes are always swapped out; in fact, only a portion of them are sometimes swapped out, and that also when the memory space is found really inadequate to support the existing working environment.

This scheduler can be invoked when memory space becomes available due to vacating of memory space by departing processes or when the supply of ready processes falls below a specified limit. In that situation, swapped-out processes are once again brought back into the main memory at the right point in time by the medium-term scheduler working on its own queue, allowing the selected swapped-out process to resume from the point it left and continue the remaining part of its execution. The process then undergoes a transition of state from suspended to ready. The aim of long-term and medium-term scheduling is primarily for performance improvement related to degrees of multi-programming, where as medium-term scheduling itself is an issue related to memory management. Chapter 5 discusses the intricacies of space management and describes policies for medium-term scheduling.

2.3.4.3   The Short-Term Scheduler: The Process Scheduler

When a job enters the ready queue and spawns into processes, it awaits the processor allocation being done by the **short-term scheduler**, also referred to as **process/processor scheduler**. Short-term scheduling using a chosen set of criteria decides how to share and distribute the computer resources (processor) among all the ready processes that currently need to be carried out in order to maximize system performance. Such decisions may be made frequently (e.g. tens of times each second) in order to provide good service to all the existing processes. Since this scheduler imposes a state transition of processes from *ready to running*, it must be invoked for every process switch (to be discussed in Chapter 4) to select the next process to be run. Most of the OS services under process management thus require frequent invocation of the short-term scheduler as part of their processing. For example, creating a process, deleting a process from the ready list when it finishes, and rescheduling the entire system requires a call to this scheduler, and resuming a suspended process and then adding one as a new entry in the ready list requires a call to this scheduler to determine whether the new one should also become the running process, and, if so, rescheduling and other related actions are then performed.

When the medium- or long-term scheduler schedules a process or a process waits for an I/O event to complete, the process arrives within the control of the short-term scheduler. Processes generally alternate between a computing burst, during which they are in the domain of short-term scheduler, and an I/O burst, during which they are in a wait list. In addition, the short-term scheduler is always invoked to determine whether any significant changes in the global state (such as a running process being suspended or one or more suspended processes needing to be brought back to a ready state) of the system have really happened due to the occurrence of an event, namely *interrupt and I/O completions*, *sending and receiving of signals*, *most operational system calls*, *clock ticks*, and many such others. If it is, the scheduler then takes the appropriate actions to reschedule.

In the case of interactive environments, a user interacting with a process would ideally like to get an immediate response to every command. Interactive programs often directly enter the ready queue just after submission to the OS without being handled by the other schedulers; this scheduler must then take appropriate measures to safeguard the system environment from any unforeseen situation, especially preventing the system from being saturated with a constant influx of such programs. In effect, short-term scheduling is one of the major issues in determining the principles and design of an operating system that should be carefully defined in order to attain certain pre-defined criteria to fulfill its main objectives. This issue will once again be discussed in detail in the area of process scheduling in Chapter 4.

2.3.4.4   Organization of Schedulers: Level Concept

Figure 2.10 shows the three levels of scheduling. Within the domain of short-term scheduling, a process may be either running or ready to run. The short-term scheduler is in charge of deciding which ready process should remain running at any instant. Within the domain of medium-term scheduling, a process may be running (that is, it may have entered the domain of the short-term scheduler), may be ready to run, or may be waiting for some resource like I/O. The medium-term scheduler is in charge of deciding when ready processes should be allowed to enter the domain of the short-term scheduler and when they should leave that domain. This decision is based on an attempt to prevent over-commitment of space, as will be discussed in Chapter 5, as well as a desire to balance compute-bound processes with I/O-bound processes. The long-term scheduler, however, distinguishes only between ready and running processes.

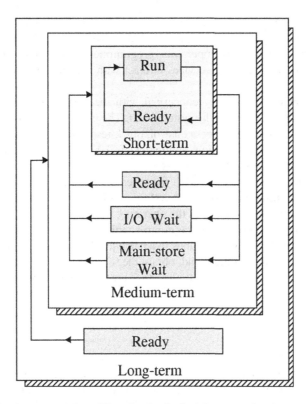

FIGURE 2.10   Level–wise presentation of three levels of schedulers, namely; short-term scheduler, medium-term scheduler, and long-term scheduler.

2.3.4.5   Processes: Long and Short

We have already seen the distinction between compute-bound and I/O-bound processes. From the point of view of the short-term scheduler, a compute-bound process remains in view for a long time, since it does not terminate quickly and seldom waits for I/O. For this reason, compute-bound processes are legitimately called **long processes**.

In contrast, an I/O-bound process enters and leaves very quickly, since it disappears from the view of the short-term scheduler as soon as it starts waiting for I/O. Interactive programs that interact heavily with the user tend to be I/O bound and often directly enter the ready queue just after submission to OS. In general, the user issues a command which is interpreted and gets executed. Shortly thereafter, the process is ready to receive the next command. The user, however, is still puzzling over the response to the previous command. Thus, the process spends most of its time waiting for the user to submit the next command and only a little time for computing to respond the command. Text editor programs and system commands usually exhibit this sort of behavior. Other I/O-bound processes are not interactive at all but spend a lot of time fetching data from devices (read) or sending data back (write), performing very little computation in between. Both kinds of I/O-bound processes are similar in that small amounts of computation are sandwiched between longer periods of waiting. For this reason, they are naturally called **short processes**.

More details about this topic are given on the Support Material at www.routledge.com/9781032467238.

2.4   OPERATING SYSTEM: SUPPORTS AND SERVICES

The services provided by the operating system as perceived by different classes of users can be broadly categorized into two different classes: *user-related services* and *system-related services*.

User-related services make the computer system more convenient, easy to program, and also friendly to the users and support them in executing their tasks using the environment consisting of machine resources and people, like operators, programmers, and system administrators. While the program is under execution, these services interact with the operating system to make use of system-related services.

System-related services are mainly concerned with the control and management of system resources for the efficient operation of the system itself. The user often makes use of these services for support like resource allocation, access control, quick response, resource isolation with protection, proper scheduling, reliable operation, and many similar functions and aspects offered by different resource managements, as already discussed.

Operating system users generally use both these services and are commonly divided into two broad classes: **command language users** and **system call users**. Command language users, informally, are those who invoke the services of the operating system by means of typing in commands at the terminal or by embedding commands as control cards (like $FTN, $RUN, etc., as discussed in the previous chapter) or embedding commands in a batch job. We will discuss this issue later in this chapter. System-call users, on the other hand, obtain the services of the operating system by means of invoking different system calls during runtime to exert finer control over system operations and to gain more direct access to hardware facilities, especially input/output resources. System calls are usually embedded in and executed during runtime of programs.

2.4.1 SYSTEM CALLS

System-related services are offered by the operating system while a program (both user and OS program) under execution interacts with the operating system. User programs, while attempting to perform certain kinds of resource management functions, communicate with the operating system to get these services by way of issuing special "extended instructions" provided by the operating system. This set of extended instructions, known as **system calls** or **supervisor calls** (SVCs), are specialized hardware instructions that interface between the operating system and user program and are usually not available to the ordinary user. Systems and application programmers often directly invoke system-related services of the operating system from their programs by means of issuing system calls, sometimes also called **application programming interfaces** (APIs), to control and willfully manage their own program during runtime. System commands issued by command-language users are essentially system programs that are normally converted into and executed as a series of system calls. Since the system calls act much like *subroutine calls*, but control is always transferred to the operating system only, it usually provides a common means to enter the operating system arena.

Most contemporary computer systems provide some hardware support to protect operating systems from user processes by defining a privilege level that changes whenever the OS–user boundary is crossed. That is why every modern computer has at least two states of execution; *problem state* (user state, slave state) and *supervisor state* (executive state, master state). Operating system services (reading or writing files, for example) can only be accessed when the CPU is in supervisor state, but user programs must run in user state. The processor can correctly execute system call programs while in supervisor state under the control of the operating system and not by any other program. Thus, switching state from user to supervisor is required for executing system call programs, and this change can be made by using software interrupts. To service software interrupts, the interrupt table is accessed by the OS to point to the OS program code that changes the system to supervisor state and also calls the appropriate OS routines (ISRs). The OS routines, for example, may start the I/O processors, change the protection rights of parts of memory, change the interrupt status of the machine, or many such system-related things as needed. (The correct routine to be called can either be directly determined by the software interrupt number or by one of the parameters attached to the system call.) This table and the ISRs must be protected by the OS. Software interrupts are discussed in more detail later in this chapter.

After executing the required system-related operations while in supervisor mode, the control is again returned to the user program for further resumption; hence, a change in state, from supervisor state (mode) to user state (mode), is once again required. The operating system must execute a privileged instruction for such switching of the state to return to the user state before entering the user program. While the intent of system calls and interrupt processing is primarily for efficient use of system resources, but they themselves are expensive with regard to consumption of processor time, leading to a little bit of degradation in overall system performance.

2.4.1.1 System Call: How It Works

Each system call at the time of its invocation provides at least one operand attached to it that gives the identity of the desired operating system service. Corresponding to each system call, there is a **library procedure** that the user program can call. This procedure puts the parameters as provided by the system call in a specified place, such as in the machine registers, and then issues a **trap** instruction (a kind of protected procedure call) to cause a software interrupt that eventually starts the operating system. The purpose of the library procedure is to hide the details of the *trap* instruction that makes the system calls look like ordinary procedure calls (subroutine calls).

When the operating system gets control after the trap, it examines the parameters to see if they are valid and, if so, performs the work requested. When the work is finished, the operating system puts a *status code* in a register, telling whether it succeeded or failed, and executes a *RETURN FROM TRAP* instruction to send control back to the library procedure. The library procedure then returns control to the caller in the usual way with a status code as a function value. This is illustrated in Figure 2.11. Sometimes additional values are also returned through parameters.

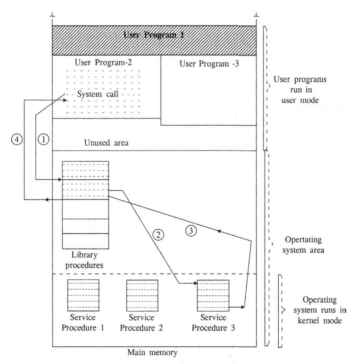

(1) System call corresponds to a library procedure.
(2) After doing some homework, trap instruction of library procedure locates and calls service procedure.
(3) Control is returned to the library procedure.
(4) Control is returned to the user program.

FIGURE 2.11 Mechanism and flow of control when a system call works in the operating system.

However, different operating systems provide various numbers and types of system calls that span a wide range. The system calls are mostly used to create processes, manage memory, control devices, read and write files, and do different kinds of input/output, such as reading from the terminal and writing on the printer/terminal.

A description regarding the working of a system call in relation to Figure 2.11 is given on the Support Material at www.routledge.com/9781032467238.

A few system calls in the UNIX operating system are:

- Process management system calls: *fork*, *join*, *quit*, *exec*, and so on.
- Memory management system calls: *brk*.
- File and directory system calls: *creat*, *read*, *write*, *lseek*, and so on.
- Input/output system calls: *cfsetospeed*, *cfsetispeed*, *cfgetospeed*, *cfgetispeed*, *tcsetattr*, *tcgetattr*, and so on.

A few system calls in the Windows operating system are:

- Process management system calls: *LOAD_AND_EXEC*, *END_PROG*, *LOAD_OVERLAY*, *GET_CHILD_STATUS*, and so on.
- Memory management system calls: *ALLOC_MEMORY* (n bytes), *SET_MEM_BLK_SIZ* (size, addr), FREE_ALLOCATED_MEM, and so on.
- File and directory system calls: *CREATE*, *OPEN*, *CLOSE*, *READ*, *WRITE*, *RENAME_FILE*, *DELETE_FILE*, *GET_CUR_DIR*, *GET_FILE_DATE*, and so on.
- Input/output system calls: *IOCTL* and a large number of different calls.

Operating system design based on a system call interface has the interesting property that there is not necessarily any OS process. Instead, a process executing in user mode gets changed to supervisor mode when it intends to execute a core program of operating system services (kernel code) and back to user mode when it returns from the system call. But, if the OS is designed as a set of separate processes, it is naturally easier to design and implement it so that it can get control of the machine in special situations. This is more conducive than the case if the core operating system (kernel) is simply built with only a collection of functions executed in supervisor mode by user processes. Process-based operating system design has nicely exploited this concept. This is discussed in Chapter 3.

2.4.2 PROCEDURE CALLS

Not all machines in the early days were equipped with system calls; rather operating system services were usually obtained by calling different procedures at the right point in time. However, contemporary modern computer systems, while using numerous system call facilities, do also use procedures and call them in different ways to perform different tasks.

A procedure call, in its simple form, assumes that the operating system is designed and implemented as a collection of coded routines in the form of procedures, each of which can call any of the other ones whenever it needs to. When this technique is used, each procedure in the system must have a well-defined interface in terms of parameters and results. The services provided by these procedures are requested by putting the parameters in well-defined places, such as in registers or on the stack, and then executing the needed procedure call instruction. Users can also invoke these OS routines by using standard procedure calls and passing appropriate parameters. This method is simple and usable on almost all computer systems, and the common technique employed to control the execution of procedure calls and subsequent returns is by making use of a stack, which is provided virtually on all computer systems. In spite of having almost no complexity in implementation, procedure calls are still not found suitable to use OS services, mainly due to the following reasons:

- Procedure calls are generally considered not appropriate to manage protection hardware when a *change in the privilege level* occurs due to transfer of control from a caller to a callee who is located on the other side of the OS–user boundary.
- Procedure calls mostly require direct addressing that must specify the actual address of the respective OS routine while invoking specific OS services in the user program for the sake of linking and binding to create the load module. It expects that the programmer at the time of implementation has sufficient knowledge and expertise in this area, but this is actually rare.

However, the concept of generic procedure call mechanism was later extended in a different way to realize a widely used technique known as a *remote procedure call* mechanism that is used to call procedures located on other machines in a client–server environment. This call mechanism, however, resides at the higher level of the operating system. In spite of having many complications and hazards in the implementation of RPC, most of them have been successfully dealt with, and this technique is popular and still in heavy use in client–server environments that underlie many distributed operating systems.

A brief explanation relating to shortcomings of procedure calls used to obtain OS services is given on the Support Material at www.routledge.com/9781032467238.

2.4.3 PROCESSOR MODES: MODE BIT

The mode bit available inside the processor is used to separate the execution of OS-related work from the user-related application work carried out by the processor. This bit can be set either to supervisor mode (state) or user mode (state). In supervisor mode, the processor can only execute hardware instruction (OS instructions) called *supervisor, privileged*, or *protected* instructions (don't confuse it with supervisor call instructions) that are different from the normal user mode instructions. But in user mode (state), the processor can execute only a subset of the hardware instructions plus all the other instructions of the application programs.

To make a system request, the supervisor call instruction (a special type of hardware instruction), sometimes called *trap instruction*, is issued from an application program running in user mode, and the result of the execution of this call instruction *sets the mode bit* of the processor to supervisor mode and then performs a branching to its corresponding operating system routines (ISR) located in a pre-defined secure place in the system area, protected from any user access. Since the OS code is located in the system area, this code can only be accessed and invoked via a trap. That is, a trap produces the same effect as a vectored interrupt. When the operating system completes the execution of a supervisor call, it once again resets the mode bit (by way of executing the "Return From Trap" instruction included in the operating system routine) to user mode prior to returning control to the user program. Figure 2.12 illustrates a simple mechanism which provides a safe way for a user-mode process to execute only pre-defined system software while the mode bit is set to supervisor mode.

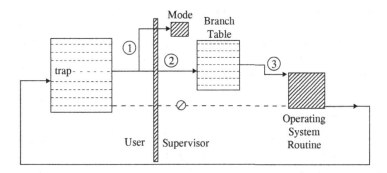

FIGURE 2.12 For trap–Instruction operation, change in mode of CPU from user–mode to supervisor—mode.

The mode bit can be used in defining the domain of memory that can be accessed when the processor is in supervisor mode versus while it is in user mode. If the mode bit is set to supervisor mode, the process executing on the processor can access either the supervisor partition (system space) or user partition (user space) of the memory. But if user mode is set, the process can reference only the user-reference space.

The mode bit also helps to implement protection and security mechanisms on software by way of separating operating system software from application software. For example, a protection mechanism is implemented to ensure the validity of processor registers or certain blocks of memory that are used to store system information. To protect these registers and memory blocks, privileged load and store instructions must be used to willfully manipulate their contents, and these instructions can only be executed in supervisor mode, which can only be attained by setting the mode bit to supervisor mode. In general, the mode bit facilitates the operating system's protection rights.

2.4.4 SOFTWARE INTERRUPT

The software interrupt (SWI) instruction is another simple and powerful tool for the invocation of operating system services and to accomplish similar other purposes relating to various system activities. Due to its simplicity and easy-to-use nature, these instructions became well-accepted and gradually used in an increasing number of various types of computer systems, including modern microprocessors with emerging technologies. A software-interrupt instruction processing essentially follows the same mechanisms as the hardware interrupt-processing sequence, as already described in previous sections. Basically, a software interrupt creates the same effect as if an external interrupt has occurred. Numerous types of SWI instructions are available that mainly depend on the specific computer architecture and its supporting interrupt handling hardware.

When it is used in application program to invoke the operating system to gain the operating-system services, it switches the processor to privileged mode and then saves the context (all information related to the state of the interrupted process) and finally transfers the control directly to the related OS routines. The loading of the address of the corresponding OS service routine into the interrupt vector attached to the SWI instruction can be performed by the operating system or some other program in a way similar to a system call instruction. Here, the user needs only to know the number or the "interrupt level" of the corresponding OS service. As a result, the linking and binding of the SWI instruction while creating the load module is straightforward, and object-code portability can be easily obtained. Moreover, if the SWI instruction can be designed with only a single interrupt vector as an entry point to the operating system, it can be even utilized to emulate the system call. Of course, the drawbacks arising due to having only a single entry point in an SWI instruction have been, however, removed by way of dedicating a separate vector to each and every individual operating-system service.

Another attractive feature of an SWI instruction is that it can be used to simulate hardware interrupts in order to test and debug numerous interrupt-related codes, whereas in reality, creating such codes for the purpose of testing are difficult to build. An SWI instruction can also be used to test and examine an interrupt-driven event-recognition sequence by issuing it from a sample program to simulate an interrupt as if it is coming from a physical device and causing the event. In spite of having lot of merit, it is always advisable that sufficient safeguards be taken to prevent all sorts of potentially hazardous uses of the SWI instructions.

2.4.5 MESSAGE PASSING

When the user requests an operating system service using the message passing approach, the user process then constructs a message X_i that describes the desired service as requested. Then, it uses a *send* function to pass the message to a trusted OS process that offers the service. The *send* function serves the same purpose as the system call (trap) rather than language constructs; it carefully

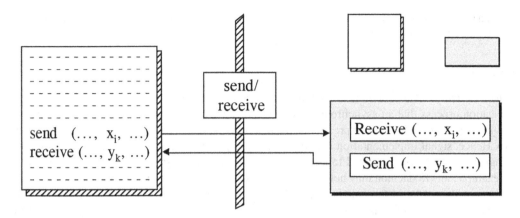

FIGURE 2.13 Message Passing mechanism in uniprocessor modern operating systems.

checks the message, switches the processor to supervisor mode, and then delivers the message to an appropriate OS process that implements the target function. Meanwhile, the user process waits for the outcome of the service thus requested with a message *receive* operation. When the OS process completes the operation, it passes a message Y_k in regard to its operation back to the user process by a *send* function that is accepted by the user process using its *receive* function, as shown in Figure 2.13. These *send* and *receive* functions can easily be put into a library procedure, such as:

send (destination, . . ., message, . . .); and
receive (source, . . ., message, . . .);

The former sends a message to a given destination, and the latter receives a message from a given source (or from any source, if the receiver does not care).

Message systems also have to deal with the question as to how processes are to be named so that the process (*destination* or *source*) specified in a *send* or *receive* call is unambiguous. Often a naming scheme is suggested and is used. If the number of concurrently active processes is very large, sometimes they are also named by grouping similar processes into *domains*, and then process addressing requires injection of the domain name into the process name to form a unique process name. Of course, the domain names must also be unique. *Authentication* is also an issue of importance in message-passing systems.

Messages are also used in the area of interrupt management to synchronize interrupt processing with hardware interrupts. For this, some services are provided that manipulate the interrupt levels, such as enabling a level, say, by means of an ENABLE system call.

However, one of the major objectives of the design of a message passing scheme is to ultimately enhance the level of system performance. For instance, copying messages from one process to another is always a slower activity than doing it with a system call. So, to make this message-passing approach efficient, one such suggestion out of many, for example, is to limit the message size to what could fit in the machine's registers and then carry out message passing using these registers to speed up the execution.

The distinction between the system call approach and message passing approach has important consequences regarding the relative independence of the OS behaviors from application process behaviors and thereby the resulting performance. This distinction has significant bearing in the design issues of the operating system and also an immense impact on the structural design. As a rule of thumb, operating system design based on a system call interface can be made more efficient than that requiring messages to be exchanged between distinct processes, although the system call is implemented with a trap instruction that incurs a high overhead. This efficiency is benchmarked considering the whole cost of process multiplexing, message formation, and message copying versus the cost of servicing a trap instruction.

2.4.6 SIGNALS

Signals are truly OS abstractions of interrupts. A signal is often used by an OS process to notify an application process that an asynchronous event has occurred. It often represents the occurrence of a *hardware event*, such as a user pressing a delete key or the CPU detecting an attempt to divide by zero. Hence, signal implementation is likely to use a trap instruction if the host hardware supports it. Signals also may be generated to notify a process about the existence of a *software condition*. For example, an OS daemon may notify a user process that its write operation on a pipe cannot succeed, since the reader of the pipe has been deleted. In addition, signals may also be generated by external events (some other process writes to a file or socket) or internal events (some period of time has elapsed). A signal is similar to a hardware interrupt but does not include priorities. That is, all signals are treated equally; signals that occur at the same time are presented to respective process one at a time, with no particular ordering. Processes can generally define handler procedures that are invoked when a signal is delivered. These *signal handlers* are analogous to ISRs in the OS.

In fact, **signals are the software analog of hardware interrupts** but do not provide priorities and can be generated by a variety of causes in addition to timers expiring. Many traps detected by the hardware, such as executing an illegal instruction or using an invalid address, are also converted into signals to the guilty process. Signals are also used for interprocess synchronization as well as for process-to-process communications or to interact with another process in a hurry.

Signals can also be used among application-level processes. Each signal has a type (called a "name") associated with it. Contemporary UNIX systems including Linux have different types of built-in signals. A few UNIX signals are:

Value	Name	Description
01	SIGHUP	Hang up; sent to process when kernel assumes that the user of that process is doing no useful work
02	SIGINT	Interrupt
03	SIGQUIT	Quit; sent by user to indicate halting of process and start production of core dump

2.4.7 LOCKS

Lock is simply an area in common virtual storage and is usually kept resident permanently in main memory. Apart from their other uses, locks can often be employed to enforce mutual exclusion between processes at the time of interprocess synchronization (discussed later in Chapter 4) for access to shared system resources. A lock contains bits which can be set to indicate that the lock is in use. Locks normally come in two classes, and are of many different types (see Chapters 7 and 9). The classes are:

- *Local*: Across all tasks in a single address space.
- *Global*: Across all address spaces.

Some of the types are:

Spin: The processor, while executing a *test-and-set–lock* type of instruction (TSL instruction in IBM machines), constantly tests the lock sitting in a tight loop and thus waiting only for the lock to set it to guard some of its activity. In fact, while waiting, the processor is

not doing any productive work but only testing the lock, thereby suffering critically from
busy-waiting. The lock used for this purpose is known as a spin lock.

Suspend: The task waiting for an event to occur is made suspended, or the task in a ready
state is explicitly suspended for various reasons; thereby to eliminating undesirable useless
busy-waiting.

Spin locks are used to avoid a race condition at the time of interprocess synchronization for critical sections that run only for a short time. A suspend lock, on the other hand, is used for the same
purpose but is employed for considerably long critical sections when a required (denied) process is
suspended and another suitable process is then dispatched to utilize the costly CPU time for the sake
of performance enhancement. Local locks are usually always suspend locks, whereas global locks
can be both spin and suspend locks.

Locks can be arranged in a hierarchical level, and many large systems employ this strategy to
prevent the circular-wait condition of deadlocks (to be discussed later in Chapter 4). A hierarchical
arrangement implies that a processor may request only locks higher in the hierarchy than locks it
currently holds.

2.4.8 PIPES

A pipe is an excellent facility introduced by UNIX to connect two processes together in a uniprocessor computing system. When process A wishes to send data to process B, it simply writes on the
pipe as though it were an output file. Process B can then get the data by reading the pipe as though it
were an input file. Thus, communication between processes looks very similar to ordinary file reads
and writes. A pipe is essentially a unidirectional channel that may be written at one end and read
at the other end for the sake of communication between two processes. In fact, a pipe is a *virtual
communication channel* to connect two processes wishing to exchange a stream of data. Two processes communicating via a pipe can reside on a single machine or on different machines in network
environment. Apart from its many other uses, it is a powerful tool that was exploited by UNIX in
its earlier versions to primarily carry out inter-process communications; for example, in a producer–
consumer problem, the producer process writes data into one end of the pipe and the consumer
process retrieves it from the other end, as shown in Figure 2.14. In fact, when the pipe is in use, only
one process can access a pipe at any point in time, which implicitly enforces the mutual exclusion
with synchronization between the processes communicating via pipe. This form of communication is conceptually very similar to the message-passing facility, allowing asynchronous operations
of senders and receivers (producers and consumers), as well as many-to-many mapping between

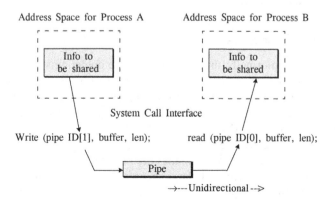

FIGURE 2.14   Overview of the mechanisms when information flows through UNIX pipes.

senders and receivers. But the major differences are that the pipe facility does not require explicit synchronization between communicating processes as the message system does and also does not even require explicit management and formation of messages. Moreover, the pipe is handled at the system-call level in exactly the same way as files and device-independent I/O with the same basic set of system calls. In fact, a pipe can be created or an already existing pipe can be accessed by means of an OPEN system call. A writer-process writes data into the pipe by means of WRITE calls, and a reader-process consumes data from the pipe by means of READ calls. When all data are transferred, the pipe can be closed or destroyed depending on whether further use of it is anticipated.

A pipe is represented in the kernel by a file descriptor. When a process wants to create a pipe, it issues a system call to the kernel that is of the form:

```
Int pipeID [2];
.........
.........
pipe (pipeID);
```

The kernel creates the pipe with a fixed size in bytes as a kernel First–In–First–Out data structure (queue) with two file identifiers. In Figure 2.14, *pipeID* [0] is a file pointer (an index into the process's open file table) to the read-end of the pipe, and *pipeID* [1] is the file pointer to the write–end of the pipe. The pipe's read-end and write-end can be used in most system calls in the same way that a file descriptor is used. The automatic buffering of data and the control of data flow within a pipe are performed as byte streams by the operating system.

UNIX pipes do not explicitly support messages, although two processes can establish their own protocol to provide structured messages. There are also library routines that can be used with a pipe for communication using messages.

The pipe can also be used at the *command-language level* with the execution of a pipeline statement, such as, **a b;**, that is often used to generate output from one program to be input to another program. This is an additional form of inter-program communication that is established without any special effort of reprogramming and also without the use of any temporary files.

Pipes are differentiated by their types. There are two types of pipes: *named* and *unnamed*. Only related processes can share unnamed pipes, whereas unrelated processes can share only named pipes. In normal pipes (unnamed pipes), the pipe-ends are inherited as open file descriptors by the children. In named pipes, the process obtains a pipe-end by using a string that is analogous to a file name but which is associated with a pipe. This enables any set of processes to exchange information using a "public pipe" whose end names are file names. Moreover, when a process uses a named pipe, the pipe is a system-wide resource, potentially accessible by any process. Named pipes must be managed in a similar way, just as files have to be managed so that they are not inadvertently shared among many processes at one time.

2.4.9 COMMAND LANGUAGE USERS

Command language users, informally, are those who invoke operating system services by issuing instructions to the OS known as *commands* that are written using a typical language known as command language. Those commands are issued by typing in at the terminal; given in the form of job control cards using job control language (JCL), mainly in mainframe systems; or embedded in a batch job. For each command, there exists one system program, consisting of instructions apart from a series of system calls, and whenever a command is issued, the corresponding system program is executed. Operating system commands are obviously different for different operating systems and are usually system-specific, but they appear to cover a common range and functionality that are mostly similar in different operating systems. The type of the commands to be offered, and subsequently the design of the command set, are settled as soon as the design of the OS is finalized.

Many large complex operating systems have more elaborate, versatile forms of command facilities and OS software support and services to assist the different types of users across a diverse spectrum.

System commands provide an interface to the operating system for the user so that the user can directly issue these commands to perform a wide range of system-related functions from user mode. This interface actually separates the user from operating system details and presents the operating system simply as a collection of numerous services. The *command language interpreter*, an operating system program (called the *shell* in UNIX), accepts these user commands or job control statements, interprets them, and creates and controls processes as needed.

2.5 DESIGN FACTORS AND RELATED ISSUES

An OS offers many services in addition to providing mechanisms for managing resources used by the community of processes so that these resources can be allocated on request in numerous ways such that their allocation will not result in any improper or unintended behavior of the entire system. While fulfilling all these basic requirements for management facilities and users' ease and convenience, a number of other factors need to be seriously considered that have a significant influence and immense impact in the continuous evolution and ever-changing design of operating systems.

• *Performance*:

While the OS creates an abstraction to provide a pleasant environment in a cost-effective manner to users, that may also sometimes slow down the execution, leading to a substantial degradation in the overall performance of the computer system. Performance is generally determined and measured in terms of certain factors, such as throughput, response time in the case of an interactive system, and also speed of execution, which although mostly depends on the related hardware platform, but in many situations is influenced by the design and working of the associated operating systems.

Most OS designer incline to continuously adding lucrative features without looking into their performance. But, when each such new feature would be injected additionally into the exiting OS design, it must be tested and evaluated with respect to its contribution to the functionality of the system against its impact on the computer's performance. Such considerations thus sometimes also insist the designers even to sacrifice an otherwise excellent function to incorporate. In addition, an invention in hardware technology often provokes designers to add features to the existing design that may look lucrative but ultimately make the system comparatively inefficient.

However, there is no universally acceptable method to determine the performance level of an OS. In some situations, an OS may appear to be offering good performance, but the same OS in other situations might look worse. So, before attempting to design an operating system, the target users and the application environment to which the OS will be dedicated, along with other tradeoffs of the functionality versus its actual performance, should be carefully analyzed with due importance and judged accordingly.

• *Protection and Security*:

Users implement security using different degrees of protection facilities offered by a modern OS for different management, objects, users, or applications to safeguard all types of resources from unauthorized accesses and threats.

• *Correctness and Reliability:*

Since all software in the computer is executed by the hardware with the support and services offered by the OS, the correctness and reliability of the underlying OS are to be ensured at the time of its design and also when injecting new features into its existing design for required enhancements.

• *Maintainability and Upgradability:*

As the complexity and the volume of the OS software are gradually increasing to accommodate a constantly growing number of users from a diverse spectrum of disciplines working on numerous hardware platforms, the design of the OS should be made easily maintainable. Maintainability is also closely related to upgradeability, which states that the release of a new version of an existing OS should include downward compatibility to confirm the upgradeability of its older version. Maintainability often means a compromise, even accepting relatively inferior performance, but to what extent it will be tolerated is actually driven by tactical decisions being made by the designers at the time of OS design.

• *Market Demand and Commercial Influence:*

With the continuous increase in the number of computer users and developers along with the constant emergence of new avenues in the area of computer applications supported by relentless developments in the field of hardware and software technologies ultimately paved the way for the different types of operating systems to evolve in advanced forms to drive the newer hardware along with offering more convenient user interface. Of course, downward compatibility of the evolving OS must be maintained. Sometimes an innovation in the design of an operating system awaits the implementation of a suitable technology. Market forces and large manufacturers, by their dominance, also promote certain features that eventually steer, control, influence, and subsequently direct the choices of the users. However, the most radical commercial development in the implementations of forthcoming new OS is the Open Systems Foundation (OSF-1) approach that was based on Mach OS and was originally designed as a multiprocessor operating system. It was initially targeted to implement different parts of the OS on different processors in the multiprocessor system and ultimately became successful. In fact, today's common trend in research and development of operating systems is to implement some variant of a UNIX/Linux interface, especially toward microkernel implementations for all types of computers as well as a fitting OS for the various types of emerging cluster architectures to handle a diverse spectrum of distributed application areas. An all-out attempt in the development process of more innovative system software is also observed that could negotiate the challenge of newer (upcoming) environments.

• *Open Systems and Design Standards:*

Due to the resurgence of electronic technology since the late 1970s, the renaissance in the architectural evolution of computers and the corresponding development of various types of operating systems and other system software to drive these constantly emerging more intelligent machines have progressed through various forms and ultimately culminated in the arrival of distributed hardware equipped with multiple processors in the form of various types of multiprocessors and multicomputers as well as cluster architectures driven by fitting modern distributed operating systems.

As the working environments constantly expanded with the continuous introduction of various types of computers with dissimilar architectures and run by individually dedicated operating systems, there was, thus, no compatibility between them, which eventually caused havoc in the user domain. To remedy this, there was a keen desire to have technology that would, by some means, bring about an imposed compatibility between different environments. Consequently, this gave rise to the birth of what is commonly known as *open system technology*, which finally succeeded in consolidating entire computing environments.

The ultimate objective of open system architecture is, however, to allow the end users to work on any computer irrespective of its architecture and associated dedicated operating system. It also enables the end users to carry out information-processing tasks from their own domain in an environment of a network of heterogeneous computers with different architectures but interconnected through a standardized communication facility. The fundamental requirements now converge to implement such a distributed system so that information can be shared and distributed across the network and yet available to each and every user in a legible form, of course obeying the underlying specific security policy. Open systems in a network of computers never encroach in the internal functioning of individual systems, it is rather mainly concerned more with the capability of the systems to cooperate in the exchange of information to accomplish the respective tasks.

One of the main goals for an open system to achieve is *portability*, which means that the application programs developed on one kind of hardware platform can be moved (ported) to run on a dissimilar one with almost no change; that is, they are hardware-independent. This implicitly demands the provision of a standard set of facilities at the *operating system level*. Another aspect is *application integration*, which specifies that the application program should present a common interface to users in order to effectively exchange data. This, in turn, suggests a *standardized operating system* in regard to having a consistent set of abstract device management and information management. Many other similar issues thus need to be settled before making any attempt to design generalized open system software that could drive a broad spectrum of distributed hardware as a whole.

Most of the efforts thus attempted already succeeded in implementing standardization that addresses most aspects of open system technology. Particularly, the POSIX project in this regard is worthwhile to mention, and it has broadened the base of OS implementation beyond that of pure UNIX by putting more emphasis on standardizing the user-interface to the OS rather than organizing its implementation. Later, the POSIX committee further refined this standard after a great many arguments and counterarguments and finally produced a standard known as **1003.1**. Virtually all manufacturers are now committed to providing standardized communications software that behaves in conformance with certain predefined rules to support their customers with the ability to communicate comfortably with other open systems.

SUMMARY

This chapter explains why operating systems are needed and gives an overview of the objectives and functions which serve to define the requirements that an operating system design is intended to meet. Here, the concepts and the general characteristics of the overall organization of an operating system have been explained. The major issues that influence the design of generic multitasking operating systems, as well as expansion in the area of fundamental requirements to support hardware abstraction, resource sharing, and needed protection have been discussed. Many other critical issues that need to be resolved have been identified. The concept of process is a central theme to all the key requirements of the operating system, and its view from different angles has been featured. A brief description of the different supports and services that are offered by operating systems in the form of user-accessibility and that of system-related subjects has been presented. The chapter ends with an introduction to the most important factors that have an immense impact in the design of generic operating systems.

EXERCISES

1. "Certain specific responsibilities are performed by an operating system while working as a resource manager"—state these and explain.
2. "The conceptual design of an operating system can be derived in the form of a collection of resource management". What is this different management that is found in any generic operating system? What are the basic responsibilities performed by the different management individually?
3. Which of the four basic OS modules might be required on a computer system? Why are these modules not multi-programmed?

4. State and explain the concept of a process. Distinguish between a process and a program. Is this difference important in serial (single-process) operating systems? Why or why not?

5. "Processes by nature can be classified into two types". State and explain these two types and show their differences.

6. "A process can be viewed from different angles". Justify the statement with adequate explanation. What are the salient features that exist in these different visions?

7. The CPU should be in privileged mode while executing the OS code and in user mode (i.e. non-privileged mode) while executing a user program. Why is a change in mode required? Explain how this change in mode is carried out.

8. What is an interrupt? What are the different classes of interrupts that are commonly found in any generic operating system?

9. Explain why an interrupt is considered an essential element in any operating system. Explain an interrupt from a system point of view.

10. How is an interrupt viewed from the domain of a user program? Explain with an appropriate diagram.

11. What is meant by interrupt processing? What are the different types of actions being taken to process an interrupt? Explain the various processing steps that are involved in each of these types.

12. What does interrupt servicing mean? State and explain the different courses of action being taken by an operating system in order to service an interrupt.

13. "Interrupts are required to be interrupted in certain situations". Explain at least one such situation with an example. Discuss how this situation is normally handled.

14. The kernel of an OS masks interrupts during interrupt processing. Discuss its merits and drawbacks.

15. State and explain vectored interrupts and non-vectored interrupts.

16. What is a trap? How can it be differentiated from an interrupt?

17. Sharing of resources is required for concurrent processing in order to attain performance improvement. Explain space-multiplexed sharing and time-multiplexed sharing in this context.

18. What is meant by protection of hardware resources? Why is protection required for such resources? How is protection achieved for each individual resource?

19. Why is scheduling of system resources required for concurrent execution in a computer system?

20. What are the different classes of resource scheduling used in a computer system? State in brief the numerous responsibilities that are performed by these different classes of schedulers.

21. Point out the responsibilities that are performed by a short-term scheduler. Explain how the action of a medium-term scheduler affects the movement of a short-term scheduler.

22. "The operating system provides numerous services that can be broadly categorized into two different classes". What are these two classes? State and explain in brief the services that they individually offer to common users normally.

23. Define system calls. How can a user submit a system call? State and explain the working principle of a system call. What is the difference between a system call and a subroutine call?

24. Various types of service calls are usually incorporated that the kernel may provide. Suggest a few of them that every kernel should have.

25. How can a device submit a service call? Does a service call always require a context switch? Does it always require a process switch?

26. System call and interrupt are closely related to each other. Justify this relationship, if there is any, with reasons.

27. Define a procedure call. How does it differ from a system call?

28. "A procedure call is simple, usable, and has almost no complexity in implementation on almost all computer systems; still it is not preferred in contemporary systems to use OS services". Would you agree? If so, give reasons in favor of your stance.

29. State some factors that might differentiate between the time to do a normal procedure call from an application program to one of its own procedures compared to the time to perform a system call to an OS procedure.

30. What is the difference between a command and an instruction? Discuss the various types of system commands that are available in a generic operating system. How is the command executed in a system?

31. A command-language interpreter is not considered a part of an operating system. Justify.

32. "The processor works in two modes". What are these two modes? Why are these two modes required? Explain how the switching of modes is carried out by the processor.

33. What is a software interrupt? In what way does it differ from a hardware interrupt? Discuss its salient features and the distinct advantages of using it.

34. Discuss the working methodology of a message-passing technique. Message-passing techniques are an important constituent of an operating system. Give reasons in favor of this statement. What are the drawbacks of this technique? What is the difference between a system call approach and a message-passing approach?

35. What is the role of a signal in the working of an operating system?

36. What are locks? What are the basic functions that a lock performs? What are the different classes and different types of locks commonly used in an operating system? What are their specific usages?

37. Discuss in brief some of the factors that influence the design of an operating system at the time of its development. Explain their role in arriving at a specific trade-off.

3 Operating Systems
Structures and Designs

Learning Objectives

- To illustrate the step-wise evolution of different design models of operating systems based on numerous design objectives.
- To explain the structure, design, formation, and subsequent realization of primitive mono-lithic systems, then improved hierarchical and extended machines, and subsequently different types of modular layered systems, mainly for large mainframe machines.
- To describe a revolutionary approach in the design and development of operating systems for virtual machines.
- To describe the introduction of a new direction in the design and development of different operating systems, leaving its traditional concept for the emerging client–server model systems.
- To articulate the arrival of a new dimension in the design and development of operating systems using a kernel-based approach.
- To demonstrate the novel concepts in the design and development of operating systems based on monolithic kernels and microkernels and subsequently hybrid kernels.
- To briefly discuss the basic design issues and salient features of generic modern operating systems, including distributed operating systems.

3.1 EVOLUTION OF SYSTEM STRUCTURE

An operating system mainly acts as a resource manager, keeping the status of resources to properly allocate/deallocate them to provide services to users. It also keeps track of the states of all executions to efficiently control the ongoing working environment. When multiple *competing processes* attempt to simultaneously gain accesses to available shared and distributed resources, the OS then acts as an arbiter by way of separating them dynamically. But when *cooperating* processes intend to interact with one another to fulfill their own targets, the operating system facilitates *sharing* of objects with appropriate protection. Many other issues still require the intervention of the operating system at the right point in time to resolve. To equip the OS to perform all these responsibilities, certain strategic design objectives are thus required to be framed on the basis of a set of well-defined policies. The ultimate aim is, however, to form a workable OS structure that is reasonably manageable and easily maintainable and also equally upgradeable. Different structures of operating systems thus gradually evolved over the years with continuous improvements in structural design as more and more demanding features have been regularly added to exploit the constantly growing potential of underlying increasingly complex and versatile hardware. A few representatives of them are given here to indicate some of the ideas and thoughts that have been introduced and subsequently implemented.

3.1.1 MONOLITHIC SYSTEMS

An operating system can be developed *without* having any structured organization, but just as a collection of procedures with well-defined interfaces in terms of parameters and results. Each procedure is visible to every other one, and it can freely call any of them to get its service. This scheme,

DOI: 10.1201/9781003383055-3

when realized, gives rise to what is called a **monolithic system**. Here, processing, data, and user interfaces; all reside on the same system with OS code to be simply executed as a separate entity in privileged mode. All the individual procedures or files containing the procedures of the OS are compiled and then bound together into a single object file with a related linker (linkage editor). The monolithic structure of the operating system, however, suggests the following organization for its implementation.

1. A main program within the operating system that invokes the requested service procedure (table search).
2. A set of service procedures that carry out the execution of requested system calls.
3. A set of utility procedures that do things such as fetching data from the user program and similar other things. These are needed by several service procedures during their execution.

This concept was exploited in developing the first **simple batch operating systems** in the mid-1950s and was implemented in the IBM 704 after refinement, and then by the early 1960s, even larger mainframe computers used this approach with considerable success. It was then implemented as the IBSYS operating system by IBM for its 7090/7094 computers. But when this design was implemented on PC-DOS and later on MS-DOS and subsequently on earlier Windows-based OSs on PCs, it worked poorly with multiple users. Even large operating systems when designed as a collection of monolithic pieces of codes were observed not suitable from their organizational point of view.

For more details about monolithic systems, see the Support Material at www.routledge.com/9781032467238.

3.1.2 HIERARCHICAL AND EXTENDED MACHINES

Generalization of monolithic design considering the OS mainly a manager of resources and then organizing the components of different managers of resources in respective hierarchical levels (layers) with an inter-relationship ultimately gave rise to an improved workable structure of this operating system.

This operating system provides some basic hardware instructions (key operating system functions) that run on the bare machine (hardware) called the **kernel** (core of the OS). Other types of instructions to perform different kinds of resource management functions together with the kernel are called the instruction set of the **extended machine**. The inner extended machine (kernel) is composed of routines that manage central storage, time, devices, and other resources. It responds to requests issued by processes and services interrupts raised from devices. In fact, the kernel runs only when it is invoked either from above by a process or below by a device. If no process is ready to run and no device needs attention, the computer sits idle. User programs run on the outer extended machine. The instructions that relate to different kinds of resource management functions (outer extended machine) can also be issued from a user program by raising special **supervisor call** (system call) instructions which act much like subroutine calls, but transfer control to the operating system rather than to one of the user subroutines.

The basic organization of this operating system, as shown in Figure 3.1, thus consists of two main parts: the *inner extended machine*, which is a low-level interface to the bare hardware and is a mechanism-dependent, hardware-dependent one. The other part is the *outer extended machine* that provides the other requirements of the specific OS in essentially the same way as user processes. There are at present no firm rules to indicate how many levels should be used, what modules should go into which levels, what should constitute the kernel, and so on. It entirely depends on the design objectives of the operating system and what support and services it will provide to users. However, this approach ultimately exhibited a lot of distinct advantages that eventually opened a new horizon with many innovative ideas that summarily had an immense impact on the evolution of different

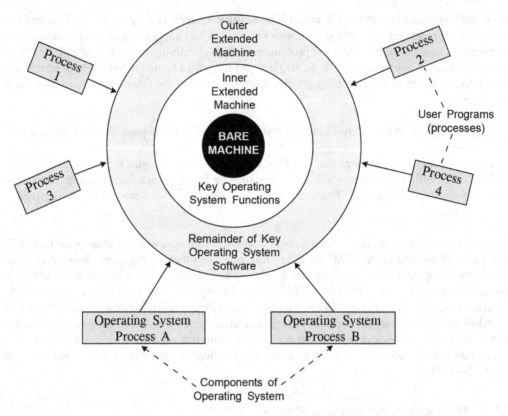

FIGURE 3.1 Design of the earlier operating systems in the form of Extended machine concept using hierarchical levels.

forms of generalized design and development of more modern operating systems for the days to come. For more details about this topic, see the Support Material at www.routledge.com/9781032467238.

3.1.3 LAYERED SYSTEMS—MODULAR HIERARCHICAL DESIGN

To negotiate constantly growing user density across a diverse spectrum of disciplines associated with numerous demands along with the continuous emergence of more complex, sophisticated, and versatile hardware, the operating system too has been continuously enhanced to drive more intelligent hardware and also to incorporate newer support and services that ultimately made it more complex, and its size also gradually increased. As a result, it was decided to make an abrupt change in its design approach in favor of structuring it in modules with relatively low degrees of interfacing between all such well-designed modules. The modular concept, however, started gaining more importance with passing days. This design approach ultimately facilitated easy maintainability and smooth upgradability and also supported encapsulation of data where objects may be manipulated exclusively within the module by means of a set of acceptable operations specified for that particular object type.

The structuring of the OS in the form of modules organized in hierarchical layers/levels eventually permitted the design to divide and separate the OS functions according to their importance, complexity, characteristic time scale, and of course, level of abstraction. The OS was then viewed as software clothing designed as series of levels or layers (like wafers arranged one above another) arranged hierarchically that wrapped around the bare hardware. However, the ordering of layers is such that some parts of the operating system belong to lower levels. The lower the level, the higher the power, and it is away from the user and closer to the core hardware and thus can then directly interact with the hardware over a far shorter time scale. Other parts of the operating system belong to higher levels which are away from the hardware and closer to the user. Some of these upper parts of the operating system allow the user to communicate directly with the operating system via commands that interact with the peripheral hardware over a longer duration of time. A representative modular hierarchical layer/level-structuring approach in designing an operating system as discussed is depicted in Figure 3.2.

In a strictly hierarchical implementation, a given level can exploit facilities including the objects and operations provided by all downward intermediate levels (up to bare hardware) by way of simply

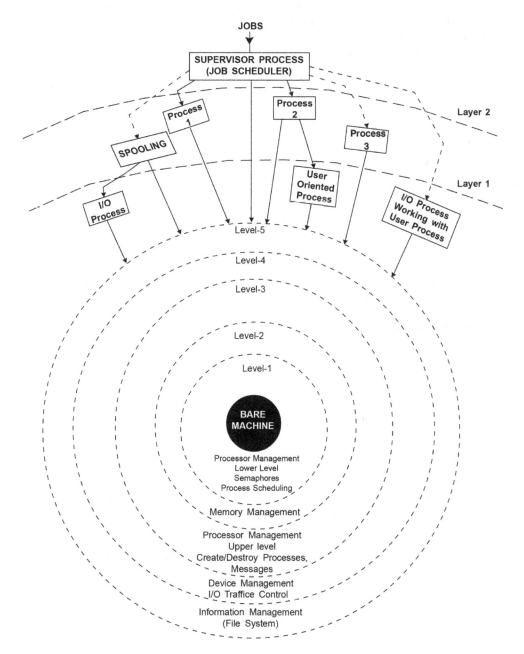

FIGURE 3.2 Generalized modular hierarchical layer/level structuring approach in designing an operating system used in large mainframe systems, and implemented in mid of 1960s.

calling upon the services they offer but without the details of their operations. Each level, however, already has its own existing set of primitive operations and related hardware support and cannot make use of anything of its higher levels. This modular hierarchical structuring approach also supports the concept of *information hiding*, where the details of data structures, processing algorithms, and mode of working of each and every module are totally confined within that module at its respective level. Externally, a module is observed to only perform a set of specific functions on various objects of different types. The internal details of its way of working are neither visible nor available and truly not of concern to the users enjoying the services provided by the respective module.

Over time, these design principles, realized in the form of hierarchical layers/levels, ultimately became a universal approach for being nicely matched with the working environment but greatly varying in methods of implementation among contemporary operating systems. The model as proposed by Denning and Brown (DENN 84) did not correspond to any specific operating system, but this representative structure (Figure 3.2) otherwise served to gain an overview of an operating system when designed and developed in the form of a hierarchical model. This model is summarized by layer/level with a few respective objects and their corresponding operations in Table 3.1.

TABLE 3.1
Leveled Operating System Design Hierarchy

Level	Name	Objects	Some Operations
5	**Information Management**		
	Command language interpreter (Shell)	User programming environment	Statements in command (shell) language
	User processes	User processes	Quit, kill, suspend, resume
	Supervisor process module		
	Job scheduler	Jobs	Scheduling of jobs
	Directories	Directory	create, destroy, open, close, read, write
	File systems	Files	create, destroy, open, close, read, write
4	**Device Management**		
	Keep track of status of all I/O devices.	External devices	create, destroy, open, close, read, write
	I/O Scheduling	External devices	
	Initiate I/O process	External devices	
	Communication	Pipes	create, destroy, open, close, read, write
3	**Processor management upper level**		
	Start process, stop process	Processes	create, destroy, send and receive,
2	**Memory Management**		
	Allocate memory	Segments, Pages,	allocate, free, fetch, read, write
	Release (free) memory		
	Local secondary store	blocks of data, device channels	read, write, allocate, free
1	**Processor management lower level**		
	P, V primitives	Semaphore	Interprocess comm.
	Process scheduling	Processes	suspend, resume, wait and signal
0	Procedures	Procedure call, call stack	call, return, mark stack
	Interrupts	Interrupt-handling programs	invoke, mask, retry,
	Instruction sets	Microprogram program interpreter, scalar and array data, evaluation stack.	load, store, branch, add, subtract
	Electronic circuits	Fundamental components like registers, gates, buses	activate, complement, clear, transfer

3.1.3.1   Case Study: IBM MVS System

Multiple virtual storage (MVS); a top-of-the-line most complex and immensely powerful operating system was introduced by IBM along with its versatile successor systems, like OS/390 and finally the largest z/OS to drive their different series of most advanced third-, fourth-, and fifth-generation mainframe and multiprocessor systems, like S/370, S/3000, and S/390 series of machines, and also for large server computers. Although MVS has often been looked as a modular-leveled (monolithic, centrally controlled) information-processing system, IBM later restructured it (and successor systems) as a "large server" in a network-oriented distributed environment using a three-tier application model. However, the evolution path of MVS actually highlights the design concept of a modular-leveled approach to an operating system that was eventually implemented in the development of MVS, a relevant representative system of this category in reality.

For more details about layered systems and their implementation and the MVS operating system, see the Support Material at www.routledge.com/9781032467238.

3.1.4   Virtual Machine Operating Systems—A Revolutionary Approach

The real essence of this layer/level concept in the design of an OS, however, was religiously implemented by IBM in their initial versions of DOS/360 and later in OS/360 and many such operating systems for their series of S/360 and S/370 computing systems. The overwhelming success of these products eventually provoked other contemporary manufacturers like Burroughs, DEC, NCR, ICL, and others to come out with their own operating systems developed almost in the same line as DOS/360 and OS/360. IBM also kept constantly enhancing these products, releasing many different versions with numerous additional features. At the other end, due to the revolution in electronic technology, series of more advanced computer systems had been regularly coming out with more intelligence and power, and lower size and cost that were capable of fulfilling various newer demands of the users. Consequently, more and more advanced operating systems were then needed that were mostly realized by simply carrying out repeated modifications and upgrading the existing older ones to drive these continually changing, more sophisticated computer systems. All these together, however, eventually created a major upheaval in computing environments. A user's application program while was executable under an older operating system, but found unusable under the new operating system (enhanced version) without modification, and that modification sometimes might be again quite extensive and also expensive. IBM faced this problem most critically. An IBM installation with different versions of operating systems in the machine often required repeatedly changing operating systems to meet all its users' needs. To avoid these operational difficulties, IBM developed a radically different form of system architecture for its S/360 and S/370 series of computers called virtual machines (VMs), which was finally accepted and widely used for being an amazing product.

Until then, it was mandatory that one piece of complete hardware was to be driven by one dedicated operating system supporting many individual users. But a VM is an arrangement that was designed to emulate multiple computer systems. The ultimate objective of the VM was to multiplex all the system resources among users located under different operating systems in such a way that each user seemed to have undivided access to all the machine's resources. In other words, each user is assumed to have a separate copy of the entire machine; each such copy was termed a *virtual machine*.

Each VM, although logically separated from all others, but is essentially the same as to have a true piece of the total hardware and as such is able to run its own operating system, exactly like that on a real hardware system. Consequently, different VMs run on a single piece of hardware and are controlled by different operating systems per their own choice to satisfy their individual requirements. This scenario is depicted in Figure 3.3, where several different operating systems are run concurrently over a single piece of hardware. Virtual machines ultimately insulate many users from one another or one user from many different types of hardware.

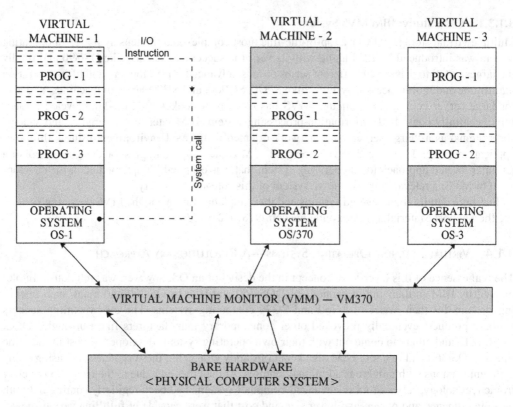

FIGURE 3.3 Virtual machines that run on a single piece of hardware, but each such machine has its own dissimilar operating system, and the role of the virtual machine monitor (VMM) in this regard to keep them operationally integrated.

The heart of the system, the *virtual machine monitor*, runs on the bare hardware (physical hardware) and creates the required VM interface, providing multitasking concurrently to several VMs of the next layer up. A VMM is essentially a special form of operating system that multiplexes only the physical resources among users, offering each an exact copy of the bare hardware, including kernel/user mode, I/O interrupts, and everything else the real machine has, but no other functional enhancements are provided. These VMs should be considered neither *extended machines* (in which policy-dependent and hardware-dependent parts have been completely separated) nor *microkernels* (to be discussed later at the end of this chapter) with different modules of programs and other features.

A VMM is actually divided into roughly *two equal major components*: **CP** (*control program*) and **CMS** (*conversational monitor system*) that greatly simplify the design of the VMM and its implementation. The CP component is located close to the hardware and performs the functions of processor, memory, and I/O device multiplexing to create the VMs. The CMS, placed above the CP, is a simple operating system that performs the functions of command processing, information management, and limited device management. In fact, the CP and CMS are typically used together, but the CMS can be replaced by any other OS, such as OS/360, DOS, OS/VS1, or OS/VS2. Virtual machines, however, have **many uses and distinct advantages**:

- **Concurrent execution:** Running of dissimilar operating systems simultaneously by different users on one physical machine.
- **Elimination of certain conversion problems:** Users can run any program under any of the installed OSs and can even use more than one installed OS simultaneously on the same piece of hardware.

- **Software development:** Programs can be developed and debugged for machine configurations that are different from those of the host. It can even permit developers to write real operating systems without interfering with other users.
- **Test of network facilities:** It can test network facilities, as will be discussed later, by simulating machine–machine communication between several VMs under one VM monitor on one physical machine.
- **Evaluation of program behavior:** The VMM must intercept certain instructions for interpretive execution rather than allowing them to execute directly on the bare machine. These intercepted instructions include I/O requests and most other supervisory calls.
- **Reliability:** The VMM typically does not require a large amount of code or a high degree of logical complexity. This makes it feasible to carry out comprehensive check-out procedures and thus ensures high overall reliability as well as integrity with regard to any special privacy and security features that may be present. Isolating software components in different VMs enhances software reliability.
- **Security and privacy:** The high degree of isolation between independent VMs facilitates privacy and security. In fact, privacy between users is ensured because an operating system has no way of determining whether it is running on a VM or on a bare machine and therefore no way of spying on or altering any other co-existing VMs. Thus, security can be enhanced by isolating sensitive programs and data to one dedicated VM.

3.1.4.1   Drawbacks

The VM had a lot of distinct advantages, and it could also be configured with *multiple processors*, but it was unable to provide all of the controls needed to take full advantage of modern multiprocessor configurations. However, it also suffered from several other serious drawbacks; one of these is that the failure of a single piece of hardware, or any malfunction of the VMM-interface simultaneously supporting many VMs would ultimately cause a crash of the entire environment. Moreover, this hardware was very expensive and also gigantic in size. In addition, the VMM-interface is still a complex program, since simulating a number of virtual 370s or compatible machines is not that simple to realize, even with compromises for moderate efficiency and reasonable performance. Last but not least, the inclusion of each additional layer offers a better level of abstraction for the sake of multiplexing and to simplify code, but that starts to affect the performance to some extent, as many interactions may then happen between such layers.

Virtual-machine operating systems are too complex, and most instructions are directly executed by the hardware to speed up the execution. In fact, virtual-machine operating systems cannot be implemented on computers where dangerous instructions (such as I/O manipulating address-translation registers, discussed in Chapter 5, or the processor state, including interrupt-return instructions and priority setting instructions) are ignored or fail to trap in a non-privileged state, as was found in PDP-11/45.

Some Famous Virtual Machine Interfaces

- IBM's VMs: The first popular VM interface
- VM line

    ○ CP-40/CMS 1967,   CP-67/CMS 1967,   VP/CSS 1968
    ○ VM/370 1972,   VM/SP 1980,   VM/ESA 1988

- z/VM 2000
- VMWare: Multiple OS on a single machine IBM VM under Linux
- Java Virtual Machine (JVM):   Hardware hiding, implemented at a little
    (—Java, Nice, Net REXX)   bit higher level over OS

A Representative List of Hardware with Virtual Machine Support

- IBM System/370, System/390, and z-Series mainframes
- Intel Vanderpool
- Freescale PowerPC, MPC8572, and MPC8641D (Motorola)
- AMD Pacifica
- Boston Circuits gCore (grid-on-chip) with 16 ARC 750D cores and time-machine hardware virtualization module
- X86 virtualization # Hardware support in X-86 processors

For more details about this topic, see the Support Material at www.routledge.com/9781032467238.

3.1.5 NETWORKS OF COMPUTERS: CLIENT–SERVER MODEL: A NEW DIRECTION

The serious drawbacks of architectural VMs, as discussed, ultimately paved the way for them to fizzle out, but their successful implementation opened a new horizon in the operating system design concept. It introduced the idea that the operating system can be developed even by way of moving a large part of conventional operating system code into a higher layer known as CMS (see virtual machine). A modern trend then started to emerge in organizing an operating system, exploiting this idea of *moving a large part of the OS codes up into higher layers even further, leaving only minimal (core) operating system codes, known as a* **kernel**. A kernel is essentially a protected, trusted subsystem containing a set of programs consisting of the most-used and fundamental components of the operating system. This kernel usually keeps track of the active processes and manages scheduling and context switching (to be discussed in Chapter 4), exception and interrupt handling, multiprocessor synchronization and communication. The remaining portion of the operating system functions are implemented in *user processes* known as the **client process** that issues a request for a service (e.g. reading a block of a data file) to a **server process** which services the request, performs the task as requested, and sends back the answer and control. However, the ultimate was the birth of a new concept, historically known as **client–server model** (not to be confused with client–server architecture).

In the client–server model, the primary task of the kernel is to handle communication between clients and servers. By way of splitting up the operating system into parts where each part handles only one facet of the system, such as process services, memory services, terminal services, and file services, and so on; each part becomes small, manageable, and hence easily maintainable. Moreover, because all the server processes run as user-mode processes and not in kernel-mode, as depicted in Figure 3.4, they do not have direct access to the hardware. As a result, if a bug in any of the servers is triggered, the same server may crash, leaving the other servers mostly unaffected, and hence, this will not usually cause the entire system as a whole to collapse.

The client–server model is also fairly adaptable to use in **distributed systems** in which the computing environment may be composed of large number of CPUs (or a set of personal computers or large systems) used as clients with shared/distributed memory systems connected by a high-speed communication network (or LAN) with server (one or a set of large hosts, such as a mainframe), as shown in Figure 3.5, in contrast to the conventional **centralized systems** consisting of a single CPU, its memory, peripherals, and some terminals. Under this environment, the application processing is divided (not necessarily evenly) between the client and server, and it is actually initiated and partially controlled by the client and then executed most efficiently either locally or in a cooperative manner with the server, keeping the client completely unaware of it, but a reply will come back and be received by the client in an ongoing user interaction. However, depending on the type of application and the design of the client–server operating-system software being used, the actual client–server interaction with respect to data transmission and its subsequent processing are to be carried out by and between the client and server in the most desirable befitting manner.

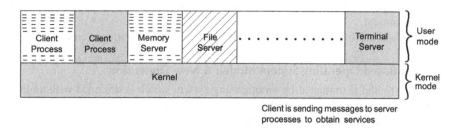

Client is sending messages to server
processes to obtain services

FIGURE 3.4 A generic operating system model runs on single system (uniprocessor) when used in client–server environment in the premises of computer networks.

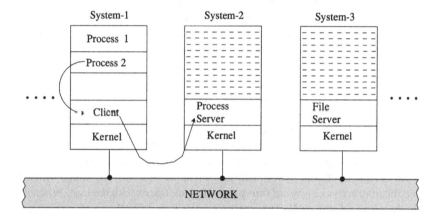

FIGURE 3.5 A generic operating system model runs on multiple systems (multiple–processor) when used in client–server environment in the premises of distributed systems.

In multi-user/multi-access environments, the client–server model also nicely fits. It facilitates the interactions that are made by and between the concurrently executing software processes issued by multiple users (clients) either working on different portions of a large program (multi-access, e.g. reservation systems) or with their individual different programs (multi-user). The interaction between the client and server processes is, however, a *cooperative, transactional exchange*, in which the client is **proactive** and the server is **reactive**.

The client–server operating system sometimes follows a different approach where the kernel is built to have a minimal amount of *mechanism* but leaves all *policy* decisions up to the server in the user space (see Figure 3.4). Here, the kernel blindly executes the task requested from the server without checking its validity and leaves the entire burden to the receiving end to accept or reject policy-wise. This separation of mechanism from policy is an important concept; it appears again and again in the design of operating systems while implementing various functions.

The client–server arrangement today provides a common model and a natural base for **distributed computing** using networks of computers over a wide geographical area supported by a **distributed operating system** that casts a *single-system image* of the entire arrangement to its users. Recently, client–server arrangements in computer networks consisting of standalone computers with their own individual different operating systems supported by **network operating systems (NOS)** and additional **middleware** (cluster architecture) provide **cloud computing**, another form (a sibling) of distributed computing that mainly aims towards virtualization of resources. But, whatever the forms, the ultimate end is primarily targeted, apart from many other reasons, to balance the load of the entire arrangement in a fitting way to realize greater efficiency and better performance in a distributed environment.

For more details about this topic, see the Support Material at www.routledge.com/9781032467238.

3.1.5.1   Kernel-Based Operating System Model: A New Dimension

The client–server model is managed by an operating system which is designed with an innovative concept popularly known as *kernel–shell* design. Under this concept, an operating system can be designed by way of dividing it into two distinctly separated major pieces: one part of the OS critical to its correct operation executes in privileged mode, referred to as supervisor mode, is called the **kernel**, or **nucleus**, while its other part, the generic system software, runs in user mode, similar to all application programs, and is called the **shell**, which talks to the user. This fundamental difference is the irrefutable distinction between the operating system and other system software, and this dual mode of processor execution is assisted by the *mode bit* present in the processor (as discussed in Chapter 2). In fact, much of the logic in the structure and implementation of the operating system design process is centered on the design of its kernel, which typically consists of a number of public and private routines, including its private system data structures. Users can only call on the OS's public routines when they intend to perform system-related work.

The design objective of the kernel is well defined. It operates as *trusted software*, kept totally protected from any undesirable attempt from the user space. While most of the functions present in the kernel may be easy to implement and also run fast, the procedure to implement trap mechanisms and authentication is too expensive and leads to graceful degradation in the overall performance of the entire system. In the event of concurrent execution of processes usually supported at the user-process level, the kernel itself typically turns interrupts off whenever they enter in order to preserve the integrity of system data and implements synchronization between the processes.

The other part of the operating system run in user mode is called the **shell**, which includes a program called the *interactive command interpreter* that interfaces with the user. When a user types a command at the terminal, the shell reads and interprets it and finally invokes the corresponding system services (programs) available in the kernel to carry out those commands. Programs when run communicate directly with the kernel and do not talk to the shell. In addition, the shell also does I/O redirection and allows the user to have pipes and filters. In fact, the shell actually maintains several variables that determine the entire operating environment.

When a new function is to be added in the kernel of the OS, it should be trusted software to be executed in *supervisor space* with access to other parts of the kernel. However, programs that are added to extend the operating system functionalities and implemented in *user mode* should not have any access to anything lying within the domain of the kernel, but those added programs can normally invoke the kernel functions as usual. The kernel, however, does not rely on the correctness of these added parts for correct operation of the OS.

When a user logs in (boots the system), the system invokes a copy of the shell to handle interactions caused by the user. Although the shell is the standard system interface, it is possible to add any other user-specified process to coexist with the system shell that, in turn, offers quite different views and dissimilar working environments for different users of the same system.

The kernel handles multiple users and processes, manages memory systems, and does all I/O management, including file management for the entire computing system. Some of the typical functions performed by an operating-system kernel with respect to management of different resources are:

Processor/Process Management

- Process creation and termination
- Process scheduling and dispatching

- Process switching
- Process synchronization at the time of inter-process communication
- Process control block management

Memory Management

- Allocation of memory to processes
- Swapping
- Page and segment management

Device or I/O Management

- Buffer management
- Allocation of devices to processes and allocation of I/O channels

File Management

- File creation and deletion
- Operations on file
- Directory creation and removal
- Operations on directories

Execution-Support Functions

- Interrupt handling
- Procedure handling
- Accounting
- Monitoring and supervision

For more details about this topic, see the Support Material at www.routledge.com/9781032467238.

3.1.5.2 Case Study: UNIX System

The kernel–shell concept has been successfully converted in design and implementation for many operating systems, but its true flavor and elegance have been observed to be best in the implementation of UNIX (see also Chapter 1). As with other operating systems, UNIX is also a layered operating system but differently structured, as shown in Figure 3.6 with a general layer-wise description. The bare hardware is here surrounded by the operating-system software, often called the **system kernel** or simply the **kernel** to emphasize its isolation and separation from the user and applications. The kernel controls the hardware and provides operating-system services by means of a system call interface that allows user programs to create and manage files and other resources. The way these system calls are implemented internally may differ between various UNIX versions. UNIX also consists of a number of *user services and interfaces* that can be grouped into the **shell**, other interface software, and the components of the C compiler (this includes assembler, compiler, loader). The remaining layer that resides outside this domain and above it consists of user applications and user interface to the C compiler.

User programs can invoke operating-system services, either directly or through library programs, by way of using system calls with respective arguments intercepted by the system call interface that ultimately issues trap instructions to switch from user mode to kernel mode to initiate UNIX. Since there is no way to write a trap instruction in C, a library is provided with one procedure written in assembly language per each system call that can be called from C. It needs to be clearly mentioned

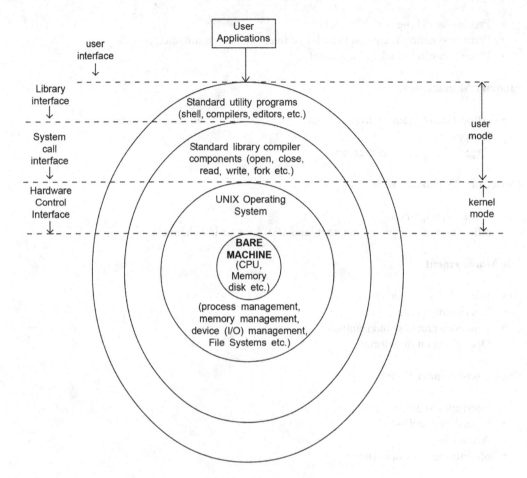

FIGURE 3.6 Operating system design based on kernel–shell concept implemented best in UNIX using layered implementation, but differently structured.

at this point that it is the *library interface*, not the *system call interface*, that has been brought to an acceptable standard with the specification defined by POSIX 1003.1 to implement standardization in different versions and forms of UNIX.

The kernel in UNIX is not really well structured internally, but two parts are more or less distinguishable. At the very bottom is the **machine-dependent kernel** that consists of a few modules containing *interrupt handler*, the *low-level I/O system device drivers*, and part of the *memory management software*. Since this directly drives the hardware, it has to be rewritten almost from scratch whenever UNIX is *ported* to (installed on) a new machine. In contrast, the **machine-independent kernel** is the same on all machines, because it *does not depend* closely on the particular hardware it is running on. This code includes *system call handling, process management, scheduling, pipes, signals, paging and swapping, the file system*, and the *high-level part of the I/O system* (disk strategy, etc.).

In fact, files and I/O devices are treated in a uniform manner by the same set of applicable system calls. As a result, I/O redirection and stream-level I/O are fully supported at both the command-language (shell) and system-call levels. Fortunately, the *machine-independent part* is much larger than the *machine-dependent part*, which is why it is relatively straightforward to *port* UNIX to a wide range of different or new hardware. It is interesting to note at this point that portability was not one of the design objectives of UNIX. Rather, it came as a consequence of coding the system with a comparatively high-level and/or in a high-level language. Having realized the importance of portability, the designers of UNIX have then decided to confine hardware-dependent code to only a few modules in order to facilitate easy porting. In fact, today's UNIX systems in many respects tend to disloyal to the original design philosophy so that they can better address increasing functionality requirements.

All versions of UNIX (as shown in Figure 3.6) provide an operating system (kernel), standard system call library, and large number of standard utility programs. Some of these utility programs maintain the standard as specified by POSIX 1003.1, and others that differ between UNIX versions that are invoked by the user include the command language interpreter (shell), compilers, editors, text-processing programs, and file-handling utilities. Out of the three interfaces to UNIX (as shown in Figure 3.6): the *true system call interface*, the *library interface*, and the *interface* formed by the set of standard utility programs along with the shell (*user interface*), this last one is not part of UNIX, although most casual users think so.

The huge number of utility programs can be again divided into *six categories*: *file and directory manipulation commands, filters, compilers and program development tools, text processing, system administration*, and *miscellaneous*. Moreover, the filters that have almost nothing to do with the operating system and are also usually not found in other existing contemporary operating systems can be easily replaced without changing the operating system itself at all. In fact, this and other flexibilities together precisely contribute much to making UNIX popular and allow it to survive so well even in the flood of numerous changes continuously going on in the domain of underlying hardware technology over time. Some popular UNIX-like operating systems are:

- UNIX-like systems on IBM mainframes
  - UTS 1981
  - AIX/370 1990
  - AIX/ESA 1991
- HP–UNIX
- Linux 1999

For more details about this topic, see the Support Material at www.routledge.com/9781032467238.

3.1.6 Comparing MVS and UNIX: Concepts and Terms

MVS is a layer/level-based top-of-the-line complex and powerful operating system from IBM with a versatile successor system, OS/390, and finally the largest z/OS to drive the different series of advanced third-, fourth-, and fifth-generation mainframe multiprocessor systems, like the S/370 series, S/3000 series, and S/390 series machines and also large server computers. IBM's AIX operating system is a distributed UNIX operating system that came on the heels of development of the LOCUS operating system. IBM's OS/390 UNIZ is another UNIX-like operating system developed mainly for server-based large distributed computing systems. A comparison (dedicated OS versus UNIX) based on different attributes offered by these operating systems and their facilities along with the related concepts behind them, is given in Table 3.2 on the Support Material at www.routledge.com/9781032467238. The table is organized in a random order; the disparate nature of the tasks and concepts that are used in the table makes logical ordering and consistent phrasing difficult.

3.1.7 Monolithic Kernel

It has been seen that partitioning OS kernel programs in separate modules with respect to their different resource management needs (as described in the previous section), along with their related data structures, including resource queues, process descriptors, semaphores, deadlock information, virtual memory tables, device descriptors, file descriptors, and the like, is very difficult. The reason is that each module depends on certain information that is encapsulated in other modules. Moreover, the performance of a partitioned OS might be too inefficient for hardware with limited computing power or information transfer bandwidth. It was thus decided to implement the OS kernel as a single *monolith*.

A **monolithic kernel** organization means that almost all of the kernel (main or major) functions: process and resource management, memory management, and file management, are implemented in a single unit. A monolithic kernel, as shown in Figure 3.7, running in kernel space in supervisor mode consists of all software and data structures that are placed in one logical module (unit) with no explicit interfaces to any parts of the OS software. In common with other architectures (microkernel, hybrid kernel, discussed later), the kernel here also provides a high-level virtual interface to its upper level with a set of primitives or system calls that implement the operating system services, such as process management, concurrency, and memory management, using one or more components (parts) that then interact with the bare hardware.

Although every component servicing its respective operations is separate within the unit, the code integration between them is very tight and difficult to develop correctly, and, since all the modules run in the same address space, a bug in one module can collapse the entire system. Still, when the implementation is complete and trustworthy, the tight internal integration of components in turn allows the low-level features of the underlying system to be excellently utilized and summarily makes a good monolithic kernel highly effective and equally efficient.

Under this system, the user gets operating system services by issuing necessary instructions (special trap instructions) known as *system calls* (*supervisor calls*) or *kernel calls* with appropriate parameters in well-defined places, such as in registers or on the stack. When these instructions are executed, the machine is switched from *user mode* to *kernel mode*, also known as *supervisor mode*, and control is then transferred to the kernel (operating system), which examines the given parameters associated with the call and then loads the corresponding service procedure, which is then executed. After completion, control is then sent back to the user program to resume its ongoing operation.

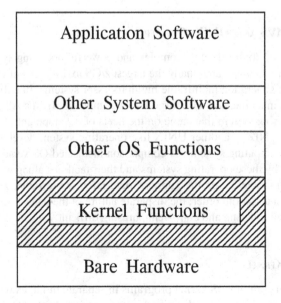

FIGURE 3.7   An overview of an operating system design based on Monolithic kernel concept.

Some Important Examples of Monolithic Kernels

- MS-DOS, Microsoft Windows 9x series (Windows 95, Windows 98, and Windows 98SE), and Windows Me
- Traditional UNIX kernels, such as the kernels of the BSDs and Solaris
- Linux kernels
- Mac OS kernels, up until Mac OS 8.6
- OpenVMS
- XTS-400
- Some educational kernels, such as, Agnix
- Syllable (operating system)

Monolithic kernels are further discussed in different sections at the end of this chapter and are also referred to in Chapter 9, "Distributed Systems".

For more details about this topic, see the Support Material at www.routledge.com/9781032467238.

3.1.7.1 Case Study: MS-DOS System

MS-DOS was a *kernel*-based (essentially *monolithic kernel*, although it did not use supervisor mode in the CPU) single-user, single-process operating system structured in **three** layers:

1. **BIOS** (basic input output system)
2. The **kernel**
3. The **shell**, COMMAND.COM

The **BIOS** is a collection of low-level device drivers that serves to isolate MS-DOS from the details of the hardware. BIOS procedures are loaded in a reserved area in the lowest portion of main memory and are called by trapping to them via *interrupt vectors*. The basic OS **kernel** was wholly implemented in the read-only memory's (ROM) resident BIOS routines, and two executable files, **IO.SYS** and **MS-DOS.SYS** (Chappell, 1994). IO.SYS (called **IBMBIO.COM** in IBM) is a hidden file and is loaded in memory at the time of booting, just above interrupt vectors. It provides a procedure call interface to the BIOS so the kernel can access BIOS services by making procedure calls to IO.SYS instead of traps to the ROM. This file holds those BIOS procedures, not in the ROM, as well as a module called **SYSINIT** which is used to boot the system. The existence of IO.SYS further isolates the kernel from hardware details. The **MS-DOS.SYS** (which IBM calls **IBMDOS.COM**) is another hidden file which is loaded in memory just above IO.SYS and contains the *machine-independent part* of the operating system. It handles process management, memory management, and the file system, as well as the interpretation of all system calls.

The third part of what most people think of as the operating system is the **shell**, **COMMAND. COM**, which is actually not part of the operating system and thus can be replaced by the user. In order to reduce memory requirements, the standard COMMAND.COM is split into **two pieces**: a *resident portion* that always resides in memory just above MDDOS.SYS and a *transient portion* loaded at the high end of memory only when the shell is active. It can be overwritten by the user programs if the space is needed. Later, MS-DOS reloads COMMAND.COM afresh from disk if it is changed.

As the device-dependent code is kept confined to one layer, porting MS-DOS is theoretically reduced to only writing or modifying the BIOS code afresh for the new hardware. Later releases of MS-DOS had UNIX-like features. At the command level (shell), MS-DOS provides a hierarchical file system, I/O redirection, pipes, and filters. User-written commands can be invoked in the same way as standard system commands, thereby providing the needed extension of the basic system functionality.

For more details about this topic, see the Support Material at www.routledge.com/9781032467238.

3.1.8   CASE STUDY: MONOLITHIC KERNEL-BASED OPERATING SYSTEM

- **The Traditional UNIX Kernel**

The original UNIX philosophy was to keep kernel functionality as limited as possible with a minimal OS to only implement the bare necessities while emphasizing the other system software to implement as many normal additional OS functions as possible. In fact, the original UNIX kernel, as shown in Figure 3.8, was small, efficient, and monolithic, providing only basic machine resource management and a minimal low-level file system, along with kernel (OS) extension facilities for creating specific computational environments. The device management functions were separately implemented in device drivers inside the kernel that were added to the kernel at a later time. Thus, the kernel would often need to be extended by way of reconfiguring it with the code of new device drivers whenever new devices were added without disturbing the existing main kernel at all. The file organization implemented byte-stream files using the *stdio* (standard I/O) library to format the byte stream.

Early monolithic UNIX kernels provided *two* significant interfaces, as shown in Figure 3.8. The first one was between the kernel and user space programs, such as applications, libraries, and commands. The second one was within the kernel space and that between the main part of the kernel and the device drivers using the interrupt handler as the interface between the device and the kernel. However, the UNIX kernel, after repeated modifications and enhancements, ultimately emerged as a medium-sized monolithic monitor in which system calls are implemented as a set of co-routines. In general, once the kernel co-routine starts its execution, it continues with the processor until completion unless it is preempted by an interrupt. Some system processes, however, also are available to service device interrupts.

The UNIX kernel, after being expanded, ported, and re-implemented many times, gradually became large and complex and eventually deviated from the original design philosophy to emphasize other expansions so that it could better address increasing functionality requirements,

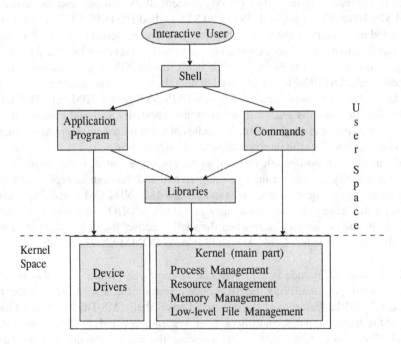

FIGURE 3.8   An overview of traditional UNIX operating system implementation using the design based on Monolithic kernel concept.

particularly in the area of *network* and *graphic device support*. Graphic devices are largely handled in user space, and networks are addressed explicitly by the expanded system call interface.

Modern monolithic kernels, when used in distributed systems, are essentially today's centralized operating system augmented with networking facilities and the integration of remote services. Most system calls are made by trapping the kernel, which services and executes the calls and then returns the desired result to the user process. With this approach, most machines in a network have disks with a traditional kernel and manage their own local file systems. Many distributed systems that are extensions or imitations of UNIX use this approach to a large extent.

For more details about this topic, see the Support Material at www.routledge.com/9781032467238.

- **The Linux Kernel**

The **Linux kernel** uses the same organizational strategy as found in other UNIX kernels but religiously sticks to a minimal OS (original principle of UNIX) that also accommodates the current technology in its detailed design with *monolithic kernel* organization. Similar to UNIX, Linux also provides an interface within the kernel between the main part of the kernel and the device drivers. This facility accommodates any modification or incorporation of additional device drivers or file systems to the existing kernel that are already *statically* configured into kernel organization. But the problem with Linux in this regard is that the development of Linux is mostly global and carried out by a loosely associated group of independent developers. Linux resolves this situation simply by providing an extra mechanism for adding functionality called a **module**, as shown in Figure 3.9. Whereas device drivers are statically configured into a kernel structure, modules can be dynamically added and deleted even when the OS is in action. Modules can also be used to implement dynamically loadable device drivers or other desired kernel functions.

Linux is designed and structured as a collection of relatively independent blocks or modules, a number of which can be loaded and unloaded on demand, commonly referred to as *loadable modules*. In essence, a module is an executable file that implements a specific function, such as a file system, a device driver, or some other feature of the kernel's upper layer. These modules can even be linked to and unlinked from the kernel at runtime. A module cannot be executed as its

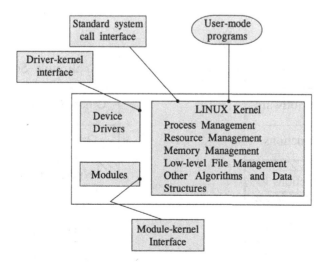

FIGURE 3.9 An overview of traditional Linux operating system implementation based on Monolithic kernel concept, showing the placement of Linux kernel, device drivers, and modules.

own process or thread; rather it can be executed in kernel mode on behalf of the current process. However, a module can create kernel threads for various purposes as and when needed. This modularity of the kernel (as also is found in FreeBSD and Solaris) is at the binary (image) level, not at the kernel architecture level. These two are completely different but are sometimes confused. Modular monolithic kernels are not to be confused with the architectural level of modularity inherent in microkernels or hybrid kernels. By virtue of having a modular structure, the Linux kernel, in spite of being monolithic, has overcome some of its major inherent difficulties in developing and evolving the modern kernel.

For more details about this topic, see the Support Material at www.routledge.com/9781032467238.

3.1.9 MICROKERNEL: THE EXTENSIBLE NUCLEUS

While a monolithic kernel puts almost all of the kernel (main or major) functions in a single unit and provides good *portability* and *flexibility*, but since it is constantly expanded and re-implemented many times to enhance its functionality, it gradually gets large and complex, which starts to severely affect not only its *portability* and *flexibility* but also hampers its *extensibility* and to a large extent its *reliability*. The viable alternative, however, came out exactly following the extended machine approach implemented in the design of OSs as already described in the beginning of this chapter that eventually gave rise to the innovative idea of an *extensible nucleus* in the organization of the kernel. This strategy, when implemented, actually uses a common set of skeletal facilities, as shown in Figure 3.10(b), that defines two types of modules for any particular OS.

1. The skeletal hardware-dependent, mechanism-dependent but policy-independent modules to manage total core operating system functions.
2. The policy-specific, policy-dependent, hardware-independent modules to provide less-important essential services but major applications of the OS, such as scheduling of CPU, I/O, and memory handling.

The first (No. 1) implements the extensible nucleus or **microkernel** that provides a low-level uniform VM interface with some form of process and memory management, usually with only the bare essentials of device management. In this way, it overcomes the problems concerning *portability*, *extensibility* (*scalability*), *flexibility*, and *reliability*. While this part does not provide complete

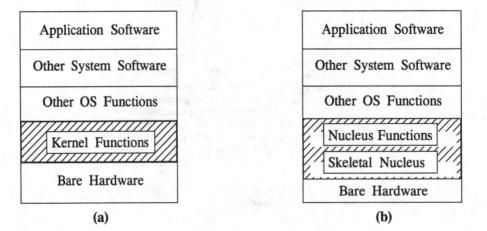

(a)   (b)

FIGURE 3.10 A formal design concept of structural organization of an operating system using (a) monolithic kernel approach, and (b) microkernel (extensible nucleus) model separately.

functionality, but it creates an environment in which the second part, that is, policy-dependent part of the operating system, can be built to meet all the needs and requirements of the application domain. The second part essentially reflects the actual requirements and functions of the specific OS that are implemented as *server processes* (*kernel processes*), resides and operates on top of the microkernel (at the upper level of the microkernel) along with user processes, performs interrupt handling, and provides communication between servers and user processes by means of message passing as shown in Figure 3.11. Processes here need not to be distinguished at all between kernel-level and user-level services because all such services are provided by way of message passing.

The microkernel is viewed differently and thus implemented in a different way by different operating systems, but the common characteristic is that certain essential core services must be provided by the microkernel, and many other services that traditionally have been part of the operating system are now placed as external subsystems (the second item in the list) that interact with the kernel (microkernel) and also with each other. These subsystems usually include file systems, process services, windowing systems, protection systems, and similar others (Figure 3.11).

But whatever the design strategy followed in the architecture of the microkernel (extensible nucleus), its emergence consequently gave rise to two fundamentally new directions and dimensions in the operating system design: **multiple OSs–single hardware** and **single OS–multiple hardware**, as shown in Figure 3.12. The first approach, as shown in Figure 3.12(a), concerns the direction that allows policy-dependent parts of different OSs to run on a VM interface used to implement policy-specific extensions built on a single hardware platform that complement the extensible kernel (nucleus) and form a complete operating system at each end. In fact, the IBM VM system designed in the 1970s mostly followed the same line, at least conceptually but implemented differently, and had the intent to inject the extensible nuclei factor into the design of an operating system that eventually culminated in the emergence of the microkernels of the 1990s.

The second approach appeared to be the reverse of the first and relates to the **portability** of an OS, as shown in Figure 3.12(b). Here, the nucleus (microkernel) is so designed that it can be run on different types of hardware and provides a high degree of flexibility and modularity. Its size is

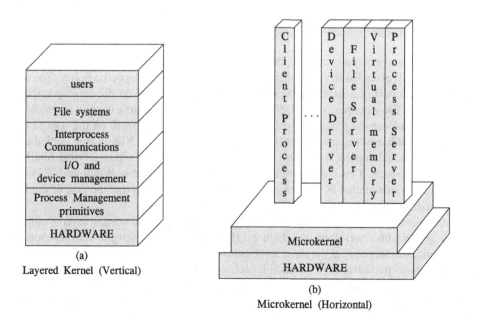

FIGURE 3.11 A typical kernel architectural design of an operating system using vertically layered kernel and horizontally layered microkernel.

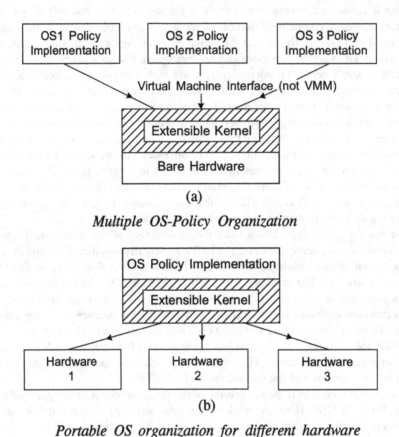

(a)

Multiple OS-Policy Organization

(b)

Portable OS organization for different hardware

FIGURE 3.12   Basic design concept of operating systems using microkernel (extensible nucleus) for the environments: a) different multiple OS when used on a single piece of hardware, and b) single portable OS when used on different hardware organization.

relatively small, and it actually consists of the skeletal policy-independent functions (bare hardware functions) that are extended with specialized servers to implement a specific policy. The remaining policy-dependent part of a specific OS, which is much larger, runs on the corresponding nucleus and is portable. For example, when UNIX is installed on new hardware, the extensible nucleus (hardware dependent/policy independent) of UNIX is configured afresh on the spot to match the existing available hardware, and the policy-dependent portion of UNIX is then copied to make it a completely runnable operating system to drive the specific hardware in a broad family of various hardware products. This well-publicized approach was exploited in Windows NT in which the nucleus kernel is surrounded by a number of compact subsystems so that the task of implementing NT on a variety of hardware platforms is carried out easily.

The microkernel design ultimately tended to replace the traditional vertical layered concept of an operating system with a horizontal one (Figure 3.11) in which the operating-system components external to the microkernel reside at the same level and interact with each other on a peer-to-peer basis by means of messages passed through the microkernel, as shown in Figure 3.13. The microkernel here validates messages, passes them between components, and grants access to the hardware. This structure is, however, most conducive to a **distributed processing environment** in which the microkernel can pass messages either locally or remotely without necessitating changes in other operating-system components. Microkernels are further explored in some detail in Chapter 9, "Distributed Operating Systems".

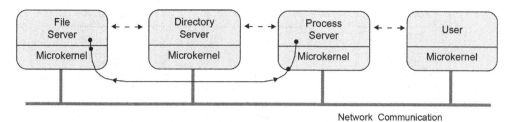

FIGURE 3.13 A formal design approach of operating systems using horizontally structured microkernel for the distributed processing environment.

A microkernel architecture is very advantageous in the context of developing an **object-oriented operating system (OOOS)** in which objects are the components of the OS used as building blocks with clearly defined interfaces that can then be interconnected with one another to form complete software. This approach, however, ensures *extensibility*; any modifications and/or additions of new features then require only certain changes to the respective objects and/or include extra objects, respectively, and thereby facilitate avoiding extensive changes in the existing form. Operating systems such as Windows though do not rely exclusively or fully on object-oriented methods but have injected object-oriented principles into their microkernel design.

In spite of microkernels having several distinct advantages, one of its serious **drawbacks** is that some functionalities of a traditional kernel are split between a microkernel, and the remainder are implemented as a collection of OS functions that use the microkernel, thereby causing the familiar stratification problem. For example, a traditional kernel includes the complete process management function which performs creation, scheduling, and dispatching of processes, whereas a microkernel might include only process creation and dispatching, and process scheduling may reside at higher level but run as a process under the microkernel. Consequently, communication between the parts may eventually cause a graceful degradation in overall system performance.

For more details about this topic, see the Support Material at www.routledge.com/9781032467238.

3.1.9.1 Case Study: Microkernel-Based OS: Windows NT

Windows NT is a commercial OS, first released for public use in July 1993 (Solomon, 1998) with the aim of being an *extensible*, *portable*, *reliable* and *secure* OS for contemporary computers, including symmetric multiprocessors.

Windows NT is designed using the extensible nucleus software model (*microkernel* approach) in which only the most essential OS functions are implemented in a small nucleus of code, the *microkernel*. Additional mechanisms are then implemented as an OS (NT Executive) on top of the nucleus to define policies as needed. The key mechanisms (such as scheduling policy, protection mechanisms, etc.) are carefully designed and tested as one trusted subassembly that can then be used to implement many different policies and mechanisms.

As depicted in Figure 3.14, the *NT kernel* provides the essential low-level mechanisms as a layer of abstraction on top of the hardware. By abstraction, it is meant that the individual hardware resources are invisible to application programs and are accessed via conceptual models, such as file systems for disk storage, virtual address spaces for memory, schedulers for task management, and sockets for network communication. The kernel provides objects and threads as computational abstraction (see Chapter 4 for threads and objects) on top of the hardware abstraction layer (HAL) and the bare hardware. Software that uses the NT Kernel can be defined using objects and threads as primitive; that is, these abstractions appear to NT Kernel client software as natural parts of the hardware. To implement objects and threads, the kernel must manage hardware interrupts and exceptions, perform processor scheduling, handle multiprocessor synchronization, and perform similar other tasks.

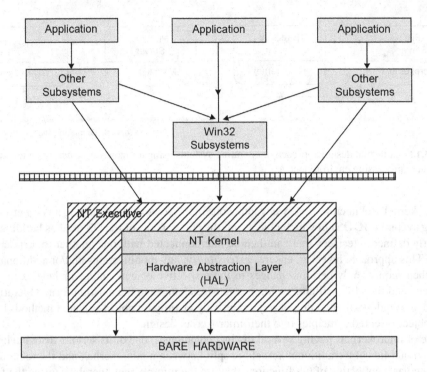

FIGURE 3.14 A schematic block diagram of representative Windows NT operating system organization.

The *NT Executive* (Figure 3.14) is designed as a layer of abstraction of the NT Kernel and builds on the NT Kernel to implement a full set of policies, specific mechanisms for general objects, and various services that Windows NT offers, including process, memory, device, and file management. Since Windows NT builds on an object-oriented approach, it does not strictly adhere to the classic separation of OS functionalities as observed in a layered architecture while creating its different modules. Instead, the NT Executive is designed and implemented as a modularized set of elements (Solomon, 1998): object manager, process and thread manager, virtual memory manager, and so on at the source code level.

While the NT Kernel and Executive are designed and programmed as separate modules, they are actually combined with the *kernel executable* when Windows NT is built. This combined module, along with the underlying HAL, provides the essential core elements of the OS and implements the full NT operating system, though this nucleus can be extended again by the subsystems that provide specific OS services.

For more details about this topic, see the Support Material at www.routledge.com/9781032467238.

3.1.10 Hybrid Kernel

Hybrid kernel (quasi-category) architecture is based on the idea of combining several notable aspects of both microkernels and monolithic kernels, but has a structure similar to a microkernel, yet implemented as a monolithic kernel. In contrast to a microkernel, all (or nearly all) services in a hybrid kernel are in kernel space, similar to a monolithic kernel, and hence, there is no performance overhead, such as message passing and context switching between kernel mode and user mode, that is typically associated with microkernel. Side by side, none of the benefits of services are obtained if they are not implemented in user space. However, the best-known example of a hybrid kernel is the NT-based kernel inside **Windows 2000, Windows XP, Windows Server 2003, Windows Vista**, and **Windows Server 2008**. The Windows NT-based operating system family architecture essentially consists of two layers (user mode and kernel mode), with many different modules within both of these layers.

For more details about this topic, see the Support Material at www.routledge.com/9781032467238.

3.1.10.1 Case Study: Windows NT-Based Kernel

NT-based Windows is classified as having a hybrid kernel (or a macrokernel) rather than a monolithic kernel, because the emulation subsystems run in user-mode server processes rather than in kernel mode, as is found in a monolithic kernel. Furthermore, the OS functionalities are separated from the general kernel design to attain a large number of design goals (closely resembling the design goals of Mach OS). This is again contrary to the principle of a monolithic kernel.

Conversely, it is said that NT is not even a microkernel system. The reason behind is that nearly all of its subsystems providing system services, including the entire Executive, run in the same address space as the kernel itself, as would be the case with a monolithic design. This strategy, in turn, offers superior performance, mainly as procedure calls are made here direct for being located in same memory space rather than using of IPC for communication among subsystems.

The Windows NT design included a collection of modules that communicate via well-known interfaces with a small microkernel limited to core functions, such as first-level interrupt handling, thread scheduling, and synchronizing primitives. Its other design goals include support for diverse architectures and a kernel with abstractions, general enough to allow multiple operating system functionalities to be implemented on top of it and also object-oriented organization.

In NT, the list of subsystems run in user mode is far shorter than those run in kernel mode. The user-mode subsystems include one or more emulation subsystems, each of which provides operating system functionality to applications. These subsystems are not devoted to a particular OS personality but rather to the native NT API (or Native API). For performance reasons, some of these emulation subsystems run in kernel mode in NT version 4.0 and onward.

For more details about this topic, see the Support Material at www.routledge.com/9781032467238.

3.1.11 Exokernel

The exokernel concept started to bloom around 1994, but as of 2005,[update] exokernels were still a research effort and have not been used in any major commercial operating systems. However, an operating system kernel was developed by the MIT Parallel and Distributed Operating Systems group. One of the targets of this kernel design is always to keep individual hardware resources invisible from application programs by making the programs interact with the hardware via a conceptual model. These models generally include, for example, file systems for disk storage, virtual address spaces for memory, schedulers for task management, and sockets for network communication. These types of abstractions, in general, although make the hardware easy to use in writing programs, but limit performance and stifle experimentation in adding new abstractions. This concept has been further redefined by letting the kernel only allocate the physical resources of the machine (e.g. disk blocks, memory pages, processor time, etc.) to multiple executing programs and then letting each program make a link to an operating system library that implements familiar abstractions, or it can implement its own abstractions.

The notion behind this radically different approach is to force as few abstractions as possible on developers, enabling them to make as many decisions as possible about hardware abstractions. Applications may request specific memory addresses, disk blocks, and so on. The kernel only ensures that the requested resource is free and the application is allowed to access it. Resource management need not be centralized; it can be performed by applications themselves in a distributed manner. This low-level hardware access allows the programmer to implement custom abstractions and omit unnecessary ones, most commonly to improve a program's performance. Consequently,

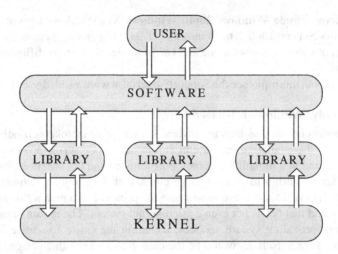

FIGURE 3.15   A typical schematic graphical overview of exokernel used in the design of modern operating systems.

an exokernel merely provides efficient multiplexing of hardware resources, but does not provide any abstractions, leaving the programmers to choose what level of abstraction they want: high or low.

An application process now views a computer resource in its raw form, and this makes the primitive operations extremely fast; 10–100 times faster than when a monolithic UNIX kernel is used. For example, when data are read off an I/O device, it passes directly to the requesting process instead of going through the exokernel. Since traditional OS functionalities are usually implemented at the application level, an application can then select an OS function from a library of operating systems, as shown in Figure 3.15. The OS function can then be executed as a process in non-kernel mode, exploiting the features of the Exokernel. This kernel is tiny in size, since functionality is limited to only ensuring protection and multiplexing of resources, which are again much simpler than conventional microkernels' implementation of message passing and monolithic kernels' implementation of abstractions. Exokernels and nanokernels are sometimes considered more extreme versions of microkernels.

For more details about this topic, see the Support Material at www.routledge.com/9781032467238.

3.2   MODERN OPERATING SYSTEMS: DESIGN ISSUES AND SALIENT FEATURES

Operating systems have been relentlessly evolving since the 1950s through various stages of development, constantly offering innovative features from a primitive form of batch systems to sophisticated multimode, multiuser, and finally different forms of modern distributed systems that took a considerable period of the last sixty-odd years to emerge. In recent years, vibrant hardware technological developments introduced multiple processors (CPUs) in the machines in the form of multiprocessors and multicomputers (networks of computers), along with varieties of memory devices with increasing capacity and speed but tiny size; numerous types of I/O devices of diverse technology; and high-speed network attachments that ultimately make systems immensely powerful and equally versatile. With the variants of these systems, new concepts popularly known as *parallel processing* and *distributed computing* in various forms were introduced that successfully handled many diverse, long-standing, unresolved problems in the application domain. To manage these enormously intelligent systems, many new design elements have been introduced, both in new operating systems and new versions of existing operating systems that ultimately resulted in a major change in the concept, design, and nature of traditional operating systems. In the application domain, the introduction of many new aspects, including internet and Web technology, multimedia applications, the client/server model of computing, cloud computing on quasi-distributed systems, and true distributed computing, have also had an immense impact on the existing concept and design of operating systems. In addition, internet access for computers as well as LAN and WAN implementations to build clusters of computers have made systems totally exposed and consequently have invited increased potential security threats and more sophisticated attacks that eventually had an enormous impact on design issues of emerging operating systems.

To address and accommodate all these issues, extensive modifications and enhancements in the existing structure of operating systems were found inadequate; it actually demanded fresh thoughts and new methods in organization of operating systems. As a result, numerous forms of structures and designs of different operating systems with various design elements have been released for both scientific and commercial use. Most of the work that led to such developments can now be broadly categorized into the following areas:

- Various forms of kernel/shell architecture.
- The thread concept and its refinement.
- Object concepts and object-oriented concept and designs.
- Numerous forms of multiprocessing on different multiprocessor and multicomputer architectures.
- Network operating systems in computer networks and client/server models.
- Cluster architecture, mainly for cloud computing.
- Distributed operating systems to drive distributed computing environments.

Operating systems developed in recent years with the kernel–shell concept can be classified into two major distinct categories: **monolithic kernel** and **microkernel**. Each category has already been discussed in detail in previous sections.

Threads are a relatively recent development in the design of the operating system as an alternative form of a schedulable and dispatchable unit of computation in place of the traditional notion of process. A *thread* is an entity that executes sequentially with a single path of execution using the program and other resources of its associated process which provides the environment for the execution of threads. Threads incorporate some of the functionalities that are associated with their respective processes in general. They have been introduced mainly to minimize the system overhead associated with process switching, since switching back and forth among threads involves less processor overhead than a major switch between different processes. Threads have also been found to be useful for structuring kernel processes. Similar to a uniprocessor machine, threads can also be implemented in a multiprocessor environment in a way similar to a process in which individual threads can be allocated to separate processors to simultaneously run in parallel. The thread concept, however, has been further enhanced and gave rise to a concept known as **multithreading**, a technique in which the threads obtained from dividing an executing process can run concurrently, thereby providing computation *speedup*. Multithreading is an useful means for structuring applications and kernel processes even on a uniprocessor machine. The emerging thread concept is distinguished from the existing process concept in many ways, the details of which are discussed in Chapter 4 ("Processor Management") as well as in subsequent chapters.

An **object** is conceived of as an autonomous entity (unit) which is a distinct software unit that consists of one or more procedures with a set of related data items to represent certain closely correlated operations, each of which is a sibling unit of computation. These procedures are called *services* that the object provides, and the data associated with these services are called *attributes* of the object. Normally, these data and procedures are not directly visible outside the object. Rather, various well-defined interfaces exist that permit software to gain access to these objects. Moreover, to define the *nature* of objects, the idea of **class** is attached to an object to define its behavior, just as a program defines the behavior of its related process. Thus, a class behaves like an abstract data type (ADT) that maintains its own state in its private variables.

Thus, the unit of a "process model" is now used to exploit objects as an alternative schedulable unit of computation in the design of operating system and other related system software. Objects react only to messages, and once an object is created, other objects start to send it messages. The newly created object responds by performing certain computations on its internal private data and by sending other messages back to the original sender or to other objects. The objects can interface with the outside world only by means of messages. Objects are discussed in more detail in Chapter 4.

The introduction of the kernel–shell concept in the design of the operating system together with the inclusion of the thread model established the multiuser environment with increasing user traffic load in virtually all single-user personal computers and workstations, realized by a single general-purpose microprocessor, but ultimately failed to rise to the desired level in performance. At the same time, as the cost of microprocessors continues to drop due to the constant advent of more sophisticated electronic technology, it has paved the way for vendors to introduce computer systems with multiple low-cost microprocessors, known as **multiprocessors**, that require only a little more additional cost but provide a substantial increase in performance and accommodate multiple users.

The structures and designs of multiprocessors, although they differ in numerous ways, mainly shared memory (UMA) architecture and distributed shared memory (NUMA) architecture, but they can also be defined as an independent stand-alone computer system with many salient features and notable characteristics and do possess a number of potential advantages over the traditional uni-processor system. Some of them, in particular, are *performance, reliability, scalability, incremental growth*, and also *ease of implementation*.

The operating systems used in multiprocessors are thus totally different in concept and design from the traditional uniprocessor modern operating system, and also from each other due to differences in their hardware architectures. They hide the presence of the multiple processors from users and are totally transparent to users. They provide specific tools and functions to exploit parallelism as much as possible. They take care of scheduling and synchronization of processes or threads across all processors, manage common and or distributed memory modules shared by the processors, distribute and schedule existing devices among the running processes, and provide a flexible file system to handle many requests arriving almost simultaneously in the working environment.

In spite of having several potential merits, multiprocessors of different kinds with different forms and designs suffer from several shortcomings along with the related cost factors that ultimately have been alleviated with the introduction of another form of architecture with multiple processors, known as **multicomputers** (Chakraborty, 2020). This architecture is essentially built up with a set of stand-alone full-fledged computers, each with its own resources, but they are connected to high-speed network interfaces (networks of computers) that eventually gave rise to computer networks, and/or offering the appearance of a single system image, depending on how the arrangement is driven. This supports high processor counts with memory systems distributed among the processors. This yields cost-effective higher bandwidth that reduces latency in memory access, thereby resulting in an overall increase in processor performance. Each of these machines in a computer network may be locally driven by its own OS supported by NOS for global access, or these machines are together driven by a completely different type of operating system, known as a **distributed operating system**, that offers an illusion of a single-system image with a single main memory space and a single secondary memory space, plus other unified access facilities, such as a distributed file system. The distributed operating system dynamically and automatically allocates jobs to the various machines present in the arrangement in a transparent way for processing according to its own policy and strategy. These arrangements, along with the respective operating systems, are becoming increasingly popular, and there are many such products available in the market from different vendors.

The object concept has been gradually refined and continuously upgraded over time to ultimately culminate in the contemporary **object-oriented technologies** that have been exploited to introduce an innovative concept in the design of operating systems. One of the salient features of this object-oriented design is that it facilitates modular programming disciplines that enable existing applications to extend by adding modules as and when required without affecting the existing logic and semantics. When used in relation to the design and development of operating systems, this approach can create modular extensions to an existing small kernel by means of adding needed objects to it. Object-oriented design and structure enable developers to customize an operating system (and, in fact, any other product) with ease without disrupting system integrity. This approach used in design has really enriched programming methodology and is considered an important vehicle in the design and development of both centralized and distributed operating systems.

For more details about this topic, see the Support Material at www.routledge.com/9781032467238.

SUMMARY

We have already described the concept and step-wise evolution of the generic operating system from its very primitive form to the most sophisticated modern one, its basic characteristics, the common principles it follows, the numerous issues linked to it to explain the different functions it performs, and the common services it usually provides while driving the bare hardware on behalf of the user. With the constant introduction of more intelligent and sophisticated hardware platforms, many different operating systems have continuously emerged over the last fifty-odd years. This chapter illustrates the step-wise evolution of different design models based on numerous design objectives and their subsequent realization, along with the formation of associated structures of different operating systems proposed over this period. The dynamism of computer systems was abstracted gradually by operating systems developed in terms of monolithic design, extended machine concept, and then versatile layered/leveled concepts and designs. Later, the evolution of VMs and their subsequent impacts facilitated redefining the concepts and designs of newer operating systems with an innovative form of the kernel–shell concept that eventually became able to manage networks of computers and computer network implementations. The kernel–shell concept was further reviewed and redefined from its monolithic kernel form to the more classic microkernel and later hybrid kernel forms to manage more sophisticated computing environments, including demands from diverse spectra of emerging application areas. A general discussion of the implementations of different models of operating systems is presented here with an illustration of popular representative operating systems as relevant case studies for each design model. This chapter concludes by giving an idea of modern operating systems used in both uniprocessor and multiple processor environments (both multiprocessors and multicomputers), including the requirements they fulfill and the salient features they possess. In short, this chapter lays a foundation for a study of generic operating system structures and designs that are elaborately discussed in the rest of this book.

EXERCISES

1. What is meant by a monolithic structure of an operating system? What are the key features of such a design? What are the main drawbacks of this design?
2. What are the factors that influenced the concept of an extended machine? How have these ultimately been implemented in the design of the extended machine?
3. What paved the way to design operating systems with layered structures? How does this design concept negotiate the complexities and requirements of a generalized operating system?
4. State the strategy in the evolution of hierarchical-level design of an operating system. How does this concept achieve the generalization that a versatile operating system exhibits?

5. State the levels and explain the functions that each level performs in the hierarchical-level design of an operating system.
6. What are the factors that accelerate the evolution of a virtual machine? State the concepts of a virtual machine. Why it is so called? Is a virtual machine a simple architectural enhancement or a first step towards a renaissance in the design of an operating system? Justify your answer with reasons.
7. What is the client–server model in the design of an operating system? What are the salient features of a client–server model from a design point of view? What are the reasons that make the client–server model popular in the user domain?
8. Discuss the environment under which the client–server model is effective. State and explain the drawbacks of a client–server model.
9. "The kernel–shell model in the design of an operating system is a refinement of the existing extended machine concept"—give your answer in light of extended machine design.
10. What are the typical functions that are generally performed by a kernel in the kernel–shell model of an operating system? What is meant by shell in this context? What are the functions that are usually performed by a shell in the kernel–shell design of an operating system? What are shell scripts? Why the shell is not considered a part of the operating system itself?
11. State and explain the features found in the design of a monolithic kernel.
12. "The virtual machine concept of the 1970s is the foundation for the emergence of the microkernel of the 1990s". Would you agree? Give reasons for your answer.
13. "The introduction of the microkernel concept in the course of design of a distributed operating system is a radical approach". Justify.
14. Briefly explain the potential advantages that are observed in a microkernel design compared to its counterpart; a monolithic design.
15. Give some examples of services and functions found in a typical monolithic kernel-based operating system that may be external subsystems in a microkernel-based operating system.
16. Explain the main performance disadvantages found in a microkernel-based operating system.
17. Explain the situation that forces the modern operating system to evolve. State the key features that a modern operating system must include.

SUGGESTED REFERENCES AND WEBSITES

Chakraborty, P. *Computer Organization and Architecture: Evolutionary Concepts, Principles, and Designs*, Boca Raton, FL, CRC Press, 2020.
Solomon, D. A. *Inside Windows NT*, Second Edition, Redmond, WA, Microsoft Press, 1998.

4 Processor Management

Learning Objectives

- To envisage the process model and its creation as an unit of execution, its description with images, the different states it undergoes, and finally its uses as a building block in the design and development of generic operating systems.
- To define and describe threads, a smaller unit of execution, along with their specific characteristics, the different states they undergo, and their different types.
- To introduce the concept of multithreading and its implementation in the design and development of modern operating systems.
- To portray a comparison between the process and thread concepts.
- To define and describe objects, a bigger unit of execution, along with a description of object-oriented concepts in the design and development of a few modern operating systems.
- To demonstrate numerous CPU scheduling criteria and the respective strategies to realize various types of CPU-scheduling algorithms, including the merits and drawbacks of each of these algorithms.
- To describe the different forms and issues of concurrent execution of processes and describe the needs of interprocess synchronization.
- To articulate possible approaches using hardware and software solutions to realize interprocess synchronization.
- To describe some useful synchronization tools, such as semaphores and monitors, including their respective merits and drawbacks.
- To demonstrate a few well-known classical problems relating to interprocess synchronization and also their solutions using popular synchronization tools.
- To describe the purpose and elements of interprocess communications.
- To demonstrate different models using message-passing and shared-memory approaches to implement interprocess communications.
- To explain various schemes used to realize interprocess communications.
- To illustrate the approaches used to realize interprocess communication and synchronization in Windows and UNIX operating systems.
- To explain deadlock and the related reasons behind its occurrence, along with different approaches to detect and avoid such deadlock.
- To discuss starvation and the reasons behind it, along with the description of different strategies to detect and avoid it.

4.1 INTRODUCTION

The operating system (OS) controls and monitors the entire computing system. It consists of a collection of interrelated computer programs, a part of which when executed under its control by the processor directs the CPU in the use of the other system resources and also determines the timing of CPU's execution of other programs. While allowing the processor to do "useful" work for users, the OS relinquishes control to the processor and then takes control back at the right point of time to manage the system and prepare the processor to do the next piece of work. The execution of an individual program consisting of a sequence of instructions is sometimes referred to as a *process* or *task*. The part of the OS program that implements certain mechanisms to constantly control, manage, and supervise the activity of the processor in executing different systems as well as user programs is

DOI: 10.1201/9781003383055-4

the subject of processor management. The terms processor management and process management are used sometimes interchangeably. In a well-designed, versatile operating system, a substantial amount of the execution time (sometimes more than 80%) is used only to execute the OS program.

4.2   THE CONCEPT AND IMPLEMENTATION OF PROCESS MODEL

Once the operating system accepts a program, it may create several *processes*. A process is essentially an activity of some kind. To carry out the activity, an operation(s) is required. To realize the operation, instructions (primitive machine instructions) must be executed. So a process can be defined as an instance of instructions (program) under execution. The notion of a process is central to almost all operating systems and is a vital concept in defining and designing an operating system. The concept and different views of the process were discussed in detail in Chapter 2. A process can be viewed as being composed of (or is said to "own") tangible elements: an executable program associated with a set of resources and related data to realize the respective process, the *process descriptor* (also called *process control block* or other names in some systems) to represent the *state* (*attribute*) of the process for keeping track of the process, OS descriptors of resources allocated to the process (such as *file descriptors* in UNIX terminology or *handles* in Windows), *security attributes* to indicate the process owner, and the process's set of permissions.

The processor manager (or process manager), a part of the operating system consisting of programs and a related set of algorithms and data structures, monitors and controls the process. A single processor may be shared among several processes by means of a scheduling algorithm (short-term scheduling), or a particular process can also be shared by more than one user at the same time. The behavior of an individual process can be characterized by listing the sequence of its instructions (Hoare's approach), and this listing is referred to as a *trace* of that process. The behavior of the processor can be characterized and explained by analyzing the way in which the different traces of various processes are interleaved. Once the process manager creates a new process and its process descriptor, it then allocates the set of required resources and initializes the respective OS data structures needed by the process. The new process is now ready to begin executing its own program and usually starts to compete with the already existing ready-to-execute processes or with the only executing process (quite natural in a multitasking OS) to gain access to the one available CPU. The processor manager in this situation negotiates the chaos using its own underlying policy, and the related strategy is then imposed to manage CPU multiplexing. Another situation may occur when two or more processes compete to access shared resources (such as main memory space or files); the process manager will then use appropriate mechanisms and also provide synchronization tools that the community of processes can use to accomplish orderly sharing among themselves. Sometimes a process also refuses to share its resources, and no other process is then allowed to access the resource. All these issues are properly handled and considered the major objectives in defining and designing the processor management module. These are further detailed in many of the following sections.

For more details about this topic, see the Support Material at www.routledge.com/9781032467238.

4.3   PROCESSOR MANAGEMENT FUNCTIONS

Processor management (or process management) is concerned with the management of the physical processors, specifically the assignment of processors to processes when created after the job scheduler has moved a job from *hold* to *ready*. Process management must perform the following functions:

1. Keep track of the resources (processors and status of the process) using one of its modules called the *traffic scheduler*.
2. In the presence of multiple processes (as in multitasking), it decides which process gets the processor, when, and how long. This is carried out by one of its modules known as the *processor scheduler* (also viewed as a micro-scheduler).

3. Allocate the resource (processor) to a process by setting up necessary hardware registers using one of its modules, often called the *dispatcher*.

4. Control the progress of the processes towards completion at a specified rate. The process status during this period is kept track of by one of its modules often called the *traffic controller*.

5. Act properly on exceptional conditions if they arise during the execution of a process, including interrupts and arithmetic errors.

6. Provide mechanisms to communicate among processes, if required, thereby implementing process synchronization. This responsibility is performed by the traffic controller.

7. Reclaim the resource (processor) when the process relinquishes processor usage, terminates, or exceeds the allowed amount of usage.

It is to be noted that the job scheduler is a part of processor management, since the record-keeping operations for job scheduling and process scheduling are very similar.

For more details about this topic, see the Support Material at www.routledge.com/9781032467238.

4.4 STRUCTURE OF PROCESSOR MANAGEMENT

The assignment of processors to processes is mainly done by job scheduling, process scheduling, and synchronization. In summary, processor management operates on two levels: assigning processors to a job and assigning processors to processes. On the job level, processor management is concerned with job scheduling, sometimes called *first-level scheduling*, which may itself be a separate process. Once a job is scheduled, the system must then perform all the functions relating to the process, and these functions may be requested by users' processes, the job scheduler, and other processes and thus may be common to all address spaces (processor management upper level). In a multiprogramming environment, the process scheduler and the synchronization mechanisms may be called by all modules of the system. Thus, they form the very center (core) of the kernel of the system (processor management lower level). This approach in modeling system structure is the basis of most of the operating system.

Although the job scheduler (long-term scheduler) and processor scheduler (short-term scheduler) primarily differ in many ways, they may sometimes interact. The process scheduler may choose to postpone or rollout a process that requires it to go through macro-level job scheduling again in order to complete. This is especially true in a time-sharing system. In fact, the job scheduler is like a coordinator of the contest that only decides who will enter the contest, but the process scheduler decides which participant will ultimately win access to the processor.

For more details about this topic, see the Support Material at www.routledge.com/9781032467238.

4.5 PROCESS–STATES MODEL

A process is the smallest individually schedulable entity consisting of code in machine instructions and data, characterized by *attributes* and *dynamic states*. During the life cycle of a job, processes may undergo a variety of states that indicate the nature of the current activity. The OS manifests the execution of a typical process in the course of its activity in terms of a progression through a succession of states. The following typical process states are possible on all kinds of computer systems, and the OS will take a process through all its states. In most of these states, processes are "stored" in main memory. These states and the transition of states (i.e. when a process switches from one state to another) are handled by routines within the operating system. The different states that a process can undergo in the life cycle of a job from the instant a job is first submitted up to its completion are *submit*, *hold*, *created* (new), *ready* (waiting), *run* (active), *blocked* (sleeping), *complete* (exit). All possible transitions of states of a process during the life cycle of a job are illustrated in Figure 4.1.

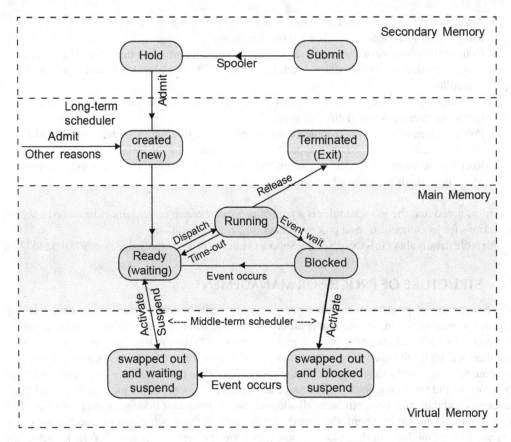

FIGURE 4.1   A schematic view of the various process states and their interrelations used in the design of the generic operating systems.

It is quite natural that, at any instant, a number of processes may be in a ready state, and as such, the system provides a *ready queue* in which each process, when admitted, is placed in this queue. Similarly, numerous events cause running processes to block, and processes are then placed into a *blocked queue* and each one is then waiting until its individual event occurs. When an event occurs, all processes in the blocked queue that are waiting on that particular event are then moved to the ready queue. Subsequently, when the OS attempts to choose another process to run, it selects one from the ready queue, and that process then enters the run state.

For more details about this topic, see the Support Material at www.routledge.com/9781032467238.

4.5.1   ADDITIONAL PROCESS STATES: SUSPENDED STATE

Many operating systems concentrate only on the three major states, ready, running, and blocked, and a particular process usually cycles through these three states a number of times before being completed or terminated and ultimately departing the system.

4.5.1.1   Swapping: Importance

Now too many ready processes are in main memory awaiting execution. A good number of blocked processes are also in main memory, waiting for an event to occur. Both these types of processes remaining idle occupies a substantial amount of costly memory space and forces the processor to remain idle for want of a sufficient number of eligible running process within the limited size of main memory. Out of many acceptable solutions, the most convenient and workable solution to negotiate this situation is *swapping*, which involves moving part or all of a process from main memory to virtual memory in disk by the mid-term scheduler, thereby freeing up the occupied memory space for the use of the existing running processes or providing an option for a newly created process/processes ready to admit. A queue can then form in virtual memory to keep track of all such temporarily swapped-out processes, called *suspended*.

When there are no more ready processes and the OS intends to choose another ready process to run, it can then use one of two options to pick a process to bring into main memory: either it can bring a previously suspended process already in the queue, or it can admit a newly created process in the ready state. Both approaches, have their own merits and drawbacks. The problem is that admitting a new process may increase the total load on the system, but, alternatively, bringing a *blocked process* back into memory before the occurrence of the event for which it was blocked would not be useful because it is still not ready for execution (the event has not yet occurred). One of the probable solutions may be to specifically consider the states of the processes when they have been swapped out and thus suspended. The suspended processes were actually in two different states: (i) a process was in a ready state but not running, waiting for its turn for the CPU, and (ii) a process was in a blocked state, waiting on an event to occur. So, there are two additional suspended states, *ready-suspend* and *blocked-suspend*, along with the existing primary process states already described. The state transition model is depicted in Figure 4.1.

Usually, when there is no ready process available in memory, the operating system generally prefers to bring one *ready-suspend* process into main memory rather than admitting a newly created process that may increase the total load of the system. But, in reality, there may also be other situations that might need completely different courses of action. In addition, a process in the *blocked-suspend* state is usually moved to the *ready-suspend* state when the operating system comes to know from the state information relating to suspended processes that the event for which the process has been waiting has occurred.

In a more complex versatile operating system, it may be desirable to define even more states. On the other hand, if an operating system were designed without the process concept in mind, it might be difficult for an observer to determine clearly the state of execution of a job at any point in time.

For more details about this topic, see the Support Material at www.routledge.com/9781032467238.

4.5.2 SUSPENDED PROCESSES: THEIR CHARACTERISTICS AND IMPORTANCE

A suspended process may be in main memory but not readily available for execution and thus may be swapped out of main memory for various reasons irrespective of whether it is waiting for an event to occur. However, a suspended process possesses several distinct characteristics, and its eviction from main memory at the right point in time has several advantages for the computing environment.

For more details about this topic, see the Support Material at www.routledge.com/9781032467238.

4.6 PROCESS DESCRIPTION

When a user program is submitted for execution, the operating system creates the processes, changes the states of various other coexisting processes, and allocates the available resources as requested at the appropriate time. To control the processes and keep track of the status of the resources, the operating system constructs and maintains four different tables, *process tables*, *memory tables*, *device (I/O) tables*, and *file tables*, to record various information relating to managing four different resources constituting the computing system. Most operating systems create these tables, but the contents and details of information present in each type of table area major design aspect that may differ from one operating system to another. Figure 4.2 shows a simplified form of the arrangement of all these tables, but in reality, the situation is more complex, and these tables must be linked or cross-referenced in some fashion.

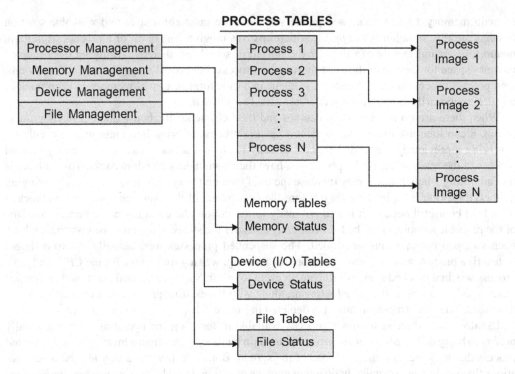

FIGURE 4.2   Model structure of different control tables used in the design of the generic operating systems.

Process Table: This table is an array of structures, one entry with several fields containing all the information of each currently existing process, up to a maximum number of processes (entries) that the OS can support at any point in time. It is linked or cross-referenced in some fashion with the other tables relating to management of other resources to refer them directly or indirectly. An entry is made in this table when the process is created and is erased when the process dies. Although the process table is ultimately managed by the process manager, various other OS queries may change the individual fields of any entry in the process table. A fundamental part of the detailed design strategy for the process manager is reflected in the design of the process table data structure which largely depends on the basic hardware environment and differs in design approaches across different operating systems.

More details about this topic are given on the Support Material at www.routledge.com/9781032467238.

A case study showing the scheme of a UNIX process table entry is given on the Support Material at www.routledge.com/9781032467238.

4.7 PROCESS IMAGE: PROCESS TOTALITY

A process consists of a program or a set of programs associated with a set of data attached to local or global variables and other defined constants. Moreover, when this program is executed, it requires a stack, which is used to keep track of procedure calls and parameter passing between procedures. The collection of program, data, and stack together is known as a *process data block* (PDB). In addition, associated with each process are a number of attributes used by the operating system for process control. The collection of all attributes is referred to as *process control block* (PCB). The combination of *process data block* and *process control block*, along with any other address space that the process shares with other processes, together form the *process image* which is stored in noncontiguous blocks in virtual memory (secondary memory) for active processes and tracked by the respective process table. But a small portion of the process image containing vital information for the use of the operating system is maintained in main memory at the same time. Figure 4.3 shows a model structure of

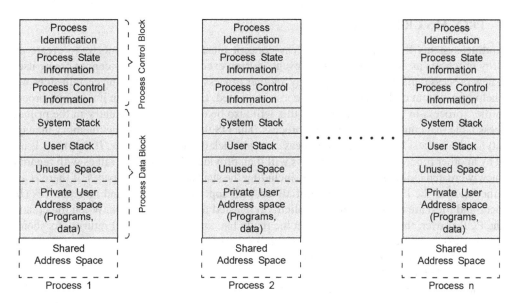

FIGURE 4.3 A schematic design of process images created by the operating system stored in virtual memory.

process images in virtual memory using a continuous range of addresses, but in actual implementation, this may be different. It entirely depends on the memory management scheme being employed and the way the control structures are organized in the design of the operating system.

More details about this topic, see the Support Material at www.routledge.com/9781032467238. A case study showing the scheme used in the creation of a UNIX process image is given on the Support Material at www.routledge.com/9781032467238.

4.7.1 PROCESS DATA BLOCK AND PROCESS CONTROL BLOCK

A process data block is a local storage area in user space for each user process, a portion of which is used for a *user data area* that includes a program, program data, and a user stack. The other portion of the PDB is used for the user program to be executed to give rise the process and the system stack which is used to store parameters and calling addresses for procedure and system calls. In systems with virtual memory (to be discussed in Chapter 5), PDB is usually allotted a page frame in main memory.

A process control block, or a *process descriptor, task control block* (TCB), or *task descriptor,* is a data structure with fields containing all information relating to the attributes of a particular process needed by the operating system to keep track of a single process to control its execution and management of resource usage. A process is recognized by the operating system only when it has a PCB created in the operating system area of memory. When the process terminates, its PCB is deleted, and the area is released for the new PCBs, if needed. Information stored in a PCB can be generalized into three categories: (i) process identification, (ii) processor state information, and (iii) process control information. Each category is again divided into one or more fields, and a PCB typically may include some or all of the fields. Some of the fields are used by the processor manager, some are used by the memory manager, and so on. Since many fields in the process control block keep changing continually over time, all PCBs thus need to be manipulated and constantly updated rapidly by the operating system. In many systems, special hardware registers are, therefore, provided to point to the PCB of the currently executing process. Special machine instructions are also provided to quickly store the contents of CPU registers into the PCB and load them back from PCB to CPU registers.

For more details about this topic, see the Support Material at www.routledge.com/9781032467238.

4.8   PROCESS CREATION

Operating systems that support the process concept must provide some means to create and destroy processes as needed to negotiate events during execution. A process cannot create itself, so a new process (*child*) must be created by another process (*parent*) following certain steps with the help of a system call. When a new process is created, the OS will assign it a unique process identifier (process-id and/or user-id), and this will also be entered as a new entry in the primary process table that contains one entry per process. The OS then allocates space (memory management) for the process data block and process control block of the new process. If a process is created by another process, the parent process will then provide all the needed values with regard to the newly created child process to the OS, including the sharing of address spaces, if there is any. All the fields in the PCB will then be initialized with appropriate values, and no resources (I/O devices and files) are allocated unless explicitly requested for these resources. When the creation of the PCB is over, the PCB is then put on the ready list, and the system call returns. As soon as a new process is created, the respective scheduling queues must be modified and updated. The other data structures associated with creation may be either created afresh or modified or may even be expanded, if needed.

For more details about this topic, see the Support Material at www.routledge.com/9781032467238.

4.9   PROCESS CREATION METHODS

There are two main models of process creation:

1. The classical method, fork/join/exec, as proposed by Conway in 1963, postulated three operating system primitive functions named fork, join, and quit, and later Dennis and Van Home defined a variant of them in 1966.
2. The other model that modern systems use is a *spawn* command (*fork*, *CreateProcess*, or other similar names).

When the *fork* (*label*) command is executed, it results in the creation of a second process within the same address space as the original process, sharing the same program and all information, including the same variables. This new process then begins execution of the shared program at the statement with the specified *label*. The original process executing *fork* continues its execution as usual at the next instruction, and the new processes then coexist and also proceed in parallel. *Fork* usually returns the identity of the child to the parent process to use it to henceforth refer to the child for all purposes. When the process terminates itself, it uses the *quit()* instruction, and consequently, the process is destroyed, its process control block is erased, and the memory space is released. The *join (count)* instruction is used by a parent process to merge two or more processes into a single one for the sake of synchronization with its child (children). At any instant, only one process can execute the *join* statement (system call), and its execution cannot then be interrupted: no other process is allowed to get control of the CPU until the process finishes executing. This is one major strategy that a code segment implements in order to install *mutual exclusion* (to be discussed later).

Modern systems use the *spawn* command (*fork*, *CreateProcess*, or other similar names) that creates a child process in a separate address space for execution, thereby enabling every child and sibling process to have its own private, isolated address space. This, however, also helps the memory manager to isolate one process's memory contents from others. Moreover, the child process also ought to be able to execute a different program from the parent, and this is accomplished by using a mechanism (usually the new program and arguments are named in the system call) that enables the child to redefine the contents of its own address space. A new process is thus created, and that program now runs directly. One of the drawbacks of this model is that any parameters of the child process's operating environment that need to be changed should be included in the parameters to *spawn*, and *spawn* has its own standard way to handle them. There are, of course, other ways to handle the proliferation of parameters to solve this problem.

An important difference between the two systems is that while *spawn* creates a new address space derived from the program, the *fork* call must create a copy of the parent address space. This can be wasteful if that address space will be deleted and rewritten after a few instructions. One solution to this problem may be a second system call, *vFork*, that lets the child process use the parent's memory until an *exec* is made. We will discuss other systems to mitigate the cost of *fork* when we talk about memory management. However, which model is "better" is an open issue. The tradeoffs here are *flexibility* vs. *overhead*, as usual.

For more details about this topic, see the Support Material at www.routledge.com/9781032467238. A case study showing the creation of cooperating processes by using *fork*, *join*, and *quit* is given on the Support Material at www.routledge.com/9781032467238.

A case study showing the mechanisms in process creation in UNIX is given on the Support Material at www.routledge.com/9781032467238.

4.10 PROCESS HIERARCHY AND DAEMON PROCESSES

A process (parent) can create one or more other processes, referred to as child processes, and each child process has exactly one parent process. Whenever a process spawns a child, a leaf node is added to the tree, and the child process is then identified and named by its *pid*, which is then given to the respective parent. The initial process is the root of the tree of all processes. The child process also, in turn, can create their own child processes, and in this way, an original process can build up an entire tree of children, grandchildren, and further descendants, giving rise to a process tree structure. In a multiple-process operating system, this hierarchy is implicitly defined among the set of processes to implement the environment. In fact, the basis of the hierarchy evolves from the process-creation mechanism. The community of processes present in the hierarchy are, however, agreed on certain basic tasks.

Daemon Process: In a large system, each user may have several active processes at any instant, and there may be hundreds or even thousands of processes running at any point in time. In fact, on most single-user workstations, even when the user is absent, dozens of background processes are running. These processes are called *daemons* and are started automatically as soon as the system is booted.

For more details about this topic, and also about daemon processes, see the Support Material at www.routledge.com/9781032467238.

4.11 PROCESS SWITCH: CHANGE OF PROCESS

The traditional multiprogramming/multitasking operating systems are mostly *event-driven*, and while responding to various system events, the OS may take actions that cause *changes in process states*. For example, at any instant, a running process may be interrupted for some reason, and the operating system then assigns another process to the *run state* and transfers control over to that process. Such a transition from one memory-resident process to another in a multitasking system is called a *process switch* or *task switch* and may eventually lead to reassignments of system resources, including reallocation of the processor.

A process switch is not unusual; rather it may be triggered at any time in response to events that change system state. When such an event occurs, the intervention of the operating system is required, and execution control is then transferred to the operating system, and an operating system program is executed to process the event. It is important to note that although *servicing of the event* that caused the change in state to happen often takes place at this point, it is a different issue and is generally not considered a part of the process switch. However, the activities involved in process switching are quite complex and sometimes require a joint effort of both hardware and software.

Since the currently running process is to be moved to another state (ready, blocked, etc.), the operating system must make substantial changes in the global environment to effect this state transition, mostly involving the execution of the following steps:

- Save the context of the processor, including the program counter and other registers into the user stack.
- Modify and update the process control block of the currently running process, and change the state of this process to one of other states, ready, blocked, ready-suspend, or exit. Other relevant fields must also be updated, including the reason for leaving the running state and other accounting information (processor usage).
- Move the PCB of this process to the appropriate queue (ready, blocked on event *i*, ready-suspend, etc.).
- Select another process for execution based on the policy implemented in the process scheduling algorithm, which is one of the major design objectives of the operating system.
- Update the process control block of this process thus scheduled, including changing the state of this process to running.
- Update memory-management data structures. This may be required depending on how the address translation mechanism is implemented. This topic is explained in Chapter 5.
- Restore the context of the *processor* to the state at the time the scheduled process was last switched out of the running state by way of loading the previous values of the program counter and other registers.
- Finally, the operating system initiates a mode switch to reactivate the user space and surrenders control to the newly scheduled process.

It is now evident that process switching causing a change in state is considerably complex and time-consuming and, above all, requires substantial effort to carry out. Minimizing time consumption and thereby increasing the efficiency of process switching is thus considered one of the major design objectives of a process-based operating system that, in turn, requires additional hardware and its supported structure. To make this activity even faster, an innovative special process-structuring technique, historically called a *thread*, was introduced, which will be discussed later.

For more details about this topic, see the Support Material at www.routledge.com/9781032467238.

4.12   CONTEXT SWITCH: CHANGE OF CONTEXT

During the tenure of program execution, if an interrupt occurs or if an interrupt is pending, the control of execution will be immediately forced to transfer from the currently running process to a service routine (ISR) appropriate to that interrupt. Since control will once again be given back to the interrupted program after the interrupt request is serviced, the processor must do the following before attempting to service an interrupt:

- It saves the context of the current program being executed.
- It saves the current value of the program counter before reloading the program counter with the starting address of an interrupt handler program that ultimately calls the interrupt service routine (ISR).

The elements that constitute the context of the current program that must be preserved are only those that may be modified by the ISR, and, when restored, they will bring back the machine to the same state as it was in just prior to the interrupt. Usually, the *context* is assumed to mean the contents of all *processor registers* and *status flags* and maybe some variables common to both the interrupted program and ISR, if any. The mechanism involved in changing context from an executing program to an interrupt handler is called the *context switch*. Since the interrupted program is not at all aware of the occurrence of the interrupt, nor does it have any idea of the machine context that may be modified by the ISR during its execution, the ISR is entirely entrusted with the responsibility of saving and restoring the needed context of the preempted activity. Context switching is mostly hardware-centric; the save/restore operation is, no doubt, much faster than its counterpart, the software approach. But, whatever approach is considered, context switching is comparatively less costly and much faster than its counterpart, process switching, which is considerably more complex and also more expensive. Linux's well-tuned context switch code usually runs in about 5 microseconds on a high-end Pentium.

For more details about this topic, see the Support Material at www.routledge.com/9781032467238.

4.13   PROCESS-BASED OPERATING SYSTEMS

When an operating system is designed based on the different services it can render, each service essentially consists of one or a set of fundamental activities (process) that can be realized when one or a set of instructions (program) is executed. This approach, when implemented at the time of designing and developing an operating system, ultimately yields a process-based operating system. Each process or set of related processes gives rise to some sort of service that the user needs. In fact, the operating system can be conceived of as a collection of such system processes (programs) or activities in order to drive the machine on behalf of the user as well as to fulfill the user's other requirements when a user starts interacting with the system.

The design disciplines in this regard always encourage modular concepts in organizing the pool of services obtained from processes that, in turn, additionally require clean interfaces between the modules. That is why some of these system processes and the related software are usually kept resident in the core kernel and executed in supervisor or kernel mode. Other system processes that reside outside the kernel are executed in user mode, similar to a user process (program). Yet there exists a small amount of code, such as process-switching/context-switching code, that may be outside of any process when executed. Figure 4.4 illustrates a representative scheme of such a design of an operating system.

In addition, some other processes relating to a few non-critical services, such as performance monitoring and statistical information processing, as often conducted by the operating system, are conveniently kept as separate processes. Since the programs related to these processes do not provide any particular service to an active user process, they can be invoked and run only by the operating system and can be interleaved with other processes under dispatcher control via the available interfaces. Implementation of the operating system as a set of such predefined processes exhibits some distinct advantages when used in a multiprocessor or multicomputer environment in which some of these operating-system processes (services) can be migrated to dedicated processors for the sake of performance improvement.

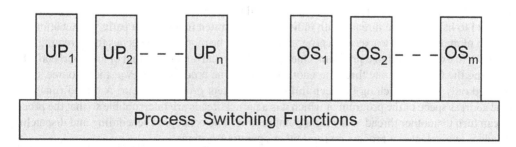

FIGURE 4.4   Different operating system services (functions) execute as separate processes used in the design of the generic operating systems.

4.14 THREADS: AN ALTERNATIVE APPROACH

Operating systems, while defined and designed in terms of processes, have several merits in which the process is considered a fundamental *unit of dispatch*, and certain processes are also additionally entrusted as *owners of resources* to control. This approach is also found especially suitable in multiprocessor or multicomputer environments in which some of the operating-system services (processes) can be shipped out to dedicated processors, thereby substantially improving system performance as a whole. But one of the major drawbacks of this process concept lies in process switching in which the activities involved in saving/restoring all the information of the currently executing process, including the resources under use, is quite complex and also expensive and eventually leads to huge overhead in relation to processor time consumption. This overhead, however, can be reduced if the resource-related overhead can be avoided, and this is possible if the currently executing process and the process to which control will be switched belong to the same application. In that situation, both processes share the same code, data, and resources; the state information of the two processes will then differ very little, only in the contents of CPU registers and stacks they are using that need to be saved/restored.

In fact, this approach places a strong demarcation between the two independent characteristics of process as already mentioned, as the *unit of dispatch* and *ownership of resources*. The portion of the process that characterize the process as unit of dispatch is then referred to as a *thread or lightweight process*, and the other portion of the process that demonstrates the process as unit of resource ownership (such as memory and files) is still being referred to as *process* or *task*. A thread can then be more specifically defined as an instance of a program in execution that uses the resources of a process. The ownership of any subset of resources can be attached to a process, but typically, at least, the *processor state* may be associated with each of the process threads in operating systems that support *threads* or "daughter" processes.

For more details about this topic, see the Support Material at www.routledge.com/9781032467238.

4.14.1 INTRODUCTION TO THREADS

The motivation of the thread model is mainly to define a thread as an alternative form of schedulable *unit of computation* to the traditional notion of process. In this model, the process is still an OS abstraction that can allocate various resources, yet it has no component that can execute a program. In fact, a thread is an entity executed sequentially using its program, and the other resources that are offered by its associated process create the environment for the execution of threads. This is depicted in Figure 4.5. We sometimes thus use the phrases "thread(s) of a process" and "parent process of a thread" to describe the relationship between a thread and its respective related process. Threads often incorporate some of the functionalities associated with processes.

A thread is said to be a dispatchable unit of work with a single path of execution within a program. It is a part of a program. If a program has more than one part that can be run independently of each other, the program can then be logically divided into more than one part through threads and is then said to have multiple threads with individually separated independent paths of execution. The creation of many threads to execute a program appears to be more advantageous than creating many processes to execute the same program. One of its primary advantages is that of low overhead while switching the CPU from one thread to another of the same process. However, the resource state is switched only when switching between threads of different processes occur. A thread runs in the same address space of the program of which it is a part. Threads are interruptible so that the processor can turn to another thread at the right point in time. The concept of scheduling and dispatching threads is equivalent to a process on most other operating systems.

The thread approach refines and divides the work normally associated with a process because there can be several threads, known as *sibling* threads, associated with a process. These threads

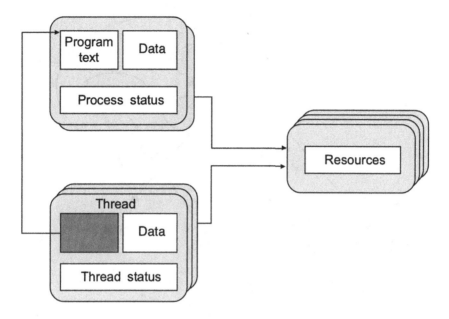

FIGURE 4.5   A schematic view of the thread concept and its relationship with its parent process.

share the program and resources of that process, thereby causing a reduction in state. In thread-based systems, a process with exactly one thread is equivalent to a traditional process. Each thread belongs to exactly one process, and no thread can exist outside a process. Here, processes or tasks are static and correspond to *passive resources*, and only threads can be scheduled to carry out program execution with the processor. Since all resources other than the processor are managed by the parent process, switching between related threads is fast and quite efficient. But switching between threads that belong to different processes incurs the full process-switch overhead as usual. However, each thread is characterized by the following (against the characteristics that are usually found associated with each process):

- **The hardware state:** Each thread must have a minimum of its own allocated resources, including memory, files, and so on, so that its internal state is not confused with the internal state of other threads associated with the same process.
- **The execution state:** Similar to a portion of the traditional process's status information (e.g. running, ready, etc.).
- **A saved processor context:** When it is not running.
- **A stack:** To support its execution.
- **Static storage:** To store the local variables it uses.
- **OS table entries:** Required for its execution.

When compared to new process creation and termination of a process, it takes far less time to create a new thread in an existing process and also consumes less time to terminate a thread. Moreover, thread switching within a process is much faster than its counterpart, process switching. So, if an application can be developed as a set of related executable units, it is then far more efficient to execute it as a collection of threads rather than as a collection of separate processes. In fact, the existence of multiple threads per process speeds up computation in both uniprocessor as well as in multiple-processor systems, particularly in multiprocessor systems, and also in applications on network servers, such as a file server that operates in a computer network

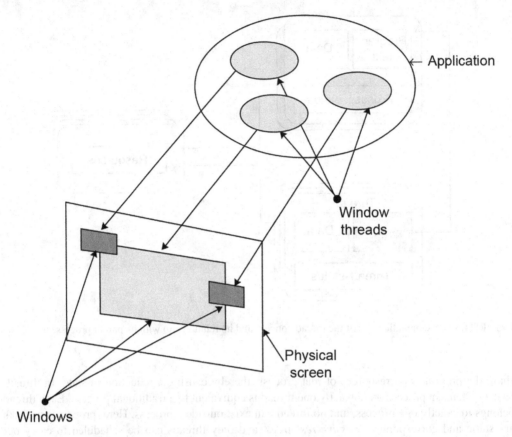

FIGURE 4.6   A broad view of an implementation and managing of virtual–terminal session windows on a physical terminal using thread paradigm.

built on a multicomputer system. Threads also provide a suitable foundation for true parallel execution of applications on shared-memory multiprocessors. Other effective uses of threads are found in communication processing applications and transaction processing monitors. Here, the use of threads simply makes the design and coding of these applications much easier to realize that subsequently perform *servicing of concurrent* requests. The thread paradigm is also an ideal approach for implementing and managing virtual terminal sessions in the context of a physical terminal, as shown in Figure 4.6, that are now widely used in contemporary commercial windowing systems.

In fact, threads exhibit a compromise between two different philosophies of operating system implementations: (i) conventional heavy state-laden process-based operating systems that offer adequate protection but can impair real-time performance, as observed in UNIX, and (ii) lean and fast real-time operating systems that sacrifice protection for the sake of time-critical performance. Threads provide, on one hand, the benefits of speed and sharing to related threads that constitute a single application, but on other hand, also offer full protection while communicating with one another in different applications.

For more details about this topic, see the Support Material at www.routledge.com/9781032467238.

4.14.2 Conventional Thread States

Since threads and processes are analogous except that threads do not have resource ownership, the different states that a thread may go through in its lifetime and the related transitions of these states are also analogous to process states and process state transitions, respectively. The different states that a thread may go through are:

- ***Ready state*** : When the thread is waiting for its turn to gain access to the CPU for execution.
- ***Running state*** : A thread is said to be in the running state when the CPU is executing it. This means that the code attached to the thread is getting executed.
- ***Waiting state*** : A thread is said to be in the waiting state if it was given a chance to execute but did not complete its execution for some reason. It may choose to go to *sleep*, thereby entering a *sleeping state*. The other possibility may be that some other thread suspends the currently running thread. The thread now enters a *suspended state*. Suspending the execution of a thread is deprecated in new versions.
- ***Dead state*** : When the thread has finished its execution.

Similar to a process scheduler, a thread scheduler in the more traditional model switches the processor (CPU) among a set of competing threads, thereby making a thread undergo its different states. In some systems, the thread scheduler is a user program, and in others, it is part of the OS. Since threads have comparatively few states and less information needs to be saved while changing states, the thread scheduler has a lower amount of work to do when actually switching from one thread to another than what is required in process switching. Hence, one of the important motivations in favor of using threads is the reduced context-switching time that enables the processor to quickly switch from one unit of computation (a thread) to another with minimal overhead. In addition, the thread manager also requires a descriptor to save the contents of each thread's registers and associated stack.

4.14.3 SINGLE-SHOT THREADS

A single-shot thread can have only three different states: *ready*, *running*, and *terminated*. When it is ready to run, it enters the *ready* state. Once it gets CPU time, it enters the *running* state. If it is preempted by a higher-priority thread, it can go back to the ready state, but when it is completed, it enters the *terminated* state. Conventional threads, however, have an extra state, the *waiting* state, which means that a conventional thread can yield the processor and wait for its time or for an event to occur. Since a single-shot thread has no waiting state, the closest thing it can do is make sure that it can be restarted before it terminates when it gets its time or an event occurs. Single-shot threads are well suited for time-critical systems where one wants to create a schedule offline. They can be implemented using very little RAM and are therefore often used in small systems. In fact, a single-shot thread behaves much like an ISR: something starts it; it is preempted by higher-priority interrupts; and when it is finished, it terminates.

4.14.4 TYPES OF THREADS

Threads can be classified into two distinct categories, kernel threads that are managed and scheduled by the kernel and user threads are managed and scheduled in user space. Whenever we use the term thread, it refers to kernel threads, whereas the term "fiber" is sometimes used to refer to user threads. While threads are scheduled preemptively, some operating systems provide a variant to threads, fibers, that are scheduled cooperatively. On operating systems that do not provide fibers, an application may implement its own fibers using repeated calls to worker functions. Since fibers are normally scheduled cooperatively, a running fiber must explicitly "yield" to allow another fiber to run. A fiber can be scheduled to run like any thread in the same process.

4.14.4.1 Kernel-Level Threads

Some OS kernels support the notion of threads and implement kernel-level threads (KLTs). There are specific system calls to create, terminate, and check the status of KLTs and manipulate them

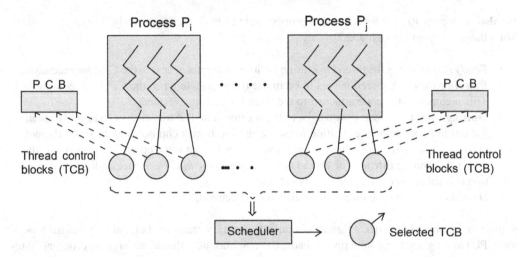

FIGURE 4.7 A schematic approach of the mechanism of kernel-level threads scheduling used in the design of thread–based operating systems.

in ways similar to those done with processes. Synchronization and scheduling may be provided by the kernel.

To create a new KLT, a process issues a system call, *create_thread*, and the kernel then assigns an *id* to this new thread and allocates a *thread control block* (TCB) which contains a pointer to the PCB of the corresponding process. This thread is now ready for scheduling. This is depicted in Figure 4.7.

In the *running state*, when the execution of a thread is interrupted due to the occurrence of an event, or if it exceeds the quantum, the kernel then saves the CPU state of the interrupted thread in its TCB. After that, the scheduler considers the TCBs of all the ready threads and chooses one of them to dispatch. It does not have to take into account which process the selected thread belongs to, but it can if it wants to. The dispatcher then checks whether the chosen thread belongs to a different process than the interrupted thread by examining the PCB pointer in the TCB of the selected thread. If so, the process switch occurs, the dispatcher then saves all the related information of the process to which the interrupted thread belongs and loads the context of the process to which the chosen thread belongs. If the chosen thread and the interrupted thread belong to the same process, the overhead of process switching is redundant and hence can be avoided.

4.14.4.1.1 Merits and Drawbacks

As the KLT is similar to a process, with the exception that it contains less state information, the programming for threads is thus almost no different from programming for processes. Moreover, this similarity facilitates assigning multiple threads within the same process on different processors in a multiprocessor system and can then be executed simultaneously on different processors, which eventually gives rise to a true parallel execution. This form of parallelism cannot be obtained with the use of user-level threads (ULTs). However, the similarities of the thread's characteristics with those of the process invite the same inherent problems: switching between threads requires the intervention of the kernel and requires substantial overhead even if the departing thread and the selected incoming thread belong to the same process. In fact, KLTs have more overhead in the kernel (a kernel thread control block) and also have more overhead in their use (manipulating them requires a system call). However, the abstraction is cleaner (threads can make system calls independently). Examples include Solaris lightweight processes (LWPs) and Java on machines that support kernel threads (like Solaris).

Many modern operating systems directly support both time-sliced and multiprocessor threading with a *process scheduler*. The OS kernel, however, also allows programmers to manipulate threads via the system call interface. Some implementations are called a *kernel thread*, whereas a *lightweight process* is a specific type of kernel thread that shares the same state and information. Absent that, programs can still implement threading by using timers, signals, or other methods to interrupt their own execution and hence perform a sort of ad-hoc time-slicing. These are sometimes called *user-space threads*.

For more details about this topic, see the Support Material at www.routledge.com/9781032467238.

4.14.4.2 User-Level Threads (Fibers)

User-level threads are implemented by a *thread library*, which is linked to the code of a process and hence are implemented entirely in user space. The programmer of the thread library writes code to synchronize threads and to context switch them, and they all run in one process. The operating system (kernel) is completely unaware of ULTs; it can only see the process. The scheduler works on processes and hence takes into account the PCBs and then selects a *ready process*; the dispatcher finally dispatches it for execution.

To create a user-level thread, a process invokes the library function *create_thread* that also creates its TCB, and the new thread is now ready for scheduling. The TCBs of all the threads are mapped onto the PCB of the corresponding process by the thread library, as shown in Figure 4.8. In the *running state*, if the thread invokes a library function to synchronize its functioning with other threads, the library function performs scheduling and then switches to another targeted thread of the process. This gives rise to a thread switch. Thus, the kernel is oblivious and remains outside the switching activities between threads but is totally aware that the process is

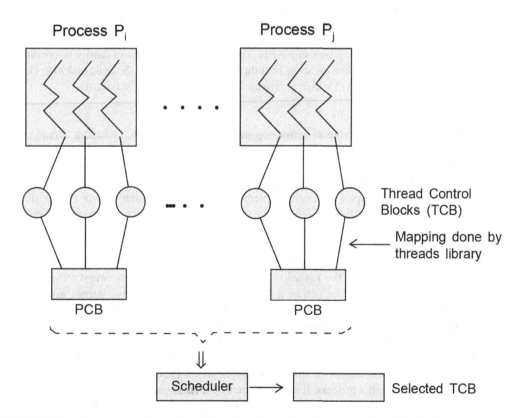

FIGURE 4.8 An overview of user-level threads and its scheduling approach used in the design of thread–based operating systems.

continuously in operation. If the thread library cannot find a ready thread in the process, it makes a system call to block itself. The kernel now intervenes and blocks the process. The process will be unblocked only when an event occurs that eventually activates one of its threads and will resume execution of the thread library function, which will now perform scheduling and switch to the execution of the newly activated thread. As the OS treats the running process like any other, there is no additional kernel overhead for ULTs. However, ULTs only run when the OS schedules their underlying process.

The thread library code is a part of each process that maps the TCBs of the threads into the PCB of the corresponding process. The information in the TCBs is used by the thread library to schedule a particular thread and subsequent arrangement for its execution. This is depicted in Figure 4.8. The scheduling algorithm can be any of those described in process scheduling, but in practice, round-robin and priority scheduling are most common. The only constraint is the absence of a clock to interrupt a thread that has run too long and used up the process's entire quantum. In that situation, the kernel will select another process to run. However, while dispatching the selected thread, the CPU state of the process should be the CPU state of the thread, and the process-stack pointer should point to the thread's stack. Since the thread library is a part of a process, the CPU executes in non-privileged (user) mode; hence, the loading of the new information into the PCB (or PSW) required at the time of dispatching a thread demands the execution of a privileged instruction (to change user mode to kernel mode) by the thread library in order to change the PCB's (or PSW's) contents and also to load the address of the thread's stack into the stack address register. It then executes a branch instruction to transfer control to the next instruction of the thread. The execution of the thread now starts.

User-level threads replicate some kernel-level functionality in user space. Examples of user-level thread systems are Nachos and Java (on operating systems that do not support kernel threads). In the case of handling Java threads, JVM is used, and the JVM is typically implemented on the top of a host operating system. JVM provides the *Java thread library*, which can be linked with the *thread library* of the host operating system by using APIs. The JVM for the Windows family of operating systems might use Win32 API when creating Java threads, whereas Linux, Solaris, and Mac OS X systems might use the *pthreads* API which is provided in the IEEE POSIX standard.

4.14.4.2.1   Merits and Drawbacks

Since the thread library is in charge of setting up thread implementation, including thread synchronization and scheduling, it keeps the kernel set aside, thereby avoiding the related overhead in the execution of needed system calls. That is why the thread switching overhead is far less than that of KLTs. This arrangement also enables each process to use a scheduling policy that best suits its nature. For example, a process implementing a multi-threaded server may perform round-robin scheduling on its threads, whereas a process implementing a real-time application may use priority-based scheduling on its threads to attain one of its major goals of response-time requirements.

But this arrangement has a few inherent drawbacks while managing threads without involving the kernel. First of all, since the kernel is unaware of the distinction between a thread and a process, if a thread were to be blocked by a system call (kernel action), the kernel would then block its parent process that would ultimately block *all* threads belonging to that process, irrespective of the fact that some other threads in the parent process may be in the ready state that could be scheduled. In order to avoid this situation, an OS would have to make adequate arrangement so that a non-blocking version of each system call is available that would otherwise make a process non-blocked. Second, since the kernel schedules a process, and the thread library schedules the threads within a process, it must ensure that at most one thread of a process would be in operation at any instant. Thus, a user-level thread cannot provide parallelism, and even the concurrency provided by them is also adversely impacted if a thread makes a system call that leads to blocking.

4.14.4.3 Hybrid Thread Models

A hybrid thread model consists of both user-level and KLTs and an associated mechanism that involves both user-level and KLTs. Different methods of associating user-level and KLTs give rise to different combinations of the low switching overhead of ULTs and the high concurrency and parallelism of KLTs. Three methods of association of user-level and KLTs are described here with their properties as follows:

> The thread library creates ULTs in a process and associates a (user) thread control block (UTCB) with each user-level thread. The kernel creates KLTs in a process and associates a kernel thread control block (KTCB) with each KLT. This is depicted in Figure 4.9, which shows different methods of associating ULTs with KLTs.

In the *many-to-one* association method [Figure 4.9(a)], all ULTs created in a process by the thread library are associated with a single KLT which is created in each process by the kernel. This method of association provides a similar effect as in mere ULTs; ULTs can be concurrent without being parallel (since they are the smallest unit of computation), thread switching incurs low overhead, and blocking of a user-level thread leads to blocking of all threads in the process. Solaris initially implemented the JVM using the many-to-one model (the green thread library). Later releases, however, changed this approach.

In the *one-to-one* association method [Figure 4.9(b)], each user-level thread is permanently mapped into a KLT. This method of association provides a similar effect as in mere KLTs. Here, threads can operate in parallel on different CPUs in a multiple processor system; however, switching between threads is performed at the kernel level and thus incurs high overhead. As usual, blocking of a user-level thread does not block other ULTs because they are mapped to different KLTs. For example, the Windows XP operating system uses the one-to-one model; therefore, each Java thread for a JVM running on such a system maps to a kernel thread. Beginning with Solaris 9 and onwards, Java threads, however, were mapped using the one-to-one model.

The *many-to-many* association method [Figure 4.9(c)] is possibly the most advantageous one. This method produces an effect in which ULTs may be mapped into any KLT. Thus, it is possible to achieve parallelism between ULTs by mapping them into different KLTs, but the system can perform switching between ULTs mapped to the same KLT without incurring high overhead. Also, blocking a user-level thread does not block other ULTs of the process that are mapped into different KLTs. Of course, this method requires a complex mechanism that has been observed in the implementation of later versions of the Sun Solaris operating system and Tru64 UNIX.

4.14.4.4 Threads and Fibers: Different Issues

When we use the term *thread*, we refer to a kernel thread, whereas *fiber* is used to refer to user threads. There are many different issues involved with these two types of threads. We have already discussed many of them in previous sections.

For more details about this topic, see the Support Material at www.routledge.com/9781032467238.

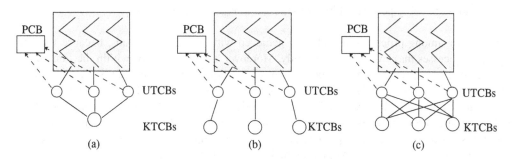

FIGURE 4.9(a), (b), (c) Different methods of associating user-level threads with kernel-level threads in the design of thread–based operating systems: (a) Many-to-one, (b) One-to-one, (c) Many-to-many.

4.14.5 THREADS: PRIORITY

Thread priorities are set by an appropriate method belonging to the thread class and are used by the thread scheduler when deciding to release a thread to run. Thread priorities are integers that specify the relative priority of one thread to another. Usually higher-priority threads get more CPU time than lower-priority threads. Priority is used to decide when to context switch from one running thread to the next, and the rules that determine when to context switch are:

- A thread can voluntarily release control by explicitly going to sleep. In such a case, all the other threads are examined, and the highest-priority ready thread is allocated to the CPU to run.
- A higher-priority thread can preempt a running thread. In this case, as soon as the higher-priority thread wants to run, it does. This is called preemptive multitasking.

However, assignment of priority to threads at the right point in time has several uses and has an immense impact on controlling the environment in which the thread runs.

For more details about this topic, see the Support Material at www.routledge.com/9781032467238.

4.14.6 MULTITHREADING

In thread-based systems, a process with exactly one thread is equivalent to a classical process. Here, the relationship between threads and processes is one to one (1: 1), and each thread of execution is a unique process with its own address space and resources. An example system of this type is UNIX System V. If there are multiple threads within a single process, it is a many-to-one (M:1) relationship, and the process defines an address space and dynamic resource ownership. Multiple threads may be created and executed within that process. Representative operating systems of this type are OS/2, MACH, and MVS (IBM large system). Other relationships, many-to-many (M:M) and one-to-many (1:M), also exist.

Breaking a single application into multiple threads enables one to impose great control over the modularity in that application and the timing of application-related events. From the job or application point of view, this multithreading concept resembles and is equivalent to a process on most other operating systems. In brief, it can be said that:

- The concept of multithreading facilitates developing efficient programs that result in the optimum utilization of the CPU, minimizing CPU idle time.
- A multithreaded program contains two or more parts that can run concurrently.
- Each part of such a program is a separate thread that defines a separate path of execution.
- Multithreading enables a single program to perform two or more tasks simultaneously. For example, a text editor can format text while it is engaged in printing as long as these two actions are being performed by two separate threads.

Concurrency among processes can also be achieved with the aid of threads, because threads in different processes may execute concurrently. Moreover, multiple threads within the same process may be allocated to separate processors (multiprocessor system) and can then be executed concurrently, resulting in excellent performance improvement. A multithreaded process achieves concurrency without incurring the overhead of using multiple processes. As already mentioned, threads within the same process can exchange information through shared memory and have access to the shared resources of the underlying process. Windows NT supports multithreading. However, multiple threads can be executed in parallel on many other computer systems.

Multithreading is generally implemented by time-slicing, wherein a single processor switches between different threads, in which case the processing is not literally simultaneous; the single

single core

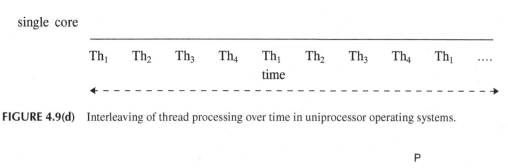

FIGURE 4.9(d)   Interleaving of thread processing over time in uniprocessor operating systems.

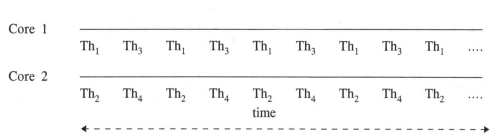

FIGURE 4.9(e)   Interleaving of thread processing over time in parallel execution on a multi-core uniprocessor operating systems.

processor can only do one thing at a time, and this switching can happen so fast that it creates an illusion of simultaneity to the end user. For instance, if the PC contains a processor with only a single core, then multiple programs can be run simultaneously, such as typing in a document with a text editor while listening to music in an audio playback program. Though the user experiences these things as simultaneous, in reality, the processor quickly switches back and forth between these separate processes.

Since threads expose multitasking to the user (cheaply), they are more powerful but even more complicated. Thread programmers have to explicitly address multithreading and synchronization.

An object-oriented multithreaded process is an efficient means of implementing a server application. For example, one server process can service a number of clients. Each client request triggers the creation of a new thread within the server.

In a single processor chip with *multiple computing cores* (*multicore*), each core *appears* as a separate processor to the operating system. With efficient use of these multiple cores, a multithreaded approach can be more effectively implemented that eventually yields overall improved concurrency. For example, consider an application with four threads. On a system with a processor with a single computing core, concurrency merely means that the execution of these threads will be interleaved over time, as the processing core is capable of executing only one thread at a time. This is illustrated in Figure 4.9(d). On a system with a processor with multiple cores, concurrency, however, means that the threads can run in parallel, as the system can assign a separate thread to each core that gives rise to parallel execution efficiently. This situation is depicted in Figure 4.9(e). Programs can now be designed in a multithreaded pattern to take advantages of multicore systems to yield improved performance.

4.14.7   THREADS AND PROCESSES: A COMPARATIVE OVERVIEW

The concepts of a process and thread are interrelated by a sense of *ownership* and *containment*.

Processes in conventional multitasking operating systems are typically independent, carry considerable state information, have separate address spaces, and interact only through system-provided interprocess communication mechanisms. Multiple threads, on other hand, typically share the state information of a single process and share memory and other resources directly but are able to execute independently. Context switching between threads in the same process is certainly faster than context switching between processes. Systems like Windows NT and OS/2 are said to have "cheap" threads and "expensive" processes. In other operating systems, not much of a difference can be observed. In Linux, there is truly no distinction between the concepts of processes and threads. However, multiple threads in Linux can be grouped together in such a way that one can effectively have a single process comprising multiple threads.

A multithreading approach allows multiple threads to exist in a single process, and this model provides a useful abstraction of concurrent execution since the threads of the program lend themselves to realizing such operation. In fact, a multithreaded program operates faster on computer systems with multiple CPUs or CPUs with multiple cores or across a cluster of machines. In this situation, threads must be carefully handled to avoid race conditions and need to rendezvous (meeting by appointment) in time in order to process data in the correct order. Threads may also require atomic operations (often implemented using semaphores) in order to prevent common data from being simultaneously modified or read while in the process of being modified. Nevertheless, improper handling of threads may lead to critical situations with adverse effects. However, perhaps the most interesting application of this approach is that when it is applied to a single process on a multiprocessor system, it yields *parallel execution*.

Operating systems generally implement threads in one of two ways: *preemptive multithreading* or *cooperative multithreading*. Preemptive multithreading is, however, generally considered superior, since it allows the operating system to determine when to make a context switch. Cooperative multithreading, on the other hand, relies on the threads themselves to relinquish control once they are at a stopping point. This can create problems if a thread is waiting for resource availability. The disadvantage to preemptive multithreading is that the system may make a context switch at an inappropriate time, causing priority inversion or other ill effects which may also be avoided by use of cooperative multithreading.

Traditional mainstream computing hardware did not have much support for multithreading. Processors in embedded systems supporting real-time behaviors might provide multithreading by decreasing the thread switch time, perhaps by allocating a dedicated register file for each thread instead of saving/restoring a common register file. In the late 1990s, the idea of simultaneous execution of instructions from multiple threads became known as *simultaneous multithreading*. This feature was introduced in Intel's Pentium 4 processor with the name *hyper-threading*.

4.14.8 THREAD IMPLEMENTATIONS

There are many different incompatible implementations of threading. These include both kernel-level and user-level implementations. User-level threads can be implemented without operating system support, although some operating systems or libraries provide explicit support for them. However, KLTs are differently implemented in different operating systems. Hybrid-level thread implementation also differ and depends mainly on the design strategy used in the development of the associated operating system, and these threads may be created either in kernel space or in user space.

For more details about this topic, see the Support Material at www.routledge.com/9781032467238.

4.14.9 CASE STUDY: SOLARIS THREADS IMPLEMENTATIONS

Solaris implements an uncommon multilevel thread mechanism to provide considerable flexibility in making use of processor resources. It exploits multithreaded architecture that makes use of four separate thread-related concepts: process, ULTs, LWPs, and KLTs. These four entities are related to one another in many different fashions. Within a process, there may be one or more than one thread (multithreaded) connected in many different ways with one or more than one LWP of the corresponding process. An LWP within a process is visible to the application, and LWP data structure can be obtained from the respective process address space. Each LWP, in turn, is always bound to exactly one single dispatchable kernel thread, which is a fundamental computational entity, and the data structure for that kernel thread is maintained within the kernel's address space. The kernel creates, runs, and destroys these kernel threads to execute specific system functions. The use of kernel threads instead of using kernel processes to implement system functions eventually reduces the overhead of switching (thread switching is much faster and less costly than process switching) within the kernel.

For more details about this topic with figures, see the Support Material at www.routledge.com/9781032467238.

4.15 OBJECTS: OBJECT-ORIENTED CONCEPT

The concept of *objects* was originally derived in simulation languages (such as Simula 67) where an object was conceived of as an autonomous entity (unit) to represent certain operations in those systems. A simulation program can be thought of as a collection of large number of these individual units of computation (objects), each of which performs small amounts of computations at a time and is closely correlated to sibling units of computation. Moreover, to define and derive the *nature* of such a simulated unit of computation (object), the idea of *class* was introduced with an object to define the behavior of the object, just as a program defines the behavior of its related process. The definition of a class includes certain facilities that an object enjoys while declaring its own data which are private to the class computation. Thus, a class behaves like an abstract data type that maintains its own state in its private variables. The simulation is then defined by specifying a set of class instances; the objects that are allowed to communicate with one another by way of only message passing.

Objects were first introduced in many *user interface systems*, such as: InterViews, which clearly illustrates the power of object-oriented programming. The growing popularity of object-oriented languages and their related programming has added a new dimension in the computing world that paved the way to design, develop, and implement operating systems by way of using objects. One such early implementation is the Spring operating system (Hamilton and Kougiouris). The object concept was gradually refined and upgraded over time and ultimately gave rise to contemporary object-oriented systems. Windows, in particular, draws heavily on the concepts of object-oriented design. Thus, the unit of a process model is now used to define objects as an alternative schedulable unit of computation. Objects reacts only to messages, and once an object is created, other objects send it messages. The newly created object responds by performing certain computations on its internal private data and by sending other messages back to the original sender or to other objects. This approach facilitates the sharing of resources and data among processes and the protection of resources from unauthorized access. The objects can interface with the outside world by means of using only messages.

In *object-oriented design*, an object is a distinct software unit that consists of one or more procedures and a collection of related items of data. These procedures are called *services* that the object provides, and the data associated with these services are called *attributes* of the object. Normally, these data and procedures are not directly visible outside the object; rather various well-defined interfaces exist that permit other software to gain access to the objects consisting of data and procedures. The data, sometimes called *variables*, are typically simple scalars or tables. Each such variable has a type, possibly a set of allowable values (constant or variable values). Access restrictions on variables may also be imposed on users, categories of users, or situations. The only way to access the data or to take any action on the data in a particular object is by invoking one of the underlying services (method) of the object. Hence, the data in the object can easily be protected from unauthorized or incorrect use (e.g. attempting to execute a non-executable piece of data). This property in the definition of the object is known as *encapsulation* and offers two distinct advantages:

- It not only protects the objects from any corruption but also safeguards against the types of problems that may arise from concurrent accesses, such as, deadlocks.
- It hides the internal structure of the object so that interaction with the object is relatively simple and standardized. Moreover, since the object is modular in concept, if the internal structure or the procedures associated with an object are modified without changing its external functionality, other objects are unaffected. This helps any modification or enhancement in the object-oriented design to be straightforward.

If a process is represented by an object, then there will be one object for each process present in a system. Clearly, every such object needs its own set of variables. But if the methods (procedures) in the object are re-entrant procedures, then all similar objects, including every new object of a similar type, could share the same procedures but with its own set of variables.

To avoid all such difficulties, the object class is redefined to make a distinction between object class and object instance. The definition of *object class* is to project it as a template that defines both the *variables* (*attributes*) and *procedures* (*services*) attached to a particular type of object. An *object instance* is an actual object that includes the characteristics of the class that defines it. The instance contains values for the variables defined in the object class. The operating system can then create specific instances of an object class as needed. For example, there is a single-process object class and one process object for every currently active process. This approach simplifies object creation and management. Objects can be defined separately both in terms of process and thread individually, giving rise to a process object and thread object. The characteristics of these objects are, of course, different and can be willfully exploited when implemented in the design and development of operating systems using both processes and threads.

Object-oriented concepts are becoming increasingly important in the design and development of operating systems. The object-oriented structure assists in the development of a general-purpose process facility to provide support for a variety of operating system environments. Objects define another mechanism to specify the behavior of a distributed system of computational units. This is done by specifying the behavior of individual units of serial computation and the model by which they are coordinated when they execute. Specialized support for the object model enables traditional sequential programmers to achieve a strong intuition about distributed computing. This help programmers take advantage of contemporary multiprocessors and also clusters of interconnected computers.

4.15.1 CASE STUDY: WINDOWS NT IMPLEMENTATION

Windows NT a representative operating system that makes extensive use of object-oriented techniques using objects defined in terms of both traditional process and contemporary threads. However, Windows NT is not a full-fledged object-oriented operating system. It is not really implemented in an object-oriented language and also does not support some common object-oriented capabilities, such as inheritance (parent–child relationship) or polymorphism. Data structures that reside completely within one executive component are not represented as objects. Nevertheless, NT illustrates the power of object-oriented technology and represents the increasing trend towards the use of this technology in operating system implementations. In spite of all these reasons, we have still used it as an example only to demonstrate how the object concept can be built up while maintaining its relationship with the existing process and thread approach at the time of its realization.

For more detailed description of this topic with related figures, see the Support Material at www.routledge.com/9781032467238.

4.16 PROCESS SCHEDULING (UNIPROCESSOR): TIME MANAGEMENT

By the term *scheduling*, we refer to a set of defined *policies* and suitable *mechanisms* to implement these policies built into the operating system that determines the order in which the work is to be performed by a computer system or by the way the computer will be used. Different types of scheduling, as already discussed in Chapter 2, are encompassed with different units of work. In many operating systems, this scheduling activity, apart from I/O scheduling, comprises three separate functions: long-, medium-, and short-term scheduling. The long-term scheduler executes rather infrequently and selects a job from a batch of jobs (hold state) to be loaded into memory (ready state) for execution. Once the job scheduler has moved a job, it creates one or more processes for this job. In a multiprogrammed operating system, more than one such job may be present in memory at a time, and hence, many such processes may share the CPU using time-multiplexing. The medium-term scheduler is executed somewhat more frequently to make a swap-in decision. The short-term scheduler (process scheduler), also known as dispatcher or low-level scheduler, executes most frequently, as the name suggests, and makes fine-grained decisions that govern the order of execution of runnable processes in memory. This module decides which process in the pool of ready processes in the memory gets a processor and when and for how long in accordance with a chosen set of criteria to optimize one or more aspects of system behavior. The process scheduler thus attempts to handle *microscopic scheduling*, the dynamic assignment of processor to process associated with each scheduled job. In this section, we will focus only on different aspects of process scheduling (processor scheduling) that is mostly carried out by a short-term scheduler.

In a batch processing environment, the scheduling algorithm is very simple: just run the next job. In a multiprogramming environment, multiple programs are waiting for service along with background jobs which are also active. Hence, scheduling algorithms will always try to achieve a target with certain decisions based on underlying policy and not provide only a suitable mechanism. The process scheduler must perform the following functions:

- Keeping track of the status of the process (all processes are either running, ready, or blocked). The module that performs this function is called the traffic controller.
- Deciding which process gets a processor: when and for how long. This is performed by the processor scheduler.
- Allocation of the processor to a process. This requires resetting of processor registers to correspond to the process's correct state and is performed by the traffic controller.
- Deallocation of the processor, such as when the running process exceeds its current quantum (time-slice) or must wait for I/O completion. This requires that all processor state registers be saved to allow future reallocation. This task is performed by the traffic controller.

Based on certain pre-defined sets of criteria, the short-term scheduler thus always attempts to maximize system performance by switching the state of deserving processes from ready to running. It is invoked whenever an event (internal or external) occurs that may eventually change the global state of the system. For any such change, the currently running process may be interrupted or preempted in favor of other existing processes, and then the next deserving process is scheduled to run. Some of the events that force changes in global system states and thereby require rescheduling include the following:

- Clock ticks: clock–time–base interrupts
- I/O interrupts and I/O completion
- Operating-system calls
- Sending and receiving of signals
- Interactive program activation

In general, whenever one of these events occurs, the short-term scheduler is invoked by the operating system to take action, mostly to schedule another deserving process with allocation of the CPU for execution. The responsibilities the short-term scheduler performs in coordination with the activities of the other two schedulers while providing process-management OS services have already been discussed in Chapter 2 and hence are not repeated here.

4.16.1 SCHEDULING CRITERIA: SHORT-TERM SCHEDULER

The scheduling mechanism is the part of the process manager whose main objective is to control and allocate the processor in such a way as to maximize system performance on the basis of a particular strategy. The strategy to be employed is influenced by certain established criteria that determine several dimensions of design objectives. There are numerous competing goals (criteria) in this regard that scheduling policies aim to fulfill. These criteria can even be viewed as being classified into several distinct but interrelated dimensions. Those are:

User-oriented criteria relate to the behavior of the system that directly affects the individual
   user or process. One such example is *response time* in interactive systems.
System-oriented criteria emphasize effective and efficient use of the CPU. An example of this
   category is throughput, which is the rate at which processes are completed.
Performance-related criteria focus on quantitative yield by the system and generally can be
   readily measured. Examples include response time and throughput.
Non-performance-related criteria are qualitative in nature and cannot readily be measured or
   analyzed. An example of this category is predictability.

However, all these dimensions can be summarized together in the following various criteria that can be used as a guideline in designing a well-defined policy:

- **Performance-Related Criteria**
  - **System-Oriented:** Throughput, processor utilization (efficiency)
  - **User-Oriented:** Response time, turnaround time, deadlines
- **Other Criteria**
  - **System-Oriented:** Fairness, waiting time, priority, resource utilization
  - **User-Oriented**: Predictability

More details on this topic are given on the Support Material at www.routledge.com/9781032467238.

4.16.2 SCHEDULER DESIGN

The scheduler is concerned with deciding on policy, not providing any mechanism. Scheduler design should start by setting a goal to be achieved. This requires selection of one or more primary performance criteria, as already described, and placing them in a relative order of preference. Based on this selected set of criteria, the scheduling policy/strategy is to be designed to maximize performance. The scheduling algorithms thus implemented are mostly based on heuristic techniques that could offer only good or near-optimal performance. Schedulers thus developed always tend to maximize the average performance of a system relative to a particular criterion. However, the worst-case scenario and controlling variance in performance should also be taken into account. For example, a user experiencing a 10-minute turnaround time for their simple batch job is frustrated even if they know the system's average turnaround time is below 5 minutes.

Unfortunately, no policy with a set of selective performance criteria is truly fair. But as the amount of available CPU time is, after all, finite, it can be shown (Kleinrock, 1975–1976) that any attempt to improve performance for one class of job (processes) is always at the expense of degraded performance for some other class. Moreover, giving one user more means giving other users less. At best, there can be a reasonable distribution of CPU time with a target of the attainment of a desired goal. There is certainly no other way out.

While a scheduling policy aims to fulfill several competing goals (criteria), some of these criteria are observed to be opposing one another. For example, to minimize response time for interactive users, the scheduler should try to avoid running any batch jobs during prime daytime even if there is a tremendous flow in incoming batch jobs. The batch users probably will not be happy with this algorithm; moreover, it violates the *turnaround* criterion. Another example is that while increased processor utilization is achieved by increasing the number of active processes, this, in turn, causes response time to decrease. The design approach varies from one environment to another, and a careful balance of all these conflicting requirements and constraints is needed to attain the desired goal appropriate to the specific environment. For example, the design objectives of a batch system environment will focus more on providing an equitable share of processor per unit time to each process (user) or better throughput and increased resource utilization. Multi-user systems are usually designed with more emphasis on minimizing terminal response time, while real-time operating systems favor a focus on the ability to quickly handle bursts of external events responsively to meet certain deadlines.

4.16.3 SCHEDULING MECHANISMS

Process scheduling is a mechanism that, on the basis of an already-defined policy in accordance with a set of chosen criteria, selects a particular process from a list of ready processes in memory (in a multitasking operating system) and then allocates CPU time to run it using time-multiplexing. Processes generally alternate between a computing burst during which they are in the domain of the process scheduler and an I/O burst while invoking an I/O operation during which they are in a wait list. When a process invokes an I/O operation, the CPU is withdrawn from that executing process, and the scheduler then allocates the CPU to another deserving process.

The scheduling mechanism is a part of the process manager. Every time a process enters the ready list, it will generally be treated as a new process, but more often it is an old process that has been brought back to the ready list from outside the domain of the short-term scheduler. It might have returned because the I/O for which it was waiting has completed, some resource it was requesting has been granted, or the medium-term scheduler has decided to favor it. Every time it leaves the ready list, either because it has terminated or due to other reasons as mentioned, the process will simply be forgotten, and it is said that the process has *departed*. It is not at all important here to consider why it has left. This narrow view will ultimately allow us to concentrate more on the fundamentals of short-term scheduling (process scheduling) that will finally determine the design and general organization of a process scheduler to implement a suitable mechanism.

Brief details on this topic are given on the Support Material at www.routledge.com/9781032467238.

4.16.4 PROCESS SCHEDULERS: DIFFERENT KINDS

Process scheduling policies are designed for fulfillment of numerous competing criteria (already discussed) to realize the specific goal of the OS in this regard. The design of a certain policy is usually determined mostly in terms of two functional characteristics: *selection* and *decision*. The *selection function* determines which process among a pool of ready process is to be selected for execution. The *decision function*, on the other hand, specifies the right instant in time when the already-decided selection function is to be launched for execution again. This function specifically targets when and for how long, meaning at what point in time (when) a process is to be selected, and this automatically implies at what instant (when) the next selection is once again to be executed, thereby limiting the execution time of the currently running process. The selection function is commonly based on priority, resource requirements, or the execution characteristics (history) of the

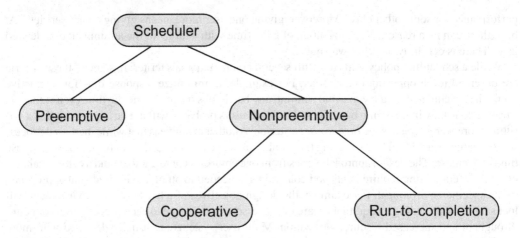

FIGURE 4.10   Different types of schedulers based on competing criteria and their interrelationships.

process, such as; time already spent in execution, time already spent in the system including execution and waiting, total service time required by the process, and similar other factors relating to specified criteria.

A *run-to-completion scheduler* means that a job, once scheduled, will be run to completion. Such a scheduler is known as a *nonpreemptive scheduler*. Another simple approach in this category is for the scheduler to assume that each process will explicitly invoke the scheduler periodically, voluntarily releasing the CPU, thereby allowing other processes to use the CPU (*cooperative scheduler*).

This nonpreemptive approach in short-term (process) scheduling allows the running process to absolutely retain the ownership of the processor and sometimes even of other allocated resources until it voluntarily surrenders control to the OS or due to a result of its own action, say, waiting for an I/O completion. This drawback could only be resolved entirely if the operating system itself could devise some arrangement that would force the running process not to continue at an arbitrary instant while engaged in involuntary sharing of the CPU. This strategy by the OS that forces temporary suspension of the logically runnable processes is popularly known as *preemptive scheduling*. Only in that situation can another ready process be scheduled.

With preemptive scheduling, a running process may be interrupted at any instant and be moved to the ready state by the operating system, allowing any other deserving process to replace it. Preemption thus generally necessitates more frequent execution of the scheduler and may even lead to a critical race condition (to be discussed later), which may be prevented only by using another method. In addition, preemption incurs more overhead than nonpreemptive methods since each process rescheduling demands a complete costly process switch. In spite of accepting all this overhead, preemptive scheduling, in essence, is generally more responsive and may still provide better service to the total population of processes for general-purpose systems, because it prevents processes from monopolizing the processor for a very long time. Today most operating systems are such preemptive multitasking systems.

The maximum time a process can keep the CPU is called the system's time quantum or time-slice length. The choice of time quantum can have a profound impact on system performance. Small time quanta give good interactive performance to short interactive jobs (which are likely to block for I/O). Larger quanta are better for long-running CPU-bound jobs because they do not make as many time-consuming process switches, thus having less overhead. If the time quantum is kept so small that the system spends more time carrying out switching of processes than doing useful work, the system is said to be *thrashing*, which is also found in other subsystems.

More details on this topic are given on the Support Material at www.routledge.com/9781032467238.

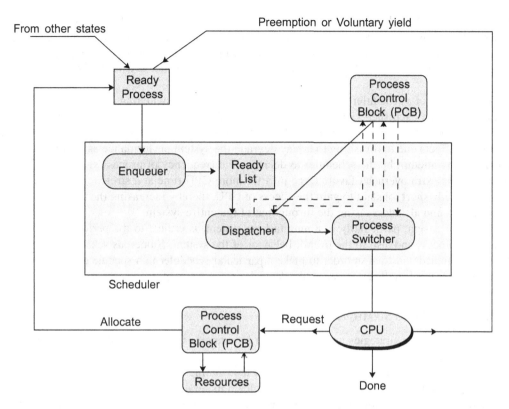

FIGURE 4.11 The role and actions of process scheduler at the time of process scheduling.

4.16.5 PROCESS SCHEDULER ORGANIZATION

The process scheduler, a part of the process manager, is in charge of controlling and allocating the CPU on which the ready processes are multiplexed. The scheduling policy determines the strategy that chooses one or more primary performance criteria, as already described, while selecting a process from a pool of ready processes for execution to maximize performance. The scheduling mechanism is derived to implement a specific already-decided policy to attain the ultimate goal of the OS and acts to remove the running process from the CPU and then selects another process from ready list on the basis of a particular strategy.

Scheduler organization is essentially composed of several different parts, depending on how it is implemented in any particular OS. Figure 4.11 shows three such conceptually distinct parts incorporated into every scheduler: the *enqueuer*, the *process switcher*, and the *dispatcher*. At an appropriate time, the scheduler switches the CPU from one executing process to another process ready for execution. The process switcher saves all the relevant information of the running process being removed from the CPU in its PCB. The running process is now changed to the ready state, and the enqueuer enters a pointer (the ready list is essentially a queue of pointers) related to this ready process in its respective PCB of a list of ready processes to update it. The dispatcher is invoked after the running process has been removed from the CPU, and it then selects one of the ready processes queued in the ready list, then allocates the CPU to the selected process.

4.16.6 SYSTEM PERFORMANCE

Apart from the contribution of hardware components, the scheduler itself can have an immense impact and can have a dramatic effect on the performance of a multitasking system. Since it is in charge of deciding the order of the processes ready for execution, it ultimately controls which and ready process is to be allocated the CPU and when to maximize CPU utilization along with the proper utilization of other resources. As a result, the perceived performance of the system is greatly influenced by the working of an appropriate scheduler matched with the existing system's environment.

The working of a scheduler also determines the frequency of switching of processes from one to another, when each such switch requires additional overhead to perform the process switch operation. Too much switching favors small or interactive jobs to get good service but may invite damaging effects due to thrashing that may degrade the system performance as a whole. On the contrary, any attempt by the scheduler to decrease the frequency of process switching in order to reduce the extra overhead favors large jobs for more CPU time at a stretch, but it will cause the other ready short jobs not to gain the access of CPU, thereby increasing the turnaround time of processes and also decreasing the throughput of the entire system.

Scheduler design, particularly in a multitasking system, is critical to the performance of each individual process and also to the overall behavior of the system. Numerous scheduling strategies have been studied and tried in order to make a particular scheduler fit a specific environment, but ultimately, it is the overall performance that depends on the choice of the strategy to be implemented.

4.16.7 SCHEDULING STRATEGIES

Different scheduling strategies are implemented by numerous scheduling algorithms, which are mainly partitioned into two major classes: *nonpreemptive* and *preemptive*. Nonpreemptive algorithms are designed so that once a process enters the running state (a processor is allocated), it is not removed from the processor until it has completed its total execution or it explicitly yields the processor as a result of its own action. Nonpreemptive algorithms are consistent with voluntary CPU sharing. Preemptive algorithms are driven by the notion of prioritized (*internal priority*) computation in which the process with the highest priority (derived from specific criteria to meet a goal) should always be the one currently using the processor. While a process is currently using the processor, a new process with a higher priority may enter the ready list, and the executing process should then be interrupted, removed, and returned to the ready list until it is once again the highest-priority process in the system, and the processor will be allocated to the newly entered higher-priority process. Incidentally, it is also possible to assign an *external priority* to each process by using a priority number that many systems use. In that situation, the scheduler always chooses a process of higher-priority over one of lower-priority and takes the same courses of action, as mentioned. However, preemptive algorithms are normally associated with systems that use interrupts (which may occur for many other reasons) to negotiate involuntary CPU sharing.

A scheduling strategy is based on the process model, and its time measurements are used to compare the performance characteristics of different algorithms. The design of the general model must be adjusted to fit each specific class of OS environments. The process model, however, does not address the resource manager's behavior except to identify the blocked state. The process scheduling model completely ignores all effects of resource competition except that for the CPU. Hence, a process in this model can be only in the running or ready state, and thus the entire time that the process might have spent in the blocked state is not taken into consideration in the performance metric.

Before describing some representative scheduling algorithms, let us identify some useful service measures (parameters) which can be taken into account at the time of defining scheduling policies. Those are:

Service time, t: The total amount of time a process needs to be in the running state before it is completed. In other words, the service time represents the amount of time the process will use the CPU to accomplish its useful work.

Wait time, W: The time the process spends waiting in the ready state before its *first* transi-
(response time) tion to the running state to receive its *first* unit of service from the processor.

Turnaround time, T : This is the duration of time that a *process p* is present; i.e. (finish time –
arrival time). The turnaround time T counts not only how long a process
p needs but also how long it sits in the ready list while other processes
are run. Once it starts, it might be preempted after some time, letting
it continue further later. The entire time a process p is on the ready list
(until it leaves our view to go to other lists) is charged to T. The process is
not visible to the short-term scheduler while it is waiting for I/O or other
resources, and therefore the wait time is not included in T.

Missed time $M : T - t$. The missed time M is the same thing, except we do not count the
(wait time W) amount of time t during which a process p is actually running. M
measures the amount of time during which p would like to run but
is prevented.

Response ratio $R : t/T$. The response ratio represents the fraction of the time that p is
receiving service. If the response ratio R is 1, then p never sits in the
ready list while some other process runs.

Penalty ratio $P : T/t$. The penalty ratio P is the inverse of R. If the response ratio R is 1/100,
then $P = 100$, and the process seems to be taking 100 times as long
as it should; the user may be annoyed. A response ratio greater than 1
doesn't make any sense. Similarly, the penalty ratio P ranges from 1
(which is a perfect value) upward.

Kernel time: The time spent by the kernel in making policy decisions and carrying them
out. This time includes context-switch and process-switch time. A well-tuned
operating system tries to keep the kernel time between 10 and 30 percent.

Idle time: The time spent when the ready list is empty and no fruitful work can be accomplished.

4.16.7.1 System Load Considerations

The values of the service measures (different guiding parameters) that would be obtained under
different policies will be influenced by many other things, such as; how many processes there are,
how fast they arrive, and what amount of time they need to run. All these things together give rise
to what are called the considerations of the load of the system at any instant, which should also be
taken into account when benchmarking different scheduling strategies.

For a brief description of this topic with figures, see the Support Material at www.routledge.
com/9781032467238.

4.16.8 Nonpreemptive Strategies

Nonpreemptive scheduling algorithms allow any process to run to completion once it is allocated
the processor and then release control to the scheduler. It never uses interrupts to make the scheduler switch to a new process and thereby avoids additional costly process switching and other related
table updating until it is inevitable. Non-preemptive policies are an example of the *hysteresis principle*; the slogan is "Resist change".

4.16.8.1 First-Come-First-Served Scheduling

First-come-first-served (FCFS), also called first-in-first-out, is the simplest nonpreemptive scheduling algorithm, which is easy to implement and easy to disparage. As each process joins the ready
queue either from the outside world or from the waiting pool, it waits there until it gains access to
the processor. This strategy assigns priority to processes in order of their arrival in the ready list,
and the priority is computed by the enqueuer by timestamping all incoming processes and then having the dispatcher select the process that has the oldest timestamp. Alternatively, the ready list can

be organized as a simple FIFO data structure (where each entry will point to a process descriptor). Processes that arrive are added to the tail of the queue by the enqueuer, and the dispatcher will take (remove) processes from the head of the queue (the oldest process in the ready queue) when the current running process stop executing. The preemptive version of this algorithm is commonly known as round-robin (RR) scheduling, discussed later.

FCFS never takes into account the state of the system and the resource requirements of the individual scheduled processes. It ignores service time requests and all other criteria that may influence performance with respect to turnaround and waiting time. In the absence of any preemption, resource utilization and the system throughput rate may be quite low. Since FCFS does not discriminate jobs on the basis of their required service time, short jobs may suffer considerable turnaround delays and waiting times when one or more long jobs are present in front of them in the system. Consequently, this scheduling may result in poor performance under a specific set of system requirements and thus has been dropped from favor.

Although FCFS is not an attractive alternative approach on its own for a single-processor system, it is often combined with a priority scheme to provide an effective scheduling mechanism. The scheduler in that situation may maintain a number of queues of processes, one queue for each priority level, and dispatch each process on a first-come-first-served basis within each queue. One example of such a system is known as *feedback scheduling*, which is discussed later in this subsection.

The characteristics of FCFS scheduling with figure is given on the Support Material at www. routledge.com/9781032467238.

4.16.8.2   Shortest Remaining Time Next Scheduling

Shortest remaining time next (SRTN) is a scheduling discipline in which the next scheduling entry, a process or a job, is selected on the basis of the shortest remaining execution time. SRTN may be implemented by means of either nonpreemptive or preemptive ways, giving rise to two different types of scheduling. The nonpreemptive version of SRTN is commonly called *shortest job (process) first* (SJF/SPF), also known as *shortest job (process) next* (SJN or SPN). The preemptive version of SRTN is usually called SRTN (or even SRT) and is also known as *preemptive shortest process next* (PSPN). We will discuss these two scheduling disciplines separately under their respective categories.

Whatever the category, in either situation, whenever the SRTN scheduler is invoked, it searches the corresponding queue (batch or ready list) to find the job or the process with the shortest remaining execution time. The difference between the two cases lies in the conditions that lead to invocation of the scheduler and, consequently, the frequency of its execution. In the case of nonpreemption, the SRTN scheduler is invoked whenever a job is completed or the running process surrenders control to the OS. In the preemptive version, whenever an event occurs that makes a new process ready, the scheduler is invoked to compare the remaining processor execution time of the currently running process with the time needed to complete the next processor burst of the newcomer. Depending on the outcome, the running process may continue, or it may be preempted and replaced by the shortest-remaining-time process. If preempted, the running process joins the ready queue as usual.

4.16.8.3   Shortest Process Next

SPN is a nonpreemptive SRTN policy in which the process requiring the shortest expected processing time is selected next. To realize this, the jobs in the ready queue may be sorted on their runtime; short processes will then jump in order towards the head of the queue past longer jobs and receive service. In this way, this method makes an attempt to shorten the average turnaround time to improve the response ratio of short processes and thereby reduce the bias in favor of long processes inherent in FCFS. Moreover, since the completed job departs the system, this discipline tends to reduce the number of waiting jobs, thereby allowing new jobs to quickly enter the queue. It is worth pointing out that SPN is only optimal when all the jobs are available in the ready queue simultaneously.

With SPN, although the overall performance in terms of response time is significantly improved, the long processes may be penalized. Moreover, if the ready list is saturated, which is often obvious, then long processes tend to remain in the ready list while short processes continuously receive service. In the extreme case, when the system has little idle time, long processes will never be served, and such starvation of long processes may ultimately be a serious liability of the scheduling algorithm. Moreover, especially for longer processes, the variability of response time is increased, and thus predictability is reduced.

Another difficulty with the SPN policy is that it requires for its working a different ingredient: explicit information about the service-time requirements or at least an estimate of the required service time of each process. But, due to the presence of many issues, it is really difficult for either the user or the scheduler to figure out which of the currently runnable processes is the shortest one. In fact, the success of SPN in practical application depends mostly on the accuracy of prediction of the job and process behavior, and that also imposes additional overhead of correctly computing a predictor calculation at runtime. That is why, in spite of having several merits, due to the presence of all these critical issues and the absence of preemption in this scheduling, this method is not usually favored as suitable for a time-sharing or transaction-processing environment.

A prediction calculation, analysis, and example figure for SPN are given on the Support Material at www.routledge.com/9781032467238.

4.16.8.4 Highest Penalty Ratio Next

Nonpreemptive scheduling policies seem to give unfair advantage either to very long processes (FCFS) or very short ones (SPN). The highest penalty ratio next (HPRN) method (some authors called it *highest response ratio next* [HRRN], but the response ratio is just the opposite or inverse of penalty ratio, as defined earlier) tries to be more reasonable and still not introduce preemption. The penalty ratio (P), which is the ratio of turnaround time to actual service time (T/t), can be taken into consideration as a figure of merit at the time of scheduling. For each individual process, all possible attempts should be made to minimize this ratio, and we would like to minimize its average value over all processes. Although this is an a posteriori measure, we can approximate it with an a priori measure as a selection criteria in a nonpreemptive scheduler. Consider the following penalty ratio (P):

$$P = \frac{T}{t} = \frac{(w+t)}{t} \quad \text{where}: \quad \begin{aligned} w &= \text{time spent waiting for the processor.} \\ t &= \text{expected service time.} \end{aligned}$$

When a new process enters the ready list, the value of w of this process is 0; hence, $P = 1$. When a new process keeps waiting in the ready list, its value of P, which starts at 1, begins to rise. After it has waited w time on the ready list, $P = (w+t)/t$.

Thus, the scheduling rule would be: When the currently running process completes or is blocked, choose the ready process with the greatest value of P for execution. This strategy is attractive because it counts the age of the processes. Although shorter jobs are favored (a smaller denominator yields a larger ratio and hence would likely be selected very soon), aging without service (increase in the value of w) also increases the penalty ratio P, so that a longer process will eventually get past competing shorter jobs. Consequently, as long as the saturation is not unreasonable, the HPRN method will not cause very long processes to starve indefinitely, since their penalty ratio by this time reaches a high value.

As with SPN/SJF, the expected service time must be estimated before attempting to use this technique. That is why, if t is not known, it can be estimated by an exponential average of service times during previous compute bursts, as stated earlier. Alternatively, we can base the HPRN method on a medium-term penalty ratio, $(M + t)/t$, where M is the total time missed while the process has languished either on the short-term ready list or on a medium-term main store wait list (but not on a I/O wait list), and t is the total CPU time used during previous compute bursts.

HPRN strikes a nice balance between FCFS and SPN. If we use the actual value of t on various types of sample process sets, it reveals that the behavior of HPRN is most similar to FCFS. Interestingly, HPRN fits neatly between FCFS and SPN: for short processes, HPRN is much like

SPN; for middle-length processes, HPRN has an intermediate penalty ratio; and for very long processes, SPN becomes worse than FCFS, but HPRN is still in the middle.

However, HPRN still has some distinct disadvantages. First of all, it is not preemptive, so it cannot beat RR or PSPN for short processes. A short process that unfortunately arrives just after a long-process started executing will still have to wait a very long time. Second, it is generally not as good as SPN (as indicated by the result of various simulations), which uses the same technique: knowledge of process length without preemption. Third, HPRN is more expensive to implement, since the penalty ratio must be calculated for every waiting process whenever a running process completes or blocks.

4.16.8.5 Priority Scheduling

Priority scheduling is carried out on the basis of external priority assigned by a positive number associated with each job. When the CPU becomes available, the scheduler allocates the CPU to the job (or process) with highest priority for its execution (it is assumed in this discussion that lower the number, the higher the priority, although some schedulers use the opposite ordering. There is no general agreement in this regard). If two or more jobs have equal priorities, FCFS is employed. Priority-based scheduling may be preemptive or nonpreemptive. Preemptive priority-based scheduling will be discussed later in this section.

Priorities can be defined internally (dynamic) or externally (static). In either case, their initial values are assigned by the operating system at process creation time or by the user at the time of submission of the job. *Internal priorities* are derived dynamically by the operating system using the measurable attributes of a process in execution within the computing environment. Memory requirement, service-time request, ratio of average CPU burst time to average I/O burst time, number of files opened, and so on are used as criteria for determining an aggregate figure of internal priorities. In SPN, we have already observed that this internal priority is derived and determined based on the length of the service-time request. *External priorities*, on the other hand, are set statically by considering factors which are external to the operating system. These priorities reflect the importance of a task that the process is to perform based on factors that the process manager can only accept as input from *users*. For example, a process's external priority might be inferred from the user identification ("important users have higher priorities"), the nature of the task ("a process should turn on a furnace when the temperature falls below a threshold value in a process control system"), or any other arbitrary criteria. A higher priority can be obtained by paying a higher rate for computer system usage.

Both nonpreemptive and preemptive priority-based scheduling have the drawback that if many high-priority processes are present in the system or keep continuously arriving, a resident ready-to-run low-priority process or request will be simply ignored and delayed indefinitely in receiving CPU service, causing it to suffer from long turnaround times or even be forced towards starvation. This starvation can, however, be compensated for if the priorities can be internally modified by a suitable strategy. *Aging* is such a strategy that tends to eliminate this starvation problem by gradually increasing the priorities internally for jobs that wait in the ready queue for a long time.

An illustrative example of this topic is given on the Support Material at www.routledge.com/9781032467238.

4.16.8.5.1 *Priority Problems—Inversion and Starvation*

When cooperating processes appear in a priority scheduling system, there can be interactions between the processes that confuse the priority system. Consider three processes, A, B, C; A has the highest priority (runs first) and C the lowest, with B having a priority in between them. A blocks and waits for C to do something. B, by this time, get its turn due to the blocking of A and will run to completion, even though A, a higher-priority process, can only continue if C runs. This is sometimes referred to as *priority inversion*. This happens also in real-time systems: the Mars Pathfinder spacecraft (see Chapter 10) suffered a failure in its operation caused by priority inversion.

Starvation is simpler to understand. Imagine a two-level priority system with an endless, fast stream of interactive jobs at first-level priority. Any CPU-bound job at second-level priority may then have to wait a longtime or might even never run, leading to what is called starvation.

The final problem with priority systems is how to determine priorities. They can be statically allocated to each program (system commands always run with priority 3), allocated by each user (root always runs with priority 3), or computed on the fly (process aging). However, all these approaches have their own merits as well as drawbacks

4.16.8.6 Deadline Scheduling

Hard real-time systems comprise time-critical processes in which each process must be guaranteed completion of execution before expiration of its deadline. In such systems, the critical performance measure is whether the system was able to meet all such processes' scheduling deadlines, and measures of turnaround and wait (missed) times are generally irrelevant here. Deadline scheduling can be considered one form of priority-based scheduling where priorities are assigned in terms of the deadlines associated with each process. In process control systems, the deadline may be established by an external sensor reading. Deadline scheduling may be preemptive or nonpreemptive. Preemptive deadline scheduling, sometimes called *event-driven scheduling* (see also Chapter 10), will be discussed later in its respective area in this chapter.

The system workload here consists of a combination of available processes, and these schedulers must have complete knowledge regarding how much time is required to execute each process (or part of a process). The scheduler will *admit* a process in the ready list only if the scheduler can guarantee that it will be able to meet each deadline imposed by the process. However, there may be several different schedules satisfying the deadline. An optimal scheduling strategy in such environments is *earliest deadline scheduling* in which the ready process with the earliest deadline is scheduled for execution. Another form of optimal scheduler is called the *least laxity scheduler* or the *least slack scheduler* that selects the ready process with the least difference between its deadline and service time (computation time). It is interesting to note that although these schedulers are sometimes optimal in single-processor systems, neither of these schedulers is optimal in multiprocessor environments.

For more details on this topic with a figure, see the Support Material at www.routledge.com/9781032467238.

4.16.9 Preemptive Strategies

In preemptive scheduling, the operating system itself could devise an arrangement that will stop the ongoing execution of the currently running process at an arbitrary instant, thereby realizing an involuntary sharing of CPU. The running process is interrupted at any time and moved to the ready state by the operating system, allowing another deserving process to replace it. This is accomplished by activating the scheduler whenever an event that causes a change in the state of the system is detected. Since, such events may occur due to many reasons (a process enters the ready state, time quantum expires, etc.), that may ultimately cause the scheduler to enforce the running process to voluntarily surrender the control of CPU. In this way, the highest-priority process among all ready processes is always allocated the CPU, and all lower-priority processes are made to yield to the highest-priority process whenever it requests the CPU. Preemptive strategies ensure quick response to high-priority processes and enforce fair sharing of the CPU among all ready processes. In fact, unlike nonpreemptive algorithms, their preemptive versions, always attempt to keep the highest-priority job in the running state at all times.

Preemption generally necessitates more frequent execution of the scheduler to reschedule processes that, in turn, always require an extra time-consuming complete process switch. In addition, suspending a running process without warning at an arbitrary instant, allowing another process to run, may lead to an adverse situation, like a race condition (to be discussed later), which requires additional non-remunerative actions using a sophisticated method to negotiate the situation. As a result, the system is sometimes observed to be spending more time switching processes than doing useful work, causing thrashing, which has an immense impact on performance metrics in all preemptive scheduling algorithms. However, the cost of such preemption may be kept low by using efficient process-switching mechanisms (as much help from hardware as possible) and by providing a large main memory to accommodate a high percentage of programs in main memory to make the process selection more effective. In spite of all this additional overhead, preemptive scheduling still is generally more responsive and may provide better service to the total population of processes for general-purpose systems because it prevents any one process from monopolizing the processor for a very long duration and provides equitable sharing of system resources to all existing users.

4.16.9.1   Round-Robin Scheduling: Time-Slice Scheduling

In preemptive scheduling, one of the most critical criteria is *time slicing*, and one of the oldest, simplest, fairest, and perhaps most widely used of all the scheduling algorithms using this time slicing is round robin, which primarily distributes processing time equitably among all n requesting processes when each n process receives approximately $1/n$ time units of processing time for every real-time unit. (This is only an approximation, since the cost of running the scheduling algorithm and time needed for process switch must also be a part of the real-time unit.)

The processor time here is divided into *slices* or *quanta*, and the duration of each time-slice is determined by a clock interrupt generated at periodic intervals. This clock (interval timer) is preferably a dedicated one, as opposed to sharing the system time base. The timer is usually set to issue an interrupt, and the periodic interval between two consecutive interrupts can be set to the desired time quantum. When this timer interrupt occurs, the time quantum of the currently executing process is over, and the scheduler is called that removes the running process from the CPU and selects the next deserving ready job from the ready list on an FCFS basis. No process is allowed to run for more than one time-slice when there are others waiting in the ready queue. If the process is running when the time-slice is over, that is, if a process needs more time to complete after exhausting its specified time-slice, the CPU is preempted and switched over to another process, and the preempted process is placed at the end of the ready queue to await further allocation. In fact, this rearrangement of the ready list effectively lowers the scheduling priority of the preempted process.

When the running process itself surrenders control to the operating system because it is either finished or blocked (due to I/O wait) before the time-slice has elapsed, a significant event is declared. The scheduler is immediately invoked and adjusts the ready list according to the implementation and resets the timer at that point to provide a fulltime quantum to the next deserving process to be dispatched to run. The last running process either departs the system (if completed) or goes out of the view of the scheduler (if blocked). The frequent setting and resetting of a dedicated interval timer requires adequate hardware support in systems that use time slicing. When an absolutely new process arrives, it is placed at the end of the ready queue, waiting for CPU allocation. In this way, the processor time is effectively allocated to processes on a rotating priority basis (hence the name *round robin*), and every one of them, in turn, gets an approximately equal amount of processor time.

Blocked processes can become ready processes at any time when the resource for which they were blocked is released by some other process and becomes available. The resource manager now allocates this newly available resource to one of the blocked processes and accordingly changes the state of that process. However, the currently executing process by this time continues its execution for the duration of its time-slice.

The ready list can be implemented as a *ring-linked list*, in which the new process is placed in the ring of n processes immediately behind the last process being executed so that the other $n - 1$ processes receive service before the new process. Another option is to implement the ready list as a queue, and the new process is always placed at the end of the queue.

Now, in regard to placement of processes in the list, this RR approach has been further modified a little bit in order to implement "fairness", which is the basic philosophy of RR scheduling. A few other variants of RR scheduling are; *inverse of remainder of quantum, limited round robin*, and the *multiple-level feedback variant of round robin*.

RR scheduling is actually very sensitive to the length of the time-slice or quantum to be chosen. If the quantum chosen is very short, then short processes will move through the system relatively quickly. But, if the chosen quantum is not very large in comparison to process switching, this will consume more time to handle system overhead, which sometimes leads to significantly lowering CPU efficiency. Thus, very short time quanta are legitimately discarded. On the contrary, if the time-slice is taken too long than the process switch, then the extra overhead due to frequent preemption will be reduced, but the last positioned user in a long queue will have to wait a longer time to get its turn, and the response time will be appreciably increased. Moreover, in this situation, most of the processes would be completed within the specified time-slice and usually surrender control to the OS rather than being preempted by an interval timer; the ultimate advantage of preemptive scheduling will be lost, and RR scheduling will eventually degenerate to simple FCFS scheduling. Therefore, the optimal value of the time-slice lies somewhere in between, but it mostly depends on the environment, which consists of both the computing system being used and the nature of the workload. This workload, in turn, is primarily determined by the type of program being submitted and also the instants of their arrivals.

Moreover, consideration of the qualitative definition of too short, short, or long duration of the time-slice is not really convincing, because a relatively short time interval in one kind of hardware system may be a comparatively long one in another in terms of the number of instructions executed by the processor (CPU speed) in the system. That is why the execution of an instruction-per-quantum measure is more realistic for comparing different systems, because the time-duration measure does not reflect the fact that processors with different speeds may generally accomplish different volumes of work within a specified time-slice.

In summary, the round robin is particularly effective in a general-purpose time-sharing or trans-action-processing system as well as in multiuser environments where terminal response time is a critical parameter. The choice of a suitable time-slice matched with the existing environment is an influencing factor in its performance metric. That is why selection of a time-slice duration is kept user-tunable and can be modified by the user at system generation (OS installation).

An example with figures relating to the operation of RR scheduling, its Gantt chart, and scheduling characteristics in tabular form are given on the Support Material at www.routledge.com/9781032467238.

4.16.9.2 Virtual Round Robin

One of the inherent drawbacks of round-robin scheduling is its relatively discriminating behavior in the treatment of I/O-bound processes, which have a shorter processor burst compared to CPU-bound processes. An environment usually consists of a mix of CPU-bound and I/O-bound processes in which an I/O-bound process during execution mostly uses the processor for a short period and then is blocked for its own request of I/O, keeps waiting for the completion of I/O operation, and then again joins the ready queue. On the other hand, a CPU-bound process during execution mostly uses a full time quantum of CPU time and then comes back once again to the ready queue. This eventually might result in poor performance of I/O-bound processes, poor utilization of I/O devices, and also a considerable increase in response time.

To minimize the effect of this drawback, a modified approach of RR scheduling called *virtual round robin* (VRR) has been suggested (Halder 91). In this, when new processes arrive, they join the ready queue managed on an FCFS basis as usual. When the time quantum of the currently running process expires, but the process has not yet completed, it is as usual returned to the same ready queue. When a process is blocked for I/O, it joins an I/O queue and stays in the I/O domain until it is released. The beauty of the this approach is the inclusion of a new FCFS auxiliary queue, and the processes which are released from their I/O activities are now moved to this queue instead of sending them as usual to the ready queue. Now, when the CPU is available and a dispatching decision is to be made, the processes in this auxiliary queue get preference over those in the main ready queue. When a process is dispatched from this auxiliary queue, it runs only for a time duration equal to the basic time quantum minus the total time it already spent when it was last selected from the main ready queue. Performance evaluation carried out by the authors revealed that this approach is indeed superior to RR scheduling in terms of processor-time distribution to implement fairness.

An example with figures relating to the operation of VRR scheduling is given on the Support Material at www.routledge.com/9781032467238.

4.16.9.3 Selfish Round Robin

The selfish round-robin method (Raphael) adds a new dimension to round-robin scheduling by giving better service to processes that have been executing for a while than to newcomers. Processes in the ready list are partitioned into two lists: *new* and *accepted*. New processes will wait. Accepted processes are serviced as usual by RR. The priority of a new process increases at rate a. The priority of an accepted process increases at rate b. Both a and b are parameters and can be adjusted to tune the method. When the priority of a new process reaches the priority of an accepted process, that particular new process becomes accepted; otherwise, when all accepted processes finish, the highest-priority new process will then be accepted.

Adjusting the relative values of a and b has a great influence on the behavior of SRR. If $b/a \geq 1$, a new process is not accepted until all the accepted processes have finished, so SRR becomes FCFS with respect to accepted and new. If $b/a = 0$, all processes are accepted immediately, so SRR becomes a RR. If $0 < b/a < 1$, accepted processes are selfish but not completely.

An example with figures relating to the operation of SRR scheduling, its Gantt chart, and scheduling characteristics in tabular form are given on the Support Material at www.routledge.com/9781032467238.

4.16.9.4 Preemptive Shortest Process Next

The scheduling algorithm PSPN/preemptive shortest job first (PSJF)/SRTN is a preemptive version of SPN/SJF/SJN that chooses to run a process which has the shortest expected remaining processing time. When a new job arrives in the ready queue, the currently running process may be preempted if the new job has a total service time requirement (CPU burst) less than the remaining service time required by the current process. The currently executing job in that situation will be preempted; it will be placed at the head of the ready queue, and the new job will take over the CPU. But if the newly arrived job has a total service time requirement greater than or equal to the remaining service time required by the currently executing job, the newly arrived job will then be placed in the ready queue as usual, and the action to be taken will be identical to that of the nonpreemptive SPN. Similar to SPN, the scheduler here also works in a consistent and predictable manner and must have some mechanism to get an estimate of processing time in order to perform the selection function. While this scheduling has a bias towards short jobs, it also tends to result in increased waiting times for long jobs, thereby causing a risk for them to suffer from starvation.

PSPN, unlike round robin, requires no additional interrupts to be generated, and therefore the overhead is reduced. On the other hand, elapsed service times must be recorded in order to compute the required remaining service times. This again gives rise to additional overhead. Moreover, PSPN incurs extra overhead due to frequent process switching and scheduler invocation while examining each and every running process and its transition to the ready state. This work would simply be a waste when the new ready process has a longer execution time than the remaining time of the currently running process. This is not very unusual. However, PSPN is better than SPN. It has an excellent penalty ratio; its turnaround time T turns out to be lower than that of SPN for all processes, including the longest processes; and the missed time M stays very low for a large majority of processes. Even for very long processes, PSPN is not much worse than RR. In fact, PSPN gives the best achievable average penalty ratio because it keeps the ready list as short as possible. It manages this feat by directing resources toward the process that will finish soonest and will therefore shorten the ready list soonest. A short ready list means reduced contention and leads to a low penalty ratio.

An example with figures relating to the operation of PSPN scheduling, its Gantt chart, and scheduling characteristics in tabular form are given on the Support Material at www.routledge.com/9781032467238.

4.16.9.5 Least Completed Next

The least completed next (LCN) policy schedules the process that has consumed the least amount of CPU time. Thus, the nature of a process (whether CPU-bound or I/O-bound) and the CPU time requirement of a process do not influence its progress in the system. The scheduling policy attempts to make all processes approximately equal in terms of CPU time consumed. So, short processes (like interactive processes) are guaranteed to complete ahead of long processes. However, this policy has the familiar drawback of long processes starving due to receiving less CPU attention. It also starts to neglect all existing processes if new processes keep arriving in the system. As a result, the execution of existing processes will be regularly postponed. In this situation, even medium-sized (not too long) processes tend to suffer from starvation or be affected by longer turnaround times. In fact, LCN provides poorer turnaround times than the RR and PSPN policies, because it favors newly arriving processes over existing processes in the system.

An example with figures relating to the operation of LCN scheduling, its Gantt chart, and scheduling characteristics in tabular form are given on the Support Material at www.routledge.com/9781032467238.

4.18.9.6 Preemptive Priority-Based Scheduling (Event-Driven)

Round-robin scheduling works on the implicit assumption that all processes are equally important. But when external factors are taken into account at the time of scheduling so that each runnable process is assigned a priority and the process with highest priority is allowed to run, the scheme is known as *priority-based scheduling*. In principle, each process in the system is assigned a priority level, whether provided statically or generated dynamically. Priorities are assigned statically considering a number of factors at the time of submission of the job. Users can also reduce the priority of their own process voluntarily using commands (like the *nice* command in UNIX) available with some OSs. Dynamically derived priorities are internal priorities assigned by the OS using measurable attributes of a process while in execution within the computing environment. Memory requirements, service-time request, ratio of average CPU burst time to average I/O burst time, number of files opened, and others are used as criteria to determine an aggregate figure of internal priorities. In this sense, many scheduling disciplines may be thought of as being priority-driven, where the priority of a process represents its chance to be scheduled next. For example, in the case of RR scheduling, the priority is its time of arrival. In SPN, the internal priority is determined based on the length of the service time request.

Priorities derived dynamically by the operating system can then be assigned to processes to fulfill desired system targets (such as increasing throughput). Highly I/O-bound processes should generally be given higher priority to let them start the next I/O request, which can then proceed in parallel with another process actually using the CPU for its computing. Assigning I/O-bound processes a lower priority means keeping them waiting a long time for the CPU, unnecessarily occupying memory with no benefit. A simple approach for good service to an I/O-bound process is to set the priority to $1/f$, where f is a fraction of the last quantum used by the process. The higher the use, that is, the higher the value of f, the lower its priority later on.

When a new job with a higher priority than that of the currently running job arrives at the ready queue, the currently running job is preempted. The new job will get the CPU, and the currently running job is placed at the head of the ready queue. (In the case of nonpreemptive scheduling, the newly arrived job with a higher priority than that of the currently running job would have been placed at the head of the ready queue, and the running job would be allowed to run to completion.)

If the newly arrived job has a priority lower than that of the currently running job, the action to be taken will be identical to that of nonpreemptive priority scheduling.

If priority-based scheduling is implemented, there remains a high possibility that low-priority processes may be effectively locked out by higher-priority ones. In general, with this scheduling scheme, no such guarantee could be given with regard to the expected time of completion of a job after its admission into the system. To get rid of this uncertainty, the usual remedy is to provide an *aging priority* in which a check prevents high-priority processes from running indefinitely. The schedulers in this situation have the option to reduce the priority of the currently running process at each clock interrupt. When this action causes the priority of the currently running process to drop below that of the next highest-priority process, a process switch occurs and the system leaves the currently executing process. Eventually, over time, the priorities of the low-priority older processes become higher than that of the running high-priority processes and will ultimately get their turn within a reasonable period of time.

Event-driven (ED) scheduling is another variant of priority-based scheduling used in real-time operating systems to schedule real-time events (processes). In such systems, all the processes are time-critical and must be executed within specific deadlines. The entire workload of the system may consist of a collection of periodic processes, executed cyclically within a specified period (deadlines), and aperiodic processes whose times of arrival are not predictable. This means certain processes arrive with different already-assigned fixed priorities and other processes with dynamically varying priorities. The scheduler always takes the highest-priority ready process whenever a significant event (arrival of an important process) occurs. Arrival of a higher-priority important process will immediately preempt the currently running process, process switching will be carried out within a very short period (a special type of hardware is used to speed up the process switching mechanism), and the new higher-priority process will be executed. Different types of schedulers under this category have been devised to negotiate all such situations, as explained in the section "Deadline Scheduling".

An example with figures relating to the operation of preemptive priority-based scheduling, its Gantt chart, and scheduling characteristics in tabular form are given on the Support Material at www.routledge.com/9781032467238.

4.16.9.7 Multiple-Level Queue Scheduling

The designs of all the scheduling algorithms explained so far have been adjusted to fit each specific class of application environments. But the practical situation in any computer center equipped with numerous devices and terminals is somewhat different. Commonly, the environment, at any instant, is composed of a heterogeneous mixture of different types of jobs, such as interactive jobs from terminal users, small but extremely time-bound jobs, and large batch jobs (almost non-interactive) requiring varied device support. No single scheduling algorithm so far known to us can be employed to fit even moderately in this environment to yield at least reasonable performance. To negotiate this situation, one approach could be taken by way of devising an algorithm that will be a combination of different scheduling disciplines; each discipline will be entrusted with what it does best. For example, large batch jobs may be subjected to FCFS or SPN, interactive programs are conducive to RR scheduling, and OS processes and device interrupts are best fitted with preemptive priority-based scheduling (Event-driven).

The realization of such a complex scheduling discipline requires thorough observation of the characteristics of the usual workload of the computing environment. One generalized approach in this regard may be to classify the jobs arriving at the computer center into several groups, where each job will be assigned to its respective group and each group will then be serviced by its best-matched scheduler. This approach is often called *multiple-level queues* (MLQs). Possible classifications of jobs to form different groups could be mainly:

- Operating-system jobs
- Interactive jobs
- Batch jobs

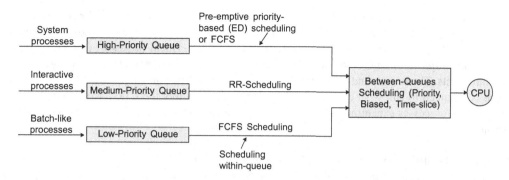

FIGURE 4.12   An illustration of actions of scheduler at the time of scheduling of processes arranged in multiple-level queue.

This would eventually result in the conventional single ready queue being partitioned into a few ready queues. As shown in Figure 4.12, three such separate ready queues are formed. A ready process may then be assigned to one of these queues on the basis of its attributes, which may be provided either by the user or the system. Multiple-level queue are thus an extension of priority-based scheduling (multiple priority-level queues) in which all processes of the same characteristics (priority) are placed in a single queue. Within each queue, jobs can be scheduled using an algorithm that is best suited for that queue considering its workload. For example, queues containing interactive jobs can be scheduled round robin, while queues containing batch jobs can be scheduled using FCFS or SPN.

Between queues, a scheduling discipline should be devised to allocate the CPU to a particular queue. Typical approaches in this regard are to use absolute priority or some form of modified time slicing injecting bias considering relative priority of the processes within particular queues. In the case of using *absolute priority scheduling* between queues, the highest-priority queue will first be handled, and all the processes from this highest-priority queue (usually consisting of OS processes) are serviced in some order until that queue is empty. This ordering of processes within the queue can be implemented using some other scheduling discipline that may be event-driven, or FCFS can also be chosen, since the queue consists of processes of similar nature and the overhead of FCFS is low. When the highest-priority queue is empty, the next highest-priority queue may be serviced using its own best-matched scheduling discipline (e.g. a queue formed with interactive jobs normally uses RR scheduling). When both higher-priority queues are empty, the next high-priority queue (e.g. consisting of batch jobs) may then be serviced using its own best-matched scheduling discipline. In this way, all queues will be handled one after another in order.

In general, during the execution of any process in any queue, if a new process arrives that is characterized as a member of a higher-priority queue, the currently running job will be preempted and the newly arrived job will start executing. This strategy ensures responsiveness to external events and interrupts, of course with an extra cost of frequent preemptions and their associated overhead.

A variant of this strategy for distributing CPU utilization across queues may be to assign a certain percentage of processor time to each queue, commensurate according to its priority. The highest-priority queue will then be given a larger portion of the CPU time, and the lowest-priority queue will be allocated a smaller portion of the CPU time.

As is expected, multiple queue scheduling, by nature, is a very general discipline that exploits all the features and advantages of different "pure" scheduling disciplines by way of combining them into one single form of scheduling. Consequently, each of these more sophisticated constituent scheduling algorithms also contributes overhead that ultimately increases the overhead of this discipline as a whole. However, distinct advantages of MLQ were observed and recognized early on by OS designers who willfully deployed it in handling environments consisting of foreground/background (F/B) jobs in timesharing systems. An F/B system, in its normal form, employs two queues: a *high-priority queue* consisting of OS, interactive, and time-critical processes (foreground) and a *low-priority queue* of batch-like and other similar processes (background) that does not service external events. The foreground queue is serviced in an event-driven manner, while the background queue is intended to run whenever no foreground process requires the CPU. Any foreground job can preempt processes executing in the background and can always take precedence over all background jobs.

4.16.9.8   Multiple-Level Queues with Feedback Scheduling

Multiple-level queues assume that the operating system has prior knowledge about the attributes (that determines the priority), such as CPU bursts and absolute priority, of a job at the time of its arrival, so that jobs can be placed in queues based on these attributes, which may be provided either by the user or the system. In practice, this is not always true. Very often, no particular priority is attached to a process when it enters the system. If the OS assigns any priority in that situation via its own way of calculation/prediction, it may or may not be accurate. Moreover, nothing is known about CPU burst time when a job is run for the first time. The lack of any such prior knowledge or merely an idea about the relative length of various processes thus restricts us to entirely rely on the algorithms where priority is derived based on "time remaining to execute" (like SPN/SJN, PSPN, HRRN, etc.). Above all, jobs are permanently assigned to one of these queues, and fixed priorities are attached to jobs once and for all. As a result, this may lead to an adverse situation that limits the effectiveness and adaptability of this scheduling.

Rather than having fixed classes (priorities) of processes allocated to specific queues, the idea is to concentrate the other way around to devise a mechanism where the priority of any process will additionally be derived based on time already spent so far in execution. As a result, the priority of a process may be changed periodically, which means jobs are not permanently assigned to any queue (in contrast to multi-level scheduling); rather, jobs move between queues, and scheduling will be done on preemptive basis. For example, each process may start with identical priority at the top-level queue. If the process is completed within a given time-slice, it departs the system after having received the royal treatment. Processes that need more than one time-slice may be reassigned by the OS to a lower-priority queue, which gets a lower percentage of the processor time. If the process still has not finished and needs yet more processor time after having run a few times in that queue, it may be moved to a lower-level queue. This approach is known as *multiple-level feedback*, meaning that the operating system allocates the processor to a process, and when the process blocks or is preempted, feeds it back into one of several priority queues. Here, the operating system allows processes to change ready sub-lists (queues).

In multi-level feedback scheduling (also called *multi-level adaptive scheduling*), a number of separate queues are maintained, similar to the case of multi-level scheduling. But, there are a number of variations with regard to the implementation of this scheme. However, a simple version is to perform preemption in the same fashion as for round robin: at periodic intervals. Our example explains this strategy with an approach that is easy to implement from a practical point of view considering jobs in general.

As usual, multiple queues are present. Within each queue, jobs are scheduled with FCFS order. Fixed priorities are assigned to each queue. Between queues, there is preemptive priority scheduling similar to ordinary multiple-level scheduling, as discussed in the last section. Each queue is assigned a time-slice or time quantum. This assigned time-slice increases gradually as one moves down between queues (Figures 4.13, 4.14, and 4.15).

When a new job enters the system from the outside world, it is always placed in the highest-priority queue. The CPU will always be allocated to the job at the head of any queue. When the CPU is assigned the job at the head of highest-priority queue, the job will hold the CPU until the end of the CPU burst or the end of the time-slice, whichever comes earlier. If the time quantum expires first,

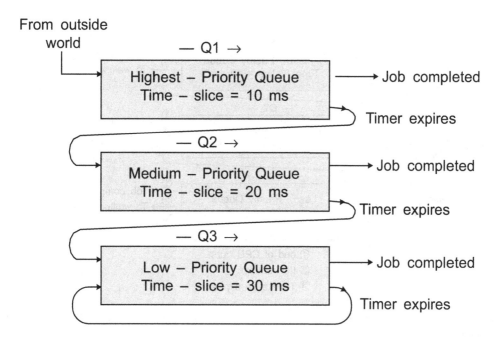

FIGURE 4.13 An illustration of actions of scheduler in Multi-level feedback scheduling for jobs with a single CPU burst.

the job is placed at the tail of the next lower queue. If the end of the CPU burst is reached before the expiry of the time-slice, and if such an end of the CPU burst is due to an issue of I/O request, the job leaves the ready queue and joins the waiting pool of jobs, remaining there waiting for its I/O completion. The job at this moment is outside the vision of the scheduler. But, if the end of the CPU burst marks the end of the job, it leaves the system as completed.

To explain the operations of multi-level feedback queues, let us first consider jobs with only one CPU burst. These jobs enter the highest-priority, Q1, from the outside world, as shown in Figure 4.13. The job at the head of this queue is assigned to the CPU. If it completes its CPU burst within the time-slice assigned to that queue, that job leaves the system as a completed job. If it cannot complete its CPU burst within the time-slice assigned to Q1, the job is then placed at the tail of the next lower-level queue, Q2 (refer to Figure 4.13).

Jobs in the second queue Q2 will only be taken up for execution when all the jobs in Q1 are finished. If a new job arrives in Q1 when a job in Q2 (the job which was at the head of Q2) is under execution, that running job in Q2 will be preempted and the newly arrived job in Q1 will get the CPU to start its execution. The newly arrived job will either leave the system from the first queue itself or enter the second queue Q2 at its tail. At this time, if no other job is available in Q1, any job that is at the head of the queue Q2 will be started, or the preempted process at the head of queue Q2 will resume execution. Similarly, jobs in Q3 will only be taken up for execution if and only if all the jobs in Q1 and Q2 are finished. If a job arrives in Q1 while a job in Q3 (the one that was at the head of Q3) is under execution, the job in Q3 will be preempted.

The entire idea is to give preferential treatment to short processes, and a job with a large CPU burst will ultimately sink down to the lowest queue. If the job at the head of the lowest queue does not complete its remaining CPU burst within the time-slice assigned to that queue, it will be placed at the tail of the same queue, as shown in Figure 4.13.

Let us now consider a more practical situation with jobs in general. Usually, each job consists of several CPU and I/O bursts. If the total CPU burst time of a job is more than its total I/O burst time, the job is called a *CPU-bound job*, and the converse of this is called an I/O-bound job. As

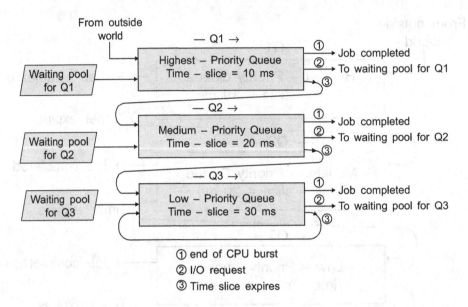

① end of CPU burst
② I/O request
③ Time slice expires

FIGURE 4.14   An illustration of actions of modified scheduler in Multi-level feedback scheduling for jobs in general.

usual, jobs that enter the system from the outside world are placed in the highest-priority queues in FCFS order. The job at the head of this queue gets the CPU first. If it issues an I/O request before the expiry of its time-slice, the job will then leave the ready queue to join the waiting pool. Otherwise, this job will naturally be placed at the tail of the next lower queue if it is not completed within the specified time-slice.

Jobs which leave the ready queue due to an I/O request will eventually become ready–to–run after completion of I/O. Now a policy is to be settled about the placement of these ready-to-run jobs at the time of their re-entry after I/O completion. The question obviously arises as to in which queue these jobs are to be placed. One strategy may be to mark each job while leaving the ready queue (due to I/O request) with the identity of the queue from which it left. When this job once again becomes ready–to–run, it will re-enter the same queue from which it left and be placed at the tail. Figure 4.14 depicts a conceptual picture of this strategy.

Placing a job once again in the same queue from which it left due to an I/O request is, however, not a judicious decision. It is also supported by the fact (as shown in Figure 4.14) that while a job having CPU burst happened to be a long burst is allowed to use only one time-slice and then it is preempted and finally it is pushed down to a lower priority queue. It will never be promoted to a higher-priority queue. Thus, a better strategy would perhaps to be one which will adapt to the changing trends with regard to CPU and I/O bursts. It is acceptable that after one long CPU burst, the remaining workload will be less, and hence, subsequent CPU bursts may be of shorter duration. Such a self-adjusting strategy is expected to be superior to a non-adapting strategy like the one we just discussed.

Following this line, one such self-adjusting strategy can be derived that will place a ready-to-run job in a queue one level above the queue from which it left due to an I/O request, because it can be logically assumed that after returning, the amount of work remaining for that job to complete its execution will be less. Figure 4.15 illustrates such a strategy. Under this strategy, jobs start to move up and down between queues.

One serious problem with this scheme is that the turnaround time of longer processes can stretch out alarmingly, leading to a situation of starvation if new jobs happen to continuously enter the

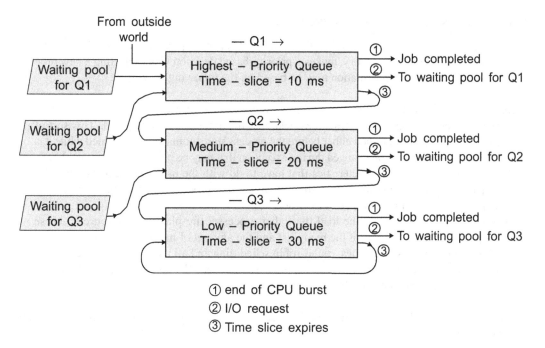

FIGURE 4.15 An illustration of actions of another type of modified scheduler used in Multi-level feedback scheduling for jobs in general.

system. To negotiate this situation, one approach could be to vary the time-slices assigned to the queues to compensate for this drawback. For example, a process scheduled from Q1 will be allowed to execute for 1 time unit, and then it will be preempted; a process scheduled from Q2 will be allowed to execute for 2 time units, and so on. In general, a process scheduled from Q_i will be allowed to execute 2^i time units before preemption. Observations with this scheme, varying execution time for different types of processes (queues), when taken at random, reveal that this scheme works quite nicely.

However, the beauty of this scheduling discipline is that it favors short processes, but at the same time, it also forces the resource-consuming processes to slowly "sink down" into lower-level queues, thereby working as filters in order to keep processor utilization high. This way of thinking is also supported by observations on program behavior that suggest that completion rate has a natural tendency to decrease with increasing service. This means that the more service a process receives, the less likely it is to be completed, even if it is given a little more service. That is why the feedback mechanism in MLQs tends to rank processes dynamically according to the actual amount of time already used, favoring to those that have received less. This is actually reflected in that when a process surrenders control to the OS before its time-slice expires (due to I/O request), it is rightly rewarded by being moved up in the hierarchy of queues.

In fact, MLQ with feedback scheduling is the most general one to incorporate many of the simple scheduling algorithms appropriate to each individual queue. Use of a feedback mechanism makes this scheduling more adaptive and responsive to the actual runtime behavior of processes, which seems to be more sensible. However, one of the major drawbacks of this class of scheduling is that it always suffers from a comparatively high overhead due to manipulation of global queue, as well as the presence of many constituent scheduling algorithms used by individual queues for their own internal scheduling, thereby contributing their own individual overhead that increases the overhead of this discipline as a whole.

4.16.10   CLASSIFICATION OF SCHEDULING POLICIES

Scheduling policies are characterized in two distinct categories, preemptive and nonpreemptive. Each policy, irrespective of category, makes a priority-based decision when selecting a new process to run. In general, priority information may be based on the following properties:

Intrinsic properties that distinguish one process from another usually include service-time requirements, storage needs, resources held, and the amount of I/O required. This sort of information may be obtained either before the process starts or may be determined while it is running and may even be changed during execution that may be placed in the process block.

Extrinsic properties are characteristics that have to do with the user who owns the process. Extrinsic properties mainly include the *urgency* of the process and how much the user is willing to pay to purchase special treatment.

Dynamic properties indicate the load that other processes are placing on resources. These properties include the size of the ready list and the amount of main storage available. Out of the commonly used policies, round-robin scheduling and all its variants are preemptive and non-intrinsic, while PSPN is preemptive and intrinsic. Nonpreemptive FCFS is non-intrinsic, and nonpreemptive SPN and HPRN use intrinsic information.

For more details on this topic with a figure, see the Support Material at www.routledge.com/ 9781032467238.

4.16.11   FAIR-SHARE SCHEDULING

All the scheduling algorithms explained so far treat the collection of all ready processes as a single pool or one that is broken down by priority of some form (such as MLQ) in which each process is assumed to be from different programs (users), and thus try to provide equitable service to all processes. But, in reality, this relationships between processes and users may be altogether different, and that should taken into consideration when scheduling the processes.

In a multiuser system, while an individual user organizes the applications or jobs as a collection of multiple groups of processes (threads), the scheduler in that situation is unable to recognize this structure and assumes them to be different individual processes. From the user's end, the concern is not how a particular process performs but how and in which order the user's group of processes that constitute a single application perform. Thus, the scheduling disciplines in this situation should primarily concentrate more on these process groupings. If applications initiated by users create different numbers of processes, an application employing more processes is likely to receive more CPU attention than an application employing fewer processes. To properly negotiate this situation, the approach taken by the scheduler is generally known as *fair-share scheduling* (FSS).

FSS can be further extended to groups of users in which each user is assumed to represent an individual single process. Scheduling decisions could then be carried out that attempt to offer each group similar service and ensure equitable use of the CPU by processes belonging to different group (users) or different applications.

Under FSS, each user is assigned a given weight of some sort that defines that particular user's share of system resources as a fraction of total utilization of those resources. Here, the scheduler, in general, monitors usage so as to give fewer resources to users who have enjoyed more than their fair share and more to those who have received less than their fair share.

Scheduling is carried out on the basis of priority in which each process is assigned a base priority. The priority is calculated together the associated priority of the process, its recent processor usage, and the recent processor usage of the group to which the process belongs. In the case of group utilization, the average is normalized by dividing by the weight of that group. The greater the weight assigned to the group, the less its utilization will affect its priority. Usually, the higher the numerical value of the priority, the lower it is.

It is to be noted that the actual share of CPU time received by a group of processes may sometimes differ from the fair share of the group due to lack of activity in its processes or in processes of other groups. Different operating systems, particularly systems using the *lottery scheduling policy* and the scheduling policy used in the UNIX operating system, differ in the way they handle this situation. Lot of work has been done in this area by many OS researchers and designers. Interested readers can consult Kay and Lauder (1988) and Woodside (1986).

For more details on this topic with computation, see the Support Material at www.routledge.com/9781032467238.

4.16.12 Hybrid Methods

Numerous types of methods can be developed by combining ones that we have already mentioned. Here are some examples.

1. Use multiple-level feedback up to a fixed number z of time-slices, then use FCFS for the last queue. This method reduces the number of process switches for very long processes.
2. Use round robin up to some number of time-slices. A process that needs more time is to be put in a second-run queue, which can be treated with SRR scheduling. Very long processes are eventually placed in a third queue that could use FCFS. RR could have absolute precedence over SRR, which, in turn, has precedence over FCFS, or each could be given a fixed percentage of total time.

4.16.13 State-Dependent Priority Methods

These three methods adjust parameters based on the current state.

1. Use RR. However, instead of keeping the quantum constant, adjust it periodically, perhaps after every process switch, so that the quantum becomes q/n, where n is the size of the ready list. If there are very few ready processes, each gets a long quantum, which avoids process switches. But if there are many, the algorithm becomes more fair for all, but at the expense of more process switching. Processes that need only a small amount of time get a quantum, and a small one may be able to finish soon. The quantum should not be allowed to drop below a given minimal value so that process switching does not start to consume undue amounts of time.
2. Offer the current process an extra quantum whenever a new process arrives. The effect of this gift is to reduce process switching in proportion to the level of saturation.
3. Some versions of UNIX use the following scheduling algorithm. Every second, an internal priority is calculated for each process. This priority depends on the external priority (set by the user) and the amount of recent time consumed. This latter figure *rises* linearly as the process runs and *decreases* exponentially as the process waits (whether because of short-term scheduling or other reasons). The exponential decay again depends on the current load (that is, the size of the ready list); if the load is higher, the CPU usage figure of a process decays more slowly. Processes with higher recent CPU usage get lower priorities than those with lower-recent CPU usage. The scheduler runs the process with the highest priority in the ready list. If several processes have the same priority, they are scheduled in RR fashion.

4.16.14 EXTERNAL PRIORITY METHODS

These three methods adjust parameters on the basis of some external priority.

1. Use RR, but let the quantum depend on the external priority of the process. That is, allow larger quanta for processes run for a user willing to pay a premium for this service.
2. The *worst service next* (WSN) method is a generalization of many others. After each time-slice, compute for each process how much it has *suffered* so far. Suffering is an arbitrarily complex figure arrived at by crediting the process for how much it has had to wait, how many times it has been preempted, how much its user is paying in premiums, and how urgent it is. The process is also debited for such items as the amount of time it has actually used and the other resources it has consumed (resources like space and access to secondary storage). The process with the greatest suffering is given the next quantum.
3. The user buys a guaranteed response ratio. At the time of scheduling, a suffering function is used that takes into account only the difference between the guaranteed response ratio and the actual response ratio at the moment.

4.16.15 OTHER SCHEDULING SYSTEMS

There are other specialized scheduling mechanisms discussed in the text and other places, and it is easy to derive many such scheduling systems from the ones that we have already discussed. In all cases, they have to be evaluated on how well they influence their figure of merit (e.g. system response time, turnaround time, throughput, etc.) and the overhead of implementing them (e.g. estimating runtime). However, it can be concluded that for every scheduling strategy, there is always a counter-strategy.

4.16.16 EVALUATING POLICIES

Since a scheduling policy decides the allocation of system resources directly or indirectly, the performance of various scheduling policies has an immense impact on the performance and effectiveness of multitasking and multiuser operating systems. Thus, the choice of a particular scheduling policy appropriate to a specific working environment is always a critical factor. In general, the unpredictable workload presented to real systems and the varying requirements of different resources by active processes being handled by individual schedulers managing specific classes of resources are highly complicated. All these and similar other factors together would generally impose too much overhead while trying to balance resource utilization at runtime. It is, hence, not only very difficult but probably impossible to draw definitive comparisons over the different scheduling disciplines because their relative performances will mostly depend on a variety of factors, such as the probability distribution of service times of the various processes, the nature and the frequency of the I/O demand, the performance of the I/O subsystem, and above all, the efficiency of the chosen scheduling discipline, including process/context switching mechanisms.

However, given a policy, when attempting to draw some general conclusions with regard to its performance; three common approaches of most interest can be used as evaluation tools: *analysis*, *simulation*, and *experimentation*.

Analysis: It involves a mathematical formulation of the policy and a derivation of its behavior. Such a formulation develops an analytic model that is mostly based on the elements of queuing theory, which are often described in the language of *queuing networks*. Queuing models are usually based on several simplifying assumptions so as to make it mathematically manageable to extract an exact, simple solution. Although in real systems, these assumptions are not always valid, they often provide only an approximation of the reality. Such an approach always ignores some relevant details and is also incapable of describing other pertinent facts. However, once a model has been built and results have been derived, the next step is to validate the model by comparing its predictions against reality. This step is easy if the model describes an actual situation, but it is harder if it describes a hypothetical situation. Nevertheless, it is an useful tool that may be used to rationally compare and study the overall behavior of the various scheduling disciplines for performance analysis.

For an illustration of this topic with a figure, see the Support Material at www.routledge.com/9781032467238.

Simulation: When analysis is inadequate or fails for being too complex, or when queuing networks do not able to effectively describe the situation, *simulation* may be used. Simulations are programs, often quite complex, that mimic the dynamic behavior of the actual system in the modeled one. In fact, simulation usually involves tracking a large number of processes through a model (such as a queuing network) and collecting statistics. Whenever a probabilistic choice is to be made, such as when the next arrival should occur or which branch a process will take, a pseudo-random number is generated with the correct distribution. It is also possible to drive the simulation with traces of real systems to better match the reality. Depending on the nature of the input to be fed to the modeled system, a simulation may be *trace-driven* or *self-driven*. A trace-driven simulation uses an input that is a trace of actual events collected and recorded on a real system. A self-driven simulation uses an artificial workload that is synthetically generated to closely resemble the expected conditions in the target systems.

Simulations, just like analytic models, must be validated to ensure that they are adequate to rationalize the situation that is being modeled. They are often run several times in order to determine how much the particular pseudo-random numbers being chosen affect the results. Simulations tend to produce enormous amounts of data that must be carefully filtered before they are used. Simulations often use extremely detailed models and therefore consume enormous amounts of computer time. Moreover, accurate simulations of comparatively complex systems are also critical in terms of design and coding. For these reasons, simulations are usually appropriate only if analysis fails.

For an illustration of this topic with figures, see the Support Material at www.routledge.com/9781032467238.

Experimentation: If simulation appears difficult and does not work, usually due to the complexity of the model, *experimentation* is the last resort and often requires a significant investment in equipment, both to build the system to be tested and to instrument it to acquire the required statistics. For example, it can be far cheaper to simulate the SPN scheduling method than to implement it properly, debug it, execute it on a user community for a while, and measure the results. Likewise, it is cheaper to simulate the effect of installing a new disk than to acquire it on rent, connect it, see how well it works, and then disconnect it after being convinced that the improvement is not cost-effective. However, experimentation almost always ensures accurate results, since by definition, it uses a truthful model.

4.16.17 Scheduling Levels

While focusing on short-term scheduling, it is to be noted that some of the short-term scheduling disciplines contain certain aspects of medium-term scheduling. Tuning the parameters of a short-term scheduling method is another form of medium-term scheduling. Moreover, since the domain of medium-term scheduling is not sharply demarcated, various reasons for waiting may lead to different blocking times that again vary considerably, thereby directly affecting short-term scheduling.

Long-term scheduling often uses some criteria while making decisions to select a specific job to admit next, and this act, in turn, sometimes directly affect the short-term scheduler. This selection at times may either overload the system with CPU-bound jobs or I/O-bound jobs, thereby leading to a situation that may summarily degrade system performance as a whole. Moreover, if too many large jobs happen to be selected for execution by the long-term scheduler using its own policy, then at times, many of these jobs must be swapped out to make room for the currently executing jobs. As a result, a sufficient number of processes on which the scheduler will work will not be available, which in turn will restrict the real benefits of a good short-term scheduler.

Long-term scheduling also blends into medium-term scheduling somewhat. The decision not to allow a process to start may be based on explicitly declared resource needs that are not currently available, in which case it can be said that the process has really started (as far as the long-term scheduler is concerned) but is still waiting for resources (as far as the medium-term scheduler is concerned).

In fact, the long-term scheduler since acts as a first-level throttle in keeping resource utilization at the desired level but influencing and regulating in many ways the decisive action to be taken by the short-term scheduler at the time of scheduling.

For more details on this topic, see the Support Material at www.routledge.com/9781032467238.

4.16.18 PERFORMANCE COMPARISON

The behavior of scheduling policies can be seen, in general, by comparing them using a simulation considering a large number of processes. In fact, a sample of 50,000 processes has been taken with service times β randomly drawn from an exponential distribution with $\beta = 1.0$, and arrival rates α similarly drawn from an exponential distribution with $\alpha = 0.8$. The saturation level (processor utilization) was therefore, $\rho = \alpha/\beta = 0.8$. Statistics were gathered on each process except for the first 100 to complete in order to measure the *steady state*, which is the behavior of a system once initial fluctuations have disappeared. The results of these simulations provide, by and large, useful insight into the general behavior of the different algorithms we have studied.

The details of this topic, using simulation with illustrative figures, are given on the Support Material at www.routledge.com/9781032467238.

4.16.19 GUIDING PRINCIPLES

The question now arises in respect to the selection of a specific scheduling algorithm from the list of policies already explained that would be found best suited in a specific environment. Here is a rule of thumb: Preemption is worth it, even with an extra switching cost. Since context must switch at every interrupt from the running process back to the kernel, it does not usually cost much extra for the kernel to make a decision and allow a different process to run. Clock devices are almost universal nowadays, from large computers down to board-level microcomputers.

The quantum size should be large enough to prevent thrashing. A process switch might cost about 50 microseconds, and other scheduling bookkeeping might occupy another 300 microseconds. If the quantum is 10 milliseconds, the scheduling mechanism occupies only about 3.5 percent of the quantum, which is quite reasonable to accept.

Some policies are more expensive than others to implement. FCFS requires only one queue for the ready list. FB requires a number of queues. WSN can require arbitrarily complex computation at every decision point. The implementer should try to balance the cost of making decisions against the advantage that a particular strategy might yield. The complexity of the scheduling program itself is also worth minimizing. Simple programs are more likely to be correct and are certainly easier to maintain.

Many operating systems use a hybrid policy, with RR and some other method for short processes, and possibly RR with a longer quantum and a lower priority for larger ones. Memory management, which we will discuss in the next chapter, also affects scheduling. Processes that need a substantial amount of storage are often given larger quanta so that they can get more work done and depart the system as quickly as possible, releasing the costly space they already occupy.

The introduction of personal computing casts a different light on scheduling activities. Here, it is not always essential to keep the computer busy 100 percent of the time, even if there is work available. It is more important to provide interactive processes with good service; even if it waits for I/O, the scheduler might then wait for a while, letting the computer sit idle, with the hope that the interactive process will soon become runnable once again and thereby avoid exercising a process switch to another one before it can start again. Similarly, an interactive process that enters a computationally intensive phase might still be considered interactive, and the scheduler might favor it instead of treating it as the equal of a background computation.

4.16.20   CASE STUDY: UNIX, LINUX, WINDOWS NT

Every operating system always targets to attain its own scheduling objectives; and in this respect, the UNIX, Windows NT, and Linux are no exception. The goals of Windows NT in this regard are different from those of UNIX and Linux. While the design objective of UNIX is more inclined towards offering fair and responsive services to its community of users, Windows NT tries to remain as responsive as possible to the needs of a single user in a highly interactive environment or even in the role of a server. Both UNIX and Windows NT employ apriority-based preemptive scheduling policy with a multiple-level queue, but UNIX employs a variant of preemptive priority-based scheduling (event driven) with a fine blend of fair-share scheduling mechanisms. Windows NT in this regard employs a comparatively flexible system of priority levels that includes round-robin scheduling within each level in multiple levels, and in other levels, dynamic priority variation is used based on their current thread activity.

The Linux scheduling mechanisms, including its revised version (version 2.6), are very similar to traditional UNIX scheduling algorithms, but its scheduling capability is greatly enhanced in subsequent versions for non–real-time processes. The Linux scheduler primarily consists of three distinct scheduling classes: SCHED_FIFO (for scheduling first-in-first-out real-time threads), SCHED_RR (for scheduling round-robin real-time threads), and SCHED_OTHER (for scheduling non–real-time threads). Linux allows individual processes to make a choice among *SCHED_FIFO, SCHED_RR*, or *SCHED_OTHER* policies. Processes using the *SCHED_FIFO* and *SCHED_RR* policies are scheduled on a fixed-priority basis, whereas processes using the *SCHED_OTHER* policy are scheduled on a time-sharing basis. An initial priority (static) for each non–real-time task is often assigned, and as the execution continues, a priority is determined dynamically, based on the task's static priority and its execution behavior. The dynamic priority is computed based mainly on how much time a process waits (waiting for an event) and how long a process runs. In principle, a task that suffers most in waiting is offered a relatively higher priority. Time-slices are assigned to a task according to its priority, and as such higher-priority tasks are obviously assigned larger time-slices.

The scheduling procedure is straightforward and efficient. When a process is ready, it is assigned to the appropriate priority queue in the active queues structure and is assigned the needed time-slice. If a task is preempted before it completes its time-slice, it is returned to an active queue. When a task uses its time-slice, but does not complete, it is placed into the appropriate queue in the expired queue structure and is assigned a new time-slice. All scheduling, however, is carried out from among the active queues structure. When the active queues structure is exhausted, expired queues only then come under consideration, and the scheduler chooses the highest-priority nonempty expired queue. If multiple tasks are present in that queue, the tasks are simply scheduled using a round-robin approach.

The details of UNIX, Windows NT, and Linux scheduling with illustrative figures are given on the Support Material at www.routledge.com/9781032467238.

4.17   INTERPROCESS SYNCHRONIZATION

4.17.1   INTRODUCTION

In the design of an operating system, the most fundamental aspect is the introduction of the process and related thread concepts. The design also supports the existence of concurrent processes, which may then be involved among themselves either in competition or cooperation. While competition among processes requires careful resource allocation and protection as well as isolation of different address spaces, cooperation, on other hand, demands adequate mechanisms in the OS for controlled usage of shared information and to synchronize the operation of the constituent processes. It is worth mentioning that OSs typically provide only the minimum mechanism to address concurrency, since there are so many ways to implement concurrency (e.g. from the point of view of programming languages, the designer's ability to set a collection of concurrent processes without interference, various methods of communication between concurrent processes without interference, etc.) but none of them have been found to dominate the area. However, as an aid to users, the OS provides a set of primitives so that interprocess synchronization can be achieved in a well-structured way without using interrupts.

Cooperating processes require the simultaneous existence of two different communicating processes that typically share some resources in addition to interacting with each other (one produces an output which is the input to the other) that, in turn, demands synchronization to preserve precedence relationships and prevent concurrency-related timing problems.

While all sorts of measures have been taken and numerous techniques have been devised for smooth execution of concurrent processes with proper synchronization for the sake of performance improvement and increased productivity, correct implementation, however, may invite other problems of different types, including a possibility of *deadlock* among concurrent processes. Deadlock will be discussed in a subsequent section later in this chapter.

The details of this topic are given on the Support Material at www.routledge.com/9781032467238.

4.17.2 CONCURRENCY: FORMS AND ISSUES

While *concurrent execution of processes* accrues major benefits in performance and efficiency, even with incurring the additional cost of a certain amount of administrative overhead due to switching between processes, on the other hand, it may invite a lot of difficulties. These concurrent processes share common resources, including shared global data, and the order in which various reads and writes are to be executed is critical to preserve system integrity and consistency. The mechanism to be used in this situation must allow at most one process to have access to such a resource at a time and let it remain in use until the completion of its operation. This approach is known as *interprocess synchronization*, without which malfunctioning at the time of concurrent execution of more than one processes cannot be avoided.

Another problem in concurrent execution of more than one process is the relative speed of the related processes involved in acquiring the shared resources. This speed is again not predictable; it depends on various factors, such as the behavior of the concerned process, the activities of other processes, and, above all, the way in which the OS handles interrupts and implements scheduling policies. One of the solutions to negotiate this predicament relating to timing factors may be the use of appropriate *timing signals* that can be exchanged among concurrent processes or threads to coordinate their collective progress. This approach is known as *interprocess signaling*, which is a rudimentary form, but is a common approach to handle interprocess synchronization.

Besides interacting with each other, the concurrent processes typically share some resources to communicate, such as shared memory, in order to exchange data, send one's output to another's input, report progress, and accumulate collective results. While accessing a shared memory, they exhibit a simple common means called *interprocess communication*. To prevent any hazard caused by timing in this situation, all such concurrent processes must be synchronized only at the time of accessing the shared resources.

Let us now identify the root of all these potential difficulties as mentioned and also to find out an alternative strategy that can combat the problems related to interprocess synchronization. This approach as being consisted of some systematic methodologies could then be injected early in the design process of OS, rather than to attempt to cure the system when it is already infested with concurrency-related timing problems.

The details of this topic are given on the Support Material at www.routledge.com/9781032467238.

4.17.3   RACE CONDITION

When two or more processes compete with one another to get access to a common shared resource during the course of their execution, they are in a race, and the situation is called the *race condition*. The result is that one of them will ultimately win the race and gain access to the resource. It will relinquish the resource only when its work is finished, leaving the state of the resource unaffected for the other processes to continue. None of the processes is aware of the existence of the others, and each is unaffected by the execution of the other processes. Such competing processes never exchange any information, but the execution of one such process may affect the state of other competing processes. The shared resources may be processor time, memory, clock, and, of course, other I/O devices. In fact, a race condition exists when the result of a computation varies, depending on the timing of the other processes. A race condition occurs when the scheduling of two processes is so critical that the various orders of scheduling them result in different computations. A race condition results from the explicit or implicit sharing of data or resources among two or more processes.

The solution to avoid the race condition can be formulated in an abstract way. The part of the program where the shared memory, variable, or resource is accessed is called the *critical section*. The critical section is one or a sequence of instructions with a clearly marked beginning and end. The critical section problem can be handled by allowing either process to enter its corresponding critical section at any time it needs to do so *except when the other process is currently in the critical section*. That is, if one could arrange matters that no two processes were ever in the critical section at the same time, we can avoid the race condition.

A process that enters its critical section must complete all the instructions therein before any other process is allowed to enter the same critical section. To implement this, it is thus required that a process explicitly request to use the shared resource prior to using it. When all use of the resource completed, the resource may then be released by the process. The *request and release* operations are usually part of the operating system facilities handled by the traffic controller. If a process requests a resource which is already in use, the process automatically becomes blocked. When the resource becomes available again as a result of a later release, the blocked process may be assigned the resource and made ready. This is often referred to as *mutual exclusion*, which enforces inter-process synchronization to ensure system integrity. Synchronization is actually a generalization of mutual exclusion. The choice of appropriate primitive operations for realizing mutual exclusion to avoid the race condition is thus a major design issue in any operating system.

The realization of mutual exclusion, on the other hand, invites two additional control problems. One severe problem is that of deadlock. This situation arises when one of the constituent processes has already acquired a resource for its use and requests another resource that is already acquired by other, and vice-versa. Both processes then keep waiting for their respective resource and are waiting forever; no constituent process can continue, and all such processes then appear dead, leading to a situation that ultimately locks the entire system. That is why it is called deadlock. Another related hazard is a situation in which the algorithm that decides to block an activity for the sake of implementing mutual exclusion continues to run for an indefinite period without arriving at a definite decision. Here, the system is very much *alive*, but looks locked, since it sits in a tight loop, only checking the status of the shared resource for the purpose of reaching a firm decision without continuing to do productive work related to other processes. Such a situation is called **livelock**. A special case of livelock is **busy waiting**, in which an activity, as an alternative to blocking, uses computational resources without making any progress. Busy waiting is, however, not vulnerable and hence is not objectionable if there is no other work worth doing during the wait. Another control problem that is fatal to concurrent processing is *starvation*. During the course of implementing mutual exclusion, one of the constituent processes which is denied access to a shared resource will naturally slow down. In an extreme case, the process may be indefinitely denied access to its requested shared resource, thereby leading to a situation of starvation, although there is no situation of deadlock.

The details of this topic are given on the Support Material at www.routledge.com/9781032467238.

4.17.4 MUTUAL EXCLUSION: REQUIREMENTS

Fundamental to successful execution of concurrent processes require the definite identification of related critical sections in which mutual exclusion of the said processes is required to be enforced. Although it is the only requirement to prevent the race condition, this is not *sufficient* for having parallel processes (multiprocessor system) co-operate correctly and efficiently using shared data. In order to derive an acceptable general solution to provide adequate support for mutual exclusion, the following **five conditions** must be met:

1. No two processes may be in their critical section at the same time in order to ensure mutual exclusion.
2. When no process is in a critical section, any process that requests entry to its critical section must be permitted to enter without delay.
3. No assumptions may be made about relative process speeds and priorities, the number of contending processes, or the availability of the number of CPUs.
4. No process running outside its critical section may block other processes.
5. No process should have to wait forever to enter its critical section, that is, to grant entrance to one of the contending processes into the critical section for only a finite duration, thereby preventing deadlock and starvation.

4.17.5 MUTUAL EXCLUSION IMPLEMENTATION

Concurrent processes can only be interleaved but cannot be overlapped, and mutual exclusion of these concurrent processes can thus be achieved in a number of ways, so that while one process is busy in its critical region, no other process will be allowed to enter the same critical region. To implement this approach to realize mutual exclusion, certain basic rules (protocols) must be observed by each process, such as:

- To negotiate protocol   (winner of the race proceeds)
- Enter critical section   (exclusive use of shared resource)
- To release protocol   (relinquish ownership)

A willing process attempting to enter a critical section first negotiates with all other concurrent processes to make sure that no other conflicting activity is in progress, and then all concerned processes are informed about the temporary unavailability of the resource. Once consensus is reached, the winning process can safely enter the critical section and start executing its tasks. After completion, the concerned process informs the other contenders about the availability of the resource, and that may, in turn, activate the next round of negotiations.

We will now turn to developing mechanisms that can be used to provide mutual exclusion and thereby synchronization. We will start with simple but conservative techniques and move toward more complex, liberal ones. In each case, we will show how certain primitives can be built to ensure mutual exclusion.

All mechanisms developed to realize mutual exclusion and synchronization ultimately depend on the synchronous nature of hardware. Some rely on the fact that processors can be made uninterruptible. These *processor-synchronous* methods work only for individual processors. Others rely on the fact that main storage can service only one access request at a time, even in a multiprocessor. These *store-synchronous* methods have a wider range of applicability.

4.17.5.1 Software Approaches: Switch Variables

Software approaches to implement mutual exclusion are based on a fundamental exclusion attribute already built into main memory (hardware) that can service only one access request at a time, even in a multiprocessor. This synchronization atomicity of main storage can be used to define a new main-storage variable called a *switch* that can then be shared by two concurrent activities to implement mutual exclusion between them. This variable allows only one or the other to enter its critical region. To mitigate the conflict that may arise due to simultaneous access to this common shared switch by concurrent independent processes, a user-made software approach can be employed to serialize the multiple accesses to the shared switch variable. When this approach is implemented; no special hardware facility, no additional OS assistance, and above all, seeking of any particular supporting attribute at the level of programming language have ever been at all assumed. Moreover, these approaches do not consider any ordering of access to be granted to the contending processes while arbitrating the conflicting situation.

4.17.5.2   Dekker's Algorithm: A Real Software-Only Mutual Exclusion Algorithm

The Dutch mathematician Dekker's approach (1965) was the first published software-only, two-process mutual exclusion algorithm. This approach cannot be easily extended beyond two generalized processes that share a common resource accessed within a critical section. Both processes are sequential and cyclic, and each of them also executes some code other than the critical section. Although the initial approach was observed to be infested with bugs, four attempts were later made in succession to rectify it and finally make it a foolproof system. In spite of having several limitations, the beauty of this approach is its simplicity while addressing the race condition as well as offering a solution, and at the same time, it highlights numerous bugs that may be encountered in developing concurrent programs.

This algorithm considers two independent and individually schedulable processes P1 and P2 that can also be interleaved in any arbitrary order. But, for the sake of simplicity and convenience, we have presented here the two processes (or threads) as a part of a single module named *mutual exclusion*. The procedure includes a global variable *turn* which actually monitors and controls access to any type of unspecified shared resource. The *turn* variable can assume only one of two values, *proc1* or *proc2*, to identify the process permitted to enter its critical section. Each process is prohibited from entering the critical section when *turn* belongs to the other. Three successive modified approaches, however, have been proposed over the already introduced initial algorithm with the previously mentioned assumption, when each such approach rectified the faults and limitations of its just predecessor, and finally the fourth one was able to overcome the shortcomings of the third one. While this fourth approach tends to be very close to the correct solution; incidentally, this new approach is again not a foolproof one, and yet appeared to have some trivial flaws in certain situations that are also not very usual. Moreover, if one of such flaws occurs, it may not be sustained for very long time. Still it is considered not to be an effective approach, and that is why the fourth approach is also hereby conclusively abandoned.

The details of each of these four approaches with their respective algorithms and their drawbacks are individually given, along with a separate correct approach, on the Support Material at www.routledge.com/9781032467238.

4.17.5.3   Dekker–Peterson's Algorithm

Dekker's algorithm, just described, published in 1965, was the only good solution for many years. Although this rather complex program solves the mutual exclusion problem, it is difficult to follow, and its correctness is tricky to prove. There were also many other ways in which the switch could be built incorrectly. However, a surprisingly simple and elegant modification of Dekker's algorithm was published by Peterson in 1981. Both algorithms can be generalized to multiple processes, but that is beyond the scope of this discussion. Here the global flag variables *p1–in* and *p2–in* indicate the position of each process with respect to mutual exclusion, and the other global variable *turn* (non-alternating switch) resolves simultaneity conflicts. The logic as used in this algorithm is able to summarily remove all the drawbacks of Dekker's algorithm.

The solution as offered in this algorithm is able to preserve mutual exclusion, considering all the critical situations that may also arise. But, while Peterson's approach is simple enough, it is not free from *busy waiting* that may summarily degrade the performance of the entire system. However, this drawback does not decline its theoretical significance but only tends to limit its direct applicability in practice. Moreover, this solution can also be generalized to any number of processes that compete over the same shared resources. This generalization can be achieved by use of a *spin switch* (Hofri, 1990).

The details of this approach with the algorithm are given on the Support Material at www.routledge.com/9781032467238.

4.17.5.4 Hardware Approach: Disable Interrupts

The process concept in the design of an operating system means that a process will remain running until it invokes an operating-system service (system call) or is interrupted. Mutual exclusion is thus guaranteed if a process is allowed to continue in its critical section by way of providing a proper guard (*lock*) so that it cannot be interrupted. Since no interrupts are allowed to arrive, the current activity will be able to complete the instructions in its critical region before any other activity starts executing in the same region. Adjusting this interruptibility of the computer gives rise to a *processor-synchronous* technique that can enforce mutual exclusion. This capability can be provided in the form of primitives defined by the innermost system kernel for disabling and enabling interrupts. A disable interrupt/enable interrupt (DI/EI) mechanism is considered a quick and easy means for ensuring indivisibility in the execution of the critical section. Some operating systems, for example, Amiga DOS, allowed processes to do this.

Interrupt disable/enable instructions are available in virtually all computers that allow interrupts to be disabled, perhaps on a selective basis. Use of these instructions was probably the most widely applicable way to implement mutual exclusion in multitasking systems running on a single-processor machine. The basic idea is quite simple. When a process wants to enter its critical region to gain exclusive access to a shared resource, it will disable all interrupts, restricting other processes from entering the same section at the same time, and re-enable them just before leaving the section to allow others to use it. Thus, once a process has disabled interrupts, it can use the shared resource, preventing any interference during the execution of the critical section. This may be accomplished by the following sequence:

    < disable interrupts >;
    < enter critical section: use protected resource >;
    < enable interrupts >;
    < remaining portion >;

Interrupt disabling, however, can cause severe problems; it actually disables clock interrupts and in turn disables the scheduler temporarily, resulting in no preemptions, thereby affecting rescheduling. In that situation, a lower-priority process could prevent a higher-priority process from continuing. It also outlaws concurrency altogether by disabling all other innocent disjoint processes not related to the blocking process. Moreover, events related to real-time processing are unable to respond efficiently; devices that need immediate service cannot be entertained until the ongoing activity in the critical region completes. In fact, attempts to disable the interrupt force the entire system virtually into a state of suspension. In addition, if the user process is given the power to handle interrupts for synchronization purposes, it may be dangerous and even totally unreliable if inappropriate moves are taken by the user that may lead to total collapse of the entire system, or the system may be trapped in a deadlock. The disabling-interrupts approach is not at all suitable for the multiprocessor systems (multiple CPUs) with shared memory, because it works only on the concerned CPU and is not applicable to other CPUs, which may cause a race condition among the processes running on them. Still, it is often convenient to entrust the kernel itself to disable interrupts for those few instructions causing a race condition. That is why it is sometimes a useful technique to disable interrupts within the kernel (implementation of semaphore WAIT and SIGNAL as system calls using DI and EI instructions at the system level only, to be discussed later in this chapter), but is not considered appropriate as a general mutual exclusion mechanism for user processes.

For more details about this topic, see the Support Material at www.routledge.com/9781032467238.

4.17.5.5   Special Machine Instructions

A more reasonable method using direct hardware support to achieve mutual exclusion is the test-and-set lock (TSL) instruction which carries out two actions, such as *reading and writing* or *reading and testing* of a single shared lock (memory location) atomically. Since these actions are performed in a single instruction fetch cycle, they are not subject to any kind of interruptions and hence are free from interference from other activities. Many computer systems, even systems with multiple processors, offer this explicit store-synchronous TSL instruction that makes mutual exclusion far easier and clearer.

- **Test-and-Set Lock Instruction**

The test-and-set lock instruction negotiates the conflicts among the contending processes by allowing only one process to receive a permit to enter its critical section. The basic idea is simple. A physical entity called *lock byte* is used as a global variable which controls the entry to the critical section (to access the shared resource). This global variable is set to *free* when the guarded shared resource is available. Each process intending to access the shared resource must obtain a permit to do so by executing the TSL instruction with the related control variable as an operand. When several concurrent contending processes compete, the TSL instruction guarantees that only one of them will be allowed to use the shared resource.

In fact, when this TSL instruction is executed, the value of the lock byte (memory word) will be read and tested, and if it is 0 (free), it is then replaced by 1 (busy) or any non-zero value and returns true, and the process may now enter its critical section. This entire sequence of operations is guaranteed to be indivisible; that is, it is to be carried out atomically; no other process/processor can access the lock (word) until the TSL instruction is completed.

The shared control variable used as a lock itself becomes a new critical section related to its testing and setting. If a process is interrupted after testing the shared control variable but before it sets it (after the *if* statement but before the assignment statement in the following declared function), the solution fails. This new, smaller critical section that manipulates the shared control variable can be handled by certain forms of needed system calls embedded in the TSL instruction. In this case, interrupts are disabled in OS code only while the variable is being manipulated, thereafter allowing them to be enabled while the main critical section is being executed. Hence, the amount of time that the interrupts are disabled is very short. When the execution of the TSL instruction is over, the shared resource becomes protected for the exclusive use of the process that calls the TSL instruction. The test and set can be defined as follows:

```
atomic function test_set (var k: integer): boolean      [k → control variable]
   begin
     if k = 0 then
       begin
         k := 1
         test_set := true
       end
     else test_set := false
   end
```

The beauty of the TSL instruction lies in the guarantee of its atomic (indivisible) action with regard to testing of the global variable and its subsequent setting at the time of entering the critical section (occupying the corresponding shared resource). The IBM System/360 family with a number of models were the first computers to include TSL instruction in hardware. Since then, the architectural design of almost all commercial computers includes explicit hardware provisions, either in a similar form to a TSL instruction or its functional equivalent for implementation of mutual exclusion. In fact, the other type of instructions, INCREMENT MEMORY and SWAP MEMORY AND REGISTER, are also available; each one, however, uses similar approaches to TSL instruction and carries out its respective indivisible operation at the time of execution to implement mutual exclusion.

4.17.5.6 Multiprocessor Implementation
The TSL instruction with modification may also be implemented in multiprocessor systems with shared memory accessible to several processors. When many concurrent processes executing on different processors attempt to execute their individual TSL instruction, as defined earlier, mutual exclusion may not be obtained. The reason is that multiprocessor systems with shared memory commonly run on a memory-cycle basis in which it is guaranteed only to have an undisturbed separate READ and WRITE cycle. In a single-processor system, these two cycles in TSL instruction are, however, actually combined and treated (executed) as a single, indivisible *read-modify-write* memory cycle. As a result, in a multiprocessor system, it is highly probable that while a TSL execution is in progress on a given processor, another processor's TSL execution may intervene between the READ and WRITE cycle of the currently running TSL instruction, and these two processes may then work on the same lock byte (shared resource) at the same time to enter the critical section, thereby creating an inconsistency in the value of the lock byte that eventually damages the ultimate objective of mutual exclusion. One way to solve this problem is to use an approach which should be carried out at much lower level, which is to implement an indivisible *read-modify-write* cycle explicitly on the system bus (not on the lock byte as is usual in TSL instruction) leading to the lock byte. Accordingly, the concerned CPU at the time of executing the TSL instruction then locks the memory bus to prohibit other CPUs or processes from accessing the lock byte (the same memory location) until it is done. In other words, each processor's TSL instruction can then only see a consistent global value of the lock byte (shared variable) as set before or after the completion of the execution of the competing TSL instructions. For example, Motorola implemented a test and set (TAS) instruction in the M68000 family of microprocessors to make them suitable for multiprocessor systems by way of using an indivisible *read-modify-write* cycle on the system bus for the purpose of TAS instruction execution to implement mutual exclusion.

• **Exchange Instruction**

A different type of instruction that uses a similar approach to TSL instruction to implement mutual exclusion is the *Exchange* (XCHG) instruction, which carries out the contents of a variable (lock byte) to be tested and subsequently set as an indivisible operation. This XCHG instruction may also be used successfully in a multiprocessor environment by providing an additional arrangement of a special LOCK prefix over the system bus that enables this instruction to enforce its atomicity (*read-modify-write* cycle on the bus) in a multiprocessor system, thereby ensuring mutual exclusion. This is found in the implementation of the Intel iAPX–86 (80 x 86) family of processors with the use of an WAIT operation. In fact, when this exchange (XCHG) instruction is executed, it exchanges the contents of a register with the contents of the lock byte (specified memory word). During execution of this instruction, access to the lock byte is blocked for any other instruction referencing that particular lock byte.

While both TSL and ECHG instructions are easy to implement, do not affect interrupts, and relieve the system from the state of any type of suspension, the performance advantages offered by them are often offset by some of their serious drawbacks. The busy waiting caused by them leads to serious degradation in the effective utilization of the system, and the busy waiting of many processes lying in a queue with arbitrary ordering may cause the possibility of acute starvation for some processes In addition, the process or processes in a state of busy waiting may hold some resource(s) that may be required by the process executing in its critical section. But access to the resource(s) will simply be denied because of the principle guiding the mutual exclusion mechanism. Consequently, the process in the critical section cannot complete its execution, and all other processes in the busy-waiting state will then remain in their existing state forever. The entire system may then simply be in deadlock. All these drawbacks that are found in hardware-based solutions summarily caused severe ill effects that greatly outweigh its many distinct advantages, and that is why a search for other effective mechanisms has been done.

For more details about these topics, see the Support Material at www.routledge.com/ 9781032467238.

4.17.5.7   Mutual Exclusion (Synchronization) without Busy Waiting

All the approaches, including disabling interrupts, as described, successfully solved the race condition by implementing appropriate mutual exclusion, but they all suffer from busy waiting, the consequence of which is often severe and damaging to the overall performance of the entire system. It also creates a critical *priority inversion problem* (a low-priority process gets CPU access and a high-priority process remains waiting in a tight loop) on systems with a priority-based scheduler. Also, the solution obtained by disabling interrupts requires explicit OS support, but is still hazardous and also sometimes has a potential dramatic effect on the I/O system. To overcome all these shortcomings, an innovative approach is conceived that creates a shared resource accessible only through the operating system to enforce mutual exclusion. Processes that attempt to enter an already-occupied critical section will then simply be put in the blocked state, similar to the way a process that attempts to gain a currently allocated resource might be blocked by the resource manager. Moreover, while a process is waiting, other processes may then continue. To make a system blocked, it, however, requires here only an extra cost of merely one or two process switch, against an unnecessary constant use of vital computational resources for being in a useless loop of busy waiting with no productive output.

For brief details on this topic, see the Support Material at www.routledge.com/9781032467238.

4.17.5.8   Semaphores

Dijkstra proposed a reliable, efficient, and specialized mechanism to implement solutions to synchronization problems, especially for mutual exclusion among an arbitrary number of cooperating processes using a synchronization tool called *semaphore*. His innovative approach was the first one to use a software-oriented OS primitive (semaphore) to accomplish process synchronization and is still considered a viable one for managing communities of competing/cooperating processes. Hence, it found its way into a number of experimental and commercial operating systems.

Competing/cooperating processes can safely progress when they hold a permit, and a semaphore can be roughly considered a permit provider. A process requests a permit from a semaphore, waits until a permit is granted, proceeds further after obtaining one, and returns the permit to the semaphore when it is no longer needed. If the semaphore does not have a permit, the requesting process is *blocked* until a permit is available. The semaphore immediately receives a permit when a process returns one. Hence, a permit request is a blocking operation, and the permit return is not. In fact, the semaphore manager only keeps a count of the number of permits available and manipulates the number accordingly.

A semaphore s is an OS abstract data type, a special variable used to synchronize the execution of concurrent processes. It has two member components. The first component, *count*, is an integer variable which can take values from a range of integers that indicates the number of permits the semaphore (*counting semaphore*) has. The second component, *wait-queue*, is a queue of blocked processes waiting to receive permits from the semaphore. The initial value of *count* is created with a fixed number of permits, and the initial value of *wait-queue* is NULL, indicating no blocked processes.

The two standard primitive atomic operations that can be invoked to access a semaphore structure are wait (or up) and signal (or down). Each primitive takes one argument, the semaphore variable s, for permit request and permit release actions. A process takes a permit out of a semaphore (the semaphore transmits a signal) by invoking the operation wait (or up) on the semaphore and inserts a permit into (or releases a permit to) a semaphore (the semaphore receives a signal) by invoking the signal (or down) operation on the semaphore. In Dijkstra's original paper, the wait (or up) operation was termed P (from the Dutch word proberen, meaning "to test") and the signal (or down) was called V (from the Dutch word verhogen, meaning "to increment"). Operating systems often distinguish between counting and binary semaphores. The value of a counting semaphore can take values from a range of integers. The value of a *binary semaphore* can range only between 0 and 1. On some systems, binary semaphores are known as *mutex locks*, as they are essentially locks that provide *mutual* exclusion.

Both of these operations include modification to the integer value of the semaphore that, once started, is completed without any interruptions; that is, each of these two operations is indivisible (atomic action). In fact, semaphore variables can be manipulated or inspected by only three available operations, as depicted in Figure 4.16 and defined as follows:

1. A semaphore variable may be initialized to a nonnegative value.
2. *wait* (s)   / * Get a permit from semaphore s * /
    {
        if (*count* > 0)   { /* permit available * /
            count = *count*—1;
        }
        else   { /* permit not available * /
                put the calling process in the *wait-queue*;
                block ; / * invoke CPU scheduler to release the CPU * /
                /* **process returns here when rescheduled with a permit it got** * /
                    remove the calling process from the *wait-queue*;
        }
        return ;
    }
3. *signal* (s)   / * Return a permit to semaphore s * /
    {
        if (not empty *wait–queue*)   { / * allocate the returning token
                                                   to a waiting process   * /
            select a process from the *wait–queue*; awaken the selected process ; }
        else   { /* put the token in the semaphore * /
            count = *count* + 1;
        }
        return ;
    }

FIGURE 4.16 An algorithm illustrating the definition of semaphore primitives (*wait and signal*).

Wait and *signal* are primitives of the traffic controller component of processor management that are embedded in the scheduler instead of built directly on the hardware.

A *wait* (s) sets the process in the queue of blocked processes, if needed, and then sets the process's PCB to the blocked state. The processor is now available, so another process is then selected by the process scheduler to run.

signal operation execution on a semaphore, as shown, first checks if there are any blocked processes waiting in the *wait-queue*. If there are, one of them is awakened and offered a permit using a scheduling discipline such as FCFS, the fairest policy to avoid indefinite delay of a process in a semaphore that may otherwise cause starvation if other processes are given preference. The process selected by the scheduler is now ready to run again. Otherwise, the semaphore member variable *count* is simply incremented by one.

There is some controversy over whether the scheduler should switch immediately to the waiting process to be activated in the domain of *signal* (Figure 4.16). An immediate switch guarantees that whatever condition awaited by that activity still holds, since the *signal* operation is in progress, and no other activity has had a chance to run. The disadvantage of an immediate switch within the *signal* domain is that it tends to increase the total number of switch processings. Moreover, the process that called *signal* may likely to call *wait* for a new region soon that may ultimately cause the said process itself to block in any case. The hysteresis principle suggests that the running process should be allowed to continue its remaining processing.

When semaphore is supported, semaphore operations as well as the declaration of semaphore variables are commonly provided in the form of system calls in the operating system or as built-in functions and types in system implementation languages.

4.17.5.9 Mutual Exclusion: General (Counting) Semaphore

The definition of *wait()* and *signal()* semaphore operations has been modified to obtain a straight-forward solution to the mutual exclusion problem. In fact, when a process executes the *wait()* operation and finds that the semaphore value (s.count) is not positive, the process is blocked, and it is then placed in the *wait-queue* (s.queue) and switched to the wait state. Control is then transferred to the CPU scheduler, which then selects another process to run. A blocked process on a semaphore *s* should be restarted by a *wakeup()* operation only when some other process executes a *signal()* operation that changes the blocked process from the waiting state to the ready state. Now, whether the CPU may continue with the running process or switch to the newly ready process depends on the policy, as already discussed in the last section (last but one paragraph). Following this discussion, Figure 4.17 suggests a more formal definition of these two primitives for semaphores:

```
type   semaphore = record
                       count : integer ;
                       queue = list of process
                       end ;
var  s : semaphore ;
wait (s) :              [ P operation ]

       s.count :=  s.count − 1
       if s.count < 0   then
           begin
               block () ;                    / * block the process * /
               place the process in s.queue
           end ;

signal (s) :           [ V operation ]

       s.count :=  s.count + 1
       if s.count ≤  0 then
           begin
               remove a process P from s.queue ;
               wakeup () ;
               place the process in ready list ;
           end ;
```

FIGURE 4.17   An algorithm illustrating the definition of general (counting) semaphore primitives (*wait and signal*).

Program/segment *mutual_exclusion*;
   ...

const *n* = ...;   (* number of processes)

var *s* : semaphore (:= 1) ;

process P (i : integer) ;
  begin
    while *true* **do**
      begin
        wait (s) ;
        < critical section > ;
        signal (s) ;
        < remaining P(i) processing >
      end [*while*]

    end ; [P(i)]

      [*main process*]

begin *[mutual_exclusion]*
  s := 1; (*free*)
  initiate P(1), P(2), . . ., P(*n*)
end [*mutual_exclusion*]

FIGURE 4.18 An algorithm that implements mutual exclusion of competing processes using semaphores.

In this implementation (Figure 4.17), semaphore values may be negative, although semaphore values are never negative under the classical definition of semaphores. In fact, if a semaphore value is negative, its magnitude actually indicates the number of processes waiting on that semaphore. This fact results from switching the order of the decrement and then the test in the implementation of the *wait()* operation.

As an illustration of the use of semaphores, let us consider that *n* different processes identified in the array P(i) share a common resource being accessed within their own critical sections, as shown in Figure 4.18. Each process ensures the integrity of its critical section by opening its critical section with a *wait()* operation and closing the critical section with a *signal()* operation on the related semaphore; that is, the semaphore is executed atomically. This means that in each process, a *wait* (*s*) is executed just before the critical section. If the value of *s* is negative, the process is suspended. If the value of *s* is 1, then it is decremented to 0, and the process immediately enters its critical section. Because *s* is now no longer positive, any other process that now attempts to execute *wait()* will make *s* negative and hence will not be allowed to enter its critical section. The process will be blocked and will be placed in the queue. When the process that already entered its critical section ultimately leaves the region, it closes its critical section with a *signal* on the same semaphore. This will increment *s* by 1, and one of the blocked processes (if any) is removed from the queue of blocked processes associated with the semaphore and put in a ready state. When it is next scheduled by the operating-system scheduler, it can then enter its critical section.

All these together firmly guarantee that no two processes can execute *wait()* and *signal()* operations on the same semaphore at the same time. This is realized (in a single-processor environment) by simply inhibiting interrupts during the time the *wait()* and *signal()* operations are executing. Once interrupts are inhibited, instructions from different processes cannot be interleaved, and only the currently running process executes until interrupts are re-enabled and the scheduler can regain control.

It is to be noted that, since the *wait()* and *signal()* operation executions by the different processes on the same semaphore must exclude one another, this situation itself is the mutual exclusion problem; hence, busy waiting with this definition of *wait()* and *signal()* operations is really not completely eliminated. In fact, we have moved busy waiting from the entry section to the critical sections of the application programs. However, the critical section [containing *wait()* and *signal()* implementations] is usually very small, and almost never occupied; hence, it does involve in limited busy waiting albeit for a shorter duration, and that also occurs rarely. But if the critical section in an application program is relatively long and is almost always occupied, busy waiting in that situation really cannot be completely avoided.

4.17.5.10   Binary Semaphore

A more restricted form of semaphore is known as *binary semaphore* and has the same expressive power as the general semaphore but is easier to implement. Here, the semaphore variable *s* is allowed to take on only two values; 0 (busy) and 1 (free). We use the *mutex* field of each semaphore to make sure that *wait* and *signal* exclude each other (*mutually exclusive*) and only for a short duration; otherwise busy waiting may occur. In fact, any access of the *value* or the *queue* field must be atomic, and this partial atomic action is required separately in implementing each of the *wait* and *signal* operations. The *wait*, activated by a process after having read the value of *mutex*, must immediately seize the semaphore variable and prevent the other concurrent *wait*s from reading it until checking its value and possibly changing it, if required, is completed. Similar actions are carried out in the case of *signal* operation. The logic of *wait(s)* should be interpreted as waiting until the semaphore variable *s* becomes *free*, followed by its indivisible setting of *s busy* before control is returned to the caller. The *wait* operation therefore implements the negotiation phase of the mutual-exclusion mechanisms. The *signal (s)* sets the semaphore variable *free* and thus represents the release phase of the mutual-exclusion protocol. Figure 4.19 depicts a formal definition of a binary semaphore.

For more details about this topic, see the Support Material at www.routledge.com/9781032467238.

```
Type binary semaphore = record
                 value ( 0, 1 )
                 queue : list of process
               end ;
var mutex : s : binary semaphore
wait B(s) :
     if  mutex = 1 then
            mutex = 0
        else begin
               block the process ;
               place the process in s.queue
     end ;
signal B(s)
     if  s.queue is empty then
            mutex = 1
        else   begin
                 remove a process P from s.queue ;
                 place the process P in the ready list ;
     end ;
```

FIGURE 4.19   An algorithm depicting the definition of binary semaphore primitives (*wait and signal*).

4.17.5.10.1   Implementation: As Lock Variable

A binary semaphore *s* can be used to implement modified lock and unlock mechanisms to implement mutual exclusion instead of using *ordinary* lock variables (Dekker–Peterson method), which eventually gives rise to busy waiting. Here, with the use of the *wait* (*s*) primitive, the process is blocked if the lock is not free, and the process is then placed in the queue of blocked processes, releasing the processor to do other useful work, thereby removing busy waiting. A *signal* (*s*) later checks the associated blocked list and selects one of the blocked processes from this list, if there are any, and wakes it up, putting it in the ready state for subsequent execution to be decided by the process scheduler.

This mechanism can also be used for other purposes, including the process waiting for I/O completion. After an I/O request has been issued, the process can be blocked by a *wait* (*x*), where *x* is a status byte associated with the I/O device. When the I/O is completed, the corresponding I/O completion interrupt occurs, and it is then converted into a *signal* (*x*).

For more details and the associated algorithm on this topic, see the Support Material at www.routledge. com/9781032467238.

4.17.5.10.2   Semaphores: Related System Calls

Semaphores are comparatively simple, yet a powerful mechanism to implement mutual exclusion among concurrent processes accessing a shared resource. To relieve users from the tedious task of devising their own synchronization mechanisms, operating systems often provide semaphores as a tool in the form of system calls so that processes that share resources (particularly parts of virtual storage) can synchronize their access with the use of these system calls. Each participating process then encloses the critical section (those sensitive statements that may be adversely affected by interleaved or concurrent execution of processes) within a *wait–signal* pair with the related semaphore variable for safe execution. The semaphore variables are manipulated only through system calls. Four fundamental system calls are needed that may have different names in different implementations: (i) *SemaphoreCreate* (initial value) initializes the semaphore with a small integer. (ii) *SemaphoreDestroy* (semaphore descriptor) informs the kernel that the given semaphore is no longer needed. (iii) *SemaphoreDown* (semaphore descriptor) performs the down (*wait*) operation on the given semaphore. (iv) *SemaphoreUp* (semaphore descriptor) performs the up (*signal*) operation on the given semaphore.

For more details about this topic, see the Support Material at www.routledge.com/9781032467238.

4.17.5.11   Semaphore: Service Ordering

Since the implementation of semaphores does not impose any definite ordering among the waiting processes to be serviced, there may be a high chance that some processes are unable to proceed due to locking of a resource by one or more other processes, leading to what is called *indefinite postponement*, sometimes referred to as *livelock*, and the affected processes then start to suffer from starvation. In fact, a biased service discipline may allow a group of processes to hinder others and attempt to permanently usurp (seize) the resource. Process starvation may, however, be avoided by imposing a simple condition on semaphore implementation: a request to enter the critical section must be granted in finite time. The scheduling algorithm that can be matched to this requirement while selecting a waiting process from the queue of blocked processes is the first-in-first-out discipline. That is why servicing of blocked processes with FIFO is sometimes also referred to as *strong implementation of semaphore*. In contrast, a *weak semaphore* is one in which all processes waiting on the same semaphore proceed in an unspecified order (i.e. the order is unknown or indeterminate).

For more details about this topic, see the Support Material at www.routledge.com/9781032467238.

4.17.5.12   Semaphore: Granularity

A semaphore allows only one process at a time to access the shared resource to implement mutual exclusion during runtime. This act imposes strict serialization of the processes that, in turn, may adversely affect the degrees of parallelism among the contending processes in systems. Apart from that, it creates other bad situations, such as the starvation of processes and deadlock in the system that, in turn, also require additional mechanisms to resolve. Hence, it is necessary to willfully control all these ill effects of serialization, and that can be accomplished by varying the *granularity of individual semaphores.*

The *finest granularity* of semaphores at one end is realized by dedicating a *separate semaphore* to guard each specific shared resource from simultaneous use by contending processes. As a result, a huge number of semaphores are required to guard all these different shared resources available in a system for the sake of synchronization. The storage requirement overhead is then also appreciable, and the total time required by these semaphores to operate contributes a huge runtime overhead due to processing of numerous *waits* and *signals.*

The *coarse granularity* of semaphores, on the other hand, can be made by assigning each semaphore to guard a collection of shared resources, possibly of similar types. This approach reduces the storage requirement and runtime overhead but adds extra cost required to negotiate an increased number of conflicts as well as enforcing rigorous serialization of processes, which may also have no other resources in common. In fact, coarse-grained semaphores, apart from creating priority inversion, may severely affect parallelism to such an extent that it often outweighs the benefits already accrued. Thus, the trade-off between coarse-grained and fine-grained semaphores must be carefully analyzed, and a satisfactory balance must then be realized on the basis of the application being handled after willful manipulation and compromise.

For more details about this topic, see the Support Material at www.routledge.com/9781032467238.

4.17.5.13   Semaphores: Properties and Characteristics

The use of semaphores provided by the operating system to ensure mutual exclusion is flexible and does not impose any constraints, even if the concurrent processes are restructured or modified. A single semaphore can also be generalized to handle more than one process in situations when several resources of the same type are used by a number of concurrent processes, by simply initializing the semaphore to the specified value of available number of resources. A general semaphore may be implemented by means of a binary semaphore. However, these two types of semaphores may differ significantly in their use, and general semaphores are observed to provide better efficiency of programs. Semaphores may also be provided as a language construct in the form of built-in functions and types in system implementation programming languages. Apart from these characteristics, semaphores also exhibit several other interesting properties, the details of which are given on the Support Material at www.routledge.com/9781032467238.

For more details about this topic, see the Support Material at www.routledge.com/9781032467238.

4.17.5.14   Classical Problems: Concurrent Programming

In the literature of operating systems, there are several well-known classical representative problems relating to mutual exclusion, synchronization, critical sections, or coordination aspects. Each can be seen as an example to theoretically explain concurrent processing and its implications. These problems mainly differ from one another in the way critical-section executions of different processes are ordered. After explaining each problem, the appropriate solution also could have been proposed based on the most popular tool, the semaphore, although other alternatives, equally good and even superior tools, are also available to solve such problems. Our aim is not at all to explore the details of all these problems individually but rather to use one such problem as a platform to explain concurrent processing and its related issues. We will thus consider here only the most common popular problem, the *producer/consumer problem*, as a representative to elucidate the essence of concurrent processing and its associated complexities. We will use this example throughout the rest of this chapter to show the power of different synchronization tools, especially of the semaphore, monitor, and messages.

4.17.5.14.1   The Producer/Consumer Problem

The producer/consumer problem is a typical example to explain the behavior of concurrent processing by cooperating processes where both mutual exclusion and synchronization are needed. The problem, in general, may be stated as follows: Given a set of cooperating processes, some of them (producers) generate (produce) some type of data items (characters, records), placing them in a shared buffer (memory) that is used (consumed) by others (consumers), usually with possible disparities in the rates of production and consumption. The solution to the problem naturally demands a suitable mechanism to implement a synchronization protocol that will allow both producers and consumers to operate concurrently at their respective service rates within the specified time-slice. Normally, data should be consumed in the order in which they are produced, although this rule is relaxed somewhat for data produced or consumed simultaneously.

4.17.5.14.1.1   Producers and Consumers with an Unbounded Buffer   Any number of producers and consumers can operate without overlap on the buffer of unbounded capacity using their respective service rates within the specified time-slice. After the initialization of the system, a producer must obviously be the first process to run in order to provide the first item for the consumer. Each time the producer generates an item, an index (*in*) into the buffer is incremented. From that point on, a consumer process may run whenever there is an item in the buffer produced but not yet consumed. The consumer proceeds in a similar fashion incrementing the index (*out*) but ensuring that it does not attempt to consume from an empty buffer. Hence, the consumer must make sure that it works only when the producer has advanced beyond it (*in>out*). Alternatively, if the consumer is considered a first process, then it begins with waiting for the first item to be produced by the producer.

A single general semaphore (**counting semaphore**) uses here a "*produced*" variable initialized with 0 as a counter to keep track of the number of items produced but not yet consumed. Since the buffer is assumed to be unbounded, the producer may run at any time to produce as many items as it can. When the producer generates an item, it is placed in the buffer, and this fact is signaled by means of the general semaphore PRODUCED; hence, no extra counter or check over the counter is required here. According to the assumption and per the nature of the problem, this implies that the consumer can never get ahead of the producer. However, this approach, in general, cannot guarantee system integrity due to having several limitations under certain situations.

The entire implementation could even be realized by a different algorithm employing a binary semaphore (in place of a general semaphore) by means of using the two primitives WAIT and SIGNAL attached to the semaphore in each critical section and calling them at the right point for mutual exclusion. In that situation, an additional variable *counter* is required which is to be incremented and decremented and to be checked at the right point in the procedure, PRODUCER and CONSUMER, to keep track of whether the buffer is empty, and if so, provisions for appropriate actions (*wait*) are to be made accordingly. But this implementation also suffers from certain limitations.

Initially, both solutions to the problem, counting semaphores and binary semaphores, are found to have shortcomings under certain situations. After detecting flaws, a refined, corrected approach to overcome the limitations of the solutions was formulated by taking appropriate actions at the right point within the existing algorithms. Although this example is not a realistic one, it can be concluded that it is a fairly representative one that demonstrates both the power and the pitfalls of the semaphore while it is in action.

The details of these two approaches to separately solve the problem with algorithms, their limitations, and finally the correct solution with refined algorithms, are described on the Support Material at www.routledge.com/9781032467238.

4.17.5.14.1.2   Producers and Consumers with a Bounded Buffer   The producer/consumer problem, initially introduced with an unbounded buffer, demonstrates the primary issues and its related solutions associated with concurrent processing with virtually no restriction over the execution of producers.

However, the unbounded buffer assumption is not a practical approach and may not be directly applicable in real-life situations where computer systems with memory (buffer) of finite capacity are used. This section will thus deal with the same producer/consumer problem, now with a bounded buffer and its solution so that it may be applicable in realistic situation where the shared buffer has a *finite* capacity. Here, the finite buffer consists of *n* slots, each capable of holding one item. It is implemented in a circular fashion by "wrapping around" from the last (highest index) to the first (lowest index) position. Two pointer variables are associated with the buffer, *in* and *out*, the former for the producer and the latter for the consumer, are used to indicate the current slots (or the next place) inside the buffer for the producers to produce an item and for the consumers to consume the next item, respectively. This is depicted in Figure 4.20. These pointer variables, *in* and *out*, are initialized to 0, incremented according to the execution of the producer or consumer, and must be expressed in terms of *modulo*, the size of the buffer. Now, the producer and consumer functions can be expressed as follows:

```
producer :
  begin
    produce pitem ;
        while ( ( in + 1 ) mod buffersize = out )) do  [ nothing ]
            buffer [ in ] := pitem
            in := ( in + 1 ) mod buffersize
        end [ while ]
  end [ producer ]
consumer :
  begin
        while in = out do  [ nothing ]
            citem := buffer [ out ]
            out := ( out + 1 ) mod buffersize
      consume citem
        end [ while ]
  end [ consumer ]
```

As usual, producers may produce items only when the shared global buffer is empty or partially filled, that is, only when there are empty spaces available in the buffer to accept items. Otherwise, new items produced might overwrite the already existing items produced earlier but not yet consumed, which may damage the processing, making it unreliable. All the producers must be kept waiting when the buffer is full. Similarly, consumers, when executing, may absorb only produced items, making the buffer empty, thereby enabling the producers to run. The consumers must wait when no items are available in the buffer; hence, they can never get ahead of producers.

At any point in time, the buffer may be empty, partially filled, or full of produced items. Let *produce* and *consume* represent the total number of items produced and consumed respectively at any instant,

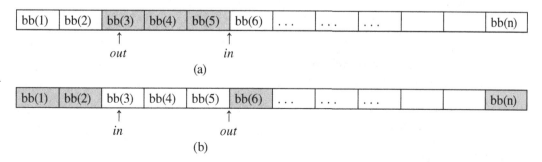

FIGURE 4.20 An algorithm illustrating the logic to solve the classical producer–consumer problem with bounded (finite) buffer used in circular fashion.

and let *item-count* be the number of items produced but not yet consumed at that instant, that is, [*item-count = produce − consume*]. Let *canproduce* and *canconsume* be two conditions indicating the current status of the buffer that can be used to control the execution of the producers and consumers, respectively, with the conditions [*canproduce*: item-count < buffersize], since the producers are allowed to run only when there are empty spaces available in the buffer, and [*canconsume*:item-count > 0], since the consumers can continue their execution if there exists at least one item produced but not yet consumed.

Figure 4.21 shows a solution to the producer/consumer problem with a bounded buffer in which two types of semaphores have been used. The general semaphores *canproduce* and *canconsume*

```
Program/segment  bb–producer–consumer
    . . .
const
    buffersize = . . .
type
    item = . . .
var
    buffer : array [ 1 . . . buffersize ] of item ;
    canproduce, canconsume : semaphore ;      [ general ]
    pmutex , cmutex : semaphore ;             [ binary ]
    in, out : ( 1 . . . buffersize ) ;
procedure  producers ;
    var pitem : item ;
    begin
        while true do
            begin
                wait(canproduce) ;
                pitem := produce ;
                wait(pmutex) ;
                buffer [ in ] := pitem ;
                in := ( in mod buffersize ) + 1 ;
                signal(pmutex) ;
                signal(canconsume) ;
                    other–producer–processing
            end [ while ]
    end [ producers ]
procedure  consumers ;
    var citem : item ;
    begin
        while true do
            begin
                wait(canconsume) ;
                wait(cmutex) ;
                citem := buffer [ out ] ;
                out := ( out mod buffersize ) + 1 ;
                signal(cmutex) ;
                signal(canproduce) ;
                consume (citem) ;
                    other–consumer–processing
            end [ while ]
    end [ consumers ]
```

FIGURE 4.21 An algorithm describing the modified solution of the classical producer–consumer problem with bounded (finite) buffer using semaphores (both counting and binary).

```
                    [ main program ]
   begin  [ bb–producer–consumer ]
      in := 1
      out := 1
      signal(pmutex) ;
      signal(cmutex) ;
      [ canconsume := 0 ; ]
      for  i := 1 to buffersize do  signal(canproduce) ;
      initiate  producers , consumers
   end  [ bb–producer–consumer ]
```

FIGURE 4.21   (Continued)

represent the two conditions to control the execution of producer and consumer processes, respectively, as already explained. Two binary semaphores *pmutex* and *cmutex* are used to protect the buffer (atomic action) while producers and consumers are active in their respective turns manipulating their index (*in* or *out*). Consequently, this solution supports multiple concurrent producers and consumers.

As shown in Figure 4.21, the producer processes, *producers*, can run only when there is any empty space in the buffer, indicated by the semaphore *canproduce*. This semaphore may initially be set to the value corresponding to the buffer size, thus allowing producers to get up to *buffersize* items ahead of consumers. Alternatively, it can also be set to 0, showing the buffer is empty at the beginning, and the producers can then proceed accordingly. However, when a consumer completes its turn, it empties a slot by consuming the item, removing it from the buffer, and signals the fact through the *canproduce* semaphore to wake up a waiting (sleeping) producer, if there is any. Similarly, the *canconsume semaphore* indicates the availability of items already produced and behaves almost in the same manner as the unbounded-buffer version of the consumers. Each time a producer process runs, it increments the value of *canconsume* [*signal* (*canconsume*)], and a consumer process decrements it by executing a *wait* operation.

Actions being taken as shown in Figure 4.21 in relation to buffer manipulations by both producers and consumers are treated here as critical sections which are kept protected with the use of the binary semaphores *pmutex* and *cmutex* to make this solution more versatile while using the global buffer. The *modulo* operator is used to implement the buffer in circular fashion. Two indices, *in* and *out*, are used by producers and consumers, respectively, to increase the *degree of concurrency* in the system. Usually, two sets of processes operate at different ends of the buffer, and they compete with their peers within the group (intra-group), but not between the groups (inter-group). This situation is handled by a single semaphore *mutex* in the solution of the unbounded–buffer case presented earlier. However, a single semaphore may unnecessarily block the producers whenever a consumer is in its critical section and vice-versa. As the indices are disjoint, two semaphores offer more concurrency, of course with a little bit of additional overhead.

4.17.5.14.2 The Readers–Writers Problem

The readers–writers problem is essentially a special case of the producer/consumer problem where producers are called the *writers* and may update (i.e. both read and write) the shared resource, and the consumers are the *readers*, which can only read the shared resource. Obviously, if two readers access the shared resource simultaneously, no adverse effect will result. However, if a writer and another process (either a reader or a writer) access the shared resource simultaneously, conflict may arise. That is why writers must have exclusive access to the shared resource while writing. In fact, the readers–writers problem has several variations, all involving priorities relating to either readers getting priority over writers or vice versa. The simplest version requires that no readers be kept waiting unless a writer has already received the access right to use the shared resource. That is, no reader should wait for other readers to complete because a writer is waiting. In other words, unlike the mutual exclusion problem, many readers are allowed to concurrently operate on a shared resource (critical section), as they do not change the content of the shared resource. Based on this discussion, a typical appropriate solution of this problem can be obtained, the details of which are, however, outside the purview of our present discussion.

4.17.5.15 Semaphores: Drawbacks and Limitations

Semaphores are a powerful, flexible, simple, and easy-to-use tool while handling concurrent processes to implement interprocess synchronization and thereby realize mutual exclusion. In spite of being immensely attractive, they suffer from severe drawbacks. Some of their notable disadvantages are:

- *Semaphores are not really structured*: They require strict adherence to related rules and regulations developed for each specific problem to solve, and failing in this may lead to corrupting or blocking the entire system. They also impose strict serialization of processes during runtime and thus require a specific form of service discipline among the waiting processes.
- *Semaphores do not support data abstraction*: They only ensure protected access to critical sections and never control the type of operations to be performed in the critical section by the contending processes. Moreover, while they perform interprocess communication via global variables which are now exposed, that in turn invites severe threats.
- *Semaphores do not have any programming-language constructs*: The user program has no liberty but can only religiously and carefully follow the synchronization protocol underlined by the semaphore. Since the compiler is not aware of the specific resource to be shared, no compilation check can be carried out to detect syntactic errors.

Besides other pertinent issues, all these drawbacks, however, encouraged designers to devise alternative appropriate suitable mechanisms that could, by and large, alleviate the notable disadvantages of using semaphores.

For more details about this topic, see the Support Material at www.routledge.com/9781032467238.

4.17.5.16 Events: An Alternative Synchronization Primitive

An *event* with a different concept is defined and developed as an abstraction of semaphore operations. The entire "event" is encapsulated to address the coordination in applications for semaphores (as opposed to the critical section problem). An event then represents the occurrence of some condition in the execution of software. Accordingly, if one process needs to synchronize its operation on the occurrence of an event, it can block itself until the event occurs. When the event occurs, another process can have the OS inform the blocked process of the occurrence. Thus, an event is analogous to a semaphore, waiting for an event is analogous to the **P** operation, and noting the occurrence of an event is analogous to the **V** operation.

As usual, an event is represented by a data structure known as an event control block, sometimes called an event descriptor. If two or more processes synchronize on an event, then they both have a way of referencing the same event descriptor. The event *wait* operation blocks the calling process until another process performs a *signal* operation. The *signal* operation resumes exactly one waiting process, if any, suspended on the event by a *wait* call. If no processes are waiting when the *signal* is issued, it is ignored. Hence, a major distinction between events and semaphores is that if no process is waiting, the result of the signal operation (i.e. the *signal* itself) is not saved, and its occurrence will have no effect. It is sometimes convenient to add a third function to the event management set, *queue*, to return the number of processes currently waiting for an event.

The rationale for these semantics is that a signal should represent the situation that an event has just occurred, not that it occurred sometime in the past. If another process detects this occurrence at an arbitrary time later (as is the case with the passive semaphore operations), the causal relationships among calls to the *wait and signal* functions are lost. These semantics, however, have a lasted bearing and far-reaching influence in the design and development of monitors, another synchronization tool described in later sections.

An example detailing this topic is given on the Support Material at www.routledge.com/9781032467238.

4.17.5.17 Critical Regions and Conditional Critical Regions

Brinch Hansen (1972) proposed a mechanism to embed semaphores in programming-language constructs called a *critical region* that can be controlled from the system's end to realize semaphore operation, thereby relieving programmers from explicitly defining the semaphore and its associated tedious legal handling. The *critical region* obviously allows several processes to access shared global variables and protects the variable by making it known to the compiler, which, in turn, can generate code that guarantees mutually exclusive access to the related data. The shared variable, say *v*, is declared in the program with a keyword *shared* and a user-definable type *T*. Processes may access this shared variable, which is protected by means of the *region* construct, which is defined as follows:

region *v* **do**;

where the sentence or sequence of sentences following *do* is executed as a critical section. At the time of generating code for a region, the compiler essentially injects a pair of *wait* and *signal* operations or their equivalents (calls to semaphore) around the critical section. Thus, mutual exclusion, as enforced by the use of the semaphore, has been properly realized by the use of *region*. Although the use of *region* may invite deadlock and also starvation of the processes waiting in the queue for the same shared variable, those can be alleviated by the compiler and with the use of appropriate scheduling algorithms on the waiting queue, respectively. Similar to a semaphore, while the critical region is used as the only facility to synchronize competing processes, it also requires busy waiting in a *wait* operation until some condition happens, in addition to its other drawbacks. To solve the synchronization problem without a busy wait, Brinch Hansen proposed a slight modification to the existing critical region, another construct called the *conditional critical region*. This construct is in all respects syntactically similar to the critical region, simply with an addition of only an extra instruction with a new keyword called *await* attached to an arbitrary Boolean condition to be used inside a critical region. This construct, when implemented, permits a process waiting on a condition within a critical region to be suspended and places it in a special queue until the related condition is fulfilled. Unlike a semaphore, a conditional critical region can then admit another process into the critical section in this situation. When the condition is eventually satisfied, the suspended process is awakened and is once again brought into the ready queue. Thus, the conditional critical region satisfies both mutual exclusion and synchronization without a busy wait.

Conditional critical regions are very easy to use for complex mutual exclusion and synchronization problems. But they are confusing and even cumbersome while keeping track of dynamic changes of the several possible individual conditions that the *await* statement requires. The common implementation of the conditional critical region normally assumes that each completed process may have modified the system state in such a way that resulted in some of the waited-on conditions being fulfilled. This incurs the additional cost involved in frequent checking of conditions. Moreover, the code that modifies shared data may be scattered throughout a program, making it difficult to keep track in a systematic manner. Due to such undesirable complex implementation, conditional critical regions are rarely supported in commercial systems directly.

For more details with algorithms and also an example on this topic, see the Support Material at www.routledge.com/9781032467238.

4.17.5.18   Monitors

The limitations as experienced in semaphore operations and the complexities involved in introducing conditional critical region approach to negotiate the interprocess synchronization problem
ultimately gave rise to introduce a new concept, proposed first by Hoare (1974) in the form of a
higher-level synchronization primitive called a monitor which was later further refined by Brinch
Hansen (1975) in a slightly different way.

The monitor is a programming-language construct that provides equivalent functionality to that
of a semaphore and has been implemented in a number of programming languages, including Ada,
Concurrent Pascal, Pascal-plus, Modula-2, Modula-3, Mesa, Concurrent Euclid, and also in a few
other languages. But they received a big boost when Arm architecture lately implemented it. *Java
synchronized classes are essentially monitors,* but they are not as pure as monitor advocates would
like, yet there is a full language-supported implementation for users to realize a synchronization
mechanism for Java threads. More recently, they have also been implemented as a program library
that, especially, enables the user to put a monitor lock on any object (e.g. to lock all linked lists).

Monitors are formed primarily to provide *structural data abstraction* in addition to concurrency
control. This means that it not only controls the timing but also determines the nature of operations
to be performed on global shared data in order to prevent harmful or meaningless updates. This
idea is realized by way of fixing a set of well-defined and trusted data-manipulation procedures
to be executed on global data in order to limit the types of allowable updates. Abstract data types
actually hide all the implementation in data manipulation. Depending on whether the users are just
encouraged or actually forced to access data by means of the supplied procedures, data abstraction
may be regarded as *weak* or *strong*, respectively. The weak form of data abstraction may be found
in an environment supported by semaphores, since it never enforces using the supplied procedures
for global data manipulation, and it therefore sometimes makes the entire system truly vulnerable
to its users.

4.17.5.18.1   Definition

A monitor is a software module consisting of a collection of procedures, an initialization sequence,
local data variables, and data structures that are all grouped together in a special kind of package
for manipulating the information in the global shared storage. The main characteristics of a monitor
are:

- The local data variables with a data structure embedded in a monitor are only accessible by the monitor's supplied procedures and not directly by any other declared external
  procedure.
- With the use of public interface, a process can enter.the monitor by invoking one of its
  private procedures.
- At any instant, only one process may be allowed to execute in the monitor, while the other
  processes that have invoked the monitor by this time are suspended and are kept waiting
  until the monitor next becomes available.

The first two characteristics encourage modularization of data structures so that the implementation
of the data structure is private, with a well-defined public interface. This has a close resemblance to
the definition of an object as found in object-oriented software. In fact, an object-oriented operating
system or a programming language can readily implement a monitor as an object with the required
special characteristics.

The third characteristic emphasizes that the monitor is able to achieve mutual exclusion, since
the data variables in the monitor can be accessed by only one process at a time. Thus, the shared
data structure can be easily protected by placing it in a monitor. If the data in a monitor represent
some resource, then the monitor ensures a mutual-exclusion facility at the time of accessing the
resource.

Since the monitors are a programming-language construct, the compiler is quite aware that they are of special types and hence can handle calls to monitor procedures differently from other procedure calls, thereby arranging for mutual exclusion. Typically, when a process calls a monitor procedure, the first few instructions of the called procedure will check to see whether any other process is currently active within the monitor. If so, the calling process will be kept suspended until the other releases the monitor. If no other process is active in the monitor, the calling process may then be safely allowed to enter. In any event, the user need not be aware of how the compiler arranges for mutual exclusion. It is enough only to know that by turning all the critical sections into monitor procedures, no two processes will ever be allowed to execute their critical sections simultaneously.

4.17.5.18.2   *Principles of Operation*

A monitor, by definition, structurally consists of a collection of private procedures and local private variables with associated data structures which cannot be accessed by any public procedure that lies outside the domain of the monitor. The public procedures are normally used as an interface to call the respective private procedures. However, a declaration of a typical monitor may have the following format, as shown in Figure 4.22.

The logic of structuring and implementation of monitors has a strong resemblance to the kernel of the operating system. As OS kernel typically consists of a number of private and public routines associated with private system data structures; the monitors likewise also contains similar type of things. Similar to OS public routines that are called by the user to perform some system-related work, monitors also do provide the same. As the kernel itself typically invalidates the interrupts whenever the system processes are executed for the sake of preserving system's integrity and to avoid synchronization problems, so monitors also allow only one process to execute inside the monitor at any instant to implement synchronization for concurrent processes.

When two or more processes want to share abstract data types, monitors make this critical data accessible indirectly and exclusively via an interface of a set of publicly available procedures. In the case of the producer/consumer problem, the shared global buffer may be declared as belonging to a monitor, and neither producers nor consumers would be allowed to directly access it. Instead, producers may be permitted to call a monitor-supplied public procedure and to provide the number of items already produced as its argument. A monitor procedure would then actually append the produced item to the buffer. Similarly, consumers may call on a monitor procedure to take a produced item out of the buffer. This is depicted in Figure 4.23. No two processes should execute *produce* and *consume* concurrently, since this may result in one of the operations being lost. In this way, a set of monitor procedures may inherently incorporate a critical section that encapsulates the shared data used by the concurrent processes and handles the buffer management and synchronization of

```
monitor–name  :  monitor
   begin
      declaration of private data ;            /* local variables used by monitor */
         procedure pub–name ( formal parameters )        /* public procedures */
            begin
               procedure body ;
               ................. ;
            end ;
         procedure priv–name                       /* private procedures */
            initialization of monitor data ;
            ................. ;
   end ( monitor–name ) ;
```

FIGURE 4.22   An algorithm showing the typical format to declare a monitor.

```
monitor    sharedBuffer {
    int  balance ;
  public ;
    produce ( int item )    ( balance  =  balance  +  item ; ) ;
    consume ( int item )    ( balance  =  balance  −  item ; ) ;
}
```

FIGURE 4.23   An algorithm explaining the use of monitor while handling a shared variable.

concurrent requests internally by means of its own codes and local variables with a specific data structure that is absolutely hidden from users. In this way, interprocess synchronizations and communications are handled by the monitor.

However, in many cases, it is observed that when a process is executing inside the monitor, it discovers that it cannot proceed until some other process takes a particular action on the information protected by the monitor. So a way is needed for an executing process to block when it cannot proceed; otherwise the process will perform an undesirable busy wait. In this situation, processes should be allowed to wait within the monitor on a particular condition without affecting other monitor users significantly. Consequently, another process may then enter the monitor to execute its own purpose. This idea of internal signaling operations was borrowed by monitors from semaphores.

In the case of the producer/consumer problem, when the producer inside the monitor finds that the buffer is full, it cannot proceed until the consumer process consumes it. So, in this situation, a mechanism is needed by which the producer process will not only be suspended but temporarily relinquish the monitor so that some other process may enter and use it. Later, when the condition is satisfied, and the monitor is again available, the blocked process needs to be resumed and allowed to reenter the monitor at the point where it left. To accommodate this situation, monitors incorporate *condition variables* to realize a solution with synchronization. This particular aspect of monitors is similar to conditional critical regions.

4.17.5.18.3   Condition Variables

A condition variable is a structure which is placed inside the monitor and is accessible as global to all procedures within the monitor. Three functions are associated with condition variables to manipulate their value. Those are:

cwait(c): Suspends execution of the invoking process on condition c until another process performs a *csignal* on the same condition. After execution of *cwait*, the monitor is then available for use by another process.

csignal(c): Resumes execution of exactly one other process suspended after a *cwait* on the same condition. If there exist several such processes, one of them is chosen; if no process is waiting, then do nothing; the signal is not saved (and will have no effect).

queue: Returns a value of *TRUE* if there exist at least one suspended process on the condition variable and *FALSE* otherwise.

Condition variables are not counters. They do not accumulate signals for later use as semaphores do. In fact, monitor *wait/signal* operations behave differently from those for semaphores. If a process in a monitor signals; that is, the process executes *csignal(x)*, the respective signaled condition queue is then inspected. If some activity is waiting in that queue, the signaler enters the queue and one waiter brought from the corresponding waiting queue is then allowed to be active (ready state) in the monitor. If no activity is waiting on the condition variable in that queue, the signaler proceeds as usual, and the signal is simply ignored and lost without creating any damage. Since a monitor condition is essentially a header of the related queue of waiting processes, one of the consequences of this is that signaling on an empty condition queue in the monitor has no effect. The monitor, however, allows only one process to enter at any point in time; other processes that intend to enter will then join a queue of suspended processes while waiting for the availability of the monitor. But when a process inside the monitor suspends itself on a certain condition *x* by issuing *cwait(x)*, the process is then placed in a queue of processes waiting on the same condition and then reenters the monitor later when the condition is met. Apart from introducing an *urgent queue* for every condition, a separate condition queue is formed, and processes that are blocked on certain conditions will then be placed in the respective queues.

When an executing process in the monitor detects a change in the condition variable *x*, it issues *csignal(x)*, which alerts the corresponding condition queue that the condition has changed. Here lies the difference in the behavior of the signal operation that distinguishes *Hoare's version* of monitor semantics from *Brinch Hansen's approach*.

With **Hoare's approach**, if a process P1 is waiting on a condition queue (for a signal) at the time when P0 issues it (signal) from within the monitor, P0 is either to be suspended (blocked) on the monitor or immediately exit the monitor, while P1 at once begins execution within the monitor. When P1 completes its execution in the monitor, P0 will once again resume its execution in the monitor. In general, this definition of monitors says that if there is at least one process in a condition queue, a process from that queue runs immediately when another process issues a corresponding signal for that condition. The process issuing the signal must either be suspended (blocked) on the monitor or immediately exit the monitor The rationale for Hoare's approach is that a condition is true at a particular instant in time when the signal occurs, but it may not remain true later, when P0, for example, finishes its execution with the monitor. In his original paper, Hoare uses these semantics to simplify proofs of the correct behavior of the monitor.

Brinch Hansen's monitor semantics incorporate the *passive* approach. (These semantics are also known as *Mesa monitor semantics* because of their implementation in the Xerox Mesa programming language. But Mesa semantics, in particular, are different; their approach is very similar to Brinch Hansen's with regard to the situation that arises due to the behavior of the *csignal* operation, but their proposed solution to the situation is different. Mesa semantics will be discussed in detail separately later in this section.) Hansen's approach is different. It states that when P0 executes a signal (as already described), appropriate for a non-empty condition queue, the signal for that particular condition is saved, and P0 is not to be suspended; rather it will be allowed to continue. When P0 later leaves the monitor, a process at the head of the respective condition queue, say, P1, will attempt to resume its execution in the monitor after rechecking the condition before it starts. He argues for rechecking due to the fact that even though *signal* indicates an event has occurred, the situation may have changed by the time P0 performs *signal* and P1 is allocated the CPU. This deliberation also favors fewer process context switches than with Hoare's approach, which will ultimately tend to enhance the overall performance of the system.

With Hoare's semantics, a situation that leads to a wait operation may be looked as:

```
. . .
if (resource–Not–Available) resource-Condition.wait
. . .
/ *Now available—continue. . ./*
. . .
```

When another process executes a *resource-Condition.signal*, a process switch occurs in which one of the blocked processes gains control of the monitor and continues executing at the statement following the *if* statement. The process performed *signal* is then blocked and delayed until the waiting process finishes with the monitor.

With Brinch Hansen's semantics, the same situation could appear as:

. . .

while (*resource–Not-Available*) *resource-Condition.wait*

. . .

/ *Now available—continue. . ./*

. . .

This code fragment ensures that the condition (in this case *resource-Not-Available*) is rechecked before the process executing *resource-Condition.wait* precedes. No process switch occurs until the process performed *signal* voluntarily relinquishes the monitor.

Mesa semantics and monitors with notify and broadcast are discussed on the Support Material at www.routledge.com/9781032467238.

4.17.5.19 Wait-Signal Monitor

Monitors are static structures with no life of their own. Consolidating all the ideas that we have discussed till now about the monitors, a sample monitor, in fact, is essentially quite simple and implements a familiar mechanism. It actually implements the *wait* and *signal* semaphore operations. *cwait* and *csignal* of monitors are very similar to the *wait* and *signal* operations, respectively, of semaphores but with one crucial difference: semaphore *wait and signal* failed because while one process was about to go to *wait* (but not *slept*) and the scheduler at that very moment if switches to other one, the semaphore later then tried to *signal* (*wake–up*) the former process, although it was not actually sleeping at that time. With monitors, this cannot happen. The inherent mutual exclusion in monitor procedures guarantees that if one process in the monitor discovers that it cannot proceed until a condition is satisfied, the process itself will be able to complete the *wait* operation inside the monitor without having to worry about the possibility that the scheduler may switch to another process just before the *wait* completes. In fact, no other process will ever be allowed into the monitor at all until the *wait* is finished, and the process will then be placed into the corresponding waiting queue.

It is also observed that the fairly simple mechanism used in a*wait-signal* monitor significantly demonstrates, at least theoretically, that semaphores can be implemented with monitors, and the reverse is also true: monitors can also be implemented by semaphores. In fact, monitors should not be considered a weaker concept than semaphores; rather the *restricted version of monitors* (monitors in which the signal is the last operation of a protected procedure) are less flexible but in many situations relieve the system to avert a possible crisis.

The details of wait-signal monitors with an algorithm are given on the Support Material at www.routledge.com/9781032467238.

4.17.5.19.1   An Implementation: Producer/Consumer Problem with Bounded Buffer

The producer/consumer problem with a bounded buffer can be solved using the full power of *monitor* with encapsulation of the critical shared data (bounded buffer). The traditional approach using semaphores to solve this problem has been modified here with the use of *condition variables* in the monitor to control the required buffer-full and buffer-empty situation in order to accommodate the usual speed disparity between producers and consumers. The bounded-buffer monitor accurately controls the shared buffer and provides the required procedures to manage a standard producer/consumer situation, besides supporting an arbitrary number of concurrent producer and consumer processes that can run in the environment in general. For the sake of maintaining similarity with the approach as already described in the semaphore-based solution of the same problem, the monitor data here also follow much the same logic and functions, except with the use of an additional variable, *count*, which keeps track of the number of items already produced but yet not consumed.

However, a user process that implements the monitor to solve the producer/consumer bounded buffer problem is obviously a separate one, and the fact is that monitors are different entities, separate from their users. More specifically, the user process need not know anything with regard to the internal details of the procedures embedded in monitors but must have full knowledge of the interface specifications required for invoking these monitor procedures at a specific point whenever needed. The rest is up to the compiler to detect the conformity of syntax and semantics of user processes with the monitor's specifications at the time of compilation, and necessary errors may be displayed if identified.

The details of a monitor-based solution with an algorithm of the producer/consumer bounded buffer problem, and also a user process using monitor to solve the same problem with an algorithm, are given on the Support Material at www.routledge.com/9781032467238.

4.17.5.20 Monitors with Notify and Broadcast: Mesa Semantics

Although numerous modifications on monitors have been proposed over the original definition as modeled by Hoare, a completely different definition of *monitor* as developed by Lampson and Redell resolved the main two drawbacks of Hoare's model with respect to the issuing of *signal* (here it is *csignal*). Those are:

*   While the process issuing the *csignal* must either immediately exit the monitor or be blocked (suspended) on the monitor, it carries the cost of two additional context switches: one to suspend the process and another to resume it again when the monitor later becomes available.
*   When a *csignal* is issued, a waiting process from the corresponding condition queue must be activated immediately, and the process scheduler must ensure that no other process enters the monitor before activation. Otherwise, the condition under which the process is going to be activated may change.

While these issues as raised in the proposed model with respect to the behavior of *csignal* operation are very similar to those as proposed by Brinch Hansen in his model, the solution approach as proposed in this model to cope the situation is quite different. This proposed model was implemented in the programming language Mesa (Lampson 80) and thus is sometimes also referred to as Mesa semantics. In Mesa, a new primitive, *cnotify*, is introduced to solve these issues by replacing the existing *csignal* primitive with the following interpretation: When a process active in a monitor executes *cnotify(x)*, it causes the x condition queue to be not only *notified* but the signaling process continues to execute rather than being blocked or exiting the monitor. The result of this notification is that the process at the head of the condition queue will be resumed later at some time when the monitor is next available. However, since there is no guarantee that another process will not enter the monitor by this time before the start of the waiting process, the waiting process thus must recheck the condition before resuming. So, at the cost of one extra rechecking of the condition variable, we are saving some processing time by avoiding extra process context switches and, above all, ignoring such constraints as to when the waiting process must run after a *cnotify*.

With the advantages of having a *cnotify* primitive to notify a waiting process following a prescribed rule rather than forcible reactivation, it is also possible to add a *cbroadcast* primitive with specific rules to the repertoire. The broadcast causes *all processes* waiting on a condition to be placed in a ready state, thereby relieving the process (using *cbroadcast*) from the burden of knowing exactly how many other processes should be reactivated.

A broadcast, in addition, can also be used in a situation when a process would have difficulty precisely figuring out which other process to reactivate. A good example is a memory manager. The memory manager has k bytes free; a process terminates, releasing an additional m bytes, but the memory manager does not know which waiting process can proceed with a total of $k + m$ bytes; hence, it uses *broadcast*, and all processes check for themselves whether it matches their requirements.

Besides all these advantages, this model also supports several other useful extensions.

Brief details of this topic with algorithms and its advantages are given on the Support Material at www.routledge.com/9781032467238.

4.17.5.21   Case Study: Monitors in Java

A Java class becomes a monitor type when the attribute *synchronized* is associated with one or more methods in the class. An object of such a class is a monitor. The Java virtual machine ensures mutual exclusion over the synchronized methods in a monitor. Each monitor contains a single unnamed condition variable. A thread then waits on the condition variable by executing the call *wait*(). The *notify*() call is like the *signal* operation. It wakes one of the threads waiting on the condition variable. The Java virtual machine does not implement FIFO behavior for the *wait* and *notify* calls. Thus, it does not provide the bounded *wait* property. The *notifyall*() call, however, activates all threads waiting on the condition variable.

4.17.5.22   Merits and Drawbacks of Monitors

Monitors have several advantages. Some of the notable ones are:

- Monitor code itself is more modular in its design structure, with all parts of synchronization protocols under one module. This facilitates easy code rectification to modify any local effects, and even a major change in the monitor code will not at all affect users' code as long as interfacing rules remain unchanged. This is in contrast to semaphores, where synchronization actions may be a part of each user process and also may span a number of processes, and thus any change in its structure and manipulation rules requires a thorough modification to all related user processes.
- Its ability to hide all the details of implementation from the users makes it quite transparent and more secure in a way similar to the ISR.
- The use of monitors supports modular programming at the time of program development to solve any related problem that, in turn, facilitates easier debugging and faster maintenance of monitor-based programs.
- Monitor code is usually more regimented, with complementing synchronizing actions found in the neighboring procedures (signal-receiving code). When semaphore is used, the pair of *wait* and *signal* operations may be spread over different processes and/or even in different modules.

Although monitors represent a significant advancement over the devices used earlier, but some of their major strengths are directly related to their weaknesses.

- While the presence of a number of monitors within an operating system may facilitate increased concurrency and provide flexibility in modular system design with ease of maintenance, management of several system resources entrusted to such separate monitors may invite deadlocks. This may especially happen when a monitor procedure calls another monitor procedure (*nested calls*).
- As the definition of monitors virtually eliminates the possibility of any access to monitor variables by external agents, it thus leaves very little scope to system implementers to combat any problems that may happen inside the monitor or outside due to the execution of the monitor.
- Since the users are bound to live only with those methods that are provided by public monitor procedures for global data manipulation, but those are often found not to meet users' requirements while accessing a given shared resource. For example, if a certain file structure is imposed by the file monitor that does only all reads and writes, then application programmers are effectively denied the freedom of interpreting the files in any other way. In many situations, it may not be acceptable to some categories of users, especially system programmers.
- Monitors never provide any control over the ordering of the waiting queues The standard policy of treating them in FIFO order is not always appropriate. Some people therefore prefer a more general mechanism for inspecting and reordering the various queues.

- The artificial use of condition variables, which introduces much complexity in monitors, is also found inconvenient to programmers for regular use.
- While a monitor requires that exclusion not be in force for very long, this hinders some applications which might require shared data for a very long time; for example, exactly this happens in the well-known *readers-writers* problem.

A detailed discussion of this topic is given on the Support Material at www.routledge.com/9781032467238.

4.17.5.23   Conclusions

Monitors have not been widely supported by commercial operating systems, including UNIX (though some versions of UNIX support mechanisms patterned after monitors), but they still are considered a powerful high-level language construct and as such are incorporated into many programming languages, including Ada, that have been useful for solving many difficult problems. Since it hides all the details of its implementation from users to make itself transparent that, in turn, also makes it more secure and enables easy code modification whenever required. Monitors act as an external functional extensions of user processes, but they differ from the traditional external procedures in that they provide additional facilities for concurrency control and also signaling that make parallel programming much less error-prone than their counterpart, the semaphore.

It is interesting to note that the structuring and implementation logic of monitors conceptually look very similar to the kernel of an operating system in all respects, and its different attributes are also very similar to those of kernels, as already described in the previous section. But the essential difference between a monitor and a kernel is that in a monitor-based operating system, there coexist a *collection of monitors* in charge of different resources where each monitor controls a particular resource or a small group of related resources. In contrast, the kernel of an operating system (monolithic implementation), in essence, is a comparatively large *single* monitor consisting of a huge number of complex programs with numerous interactions that may be sometimes difficult to debug and enhance and, above all, tedious to maintain. In addition, for being less reliable, monolithic operating systems often restrict concurrency by allowing at most one of their routines to be active at a time. On the contrary, each monitor itself implements mutual exclusion (concurrency), enforcing serial execution of procedures, and the presence of a large number of monitors simply permits unrestricted concurrency between processes that use separate monitors. In fact, monitors were originally introduced as an essential tool in structuring of OSs.

Finally, it is observed that the increasing trend in implementing concurrent applications running within an address space using threads has appreciably changed the nature and overall behavior of the general problem. While synchronization of threads running across different address spaces is in nature similar to the usual interprocess synchronization already described, it is natural to possibly implement many of the characteristics of a monitor in programmer-scheduled threads within an address space. The solutions thus targeted are then much easier to derive than semaphore-based synchronization and are easier to implement than full monitors. The reason is that the threads share a common address space, and only one thread will execute at a time in the space. Basically, the approach allows the program to control the address space while scheduling threads for execution so that a thread runs only when it does not violate a critical section. Whereas a generic solution cannot make any assumptions about the presence or absence of critical sections, thread scheduling is usually performed by the program developer while building application programs.

For more details about this topic, see the Support Material at www.routledge.com/9781032467238.

4.17.5.24   Case Study: Interprocess Synchronization in UNIX Using Semaphores

Interprocess synchronization is carried out by UNIX System V using semaphores that are implemented and executed at the kernel level. Concurrent executing processes invoke semaphore system calls in the form of a generalized *wait and signal* operations (primitives) in which several operations can be done simultaneously, and the increment and decrement operations may cause a change in the semaphore values, but that will always be greater than 1. User-specified keys are used as semaphore names. A key is associated with an array of semaphores. Individual semaphores in the array can be accessed with the help of subscripts. A process intending to gain access to a semaphore makes a *semget* system call with a key as a parameter. If a semaphore array matched with the key already exists, the kernel makes it accessible to the process that makes the *semget* system call; otherwise the kernel creates a new semaphore array, assigns the key to this array, and makes it accessible to the process.

The kernel provides a single system call *semop* for *wait* and *signal* operations. The call uses two parameters: a key and a list (*subscript, op*) of specifications, where *subscript* identifies a particular semaphore in the semaphore array and *op* is the operation to be performed. The entire set of allowable operations is prescribed in the form of a list, where each operation is defined on one of the semaphores in the semaphore array and is performed one at a time in an atomic manner. This means that either all operations as defined are performed one at a time and the process is then free to continue its execution, or none of the operations are performed and the process is then blocked. Associated with each semaphore are queues of such processes blocked on that semaphore. A blocked process is activated only when all operations, as indicated in *semop*, can succeed.

Execution of *semop* itself is also atomic in nature; that is, only one process can access the semaphore at any instant, and no other process is allowed to access the same semaphore until all operations are completed or the process is blocked. It is interesting to note that the semantics of *semop* itself facilitate avoiding deadlocks. A single *semop* either allocates all the resources that a process requires, or it is not allocated any of the resources. This attribute of *semop* resembles the all-requests-together approach, which is one way to prevent (avoid) deadlocks.

For more details about this topic, see the Support Material at www.routledge.com/9781032467238.

4.18 INTERPROCESS COMMUNICATION AND SYNCHRONIZATION

Since concurrent processing can significantly improve system performance, the operating system must provide adequate support to realize concurrent processing by way of resolving competition as well as cooperation between the processes. These, in turn, primarily require correct implementation of two functions: interprocess synchronization and also their communication. Competing processes need to be synchronized to realize mutual exclusion; cooperating processes may need to exchange information. Semaphores and critical regions are able to primarily synchronize the operation of concurrent processes but not able to convey information between them (except than the synchronization signal). Monitors also allow synchronization in the execution of concurrent processes while sharing information by using shared memory within the monitor. Moreover, both these tools as well as other similar mechanisms are based on the assumption of the availability of shared memory to accomplish sharing by all synchronizing processes, which may be running on one or more CPUs. In the case of distributed systems consisting of multiple CPUs (multicomputers), each with its own private memory and connected by a local network with no common memory, the use of semaphores is not workable. This is also true in distributed shared memory multiprocessor systems, since semaphore variables are global, and accessing such global variables can result in substantial communication delays in such systems. In the case of using monitors, the structures (local data, public procedures) of monitors are usually centralized on each CPU, making them inapplicable in such distributed systems. The designer was thus eagerly looking for some sort of a single mechanism to devise so that both synchronization and the communication functions could be realized at a time with ease in order to likely reduce the overhead with increased uniformity and greater clarity.

4.18.1 Messages

To negotiate all these issues, one approach may be to use a single mechanism, popularly known as *message passing*. Messages are a relatively simple mechanism able to implement both interprocess communication and synchronization and are often used in contemporary commercial centralized systems as well as in distributed system environments. Computer networks also normally use this attractive message passing mechanism to manage both interprocess communication and synchronization between concurrent processes that run on different nodes (machines) interconnected with one another in networks. Distributed operating systems running on loosely coupled system (multicomputers) as well as on tightly coupled systems (multiprocessor) usually also exploit messages for this purpose. Messages can also be used simply as a communication mechanism explicitly intended to copy information (even to transfer major portions of the operating systems and/or application programs) without using shared memory from one address space into another process's address space of even other nodes (machines) located remotely. Sometimes the operating system itself is involved in this communication activity, since concurrency is to be implemented across address spaces, but those are inherently guarded by the protection mechanisms of memory management in order to strictly prevent any form of malfunctioning. The OS in that situation must inject an additional mechanism by which the information can be copied from one application's address space to that of another. Applications can then use the OS as an intermediary to share information by way of copying it in these systems. Messages have been even found in use in the implementation of 32-bit *system buses*, such as Multibus II (Intel) and Futurebus (IEEE), designed for microcomputer systems that provide specialized hardware facilities for interprocessor communication with low overhead.

More details on this topic with a figure are given on the Support Material at www.routledge.com/9781032467238.

4.18.2 Message Format

A message, in essence, is a block of information formatted by a sending process so that its syntax conveys a certain meaning to the receiving process. The format of the message mostly depends on the objectives that the message should accomplish and also on the type of computer system (a single centralized computer or a distributed computing system) on which it will be run. Furthermore, there must be a protocol that both the sender and the receiver obey in this message format. A message may contain data, execution commands, or even some code to be transmitted between two or more processes. For large quantities of information to be transmitted, it can usually be placed in a file, and the message can then simply reference that file. In fact, the message format, in general, is not fixed but flexible and negotiable by each specific sender–receiver pair. A message is divided into two parts: a *header*, which contains various pieces of information about the message, and the *message body*, which contains the actual contents of the message. A representative format of a message with a possible arrangement of its fields is depicted in Figure 4.24.

The header mostly has a fixed format in a given operating system and contains such information as type, length, sender ID, receiver ID, and a data field. The type field can be used to identify messages containing specialized information, such as synchronization information and error reporting.

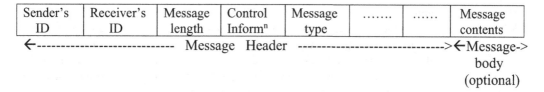

Sender's ID	Receiver's ID	Message length	Control Inform^n	Message type	....	......	Message contents

←-------------------------- Message Header -------------------------------->←Message->
body
(optional)

FIGURE 4.24 A typical message format of message-passing mechanism used in interprocess communication and synchronization.

There may also be additional fields containing control information, such as a pointer field so that a linked list of messages can be created, a sequence number that keeps track of the number and order of messages passed between sender and receiver, and sometimes a priority field. The optional message body normally contains the actual message, and the length of the message may vary from one message to another (variable-length message), even within a single operating system. However, designers of operating system normally do prefer short, fixed-length messages for the sake of minimizing processing load and to reduce storage overhead.

4.18.3 MESSAGE IMPLEMENTATION: DIFFERENT ISSUES

Systems using messages as a tool for communication and synchronization have many challenging problems and numerous issues that do not arise with semaphores or monitors, especially if the communicating processes are located on different machines connected by networks. Typical message operations are *SEND* message and *RECEIVE* message, which are provided either by the operating system or pre-declared in a system implementation language. This pair of primitives, *SEND* and *RECEIVE*, used at the time of communication between processes, like semaphores and unlike monitors, are essentially system calls rather than programming-language constructs. Systems based on message passing come in many different forms. In fact, implementation of messages is found to differ in a number of details that among other things affect the functioning and use of parameters that are associated with these *SEND* and *RECEIVE* operations. Some of the important issues relating to message implementation are described here for the sake of an overall understanding as to how message-passing mechanisms are to be realized. The important issues, in particular, are the following.

4.18.3.1 Naming: Addressing

Every message is identified by its name (address) for which it is meant. One of the major decisions in designing the naming of a message is whether the naming should be *direct* or *indirect*. *Direct naming* (*addressing*) implies that whenever a message operation is invoked, each sender must name the specific recipient (destination), and conversely, each receiver must name the source from which it wants to receive a message. The following code fragment explains the direct naming pattern of a message when a process A sends a message to process B.

```
.......
.......
process  A ;
.........
  send ( B, message ) ;
.........
.........
process B;
  receive (A, message) ;
.........
```

Here, *message* represents the contents that are to be transmitted as the actual message, and B and A in the parameters identify the destination (receiver) and the source of the message (sender), respectively. Direct naming, by nature, is a *symmetric* communication in the sense that it is a one-to-one mapping, and each sender must know the name of its receiver and vice-versa. Although this provides a safe and secure means of message communication, but it may impose a severe constraint when a service routine is implemented by the *send/receive* mechanism for public use by a community of users, since the name of each customer in this case must be known to the service routine beforehand, so it can expect the request.

4.18.3.1.1   Indirect Naming: Mailbox

An alternative approach in this regard in message communication is *indirect naming* in which messages are sent to and received from specialized dedicated repositories used only for this purpose, commonly called *mailboxes*. The association of processes (senders and receivers) to mailboxes can be either static or dynamic. Pipes in the UNIX systems in this regard can be considered an analog of mailboxes. The following code fragment illustrates the functioning of a mailbox, for example, *mailbox-1* as used here, when a process A sends a message to process B.

```
.......
.......
process A ;
.......
 send ( mailbox-1, message ) ;
.......
.......
process B ;
 receive ( mailbox-1, message) ;
.......
```

The *send* operation places the generated *message* into the named mailbox; *mailbox-1*, and the *receive* operation removes a message from the named mailbox, *mailbox-1*, and provides it to the receiving process through the private variable, *message*.

Ports also are often statically associated, in place of a mailbox, with a process for message communication; that is, the port is created and assigned to the process permanently. In particular, a port is typically owned by and created by the receiving process, and when the process is destroyed, the port is also destroyed automatically.

The placement of the mailbox with regard to its location and ownership is a design issue for the OS developer to decide. That is, should the mailbox be put in an unused part of the receiver's (process's *B*) address space, or should it be kept in the operating system's space until it is needed by the receiver (process *B*)? Figure 4.25 shows the mailbox for process *B*, which is located in the user's space. If the mailbox is kept in this manner in the user space, then the *receive* call can be simply a library routine, since the information is being copied from one part of *B*'s address space to another. However, in that situation, the translation system (compiler and loader) will have to take care to allocate space in each process for the mailbox. Under this arrangement, there remains a possibility that the receiving process may sometimes overwrite parts of the mailbox inadvertently, thereby destroying the links and losing messages.

The alternative to this approach is to keep *B*'s mailbox in the operating system's space and defer the copy operation until *B* issues the receive call. This situation is illustrated in Figure 4.26. This option shifts the responsibility of mailbox space arrangement from user process onto the OS. Consequently, it prevents any occurrence of inadvertent damage of messages or headers, since the mailbox is not directly accessible to any application process. While this option requires the OS to allocate memory space for mailboxes for all processes within its own domain, it at the same time puts a system-wide limit on the number of messages awaiting delivery at any given instant. The user processes, however, can access the mailbox only with the help of respective system calls that the operating system should provide. In addition, the operating system should have extra support for maintenance of mailboxes, such as, *create_mailbox* and *delete_mailbox*. Such mailboxes can be viewed as being owned by the creating process, in which case they terminate with the process, or they can be viewed as being owned by the operating system, in which case an explicit command, such as, *delete_mailbox* is required to destroy the mailbox.

The **distinct advantage** of using *indirect naming* (*addressing*) in message communication is that it makes the horizon totally open by decoupling the sender and receiver, allowing greater flexibility

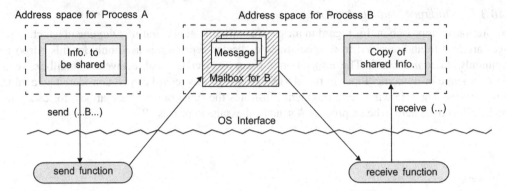

FIGURE 4.25   A schematic block diagram of message-passing mechanism using mailboxes.

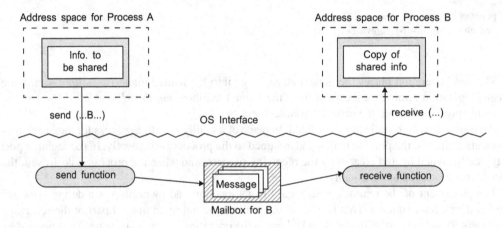

FIGURE 4.26   A schematic block diagram of message-passing mechanism using mailboxes placed in operating system space.

in the use of messages. It provides a relationship that can be *one-to-one*, *one-to-many*, or *many-to-one*, as well as *many-to-many* mappings between sending and receiving processes.

A *one-to-one mapping* is typically defined **statically** and permanently by creating a dedicated specific mailbox for the exclusive use of only two processes. This essentially establishes a private communication channel between them that insulates all their interactions from other erroneous interferences. *One-to-many mapping,* on the other hand, is provided by a mailbox dedicated to a single sender but used by multiple receivers. It is useful for applications in which a message or information is to be broadcast to a set of processes. *Many-to-one mapping* is particularly important for server processes, and it may be implemented by providing a public mailbox with numerous senders (user processes) and a single receiver (server process). If the sender's identity for any reason is felt to be important, that could be provided within the body of the message itself. In the case of many senders, the association of a sender to a mailbox may occur **dynamically**. Primitives, such as, *connect* and *disconnect*, may be used for this purpose. Modern systems thus favor the implementation of mailboxes in the domain of operating system, since it is a more versatile approach.

4.18.3.2   Copying

The exchange of messages between two processes simply means to transfer the contents of the message from the sender's address space to receiver's address space. This can be accomplished in several ways, such as by either *copying* the entire message directly into the receiver's address space or by simply *passing a pointer* to the message between two related process. In essence, message passing can be carried out *by value* or *by reference*. In distributed systems with no common memory, copying cannot be avoided. However, in centralized system, the trade-off is between safety versus efficiency.

Copying of an entire message from a sender's space to a receiver's space in message transmission exhibits several advantages. This approach keeps the two processes decoupled from each other, yet an imprint of the sender's data is made available to the receiver. The original with the sender remains unaffected irrespective of any act be by the receiver on the data at its own end. Similarly, the receiver's data also remain totally protected from any sort of direct access by the sender. Consequently, any malfunction of either process is fully localized in the sense that it can corrupt only the local copy and not the other one. The availability of such multiple private copies of data is always beneficial from a certain standpoint and is a possible alternative to its counterpart that contains a single copy of carefully protected global data, as is found in a typical monitor approach.

The message copying approach, however, also suffers from several **drawbacks**. It consumes additional processor and memory cycles that summarily lead to usage of extra system time. This asynchronous message communication is a useful feature, but due to existing memory protection schemes, it may also require that each message first be copied from the sender's space to the operating system's space (to any buffer) and from there to the receiver process's space (as already mentioned in the mailbox); that is a double copying effort and also additional support of an extra dynamic memory pool which is required by OS to operate while delivering only a single message.

Use of Pointers: To get rid of the complexities arising out of copying, an alternative approach was devised in favor of using a pointer to pass it to the message between the sender and receiver processes. Although this provides a faster solution by way of avoiding the copying of message, but it enables the receiver to get entry into the sender's addressing space that may otherwise cause a threat to security. Moreover, as a single copy of message is accessed both by the sender and the receiver, an additional mechanism is then required to synchronize their access to the message, to signal the end of any receiver operation so that the sender may reclaim it for any modification, if required.

Copy-on-write : Besides these two approaches with their merits and drawbacks, that is, multiple copies of messages with copying and a single copy of the message without copying, an alternative viable hybrid approach in the line of UNIX *copy-on-write* facility ultimately came out that was eventually taken by the Mach operating system. With *copy-on-write*, sender and receiver copies of the exchanged message are logically distinct. This allows each process to operate on the contents of the message freely with no concern for interference. However, the OS attempts to optimize performance by initially sharing a single physical copy of the message that is mapped into the address spaces of both sender and receiver. As long as both processes only read the message, a single physical copy is enough to serve the purpose. However, when either process attempts to modify the physically shared message space, the operating system intervenes and creates a separate physical copy of the message. The address-map tables are accordingly re-mapped, and each process continues with its own separate physical copy of the message. Thus, the *copy-on-write* scheme supports logical decoupling and at the same time eliminates the copying overhead in systems where the ratio of reads to writes is high.

4.18.3.3 Queuing Discipline

The simplest discipline in the arrangement of messages is queuing is normally first-in-first-out, but this may not be adequate in some situations when some messages are more urgent than others. An alternative is to allow determination of message priority on the basis of message type or account number (designation) of the sender. The other alternative when selecting a particular message from the queue is decided based on the priority given along with the message in the priority field, which is a part of control information. Another alternative is to allow the receiver to inspect the message queue and select which message to receive next.

4.18.3.4   Message Length

To decide the length of the message is a major issue in message design, and that too whether the message would be of *fixed* or *variable length*. The trade-off is one of overhead versus flexibility, and this is particularly applicable when messages are transmitted by way of copying and buffering.

Messages of fixed length are usually advantageous because the related system buffers would then also be of fixed size, which in turn makes the allocation quite simple and efficient, and the communication also would be comparatively easy in terms of timing and synchronization. But, in reality, messages are mostly of variable sizes. However, short messages with a fixed-size buffer often waste specified buffer space. Long messages with a fixed-size buffer must be properly split up to fit into the smaller buffer and then must be sent in installments, but that often causes additional overhead and also results in sequencing (ordering) problems at the receiving end.

An effective alternative may be to dynamically create buffers of variable size every time to fit the size of each instantaneous individual message. But such frequent dynamic allocation of variable-size chunks of memory at different times is not only costly in terms of CPU time usage, the constant creation of this dynamic memory pool carried out by the memory management of OS may, in turn, lead to critical problems of memory fragmentation that again require related added overhead to resolve. Fragmentation issues will be discussed later in the chapter in "Memory Management".

However, the message length issue is not so very important in those systems in which message passing is carried out via *pointers*, where a single parameter, like *size-of-window*, may be needed to include in the message itself so as to provide a different window size for each individual message transmission.

4.18.4   Message Exchange: Synchronous versus Asynchronous

Exchanges of messages between a sender and a receiver are accomplished by the *send* and *receive* operations, which use two general options:

1. The *send* operation may use synchronous and asynchronous semantics.
2. The *receive* operation may use blocking or non-blocking semantics.

When the message exchange is *synchronous*, both the sender and the receiver must arrive together to complete the transfer. In *synchronous systems*, the synchronous *send* operation incorporates a built-in synchronization strategy which blocks (suspends) the sending process until the message is successfully received by the receiving process. In fact, when a sender wants to send a message for which no outstanding *receive* is issued, the sender must be blocked until a willing receiver accepts the message. In other words, the *send* call synchronizes its own operation with the receipt of the message.

The synchronous *send–receive* mechanism has many **advantages**. First of all, it has comparatively lower overhead and easier to implement. Second, the sender knows that its message has been actually received, and there is no possibility of any damage once the *send* statement crosses over and the *send* operation is completed. Last but not least, if the sender attempts to transmit a message to a nonexistent process, an error is then returned to the sender so that it can synchronize with the occurrence of the error condition and take appropriate action. However, one of the serious drawbacks of this approach is its forcible implement of synchronous operation of senders and receivers, which may not be desirable in many situations, as exemplified by the public server processes in which the receiver and the sender processes usually run at different times.

With **asynchronous** message exchange, the asynchronous *send* operation delivers the message to the receiver's mailbox with the help of the operating system and buffers outstanding messages, then allows the sending process to continue operation without waiting, regardless of any activity of the receiver with the message (the mailbox may, however, be located within the domain of receiver's process or in the address space of operating system, as already discussed). The sending process here need not be suspended, and the *send* operation is not at all concerned with *when* the receiver actually receives the message. In fact, the sender will not even know whether the receiver retrieves the message from its mailbox at all.

The distinct **advantage** of an asynchronous *send* operation, which behaves like a "set and forget" mode of operation, substantially increases the desired degree of concurrency in the system. All the messages being sent to a particular receiver are queued by the system without affecting the sender, which also allows other senders to create new messages, if required.

Although the asynchronous *send* operation is a useful feature, its **drawbacks** may cause several adverse situations to happen. For example, if a sender transmits a message to a nonexistent process, it is not then possible for the OS to identify the specific mailbox in which to buffer the message. But the sender is completely unaware of this situation and continues after "transmitting" the message, and, as usual, does not expect a return value. The fate of this message is then simply unpredictable. Since there is no blocking to discipline the process, these types of messages keep consuming system resources, including processor time and buffer space, to the detriment of other processes and also the operating system. Moreover, as there is no mechanism that causes an alert, such as UNIX signals, there is no way for the OS to tell the sending process about the status of its operation. Therefore, additional systems are required that will block an asynchronous *send* operation in this situation until the message is actually placed in the receiver's mailbox. But there exists no such implied synchronization between the sending and receiving process, since this fundamentally opposes the philosophy behind the asynchronous *send* operation: that the sender process would not be suspended, and the receiver may retrieve the mailbox at any arbitrary time after the message has been delivered. Therefore, the non-blocking *send* places the burden entirely on the programmer to ascertain that a message has actually been received. Hence, the processes must employ "reply messages" to acknowledge the receipt of an actual message. We will discuss next an appropriate mechanism so that this approach can be properly accomplished.

Another situation may occur that sometimes becomes critical due to the inherent drawback of the asynchronous *send* operation. When a sending process starts producing messages uncontrollably that quickly exhaust the system's buffering capacity, it then creates blockage of all further message communication between other processes. One way to solve this problem may be to impose a certain limit on the extent of buffering for each sender–receiver pair or on a mailbox basis. However, in either case, this uncommon situation due to buffering of outstanding messages causes to incur additional system overhead.

Another common problem that frequently happens related to both of these implementations is starvation (indefinite postponement). This usually happens when a message is sent to a definite destination but never received. Out of many reasons, this may be due to crashing of the receiver or a fault in the communication line, or it may be that a receiver is waiting for a message which is never created. Whatever it may be, ultimately this failure to complete a transaction within a finite time is not at all desirable, especially in an unbuffered (synchronous) message system, because that may automatically block the unmatched party. To address this problem, two common forms of *receive* primitive are used: a *non-blocking* (wait less) version and a *blocking* (timed-wait) implementation.

The **blocking** form of the *receive* primitive is a blocking *receive* operation that inspects the designated mailbox. When a process (receiver) calls *receive*, if there is no message in the mailbox, the process is suspended until a message is placed in the mailbox. Thus, when the mailbox is empty, the blocking *receive* operation synchronizes the receiver's operation with that of the sending process. But if the mailbox contains one or more messages, the calling process is not suspended, and the *receive* operation immediately returns control to the calling process with a message. Note that the *blocking receive* operation is exactly analogous to a resource request in the sense that it causes the calling process to suspend until the resource, that is, an incoming message, is available.

The ***non-blocking*** form of the *receive* primitive is a non-blocking *receive* operation that inspects the designated mailbox and then returns control to the calling process immediately (with no waiting and without suspending) either with a message, if there is one in the mailbox, exactly in the same manner as in the case of blocking *receive*, or with an indicator that no message is available. As the blocking and non-blocking functions of *receive* are sometimes complementary, both these versions of *receive* are often supported in some systems.

In short, both sender and receiver together can give rise to four different types of combinations, three of which are common, although any particular system is found to even have one or two such combinations implemented.

- *Synchronous (blocking) send, blocking receive*: Both the sender and receiver are blocked until the message is delivered; this is sometimes referred to as *rendezvous* (a meeting by appointment). This combination is particularly useful when tight synchronization is required between processes.
- *Asynchronous (non-blocking) send, blocking receive*: Although the sender here may be allowed to continue on, the receiver is blocked until the requested message arrives. This is probably the most useful combination. It allows a process to send one or more messages quickly to several destinations as and when required. A process that must receive a message before it can proceed to do other useful work needs to be blocked until such a message arrives. A common example in this case is a server process that exists to provide a service or resource to other client processes which are to be blocked before the request of a service or the resource is granted by the server. Meanwhile, the server continues with its own work with other processes.
- *Asynchronous (non-blocking) send, non-blocking receive*: Neither the sender nor the receiver is required to wait.

4.18.4.1 Send–Receive Operation: A Modified Approach

A more appropriate but slightly complex approach to negotiate the problem of indefinite postponement (starvation, as already mentioned) is to incorporate a facility for setting a time limit during which a particular message exchange must be completed. Although this time limit is required to be included in both *send* and *receive* operations, but inclusion of it only in a *receive* operation is enough to serve the purpose. The modified calling sequence of the *receive* operation with inclusion of this time limit would then be:

receive (mailbox1, message, time-limit)

where *time-limit* is the maximum allowable time, expressed in clock ticks or any standard unit of time, that the receiver can wait for the message. If none arrives, the OS would then return control to the receiver and provide it with an indicator, perhaps via a special system message, that the time limit has elapsed. The sender processes can also be modified in this scheme by using an interlock mechanism within itself that is of the form:

Sender:
         ....
         send (*mailbox1, message*)
         receive (*ack, time-limit*)
         ....

Receiver:

> ....
> **receive** (*mailbox1, message, time-limit*)
>   **if** message-received-in-time   **then**
>   **send** (*ack*)

The sender sends a message, and the receiver after receiving the message will *send* back a special acknowledgement message, *ack*, for which the sender waits. If the receiver for any reason does not receive the original message, the time limit eventually will expire, and the sender then regains control (from its timed-out *receive* operation), at which point it can take appropriate remedial action. The receiver process also cannot be held captive by a late message; it is signaled and informed about the fault as soon as its own *receive* times out.

4.18.5 Design Issues: Message-Passing Systems

Monitors and semaphores are basically designed for synchronization of concurrent processes in machines that share one memory; they are data-structure oriented. As the use of separate computers in networks of computers become more prevalent, the message-passing paradigm is found more fitting to this environment. The design issues of message-passing systems in implementing synchronization and communication between concurrent processes is, however, somewhat different from its counterpart, semaphores and monitors, and as such many critical problems need to be resolved, especially when the processes run on different machines connected by a network. When the processes run on multiprocessor system, the dimension of these problems may be again altogether different and even acute. However, many issues in this regard may arise, but we will consider here only the most common ones and their remedies at the time of designing a somewhat trusted message-passing system.

To ensure **reliability**, messages are to be delivered in an orderly way to processes running on different machines without any loss, which mostly happens due to the presence of the network. To safeguard against loss of messages, the sender and receiver can both agree that as soon as a message would be received, the receiver will at once send back a special message to the sender in the form of *acknowledgement*. If the sender has not received the acknowledgement within a specified time limit, it may retransmit the message or take any other appropriate remedial action.

There may be two different reasons for a mishap while passing messages. The first one is that the message may be lost due to a transmission error; hence, the receiver does not get it, and thus the question of sending an acknowledgement does not arise. The sender does not getting its acknowledgement and will then keep trying to retransmit the message in an appropriate format for a certain number of times, but in vain with no response. After that the system must declare that there is a line fault. The second reason may be that the message itself is correctly received, but the acknowledgement is lost. The sender will not be getting the acknowledgement within the specified time interval and hence starts re-transmitting the message. The receiver will get it twice at its own end. It is thus essential that the receiver somehow be able to distinguish the old original one already received from the new message received due to retransmission of the original. Usually, this problem is handled by putting consecutive sequence numbers in each original message. If the receiver sometimes gets a message bearing the same sequence number as the previous message, it knows that the message is a duplicate one and decides to ignore it.

The **identification** of processes involved in message passing is also an issue, and thus message systems also have to deal with how processes are to be named so that the process specified in a *send* and *receive* call is unambiguous. Different operating systems, however, use different naming formats, but often a naming scheme, such as, *process@machine* or *machine:process*, is used. But when a huge number of machines are connected over a network and there is no central authority that allocates machine name (identification), it may happen that two different units give their machine the same name. This problem of conflicting names can be considerably reduced by simply grouping machines into **domains**, and then the processes can be addressed as *process@machine.domain*. Under this scheme, the domain names must be unique.

Authenticity is another issue in the design of message-passing systems. It is realized by a technique by which the authentication of interacting processes involved in communication is verified. It is surprisingly difficult, particularly in the face of threats organized by malicious, active intruders, and hence requires complex mechanisms, usually based on *cryptography*, by which a message can be encrypted with a key known only to authorized users.

In the case of a *centralized system* in which the sender and receiver exist on the same machine, the design considerations may be altogether different. The fundamental question is whether it is judicious to use a message-passing system that employs a relatively slow operation of copying messages from one process to another than that of its counterpart, the comparatively fast semaphore or monitor, for the sake of realizing better performance. As a result, much work has been carried out to effectively improve message-passing systems, and as such many alternatives have been proposed. Among them, Cheriton (1984), for example, suggested limiting the size of the message so as to fit it in the machine's register and then perform message passing using these registers to make it much faster.

4.18.6 MESSAGES: FOR INTERPROCESS SYNCHRONIZATION AND COMMUNICATION

Message-passing systems, although realized by numerous operations and also different implementations of messages between senders and receivers, are still primarily considered a useful tool for both interprocess synchronization and communication. When message-passing is carried out between two processes with no data field (empty message), it is equivalent to *signaling*. A sender process, by sending a message, then essentially passes a *timing signal* to another process, the receiver. In terms of signaling, this has the same effect as one process (sender) executing a *signal* operation and the other process (receiver) executing a *wait* on the semaphore. In this analogy, the existence of the mailbox corresponds to the presence of a unique semaphore variable. As usually happens in semaphore systems, the process undergoing a *wait* (receiver) remains suspended until the semaphore is signaled (message sent to the mailbox) by some other process. Alternatively, if the semaphore is free (mailbox contains one or more message), the process will not *wait* and is allowed to proceed without being blocked.

This signaling power of a message-passing system can be used to enforce mutual exclusion following the logic of a similar solution using semaphore. We assume here the use of the *blocking receive* and *non-blocking send* primitives. This is depicted in Figure 4.27 in which the program segment contains the representative code of a set of concurrent user processes that access a shared resource protected by the mailbox, *mutex*, which can be used by all processes to send and receive. Following the logic of semaphore implementation, it is assumed that the mailbox is created empty: it initially contains no message. This is equivalent to the semaphore being initialized by the system to *busy*. To make a message available to the first requestor, the parent process uses a *send* to send a message to the mailbox before initiating any of the users to access the resource; otherwise the first user process will be blocked due to mailbox having no message (empty). Since this message attached to *send* in the parent process is used solely for signaling purposes, its data content is immaterial, and hence we assume that it is a *null* (empty) message. When the first process wishes to use the resource, it invokes the *receive* operation (*receive* operation in process *user* in Figure 4.27) on the *mutex* mailbox. This results in the removal of the initial *null* message from the mailbox and is delivered to the process via its *msg* parameter. Once the process acquires the message, it is free to continue, and it enters the critical section. If any other process executes a *receive* on the *mutex* during that time, it will be blocked because the mailbox is empty. When its critical section is completed, the owner of the message then places a message back in the mailbox *mutex* (*send* operation in the process *user* in Figure 4.27) and continues to execute its remaining processing.

Program / segment *message–mutex* ;

     ....

     ....

const

  null = ... ;   [empty message]

  n = ... ;   [number of processes]

type

  message = **record** ..... ;

process *user* (i : integer) ;

  var

    msg : *message* ;

  begin

      while *true* **do**

        begin

          receive(mutex , msg) ;

          < critical—section > ;

          send(mutex , msg) ;

            other–remaining–processing

        end [*while*]

  end ; [*user*]

        [*parent process*]

begin [*message–mutex*]

  create_mailbox(mutex) ;

  send(mutex , null) ;

  initiate *user(1) ; user(2) ; .... ; user(n)* ;

end ; [*message–mutex*]

FIGURE 4.27 An algorithm illustrating the Mutual exclusion of competing processes by using messages.

This approach is conceptually similar to semaphore implementation. It also shows that the empty message used here only for signaling is enough to fulfill the desired purpose for synchronization. Here, a single message is passed from process to process through the system as a token permit to access the shared resource. The *receive* operation (as shown in process *user* in Figure 4.27) should be an atomic action (indivisible) in the sense while delivering the message, if there is any, to only one caller (blocked process) when invoked concurrently by several users. The process after receiving the message (as shown in process *user* in Figure. 4.27) would then be able to proceed accordingly. The other remaining waiting processes, if any, would remain blocked as usual and get their turns one at a time when the message is returned by processes (*send* operation in process *user* in Figure 4.27) while coming out of the critical section. However, if the mailbox (*mutex*) is found empty at any instant, all processes will then be automatically blocked. These assumptions hold true for virtually all message-passing facilities. The real strength of message-passing systems is, however, fully extracted when a message contains actual data and transfers them at the same time to the desired destination, thereby accomplishing the ultimate purpose of achieving both interprocess synchronization and communication within a single action.

This discussion has convincingly established the fact that messages should not be considered a weaker mechanism than semaphores. It appears from Figure 4.27 that a message mechanism may be used to realize a binary semaphore. General semaphores can similarly be implemented by simulating messages by increasing the number of token messages in the system to match the initial value of an equivalent general semaphore. For example, if there are eight identical tape drives available in a system that are to be allocated by means of messages, then eight tokens need to be initially created by sending *null* messages to the appropriate mailbox.

Message passing, however, unlike other strong contenders, is a robust and versatile mechanism for the enforcement of mutual exclusion and also provides an effective means of interprocess communication. That is why messages in different forms with numerous implementation provisions and add-on facilities are often found in use in both types of distributed operating systems, especially network operating systems.

4.18.6.1   Case Study: Producer/Consumer Problem with Bounded Buffer

Since messages can be used to emulate semaphore, it can then be possible to devise a solution to the bounded-buffer producer/consumer problem by using an algorithmic structure similar to the approach that has been used to obtain the solution of this problem using semaphores. As the buffer is bounded, the capacity of the buffer is limited by the total number of messages that are made initially available to both producers and consumers. This capacity of the buffer, in fact, determines the maximum number of items that the producer can generate at a stretch before the first item is consumed by the consumer. It is assumed here that each message as usual has a data field holding a single data item used as a data buffer. Two mailboxes, *canproduce* and *canconsume*, are taken for the purpose of message exchanges between producers and consumers.

Each producer process acquires a message from the *canproduce* mailbox; it then fills the data field of the message with the produced item and finally sends the message to the *canconsume* mailbox for the consumer to use. In this way, the number of remaining empty messages in the *canproduce* mailbox shrinks with each production. However, as long as there exists at least one empty message in the *canproduce* mailbox, the producer is allowed to continue production. The consumer behaves in the same way. It removes a message from the *canconsume* mailbox, consumes the data item therein, and then returns the empty message to the *canproduce* mailbox for the producer to work. This consumption actually increases the number of remaining empty messages in the *canproduce* mailbox. However, the producer can run only when there are empty messages, at least one message in the *canproduce* mailbox, otherwise producers are blocked and kept waiting (sleep) until a *receive* operation is carried out by the consumer to subsequently consume a message and thereafter sends an empty message to the *canproduce* mailbox for the producer to continue (wakeup). Similarly, the consumers can only proceed when there is least one item in the *canconsume* mailbox being sent by the producer that is not yet consumed; otherwise the consumers are blocked (sleep) and kept waiting until a message is generated by the producer and sent to the *canconsume* mailbox for the consumer to work on (wakeup).

This solution is quite flexible and also allows multiple producers and consumers to run concurrently as long as all have access to both mailboxes. Other than the names of the two mailboxes, all variables as used here are local. Elimination of the global buffer is the beauty of this approach that, in particular, fits both centralized and distributed processing environments.

Moreover, this approach elegantly handles the aspect of global data manipulation, a major issue in distributed systems, in the situation when all producer processes and the associated *canproduce* mailbox reside at one site and all the consumer processes and the associated *canconsume* mailbox at another. In addition, it finds no difficulty even if both sites are run under different operating systems or if the producer–consumer processes are independently developed in different programming languages under dissimilar programming environments, provided both mailboxes are globally accessible and both operating systems at their own ends can provide a compatible form of *send–receive* operation support.

For more details and a algorithm about this topic, see the Support Material at www.routledge.com/9781032467238.

4.18.7 MESSAGE USAGE: A POSSIBILITY IN INTERRUPT SIGNALING

It is known that when an interrupt occurs, the interrupt signal causes switching of a process from one to another; a signal in interprocess synchronization does the same. Moreover, interrupts are asynchronous that intimate (signal) the arrival of certain external events, and this is conceptually identical when a process in interprocess synchronization at any instant similarly signals the occurrence of a certain event, such as an attempt to use a resource or the situation when the buffer is full. That is why there exists a strong resemblance between a signal when an interrupt occurs and a signal at the time of interprocess synchronization to tackle concurrent processes. Now, we know that when message passing is carried out between two processes with no data field, this empty message is equivalent to a signal. As the message possesses signaling power, an important possibility that can now be explored is whether this ability of messages could be exploited to realize a single uniform tool that would be usable for signaling interrupts as well as handling all aspects of interprocess synchronization and communication. If it is possible, this, in turn, will then definitely reduce the workload of system developers, especially in the area of program development and its maintenance. However, lots of arguments and counter arguments (against and in favor of unification) with merits and drawbacks in favor of and against this proposal have been presented by the contending parties. But finally, it is left up to designers to decide whether they will step forward towards further exploring this approach to incorporate an innovative concept in the design of operating systems. It is also kept open to let the readers and the designers of the operating systems of tomorrow form their own views, draw their own conclusions without being prejudiced, and make informed judgments.

A brief discussion of this approach is given on the Support Material at www.routledge.com/9781032467238.

4.18.8 EQUIVALENCE OF PRIMITIVES

There are many popular alternatives for synchronizing concurrent processes: Semaphores capture the essence of process synchronization. At the most abstract level, the monitor mechanism is also considered for sharing and synchronization. Some operating systems implement event counters for this purpose where events are used as abstractions of semaphore operations, particularly to address the coordinated applications (to trigger actions by other processes) of semaphores (as opposed to critical section problems). Both semaphores and events can be used to synchronize the operation of two processes but not to convey any information between them. Event counts do not rely on shared memory, unlike other synchronization mechanisms. Campbell and Habermann (1974) introduced a method called **path expressions**. Reed and Kanodia (1979) described a different interprocess synchronization method called **sequencers**. Atkinson and Hewitt introduced a different one called **serializers**. Message passing addresses a generalized interprocess communication mechanism that implements information transmission in conjunction with synchronization. There is also a list of other methods for this purpose that is certainly pretty long, with new ones being dreamed up all the time. We are not willing at this moment to delve into any such discussions or descriptions for all of them.

Fortunately, many of the proposed schemes are, by and large, similar to others, and in fact, any of the synchronization primitives can basically be built up from any of the others. This is a prevailing truth both philosophically (all synchronization systems are truly different ways of viewing the same essential ideas) as well as practically (a user can build a system intuitive to them if the system provides another). However, all modern operating systems provide semaphores, messages, or (more likely) at least one of the synchronization mechanisms already described or even a combination of those approaches.

Since, semaphores, monitors, and messages are very popular and common mechanisms to negotiate interprocess synchronization and communication problems, we will describe here in brief their essential equivalence in order to obtain a clear understanding of the working of these primitives and how they can be implemented. Although the other primitives, as already mentioned, are equally important, we restrict ourselves from entering the domain of those primitives due to the shortage of available space and for being beyond the scope of this text.

4.18.8.1 Implementation of Monitors and Messages Using Semaphores

Let us consider that the system provides semaphores as a basic tool that can be used to build monitors and messages. Since the monitor is a programming-language construct, the compiler designer can easily implement the monitor as a language construct with the help of the existing semaphore operation in the following way: The compiler developer will first construct a collection of runtime procedures for managing monitors and put them in the system library. Whenever the compiler generates code involving monitors, necessary calls are made to the respective runtime procedure that must be included as a call statement in the object code of the user program in order to perform the necessary monitor functions. Accessing and managing each such runtime procedure can be accomplished with the available semaphore support.

Each monitor is associated with a binary semaphore, *mutex*, which is initialized to 1 to control entry to the monitor. An additional semaphore is also employed for each condition variable to work as needed by the monitor operation. This semaphore is initialized to 0. When a process enters a monitor, the compiler generates a call to a runtime procedure, such as *enter_monitor*, which actually does a *down* (*wait*) on the *mutex* associated with the monitor being entered. The calling process now enters the monitor, thereby also preventing the entry of the other processes. If the monitor is currently in use, the calling process will be blocked. When a process leaves a monitor, the compiler generates another call to a runtime procedure, such as, *leave_monitor* which actually does an *up* (*signal*) on the *mutex* associated with the monitor. It is to be remembered that *signal* must always be carried out as the last operation before leaving a monitor. The condition variables are also operated in a similar way. For example, a *wait* operation on a condition variable, *c*, is carried out as a sequence of two semaphore operations. First an *up* operation on binary semaphore *mutex* allows a process to enter the monitor and second operates a *down* on *c* to block on the condition variable.

Let us now examine how a message-passing mechanism can be implemented using the existing semaphore support. Here, each *sender* and *receiver* process is associated with one semaphore which controls the operation of the process. This semaphore is initially set to 0 to block the process. The needed mailboxes are implemented by creating a shared buffer area. Each such mailbox contains an array of message slots organized in the form of a linked list, and the messages are delivered in FIFO order. This shared buffer as a whole is entirely protected by a binary semaphore, *mutex*, to ensure that only one process can be inside the shared data structure at any instant.

For the management of mailboxes, each mailbox contains two integer variables, indicating how many message slots are full and how many are empty. In addition, each mailbox also contains the starting address of two queues: one queue contains only the process numbers of the processes that are unable to send to the mailbox, and the other queue contains only the process numbers of those processes that are unable to receive from the mailbox. The process numbers of the waiting processes are required to execute an *up* operation on the respective semaphore to activate the corresponding process.

Send and *receive* operation is carried out in the usual manner on a mailbox with at least one empty slot or one slot with a message, respectively, to insert or remove a message, and then it updates the respective counter and adjusts the links and finally exits in the usual way. The *mutex* semaphore is to be used at the beginning (*down/wait*) and end (*up/signal*) of the critical section so as to ensure mutual exclusion in terms of use of counters and pointers of the linked list by only one process at a time.

When a *send* is done, if there exists an empty slot in the destination mailbox, the message is normally put there, and the sender then checks the receiving queue of that mailbox to see if there is any waiting process. If found, the first one is removed from the queue, and the sender does an *up* on its semaphore and then comes out of the critical region. The newly activated receiver now starts and continues. If there is none, the sender comes out, doing an *up* as usual to allow the other deserving process to start.

When a *send* fails to complete due to a mailbox being full, the sender first queues itself on the destination mailbox, then does an *up* on *mutex* and a *down* on its own semaphore. Later, when a receiver removes a message from the full mailbox, an empty slot will be formed, and the receiver will then notice that someone is queued attempting to send to that mailbox; one of the sender in the waiting queue will then be activated (*wake-up*).

Similarly, when a *receive* is attempted on an empty mailbox, the process trying to receive a message fails to complete and hence queues itself in the receive queue of the relevant mailbox, then does an *up* on *mutex* and a *down* on its own semaphore. Later, when a sender, after sending a message, observes that someone is queued attempting to receive from that mailbox, one of the receivers in the waiting queue will be activated. The awakened receiver (process) will then immediately do a *down* on *mutex* and then continue with its own work.

This representative example shows that a user can build a system primitive intuitive to them if the system provides another. It can similarly be shown that semaphores and messages can be equally implemented using monitors, and likewise, semaphores and monitors can also be implemented using messages. We will not proceed to any further discussion of these two issues due to space limitations. However, interested readers, for the sake of their own information, can consult the book written by Tanenbaum on this subject.

4.18.9 Implementation: Interprocess Communication and Synchronization

4.18.9.1 IBM MVS

When the MVS operating system runs on a multiprocessor computer system with multiple processors, each of which while executing a process may cause interprocess communications to happen between these processes running on different processors, thereby making the system more complicated, and hence, the complexity of the operating system is greatly increased when compared to an usual single-processor machine. However, MVS provides two facilities for enforcing mutual exclusion with respect to the use of resources: **enqueing** and **locking**. Enqueing is concerned with *user-controlled resources*, such as files, whereas locking is concerned with MVS *system resources*, such as shared memory.

For more details and a figure on this topic, see the Support Material at www.routledge.com/9781032467238.

4.18.9.2 Windows System

The features in relation to message passing in Windows are drawn from and thus bear a close resemblance to the corresponding features of the Mach distributed operating system. Windows provides a local procedure call (LPC) facility for message passing between processes located in the same computer system. However, it provides a remote procedure call facility used for message passing in a distributed environment. In fact, it uses similar arrangements involving client and server stubs for any type of environment whether using LPC or RPC. Generally, LPC is used by a process to communicate with an environment subsystem. At present, we confine ourselves only to the features of the message-passing system of Windows used in an environment that employs LPC. The discussions with regard to message passing using RPC are temporarily postponed at this moment and will be explained later in relation to distributed operating systems (Chapter 9).

Message passing with LPC uses a similar plan of action as in a client–server model. LPC provides three types of message passing that suit the passing of small messages, large messages, and special messages used by the Win 32 GUI. The first two types of LPC use port objects to implement message passing. Each port object behaves like a mailbox. It contains a set of messages in a data structure called a message queue (already discussed in the previous section). To set up communication with clients, a server creates a port and connects it to port object. The name of the port is then announced within the system. A process that intends to communicate with a server sends a connection request to the port and becomes its client. While sending a message, a client can indicate whether it expects a reply. When the server receives the request, it returns a port handle to the client. In this way, the server can communicate with many clients over the same port.

For small messages, the message queue in the port object contains the text of the message. The length of each such message can be up to 304 bytes. As already mentioned (in "Copying"), such messages get copied twice during message passing to keep the system flexible and at the same time reliable. When a process sends a message, it is copied into the message queue of the port. From there, it is copied into the address space of the receiver. The length of the message is, however, kept limited to only 304 bytes in order to mainly control the overhead of message passing within an affordable limit, both in terms of space and time.

The second method of message passing is used for large messages. In order to avoid the overhead of copying a message twice, a message is not copied in the message queue of the port. Instead, the message is directly put into a section object. The section object is mapped in both the address spaces of the client and the server processes. When the client intends to send a message, it puts the text of the message in the section object and sends a message to the port (to signal the port) indicating that it has put a message in the section object. The server itself then views the message in the section object. In this way, the use of the section object helps to avoid the copying of the message into the server's address space.

The third type of message passing using LPC is comparatively faster and hence is called *quick* LPC. Here again, the actual message is passed in a section object that is mapped in both the address spaces of the client and the server processes. Quick LPC uses two interesting features that are not present in the other types of LPC. Here, the server creates a thread for every client. Each thread is totally dedicated to requests made by the respective client. The second feature is the use of event-pair objects to synchronize the client and server threads. Each event-pair object consists of two event objects: the server thread always waits on one event object, and the client thread waits on the other one. The message-passing mechanism proceeds as follows: The client thread submits a message in the section object; it then itself waits on its own respective event object and signals the corresponding event object of the pair on which the server thread is waiting. The server thread similarly waits on one event object and signals the corresponding event object. To facilitate error-free message passing, the kernel provides a function that ensures atomicity while signaling on one event object of the pair and waiting on the other event object of the same pair.

4.18.9.3 UNIX System

Numerous mechanisms are provided by UNIX in handling interprocess communication and synchronization problems. Some of the most important are:

- Semaphores
- Signals
- Messages
- Pipes
- Sockets
- Shared memory

While semaphores and signals are used only to realize synchronization between processes, the others, such as messages, pipes, sockets, and shared memory, provide an effective means of communicating data across processes (interprocess communication) in conjunction with synchronization.

For more details about this topic, with a description of each of the tools and supporting figures, see the Support Material at www.routledge.com/9781032467238.

4.19   DEADLOCK AND STARVATION

Concurrent execution of cooperating or competing processes in multitasking or multi–user environment always yield high overall resource utilization. Moreover, when these concurrent processes indulge parallel operations of many input/output devices, it further give rise to significant improvement in system performance. That is why, while all–out attempts have been thus made to implement such concurrency, it on the other hand, plague all these efforts, thereby creating a fertile ground for two major problems; namely, *deadlock* and *starvation*, which are mostly fatal in detrimental to overall system performance.

Deadlock is defined as the *permanent blocking* of a set of processes that either compete for system resources or cooperate with each other via communication. A deadlock, or the more striking name **"deadly embrace"**, as described by Dijkstra (1968), is actually a situation when a group of processes are permanently blocked as a result of each process having acquired at least one resource while making a request on another. This request can never be satisfied because the requested resource is being held by another process that is blocked, waiting for the resource that the first process is holding, thus making it impossible for any of the processes to proceed. Unlike other problems in the management of concurrent processes, there is no efficient solution considered a general one. Figure 4.28 illustrates a situation of deadlock among three processes on three resources that might put the system in the state as shown while being executed in the following manner:

Process 1	**Process 2**	**Process 3**
-----------------------	-----------------------	-----------------------
………..	………..	………..
request (resource 1) ;	request (resource 2) ;	request (resource 3) ;
/* Holding res. 1 */	/* Holding res. 2 */	/* Holding res. 3 */
………..	………..	………..
request (resource 2) ;	request (resource 3) ;	request (resource 1) ;

FIGURE 4.28   A schematic view of a situation of three deadlocked processes with three available resources.

Process 1 acquires *resource 1* and is requesting *resource 2*; Process 2 is holding *resource 2* and is requesting *resource 3*; Process 3 acquires *resource 3* and is requesting *resource 1*. None of the processes can proceed because all are waiting for release of a resource held by another process. As a result, the three processes are deadlocked; none of the processes can complete its execution and release the resource that it owns, nor they can be awakened, even though other unaffected processes in the system might continue. The number of processes and the number and kind of resources possessed and requested in a deadlocked situation are not important.

This example illustrates the general characteristics of deadlock. If these three processes can run serially (batch-wise) in any arbitrary order, they would then merrily complete their run without any deadlock. Deadlock thus results primarily due to concurrent execution of processes with uncontrolled granting of system resources (physical devices) to requesting processes. However, deadlocks can also occur as a result of competition over any kind of shared software resources, such as files, global data, and buffer pools. In a database system, for example, a program may have to normally lock several records it is using to avoid a race condition. If process *X* locks record *R1* and process *Y* locks record *R2*, and then each process tries to lock the other one's record in order to gain access to it, deadlock is inevitable. Similarly, deadlocks can also result from execution of nested monitor calls. All these things together imply that deadlocks can occur on hardware resources as well as also on software resources.

Even a single process can sometimes enter a deadlock situation. Consider a situation when a process issues an I/O command and is suspended awaiting its completion (result) and then is swapped out for some reason prior to the beginning of the I/O operation. The process is blocked waiting on the I/O event, and the I/O operation is blocked waiting for the process to be swapped in. The process thus goes into a deadlock. One possible way to avoid this deadlock is that the user memory involved in the I/O operation must be locked in main memory immediately before the I/O request is issued, even though the I/O operation may not be executed at that very moment but is placed in a queue for some time until the requested device is available.

Deadlock is actually a global condition rather than a local one. If a program is analyzed whose process involves a deadlock, no discernible error as such can be noticed. The problem thus lies not in any single process but in the collective action of the group of processes. An individual program thus generally cannot detect a deadlock, since it becomes blocked and unable to use the processor to do any work. Deadlock detection must be thus handled by the operating system.

4.19.1   RESOURCES: DIFFERENT TYPES

Granting exclusive accesses to either hardware objects, such as devices and memory pages, or to software objects, such as databases, files, global data, and buffer pools, are the main reasons for deadlocks to occur. These objects are commonly referred to as **resources**. A computer system is normally equipped with many different types of resources, but sets of a particular type of identical resource, such as three disk drives, is referred to as a **resource class**. Similarly, all identical tape drives available in a computer system are therefore considered in the same class. However, resources in general attached to a computer system whose allocation may cause deadlock to occur can be broadly classified into two distinct classes: **reusable** and **consumable** resources. Both these classes of resources are again operationally either **preemptible** or **nonpreemptible**.

A resource is said to be preemptable if it can be taken away from the process that owns it without injuring the process or the resource. A disk drive is a preemptable resource. A nonpreemptible resource is one that cannot be taken away from the current owner without causing ill effects or even causing the computation to fail. A printer is a nonpreemptible resource, since taking the printer away from a process and giving it to another process will result in interspersing the output. Similarly, the process block created in the kernel for an existing process is neither shared nor preempted.

Reusable resources: A *serially reusable resource*, R_k, for deadlock analysis has either one or a finite number of identical units and is characterized as one that can be safely used by only one process at a time. Such a resource is normally granted to a requesting process whenever available and is not depleted by that use. When this resource is released later by its temporary owner, it can be allocated to another requestor, if there is any. Examples of reusable resources include shared hardware and software resources, such as processors, main memory, secondary memory, I/O devices, I/O channels, files, databases, global data structures, and semaphores. A computer system may include reusable resources of different types, and each type may have a single or finite multiple number as well as a single type of resource having one or a finite multiple number. However, while systems containing only serially reusable resources and when they are already granted to and also they are offered to comply the requests issued by the deserving processes; all these together then constitute a family of resource–process graph models (discussed in a later section, "Deadlock Modeling: Graphical Representation") that can be used to define and handle deadlocks.

Generally, all the reusable resources are granted to the processes on their specific requests for a finite time and are relinquished unless deadlocked. All other issues in relation to holding of resources for an unlimited period other than the deadlock condition, such as hanging of the system due to hardware/software failure or program execution in infinite loops due to malfunctioning of a program, are assumed here to be properly taken care of by the operating system, and hence are kept set aside in this context for the consideration of only those issues that are solely related to deadlocks.

Consumable resources: These resources, by definition, significantly differ from serially reusable resources in that a process may request and acquire units of consumable resources but will never release them. Conversely, a process can release units of consumable resources without ever acquiring them. More specifically, a *consumable resource* is characterized as one that can be created (produced) and destroyed (consumed) by active processes. Common examples of consumable resources are messages, signals, interrupts, and contents of I/O buffers. In fact, there is as such no limit on the number of such resources of a particular type in a system, and that can even vary with time. For example, an unblocked producing process may create any number of such resources, as happens in the producer/consumer problem with an unbounded buffer. When such a resource is acquired by an active process, the resource ceases to exist. Since such resources may have an unbounded number of units, and moreover, the allocated units are not released, the model for analyzing consumable resources significantly differs from that of serially reusable resources. These consumable resources, however, can sometimes also cause deadlocks to occur.

For more details and figures about this topic, see the Support Material at www.routledge.com/ 9781032467238.

4.19.2 GENERAL RESOURCE SYSTEMS

Since systems, in general, consist of a combination of both reusable and consumable resources, deadlock handling mechanisms should then be derived taking both these types of resources into account. The formal definition of a general resource graph for deadlock handling, however, does not consider the resources specifically as the union of reusable and consumable types. Hence, the general resource graph would then be redefined and would include a combination of the different conditions that are separately applicable to both reusable resources and consumable resources. The deadlock handling mechanism would then conduct analysis by using reusable resource graph reductions on all reusable resources and consumable resource graph reductions on all consumable resources. Thus, in the quest for a deadlock-free state, the reusable resources must be completely isolated by reductions. However, in the case of a consumable resource graph, there must be at least a specific sequence in which each process can be shown not to be deadlocked on any consumable resource.

4.19.3 DEADLOCKS AND RESOURCES

Deadlocks, in general, occur with nonpreemptible resources. For example, if the use of a file is preempted, the process cannot assume that it can get the file to use again with the same state as before. The process would then be injured and most likely should just quit. Even worse, the process may have left the file in an inconsistent state. For example, the file may represent a load image that the preempted process was in the middle of linking. Some links are completed, and others are not. In this case, preemption injures the resource, and it might never again be usable. The incomplete linked image cannot be loaded, nor can the linking be finished. However, preemptable resources involved in potential deadlocks can normally be resolved by simply reallocating such resources from one process to another. Our focus in relation to deadlock issues is thus primarily concerned with nonpreemptible resources.

While requesting a resource, different systems, however, have different forms. In fact, the exact nature of requesting a resource is mostly system dependent, and it is mainly carried out by using system calls. When a process requests a resource, if it is available, it is then granted and allocated; the resource is afterwards used by the process, and finally, the resource is released. But if the resource is not available, it is assumed that the requesting process is then simply put to sleep.

For more details about this topic, see the Support Material at www.routledge.com/9781032467238.

4.19.4 THE CONDITIONS FOR DEADLOCKS

Coffman et al. (1971) showed that four conditions must be present for a deadlock to occur. However, the first three conditions are, in fact, related to policy decisions, but the fourth condition is fundamentally different from the other three. In truth, the fourth condition causes a situation that might occur depending on the sequencing of requests and releases of resources by the involved processes.

1. *Mutual exclusion condition*: Each resource is either currently assigned to exactly one process only or is available.
2. *Hold-and-wait condition*: Process currently holding allocated resources granted earlier can request new resources and await assignments of those.
3. *No preemption condition*: Resources previously granted cannot be forcibly taken away from a process holding it. They must be released by the respective process that holds them.
4. *Circular wait condition*: There must exist a close chain of two or more processes, such that each process holds at least one resource requested by the next process in the chain.

All four conditions must be simultaneously present for a deadlock to occur. If any one of them is absent, no deadlock is possible. Thus, one way to negotiate deadlocks is to ensure that at every point in time, at least one of the four conditions responsible for the occurrence of deadlocks is to be prevented by design.

The first three conditions are merely policy decisions for error-free execution of concurrent processes to realize enhanced performance and hence cannot be compromised. On the other hand, these three conditions are the primarily ones that can invite a deadlock to exist. Although these three conditions are *necessary* conditions for deadlock to occur, deadlock may not exist with *only* these three conditions. The fourth condition, which is a consequence of the first three conditions that might occur depending on the sequencing of requests and releases of resources by the involved processes, is actually a *sufficient* condition for a deadlock to exist and hence is considered a definition of deadlock. This states that, given that the first three conditions exist, a sequence of events may happen in such a way that leads to an unresolvable circular–wait condition, resulting ultimately in a deadlock.

4.19.5 DEADLOCK MODELING: GRAPHICAL REPRESENTATION

The four conditions that are necessary and sufficient for a deadlock to occur can be graphically represented using directed graphs (Holt, 1972). Since deadlock is entangled with processes and allocated/requested resources, two kinds of nodes are used: processes, shown as squares, and resources, shown as circles. An arc (↑) from a resource node to a process node indicates that the resource is currently held by that process. In Figure 4.29(a), resource R1 is currently assigned to process P1. Conversely, an arc (↓) from a process to a resource means that the process is currently blocked waiting for that resource. In Figure 4.32(b), process P2 is waiting for resource R2. Figure 4.32(c) shows that a deadlock occurs. Process A is waiting for resource X, which is currently held by process B. Process B is not ready to release resource X because process B is waiting for resource Y, which is held by process A. Both processes keep waiting and will wait forever. The formation of a cycle with processes and resources in the graph shows that there is a deadlock involving the processes and resources present in the cycle. In this example, it is A → X → B → Y → A.

With many processes and resources attached to a system, a resource graph can then be created in the form of the representative resource graphs shown in Figure 4.29. This graph is simply a tool that enables one to foresee if a given resource request/release sequence leads to a deadlock. The system will then inspect step by step each and every occurrence of resource requests and releases, and after checking every step, the graph is to be re-examined to see whether it contains any cycles (circuits). If so, deadlock is inevitable, and the operating system could then simply suspend the requesting process without granting the request in order to prevent or even better to avoid the impending deadlock. But if the graph contains no cycles, there is no possibility of a deadlock. The resource graph can be generalized to include multiple resources of the same type, such as seven tape drives, five disk drives, and so on.

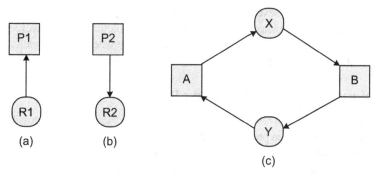

(a) Holding a resource.
(b) Requesting a resource.
(c) Deadlock occurs.

FIGURE 4.29   Graphical representation of resource allocation graphs in modeling deadlock.

In general, **four strategies** are employed for dealing with deadlocks.

1. Don't pay any attention to deadlock: simply ignore it altogether.
2. Deadlock detection and subsequent recovery.
3. Deadlock prevention by way of structurally abolishing one of the four conditions which are responsible for deadlock to happen, as already explained.
4. Dynamic avoidance by legitimate allocation of resources.

4.19.5.1   The Ostrich Approach

The simplest algorithm is the ostrich approach: put your head in the sand and assume there is no problem at all. Thus, rather than facing the problem, this approach is an attempt to evade the problem. As the number of users is increasing day by day, and as computer-related interactive activities are being more and more exposed, any sort of problem that may jeopardize the system cannot be ignored. But system engineers, in particular, though they are quite aware that this problem may crash the entire system, they usually do not assign any importance to this problem and hence are not ready to give it any special attention nor willing to assume any additional overhead in order to eliminate deadlocks for the sake of convenience or performance improvement, since they have observed that crashing of the system happens more frequently due to the failure of operating system, hardware defects, or even sometimes due to errors in system software and utilities. On the other hand, scientists and particularly designers of mainframe operating systems are very keen to eliminate or even prevent this unacceptable problem at any cost.

In order to avoid deadlock, most mainframe operating systems usually take all possible measures right at the beginning when a job is just submitted by way of decisive allocation/deallocation of resources. UNIX, on other hand, totally ignores deadlocks, even it suffers from deadlocks that may remain undetected, and lets them be automatically resolved individually. In this system, the total number of permissible processes is determined by the number of available slots in the process table. Since the process table size is finite for a finite number of resources, if the table is full at any point in time and a new process still tries to enter, the operating system then, at best, would reasonably keep the process waiting, setting it aside until its entry is justified or it can tell it to retry. Similarly, the maximum number of files to be opened at any instant is also restricted by the size of the i-node table. In fact, UNIX users would prefer to have occasional deadlocks than to abide by several inconvenient restrictions on processes in order to eliminate (prevent) deadlocks.

If the deadlock issue can be resolved without cost, there is no point to any further discussion. But the problem is that the price is reasonably high in terms of a large penalty in performance for the sake of correctness and also several unusual restrictions on processes for the purpose of convenience. Thus, there exists an unpleasant trade-off between correctness and convenience. It is obviously a matter of concern about which is more important and to whom. Under such conditions, it is difficult to arrive at any well-acceptable judicious general solution.

4.19.6   Deadlock Detection and Subsequent Recovery

In general, processes freely request resources and are then granted them whenever possible with no limit to resource access or restrictions on process actions. This liberal allocation of resources with no particular intervention may eventually invite deadlocks. That is why, checking for deadlocks are occasionally carried out either for the purpose of reclaiming resources from the already deadlocked processes, if there is any, or at the time of granting a resource whenever it is requested, or initiating a periodical examination to ascertain whether a deadlock already exists, and sometimes also performing a search for deadlock whenever certain unusual events occur. Ironically, deadlock enters sneakily with no warning of any unexpected event, and thus deadlock detection algorithms cannot automatically be started.

One of the vital aspects of this approach is to decide how frequently the detection algorithm should be run. If it is executed too often, it merely wastes system resources and performs nonproductive activities. On the other hand, if it is not run frequently enough, runtime overhead for deadlock detection can be avoided but at the expense of leaving deadlocks undetected for longer. Consequently, it can result in lower resource utilization, since deadlocked processes and allied system resources already granted will be unnecessarily tied up in a nonproductive manner until the system is restored to normalcy.

A deadlock **detection strategy**, however, runs in two phases. The first one is the *detection phase* that reveals the existence of the problem, during which the system uses appropriate algorithms in order to check if a deadlock currently exists. If it is detected, the system then goes to the second phase: *recovery from deadlock*, that is, to break the deadlock to reclaim resources held by the blocked processes and thereby release the affected processes to continue normally. This can be accomplished by employing suitable mechanisms. Sometimes removal of a deadlock using this strategy is determined manually; that is, the console operator manually invokes the detection algorithm when the system appears to be inactive for a considerable period.

Detection phase: It has already been explained that the existence of a cycle with no non-cycle outgoing path from any of the involved nodes in a general resource graph (as described in item 4 of Section 4.19.4 and shown in Section 4.19.5) constituting even with multiple resources of same type (against single resource of each type, such as one printer, one tape drive, etc.) is a sufficient condition for deadlocks to occur. Any process involved in this cycle is deadlocked. Thus, the existence of deadlocks can be determined by using any formal algorithm that detects cycles (circuits) in a directed graph (see "Graph Theory"). The algorithm inspects the graph and terminates either when a cycle is detected or no such cycle exists. The ability of the chosen algorithm is particularly important because it facilitates subsequent deadlock recovery after detection.

A simple algorithm with a figure that detects deadlock is given on the Support Material at www.routledge.com/9781032467238.

4.19.6.1   Recovery

Second phase: Once the deadlock detection algorithm has succeeded and detected a deadlock, a strategy is needed for recovery from deadlock to restore the system to normalcy. The first step in deadlock recovery is thus to identify the deadlocked processes. The next step is to break the deadlock by the following possible approaches. Incidentally, none of them are, in particular, observed to be promising.

1. Killing all deadlocked processes

One of the simplest methods to recover the system from deadlock is to kill all the deadlocked processes to free the system. This may be one of the most common solutions but not the most acceptable for many reasons, yet it is still taken into consideration in operating system design.

2. Rollback

Since the occurrence of deadlocks is most likely, system designers often keep the provision of maintaining previously defined separate periodical checkpoints for all the processes residing in the system. Checkpointing a process means that everything with regard to its runtime state, including its memory image, state of the resources being currently held by the process, and similar other important aspects, is recorded in a special file so that it can be restarted later using this information. As the execution of a process progresses, an entire collection of checkpoint files, each generated at different times, is sequentially accumulated.

When a deadlock is detected, the first step is to identify which resources are responsible for the deadlock. To recover the system, a process that holds one such resource is rolled back to an earlier moment when it did not have the resource, and then the process will be preempted so that the resources owned by the current process can now be withdrawn and finally will be assigned to one of the deadlocked processes that needs it. Later, the rolled-back process can once again be restarted from the specified point at a convenient time. The risk in this approach is that the original deadlock will recur because if the restarted process tries to acquire the resource once again, it will have to wait until the resource becomes available. This strategy thus requires that rollback and restart mechanisms be built into the system to facilitate high reliability and/or availability. In general, both rolling back and subsequent restarting may be difficult, if not impossible, for processes that cannot be safely repeated. This is true for processes that have made irreversible changes to resources acquired prior to deadlock. Common applications include reading and writing messages to the network, updating files while journalizing in transaction-processing systems (e.g. examination processing, financial accounting, and reservation systems), and checkpointing in real-time systems.

3. Preemption

At a certain point in time, it may be possible to select a process to suspend for the purpose of temporarily taking a needed resource from this suspended process and giving it to another process in order to break the existing deadlock. The selection criterion should be cost-effective, and re-invocation of the detection algorithm is then required after each preemption to inspect whether the deadlock breaks. Under certain environments, particularly in batch processing operating systems running on mainframes, this practice is very common, not to break any deadlocks but to expedite the execution of a particular process by way of offering it unrestricted resource access.

Taking a resource in this manner away from a process and giving it to another one for use, then returning it again to the former process may be a tricky at best but highly dependent on the nature of the process and the type of resource that can be withdrawn and then easily given back.

4. Killing Processes

The most drastic and possibly simplest approach to break a deadlock is to kill one or more processes successively until the deadlock no longer exists. The order in which processes are selected for killing should be on the basis of certain predefined criteria involving minimum loss. After each killing operation, the detection algorithm must be re-invoked to inspect whether the deadlock still exists. Different selection criteria can be formulated in this regard while choosing a process to kill. The process to be selected as victim should have:

- The least amount of processor time used so far
- The lowest number of lines of output generated so far
- The least total resources allocated so far
- The most estimated time remaining so far
- The lowest priority

Some of these quantities can be directly measured; others cannot. It is also difficult to assess estimated time remaining. In spite of having limitations, these parameters are still taken into account, at least as a guiding factor while selecting a process as a victim in order to break the existing deadlock.

A brief description of this approach is given on the Support Material at www.routledge.com/9781032467238.

4.19.6.2   Merits and Drawbacks

Deadlock detection and recovery, as a whole, provide a higher potential degree of concurrency than the other two commonly used approaches, deadlock prevention and deadlock avoidance, to be discussed in the following sections. While the runtime overhead caused by the deadlock detection mechanism can routinely be made into a tunable system parameter, the costly part of this approach is really the overhead of deadlock recovery once deadlocks are detected. This is mostly due to wastage of system resources already consumed by the processes that are possibly to be restarted or rolled back, if permitted, to recover the system to normalcy. In general, deadlock recovery is lucrative in systems with a low probability of deadlocks. In systems with high loads, unrestricted granting of resource requests tends to indulge in over commitment of resources, which can eventually cause deadlocks to occur very frequently. At the other end, systems with no provision for deadlock detection indirectly allow deadlocks to occur directly and also very frequently, and as the system load gradually increases, this results in a proportionate increase in wasted system resources, particularly in the situations when they are most needed.

4.19.7   DEADLOCK PREVENTION

The basic philosophy in defining the strategy to prevent deadlock is to design a system in such a way that the possibility of deadlocks occurring can be eliminated beforehand. Methods to prevent deadlock, however, fall into two distinct classes: One consists of indirect methods, in which each method will prevent one of the three necessary conditions that cause deadlock to occur, as listed earlier (conditions 1 through 3 in Section 4.19.4). The other class consists of a direct method that will prevent the occurrence of a circular wait (condition 4). If we can ensure that at least one of these conditions is prevented, then deadlocks will be structurally impossible (Havender, 1968). Let us now discuss relevant techniques so that each of these four conditions can be ultimately prevented.

1. Mutual Exclusion Condition

The first of the four conditions (Section 4.19.4), mutual exclusion, as already mentioned, is usually difficult to dispense with and cannot be disallowed. Simultaneous access by many processes to a particular resource is usually provided for the sake of performance improvement that requires mutual exclusion; hence mutual exclusion must be incorporated and supported by the operating system, even though it may invite deadlock. Some resources, such as shared or distributed databases, may at any instant allow multiple accesses for reads but only one exclusive access for writes. In this case, deadlock can occur if more than one process seeks write permission.

However, some types of device, such as printers, cannot be given simultaneously to many processes without implementing mutual exclusion. By spooling printer output (thereby avoiding implementation of mutual exclusion), several processes can be allowed to generate output at the same time. In this approach, the only process that actually requests the physical printer is the printer daemon. Since this daemon never seeks any other resources, deadlock, at least for the printer, can be eliminated. But when competition for disk space for the purpose of spooling happens, this, in turn, may invite deadlock and cannot be prevented.

Unfortunately, not all devices have the provision for being spooled. That is why the strategy being religiously followed in this regard is: avoid assigning any resource when it is not absolutely necessary, and try to ensure that as few processes as possible may claim the resource, which can be easily enforced initially at the job scheduler level at the time of selecting a job for execution.

2. Hold-and-Wait Condition

The second of the four conditions (Section 4.19.4), *hold-and-wait*, appears slightly more attractive. This condition can be eliminated by enforcing a rule that a process is to release all resources held by it whenever it requests a resource that is not currently available; hence the process, in turn, is forced to wait. In other words, deadlocks are prevented because waiting processes are not holding any resources unnecessarily. There are two possible approaches to implement this strategy.

    a. Require all processes to request all their needed resources prior to starting execution. If everything is available, the process will then be allocated whatever it requires and can then run to completion. If one or more resources are not available (busy), nothing will then be allocated, and the process will be left waiting. This approach is, however, inefficient, since a process may be held up for a considerable period, waiting for all its resource requests to be fulfilled, when, in fact, it could have started its execution with only some of its requested resources.

Apart from that, a real difficulty with this approach is that many processes cannot predict how many resources they will need until execution is started. Although sometimes exerting additional effort, estimation of resource requirements of processes is possible, but such estimation with regard to preclaiming resources usually tends to be conservative and always inclined to overestimation. In fact, preclaiming necessarily includes all those resources that could potentially be needed by a process at runtime, as opposed to those actually used. This is particularly observed in so-called data-dominant programs in which the actual requirements of resources are only determined dynamically at runtime. In general, whenever resource requirements are to be declared in advance, the overestimation problem cannot be avoided.

This estimation task appears somewhat easier for batch jobs running on mainframe systems where the user has to first submit a list (JCL) of all the resources that the job needs along with each job. The system then tries to acquire all resources immediately, and if available, allocates them to the job until the job completes its execution; otherwise, the job is placed in the waiting queue until all the requested resources are available. While this method adds a slight burden on the programmer and causes considerable wastage of costly resources, it, in turn, does prevent deadlocks.

Another problem with this approach is that the resources will not be used optimally because some of those resources may actually be used only during a portion of the execution of the related process, and not all the resources will be used all the time during the tenure of the execution. As a result, some of the resources requested in advance will be tied up unnecessarily with the process and remain idle a long time until the process completes, but only for the sake of deadlock prevention; they cannot be allocated to other requesting processes. This will eventually lead to poor resource utilization and correspondingly reduce the level of possible concurrency available in the system.

    b. The process requests resources incrementally during the course of execution but should release all the resources already being held at the time of encountering any denial due to unavailability of any requested resources. The major drawback of this approach is that some resources, by nature, cannot be withdrawn safely and given back easily at a later time. For example, when a file is under process, it cannot be stopped, because it may corrupt the system if not carried to completion. In fact, withdrawal of a resource and later its resumption are only workable if this does not damage the integrity of the system and moreover if the overhead for this act due to context/process switch is found to be within the affordable limit.

3. No-Preemption Condition

The third condition (Section 4.19.4), the *no-preemption* condition, can obviously be prevented by simply allowing preemption. This means that the system is to be given the power to revoke at any point in time the ownership of certain resources which are tied up with blocked processes. The no-preemption condition can be prevented in several ways. One such way is that if a process holding resources is denied a further request, the process must relinquish all its original resources and, if necessary, request them again, together with the additional new resources already allocated.

However, preemption of resources, as already discussed, is sometimes even more difficult than the usual approach of voluntary release and resumption of resources. Moreover, preemption is possible only for certain types of resources, such as CPU and main memory, since the CPU can be regularly preempted by way of routinely saving its states and status with the help of process/context switch operations, and memory can be preempted by swapping its pages to secondary storage. On the other hand, some types of resources, such as partially updated databases, cannot be preempted without damaging the system. Forcibly taking these resources away may be tricky at best and impossible at worst. Therefore, preemption is possible only for certain types of resources, and that too if and only if deadlock prevention is felt to be more important than the cost to be incurred for the process switch operation associated with preemption. Since this approach cannot be applicable for all types of resources in general, it is therefore considered less promising and hence is dropped from favor.

4. Circular Wait

Attacking the last one, the fourth condition (Section 4.19.4), the *circular wait*, can be eliminated in several ways: One simple way is to impose a rule saying that a process is allowed only to have a single resource at any instant. If it needs a second one, it must release the first one. This restriction, however, can create hindrance, and that is why it is not always acceptable.

Another way to prevent a circular wait is by linear ordering of different types of system resources by way of numbering them globally:

1. Printer
2. Plotter
3. Tape drive
4. CD-ROM drive
5. Disk drive, and so on

It is observed that the system resources are divided into different classes R_k, where $k = 1, 2, \ldots, n$. Deadlock can now be prevented by imposing a rule which says: processes can request and acquire their resources whenever they want to, but all requests must be made in strictly increasing order of the specified system resource classes. For example, a process may request first a printer and then a disk drive, but it cannot request first a tape drive and then a plotter. Moreover, acquiring all resources within a given class must be made with a *single request*, and not incrementally. This means that once a process acquires a resource belonging to class R_x, it can only request resources of class $x + 1$ or higher.

With the imposition of this rule, the resource allocation graph can never have cycles. Let us examine why this is true, taking two processes, A and B. Assume that a deadlock occurs only if A requests resource x and B requests resource y. If $x > y$, then A is not allowed to request y. If $x < y$, then B is not allowed to request x. Either way, deadlock is not possible, no matter how they are interleaved.

The same logic also holds for multiple processes. At any instant, one of the assigned resources will be of the highest class. The process holding that class of resource will never ask for a resource of same class already assigned (as discussed). It will either finish or, at worst, request resources of higher classes. Eventually, it will finish and release all its acquired resources. At this point, some other process will acquire the resource of the highest class and can also complete its execution. In this way, all processes will finish their execution one after another, and hence there will be no deadlock.

A slight variation of this algorithm can be made by dropping the requirement that resources are to be acquired in a strictly increasing order of the specified system resource classes and also requiring that no process request a resource with a class lower than that of the resource it is already holding. Now if a process initially requests resources with classes R_x and $R_x + 1$, and then releases both of them during the tenure of execution, it is effectively starting afresh, so there is no reason to restrict it from requesting any resource belonging to any class less than x.

One serious drawback of this approach is that the resources must be acquired strictly in the prescribed order, as opposed to specific requests when they are actually needed. This may mean that some resources are to be acquired well in advance of their actual use in order to obey this rule. This adversely affects resource utilization and lowers the degree of concurrency, since unused resources already acquired are unavailable for needed allocation to other requesting processes already under execution.

Another practical difficulty faced with this approach is to develop a particular numerical ordering of all the resources so that the specific rule can be imposed to eliminate the deadlock problem. In reality, the resources, such as disk spooler space, process table slots, locked database records, and similar other abstract resources, together with the number of usual potential resources and their different uses, may be so large that no specific ordering could be effectively possible to work out for actual implementation.

4.19.8 DEADLOCK AVOIDANCE

The deadlock problem can be resolved using another approach to avoid the situation that may cause deadlock to occur. In fact, there exists a fine demarcation line that distinguishes, at least in principle, deadlock avoidance from deadlock prevention. Truly speaking, the strategies drawn for deadlock avoidance can also be used for deadlock prevention because they ultimately prevent deadlock from occurring. Recall that deadlock prevention is realized by limiting how requests can be made and requires strict adherence to at least one of the four conditions as already discussed. Three of them (*mutual exclusion, hold-and-wait, no preemption*) are policy-related necessary conditions, and preventing one of these three conditions can indirectly prevent deadlock. The fourth condition, circular wait, is a sufficient condition, and by preventing this condition, deadlock can be prevented directly. In doing so, prevention mechanisms, finding no other alternatives, admit poor resource utilization and even compromise with degradation in the assumed level of concurrency.

Deadlock avoidance, on the other hand, is a little bit liberal, withdrawing all restrictions as imposed by these three necessary conditions, allowing them to freely occur, but in a way taking judicious measures so as to ensure that the deadlock situation never occurs. Since avoidance is a predictive approach, it relies on information about the resource activity that will be occurring for the process. However, the avoidance approach permits more resource utilization and higher concurrency in the execution of processes than what prevention usually offers.

The main strategy of deadlock avoidance lies in the decision which is made dynamically at the time of granting resource requests: grant only those requests for available resources by letting the resource manager decide whether granting a particular request is safe. If such granting of resources does not potentially lead to a situation of deadlock, it is safe, and the resource is then granted to the requestor. Otherwise, the requesting process is suspended until it is safe to grant the pending request without causing any harm. This is normally carried out when one or more requesting resources held by other active processes are released. Avoidance is basically a conservative strategy. It tends to underutilize resources by refusing to allocate them if there is any possibility for a deadlock. Consequently, it is rarely favored for use in modern operating systems.

Deadlock avoidance can be accomplished with the following two approaches:

1. **Process Initiation Refusal**: A process should not be started if its claims might lead to a deadlock. Deadlock avoidance requires all processes to declare (pre-claim) their maximum resource requirements prior to execution. In fact, when a process is created, it must explicitly state its maximum claim: the maximum number of units the process will ever request for every resource type. The resource manager can honor the request if the stated resource requirements do not go beyond the total capacity of the system or do not exceed the total amount of resources that are available at that time, and it then takes the appropriate actions accordingly.

2. **Resource Allocation Refusal**: The main algorithms to ensure deadlock avoidance are based on the policies to be adopted while allocating resources in an incremental way to requesting processes. Once the execution of a process begins, it then starts requesting its resources in an incremental manner as and when needed, up to the maximum declared limit. The resource manager keeps track of the number of allocated and the number of available resources of each type, in addition to keeping a record of the remaining number of resources already declared but not yet requested by each process. If a process requests a resource which is temporarily unavailable, the process is then placed in waiting (suspended). But if the requested resource is available for allocation, the resource manager examines whether granting the request can lead to a deadlock by checking whether each of the already-active processes could complete, in case if all such processes exercise all of their remaining options by acquiring other resources that they are entitled to by virtue of the remaining claims. If so, the resource is allocated to the requesting process, thereby ensuring that the system will not be deadlocked.

At any instant, a process may have no or more resources allocated to it. The **state** of the system is simply defined as the *current allocation of resources to all already-active processes*. Thus, the state of a system consists of *two vectors*: the total number of resources, and the total number of available resources, as well as two matrices, claim and current allocation, as already defined. A state is said to be **safe** if it is not deadlocked and there exists at least one way to satisfy all currently pending requests issued by the already-active processes following some specific order without resulting in a deadlock. An **unsafe** state is, of course, a state that is considered not to be safe. As long as the processes tend to use less than their maximum claim, the system is likely (but not guaranteed) to be in a safe state. However, if a large number of processes are found to have relatively large resource demands (at or very near their maximum claim) almost at the same time, the system resources will then be heavily under use, and the probability of the system state being unsafe happens to be higher.

Safety Evaluation: Attainment of a safe state can possibly be guaranteed if the following strategy is used: when a resource is requested by a process, make the decision while granting the request on the basis of whether the difference between the current allocation and the maximum requirement of the process can be met with the currently available resources. If so, grant the request, and the system will possibly remain in the safe state. Otherwise, refuse granting the request issued by this process, and suspend (block) the process until it is safe to grant the request, because such a request, if granted, may lead to an unsafe state culminating ultimately in a deadlock. Then exit the operating system.

When a resource is released, update the available data structure to reflect the current status of state and reconsider pending requests, if any, for that type of resource.

It is important to note that if a state is unsafe, it does not mean that the system is in a deadlock or even indicate that a deadlock is imminent. It simply means that the situation is out of the hands of the resource manager, and the fate will be determined solely by future courses of action of the processes. Thus, the main difference between a safe state and an unsafe state is that as long as the state is safe, it is guaranteed that all processes will be completed, avoiding deadlock, whereas in an unsafe state, no such guarantee can be given. That is why a lack of safety does not always imply deadlock, but a deadlock implies non-safety as a whole.

Brief details on this topic with figures and examples are given on the Support Material at www.routledge.com/9781032467238.

4.19.8.1 Merits and Drawbacks

Deadlock avoidance has the **advantage** that it acquires resources in an incremental manner as and when needed, up to the maximum declared limit. This eliminates the problem of resources being idle due to premature acquisition that leads to poor resource utilization, which is often encountered with other deadlock prevention strategies based on *process initiation refusal*, as already discussed. Moreover, it does not require preempting and rolling back processes as exercised in the *deadlock detection* approach, thereby avoiding wastage in resource usage by processes that are either restarted or rolled back, apart from incurring a huge system overhead required for such actions. It is also less restrictive and provides a comparatively high degree of concurrency compared to *deadlock prevention*.

However, it imposes a number of restrictions on its use that are considered as its **drawbacks**:

- There must be a fixed number of resources to allocate and a fixed number of active processes in the system.
- The maximum resource requirement for each process must be declared in advance.
- Claiming of resources in advance indirectly influences and adversely affects the degree of concurrency in systems.
- The resource manager has to always perceive a greater number of system states as unsafe that eventually keep many processes waiting even when the requested resources are available and able to be allocated.
- Requirement of additional runtime storage space to detect the safety of the system states and also the associated overhead in execution time for such detection.
- The active processes must be independent; that is, the order in which they execute must be free from encumbrance of any synchronization requirement.

4.19.9 THE BANKER'S ALGORITHM

A scheduling algorithm for allocation of resources that gives rise to a classic model of a state used to avoid deadlock, proposed first by Dijkstra (1965), is by far the best-known avoidance strategies. In fact, the safety evaluation portion of the entire strategy to realize deadlock avoidance that has just been discussed is nothing but the banker's algorithm. Dijkstra used this name because of the analogy of this problem to one that occurs in banking, when customers (processes) wish to borrow money (resources) following lending policies in terms of a line of credit (maximum claim for resources) declared by the banker (operating system).

The ultimate objective of this algorithm is to determine the safety of a state, that is, to find out whether some ordering of resource acquisitions exists that leads to completion of all processes. The time complexity of this algorithm is proportional to $p^2 \times r$, where p is the number of active processes and r is the number of resources present in the system. More efficient algorithms, however, are found when the system has only one instance of each type of resource, or only a single type of many resources is present in the system.

4.19.9.1 Multiple Resources of Different Types

The banker's algorithm can be generalized to handle multiple resources of different types. Let there be a set of n processes P, say P = (P1, P2, P3, P4, P5), using a set of m resources R, say R = (R1, R2,

R3, R4). The nature of the current system state S_k is determined by the pattern of resources already allocated to processes, as shown in Figure 4.30(b) as an example. At any instant, the system state can be deduced by enumerating the number of units of resource type held by each process. Let a vector E be the total number of resources in existence in the system for each type of resource R_j, as shown in Figure 4.30(a). Let $Alloc$ be a table, as shown in Figure 4.30(b), in which row i represents process P_i, column j represents R_j, and $Alloc$ (i, j) is the number of units of resource R_j held by the process P_i. Let another table $Maxc$ be the maximum claim on resource R_j by process P_i, as shown in Figure 4.30(c). Let $Need$ be a table, as shown in Figure 4.30(d), in which row i represents process P_i, column j represents R_j, and $Need(i, j)$ is the number of units of resource R_j is needed by the process P_i. This table can be generated by computing the element-wise difference of two tables, $Maxc(i, j)$ and $Alloc(i, j)$, such as;

$$Need\ (i, j) = Maxc\ (i, j) - Alloc\ (i, j) \text{ for all}, 0 < i \le n \text{ and } 0 < j \le m$$

The available resource vector $Avail$ for each type of resource R_j is simply the difference between the total number of each resource that the system has and what is currently allocated. This is shown in Figure 4.30(e) as an example.

This algorithm determines whether the current allocation of resources is safe by considering each process P_i and asking: if this process suddenly requests all resources up to its maximum claim, are there sufficient resources to satisfy the request? If there are, then this process could not be dead-locked in the state. So there is a sequence whereby this process eventually finishes and returns all its resources to the operating system. In this way, if we can determine that every P_i for all i, $0 < i \le n$ can execute, we declare the state is safe.

	R1	R2	R3	R4
E =	7	5	3	2

Total number of each type
of resource in system.
(a)

	R1	R2	R3	R4
P1	3	0	1	0
P2	0	1	0	0
P3	1	1	1	0
P4	1	1	0	1
P5	0	1	0	1

ALLOC : (Resource allocated)
(b)

	R1	R2	R3	R4
	2	1	1	0

Avail : (Number of available
resources of each type)
(e)

	R1	R2	R3	R4
P1	4	1	1	0
P2	0	2	1	2
P3	4	2	1	0
P4	1	1	1	1
P5	2	1	1	1

Maxc : (Maximum claim)
(c)

	R1	R2	R3	R4
P1	1	1	0	0
P2	0	1	1	2
P3	3	1	0	0
P4	0	0	1	0
P5	2	0	1	0

Need : (Resource still needed)
(d)

FIGURE 4.30 An analytical example detailing Banker's algorithm in deadlock avoidance with multiple resources.

Assuming that all the vectors, such as; E and *Avail* and all the tables such as *Alloc*, *Maxc*, and *Need* are present. Then

1. Find P_i such that *Need* (i, j) $\leq$ *Avail*(j) for each i, $0 < I \leq n$ and all j, $0 < j \leq m$. If no such P_i exists, then the state is unsafe and the system will eventually enter deadlock, since no process can run to completion; halt the algorithm; and exit to the operating system.
2. Assume the process of the chosen row thus obtained, requests all the resources it needs up to its maximum claim (which is certainly possible) and finishes. Mark the process as terminated, reclaim all the resources it acquired, and add all those resources to the *Avail* vector.
3. Repeat steps 1 and 2 until either all processes are marked terminated, in which case the initial state was safe, or until a deadlock occurs, in which case the state was unsafe.

In step 1, if it is found that several processes are eligible to be chosen, it does not matter which one will be selected: in any case, either at best, the pool of available resources gets larger due to release of resources indicating poor utilization of resources but at the same time enabling many other waiting processes to start and finish, thereby avoiding deadlock to occur; or at worst, the pool of available resources remain the same.

The banker's algorithm is an excellent approach, at least from a theoretical point of view. In spite of having immense importance even today, especially the in academic domain, but in practice, the banker's algorithm has been neither approved nor accepted as a workable one to implement. One of the main reasons is that the basic assumptions on which the algorithms has been derived are not sound enough to trust, and hence, has the same drawbacks that all other avoidance strategies, in general, do have. The most important one is that processes are rarely aware in advance about their maximum resource needs. Moreover, the number of processes is not fixed but varies dynamically as new users frequently enter and exit. In addition, resources that were supposed to be available can suddenly go out of reach (disk drives not functioning), thereby reducing the total number of available resources. Furthermore, avoidance is overly conservative, and there are many more things that actually prevent the algorithm from working; hence, in reality, few operating systems, if any, use the banker's algorithm for deadlock avoidance.

The Banker's algorithm used for a single type of resources is discussed on the Support Material at www.routledge.com/9781032467238.

4.19.10 Hybrid Strategy: A Combined Approach

It has been observed that all the strategies that have been discussed so far for dealing with deadlock have their own strengths and drawbacks, but none of these approaches is considered suitable for use as an exclusive method to negotiate deadlocks in a complex system. That is why, rather than to attempting to employ only one of these strategies to deal with deadlocks in general, it might be more efficient to combine different strategies into a single approach which would be able to handle different deadlock situations in order to extract maximum effectiveness. This can be accomplished by grouping all the system resources into a collection of disjoint classes and then applying the most appropriate method of handling deadlocks to resources within each particular class. One such approach that uses this strategy could be formulated as follows:

- Group all system resources into a number of different disjoint resource classes.
- Apply a resource (linear) ordering strategy, as described earlier in relation to deadlock prevention, while attacking circular wait, which can possibly prevent deadlocks between resource classes.
- Within a resource class, use an algorithm that is most suitable for that particular class.

Grouping of resources can be accomplished based on the principle being followed in the design hierarchy of a given operating system. Alternatively, this grouping can also be made in accordance with the dominant characteristics of certain types of resources, such as permitting preemption or allow-ing accurate predictions, and similar others. To describe this technique with an example, consider an usual system with the classes of resources as listed in the following, and ordering of this listing follows the same order in which these classes of resources are being assigned to a job or process during their lifetime, that is, starting from entry to the system until they exit. These resources are:

- *Swapping space*: An area of secondary storage (disk) designated for backing up blocks of main memory needed for use in swapping processes.
- *Process (job) resources*: Assignable devices, such as printers and fixed disks with remov-able media, like disk drives, tapes, CDs, and cartridge disks.
- *Main memory*: Assignable on a block basis, such as in pages or segments to processes.
- *Internal resources*: Such as I/O channels and slots of the pool of the dynamic memory.

The ultimate objective of this strategy is first to prevent deadlock between this four classes of resources simply by linear ordering of requests in the order as presented. Next, to prevent deadlock within each class, a suitable local deadlock-handling strategy is chosen according to the specific characteristics of its resources. Within each individual resource class, the following strategies, for example, may be applied:

Swapping space: Prevention of deadlocks by means of acquisition of all needed space at one time in advance is a possibility, as is found in the hold-and-wait strategy in deadlock prevention. This strategy appears reasonable if the maximum storage requirements are known, which is often the case. Deadlock avoidance is also possible, but deadlock recovery (detection) cannot be achieved, since there is no backup of the swapping space.

Process (job) resources: Avoidance of deadlocks is often effective in this category because it can be expected that processes would declare in advance the resources in this class that they may need during runtime. This is customarily done for jobs by means of providing job-control statements, which contain all such resource requirements, along with the job while it is submitted. Deadlock prevention is also possible by means of resource ordering within this class. But detection and recovery are not desirable at all due to the possibility of files that belong to this class of resources having already been modified by this time.

Main memory: With the use of swapping, prevention by means of preemption appears the most suitable strategy for main memory, because when a process is preempted, it is sim-ply swapped to secondary memory (disk), thereby freeing the space to resolve deadlock. Moreover, this approach facilitates runtime support while handling the situation when growth (and shrinking) of memory spaces already allocated to active processes takes place. Avoidance is normally not desirable because it leads to increase in runtime overhead and tends to underutilize resources. Deadlock detection although is possible but generally undesirable due to either an increase in runtime overhead for frequent detection or unused memory space held by the deadlocked processes.

Internal resources: Deadlock avoidance and even deadlock detection are not desirable, since resources of this type are frequently requested and released, resulting in frequent changes in system state that make the runtime overhead so much high, often beyond the tolerance limit. Prevention by means of resource ordering is probably the best choice for this type of resource.

4.19.11 CASE STUDY: DEADLOCK HANDLING IN UNIX

Most operating systems remain indifferent and simply ignore the possibility of deadlocks involving user processes. UNIX is no exception. However, it contains some features that address deadlocks involving processes which execute kernel code while servicing interrupts and system calls. The overall approach in this regard is simply based on deadlock prevention through resource ranking (as already described in the previous section). The related approach is to lock and unlock (release) the data structures in the kernel in a standard manner. However, there are some exceptions to this rule inherent to UNIX. Because all kernel functionalities cannot lock the data structures in the standard order, deadlocks cannot be totally prevented. We present simplified views of two arrangements that are used to avoid deadlocks.

The UNIX kernel uses a disk cache (buffer cache) to speedup accesses to frequently used disk blocks. This disk cache consists of a pool of buffers in primary memory and a buffer list with a hashed data structure to inspect whether a specific disk block exists in a buffer. The buffer list is maintained using the least recently used (LRU) replacement technique in order to facilitate reuse of buffers. The normal order of accessing a disk block is to use the buffer list with the hashed data structure to locate a disk block; if found, put a lock on the buffer and also put a lock on the respective entry in the buffer list thus obtained in order to update the LRU status of the buffer. If the requested disk block is not found in the buffer list, it is obvious that the process would then merely want to obtain a buffer for loading this requested new block. To achieve this, the process first puts a lock on the buffer list. It would then directly access the buffer list and inspect whether the lock on the first buffer in the list has already been set by some other process. If not, it then sets the lock and uses the respective buffer; otherwise it repeats the same course of action on the next entry in the buffer list. Deadlocks are possible because of this order of locking the buffer list, and the buffer is different from the standard order of setting these locks.

UNIX uses an innovative approach to avoid deadlocks. The process looking for a free buffer uses a technique that enables it to avoid getting blocked on its lock. The technique is to use a special operation that attempts to set a lock but returns with a failure condition code if the lock is already set. If this happens, the operation is repeated with an attempt to set the lock on the next buffer, and so on until it finds a buffer that it can use. In this way, this approach avoids deadlocks by avoiding circular waits.

Deadlock is possible in another situation, when locks cannot be set in a standard order in the file system function that establishes a link. A *link* command provides pathnames for a file and a directory which is to contain the link to the file. This command can be implemented by locking the directories containing the file and the link. However, a standard order cannot be defined for locking these directories. Consequently, two processes trying simultaneously to lock the same directories may get deadlocked. To avoid the occurrence of such deadlocks, the file system function does not try to acquire both locks at the same time. It first locks one directory, gets it work done in the desired manner, and then releases the lock. It then locks the other directory and does what it wants to do. Thus, it requires and acquires only one lock at any time. In this way, this approach prevents deadlocks because the hold-and-wait condition is not satisfied by these processes.

4.19.12   DISCUSSIONS: VARIOUS STRATEGIES AND THEIR IMPACTS

Dynamic sharing of resources is the main reason for deadlock. Deadlocks are especially fatal and certainly not acceptable in time-critical environments, such as factory processes or monitoring aircraft operations. However, the danger of deadlocks can be mitigated by several considerations.

First, deadlocks can often be avoided by proper design of the algorithms that share resources. For example, different parts of the kernel may share information, like process context blocks that require exclusive access, similar to holding a resource during runtime while they modify that information. A *hierarchical design* inside the kernel is often used to make sure that no deadlocks arise from using these resources. However, we have already discussed numerous mechanisms for achieving exclusive access of resources that deal with interprocess communications

Second, deadlock also causes an unacceptable situation when everyone is infinitely patient. One way to come out of this situation may be to modify the mechanism of the service (system) call issued for requesting respective resources by including an additional *timeout* parameter. If the resource

manager fails or is not willing to honor the request within the time interval specified by this parameter, it can unblock the calling process and give it a failure indication. The process could then try
again, try a different request, or even may back out of whatever action it is trying to perform, or it
can, at best, terminate if it finds no other way out.

There exist differences between deadlock prevention and avoidance. Prevention includes any
method that negates one of the four conditions already explained. Avoidance, on the other hand,
includes methods like the banker's algorithm that takes advantage of prior knowledge (such as maximum claims). This advance knowledge alerts the system beforehand while navigating the progress
diagram and still avoids dangerous regions.

The *conservative liberal metaphor* helps in rating various policies that we have seen. *Liberal
policies* have a greater potential for parallelism and throughput because they allow more flexible
navigation of the progress diagram, but they have an equal potential for deadlock and starvation.
The advance-claim algorithm provides a reasonably liberal method that is still conservative enough
to prevent deadlock. To prevent starvation as well, other conservative steps must be taken, such
as banning new arrivals or concentrating resources on particular processes. Overly conservative
methods like one-shot allocation remove all worries about deadlock and starvation but at the cost of
severe reduction of concurrency, leading to potential degradation in system performance.

Although we have devoted a considerable amount of attention to the advance-claim algorithm, it
is mostly interesting from the theoretical end and bears some academic importance but is not practicable. It can be pointed out that many applications are unable to compute reasonable claims before
they start working; they can only discover what they will need once they have made some progress.

Furthermore, resources can suddenly become unavailable if the hardware malfunctions.
Therefore, most operating systems do not implement the advance-claim algorithm. It is much more
common to grant resources to processes following the most liberal policy imaginable and acceptable. If this policy leads to deadlock, the deadlock is detected (either by the resource manager or
by disgruntled users) and broken by injuring some process(es). Hierarchical allocation has also
been used successfully, especially within the kernel, to make sure that its modules never become
deadlocked.

Our ultimate goal is to achieve the most liberal resource-allocation policy without encounter-
ing any deadlock. Serialization avoids deadlock but is very conservative. Figure 4.31 also shows
the resource-allocation policies that we have already explained. The one-shot, hierarchical, and
advance-claim algorithms put increasingly less onerous restrictions on the processes that wish to
request resources. The advance-claim algorithm also requires a certain amount of prior knowledge
about the resources required by each process. The more information of this nature we know, the

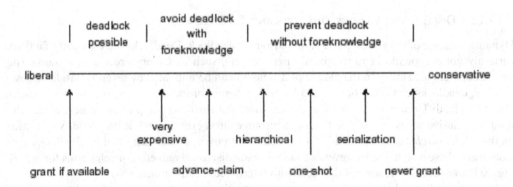

FIGURE 4.31 A pictorial representation of the liberal-conservative spectrum in rating various policies relating to deadlock problem and its solution approaches (Finkel).

closer we can get to our goal. However, the algorithms that make use of such knowledge are increasingly expensive to execute.

4.19.13 STARVATION

Deadlock arises from dynamic resource sharing. If resources are not shared, there can never be deadlock. Moreover, deadlock results due to overly liberal policies for allocation of resources. Starvation is a problem that is closely related to deadlock. In a dynamic system, it is required that some policy be formulated to decide which process will get what resource when and for how long. While some of these policies are found quite reasonable and also lucrative from the point of resource allocation to negotiate deadlock, they sometimes may give rise to a peculiar situation in which some processes are continuously postponed and denied the desired service. Even when the needed resources are available, a process is still getting blocked. It happens that it might never get a chance to run again; we call this danger **starvation**, and the said process then enters a state of starvation, even though the process is not deadlocked.

Starvation arises from consistently awarding resources to the competitors of a blocked process. As long as one competitor has the resources, the blocked process cannot continue. Starvation, in general, may result due to overly liberal policies for reassignment of resources once they are returned. When resources are released, they can be granted to any process waiting for them in the resource wait list (The short-term scheduler most likely should not switch to the waiting processes but should normally continue with the releasing processes, in accord with the hysteresis principle.) However, not all policies used for granting those resources prevent starvation as being experienced from different real-life situations. Sill, increased conservatism may be one way to prevent this problem.

A refinement of this policy is to grant resources whenever they are available after being released to those processes with low requirements, thereby allowing them to complete rather than allocating them to the first blocked process. With best hope, it can be expected that the processes we favor in this way will eventually release enough resources to satisfy the requirement of the first blocked process. More precisely, we might sort the resource wait list by the order in which processes block. When resources are freed, we scan this list and grant resources only to processes whose current request can be fully satisfied. Unfortunately, this **first-fit** policy may insist the first blocked process to eventually go into starvation if a continuous stream of new jobs with smaller requirements arrives.

One way to modify this strategy is to allow partial allocation. As many units of the resource can be granted to the first process in the list as may be done safely; the rest may be allocated (if safe) to other later processes in the list. Even this policy fails, because there may be situations in which no resources may safely be granted to the first blocked process, others may otherwise continue even then.

Another further modification could be to order the resource wait list according to some safe sequence (if there are several safe sequences, any one will do). Resources are granted, either partially or fully, starting at the head of this list. However, there is no way to guarantee that any particular process will ever reach the beginning of this list. A process may remain near the end of the safe sequence and hence be left in starvation and never be favored with the allocation of resources.

Starvation detection: The approach to detect starvation can be modeled exactly along the lines of deadlock detection. By the time deadlock is detected, it may be too late, but it is never too late to fix starvation. Starvation might be signaled by a process remaining on the resource wait list for too long, measured in either units of time or units of process completion.

Once starvation is detected, new processes may be denied resources until starving processes have completed. Of course, processes that already have resources must be allowed to get more, since they may appear earlier on belonging to the safe sequence. This approach does certainly work, but it must be tuned carefully. If starvation detection is too sensitive, new processes are banned too often, with the result that there is an overall decrease in throughput. In other words, the policy becomes too conservative. If detection reveals that it is not sensitive enough, processes, however, can normally go with starvation for a long time before they are finally allowed to run.

Starvation can be avoided by using a first-come-first-serve resource allocation policy. With this approach, the process waiting the longest units of time gets served next. In due course, any given process will eventually become the oldest, and, in turn, gets a chance with the needed resources.

Starvation control, however, has not been extensively dealt with. Holt (1972) suggested maintaining counters for each blocked process that are periodically incremented. When a counter exceeds a critical value, the scheduler has to find a safe sequence and finish jobs in that order. He also suggested partial allocations but a requirement that resources not be granted to jobs with zero holdings. The approach of banning new jobs was also introduced and considered. Another approach to handle starvation, which allocates resources according to a safe-sequence order, is found in the Boss 2 operating system for the RC4000 computer.

Fortunately, starvation is seldom a critical problem in the working of an actual operating system, because nonpreemptible, serially reusable resources, such as printers and tape drives, are mostly underused, and the existence of such idle periods tends to prevent starvation.

SUMMARY

This chapter introduces the details of processes, the characteristics of processes in terms of their different states, and their other features in order to realize already-defined functions (described in Chapter 2) that are to be performed by the processor (process) management module. The process concept, however, has been further refined and gives rise to a new construct of a relatively small executable unit known as thread. The reverse trend also has been observed. The concept of a relatively large executable unit, called object consisting of processes and threads has been started to evolve, and a new concept of object-oriented design opened a new horizon that ultimately led to the development of some contemporary powerful operating systems. We presented here some cases as examples in relation to the actual implementation of these different concepts in the development of modern operating systems.

Controlling multiple processes in a multitasking environment requires a specific discipline realized by a mechanism known as scheduling that allocates a processor or processors to each different process at the right point in time for substantial performance improvement with optimal resource utilization. Out of four types of scheduling discussed in detail in Chapter 2, one of these, I/O scheduling, will be described in Chapter 7. Out of the remaining three types of scheduling, long-term and medium-term scheduling are concerned primarily with performance concerns in relation to degrees of multiprogramming. Hence, the only scheduling that remains is short-term scheduling, also called process (processor) scheduling and discussed here in this chapter on a single-processor system. Since the presence of multiple processors in a system adds additional complexity while this type of scheduling is carried out, it is convenient to first focus on the single-processor (uniprocessor) case to describe the fundamental approaches so that more elaborate forms of handling multiple processors can be easily explained. This section focuses on the various criteria based on which different scheduling policies can framed and then addresses different strategies for the design and implementation of respective policies to derive corresponding scheduling algorithms.

Operating systems, while supporting multitasking, multiprocessing, and distributed processing, often use concurrent execution among a related group of processes that allows a single application to take advantage of parallelism between the CPU and I/O devices on a uniprocessor and among CPUs on a multiprocessor for the sake of performance improvement. However, multiple processes that compete for or cooperatively share resources (including information) introduce the potential for new problems that raise a lot of issues in software implementation. Hence, the design criteria of the OS for accommodating concurrency must address a host of these issues, including sharing and competing for resources, synchronization of the activities of multiple processes, communication among processes, and allocation of processor time to processes.

Synchronization among concurrent processes is essential for preserving precedence relation-ships and preventing concurrency-related time-critical issues. Synchronization is required in uniprocessors, multiprocessors, and multiprocessing with networks of servers and workstations. Failure to devise appropriate synchronization mechanisms and enforce their use by each process that uses common resources often results in erratic system behavior that is extremely difficult to debug. Concurrency yields increased productivity when implemented correctly, but it can equally degrade reliability when improper interprocess synchronization pollutes the entire system with elu-sive timing errors. However, if a problem is sufficiently complex, that is why it is traditionally first studied in a uniprocessor environment, and we have followed the same approach in this chapter. We first identified concurrency-related issues and then articulated some possible approaches using some hardware and software solutions to implement interprocess synchronization. The appropriate solutions in this regard that aim to realize increased productivity can either be assisted by operat-ing systems or provided by language compilers. Three such approaches are examined: semaphores, message-passing, and monitors, for interprocess communication and synchronization. A few well-known examples are cited here that demonstrate concurrency problems and also approached to their solution.

Concurrency implemented in a community of cooperating or competing processes extracts potential benefits in terms of performance, resource utilization, and system response but also invites a critical problem known as deadlock that eventually plagues all efforts to realize the benefits of concurrent processing. This chapter includes a discussion with regard to the reasons for deadlock. Then three automated strategies are discussed for negotiating deadlock: (i) detection and recovery and manual handling, (ii) prevention, and (iii) avoidance. The entire discussion on this issue is, how-ever, limited to only a single system; measures to deal with this issue with distributed computing systems are outside the scope of this book.

EXERCISES

1. Describe how processes are developed and executed in the system following its different states.
2. What is meant by process control block? Give the approximate structure of a process con-trol block with the different categories of information that it contains.
3. What are the events that are commonly responsible for a process switch occurring? Enumerate the steps usually followed when a process switch occurs.
4. What are the main drawbacks that have been faced in the design of an operating system based on the process concept? How have these drawbacks been negotiated with making changes in concepts?
5. What is meant by "thread"? What are the advantages that can be obtained by using the thread as a unit of computation?
6. What are the type of system calls that a thread should avoid using if threads are imple-mented at the user level?
7. An OS supports both kernel-level threads and user-level threads. Justify the following statements:
   a. If a candidate for a thread is a CPU-bound computation, use a kernel-level thread if the system contains multiple processors; otherwise, make it a user-level thread.
   b. If a candidate for a thread is an I/O-bound computation, use a user-level thread if the process containing it does not contain a kernel-level thread; otherwise, make it a kernel-level thread.
8. A process creates eight child processes. It is required to organize the child processes into two groups of four processes each such that processes in a group can send signals to other processes in the group but not to any process outside the group. Implement this require-ment using the features in UNIX.

- **Process scheduling**

9. State and explain the different criteria that are involved in the design strategy and design objectives of a process scheduling mechanism and its associated algorithm.
10. Assume that the following jobs to execute with a single-processor system, with the jobs arriving in the order listed here:

I	Service Time
1	60
2	20
3	10
4	20
5	50

   a. If the system uses FCFS scheduling, create a Gantt chart to illustrate the execution of these processes.
   b. What is the turnaround time for process P_3?
   c. What is the average wait time for the processes?
11. Use the process load as given in the previous example, and assume a system that uses SJN scheduling:
   a. Create a Gantt chart to illustrate the execution of these processes.
   b. What is the turnaround time for process P_4?
   c. What is the average wait time for the processes?
12. Prove that, among nonpreemptive scheduling algorithms, SJN/SPN provides the minimum average waiting time for a set of requests that arrive at the same time instant.
13. Assume that the following jobs execute with a single-processor system that uses priority scheduling, with the jobs arriving in the order listed here, where a small integer means a higher priority:

I	Service time	Priority
1	60	2
2	20	1
3	10	4
4	20	5
5	50	3

   a. Create a Gantt chart to illustrate the execution of these processes.
   b. What is the turnaround time for process P_4?
   c. What is the average wait time for the processes?
14. The SJF (aging) algorithm with $\alpha = \frac{1}{2}$ is being used to predict run times. The previous four runs of a process, from oldest to most recent, are 40, 20, 40, and 15 msec. What will be the prediction for the next time?
15. Assume that the following jobs to execute with a single-processor system that uses RR scheduling with a quantum of 10 and the jobs arriving in the order listed here:

i	Service Time	Arrival Time
1	60	0
2	20	8
3	10	8
4	20	65
5	50	75

    a. create a Gantt chart to illustrate the execution of these processes.

    b. What is the turnaround time for process p_3?

    c. What is the average wait time for the processes?

16. Devise a data structure that allows SRR to be implemented efficiently. Consider a preemptive HPRN policy. Can it be implemented exactly? If not, how would you approximate it?

17. Consider the following process arrival list:

Name	Arrival time	Service time
A	0	3
B	2	6
C	3	10
D	7	1
E	8	5
F	15	2
G	25	7

Calculate T, M, and P for each process under the following policies: FCFS, SPN, PSPN, HPRN, RR with $t = 1$, RR with $t = 5$, and SRR with $b/a = 0.5$ and $t = 1$. Assume that if events are scheduled to happen at exactly the same time, new arrivals precede terminations, which precede quantum expirations.

18. Some operating systems are used in environments where processes must get guaranteed service. Deadline scheduling means that each process specifies how much service time it needs and by what real time it must be finished. Design a preemptive algorithm that services such processes. There will be occasions when deadlines cannot be met; try to discover these situations as early as possible (before starting a process, if it cannot be finished in time).

19. A multiprogramming time-sharing operating system uses priority-based scheduling for time-critical processes and round-robin scheduling for interactive user processes. At certain times, the hardware is upgraded by replacing the CPU with a functionally equivalent model that is twice as fast. Discuss the changes that different classes of users will experience. Do some parameters of the operating system need to be changed? If so, which ones and how? Explain the expected change in the system behavior as a consequence of such changes.

20. A group of processes G_k in a system is using fair-share scheduling. When a process P_1 from G_k is selected for scheduling, it is said that "P_1 is a selection from G_k". Show that if processes do not perform I/O operations, two consecutive selections from G_k cannot be for the same process

21. State the distinct advantages that can be obtained from a multilevel feedback queuing scheduler. Which type of process is generally favored by this scheduler: a CPU-bound process or an I/O-bound process? Explain briefly why.

- **Interprocess Synchronization**

22. The processes P_0 and P_1 share variable V_2, processes P_1 and P_2 share variable V_0, and processes P_2 and P_3 share variable V_1. Show how processes can use *enable interrupt* and *disable interrupt* to coordinate access to the variables V_0, V_1, and V_2 so that the critical section problem does not arise.

23. How is mutual exclusion implemented using general semaphores? Explain the drawbacks and limitations of semaphores in general. State the properties and characteristics that a semaphore in general exhibits.

24. "A general semaphore is superfluous since it can be implemented with a binary semaphore or semaphores"—explain.

25. It is sometimes found that a computer has both a TSL instruction and another synchronization primitive, such as semaphores and monitors, in use. These two types play a different role and do not compete with each other. Explain this with reasons.

26. Two processes p_1 and p_2 have been designed so that p_2 writes a stream of bytes produced by p_1. Write a skeleton of procedures executed by p_1 and p_2 to illustrate how they synchronize with one another using P and V. (Hint: consult the producer/consumer problem)

27. Semaphores can be realized in a programming-language construct called *critical region*. Discuss the mechanism by which it can be realized. State the limitations that you may encounter.

28. An inventory manager issues the following instructions to the store manager in regard to a particular item: "Do not purchase the item if the number of items existing in the store exceeds n, and hold any requisition until the number of items existing in the store is large enough to permit the issue of the item". Using a particular item, implement these instructions with the help of a monitor.

29. You have an operating system that provides semaphores. Implement a message system. Write the procedures for sending and receiving messages.

30. Show that, using message, an interrupt signaling mechanism can be achieved.

31. Show that monitors and semaphores have equivalent functionality. Hence, show that a monitor and message can be implemented using semaphores. This will demonstrate that a monitor can be used anyplace a semaphore can be used.

32. Solve the producer/consumer problem using monitors instead of semaphores.

- **Interprocess Communication and Synchronization**

33. Suppose we have a message-passing mechanism using mailboxes. When sending to a full mailbox or trying to receive from an empty one, a process does not block. Instead it is provided an error code. The process in question responds to the error code by just trying again, over and over, until it succeeds. Does this scheme lead to race conditions?

34. What sequence of SEND and (blocking) RECEIVE operations should be executed by a process that wants to receive a message from either mailbox M1 or mailbox M2? Provide a solution for each of the following cases:
   a. The receiving process must not be blocked at an empty mailbox if there is at least one message in the other mailbox. The solution can use only the two mailboxes and a single receiving process.
   b. The receiving process can be suspended (blocked) only when there are no messages in either mailbox, and no form of busy waiting is allowed.

35. Discuss the relative time and space complexities of the individual implementations of the message facility. Propose an approach that you consider to be the best trade-off in terms of versatility versus performance.

- **Deadlock and Starvation**

36. "Deadlock is a global condition rather than a local one". Give your comments. What are the main resources that are held responsible for the occurrence of a deadlock?

37. State and explain the conditions that must be present for a deadlock to occur.

38. "A deadlock can occur even with a single process". Is it possible? If so, justify the statement with an appropriate example.

39. What are the merits and drawbacks of the recovery approach when deadlock has already occurred and been detected?

40. Discuss the merits and shortcomings of the deadlock avoidance strategy.
41. An OS uses a simple strategy to deal with deadlock situations. When it finds that a set of processes is deadlocked, it aborts all of them and restarts them immediately. What are the conditions under which the deadlock will not recur?
42. Compare and contrast the following resource allocation policies:
    a. All resource requests together.
    b. Allocation using resource ranking.
    c. Allocation using the banker's algorithm in the light of (i) resource idling and (ii) overhead of the resource allocation algorithm.
43. Three processes share four resources that can be reserved and released only one at a time. Each process needs a maximum of two units. Show that a deadlock cannot occur.
44. When resource ranking is used as a deadlock prevention policy, a process is permitted to request a unit of resource class R_x only if $rank_x > rank_y$ for every resource class R_y whose resources are allocated to it. Explain whether deadlocks can arise if the condition is changed to $rank_x \geq rank_y$.
45. A system is composed of four processes [P_1, P_2, P_3, P_4] and three types of serially reusable resources, [R_1, R_2, R_3]. The number of total existing resources are C = (3, 2, 2)
    a. Process P_1 holds 1 unit of R_1 and requests 1 unit of R_2.
    b. Process P_2 holds 2 units of R_2 and requests 1 unit each of R_1 and R_3.
    c. Process P_3 holds 1 unit of R_1 and requests 1 unit of R_2.
    d. Process P_4 holds 2 units of R_3 and requests 1 unit of R_1.
46. Can a system be in a state that is neither deadlocked nor safe? If so, give an example. If not, prove that all states are either deadlocked or safe.
47. A situation in which there are several resource classes and for each class there is a safe sequence but the situation is still unsafe—justify.
48. Can a process be allowed to request multiple resources simultaneously in a system where deadlocks are avoided? Justify why or why not.
49. What are the effects of starvation that may affect the overall performance of a system? Discuss the mechanism by which starvation can be detected and then avoided. Explain how starvation is avoided in the UNIX and Windows operating systems.

More questions for this chapter are given on the Support Material at www.routledge.com/9781032467238

SUGGESTED REFERENCES AND WEBSITES

Anderson, T. E., Bershad. B. N., et al. "Scheduler Activations: Effective Kernel Support for the User-level Management of Parallelism", *Proceedings of the ACM Symposium on Operating Systems Principles*, New York, ACM, pp. 95–109, 1991.

Birrell, A. D. "An Introduction to Programming with Threads", *Technical Report, DEC–SRC*, January, 1989. Available at www.research.compaq.com/SRC.

Brinch Hansen, P. "Structured Multiprogramming", *Communications of the ACM*, vol. 15, no. 7, pp. 574–578, 1972.

Brinch Hansen, P. "The Programming Language Concurrent Pascal", *IEEE Transactions on Software Engineering*, vol. 1, no. 2, pp. 199–207, 1975.

Buhr, P., Frontier, M. "Monitor Classification", *ACM Computing Surveys*, vol. 27, no. 1, pp. 63–107, 1995.

Campbell, R. H., Habermann, A. N. "The Specification of Process Synchronization by Path Expressions", in *Operating Systems*, Kaiser, C. (Ed.), Berlin, Springer-Verlag, 1974.

Cheriton, D. "*The V Kernel*: A Software Base for Distributed Systems", *IEEE Software*, vol. 1, no. 2, pp. 19–42, 1984.

Cheriton, D. "The V Distributed System", *Communications of the ACM*, vol. 31, no. 3, pp. 314–333, 1988.

Coffman, E. G., Elphick, M. J., Shoshani, A. "System Deadlocks", *Computing Surveys*, vol. 3, pp. 67–78, 1971.

Dijkstra, E. W. *Cooperating Sequential Processes*. Eindhoven, Technological University, 1965. (Reprinted in *Programming Languages*, F. Genuys, ed., Academic Press, New York, 1968)

Habermann, A. N. "Prevention of System Deadlocks", *Communications of the ACM*, vol. 12, no. 7, pp. 373–377, 385, 1969.

Hall, L., Shmoys, D., et al. "Scheduling to Minimize Average Completion Time Off-line and On-line Algorithms", *SODA: ACM–SIAM Symposium on Discrete Algorithms*, New York, ACM, 1996.

Havender, J. W. "Avoiding Deadlock in Multitasking Systems", *IBM Systems Journal*, vol. 7, pp. 74–84, 1968.

Hoare, C. A. R. "Monitors: An Operating System Structuring Concept", *Communication of the ACM*, vol. 17, no. 10, pp. 549–557, 1974.

Hofri, M. "Proof of a Mutual Exclusion Algorithm", *Operating Systems Review*, vol. 24, no. 1, pp. 18–22, 1990.

Holt, R. C. "Some Deadlock Properties of Computer Systems", *Computing Surveys*, vol. 4, pp. 179–196, 1972.

Isloor, S., Mersland, T. "The Deadlock Problem: An Overview", *Computer*, vol. 13, no. 9, pp. 58–78, 1980.

Kay, J., Lauder, P. "A Fair Share Scheduler", *Communications of the ACM*, vol. 31, no. 1, pp. 44–55, 1988.

Kleinrock, L. *Queuing Systems*, vols. I and II, New York, Willey, 1975–1976.

Lamport, L. "The Mutual Exclusion Problem Has Been Solved", *Communications of the ACM*, vol. 34, no. 1, p. 110, 1991.

Lampson, B. W., Redell, D. D. "Experience with Processes and Monitors in Mesa", *Proceedings of the 7th ACM Symposium on Operating Systems Principles*, New York, ACM, pp. 43–44, 1979.

Levine, G. "Defining Deadlock with Fungible Resources", *Operating Systems Review*, vol. 37, no. 3, pp. 5–11, 2003.

Levine, G. "The Classification of Deadlock Prevention and Avoidance is Erroneous", *Operating System Review*, vol. 39, pp. 47–50, 2005.

Lipton, R. On Synchronization Primitive Systems, PhD thesis, Pittsburgh, PA, Carnegie–Mellon University, 1974.

Marsh, B. D., Scott, M. L., et al. "First-class User-level Threads", *Proceeding of the Thirteenth ACM Symposium on Operating Systems Principles*, New York, ACM, October, pp. 110–121, 1991.

Mauro, J., McDougall, R. *Solaris Internals: Core Kernel Architecture*, London, Prentice Hall, 2007.

Philbin, J., Edler, J., et al. "Thread Scheduling for Cache Locality", *Architectural Support for Programming Languages and Operating Systems*, vol. 24, pp. 60–71, 1996.

Reed, D. P., Kanodia, R. K. "Synchronization with Eventcounts and Sequencers", *Communications of the ACM*, vol. 22, pp. 115–123, 1979.

Robins, K., Robins, S. *UNIX Systems Programming: Communication, Concurrency, and Threads*, Second Edition, London, Prentice Hall, 2003.

Rypka, D. J., Lucido, A. P. "Deadlock Detection and Avoidance for Shared Logical Resources", *IEEE Transactions on Software Engineering*, vol. 5, no. 5, pp. 465–471, 1979.

Schlichting, R. D., Schneider, F. B. "Understanding and Using Asynchronous Message Passing Primitives", *Proceedings of the Symposium on Principles of Distributed Computing*, New York, ACM, pp. 141–147, 1982.

Scrhrage, L. E. "The Queue M/G/I with Feedback to Lower Priority Queues", *Management Science*, vol.13, pp. 466–474, 1967.

Siddha, S., Pallipadi, V., et al. "Process Scheduling Challenges in the Era of Multi-core Processors", *Intel Technology Journal*, vol. 11, 2007.

Vahalia, U. *UNIX Internals: The New Frontiers*, London, Prentice Hall, 1996.

Woodside, C. "Controllability of Computer Performance Tradeoffs Obtained Using Controlled–Share Queue Schedulers", *IEEE Transactions on Software Engineering*, vol. SE-12, no. 10, pp. 1041–1048, 1986.

5 Memory Management

Learning Objectives

- To define the key characteristics of memory systems and basic requirements of primary memory.
- To signify the use of memory hierarchy for access-time reduction.
- To describe the basic requirements of memory management considering the sharing and separation of memory along with needed protection.
- To explain the required address translation for both static and dynamic relocation.
- To discuss the implementation and impact of memory swapping.
- To define the functions and responsibilities of memory management.
- To mention the different memory management schemes being used along with their comparison parameters.
- To describe the contiguous memory allocation schemes including different methods of memory partition (both static and dynamic), and various techniques used in their management with each of their respective merits and drawbacks.
- To implement noncontiguous memory allocation schemes using paged memory management along with its related issues and respective merits and drawbacks.
- To describe the various segmented memory management schemes and their related issues, including the support needed from the underlying hardware.
- To illustrate different kernel memory allocation schemes along with real-life implementations as carried out in UNIX and Solaris.
- To demonstrate the implementation of virtual memory with paging and its different aspects with related issues, along with its actual implementation in VAC (DEC), SUN SPARC, and Motorola systems.
- To illustrate the significance of the translation lookaside buffer (TLB) and its different aspects in the performance improvement of paged memory management.
- To demonstrate segmentation and segmentation with paging in virtual memory and also its actual implementation in real-life in the Intel Pentium.
- To examine the various design issues that appear in the management of virtual memory and subsequently their impacts on its overall performance.
- To describe in brief the real-life implementations of memory management carried out in UNIX, Linux, Windows, and Solaris separately.
- To explain the objectives, principles, and various design issues related to cache memory.

5.1 INTRODUCTION

The one single development that puts computers on their own feet was the invention of a reliable form of memory: the core memory. A journey through the evolution of computers convincingly establishes the fact that due to important breakthroughs in the technological advancement in electronic industry, the size and the speed of the memory itself has constantly increased and greatly paved the way for succeeding generations of computers to emerge. Still, at no point in time in the past and even today, with sophisticated technology, is there ever enough main memory available to satisfy current needs. In addition, as technology constantly advances, the speed of CPUs increases at a much faster rate than that of memory, causing a continuous increase in the speed disparity between CPU

DOI: 10.1201/9781003383055-5

and memory, thereby adversely affecting the performance of the computer system as a whole. To negotiate such situations of space scarcity and speed disparity, computer memory came out with perhaps the widest range of type, technology, organization, and performance as well as its cost to keep the cost/performance of a computer system within an affordable limit. A typical computer system thus equipped with a diverse spectrum of memory subsystems maintaining a well-defined hierarchy; some are internal to the system to hold information that is directly accessible and referenced by the CPU, called *primary memory* or *physical memory*, and some are external to the system to store information, called *secondary memory*, accessed by the CPU via an I/O module. When data and programs are referenced by the CPU for execution, they are loaded in primary memory from this secondary memory; otherwise they remain saved in secondary memory (on a storage device). Discussions of secondary memory are outside the domain of this chapter and will be provided in Chapter 6, "Device Management".

While primary memory has faster access times than secondary memory, it is volatile, and secondary memory, on the other hand, is comparatively slower in operation but is a long-term persistent one that is held in storage devices, such as disk drives, tape drives, and CD-ROM. However, all processes (programs) must be resident in a certain portion of primary (main) memory before being activated. In other words, anything present in primary memory is considered active. The primary memory is therefore part of the *executable memory* (and is also sometimes called executable memory), since the CPU can fetch information only from this memory. Information can be loaded into CPU registers from primary memory or stored from these registers into the primary memory. As the size of the main memory in any computer system, whether large or small, is limited, a challenge is always faced at the time of application program development in respect to the size of the programs to be developed so that these programs or parts of them along with all associated information could be accommodated in the available primary memory when they will be used by the CPU, and this information is then written back to the secondary memory soon after it has been used or updated. If this challenge could be met, the execution time of a process could then be reduced substantially. However, from now, we will always refer to primary memory or main memory by the term "memory or core memory"; otherwise we will specifically use the term "secondary memory".

Memory in a uniprogramming system is basically divided into two parts: one part permanently holds the resident portion (kernel) of the operating system, while the other part is used by the currently active programs. In a multiprogramming/multitasking environment, this division of memory is even more complex; the user part (non-OS part) of memory is once again subdivided here to accommodate multiple processes (programs). The task of this subdivision and many other responsibilities, such as allocation of finite sizes of memory to requesting processes, assistance in managing the sharing of memory, minimizing the memory access time, and others, are carried out statically/ dynamically by the operating system, and this activity is known as ***memory management***. In the hierarchical design of a layered operating system, as described in Chapter 3, memory management belongs to Level 2. The supporting operations of the secondary memory lie in the basic I/O system (devices) located in Level 4 in the hierarchical design of OS that shuttles portion of address spaces between primary and secondary memory while responding to requests issued by the memory manager, and those are examined in details in the chapter on device management.

Design of effective memory management is therefore an important issue, since the overall resource utilization and the other performance criteria of a computer system are greatly influenced and critically affected by the performance of the memory management module, not only in terms of its effectiveness in handling merely memory but also as a consequence of its impact on and interaction with the other resource managers.

In this chapter, we will present the principles of managing main memory and then investigate different forms of memory management schemes, ranging from very simple to highly sophisticated. The ultimate objective is, however, to provide needed memory spaces to each individual program for its execution. We will start at the beginning from the point of the simplest possible memory management system and then gradually proceed to more and more elaborate forms of advanced ones. An attempt is made to explore the salient features of these different types of memory management schemes: their merits, their drawbacks, their limitations, and above all their implementations in contemporary representative computer systems whenever possible.

5.2   KEY CHARACTERISTICS OF MEMORY SYSTEMS

Location: It consists of internal processor memory, main memory, and external memory

Storage Capacity: Memory consists of a number of *cells*, each of which can store a bit of information that contains a binary 0 or a 1. An 8-bit cell is called a *byte*. One byte can store one character. Bytes are grouped into *words*, which is commonly the natural unit of organization of memory. Common word lengths are 8, 16, 32, 48, and 64 bits (1, 2, 4, 6, and 8 bytes, respectively). Each location (word) containing the same number of bits is identified by what is called its *address* by which programs can refer to it. If a location address consists of n (e.g. 32) bits, then the number of locations that can be addressed is 2^n (2^{32}), which is the size of the memory.

Addressable Unit: Each location (addressable unit) in memory is identified (referred to) by its address. In many systems, the addressable unit is the word, and in some systems, the addressable unit is a byte. If an address contains m bits, the maximum number of locations (bytes) directly addressable is 2^m (byte-oriented) that can store a maximum of 2^m characters, which is the size of memory. If bytes are grouped into words and if a word consists of 4 bytes, (i.e. 32 bits), and this word is taken as an addressable unit, then with the same m-bit address, a memory of size $2^{m+2}(4.2^m = 2^{m+2})$ bytes can be addressed; that is, the same length of address bit can address a memory of greater capacity if it is accessed in terms of word units. This is an important factor to be considered at the time of memory organization. For example, a computer with a 16-bit word has 2 bytes/word, whereas a computer with a 32-bit word has 4 bytes/word. The significance of a word is that most instructions operate on entire words. Thus, a 16-bit machine will have 16-bit registers and instructions for manipulating 16-bit words.

More details on this topic are given on the Support Material at www.routledge.com/9781032467238.

5.3   PRIMARY MEMORY: ESSENTIAL REQUIREMENTS

Memory is a vital resource without which programs (processes) and data would have no room for their execution. Hence, memory design and its organization is an important issue that has an immense impact on the entire design of both software and hardware. However, the design principle must fulfill some basic requirements. First, the memory capacity must be as large as possible apart from using larger virtual memory to support it. Second, the memory access time must be as small as possible, close to the processor speed to make processor–memory handshaking faster so that the processor can operate at its optimal speed. Last, the cost of the memory must be within an affordable limit and must be reasonable in relation to that of other components of the computer system.

Realization of faster single memory (similar to the register used as internal processor memory) is relatively very expensive; hence, modern CPUs typically contain a handful of registers (a modern RISC processor contains around 100 such registers) to reduce frequent CPU–memory interactions. Also, the computer system of today is typically equipped with a variety of memory units of very different physical characteristics and costs using a hierarchy of memory to negotiate this issue. With the advent of modern technology, access times (speed) for the primary memory unit have substantially decreases but are still 1 to 4 times longer than the time to reference a register. Size-wise, the primary memory of today may have a few gigabytes, roughly a few million times more executable memory than that of CPU registers. Although these numbers change rapidly due to the continuous evolution of newer electronic technology, but the speed and size ratios still tend to remain relatively unchanged.

More details on this topic are given on the Support Material at www.routledge.com/9781032467238.

5.4 MEMORY HIERARCHIES: ACCESS-TIME REDUCTION

To achieve optimal performance, the memory system must be large enough and also be able to keep up with the CPU speed. But relatively fast memory with moderate size is comparatively expensive. That is why computer memory exhibits the widest range of *types*, *technology*, *organization*, *performance*, and also *cost*. Technology-wise, the *three key characteristics* of memory, **capacity**, **speed** (access time), and *cost*, are considered as a tradeoff. From an application point of view, large-capacity memory with low-cost per bit is an essential requirement. But to meet performance requirements, an expensive, relatively low-capacity memory with fast access time is also a must. To accommodate these diverse requirements in the design, a compromise is thus made which dictates that instead of using a single memory component or technology, a **memory hierarchy** using different types of memory components is to be employed to create the illusion of a large and fast memory, and that too at a low cost to realize cost-effective performance. A typical memory hierarchy is thus built based on trade-off parameters, such as; *capacity*, *access time*, *cost/bit*, and *frequency of access by CPU*. If the memory can be organized in this manner using different memory components, and if the instructions and data can be distributed across these different memory components, it is intuitively clear that this scheme will offer a desired level of performance with a substantial reduction in overall costs. However, it is to be noted that memory management is concerned with handling only executable (primary) memory and providing mechanisms to manually move information across the hierarchy. A virtual memory system automates the movement of information between the secondary and primary memories. The file manager provides mechanisms to administer secondary memory according to the users' demand. Since construction of a memory hierarchy in this fashion using different types of memory components is a matter of computer organization and architecture, interested reader can consult Chakraborty (2020) or any other standard textbook on this subject.

More details on this topic with figures are given on the Support Material at www.routledge. com/9781032467238.

5.5 MEMORY MANAGEMENT: SOME BASIC REQUIREMENTS

Memory management has evolved with the evolution of operating systems and hardware technology, and it resides at Level 2 in the hierarchical design of layered operating system, as described in Chapter 3. The memory manager usually performs a lot of responsibilities; a few of them are: allocation of a finite capacity of memory to simultaneously requesting processes with adequate protection, assistance in managing the sharing of memory and minimizing memory access time, and similar tasks that are carried out statically or dynamically. Different memory management schemes in this regard have been designed that differ in policies as well as in underlying mechanisms, but memory management as a whole must satisfy at least some specific requirements in order to carry out fault-free execution of programs. Some of the critical requirements are the following.

5.5.1 SEPARATION AND SHARING: IMPORTANCE AND DIFFERENT APPROACHES

Separation of address spaces and sharing of memory are, in fact, two conflicting aspects of multiple coexisting active processes in a multitasking environment. Each process's address space must be isolated (separated) to ensure its integrity and safeguard its contents (protection), and at the same time, the cooperating processes should be allowed to have controlled access to common areas of memory (sharing) without damaging the necessary separation. Different strategies in this regard have been devised by different memory management systems in contemporary operating systems to fulfill these crucial requirements, at least to an acceptable extent for the sake of interprocess cooperation as well as to minimize the waste in memory space by avoiding redundancy.

5.5.2 PROTECTION: IMPORTANCE AND IMPLEMENTATION

Protection mechanisms in multiple coexisting active processes with separation in the address spaces commonly ensures that a program in one process cannot refer to any information of another process by any form of branching, and/or a process cannot normally access the data area of another process, but sharing of data, of course, can be allowed by means of some special arrangements. The resident portion of the OS should also be kept isolated and protected from any unauthorized intentional or unintentional tampering attempted by user processes. Memory protection is thus urgently required and must be implemented at the hardware level (processor or memory) rather than by the software (operating system). Many different methods to implement memory protection have been improvised using the hardware facilities available in the system, and many refinements to those approaches have also been made. Each such method, however, has been found to have several merits and also certain critical drawbacks, as usual.

5.5.3 RELOCATION: ADDRESS TRANSLATION

In a multitasking/multi-user environment, the available main memory, limited in size, is generally distributed among a number of active processes of different sizes, fitting them without overlap or wasting space. It is not possible to also predict which programs of what sizes are to be executed concurrently and how long they will run. Moreover, swapping in/out of active processes often to/from memory for the sake of performance improvements usually changes their physical location from their earlier positions in memory. Due to all these reasons and more, it was decided that a program must be allowed to load anywhere in memory whenever there is room for it. Consequently, the actual starting address of a program is not fixed and is therefore not known until load time. This act of placing a program anywhere suitable in memory irrespective of its previous location while it was compiled and linked or even swapped out is known as *relocation*, and it is carried out by a system program at the time of actual loading.

Act of such relocations require appropriate changes in certain address portions in the program to match them with the current location after relocation. The processor hardware and operating-system software must then somehow translate (map) such memory references found in the program code into actual physical memory addresses that reflect the current location of the program in main memory. Memory-protection hardware also carries out various checks along with the required address translation. Although memory relocation makes management more efficient, flexible, and versatile, it is overall an expensive mechanism that will eventually lead to graceful degradation in performance caused by the added operational overhead. Different memory management schemes have thus evolved with different targets that differ in the relative complexity of address translation and the associated memory protection and consequently in the amount of generated runtime overhead that they usually pay. However, address translation, sometimes called *memory mapping* or *program relocation*, converts the logical address generated by a program into a corresponding physical address, and it arises in three different situations: *object code generation* (compilation), *linking and loading*, and *execution time*. Depending on when and how this mapping takes place in a given relocation scheme, two basic types of relocation are observed: *static relocation* and *dynamic relocation*.

5.5.3.1 Static Relocation

- **At program generation time:** The source program and its other modules written by different people, usually at different times, are compiled separately to create the respective object codes, and those are then linked together (by a system program called a *linker*) to form a single module (load module) that can then straightaway be loaded into memory and directly executed. While the single load module is created as output, each location-sensitive address within each object module must then be changed (relocated) from its symbolic addresses to a reference to the starting address location of the created load module. This form of relocation refers to *static relocation* performed by a *relocating linker*, when different object modules are combined by the linker to create a load module. At loading time, the created load module (executable program) is now loaded by an *absolute loader* into memory starting strictly at the location pre-defined and specified in the header of the load module with no address translation (relocation) at the time of loading. If the memory area specified in the header of the load module is not free, then the program has to wait for the specific memory slot to become free, although there are other slots available in memory. A *relocating loader*, however, removes this drawback by loading an executable module to any available slot and then translates all location-sensitive information within the module correctly to bind to the actual physical location in which this module will be loaded. Since the software relocation involves considerable space and time complexity, systems with static relocation are commonly and practically not favored over only static binding of modules.

5.5.3.2 Dynamic Relocation
- **At execution time:** Dynamic relocation is carried out, which implies that address translation (mapping) from the logical (virtual) address space to the physical address space is to be performed using a base register provided by the CPU. The executable program code to be run in systems with dynamic relocation is prepared by a compiler or an assembler assuming that the program is to be loaded at location 0 in main memory without any relocation adjustments. Executable code stored on the secondary storage when loaded into main memory is without any address translation at some available memory slot which is large enough to hold the program, and the starting address of this given memory slot is saved in the PCB of the program belonging to the memory manager. The operating system simply sets the base register to this starting physical load address, called the *base address*, which is obtained from the PCB area of the executing program. Each memory reference generated by the executing process is then mapped into the corresponding physical address which is obtained by simply adding the contents of the base register to the present address of the current memory reference.

5.5.3.3 Advantages
The notable feature of this scheme is that the relocation process is free from any additional memory management strategies and is simply an hardware-only implicit base addressing implemented only at runtime (final stage). Moreover, here the logical (virtual) address space in which the processor-generated addresses prior to relocation are logical (virtual) addresses is clearly separated from the physical address space containing the corresponding physical addresses generated by the mapping hardware used to reference the physical memory. This attribute nowadays facilitates designing a flexible form of an on-chip (earlier an optional off-chip) advanced memory-management unit (MMU) within the microprocessor CPU for the purpose of generating physical addresses along with other supports. Another distinct advantage is that it gives the OS absolute freedom by permitting it to freely move a partially executed program from one area of memory into another, even in the middle of execution (during runtime) with no problem accessing information correctly in the newly allotted space. This feature is also very useful, particularly to support swapping programs in/out of memory at any point in time. Consequently, this approach demands extra hardware to provide one or more base registers and some added overhead also involved in the additional computations required in the relocation process. Contemporary architectures, however, address these issues

supporting implicit base addressing; they provide a dedicated adder to allow address calculation to proceed in parallel with other processor operations, and with this overlapping, they minimize the impact on the effective memory bandwidth to an affordable limit.

5.5.4 SWAPPING: IMPACT AND IMPLEMENTATION

Swapping is an activity carried out by memory management that temporarily removes part or all of a partially executed preempted or suspended process from main memory to a specified area on a disk (swap area/backing store) for the sake of creating space which can now be allocated to another deserving process waiting to enter the system for the purpose of better utilization of system resources. Movement of information of this type between memory and disk (swap area) is handled by the upper level of the two-level scheduler (medium-term scheduler), known as the *swapper*. The processes selected for swapping out are blocked (on a memory request) by the memory manager, and then their occupied memory spaces are made free (deallocated). The context block of a swapped-out process should indicate where it has been placed in the backing store. The context block itself is usually not swapped out. However, swapping should not be carried out very often since it involves lot of intricacy and additional overhead. Still, many different forms of modified swapping are observed in virtual memory systems based on paging or on segmentation.

The policy design and the mechanisms to implement swapping require some specific provisions and necessary support from the operating system end. However, the major responsibilities performed by a swapper mainly consist of:

- Selection of processes to be swapped out
- Selection of processes to be swapped in
- Allocation, administration, and management of swap space

While selecting a victim for swapping out, the swapper takes many relevant factors into account, such as the current status, memory residence time, size of each resident process, consideration of age to avoid thrashing, and similar other vital factors that could influence the performance of the system as a whole. The selection of a process to be once again *swapped in* is usually based on the fulfillment of certain criteria: the priority of the process and the amount of time it spent in secondary storage (aging); otherwise this may invite the problem of starvation, the availability of resource for which it was swapped out, and finally the fulfillment of minimum disk-resident time requirement from the instant of its being swapped out. This is specifically required in order to exert control over forthcoming thrashing.

- **Swap file:** When a partially executed process is swapped out, its runtime *process image*, along with the runtime states consisting of the contents of the active processor registers, as well as its other data and stack locations, are temporarily saved in a swap file. One of two types of swap files is commonly used for this purpose and must be created, reserved, and allocated statically/dynamically before or at the time of process creation. Those are:
  - A system-wide single swap file in a special disk (usually in system disk) for all active processes, to be created at the time of system generation.
  - A dedicated swap file for each active process that can be created either statically at the time of program preparation or dynamically at the time of process creation.

However, each of these two approaches has its own merits and also certain drawbacks.

- **Policy decisions:** Swapping of a process is sometimes urgently needed and is thus favored, even after accepting that the cost of swapping is appreciable. That is why the operating system often enforces certain rules to designate a process as not swappable if it belongs to a given class of privileged processes and users. All other processes, however, may be treated as swappable by default. Sometimes, the memory management (operating system) decides the policy and implements it on its own when it finds that a relatively large process in memory remains blocked over a considerable duration of time, when the other waiting processes that deserved to be run can be placed there for the sake of performance improvement.

- **Relocation:** In systems that support swapping, re-placement of a swapped-out process in main memory when it is once again reloaded as a result of swap-in is carried out using dynamic allocation (already explained in the last section) whenever a suitable size of memory anywhere is found. Of course, this approach has comparatively high overhead and also requires some sort of additional hardware facilities.

5.5.5 LOGICAL ADDRESSES AND LOGICAL ORGANIZATION

The sequence of instructions and associated sets of data of a program have individual respective addresses within a program address space called *logical addresses* which are used to identify or locate them and usually are relative to the start of the program. A programmer assumes that the program starts from 0 and extends to a maximum of $N-1$, where N is the maximum number of locations available in memory. A user presumes that most programs and their associated data are organized in the form of some sort of module (*logical organization*) written and compiled independently and that they may be placed at different locations in memory during runtime. Memory management, by some means, must ensure that all interactions between the modules are correctly maintained during runtime with needed protection, if there is any.

5.5.6 PHYSICAL ADDRESSES AND PHYSICAL ORGANIZATION

The actual address of a physical location in memory used by the CPU to access that particular memory location is called the *physical address* (or absolute address). Programs when written occupy contiguous memory locations in logical address space starting from address 0. When a program is ultimately run in the physical address space, this logical address space, by some means, has to be converted into actual physical address space and must be associated and bound to physical memory locations in the same way as indicated by the logical addresses generated by the program. When a program is saved in a secondary storage device (say, on a disk), only the contents of the memory with no address information are really saved. When it is once again loaded back into main memory at a later time for execution, it can be loaded anywhere in memory, wherever there is room for it. In this situation, the actual starting address of a program is not fixed and is therefore not known until load time. To run it successfully, all the location-sensitive addresses within the program must be modified accordingly as per the actual physical starting address of the program being loaded in main memory.

For more details on this entire section, with respective figures, see "Memory Management: Some Basic Requirements" and "Memory Management: Some Fundamental Responsibilities" on the Support Material at www.routledge.com/9781032467238.

5.6 MEMORY MANAGEMENT: FUNCTIONS AND RESPONSIBILITIES

The *memory manager* consists of a number of modules which are basically concerned with the management of primary memory directly accessible by the processor. Besides many others, it is mainly concerned with *five* basic functions.

- Allocation of physical blocks of storage to requesting processes as needed and keeping track of the status of each location of primary memory, either allocated or free, in a coherent way by creating appropriate data structures. It also provides mechanisms that allow information to migrate up and down in the memory hierarchy.

- Determining allocation policy for memory, that is, deciding to which process it should go, how much, when, and where. If primary memory is to be shared by one or more processes concurrently, then memory management must determine which process's request needs to be served.
- The allocation policy adopted by memory management along with the memory organization scheme being employed has a direct impact in the overall utilization of system resources. The overall system performance is also greatly affected by the way in which the memory-management policy and the job-scheduling policy influence each other while allocating memory to different processes. The ultimate objective of memory management and job scheduling is to minimize the amount of memory wastage and maximize the number of processes that can be accommodated in the limited available memory space.
- Allocation technique—once it is decided to allocate memory, the specific locations must be selected and allocation information updated.
- Deallocation technique and policy—handling the deallocation (reclamation) of memory. A process may explicitly release previously allocated memory, or memory management may unilaterally reclaim the memory based on a deallocation policy. After deallocation, status information must be updated.
- Handling the virtual memory mechanism—keeping track of virtual memory allocation and also interacting with mass storage (device) handlers; to manage swapping on predefined policies between main memory and disk when main memory is not large enough to hold all the processes.

Apart from all these, memory management provides mechanisms that allow information to migrate up and down the memory hierarchy with the necessary binding of addresses, which is an essential requirement for information movement. It also employs numerous strategies to distribute a limited size of memory to many processes to load only once, thereby enhancing memory utilization. While distributing memory, it also ensures the protection (integrity) of each active process when many such processes coexist in memory. To address all these issues, memory management must fulfill certain fundamental requirements in order to satisfy the basic demands of the operating environment.

5.7 DIFFERENT MEMORY-MANAGEMENT SCHEMES: COMPARISON PARAMETERS

Memory management modules should be as small as and also simple to fulfill the ultimate target of increasing user flexibility and system efficiency. Several approaches to memory management have been devised based on *contiguous allocation* as well as *noncontiguous allocation* of memory. **Contiguous allocation** means that each logical object is placed in a set of memory locations with strictly consecutive addresses. A common approach with contiguous allocation is found in partitioned memory management, both static and dynamic approaches, which will be discussed later in this chapter. **Noncontiguous allocation** means that memory is allocated in such a way that parts of a single logical object may be placed in noncontiguous areas of physical memory. Address translation is performed during the execution of the instruction that establishes the necessary correspondence between a contiguous virtual address space (in virtual memory) and the possibly noncontiguous physical addresses of locations where object item resides in physical memory at runtime. Paging is such a memory-management scheme that exhibits noncontiguous allocation of physical memory, removing the obligatory requirement of contiguous allocation of physical memory. The various types of techniques used to implement different memory management strategies are:

- Single contiguous memory management
- Fixed-partitioned memory management

- Dynamic (relocation) partitioned memory management
- Paged memory management
- Demand-paged memory management in the case of virtual memory
- Segmented memory management
- Segmented and demand-paged memory management
- Memory management with swapping and paging

Each of these strategies while implemented exhibits some merits as well as certain drawbacks. Therefore, a comparison of these schemes involves analysis of each scheme informally with respect to certain essential parameters, such as:

- Wasted memory
- Overhead in memory access
- Time complexity

A brief discussion of this topic is given on the Support Material at www.routledge.com/9781032467238.

5.8   MEMORY MANAGEMENT SCHEMES

In the early days, different memory management strategies and related algorithms were mainly realized exploiting the facilities offered by different hardware schemes used in memory organization. This situation has been, however, gradually changing with the introduction of separate memory management hardware units, and later on-chip MMUs in high-end microprocessors and RISC chips. On each such processor, the operating system designers developed a specific memory management scheme fitting the hardware facilities available to them. Alternatively, they could develop the most appropriate type of memory management scheme and then choose the specific hardware platform that was best suited. Whatever the line of thought, however followed, several approaches to memory management were devised that are broadly classified as being contiguous allocation or noncontiguous allocation of memory. Memory management initially evolved with the concept of contiguous allocation, and noncontiguous allocation came much later. That is why, following chronological order, the discussions here start first with various strategies of memory management relating to contiguous allocation of memory.

5.8.1   CONTIGUOUS MEMORY ALLOCATION

Contiguous allocation means that each logical object (or a process) is entirely placed in a set of memory locations with strictly consecutive addresses in a single contiguous area in memory before the start of its execution (*static*). This strategy, however, subsequently gave rise to partitioning the available physical memory, and fitting partitions, if available, are then allocated to different memory requests. The partition approach itself again comprises two distinct classes: one is to define and carry out the partition statically, say, during system generation or system installation (booting) at the beginning of the day, and the other may be defined to carry out the partition dynamically (without having any physical partition in advance) in response to user demands as and when those arrive. Different schemes as proposed in this regard raise numerous types of different practical issues that have been identified and then properly addressed to arrive at a fruitful solution. We now describe some of these popular schemes in brief in the following sections in chronological order of their appearance.

In the early days, the **bare machine** had only the hardware, with no operating system (hence, no memory management or MMU) or any other supporting software or utilities. The entire machine was ultimately under the absolute control of the user, who had to write each and every program for their own applications as well as to drive and control the machine, and all these were written in absolute binary that was not only tedious to design but laborious to develop and equally error-prone.

A brief discussion of this topic with a figure is given on the Support Material at www.routledge.com/9781032467238.

5.8.1.1   Single-User: The Resident Monitor

The next simplest approach to memory management is the *single-user fixed partitioning* found in the *resident monitor* (the first true operating system) approach, the forerunner of the modern operating system, already discussed in Section 1.6.2.1. In this system, memory management distinctly divides the entire memory into two contiguous areas (partitions). One of them is permanently allocated to the resident portion (core) of the operating system (monitor) at one extreme end of memory, whether top or bottom, and the other part of the OS; such as, the command-line interpreter and loader, are sometimes placed at the opposite end of the memory. This leaves a single, large contiguous area of free memory (second partition) in between for transient programs to use one after another, with all machine resources dedicated to one such single user (one program). The OS (resident monitor) here keeps track only of two addresses, which are the first and the last locations available for the user processes. The PC-DOS operating system, the predecessor of popular MS-DOS, has followed this approach in general.

When a transient process attempts to enter the system, the operating system used to check the size of the requesting process and whether it is within the bounds of the available user memory. Otherwise, loading of the program cannot be successfully completed, and instead, a trap is generated in the operating system that in effect flashes an error message to the user. But, if it is allowed to load, the process gets control from the operating system and starts executing until completion or abnormal termination due to the occurrence of an error condition. After completion, the process relinquishes its control and transfers it to the operating system that, in turn, loads another fitting program in waiting. Single-process monitors creating single-process environments hardly ever support *sharing* of code and data in memory. Although the resident monitor is basically a single-user operating system, a certain level of multiprogramming can be simulated with the resident monitor by swapping out an active process waiting for a long time for its I/O completion, and meanwhile a new process or an already swapped-out process can be entered from the backing store to make use of the CPU idle time. Of course, swap time (process switch time) should be here considered an essential parameter that often influences the decision about whether the swapping is really profitable as far as CPU utilization is concerned. Many different approaches in this regard have been improvised and subsequently implemented. Last, this system must have a proper protection mechanism in memory to safeguard the resident monitor from any accidental or malicious tampering by user processes, failing which may lead to total collapse of the entire operating environment. The required protection mechanism is commonly realized by some sort of hardware assistance; two such mechanisms are generally in use: one is the use of a *fence register*, and the other is to employ *protection bits*, discussed in the last section.

The distinct advantages of the resident monitor scheme in its pure form are that it is simple to use, easy to implement, and usually requires as little as 1 Kbytes, or even a little bit more for a relatively sophisticated one. Its main drawbacks are mainly poor utilization of memory, poor utilization of processor due to needless waiting for I/O, and user jobs being limited to the size of available main memory, with the exception perhaps of an overlay mechanism. However, due to the advent of advanced hardware technology, the resident monitor approach has overcome a few of its limitations, and thus was later modified accordingly. But its major impact is that it laid the foundation and paved the way in the development of modern single-user operating systems used in the early version of today's microcomputers.

More details on this topic with a figure are given on the Support Material at www.routledge.com/9781032467238.

5.8.1.2   Partitioned-Memory Management

Multiprogramming is supported by many memory-management schemes using numerous techniques. One such is *partitioning*, which has been used with several variations in some now-obsolete operating systems. This approach basically implies dividing the available physical memory into several partitions, which may be of the same or different sizes, each of which may be allocated to different processes. While allocating a partition of the memory to a process, many different strategies could be taken that depend on when and how partitions are to be created and modified. These strategies, in general, have different targets to achieve, with their own merits and drawbacks. This approach is again differentiated mainly in two ways: one that divides primary memory into a number of fixed partitions at the time the operating system is configured before use, and the other one that keeps entire memory as it is and dynamically partitioned it into variable-sized blocks according to the demand of the programs during their execution. In this section, we will discuss fixed partitioning with static allocation and variable partition with dynamic allocation.

5.8.1.2.1 Fixed Partition: Static Allocation

In fixed partitioning, the memory is divided into a number of fixed-size partitions at some time prior to the execution of user programs, and those partitions remain fixed thereafter. The number and sizes of individual partitions are usually determined at the time of system generation and mostly depend on the capacity of the available physical memory and also the typical size of processes that are most frequently handled in a given installation. Since only one process can reside and run in any partition at any point in time, the maximum number of distinct partitions at any instant sets the upper limit of degrees of multiprogramming that can be used. This type of partitioning memory considering specific sizes of partitions and thereby creating a definite number of partitions has a strong impact on the overall performance of the system. That is why some systems carry out willful manual partitioning, mainly by the operator, when the system is started up at the time of loading the operating system (booting) and not changed thereafter, or at any time when the system is running, the partition size is redefined according to the prevailing situation without going through further rebooting.

The memory is partitioned into the same or different desirable sizes to accommodate both small or large jobs in which one partition is kept reserved for the resident portion of the operating system. Each such a partition can hold only one process at any instant, and the CPU then switches from one process to another in different partitions either in time-sharing fashion or another manner. Once the partitions are created and defined, the memory manager has to keep track of the attributes of all the partitions, including their current status, such as free or allocated, by using a data structure called a *partition description table* (PDT). When a process in one partition completes its execution, the status field for that partition in the PDT is changed to 'Free', and the OS can place a suitable new job from the waiting job queue in that partition, and the status field of the selected entry in the PDT is then marked 'Allocated'. The process control block of the process is accordingly updated. In brief, whenever the operating system attempts to place a new job in the memory partition, either the PDT is searched for a suitable partition to match, or the job queue is searched for a suitable job to match the available partition.

- **Allocation strategy:** A fixed-partition system requires that a process address space size (known from the process image) correlate with a partition of adequate size. Out of many available partitions, selection of a particular partition for allocation to a requesting process can be made in several ways; two common approaches are the *first fit* and *best fit*. The first-fit approach selects the first free partition large enough to fit the requesting process for allocation. The best-fit approach, on the other hand, requires the smallest free partition out of many such that meets the requirements of the requesting process. Both algorithms need to search the PDT to find a free partition of adequate size. However, while the first-fit terminates upon finding the first such partition, the best-fit continues to go through the entire table to process all qualifying PDT entries to find the most appropriate (tightest) one. As a result, while the first-fit attempts to speed up the execution, accepting costly memory wastage within the partition; the best-fit aims to optimize memory utilization, sacrificing even execution speed. However, the best-fit algorithm can be made profitable if the free partitions in the PDT are kept sorted by size; then the PDT could intuitively find a suitable partition fitting the requesting process quickly, thereby making the execution speed much faster. It is to be noted that the best-fit algorithm discriminates against small jobs as being unworthy of occupying a whole partition in order to attain better memory utilization, whereas usually, it is desirable to give the smallest jobs (assumed to be interactive jobs) the best service, not the worst.

• **Allocation method:** The job scheduler chooses one job from the job queue for execution in response to the request issued either from the user end or due to the availability of one or more free partitions reported by the memory manager. In some situations, there may be a few free partitions, but none is found to accommodate the incoming job; the job in question will then have to wait until such a partition is available. Another job fitting the available partition will then be taken from the job queue for execution in order to keep the memory utilization high, even disobeying the ordering of process activations intended by the scheduling algorithm that, in turn, may affect the performance of the system as a whole. Another situation may happen when a high-priority job is selected for execution but no matching partition is available: the memory manager then decides to swap out one suitable process from memory to make room for this incoming job, even accepting the additional overhead, but its justification should be carefully decided beforehand. It is interesting to observe that although memory management and processor scheduling reside in separate domains of the operating system with different types of responsibilities and targets, operation of the one may often affect and influence the normal operation of the other when static partitioning of memory is employed. However, the actions of memory management should be coordinated with the operation of processor scheduling in such a way as to extract the highest throughput while handling an environment consisting of conflicting situations.

• **Allocation Schemes:** Although a number of allocation schemes are available for this kind of systems, *two main approaches* are common:

1. Fixed memory partition with *separate input job queues* for each partition.

2. Fixed memory partition with *single input job queues* for all the partitions.

Each of these approaches has precise merits in some situations and also specific drawbacks in other situations.

• **Protection:** Different partitions containing user programs and the operating system should be protected from one another to prevent any kind of damage that may be caused by accidental overwrites or intentional malicious encroachment. Adequate protection mechanisms are thus required that can be realized in many different ways, described in the last section.

• **Swapping:** Swapping is carried out in this system mainly to negotiate an emergency, such as a high-priority job that must be immediately executed, or in situations when a job is waiting and idle for resources needed for its execution, thereby preventing other intended jobs from entering. Swapping- in is also done for an already swapped-out job in order to increase the ratio of ready to resident processes and thereby improve the overall performance of the system. There are also other situations when swapping is urgently needed. The mechanisms required to implement swapping were discussed in a previous section.

• **Fragmentation:** In a fixed-partition system, allocation of a process in a partition of adequate size causes an amount of memory space to remain unused internally within the partition when the process is loaded. This phenomenon is called ***internal fragmentation***, or sometimes ***internal waste***. The extent to which internal fragmentation causes memory wastage in a given system varies depending on several factors, such as the number of partitions, the size of each individual partition, frequency of execution of processes of a specific size, and average process size and variance. This waste also tends to increase due to the provision of one or two large partitions, usually required for large processes, but they mostly arrive infrequently, thereby causing these partitions to be mostly underutilized or poorly utilized. However, the sum of all such internal fragmentations that occur in each partition sometimes even exceeds the size of a specific partition. Since internal fragmentation in fixed-partitioned system is inevitable and cannot be avoided, an efficient memory management strategy would thus always attempt to keep this internal fragmentation to a minimum affordable limit, of course, with no compromise in any way with the overall performance of the system.

- **Conclusion:** Fixed-partition memory management is one of the simplest possible ways to realize multiprogramming with modest hardware support and is suitable for static environments where the workload can be ascertained beforehand. But the negative impact of internal fragmentation is one of its major drawbacks. It is equally disadvantageous in systems in which the memory requirement of the job is not known ahead of time. Moreover, the size of the executable program itself faces severe restrictions imposed by partition size. In addition, programs that grow dynamically during runtime may sometimes find this system unsuitable due to nonavailability of needed space in the partition thus allocated, and no operating system support is available at that time to negotiate this situation. Another pitfall of this system may be of fixing the number of partitions that limits the degree of multiprogramming, which may have an adverse effect on the effective working of short-term (process) scheduling and may create a negative impact on the overall performance of the system. With the use of swapping mechanisms, this situation may be overcome by increasing the ratio of ready to resident processes, but that can only be achieved at the cost of additional I/O overhead. Due to all these issues and others, timesharing systems as a whole thus required operating system design to move away from fixed-partition strategies indicating a move towards handling of dynamic environments that could use memory spaces in a better way.

Still, fixed-partition memory management was widely used in batch multiprogramming systems in the early days, particularly in OS/360, a versatile operating system used on large IBM mainframes for many years. This system was a predecessor of OS/MVT (multiprogramming with variable number of tasks) and OS/MFT, which, in turn, is a predecessor of MULTICS that ultimately became converted into today's UNIX.

More details on this topic with figures are given on the Support Material at www.routledge.com/ 9781032467238.

5.8.1.2.2 Overlays

An **overlay** mechanism used in software development is a technique by which a program larger than the size of the available small user area (partition) can be run with almost no restrictions in relation to the size of the offered area, without getting much assistance from the operating system in this regard. In the overlay technique, a user program can be subdivided by the developer into a number of modules, blocks, or components. Each such component is an entity in a program that consists of a group of logically related items, and each could fit in the available memory. Out of these components, there is a main component (root segment) and one or more fixed-size components known as overlays. The root segment is always kept resident in the main memory for the entire duration of program execution. The overlays are kept stored on a secondary storage device (with extensions either .ovl or .ovr) and are loaded into memory as and when needed. Overlay 0 would start running first; when it was done, it would call another overlay. Some overlay systems were highly complex, allowing multiple overlays to reside in memory at any point in time.

In most automatic overlay systems, the developer must explicitly state the overlay structure in advance. There are many binders available that are capable of processing and allocating overlay structure. An appropriate module loader is required to load the various components (procedures) of the overlay structure as they are needed. The *portion* of the loader that actually intercepts the calls and loads the necessary procedure is called the **overlay supervisor** or simply the *flipper*. The root component is essentially an overlay supervisor that intercept the calls of the executing resident overlay components during runtime. Whenever an inter procedure reference is made, control is transferred to the overlay supervisor, which loads the target procedure, if necessary.

The hardware does not support overlays. Checking every reference would be unacceptably slow in software. Therefore, only *procedure calls* are allowed to invoke new overlays. Procedure invocation and return are, however, more expensive than they usually would be, because not only must the status of the destination overlay be examined, but it may also have to be brought into secondary storage. However, the software, such as translators, like compilers and assemblers, can be of great assistance in this regard.

The overlay concept itself opened a wide spectrum of possibilities. To run the program, the first overlay was brought in and ran for a while. When it finished, or even during its execution, it could read in the next overlay by calling it with the help of the overlay supervisor, and so on. The supervisor itself undertakes the task of necessary input–output to remove the overlay or overlays that occupy the place the desired one needs to be loaded and then bring the required overlay into that position. To implement the overlay mechanism, the programmer had a lot of responsibilities, such as breaking the program into overlays, deciding where in the secondary memory each overlay was to be kept, arranging for the transport of overlays between main memory and secondary memory, and in general managing the entire overlay process without any assistance from the hardware or operating system. If, by some means, the entire burden of the overlay mechanism and its related management responsibilities could be shifted onto (entrusted with) the operating system, relieving the programmer from hazardous bookkeeping activities, we would nearly arrive at the doorstep in the emergence of an innovative concept now called **paging**. Paging is discussed in detail in a later section in this chapter.

An overlay mechanism is essentially a more refined form of a **swapping technique** which swaps only portions of job's address space and is called *overlay management*. Overlays work well only with applications where the execution of the program goes through well-defined phases, each of which requires different program units. Thrashing can result from the inappropriate use of overlays. Overlays, normally used in conjunction with single contiguous, partitioned, or relocatable partitioned memory management, provide essentially an approximation of *segmentation* but without the segment address mapping hardware. Segmentation is discussed in a later section in this chapter.

In spite of being widely used for many years with several merits and distinct advantages, the overlay technique is critically constrained due to the involvement of much work in connection with overlay management. To get out of it, a group of researchers in Manchester, England, in 1961 proposed a method for performing the overlay process automatically with no intimation even to the programmer that it was happening (Fotheringham, 1961). This method is now called *virtual memory*, in which all management responsibility is entrusted to the operating system, releasing the programmer from a lot of annoying bookkeeping tasks. It was first used during the 1960s, and by the last part of the 1960s and early 1970s, virtual memory had become available on most computers, including those for commercial use. Nowadays, even microprocessor-based small computer systems have highly sophisticated virtual memory systems. Virtual memory is discussed in detail in later sections in this chapter.

More details on this topic with a figure are given on the Support Material at www.routledge.com/9781032467238.

5.8.1.2.3 *Dynamic Linking*

The appearance of overlay concept eventually blooms out many sparkling ideas to emerge. One of them is that, instead of having an overlay structure, a mechanism could be developed by which linking of external references and subsequent loading are postponed until execution time. That is, the translator (assembler/compiler) produces object code containing text, binding, and relocation information from a source language deck. The loader loads only the main program. During runtime, if the main program should execute a transfer instruction to an external address or refer to an external variable, the loader is called and the segment containing the external references will only then be loaded and linked to the program at the point where it is first called. This type of function is usually called *dynamic linking, dynamic loading,* or *load-on-call* (LOCAL).

Dynamic linking and subsequent loading are powerful tools that provide a wide range of possibilities concerning use, sharing, and updating of library modules. Modules of a program that are not invoked during the execution of the program need not be loaded and linked to it, thereby offering substantial savings of both time and memory space. Moreover, if a module referenced by a program has already been linked to another executing program, the same copy can be linked to this program as well. This means that dynamic linking often allows several executing programs to share one copy of a subroutine or library procedure, resulting in considerable savings both in terms of time and memory space. Runtime support routines for the high-level language C could be stored in a *dynamic link library* (files with extension .dll). A single copy of the routines in this library could be loaded into memory. All C programs currently in execution could then be linked to this one copy instead of linking a separate copy in each object program. Dynamic linking also provides an interesting advantage: when a library of modules is updated, any program that invokes a new module starts using the new version of the module automatically. It provides another means to conserve memory by overwriting a module existing in memory with a new module. This idea has been subsequently exploited in virtual memory, discussed in the following section.

In an object-oriented system, dynamic linking is often used to refer software object with its allied methods. Moreover, the implementation of the object can be changed at any time without affecting the program that makes use of the object. Dynamic linking also allows one object to be shared by several executing programs in the way already explained.

Dynamic linking is accomplished by a dynamic loader (a constituent of the OS services) which loads and links a called routine and then transfers the control to the called routine for its execution. After completion (or termination) of the execution, the control is once again sent back to the OS for subsequent necessary actions. The called routine, however, may be still in memory if the storage page supports that, so a second call to it may not require another load operation. Control may now simply be passed from the dynamic loader to the called routine. When dynamic linking is used, the association of an actual address with the symbolic name of the called routine is not made until the call statement is executed. Another way of describing this is to say that the binding of the name to an actual address is delayed from load time until execution time. This delayed binding offers greater flexibility as well as substantial reduction in storage space usage, but it requires more overhead since the operating system must intervene in the calling process. It can be inferred that this delayed binding gives more capabilities at the expense of a relatively small higher cost.

More details on this topic with figures are given on the Support Material at www.routledge.com/9781032467238.

5.8.1.2.4   Sharing of Programs

Programs can be shared in two ways: *static sharing* and *dynamic sharing.* In static sharing, the program to be shared undergoes static binding by a linker that injects a copy of the shared program in each of all the other programs that want to use it. Static binding is done to create the load module (executable module, .exe file) before the execution of a program begins. The identity of the shared program is then lost in each of the load modules thus produced by the linker. If more than one such load module at any instant are present simultaneously in memory, then more than one copies of the same shared program are in memory at the same time. However, static sharing of a program is easy to implement but adversely affects memory usage causing wastage by having multiple copies of the shared program during the execution of the programs that use the shared program.

Dynamic sharing implies that a single copy of the shared program can be used by several other programs during their execution when they require it. It is done by dynamic linking carried out by a dynamic linker (loader, a part of OS). Here, the shared program has a different identity (a different file extension, .dll) and it is known to OS. When this shared program is called for the first time by any other calling program, a copy of the shared program is then brought in main memory from secondary storage, and it is then linked to the calling program at the point where the call occurs. When another calling program needs to use the same shared program, the kernel first checks whether a copy of the shared program is already available in memory. If so, the kernel then links the existing shared program to this new calling program. Thus, there exists only one copy of the shared program in main memory, even when it is shared by more than one program. While dynamic sharing conserves memory space, it is at the cost of complexity in its implementation. Here, the kernel has to always keep track of shared program(s) existing in memory and perform the needed dynamic linking. The program be shared also has to be coded in a different way. It is written as a *reentrant program* to negotiate the mutual interference of programs that share it.

> **Reentrant programs:** When a shared program is dynamically shared by other sharing programs, the data created by one executing sharing program and embedded in the shared program should be kept protected by the shared program from any interference that may be caused by any of the other sharing programs while in execution. This is accomplished by allocating a separate data area dynamically for each executing sharing program and holding its address in a CPU register. The contents of these registers are saved as part of the CPU state when a process switch occurs and once again reloaded into the CPU registers when the program is brought back into main memory. This arrangement and related actions ensure that different invocations of the shared program by individual sharing programs will not interfere with one another's data.

More details on this topic with figures are given on the Support Material at www.routledge.com/ 9781032467238

5.8.1.2.5   Variable Partition: Dynamic Partition

To alleviate the critical internal fragmentation problem and several other acute constraints attributed by fixed-size partition static allocation scheme, it was then required to redesign the memory manager so that instead of creating the partitions before the arrival of the processes, it could create the partition dynamically by allocating space from the currently existing state of the system to fit the requirement of each requesting process at the time of its arrival. Likewise, when a process is completed, terminated, or even swapped out, the vacated space is returned to the pool of free memory areas so that the memory manager can proceed with further allocation of partitions from the available total memory areas whenever needed. In fact, the memory manager may continuously create more partitions to allocate the required amount of memory to newly arriving processes until all the physical memory is exhausted. Truly, there is no restriction on the maximum number of jobs that can reside in memory nor even on their sizes at any point in time, except the occurrence of some peculiar situations arising from certain restrictions on the part of OS design, particularly the limitations of available PCB queue lengths and other data structures used by the operating system.

This differently defined memory management scheme is known as **dynamic partition** or **variable partition**, meaning that the partitions are to be created to jobs' requirements during job processing. Various types of approaches exist to accomplish dynamic partition allocation. Numerous specifications of data structures are needed to support dynamic definition and allocation of partitions. Tables must be made with entries for each free area and each allocated partition specifying the size, location, and access restriction to each partition.

- **Operation Methodology:** Initially the entire user area in memory is free and treated as a single big hole for allocation to incoming processes. Whenever a request arrives to load a process, the memory management then attempts to locate a contiguous free area of memory to create a partition whose size is equal to or a little bit larger than the requesting process's size declared at the time of its submission or otherwise available (from the process image file). If such a free area suitable for the requesting process is found, the memory management then carves out a contiguous block of memory from it to create an exact-fit partition for the process in question, and the remaining free memory, if any, is then returned to the pool of free memory for further allocation later on. The block of memory or the partition thus created would then be loaded with the requesting process and is declared allocated by registering the base address, size, and the status (allocated) in the system PDT or its equivalent, as we will see next. As usual, a link to or a copy of this information is recorded in the corresponding process control block. The process is now ready for execution. If no such suitable free area is available for allocation, an appropriate error message is shown to user, or other appropriate actions are taken by the operating system. However, after successful allocation of a partition to a deserving process, if another request arrives for a second process to load, the memory management should then start attempting to locate a suitable free area immediately following the area already allocated to the first process. This allocation, if possible, once made, is then recorded in the modified PDT (an extension of the previously defined PDT). In this way, successive memory allocation to requesting processes is to be continued until the entire physical memory is exhausted, or any restriction is imposed by the system on further admission of any other process. Although all these partition-related information including free memory areas are essentially remained unchanged as long as the process(es) resides in memory, but may sometimes need to be updated each time a new partition is created or an existing partition is deleted.

When adequate room is not available for a new process, it can be kept waiting until a suitable space is found, or a choice can be made either to swap out a process or to shuffle (*compaction*, to be discussed later) to accommodate the new process. Generally, shuffling takes less time than swapping, but no other activity can proceed in the meantime. Occasionally, swapping out a single small process will allow two adjacent medium-sized free pieces to coalesce into a free piece large enough to satisfy the new process. A policy to decide whether to shuffle or swap could be based on the percentage of time the memory manager spends in shuffling. If that time is less than some fixed percentage, which is a tunable parameter of the policy, then the decision would be to shuffle. Otherwise, a segment would be swapped out.

When a resident process is completed, terminated, or even swapped out, the operating system demolishes the partition by returning the partition's space (as defined in the PDT) to the pool of free memory areas and declaring the status of the corresponding PDT entry "FREE" or simply invalidating the corresponding PDT entry. For a swapped-out process, in particular, the operating system, in addition, also invalidates the PCB field where the information of the allocated partition is usually recorded.

As releasing memory due to completion of a process and subsequent allocation of available memory for the newly arrived process continues, and since the sizes of these two processes are not the same, it happens that after some time, a good number of tiny holes is formed in between the two adjacent partitions, not large enough to be allocatable that are spread all over the memory. This phenomenon is called *external fragmentation* or *checkerboarding*, referring to the fact that all the holes in the memory area are external to all partitions and become increasingly fragmented, thereby causing only a simple waste. This is in contrast to *internal fragmentation*, which refers to the waste of memory area within the partition, as already discussed earlier. *Concatenation* or *coalescing*, and *compaction*, to be discussed later, are essentially two means that can be exploited to effectively overcome this problem.

- **Memory Allocation Model:** Under this scheme, when a process is created or swapped in, the memory of a particular size that is allocated may not be sufficient when the process is under execution, since its data segments can grow dynamically and may even go beyond the allocated domain. In fact, the allocated memory used by an executing process essentially constitutes of the following:

1. Program code with static data to be executed.
2. Program-controlled dynamic data (PCD data) generated during execution.
3. A stack used by program that may grow during execution.

The executable *program code and its associated static data components* are more or less constant in size, and this size information can be obtained from the directory entry of the program file. The stack contains program data and also other data consisting of the parameters of the procedures, functions, or blocks in a program that have been called but have not yet been exited from, and also return addresses that are to be used while exiting from them. These data are allocated dynamically when a function, procedure, or block is entered and are deallocated when it exits, making the stack grow and shrink accordingly. The other kind of data that can grow dynamically are created by a program using features of programming languages, such as the new statements of Pascal, C++, and Java or the *malloc* and *calloc* statements of C. Such data are called program controlled dynamic data. Normally, PCD data are allocated memory using a data structure called a *heap*. As execution proceeds, the size of the stack, the PCD data, and their actual memory requirements cannot be predicted, as they constantly grow and shrink. That is why a little extra memory is allocated for these two dynamic components whenever a process is newly created, swapped in, or moved (to be discussed in next section), as shown in Figure 5.1(a) using two such processes.

To realize flexibility in memory allocation under this approach, an alternative form of memory allocation model, as depicted in Figure 5.1(b), is developed to accommodate these two dynamic components. The program code and its allied static data components in the program are allocated adequate memory per their sizes. The stack and the PCD data share a single large area at the top of its allocated memory but grow in opposite directions when memory is allocated to new entities. A portion of memory between these two components is thus kept free for either of them. In this model, the stack and PCD data components, however, do not have as such any individual size restrictions. Still, even if it is found that the single large area as offered to both stack and PCD data is not adequate and runs out, either the process will have to be moved to a hole with enough space (discussed next in *dynamic allocation*) or swapped out of memory until a befitting hole can be created, or it ultimately may be killed.

A program during execution when calls its needed procedures from the runtime library offered by the programming languages, these library routines themselves perform allocations/deallocations activities in the PCD area offered to them. The memory management is not at all involved in these activities, and in fact, it just allocates the required area for stack and PCD, and nothing else.

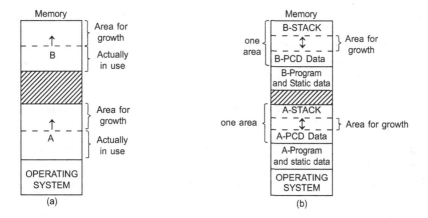

FIGURE 5.1 In variable–partitioned memory management, memory space allocation for; a) a growing data segment, and b) as one free area for both a growing stack and a growing data segment.

- **Dynamic Allocation:** Sill, the executing process often runs out of already-allocated space and then requests more memory for its ongoing computation. One simple way to negotiate this situation may be that the memory manager could then block the process until more adjacent space becomes available. But this strategy is not favored for many interactive users, since it might involve very long waits for service. Alternatively, the memory management could find a larger hole that matches the requirement and then move the process to the new hole, thereby releasing the currently used space. However (similar to compaction, to be discussed later), the system would then require some means of adjusting the program's addresses accordingly when it moves to the new address space, and the additional overhead linked with it should be taken into account when such an attempt is made for the sake of tuning the performance.

More details on this topic with figures are given on the Support Material at www.routledge. com/9781032467238.

- **Space Management:** In dynamically partitioned memory management, the memory manager needs to constantly keep track of all the allocated partitions and free spaces (partitions); the attributes of all these partitions always keep changing due to the dynamic nature of the scheme that eventually requires a data structure different from that used in a fixed-partitioned scheme.
  1. **Partition Description Table (PDT):** In variable-partitioned scheme, a modified PDT is used that keeps track only of allocated partitions and contains an entry for each such allocated partition which consists of two fields, the base address and the size. The system refers to each of these entries (processes) using their addresses. Each entry in the PDT is linked to the corresponding process's PCB. When a process is completed or terminated (aborted), the corresponding entry in the PDT along with its PCB is deleted. When a process is swapped out, the corresponding entry in the PDT along with the link in its corresponding PCB is removed. This space in the PDT now obtained can subsequently be used for newly created partitions offered to other incoming processes, and this information is accordingly recorded in the respective data structures (including the PCBs) of the newly arrived processes. However, the size of the PDT is limited by the maximum number of PCBs that the operating system provides in its design.

     To keep track of the free partitions that are constantly created when a job completes (terminates) or is swapped out, which are subsequently used up due to allocation of a newly arrived job, a linked list of all such available free partitions with all their information is thus maintained in the form of a separate free list for the purpose of re-allocating them efficiently. The free list is usually arranged in order of increasing memory address, and each entry in the free list will then contain the size of the current free space itself and a pointer to the next free location. An alternative approach may be to store this information within the current free space (hole) itself without creating a separate list. This approach normally uses the first two words within each free partition for this purpose. A pointer to the first free partition is stored in a variable HEAD. This approach, however, does not impose any additional memory overhead.

     More details on this topic with figure are given on the Support Material at www. routledge.com/9781032467238.

  2. **Bit Maps:** The entire memory here is conceived and divided up into allocation units. This unit may be considered as small as consisting of only few words, or may be as large as several kilobytes. When space is allocated to a job, it should be given in terms of an integral multiple of consecutive units. Corresponding to each allocation unit is a bit in the bit map, which is 0 if the unit is free and 1 if it is allocated (or vice-versa). The bit map is created using contiguous words, and the bits in the bit map are packed into these words. When a piece of memory is freed, the corresponding bits in the bit map are reset to 0 (or 1). A series of consecutive 0 bits (or 1) in the bit map is equivalent to a

corresponding free space of respective size. Hence, it is not necessary to join the pieces to their neighbors explicitly.

- One of the important design issues related to this scheme is the size of the allocation unit to be chosen. The smaller the allocation unit, the closer space to be allocated to the job's required space and hence the less the memory wastage in internal fragmentation, but the size of the bit map in that case will be larger. If the allocation unit is chosen to be large, the size of the bit map will be small, but there remains a possibility that an appreciable amount of memory may be wasted in internal fragmentation, particularly in the last allocated unit of each process, if the process size is not an exact multiple of the allocation unit. Hence, the tradeoff must be in the selection of the proper size of the allocation unit that should lie somewhere in between.
- Implementation of the bit map approach is comparatively easy with almost no additional overhead in memory usage. The bit map provides a simple way to keep track of memory space in a fixed-sized memory because the size of the bit map depends only on the size of memory and on the size of the allocation unit. However, the main drawback of this approach is that when a job is required to be brought into memory, the memory manager must search the bit map for the needed free space to find a stream of needed consecutive 0 (or 1) bits of a given length in the map, which is always a slow operation. So, in practice, at least for this type of memory allocation strategy, bit maps are not often used and consequently fell out of favor.
- More details on this topic with a figure are given on the Support Material at www.routledge.com/9781032467238.

3. **Linked Lists:** Another common approach to keep track of memory usage is by maintaining a linked list of allocated and free memory segments, where a segment represents either a process or a hole (free area). Each entry in the linked list specifies a process (P) or a hole (H), the address at which it starts, the length (the number of allocation units), and a pointer to the next entry. The entries in the list can be arranged either in increasing order by size or in increasing order by address. Keeping the linked list sorted in increasing order by address has the advantage that when a process is completed, terminated, or even swapped out, updating the existing list requires only replacing a P with an H. This process normally has two neighbors (except when it is at the very top or bottom of memory), each of which may be either a process or a hole. If two adjacent entries are holes, they can then be concatenated (coalesced) into one to make a larger hole that may then be allocated to a new process, and the list also becomes shorter by one entry.

It is sometimes more convenient to use a *double-linked list* to keep track of allocated and free memory segments rather than a single-linked list, as already described. This double-linked structure makes it much easier for the departing process to locate the previous entry and see if a merge is possible. Moreover, the double-linked list of only *free areas* (free list) is otherwise advantageous too, since this organization facilitates addition/deletion of new memory areas to/from the list. In addition, if the entries in this list can be arranged in increasing order by size, then the "best possible" area to satisfy a specific memory request can be readily identified.

More details on this topic with figures are given on the Support Material at www.routledge.com/9781032467238.

- **Allocation Strategy:** At the time of memory allocation, two fundamental aspects in the design are: *efficient use of memory* and the *effective speed of memory allocation*. Efficient use of memory is again primarily associated with two issues:
  1. *Overhead in memory usage*: The memory manager itself uses some memory to accomplish its administrative operations, while keeping track of memory segments, and the memory usage by a requesting process, to only keep track of its own allocated memory as well.
  2. *Effective use of released memory*: When a memory segment is released by a process, the same can be reused by fresh re-allocation.

Efficient use of memory is an important factor because the size of a fresh request for memory seldom matches the size of any released memory areas. Hence, there always remains a possibility that some memory area may be wasted (external fragmentation) when a particular memory area is re-allocated. Adequate care should be taken to reduce this wastage in order to improve memory utilization and to avoid additional costly operation like compaction (to be discussed later). Common algorithms used by the memory manager for selection of a free area for creation of a partition to accomplish a fresh allocation for a newly created or swapped-in process are:

- **First fit and its variant next fit**
- **Best fit**
- **Worst fit**
- **Next fit**
- **Quick fit**

The simplest algorithm is **first fit**, where the memory manager scans along the free list of segments (holes) until it finds one big enough to service the request. The hole is then selected and is broken up into two pieces: one to allocate to the requesting process, and the remaining part of the hole is put back into the free list, except in the unlikely case of an exact fit. First fit is a fast algorithm because it searches as little as possible. But the main drawback of this approach is that a hole may be split up several times, leading to successively smaller holes not large enough to hold any single job, thereby resulting in waste. Moreover, there is a possibility that a sufficiently large hole may be used up by this technique that may deprive a large process from entering that is already in the job queue but came at a later time.

Best fit is another well-known algorithm in which the entire list is searched and then selects the smallest hole that is adequate in size for the requesting process. Rather than breaking up a big hole which might be needed later, best fit tries to optimize memory utilization by selecting one close to the actual needed size, but it then constantly generates so many tiny holes due to such allocation that these holes eventually are of no further use. Best fit is usually slower than first fit because of searching the entire list at every allocation. Somewhat surprisingly, it also results in more wasted memory than first fit and its variant, next fit (to be discussed next), because it tends to constantly fill up memory with so many tiny, useless holes. First fit, in this regard, usually generates comparatively large holes on average.

Next fit is basically a minor variation of first fit. It works in the same way as first fit does, except that it always keeps track of the position in the linked list when it finds a suitable hole. The next time it is called, it starts searching the list for a suitable hole from the position in the list where it left off, instead of always starting at the beginning, as first fit does. Simulations carried out by Bays (1977) reveals that next fit usually gives a little worse performance than first fit. However, the next fit technique can also be viewed as a compromise between first fit and best fit. While attempting a new allocation, next fit searches the list starting from the next entry of its last allocation and performs allocation in the same way as first fit does. In this way, it avoids splitting the same area repeatedly as happens with the first fit technique, and at the same time it does not suffer from allocation over-head as found in the best fit technique, which always starts searching from the beginning of the list.

Worst fit is the opposite of best fit. It always take the largest available hole that exceeds the size of the requesting process. Best fit, in contrast, always takes the smallest possible available hole matched with the size of the requesting process. The philosophy behind the worst fit technique is obviously to reduce the rate of production of tiny, useless holes that best fit constantly generates. However, studies based on simulation reveal that worst-fit allocation is not very effective in reducing wasted memory, particularly when a series of requests are processed over a considerable duration of time.

Quick fit is yet another allocation algorithm which normally maintains separate lists of some of the most common sizes of segments usually requested. With this form of arrangement and using quick fit, searching a hole of the required size is, no doubt, extremely fast but suffers from the same drawbacks similar to most of the other schemes that sort by hole size; particularly when a process completes or terminates or is swapped out, finding its neighbors to see whether a merge is possible is extremely tedious. If merging cannot be carried out, it is quite natural that the memory will quickly fragment into a large number of tiny, useless holes.

While working with experimental data, Knuth concluded that first fit is usually superior to best fit in practice. Both first fit and next fit are observed to perform better than their counterpart, best fit. However, next fit has a tendency to split *all the areas* if the system is in operation for quite a long time, whereas first fit may not split all of the last few free areas, which often helps it allocate these large memory areas to deserving processes.

To implement any of these methods, the memory manager needs to keep track of which pieces of physical area are in use and which are free using a data structure known as ***boundary tag*** (discussed later in "Merging Free Areas"). In this structure, each free area has physical pointers that link all free areas in a doubly linked list. They do not have to appear in order in that list. Also, each such area, whether free or in use, has the first and last words reserved to indicate its status (free or busy) and its length. When a free block is needed, the doubly linked list is searched from the beginning or from the last stopping point until an adequate area is found. If found, it is then split up; if necessary, to form a new busy piece and a new free piece. If the fit is exact, the entire piece is removed from the doubly linked free list. When a piece is returned to free space, it is joined to the pieces before it and after it (if they are free) and then put on the free list.

All four algorithms as presented can be further sped up by maintaining distinctly separated lists for processes and holes, and only the hole list can be inspected at the time of allocation. The hole list can again be kept sorted in ascending order by size that, in turn, enables the best fit technique to work faster, ensuring that the hole thus found is the smallest possible required one. With this arrangement, both first fit and best fit are equally fast, and next fit is simply blunt. On the other hand, this arrangement invites additional complexity and subsequent slowdown when deallocating memory, since a now-free segment has to be removed from the process list and inserted appropriately into the hole list, if required, with concatenation.

Various other algorithms are also found, particularly to counter situations when the size of the requesting processes, or even the probability distribution of their need and process lifetimes, are not known to the system in advance. Some of the possibilities in this regard are described in the work of Beck (1982), Stephenson (1983), and Oldehoeft and Allan (1985).

An Example: Illustration of All Four Techniques

For example, take a part of memory with a free list that contains three free areas of size 200, 150, and 500 bytes respectively. Processes make allocation requests for 130, 50, and 300 bytes in sequence. The four techniques are employed separately to satisfy these requests.

The solution to this example with a figure is given on the Support Material at www.routledge.com/9781032467238.

- **Impact of External Fragmentation: An Estimation:** External fragmentation causing memory wastage is obvious in systems with dynamic partitioning of memory irrespective of the allocation strategy (first fit, best fit, etc.) being used while partitioning the memory. The primary reason for fragmentation is that the pattern of returns of free areas due to different lifetimes of resident objects is generally different from the arrival pattern of objects and hence the order of their allocations. Merging adjacent free areas reduces the amount of wasted memory to minimize fragmentation and its impact but is unable to solve this problem. However, sometimes after the commencement of operation, the system using dynamic allocation of memory tends to attain a state of equilibrium in which the memory wasted by a given allocation scheme can be estimated and can then be used for the purpose of comparison. With an appropriate calculation using simulation, it can be shown that, averaged over time, there must be half as many holes as processes in the memory region. This result is sometimes known as the **fifty (50) percent rule**. The rule highlights that approximately one-third of memory, or around 33 percent, is wasted due to fragmentation, even though adjacent free areas are continuously merged whenever possible. However, this rule can be derived in many other different ways; one such useful derivation of it is the **unused memory rule**, whose explanation with mathematical computation is outside the scope of this discussion.

The details of this topic with mathematical computation are given on the Support Material at www.routledge.com/9781032467238.

- **Merging Free Areas:** External fragmentation results in the production of many useless tiny holes that may give rise to substantial wastage in memory, which eventually limits the system in satisfying all the legitimate demands that could otherwise be possibly met. Consequently, it affects the expected distributions of available memory among the requesting processes. Merging of free areas including many useless tiny holes is thus carried out to generate relatively large free areas that can now hold processes, thereby providing better memory utilization to improve system performance as well as neutralizing the evil effects caused by external fragmentation.

Merging can be carried out whenever an area is released, and it is accomplished by checking the free list to see if there is any area adjacent to this new area. If so, this area can be merged with the new area, and the resulting new area can then be added to the list, deleting the old free area. This method is easy to implement but is expensive, since it involves a search over the entire free list every time a new area is added to it. Numerous types of techniques already exist to accomplish merging in various ways. Two generic techniques to perform merging that work most efficiently, *boundary tags* and *memory compaction*, will now be discussed.

- **Boundary tags**: Using boundary tags, both the allocated and free areas of memory can be tracked more conveniently. A *tag* is basically a status descriptor for a memory segment consisting of an ordered pair (allocation status, size). Two identical tags containing similar information are stored at the beginning and the end of each segment, that is, in the first and last few bytes of the segment. Thus, every allocated and free area of memory contains tags near its boundaries. If an area is free, additional information, *the free list pointer*, follows the tag at the starting boundary. Figure 5.2 shows a sample of this arrangement. When an area becomes free, the boundary tags of its neighboring areas are checked. These tags are easy to locate because they immediately precede and follow the boundaries of the newly freed area. If any of the neighbors is found free, it is immediately merged with the newly freed area. Three possibilities (when the new free area has its left neighbor free, when the new free area has its right neighbor free, and when the new free area has both neighbors free) may happen at the time of merging, which is depicted on the Support Material at www.routledge.com/9781032467238.

The details of this topic with a figure and explanation are given on the Support Material at www.routledge.com/9781032467238.

- **Memory Compaction:** In the variable partitioned memory management scheme, the active segments (processes) are interspersed with the holes throughout the entire memory

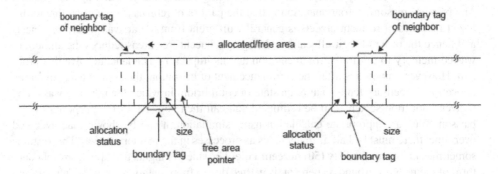

FIGURE 5.2 In variable–partitioned memory management, use of boundary tags and free–area pointer to coalesce the free spaces to minimize the external fragmentation.

in general. To get out of it, one way may be to relocate some or all processes towards one end of memory as far as possible by changing memory bindings such that all the holes can come together and be merged to form a single one big segment. This technique is known as *memory compaction*. All location-sensitive information (addresses) of all involved processes has to be relocated accordingly. If the computer system provides a relocation register (base register), relocation can be achieved by simply changing the contents of the relocation register (relocation activity, already discussed separately in the previous section). During compaction, the processes involved (those processes to be shifted) must be suspended and actually copied from one area of memory into another. It is, therefore, important to carefully decide when and how this compaction activity is to be performed. Figure 5.3 is self-explanatory and illustrates the use of compaction while free areas are to be merged.

Now the question arises of how often the compaction is to be done. In some systems, compaction is done periodically with a period decided at system generation time. In other systems, compaction is done whenever possible or only when it is needed, for example, when none of the jobs in the job queue finds a suitable hole, even though the combined size of the available free areas (holes) in a scattered condition exceeds the needs of the request at hand. Compaction here is helpful and may be carried out to fulfill the pending requirement. An alternative is with some systems that execute memory compaction whenever a free area is created by a departing process, thereby collecting most of the free memory into a single large area.

When compaction is to be carried out, it is equally important to examine all the possible options for moving processes from one location to another in terms of minimizing the overhead to be incurred while selecting the optimal strategy. A common approach to minimize the overhead is always to attempt to relocate all partitions to one end of memory, as already described. During compaction, the affected process is temporarily suspended and all other system activities are halted for the time being. The compaction process is completed by updating the free list (in linked-list approach) and the affected PDT entries. As the compaction activity, in general, is associated with excessive operational overhead, dynamic partition of memory is hardly ever implemented in systems that do not have dynamic relocation hardware.

Details on this topic with a figure and explanation are given on the Support Material at www.routledge.com/9781032467238.

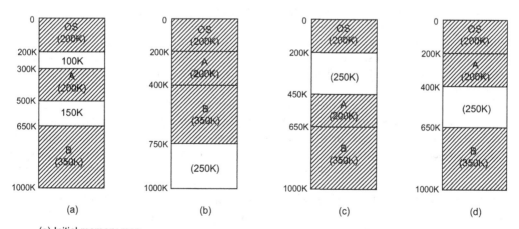

(a) Initial memory map.
(b) A and B merged, Total 250K moved to compact.
(c) From (a), when A moved downwards, total 250K moved to compact.
(d) From (a), when A moved upwards, total 250K moved to compact.

FIGURE 5.3 In variable–partitioned memory management, compaction of memory is used to reduce the effect of external fragmentation. An example of memory compaction is shown with different configuration in memory usage.

- **Space Management with the Buddy System:** Memory management with linked lists sorted by hole size made the allocation mechanism very fast, but equally poor in handling merging after deallocation of a process. The buddy system (Knuth, 1973), in fact, is a space (memory) management algorithm that takes advantage of the fact that computers use binary numbers for addressing, and it speeds up the merging of adjacent holes when a process is deallocated. This scheme performs allocation of memory in blocks of a few standard sizes, essentially a power of 2. This approach reduces the effort involved in allocation/deallocation and merging of blocks, but it is extremely inefficient in terms of memory utilization, since all requests must be rounded up to the nearest power of 2, which summarily leads to a substantial amount of internal fragmentation on average, unless the requirement of the requesting process is close to a power of two.

The entire memory is here split and recombined into blocks in a pre-determined manner during allocation and deallocation, respectively. Blocks created by splitting a particular block into two equal sizes are called *buddy blocks*. Free buddy blocks can later be merged (coalesced) to reconstruct the block which was split earlier to create them. Under this system, adjacent free blocks that are not buddies are not coalesced. Thus, each block x has only a single buddy block that either precedes or follows x in memory. The size of different blocks is 2^n for different values of $n \geq t$, where t is some threshold value. This restriction ensures that memory blocks are not uselessly small in size.

To control the buddy system, memory management associates a 1-bittag with each block to indicate the status of the block, that is, whether allocated or free. As usual, the tag of a block may be located within the block itself, or it may be kept separately. The memory manager maintains many lists of free blocks; each free list consists of free blocks of identical size, that is, all blocks of size 2^k for some $k \geq t$, and is maintained as doubly linked list.

Operation methodology: Allocation of memory begins with many different free lists of block size 2^c for different values of $c \geq t$. When a process requests a memory block of size m, the system then inspects the smallest power of 2 such that $2^i \geq m$. If the list of blocks with size 2^i is not empty, it allocates the first block from the list to the process and changes the tag of the block from *free* to *allocated*. If the list is found empty, it checks the list for blocks of size 2^{i+1}. It takes one block off this list and splits it into halves of size 2^i. These blocks become *buddies*. It then puts one of these blocks into the free list for blocks of size 2^i and uses the other block to satisfy the request. If a block of size 2^{i+1} is not available, it looks in the list for blocks of size 2^{i+2}. It then takes one block off this list and, after splitting this block into two halves of size 2^{i+1}, one of these blocks would be put into the free list for blocks of size 2^{i+1}, and the other block would be split further in the same manner for allocation as already described. If a block of size 2^{i+2} is not available, it starts inspecting the list of blocks of size 2^{i+3}, and so on. Thus, several splits may have to be carried out before a request can be ultimately met.

After deallocation of a process that releases a memory block of size 2^i, the buddy system then changes the tag of the block to *free* and checks the tag of its buddy block to see whether the buddy block is also free. If so, it merges these two blocks into a single block of size 2^{i+1}. It then repeats the check for further coalescing transitively; that is, it checks whether the buddy of this new block of size 2^{i+1} is free, and so on. It enters a block in the respective free list only when it finds that its buddy block is not free.

Buddy systems have a distinct advantage over algorithms that sort blocks (multiples of block size) by size but not necessarily at addresses. The advantage is that when a block of size 2^x bytes is freed, the memory manager has to search its buddy block only from the free list of 2^x block to see if a merge (coalesce) is possible. While other algorithms that allow memory blocks to be split in arbitrary ways, all the free lists (or a single list of all holes) must then be searched to find a merge which is more time consuming; the buddy system in this regard exhibits a clear edge over the others.

The serious drawback of this approach is that it is extremely inefficient in terms of memory utilization. The reason is that all the requests must be rounded up to a power of 2 at the time of allocation, and it happens that the sizes of most of the requesting processes are not very close to any power of 2. This results in a substantial amount of internal fragmentation on average, which is simply a waste on the part of memory usage, unless the size of a requesting process comes close to a power of 2.

Various authors (notably Kaufman, 1984) have modified the buddy system in different ways to attempt to get rid of some of its problems. The UNIX 5.4 (SVR 4) kernel uses this basic approach for management of memory that is needed for its own use and, of course, adds some modifications to the underlying existing strategy (a new one is the *lazy buddy allocator*). A brief discussion of this modified approach is provided in a later section.

The details of this topic with a figure and explanation are given on the Support Material at www.routledge.com/9781032467238.

Space Management with Powers-of-Two Allocation: This approach construction-wise resembles the buddy system but differs in operation. Similar to the buddy system, the memory blocks are also always maintained as powers of 2, and separate free lists are maintained for blocks of different sizes. But here an additional component is attached to each block that contains a header element, which is used for two purposes. This header element consists of two fields, as shown in Figure 5.4. It contains a status flag which indicates whether the block is currently *free* or *allocated*. If a block is free, another field in the header then contains size of the block. If a block is allocated, the other field in the header then contains the address of the free list to which it should be added when it becomes free.

When a requesting process of size m bytes arrives, the memory manager starts inspecting the smallest free block that is a power of 2 but large enough to hold m bytes, that is, $2^i \geq m$. It first checks the free list containing blocks whose size is the smallest value x such that $2^x \geq m$. If the free list is empty, it then checks the list containing blocks that are the next higher power of 2 in size, and so on. An entire block is always allocated to a request; that is, no splitting of blocks is carried out at the time of allocation. Thus, when a process releases a block, no effort is needed to merge (coalesce) adjoining blocks to reconstruct larger blocks: it is simply returned to its free list.

Operation of the system starts by creating blocks of desired sizes and entering them in the corresponding free lists. New blocks can be created dynamically whenever the system runs out of blocks of a requested size or when no available block can be allocated to fulfill a specific request. The UNIX 4.4 BSD kernel uses this approach for management of memory that is needed for its own use and, of course, adds some modifications to the underlying existing strategy (a new one is the *McKusick–Karels allocator*). A brief discussion of this modified approach is provided in a later section.

Status	*size / address*
Free or	Size of block or
Allocated	Address of free list

FIGURE 5.4 In variable–partitioned memory management, space management is also done with allocation of space which is a powers-of-two in size, and a specimen of header element used in each such allocated space is shown.

5.8.1.2.5.1 Comparison of Different Allocation Schemes Different allocation strategies can be compared by considering their merits and drawbacks based mainly on two parameters: *speed of allocation*, and *efficient utilization of memory*. In terms of allocation speed, the buddy system and powers-of-two allocation scheme are superior to first-fit, best-fit, next-fit, and worst-fit schemes since they do not require searching the free lists. The powers-of-two allocation scheme, in turn, is faster than the buddy system because it does not need to perform the splitting and subsequent merging. However, effective memory utilization can be achieved by computing a memory utilization factor that can be defined as:

$$\text{Memory utilization factor} = \frac{\text{Memory in use}}{\text{Total memory committed}}$$

where *memory in use* is the amount of memory in actual use by the requesting processes, and *total memory committed* includes allocated memory, free memory available with the memory manager, and memory used by the memory manager to store its own data structures to manage the entire memory system. The larger the value of the utilization factor, the better the performance of a system because most of the memory will then be in productive use, and the converse is the worst.

In terms of this utilization factor, both the buddy system and powers-of-two allocation scheme stand to the negative side because of an appreciable internal fragmentation in general. These schemes also require additional memory to store the list headers and tags to control their operations and keys for protection. The powers-of-two allocation scheme, in addition, suffers from another peculiar problem. Since it does not merge free blocks to reconstruct large blocks, it often fails to satisfy a request to hold a job of sufficiently large size even when free contiguous blocks of smaller sizes are available that could satisfy the request if they could be merged. In a buddy system, this situation rarely occurs, and it could happen only if adjoining free blocks are not buddies. In fact, Knuth (1973) reports that in simulation studies, a buddy system is usually able to achieve 95 percent memory utilization before failing to fulfill a specific requirement.

On other hand, the first-fit, next-fit, and best-fit techniques although provide better memory utilization, since the space in an allocated block is mostly used up, but the first-fit and next-fit techniques may sometimes give rise to the appreciable internal fragmentation which is inherent in the nature of these two techniques. However, all these techniques also suffer from external fragmentation since free blocks of tiny sizes are continuously generated that are too small to satisfy any standard requests.

5.8.1.2.6 Comparison: Dynamic Partition versus Fixed Partition

In summary, both fixed partitioning and dynamic partitioning schemes exhibit merits as well as drawbacks. However, fixed partitioning is generally suitable for static environments where the workload can be ascertained beforehand with known sizes of frequently executing processes, and that is why it was widely used in batch multiprogramming systems. Dynamic partitioning is likely more conducive in environments where the workload is unpredictable or less well behaved. In fact, a compromise has been made in some systems in which a combined scheme has been used that supports both static and dynamic partitioning of memory at the same time. This means, a *portion of memory* maybe divided into a certain number of fixed partitions which can be used by the resident portion of the operating system and its supporting routines, like device drivers and portions of the file systems. The remaining portion of memory may then be used to allocate other processes by using dynamic partitioning.

Point-wise comparisons of these two approaches are briefly given on the Support Material at www.routledge.com/9781032467238.

5.8.1.2.7 Contemporary Allocation Strategies

Modern memory management techniques all use some form of variable partitioning in the form of allocating fixed-sized blocks (called "pages", to be discussed in later sections) that greatly simplifies the overall memory management and makes the management of the free list trivial. In contrast, the older dynamic partition approach uses *variable-sized blocks* of memory that require additional overhead to manage the memory and its optimal utilization. Under this scheme, the request for additional memory from the process during runtime is fulfilled either by unloading the part of the program (or the entire program) to a fitting area in memory, or the program is allowed to grow, allocating the memory from the free list as it did with the original request when the process was started. However, in conjunction with variable-sized memory allocation, modern operating systems combine the program translation mechanisms (systems) and the associated advanced hardware support to provide an innovative alternative approach with space binding by using the loader (dynamic linking loader) to rebind addresses www.routledge.com/9781032467238.

Brief details of this topic are given on the Support Material at www.routledge.com/9781032467238.

5.8.2 NONCONTIGUOUS MEMORY ALLOCATION

Contiguous allocation of memory involving both unequal fixed-size and variable-size partitions is inefficient mainly in the overall utilization of memory, thereby causing a critical negative impact of substantial memory wastage due to internal and external fragmentation of memory. Although this problem can be solved by an expensive memory compaction approach, sometimes it is also inconvenient. When the requirement of contiguous allocation of memory is relaxed, and several non-adjacent memory areas are allocated to a process to run, such a scheme of allocation of memory is called *noncontiguous allocation*. Here, none of these scattered areas is large enough to hold the entire executable code (including code, data, and stack) but still be able to run in noncontiguous locations. Out of several advantages obtained from this scheme, the most notable one is that a memory area which is not large enough to hold an entire process can still be used, thereby minimizing the ill effect of external fragmentation. This, in turn, also relieves the system from carrying out the expensive processing of merging free memory areas (memory compaction) that eventually reduces the add-on OS overhead.

To illustrate how a noncontiguous allocation (multiple partition) is carried out to load a process and subsequently its execution, let us consider how a process P of size 120K, as shown in Figure 5.5(a), is to be initiated. Four free memory areas of 30K, 50K, 80K, and 70K are at present available in the memory, as shown in Figure 5.5(b). It is assumed that process P is accordingly split into three components, P(1) = 30K, P(2) = 50K, and P(3) = 40K, so as to fit into three available non-adjacent free areas, 30K, 50K, 80K, and loaded into them as shown in Figure 5.5(c). After allocating 40K (P3) into the free area of 80K, a new free area of 40K will be generated. The area 70K located between process C and process D remains unused and could be allocated to some other process or to the component of some process with size ≤ 70K. The logical address space of process P extends from 0 to 120K, while the physical address space extends from 0 to 690K. Suppose that an instruction being referenced in process P has the address 55K. This is the logical address of the instruction. The process component P(1) in Figure 5.5(c) has a size of 30 Kbytes. Therefore, the referenced instruction will be available in component P(2) since the size of component P(2) is 50K and will be situated at an offset of (55K − 30K) = 25 Kbytes from the beginning of P(2). Since P(2) is loaded in memory with the start address 400

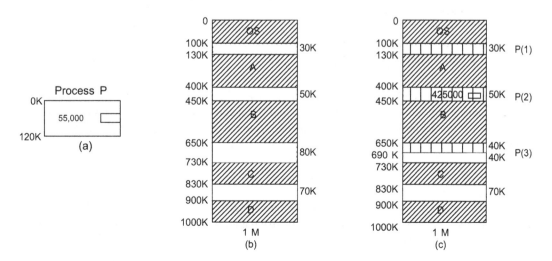

FIGURE 5.5 An example of noncontiguous–memory allocation scheme for a representative process P is illustrated.

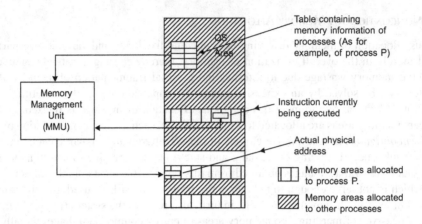

FIGURE 5.6   A schematic representation of address translation used in non–contiguous memory allocation scheme is shown.

Kbytes, the physical address of the referenced instruction will be (400K + 25K) = 425 Kbytes, as shown in Figure 5.5(c).

- **Logical addresses, physical addresses, and address translation:** In the case of non-contiguous allocation, there is a clean separation between user's logical address space and actual physical address space. The logical address space is the *logical view* of the process, and the real view of the active process in the memory is called the *physical view* of the process. During execution, the CPU issues the logical address and obtains the physical address of the corresponding logical address. The OS stores information about the memory areas allocated to different components of a process (here the process P) in a table created, managed, and controlled by the memory management unit. The table includes the memory start addresses and the sizes of each of the components of the process (here it is made of three components P(1), P(2), and P(3) of the process P). This is depicted in Figure 5.6. The CPU always sends the logical address of each constituent (instruction or data) of the process to the MMU, and the MMU, in turn, uses the table containing memory allocation information to compute the corresponding actual physical address, which is also called the *effective memory address*. The computing procedure using memory mapping hardware to derive the corresponding effective memory address from a logical address at execution time is called ***address translation***.

In general, a logical address issued by the CPU mainly consists of two parts: the *id* of the process component containing the issued address and the specific byte within the component (offset) indicating the particular location. Each referenced address will then be represented by a pair of the form:

$(comp_k, offset_k)$

Where offset $offset_k$ is the displacement of the target location from the beginning of the process component $comp_k$. The MMU computes the effective memory address of the target location $(comp_k, offset_k)$ using the formula:

Effective memory address of logical address $(comp_k, offset_k)$
   = starting address of memory is allocated to $comp_k + offset_k$ within $comp_k$.

The OS (memory management) records the required memory information concerning any process (here, process P) in the table as soon as it schedules a process and provides that to MMU in order to carry out the required address translation whenever it is needed.

Logical and physical organization in relation to this topic with a figure are given on the Support Material at www.routledge.com/9781032467238.

5.8.2.1   Implementation of Noncontiguous Memory Allocation

Noncontiguous memory allocation is implemented by two popular approaches:

* Paging
* Segmentation

5.8.2.1.1   Simple Paging: Paged Memory Management

In case of contiguous memory allocation, the *relocatable partition* approach while uses memory compaction manifests the fact that the address space seen by a job is not necessarily the same when the program is actually executed. The multiple partition algorithms used in noncontiguous allocation while were able to relax the *contiguity requirement*, but it did not always decrease fragmentation. The overlay concept first introduced the novel idea that a program can be subdivided into a number of mutually exclusive modules and that all the modules forming the program are not needed at the same time in main memory to start the execution. The presence of only a few modules in memory can easily begin the execution. Moreover, *the different modules present in an application could be treated as a separate unit that may be swapped in or out during the execution of the program.*

All the nice features of these different existing memory management schemes, when combined into one scheme of memory management, give rise to an innovative approach of memory management, historically known as *paged memory management*. The paging system was first introduced in the ATLAS computer at the University of Manchester. It not only discards the mandatory requirement of contiguous allocation of physical memory but also solved the fragmentation problem without physically moving partitions. Paged memory management has been best exploited in an environment with the use of *virtual memory*, which will be discussed in a later section.

A paging scheme also uses the notion of a process component (a part of a total process) discussed in the last section. Here, each process is divided into small fixed-sized components of the same size. Each such component is called a **page**, which is always a power of 2. The size of a page is defined and specified in the architecture of memory organization and of the computer system. The entire memory can accommodate an integral number of pages in it. Memory allocation is performed in terms of a page as unit, meaning each such memory allocation is the same as the page size. As the pages are all the same size, no unused space in memory can be smaller than a page in size. Consequently, external fragmentation does not arise at all in the system. It can also be shown that the wasted space in memory due to internal fragmentation for each process will consist of only a fraction of the last page of a process at best.

The operating system partitions the entire memory into equal fixed-size chunks of relatively small areas called **page frames**. Each page frame is same in size as a page (say, x bytes). Processes always use numeric logical addresses, and each such logical address is decomposed by the MMU into the pair (p_k, b_k), similar to $(comp_k, offset_k)$, as explained in the last section, where p_k is the page number and b_k is the offset within p_k ($0 \leq b_k < x$). The physical address space of the process consists of page frames that may be scattered and non-adjacent throughout the memory allocated to pages of the process. In fact, paging is supposed to be entirely transparent to the user

When a process of size s is required to be loaded, the operating system must allocate n free page frames so that $n = s/p$, where p is the page size and the value of n will always be an integral number. If the size s of a given process is not an exact multiple of a page size, the last page frames may be partly unused. This phenomenon is sometimes called **page fragmentation** or **page breakage**. The allocation of memory then consists of simply finding any n free page frames, which may not be necessarily contiguous, and the policy for page frame allocation has practically no impact on memory utilization, like first-fit, best-fit, and so on, since all frames fit all pages and any such fit in any order is as good as any other.

Thus, we observed that simple paging, as described here, is very similar to a fixed-partition mechanism. The differences are that, with paging, the partitions are rather small and obviously of a fixed size, a program may occupy more than one partition, and these partitions also need not be contiguous.

The consequences of making each page frame the same in size as a page are twofold. First, a page can be directly and exactly mapped into its corresponding page frame. Second, the offset of any address within a page will be identical to the offset in the corresponding page frame; no additional translation is required to convert the offset within a page in the logical address to obtain the offset of the corresponding physical address; only one translation is required, and that is to convert a page in the logical address into the corresponding page frame to derive the required physical address.

Using a page size of a power of 2 has two important effects: the logical addressing scheme is much easier and convenient to use for the programmer and is also transparent to the developer of all system utilities like the assembler, the linker, and the database management system. Second, it is relatively easy to implement a mechanism in hardware that can quickly carry out the required address translation during runtime.

An example of a simple paging system with illustrations is given on the Support Material at www.routledge.com/9781032467238.

- **Address translation:** The mechanism to translate a logical address into its corresponding physical address uses the following elements:

s: Size of a page.
l_i: Length of logical address.
l_p: Length of physical address.
n_p: Maximum number of bits required to express the page number in a logical address.
n_o: Maximum number of bits required to express the offset within a page.
n_f: Maximum number of bits required to express the page frame number in a physical address.

Since the size of a page s is a power of 2, then $s = (2$ to the power $n_o)$. Hence, the value of n_o depends on the size of the page, and the least significant n_o bits in a logical address give the offset b_i. The remaining bits in a logical address form the corresponding page $p_i = n_p = l_i - n_o$. The values of b_i and p_i can be obtained by grouping the bits of a logical address as follows:

$$\overleftarrow{\qquad n_p \qquad} \rightarrow \overleftarrow{\quad n_o \quad} \rightarrow$$
$$p_i \qquad\qquad b_i$$

The effective memory address (physical address) is then generated using the following steps that are needed for address translation.

- Extract the page number p_i as the leftmost n_p bits of the logical address.
- Use the page number as an index into the process page table to find the corresponding page frame number. Let it be q_i, and the number of bits in it is n_f.
- The remaining rightmost n_o bits in the logical address that are the offset within the page are then simply appended (concatenated) on the right side of the of n_f as already obtained to construct the needed physical address.

Since each page frame is identical in size to a page, n_o bits are also needed as offset b_i to address the location within a page frame. The number of bits needed to address a page frame in an effective memory address is $n_f = l_p - n_o$. Hence, an effective memory address (physical address) of a targeted byte b_i within a page frame q_i can be represented as:

$$\xleftarrow{\hspace{1cm}} n_f \xrightarrow{\hspace{1cm}} \xleftarrow{\hspace{1cm}} n_o \xrightarrow{\hspace{1cm}}$$

$$\underline{\hspace{3cm}\hspace{3cm}}$$

$$q_i \qquad\qquad\qquad b_i$$

The processor hardware after accessing the page table of the currently executing process carries out this logical-to-physical address translation. The MMU can then derive the effective memory address by simply concatenating q_i and b_i to generate the physical address l_p number of bits.

Conclusively, it can be stated that with simple paging, main memory is divided into many small frames of equal size. Each process is then divided into frame-size pages. When a process is loaded into memory for execution, all of its pages, if possible, are brought into available frames, and accordingly a page table is set up to facilitate the needed address translation. This strategy, in effect, summarily solves many of the critical issues causing serious problems that are inherent in a partitioned-memory management approach.

An example of address translation with illustration is given on the Support Material at www.routledge.com/9781032467238.

- **Protection:** Under the paging scheme, the dedicated page table for the running process is used for the purpose of address translation that prevents any memory reference of the process from crossing the boundary of its own address space. Moreover, use of a page table limit register which contains the highest logical page number defined in the page table of the running process together with the page table base register which points to the start address of the corresponding page table of the same running process can then detect, arrests, and confirm any unauthorized access to memory beyond the prescribed boundaries of the running process. Moreover, protection keys can also be employed in the usual way with each memory block (page frame) of a specific size. In addition, by associating access-right bits with protection keys, access to a page may be made restricted whenever necessary, and it is particularly beneficial in situations when pages are shared by several processes.

  A brief description of this topic is given on the Support Material at www.routledge.com/9781032467238.

- **Sharing; Shared Pages:** Sharing of pages in systems with paged memory management is quite straightforward and falls into two main categories. One is the *static sharing* that results from static binding carried out by a linker or loader before the execution of a program begins. With static binding, if two processes X and Y statically share a program Z, then Z is included in the body of both X and Y. As a result, the sizes of both X and Y will be increased and will consume more memory space if they exist in main memory at the same time.

The other one is the *dynamic binding* that removes one of the major drawbacks of static binding, particularly in relation to redundant consumption of memory space. This approach can be used to conserve memory by binding (not injecting) a single copy of an entity (program or data) to several executing processes. The shared program or data still retains its own identity, and it would be dynamically bound to several running processes by a dynamic linker (or loader) invoked by the memory management. In this way, a single copy of a shared page can be easily mapped to as many distinct address spaces as desired. Since each such mapping is performed with a dedicated entry in the page table of the related sharing process, each different process may have different access rights to the shared page. Moreover, it must be ensured by the operating system that the logical offset of each item within a shared page should be identical in all participating address spaces since paging is transparent to the users.

A brief description of this topic with a figure is given on the Support Material at www.routledge.com/9781032467238.

5.8.2.1.1.1 Conclusion: Merits and Drawbacks   A paging system is entirely controlled and managed by the operating system that outright discards the mandatory requirement of contiguous allocation of physical memory; pages can be placed into any available page frame in memory. It practically eliminates external fragmentation and thereby relieves the operating system of the tedious task of periodically executing memory compaction. Wasted space in memory due to internal fragmentation for each process is almost nil and will consist of only a fraction of the last page of a process. Since this system is quite simple in allocation and deallocation of memory, the overhead related to management of memory is appreciably lower in comparison to other schemes. Using a small size in the page, the main memory utilization may be quite high when compared to other schemes and that too in conjunction with process scheduling may optimize the usage of memory even more.

The paging system, however, also suffers from certain drawbacks. It increases the space requirement overhead for the purpose of management of memory, and more time is spent to access the entities. Those are:

- Creation of a memory-map table to keep track of the entire memory usage available with the computer system.
- Creation of a page-map table per process. The storage overhead of the page-map table, also known as *table fragmentation*, may be quite large in systems with small page size and large main memory.
- Although it is not a significant amount, it still wastes memory due to internal fragmentation that may happen in the last page of a process. If a good number of processes exist in the system at any instant, this may result in appreciable wastage in the main memory area.
- The address translation process is rather costly and severely affects the effective memory bandwidth. Of course, this can be overcome by incurring extra cost with the use of additional dedicated address translation hardware.

In addition, it is generally more restrictive to implement sharing in a paging system when compared with other systems, in particular with segmentation. It is also difficult to realize adequate protection within the boundaries of a single address space.

5.8.2.1.2 Segmentation: Segmented Memory Management

If the average size of a request for memory allocation can be made smaller, the internal fragmentation and its effect will be almost eliminated; external fragmentation and its negative impact may still remain, but it will be mostly less. Since the operating system cannot contribute much in any way to reduce the average process size, there may be a way to reduce the average size of a memory request by simply dividing the address space of a process into chunks that are relatively small. This novel idea was first introduced by the overlay concept in which a program can be subdivided into a number of mutually exclusive modules, and *the different module during the execution of the program could be treated as a unit* that may be swapped in or out during runtime. However, the overlay approach suffers from the constraint that the to-and-fro journey of the module is always confined within the domain of a specific area of overlay allocated in main memory. If this obligation can be waived so that the module is allowed to be loaded (or swapped in) into any noncontiguous area of memory, then this modified strategy would give rise to another attractive memory management scheme called *segmentation*.

A user program can be subdivided into a number of blocks (components), and each such block is called a ***segment***. A segment is an entity in a program that consists of a group of logically related items together, can be loaded as a unit into any location of memory for execution, and can even be shared by other programs. Segments are a user-oriented concept exploited in the logical division of a process that consists of a set of segments in which individual segments are generally of different sizes, but within the confine of a certain permissible maximum length (size limit). Although different segments of a process may be loaded in separate, noncontiguous areas of physical memory (i.e. base address of segments are different), but entities belonging to a single segment must be placed in contiguous areas of physical memory. Thus, segmentation can be described as a hybrid (dual) mechanism that possesses some properties of both contiguous (with regard to individual segments) and noncontiguous (with respect to address space of a process) approaches to memory management. Moreover, the segments thus generated are, in general, individually relocatable.

From the operating system's point of view, segmentation is essentially a multiple-base-limit version of dynamically partitioned memory. Memory is allocated in the form of variable partitions; the main difference is that one such partition is allocated to each individual segment. It is normally required that all the segments of a process must be loaded into memory at the time of execution (except in the presence of overlay schemes and virtual memory, which will be described later). As compared to dynamic partitioning, a program with segmentation may occupy more than one partition, and these partitions also need not be contiguous.

- **Principles of Operation:** The programmer declares the segments while coding the application. The translator (compiler/assembler) generates logical addresses of each segment during translation to begin at its own logical address 0. Any individual item within a specific segment is then identified by its offset (displacement) relative to the beginning of the segment. Thus, addresses in segmented systems have two components:
  - Segment name (number)
  - Offset (displacement) within the segment

Hence the logical address of any item in the segmented process has the form (s_k, b_k), where s_k is the id of the segment (or segment number) in which the item belongs, and b_k is the offset of the item's specific location within that segment. For example, assume that there is an instruction corresponding to a statement, call hra.cal, where hra.cal is a procedure in segment hraproc, may use the operand address (hraproc, hra.cal), or may use a numeric representation for s_k and b_k for that specific statement.

- **Address Translation:** Analogous to paging, since the logical address of a segmented system consists of a two-dimensional (two-part) representation, like (s_k, b_k), an address translation mechanism is then needed to convert this representation into its corresponding unidimensional physical equivalent. When a segmented process is loaded, the operating system attempts to allocate memory for the supplied segments present in the process and may create partitions to suit the needs of each particular segment. The base address of memory (as obtained while partition is created) and the size (specified in the load module) of a loaded segment are recorded as tuple called the *segment descriptor*. All segment descriptors of a given process are collected in a table called the *segment descriptor table* (SDT). The base address is recorded so that actual physical address of any item in a specific segment can be calculated during runtime. The size of the segment is recorded so as to assure that invalid addresses, if referenced, will not be allowed during execution. When segment numbers and relative offsets within the segments are defined, two-component logical addresses uniquely identify all items within a process's address space.

Figure 5.7(a) illustrates the logical view of a load-module sample of a process P with all its segments. Figure 5.7(b) depicts a sample placement of this already-defined segments into physical memory with the resulting SDT [Figure 5.7(a)] already formed by the operating system in order to facilitate the needed address translation. Each segment descriptor (entry) in this table shows the physical base address of the memory area allocated to each defined segment, and the size field of the same segment descriptor is used to check whether the supplied offset in the logical address is within the legal bounds of its enclosing segment. Here, the name of the segment is also included

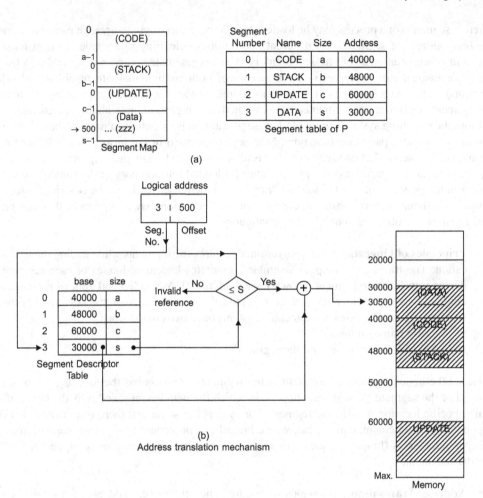

FIGURE 5.7 A schematic representation of an example showing different memory segments and related address translation mechanism used in segmented memory management.

in the respective segment descriptor but only for the purpose of better understanding. The MMU uses this SDT to perform address translation and uses the segment number provided in the logical address to index the segment descriptor table to obtain the physical base (starting) address of the related segment. The effective memory address is then generated by adding the offset b_k of the desired item to the base address (start address) of s_k of its enclosing segment. Thus, the address translation mechanism in the segmentation approach is definitely slower in operation and hence more expensive than paging.

Apart from the comparatively high overhead while carrying out address translation, segmentation of address space incurs extra costs due to additional storing of quite large segment descriptor tables and subsequently accessing them. Here, each logical address reference requires two physical memory references:

• Memory reference to access the respective segment descriptor in the SDT.
• Memory reference to access the target location in the physical memory.

In other words, segmentation may reduce the effective memory bandwidth by half in comparison to the actual physical memory access time.

A brief description of this topic with an example is given on the Support Material at www. routledge.com/9781032467238.

- **Hardware Requirements:** Since the size of the SDT itself is related to the size of the logical (virtual) address space of a process, the length of an SDT may vary from a few entries to several thousand. That is why SDTs may themselves be often assigned a separate special type of segment (partition) of their own. The accessing mechanism of SDT is often facilitated by means of a dedicated hardware register known as a segment descriptor table base register (SDTBR), which is set to point the base (starting) address of the SDT of the currently running process. Another dedicated register called the segment descriptor table limit register (SDTLR) is set to mark the end of that SDT as indicated by SDTBR. This register actually limits the exact number of entries in the SDT, as there are an actual number of segments defined in a given process. As a result, any attempt to access a nonexistent segment (that may have a specific segment number) may be detected and access will then be denied with exceptions.

When a process is initiated by the operating system, the base and limit of its SDT are normally kept in the PCB of the process. Upon each process switch, the SDTBR and SDTLR are loaded with the base and length, respectively, of the corresponding SDT of the new running process. Moreover, when a process is swapped out, all the SDT entries in relation to the affected segments are invalidated. When a process is again swapped back in, the SDT itself is swapped back with required updating of the base fields of all its related segment descriptors so as to reflect the new load addresses. Since this action is an expensive one, the swapped out SDT itself is generally not used. Instead, the SDT of the swapped-out process may be discarded, and a new up-to-date SDT is created from the load-module map of the swapped-in process when it is once again loaded back in memory. In the case of memory compaction, if supported, when it is carried out, the segments of a process are relocated. This requires updating of the related SDT entries for each segment that is moved. In such systems, some additional or modified data structures and add-on hardware support may be needed so as to identify the related SDT entry that points to the segment scheduled to be moved.

Segment Descriptor Caching: To reduce the duration of time required for the slow address translation process in segmented system, some designers suggest keeping only a few of the most frequently used segment descriptors in registers (segment descriptor register, SDR) in order to avoid time-consuming memory access of SDT entries for the sake of mapping. The rest of the SDT may then be kept in memory in the usual way for the purpose of mapping. Investigations of the types of segments referenced by the executing process reveal that there may be functionally three different categories of segment, instructions (code), data, and stack. Three dedicated registers (for the purpose of mapping) may thus be used, and each register will contain the base (beginning) address of each of such respective segment in main memory and its size (length). Since, in most machines that use segmentation, the CPU emits a few status bits to indicate the type of each memory reference, the MMU can then use this information to select one of these registers for appropriate mapping.

Segment descriptor registers are initially loaded from the SDT. In a running process, whenever an intersegment reference is made, the corresponding segment descriptor is loaded into the respective register from the SDT. Since in a running process, different segments appear at different times, SDRs are normally included in the process state. When switching of process occurs, the contents of the SDRs of the departing process are stored with the rest of its context. Before dispatching the new running process, the operating system loads the SDRs with their images, recorded in the related PCB. Use of such hardware-assisted SDRs has been found to accelerate the translation process satisfactorily; hence, they are employed in many segmented architectures, including Intel's iAPX-86 family of machines.

- **Protection:** Separation of the address spaces of distinctly different processes, placing them in different segments in disjoint areas of memory, primarily realizes protection between the processes. In addition, the MMU at the time of translating a logical address (s_k, b_k) compares b_k with the size of the segment s_k, available in a field of each and every SDT entry, thereby restricting any attempt to break the protection. However, protection between the segments within the address space is carried out by using the type of each segment defined at the time of segment declaration depending on the nature of information (code, data, or stack) stored in it. Access rights to each segment can even be included using the respective access-rights bits in the SDT entry. Since the logically related items are grouped in segmentation, this is one of the rare memory-management schemes that permit finely grained representation of access rights. The address mapping hardware at the time of address translation checks the intended type of reference against the access rights for the segment in question given in the SDT. Any mismatch will then stop the translation process, and an interrupt to the OS is issued.

One of the more sophisticated mechanisms to implement protection is to use a ring-protection structure (similar to level structure of operating system, Chapter 3) in which lower-numbered or inner rings enjoy greater privileges than high-numbered or outer rings. Typically, ring 0 is reserved for kernel functions of the operating system. All applications usually reside at a higher level. Some operating system services or utilities may occupy an intermediate-level ring. A ring system obeys the following two basic principles:

1. A program may access only data that reside on the same ring or on a ring with lower privilege.
2. A program may call services residing on the same or a more privileged ring.

- **Sharing: Shared Segments:** Ease of sharing is the appealing beauty of the segmentation approach. Shared entities are usually placed in separate dedicated segments to make sharing flexible. A shared segment may then be mapped by the appropriate segment descriptor tables to the logical address spaces of all processes that are authorized to use it. The intended use of based addressing together with offsets facilitates sharing, since the logical offset of a given shared item is identical in all processes that share it. Each process that wants to use a shared object (segment) will have a corresponding SDT entry in its own table pointing to the intended shared objects that contains information including the base address, size, and their access-right bits. This information is used at the time of address translation. Different process may have different access rights to the same shared segment. In this way, segmented systems conserve memory by providing only a single copy of the objects shared by many authorized users rather than having multiple copies. The participating processes that share a specific object keep track of their own execution within the shared object by means of their own program counter, which is saved and restored at the time of each process switch.

Sharing of segments, however, often invites some problems in systems that also support swapping. When swapping out shared objects or any one of the participating processes which are authorized to reference the shared objects are swapped in, they are always placed in currently available locations that may be different from their previously occupied locations. The OS should at least keep track of construction of the SDT before and after swapping of both shared segments and processes that use them. It must ensure proper mapping of all logical address spaces of participating processes to the shared segments in main memory.

A brief description of this topic with a figure is given on the Support Material at www.routledge.com/9781032467238.

5.8.2.1.2.1 Conclusion: Merits and Drawbacks Segmentation is one of the basic tools of memory management and permits the logical address space of a single process to break into separate logically related entities (segments) that may be individually loaded in noncontiguous areas of physical memory. The sizes of the segments are usually different, and memory is allocated to the segments according to their sizes, thereby mostly eliminating the negative effect of internal fragmentation. As the average segment sizes are normally smaller than the average process sizes, segmentation can reduce the amount of external fragmentation and its bad impact as happens in dynamically partitioned memory management. Other advantages of segmentation have also been observed that include dynamic relocation, adequate protection both between segments and between the address spaces of different processes, easy sharing, and sufficient flexibility towards dynamic linking and loading.

However, one of the shortcomings of the segmentation approach is its address translation mechanism. Address translation of logical-to-physical address in such systems is comparatively complex and also requires dedicated hardware support that ultimately enables a substantial reduction in effective memory bandwidth. In absence of overlay and virtual memory, another drawback of segmentation is that it cannot remove the problem that limits the size of a process's logical address space by the size of the available physical memory. However, this issue has been resolved, and the best use of segmentation was realized as soon as virtual memory was introduced in the architecture of computer systems, which will be discussed in the following sections. Contemporary segmented architectures, implemented on the platform of modern processors, such as Intel X-86 or the Motorola 68000 series, support segment sizes on the order of 4 MB or even higher.

5.8.2.1.3 Segmentation versus Paging

Segmentation and paging differ both in approach (strategy) as well as in implementation. Segmentation is usually visible, and segments are a user-oriented concept, providing a means of convenience for organizing and logical structuring of programs and data. Paging, on the other hand, is invisible to the programmer and concentrates more on the management of physical memory. In a paged system, all pages are of fixed size in contrast to segments, which have variable size, and all page addresses form a linear address space within the logical address space. Since segments are usually of unequal sizes, there is no simple relationship between logical addresses and their corresponding physical addresses, whereas in paging, such a straightforward relationship does exist.

Each segment table entry therefore contains a complete physical memory address rather than a simple frame number, as in a paged memory system. The offset byte number b_k is added to this address to compute the effective physical address. This step involves an addition cycle rather than mere concatenation as observed in paging. In addition, with a paged memory system, a logical (virtual) address kkkk is specified as a single number. After knowing the number of bits used to represent the page number and byte offset, the MMU extracts p_k and b_k from kkkk automatically. The logical address space is thus single-dimensional. If a CPU register holds the address of the last byte of a page, adding 1 to this address makes it "spill over" into the next page. This does not usually happen in a segmented memory, since the last byte of one segment and the first byte of the next segment may (usually) not be necessarily adjoining bytes in the process. This difference bears important aspects that leads to significant implications at the time of allocation of main memory. This comparison equally holds in systems with virtual memory support.

Placement strategies based on the methods of finding a suitable area of free memory to load an incoming page/segment are somehow manageable in paging systems, but are quite complex in segmented systems, since the segments are usually of variable sizes, and within segments, memory contiguity requirements complicate the management of both main and secondary memories. That is why pure segmentation systems are increasingly rare in use.

5.8.2.1.4 Segmentation with Paging

When the segments are large, it may be inconvenient and even impossible to accommodate them entirely in the allotted limited main memory. This leads to the idea of dividing each segment into pages, and an integral number of pages is then allocated to each segment so that only those pages that are actually needed have to be around. Paging and segmentation thus can be combined to gain the advantages of both, resulting in simplifying memory allocation and speeding it up, as well as removing external fragmentation. A page table is then constructed for each segment of the process, and a field containing the address pointing to the respective page table is kept in the segment descriptor in the SDT. Address translation for a logical address in the form (s_k, b_k) is now carried out in two stages. In the first stage, the entry s_k in the SDT is searched, and then the address of its page table is obtained. The byte number b_k, which is the offset within the segment, is now split into a pair (ps_k, bp_k), where ps_k is the page number within the segment s_k, and bp_k is the byte number (offset) within the respective page p_k. The page table is now used in the usual way to determine the required physical address. The effective address calculation is now carried out in the same manner as in paging: the page frame number of ps_k is obtained from the respective page table, and bp_k is then concatenated with it to determine the actual physical address.

Figure 5.8 shows process P of Figure 5.7 in a system that uses segmentation with paging. Each logical address is thus divided here into three fields. The upper field is the segment number, the middle one is the page number, and the lower one is the offset within the page. The memory map, as shown in Figure 5.8, consists of a segment table and a set of page tables, one of each segment. Each segment is paged independently, and the corresponding page frames again need not be contiguous. The internal fragmentation, if exists, occurs only in the last page of each segment. Each segment descriptor in the SDT now contains the address that points to the respective page table of the segment. The size field in the segment descriptor, as usual, prevents any invalid reference,

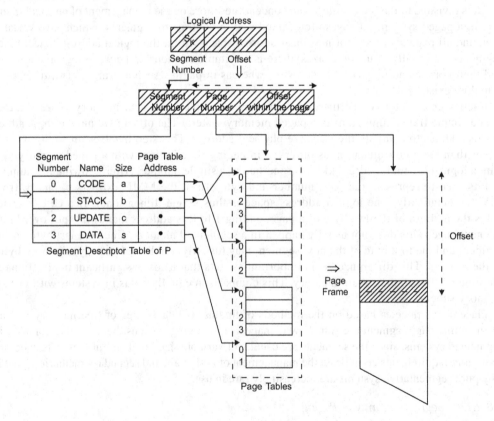

FIGURE 5.8 A schematic representation of segmentation with paging approach used in segmented–paged memory management.

which facilitates memory protection. Different tradeoffs exist with respect to the size of the segment field, the page field, and the offset limit. The size of the segment field being set puts a limitation on the number of segments that can be declared by users within this permissible range, the page field that defines the number of pages within each segment determines the segment size, and the size of the offset field describes the page size. All three parameters are entirely determined by the design of the operating system, which depends mostly on the architecture of the computer system being employed.

5.8.3 MEMORY ALLOCATION STRATEGY: FOR OS KERNEL USAGE

The kernel continuously creates and destroys many data structures at different times during the course of its operation to manage and monitor user and system processes. These data structures are mostly small tables, arrays, buffers, and control blocks (such as process control block [PCB], I/O control block [IOCB], file control block [FCB], and event control block [ECB]) that are employed to monitor the computing environment, including the allocation, execution, and managing of processes as well as controlled use of resources in the system. These data structures are created only when the respective situations occur and consume memory space, and thus usage of memory and the related memory operation time together with the CPU time used by the OS constitute the OS overhead, which is a measure in the performance of the OS. Therefore, creation, maintenance, and deletion of the needed data structures by the kernel as well as its other associated operations related to memory usage must be fast, efficient, and also effective.

In fact, the lifetimes of these data structures are tied to lifetimes of related entities like processes, events, or activities like I/O operation and file operation. Hence, these data structures do not possess any predictable relationship with one another. This feature rules out the use of the kernel *stack* for creation of these data structures and subsequent use of them. The kernel in this situation must use a *heap*. Since the sizes of control blocks are mostly known while designing the OS, the kernel uses this feature to make memory allocation and management simple and efficient. When one control block is destroyed, the respective memory space is released, and it can then be allocated to create a similar control block in near future. To take advantage of this approach, a separate free list can be maintained for each and every type of control block to facilitate quick and effective allocation. For other types of data structures, such as buffers and small tables, which are mostly of variable sizes, the kernel requires dynamic memory allocation. For example, the *allocb* routine in UNIX allocates STREAMS buffers of arbitrary size.

5.8.3.1 Case Study: Kernel Memory Allocators in UNIX and Solaris

As the design goal of UNIX is to be platform (machine) independent, its memory-management scheme will vary from one system configuration to another. Earlier versions of UNIX simply used variable partitioning with no provision of virtual memory (to be discussed later) support. Current implementations of both UNIX and Solaris, however, use noncontiguous memory allocation with paging in the presence of virtual memory.

In both UNIX SVR4 and Solaris, there are actually two separate memory-management schemes. The *paging system* in the presence of virtual memory is an established, effective memory-management scheme that allocates an integral number of required page frames in main memory to processes and also to disk block buffers to effectively use each page profitably. This paged virtual memory scheme is, however, less suited as a memory management scheme for memory allocation to the kernel. One of the main reasons is that the kernel frequently generates and destroys small tables, arrays, and buffers as well as creating many objects (such as process structures, vnodes, and file descriptor blocks) dynamically at different times as and when needed during the course of execution. Each of these entities while requires dynamic memory allocation, but most of these entities are significantly smaller than the usual machine page size, and therefore, the paging mechanism would be ineffective and not appropriate for such dynamic kernel memory allocation. That is why a separate *kernel memory allocator* is used, and three such kernel memory allocators are worth mentioning:

- McKusick–Karels allocator
- Lazy buddy allocator
- Slab allocator

The details of each of these three allocation strategies, with computations, are separately given on the Support Material at www.routledge.com/9781032467238.

5.9 VIRTUAL MEMORY

In the memory management schemes, both fixed and dynamic partitioning have the requirement of contiguous allocation of physical memory, while noncontiguous allocation schemes relieve the system of this stringent obligation. But both contiguous and noncontiguous allocation schemes, of course, require the entire executable code to be resident in the main memory before the execution begins, that ultimately limits the maximum possible size of the job which depends on the available space in the physical memory at program execution time. A noncontiguous allocation policy in the form of a paging and segmentation approach, however, divides a process into a number of components (pages and segments), and these process components do not need to be located in the contiguous memory area during execution. Moreover, these process components are referenced by their logical addresses that are dynamically translated by the MMU into the corresponding actual physical addresses for execution during runtime. This provides total freedom in swapping a process in and out of main memory at different times, even during the tenure of execution, and it can be placed once again accordingly in any region of main memory at that moment. Subsequent developments combining paging and segmentation manifests that it is not even essential that all of the pages or segments of a process be resident in main memory during runtime.

When a new process gets started, the operating system initiates the execution by bringing only one or a few process components into memory that include the initial part of the program and related data pieces to which those instructions refer. Other portions are brought into memory as and when a need arises, either into a free area in memory or by replacing a portion of the component already existing in memory but not currently in use. The execution continues, and the processor keeps track of the availability of all memory references by using the respective page or segment table. If the processor encounters a logical address that is not available in main memory, the execution is temporarily halted, and the processor generates an interrupt indicating that a memory access fault occurred. The operating system now takes control, puts the interrupted process in a blocked state, and attempts to fetch the needed portion of the process into main memory that contains the required logical address which causes the access fault so that the execution of the process can continue. By this time, the OS can initiate another process to run to make use of available CPU time while the interrupt servicing is in progress. Once the needed portion of the process is brought into main memory, the OS then places the affected blocked process back into the ready state.

Although this approach requires a lot of additional administrative overhead when implemented, but offers two distinct advantages that ultimately result in increased system utilization.

- Only a part of the process and not the entire one gets loaded to begin its execution, that ultimately enables main memory to accommodate many other processes, thereby eventually increasing the degrees of multiprogramming that, in turn, effectively increases processor utilization.

- The mandatory requirement in the size of the program that must be restricted by the size of the available memory has now been waived without use of any sort of overlay strategy. The user now perceives a potentially larger memory allocated in a specific area on the disk, and the size of such memory is related to disk storage. The operating system, in association with related hardware support, automatically loads parts of a process during runtime from this area into main memory for execution as and when required, and that too without any participation of the user or any notification to the user.

The whole responsibility is now shouldered by the operating system in order to create an illusion to the user while providing such an extremely large memory store. Since this large memory is merely an illusion, it is historically called *virtual memory*, in contrast with the main memory, known as *real memory*(physical memory), which is the only place the actual execution of a process can take place. The details of virtual memory management are generally transparent to the user, and the virtual memory manager creates the illusion of having a much larger memory than may actually be available. It appears as if the physical memory is stretched far beyond the actual physical memory available on the machine. *Virtual memory can thus be defined as a memory hierarchy consisting of the main memory of computer system and a specified area on disk that enables the execution of a process with only some portions of its address space in main memory.* The virtual memory model loads the process components freely into any available areas of memory, likely to be non-adjacent, for execution. The user's logical address can then be referred to as a *virtual address*. The virtual address of every memory reference used by a process would be translated by the virtual memory manager (the part of the OS responsible for memory management) using special memory mapping hardware (a part of the MMU) into an actual address of the real memory area where the referenced entity physically resides. This is done on behalf of the user in a way transparent to the user. This model almost totally solves the memory fragmentation problem since a free area of memory can be reused even if it is not large enough to hold an entire process.

While the other memory management techniques attempted to approximate 100 percent memory utilization, the implementation of the virtual memory concept attains a utilization logically greater than 100 percent. That is, the sum of all the address spaces of the jobs being multiprogrammed may exceed the size of physical memory. This feat is accomplished by removing the requirement that a job's entire address space be in main memory at one time; instead, only portions of it can be loaded, and the image of the entire virtual address space of a process rests on the disk. In traditional memory management schemes, the user's logical address space starts from 0 to a maximum of N, the size of the actual physical memory available to the user. Under virtual memory management, the user's logical address space starts from 0 and can extend up to the entire virtual memory space, the size of which is decided by the machine's addressing capability or the space available on the backing store (on the disk, to be discussed). For a 32-bit system, the total size of the virtual memory can be 2^{32}, or approximately 4 gigabytes. For the newer 64-bit chips and operating systems that use 48- or 64-bit addresses, this can be even higher.

Virtual memory makes the job of the application programmer much simpler. No matter how much memory the application needs, it can act as if it has access to a main memory of that size and can place its data anywhere in that virtual space that it likes. Moreover, a program may run without modification or even recompilation on systems with significantly different sizes of installed memory. In addition, the programmer can also completely ignore the need to manage moving information back and forth between different kinds of memory. On the other hand, the use of virtual memory can only degrade the execution speed and not the function of a given application. This is mainly due to extended delays caused in the address translation process and also while fetching missing portions' of a program's address space at runtime.

Brief details about this topic are given on the Support Material at www.routledge.com/ 9781032467238.

5.9.1   BACKGROUND AND HISTORY

Before the development of the virtual memory technique, programmers in the 1940s and 1950s had to manage two-level storage (main memory or RAM and secondary memory in the form of *hard disks* or earlier *magnetic drums*) directly. Virtual memory was developed in approximately 1959–1962 at the University of Manchester for the Atlas Computer and completed in 1962. However, Fritz-Rudolf Güntsch, one of Germany's pioneering computer scientists and later the developer of the Telefunken TR 440 mainframe, claims to have invented the concept sometime in 1957. However, in 1961, Burroughs finally released the B5000, the first commercial computer with virtual memory. Still, the inclusion of virtual memory and its acceptance were strongly challenged, and the debate in favor of its usefulness continued until 1969, when an IBM research team led by David Sayre showed that the virtual memory overlay system worked consistently better than the best manually controlled systems. In the 1970s, minicomputer models, such as VAX models running the VMS operating system, implemented virtual memory, and by the early 1970s, the triumph of virtual memory started. From then it became available on almost all computers. Early personal computers in the 1980s were developed without virtual memory, mainly on the assumption that such issues were only applicable to large-scale commercial computers. Virtual memory was finally introduced for Microsoft Windows in Windows 3.0 (1990) and the Apple Macintosh starting with System 7 (1991). Nowadays, almost all microprocessors, including the Intel X-86 series and Motorola 68000 series, have highly sophisticated virtual memory systems.

Brief details on this topic are given on the Support Material at www.routledge.com/9781032467238.

5.9.2   VIRTUAL MEMORY AND LOCALITY

According to the principle of locality, execution of a program over any short period of time is observed to be confined to a small section of the program (e.g. a loop or a subroutine) and accesses perhaps only a small portion of data (a few arrays of data). Moreover, many programs are observed to have the tendency to favor specific portions of their address spaces during execution, thereby supporting the principle of locality. Experiments with processes in virtual memory environments unconditionally confirm this principle of locality, indicating that during the lifetime of the process, references are mostly confined to a subset (a few components) of a program. If these components of a process can be made resident for most of the time in memory during the execution of a program, then the principle of locality suggests that a virtual memory scheme may work most effectively. Since unused components are not present in main memory, swapping them in and out of memory is not often required and consequently lowers the rate of back-and-forth journey (**thrashing**) of the process components from and to the disk. This ultimately saves a substantial amount of time that summarily leads to a notable increase in the overall performance of the virtual memory system. In fact, in the steady state, practically all the main memory will then be occupied with useful process components of different programs so that the processor and the operating system can have direct access to as many processes as possible. The virtual memory handler actually uses special techniques that essentially ensure exploitation of the principle of locality of reference. In fact, the feasibility and practicality of virtual memory implementation primarily depend on two basic ingredients: first, to control the amount of memory allocated to a process to accommodate all its useful components, and second, the decisions about which parts (components) of a process are to be kept in memory, when to bring them, and where to place them. Both these tasks are, however, policy-dependent, and are thus performed by the software components of the virtual memory handler.

Brief details on this topic are given on the Support Material at www.routledge.com/9781032467238.

5.9.3 Basic Concepts

Virtual memory is normally created in a fixed disk drive or in a specific reserved area on a disk drive. The virtual address space of a process containing its various components often exceeds the size of the available real memory. For the sake of multitasking, the real memory is then used by the currently needed components of different processes that are not necessarily in contiguous locations, as shown in Figure 5.9. Information about the memory areas where these components reside is maintained in a data structure of the virtual memory handler and is used by the MMU at the time of address translation. Other components of each of the processes to be executed are brought from the virtual memory into real memory as and when they are needed, and this operation is carried out as quickly as possible.

During execution, if information (an instruction or data) contained in a particular process component is required which is not present in memory, the execution is then temporarily halted, and the processor generates an interrupt indicating that a memory access fault occurred. The OS then takes the control, puts the interrupted process in a blocked state, and attempts to bring the needed process component into memory from the disk that contains the required virtual address which caused the access fault so that the execution of the blocked process can continue once again. For this purpose, the OS issues a disk I/O request. Once the needed component of the process is brought into main memory from the disk, the I/O issues an interrupt that enables the OS to get back control. The OS then places the affected blocked process back into the ready state and relinquishes control in favor of the processor to resume its ongoing execution with the user processes.

The new component being brought from the virtual memory has to be accommodated somewhere in memory. If a free area is available, it can be placed there. In the absence of a free area, the virtual memory handler replaces a component from memory, often belonging to the same process, that is not in current use in order to make room for the new component to load. The component selected for replacement might have been modified by this time after its admission in memory. The contents of the component in memory will be different from its original image in the virtual memory. In this situation, the component to be replaced is written back to its position in virtual memory, often without overwriting (depending on policy) the original image, as shown in Figure 5.10. If the content of the component selected for replacement remains unchanged, it can simply be rejected,

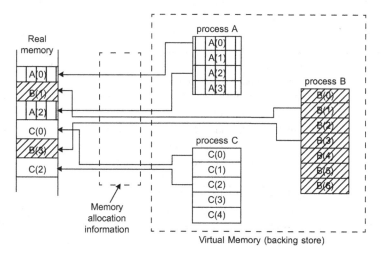

FIGURE 5.9 A schematic representation of basic operations of virtual memory management system, showing presently required portions of currently executing processes loaded into main memory.

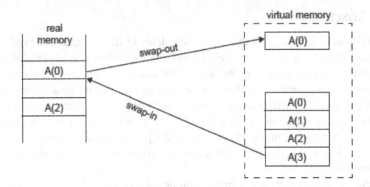

FIGURE 5.10   In virtual memory management system, a new component is swapped in main memory from virtual memory, whenever required, by way of swapping out an existing component from main memory, not in use, to make room.

and the new component brought from virtual memory can be immediately loaded in its place in memory. In this case, the overhead involved in writing back the component on the virtual memory is simply avoided, thereby saving a considerable time that may summarily result in an appreciable improvement in overall system performance.

5.9.4   VIRTUAL MEMORY IMPLEMENTATION

Two fundamental approaches used for successful implementation of virtual memory have been observed:

- Paging
- Segmentation

Paging and segmentation differ both in approach (strategy) as well as in implementation, particularly in the manner in which the boundaries and size of process components are derived. Under the paging scheme, each process component is called *a page*, and all pages are identical in size. Page size is determined by the architecture of the computer system. Page demarcation in a process is implicitly also carried out by architecture. Paging is therefore invisible to the programmer. In segmentation, each process component is called *a segment*. Segments are a user-oriented concept declared by the programmer to provide a means of convenience for organization and logical structuring of programs and data for the purpose of virtual memory implementation. Thus, identification of process components is performed by the programmer, and, as segments can have different sizes, there exists no simple relationship between virtual addresses and the corresponding physical addresses, whereas in paging, such a straightforward relationship does exist. Paging and segmentation in virtual memory systems, therefore, have different implementations for memory management and different implications for effective memory utilization.

Paging and segmentation schemes when implemented in virtual memory system give rise to two different forms of memory management, *paged virtual memory management* and *segmented virtual memory management* respectively. Some operating systems often exploit a mechanism by combining segmentation and paging approaches called, *segmented paged memory management*, to extract the advantages of both approaches at the same time. Obviously, the address translation mechanisms of these schemes also differ from one another and are carried out by means of either page-map tables, segment descriptor tables, or both.

5.9.4.1   Paging

Paging is an obvious approach associated with systems providing virtual memory, although virtual memory using segmentation is also equally popular and will be discussed later. Paging is considered

Prot.   Other
P   R   M   info   info   page Frame No. #

FIGURE 5.11   In virtual memory management system with paging, a representative Page Table Entry is shown.

the simplest and most widely used method for implementing virtual memory, or, conversely, the paging approach is found best implemented in virtual memory. In simple paging (without virtual memory), as already discussed, when all the pages of a process are loaded into main memory, the respective page table for that process is created and then loaded into main memory. Each page table entry contains the page frame number of the corresponding page in main memory. The same approach is also employed for a virtual memory scheme based on paging but with an important exception: in virtual memory systems, only some portions of the address space of the running process are always present in main memory, and the rest need not be required to be in main memory. This makes the page table entries more complex than those of simple paging.

As shown in Figure 5.11, the page table entry, in addition, contains a *present* (P) or *valid bit*, indicating whether the corresponding page is present in main memory. If the bit indicates that the page is in main memory, then the page table entry also includes the page frame number of that page. The *referenced bit* (R) indicates whether the page already present in memory is referenced. The bit R is set whenever the page is referenced (read or written). The page table entry also contains a *modify* or *dirty bit* (M) to indicate whether the contents of the corresponding page have been altered or modified after loading in main memory. If the contents of the page remain unchanged, it is not necessary to write back the page frame of this page on the backing store when its turn comes to replace the page in the frame that it currently holds. The associated overhead can then be avoided. The *protection information* (*Prot info*) bit for the page in the page table indicates whether the page can be read from or written into by processes. *Other information* (*Other info*) bits are kept for the page in the page table for storing other useful information concerning the page, such as its position in the swap spaces. In addition, other control bits may also be required in the page table for various other purposes if those are managed at the page level.

5.9.4.1.1 Address Translation

During the execution of a program, the CPU always issues virtual addresses, but it has to be run in real address space. Thus, an address mapping is required that will convert these virtual addresses to the corresponding physical addresses. In paging systems, this address translation is performed at the page level. In particular, each virtual address consists of two parts: the (virtual) page number and the offset within the page, as shown in Figure 5.12. Since pages and page frames have identical sizes, offsets within each are identical and need not be converted. Thus, in a paging system, only the address translation of (virtual) pages to its corresponding page frames in memory is required, and that is performed with the aid of a mapping table, called the *page-map table* (PMT) or simply *page table*. The PMT is created at process loading time to establish the correspondence between the virtual and physical addresses. Since PMTs of different processes are of variable lengths, depending on the size of the processes, it is not expected that they will be held in registers. Instead, the PMT must be in main memory while in use.

A sample format of the PMT corresponding to the assumed placement of pages in physical memory, along with the needed hardware implementation for address translation, is shown in Figure 5.12. As indicated, there is one PMT entry for each virtual page of a process. Besides other information, the content of each entry is the number of page frames (composed of the high-order, page-level bits) in the physical memory where the corresponding virtual page is actually located.

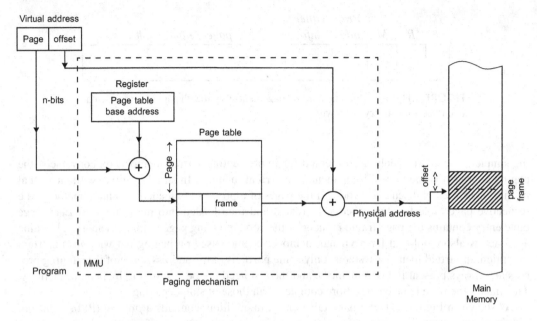

FIGURE 5.12 A schematic block diagram of address translation mechanism used in the management of virtual memory with paging system.

Since the offsets of the virtual addresses being issued by the CPU are not mapped, the high-order bits of the physical address are obtained after translation; that is, the page frame number needs to be stored in a PMT. All other PMT entries are similarly filled with page frame numbers of the locations where the corresponding pages are actually loaded.

The address translation mechanism in paged systems is illustrated in Figure 5.12. When a particular process is running, a register holds the starting (base) address of the page table for that currently running process. The page number (p_k) of a virtual address is used to index that page table to obtain the corresponding frame number. This is then combined (concatenate) with the offset portion (b_k) of the virtual address to produce the desired real (physical) address. It is obvious that the field containing the page number in the virtual address is longer than the field containing the frame number.

In general, each process, even of average size, can occupy huge amounts of virtual memory, and there is only one page table for each process. If the size of the pages is considered moderate, a good number of page table entries are still required for each process. Consequently, the amount of main memory devoted to page tables alone could be substantially high and may severely affect and limit the space requirements for the execution of users' applications. In order to overcome this problem, most virtual memory management schemes hold page tables in virtual memory instead of storing them in main memory. When a process is under execution, only a part of its page table containing few page table entries, including the currently executing page, are made available in main memory.

5.9.4.1.2 Page Faults: Related Actions

While performing address translation for a virtual (logical) address constituting of page number p_k and offset b_k, the MMU checks the valid bit P (as shown in Figure 5.12) of the page table entry of p_k. If it indicates that p_k is not present in memory, the MMU raises an interrupt called a *page fault* or *missing page interrupt*, and the related process that suffers a page fault is eventually blocked by the memory management until the required page is loaded into memory. The interrupt handler now gets control and finds that the interrupt is related to a page fault. It then invokes the virtual memory handler and passes it the page number p_k that caused the page fault. The virtual memory handler then consults the page table to get the *other-info* field (as shown in Figure 5.12) of the page table entry of page p_k that contains the disk block address of page p_k. After getting this address, the virtual memory handler looks up the free-frames list to find a currently free page frame. If no such free page frame is available, some other actions (to be discussed later) are taken so that a free page frame can be obtained. However, it now allocates the free page frame to page p_k and starts an I/O operation to load p_k in the free page frame. Note that page I/O is distinct from I/O operations performed by processes, which are called *program I/O*. When the I/O operation is completed, the system updates page p_k's entry in the page table by setting the valid bit to 1, putting the free page frame number in the page frame # field of page p_k, and also marking the frame as being in a normal state. This ends the related procedures to be followed when a page fault occurs that ultimately bring the page p_k into memory.

The faulting instruction is now brought back to the state when the page fault occurred. All other actions that are required after interrupt servicing are then accordingly carried out to resume the execution of the faulting instruction, assuming that nothing has happened.

A brief description of this topic is given on the Support Material at www.routledge.com/ 9781032467238.

5.9.4.1.3   *Multi-Level Page Tables: Hierarchical Address Translation Tables*

As technology rapidly advances, the cost of the components constantly dropped, eventually making it possible to provide a comparatively large 32-bit (2^{32} = 4 GB) virtual address space on almost all contemporary computers, including the microcomputers of today. If this virtual address space is considered with 4K (2^{12}) page size, then the size of the page table will be large enough, with 2^{20} entries ($2^{32} \div 2^{12} = 2^{20}$) in its page table. In order to reduce the memory requirements of such a huge page table (sometimes containing thousands of pages) in memory all the time, many computers use a *multi-level page table* by *paging the page table* itself and loading its pages on demand just like pages of a process. In fact, those page tables that are only needed at any instant should be kept in memory, and the rest would remain in virtual memory as usual. In this two-tiered arrangement, a higher-level page table contains entries (pages) pointing to the page tables, and each page table contains entries of different pages of a process. If the size of the higher-level page table itself is found too large, it could be then expanded to three, four, or even more levels to further reduce the memory commitment for page tables. Although implementation of additional levels offers more flexibility, but it is doubtful, due to additional complexity and time consumption associated with increases in page table levels, whether it is worth it to go beyond three levels.

- **Two-Level Paging:** Under this scheme, there is a *page directory* (like that shown in Figure 5.19) in which each entry points to a page table. Typically, the maximum size of a page table is kept restricted to be equal to one page. This strategy is used by the Pentium processor, for example. Here, an approach with a two-level paging scheme is considered, which employs typically a 32-bit addressing, using byte-level addressing, the page size assumed 4 Kbytes (2^{12}) and the virtual address space taken as 4 Gbytes (2^{32}). The number of pages now required to address this virtual memory is 2^{20} ($2^{32} \div 2^{12} = 2^{20}$) pages. If each page table entry is taken as 4 bytes (2^2) in length, then the page table consisting of 2^{20} page entries requires 4 Mbytes (2^{22}). The root directory is kept in one page (4 Kbytes = 2^{12}) with each entry 4 bytes (2^2) in length, so it consists of 2^{10} entries, and each such entry points to one user page table, which again consists of 2^{10} page table entries. In this way, the total 2^{20} virtual pages are mapped by the root page table with only 2^{10} entries. It is to be noted that the root page table consisting of one page is always kept resident in main memory.

Brief details about this topic are given on the Support Material at www.routledge.com/ 9781032467238.

5.9.4.1.3.1 Case Study: Two-Level Paging: VAX (DEC Systems) The 32-bit virtual addresses used in VAX providing a virtual space of size $2^{32} = 4$ gigabytes are split into three fields in which the high-order 2 bits (value = 00, 01, 10, 11) signifies the nature of the use (user space, OS space, etc.) of the respective virtual space. With the use of the leftmost 2 bits in the virtual address, the entire virtual space is actually partitioned into ($2^2 =$) four sections, and the size of each section is $2^{32} \div 4 = 2^{30} = 1$ Gb. Each such section starts from 0, 1, 2, and 3 Gb with the values of this 2 high-order bits in each sections are 00, 01, 10, 11 respectively. The page size is taken as 512 (= 2^9) bytes, and hence, the number of bits used to express offset within the page is then of 9 bits. The number of bits used in each entry (32 bits = 4 bytes in length) of the page table to express the number of virtual pages is, therefore, 32—(2 + 9) = 21 bits. Hence, the number of pages present in the system 2^{21} (= 2 million) pages, and as each page entry in the page table is 32 bits (or = 4 = 2^2 bytes) in length, that ultimately makes the size of the page table equal to $2^{21} \times 4$, or 2^{23} bytes (= 8 Mbytes), which is quite large. While managing to keep this huge size of page table in memory, designers eventually opted for a two-level page table scheme that allows user page tables to be themselves paged out when they are not currently needed.

The paging structure and address translation mechanism of VAX are quite complicated but possess several distinct advantages. But it imposes the need for two memory references to the page tables on each user memory reference; the first one is to the system page table, and the second is to the user page table, thereby causing a serious drawback due to repeated memory visits, which are quite time consuming. However, this shortcoming has been overcome with the use of special hardware (associative memory, to be discussed later) support that enables bypassing the path most of the time, making it much lucrative and also practicable.

The details of this topic with a figure are given on the Support Material at www.routledge.com/9781032467238.

5.9.4.1.3.2 Case Study: Three-Level Paging: Sun SPARC The architecture of SPARC, a RISC processor introduced by SUN Microsystems, uses a three-level page table to realize a three-level paging mechanism. Under this scheme, when a process is loaded into memory, the operating system assigns it a unique context number, similar to a process-id, which is kept reserved and fixed for the process during its entire lifetime. A context table is built up with all the context numbers assigned to the processes available in the system and is permanently resident in hardware. In this way, it helps to avoid reloading the tables when switching from one process to another. MMU chips usually support such 4096 contexts in almost all models.

When a memory reference is issued, the context number and virtual address are presented to the MMU, which uses the context number as an index into its context table to find the top-level page table number for that context (which is the context of currently executing process). It then uses *Index1* to select an entry from the top-level page table. The obtained entry then points to the next level page table, and so on until the target page is found. If, during this translation process, any entry in the respective page table is not found, the mapping cannot be completed and a page fault occurs. The running process must then be suspended until the missing page-table page is brought in, and the affected instruction once again can be restarted. Too many memory references to access the respective page tables (three levels) on each user memory reference, however, make the system very slow due to repeated visits to slower memory. Hence, to speed up the lookup, special hardware with associative memory is provided.

A brief description of this topic with a figure is given on the Support Material at www.routledge.com/9781032467238.

5.9.4.1.3.3 Case Study: Four-Level Paging: Motorola 68030 The four-level paging scheme used by Motorola on its 68030 chip is highly flexible and sophisticated. The beauty of this scheme is that the number of levels of page tables is programmable, from 0 to 4, controlled by the operating system. Moreover, the number of bits in the virtual address to be used at each level is also programmable. This chip determines the value of the field widths that are written to a global translation control register (TCR). In addition, since many programs use far less than 2^{32} bytes of memory, it is possible to instruct the MMU to ignore the uppermost n insignificant bits. It should be noted that the operating system need not use all four levels if the job can be executed with fewer. Many other attractive features are found in this memory management scheme, but, at present, we restrict ourselves not to proceed anymore to enter any further details of its paging and associated address translation mechanism. Our sole intention is only to show that four-level paging is possible and that it is implemented in practice for commercial use. Interested readers can go through the respective manuals to get a clear understanding of its implementation and related operations.

5.9.4.1.4   Inverted Page Table

Use of multi-level page table organization to perform virtual address translation in a large virtual memory has produced alluring benefits along with overcoming the slower lookup process by using additional specialized hardware to make it faster. But, with the advent of RISC chips offering 64-bit virtual addresses spaces, it becomes really acute to organize such gigantic page tables, even with the deployment of a multi-level paging scheme in page table organization. It then insists to review the situation afresh, which eventually gives rise to the introduction of some other innovative approach. In traditional paging schemes of all forms, the page tables per process are created and kept sorted by virtual page number. For any virtual page x obtained from the issued virtual address, the corresponding page frame is then obtained from an entry in the respective page table that is used to form the target physical address.

In the new alternative approach, the page table is organized on the basis of page frames. Here, the ith entry of the page table refers to the page frame i that contains information about the page currently occupying the page frame i. As a result, the number of entries in this table (i.e. the size of page table) is equal to the number of page frames in physical memory, irrespective of the number of pages in the virtual address space as well as of the number and sizes of processes being executed. Since the size of the memory is fixed in a computer system, which is much small in comparison to the size of the virtual address space, only a fixed portion of memory is required to store this smaller table. This structure of the page table as shown in Figure 5.13 is historically called an ***inverted page table*** (**IPT**). The page table's structure is called *inverted* because it indexes page table entries by frame number rather than the usual virtual page number. Figure 5.13 illustrates a specimen implementation of the IPT approach.

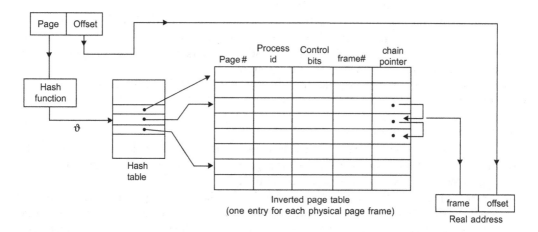

FIGURE 5.13   A formal design approach of inverted page table structure and related address translation mechanism employing a hash table used in the management of virtual memory with paging system.

Each entry in the page table includes the following:

Page number: This is the page number portion of the issued virtual address.

Process-id: The process that occupies this page. The combination of page number and process-id uniquely identifies a page within the virtual address space of a particular process.

Frame number: This is the page frame in memory which is owned by that particular process indicated by page number and process-id.

Control bits: This field includes many flags, such as valid, referenced, and modified, protection, and locking information.

Chain pointers: This field is null (often indicated by a separate bit) if there are no chained entries for this entry. Otherwise, this field contains the index value of the next entry in the chain.

In Figure 5.13, each entry of IPT contains the process-id (P) and page number (p); the pair (P, p) is then used to carry out the required address translation. P is obtained when the scheduler selects a process for execution: it copies the id of the process (P) from its PCB into a register of the MMU. The page number portion (p) is taken from the virtual address as issued. This page p is then searched in IPT using a hashing mechanism that generates a hash value v from the supplied page number p. This hash value is then used as a pointer to the IPT. If the IPT entry as indicated by the pointer contains the page p, then this page exists, and the corresponding page frame number f present in the indicated IPT entry is copied for use in address translation. With this type of hashing, collision may occur when more than one virtual address may map into the same hash table entry. A chaining technique (coalesced chaining) is thus used here for managing this overflow. The hashing technique used, however, normally results in chains of table entries that are typically short; hardly between one and two entries. These table entries are individually visited following the chain when searching of a particular page is carried out in order to obtain the corresponding page frame number before finally declaring a page fault. Address translation in this way is then completed by combining the frame number f thus obtained with the offset b present in the virtual address.

When a page fault occurs, the needed page is brought using a conventional page table that may be stored on disk instead of in main memory. This overhead is possibly unavoidable given the large size of the page table to handle the large amount of information in the system. An IPT is often organized with the use of associative memory to speed up the look-up operation. On a hit, the IPT is not needed. Only when a miss occurs, the page table is then consulted to find a match for the virtual page as required by the issued virtual address. The hash table look-up as described can be done either in hardware or by the operating system. As the software mechanism for look-up is comparatively slow, and if the look-up is done in software, care should be taken that this look-up not happen very often. Many systems, however, use IPTs, including the versatile **IBM RS 6000** and **AS 400** (now called P-series) systems. The Mach operating system on the **RT-PC** also uses this technique. Variations in the approaches as well as implementations of IPTs have also been observed on the **PowerPC**, **UltraSPARC**, and **IA-64** (Intel) architectures.

A brief description of this topic is given on the Support Material at www.routledge.com/9781032467238.

5.9.4.1.5   Translation Lookaside Buffer

In almost all paging schemes, every virtual memory reference, in principle, actually causes two physical memory accesses: one for accessing the page table entry and one to subsequently fetch the desired information. This ultimately results in doubling the memory access time, thereby causing a 50 percent reduction of the memory bandwidth. Due to the *locality of references*, it has been observed that a small fraction of page table entries are heavily in use, and the rest are relatively rare. Based on this fact, most virtual memory schemes thus provide high-speed associative memory used as a cache for storing a subset of frequently used page table entries that ultimately helps to avoid repeated costly memory visits to access the page table. This extra high-speed memory is used as

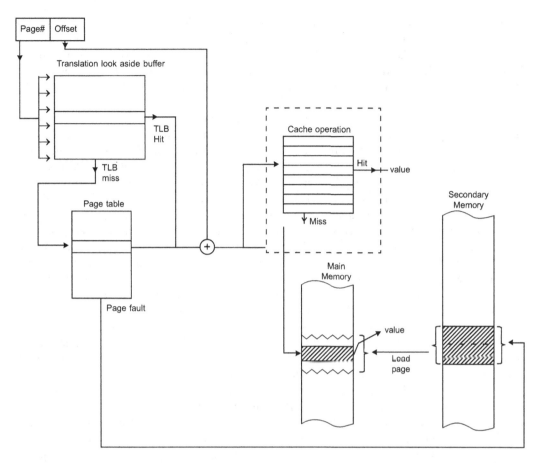

FIGURE 5.14   A schematic block diagram in which use of Translation Lookaside Buffer along with cache operation used in the management of virtual memory with paging system.

a buffer and functions in the same way as a memory cache, dedicated to the use of only address translation mechanism; it is called a **translation lookaside buffer** (**TLB**). Each entry in the TLB must include the page number as well as the complete information of a page table entry. The search is carried out to inspect a number of TLB entries simultaneously to determine whether there is a match on page number. This technique is often referred to as *associative mapping*.

Given a virtual address, the processor will first inspect the TLB for the desired page table entry, as shown in Figure 5.14. If it is present (*TLB hit*), then the frame number from the entry is retrieved, and the physical address is formed in the usual manner. But, if the desired page table entry is not found (*TLB miss*), then the process will use the page number portion of the virtual address to examine the corresponding page table entry. If the "present or valid bit" is set, then the page is in main memory, and the processor can retrieve the respective frame number from the corresponding page table entry to form the physical address. If the present bit is not set in the page table, then a page fault will occur, the necessary actions will be taken to load the needed page in memory to resolve the page fault, and page table updating will be carried out in the usual manner, as already discussed. However, once the physical address is generated, and if the system supports memory cache system (not the TLB cache), the cache is then consulted to see if the cache block containing that word is present. If so, it is the content of the address thus referenced and hence is returned to the CPU for subsequent processing. If the cache does not contain that word (cache miss), the word is retrieved from main memory as usual.

Associative memory is expensive; hence, its size is relatively small to accommodate this additional cost. It can contain only a few entries of the recently used pages referenced by a process as well as the ones most likely to be needed in the near future. Whenever the search for a page in the TLB fails, the hardware arranges the page from elsewhere as already described and stores it in the TLB. This may sometimes require displacing an existing entry from the TLB to make room for the new one.

The presence of a TLB, however, can accelerate (speedup) the address translation, which can be shown by appropriate computations. But this performance improvement as obtained, on average, cannot be achieved due to a lot of hindrances including the decrease in the locality of references within a process, caused by many different practical factors. Moreover, while the effective multithreading approach is used in applications for yielding better performance, it may also result in abrupt changes in the instruction stream, thereby causing the applications to almost spread all over the entire address space, that eventually declines the locality of reference and its profitable use. As a result, with increasing requirements for memory by executing processes, and as locality of references decreases, it is natural that, using a TLB of limited size, the hit ratio of TLB accesses tends to decline. Eventually, the presence of the TLB can itself create a potential bottleneck in performance. While the use of a larger TLB with more entries can improve TLB performance, but TLB size cannot be increased as often as memory size is made, since the TLB size is closely related to the other aspects of hardware design, namely, cache memory and main memory, as well as the number of memory accesses per instruction cycle, which may create additional issues required to be resolved. An alternative approach may be to use a larger page size (*superpage*) so that each page table entry in the TLB can address a larger block of memory. But the use of a larger page size itself, can lead to performance degradation for many reasons (to be discussed later).

Among many other alternatives, the use of **multiple page sizes** on the whole provides a reasonable level of flexibility for the effective use of a TLB. For example, program instructions in a process that occupies a large contiguous region in the address space may be mapped using a small number of large pages rather than a large number of small pages, while the threads, stacks, and similar other smaller entities could then be mapped using the small page size. Still, most contemporary commercial operating systems prefer and support only one page size irrespective of the availability of hardware support. One of the main reasons behind this is that many issues of the operating system are closely interrelated to the underlying page size, and thus a change to multiple page sizes may be a complex proposition.

However, TLB is still an important and most expensive component in the address translation process that is managed using probabilistic algorithms, in contrast to the deterministic mapping of the register-assisted type, as already described. The typical strategies followed for TLB management in paging systems, such as fetch, allocation, and replacement policies, are all OS issues and hence are to be carefully designed, and the entries are to be properly organized so as to make the best use of the limited number of mapping entries that the costly small TLB can hold. In fact, the solutions to all these issues must be incorporated in the TLB hardware, although that makes the TLB too machine specific, but it is then to be managed in identical ways that any form of hardware cache design usually follows.

A brief description of this topic is given on the Support Material at www.routledge.com/9781032467238.

5.9.4.1.6 Superpages

Continuous innovation in technology in electronics engineering since the 1990s has abruptly modified and enhanced the traditional design and architecture of computer systems as well as their resources, mainly increasing capability, reducing size and cost, and increasing speed. Moreover, as user density has constantly increased, introducing a diverse spectrum of application areas, the number and size of processes executed by computer systems have rapidly grown. The increase in sizes of memory and processes has created critical problems in the profitable use of TLBs, since the size of TLBs cannot be increased equally and proportionately to the similar increase in memory and cache size, mainly due to cost. As a result, *TLB reach*, which is the product of page size and the number of entries in a TLB, has increased only marginally, but the ratio of TLB size to memory size has gone down by a factor of over 1000, which consequently lowers TLB hit ratios, thereby causing severe degradation in the overall performance of the system. In addition, processor caches have also become larger than TLB reach. This badly affects cache performance because access to instructions or data in a cache may be slowed due to frequent TLB misses and subsequent look-ups through page tables. However, to mitigate all these issues, one possible way may be to use a larger page size (superpage) so that TLB reach becomes larger. But, this approach, in turn, may invite some problems, namely larger internal fragmentation and more page I/O, apart from issues of additional cost.

A **superpage** is similar to a page of a process, except that its size is a power-of-two multiple of the size of an usual page, and its start address in both the logical and physical address spaces is aligned on a multiple of its size. In spite of having some drawbacks (already discussed in last section), this feature increases TLB reach, which, in turn, offers a higher TLB hit ratio without expanding the size of the costly TLB.

The sizes and number of superpages to be allocated in a process are generally adapted according to the execution characteristics of a process. The memory manager in some situations may combine pages of a process into a superpage of appropriate size if the pages are accessed very often and satisfy the contiguity requirement as well as the address alignment in the logical address space. This action is called a ***promotion***. For example, program instructions in a process that are often accessed and occupy a large contiguous regions in the address space may be mapped using a small number of superpages rather than a large number of small pages. A promotion thus increases TLB reach and releases some of the TLB entries that were assigned to individual pages of this new superpage. On the contrary, if the memory manager ever observes that some pages in a superpage are not used regularly, it may decide to disband the superpage into its individual pages. This action is called ***demotion*** that now enables memory manager to release some memory space which can then be used to load other useful pages that eventually may reduce the page fault frequency and thereby increase the desirable hit ratio. Several multiprocessor architectures, including Pentium, IA–64, Alpha, UltraSPARC, and MIPS 4000, support a few superpage sizes and allow a TLB entry for a page or superpage.

5.9.4.1.7 Protection

Most of the issues in regard to protection in paged virtual systems have already been discussed previously in Section 5.8.2.1.1. Those are mainly:

- Protection against exceeding the size of a page.
- Protection by including *access* bits in page table entries to restrict the access rights to specified pages.
- Protection keys to guard the pages in question.

Protection in paged virtual memory, however, is analogous to that of the logical and physical address spaces, as discussed earlier in the section on simple paging.

5.9.4.1.8 Sharing: Shared Pages

Most of the issues in relation to sharing pages in paged virtual systems have already been discussed previously in Section 5.8.2.1.1. However, the virtual memory handler creates necessary entries in the page table of the calling program for pages of the called shared program and sets a flag in each of such page table entries to indicate that it is a shared page. When the shared program is called, the dynamic linker changes all location-sensitive addresses of the shared program being called. When a reference to an address that belongs to the shared program creates a page fault, the virtual memory handler checks whether the required page of the shared program is already in memory. If so, it puts the page frame number of the page in the relevant entry of the said page table; otherwise the page fault will be resolved in the usual way with necessary modification to the relevant entry of the respective page table.

Management of pages involved in sharing could be implemented in a better way by maintaining the information of all shared pages in a separate *shared page table* and collecting all page reference information for all shared pages to store as page entries in this table. This arrangement will facilitate better management of this table separately for mapping shared pages. A related version of this technique is used in the **Windows operating system**.

A brief description of this topic with a figure is given on the Support Material at www.routledge.com/9781032467238.

5.9.4.2 Segmentation: In Virtual Memory

The segmentation strategy in the virtual memory environment also follows the same methodology used in simple segmentation (Section 5.8.2.1.2) that exploits a similar type of segment table, as shown in Figure 5.15, but here the segment table entries are more elaborate and also complex. One of the main reasons is that only some of the segments in a process may be in memory at any instant; an extra bit P is thus needed in each table entry to indicate whether the corresponding segment is currently *present* in main memory. If the bit is set, it indicates that the segment is in memory, so the entry also includes the starting address, the length of that segment, and other related control information. Another control bit M in the table entry is a *modify bit* that indicates whether the contents of the corresponding segment have been altered or modified since the segment was last brought into memory. If the contents of the segment in the frame remain unchanged, (i.e. the segment is not dirty), then it is not necessary to write this segment back to the backing store when the time comes to replace this segment in the frame that it currently holds. The associated overhead in this regard can be avoided. Other information bits are kept for the segment in the segment table for storing

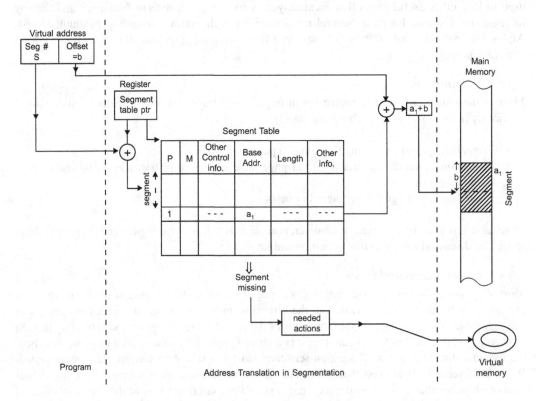

FIGURE 5.15 A schematic representation of segmentation used in virtual memory implementation.

other useful information concerning the segment, such as its position in the swap spaces. In addition, other control bits may also be required in the segment table for various other purposes, such as protection or sharing, if those are mapped and managed at the segment level.

Under segmentation, the virtual (logical) address space is inherently two-dimensional in nature. A logical address $kkkk$ is specified as a pair (s_k, b_k), where s_k is the segment number (name) and b_k is the offset within the segment. If n bits are used to represent s_k, then a process can contain a maximum of 2^n segments. If m bits are used to represent b_k, then the maximum size of a segment is 2^m bytes or words. Once again it is to be noted that the size of individual segments is not fixed, and they are usually unequal but bounded within the limit of maximum size.

When a specific process is executed, the address translation starts using a register that holds the starting address of the segment table of that particular process. The segment number (s_k) present in the virtual address as issued is used to index this table and look up the corresponding beginning memory address of the segment. This address is then added to the offset portion (b_k) of the virtual address to produce the desired physical address, as shown in Figure 5.15. When the required segment as indicated by the segment number (s_k) in the virtual address is not present in memory, a "missing segment" fault is raised that activates certain actions to load the required segment in memory. If sufficient free memory is available, then the needed segment is loaded. Otherwise a segment-out operation (s) may have to be carried out in order to make room for the new segment to load before actual loading of the segment begins. Replacement of segments is a policy decision which is carried out by the memory management only at the time of each replacement.

Since segments do not have fixed size, removing one segment from memory may not be sufficient for loading another segment (as opposed to paged virtual memory systems). So, many segments may need to be removed to make room for a new segment to load. Different segment sizes may be critical, but this also invites external fragmentation, which can, however, be negotiated either by means of memory compaction or by first fit/best fit strategies.

Segmented virtual memory, by virtue of its inherent two-dimensional nature, exhibits a nice feature. It permits a segment to grow or shrink dynamically in size. A segment can simply be allowed to grow in its present location if the adjoining memory area is free. Otherwise dynamic growth of a segment can be tackled by shifting it to a larger memory area with required relocation, thereby releasing the memory area already occupied by it.

5.9.4.2.1 Protection and Sharing

Protection and sharing in segmented virtual memory environments are analogous to the logical and physical address spaces, as discussed earlier (see Section 5.8.2.1.2).

5.9.4.3 Segmentation with Paging

Both segmentation and paging implementations in virtual memory have merits as well as drawbacks, and neither is superior to the other when compared on trade-off characteristics. Moreover, when the segments are large, it may be inconvenient and even impossible to accommodate them entirely in the allotted limited main memory. This leads to the idea of dividing each segment into pages, and an integral number of pages is then allocated to each segment so that only those pages that are actually needed are used. Paging and segmentation approaches thus are combined by providing the necessary processor hardware and support of operating system software in order to extract the maximum benefits of both. This ultimately gave rise to a popular scheme known as *segmentation with paging* (segmented paging scheme), which essentially uses segmentation from the user's point of view, but each segment is divided into pages of fixed size in order to realize more effective memory management as opposed to assigning a contiguous larger block of memory to an entire segment. In this way, this combined system enjoys most of the advantages of segmentation by retaining it and at the same time eliminates the complicated issues of effective placements of segments in main memory for optimal utilization of memory, as well as realizing better management of secondary storage (virtual memory) by using a paging scheme. Under this scheme, only the needed portion of executing programs is maintained in memory in terms of pages rather than segments. The page faults are serviced as usual as in paged virtual memory systems.

In this combined scheme, a user's address space (virtual memory) is divided into a number of segments per the choice of the programmer. Each segment, in turn, is divided into a number of fixed-size pages, each page equal in length to page frames in main memory. In the case of a segment shorter in length than a page, the segment holds the entire page. It is important that from the programmer's point of view, this scheme is nothing but true segmentation, and the logical (virtual) address is still in the form (s_k, b_k), where s_k is the segment number and b_k is the segment offset, which is the byte number within the segment. From the system's point of view, the segment offset b_k is viewed as being split into a pair (p_k, b_k), where p_k is the page number within the segment s_k and b_k is the byte number (offset) within the respective page p_k. So, the generalized logical address in combined segmentation with paging systems has the form (s_k, p_k, b_k), where the symbols have their usual significance, as already described.

Address translation in this system is carried out in two stages, as shown in Figure 5.16. In the first stage, when a particular process is in execution, a register holds the starting address of its segment table. From the virtual address as presented, the processor uses the segment number portion s_k to index the process segment table to obtain the particular segment table entry that will indicate the start of the respective page table (out of a number of existing page tables, one per process segment) for that segment. If the *present bit* in the segment table entry as obtained is not set, the target segment is absented from real memory, and the mapping hardware generates a segment-fault exception, which is processed as usual. Otherwise, if the *present bit* is set, then in the second stage, the page number portion p_k of the virtual address is used to index the corresponding page table (as obtained from segment table entry) to find a specific page table entry. If the *present bit* in the page table entry as obtained is set, the corresponding frame number is looked up. This frame number is then combined with the offset number b_k of the virtual address to generate the real target address. If the present bit in the page table is not set, the target page is absent from real memory, and the mapping hardware generates a page-fault exception, which is processed as usual. At both stages of mapping,

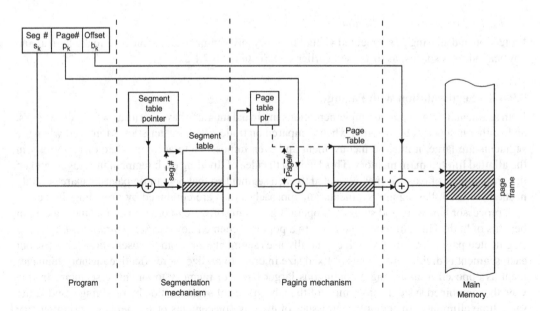

FIGURE 5.16 A representative block diagram of address translation mechanism used in the management of virtual memory with segmented paging system.

the length fields in the respective table are used to confirm that the memory references of the running process are not violating the boundaries of its address spaces.

With both the segment table entry and the page table entry having the same usual formats, many variations of this powerful scheme are possible depending on the types of information that are to be included in the respective tables. While the combination of segmentation and paging is certainly appealing, the address translation here involves two levels of indirection to complete the mapping of each virtual address: one through the segment table and the other through the page table of the referred segment. Hence, it requires two memory references if both tables are held in main memory, which may eventually reduce the effective memory bandwidth by two-thirds. This may be too much to tolerate even with all the added benefits. To help the operating system to speed up the translation process, address translation buffers (similar to TLB, as already explained) may be employed for both the segment and page table references. Alternatively, a single set of address translation buffers may be exploited, each containing a pair (s_k, p_k) and the corresponding page frame number.

Memory sharing can be achieved in the usual way as performed in a segmented virtual memory scheme. *Memory protection* is carried out at the level of segments by including the protection information with each entry of the segment table. Address translation buffers may contain access validation information as copied from the segment table entries. If the access validation could be performed at the level of the segment, access validation at the page level is then not needed.

Further brief details on this topic are given on the Support Material at www.routledge.com/ 9781032467238.

5.9.4.3.1 Case Study: Segmentation with Paging: Intel Pentium

The Pentium, a 32-bit microprocessor, introduced in 1993, is equipped with direct hardware support for both segmentation and paging. Its real address space can be as large as 4 GB (2^{32} bytes); however, the virtual address space can be an extremely large 64 TB (64 terabytes = 2^{46} bytes). An on-chip MMU has a segmentation unit that performs address translation for segments ranging in size from 1 to 2^{32} bytes. A separate paging unit handles address translation for pages of 4 KB or 4 MB. The segmentation and paging unit both contain individual TLBs to reduce the delay in this two-stage address translation process.

Any of the following four memory management mechanisms can be implemented under program control:

1. unsegmented and unpaged
2. segmented and unpaged
3. unsegmented and paged
4. segmented and paged

The output of the paging unit is a 32-bit*real address*, while the output of the segmentation unit is a 32-bit word called a *linear address*. If both segmented and paging mechanisms are used, every memory address generated by a program goes through a two-stage translation process:

Virtual address A_V → Linear address N, → Real address A_R
Without segmentation, $A_V = N$; without paging, $N = A_R$

By using the pipeline approach, overlapping the processing in the formation of virtual, linear, and real addresses as well as overlapping the memory addressing and fetching operation, the total amount of delay can be once again reduced to a large extent so that the next real address is ready by the time the current memory cycle is completed. In fact, the on-chip MMU has a segmentation unit that processes the virtual address A_V, translating it to produce a linear address N as output, which is then fed to a paging unit that processes the linear address N to produce a real address A_R.

A brief description of this topic with a figure is given on the Support Material at www. routledge.com/9781032467238.

5.9.5 Virtual Memory Management: Design Issues

Virtual memory, in general, is probably best exploited when organized using a segmentation with paging approach, and in this situation, most of the memory (virtual memory) management issues that are frequently faced by designers are related to the issues associated with paging. However, the key aspects here to be considered as listed below may actually be related to both segmentation and paging. In fact, the different strategies adopted to manage each of these key aspects of different natures always aim to reduce mostly the rate of page faults, because page faults, besides other issues, mainly invite considerable overhead that eventually causes severe degradation in overall system performance. Unfortunately, there exists no specific policy associated with any aspect that works best. Moreover, if a specific policy is found to work well with a particular aspect, the same one may have a negative impact on another policy employed for a different aspect. In addition, the performance of a set of derived policies depends largely on certain factors, such as the size of main memory and virtual memory, as well as their relative speed, the number of active processes in the system, and above all the execution pattern of each individual programs, which is again simply unpredictable and mostly depends on the type of application and the programming language used to code it, along with the intelligence of the compiler employed to translate it. Conclusively, it can be inferred that no set of policies is ever found to be universally acceptable. However, designers always still attempt to derive a set of policies that work well on average over a wide range of smaller systems that execute a diverse spectrum of applications. For large mainframe systems, the situation is even more acute, and that is why their operating systems are designed with the provision of adequate additional monitoring and control mechanisms that will enable the console operator to intervene in the execution in a crisis in order to tune the underlying policies embedded in the operating system to achieve satisfactory results within the confine of the existing environment. However, it can be inferred that the task of memory management in a paging environment is becoming immensely complex. The key aspects shown in Table 5.1 are considered part of the design issues used in deriving the memory management policies in virtual memory environment.

A brief description of this topic is given on the Support Material at www.routledge.com/9781032467238.

TABLE 5.1

Operating System Policies on Aspects for Virtual Memory Implementation

- **Page Size**

- **Fetch Policy**
  Prepaging
  Demand paging
  Anticipatory paging

- **Replacement Policy**

- **Replacement algorithms**
  Optimal
  Not–Recently–Used (NRU)
  First–in–First–Out (FIFO)
  Clock
  Least–Recently–Used (LRU)
  Least–Frequently–Used (LFU)
  Page Buffering

- **Working set theory**

- **Working set Management**
  Working set size
  Fixed
  Variable
  Replacement Scope
  Local
  Global
  Page–fault–frequency

- **Cleaning Policy**
  Precleaning
  Demand

- **Placement Policy**

- **Load Control**
  Degree of
  multiprogramming

5.9.5.1 Page Size

The page size, usually decided by the OS designers, is a vital parameter with an immense impact on both storage utilization and the effective memory data-transfer rate, and it eventually becomes a factor in the management of virtual memory and its performance. In fact, whatever the page size, half of the allocated final page will remain unused (internal fragmentation). To minimize such waste, a smaller page size is thus always favored. But small pages need a larger page table, which, in turn, will consume a good amount of memory space. Moreover, transferring pages to and from virtual memory (disk) normally happens a page at a time, where transfer of a small page takes almost as much time as transferring a large page, and this happens more and more as the size of the page is smaller, ultimately giving rise to a substantial amount of delay with each operation. This particular fact argues in favor of having a larger page size. In addition, large pages tends to reduce table fragmentation.

In general, the page-size trade-off is mostly technology dependent, and the decision in this regard tends to vary as the price and performance of individual components change. In addition, the page table on some machines is loaded into hardware registers or an on-chip cache (TLB) at the time of each and every process switch. On these machines, having a small page size requires relatively more space to accommodate the page table, and the time required to load the page table is also longer. However, if the page size is small, the hit ratio tends to increase with more pages available in memory, but it tends to decrease if the page size increases as fewer pages will then be present in a given size of memory. In fact, the effect of page size on hit ratio, which largely determines the **performance** of virtual memory, is complex and depends mostly on the *page reference stream* and the *amount of space available* in memory

Early implementation of virtual memory used a larger page size, mainly to reduce the cost of hardware support. In the late 1970s, a reverse swing was observed; the VAX architecture (one of the finest in those days) adopted a small page size of 512 bytes, probably focused more on making the best use of the then new and very expensive semiconductor RAM. In the early 1990s, the trend once again favored using larger page sizes, mainly due to a drop in hardware costs, with 4 KB being typical. This was observed in MMUs and also in UNIX implementation. From this time onward, the page size has gradually become larger, and this change has occurred mainly in response to the increased capacities and affordability (sharp drops in price due to innovation in advanced hardware technology) of RAM, while disk and network access times have improved only incrementally. Most computers today thus use page sizes ranging from 2 to 8K, while the Pentium supports page sizes of 4K or 4 MB.

A brief description with mathematical computation for a justified value of page size is given on the Support Material at www.routledge.com/9781032467238.

5.9.5.2 Fetch Policy

The fetch policy decides when a page is to be brought from the backing store to primary memory. Basically, there are two different strategies relating to fetching: *demand paging* and *prepaging*.

Demand paging: Here, processes are allowed to start up with none of their pages in memory, and thus a page fault occurs, since the respective page containing the first instruction to be executed is not present. Subsequently, other page faults associated with it usually follow quickly, causing a flurry of page faults. As a result, within a short span, more and more pages, which are currently needed and also required for near-future references, are now in memory. Over time, the execution gradually attains a stable state, after which only a few page faults may then occur. This strategy is so named because pages are loaded only on demand, not in advance. Demand paging actually slows down processing because of repeated page faults that result in considerable delay. However, it exhibits many other advantages. Here, a page will be admitted into the system only when there is an explicit demand for that specific page. This characteristic matches well with the program behavior in which a program with a particular set of data may not always be using all its pages for a particular run. Consequently, this results in better memory utilization, thereby increasing degrees of multi-programming, demonstrating better CPU utilization, and ultimately producing higher throughput.

Another method in this category called **clustering** brings an additional few adjacent pages in at the same time as the required one with the expectation that the pages nearby will have a higher probability of being accessed soon. If adjacent pages in the virtual store are kept in adjacent locations on the backing store, the cost of bringing in a group of pages might be only slightly higher than bringing in just one. The source of this efficiency is discussed in Chapter 6, "Device Management". However, if these additional pages are not needed, they will simply be thrown out soon, since they have not been touched.

Prepaging: Here, pages are loaded *before* letting processes run. This strategy makes use of the characteristics of most of the secondary memory devices, such as disks, in which the pages of a process are stored contiguously. Under this strategy, these contiguous pages can be brought in at one time rather than one at a time, thereby reducing the repeated disk access time (seek time + latency time), making this procedure more efficient as a whole. This strategy, of course, may fail or be ineffective if most of the extra pages that are being brought in are of no use. Observations on different forms of prepaging, however, do not yet confirm whether it matches with the normal working environment.

Anticipatory fetching: This attempts to determine in advance which pages will be referenced within a short period. Those pages will then be brought into memory before they are actually referenced.

Adviced paging: This is another method in which the process may inform the memory manager through a service call that a particular page is about to be accessed and thus should be brought in or that a particular page will not be used again for a long time and might as well be paged out. Such a call would have this form: *Page Advice (starting address, ending address, direction)*, which tells the memory manager that the process is about to use the region in virtual space between the two addresses, so it might swap in the relevant pages (if *direction* is 'in') or that this region will not be accessed for a considerable period (if *direction* is 'out').

Advised paging, however, takes advantage of the programmer's or compiler's knowledge of how the program works, knowledge that can be more accurate than that of the memory manager. However, the programmer has no knowledge at all of the other processes that are competing in the ready list, but the memory manager does know. It would be foolhardy for the memory manager to put too much credence in advice. At best, the memory manager might turn off the reference bit for a page that the process claims will be not used for a while, making it a candidate for page-out. For bringing in, the advice should most likely be ignored.

5.9.5.3 Replacement Policy

This strategy is concerned with deciding to select a page frame in memory to be replaced to make room for an incoming referenced page of an active process when no free area is available in the primary storage. This is required; otherwise the process suffering from page fault may be suspended for indefinite period until a memory area becomes available. Suspending such processes for no fault of their own would even have further adverse effects on their rescheduling and turnaround times that ultimately may degrade the performance of the entire system. Moreover, the presence of all such suspended inactive processes occupying their already-allocated page frames may likely lead to reduced availability of free frames for the other active processes to use. That is why the page replacement decision is an important activity in the management of a paged virtual memory system.

A page frame selected for eviction by the replacement strategy may have had the contents modified after its arrival into memory from its respective page in virtual memory. When such a modified page is selected for eviction, it must be written back to disk onto its earlier obsolete copy to have its latest version. However, when a frame selected for eviction has not been modified during its stay in memory, it can simply be discarded, since its exact copy is already available on the disk. Thus, the status of the page frame in this regard is required to be maintained, and this is done by the hardware using a modified bit (dirty bit) in the page table. When a page is loaded into memory, this bit is cleared (bit = 0) by the mapping hardware, and it is set by the mapping hardware whenever the page is written to (modified). Whenever a frame is selected for eviction by the replacement strategy, this bit provided by the hardware is consulted for taking fitting action; otherwise all evicted pages would be unnecessarily copied to disk regardless of whether they have actually been modified, thereby having an adverse effect on the management of virtual memory and the performance of the entire system.

While it would be possible to select a page at random to replace at each page fault, better system performance can be attained if certain criteria are considered at the time of making the decision to replace a specific page. A page replacement decision is sometimes found difficult, since it involves several interrelated aspects that need to be addressed. Those are:

- How many page frames are allowed to be allocated to each active process.
- Whether the replacement should remain confined within the set of pages belonging to the requesting process that caused the page fault or involve all the page frames in main memory, which may sometimes increase the number of page frames already allocated to the process.
- What criteria should be used to select a particular page for replacement when a new item is to be brought in and there is no free frame.

Out of these three aspects, the first two lie in the domain of *working set management*, which will be discussed in the following subsection. The third one is, of course, concerned with *replacement policy*, which is the subject of this subsection.

Replacement of a page is a policy decision which is often influenced and based on ***page-reference strings*** (memory reference information) derived from the actual memory references made by an executing program, and it can be kept track of with the assistance of the page table. The behavior of the various replacement policies can be suitably exhibited by means of the page-reference strings. Most of the policies that attempt to select a page for removal should choose the page likely to have a remote chance of being referenced in the near future. The principle of locality can be used as a guideline to reveal that there is a relationship between recently referenced history and near-future behavior. Thus, the design methodology of most of the policies relies on an objective in which future program behavior can be predicted on the basis of its past pattern. The related page-in and page-out in this regard is reflected in the respective page table.

Locking Page Frames: All the replacement policies have some limitations and must abide by certain restrictions at the time of selecting a page for replacement. Some of the page frames (e.g. kernel of the OS and key control structures, I/O buffers in memory engaged in I/O operation, etc.) needed to be *locked* in memory, and the corresponding page stored in that frame cannot be replaced. A few other frames with time-critical aspects may also be locked into memory. All the frames of these types are to be kept outside the domain of replacement activity. Locking is usually achieved by associating a bit to be set as locked (*lock bit*) with each such frame, and this bit can be included with each page table entry in the current page table.

A brief description of locking page frames is given on the Support Material at www.routledge.com/9781032467238.

Shared Page Frames: In a timesharing system, it is very common that several users are running the same program (e.g. a compiler, a database, a text editor) using shared pages to avoid having multiple copies of the same page in memory at the same time. These shared pages are typically read-only pages that contain program text and not pages that contain data. The problem arises when the pages of a specific program are removed (page-out) along with the pages it is sharing that may, in turn, ultimately cause a large number of page faults to occur when other active programs in memory require those shared pages. Likewise, when a program is completed or terminated, it is essential to inspect all the page tables to find those shared pages that are still in use by other active programs so that their disk space (virtual memory) will not be freed by chance. Such checking over all the page tables is usually too expensive. Hence, special data structures or additional hardware support are needed to keep track of all such shared pages.

5.9.5.4 Replacement Algorithms

A large number of page replacement algorithms are available. The best possible page replacement algorithm is easy to describe but difficult and perhaps impossible to implement. Much work has been done on this subject, and more than 300 papers have been published (Smith, 1978). Still, there are only a few basic interesting algorithms available that have been used for the selection of a page to replace. We will describe only a few of them. Each operating system, however, obviously has its own page replacement scheme.

5.9.5.4.1 Optimal Replacement

Optimal page replacement always attempts to make the page replacement decision in such a way that the total number of page faults during the execution of a program is as low as possible. This algorithm by Belady ensures that no other sequence of page replacement decisions can generate a smaller number of page faults and hence was proven to be optimal. In order to realize optimal page replacement at each page fault, this replacement policy should consider all possible alternative page replacement decisions, analyze their impact on future page faults, and then select the best possible alternative. Belady formulated a simple rule by which this can easily be achieved: At each page fault, select a page for replacement whose next reference is farthest in the page reference string.

Belady's formulation of this algorithm itself makes it unrealizable, because at the time of page fault, the operating system has no way of knowing in advance when each of the pages will be referenced next. However, from an academic point of view, by running a program on a simulator and keeping track of all page references, it is possible to implement optimal page replacement on the *second run* by using the page reference information already collected from the first run with the simulator. It should be noted that the page reference history as collected, based on which this algorithm operates is confined only to that specific program. The significance of this algorithm is purely theoretical, and it is of no use in practical systems. However, this method can serve as a yardstick for comparisons and for evaluating other page replacement algorithms.

Another way to implement this approach with a close approximation may be carried out as follows: When a page fault occurs, some set of pages is in main memory. One of these pages may be referenced at the very next instant; some of the other pages may not even be needed until a large number of instructions later. Each page thus can be labeled with the number of instructions that would be executed before that page is first referenced. The optimal page replacement algorithm uses this label and simply says the page with the highest label will be selected for removal.

An example to illustrate this approach with a figure is given on the Support Material at www. routledge.com/9781032467238.

5.9.5.4.2 Not Recently Used Page Replacement Algorithm (NRU)

In computer systems that do not provide sufficient information with regard to the last use of a page, this method provides a mechanism that could achieve an equivalent effect. The operating system in most computers with virtual memory keeps track of the status of pages in memory, whether used or unused, with the help of *two status bits* associated with each page in the page table, as shown in Figure 5.11. The bit R is set when the page is referenced (read or written), and the bit M is set when the page is only modified (i.e. written to).

It is important that these bits be updated on every memory reference, so it is essential that they be set by the hardware. Once a bit has been set to 1, it remains 1 until the operating system resets it to 0 in software. If the hardware does not have these bits, they can be simulated by the software under the control of the operating system (memory management). However, the number of references made to a page or the order in which these references were made will not be known.

The R and M bits combined can be used to build a simple effective page replacement algorithm. When a process is started, both these page bits are initially set to 0 by the operating system for all its pages. *Periodically* (e.g. on each clock interrupt), the R bit is cleared (set to 0) to distinguish pages that have *not been referenced recently* from those that have been. At each page fault, the operating system scans all the pages and divides them into four distinct categories based on the current values of the R and M bits.

Class 0: Not referenced recently, not modified (R = 0, M = 0; number = 00)
Class 1: Not referenced recently, modified (R = 0, M = 1; number = 01)
Class 2: Referenced recently, not modified (R = 1, M = 0; number = 10)
Class 3: Referenced recently, modified (R = 1, M = 1; number = 11)

At first glance, although class 1 pages seem impossible, they occur when a class 3 page has its R bit cleared by a clock interrupt. Clock interrupts, however, do not clear the M bit because this information is only needed to decide whether the page has to be rewritten to disk at the time of its removal for the sake of immediate time saving.

The not-recently used (NRU) algorithm removes a page at random from the lowest numbered non-empty class. This algorithm implicitly indicates that it is always appropriate to remove a modified page that has not been referenced (R = 0, M − 1) in at least one clock (typically 20 msec.) than a clean page that is in heavy use (R = 1, M = 0).

The distinct advantage and possibly the main attraction of NRU is that it is easy to understand, efficient to implement, and offers a performance that, while certainly *not optimal*, is often *adequate*. Variations of this scheme are in use in **different versions of UNIX**.

5.9.5.4.3 *First-In, First-Out (FIFO) Algorithm*

FIFO is another *low-overhead* and *simplest* paging algorithm that selects a page for removal that has been in memory for the longest time, based on the consideration that it would have fallen out of use. This assumption is often found wrong. Moreover, the pages that are replaced due to only along stay in memory would often contain those regions of program or data that are heavily in use for the longest times throughout the tenure of a program execution. Removal of these pages may be expensive for repeated page-in and page-out by the FIFO algorithm. However, the implementation of FIFO can be carried out in many different ways.

In one method, an additional field can be introduced in the page table that records the time of arrival of a page when it is brought into memory. At the time of page replacement, the memory manager scans these entries in the page table and selects the oldest among the existing pages. In the second method, a linked list can be used to maintain the FIFO queue of page numbers according to their arrival, and the new page numbers are added only at the end of this queue. The page to be replaced is the one which is at the head of this queue. Another way may be that the columns in the page table are kept ordered (like a queue) so that the oldest page is always at the bottom and the newest page is at the top. In a page fault, the page at the tail is removed, and the new page is to be added to the top of the list. In actual implementation of FIFO removal, the clock value indicating when a page was loaded can be stored, and for removal, a search can be made for the oldest time. However, FIFO has **three key disadvantages**:

1. If a page is frequently and continually used, it will eventually become the oldest and will be removed even though it will be needed again immediately.
2. Some strange side effects can occur contrary to normal expectations.
3. Others algorithms have been found more effective.

The most noted side effect, called the *FIFO anomaly*, or **Belady effect**, is that under certain circumstances, adding more physical memory can result in poorer performance when one would expect a larger memory to result in a better performance. The actual page traces that result in this anomaly are, of course, very rare. Nevertheless, this perverse phenomenon coupled with the other objections noted has ultimately caused FIFO in its pure form to drop from favor.

Brief details about this section with examples and figures are given on the Support Material at www. routledge.com/9781032467238.

5.9.5.4.3.1   *FIFO Approximations*

- **Second Chance Page Replacement:** A simple modification to FIFO is called *second chance*. Here, the page table is provided with two additional fields: a reference bit (R) field and a time-of-arrival field. This replacement scheme avoids the problem of throwing out a heavily used page by inspecting the R bit of the oldest page. The R bit is set to 1 when a page is referenced. The R bit is set to 0 periodically over a suitable interval of time in software. When a page replacement is required, the memory manager scans the page table entries to look for the page with the smallest value in the time-of-arrival field (the oldest page) and also examines its reference bit R. If R is 0, the page is both old and unused, so it is replaced immediately. If the R bit of the oldest page is 1, the page will not be replaced. Instead, its R bit is cleared to 0, its load time is updated to the current time, and the page is put at the end of the list of pages as if it had just arrived in memory. Then, the search continues for the next oldest page in a similar way from the front of the list. In the worst case, when all the pages have their referenced bit set 1, each one will then be appended one after another to the end of the list, setting its R bit to 0, and the second chance in that situation will then simply degenerate into pure FIFO.

- **Clock Page Replacement:** Second chance is reasonable in approach, but it is equally inefficient, at least operationally, because it is constantly moving pages around on its list. A better approach is to keep all the pages on a circular list in the form of a clock. At any time, the hand of the clock will be pointing to a potential victim in the circular list. When a page is first loaded into a frame in memory, the reference bit (R bit) in the page table for that frame is set to 1. When the replacement of a page is needed, the page being pointed to by the hand is inspected. If the R bit of this page is 0, the page will be selected for replacement and evicted, the new page is inserted into the clock in its place, and the hand is then advanced one position. If the R bit of the page is 1, it will be cleared (set to 0), the hand is advanced to the next page, and so on, until a page is found with R = 0. If all of the frames have an R bit of 1, then the pointer will make one complete cycle through the buffer, setting all the R bits to 0, and come to a stop at its original position, then finally replace the page in that frame. Not surprisingly, this algorithm is called a *clock* policy because the page frames can be visualized as laid out in a circle. It differs from the second chance algorithm only in the implementation. A number of operating systems, including Macintosh, have employed different variants of this simple clock policy.

- **Modified Clock Algorithm**: The clock algorithm can also be modified to make it more effective by including a modify bit M in each page table entry along with the usual reference bit R. If the M bit is set, then the respective page is required to be written back into secondary memory when its turn comes for replacement. Usually, all processors that support paging provide this bit with every frame of main memory. However, if the hardware does not have these bits, they can be simulated by the software under the control of operating system. R and M bits in combination can be used to build the needed page replacement algorithms in a way similar to the NRU algorithm already described. The notable difference of this algorithm from NRU is that the referenced bit R is here reset *at each page fault* and when page replacement is required. In NRU, the R bit is always cleared *periodically* (e.g. on each clock interrupt) to distinguish pages that have *not been referenced recently* from those that have been, and this is done irrespective of any occurrence of page fault.

Brief details of this section with examples and figures are given on the Support Material at www. routledge.com/9781032467238.

5.9.5.4.4 Least Recently Used (LRU) Page

One of the most popular page removal techniques with a good approximation of the optimal algorithm is called *least recently used*. This algorithm is based on the observation that pages that have been heavily used during the execution of last few instructions will have the chance to be used once again in the next few, according to the *theory of locality*. It thus legitimately selects a page for removal that has *not been referenced* for the longest time. FIFO, in contrast, removes the page that *has been in memory* for the longest time, regardless of how often and when it was referenced. The LRU policy is thus based on the theory that if a page is referenced, it is likely to be referenced again soon. Conversely, if it has not been referenced for a long time, it is unlikely to be needed in the near future. Hence, according to the LRU policy, when a page fault occurs, throw out the page that has been unused for the longest time. In LRU, the number of page faults is a non-increasing function of the number of frame allocation. Thus, it is possible for the LRU policy to combat thrashing (the to and fro journey of pages) by simply increasing the number of frames in main memory.

Hence, an LRU page trace analysis can put the most recently referenced page on the top of a list M of all the frames in use. The least–recently used page thus falls to the bottom of the M list and is a candidate for removal. LRU has been found to possess many interesting theoretical properties; in particular, it is a member of a class of removal techniques called *stack algorithms*. This algorithm functions in such a way that increasing memory size can never cause the number of page faults (page interrupts) to increase, in contrast to the FIFO anomaly, and as such this algorithm *guarantees* that it never suffers from Belady's anomaly. The details of the stack algorithm are beyond the scope of this book. The interested reader can find more details in Mackawa et al. (1987).

Implementation of theoretically realizable LRU is not so easy. It is necessary to maintain a *linked list of all pages* in memory with the most recently used page at the front and the least recently used page at the rear. The difficulty is that the list must be updated on every memory reference. Finding a page in the list, deleting it, and then moving it to the front to post the newer one is an expensive, time-consuming operation. Either additional special hardware is needed or it must be realized with a cheaper approximation in software. But, even with hardware, switching and manipulating a linked list on every instruction is prohibitively slow.

However, there are other ways to implement LRU with special hardware. One such way is to equip the hardware with a 64-bit counter C, which is automatically incremented after each instruction is referenced. Furthermore, each page table entry must also have a field large enough to store the contents of counter C. After each memory reference, the current value of C is stored in the page table entry for the page just referenced. At the time of page replacement, all the counter values in the page table are examined to find the lowest one. That page is the least recently used and a candidate for removal.

Incidentally, there are also other hardware-based ways to implement LRU. But, whatever implementation mechanism is employed, exact LRU is unfortunately expensive to implement. Additional hardware could certainly be designed and built to accomplish it, but it would be quite costly. Luckily, an exact implementation is not needed at all, because a simple variant of it works almost as well.

Brief detail on this section with examples and figures are given on the Support Material at www.routledge.com/9781032467238.

5.9.5.4.5 Least Frequently Used (LFU) Page

Here, an additional field (a software counter), initially set to 0, is associated with each entry (page) in the page table that keeps count the number of times the respective page is referenced. Whenever a page is *referenced*, the content of this field is incremented by 1. At the time of page replacement, the page with the lowest value in this field will be chosen for removal. The logic behind the replacement of a page with the lowest value in this field is really the replacement of the least actively used page, which certainly is a proper choice.

Keeping the implementation arrangement of LFU intact, only a slight modification in its operation gives rise to another algorithm, known as the **Not Frequently Used** (NFU) algorithm.

Here, at *each clock interrupt*, the memory management scans all the frames in memory. For each page, the R bit, which is either 0 or 1, is added to the content of this additional field (counter). In effect, the counter aims to keep track of how often each page has been referenced. When it comes time to replace a page, the page with the lowest value in this field will be chosen for replacement.

One of the serious drawbacks found with both LFU and NFU in certain situation that arises because of their keeping track of everything and not forgetting anything For example, when a multi-pass compiler runs, pages that were heavily used during pass 1 may still have a high count well into later passes. In fact, pass 1 usually has the largest programs and the longest execution time of all passes; the pages containing codes for subsequent passes when executed will always have lower counts than the pass 1 pages. Consequently, memory management, during the execution of pass 2 or subsequent passes, will remove useful current pages instead of pages (of pass 1) that are now no longer in use. However, NFU can be modified in several ways. A small modification to NFU gives rise to a modified algorithm known as *aging*, which is able to simulate LRU quite well.

5.9.5.4.6 Most Frequently Used (MFU) Page

In this case, the page with the largest value in the field (counter) that keeps count of the number of references is replaced. The logic that works behind this is that the page with the smallest value in the field (counter) might have been brought in just recently and expected to remain in use in the near future.

5.9.5.4.7 Belady's Anomaly and LRU

Belady's anomaly shows that offering more page frames sometimes (not always) causes more page faults, which is against expectations. In contrast, it can be shown in LRU that the number of page faults is a non-increasing function of the number of frame allocations. Thus, it is possible with this LRU policy to combat thrashing (to and fro journey of pages) by simply increasing the number of frames in main memory.

An example and its corresponding figures are given on the Support Material at www.routledge.com/9781032467238.

5.9.5.4.8 Ad Hoc Algorithm: Page Buffering

The optimal policy is simply impossible to implement, and although LRU and the clock policy (which is a close approximation to LRU) are superior to FIFO, but they both require additional hardware support that FIFO does no need. Moreover, they both involve much complexity and overhead that FIFO does not. In addition, there is a common factor for all algorithms that the cost of replacing a page that has been modified is always greater than replacing one that has not been, because the modified page must be written back to secondary memory.

Keeping all these facts in view, an innovative strategy can be designed using a simpler paging algorithm called *page buffering* that can summarily improve paging performance. This strategy exploits the pure FIFO algorithm for the replacement of pages, but subsequent actions are different and are implemented also in a different way. Instead of throwing a replaced page out of memory, this strategy, for the sake of performance improvement, assigns the replaced page to one of two lists: the *free page list* if the page has not been modified or *the modified page list* if the page is modified. It is to be noted here that the replaced page is not physically removed from main memory; instead, the entry for the page in the page table is deleted and placed in either the free or modified page list.

The distinct advantage of this mechanism is that the page to be replaced remains still in memory. If the page is further referenced in the near future, it can be returned immediately to the resident set with only a little effort. Effectively, the free and modified page lists act here like a cache of pages. The modified page list, however, serves another useful function: When the device is idle, modified pages are usually written out in clusters rather than one at a time, and the modified bit of those pages is then set to 0, indicating that these frames are now available for use at the time of page replacement. This significantly minimizes the number of I/O operations and thereby reduces the total amount of time required for disk handling. The powerful **VAX VMS** (DEC system) is a representative operating system that uses this approach, and a few other operating systems, including the **Mach operating system** (Rash 88) use this approach with a few variations.

Brief details on this topic are given on the Support Material at www.routledge.com/9781032467238.

5.9.5.4.9 Comparison

The results of an experiment as reported in Baer (1980) compares the four algorithms, FIFO, Clock, LRU, and OPT, and are depicted in Figure 5.17. While conducting the experiments, it was assumed that the number of pages assigned to a process is fixed. The experiments were carried out by running a FORTRAN program considering 0.25×10^6 references, using a page size of 256 words. The experiment was run with different frame allocations, 6, 8, 10, 12, and 14 frames, and the page faults caused by these four algorithms were counted separately for each of these allocations of frame one at a time. Interesting situations were observed. With small allocations, the differences among the four policies were impressive, with FIFO having page faults almost double OPT. The curves show that, to realize efficient run, we would prefer to be on the right of the knee of the curve (which shows a small page fault rate) but at the same time keep a small frame allocation (as far as left of the knee of the curve). These two conflicting constraints, while combined as a compromise, suggest that the most desirable, realistic mode of operation would be around the knee of the curve.

Finkel also conducted a similar experiment in order to find the performance of various replacement algorithms using 100 pages with 10,000 synthesized page references. He employed an exponential distribution for the probability of referencing a specific page so as to approximate the principle of locality. This experiment also revealed identical results as those reported in Finkel (1988). The outcome of this experiment confirmed that the maximum spread of page faults here was about a factor of 2. Apart from that, many other interesting and important conclusions were also derived from his experiment.

5.9.5.5 Working Set Theory

The set of pages that a process is currently using is mostly determined by the program's locality at that instant. This set of pages is called the *working set* of the program at that time. The working set concept was introduced and popularized by Denning (1968, 1970, 1980) and has had a profound impact on the design of virtual memory management. He showed that the behavior of a program

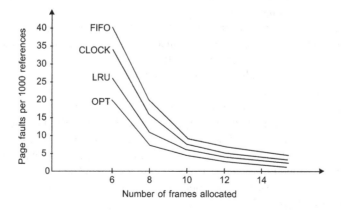

FIGURE 5.17 Graphical representation of comparison of four popular and commonly used replacement algorithms with fixed number of local page allocation.

during its execution inspired the working set theory to evolve, the basis of which is mainly the following:

- An executing process prefers only a subset of its pages at any interval in time.
- The typical patterns of the memory reference of an executing process exhibit a strong relationship between the recent-past and immediate-future memory references.
- On average, the frequency with which a particular page is referenced mostly changes slowly with time.

The notion of a working set, however, assists the virtual memory handler in deciding how many real page frames to be allocated to a given process and which pages of the process should be resident in memory at any given time to realize satisfactory performance by the process. In fact, when a program begins its execution and starts referencing more and more new pages, it actually builds up a working set gradually. Eventually, the process, due to the principle of locality, should finally stabilize on a certain set of pages. Subsequent transient periods indicate a shift of the program from its existing locality to a new locality during its execution. It is interesting to note that during this transient phase, when the new locality has already started, some of the pages of the old locality still remain within the new evolving working set, causing a sudden increase in the size of the working set as new pages are continually referenced. Thereafter, within a short duration of time when the pages of the old locality start to be replaced by the referenced pages of the new locality, the working set size again begins to decline and finally stabilizes when it contains only those pages from the new locality. Since the future references of the pages are not known, the working set of a program can be defined as the set of pages already referenced by the executing program during a predefined recent-past interval of time. This set is then probably able to predict the domain of future references.

The *working-set principle* is basically a guideline for two important aspects of paging systems: *allocation* and *replacement*. It states that:

- For a program to run smoothly, its working set must be in memory.
- A page of an active process may not be removed from memory if it is a member of the working set of the process.

The working set of each process is thus always monitored to ensure that it should be in memory so that the process can run without causing many faults until it moves to another execution phase (another locality) or completes. If the available memory is not large enough to accommodate the entire working set, the process will then naturally cause many page faults to occur and consequently is said to be **thrashing**, ultimately requiring the system to spend most of its time shuttling pages between main and secondary memory. However, the two requirements, as mentioned, cannot always be religiously met due to various reasons, particularly when the degrees of multiprogramming are relatively high for the sake of performance improvement. Still, many paging systems try to keep track of each process's working set and attempt to hold it in memory as far as possible during the execution of the process. This approach, called the **working set model** (Denning, 1970), is mainly designed to greatly reduce the page-fault rate.

Strict implementation of the working set model is a costly affair, and that is why a close approximation of the realizable definition of the working set is attempted instead. For example, when a program is under execution, after a predefined interval of time, the referenced bits of its resident pages can be recorded and then cleared. Status (settings) of those bits prior to cleaning can be saved in counters or bit arrays, which may be provided with individual page entries in the page table. Using this counter or bit arrays, the working-set approximations can be made as a list of pages that have been referenced during recent past.

Using this working-set approach, the *clock algorithm* can be effectively modified to improve its performance. In clock algorithm, normally, when the hand points to a page whose R bit is zero, the page is evicted. The improvement is in effect to further check to see if that page is part of the working set of the currently active process. If it is, the page is spared and kept out of eviction. This algorithm is called **Wsclock**.

5.9.5.6 Working Set Management

Working set theory is simply a guideline to the operating system with respect to page allocation and page replacement. It helps the system decide:

- how many real page frames to be allocated to a given process, that is, what will be the size of the *working set*,
- which pages of the process should be resident in memory; in other words, what will be the *scope of replacement*.
- **Allocation Policy: Working Set Size:** With the limited size of memory in the system, the operating system must decide how much memory is to be allocated, that is, how many pages of a particular process are to be brought into memory for smooth execution. Several interrelated factors are to be considered that influence the performance of the system:
  - The smaller the number of page frames allocated to a process, the greater the degree of multiprogramming that will eventually improve the performance of the system.
  - If a relatively small number of page frames is allocated to a process, then despite the principle of locality, it may result in a high rate of page faults, resulting in severe degradation in the performance of the system.
  - The more page frames allocated to a process, intuitively, the fewer page faults a program will experience, which may result in a better performance. But observations reveal that beyond a certain number of page frames allocated to a process, any additional allocation of frames will have no noticeable effect on the page fault rate for that process, mainly because of the principle of locality.

Considering all these factors and others and making a compromise among several conflicting requirements, two different types of allocation policies have evolved that control the working set size. A **fixed-allocation policy** offers a fixed number of frames to a process during its entire tenure of execution. This number must be decided ahead of time; is often decided at initial load time; and may be determined based on the size, types, and other attributes of the process or even on advice issued from the user end. With this policy, whenever a page fault occurs and replacement of page is required in the execution of a process, one of the pages of that particular faulting process must be selected for replacement to make room for the new page to hold. This policy behaves quite well with those processes with high degree of principle of locality, showing an exceptionally low page fault rate and thereby requiring only a small number of page frames.

The other allocation policy is known as the **variable-allocation policy**, in which the number of page frames allocated to a process frequently varies during the entire tenure of its execution. This policy is suitable for those processes that exhibit a weak form of principle of locality during execution and constantly tend to result in high levels of page faults, thereby continually expanding their working set size. The variable-allocation policy appears to be the more powerful one, but, on the other hand, it often develops thrashing due to snatching page frames from other active processes that subsequently may create unnecessary extra page faults at their end through no fault of their own. For this reason, the intervention of the operating system is required every time to assess the behavior of the active processes that, in turn, demand adequate software intelligence to be embedded in the operating system as extra overhead with the support of additional hardware mechanisms required.

However, both allocation policies as described are closely related to replacement scope.

- **Replacement Scope:** When a process gets a page fault, and there is no free page frame in memory, then if the policy chooses the victim only from the resident pages of the process that generates the page fault, it is called a **local replacement policy**. In this case, the algorithm religiously obeys the fixed-allocation policy. All the replacement algorithms already discussed in the preceding subsection use this policy. On the other hand, if the policy considers all unlocked pages in main memory as candidates for replacement irrespective of which process owns the particular page to be evicted, it is known as a **global replacement policy**. This algorithm implies a variable-allocation policy. The clock algorithm is commonly implemented as a global replacement policy, since it considers all residential pages in a single list while it selects. The problem with this global replacement policy (variable-allocation) is actually the selection of a frame from all the unlocked frames in memory using any of the replacement policies, as already discussed. The page to be selected for replacement can belong to any of the resident process; there is as such no definite guideline to determine which process should lose a page from its working set. Consequently, the process that loses its page may suffer from reduction in working set size that may affect it badly. One way to combat this potential problem is to use page buffering (as already discussed). In this way, the choice of which page to replace becomes less important, because the page can normally be reclaimed at any instant if it is referenced before the next time a block of pages is overwritten.

A **local replacement with variable allocation** policy can alleviate the problems faced by the global replacement strategy. The improvement or enhancement that can be made over the existing *local replacement with fixed allocation* policy is to reevaluate the number of page frames already allocated to the process at a specific interval of time and then change it accordingly to improve the overall performance. However, such planned attempt to be taken periodically for making decisions whether to increase or decrease the working set size of active processes actually requires a thorough assessment of their likely future demands of pages. Such an evaluation activity, in fact, is not only a time-consuming proposition, but it makes this approach more complex than a relatively simple global replacement policy. Still, it may probably yield overall better performance. However, the key to the success of this strategy is to determine the working set size at any instant that dynamically changes and also the timing of reevaluation to effect such changes. One particular strategy that seems to have received much attention in this area is the **working set strategy**. A true working set strategy would be difficult to improvise and equally hard to implement for all practical purposes for each process, but it can serve as a yardstick for comparison.

Local replacement policies tend to localize effects of the allocation policy to each particular process. They are easier to analyze and simple to implement with minimal overhead. But their major drawbacks are: when the working set grows, thrashing is inevitable, even if there are plenty of free page frames. If the working set shrinks, local algorithms simply waste memory. If the amount of allocations (number of page frames) tends to be too small, there will be a high probability of increased page fault rate. If the amount of allocations (number of page frames) tends to be unnecessarily large, the degree of multiprogramming will then be considerably reduced, thereby adversely affecting the performance of the entire system.

Global replacement policies, on the other hand, increase the correlation and the degree of coupling between replacement and allocation policies. In particular, pages allocated to one process by the allocation algorithm may be snatched away by a global replacement algorithm. This algorithm is more concerned with the overall state of the system and much less interested in the behavior of each individual process. By offering more page frames and thereby varying the number of frames in use by a given process, global replacement may badly affect the regions, based on which the logic and the attributes of the replacement algorithms are derived. Moreover, research results reveal that the relationship between the frequency of page faults and the amount of real memory (number of page frames) allocated to a program is not linear. Despite all these facts, global replacement, not unnaturally, is still considered close to optimal.

From this discussion, the important conclusion is that each program has a certain threshold regarding the proportion of real (page frame) to virtual pages. An amount of allocation below this threshold causes page faults to increase very quickly. At the high end, there seems to be a certain limit on the number of real pages above which any additional allocation of real pages results in very little or almost no noticeable performance improvement. It is thus suggested to allocate memory in such a way that each active program will get an amount that lies between these two extremes. In fact, these upper and lower bounds should probably not be fixed, they are mostly program-specific and thus dynamically derived on the basis of the faulting behavior of the program at the time of its execution. Therefore, it is more judicious to keep track of the behavior of the active program rather than uselessly chase increasing the degree of multiprogramming for the sake of performance improvement. Therefore, improvising a good design of an allocation algorithm that will be stable and at the same time will not be inclined toward thrashing can be achieved by *monitoring the page fault rate rather than keeping track of the working set size directly.*

Thus, the proposed algorithm will be based on the principle that a program that frequently experiences a large number of page faults, i.e. having a high page-fault rate which is above some maximum threshold, should be allocated more frames, if possible, without degrading the system or otherwise suspended it to allow other active processes to run smoothly. Similarly, for a program that exhibits a low page-fault rate below some minimum threshold, a few pages may be taken away from that process without causing any appreciable effect. Moreover, the number of frames to be allocated may be determined by the amount of available free memory, its priority, and other similar influencing factors. However, when designing an algorithm to implement this approach, one practical difficulty is that it requires prior knowledge about the size of the working set of the process, in particular which specific pages the process would really need at any instant during the course of its execution. However, this problem has been addressed and has a solution using a strategy known as the **page-fault frequency** algorithm that implements this approach.

Brief details on this section with a figure are given on the Support Material at www.routledge. com/9781032467238.

5.9.5.7 Page-Fault Frequency (PFF)

The page-fault frequency (PFF) algorithm is applied to the allocation module to monitor and control the page replacement activities. The PFF algorithm uses a parameter F (*critical page fault frequency*) that may be defined as follows:

$$F = 1/T$$

where T is the *critical interpage fault time*, that is, the time between two consecutive page faults of a particular process and is usually measured in number of page faults per millisecond. The operating system defines a system-wide (or sometimes per-process) critical page fault frequency F.

To implement this algorithm, it requires a reference bit (R) to be associated with each page in memory. When a page is accessed, its reference bit is set to 1. When a page fault occurs, the operating system notes the virtual (process) time since the last page fault for that process. This could be accomplished by maintaining a counter of page references. The operating system stores the time of the most-recent page fault in the related process control block. Now, if the amount of time since the last page fault occurred is less than T ($= 1/F$) ms, the process is operating *above* the PFF threshold F, and a new page is added to the resident set of the process from the pool of free pages to hold the needed page. This triggers a growth in the resident set size. Otherwise, the process is operating *below* the PFF threshold F, and a page frame occupied by a page whose referenced bit and modified bit are not set is freed to make room for the new page. At the same time, the operating system sweeps and resets referenced bits of all resident pages. The pages that are not–referenced, unmodified, or not–shared since the last sweep are then released, and these freed page frames are returned to the pool of free pages for future use.

PFF may be implemented as a global or local policy, although in its original proposal, PFF was described as a global policy. This strategy can be further extended for the sake of completeness; some other policies are additionally needed to maintain the size of the pool of free frames within the specified limits. Modified pages should be written back to disk in an appropriate manner. Moreover, if the PFF algorithm is supplemented with page buffering, the resulting performance is quite appreciable.

Implementation of PFF in this manner faces several problems. First, resetting of reference bits at the end of an interval would encroach on the page replacement decisions. If a page fault occurs in a process soon after the required actions being taken and the working set was determined, most pages of the process in memory would have their reference bits off, so memory management cannot differentiate between these pages for the purpose of page replacement. The consequences are even severe if processes either remain blocked or do not get an opportunity to execute for an entire interval; their allocation would then shrink unnecessarily. As a result, it will be difficult to decide on the needed size of the working set window. To alleviate this problem, an alternative is to use a working set window for each process individually. But this would rather invite additional complications in the operation of memory management and further increases its overhead. Moreover, it would not address the issues of interference with page replacement decisions. Apart from these, there are also other problems, such as the PFF approach possibly not performing properly during the transient periods (as already stated) when there is a shift from an existing locality to a new locality. This problem, however, has been resolved by modifying the existing PPF approach accordingly.

More about this section is given on the Support Material at www.routledge.com/9781032467238.

5.9.5.8 Cleaning Policy: Paging Daemons

All the strategies and policies that are devised for different aspects of a paging system mainly aim to increase the performance efficiency of the paging system. But they can only work well when plenty of free page frames are available that can be claimed when page fault occurs. To ensure a plentiful supply of free page frames, many paging systems employ a *cleaning policy* that is mostly concerned with deciding when a modified page should be written out to secondary memory. A cleaning policy is essentially the opposite of a fetch policy. Two types of cleaning policy are in common use: *demand cleaning* and *precleaning*.

With **demand cleaning**, a page that is modified is written out to secondary memory only when it has been selected for replacement and is thus evicted from memory. A **precleaning** policy writes modified pages to secondary memory before their page frames are actually needed, and those pages can be written out in batches. In fact, many paging systems have a background process called a *paging daemon* that sleeps most of the time but is awakened periodically to inspect the state of memory. When only a few free page frames are available, the paging daemon starts working, selecting pages to evict using the chosen page replacement algorithm. If these pages have been modified since being loaded, they are written out to disk.

No policy is foolproof, and in fact, both policies have some drawbacks when strictly followed. With precleaning using paging daemons, while a page is written out, it remains in memory until the page replacement algorithm decides that it is to be removed. This facilitates that in the event when one of the evicted pages is once again needed before its frame has been overwritten, it can be reclaimed simply by restoring the status of the page in the page table and at the same time removing the page from the pool of free page frames. Precleaning always ensures a supply of free page frames and obviously yields better performance than visiting all of the memory and then trying to find a frame at the moment it is needed. At the very least, precleaning using paging daemons ensures that all the free frames are ready to use, so they need not be written to disk in a big hurry when they are required. But this act, instead of offering advantages, often turns out to be a serious drawback. Precleaning allows the writing of pages in batches, and it makes little sense to write out hundreds or thousands of pages when the majority of them have been modified again before they are actually replaced and finally evicted. The precleaning action in this situation is thus redundant that simply waste the limited transfer capacity of the busy secondary memory with unnecessary cleaning operations.

With demand cleaning, on the other hand, the modified page is first written back to the secondary storage before the reading in of a new page begins. Although this approach may reduce redundant page writes (as in precleaning), it goes through two page transfers when a page fault occurs that causes the faulty process to remain blocked for a considerable duration. This may, however, result in a noticeable decrease in processor utilization.

The use of the *page buffering* technique can offer a better approach in page cleaning. The strategy to be followed is: Clean (remove) only those pages that need to be replaced. The cleaning and replacement operations are to be separated out, and they are treated individually. As usual with page buffering, the replaced pages can be placed on two lists: modified and unmodified. The pages on the modified list can be periodically be written out in batches and moved to the unmodified list. A page on the unmodified list is either reclaimed if it is referenced or thrown out from the list when its frame is assigned to another page. In this way, a good number of redundant page writes can be avoided, which is a compromise between two extremes.

5.9.5.9 Placement Policy

A placement policy determines where in main memory the program or part of a program is to be placed. In contiguous memory allocation, this is of course a vital issue and is handled with various strategies, such as first-fit, next-fit, and best-fit. In the case of noncontiguous memory allocation, such as pure paging or paging combined with segmentation, the need of any strategy to choose a specific portion of memory for the purpose of placement of particular information is simply irrelevant. The reason is that wherever the information is placed in any portion of memory, be it noncontiguous, the address translation hardware and the memory access hardware can perform the address translation mechanism and other related functions with equal efficiency that the page-frame allocation mechanism ultimately does.

In multiprocessor environments, the architecture of the computer system comprises multiple CPUs capable of independently executing different tasks, and several different memory modules exist to support the activities of these CPUs. There exist various types of interconnections (as opposed to uniprocessors) between CPUs, and these different memory modules are not always necessarily located centrally, but how these memory modules will be interconnected to different CPUs is an important issue to be addressed when designing such computer systems. Many different forms of design and architecture of such systems have gradually evolved. On the so-called NUMA multiprocessor, the distributed memory of the machine, also shared, can be referenced by any processor (CPU) on the machine, but the time required to access a particular physical location varies according to numerous factors, including the distance between the specific processor and the particular memory module that is accessed. Hence, the execution performance largely depends on the extent to which data reside close to the processors that use them. Numerous approaches have been devised to address this issue. For NUMA systems, it is desirable that an automatic placement strategy be devised so that the pages can be assigned to a memory module that can ensure possibly the best performance.

5.9.5.10 Load Control

Load control determines how many processes (degrees of multiprogramming) will be allowed to be in main memory at any instant. This policy is critical to devise and equally difficult to implement for effective management of main memory. On the one hand, while it advocates for only few processes to be in the system at any point in time, in many situations, it essentially reduces processor utilization by limiting process scheduling when most of the resident processes may be blocked, and much time will then be spent as overhead to resolve the situation (possibly by swapping) for effective processor utilization. On the other hand, if the policy accepts too many processes in memory at any instant, on average, the size of the resident set of each process may not be supported by the available size of memory, which eventually may cause frequent page faults to occur, leading to severe degradation in system performance.

It is intuitive that, as the degree of multiprogramming increases from a small value, processor utilization is likely to increase and actually rise sharply because there are many active processes present in the system to use the processor. But the danger of this gradual increase in the degree of multiprogramming is that after a certain point, any attempt to further increase the degree of multiprogramming (the number of resident processes) may cause an adverse effect, mainly due to non-availability of adequate memory space to hold the average resident set of all the active processes. From this point onward, the number of page faults rises abruptly, and consequently processor utilization then begins to fall drastically.

However, there are a number of approaches that resolve the problem of load control by determining how many active programs are to be resident in the existing system at any instant to yield the best performance. In fact, the *working set theory* or the *page-fault frequency algorithm* (especially the principle on which the algorithm is based) implicitly determine load control. It simply states that those processes are allowed to continue their execution if their resident set size is relatively large, and the needed memory should be provided to the resident set of each process to remain active. So this policy automatically controls and dynamically determines the number of active processes in the system at any point in time.

Denning and his colleagues proposed another approach known as the $L = S$ *criterion*, which adjusts the degree of multiprogramming so that the mean time between page faults (L) equals the mean time required to process a page fault (S). Numerous experiments based on this criterion to study performances reveal that this is the point at which processor utilization reaches a maximum.

Another approach devised by Carr (1984) describes a technique adapting the clock page replacement algorithm (Figure 5.73 on the Support Material at www.routledge.com/9781032467238) using a global scope. This approach is based on monitoring the rate at which the hand traverses the circular buffer of frames. If the rate of traversal is below a given lower threshold, the degree of multiprogramming can be safely increased. On the other hand, if the rate of traversal exceeds a given upper threshold, it indicates either a high page-fault rate or limited number of pages available for replacement, which implies that the existing degree of multiprogramming is too high and should not be increased any more.

To effect load control, the degree of multiprogramming is sometimes required to be increased or decreased. It can be increased by simply bringing in few more processes in the existing system and activating them. On the other hand, it is decreased using a common approach of merely suspending one or more currently resident processes and then swapping them out of main memory. The main categories of processes that can be suspended are: largest process, frequent faulting process, lowest-priority process, last process activated, and processes with largest remaining time.

Like many other areas of operating system design that are mostly policy-dependent, the design issue related to the management of virtual memory is quite complex, because most of the issues in this area are closely interrelated to one another, and in many situations, they are conflicting. The policy to be adopted here to achieve one's goal is to be carefully selected, because it requires adequate support of both hardware and software and has a bearing on many other design factors related to other areas of the OS. A policy employed in this area may sometimes be lucrative, but it may have a negative impact in the operation of other areas of the OS. In addition, the design is often influenced by the characteristics of the program to be run on the system.

5.10   CASE STUDY: MEMORY MANAGEMENT IN UNIX AND SOLARIS

UNIX is intended to be machine independent with a high degree of portability and is available for machines with a diverse spectrum of system architectures and a variety of classes of processors ranging from microprocessors to supercomputers, along with widely different memory management units ranging from essentially nothing (IBM PC) to sophisticated paging hardware. Consequently, the memory-management scheme will vary from one system to the next. Early versions of UNIX used a simple variable-partition scheme with no virtual memory support. But current implementations of UNIX and Solaris make use of virtual memory with paging. Unfortunately, most computer systems are unable to provide adequate hardware support for good virtual memory management, and it is thus left to the virtual memory handler to make virtual memory practical and effective. This section refers to some common features of UNIX virtual memory along with a few attractive techniques used in different versions of UNIX implementation that overcome deficiencies in hardware support. A brief description of those, with figures, is covered on the Support Material at www.routledge.com/9781032467238 to provide a clear view of the practical issues related to virtual memory implementation rather than to study in detail the virtual memory handler of a specific UNIX version.

The memory model of UNIX (SVR4) and Solaris supports a **paging system** for allocating page frames to processes and also allocating page frames to disk block buffers. Another memory management scheme along with the paging system, known as *kernel memory allocator* is employed for kernel memory allocation that has already been discussed in previous section.

UNIX uses the idea of a unit called a *region* (or *segment*), which is a contiguous area in virtual address space comprising one or more pages that can be treated as a distinct entity. Every *process* (task) has an address space consisting of three separate regions, *text or code, data*, and *stack*; each region occupies a contiguous area of virtual memory, but separate regions belonging to a single task may be placed in noncontiguous areas of virtual memory. UNIX systems support shared text segments, but data and stack segments are never shared. Since text segments are never modified, only data segments, user stacks, and swappable parts of process control blocks are actually copied to the swap area in secondary memory.

- **Page Table:** UNIX manages paged virtual memory by means of a number of data structures that are more or less machine independent, but minor modifications may be needed for some hardware platforms. The data structure used for page table is one page table for each process, with one entry for each page in the virtual memory for that process. A specimen page table entry usually contains fields such as page frame number, age, modify, referenced, copy-on-write, valid, and protect. The page table, however, differentiates between three kinds of pages: resident, un-accessed (age), and swapped-out. A resident page is available in memory that has been loaded on demand in response to a page fault. An un-accessed page has not been referenced even once during the execution of the process and hence has never been loaded in memory. A swapped-out page is available in swap space. If such a page is referenced, a page fault would occur that loads this page back into memory from its location in the swap area.

To conserve memory space and swap area, the UNIX virtual memory handler uses the *copy-on-write* technique when a UNIX process (task) creates a child process via the FORK directive. The parent process and its child process share a single physical copy of the data region. When either of them wants to modify data, a new physical page frame is provided to selectively replicate parts of the data space rather than the entire data space, and a separate physical copy of the original page prior to modification is made for the other party. This process of incremental page copying on an as-needed basis is often referred to as *copy-on-write*. It reduces the copying overhead as well as conserving memory, but it requires a somewhat more complex implementation of the mapping tables. The actual mechanism used to implement the copy-on-write technique is given on the Support Material at www.routledge.com/9781032467238.

- **Hierarchical (multi-level) mapping tables:** UNIX uses tables that facilitate implementation of the vital strategy of using allocations of noncontiguous regions for different segments of a particular process in virtual address space and the important copy-on-write technique more efficiently. For example, a parent and a child process while sharing a region need only maintain private first-level tables that contain pointers to a single shared copy of the second-level page table in which the actual page table entries are stored.

- **Page Frame Data Table:** Similar to a page table, this table describes each frame of real memory and is indexed by frame number (similar to page numbers in page tables) and ultimately facilitates the effective operation of the page replacement algorithm. Each entry of this page frame data table contains information such as page state, logical device, block number, reference count, and pointer.

- **Page Replacement:** Different versions of UNIX use variations of the NRU page-replacement algorithm (as discussed before) based on a global replacement policy that works better with maintenance of longer page usage histories. UNIX maintains a list of free pages to reduce the page replacement overhead and offers the first page in the free list when it needs to load a new page. To add new pages to this free list, it exploits the clock algorithm with one or two hands (used in UNIX SVR4) to identify the inactive eligible (not locked) pages to be taken out from memory using their reference (R) bit. The mechanisms used to implement one-handed clock and two-handed clock algorithms in this regard are separately described on the Support Material at www.routledge.com/9781032467238.

- **Paging Daemon:** This is a vital module attached to the cleaning policy adopted by the virtual memory handler of the UNIX system. It is a background process that sleeps most of the time but starts working when it finds that the number of frames in the free list has fallen below the low threshold and goes to sleep when it detects that this number exceeds the high threshold. The monitoring activity carried out by UNIX on daemon operation, and the way the paging daemon itself operates to support the page replacement activities are simply enormous. The details of the working procedures that the daemon follows are given on the Support Material at www.routledge.com/9781032467238.

- **Swapping:** In UNIX, swapping is delegated to a separate kernel process, a scheduler known as a **swapper**, which is always process 0 in the system. However, swapping from memory to disk is generally initiated when the kernel runs out of free memory on account of many events or meeting specific conditions. When it is found that swap-out is necessary, the swapping activity is carried out by the **page-out daemon** that activates the swapper and, according to its own defined policy, swaps out selected processes to produce a sufficient number of free page frames. The swapper also periodically checks to see whether sufficient free memory is available to swap-in processes selected per the defined policy. Free storage in memory and on the swap device is always tracked by using an appropriate data structure.

- **Swap-Use Table:** For each swap device, there is one swap-use table. Each entry in this table is for each page on the device that contains information such as page/storage unit number, and reference count.

- **Disk Block Descriptor:** This table describes the disk copy of the virtual page. Each entry in this table is for each page associated with a process that contains certain information, such as swap device number, device block number, and type of storage.

- **Kernel Memory Allocator:** This portion was already described earlier in detail.

More details about this section with figures are given on the Support Material at www.routledge.com/9781032467238.

5.11 CASE STUDY: MEMORY MANAGEMENT IN LINUX

Linux has a close resemblance to UNIX, but since it attempts to accommodate a wide spectrum of diverse hardware platforms, its memory management scheme as implemented is quite complex. However, this narrative mainly covers a brief overview of some common features of Linux virtual memory management with respect to two major areas, *process virtual memory* and *kernel memory allocation*. Here, the ultimate objective is to provide a clear view of the practical issues in virtual memory implementation rather than to study in detail the virtual memory handler of a specific Linux version.

Virtual Memory

- **Virtual Address Mapping:** The design of Linux was actually intended to drive the 64-bit Alpha processor, which provided the needed hardware support for three levels of paging. It uses a hierarchical *three-level page* table structure that is platform- independent. This page table structure consists of the following types of tables. Each individual table has a size of one page. The three levels are:
  - **Page global directory:** Each active process has a single page global directory, and this directory must be resident in one page in main memory for an active process. Each entry in this directory points to one page of the page middle directory.
  - **Page middle directory:** Each entry in the page middle directory points to one page in the page table. This directory may span multiple pages.
  - **Page table:** As usual, each entry in the page table points to one virtual page of the process. This page table may also span multiple pages.

The virtual address of Linux is thus viewed as consisting of four fields to address this three-level page table structure; three of these are for the three levels, and the fourth one is the offset (byte number) within a page. The leftmost field is used as an index into the *global page directory*. The next leftmost field is used as an index into the *page directory*. The third field serves as an index into the *page table*, and the fourth field offers the *offset* within the selected page frame in main memory. Sixty-four-bit Linux also accommodates two-level hardware (32-bit Intel X-86/Pentium processor) support by defining the size of the *page middle directory* as one. Note that all references to the extra level of indirection in addressing are handled at compilation time rather than at runtime. This not only makes it a platform-independent, but while running on a platform with two-level paging hardware, using of three-level generic Linux would not incur any additional cost as performance overhead.

Similar to UNIX, the virtual (logical) address space of a process can consist of several **regions**, but each such region can have different characteristics of its own and is handled separately using separate policies for loading and replacement of pages. A page in a **zero-filled memory region** is filled with zeroes at its first use. A **file backed region** assists in mapping files in memory with ease. The page table entries of its pages point at the disk buffers used by the file system. In this way, any update in a page of such a region can be immediately reflected in the file that can allow concurrent users to use it with no delay. A **private memory region** is handled in a different fashion. When a *fork* system call creates a new child process, this new process is given a copy of the parent's page table. At this time, the copy-on-write policy is enforced on the pages of a private memory region. When a process modifies such a page, only then is a private copy of the page made for it.

- **Page Allocation:** Linux uses a page size of 4 Kbytes. It uses a buddy system allocator for speedy allocation/deallocation of contiguous page frames (for mapping of contiguous blocks of pages) with a group of fixed-size consisting of 1, 2, 4, 8, 16, or 32 page frames. The use of the buddy system allocator is also advantageous for traditional I/O operations involving DMA that requires contiguous allocation of main memory.
- **Page Replacement:** Linux essentially uses the *clock algorithm* described earlier (see Figure 5.73 on the Support Material at www.routledge.com/9781032467238), with a slight change that the *reference bit* associated with each page frame in memory is replaced by an 8-bit *age variable*. Each time a page is accessed, its age variable is incremented. At the same time, in the background, Linux periodically sweeps through the global page pool and decrements the age variable for each page while traversing through all the pages in memory. By this act, lower

the value of age variable of a page, the higher its probability of being removed at the time of replacement. On the other hand, a larger value of the age variable of a page implies that it is less eligible for removal when replacement is required. Thus, the Linux system implements a form of the least frequently used policy (**LFU**), already described earlier.

A Linux system always tries to maintain a sufficient number of free page frames at all times so that page faults can be quickly serviced using one of these free page frames. For this purpose, it uses two lists called the **active list** and **inactive list** and takes certain approved measures to maintain the size of the active list at two-thirds of the size of the inactive list. When the number of free page frames falls below a lower threshold, it executes a series of actions until a few page frames are freed. As usual, a page frame is moved from the inactive list to the active list if it is referenced.

Kernel Memory Allocation

Kernel memory allocation in Linux also uses the **buddy algorithm** in units of one or more pages, in a way similar to the page allocation mechanism used for virtual memory management of users. Here, the minimum amount of memory allocated is one page. To satisfy the request for odd sizes of small and short-term memory requirements sometimes needed by the kernel, the memory allocator implements a different approach in addition to the existing one. To provide these small chunks of memory, Linux often uses a scheme known as **slab allocation** (the slab allocator was discussed earlier) that offers a small chunks of memory space less than the size of a page within an allocated page. The size of the slab is always a power of 2 and depends on the page size. On a machine based on the Pentium X-86 processor, the page size is 4 Kbytes, and the different sizes of slabs that can be allocated within a page may range from 32 to 4096 bytes.

The slab allocator assigns all kernel objects (each object is a data structure) of the same class together to form a pool. A pool may consist of many slabs, and each slab may contain many small objects. However, all the objects in a slab are of only one kind. Linux maintains a set of linked lists, one for each size of slab. Slabs may be split and aggregated in a manner similar to the buddy algorithm and may be moved between lists accordingly. However, the algorithm used in slab allocation in Linux is relatively complex. The details of it are beyond the scope of this book. A thorough description of it can be found in Vahalia (1996).

Brief details on this topic with a figure are given on the Support Material at www.routledge. com/9781032467238.

5.12 CASE STUDY: MEMORY MANAGEMENT IN WINDOWS

The memory manager of Windows is designed to operate over a wide spectrum of platforms with different system architectures. It provides both 32-bit and 64-bit logical addresses. With 32-bit addressing, it can allow a maximum of 2^{32}, that is, 4 Gbytes, of address space per process. In fact, the address space of a process is 2 Gbytes, with an option that allows user space to be extended to 3 Gbytes; the remainder of the logical address space is reserved for the use of the OS shared by all processes. This feature enables the system architecture to include few gigabytes of RAM that can comfortably support execution of larger memory space-intensive applications. The default virtual address space as seen by a user process as shown in Figure 5.18 consists of *four regions*.

- 0x00000000 to 0x0000FFFF: Set aside to help programmers catch NULL-pointer assignments.
- 0x00010000 to 0x7FFEFFFF: Available user address space that is divided into pages for loading into main memory.
- 0x7FFF0000 to 0x7FFFFFFF: This space is inaccessible to the user and is used by the system as a guard page that enables the operating system easier to check on out-of-bounds pointer references.
- 0x80000000 to 0xFFFFFFFF: This space is dedicated for system use. It mainly contains the Windows microkernel, other executive systems, and device drivers.

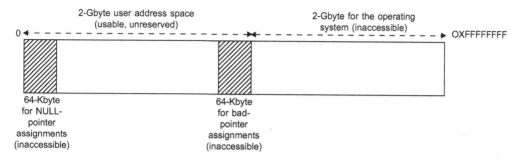

FIGURE 5.18   A block diagram of Windows default virtual address space used in virtual memory management of Windows (32-bit addressing).

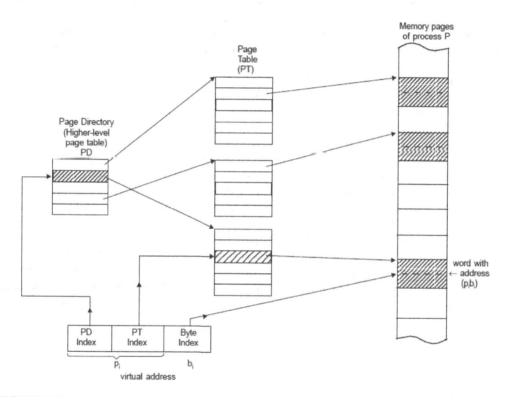

FIGURE 5.19   A representative diagram, showing two-level page table organization of Windows (32-bit addressing) used in the management of its virtual memory.

Paging:

Windows allows a process to occupy the entire user space of 2 Gbytes (minus 128 Kbytes) when it is created. This space is divided into fixed-size pages. But the sizes of pages may be different, from 4 to 64 Kbytes depending on the processor architecture. For example, 4 Kbytes is used on Intel, PowerPC, and MIPS platforms, while in DEC Alpha systems, pages are 8 Kbytes in size.

   Address Translation: Windows provides various types of page table organization and
   uses different page table formats for different system architectures. It uses two-level,
   three-level, and even four-level page tables, and consequently the virtual addresses used
   for addressing are also of different formats for using these differently organized page
   tables.

←10 bytes→ ←10 bytes →   ← 12 bytes →

PD index	PT index	byte index (offset)

FIGURE 5.20   A representative virtual (logical) address format of Windows (32-bit addressing) used in the management of its virtual memory.

However, on an Intel X-86 architecture, windows uses a two-level page table organization, as shown in Figure 5.19. The higher level page table is called a *page directory* (PD), with a size of 1 page (4 Kbytes) that contains 1024 entries of 4 bytes each. This requires 10 bits (2^{10} = 1024) in the virtual address to identify a particular entry in page directory. Each such entry in the PD points to a page table (PT). The size of each page table is also 1 page that contains 1024 page table entries of 4 bytes each. This also requires 10 bits (2^{10} = 1024) in virtual address to identify a particular entry in a page table. Each such entry in the PT points to a page frame in main memory. The size of each page frame is 4 Kbytes (2^{12} = 4 K); hence 12 bits is required in the virtual address to identify information within a page frame. Each 32-bit virtual (logical) address is thus split into three components, as shown in Figure 5.20.

At the time of translating such a 32-bit logical address, the *PD index* field is used to locate the corresponding page table. The *PT index* field is then used to select the corresponding page within the page table. This page points to a particular page frame in main memory. The *byte index* is then concatenated with the address of the page frame to obtain the desired physical address.

Each page table entry in question is 32 bits (4 bytes). Out of these 32 bits, only 20 bits are used to identify the page frame containing a page. The remaining 12 bits are used for the following purposes: 5 bits contain the protection field, 4 bits indicate the *paging file* (e.g. the disk file to which pages are to be written when removing them from memory) that contains a copy of the page, and 3 bits specify the *state* of the page.

If the page is not in memory, the 20 bits of its page table entry specify the offset into the paging file to identify the page. This address can be used to load the page in memory. If this page is a text (code) page, a copy of it already exists in a code file. Hence, this type of page need not be included in a paging file before it is loaded for the first time. In this case, 1 bit indicates the page protection, and 28 bits point to a system data structure that indicates the position of the page in a file containing the code.

Use of the page state in the page table simplifies the accounting in page handling. A page can be in one of three states:

Available: Pages not currently used by this process.
Reserved: A set of contiguous pages that the virtual memory manager sets aside for a process but does not count that against the process's memory quota until used. When a process or thread needs to write to memory, some space from reserved memory can then be quickly allocated to them.
Committed: Pages for which the virtual memory manager has set aside space in its *paging file*. In this way, it keeps control over the free disk space being set aside for a particular process that can also be used by other processes if needed. A page frame can be in any one of eight states (requiring 3 bits to specify). Some of these states may be as follows:
Valid: The page is in active use.
Free: The page is not in active use.
Zeroed: The page is cleaned out and available for immediate use.

Standby: The page has been removed from the working set of the process to which it was allocated, but it can be brought back (reassigned) to the process if it is referenced again.

Modified: The page is dirty and yet to be written out.

Bad: The page cannot be accessed due to hardware failure.

- **Page Sharing:** At the time of handling the sharing of pages, the pages to be shared are represented as *section objects* held in a section of memory. Processes that share the section object have their own individual *view* of this object. A view controls the part of the object that the process wants to view. A process maps a view of a section into its own address space by issuing a system (kernel) call with parameters indicating the part of the section object that is to be mapped (in fact, an offset), the number of bytes to be mapped, and the logical address in the address space of the process where the object is to be mapped. When a view is accessed for the first time, the kernel allocates memory to that view unless memory is already allocated to it. If the memory section to be shared has the attribute *based*, the shared memory has the same virtual address in the logical address spaces of all sharing processes.

Sharing of pages is supported by the copy-on-write feature. As usual, a single copy of the shared page is used by all sharing processes until any sharing process attempts to modify it. If a process wants to modify the shared page, then a private copy of the page is created for it. Copy-on-write is implemented by setting the *protection field* of the page in the page table entry to *read-only*. A protection exception is raised when a process attempts to modify it, which is resolved by the virtual memory manager by making a private copy of the page for use by the process.

Sharing of pages also uses a distinct feature which relates to a "level of indirection" to simplify its implementation. Usually, all sharing processes individually include the shared pages in their own page tables, and all these entries of shared pages in all these page tables would have to be modified when a page is loaded or removed from memory. To avoid this complication and to reduce the time-consuming overhead, a level of indirection is included while accessing page table entries for shared pages. A provision of an *indirection bit* is kept, which is set in the page table entries of the shared pages in each sharing process's page table. The page table entry of the shared page points to a *prototype page entry*, which points to the actual page frame containing the page. When a shared page is loaded or removed from memory, only the prototype page entry needs to be modified.

- **Replacement Scope:** Windows uses the *variable allocation, local scope scheme* (see replacement scope, described earlier) to manage its resident set. As usual, when a process is first activated, it is allocated a certain number of page frames as its working set. When a process references a page not in main memory, the virtual memory manager resolves this page-fault situation by adjusting the working set of the process using the following standard procedures:

- When a sufficient amount of main memory is available, the virtual memory manager simply offers an additional page frame to bring in the new page as referenced without swapping out any existing page of the faulting process. This eventually results in an increase in the size of the resident set of the process.

- When there is a dearth of available memory space, the virtual memory manager swaps less recently used pages out of the working set of the process to make room for the new page to be brought into memory. This ultimately reduces the size of the resident set of the process.

5.13   CACHE MEMORY

The processor executes information which is primarily fetched from main memory; hence, both the *size* and the *speed* of the main memory are always key factors in the performance of the system as a whole. The introduction of virtual memory has certainly resolved the space scarcity problem in main memory and thereby relieved the programmer by removing the restrictions imposed on the size of the address spaces of individual processes. But it also increases the execution time of the processes due to frequently needed dynamic translation of virtual addresses to physical addresses done by memory management, thereby causing a graceful degradation in overall system performance. In addition, the frequent occurrences of page faults require servicing of related interrupts that are again an added time-consuming event. As a result, the performance of the system is even more affected.

As electronic technology continuously advances, CPU speed increases rapidly, and the speed of memory also increases, but relatively modestly due to its inherent design. As a result, the CPU–main memory speed disparity (gap between their speeds) has gradually increased instead of being reduced. This has become more predominant, especially at the time of their handshaking. In fact, the rate at which the processor can operate in a system is clearly hindered by the memory cycle time (the time it takes to read/write one word from or to memory), which eventually causes significant problems, leading to severe bottleneck in the operation of the system over the years. If the memory could be built up with the same technology as the processor registers, the memory cycle times would then be closely comparable to processor cycle times. But this proposition may be too costly. Hence, to obtain an acceptable solution, balance is required between these conflicting parameters of memory, such as size, speed, and cost. A technique has been improvised that combines a small amount of costly faster memory with a larger size of comparatively slow and less costly main memory to attain a speed almost on the order of fast memory as well as the capacity of fairly large memory at an affordable price. This relatively small, comparatively fast, and a slightly costly memory placed between the processor and main memory that operates on the principle of locality is historically known as **cache memory** (from the French word *cache*, meaning to hide). Cache is considered the fastest component in the memory hierarchy, and approaches nearly the speed of CPU components. Cache memory was first commercially introduced in the IBM 360/85 system in 1968. The insertion of this element into the memory hierarchy has dramatically improved the performance of the entire system as a whole.

The evolution of cache memory and its organization is purely a subject of computer organization and architecture. In fact, cache memory is solely used as a supporting module to main memory for improved performance (speed) during execution. Hence, this small, fast, and costly cache memory is placed between a processor and main memory and acts as a buffer, creating a two-level internal memory. In fact, cache–main memory handshaking is similar to that of main memory–virtual memory, at least in principle. But the cache is controlled and managed by the MMU and is also transparent to the programmer. Depending on the speed and application environment, the cache can also be implemented at one or multiple levels in the organization of the computer.

While cache is now considered a vital resource, it is not visible to the operating system (the resource manager), which is why it is called the cache (to hide) and hence lies outside the jurisdiction of operating-system activities. Since it lies within the memory hierarchy of the entire memory system of a computer, it often interacts with other memory-management hardware, and thus appears to be linked indirectly with the working of the operating system. Moreover, failure of the cache line (similar to a page fault) has an impact on memory management and thereby imposes an additional overhead on the operating system as a whole. Since cache memory has been introduced on the heels of virtual memory, many of the principles and strategies used in virtual memory schemes are equally applied in cache memory. In fact, the policy, management, and strategies used to monitor the cache are implemented within an additional in-built hardware called the **cache controller**, associated with the cache memory chip.

Since, the cache is invisible to the operating system, its presence or absence in the computer system does not affect the designs of operating systems or their implementations to realize different necessary activities. In fact, the design of the cache, its principles of operation, and its other working activities do not have any impact on the working of the underlying operating system, and hence are not included in the regular functioning of the operating system. Therefore, cache memory, as a whole, is kept set aside from the purview of any types of operating systems, in general.

Brief details on this section, with all related issues supported by figures, are given on the Support Material at www.routledge.com/9781032467238.

SUMMARY

This chapter presents the principles of managing the main memory, then investigates different forms of memory management schemes, ranging from very simple contiguous allocation of memory, including static (fixed) partition, dynamic (variable) partition, and overlay, to highly sophisticated noncontiguous allocation of memory, including paging, segmentation, and segmentation with paging. In allocating space for processes using each of these schemes, various issues relating to management of memory were discussed. Static partition of memory, its allocation/deallocation, and space management are relatively simple and straightforward, although they suffer from critical internal fragmentation. Dynamic creation of partitions according to specific needs and also to eliminate the problem of internal fragmentation requires more complex algorithms; particularly deallocation of partitions and coalescing of free memory are needed to combat external fragmentation. The need for occasional compaction of memory is also a major issue in the increased time and space complexity of dynamic partitioning. However, both static and dynamic partitioning require almost identical hardware support to fulfill their aims. Sharing, in fact, is quite restrictive in both systems.

Since physical memory in paging as well as in segmented systems retains its linear-array organization, an address translation mechanism is needed to convert a two-dimensional virtual-page address or virtual-segment address into its unidimensional physical equivalent. Both paging and segmentation in dynamically partitioned memory reduce the impact of external fragmentation, and the other advantages they mainly offer include dynamic relocation with needed dynamic linking and binding, fine-grained protection both within and between address spaces, and ease of sharing.

The introduction of virtual memory alleviated to a large extent the main memory space scarcity problem and also removed the restrictions on the size of address spaces of individual processes due to limited capacity of the available physical memory. With virtual memory, paging simplifies allocation and deallocation of physical memory. Translation of virtual to physical addresses during runtime, usually assisted by the hardware, is used to bridge the gap between contiguous virtual addresses consisting of pages and discontinuous physical addresses comprising page frames. Virtual memory is commonly implemented using segmentation with paging in which demand paging is used, which allows a process to run only with pages on demand. Since the capacity of main memory is far less than that of virtual memory, it is often necessary to replace pages from memory to make frames free for new pages. Numerous page-replacement algorithms are used, out of which LRU replacement is an approximation of optimal page replacement but is difficult to implement. However, the second-chance algorithm along with a few others are close approximations of LRU replacement. Besides, when a policy relating to fixing of number of frame-allocation to a process is formed, it exploits either local page replacement, or dynamic using global page replacement. In addition, the working-set model approach is introduced as a guideline that shows the minimum number of page frames required for an executing process to continue with fewer page faults.

Kernel processes typically require memory to be allocated using pages that are physically contiguous. The McKusick–Karels allocator, lazy buddy allocator, and slab allocator are only a few methods described here that are used for this purpose in which memory wastage due to fragmentation is negligible and memory requests can also be satisfied speedily.

Last, the salient features of memory management implemented in reality by popular, commercially successful operating systems such as UNIX, Linux, Windows, and Solaris are illustrated here as case studies to explain the realization of different aspects of memory management that were theoretically discussed.

EXERCISES

1. What are the functions performed by the memory manager? What is meant by memory allocation? What are the physical address and logical address?
2. What is meant by address translation? What are the different situations when address translation takes place? Explain how address translation takes place at: **a.** program generation time, **b.** loading time, **c.** execution time
3. Name the different memory management schemes that are commonly mentioned. What are the parameters used while making a comparison between them?
4. State the policy-decisions that are made to guide swapping actions. "Swapping, in turn, invites relocation": give your comments.
5. Explain with a diagram the multiple-user fixed partition scheme of memory management with a partition description table. Give its merits and drawbacks.
6. What are the different approaches taken by the operating system in dynamic partitioning memory management while allocating memory to processes? Compare and contrast the merits and drawbacks of these approaches in light of keeping track of allocated partitions as well as free areas.
7. What is meant by fragmentation of memory? State and explain the different types of fragmentation observed in contiguous allocation of memory.
8. What is meant by compaction? When does it take place? What is the effect of compaction? What is the overhead associated with compaction? Selective compaction of memory in certain situations performs better than brute-force straightforward compaction: Give your comments.
9. What is a bit map? How it can be used for keeping track of allocated and free space in main memory in a dynamic partition approach? Discuss its merits and drawbacks.
10. A dynamic memory partitioning scheme is being used, and the following is the memory configuration at any given instant:

	15K		20K		60K		20K		45K	
	H1		H2		H3		H4		H5		H6
P1		P2		P3		P4		P5		P6	
20K		40K	50K		10K		30K		35K		40K

The Ps are the processes already allocated with blocks; the Hs are the holes and are free blocks. The next three memory requests are for 35K, 20K, and 10K. Show the starting address for each of the three blocks using the following placement algorithms:

   a. First–fit
   b. Next–fit (assume the most recently added block is at the beginning of memory)
   c. Best–fit
   d. Worst–fit

11. What is meant by overlay? Explain with a diagram the implementation of an overlay mechanism. What are the responsibilities performed by an overlay supervisor? "The concept of overlay opens a new horizon in the emergence of modern approaches in memory management". What are those innovative approaches? How they have been conceptually derived from the implementation of an overlay mechanism?
12. Discuss memory fragmentation and its impact on the buddy system. Explain why free lists in a buddy system are made to be doubly linked.
13. What are the distinct advantages that can be obtained in a power-of-two allocation system over its counterpart buddy system?
14. Discuss the basic principle involved in noncontiguous memory allocation strategy. State the distinct advantages that can be accrued from this strategy.

15. State and explain the salient features of a simple paging system. How is address translation carried out in a simple paging system?

16. Suppose you have a processor that supports 64-bit address space and 4 KB frame size. How many levels of paging do you need in that system if each page table/directory is restricted to a single frame? You may assume each page table entry (page descriptor) is 8 bytes.

17. State and explain segmentation in light of its principles of operation. What hardware support is required to implement segmentation? What is a segment descriptor table? When is it created? Where is it stored?

18. Why is it said that the segment numbers are visible to processes (in a segmentation scheme), but page numbers are invisible/transparent to processes (in a paging scheme)?

19. Consider a simple segmentation system that has the following segment table:

Segment	Base	Length (bytes)
0	220	500
1	2300	50
2	750	100
3	1229	570
4	1870	110

For each of these logical addresses: **a.** 0, 390; **b.** 2, 90; **c.** 1, 19; **d.** 0, 590; **e.** 4, 22; **f.** 3, 590; **g.** 3, 253, determine the corresponding physical address. Also check whether there is an invalid address specification for a segment fault to occur.

20. What is demand segmentation? Why is it difficult to implement compared to demand paging?

21. What is the difference between simple paging and virtual memory paging? What elements are typically found in a page table entry? Briefly define each element. Define briefly the alternative page fetch policies.

22. What is the purpose of a translation lookaside buffer (TLB)? Page tables are stored in physical memory, which has an access time of 100 ns. The TLB can hold eight page table entries and has an access time of 10 nanosec. During execution of a process, it is found that 85 percent of memory references are found in the TLB and only 2 percent of the references lead to page faults. The average time for page replacement is 2 ms. Compute the average memory access time.

23. How is a TLB different from hardware cache memory used to hold instructions/data?

24. A machine has 48-bit virtual addresses and 32-bit physical addresses. Page sizes are 8K. How many entries are needed for a conventional page table? For an inverted page table?

25. Assume that a 32-bit address uses a two-level page table. Virtual addresses are split into a high-ordered 9-bit top-level page table field, ant 11-bit second-level page table field, and an offset. How large are the pages and how many are there in the virtual address space?

26. If an instruction takes 1 microsec and a page fault takes an additional n microsec, develop a formula for the effective instruction time if page faults occur every k instructions.

27. What different page replacement policies are commonly used? Write two page replacement policies for virtual memory.

28. What is the relationship between FIFO and the clock page replacement algorithm? Explain why the two-handed clock algorithm for page replacement is superior to the one-handed clock algorithm.

29. Consider the following page reference string. 1, 2, 3, 4, 2, 1, 5, 6, 2, 1, 2, 3, 7, 6, 3, 2 Using four frames that are all initially empty, how many page faults will occur under **a.** FIFO, **b.** Second-chance, **c.** LRU, **d.** NRU, **e.** Optimal?

30. To implement the LRU approach, what are the modifications required in the page table. Show that the LRU page replacement policy possesses the stack property. Discuss an alternative approach that can implement the LRU approach.

31. What is meant by thrashing? How can it affect the performance of a system? Describe a strategy by which the thrashing can be minimized.

32. What is the difference between a working set and a resident set? Explain with reasons and preferably with the help of examples why the working set size of a process may increase or decrease during the course of its execution.

33. What is the advantage of a page fault frequency algorithm over the estimation of the working set using the window size? What is its disadvantage?

34. State the different types of allocation policy and different types of replacement scope. How is the former related to the latter?

35. Is it possible to page out page tables from the kernel space to the swap device? Justify your answer.

36. "In a virtual memory system using a segmentation-with-paging scheme, the involvement of segmentation is limited to sharing. It does not really have any role in memory management". Justify and comment on this.

More questions and problems are given at the end of the chapter on the Support Material at www. routledge.com/9781032467238.

SUGGESTED REFERENCES AND WEBSITES

Baer, J. L. *Computer Systems Architecture*, Rockville, MD, Computer Science Press, 1980.

Bays, C. A. "Comparison of Next–fit, First–fit, and Best–fit", *Communications of the ACM*, vol. 20, no. 3, pp. 191–192, 1977.

Beck, L. L. "A Dynamic Storage Allocation Technique Based on Memory Residence Time", *Communication of the ACM*, vol. 25, pp. 714–724, 1982.

Bonwick, J., Adams, J. "Magazines and Vmem: Extending the Slab Allocator to Many CPUs and Arbitrary Resources", *Proceedings of the 2001 USENIX Annual Technical Conference*, pp. 15–34, 2001.

Carr, R. *Virtual Memory Management*, Ann Arbor, MI, UMI Research Press, 1984.

Chakraborty, P. *Computer Organization and Architecture: Evolutionary Concepts, Principles, and Designs*, Boca Raton, FL, CRC Press, 2020.

Denning, P. J. "The Working Set Model for Program Behavior", *Communications of the ACM*, vol. 11, no. 5, pp. 323–333, 1968.

Denning, P. J. "Virtual Memory", *Computing Surveys*, vol. 2, no. 3, pp. 154–189, 1970.

Denning, P. J. "Working Sets: Past and Present", *IEEE Transactions on Software Engineering*, vol. SE–6, no. 1, pp. 64–84, 1980.

Finkel, R. A. *An Operating Systems Vade Mecum*, Second Edition, Englewood Cliffs, NJ, Prentice Hall, 1988.

Fotheringham, J. "Dynamic Storage Allocation in the Atlas Computer Including an Automatic Use of a Backing Store", *Communications of the ACM*, vol. 4, pp. 435–436, October, 1961.

Kaufman, A. "Tailored-list and Recombination-delaying Buddy Systems", *ACM Transactions on Programming Languages and Systems*, vol. 6, pp. 118–125, 1984.

Knuth, D. E. *The Art of Computer Programming, Vol. 1: Fundamental Algorithms*, Second Edition, Reading, MA, Addison–Wesley, 1973.

Maekawa, M., Oldehoeft, A. E., Oldehoeft, R. R. *Operating Systems: Advanced Concepts*, Menlo Park, CA, Benjamin/Cummings, 1987.

Oldehoeft, R. R., Allan, S. J. Adaptive Exact-fit Storage Management", *Communication of the ACM*, vol. 28, pp. 506–511, 1985.

Smith, A. J. "Bibliography on Paging and Related Topics", *Operating Systems Review*, vol. 12, pp. 39–56, 1978.

Stephenson, C. J. "Fast Fits: A New Method for Dynamic Storage Allocation", *Proceedings of the 9th Symposium on Operating Systems Principles*, New York, ACM, pp. 30–32, 1983.

Vahilia, U. *Unix Internals*, The New Frontiers, Prentice Hall, 1996.

6 Device Management

Learning Objectives

- To illustrate the general characteristics of different types of I/O devices.
- To describe the I/O modules containing the I/O (device) controllers that connects the I/O devices to the hardware platform.
- To describe generic I/O system organization to realize different types of I/O operations.
- To discuss physical I/O operation at the device level.
- To describe the device management module along with its objectives and functions.
- To explain logical structuring of physical I/O and to organize its functions.
- To outline the design principles of a generic device manager with constituents including I/O schedulers, interrupt handlers, and device drivers.
- To describe different types of I/O buffering and its impact on system performance.
- To describe the clock device along with the required hardware and software (clock device drivers).
- To discuss the organization of magnetic disk I/O devices along with their physical characteristics and different components being used.
- To describe disk I/O operation along with its parameters.
- To describe disk management in the context of its formatting and data organization.
- To explain the disk-arm scheduling policies (disk-access time management) and the different traditional methods used to implement these policies.
- To describe different types of RAID arrangements of disks.
- To define the disk cache and its design considerations to improve the overall system performance.
- To discuss the page cache and disk cache along with their merits and drawbacks.
- Case study: to briefly describe individually the device management implemented in UNIX, Linux, and Windows.

6.1 INTRODUCTION

All types of computers include a set of I/O modules as one of their fundamental resources following the Von Neumann design concept. Computer devices of different classes often come with numerous brands and models from different vendors using diverse technologies. All such details are, however, kept hidden from the internal working of the system, and that is why it is said that I/O is **transparent** with respect to brand, model, or physical device type. Various types of such I/O (peripheral) devices in the form of I/O modules are interfaced to the main system for migration of data from the outside world into the computer or from the computer to the outside world. Each such I/O module is made up of its own logic that on the one hand works in tune with the main system (CPU and main memory) and on other hand establishes a physical connection with the outside electro-mechanical peripheral devices to execute the physical I/O operation.

With the continuous introduction of more advanced technology, processor speed has enormously increased, and memory access time has decreased, mostly by the intelligent use of one, two, or even more levels of internal cache to manage growing processor speed. But the speed of the I/O modules has not improved to the extent (due to being mostly electro-mechanical) as to cope with

DOI: 10.1201/9781003383055-6

this faster processor-memory bandwidth. As a result, it causes a severe bottleneck when interacting with the rest of the system that creates a strong challenge in the overall performance of the machine, particularly in the case of most important I/O module, disk storage. Even today, the speeds of I/O devices themselves, and I/O speed in general, are comparatively far lower than the overall speed of the processor–memory cluster. That is why modern computer systems provide adequate hardware assistance in the I/O area with proper support of event management mechanisms (such as interrupts) so that I/O operations can be overlapped with those of the CPU by allowing the CPU to continue with its own work while I/O operations are in progress in parallel in order to reduce the impact of slower I/O on the overall performance of the system. Along these lines, constant development in the design of more intelligent I/O modules and their allied interfaces continue, ultimately culminating in the introduction of a separate I/O processor to handle I/O modules on its own, thereby totally decoupling I/O activities from the clutch of the main system. But if there is an I/O processor, many standard issues in relation to the central processing unit, such as scheduling and interprocess synchronization, are equally applicable to the I/O processor for its proper function. A large computer system, nowadays, is thus equipped with such powerful I/O modules that an I/O module itself can be treated as if it is a completely standalone, full-fledged computing system.

In fact, the operation and working of all these numerous types of relatively slow I/O modules, in particular generic devices such as disks, tapes, printers, and terminals, are monitored and controlled by the operating system with respect to managing the allocation, isolation, sharing, and deallocation of these devices according to the prescribed policies as designed. The portion of the operating system performing all these responsibilities is known as the **I/O system**, **device management**, or sometimes **I/O management**. An amazingly large proportion of the instructions in the operating system, often 50 percent, are devoted only to handling devices. Although device management has gradually gained considerable importance due to the continuous increase in user density (the user interacts with the system only through I/O devices), it is still a relatively simple part of the overall OS design, because it is essentially defined mostly by the hardware design.

Brief details on this section are given on the Support Material at www.routledge.com/9781032467238.

6.2 I/O DEVICES: GENERAL CHARACTERISTICS

A typical computer system is equipped with numerous types of I/O devices (mainly electro-mechanical) of the widest range of type, technology, organization, performance, and also cost to keep the computer system within an affordable limit. These devices may again be grouped into different classes, such as devices used for *storage of information* (magnetic disk, tape, CD-ROM, etc.), *human readable* devices (printers, video display units, keyboards), and other devices, such as; a mouse, modem (used for communication), network interface, or digital line driver. Other machine-readable devices include clocks, sensors, actuators, and controllers. In fact, enough varieties are also observed within each class of these devices, ranging from slow, cheaper ones to fast, expensive ones. However, the key parameters among many such differences are mainly: **unit of transfer** (stream of characters/bytes or larger chunks of blocks), **data rate** (bits per sec; bps), **data representation** (character code and parity conventions), **control mechanism** (used to drive the device), and *error conditions* (nature and tolerance of errors). Moreover, the way a device is to be used also has an impact on the underlying policy and strategy of the operating system and its associated utilities. For example, a disk used for files requires the support of a file management system, whereas the same disk used in a virtual memory scheme depends largely on the hardware and software mechanisms controlling the virtual memory system. Similarly, it is applicable to terminals (when used for an ordinary user, by a console operator, or by a system administrator). These varied attributes in the characteristics of I/O devices pose a difficult situation for both the operating system and the user processes while attempting to implement a uniform and consistent approach to I/O handling.

Brief details on this topic are given on the Support Material at www.routledge.com/9781032467238.

6.3 TYPES OF I/O DEVICES

I/O devices can be roughly divided into two categories: (i) **block-oriented devices** and (ii) **character (stream)-oriented devices**. A block-oriented device is one that stores information in fixed-size blocks; each such block has its own address, and read/write are done one block at a time at random independently of all others. Hard disk, CD-ROM, and tape are examples of block-oriented devices with block sizes commonly ranging from 128 to 4096 bytes. Only blocks of tape devices are accessed sequentially. A character (stream)-oriented device operates only on a stream of characters. It is not addressable. Terminals, line printers, communication ports, network interfaces, mice, and other pointing devices, and most other devices that are not secondary storage are usually character (stream)-oriented devices. There are still other devices that do not belong to any of these categories. **Clocks**, for example, are neither block addressable, nor do they generate or accept character streams. All they do is to cause interrupts at well-defined intervals. Memory-mapped screens, also do not fit this model. Still, the model of a block or character devices is so general enough that it can be used as a basis to define and design operating system software to be *device independent* while dealing with I/O.

6.4 I/O CONTROLLERS: DEVICE CONTROLLERS

The specific piece of hardware organized to carry out specific algorithms to constantly monitor a device carrying out its basic tasks is called an *I/O controller* or *device controller* or *adapter*. It provides a means of more modular and general design for controlling devices. One end of the controller is connected to the main system, and the other end is connected to the mechanical device by a cable. Nowadays, many controllers can individually handle two, four, or even more identical devices at the same time.

As shown in Figure 6.1, there is a lower-level device-specific interface between controllers and devices known as the **controller–device interface** (*or* **hardware controller**) that physically drives the device under the control of the software (high-level software interface) located in a level just above this interface (generic device controller) in the form of command to realize the desired operation. At the device end, this must be compatible with the respective operation to be carried out by a specific device. Note that these are totally *device-dependent* and typically quite different from the standard traditional computer logic levels. Thus, standardization is required here so that devices manufactured by one vendor can be connected to a controller manufactured by another. Official standards, such as, ANSI, IEEE, or small computer serial interface (SCSI) or a de facto one are examples of such an interface. The presence of the controller–device interface creates a line of demarcation between the controller and device, because the operating system nearly always deals with the controller, not the device.

Similarly, as shown in Figure 6.1, there is also an interface known as the **controller–bus interface** that lies above the generic device controller and the bus of the main system to connect the

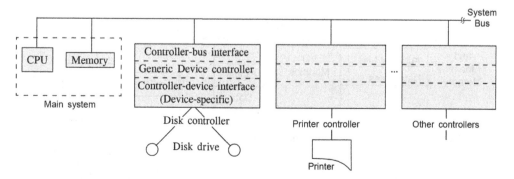

FIGURE 6.1 An illustration of a representative model for connecting device I/O controllers and I/O devices with the main system.

controller to the bus so that a device can be attached to a computer and then interoperate with other facilities in the main system. Nearly all small computers use the single bus model, as shown in Figure 6.1, for communication between the main system and controllers. Large systems often use multiple buses and specialized *I/O processors* (*I/O channels*) to relieve the CPU to a great extent from the burden of its required involvement in I/O activities.

The operation of the device controller (at one end with the device and at other end with the main system) is manipulated by the software. The high-level software interface to a device controller is a middle layer, the **generic device controller** that defines the interaction between the software and the controller. It states how software manipulates the hardware controller to cause the device to perform I/O operations. This software interface generally provides a uniform abstraction of I/O devices to software engineers. In particular, it makes every device appear to be a set of dedicated registers. These registers are accessible either directly as part of a physical store or indirectly via I/O instructions provided by the hardware. A set of such dedicated registers is usually called an **I/O port**.

Controllers often incorporate a small amount of memory (hardware) called a *buffer* to temporarily hold data after it is read from the device or sent from the main system for subsequent needed actions. With its various forms, it plays a vital role (to be discussed later) in I/O operation and is mainly used to overlap the operation of the device and that of the main system to smooth out peaks in I/O demand.

More about this with a figure is given on the Support Material at www.routledge.com/ 9781032467238.

6.5 I/O SYSTEMS: I/O MODULES

The I/O system performs the task of transferring information between main memory or the CPU and the outside world. It includes *I/O modules, a link,* and the *external I/O devices.* This link is used to communicate *control, status,* and *physical data* between the I/O modules and the external devices. *Data* are in the form of set of bits to be sent to or received from the I/O modules. *Control signals* determine the function that the device will perform. *Status signals* indicate the *state* of the device, whether the device is ready for operation. The I/O module thus includes a *control unit* that carries out all these responsibilities while operating the device, and the related software is designed to execute I/O operation. Figure 6.2 shows a model of an I/O system in which the I/O module stands as a mediator between the high-speed CPU or memory and the much slower electro-mechanical devices of different types.

For computers used in process control environments like assembly line processing, industrial processes, etc., the *status condition* of the process being sent is in the form of a status signal

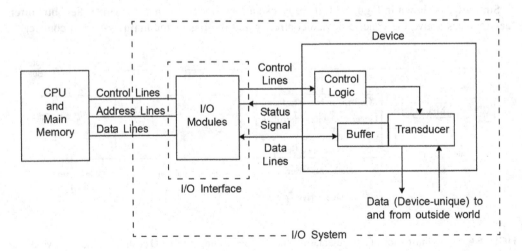

FIGURE 6.2 A generic representative model of an I/O system including I/O interface and external device.

as *input*, and the corresponding *control signal* is obtained as *output* to monitor and control the process.

Brief details on this section with a figure are given on the Support Material at www.routledge.com/9781032467238.

6.6 I/O SYSTEM ORGANIZATION: TYPES OF I/O OPERATION

I/O organization consisting of I/O systems lies in the domain of computer organization and architecture (Chakraborty, 2020). The I/O system again depends on the intelligence of its attached I/O module, the amount of hardware available to communicate with its peripherals, and also the number of peripherals attached to it. In fact, I/O systems are usually distinguished by the extent to which the CPU is required to get involved in the execution of less important I/O-related activity. The CPU actually executes the I/O instructions and may accept the data temporarily, but the ultimate source or destination is the memory unit while transfer of information takes place to and from external devices. However, the ultimate target of the I/O organization as gradually evolved is to relieve the CPU as much as possible from the relatively inferior time-consuming I/O-related activity and eventually to totally release the CPU, isolating it from I/O-related tasks as a whole. To achieve this goal, the evolution process in I/O organization that have passed through a series of developments starting from its most primitive form to the ultimate emergence of its latest modern version can be categorized in sequence as follows:

1. Programmed I/O (PIO)
2. Interrupt-driven I/O
3. DMA
4. I/O channel
5. I/O processor (IOP)

More details about this section are given on the Support Material at www.routledge.com/9781032467238.

6.7 PHYSICAL I/O OPERATION: DEVICE-LEVEL I/O

The I/O operation carried out by the system on devices is implemented by issuing a specific I/O instruction that contains the respective device address [like *controller_id* (*c*), *device_id* (*d*)] and the *address* (*addr*), where *addr* is the starting address of the location that contains the command for the required I/O operation, such as start, open, read, write, or close. The entire I/O function can then be formulated in a general way that executes the following operations in sequence:

* Initiating an I/O operation
* Checking device status
* Performing I/O operations
* Completion of an I/O operation
* Handling interrupts

More detail about this section are given on the Support Material at www.routledge.com/9781032467238.

6.8 DEVICE MANAGEMENT: OBJECTIVES

Device management directly manipulates hardware devices, providing the first-level abstraction of these resources used by applications to perform I/O. One of the major requirements in the design of device management is to efficiently operate and utilize various types of I/O devices available in the system to realize optimized I/O device performance, thereby ensuring overall improved efficiency of the operating system. It should also implement a generalized approach for different types of I/O devices with numerous patterns of characteristics present in the system to make it convenient while performing device-level I/O. This requires generality while handling different types of I/O devices and is achieved by defining certain methods that treat all these devices, such as disks, tapes, printers, and terminals, in the same uniform manner for the sake of simplicity and also freedom of handling various errors arising from all these devices. In fact, the overall generality can be mostly realized if physical I/O function can be structured logically in a modular fashion. This concept is considered one of the keys in the design of device management software, and is explained in detail later (Section 6.10).

Brief details on this topic are given on the Support Material at www.routledge.com/9781032467238.

6.9 DEVICE MANAGEMENT: FUNCTIONS

The device management monitors and controls the devices, and while attempting to provide efficiency in device utilization and generality in device handling, it performs the following basic functions:

1. When initiating an I/O operation, the status of the device is to be checked. The status of all devices is being kept track with a special mechanisms using a database known as a **unit control block** (UCB) associated with each device. The module that keeps track of the status of devices is called the **I/O traffic controller**.
2. In multiprogramming/multi-user environment, it decides the policy to determine which process from the waiting queue pending on a physical device gets a device, when, and for how long. A wide range of techniques are available for implementing these policies that is based on the objective of improved system performance. In general, three basic techniques are followed. Those are:
   a. *Dedicated*: a technique whereby a device is assigned to a single process.
   b. *Shared*: a technique whereby a device is shared by many processes.
   c. *Virtual*: a technique whereby one physical device is simulated on another physical device.
3. Allocating: physically assigning a device to a process.
4. Actions with regard to completion of I/O (interrupt servicing), error recovery, if there is any, and subsequently deallocating a device. Deallocation (policy-wise and technique-wise) may be done on either a process or a job level. On the job level, a device is assigned for as long as the job exists in the system. On a process level, a device may be assigned for as long as the process needs it.

In order to realize these basic functions, device management uses certain data structures that constitute the physical input–output control system (IOCS). Those are:

- Physical device table (PDT)
- Logical device table (LDT)
- Unit control block (UCB)
- I/O queue (IOQ)

The **physical device table** (PDT) is a system-wide data structure that contains information on all physical devices present in the system. Each row of this table contains the information on one physical device that consists of several fields; some notable ones are *device address*, *device type*, and *IOQ pointer*. The **logical device table** (LDT) is a per-process data structure that describes assignments to the logical devices used by the process. One copy of the LDT exists for every process in the system, and this copy is accessible from the PCB of the process. Both the PDT and LDT are fixed tables and are accessed by device numbers as keys. The **unit (device) control block** (UCB) is a data structure that represents a unit (device) in the operating system. This data structure contains all information that describes the characteristics of the device pertaining to the generic set of I/O operations that are supported by the I/O system. When a device is configured to the system, a UCB is created and inserted into the device list. An UCB is allocated only on demand when a process initiates an I/O operation and is destroyed when the I/O operation completes or terminates. The **I/O queue** (IOQ) is a waiting list of all processes pending for an I/O operations on a physical device when this device is busy with some other process. This wait queue contains a pointer to the corresponding UCB that, in turn, points to the corresponding queue of process control blocks of processes waiting for device access.

The PDT, LDT, and IOQ data structures reside within the kernel. The process creates a UCB on demand in its own address space, initializes its fields, and uses some of its fields (*device switch pointer*, etc.) as parameters in the physical call to device-specific I/O routines (device drivers) lying in the kernel space specified by the I/O request. The presence of the UCB in the address space of a user's process avoids many complexities, such as checking the status of an I/O operation, like "Get status info", without having to invoke the implicit system call required to enter the kernel space.

More details about all these tables with respective figures are given on the Support Material at www.routledge.com/9781032467238.

6.9.1   DEDICATED, SHARED, AND VIRTUAL DEVICES

I/O devices can be broadly classified into two distinct categories, ***dedicated devices*** and **shared devices**. Examples of *dedicated devices* are magnetic tapes and printers that are difficult to share between processes. A dedicated device is assigned to a job for the job's entire duration (job-level assignment) and is normally released by the system after the completion of the job. As long as the device is assigned to a job, no other users can get access to the device. A dedicated assignment is only effective if it is used by the job continuously. Otherwise poor utilization of devices may cause problems that eventually lead to severe degradation in the performance of the I/O system and the system as a whole.

Most direct access storage devices are *sharable devices*. Examples of shared devices are disk of all types and drums. Several processes can share access to a disk almost at the same time, because of the inherent direct-access nature of the disk system. If two or more processes simultaneously request a disk operation on a particular disk, all the requests will be accepted, and a scheduling mechanism based on a certain policy must then be employed to handle them in a specified order. Proper scheduling of disk access to service various requests arriving from different users is a major criteria in the performance of the entire system.

While processes have the benefit of virtual storage, they also have the benefits of **virtual devices**. These devices are actually simulated by the operating system, with data essentially kept either in the main store or on other devices, typically large disks. An example is the *spooling* systems, in which printer output is actually sent to a disk that waits for the printer to become available. The disk in this situation behaves like a virtual printer. When virtual devices are provided, the operating system must transparently deal with physical devices without any interference from processes. With the use of virtual devices, **dedicated devices** can be converted into **shared devices** through different techniques, such as spooling. For example, the output of a process to a printer can be spooled onto a disk, allowing the same printer to be used by another process simultaneously. Later, when the printer becomes available, all the spooled output of different users can be sent to the printer one after another to get the hard copy printout. Since a disk can be shared, it effectively converts a dedicated device into a shared one, changing a single printer into many virtual printers.

6.10   PHYSICAL I/O FUNCTION ORGANIZATION: LOGICAL STRUCTURING

The bewildering variety of only one class (e.g. hard disk, tapes, or CD-ROM) of device manufactured by different vendors using different types of technology requiring completely different controlling programs (device controllers) for their operation and to attach these numerous devices to computers is one of the grand challenges of OS designers and developers. Each brand of disk, channel, tape, or communication device has its own control protocol, and new devices with diverse characteristics are frequently introduced in the market. It is thus essential to reduce this variety to some sort of order; otherwise, whenever a new device is to be attached to the computer, the operating system (device management) will have to be completely reworked to accommodate it. In order to get rid of this problem, it is required to organize the physical I/O function into a regular structure, at least at some level inside the kernel, that can work well across a wide range of different class of devices. The device-specific parts of device control can then be sequestered into well-defined modules. This idea eventually gave rise to the concept of organizing the physical I/O function into an appropriate logical structure.

The concept of hierarchical-level structuring as implemented in the design of an operating system (Chapter 3) can also be similarly mapped in the design of device management (I/O software) to realize the desired I/O functions. The ultimate objective of implementing this approach in the design of device management is to organize the software, decomposing it into a series of layers in which each layer in the hierarchy is entrusted with performing small manageable subfunctions of the whole. Each such layer has its own form of abstractions and relies on the next lower layer, which performs more primitive functions, but it hides the details of these functions and the peculiarities of the hardware associated with the next lower layer. At the same time, it offers services to the next higher layer, and this upper one is more concerned with presenting a relatively clean, regular interface to the users. Conclusively, at the outset, this layered concept in the design and subsequent realization of device management still nicely matches with the environment, fulfills its primary requirement to interact at one end directly with the computer hardware, and communicates with the user processes through its other end. However, the number of layers involved in the organization used by most device management systems (not all) may vary from one device to another depending on the class of device and the application. Three such representative classes of devices present in the system are *local peripheral devices* (console, printer, etc.), *communication devices* (involved in network architecture using the ISO-OSI model or TCP/IP), and *file-based secondary devices* (storage devices supporting the file system). The layering in the design of the device management of each of these classes is obviously different.

Brief details on different types of layering in the organization of these three different classes of devices with respective figures are given separately on the Support Material at www.routledge.com/9781032467238.

6.11 DEVICE MANAGER: ITS CONSTITUENTS AND DESIGN PRINCIPLES

Each OS defines an architecture for its own device management system, but that usually varies among systems, and as such there exists no universal organization. However, the design of a generalized device management system can be obtained following the concept described in the last section by logically structuring the physical I/O operation. In fact, this principle can be used as a guideline by mapping each layer of the logical structure into a corresponding software module, and in this way, the entire device management software can be developed that actually comprises of various constituent software at different levels, each one at certain level performing a specific responsibility that ultimately gives rise to realize the entire I/O functions and facilities.

Figure 6.3 illustrates a representative device management system design in a comprehensive and efficient way by structuring I/O software into different layers and indicates the principal functions that each layer performs. It is interesting to note that each layer in Figure 6.3 has an almost one-to-one correspondence with each of the lower three layers as shown in Figure 6.8 on the Support Material at www.routledge.com/9781032467238. For example, logical I/O (Figure 6.8a on the Support Material at www.routledge.com/9781032467238) corresponds to device-independent software (Figure 6.3). Similarly, device I/O corresponds to device drivers, and control I/O corresponds to scheduler and interrupt handler. The module user-level I/O software at the top of device management is a part of device management but resides outside its domain and is critically linked to user

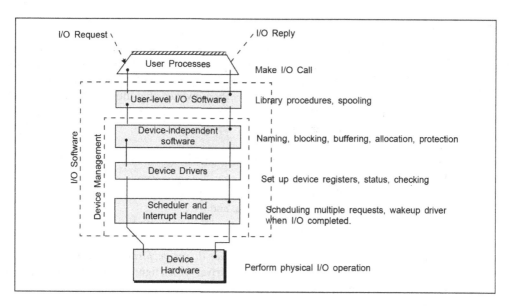

FIGURE 6.3 Pictorial representation of layered structure of the generic Device Management system (I/O system) and the main function of each layer.

software and even runs outside the kernel. For example, when a user program attempts to read a block from a file, device management (operating system) is invoked to carry out the operation. The device-independent software first searches the cache, for example, to find whether the block is available. If the desired block is not present in the cache, it calls the device driver, which, in turn, issues the appropriate request to the hardware. The process is then blocked (sleep) until the related disk operation is completed.

When the related disk operation is over, the device hardware generates an interrupt. The interrupt handler takes control, runs the respective interrupt service routine to resolve the interrupt that extracts the status from the device, checks whether the related disk operation is successfully completed, and if so finally wakes up the sleeping process to finish the I/O request and let the user process continue again. We now discuss each individual layer separately, as shown in Figure 6.3, one after another starting from the bottom, and show how the various layers of device management fit together.

6.11.1 Scheduler and Interrupt Handler

When an I/O instruction in a user process is executed, an I/O request is issued. It is handled by device-independent software to identify the needed device driver, and the respective device driver process is then started. When the device driver issues an I/O command to access the respective device (hardware) for needed I/O operation, the driver process itself is blocked until the respective I/O operation is completed and the interrupt occurs. The scheduler will now come into action to schedule the already-received driver's request in a queue if multiple requests have already arrived for the same device; otherwise the driver's request is immediately attained. The **I/O scheduler** uses certain pre-defined policy to decide when an I/O module (or the IOP) is to be assigned to a request and sets up the path to the device. When the request is scheduled, its turn comes, it gains access to the device, and the needed I/O operation starts. After the completion of the I/O operation, an interrupt will be issued by the device controller of the respective device and is received by the interrupt handler, which services the interrupt using the respective ISR located very close to the hardware that, in turn, activates the blocked driver process. In this way, control flows upwards and ultimately allows the user process to continue its execution with the next instruction.

6.11.2 DEVICE DRIVERS

I/O instruction of very different sorts of requests, such as; *open*, *read*, *write*, and *close*, from user processes goes to the device-independent software that converts it to device-dependent code consisting of specific I/O operation code, including the device as requested, which ultimately goes to the layer *device drivers*. The specific device driver is then invoked that ultimately carries out the needed I/O operation with the help of the device controller attached to the requested device. The functions that the I/O device driver performs are:

- to determine the I/O command or create the channel program in order to perform the desired I/O operation,
- to initiate I/O to the particular device through the respective I/O modules,
- to handle the interrupts arrived from the device, and
- to optimize its performance.

In summary, from the user's end, it appears that *the device driver performs the entire physical I/O*.
   The details of I/O operations executed by the device driver with a figure are given on the Support Material at www.routledge.com/9781032467238.

6.11.2.1 Case Study: UNIX Device Drivers

The beauty of UNIX lies in its explicit attempts to simplify the application programming model for files and devices as similar as possible. The upper part (as shown in Figure 6.10 on the Support Material at www.routledge.com/9781032467238) of the UNIX device driver (API) uses operation names similar to the file interface, although they apply to physical devices rather than to an abstraction of storage. Device drivers here are intended to be accessed by user-space code. If an application accesses a driver, it uses one of two standardized interfaces: the *block-oriented device interface* or *character-oriented device interface*. Both interfaces define a fixed set of functions, such as; *open*, *read*, *write*, *close*, and *select*. Any driver can implement a subset of the functions appropriate for that particular device according to the device characteristics, the strategies of driver design, and the requirements of the driver. When an application in the user space calls the driver, it performs a system call. The kernel then looks up the entry point for the device in the block or character *indirect reference table* (the *jump table*), then calls the entry point. The exact semantics of each function depends on the name of the device and the intent of the driver design. Hence, the function names provide only a purpose for each. In the UNIX family of systems, the logical contents of the jump table are kept in the system in the /dev directory. However, a UNIX driver comprises three main parts:

- System initialization code
- Code to initiate device operations
- Device interrupt handlers

The *initialization code* is run when the system is bootstrapped. It scans and tests for the physical presence of the devices and then initializes them. The upper part of the device driver (API) implements functions for a subset of entry points (as shown in Table 6.1). This part of the code also provides information to the kernel (the lower part shown in Figure 6.10 on the Support Material at www.routledge.com/9781032467238) as to which functions are implemented. The *device interrupt handler* is called by the system interrupt handler that corresponds to the physical device causing the interrupt.
   The devices and the respective drivers are usually installed by the system people following certain steps. The information required at the time of installing a driver can be incorporated into a configuration file and then processed by the configuration builder tool, */etc/config*, to build a *makefile* capable of building the kernel.
   Table 6.1 containing BSD UNIX driver entry points is given on the Support Material at www.routledge.com/9781032467238.

6.11.3 Device-Independent Software

The design of device management is different in different operating systems, particularly in describing how a specific operating system will identify its device resources so that the respective device driver can be invoked to execute the prescribed I/O operations. In spite of having many differences, almost all contemporary operating systems hide all device-specific aspects and peculiarities from users and provide an abstraction of physical devices by a standard symbolic name known as a logical device to the users. Some systems often extend this view to the entire I/O system by treating I/O devices as files (where all I/O devices appear to users as a set of files, augmenting the fundamental notion of the file as a linear array of character or records), possibly with some special attributes. For example, a text file may be printed using a COPY operation where the destination "file" is a printer device. Whatever it may be, this approach enables the user to access and manage both I/O devices and usual files through a single unified system call and file manipulation services. This is often called device-independent I/O. The ultimate aim of this concept is to relieve the user process from the burden of explicitly mentioning the devices, irrespective of its actual physical identity. Device independence actually facilitates program portability and the added flexibility of changing devices and files specifications even at runtime.

Implementation of this approach requires adequate support from the device management of the operating system, and that is accomplished by the device-independent software module, which is assumed to be the first level of the device management system. This level performs its responsibilities by creating a useful interface that maps the logical devices used in I/O instructions issued in the user space to each of their specific machine-recognizable patterns, adding many device-related attributes that can ultimately be executed by the respective physical devices using their own device drivers and the particular device controller. In addition, the device-independent software performs the I/O functions that are common to all devices and provides a uniform interface to its upper layer, the user-level software, irrespective of the type of the devices.

In different operating systems, the design of the device-independent software may be different, causing device management itself to be different. However, the specific responsibilities (functions) that the device-independent software usually performs that are common to most of the operating systems are the following. But the exact boundary between device-independent software and device-dependent software (a device driver that resides just at its lower level) depends on its design criteria and therefore is system dependent. One possible reason for such differences in its design is that some functions that could be carried out in a device-independent way may actually be done in the drivers for the sake of increasing efficiency or to meet some other goal. However, the functions that are typically common in most device-independent software are:

- Uniform interfacing for its upper layer, user-level software
- Uniform interfacing for its lower layers, device drivers
- Device naming
- Ensuring device-independent block size
- Providing storage allocation on block devices
- Allocating and releasing dedicated devices
- Device protection
- Error handling
- Buffering

Uniform naming of devices helps to identify the particular physical device and locate the respective driver. Symbolic device names may be used as parameters when invoking the respective drivers as well as the specific operation (read or write) it will carry out on the device.

Brief details on the different functions of this software are given on the Support Material at www.routledge.com/9781032467238.

6.11.4 User-Level I/O Software

I/O software that is responsible for managing and controlling devices is mostly confined within the domain of operating system and works in supervisor mode. However, a small portion of it that consists of libraries is closely related to user programs, and when linked with user programs during runtime, all these programs start running outside the kernel. In UNIX systems, system calls, including I/O system calls, are normally made by library procedures. For example, when a C program contains a call like

read (id, no_of_bytes, in_buffer)

the corresponding library procedure in binary form is brought into memory and will be linked with the calling user program at runtime. All other similar procedures that involve I/O are collectively contained in a standard I/O library, which is clearly a part of the operating system, but all run as part of the user programs outside the boundary of the operating system. Still, there is other user-level software that is related to any such library procedure. **Spooling** is such an I/O function related to dedicated devices, such as; a printer, that permits any user process to open a character-special file for the printer and then fill the file with data to be printed, if the printer device is either busy or not available. A spooling mechanism is also often used in the network environment when transferring a file over the network.

Brief details on this topic are given on the Support Material at www.routledge.com/9781032467238.

6.12 I/O BUFFERING

To accomplish an I/O operation, the simplest way is to issue an I/O command and then wait for the data to become available. This waiting may either be busy-waiting (continuously testing the device status) or, more practically, blocking of process on an interrupt until the entire I/O is completed and subsequent arrival of an interrupt from the device-end declaring the completion of I/O that unblocks the said process, apart from quite slow operation of the devices themselves. All these together create a hindrance in the overall execution of the process and also badly affect the other operating-system declared policies. The I/O wait time could only be reduced if the data are made available in memory whenever the process needs it and, if possible, if the input can be transferred in advance of requests being made and the output can be transferred sometime after the request is made. The basic approach in this regard would be to overlap the processing of one record with the reading of the next record (or writing of the previous record) that eventually could reduce the I/O wait time literally zero if I/O for the next (previous) record were completed by the time the previous (next) record is processed. To achieve this goal, the technique used is known as **buffering**. Different forms of buffering schemes exist that are supported by different operating systems to attain different objectives, but all of them necessarily aim to ultimately improve the performance of their own system.

An *I/O buffer* is usually a memory area temporarily used to store data involved in an I/O operation. Buffering is a technique which uses this I/O buffer to provide overlap of the I/O and allied subsequent CPU (or IOP) activities in a process that essentially reduces the I/O wait time. This means that the device manager, by means of using this technique, can keep slower I/O devices busy during times when a process does not really require I/O operations. As already mentioned, this can be achieved by

- *Input buffering*: *Pre-fetching* an input record by having the input device read information into an I/O buffer before the process requests it, or
- *Output buffering*: *Post-writing* an output record from an I/O buffer to the I/O device while the process continues its own execution.

Input buffering can be started to read the next record on an I/O buffer sometime before the record is needed by the process. This may be carried out while the CPU (IOP) is processing the previous record. By overlapping a part of I/O operation time with CPU (or IOP) processing time, the actual time needed for completion of an I/O operation would be comparatively less and lead to less wastage. In the case of output buffering, the record to be written is simply copied into an I/O buffer when the process issues a write operation. Actual output can be conveniently performed from this I/O buffer to the destined location sometime later. It can also be overlapped with processing or a part of processing for the next record.

The use of two system buffers, called **double buffering**, in place of a single buffer in the I/O operation can make the buffering mechanism even more efficient and effective, although there exists a distinct difference in the operation of a double buffer from that of a single buffer. But, sometimes it is found that even double buffering is not enough to reasonably reduce the problem of I/O waiting, especially in situations when the process enters rapid I/O bursts. That situation requires more than two buffers to smooth out I/O operation, and that is why **multiple buffers** are employed to handle this environment.

While the buffering technique intuitively always attempts to smooth out peaks in I/O demand, the effect of buffering on performance depends mostly on the process's characteristics. In the case of an I/O-bound process, use of buffers often yields substantial performance improvement, whereas for a CPU (compute)-bound process, the situation is exactly the reverse. However, in either case, no amount of buffering is adequate to allow an I/O device to keep pace with a process indefinitely, particularly in situation when the average demand of the process becomes greater than the I/O device can support. Nevertheless, generally in a multiprogramming environment, it has been observed that, within the system, there is a nearly homogeneous mixture of various I/O-bound and CPU-bound processes to service. Buffering technique thus emerges as a powerful tool that can ultimately increase the performance of each individual process, and thereby enhance the efficiency of the operating system as a whole.

Different forms of I/O buffering and their operations with figures are given on the Support Material at www.routledge.com/9781032467238.

6.13 CLOCK

In computer systems, the timing order in which events are to happen is critical, and the hardware in computers uses clocks that are different from usual clocks to realize synchronization. **Clocks**, also called **timers**, mainly prevent one process from monopolizing the CPU, among other things. The *clock software* generally takes the form of a device driver, even though a clock is neither a block device, like a disk, nor a character device, like a terminal or printer. A clock in this context is a circuit that emits series of pulses with a precise pulse width and specified interval between consecutive pulses. The interval between corresponding edges of two consecutive pulses is called the *clock cycle time*. Pulse frequencies are commonly between 1 and 100 MHz or correspond to clock cycles of 1000 nsec to 10 nsec. To achieve high accuracy, the clock frequency is usually controlled by a crystal oscillator. The existing clock cycle can also be divided into subcycles. A common way of providing finer resolution than the basic clock is to tap the primary clock line and insert a circuit with known delay in it, thereby generating secondary clock signal that is phase-shifted from the primary (basic clock) one.

6.13.1 CLOCK HARDWARE

Clocks come in several styles. However, clocks used in computers are commonly of two classes. The simplest, a **line clock**, is tied to the 110- or 220-volt power line and causes an interrupt on every voltage cycle, at 50 or 60 Hz (i.e. the 50th or 60th part of a second). The other kind of clock in this class is built using an additional hardware circuit that generates a periodic signal of high accuracy. The other class of clock are **programmable clocks**, which typically have several modes of operation, *one-shot mode*, and *square-wave mode*. However, irrespective of its class, the time interval between two consecutive interrupts caused by the clock during its operation is called a **clock tick**.

The **advantage** of a programmable clock is that its interrupt frequency (the time interval between two consecutive interrupts) can be controlled by software. If a 1-MHz crystal is used, then the counter will be pulsed every microsecond. With a 16-bit register, interrupts can be programmed to occur at rates from 1 to 65535 microsec. Programmable clock chips, however, usually contain two or three independently programmable clocks and have many other options as well.

To implement a **time-of-day clock**, the software asks the user for the current time, which is then *translated* into the number of *clock ticks*. At every clock tick, the real time is incremented by one count. To prevent the current time from being lost when the computer's power is turned off, some computers store the real time in a special register powered by a battery (battery backup).

The hardware design of a clock with a figure is given on the Support Material at www.routledge.com/9781032467238.

6.13.2 Clock Software (Clock Device Drivers)

The hardware of the clock is responsible only for generating interrupts at known intervals. Everything else involving time must be done by the software, **the clock driver**. The exact duties of the clock driver vary among operating systems but usually include most of the following:

1. Maintaining the time of day.
2. Allowing processes to run only for the specified time they are assigned to.
3. Handling the ALRAM system call made by user processes.
4. Accounting for CPU and other resource usage.
5. Providing *watchdog timers* for parts of the system itself.
6. Doing profiling, monitoring, and statistics gathering.

Discussions on each mentioned point with figures are given on the Support Material at www.routledge.com/9781032467238.

6.14 MAGNETIC DISK I/O

Disk is slower, cheaper, and usually much larger secondary (serial) memory using direct-access in contrast to random-access primary memories that hold the bulk of information, which is also *persistent*, meaning that the stored information is not lost even when the power is turned off. Its read–write circuitry is shared among different storage locations. The information is read from and written to the device a chunk of bytes or words at a time. These bytes or words are usually grouped into larger units called **blocks**. Hence, the disk is called a block-oriented device. In fact, the size of a block in a disk is mostly determined by the characteristics of the device and its controller. However, the disk is the most important secondary device, the performance of which greatly influences the computer environment as a whole, and is a major factor that has an immense impact on the performance of the entire system. We will describe here some of the major physical characteristics of the disk and will then highlight some of the key issues and a few of the most important approaches that can possibly enhance disk performance as a whole.

Brief details on this topic are given on the Support Material at www.routledge.com/9781032467238.

6.14.1 Physical Characteristics

There are some typical important physical characteristics that make a difference among the various types of magnetic disks. Although this area actually lies in the domain of computer organization and architecture (Chakraborty, 2020), we will here mention all these in a nutshell for the sake of completeness.

- **Head/storage media movement:** Fixed-head disk, movable-head disk
- **Platters:** Single-platter, multiple-platter

- **Sides:** Single-sided, double-sided
- **Portability:** Non-removable disk, removable disk
- **Head mechanisms:** Contact (magnetic tape), fixed gap, aerodynamic gap (Winchester)

Brief details on this topic are given on the Support Material at www.routledge.com/9781032467238.

6.14.2 DISK COMPONENTS AND ORGANIZATION

Every disk is physically a flat circular object called a *platter* coated with an emulsion of magnetic material that is rotated around its own axis. As shown in Figure 6.4, the surface is organized by drawing a set of fixed paths or **tracks**, which are concentric sets of rings (or sets of parallel lines in tapes), and each track consists of a sequence of cells, each cell capable of storing 1 bit of information. Each track is the same width as the head. There are thousands of tracks per surface. Adjacent tracks are separated by gaps known as **intertrack gaps** (Figure 6.4). The read–write head, fixed on an arm, can move radially over the platter due to the radial movement of the arm to perform read/write serially along a track on a surface. Each track is logically divided into several **sectors**, defined as an angular portion of the track that stores a physical block of information. Sectors may be of fixed or variable length, but they are always a power of 2 to optimize use of the disk surface as well as to ease the recording mechanism. In most contemporary systems, fixed-length sectors are used, with 512 (= 2^9) bytes being the nearly universal sector size for the sake of operational ease. However, the number of blocks stored on the disk is determined by the number of tracks with the number of sectors on each track present in the disk platter. Drawing of tracks on the surface, along with fixing the *start* and *end* *points* of every track and every sector, is done by means of generating control data (the system's own data) on the disk accomplished at the time of formatting the disk. Hence, the disk cannot be used without formatting. These extra data recorded on the disk are used by the disk drive and not accessible to the user. In addition, adjacent sectors are also separated by **intersector** (similar to intertrack) gaps.

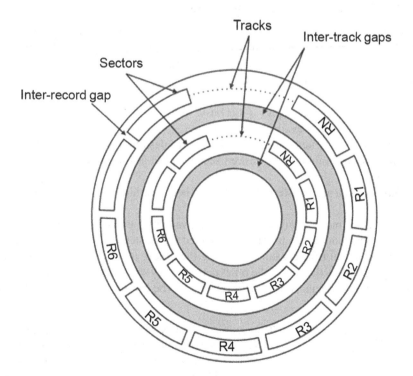

FIGURE 6.4 A representative scheme showing data layout arrangement in magnetic disk (hard disk).

Higher disk capacities are obtained by mounting many platters vertically, spaced at a definite distance from each other on the same spindle to form a *disk pack*. The disk pack is provided with a single movable arm with many fixed branches. The number of branches present in such an arm depends on the number of platters available in the disk pack. Each branch of the arm holds two read/write heads, one for the lower circular surface of a platter and the other for the upper circular surface of the next platter of the disk pack. Because of engineering economics for devices, the read/write heads attached to different branches of a single movable arm are positioned over a particular track on both sides of different platters (except possibly the topmost and the bottommost one) while the media rotates under/over the heads. All these identically positioned tracks (both top and bottom surface of each platter) on different platters' surfaces together constitute what is called a **cylinder** of the disk. This notion of a cylinder is an important property in the I/O operation of a disk pack. If the records can be organized to be placed in the same cylinder (identical tracks on different platters), the I/O operations on such records can then immediately be carried out without further movement of the heads, thereby saving a substantial amount of time needed for the mechanical movement of the heads for the correct placement. The disk pack can now be looked upon as consisting of a set of concentric cylinders between the innermost cylinder, which consists of the innermost tracks of all surfaces, and the outermost cylinder, which consists of the outermost tracks of all surfaces.

A physical disk record is normally stored in the disk pack on one track in one sector on one surface of the disk or may be extended on other sectors that may be on the same surface or on the other side of the platter or even on different platters depending on the nature of formatting, which does sector numbering (or *interleaving*). A *record's address* is usually specified as (*cylinder number, surface number, record number*), and the commands supported by a disk device are **read/write** [*record–address, addr* (*I/O-area*)] and **seek** (*cylinder number, surface number*).

More about this topic with related figures is given on the Support Material at www.routledge.com/9781032467238.

6.15   DISK I/O OPERATION: PARAMETERS

An I/O operation on a record using a record address actually depends mostly on the computer system, the nature of the I/O channel and disk controller hardware, and also on the operating system being used. However, the following steps are, in general, involved when information is transferred to and from any disk after initiation of a disk I/O operation.

1. Wait until the device is available, if it is busy.
2. Wait until the channel is available, if it is busy.
3. Wait until the read–write head is positioned on the desired track.
4. Wait until the beginning of the desired sector on the accessed track comes under read–write head.
5. Wait until the data are transferred serially and not in parallel to and from the disk.

Each step will consume a certain amount of time (wait time), except for the first one, if the disk is readily available. The total duration of time consumed by the steps 2 to 5 is considered *device busy time*. However, the actual time consumed to bring the disk to a position to begin the data transfer operation in any disk I/O is the sum of the times consumed by steps 3 and 4, and this is mandatory for any disk I/O operation to begin. However, the total time to be consumed for any disk I/O operation is:

$$
\begin{matrix}
\text{Total time required to} \\
\text{transfer an information in} \\
\text{I/O operation}
\end{matrix}
=
\begin{matrix}
\text{Time required to place the} \\
\text{head at the beginning of the} \\
\text{target location [step 3 + 4]} \\
(\textit{Access time})
\end{matrix}
+
\begin{matrix}
\text{Time required only to} \\
\text{transfer the actual} \\
\text{information (step 5)} \\
(\textit{Transfer time})
\end{matrix}
$$

The wait time in step 3 is the time required by the movable-head disk system to position the head at the right track to perform the needed data transfer. This is known as **seek time**. When step 3 is over, that is, the track is selected, and the head is positioned on the right track, step 4 starts. The wait time in step 4 is the time consumed by the disk controller until the target sector (which may be on the wrong part of the moving track) arrives just under the head so that data transfer can start. The average time needed for this movement to occur is called the **rotational delay** or **rotational latency**. After consuming these two mandatory times (steps 3 and 4), known as **access time**, the current position of the disk and the head can start physical data transfer. Now, the data transfer starts (step 5) as the sector moves serially under the head. The time required for the transfer of all the needed information is the **transfer time**. This transfer time varies depending on the amount of information to be transferred (say, 40 bytes or 15 words) as well as on the **data transfer rate** that the specific disk and its controller can provide. However, the data transfer rate can never be reduced by adopting any kind of policy/strategy unless the electronic technology used in the disk is modified. That is why, apart from the size of the disk to take into account, the *access time* as well as its *transfer time* are considered vital parameters at the time of selection.

Apart from the delays caused by the *access time* as well as the *transfer time*, there may be several other delays caused by *queuing* normally associated with a disk I/O operation in situations when a process issues an I/O request, but most of the time, it has to wait first in a queue for the device to be available (step 1). Another form of delay may occur, particularly with some mainframe systems that use a technique known as *rotational positional sensing* (RPS).

Seek Time (t_S): This time is required by the disk to place its movable arm on the required track and mostly depends on two key factors; the initial startup time of the arm that is required for its movement and the time taken by the arm to pass over the tracks radialy to reach the target track once the access arm has taken up speed. The average seek time is t_S to place the head on the right track.

Rotational Delay: This delay mostly depends on the speed of rotation of the disk. Let the disk is rotating i.e. each track is rotating at the speed of r revolutions per second. The start of the block to be transferred may be just under the head or at any position on the track. Hence, on average, half a revolution is required to get to the beginning of the desired sector under the head. This time is the latency time, which is equal to $(2r)^{-1}$ seconds.

Transfer Time: The transfer time to and from the disk mostly depends on the data transfer rate in which the rotation speed of the disk is a dominating factor. To make a rough estimate of this transfer time, let us assume that each track has a capacity of N words that (i.e. the disk) rotates at the speed of r revolutions per second. The data transfer rate of the memory is r.N words per second. The size of the block to be transferred is n words. The time required to transfer n words is $n \times (r.N)^{-1}$ seconds. Hence, once the read–write head is positioned at the right track at the start of the desired block, the physical time to be taken only to transfer the desired block is $n \times (r.N)^{-1}$ seconds.

Hence, the total time required to transfer an information of a block of n words in a disk I/O operation can be expressed as

$$t_B = t_S + (2r)^{-1} + n \times (r.N)^{-1} \text{ seconds}$$

where the symbols here have their usual significances, as already mentioned.

More about this topic is given on the Support Material at www.routledge.com/9781032467238.

6.16 DISK MANAGEMENT: DATA ORGANIZATION AND FORMATTING

Data are organized on the sectors of the concentric tracks on the disk surface. In an I/O operation, data are transferred in a single block to and from memory using the buffering technique. In a read operation, the data transfer starts only after the entire block of data is read off the device. When this transfer is started and is in progress, the disk is continually revolving, and one or more sectors may pass under the head by the time the transfer is completed. Hence, an attempt to read just the next consecutive sector cannot succeed in the same revolution of the disk. In the case of a write operation, the effect is the same: data transfer from the disk buffer takes place before writing of the data on the disk is initiated, and consequently data cannot be written into just the next consecutive sector in the same revolution. In both cases, the throughput of the disk device is severely affected.

To avoid this problem caused by data transfer time, it may then be necessary to read one block and then skip one, two, or even more blocks. Skipping blocks to give the disk drive enough time to transfer data to and from memory is called **interleaving**. This technique separates consecutively numbered sectors on a track by putting other sectors between them. The expectation is that the data transfer involved in reading/writing a sector can be completed by the time before the next consecutively numbered sector passes under the head. Interleaving is realized when the disk is formatted, taking into account the *interleave factor* (*inf*), which is the number of sectors that separate consecutively numbered sectors on the same track of the disk. Numbering of sectors in this way by choosing a suitable interleaving factor would at least enable the disk drive to read consecutively numbered sectors with ease and still achieve the maximum speed, of course within the limits of the underlying hardware capability.

Another problem is observed when the first sector of any platter is to be read immediately after reading the last sector of the previous platter in the same cylinder. The read operation in this case is required to be switched between heads positioned on different platters. As a result, a delay is caused, known as **head switching time**. This is sometimes predominant, particularly in the processing of sequential file when the last sector on a platter has been read before the next read operation starts. Such **head skewing** staggers the start of tracks on different platters in the same cylinder. One possible solution is that the times when the last sector of a track and the first sector of the next track in the same cylinder pass under their respective heads must be separated by the head switch time. Still, one more problem is found in situations in which the head is required to be moved to the next cylinder, and this naturally consumes the needed seek time. **Cylinder skewing** is analogous to head skewing and similarly staggers the start of a track on consecutive cylinders to allow for the seek time.

However, interleaving is not as important in modern disks, which are equipped with sophisticated controllers that can transfer data to and from memory at faster speeds and high rates. Modern disks are more concerned with head and cylinder skewing. Still, sector interleaving is important, since it offers an insight that provides a means to optimize disk throughput as far as possible by way of data staggering.

More about this topic with a figure is given on the Support Material at www.routledge.com/9781032467238.

6.17 DISK ACCESS TIME MANAGEMENT: DISK ARM SCHEDULING POLICIES

The performance of a disk driver is ultimately concerned with the time to read or write a disk block, which again depends on three main elements, as already described: the *seek time*, the *rotational delay*, and the *actual transfer time*. Here, the third one entirely depends on both the data transfer rate and the amount of information to be transferred and hence is not considered a factor in disk management. The second one, rotational delay, is caused when accessing a specific sector, and this sector access involves selection of tracks, which is linked to seek time. Moreover, seek times are usually an order of magnitude greater than rotational delay, and if track selection takes place at random, then the average seek time abruptly increases and the performance of the disk system will then drop drastically. That is why for most disks, *the seek time dominates*, so at the time of disk management, *attempts should be made to ultimately reduce the average time spent on seeks*, which can consequently improve the system performance substantially. Minimization of rotational delay, on the other hand, has very little effect on overall system performance.

The seek time for a specific disk block to service an I/O request depends on the position of the block relative to the current position of the disk heads. In a multitasking environment, there will normally be a number of I/O requests arriving from various processes to a single disk that are maintained in a queue and are serviced successively. This often requires access to random locations (tracks) on the disk, even if the items are selected (scheduled) from the queue at random. Consequently, in a multitasking environment, the total seek time involved in servicing all I/O requests for a particular device abruptly increases. This indicates that the order in which these items are to be selected to perform their individual I/O operations eventually determines the total seek time needed to service all the I/O requests after visiting all the required tracks. Moreover, when the same disk pack is used both for secondary store (files) and backing store (swap space), the swap space should be kept on the tracks halfway between the center and the edge, because the items in this location can then be accessed with the lowest average seek time. However, the main objective ultimately aims to always bring down the total seek time as much as possible so as to increase the throughput (which is the number of I/O operations performed per second) of a disk that, in turn, *depends on the order* in which I/O requests are to be serviced.

Therefore, it is necessary to introduce suitable ordering in disk I/O operations that will ultimately give rise to some specific *disk* (track) *scheduling policy* to be obeyed by the physical IOCS and the device drivers. Since scheduling policies always attempt to minimize the wasted time in executing lengthy seeks, they will inevitably improve the throughput as well as the overall system performance, but individual requests sometimes may be affected adversely. In general, disk-head scheduling is defined based on the following assumptions:

- There is only one disk drive. If there are several, each is to be scheduled independently.
- All requests are for single, equal-sized blocks.
- Requested blocks are randomly distributed on the disk pack.
- The disk drive has only one movable arm, and all read/write heads are attached to that one arm.
- Seek latency is linear in the number of tracks crossed (this assumption fails if the disk controller has mapped tracks at the end of the disk to replace ones that have bad sectors).
- The disk controller does not introduce any appreciable delays.
- Read and write requests take identical time to service.

Disk scheduling requires a careful examination of pending requests to determine the most efficient way to service all the requests. A disk scheduler examines the positional relationship among waiting requests. The queue of requesting processes is then reordered so that the requests can be serviced with minimum head movement. We now examine some of the common disk scheduling policies that aim to optimize the total seek time for a number of I/O requests available in the queue at any instant. We assume a disk of 100 tracks or cylinders and that the disk request queue has random requests in it. Assume that a queue of requested tracks in the order as received by the disk scheduler is 20, 15, 30, 10, 45, 55, 35, 5, 95, 85. The various scheduling algorithms will now be explained based on this request queue, and each algorithm will use this queue to show its respective performance.

6.17.1 RANDOM SCHEDULING

If the item to be serviced is selected from the queue in any random order, it is called random scheduling. Under this policy, it can be expected that the tracks to be visited to service individual requests will also occur randomly, thereby yielding poor performance most of the time. Random scheduling is otherwise useful as a benchmark against which other policies can be ranked (evaluated).

6.17.2 First-In-First-Out/First-Come-First-Serve

The simplest form of disk scheduling is FIFO or FCFS scheduling, which processes items from the queue starting from the current item and proceeding in sequential order. As the requests arrive, they are placed at the end of the queue one after another according to their time of arrival. This policy is easy to implement and reasonably fair, because it ensures that every request will eventually be honored, and all the requests are serviced in the order they are received. However, every request here is likely to suffer from a seek operation.

Figure 6.5 shows the working of FIFO considering the queue as already mentioned. Initially, the read/write head is on cylinder 20. In FIFO scheduling, the head will now move from cylinder (track) 20 to cylinder 15, then from 15 to 30, then to 10, and so on, as shown in Figure 6.5. If t is the time taken to move the head from one track to the adjacent track, the total seek time in processing all the requests in the queue is:

$$5t + 15t + 20t + 35t + 10t + 20t + 30t + 90t + 10t = 235t$$

If there are only a few I/O requests in the queue, and if many of the requests are clustered closely in a disk region, then FIFO is expected to exhibit a moderately good performance. On the other hand, if there are many requests in the queue that are scattered, then the performance of FIFO will often become an approximation of random scheduling, and this performance may not always be acceptable. Thus, it is desirable to look at a more sophisticated scheduling policy that could yield a reasonable result. The principle and working of a number of such algorithms will now be considered and discussed.

Although FCFS is not an attractive approach on its own, but its refinements once again illustrate the law of diminishing returns. However, there are many alternatives to FCFS, and they are all much better. For example, the **Pickup** method keeps the requests in FCFS order to prevent starvation, but on its way to the track where the next request lies, it "picks up" any requests that can be serviced along the way.

6.17.3 Priority

The system that is designed on the priority principle will not consider the scheduling mechanism policy to lie under the domain of device management software. The aim of this approach is mostly

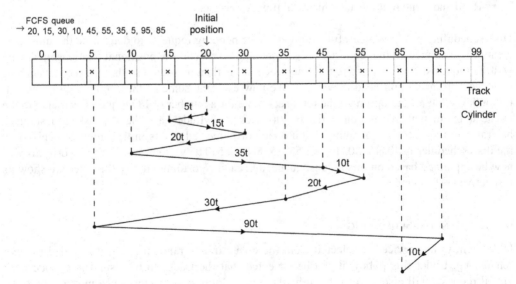

FIGURE 6.5 A representative sample example showing the implementation of disk–arm scheduling using FCFS (First Come First Serve) scheduling algorithm in magnetic disk.

to satisfy other objectives rather than to optimize disk throughput (performance). As in process scheduling, here also short batch jobs and interactive jobs are often given higher priority than longer jobs that require a longer time to complete their computations. In this way, this policy allows a lot of short jobs to leave the system quickly after finishing their tasks and thus may exhibit a good interactive response time. Consequently, this approach requires longer jobs to wait long times and even excessively long times if there is a continuous flow of short batch jobs and interactive jobs, which may eventually lead to starvation. In addition, this policy could sometimes lead to countermeasures on the part of users, who may split their original jobs into smaller pieces to beat the system. Furthermore, when this policy is employed for database systems, it tends to offer poor performance.

6.17.4 LAST-IN-FIRST-OUT

This policy always immediately schedules the most-recent request irrespective of all the requests already lying in the queue. Surprisingly, it is observed to have some merit, particularly in transaction processing systems, in which offering the device to the most recent user could result in little or almost no arm movement while moving through a sequential file. Exploiting the advantage of this locality, it improves disk throughput and reduces queue lengths as long as a job actively uses the file system. On the other hand, the distinct disadvantage of this approach is that if the disk remains busy because of a large workload, there is a high possibility of starvation. Once a job has entered an I/O request and been placed in the queue, it will fall back from the head of the line due to scheduling of the most-recent request, and the job can never regain the head of the line unless the queue in front of it empties.

FIFO, priority, and last-in-first-out (LIFO) scheduling policies are all guided by the desire of the requestor. In fact, the scheduler has no liberty to make any decision to schedule an item that may be appropriate to the existing position of the arm to optimize the throughput. However, if the track position is known to the scheduler, and the scheduler is free to select an item based on the current position of the arm, the following strategies can then be employed to carry out scheduling based on the items present in the queue, as requested.

6.17.5 SHORTEST-SEEK (SERVICE)-TIME-FIRST

In shortest-seek (service)-time-first (SSTF) scheduling, the request closest to the current head position is serviced first. In other words, the request that requires the least movement of the disk arm from its current position is serviced, thereby spending the minimum seek time. Always choosing the minimum seek time per individual request does not, of course, give any guarantee the average seek time will be minimized when a number of I/O requests (and thereby several arm movements) are serviced. However, this algorithm in all situations should always offer better performance than FIFO.

To explain the working of this policy, we are using the same queue as used in our last example of FCFS. The request for track 20 arrives first. While this request is being processed, other requests arrive and are queued up. For selection of the next request to be processed, the request which involves the least head movement is selected. Here, the I/O request involving track 15 is likely the right choice. After processing this request, the next request that involves the least head movement from the current head position (track 15) is now the request involving track 10 even though the request involving track 10 has arrived after the already-received request involving track 30. Successive choices are shown in Figure 6.6. The total seek time in this case is:

$$5t + 5t + 5t + 25t + 5t + 10t + 10t + 30t + 10t = 105t$$

Note that when the scheduling algorithm changes from FCFS to SSTF, there is a considerable reduction in seek time, from 235t to 105t. In fact, this algorithm, on average, cuts the total arm motion almost in half compared to FCFS.

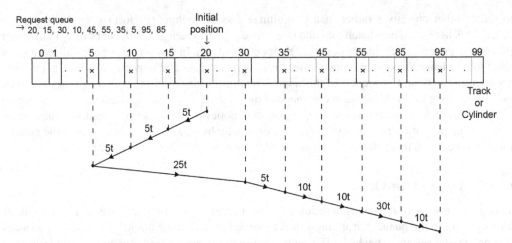

FIGURE 6.6 A representative sample example showing the implementation of disk–arm scheduling using Shortest Seek Time First (SSTF) scheduling algorithm in magnetic disk.

The SSTF policy is analogous to the shortest job first (SJF) policy of process scheduling. Hence, it achieves good disk throughput, but similar to the SJF algorithm, SSTF can cause starvation for some I/O requests. If a request is consistently bypassed, the disk must be incapable of keeping up with the disk requests in any case.

In a real situation, more requests usually keep coming in while the requests shown in Figure 6.6 are being processed. Consider the situation if, after moving to track 30 and while processing this request, a new request for track 25 arrives. So, after completing the request for track 30, it will take up the newly arrived request for track 25 (due to less arm movement), keeping the scheduled existing request for track 10 in the queue waiting. If another new request for track 15 then arrives while the request for track 25 is under process, then the arm will next go to track 15 instead of track 10. With a heavily loaded disk, it is observed that the arm will tend to stay in the middle of the disk most of the time, so requests at either extreme will have to wait indefinitely until a statistical fluctuation in the load causes there to be no requests near the middle. Thus, all requests that are far from the middle may suffer from starvation and receive poor service (not being attended). So the goals of minimal response time and fairness are in conflict, though overall throughput of the disk increases. This kind of starvation is not as bad as the underlying problem, in which it is very likely that the main memory allocation policy itself will cause thrashing.

However, SSTF always has the advantage of minimizing the total seek latency and saturating at the highest load of any policy. On the negative side, it tends to have a larger wait-time variance. Since this policy allows the arm to move in two directions at the time of selecting an item to service, a *random tie-breaking* algorithm may then be used to resolve cases of equal distances. In addition, SSTF and various other scan policies can be implemented more effectively if the request queues are maintained in sorted order by disk track number.

6.17.6 SCAN

In SSTF scheduling, the least movement of the arm in both directions for the purpose of selecting the right item is one of the reasons for starvation problem and can result in increasing seek time. Scan scheduling has been introduced to alleviate these problems of SSTF. In this method, the disk heads are required to move in one direction only, starting from one end of the disk (platter) and moving towards the other end, servicing I/O operations en route on each track or cylinder before moving on to the next one. This is called a *scan*. When the disk heads reach the last track in that direction (other end of the platter), the service direction of the head movement is reversed and the scan proceeds in the opposite direction (reverse scan) to process all existing requests in order,

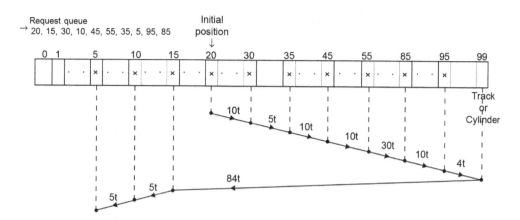

FIGURE 6.7 A representative sample example showing the implementation of disk–arm scheduling using SCAN scheduling algorithm in magnetic disk.

including new ones that have arrived. In this way, the head continuously scans back and forth across the full width of the disk.

Let us now explain the SCAN scheduling technique with our example queue of the previous two sections. Before applying SCAN, we should know the direction of the head movement as well as the last position of the read/write head. Let us assume that the head will be moving from left to right and the initial position of the head is on track 20. After servicing a request for track 20, it will service a request for track 30, then track 35, and so on, until it services the request for track 95. After that, it continues to move forward in the same direction until it reaches the last track in that direction (track number 99), even though there is no request to service. After reaching 99, the head movement will then be reversed, and on its way, it will service requests for track 15, then track 10, and then track 5. Figure 6.7 shows the sequence of operation using the SCAN algorithm. The total seek time here is:

$$10t + 5t + 10t + 10t + 30t + 10t + 4t + 84t + 5t + 5t = 173t$$

Time 4t indicates the time taken to move the head from track 95 (last request) to the last track (track number 99). As the head moves from left to right, servicing the requests on its path, new requests may arrive for tracks both ahead and behind the head. The newly arrived requests that are ahead of the current position of the head will be processed as usual as the head reaches the track of new requests during its forward journey. The newly arrived requests that are behind the head will be processed during the reverse journey of the head along with the pending older requests en route in order lying in the queue. These newly arrived requests may be processed before existing older ones, depending on the track position that the new items have requested. The older requests in this situation may have to wait longer than the newly arrived ones, leading to an increase in their response times.

It is to be noted that the SCAN policy is biased against the area most recently traversed. Thus, it does not exploit locality as an SSTF or even LIFO attribute. It is also interesting to observe that the SCAN policy favors those jobs whose requests are for tracks nearest both innermost and outermost tracks and equally inclined to the latest-arriving jobs. The first issue can be avoided by a circular SCAN, or C-SCAN, policy, while the second issue can be addressed by the N-step-SCAN policy.

6.17.7 LOOK OR ELEVATOR ALGORITHM

This algorithm is a slight variant of the existing SCAN algorithm. Here, the disk head keeps moving in the same direction until there are no more outstanding requests in the current direction. In practice, it appears more sensible, since the head only goes as far as the final request in each direction. The disk head at this point switches directions (instead of moving forward until the last

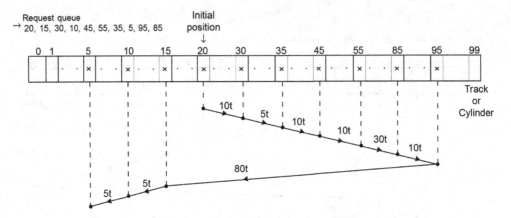

FIGURE 6.8   A representative sample example showing the implementation of disk–arm scheduling using elevator scheduling algorithm in magnetic disk.

track of the disk in that direction, as with SCAN) and then starts traversing in the reverse direction until the last request in this direction is met. This algorithm is known both in the disk world and the elevator world as the *elevator algorithm*. Often this algorithm is also called the *LOOK algorithm*, since it looks for a request before continuing to move in a given direction. The working of this algorithm requires the associated software to maintain 1 bit: the current direction bit, *UP* or *DOWN*. When a request completes, the disk or elevator driver checks the bit. If it is *UP*, the arm or cabin is moved to the next higher pending request, if any. If no request in the same direction is pending at higher position, the direction bit is reversed, and it is set *DOWN*; the movement of the head or cabin starts to move in the reverse direction to the next lower requested position, if any.

Figure 6.8 shows the sequence of operation of the elevator algorithm with the same example queue of the previous two sections The total seek time here is:

$$10t + 5t + 10t + 10t + 30t + 10t + 80t + 5t + 5t = 165t$$

6.17.8   Circular SCAN or C-SCAN

This scheduling policy performs a scan as in SCAN scheduling that again restricts scanning to *one direction* only. In fact, it is a variant of SCAN designed to produce a more uniform wait time. As with SCAN, the read/write head moves from one end to the other, servicing requests en route in order. Once it reaches the other end in one direction, it immediately jumps, returning to the beginning of the opposite end without servicing any request on the return trip, and the scan begins once again and the head starts moving again to the other end.

Figure 6.9 shows CSCAN scheduling for our representative example queue. The total seek time in this case is:

$$10t + 5t + 10t + 10t + 30t + 10t + 4t + 100t + 5t + 5t + 5t = 194t$$

C-SCAN reduces the maximum delay experienced by new requests. With SCAN, if the expected time for a scan from the inner track to the outer track is T, then the expected service interval for tracks at the periphery is 2T. With C-SCAN, this interval is on the order of $T + S_{max}$, where S_{max} is the maximum seek time.

6.17.9   C-LOOK

Similar to LOOK, which is a variant of SCAN algorithm, the C-LOOK algorithm is a variant of C-SCAN in the same fashion. Here, the disk head also keeps moving in the same direction until there are no more outstanding requests in the current direction. Once it reaches the last request in one direction, it

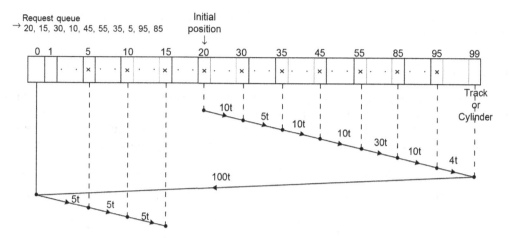

FIGURE 6.9 A representative sample example showing the implementation of disk–arm scheduling using Circular Scan or C-SCAN scheduling algorithm in magnetic disk.

immediately switches its direction and returns to the first-positioned request at the opposite end without servicing any request on the return trip, and the scan once again begins moving towards the other end.

In practical situations, it is observed that one or a few processes sometimes have high access rates to one specific track, thereby almost monopolizing the entire device by repeated requests to that track. High-density multi-platter disks, in particular, are likely to be very inclined to this type of functioning than their counterpart lower-density disks and/or disks with only one or two surfaces. To alleviate the problem of head movement remaining almost fixed on a specific track while responding to successive requests, the disk request queue can be segmented such that only one such segment is permitted to be processed entirely at a time. The N-step-SCAN and FSCAN policies use this approach.

6.17.10   N-step-SCAN

The N-step-SCAN policy usually segments the disk request-queue into sub-queues, each of length N. Sub-queues are processed one at a time using the SCAN algorithm. While a queue is being processed, new requests may arrive, and those must be added to some other queue. If fewer than N requests are available at the end of a scan, then all of them are processed with the next scan. For large values of N, the performance of N-step-SCAN tends to approach that of SCAN.

6.17.11   FSCAN

This policy is similar to N-step-SCAN but uses only two sub-queues. All of the requests already arrived are in one of the queues. The other queue remains empty. The processing of the filled-queue begins using the SCAN algorithm, and during the processing of this filled-queue, all new requests that arrive are put into the other queue. This queue will be serviced only after the completion of the queue under process. In this way, service of the new requests is deferred until all of the old requests are processed, thereby attempting to produce uniform wait times for all the requests on average.

6.17.12   Deadline Scheduling

The strategy and implementation mechanism of this approach are discussed in detail in "Device Management in Linux".

6.17.13   Anticipatory Scheduling

The strategy used in this approach is a further extension of the existing deadline scheduling method to negotiate the problems arising from the presence of synchronous I/O and has been efficiently implemented in advanced version of Linux (Linux 2.6). Its details can be seen in "Device Management in Linux".

6.18 RAID

Over a couple of decades, the speed of disk storage devices by far exhibited the smallest improvement when compared to that of processors and main memory due to continuous advances in electronic technology. Yet there has been a spectacular improvement in the storage capacity of these devices. However, magnetic disks inherently have several drawbacks. The most important of them are:

- They have relatively slow data-transfer rates.
- Their electromechanical construction is such that they are prone to both transient and catastrophic failures.

Computer users thus constantly clamor for disks that can provide larger capacity, faster access to data, high data-transfer rates, and of course, higher reliability. But those are generally expensive. Alternatively, it is possible to arrange a number of relatively low-cost devices in an array in which each one can act independently and also work in parallel with others to realize a considerable high performance at a reasonable cost. With such an arrangement of multiple disks, separate I/O requests can also be handled in parallel, as long as the data are located on separate disks. On the other hand, a single I/O request can be executed in parallel if the block of data to be accessed is distributed across multiple disks. Based on this idea, a storage system was proposed using small relatively inexpensive multiple disks (alternative to a single large one), called a *redundant array of inexpensive disks* (RAID), which offered a significant improvement in disk performance and also in reliability. Today, RAID technology is more appropriately called a *redundant array of independent disks*, adopting the term *independent* in place of *inexpensive* as accepted in the industry.

The presence of multiple disks using a RAID arrangement in the configuration opens a wide variety of ways to organize data, and redundancy can also be included to improve reliability. However, it raises difficulties in developing schemes for multiple-disk database design that can be equally usable on a number of different hardware platforms and operating systems. Fortunately, the industry has agreed on a standardized scheme to overcome this difficulty using RAID, which comprises seven universally accepted levels from zero through six, besides a few additional levels that have been proposed by some researchers. These levels do not indicate any hierarchical relationship; they rather designate different architectures in design that exhibit the following common characteristics:

- RAID consists of a set of physical disk drives, but to the operating system, it is recognized as a single logical disk drive.
- Data are distributed in different fashions across multiple physical disk drives present in the array.
- Redundant disk capacity is used to store parity information, which enables recovery of data at the time of any transient or catastrophic failure of a disk.

Different RAID levels differ essentially in the details of the second and third characteristics as mentioned above. But, only the third characteristic, however, is not supported by RAID 0 and RAID 1.

The RAID arrangement distributes the data involved in an I/O operation across several disks and performs the needed I/O operations on these disks in parallel. This feature can consequently provide fast access or a higher data transfer rate, but it depends on the arrangement of disks employed. The performance of any of the RAID levels critically depends on the request patterns of the host system and the layout of the data. High reliability is achieved by recording redundant information; however, the redundancy employed in a RAID arrangement is different by nature from that employed in conventional disks. A traditional disk uses a cyclic redundancy checksum (CRC) written at the end of each record for the sake of providing reliability, whereas redundancy techniques in a RAID employ extra disks to store redundant information so the original data can be recovered even if some disks fail. Recording of and access to redundant information does not consume any extra I/O time because both data and redundant information are recorded/accessed in parallel.

Disk striping: RAID technology uses a special technique known as *disk striping* that provides a way to achieve high data transfer rates during an I/O operation. A *disk strip* is a unit of data on a disk, which can be a disk block, a sector, or even an entire disk track. Identically positioned disk strips on different disks form a *disk stripe*. A file may be allocated an integral number of disk stripes. The data located in the strips of the same stripe can be read/written simultaneously because they reside on different disks. If the array contains *n* disks, the data transfer rate is expected, at least theoretically, to be *n* times faster than that of a single disk. However, the real data transfer rates as obtained by this arrangement may not be exactly equal to *n* times due to the presence of several factors that prevent parallelism of I/O operations from occurring smoothly. In fact, the implementations of disk striping arrangements and the redundancy techniques employed differ significantly from one level to another in the proposed various RAID organizations. Two main important metrics that determine the performance differences among these levels are:

- *Data transfer capacity (rate)*, or ability to move data, and
- *I/O request rate*, or ability to satisfy I/O requests.

There are all together seven different RAID schemes, RAID 0 through RAID 6, each with its own disk arrangements and specific data organizations along with allied redundancy techniques. . However, RAID level 0 +1, and RAID level 1 + 0 are actually hybrid organizations based on RAID 0 and RAID 1 levels, and RAID level 5 is the most popular RAID organization.

A comparison of the seven different levels of RAID organization on vital metrics in tabular form and also more details of this topic with a figure are given on the Support Material at www.routledge.com/9781032467238.

6.19 DISK CACHE

The principle used in memory cache can be applied equally to disk memory to effectively improve disk access time that, in turn, enhance the performance of the entire system. A *disk cache* is essentially a buffer (dedicated area) in relatively fast main memory for specified disk sectors. This cache usually maintains a copy of some of the most recently used sectors of the disk containing file data and metadata. When an I/O request is initiated on a file, the file system checks whether the requested disk block exists in the disk cache (main memory). If so, the request results in a cache hit and is responded to via the disk cache, thereby effectively eliminating the delays and overhead associated with disk access, and a quick response via memory to the requesting process. Alternatively, if the requested block is not in the disk cache, a disk-cache miss occurs, and an I/O operation then involves in two copy operations, one between the requested disk block in disk and the disk cache, and the other between the disk cache and the target memory location in the address space of the process that initiated the I/O operation. As a result, the entire I/O operation becomes expensive to complete. But, because of the principle of locality of reference, it is expected that when a block of data is fetched into the disk cache to meet any single I/O request, it is highly probable that the same block may be referenced in the near future.

6.19.1 DESIGN CONSIDERATIONS

Several design issues in disk cache need to be addressed that influence its performance along with several other aspects that may affect the performance of the entire system. Besides other targets, the ultimate objective is to obtain a high hit ratio by committing only a limited amount of memory to the disk cache.

When an I/O request has a hit in the disk cache, the block of data in the disk cache (within main memory) is either transferred to the target memory location assigned by the user process or using a shared memory approach in which a pointer is passed to the appropriate slot in the disk cache, thereby avoiding a memory-to-memory transfer and also allowing other processes to enjoy shared accesses over the entire disk cache.

The next design issue is the *replacement strategy*, similar to the memory cache, which is required when a new block is brought into the disk cache to satisfy an I/O request but there is no room to accommodate it; one of the existing blocks must be replaced. Out of many popular algorithms, the most commonly used algorithm is **least recently used (LRU)**. In fact, the cache can be logically thought of as consisting of a stack of blocks, with the most recently referenced block on the top of the stack. When a block in the cache is referenced, it is taken from its existing position in the stack and put on the top of the stack. When a new block is fetched from secondary memory, the block at the bottom of the stack is removed to make room for the new one, and the incoming new block is pushed on the top of the stack. In fact, it is not necessary to actually move these blocks around in main memory; only a stack of pointers could be associated with the disk cache to perform these operations. The replacement strategy, however, can employ another useful algorithm known as **least frequently used (LFU)**, which selects to replace the lowest–referenced block in the set.

Disk caching, in principle, is ultimately involved in both reads and writes. The actual physical replacement of an entry from the disk cache can take place either on *demand* or *preplanned*. In the former case, a block is replaced and written to disk only when the slot (room) is needed, but if the selected block is only read, it is not modified; hence, it is simply replaced, and it is not necessary to write it back to the disk. For preplanned, the disk block may be continually modified by the running processes and remain in the disk cache (if slot is not required), and instant writing to disk for immediate upgrade is temporarily postponed to perform later at a convenient time. This mode is related to *write-back* blocks, similar to memory cache, in which a number of slots are released at a time. This mode of writing is known as **delayed write** in UNIX. The main drawback of this approach is due to volatile main memory that may create potential corruption of the file system, since unwritten buffers might be in memory that may be lost due to sudden power failure or system crashes for any other reason.

Disk caches, unlike memory caches, are often implemented entirely in software, possibly with indirect assistance from memory management hardware when disk blocks are intelligently mapped in memory. This concept and basic principle of operation of disk cache, more specifically a *unified disk cache* (as explained later) to handle I/O operations, is implemented in UNIX as a *buffer cache*, which is discussed in detail later ("Device Management in UNIX").

More details on this topic are given on the Support Material at www.routledge.com/9781032467238.

6.20 PAGE CACHE

Like disk cache, the operating system along with disk cache also implicitly or explicitly maintains another cache, called the *page cache*. It usually contains all code and data pages that exist in memory, including any memory-mapped files. When a page fault occurs, the required new page is loaded into this cache. The page size is typically a few disk blocks, so this operation involves reading a few blocks from a program file or a swap file. This is essentially a file I/O. When disk blocks are fetched from disks, they are first placed into the disk cache and then copied into the page cache. When a modified page is removed from memory, it is first copied into the disk cache, and from there, it is written to the disk according to the convenience of the operating system sometime in the future. But the serious drawbacks of this approach that adversely affect the performance of the system are: double copying of data in pages and two copies of the pages may exist in memory for sometime until either the copy in the disk cache or the copy in the page cache is overwritten. Moreover, the amount of memory to be allocated for each such cache cannot be predicted beforehand but should be judiciously decided to avoid memory wastage. To alleviate all these problems, the concept of a unified data cache has been introduced.

6.21 UNIFIED DISK CACHE

Both disk cache and page cache in the system can be merged, giving rise to the concept of a *unified disk cache* for the use of both paging and disk I/O. However, all the strategies to individually handle page cache and disk cache (as already discussed) are implemented together in a unified disk cache that allows the size of individual caches to vary at will, of course within the limit of committed memory to suit each one's various types of demands. The file system converts the address issued by any I/O operation into a corresponding page number and an offset within the page. This page number is then passed to the unified cache so that it can load the respective page from the disk in a manner similar to page cache. This unified disk cache approach was implemented in Sun OS 4.0. Later, it was employed in UNIX SVR 4 (System V, release 4). LINUX implementations from version 2.4 onward also exploit the unified disk cache approach.

- **Merits and Drawbacks**

The disk caching technique exhibits a lot of advantages as well as serious drawbacks. Some of the *potential advantages* are:

- Elimination of a number of time-consuming repeated disk accesses.
- Improved effective disk-access time.
- Improved response time to applications.
- Reduced server and network loading with client disk caching in distributed systems running over networks of computers (not computer networks).

The *main disadvantage* of disk caching is due to its use of a delayed write policy, which may result in potential corruption of the file system if the power fails or system crashes occur due to other reasons. Moreover, it is sometimes critical to decide on the amount of memory to be committed to disk caches to realize satisfactory performance and set other parameters to implement it favorably. Failing this, it may result in poor performance in systems using disk caches in comparison to that of non-cached systems in certain situations.

Considering all these aspects, the use of the disk caching technique is still relatively advantageous, and it is also used by Berkley implementers with variants of UNIX. It has been claimed that elimination of 85% of disk accesses can be achieved when disk caching technique is used, in comparison to that of in same systems with no buffer cache.

6.22 CASE STUDY: DEVICE MANAGEMENT IN UNIX

UNIX treats each individual I/O device; disk drives, tape drives, printers, terminals, and communication lines, as a special file. All types of I/O operations related to a device are carried out by the respective special file associated with that device. These files are managed by the file system and are used in the same manner as user data files. This arrangement helps to provide a clean, uniform interface to both processes and users. Thus, the file subsystem that manages files located on secondary devices also serves as a process interface to devices. Figure 6.10 shows a scheme of the logical structure of I/O facility in UNIX.

All types of UNIX files are only byte-stream sequential files without any structure. These files, when involved in any I/O operation, follow one of two modes, **buffered** or **unbuffered**. Buffered I/O uses system buffers. Unbuffered I/O typically includes the DMA facility (DMA also uses a buffer but of its own at the level of device controller, not provided by the operating system), which

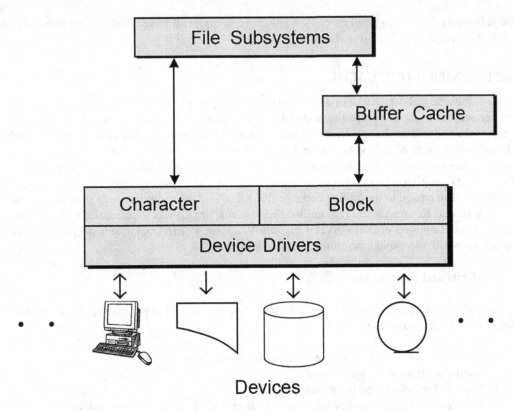

FIGURE 6.10   A formal design concept in logical structuring of I/O facility in UNIX.

supports I/O to take place directly between the I/O module and the memory area assigned to the I/O process.

Buffered I/O

The buffering technique is used at the operating-system level in I/O operations on both block- and character-oriented devices. Although different forms of buffering schemes exist, UNIX uses the I/O buffering technique in its own way using two types of buffers: **system buffer caches** and **character queues**, in order to improve the performance of each individual process and thereby enhance the efficiency of the operating system as a whole.

- **Buffer Cache:** UNIX implements a disk cache approach; essentially a unified disk cache to handle disk I/O operations, called here a *buffer cache* managed by the kernel. It is a dedicated part of main memory blocks used mainly to store recently used disk blocks. The size of the entire buffer cache is typically determined during system configuration, but the size of each buffer in buffer cache is the same as that of a disk block (sector). A buffer is allocated to a disk block that can be shared by all other processes, thereby enabling different processes to avoid repeated disk accesses for the same data. Similarly, many accesses made by a single process for some data more than once need not access the disk regularly. Since both the buffer cache and the user process I/O area are in main memory, the transfer of data between the buffer cache and the user process is simply a memory-to-memory copy, and moreover, it is always carried out using DMA, which uses only bus cycles, leaving the processor free to do other useful work. Each buffer in the buffer cache is either locked for use by other process(es) or free and available for allocation. Buffer cache management maintains three lists, *Free list*, *Driver I/O queue*, and *Device list*, to manage these buffers.

When a large volume of data is processed, to minimize the disk-access delay, pre-fetching of data block on a per-process basis is carried out by initiating an I/O for the next disk block of the file. Since records are usually ordered in blocks, an entire disk block I/O operation (read/write) is relatively faster even when only a specific byte in it is required.

- **Character Queue:** Block-oriented devices, such as tape and disk, are conducive to the buffer cache approach. Character-oriented devices, such as printers and terminals, can also be made suitable by a different form of buffering. A character queue is either written by the process and read by the device or written by the I/O device and read by the process. In both cases, the producer–consumer model explained in Chapter 4 is used. Since the character queues may only be read once, hence, as each character in this queue while is read and after its use, it is effectively destroyed. This is in contrast to the buffer cache, which can be read multiple times.

Unbuffered I/O

Unbuffered I/O is simply DMA that operates between devices (I/O module) and the reserved memory area assigned to a process. This is probably the fastest mode of I/O operation. However, the process executing unbuffered I/O is locked in memory and cannot be swapped out. This commitment may sometimes adversely affect the overall performance of the system, since a part of the memory is always tied up that limits the advantages of swapping.

Conclusion

Disk drives are considered the most important devices for all contemporary modern operating systems, including UNIX, due to their immense potential to provide reasonably high throughput. I/O involving these devices may be unbuffered or buffered via buffer cache. Tape drives are operationally different but functionally similar to disks; hence, they use similar I/O schemes. In large UNIX installations, more than 100 disk blocks may be buffered.

Terminal when involved in I/O is, by virtue, relatively quite slow in operational speed at the time of exchange of characters; character–queue approach is thus found to be most suitable for this device. Communication lines similarly require serial processing of bytes of data for input or output and hence can best be managed by the use of character queues. Likewise, I/O involving printers will generally depend on the speed of the printer. Slow printers generally use character queue, while a fast printer might employ unbuffered I/O; since the particular bytes of data proceeding to a printer are never reused, using a buffer cache for this device would mean useless overhead.

More details on this topic, including the general organization of the buffer cache and its operation, with a figure, are given on the Support Material at www.routledge.com/9781032467238.

6.23 CASE STUDY: DEVICE MANAGEMENT IN LINUX

The organization of Linux IOCS (kernel facility) bears a close resemblance to that of other UNIX implementations, including SVR4. Thus, all types of block, character, and network I/O devices are supported by Linux and are similarly treated like files. The Linux kernel, as in UNIX, associates a special file with each individual device driver. A buffer cache is here used to speedup file processing. However, I/O kernel specifics in many Linux versions are different from that of UNIX. We mention some of them here before looking at several I/O features that contemporary Linux usually provides.

- Linux kernel modules are essentially dynamically loadable. So a device driver has to be registered with the kernel when installed and de-registered at the time of its removal.
- For devices, the *vnode* (similar to *inode* in UNIX) of the virtual file system (VFS) contains pointers to device-specific functions for the file operation, such as; *open, read, write,* and *close*.
- Similar to UNIX, each buffer in the disk cache also has a buffer header, but it is allocated in a slab offered by the slab allocator (already discussed).
- Modified buffers in the disk cache are written out when the cache is full, when a buffer is in the cache for a long time, or when a file directs the file system to write out its buffers in the interest of synchronization to yield better system performance.

Disk Scheduling

In Linux 2.4, the default disk scheduler, known as the **Linux Elevator**, is basically a variant of the LOOK algorithm discussed in Section 6.17.7. Linux 2.6, however, used innovative approaches in this area, replacing the one in its older version, 2.4, to further enhance I/O scheduling performance. Thus, the Elevator algorithm used in Linux 2.4 was augmented by two additional advanced algorithms, **deadline I/O scheduling** and the **anticipatory I/O scheduler**.

1. **The Elevator Scheduler** (Linux 2.4): The scheduler maintains a single queue sorted on the block number of all pending I/O requests (both read and write). As the disk requests are serviced, the drive as usual keeps moving in a single direction, servicing each request encountered on its way until there are no more outstanding requests in the current direction. To improve disk throughput, this general strategy is refined: it combines the new requests that arrive with the existing queue of pending requests whenever possible and uses four types of specific actions (actions to be taken in order, as explained on the Support Material at www.routledge.com/9781032467238) while attempting to carry out this merging.

In fact, Linux 2.6 provides four I/O schedulers. The system administrator can select the one that best matches the nature of the workload in a specific installation. However, the No-Op scheduler is simply an FCFS scheduler. The other three schedulers are the following.

2. **Deadline Scheduler** (Linux 2.6): The two critical problems as faced by the elevator scheduler are: requests from distant blocks may experience continuous delay, thereby resulting in starvation due to the arrival of a continuous stream of new requests in close vicinity to the currently servicing request. The second problem has the potential to be even more acute and is related to the operational differences between read and write requests. While a read operation takes less time, if the data do not exist in the buffer cache, a disk access is required, and consequently the process can get blocked until the read operation is completed. But the process issuing a write request does not get blocked, since a write request actually copies data into a buffer (memory-to-memory copy), and the actual write operation takes place sometime later as time permits. If such a stream of write requests (e.g. to place a large file on the disk) arrives, it then blocks a read request for a considerable time and thereby blocks a process. Therefore, to provide better response times to processes, the IOCS adopts a design strategy allowing read operations to perform at a higher priority than write operations.

The deadline scheduler also uses an elevator (LOOK) scheduling approach as its basis and incorporates a feature to avoid large delays (first problem) in order to alleviate both these problems.

It employs three queues. The first one is, as before, the *elevator queue* containing the incoming requests sorted by track number, and the scheduler normally selects a request based on the current position of the disk heads. In addition, the same request is placed either at the tail of a *read FIFO queue* (second queue) for a read request or a *write FIFO queue* (third queue) for a write request. Thus, the read and write queues separately maintain lists of requests in the sequence in which these requests arrived. Since elevator scheduling faces an inherent problem when a process performs a large number of write operations in one part of the disk, I/O operations in other parts of the disk would be constantly getting delayed. Moreover, if a delayed operation is a read, it would cause further substantial delays in the requesting process. To prevent such exorbitant delays, the scheduler assigns a deadline (expiration time) with a default value of 0.5 seconds to a *read request* (higher priority) and a deadline of 5 seconds to a write request. Each deadline for a read and write request is attached to each request in the respective FIFO queue.

Normally, the scheduler dispatches requests from the sorted queue. When the task in relation to a request is completed, it is removed from the head of the sorted queue and also from the respective FIFO queue. However, when the item at the head of one of the FIFO queues becomes older and its deadline expires, then the scheduler next dispatches this request from that FIFO queue, plus a couple of the next few requests from this queue, out of sequence before resuming normal scheduling. As each request is dispatched, it is also removed from the sorted queue. In this way, the deadline scheduler scheme resolves both the starvation problem and the read versus write problem.

3. **Completely Fair Queuing Scheduler** (Linux 2.6): This scheduler maintains a separate queue of I/O requests for each process, and performs round robin between these queues. The ultimate objective of this approach is to offer a fair share that consequently avoids large delays for processes (see "UNIX Fair Share Scheduling", Chapter 4).
4. **Anticipatory Scheduler** (Linux 2.6): Both the original elevator scheduler and the deadline scheduler, like the other disk scheduling algorithms already discussed, keep dispatching a new request that appears close to the currently executing request as soon as the currently executing request is completed so as to obtain a better disk performance. Typically, a process that performs synchronous read requests gets blocked (sleep) until the read operation is completed and the data are available. Then it wakes up. This process usually issues the next I/O operation immediately after waking up. When elevator or deadline scheduling is used, the small delay that happens between receiving the data for the last read and issuing the next read would cause the disk heads to probably pass over the track that contains the data involved in the next read operation. This may cause the scheduler to turn elsewhere for a pending request and dispatch that request. By virtue of the principle of locality, it is probable that successive reads from the same process will be to disk blocks that are close one another. As a result, the next read operation of the process could be serviced only in the next scan of the disk, causing more delays in the process and more movement of the disk heads. This problem can, however, be avoided if the scheduler were to delay a short period of time after satisfying a read request to see if a new nearby read request is made, so that this next read request could be immediately serviced, and in this way, the overall performance of the system could be enhanced. This strategy, as proposed, is exactly followed in anticipatory schedulers and implemented in Linux 2.6.

The anticipatory scheduler uses deadline scheduling as its backbone but also adds a feature to handle synchronous I/O. When a read request is dispatched, the anticipatory scheduler causes the scheduling system to delay for up to 6 milliseconds depending on the configuration. During this small delay, there is a high chance that the application that issued the last read request will issue another read request to almost the same region of the disk. This next read operation can then be serviced immediately in the same scan of the disk. If no such read request occurs, the scheduler resumes its normal operation using the prescribed deadline scheduling algorithm.

Experimental observations on reading numerous types of large files while carrying out a long streaming write in the background and vice-versa reveal the fact that the anticipatory scheduler exhibits dramatic performance improvement over the others.

Linux Page Cache

In earlier versions of Linux, up to version 2.2, the kernel used to maintain a page cache (already discussed in the last subsection) for all reads and writes of regular files from the file system as well as for virtual memory pages and a separate buffer cache for block I/O. Releases of Linux from version 2.4 onward started to use a single *unified page cache* (already discussed in the last subsection) replacing the separate existence of two different caches, the disk cache and page cache, to handle all possible traffic between the disk and main memory.

6.24   CASE STUDY: DEVICE (I/O) MANAGEMENT IN WINDOWS

The Windows I/O manager is responsible for all I/O and provides a uniform interface to all types of drivers. The I/O manager essentially consists of the NTFS and the device driver for the disks. All information read from or written to the device is managed as a stream of bytes called a virtual file. The I/O manager consists of basically **four modules**:

- **Cache manager:** Windows uses a centralized cache manager to provide a caching service in main memory to all file systems of the I/O manager, the virtual memory manager, and network components. The part of the file held in a cache block (256 Kbytes) is called a *view*, and a file is considered a sequence of such views. Each view is described by a *virtual address control block* (VACB), and an array of such VACBs is set up by the cache manager when the file is opened. This VACB actually helps quickly determine whether a needed part of a file is in the cache at any instant, and also readily tells whether a view is currently in use.

When an I/O request is issued, the I/O manager passes it to the cache manager, which consults the VACB array for the file to ascertain whether the request is already a part of some view in the cache. If so, it readily serves the request and takes appropriate actions on respective VACB. Otherwise, it allocates a cache block and maps the view in the cache block. If the request is a read one, it copies the required data in the caller's address space, maybe with the help of the VM manager. In addition, if a page fault occurs during the copy operation, the VM manager invokes the disk driver through NTFS to read the required page into the memory, and that is performed in a non-cached manner.

The buffering of a file is carried out by the cache manager, which analyzes the requests (read/write), and if it observes that the previous few requests (read) indicate sequential accesses to a file, it then starts prefetching subsequent data blocks. In the case of file updates (writing), the data to be written into a file are reflected in the view of the file held in the cache manager, which exploits two typical services to improve overall performance:

- **Lazy write:** The system performs updates in the cache only, not on the disk. Later, when demand on the processor is low, the cache manager periodically nudges the VM manager to write out the changed data to the disk file. If a particular cache block is once again referenced and updated in the meantime, there is a substantial savings, since disk access is not required.
- **Lazy commit:** This is for transaction processing and is very similar to the lazy write. Instead of immediately marking a transaction as successfully completed, the system

caches the committed information and later writes it at its convenience to the file system log by a background process.

- **File system drivers:** The I/O manager treats a file system driver as just another device driver and routes certain volumes of messages to the appropriate software driver (such as *intermediate* and *device drivers*) for that particular device adapter (controller) to implement the target file system.
- **Network drivers or filter drivers:** Windows uses network drivers to support its integrated networking capabilities and enable distributed applications to run. This driver can be inserted between a device driver and an intermediate driver, between an intermediate driver and a file system driver, or between the file system driver and the I/O manager API to perform any kind of function that might be desired. For example, a network redirector filter driver can intercept file commands intended for remote files and redirect them to remote file servers.
- **Hardware device drivers:** These drivers access the hardware registers (controller's registers) of the peripheral devices through entry points provided in Windows Executive dynamic link libraries (.dll). A set of these library routines exist for every platform that Windows supports; because the routine names are the same for all platforms, the source code of Windows device drivers is portable over different types of processor.

Windows supports both **synchronous** and **asynchronous** I/O operation. With synchronous I/O, the application is blocked (sleep) until the I/O operation completes. In the case of asynchronous I/O, an application initiates an I/O operation and then can continue with other processing while the I/O operation is in progress in parallel.

Windows supports two types of RAID configurations:

- **Hardware RAID**, in which separate physical disks are combined into one or more logical disks by the disk controller or disk storage cabinet hardware. In hardware RAID, redundant information is created and regenerated entirely by the controller interface.
- **Software RAID**, in which noncontiguous disk space is combined into one or more logical partitions by the fault-tolerant software disk driver, FTDISK. The software RAID facility is available on Windows servers, which implement RAID functionality as part of the operating system, and can be used with any set of multiple disks. It implements RAID 1 and RAID 5. In the case of RAID 1 (disk mirroring), the two disks containing the original and mirror partitions may be on the same disk controller or on different disk controllers. When they are on different disk controllers, it is often referred to as **disk duplexing**.

SUMMARY

Device management comprising I/O subsystems controls all I/O devices that implement a generic device interface for the rest of the operating system to access the I/O devices with relative ease. It allocates devices to processes, schedules I/O requests on the devices, and deallocates the devices when they are not needed. It also maintains data caches and page caches to hold data from block as well as character devices. It, along with numerous device drivers, occupies a major part of the operating system. I/O devices are connected to the host system through I/O controllers, each of which is interfaced with the operating system by a respective device driver. This driver converts the complex hardware interface to a relatively simple software interface for the I/O subsystem to easily use. A representative UNIX device driver is presented as a case study. Different types of I/O operation, programmed I/O, interrupt-driven I/O, DMA, I/O channels, and finally I/O processors are described. Clocks, also called timers, are discussed with clock software that generally takes the form of a device driver, even though a clock is neither a block device, like a disk, nor a character device, like a terminal or printer. This chapter also presents in brief the magnetic disk with its physical characteristics and different components' organization, along with the major parameters that are involved in disk operation. Disk management in relation to formatting and subsequent data organization is described. I/O requests are handled by a disk scheduler, and different types of disk-arm scheduling policies with illustrative examples, along with their merits and shortcomings, are described. RAID technology is discussed that uses many identical disks in parallel as an array and is viewed as single "logical disk" controlled by a single "logical controller". RAID enhances disk performance and reliability to a large extent. Disk cache, along with its design considerations, as well as page cache, and finally the combination of the two to form a unified cache was described, with its merits and drawbacks. Finally, device management as implemented in UNIX, Linux, and Windows is described figures in brief to illustrate how this management is actually realized in practice in representative commercial systems.

EXERCISES

1. The transfer rate between a CPU and its attached memory is higher by an order of magnitude than mechanical I/O transfer. How can this imbalance cause inefficiencies?

2. Explain the architectures of device controllers with the help of a block diagram. What are the specific functions that a device controller performs?

3. What is meant by device-level I/O? Discuss the steps it follows while carrying out an I/O operation physically.

4. Why is device management becoming more important as a constituent in the design of a contemporary operating system? State and explain the main functions that device management must perform, mentioning its common targets.

5. With an approximate structure of a device (unit) control block, explain how it is used by the operating system while managing devices. Discuss the functions that are performed by its main constituents.

6. What are interrupts? When a device interrupts, is there always a context switch?

7. What are device drivers? Explain with a diagram the general functions usually carried out by a device driver. What is meant by reconfigurable device drivers? Explain why modern operating systems use such device drivers.

8. What is meant by "device independence"? What is the role played by device-independent software? What is its usefulness? What are the main functions that are typically common in most device-independent software?

9. What is meant by buffering technique as used by an operating system? Should magnetic disk controllers include hardware buffers? Explain your answer.

10. Why would you expect a performance gain using a double buffer instead of a single buffer for I/O?

11. Using double buffering exploited by the operating system, explain the impact of buffering on the runtime of the process if the process is I/O-bound and requests characters at a much higher rate than the device can provide. What is the effect if the process is compute-bound and rarely requests characters from the device?

12. In a certain computer system, the clock interrupt handler requires 2 msec. (including process switching overhead) per clock tick. The clock runs at 60 Hz. What fraction of CPU is devoted to the clock?

13. State the main physical characteristics of a magnetic disk. How are data normally organized in such a disk?

14. Write down the procedures and steps followed in an I/O operation involving a magnetic disk when transferring information to and from the disk after the initiation of an I/O operation.

15. What are the parameters that influence the physical disk I/O operation? How are they involved in such an operation? Compute the total time required to transfer the information

of a block of n words in a disk I/O operation when the disk has a capacity of N words per track and each track is rotating at the speed of r revolutions per second. Write down the assumptions made, if any.

16. What is meant by interleaving? When and how is the interleaving on a disk carried out? What is the role of interleaving in the organization of data on a disk? How does interleaving facilitate data access on a disk?

17. If a disk controller writes the bytes it receives from the disk to memory as fast as it receives them, with no internal buffering, is interleaving conceivably useful? Discuss with reasons.

18. Explain the notion of interleaving: how it works and how it at affects the logical-to-physical translation of disk addresses. Should the knowledge of interleaving be confined only to the related disk driver? Explain with reasons.

19. A disk is double interleaved. It has eight sectors of 512 bytes per track and a rotation rate of 300 rpm. How long does it take to read all the sectors of a track in order, assuming that the arm is currently positioned correctly and ½ rotation is needed to get sector 0 under the head? Compute the data rate. Now carry out the problem with a non-interleaved disk with the same characteristics. Compare and contrast interleaving and non-interleaving in this regard.

20. Calculate how much disk space (in sectors, tracks, and surfaces) will be required to store logical records each of 120 bytes in length blocked 10/physical record if the disk is fixed sector with 512 bytes/sector, 96 sectors per track, 110 tracks per surface, and 8 usable surfaces. The file contains 4440 records in total. Do not consider any file header record(s) or track indexes, and assume that records cannot span two sectors.

21. Discuss the delay elements that are involved in a disk read or write operation. Out of those, which element would you consider the most dominant and why?

22. What does disk scheduling mean? Why is it considered an important approach that requires the operating system to include it?

23. What scheduling algorithm is used by contemporary Linux operating system? Discuss the strategy and principles of its operation.

24. The head of a moving-head disk system with 200 tracks numbered 0 to 199 is currently serving a request at track 15 and has just finished a request at track 10. The queue of pending requests is kept in the order 8, 24, 16, 75, 195, 37, 55, 75, 153, 3. What is the total head movement required to satisfy these requests for the following disk scheduling algorithms? **a.** FCFS, **b.** SSTF, **c.** SCAN, **d.** LOOK, **e.** C-SCAN, **f.** C-LOOK.

25. Disk requests arrive to the disk driver for cylinders 10, 22, 20, 2, 45, 5, and 35, in that order. A seek takes 6 msec. per cylinder movement. How much seek time is needed for: **a.** FCFS, **b.** SSTF, **c.** SCAN, **d.** LOOK, **e.** C-SCAN, **f.** C-LOOK?

26. Discuss the impact of disk scheduling algorithms on the effectiveness of I/O buffering.

27. An input file is processed using multiple buffers. Comment on the validity of the following statements:
    a. "Of all the disk scheduling algorithms, the FCFS strategy is likely to provide the best elapsed time performance for the program".
    b. "Sector interleaving is useful only while reading the first few records in the file; it is not so useful while reading other records".

28. Define RAID. How does RAID handle several inherent drawbacks of a disk accessed for data transfer? What are the common characteristics that are observed in all RAID levels? Compare and contrast the performance of the seven RAID levels with respect to their data transfer capacity.

29. What are the implications of using a buffer cache? Describe implications of the UNIX buffer cache for file system reliability. UNIX supports a system call *flush* to require the kernel

to write buffered output onto the disk. Do you suggest using *flush* to improve the reliability of your files?

30. State and explain the different types of RAID configuration used in Windows.

SUGGESTED REFERENCES AND WEBSITES

Chakraborty, P. *Computer Organization and Architecture: Evolutionary Concepts, Principles, and Designs*, Boca Raton, FL, CRC Press, 2020.

7 File Management

Learning Objectives

- To introduce the concept of permanently storing information in the form of files.
- To describe the generic file system, a major part of the operating system that entirely handles all types of files, including their naming, structuring, operations, and different types of accesses made on various kinds of files.
- To elucidate different types of file services that a respective file server provides.
- To outline the file control block while handling the files.
- To discuss the file management system, including its requirements, design issues, design principles, and functions.
- To explain the different types of file organizations along with their individual related specific accesses.
- To define the file directory and describe its different types of structures.
- To introduce the concept of file sharing by way of forming a graph directory structure.
- To define records and blocking of the records that constitute the file.
- To discuss different issues and approaches to file allocation and subsequent different methods employed to store files in secondary devices.
- To describe different techniques that manage free spaces in secondary storage.
- To illustrate a physical representation of file organization.
- To explain the various methods in implementing file system reliability.
- To define and describe the virtual file system (VFS) and pipes.
- To introduce and describe the log-structured file system.
- Case study: to describe individually and separately in brief the file management systems implemented in UNIX, Linux, and Windows.

7.1 INTRODUCTION

All computer systems ultimately process information, and storing this information in main memory within a specific process's address space is only a temporary measure at best for the duration the process remains active; the information is automatically lost when the process terminates or the computer is turned off or crashes. Also, adequate memory space is not available for this purpose. In addition, information confined within a specific process's address space cannot be accessed by other processes intending to simultaneously share it (or a part of it). All these facts, along with many other issues, dictate that information to be stored must be made independent, sharable, and also on a long-term basis. In other words, the essential requirement is that the storage space must be large enough to permanently store the bulk of information, must be independent of any specific process, and must survive for a long time except in the event of catastrophe. All these requirements can be satisfied only if the information is stored on secondary devices, such as disk, tape, or any other external media using a specific form of units called *files*. Processes can then operate independently on these files at will. Files produced in this way must be persistent and have a life outside of any individual application that uses them for input/output as well as irrespective of the state of the process that uses it. A file will then exist permanently unless and until it is explicitly removed by its owner.

The concept of a file is a central theme in the vast majority of computer applications, except for real-time applications and some other specialized applications which seldom use files. In general,

DOI: 10.1201/9781003383055-7

applications use one or more files to input information, process data, and finally produce output virtually in the form of files that are permanently saved for further future use. The ultimate objective of having files in this manner is to enable the owner of the file to access it, modify it, and save it and also to authorize them to protect the file's integrity. To implement the underlying objectives, a part of the operating system is solely entrusted with managing and controlling files and their contents located on secondary storage. This part known, as the file management system, is primarily concerned with structuring, naming, accessing, using, and protecting files, along with other major topics related to files.

Files are usually stored on any type of physical devices, such as disk drives, magnetic tapes, and similar other peripheral devices or semiconductor memory. These storage devices vastly differ in the nature of their physical organization as well as operations. To relieve the users from all the peculiarities of the underlying storage devices, the operating system hides everything and provides the user a uniform logical view of the stored information for the sake of convenience. Irrespective of the specific storage volume that contains a given file, the file is designated as online or offline. When the combined size of all files in use in the system exceeds the online capacity of the available storage devices, then volumes (disks or tapes media) may be dismounted, and new volumes are added to allow ongoing file operations to continue. This chapter, however, emphasizes mostly the management of online files, or abbreviated as files.

The file management system is supposed to hide all device-specific aspects of where the file resides and offer a clean abstraction of only a simple, uniform space of named files. Some systems extend this view with a further abstraction of even an input/output system in which all I/O devices appear to the user as a set of files. However, the primary concern is after all the various services that the file management system offers for both usual files and files related to I/O device management. There are lots of other issues related to the file management system that are differently implemented by different operating systems. This chapter will only discuss all the topics related to file and file management systems (FMS) common to any generic operating system. At the end, the FMS of contemporary representative popular operating systems, such as UNIX, Linux, and Windows, are separately discussed in brief to give an overview of different types of actual FMS that are implemented in practice.

More details on this topic are given on the Support Material at www.routledge.com/9781032467238.

7.2 FILES

A file is essentially a container for a collection of logically related pieces of information that are physically stored normally on any type of peripheral device for long-term existence but presented by most operating systems as device-independent. A file often appears to users as a linear array of characters or record structures with a collection of similar records stored somewhere in the system. To users and applications, a file is treated as a single entity and may be referenced by name. Files can be created, read, written, and even removed using various system calls. File thus created can also include access permissions (at file level) that allow controlled sharing by many concurrent processes. In some sophisticated systems, such access controls can be enforced at the record level or even lower at the field level. A file can be used for read/write only after it is *open*, and similarly, after its use, it should be *closed* using system calls.

7.3 FILE SYSTEMS

Files are managed by operating systems. The naming, structuring, accessing, using, protection, and implementation of files, with little or no interpretation of information stored within them, are the major tasks of the operating system. The way in which these tasks are achieved by the operating system is different for different operating systems and is an attribute of the operating system injected into it at the time of its design. The part of the operating system entrusted with the responsibility of dealing with files is known as the *file system*. It hides all peculiarities and device-dependent details from the users and provides them with a consistent and simple logical picture of the stored information. However, a file system maintains a set of attributes associated with the file that include owner, creation time, time last modified, access privileges, and similar other information.

The file system viewed from the user's end mainly consists of:

1. What constitutes a file
2. How files are named
3. What different types of operations are allowed on files
4. How files are to be protected with access privileges

The file system viewed from designer's end consists mainly of:

1. How the files will be stored
2. Whether linked lists or bit maps are used to keep track of free storage, how many sectors there are in a logical block, and so on
3. What runtime calls would manipulate most of the files and directories
4. How an executing program would bind a given file at runtime if it intends to access it [OPEN system service (call)]
5. What arrangements optimize access to actively used files shared by many concurrent processes [by means of the OPEN system service (call)]

and similar other relevant things.

A file is stored on device as a linearly addressed block of bytes. The file system provides an abstraction from storage blocks to appropriate data structures suitable for use by application programs. At the least, the file system provides an abstraction that links (maps) blocks of the stored element together to form a logical collection of information, commonly called *stream-block translation*. Consequently, such a translation conceptually allows one to store (and retrieve) an arbitrary stream of linearly addressed bytes on the block-oriented storage system (disk-like or tape devices). When the data are retrieved, they will be read block by block, converted into a stream of bytes, and then converted back into the application-level data structure. If an OS (file system) provides only stream-block translation facilities, it is said to provide a **low-level file system**. UNIX, Linux, and Windows belong to this category. On the other hand, if the OS (file system) provides record-stream translation facilities, it is said to have a **structured** (or **high-level**) **file system**. IBM mainframe operating systems (OS/370 or MVS) and to some extent Apple Macintosh system belong to this category.

File systems that support multimedia documents for storage and retrieval of information must be able to handle the information that represents, for example, numerical data, typeset textual data, graphics, images (videos), and audio information. Ordinary low-level file systems are not designed to accommodate these types of multimedia documents because different types of media potentially require different access mechanisms and modification strategies for efficient handling of I/O. For example, the technique for efficient access of an image significantly differs from that of accessing a textual data. In fact, application domains require the OS to provide flexible, high-performance access methods suitable for use with multimedia data, where the methods are defined by the programmers themselves.

More details on this topic with a figure are given on the Support Material at www.routledge.com/9781032467238.

7.3.1 FILE NAMING

File systems shield the user from the details of how and where the information is stored and how the physical devices actually work. This abstraction mechanism is realized and managed by one of the ways, such as, naming a file. When a process creates a file, it gives the file a name. When the process terminates, the file still exists and can be accessed by other processes using its name. The exact rules for file naming vary somewhat from system to system, but almost all operating systems allow strings of letters or a combination of letters and digits or even special characters as valid file names. Some file system distinguish between uppercase letters and lowercase letters, whereas others do not. UNIX falls into the first category.

Many operating systems support two-part file names with the two parts separated by a period, like ABC.TXT. The part following the period is called the file extension and usually indicates something about the file. Here, .TXT simply reminds the owner that it is a text file rather than conveying any specific information to the computer. On the other hand, a COBOL compiler will require that a file submitted for compilation must have the extension .COB; otherwise it will not be accepted for compilation. Different operating systems follow different conventions in file naming both with respect to length of file name as well as the length and number of extensions to be used in a file name. For example, in MS-DOS, file names are 1 to 8 characters plus an optional extension of 1 to 3 characters. In UNIX, the size of the extension, if any, is up to the user, and a file may even have two or more extensions, as in prog.c.z, where c indicates that it is a C program file and z is commonly used to indicate that the file (prog.c) has been compressed using the Ziv–Lemple compression algorithm.

Brief details on this topic are given on the Support Material at www.routledge.com/9781032467238.

7.3.2 FILE STRUCTURE

When applications operate on data, they rely on the structure present in the data, represented as collection of records, each of which contains typed fields of information. For example, a collection of all employee information is a file in which all the information relating to each individual employee is a record in the file; the employee's record may contain different fields, such as name, address, basic pay, DA, and so on. There may also have application domain-specific structure in the data in the files that reflects numerical/non-numerical data, images, and audio information. Files can be structured in any of several ways decided by the operating system under which it is running.

When the file is structured as a sequence of fixed length records, the read operation returns one record, and the write operation overwrites or appends one record. However, the length of this fixed-length record can also be changed by defining the record length as needed, and it is declared accordingly in the respective application program. On the other hand, the files can also be defined in an unstructured sequence of bytes. In effect, the operating system does not know or even care what is in the file. All it sees is a stream of bytes. Any meaning must be imposed by user-level application programs. Both UNIX and Windows (NTFS) use this approach. Since the operating system regards files as nothing more than byte sequences, this approach provides maximum flexibility. User programs can put anything they want in a file and can name them any way they like. For users who want to do unusual things, this approach can be very important; the operating system, however, does never interfere in this regard.

Another kind of file structure to represent a file consists of a tree of records, not necessarily all the same length, each containing a key field in a pre-defined position in the record. The tree is stored on the key field to enable rapid searching for a particular key. The basic operation here is to get the record of a specific key, but "next record" can also be available. Furthermore, when new records are added, they are accordingly placed by the operating system. This type of record-based arrangement makes the file system most flexible and hence is widely used in large mainframe systems engaged in bulk volume commercial data processing.

Brief details on this topic with a figure are given on the Support Material at www.routledge.com/9781032467238.

7.3.3 FILE TYPES

All contemporary operating systems support several types of files. They have *regular files*, *directories*, *character-special files*, and *block-special files*. For example, UNIX and Windows have regular files and directories. UNIX also uses character-special and block-special files. Windows also has metadata files. We will define metadata in the section "File Attributes".

- **Regular files** are generally ASCII files (text) or binary files containing user information. The distinct advantage of ASCII files is that they can be displayed and printed as it is, and they can be edited with an ordinary text editor. Furthermore, if a large number of programs are ASCII files for input and output, it is easy to connect the output of one program to the input of another (as found in UNIX pipes).
- **Binary files** just means that they are not ASCII files. Listing them on a printer or displaying them on a terminal gives an incomprehensible listing, apparently full of random junk. Usually they have some internal structure. Although the file is nothing but a sequence of bytes, the binary file, if it is an executable file, must have a definite format that is differently defined in different operating systems. In general, it has five sections: the first section is a header which consists of a magic number identifying the file as an executable file as well as other necessary related information, and the other sections are text, data, relocation bits, and a symbol table, as shown in Figure 7.1a.
- Another example of a binary file is an **archive** found in many contemporary modern operating systems. A representative format of such a file is depicted in Figure 7.1b. It consists of a collection of library procedures (modules) already compiled but not linked. Each one is prefaced by a header telling its name, creation date, owner, protection code, and size. Similar to an executable file, the module headers are full of binary numbers.

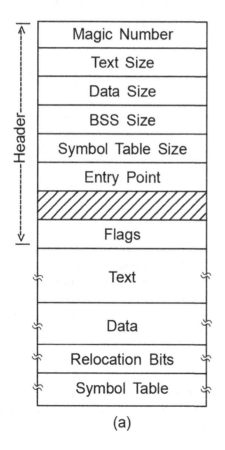

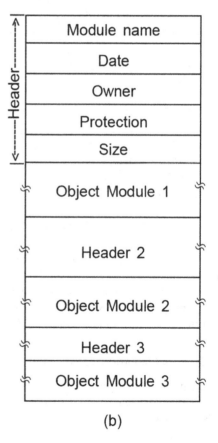

FIGURE 7.1   A pictorial representation of the formats of an (a) executable file and (b) archive file created by a generic modern operating system.

All operating system must recognize one file type: their own executable file, but some recognize more. They sometimes even go to the extent of inspecting the creation time of an executable file. Then it locates its corresponding source file and sees if the source has been modified since the binary file was made. If it has, it automatically recompiles the source. In UNIX, the term "make program" has been built into the shell. Here, file extensions are mandatory so as to enable the operating system to decide which binary program was derived from which source.

- A **directory** is a system file associated with the file management system for maintaining the structure of the file system and consists of a collection of files and directories. Directories and their various types of structures will be discussed later.
- **Character-serial files** are related to input/output and are used to model serial I/O devices, such as terminals, printers, and networks. **Block-special files** are used to model disk-like media, tapes, and so on.

7.3.4 FILE ATTRIBUTES

Every file has a name for its identification and data. In addition, all operating systems attach various types of other information to files, such as, the date and time the file was created and the file's size. These extra items are called the file's attributes, or **metadata**. The different types of attributes that are offered by the file manager (operating system) vary considerably from one operating system to another. Some of the most common attributes are discussed here, but other ones also exist. No existing operating system provides all of these, but each one present in some system (or is able to be provided on request). The file system maintains a data structure for each file called a **file descriptor** in which it stores detailed information relating to the current attributes of the file. Common attributes that are maintained are:

External name, owner, user, current size, maximum size, record length, key position, key length, time of creation, time of last change, time of last access, read-only flag, hidden flag, ASCII/binary flag, system flag, archive flag, temporary flag, random access flag, lock flags, current state, sharable, protection settings, password, reference count, storage device details, and so on.

Most minicomputer and microcomputer (desktop computer) by this time get enough matured, and thus do not require all these items in their file systems to handle the files.

Brief details on file descriptors with these attributes are given on the Support Material at www.routledge.com/9781032467238.

7.3.4.1 Case Study: UNIX File Descriptor

The UNIX file descriptor is called an **i-node** (an abbreviation for *index node*). The i-node for a file is kept with the file on the storage device. The i-node lists the file's attributes and disk addresses of the file's block. The way in which the i-node is used to locate the file's block will be discussed in a later section. The i-node is augmented with other information when the file is actually opened.

A representative BSD UNIX i-node file descriptor is given (Table 7.1) on the Support Material at www.routledge.com/9781032467238.

7.3.5 FILE OPERATIONS: SYSTEM CALLS

Different file systems provide different types of operations on files for storing and retrieval of data. Typical functions (operations) that are most common and must be supported using respective system calls include the following:

Create/Creat: A new file is defined and created with no data, positioned within the structure of files. The purpose of the call is to announce that the file is being created and to set some of the attributes.

Delete: A file is removed from the file structure and destroyed when it is not required. In addition, some operating systems automatically delete any file that has not been used in *n* days.

Delete_One: This deletes an existing record from the currently positioned location of the file, sometimes for the purpose of preserving the existing file structure.

Open: This function opens the file before being used and allows the system to fetch the attributes and to reflect in the file descriptor that the file is in use. It locates the address of the referenced file by searching through the directories, lists disk addresses of the file in main memory, allocates buffers in the main memory, and establishes a runtime connection between the calling program and called file to perform subsequent operations on the file. A possible format of the OPEN system call is:

OPEN (file-name, access-mode)

While invoking the OPEN service, the user specifies the file name and the access mode. The file system verifies the user's authority to access the file in the intended mode before opening the file.

Close: The file should be closed with respect to a process to free up internal table space used to keep attributes and disk addresses, if permissible. The process may no longer perform functions on the file until the process opens the file once again. Many systems encourage this by imposing a maximum number of open files on processes.

Read: This system call (operation) copies all or a portion of the data (a byte or a block of bytes) beginning at the current file position from a file into the respective buffer of the corresponding file. The caller must specify the amount of data needed. If the file position is L bytes from the end when read is invoked, and the number of bytes to be read is greater than L, an end-of-file condition is returned. The possible format of a READ system call is:

READ (file-name, no-of-bytes, in-buffer)

Write: Data are written to the file at the current position. If the current position is the end of the file, the file's size increases. If the current position is anywhere within the file, existing data are overwritten and lost forever. One possible format of a WRITE system call is:

WRITE (file-name, no-of-bytes, out-buffer)

Rename: This system call changes the name of an existing file.

Seek: For random access files, a method is needed to specify from where to take the data. One common approach is a system call *seek* that repositions the current position to a specific place in the file. After the call has completed, data can be read from or written to that specific position. No I/O can be invoked when a Seek call is executed. A representative format of SEEK system call is:

SEEK (file-name, logical position)

Many other useful operations are provided by almost all file systems. However, the nature of operations that are to be performed on a file entirely depend on, and have an impact on the organization of the file.

Brief details on many other common useful operations for files are given on the Support Material at www.routledge.com/9781032467238.

7.3.6 FILE ACCESS

The mechanism by which a file is (or its records are) accessed is closely related to the organization of the file. The file organization itself simply means how the records of a file are logically structured in the file. The "record access pattern" thus depends on the file organization that describes the order in which records in a file are accessed by a process. The application programmer defines the format for logical records and also the access routines for reading and writing records. The file system invokes the programmer-supplied access routines when reading from and writing to the file. Different types of organization of files and their related access mechanism exist, and each one is equally popular, but the selection of a particular one mostly depends on the environment and the type of the application that uses the file. Since file organization and file access are directly linked to one another, they will be discussed separately in detail in the following subsection.

7.4   FILE SERVICE: FILE SERVERS

The file system always provides the user with a higher-level abstraction and also a uniform logical view of the information stored in the form of a file on secondary storage devices. This view is actually provided by the file system using some of its services. The file service is essentially the specifications of what the file system offers to its users. It describes the primitives available with the actions they perform and similar other things. To the users, the file service precisely defines what services they can count on, but it says nothing about how it is implemented. In effect, the file service specifies the file system's interface to the clients. Depending upon the mode in which the file system services are invoked, the users of the file system can be grouped into two distinct categories: *command language users* and *system call users*.

Command language users are interactive users who type commands on the keyboard that the file system can recognize and get numerous services that the file system offers. These services include listing the contents of the file/directory, making new directories, copying/deleting a file, changing a directory, changing the name of a file, changing the access control permission of a file, and many other useful services. The same services, however, can also be obtained in batch mode by invoking the existing command files (batch files) from the keyboard.

The second category of users are those who get file services from the file system by using programs, application programs as well as system programs. Programs include simple statements (relating to the available file services) that are interpreted by the file system and then invoke services through a set of related runtime system calls for the manipulation of files. The services that a file system usually provides to its system call users can be broadly classified as follows:

- **File-related services:** create files, open files, read files, write into files, copy files, rename files, link files, delete files, seek records, and so on.
- **Directory-related services:** make directory, list directory, change directory, rename directory, and so on.
- **Volume-related services:** initialize the volume, mount the volume, dismount the volume, verify the volume, backup the volume, compact the volume, and so on.

A file server is essentially just a user process, or sometimes a kernel process, running on a machine that implements the file services. A system may have one file server or several servers, each one offering a different file service, but the user should not be aware of how many file servers there are or what the location or function of each one is. All they know is that when they call the procedures specified in the file service, the required work is performed somehow. A system, for example, may have two services that offer UNIX file service and Windows file service, respectively, with each user process using the one appropriate for it. It is hence possible to have a terminal with multiple windows, with UNIX programs running in one window and Windows programs running in another window, with no conflicts. The type and number of file services available may even change as the system gradually improves.

7.5 FILE CONTROL BLOCKS

When a file-related operation, such as OPEN, READ or WRITE, is required, the file directory in which the file is stored on the secondary device (disk) is searched. The directory information associated with an actively used file is always kept in the main memory using a data structure called a **file control block** (**FCB**). A FCB usually contains all information derived from a variety of sources concerning file processing activity, like symbolic filename, system-assigned identity, type, starting disk address, size, access permits, and similar information that may be required in processing file-related services. When a program is compiled, the compiler creates the FCB in its object code and records all this information in the FCB.

When an executing program issues the file-service system call OPEN to access a specific file before beginning a file-related operation, the FCB of the file is created in a specified area in main memory, possibly in a place in the process control block (PCB) of the process. When the OPEN call is executed, the operating system finds the related file in the file directory and copies all the required information about the file from the respective file directory into FCB. The recorded file-access permission as given in FCB is then checked with the requested access mode given in the OPEN system call to verify the user's authority to access the file. If it matches, the program would continues; otherwise the execution of the program will be aborted. A buffer area is then accordingly created and kept reserved, and the starting address of this buffer area is stored in the FCB in the buffer address place. The current file position is set 0 when the file is opened. In this way, several files can be opened by a single program. But the number of files that can be opened at any instant by any single process is restricted by the operating system, since the FCB is placed in the PCB, and the PCB is of fixed size.

In the case of a *shared file*, the same file can be opened by several programs, even if it is already opened. At the time of opening a file, each program creates a FCB for the same file with its own connection-identity, current–file–position, and buffer. Thus, different programs can access the same file at different file offsets. One program may be reading and processing a specific record of a file while another program may be reading and processing another record of the same file. When one program closes the file, its corresponding FCB and the connection–identity are removed, and the related buffer is released. However, the other programs can still continue their needed operations on the same file.

Brief details of this topic with a figure are given on the Support Material at www.routledge.com/9781032467238.

7.6 FILE MANAGEMENT SYSTEMS: REQUIREMENTS

The file management system is a part of the operating system consisting of a set of system software that provides services needed by the users and applications for controlling and using their files, thereby relieving the users from the tedious task of developing every time the different types of special-purpose software on their own for each of their applications to execute. To perform these responsibilities, the file management system must fulfill certain minimum requirements that include the following:

- To provide a mechanism in storing data in such a way so that the users can perform different types of operations (as mentioned before) on their files.
- To ensure the validity of data stored in the files.
- To offer the users the needed I/O support while using various types of different storage devices.
- To provide a standardized set of I/O interface routines while actual physical devices are to be used.
- To provide needed I/O support to multiple users for the purpose of sharing and distribution of files in the case of multi-user systems.

- To safeguard the data as far as possible from any sort of accidental loss or damage.
- To attain optimum I/O performance both from the standpoint of the system with respect to overall throughput, as well as from the user's point of view in terms of response time.

7.7 FILE MANAGEMENT SYSTEMS: FUNCTIONS AND DESIGN ISSUES

A representative conceptual level–wise hierarchical approach is depicted in Figure 7.2 that demonstrates the involvement and working of the file management system while providing necessary support in the input–output operations of users and application programs by means of performing various functions. The essence of this structure is to exhibit a clear separation between process-level which is concerned to provide efficient implementation of an I/O operation (file processing) and device-level (physical input–output control system) which aims to provide high device throughput. The division of layers as considered here is somewhat arbitrary, and the number of layers with their interfaces that are actually used varies across different systems in practice, and hence, may use various other approaches.

Users and application programs often interact with the file system by issuing legible commands or instructions provided by the file system in order to execute certain permissible operations on files. In response, the file system, before performing any operation on file, must identify and locate the selected file (or directory and then the file) and consult with its already-recorded associated attributes to decide whether the operation as issued is allowed. In this way, the file system ensures access control (sharing and protection) on particular file to only authorized users in shared systems (for both single as well as multiple users). The basic operations that a user or application may intend to perform on a file are carried out at the record (or character) level. The user or application views the file as having some sort of structure that organizes the record (or a stream of characters). To translate the user-supplied commands or instructions into corresponding specific file manipulation commands, the file management system employs the related access method applicable to this existing file structure that provides efficient file processing.

The physical I/O, however, is done on a block-basis, while users and applications are only concerned with records (or a stream of characters). Therefore, the records of a file must be blocked for

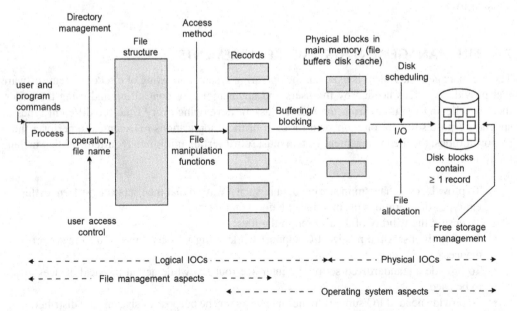

FIGURE 7.2 A block diagram of a representative scheme of file management system with its required elements used in a generic modern operating system.

output and unblocked after input. To support block-I/O of files, several functions are needed, and those are carried out at the physical I/O level (physical IOCS). The physical IOCS layer, which is a part of the kernel in most operating systems, implements device-level I/O (discussed in Chapter 6). We assume that the physical IOCS is invoked through system calls, and it also invokes other functionalities of the kernel through system calls. The part of physical IOCS which belongs to the operating system implements different policies and strategies by using several modules, such as disk scheduling and file allocation, to achieve many different targets, including high device-throughput. These modules, in turn, invoke physical IOCS mechanisms to perform actual I/O operation. In fact, process-level mechanisms that implement file-level I/O use physical IOCS policy-modules to realize efficient device-level I/O. Finally, blocking and I/O buffering although are shown as separate layers in the interest of clarity, but sometimes they exist in the access-method layer and are available only to access-method policy-modules and not allowed to access directly from the file system layer.

This hierarchical level–wise division at least suggests what would be the concern of the file management system, and which would go in the domain of the operating system kernel. In fact, this division proposes that the file management system should be developed as a separate system utility that would use the kernel support to realize the needed file-I/O operations.

7.8 FILE MANAGEMENT SYSTEMS: DESIGN PRINCIPLES

File system design principles can be described in many ways, and principles themselves differ significantly from one system to another depending on the objectives, but the basic principle involved in the organization of system software to conceptually derive any file system follows a standard methodology consisting of a series of hierarchical layers. Each layer, in turn, can be realized by using one or more software modules in order to achieve a specific target. However, a reasonable representative structure of such an organization is depicted in Figure 7.3.

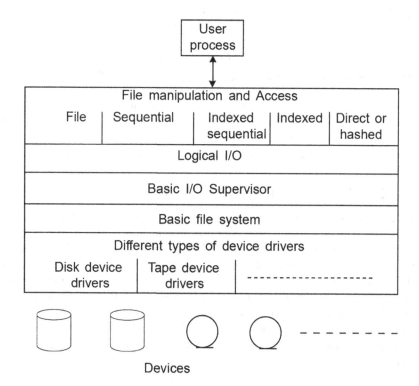

FIGURE 7.3 A schematic block diagram of a representative file system software architecture of a generic modern operating system.

At the lowest level is the *device driver*, which is a physical IOCS that communicates directly with hardware peripheral devices or the associated controllers or channels to implement certain mechanisms at the device level, such as I/O initiation on a device, providing I/O operation status, processing the completion of an I/O request, and recovery of error, if any. The policy employed by the device driver is to optimize the performance of the related I/O device. Device drivers are commonly considered part of the operating system.

The next higher level is referred to as *basic file system*, which is also a part of physical IOCS. This level is the first interface that deals with blocks of data defined outside the computer system environment that are to be exchanged with secondary devices, mostly disk or tape systems. It is thus involved only in the placement of those blocks on secondary storage devices and the buffering of those blocks in main memory. It is not at all concerned about the content or meaning of the data, nor the structure of the files involved. The basic file system (a part of physical IOCS) is also considered part of the operating system.

The *basic I/O supervisor* is responsible for implementing certain mechanisms at the file level, such as file-I/O initiation and termination. It selects the device on which the prescribed file resides to perform file-I/O and is also concerned with scheduling device access (such as disk or tapes) to optimize file access performance. To achieve all this, specific structures are maintained that control file-I/O by way of dealing with device-I/O and other related aspects, and file status. Assignment of I/O buffers and allocation of secondary memory space are also carried out at this level, but the actual placement is done at the next level. The *basic I/O supervisor* is also considered part of the operating system.

Logical I/O is entirely related to users and applications. This module deals with everything with the records of a file with respect to their organization and access. In contrast to the basic file system that deals with blocks of data, logical I/O is concerned with the file records that are defined and described by users and applications. The structuring of a directory to enable a user to organize the data into logical groups of files as well as the organization of each individual file to maintain basic data about files are provided at this level. In fact, logical I/O is engaged to the extent of providing general-purpose record I/O capability.

Access method is perhaps the first level of the file management system that directly interacts with the user. This level provides the primary standardized interface between the application and the file system and consequently with the devices that physically hold the data. Different types of access methods exist that describe different ways of accessing and processing the data residing in a particular file. Each type of access method, in turn, tells something about the corresponding file structure that can be the best fit for effective storing of data. Some of the most commonly used access methods are shown in Figure 7.3, and those are explained separately in a later subsection.

7.9 FILE ORGANIZATION AND ACCESS: STRUCTURED FILES

File organization defines the logical structuring of records in a file in a way that determines how they are to be accessed to efficiently make use of the I/O medium. This, in turn, demands certain important criteria while choosing a specific file organization that mainly include: minimal storage area, short access time, ease of handling, easy maintenance, and above all reliability. However, these criteria appear to conflict with one another. For example, minimal storage area demands minimum redundancy in the data. On the other hand, redundancy is a useful way to increase the speed of data access. An example of this is the use of indexes. Hence, including all these criteria equally and favorably in any file organization is simply impossible, and therefore, which of these criteria are to be given more priority is to be decided beforehand in order to fulfill targeted objectives when designing a suitable file organization.

Many different types of file organization exist in reality. A file system usually provides several alternative file organization methods so that a program can select a specific file organization that best fits its environment and suits its requirements. However, we confine ourselves to the discussion of only five fundamental organization schemes. Most real-life systems use structures that fall into one of these categories or some other structures that may be realized with a combination of these organization types. The five fundamental organization methods for files are:

- The pile
- The sequential file
- The indexed-sequential file
- The indexed file
- The direct or hashed file

7.9.1 The Pile

The pile is perhaps the simplest form of file organization. It saves data in any manner, mostly in the order in which they entered. Each record simply consists of one burst of data. The records may have different fields, different numbers of fields, or even similar fields in different orders. Each field here contains everything, such as field name, length, contents, and type, and all these are included as sub-fields indicated by delimiters within the field. A schematic representation of a pile is shown in Figure 7.4a. As this form has no specific structure, record access in a pile file is carried out by passing through each individual record, which is an exhaustive search. To find a record that contains a particular field with a particular value, or to find all records that contain a particular field, in any case, it is necessary to inspect each record in the pile until the desired record is found or the entire file has been examined.

This type of file organization is most suitable in situations when the collected data are not easy to organize. From the point of view of space usage for storing data that vary in size and structure, this type of organization seems to be useful. But one of its major drawbacks is that it often requires exhaustive searches for some types of file operations. For having limited scope in handling only some specific environments, this type of file organization is otherwise unsuitable for most applications and hence has fallen out of favor.

7.9.2 The Sequential File

Many applications need to convert information from a simple byte stream into a stream of records with application-specific data structures. They format each information in a unit called a *record*, the various parts of which are called the *fields* of the record. The most common form of file structure that contains a collection of named sequences of logical records arranged in a particular order is known as *sequential file*. In this file, all records are of the same length with a fixed format, consisting of the same number of fixed-length fields in a specified order, as depicted in Figure 7.4b. Here, the physical organization of the file on the media directly matches the logical organization of the file. Each record is allocated with k bytes to contain all its information plus an additional H bytes for record descriptor information. The name of the field, length, and type of each field are attributes of this file organization.

One of the fields (usually the first field, but not always) in each record is referred to as the *key* field (primary), and that is applicable for all the records in the file. The significance of the key field is that it uniquely identifies a record, and the values of the key field are usually different for different records (if the same for some records, then another particular field known as the secondary key will be considered for unique identification). The file is organized with the records that are stored in any specific key sequence (mostly sorted on keys). Similar to byte-stream files, here access to the file is defined by a file position and the position that indexes records arranged on keys in the file instead of bytes.

Sequential files are highly conducive to and generally optimum for batch processing applications in which accessing and subsequent processing of the records in a file are involved in order (sequence), starting from any specific position (usually from the beginning), but are not

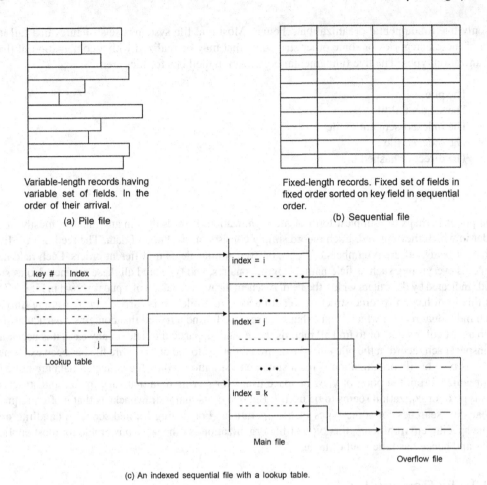

Variable-length records having variable set of fields. In the order of their arrival.

(a) Pile file

Fixed-length records. Fixed set of fields in fixed order sorted on key field in sequential order.

(b) Sequential file

(c) An indexed sequential file with a lookup table.

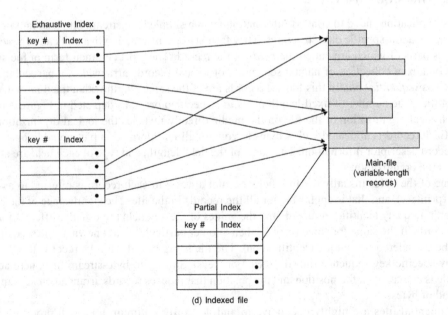

(d) Indexed file

FIGURE 7.4 Representative block diagrams of different types of commonly used file organization employed in generic modern operating systems.

normally skipped around or processed out of order. Sequential files can be built on most I/O devices; hence these files are not critically dependent on device characteristics. Consequently, a sequential file can be migrated easily to a different kind of device. Since sequential files can be rewound, they can be read as often as needed. Therefore, sequential files with large volume are mostly convenient when the storage medium is magnetic tape, but they can be stored easily on any type of disk media.

Sequential files exhibit poor performance for interactive applications in which queries and updates of individual records when carried out require a sequential search of the file, record by record, for a key match to arrive at the desired record, if present. Consequently, it causes a substantial delay in accessing the target record if the file is a relatively large one. Additions/deletions to the file also pose similar problems. However, the procedure normally followed in this case is to create a separate transaction file with the new records to be added/deleted, sorted in the same order on the key field as the existing master file. Periodically, a batch update program is executed that merges the new transaction file with the existing master file based on the keys to produce a new up-to-date master file, with the existing key sequence remaining unchanged.

7.9.3 Indexed Sequential Files

The drawbacks in handling sequential files, particularly when the file operation is concerned with a specific single record rather than with every record in the file, was overcome with the introduction of another popular approach known as an indexed sequential file. This file system maintains the key characteristics of the sequential file and is able to read from or write to a specific record independent of the record's location in the file. While providing this capability, this file system also retains the ability to access records sequentially.

Records in an indexed sequential file are organized in sequence based on a key field, and each record header includes an integer index field. This file system uses two additional features: an index file, which is usually a simple sequential file that provides a quick lookup capability to reach the close vicinity of the desired record in the main file by way of randomly accessing the main file, and an overflow file, which is integrated to the main file and contains records that can be located by following a pointer from its predecessor record. The way the overflow file is employed is described later in this chapter.

A schematic view of an indexed sequential file organization is shown in Figure 7.4c. Several levels of indexing can be employed to locate a record in the main file with an indexed- sequential structure. But, in its simplest form, a single level of indexing is commonly used. The index file contains records, and each record consists of two fields: a key field, which is the same as the key field in the main file, and a pointer to the main file. To locate a specific record in the main file, the index file is searched to find the highest key value that is equal to or precedes the desired key value. Using the respective pointer as indicated in the index file entry thus obtained, the target area in the main file is accessed, and then the search continues sequentially in the main file until the desired record is obtained, if present.

Indexed sequential files are widely used in business computing for files that contain very large numbers of records, particularly if the records are often referenced in a non-sequential manner. To get an estimate of its effectiveness, consider a sequential file with 1 lakh records. To search a record for a particular key value requires on average one-half lakhs or 50,000 record accesses. Now, consider this file an indexed-sequential one with an index file that contains 500 entries with the keys in the index more or less evenly distributed over the main file. To search a record for a particular key value in this file will now take on average 250 accesses to the index file followed by 100 accesses (number of records per block in main file = 100,000/500 = 200; now 200/2 = 100) to the main file. The average search length now becomes 250 + 100 = 350, which is a sharp drop from the 50,000 of its corresponding sequential organization; a straightaway profitable proposition than its counterpart, the ordinary sequential file.

However, addition of records to this file is carried out in a different way. Each record in the main file contains a link field offered by the file system, not visible to the application, used as a pointer to the overflow file. When a new record is to be inserted into the file, it is added to the overflow file. The record in the main file that immediately precedes the new record in logical sequence is accordingly updated to contain a pointer that will indicate the new record in the overflow file. If the immediately preceding record is itself in the overflow file, then the pointer associated with that record will be updated accordingly. Similar to the sequential file, the indexed sequential file also is occasionally merged with the overflow file in batch mode.

While preserving all its merits over sequential organization, indexed-sequential organization also has a sequential nature without sacrificing anything and permits sequential processing, particularly when the application requires processing almost every record in the file that is indexed sequentially. To process the entire file sequentially, the records of the main file are processed in sequence as usual until a pointer to the overflow file is found. In that situation, accessing and subsequent processing then continue in the overflow file until a null pointer is encountered, at which time accessing of the main file is resumed once again from the point where it left off.

When the main file is huge, the index file becomes larger, and searching for a key over such a larger index file may be expensive. In order to realize greater efficiency in access for such a large main file, multiple levels of indexing can be employed. Here, the lowest level of the index file is operated as a sequential file, and a higher-level index file is created for that file. Searching for a record in the main file starts from the lowest level and continues to move to the upward levels until the target record in the main file is obtained, if present. In this way, a substantial reduction in average search length can be attained. But searching many index files one after another at different levels may also be time-consuming and add proportionately to the total access time. This aspect should be taken into consideration while designing a multi-level indexed sequential file that determines how many different levels of index file will be created, and this may be one of the trade-offs in the design considerations.

7.9.4 INDEXED FILES: INVERTED FILES

In spite of having several advantages, indexed sequential files, like their predecessor, sequential files, suffer from certain limitations. One major limitation is that effective access to the record and subsequent processing of the file are mainly confined to that based on a single field (key) of the record constituting the file. When it is necessary to search for a record on the basis of an attribute other than the key field, it appears that neither form of sequential organization is helpful. In fact, many applications demand this flexibility while organizing their respective files.

In the case in which the application needs to search with different criteria, such as name of the customer or account number in a personnel inventory file, it suggests that each record might have two or more index fields. One field links the records together by name and the other by account number. This means that a composite structure is needed that employs each type of field that may be the subject of a search. This can be implemented by preparing one index table with names and another with account numbers. Searches can take place on the appropriate table, and the record can be accessed from the respective storage device. A schematic representation of an indexed file organization is shown in Figure 7.4d. The net effect is that there is no restriction on the placement of the records as long as a pointer present in at least one index refers to that record. Moreover, variable-length records are also supported by this organization.

Indexed files can thus be generalized to support multiple index fields, each with its own index into the records. Two types of indexes are used. An exhaustive index file contains one entry for every record in the main file. This index file itself is normally organized as a sequential file for convenience of searching. A partial index file contains entries to records where the field of interest exists. With the main file having variable-length records, some records may not contain all the fields, thereby saving storage space. However, the table storage requirements are increased. The overhead to manage the indexes also increases, as the addition of a new record to the existing main file requires that all of the respective index files must be updated. Similarly, record deletions can be expensive, because of removal of dangling pointers from the respective indexes. Above all, access times can be appreciably reduced by using this file organization.

Index files are important mostly with applications which are query-based, interactive in nature, and time-critical. Here, exhaustive processing of records rarely happens. Representative examples of such application areas are railway reservation systems, banking operations, and inventory control systems.

7.9.5 The Direct (or Hashed) File

Direct file organization provides the capability to directly access any record of known address from a block of disk-like media. Similar to sequential and index-sequential files, a key field here is also required to be associated with each record by which the record is directly (randomly) accessed. Hence, access to a record is independent of which record was accessed prior to it, so there is no notion of any sequential ordering of records. Direct access avoids any form of sequential access, which makes it both convenient and efficient.

In direct access organization, the process provides a key value which is transformed by this organization to the key value to generate a (track-no, record-no) address. The disk heads are now positioned on track-no track before issuing any read/write command on record-no record. The direct file may sometimes make use of hashing technique on the key value to make this organization even more attractive. One of the hashing techniques, such as linear hashing or coalesced chaining, can be employed for this purpose.

Direct file organization provides **high efficiency** in access when fixed-length records are used and records are accessed and processed one at a time at random. Representative examples are employee inventory, examination processing, pricing tables, and directories. In spite of having several merits, this organization, however, exhibits two main drawbacks when compared to a sequential file:

- Record address computation consumes some CPU time.
- Dummy records sometimes need to be inserted to make this organization more versatile, which may lead to poor utilization of I/O media.

Another drawback observed in the use of direct files is **excessive device dependence**. Characteristics of an I/O device are explicitly assumed and used by the file system while address calculation is carried out. Rewriting the file on another device with different characteristics, such as different track capacity, implies modification of the address calculation method and its related formulas. In addition, it is also observed that sequential processing of records in a direct file is a *detrimental* one when compared with similar processing of records carried out on a sequential file or even on an indexed-sequential file.

7.9.6 Access Methods

An access method is a module of the IOCS that implements access to a class of files using one of the specific file organizations mentioned previously. There exist several access mechanisms when accessing records in a file, but whether the mechanism to be used is a sequential search or an address translation method is entirely determined by the organization of the corresponding file. In fact, the access method used for a file mostly complements the organization of the file, and it is thus always chosen in such a way to favorably exploit the file organization while accessing records from the respective file. In addition, the file access mechanism may use advanced techniques in I/O programming to make file processing more efficient and effective. Two popular techniques are buffering, which was discussed in Chapter 6, and blocking of records, which is discussed in the following section.

7.10   FILE DIRECTORIES

A file system includes various files owned by several users. Any file management system uses the concept of the directory as a way of grouping collections of files (mostly related files) together to keep track of files. Thus, a directory contains information about a group of files, usually related files, and may even contain other directories. In fact, a directory itself is actually a file and can be viewed essentially as a symbol table in which each entry concerning one file is a record occupying one row of the table. As shown in Figure 7.5, each record consists of different types of fields containing various information that includes attributes, location, type, ownership, flags, and usage information, as well as the manner in which it may be accessed by other users in the system. Much of this information, especially that related to storage, is managed by the operating system. Some of the information available in directories is generally provided to the users and applications indirectly by the system routines. However, each such field, in turn, contains several fundamental fields, such as; name of the file, file type, and file organization.

The directory will be created before putting files into it. A directory can similarly be removed when it is not required. Various types of system calls are provided to create a directory, to remove a directory, to put an existing file in a directory, and to remove a file from a directory. Directory entries may be either files or directories. All these give rise to the total entity of the file system.

Brief details of different elements in a file directory (Table 7.2) are given on the Support Material at www.routledge.com/9781032467238.

7.10.1   STRUCTURE

A file system normally contains several directories. The format of the directory and the types of information to be kept in each directory entry (an example is shown in Table 7.2 on the Support Material at www.routledge.com/9781032467238) differ widely among various operating systems. Some of this information may often be included in a *header record* associated with the file, thereby reducing the amount of storage required for the directory that makes it convenient to keep it in main memory either partly or entirely for the sake of performance improvement. However, the directory structure of the file system broadly falls into two categories. The simplest form of the structure for a directory is a **single-level directory** or **flat directory**. The other one, based on a more powerful and flexible approach, is almost universally adopted, the **hierarchical** *or* **tree-structured** directory.

7.10.1.1   Single-Level (Flat) Directories

Some operating systems in the early days (in single-user systems) used one master directory containing a list of entries, one entry for each file, for all files present in a given storage volume. This structure could be viewed as a simple sequential file, with the name of the file serving as the key and the other information (attributes) of the corresponding file forming each such record. Each file in the directory should have a unique name. The file name, file name extension, and version number (if supported) will uniquely identify a file. Since all file names appear in a single directory, it is said that the directory has *one level*. As all file names are searched by the same method, we say, the directory is *flat*. Such a directory structure is shown in Figure 7.6, with a number of entries

Preliminary Info	Location Info.	Access Control Info.	Flags	Usage Info.
. . . .	. . . .	. . . .	. . . . . .	. . . .

FIGURE 7.5   A pictorial representation of a typical directory entry used in generic modern operating system.

Thesis	attributes
Student	attributes
News	attributes
Mail	attributes

(a)

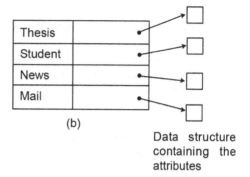

(b)

Data structure
containing the
attributes

FIGURE 7.6 Schematic block diagrams of representative structuring of one-level (flat) directories used in generic modern operating systems; (a) Attributes in the directory entry, and (b) Attributes lying elsewhere outside directory.

containing file names and other attributes; one entry per file is stored in a master directory. Two possible structures may exist. One approach as shown in Figure 7.6a, in which each entry contains the file name and all other attributes, including the disk addresses where the data are stored. The other possibility is shown in Figure 7.6b. Here, the directory entry holds the file name and a pointer to another data structure where the attributes and the disk addresses are found. Both these systems are equally and commonly used.

When a file is opened, the file management searches its directory until it finds the name of the file to be opened. It then extracts the attributes and disk addresses, either directly from the directory entry or from the data structure pointed to, and puts them in a table in main memory. All subsequent references to the file then use this table to get the required information of the file.

While flat directories are very conducive to single-user systems, they have some major drawbacks even in those systems, particularly when the total number of files is huge enough that it poses trouble in unique naming of the files, and searching a directory for a particular file requires significant time. Moreover, there is no provision for organizing these files in a suitable way, such as type-wise, application-wise, or user-wise, for multiple users or in a shared system. Last but not least, since a flat directory has no inherent structure, it is difficult to conceal portions of the overall directory from users, even if it is sometimes critically required. Thus, the flat directory as a whole is most inconvenient and inadequate when multiple users share a system or even for single users with many files of different types.

- **Two-Level Directories**

The problems being faced by flat directories have been alleviated with the use of a two-level directory structure in which there is a *master file directory* (MFD), and every account is given a private directory, known as a *user file directory* (UFD). The master directory has an entry for each user directory, providing the address and access control information. Each user directory is a simple list of the files of that user in which each file is described by one entry. A user who wants to separate various types of files can use several accounts with different account names. Although this structure certainly offers some distinct advantages compared to the straightforward flat directory structure, it still provides users with no help in structuring a collection of a large number of files, in general.

Brief details on this topic with a figure are given on the Support Material at www.routledge.com/ 9781032467238.

7.10.1.2 Hierarchical Directories

To find a generalized solution to this problem, the two-level directory structure was extended to an arbitrary number of levels that can be implemented in many interesting ways to provide better support to users. This ultimately gave rise to a more powerful, flexible, and almost universally accepted approach, the *hierarchical* or *tree structure*, which is basically an uprooted tree. Here, the root of the tree is a master directory that may have two types of nodes: directories and ordinary files. A directory can have children (sub-nodes); a non-directory cannot. Directories may be empty, and are usually user directories. Each of these user directories, in turn, may have subdirectories and files. Files are not restricted to a particular level in the hierarchy; that is, they can exist at any level. However, the top few levels of the directory structure usually tend to have a lot of directories, but ordinary files can reside there, too. Now, the obvious question thus arises as to how this hierarchical structure will be organized.

- The first aspect concerns the number of levels when the file system may provide a **fixed multi-level directory** structure in which each user has a user directory (UD) containing a few directories, and some of these directories may contain other directories, too. A user can then group the files based on some functionally related meaningful criterion, such as the name of activities to which they pertain. However, this approach is not adequate and relatively lacks flexibility, since it provides a fixed number of levels in the hierarchy and a fixed number of directories at each such level.
- The second approach provides more generalization with better flexibility in which a directory is treated as a file, and it can be created in a similar way to how a file is created. Here, the directory may appear as an entry in another directory with its flag field (Figure 7.5) with a value D to indicate that it is a directory file. The root directory as usual contains information about the user directories of all users. A user creates directory files and ordinary files to structurally organize their information as needed. Figure 7.7 shows the directory tree for a user (say, Y), and in this way, the directory trees of all such users together constitute the directory tree of the file system.
- The next aspect is *naming*, by which files can be unambiguously accessed following a path from the root (master) directory down various branches until the desired file is reached. The path that starts from the root directory and then traverses in sequence through the directory hierarchy of the file system up to the targeted file will constitute a pathname consisting of the directory names thus traversed in sequence for the file, known as the **absolute pathname**.

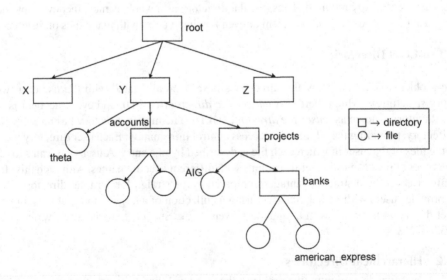

FIGURE 7.7   A representative sample example showing the implementation of a tree–structured directory for files used in generic modern operating system.

Several files with the same file name belonging to different directories are permitted, since they have unique pathnames or differ in their absolute pathnames. While absolute pathname can uniquely locate the desired file, it often appears inconvenient to spell out the entire pathname to locate a file every time it is referenced. Alternatively, the pathname for a file can be started from the user's current directory and then traverse down various branches until the desired file is reached, called a **relative pathname**, which is often short and convenient to use. However, relative pathname can sometimes be confusing because a particular file may have a different relative path name from different directories. Moreover, a user during execution may change the current directory to some other working directory by navigating up or down in the tree using a change–directory command. To facilitate this, each directory stores information about its *parent directory* in the directory structure.

Brief details on naming are given on the Support Material at www.routledge.com/9781032467238.

7.11 GRAPH DIRECTORY STRUCTURE: FILE SHARING

The use of a tree structure in organizing the directory structure of a file system certainly exhibits several advantages by providing each file exactly one parent directory, creating a total separation of different users' files, thereby offering complete naming freedom to users. However, this directory structure is inadequate and rather cumbersome when the file is required to be shared. In multi-user systems, there is always a high requirement to allow files to be shared among a number of users. Many issues arise in this regard; the most noted ones are:

- How the shared files can be accessed more conveniently by users in the existing tree-type directory structure.
- How the access rights to the file to be shared are to be offered to the other users.
- The management of simultaneous access over shared files by different users.

Use of the tree structure leads to a fundamental asymmetry when different users access a shared file. The file would always exist in some directory belonging to one of the users who can access it with a shorter pathname than other users. A user wishing to access a shared file of another user can do so by visiting a longer path through two or more directories. This problem can be resolved by organizing the directories in an acyclic graph structure in which a file can have many parent directories; hence, a shared file can be pointed to by directories of all those users who have rights to access it. To implement this, links can be used, which gives rise to the construction of an acyclic graph structure.

- **Links:** A link (sometimes called a **hard link**) is a directed connection between two existing files (a directory is also a file) in the directory structure. The link is created using the appropriate command in which a link name is given that links the target shared file (or directory) to be accessed. Once the link is established, the target file can be accessed as if it were a file with a name (link name) in the current directory. The link name entry in the current directory is identified by the value L in its flag field.

When the link mechanism is used, the file system normally maintains a *count* indicating the number of links pointing to a file. The UNIX file system uses *inodes* that contain a field to maintain a *reference count* with each file to indicate the number of links pointing to it. The content of this count field (*reference count*) is incremented or decremented when a new link is added or deleted, and the concerned directories and shared file are also required to be accordingly manipulated. A file can be deleted only if its reference count is 0. Thus, if a file has many links to it, it cannot be deleted even if its owner intends to do so by executing a delete operation.

A major limitation in using hard links for file sharing is that *directories* and *inodes* are data structures of a single file system (partition), and hence cannot point to an *inode* on another file system. Moreover, a file to be shared can have only one owner and one set of permissions, and thus all the responsibilities relating to the file are entrusted only to its owner, even including the disk space held by it.

An alternative way to share files is to create a **symbolic link**, which is itself a file and contains a pathname of another file. Thus, if a file X is created as a symbolic link to a shared file Y, then file X will contain the pathname of Y provided in the link command. The directory entry of file X is marked as a symbolic link, and this way the file system knows how to interpret its contents. Symbolic links can create dangling references when files are deleted. One interesting feature of this kind of link is that it can work across mounted file systems. In fact, if a means is provided for pathnames to include network addresses, such a link can then refer to a file that resides on a different computer. UNIX and UNIX-like systems call it a **symbolic link**, whereas in Windows, it is known as **shortcut**, and in Apple's Mac OS, it is called **alias**. However, one of the disadvantages of symbolic links is that when a file is deleted, or even just renamed, the link then becomes an orphan.

- **Access Rights:** The file system should provide an adequate and a sufficiently flexible mechanism for extensive sharing of files among many different users, of course, providing suitable protection mechanisms to amply secure and control the usage of these shared files. Typically, the file system provides a wide range of access rights to the users of shared files. Different types of access rights are provided by different operating systems (file systems); however, the rights being offered normally constitute a hierarchy in the access control list (to be discussed later), meaning that each such right implies those that precede it. Thus, for example, if a particular user is offered the right to append a specific file, it is implied that the same user can automatically enjoy the rights that precede it, such as acquaintance, execution, and reading.
- **Concurrent Access:** When different users with the same access rights on a particular file attempt to execute one of the permitted operations on the file simultaneously, the file management system must impose certain rules in order to keep them mutually exclusive for the sake of needed interprocess synchronization (already discussed in Chapter 4). Several useful methods are available to negotiate such situations, and one such simple approach may be to lock the entire file while it is under use, thereby preventing other users from accessing it simultaneously. Another approach may be relatively fine-grained control in which the respective record(s) under use is only locked and not the entire file. Manipulation of files with the same command being issued simultaneously by different users may also lead to a situation of deadlock. But those situations can be easily handled by the file management system using additional simple methods that can ensure prevention of deadlocks (already discussed in Chapter 4).

Brief details on links with a figure, and also different access rights, are given on the Support Material at www.routledge.com/9781032467238.

7.12 BLOCKING OF RECORDS: LOGICAL TO PHYSICAL

A structured file is organized, accessed, and processed in terms of logical units known as *records* defined by the creator, whereas a *block* is the physical record that is the unit of data transfer to or from an I/O medium. To perform I/O, the records must be organized in terms of blocks. A file is said to exploit blocking of records if a physical record (block) contains more than one record (logical record). The number of logical records contained in one physical record is called the **blocking factor** of a file. The blocking factor thus depends on the length of the block, which is decided mostly by the file management system, and also on the size of the record, which is defined by the user. If records are blocked, and m is the blocking factor, then a read operation on a file transfers m logical records to the memory at a time. Consequently, the total number of I/O operations required for processing a file is substantially reduced, thereby improving not only the file processing efficiency but also utilization of space on secondary storage and thereby throughput of a device. On the other hand, actions for extracting a particular logical record from a block thus accessed for processing are collectively called **deblocking** actions. However, many issues now need to be addressed, apart from deciding what size of block is suitable for overall use.

First, the block may be considered *fixed* or *variable length*. Fixed-length blocks offer several advantages, such as; making data transfer easy to or from a secondary device, straightforward buffer allocation in main memory and memory commitment for file buffers, and simple organization of blocks in secondary storage that requires no additional overhead.

The second consideration is about the size of the block to be chosen, which, in turn, is related to the blocking factor when compared to the average size of a record. Intuitively, the larger the block, the more *sequential* records can be handled in one I/O operation, thereby resulting in a reasonable reduction in the total number of I/O operations needed to process a file. However, if the records are being accessed *randomly* with no particular locality of reference, then larger blocks result in the unnecessary transfer of useless records. Moreover, larger blocks require larger I/O buffers, and management of larger buffers itself creates other difficulties. Another serious drawback of using a larger block irrespective of any type of access is that if such a block fails in an I/O operation, it requires all the records that are now quite large in number contained in the block to be created afresh, thereby requiring more additional overhead in order to make the file workable again. In general, for a given size of a block, there are three methods of blocking.

7.12.1 Fixed Length Blocking

Here, the block size is usually an integral multiple of fixed-length record size. Sometimes the record size is even slightly increased by adding a small unused space at its end to make the record size an exact divisor of the block size. This unused additional space can also be used by the record in the future in many ways if needed. In summary, the fixed-length blocking approach is the most common one, especially for sequential files with fixed-length records, and offers a lot of advantages, as already discussed.

7.12.2 Variable-Length Spanned Blocking

Here, variable-length records are stored after being packed into blocks with no space remaining unused. Consequently, some records may span over two blocks, with the continuation indicated by a pointer to the successor block. However, this approach, while providing better storage usage and no constraint on the size of records, causes difficulties at the time of implementation, mainly in updating of records, which is tedious and also time-consuming irrespective of the type of organization being used. Also, for records that are spread over two blocks, each one requires two expensive I/O operations.

7.12.3 Variable-Length Unspanned Blocking

In this method, variable-length records are stored, but spanning is not allowed. As a result, there may be unused (wasted) space in most of the blocks, because the next record is often larger than the available unused remaining space. This approach results in wastage of space and thereby requires limiting record size to be nearly the size of a block. In virtual memory environments, while the small page is used as the basic unit of data transfer operation, this method is often implemented by combining multiple pages to create larger blocks as units for the sake of efficient I/O operation. In fact, this approach is profitably employed for VSAM files used in the IBM OS/370 ESA and in the OS/390 versatile operating system to drive large IBM mainframes. However, irrespective of different blocking schemes, as mentioned, the effect of blocking is unaltered even while the spaces on secondary devices are managed by different file allocation schemes.

7.12.4 CHOICE OF BLOCKING FACTOR

The right choice of a blocking factor could be considered a dominant parameter in I/O processing carried out by the file management system. To demonstrate this, let us consider that s_r and s_b represent the size of a record (logical record) and block (physical record), respectively; then $s_b = m \cdot s_r$, where m is the blocking factor. The total I/O time per block $(t_{io})_b$, and the I/O time per record $(t_{io})_r$, can then be computed as

$$(t_{io})_b = t_a + m \cdot t_x \ldots \text{(a)}$$
$$(t_{io})_r = (t_a / m) + t_x \ldots \text{(b)}$$

Where t_a and t_x are the access time per block and transfer time per record, respectively. If $t_a = 8$ msec., data transfer rate = 1000 Kbytes/sec, record length $s_r = 200$ bytes. So the transfer time per record (logical record), that is, $t_x = 200/1000$ msec. = 0.2 msec. The values of $(t_{io})_b$ and $(t_{io})_r$ can be computed using Equations (a) and (b) for a given value of m.

If the CPU time spent in processing a record t_p is 2.5 msec. and m = 4, then $(t_{io})_r < t_p$. This shows that the next record is available to the CPU before the processing of the current record is completed, thereby totally eliminating CPU idle time waiting for the next record to arrive. In fact, proper blocking of records and related buffering, when combined, ensure that the process does not suffer any I/O waits after the initial start-up phase.

Brief details on this topic, with Table 7.3, are given on the Support Material at www.routledge.com/9781032467238.

7.13 MANAGEMENT OF SECONDARY STORAGE

Disk being a prime secondary storage device, a major issue is its space management which is carried out efficiently and reliably by the file management system, primarily following the line similar to those used in memory management. Like a file, which is considered to consist of a collection of logical blocks containing long sequences of bytes, the disk space is also divided into logical disk blocks, and the size of the logical block is the same as the logical disk block. The size of this logical disk block, on the other hand, is also equal to the size of the logical sector.

Disk blocks are consumed by files, and as files are manipulated by the file management system, so are disk blocks allocated/deallocated to files. This, in turn, gives rise to several issues. First, limited space on secondary storage must be properly allocated to files, and second, it is necessary to keep track of the available free space for additional allocations due to growth of existing files as well as for fresh allocations to new files. Moreover, when a file is deleted, the disk blocks occupied by the file are to be released, and this space must then be added to the existing free space by using a suitable strategy. All these issues are closely interrelated to one another; that is, the approach taken for file allocation may have an impact on the approach taken for free space management. On the other hand, all the free space management strategies may not go well with all the file allocation strategies. In addition, it has been observed that there is a strong interaction between file structure and allocation policy.

Brief details on this topic are given on the Support Material at www.routledge.com/9781032467238.

7.14 FILE ALLOCATION: DIFFERENT ISSUES AND APPROACHES

When allocating space to a file, different strategies involving several issues have been tested; some primary issues are:

*   What is the amount of space to be allocated to a file when a new file is first created? Whether the maximum space is to be provided at a lot that is requested at the time of its creation?

- The other approach suggests allocating space to store an entire file as a collection of pieces, each one with contiguous areas; these pieces themselves may not normally be contiguous. Now, the obvious question is, what will be the size of these pieces used as a unit for file allocation? The size of a piece can range from a single disk block to even the entire file.

Whatever method of allocation is considered, the key issue in storing files is how to keep track of the space allocated to a file and what sort of data structure or table is to be used for this purpose. Various methods are, however, used in different systems. An example of such a data structure is the *inode* used in UNIX or *file allocation table* (FAT) used in Windows and some other systems.

7.14.1 STATIC (PRE-ALLOCATION) AND DYNAMIC ALLOCATION

Early file systems used to allocate a large enough single contiguous disk area to a file. This scheme is simple to implement, and only the disk address of the first block (starting address) of the file is required to handle the entire file. The performance is also superb due to inherent speedy access of the file from the disk. However, *contiguous allocation* also suffers from several critical drawbacks. Under this scheme, the space to be allocated to a file is usually its maximum size or an estimate of it (a reliable estimate is, however, difficult to achieve) or often inclined to an overestimation in file size due to apprehension about running out of space. Whatever it may be, it eventually invites a handful of waste in secondary storage space and both internal and external fragmentation of disk space that might have been otherwise used. Compaction of the disk removes external fragmentation, but it is usually prohibitively expensive. Besides, a contiguous allocation scheme also faces other difficulties (due to the presence of bad blocks) and requires complicated arrangements when allocating spaces to a disk.

Contemporary FMS avoid all these problems by adopting the noncontiguous memory allocation model (see Chapter 5) to disk space allocation. This approach avoids external fragmentation. Fixed-sized or variable-sized disk blocks are allocated on demand at the time of file creation or updating a file. This reduces the average fragmentation (internal) per file to half the size of a disk block (in the last allocated disk block). As usual, access to data requires the equivalent of "address translation" (see Chapter 5) that needs appropriate data structures or tables containing several information, particularly about disk blocks allocated to a file.

Brief details on this topic are given on the Support Material at www.routledge.com/9781032467238.

7.14.1.1 Different Options

Noncontiguous allocation is closely related to the size of the piece of disk area to be allocated to a file. At one end, a piece may be taken that is large enough to hold the entire file. At the other end, space is to be allocated on disk one block at a time. Whatever it may be, selection of the size of a piece is a critical one, and several factors decide the tradeoff between efficiency with regard to a single file operation versus the entire system's efficiency as a whole. The factors suggested by Wiederhold (1987) in this regard, as listed in the following, are of primary importance. These factors are interrelated to one another but are to be minutely considered individually at the time of deciding the tradeoff.

- Having a large piece provides contiguity of space that eventually increases performance while writing a file in a single blow as well as for read/modify operations in transaction-oriented processing systems.
- Using a large number of small pieces provides allocation flexibility and better space utilization but at the same time increases the size of the tables employed to manage the allocation information.

Now, the consideration is whether fixed-size or variable-sized pieces of the disk area are to be used in each of these two approaches; such as, small number of moderately large pieces or large number of small pieces. However, considerations of the size of the pieces as well as the number of pieces to be used altogether on permutations give rise to several options, each of which is equally conducive to both pre-allocation and dynamic allocation, but each one, in turn, has also its own merits and similarly drawbacks. While moderately large and variable-sized contiguous pieces of disk area normally provide better performance with less wastage of space (fragmentation), managing these pieces with the existing free spaces and minimizing of fragmentation raises some issues. Those can be resolved by adapting the noncontiguous memory allocation model (see Chapter 5) to disk space allocation. The most viable alternative strategies in this regard are, first fit, best fit, and nearest fit. Each of these strategies has its own strengths and drawbacks; hence, it is very difficult to decide which one is superior, because numerous factors interact with one another in a critical fashion. The factors that influence choosing a particular strategy are types of files, structure of files, access mechanism to be employed, disk buffering, disk caching, disk scheduling, and many other performance metrics in the system that are closely associated with I/O operation.

Brief details on this topic are given on the Support Material at www.routledge.com/9781032467238.

7.15   FILE ALLOCATION: DIFFERENT METHODS

After considering all the issues, as discussed, two distinct categories relating to space allocation to a file ultimately emerge: *contiguous allocation* and *noncontiguous allocation*. Noncontiguous allocation uses two common methods: *chained* (or linked) *allocation* and *indexed allocation*.

7.15.1   CONTIGUOUS ALLOCATION

This method is used mostly in a pre-allocation strategy in which a single contiguous set of blocks is allocated to a file. Thus, adjacent logical blocks occupy adjacent physical blocks. It is simple to implement and easy to maintain, because the FAT for keeping track of file blocks needs just a single entry for each file, showing only the address of the starting block and the length of the file. This method is excellent for processing individual sequential files in which multiple physically adjacent blocks can be accessed at a time with minimum disk head movement resulting in faster access, thereby yielding notable improvement in I/O performance. No other scheme even comes close. Multi-sector transfers also are conducive, since there is no intervening disk access. Random access to contiguous blocks is also quite easy and fast, because the address of the required disk block can be easily calculated on the basis of the file's starting address recorded in the directory. For example, if the address of the starting block of a file is n and the kth block is required, its address on secondary storage is simply $n + k - 1$, and this can be accessed from the disk very quickly. However, the performance of multi-sector transfers in random-access mode depends mostly on the number of consecutive blocks that are accessed between successive seek operations.

The *second approach* in the implementation of a contiguous allocation scheme is that once the initially allocated space is full, the file system searches for another bigger contiguous free area. The partially created file is then copied into this area, and the remaining space of this newly allocated area can then be used by the file if it grows. The initially allocated area is released. All these activities are, however, carried out by the file system in a way transparent to the user with no notification, except that a slight delay may be experienced.

A *third method* of contiguous allocation is that once the initially allocated space is full, the rest of the file will be placed in some other contiguous free area, commonly called *overflow*. This overflowed file can later be reconstructed offline by another operation, such as COMPACT.

The contiguous allocation scheme has its own merits and drawbacks, already discussed in detail in a previous section. External fragmentation is an obvious consequence of the contiguous allocation scheme that makes it difficult for the file system to find a sufficient number of contiguous blocks to satisfy the new requests. It will then be necessary to perform a compaction (defragmentation) algorithm to coalesce the scattered free space on the disk to a contiguous space for further use.

Briefs detail on this topic with figures are given on the Support Material at www.routledge.com/9781032467238.

7.15.2 Noncontiguous Allocation: Linked (or Chained) Allocation

The major problem of contiguous allocation is fragmentation of both types, especially external fragmentation, which consequently reduces the percentage of disk space usage. However, one solution to this predicament is linked allocation, which is essentially a disk version of a linked list and hence does not require the file size to be declared in advance.

Here, disk space is allocated on an individual block basis, and a file is represented by a linked list (or chaining) of allocated disk blocks together. Each block contains two fields: the data which is to be written into the file and the control information, which contains the address of the next disk block (i.e. a pointer to the next block in the chain) allocated to the file. Here, the directory (FAT) needs just a single entry for each file, showing the starting block (the Loc info. field of the directory entry for the file points to the first disk block; see Figure 7.5) and the length (number of blocks) of the file. Other blocks are accessed one after another by following the pointer given in the current block using the classical linked allocation mechanism. Although this method supports pre-allocation, it is more common to simply allocate blocks on an as-needed basis. When an additional disk block is needed to append new information to a file, any free block can be added to a chain, even in the middle of an existing file, a feature not offered by any other space allocation policies. Searching (or selecting) an individual block of a file requires only tracing through the chain to the target block. There is almost no external fragmentation, if any; it is only on the last allocated block and then only half the size of the block, on average. To delete a file, the list of disk blocks allocated to the file is taken off and is simply added to the list of free blocks. In this way, it saves a lot of processing time required for file deletion.

This type of organization of files is most suitable and efficient for sequential file processing in both single-user and multi-user shared systems, but random access is extremely slow because locating a given block requires accessing all the intervening blocks in the chain. Moreover, as there exists no principle of locality, if it is required to access several blocks of a file at a time (as in sequential processing), then a series of accesses to different parts of the disk are required, which eventually increases the disk I/O. This problem has been resolved in some systems by periodically consolidating files (reordering allocated blocks to consecutive blocks and then chaining). In addition, the use of a pointer associated with each disk block of a file to indicate its own next block leaves an amount of space in a block for data storage that is no longer a power of two because the pointer takes up a few bytes. While it is not fatal to have such a peculiar size, it is less efficient because many programs are used to read and write in blocks whose size is a power of two. Another serious drawback of linked allocation is its sensitivity to chaining to damaged pointers.

Reliability with this organization is also poor due to its sensitivity to chaining to damaged pointers, which can make the remaining blocks inaccessible, leading to total loss of data in the entire file, and recovering chained files is an extremely painful experience. Similarly, if a pointer in the free list is corrupted, the operation of the file system may be disrupted. However, some designs negotiate this problem by storing pointers in a separate dedicated file and making redundant copies of it to counter this fatal situation and allow subsequent safer recovery. This idea of keeping a copy of the list of chains of the active files into the main memory facilitates faster access, especially for random file access. Some versions of the popular MS-DOS operating system use a similar approach.

More on this topic with figures is given on the Support Material at www.routledge.com/9781032467238.

7.15.3 INDEXED ALLOCATION

Many of the negative factors experienced with contiguous and noncontiguous chained allocation methods are duly addressed in the indexed allocation method. In its simplest form, the directory (FAT) entry of each file points to a separate one-level index known as a *file map table* (FMT) for each file. The index in the FMT has one entry for each portion allocated to the file, and each corresponding allocated disk block contains a single field: the only data field. Typically, the file indexes (FMTs) are not physically kept as part of the directory (FAT). Rather, the file indexes (FMTs) for a file are kept in a separate block, and the *loc.* info field (see Figure 7.5) of a directory entry points to the FMT for a file, as shown in Figure 7.8.

Allocation of disk space to a file is performed on an as-needed basis when a file is created or updated using either fixed-size blocks, as shown in Figure 7.8, or variable-sized blocks (with two fields in FMT, the starting address of the block and the length of the respective block). Allocation by fixed-size blocks eliminates fragmentation, whereas allocation by variable-sized blocks improves locality (access to successive blocks). Whatever the case, the file consolidation operation may also need to be carried out periodically to reduce the size of the index in the case of variable-sized blocks, but it shows no effect in the case of fixed-size block allocation. To locate a free block, the disk status map (DSM) or free list (to be discussed in next section) is searched, and if this free block is allocated to a file, the address of this block is added to the FMT of the respective file. Deallocation is performed when the file is deleted, and all disk blocks pointed to by the FMT of the file are marked free before the FMT and the directory entry of the file are erased. Indexed allocation supports both sequential access and direct access to the file, be it small, medium, or large, and therefore is accepted as the most common and useful form of file allocation.

Generally, for a small file, the FMT itself can be accommodated in the directory entry to realize improved efficiency with better accessibility. But for a medium or large file, the FMT is quite large; hence, multi-level indexed allocation is commonly used. The directory entry still contains a part of the FMT. The first few entries in the FMT, say, k entries, may point directly to data blocks as is found in traditional indexed allocation. Other entries of FMT point to special blocks, commonly called *index blocks*, which contain pointers to data blocks that are accessed through two levels of indirection. The first level of indirection is from the FMT to the respective index block, and the second level of indirection is from the index block to the target data block. This type of arrangement is quite useful for small files, as the FMT itself is found in the directory entry, and even for medium-sized files containing k or fewer data blocks which can be accessed directly through FMT with no need for any index blocks. Only moderately large and very large files have to visit multiple levels of

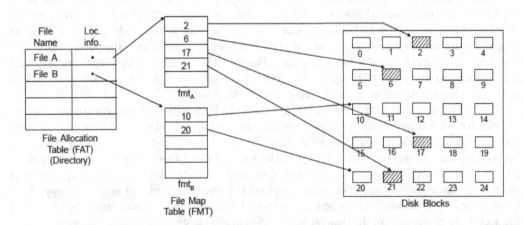

FIGURE 7.8 A schematic block diagram illustrating the mechanism of indexed allocation method used in file management of a generic modern operating system.

indirection in which one disk access per level of indexing is required to reach the target data block and thus face a marginal degradation in their access performance. However, successive accesses to file blocks within the addressing range of the current index blocks need not face this overhead if recently used index blocks are kept in memory. Naturally, sequential access is more likely to benefit from buffering of index blocks. However, the nature of noncontiguous allocation is such that it is unlikely to find adjacent logical blocks in consecutive physical disk blocks (or sectors). In order to reduce latency in disk access, systems using noncontiguous allocation occasionally make their file contiguous by means of performing defragmentation or consolidation or by another similar useful approach.

Conclusion: File organization using indexed allocation is less efficient for sequential file processing when compared to the linked allocation scheme, since the FMT of a file has to be accessed, and then a series of accesses to different parts of the disk are required that eventually increases the disk I/O. Random access, however, is comparatively more efficient, since the access to a particular record can be carried out directly by way of obtaining the specific address of the target block from the FMT. Reliability in indexed allocation is comparatively less damaging than linked allocation. This is because any corruption in an entry of an FMT or DSM may lead to a situation of limited damage.

Indexed allocation with variable-length blocks and multiple-level index allocation with figures are given on the Support Material at www.routledge.com/9781032467238.

7.16   FREE SPACE MANAGEMENT: DIFFERENT TECHNIQUES

Spaces on the disk not currently allocated and spaces released by a file when it is deleted together constitute the free space on the disk. Free space management is closely related to each of the file allocation techniques just described and is a major issue in the performance of a system as a whole. While file allocation techniques are mostly concerned with the *FAT*, free space management needs a different type of table known as a *disk allocation table*. Various techniques related to free space management exist, but we will describe here only a few popular techniques that have been used in many reputed contemporary system.

7.16.1   DISK STATUS MAP OR BIT TABLES

The status of disk blocks can be recorded by adapting the bit map scheme used for noncontiguous memory allocation in memory management (see Chapter 5). While managing disk block status, a table called the DSM or bit tables is used. The DSM is similar to a bit map; it has one entry of only one bit for each disk block that indicates whether the disk block is free or has been allocated to a file. When the bit is 1 in an entry, it indicates that the corresponding disk block is allocated. Similarly, when the bit is 0 in an entry, it indicates that the corresponding disk block is free to use. Figure 7.9 illustrates a DSM. Every time a new block needs to be allocated to a file, the DSM is consulted. An alternative to the use of a DSM may be to use a free list of disk blocks (to be discussed in the next section).

This method is easy to implement, and it is relatively simple to locate one or a contiguous group of free blocks, and subsequent allocation and deallocation of blocks can be carried out quickly by setting and resetting the corresponding bits of the map. It also performs equally well with any of the file allocation techniques just described. But the size of a bit map for even a moderate size of disk is so large that it cannot be stored even in today's most common memory sizes for speedy operation. Moreover, searching of bit tables while in memory is so time-consuming that it badly affects the overall system performance to an unacceptable degree on average. On the other hand, if the same bit table is stored on disk, it would require such a large number of disk blocks that searching of this amount of disk space every time a block is needed is a huge time-consuming operation that cannot be afforded. So, this proposition is outright rejected, and a bit table resident in main memory is indicated. In fact, systems that employ bit tables in main memory maintain auxiliary

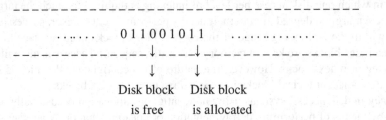

FIGURE 7.9 An example relating to management of disk free space using disk status map (DSM) or bit tables employed by a generic modern operating system.

data structures that summarize the contents of the bit tables by logically dividing them into almost equal-sized subranges, and a summary can be made for each such subrange that mainly includes the number of free blocks and the maximum-sized contiguous number of free blocks. When the file management needs a particular number of contiguous blocks, it can go only through the summary table to find an appropriate subrange and then search that particular subrange to find the desired one.

7.16.2 Chained Free Blocks and Groups of Blocks

Systems with noncontiguous allocation follow a philosophy which presumes that the files usually grow incrementally and thus allocate only a single block or groups of blocks to them in the form of pieces. Chaining of free pieces is rather simple and convenient. These pieces may be chained together by using only a pointer and length-value in each free piece. Allocation of free spaces by variable-length pieces may be carried out using the first-fit algorithm. The headers from the pieces are fetched one at a time to determine the suitable free piece in the chain. After obtaining the required piece, pointers and length values are adjusted. One of the distinct advantages of this method is its negligible storage overhead, because there is no need to have a disk allocation table, merely to use a pointer to indicate the beginning of the chain and the length of the first piece. Since disk space needed for pointers and length-value is usually less than 1 percent, its impact on disk utilization is of little practical concern. This method is thus suited to all types of file allocation techniques. Another advantage of this approach is that new free pieces obtained upon deletion of files can be appended to the existing free chain by simply updating the link of the tail block, and this can be performed with only a single disk access.

When free space management is performed on a *block-basis*, and if allocation is made one block at a time, simply choose the free block at the head of the chain and adjust the first pointer or length-value accordingly. One serious problem is that every time a block is allocated, it is necessary to read the block first to recover the pointer to the now-new first free block before writing data to that block. If many such individual blocks need to be allocated one at a time for a file operation, this may slow down the file creation process to a great extent and make the file highly fragmented. Consequently, deletion of a highly fragmented file requires one disk access per each block freed to update the pointers that, in turn, makes the entire file-deletion process very time-consuming. Block-basis allocation, however, does not give rise to any external disk fragmentation; hence, disk compaction may not be needed. Moreover, chaining on a block-basis allows easy handling of bad blocks by simply overwriting them from both file and free chains.

7.16.3 Indexing

Indexing of free space may be cumbersome. This approach treats the free space as a file and similarly uses an index table as already described in the file allocation method. In a freshly initialized volume with a very large number of free blocks, this approach requires multiple levels of indexing when it intends to access many or all of them, thereby consuming an unacceptable amount of processing time. As new files are gradually created, the number of free blocks may automatically be decreased, but allocations and deallocations of blocks may require high overhead due to multiple levels of indexing. That is why some designs propose keeping at least one index block of the free list in memory that can speed-up the allocation of up to n free blocks, where n is the number of indices in an index block. However, the outcome obtained is still not acceptable. For the sake of efficiency, the index should be maintained on the basis of variable-sized pieces rather than on a block-basis. This requires only one entry in the index table for every free piece on the disk. This approach appears to mostly offer adequate support for all types of file allocation methods.

7.16.4 FREE LIST OF BLOCKS

This approach can be viewed in two ways:

- free space in the form of each individual block-basis, and
- free space as a collection of different clusters of contiguous free blocks.

In an individual block-basis approach, each free block is identified by assigning it a serial number (or by its address), and the list of numbers (or addresses) of all free blocks can then be recorded in a separate list. With a disk of common size today, the size of the number (or address) to represent (identify) each free block in the free list will require in the range of 32 bits ($2^{32} = 4$ GB). Such a huge free list cannot be maintained in main memory and hence must be stored on disk. Now, the problem is that every time a free block is needed, a corresponding slower disk access will then be required, and this will eventually affect the overall system performance adversely. To avoid this problem, some designers suggest two effective techniques that store a small part of the list in main memory so that the block request can be quickly responded to.

One such technique is to fetch a part of the list into main memory and treated it as a *push-down stack*. Whenever a new block is required to be allocated, it is popped off the top of the stack, and similarly when a block is deallocated, it is pushed on to the top of the stack. In this way, all the requests can be responded to with no delay except in the situation when the stack (part of the list) in memory is either full or exhausted. At that time, only one appropriate transfer of a part of the list between disk and memory is required to resume stack operations. The other technique is similarly to fetch a part of the list into main memory, and it would now be treated as a FIFO queue and be operated in a similar way to a push-down stack but obeying the traditional queue operations. To make each of these approaches more attractive and effective, a background process (or thread) can be slowly run whenever possible to sort the list in memory by serial number (or by address) to enable each of these approaches to be applicable for contiguous allocation of blocks as far as possible.

The second approach is allocation of free space from a collection of different clusters of contiguous free blocks, and it requires keeping track of such clusters and also implementation of a policy for allocation and deallocation of blocks. Addresses and sizes of free disk areas can be maintained as a separate list or can be recorded in unused directory entries. For example, when a file is deleted and subsequently deallocated, its entry in the basic file directory can be marked as unused, but its address and size in terms of blocks can be left intact. At the time of creation of a new file, the operating system can inspect unused directory entries to locate a free area of suitable size to match the current request. The first-fit and best-fit algorithms could be used for this purpose. Depending on the portion of the directory that is kept in main memory, the trade-off between first-fit and best-fit may go either way. While first-fit may sometimes give rise to a substantial amount of internal fragmentation, it requires fewer entries of the directory to be looked up and may be preferable when very few directory entries are available in main memory and most of the directory entries are on the disk. On the other hand, if most of the directory entries are available in main memory, the best-fit algorithm provides a better performance since it tends to reduce internal fragmentation by carrying out a closer match of the requested size to the size of the allocated disk area.

Brief details on this topic are given on the Support Material at www.routledge.com/9781032467238.

7.17   FILE ORGANIZATION: PHYSICAL REPRESENTATION

There are many ways to organize files on disk. A few principles seem to be universal.

* Disk blocks have numbers, and complex structures can be placed on the disk by having data in one block refer to another block by number.
* Each file is described by a *file descriptor*, which tells how the file is physically arranged on the disk.
* Each physical disk is described by a *disk descriptor*, which tells how the disk is arranged into areas and which parts are currently unused. The disk descriptor is stored at a well-known location on the disk.
* Information may be stored redundantly on the disk to allow programs to try to restructure the disk if it gets confused. Confusion is the typical result of unscheduled operating-system failures, because the structure may be undergoing modification at the time of the failure. Even worse, the disk may be in the middle of writing a block when failure occurs. Restructuring a garbage disk is called **salvaging**.
* The basic unit of allocation is the single disk block, although entire tracks or cylinders may be allocated at a time to keep large regions in a file contiguous on the disk. This attempt to keep files in local regions on the disk is called **clustering**. It is based on the cache principle, since it is faster to read or write on the disk at cylinders close to the current position, and the most likely request to come after one file request is another request on the same file. Clustering may also be attempted to keep files that are in the same directory positioned close together on the disk. Another form of clustering, called **skewing**, that spaces consecutive blocks of a file by a few sectors apart. As a result, a typical process reading the entire file will find the next file block under the disk read/write head at the time it needs it. Some disk controllers *interleave* sectors to place consecutively numbered ones some distance apart from each other on the same track. In this case, the file manager most likely should not attempt skewing.
* Searching file structures and allocating free blocks would be too time consuming if the information were stored only on the disk. In accordance with the cache principle, some structure and allocation information may be duplicated in the main store. But, as is typically the case with caches, the cached (main-store) data and the actual (disk) data will possibly be out of step. Operating system failures (crashes) then become even more serious than they seem to be, because they may lose recent changes. To mitigate the danger, all main-store caches are occasionally (perhaps every minute) archived to the disk. Perhaps the worst time for a catastrophic failure is during archiving.

The facilities provided by the file service mostly determine the structures that must be used. For example, direct access of arbitrary positions in a file requires different structures than sequential access. Hierarchical directories and flat directories require different structures. Different methods of access control also need different structures.

7.18   FILE SYSTEM RELIABILITY

The file system never provides any protection to data against physical damage to the devices and media but can only help to secure the information. Consequently, damages with a file system, if result in irrevocable lost for some reasons, then restoring all the information will be not only time-consuming and painstaking, but equally difficult, and in many situations, seems to be practically impossible, and may even be catastrophic. However, there are some commonly used methods, such as bad block management, and backups, that help to offer safeguards to the file system. That is why the reliability of the file system is urgently sought. The file system is said to be reliable if it can guarantee that the functions of the file system will work correctly despite the different types of faults that may occur in the system. The reliability of file system concerns two main aspects:

- To ensure correctness of all types of file operations.
- To adequately guard against any type of error that may damage the data and thereby cause loss of data in files.

Reliability is closely associated with the terms **fault** and **failure**. A *fault* is commonly a defect in some part of the system causing an error in the system state. When an error causes unexpected behavior or an unusual situation in the system, it is termed a failure. In other words, a fault is the cause of a failure. For example, crashing of I/O devices due to a power outage or corruption of a disk block is a fault, whereas inability of the file system to read such a block is a failure. Faults are of various types, and any one of them may affect the entire computer system or hardware components such as processor, memory, I/O devices, and communication links. But we will concentrate here only on some of those issues of fault and the respective approaches to prevent them that are related to FMS.

Reliability problems in file systems that are most common are mainly system crashes due to power interruptions and data corruption by viruses leading to loss of data in files or loss of file system control data (various data structures needed by the file system, to be described in the following discussion) stored on disk. If the control data are either lost or become inconsistent, the injury is fatal, and the file system may not be able to work at all. On the other hand, damage caused by loss of only data in a file due to data corruption is relatively less serious, since it is limited to only a single file.

Brief details on this topic are given on the Support Material at www.routledge.com/9781032467238.

7.18.1 FILE SYSTEM INTEGRITY: IMPORTANCE

Integrity of the file system ensures the correct and consistent operation of the file system. Loss of integrity arises mostly due to the loss of or damage to the control data of the file system that mainly includes the table of active files, namely FCBs of open files, parts of the free list of disk blocks or DSM, and file map tables of open files. Some of these control data, like the file map table and others, are written back to disk only when a file is closed. Other control data, like the DSM and free lists, may be copied to disk by the system only periodically. Such an arrangement may lead to a situation in which disk copies of control data at any instant may not be identical to their corresponding memory contents during system operation; hence, the latest control data may be lost due to erasure of memory if the power fails. Similarly, control data not being maintained in memory are lost when a disk crashes.

Brief details on this topic with an example are given on the Support Material at www.routledge.com/9781032467238.

7.18.2 RELIABILITY IMPLEMENTATION: DIFFERENT TECHNIQUES

File management systems (operating systems) often use two popular approaches to ensure file integrity, thereby ensuring that the data are reliably stored over a period of time. Those are:

Recovery: This is a classic approach implemented using different techniques when a failure occurs. It attempts to restore the damaged data in files and inconsistent control data of the file system to some near-past consistent state so that the file system can once again resume its normal operation from the new state. While this action rescues files from a damaged state, deviations from the expected behavior may also be observed. Appropriate manipulation measures in system operation can then accordingly be taken by noticing the deviations that happened.

Fault tolerance: This is another effective approach that uses some commonly used techniques in order to guard the file system against any loss of integrity. Its objective is to keep the operation of file system consistent, uninterrupted, and perfectly correct, even in the event of failure, at all times.

7.18.2.1 Recovery Techniques

One effective method often used to recover a file system in the event of failure is periodically making a backup of all user and control data in the file system. When a system failure occurs, the file system is restored to the state recorded in its latest backup. However, all the actions performed between the last backup and the instant of failure are not really recoverable and are lost. So all the actions executed during this interval are required to be executed afresh just after recovery to bring the file system to the correct state. This approach requires two main kinds of overhead: one due to creating backups at regular intervals, thereby investing both extra time and extra space, and the other for reprocessing the part of the files whose updates were lost, which mainly means extra time. But, for a large disk, blindly backing up the entire drive including unused disk blocks on any specified device, called a physical dump (**full backup**), is awkward and heavily time consuming. Although the full-backup approach has been further modified to make it reasonably acceptable, and many variants of it have been devised to make it more foolproof using extra devices, still due to many adverse reasons coupled with other issues makes this approach ultimately to fell out of favor.

An alternative approach to a full backup of the entire file system at regular intervals is to make **incremental backups**, which are dumps (copy) of only those files and data structures that have been modified since the last full or incremental backup was created. This approach reduces both space and time overhead to an acceptable level.

An effective and elegant way to reduce overhead is to use a *combination (hybrid) of incremental and full backups* of a file system. Here, the file system creates full backups at relatively large intervals of time, such as a few days or a week. Incremental backups are created at shorter intervals, such as at every file close operation, and are discarded when the next full backup is made. Although this approach sounds good and appears foolproof, it increases both space and time overhead because of the creation and coexistence of both full and incremental backups, and, in addition, some files may exist in more than one incremental backup.

Brief details on this topic with a figure are given on the Support Material at www.routledge.com/9781032467238.

7.18.2.2 Fault-Tolerance Techniques

Another important way the reliability of a file system can be improved is implementing techniques which provide adequate prevention that can:

- safeguard loss of data due to malfunctioning of devices caused by physical damage to the devices or media or by other types of faults caused by numerous reasons.
- ensure file system consistency by preventing inconsistency of control data resulting from system crashes.

These techniques are commonly known as *fault-tolerance techniques* that primarily attempt to implement some precautionary measures which can safeguard the file system from any unforeseen damage. Two such techniques, *stable storage* and *atomic actions*, can be mentioned in this regard.

- **Stable storage:** This simple technique, named **disk mirroring** by Lampson, uses redundancy by creating two copies of a record, called its primary and secondary copy, that are maintained on disk to negotiate only a single failure occurrence. This disk mirroring is quite different from the disk mirroring technique used in RAID, as described in Chapter 6. For a file write operation, it updates both copies: the primary copy first, followed by the secondary copy. For a file read operation, the primary copy of the disk block(s) is first accessed. If it is all right, there is no problem, but if it is not readable, the secondary copy is accessed. While this technique guarantees total survival even after a single failure and is thus applied to all the files for general use in the file system, it is very expensive; still, it can be made profitable when processes selectively use it to protect their data. However, one of the serious drawbacks of this approach is that it fails to indicate whether a value is the old or new version (both the copy contains old version when the failure occurs before the primary copy is updated, both the copy contains new version when the failure occurs after both copies have been updated). So the user is confused and cannot ascertain definitely whether to re–execute the operation which was ongoing at the time of failure while restoring the system to normalcy. The atomic action described next, however, addresses this issue and accordingly overcomes this problem.
- **Atomic action:** An action may consist of several sub–actions, each of which may involve in some operation that intends to manipulate either control data (data structures) of file system or updating data of files. Any failure during the course of such an operation interrupts its execution and eventually may make the file system inconsistent and cause errors. For example, consider an inventory control system that involves transferring spares from one account to another. If a failure occurs during the transfer operation, it interrupts its execution; spares may have been debited from one account but not credited to the other account, or vice-versa. The inventory control file system would then be in an inconsistent and erroneous state. The ultimate objective of atomic action (very similar in nature to the atomic action used in interprocess synchronization, as described in Chapter 4) aims to avoid all such ill effects of system failure. In fact, any action X_i consisting of a set of sub-actions $\{x_{ik}\}$ is said to be an atomic action if, for every execution of X_i, either

1. Executions of all sub-actions in $\{x_{ik}\}$ are completed, or
2. Executions of none of the sub-actions in $\{x_{ik}\}$ are completed

An atomic action succeeds when it executes all its sub-actions without any interruption or interference. In that situation, it is said to commit. An atomic action fails if a failure of any type occurs or an abort command is executed before all its sub-actions are completed. If it fails, the state of file system, the state of each file, and each variable involved in the atomic action should remain as it was prior to the beginning of the atomic action. If an atomic action commits, it is guaranteed that all the actions already taken by it will survive even if a failure occurs.

Brief details on the implementation of atomic actions with an algorithm are given on the Support Material at www.routledge.com/9781032467238.

7.19 VIRTUAL FILE SYSTEMS

The objectives of a file system are to meet a diverse spectrum of requirements as demanded from both the system and the users: high reliability, efficient and effective response, easy and fast access to files located on other computer systems, and above all a friendly interface for the sake of convenience. It is obvious that no file system design can offer all these features at the same time, and that is why an operating system (file management system) aims to provide a **virtual file system (VFS)** that enables several different file systems to operate simultaneously to realize different useful features.

A VFS is an abstraction that supports a generic file model and is implemented using a VFS layer that resides between a process and a file system to support many different file systems simultaneously

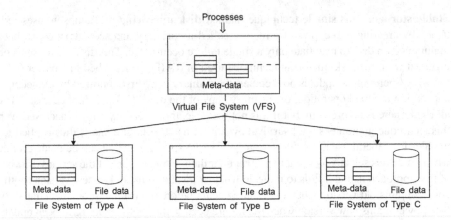

FIGURE 7.10   A generalized block diagram illustrating a schematic representation of virtual file system used in a generic modern operating system.

(similar to the virtual machine layer that resides between the operating systems and bare hardware to support many different operating systems running simultaneously on the same piece of hardware), as shown in Figure 7.10. The VFS layer also has two interfaces: the upper interface that interacts with the processes above and the lower interface for the target file systems lying below. Any file system that conforms to the specification of VFS file system interface can be installed to run under VFS. This feature helps to add a new file system easily to the existing environment. The VFS process interface (upper interface) provides functionalities to perform generic *open, close, read, write,* and other common operations on files, and **mount** and **unmount** operations on file systems. These functionalities are invoked through respective system calls. The VFS file system interface (lower interface) determines under which file system a particular file actually belongs and invokes the respective functionalities of the corresponding file system as needed. This interface also invokes functions of the specific file system to implement mount and unmount operations.

As shown in Figure 7.10, many different file systems initiated by different processes can be run simultaneously using the VFS interface. In addition, the VFS can also be used to compose a heterogeneous file system. For example, a user can mount a file system of type A in a directory of a file system of type B. This feature is particularly useful with removable media like CDs; it permits a user to mount the file system that resides in a CD in his current directory and access its files without any concern for the fact that the file data are recorded in a different format. This feature is also important when used in a distributed environment for mounting a remote file system into a file system of a different type. For example, the Sun Network File System (NFS) uses a VFS layer to permit mounting of different file systems and provides sharing of these different file systems in nodes operating under the Sun OS operating system, which is a version of UNIX.

The VFS, in essence, does not contain any file data; rather it contains merely data structures that constitute VFS metadata. Each file system that runs under it contains its own metadata and file data. The VFS layer implements a complete system-wide unique designator for each file by creating a key data structure of the file used by VFS. This data structure is known as virtual node, popularly called *vnode*. The *vnode* is essentially a representation of a file in the kernel. It can be looked upon as a file object with the following three parts:

- File system-independent data
  - such as a *file id* that is unique within the domain of the VFS, which may be an individual computer system or a network;
  - the file type, such as directory, data file, or special file;
  - other fields, such as open count, lock, flags, and so on;

- File-system-specific data, such as the file map table;
- Addresses of functions in the file system which contains this file. These functions implement the *open, close, read*, and *write* operations on files of this type.

Eliminating the VFS layer from this approach will indicate that all the processes will be running under one file system, and in that case, all the nodes will be treated as physical nodes. Many contemporary modern operating systems have provided VFSs since the 1990s. Some of the notable ones among them are UNIX SVR4, UNIX 4.2 BSD, Linux, and Sun OS.

7.20 PIPES

A pipe is a sort of pseudo-file that can be used to connect two processes together. When process P1 wants to send data to process P2, it writes at one end of the pipe as though it were an output file. Process P2 can read the data by reading from the other end of the pipe as though it were an input file. Thus, communications between processes looks very much like ordinary file reads and writes. The pipe acts here as a virtual communication channel to connect two processes wishing to exchange a stream of data. That is why some systems often implement interprocess communication mechanism via pipe, which is similar to messages but can be programmed using the standard set of file and I/O services. It can also be used to link external devices or files to processes. The two processes communicating via a pipe can reside on a single machine or on different machines in a network environment.

The operating system usually provides automatic buffering for the data within a pipe and implicit synchronization between the processes communicating via a pipe. A user, for example, intending to write on a pipe may be delayed while the pipe is full, and similarly a process wishing to read from an empty file may be suspended until some data arrive. Pipes can be handled at the system-call level in exactly the same way as files and device-independent I/O, and, in particular, can use the same basic set of system calls that may also be used for handling devices and files. This generality in approach enables pipes to use even at the command-language level that can establish an additional form of inter-program communication. That is why pipes are often found in use to output from one program or device to input to another program or directly to a device without any reprogramming or the use of temporary files. By allowing this form of redirection, applications that are not specifically developed to work together, such as a spellchecker and a text formatter, can be combined to perform a new complex function without any reprogramming. In this way, several independent utilities can be cascaded, which can then enable users to construct powerful functions out of simple basic utilities, functions that can even go beyond the limit of their designers' vision. The pipe is, therefore, a powerful tool that is exploited in many operating systems, including UNIX. More about pipes can be found in Chapter 2 and in Chapter 4, where it is explained in detail.

7.21 FILE SYSTEM PERFORMANCE

The performance of a file system depends on various factors; each such factor, in turn, requires the appropriate techniques to yield good performance. When all such techniques are incorporated into the design of a file system, it is expected that the developed file system can offer relatively good performance. Some common and notable factors that can influence the performance of a file system are listed in Table 7.1 along with the corresponding techniques that are generally used to enhance the performance of each of these factors individually. However, all the techniques mentioned in the table are also described separately in detail in the preceding sections.

Caching and *buffering* are the most common techniques used to speed up access to metadata and file data. A *file map table* is usually buffered in memory when the file is first opened, but buffering may not be feasible if the FMT (or FAT) is large in size; in that case, only the active part of it may be cached in memory. Directories (may be partly) are usually cached in memory when accessed for the

TABLE 7.1

Factors Influencing File System Performance

Factor	Techniques Used to Address the Factor
• Accessing file map table or FAT	• File map table cache in main memory
• Directory access	• Hash tables, B+ trees
• Accessing a disk block	• Disk block cache in main memory
• Accessing data	Disk scheduling
• Writing data	Cylinder groups and extents
	Disk block cache in device
	• Blocking and buffering data
	• Different approaches to when the computed data is to be written on disk

first time. When a directory is used to resolve a pathname, it is retained in a memory cache known as the **directory names cache** to speed up future references to files located in it. *Disk-arm movement* is an important issue when a disk block is accessed and, in turn, becomes a dominant factor in the performance of file system. To minimize this movement, several useful techniques are used with respect to accessing the free blocks and subsequent allocation of them. Sometimes a free list is also arranged in the form of block-clustering by grouping consecutive blocks to considerably improve disk I/O performance. Some modern systems, especially Linux, use this approach. When allocating blocks, the system attempts to place consecutive blocks of a file in the same cylinder.

Another performance bottleneck in systems that use *inodes* or anything equivalent to *inodes* is that reading even a short file requires two disk accesses: one for the *inode* and one for the data block. Usually *inodes* are placed near the beginning of the disk, so the average distance between an *inode* and its blocks will be about half the number of cylinders, thereby requiring appreciably long seeks. To improve the performance, *inodes* are placed in the middle of the disk instead of at the beginning, thereby reducing the average seek between the *inode* and its pointed first block by a factor of two. Another approach may be to divide the disk into cylinder groups, each with its own *inodes*, blocks, and free list (McKusick, et al., 1984). When creating a new file, any *inode* can be chosen, but an attempt is made to locate a block in the same cylinder group as the *inode*. If no such block is available, then a block close to the cylinder group is used.

Still, an important issue remains; at what time the data is to be written back from the cache (or memory) to the disk. The notion of *delayed writes* (write-back) tends to improve the effective speed of writing and response time, eliminate redundant disk writes, and also reduce the network and server load in distributed systems, but, of course, sometimes at the cost of gross data loss in the event of system failure. In this regard, UNIX uses a system call, *sync*, that forces all the modified blocks out onto the disk immediately. In fact, when the UNIX system is started up, a program, usually called *update*, is started up in the background to sit in an endless loop issuing *sync* calls, sleeping for 30 seconds between two successive calls. As a result, no more than 30 seconds of work is lost if a system crash occurs. This sounds quite comfortable for many users. The Windows approach is normally to use write-through caches that write back all modified blocks to the disk immediately. When a large file is handled, the disk I/O time taken by Windows is thus appreciable.

As technology advances, operating systems are also gradually modernized, and these advanced systems provide device-independent I/O, where files and logical I/O are treated by a single, unified set of system services at both the command-language and system-call levels. In such systems, user processes can be interchangeably connected to pipes, files, or I/O devices. This facility is often coupled with runtime binding of processes to devices that summarily makes compiled programs insensitive to configuration changes and provides considerable flexibility in managing resources and thereby speeding up computer systems. Moreover, the recent trend to further enhance file system performance is to implement all the speed-up techniques in hardware that were previously realized by software. In addition, modern I/O device technology also incorporates some of the techniques mentioned in Table 7.1. Thus, SCSI disks provide disk scheduling in the device itself. RAID units, as already discussed in previous section, today contain a disk block buffer which can be used to both buffer and cache disk blocks.

More details on this topic are given on the Support Material at www.routledge.com/9781032467238.

7.22   LOG-STRUCTURED FILE SYSTEMS

With the advent of modern technology, CPU speed is continuously getting faster, the size of memory is growing exponentially, their speed is moderately increasing, and disks are also getting much bigger and cheaper but not much faster in operation. The net effect of these factors all together creates an overall performance bottleneck arising from the considerably slower disk I/O operation that eventually has a negative impact on the performance of current file systems. Many innovative ideas have emerged, and finally the research carried out at Berkeley made an attempt to alleviate this problem by designing a completely new form of file system, known as a log-structured file system (LFS). This section briefly describes the working of an LFS. For more details, the paper by Rosenblum and Ousterhout (1991) can be consulted.

As CPUs get faster and RAM gets larger, the size of disk caches have consequently also rapidly increased to improve overall performance. These facts primarily influence the design of LFS to evolve which claims that it is now feasible to satisfy a substantially large fraction of all read requests, which normally go to a disk, can now be directly obtained from the file system–cache with no disk access needed, thereby ultimately reducing the total number of disk accesses required for read operations. This observation led to the conclusion that in the future, most disk accesses will be mainly confined to disk-write operations and the associated disk head movement. It also indicates that the read-ahead policy used by some file systems to fetch blocks before they are actually needed does not really contribute much to file system performance.

While disk head movement can be minimized to improve disk performance through disk scheduling and also with the use of cylinder groups at the time of disk space allocation for files, they are found useless or less effective, particularly when files located in different parts of a disk are processed simultaneously in a shared computing environment. For example, in a UNIX system, write operations to a disk take only about 10% of the disk time, and the rest of the time is mostly spent in disk arm movement that mainly causes poor disk throughput. However, this problem arising mainly from disk head movement has been properly addressed, and to minimize the needed disk head movement, the concept of a log-structured file system has been introduced, which uses a radically different file organization.

In LFS, all writes are initially buffered in memory, and periodically all the buffered-writes of file data of all files together are written to the disk in a single sequential structure that resembles a journal. This is called the **log file**. When an update or write operation is performed on any file, the new data are simply added to the end of the log file. Hence, little disk head movement is involved in this operation. The file system keeps and writes special index blocks into the log file that contain metadata (pointer, file structure, etc.) about the location of each file's data in the log file. The index blocks are consulted when the file data have to be read off the disk. Thus, little disk head movement is required for reading data that were written into a file recently; however, older data require more disk head movement. Measurements and performance studies on the Sprite log-structured file system revealed that disk head movement accounted for only 30 percent of the disk time consumed during file processing. Its performance was observed to be superior to its counterpart traditional file systems for small writes.

Figure 7.11 illustrates in a simplified way the arrangement made in a log-structured file, at least schematically, and assuming quite a few things that are usually involved in the working of a file system. For the sake of simplicity, we first assume that the metadata and file data blocks of a single

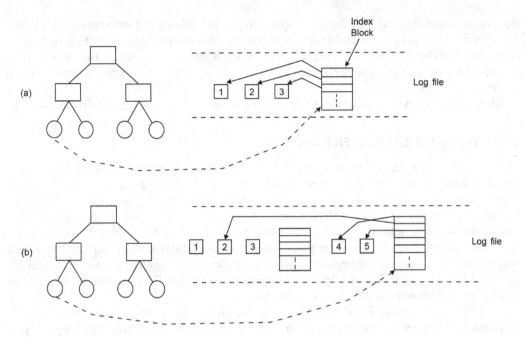

FIGURE 7.11 A representative scheme of file–update mechanism used in a log–structured file system employed by a generic modern operating system.

file are in the log file, and the data blocks in the log file are numbered as shown in Figure 7.11(a). In actual implementation, the index block contains the pointer that points to the respective file data blocks. The directory entry of a file points to the respective index block in the log file; it is assumed here that the index block contains the FMT (FAT) of the file. When the file data contained in block 1 is modified (updated), the new values are written into a new disk block, say, block 4. This is depicted in Figure 7.11(b). Similarly, when the data in block 3 are updated, some of its file data are written into disk block 5. The file system now writes a new index block that contains the updated FMT of the file and sets the FMT pointer in the directory of the file to point to the new index block. The new FMT now contains pointers to the two new data blocks and to data block 2, which has not been changed, as shown in Figure 7.11(b). The old index block and disk blocks 1 and 3 are now released.

Since disk files are written as a sequential-access file, all the finite disks will be quickly occupied by the log file, leaving almost no space for new segments to write, although there may still be many blocks that are no longer needed. As shown in Figure 7.11b, if a file is updated, a new index block is written, but the old one, though currently of no use, will still occupy space in previously written areas.

To deal with this problem, LFS exploits the service of a *cleaner thread* that scans the log circularly to compact it, similar to memory compaction (see Chapter 5). It starts out by reading the summary of the first segment in the log to see which index blocks are still current and file blocks are still in use. If they are not, that information is discarded, and the spaces occupied by them will be released. The index blocks and file blocks that are still in use go to memory to be written out in just the next available segment. The original segment is then marked as free, and the log can use it to store new data. In this way, the cleaner moves along the log, removing old segments from the back and putting any live data into memory for rewriting in the next segment. Consequently, a large free area on the disk is available for the log file. The entire disk can now be viewed as a big circular buffer, with the *writer thread* adding new segments to the front and the *cleaner thread* removing old ones from the back. This operation involves considerable disk head movement that determines the disk usage; however, the cleaner and writer threads perform their operations (i.e. compaction) as a background activity without affecting the actual file processing activities. Performance results reveal that all this complexity is worthwhile. Measurements offered in the paper mentioned in the beginning of this section show that LFS clearly outperforms UNIX by an order of magnitude on small writes while exhibiting performance as good as or even better than UNIX for reads and large writes.

7.23 CASE STUDY: FILE MANAGEMENT SYSTEMS IN UNIX

The UNIX file system originated, from and was greatly influenced by its predecessor, the MULTICS file system (Chakraborty, 2020). Different versions of UNIX differ in features of the file system, but only a brief discussion of some of the common features available to almost all UNIX versions is given here.

Files: In UNIX, a file is nothing but a sequence of bytes (byte-stream), and as such is only streams of characters with no specific structure. Each individual file must completely reside on a single volume. Sequential access is supported for all files; random access is possible only to files stored on block-structured devices.

Types of Files: In UNIX, there are six types of files: regular or ordinary (ASCII files), directory (tree-structured hierarchically organized), special (physical devices mapped to file names), pipes (named), links (an alternative file name for an existing file), and symbolic links (data files containing the name of the file it is linked to).

Inodes, File Structures, and File Descriptors: The generic arrangement of file processing is mostly organized around the use of directory entries, FCBs, and internal ids with the use of data structures such as *inodes*, file structures, and file descriptors.

In UNIX, the directory entry is 16 bytes (in System V and Version 7): the *inode* is 2 bytes, and the file name is contained in the remaining 14 bytes. An *inode* is a control structure that contains key information about a particular file. Several file names may be associated with a single *inode*, but an active *inode* is associated with exactly one file, and each file is controlled by exactly one *inode*. The *inode* data structure is maintained on disk, and there is an *inode* table or *inode* list that contains the *inodes* of all the files in the file system. When a file is opened, its *inode* is brought from disk into main memory and stored in a memory-resident *inode* table.

The file structure contains two fields: current position in an open file, which is in the form of an offset from start of the file, and a pointer to the *inode* for the file. A file descriptor points to a file structure. Its use is very similar to that of the internal id of a file in the generic arrangement. Figure 7.12 shows the arrangement of file descriptor, file structure, and *inode* in memory. A directory-lookup cache holds information concerning a few files on an LRU basis which is searched at the time of opening a file. A successful search can relieve the system from tedious and time-consuming directory lookups. When a file is opened, the file descriptor is passed to the process that opened the file. When a process creates a child process, a table of descriptors is created for the child process, and

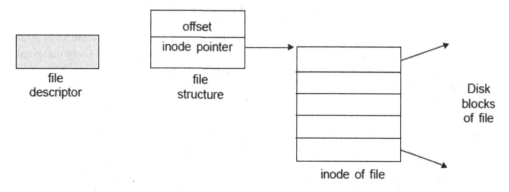

FIGURE 7.12 A schematic block diagram consisting of relevant data structures used in UNIX file management system.

the file descriptors of the parent process are copied into it. Thus, many file descriptors may share the same file structure. Processes owning the descriptors share the file offset.

- **Disk Space Allocation:** Each file has a FAT analogous to FMT, and this information is obtained from the contents of the *inode*. File allocation is carried out dynamically on a block basis; hence, the allocated blocks of a file on disk are not necessarily contiguous. An indexed allocation method is used to keep track of each file, with part of the index stored in the *inode* of the file. The *inode* includes 39 bytes of allocation address information which is organized as thirteen 3-byte addresses or pointers. The first 10 addresses point to the first 10 data blocks of the file. If the file is still longer than 10 blocks long, then one or more levels of indirection is used.

The total number of data blocks in a file depends on the size of the fixed-size blocks in the system. In UNIX System V, the length of a disk block is 1 Kbyte (2^{10}), and thus each such block can hold a total of 256 (2^8) block addresses; each block address is of 4 bytes (= 2^2). Hence, the maximum number of disk blocks that can be addressed using triple levels of indirection are 256 $\times$ 256 $\times$ 256 = 2^{24} disk blocks. Each disk block is 1 Kbytes = 2^{10} bytes. Hence, the maximum size of a file with this scheme is $2^{24} \times 2^{10}$ bytes = 2^{34} bytes = 16 Gbytes. Similarly, two levels of indirection needs 256 $\times$ 256 = 2^{16} disk blocks, that is, $2^{16} \times 2^{10}$ bytes = 64 Mbytes, and with a single level of indirection, the maximum size of the file would be 256 = 2^8 disk blocks, that is, $2^8 \times 2^{10}$ bytes = 256 Kbytes, and the direct (i.e. zero level of or no indirection) would require simply 10 $\times$ 1 Kbytes = 10 Kbytes.

For file sizes smaller than 10 Kbytes, this arrangement is as efficient as the flat allocation discussed in a previous section. Such files also have a small allocation table that can fit into the *inode* itself with no indirection. Not much bigger files, while using one level of indirection, may be accessed with little extra overhead, but as a whole, reduce processing and disk access time. Two or more levels of indirection permit files to grow to very large sizes, virtually satisfying all applications, although their access involves extra time consumption while traversing through the different levels of indirection in the FAT.

- **Free Space Management:** In its simplest form, the UNIX file system maintains a list of free disk blocks in a way similar to linked allocation in which each block points to the next block in the list. To avoid the high overhead inherent in this approach, UNIX employs an indexed allocation scheme but implemented differently. Here, free space is managed by means of a chained list of indices to unused blocks. In particular, approximately 50 pointers to free blocks are collected in one index block. The index blocks in the free list are chained together so that each points to the id of the next one in line in the free list. The first index block is normally kept in main memory. As a result, the system has immediate access to addresses of up to 50 free blocks and to a pointer to an index block on the disk that contains 50 more pointers to free blocks. With this arrangement, the overhead of adding disk blocks to the free list when a file is deleted is greatly minimized. Only marginal processing is needed for files smaller than 10 Kbytes (or multiples of 10 Kbytes depending on the size of data blocks) in size. However, while disk blocks are added and deleted from the free list, race conditions may occur, and that is why a lock variable is used with the free list to avoid such situations.
- **Sharing of Files:** UNIX provides file sharing with the use of a single file image. As illustrated in Figure 7.12, every process that opens a file points to the copy of its *inode* using its file descriptor and file structure. Thus, all processes that share a file use the same copy of the file; changes made by one process are at once visible to other processes sharing the file. As usual, race conditions may exist while accessing an *inode*; hence, to ensure mutual exclusion, a lock variable called an **advisory lock** is provided in the memory copy of an

inode that is supposed to be heeded by processes; however, the file system does not enforce their use. A process attempting to access an *inode* must go to sleep if the lock is set by another process. Processes that concurrently use a file must do their own planning to avoid race conditions on the data contained in the file.

- **Directories:** Directories are tree-typed and hierarchically organized. A directory is also simply a file that contains a list of file names and/or other directories plus pointers (*inode* number) to associated *inode*s. When the file or directory is accessed, the file system must take its *inode* number from the related directory and use it as an index to the respective *inode* table to locate its disk blocks.
- **Volume Structure:** A UNIX file system resides on a single logical disk or disk partition, and all such disks that contain UNIX file systems have the layout depicted in Figure 7.13, with the following elements:
  - **Boot Block:** Block 0 is not used by UNIX and often contains code to boot the computer.
  - **Superblock:** Block 1 is the superblock that contains critical information about the layout of the file system, the number of *inode*s, the number of disk blocks, and the start of the list of free disk blocks (typically a few hundred entries). Damage to or destruction of the superblock will render the file system unreadable.
  - **Inode Tables:** The collection of *inode*s for each file. They are numbered from 1 to some maximum.
  - **Data Blocks:** All data files and directories/subdirectories are stored here.
- **Multiple File Systems:** Many file systems can exist in a UNIX system. When a physical disk is partitioned into many logical disks, a file system can be constructed on each of them and can exist only on a single logical disk device. In other words, a logical disk contains exactly only one file system. Hence, files also cannot span different logical disks. While a disk is partitioned, it provides some protection and also prevents a file system from occupying too much disk space. Each file system consists of a superblock, an *inode* list, and data blocks. The superblock itself contains the size of the file system, the free list, and the size of the *inode* list. The superblock, which is the root of every file system, is maintained by UNIX in main memory for the sake of efficiency. The superblock is copied onto the disk periodically. Some part of the file system may be lost if the system crashes after the superblock is modified but before it is copied to the disk. Some of the lost state information can be reconstructed by the file system, such as the free list, by simply analyzing the disk status. This is, of course, carried out as part of the system booting procedure.

A file system can be mounted in any directory in a logical disk device by using a file system program **mount** with the parameters of a *device-special file name* (for the file system) and the *pathname* of the directory in which it is to be mounted. Once the file system is mounted, the root of the file system has the name given by the pathname, and the superblock of the mounted file system is then loaded in main memory. Disk block allocation for a file in the mounted file system must now be

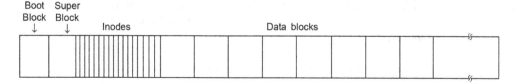

FIGURE 7.13 A schematic block diagram showing a representative layout of volume structure of a disk used in traditional UNIX system.

performed within the logical disk device on which the file system exists. All the files in a mounted file system are then accessed in the usual way.

- **Other Features:** UNIX provides extensive buffering of disk blocks in order to reduce physical I/O and effective disk access time. However, buffers are not allocated at the level of a file or a process. This arrangement facilitates implementation of concurrent file sharing with the use of only a single file image and also reduces the disk access overhead when a file is processed simultaneously by two or more processes. UNIX supports two kinds of links: a hard link, already described in Section 7.11, and a symbolic link, which was described in Section 7.11.

More details on this topic are given on the Support Material at www.routledge.com/9781032467238.

7.24   CASE STUDY: FILE MANAGEMENT SYSTEMS IN LINUX

The file management system of Linux provides versatile and a powerful file handling that supports a wide variety of many different FMS and file structures. This approach makes use of a VFS, as already described in Section 7.19, which presents a single, uniform file system interface to user processes and provides a common file model that is capable of representing the general features and behavior of any conceivable file system. The Linux file model closely resembles the UNIX file model and is implemented using UNIX-like data structures, such as superblocks and *inodes*. The standard file system of Linux is called **ext2**. The file system **ext3** incorporates journaling, which provides integrity of data and metadata and fast booting after an unclean shutdown.

The **VFS in Linux** is an object-oriented scheme. It assumes that files are objects in a computer's mass storage memory that share basic properties regardless of the target file system or the underlying processor hardware. Files have symbolic names and other related attributes that enable them to be uniquely identified within a specific directory in the file system. The VFS scheme actually maps and translates the functions that the user has submitted to the corresponding target file system activities.

The key components of Linux file system are depicted in Figure 7.14, in which a VFS layer is placed between a process and a file system that, in turn, simultaneously support many different file systems. In a VFS file scheme, when a user process issues a file operation, such as *read* or *write*, which is basically a file system call, the VFS converts this into an internal (to the kernel) file system call that is passed to a mapping function for a specific target file system (e.g. HP FS). In most cases, this mapping function simply maps the file system functional calls from one scheme to another. The original user file system call is simply translated into a call that is native to the target file system. The target file system software is then invoked and converts the file system request into device-oriented instructions which are passed to a device driver by means of page cache functions. The requested operation is then performed under its control and secondary storage. The results of the execution are communicated back to the user in a similar manner. VFS is truly independent of any file system, so the implementation of a mapping function must be part of the implementation of a file system on Linux. Any file system that conforms to the specification of the VFS-file system interface can be installed to run under it. This feature enables a new file system to be added easily in the environment.

Since VFS is written in C, rather than a traditional object-oriented programming language (such as C++ or Java), VFS objects are implemented simply as C data structures. Each object contains both data and pointers to the file-system-implemented functions that operate on data. VFS objects are essentially of four types:

- **Superblock object:** This represents a specific file system that is mounted.
- **Inode object:** This represents a specific file.
- **Dentry object:** This represents a specific directory entry.
- **File object:** This represents an open file associated with a process.

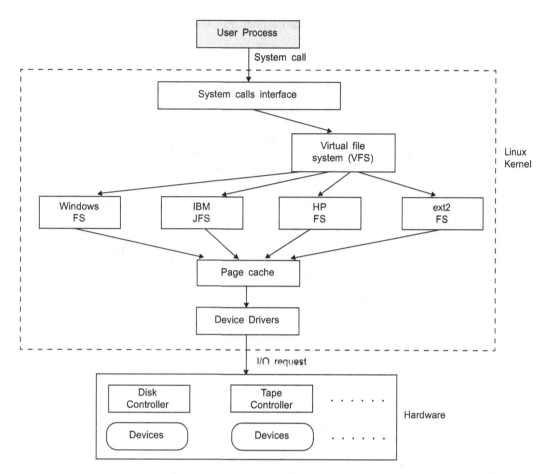

FIGURE 7.14 A schematic representation of Linux virtual file system used in today's Linux operating systems.

Since the Linux file management scheme is mostly derived from the concepts used in UNIX file systems, the Linux file system, similarly to UNIX, also employs a tree-typed hierarchical organization of directories, in which each directory may contain files and/or other directories. A path from the root through the tree consists of a sequence of directory entries, ending in either a *directory entry* (dentry) or a file name. Thus, file operations can be equally performed on either files or directories.

- **The Superblock Object:** This object stores information describing a specific file system. Typically, the superblock corresponds to the file-system superblock or file-system control block, which is stored in a specific sector on a disk. The superblock object consists of a number of key data items, including a list of superblock-operations that refer to an operation-object which defines the object methods (functions) that the kernel can invoke against the superblock-object. Some of the notable methods defined for the superblock-object are read_inode, write_inode, remount_fs, write_super, and clear_inode.
- **The Inode Object:** As in UNIX, an *inode* is associated with each file. The *inode-object* holds all the information about a named file except its name and the actual data contents of the file. Items contained in an inode-object include owner, group, permissions, access times for a file, size of data, and number of links. However, the inode-object also includes an *inode*-operations-object that describes the file system's implemented functions that the

VFS can invoke on an *inode*. A few of the methods (functions) defined for the inode-object include the following:

- *create*: Create a new *inode* for a regular file associated with a dentry object in some directory.
- *lookup*: Search a directory for an *inode* corresponding to a filename.
- *mkdir*: Create a new *inode* for a directory associated with a dentry object in some directory.
- **The Dentry Object:** A dentry (directory entry) is simply a specific component in a path. The component may be either a directory entry or a file name. When a file is opened, the VFS transforms its directory entry into a dentry object. Dentry objects facilitate access to files and directories and are cached (in a dentry cache) so that the overheads of building them from the directory entry can be avoided if the file is opened repeatedly during a computing session.
- **The File Object:** The file object is used to represent a file opened by a process. The object is created in response to the *open()* system call and destroyed in response to the *close()* system call. The file object consists of a number of items, including the following:
  - dentry object associated with the file
  - file system containing the file
  - file object usage counter
  - user's user-ID
  - user's group-ID
  - file pointer, which is the current position in the file from which the next operation on the file will take place

The file object also includes an *inode*-operations-object that describes the file system's implemented functions that the VFS can invoke on a file object. The methods (functions) defined for file object include *read, write, open, release,* and *lock*.

- **Locks:** The standard file system of Linux is **ext2**, which was influenced by the design of UNIX BSD. This ext2 provides a variety of file-locks for process synchronization. **Advisory locks** are those that are supposed to be heeded by processes to ensure mutual exclusion; however, the file system does not enforce their use. UNIX file-locks belong to this category of locks. **Mandatory locks** are those that are checked by the file system; if a process attempts to access data that is protected by a mandatory lock, the process is blocked until the lock is reset by its holder. A **lease** is a special kind of file-lock which is valid for a specific amount of time after which another process that tries to access the data protected by it can get it. It is implemented in the following way: if a process attempts to access data protected by a lease, the holder of the lease is alerted by the file system. It now has a stipulated interval of time to finish accessing the file and then frees the lease. If it fails to do so, its lease is broken and access to the data protected by the lease is awarded to the process that was attempting to access it.
- **Disk Space Allocation:** ext2, similar to UNIX BSD's fast file system, employs the notion of a block group consisting of a set of consecutive disk blocks to reduce the movement of disk heads when file data are accessed. It uses a bitmap to keep track of free disk blocks in a block group. When a file is created, it tries to allocate disk space for the *inode* of the file within the same block group that contains its parent directory and also includes the file data within the same block group. Every time a file is extended due to the addition of new data, it searches the bitmap of the block group to find a free disk block that is close to a target disk block. If such a disk block is found, it checks whether a few adjoining disk blocks are also free and preallocates a few of these to the file with the assumption of its forthcoming requirements.

If such a free disk block is not found, it preallocates a few contiguous disk blocks located elsewhere in the block group. In this way, it is comfortably possible to read large sections of data without having much movement of the disk head. When the file is closed, preallocated but unused disk blocks are also released. This strategy of disk space allocation that makes use of (almost) contiguous disk blocks for contiguous sections of file data provides notably increased performance in file access, even when files are created and deleted at a high rate.

More details on this topic are given on the Support Material at www.routledge.com/9781032467238.

7.25 CASE STUDY: FILE MANAGEMENT SYSTEMS IN WINDOWS

Windows provides a number of file systems, including the FAT, which are mostly based upon the MS-DOS file system and inherit many of its properties. In addition, the developers of Windows also designed Windows NT, Windows XP, Windows Vista, and Windows 2000 and their continuously upgraded versions. All these upgraded systems have a native file system, NTFS, that has different properties and is designed to meet different objectives. NTFS is mainly intended to meet the high-end requirements of file systems for servers and workstations so that it can provide support to network applications for large systems of corporate entities and client–server applications for file servers, compute servers, and database servers. This section provides an overview of NTFS.

- **Salient Features of NTFS:** The design objective of NTFS is to offer adequate flexibility; although it is built on a simple file system model but is itself a powerful file system. Some of the notable features of NTFS include the following:
  - **Large disk device and large files:** It supports a very large disk device and very large files.
  - **Security:** It uses security descriptors containing many security attributes as well as providing features such as a sophisticated protection system, encryption, and data compression.
  - **Recoverability:** NTFS can restore the damaged data in files and also metadata by reconstructing disk volumes in the event of any type of system crashes. To provide full recoverability, including user data, it requires to incorporate much more elaborate and resource-consuming recovery facilities. Moreover, it employs redundant storage (backup) for critical file-system data that describes the structure and status of the file system. In addition, it may use a RAID architecture to avoid any loss of user files.
  - **Multiple data streams:** In NTFS, a file is a collection of attributes, and each attribute is considered an independent byte stream. The data in a file are also treated as a stream of bytes while it is even considered to be an attribute. In NTFS, it is possible to define multiple data streams for a single file. Use of such multiple data streams provides enormous flexibilities; for instance, a large graphic image may have a smaller thumbnail associated with it. Such a stream at one end can contain a maximum of 248 bytes, and at the other end, at least, only a few hundred bytes.
  - **Indexing of attributes:** The descriptions of the attributes associated with each file are organized by NTFS as a relational database so that they can be indexed by any attribute.
- **NTFS Volume:** NTFS considers disk storage in the following way:
  - **Sector:** It is the smallest possible storage unit on the disk. Its data size in bytes is a power of 2 and is almost always 512 bytes.
  - **Cluster:** A collection of one or more contiguous (one after another on the same track) sectors, and its size in terms of sectors is always a power of 2.

- **Volume:** A volume is usually a logical partition on a disk or all of a single physical disk, or it can even be extended across multiple physical disks consisting of one or more clusters and controlled by a file system. A volume at any instant consists of file system information, may have a collection of files, and may have any additional unallocated space remaining on the volume that can be allocated to files. A *bitmap* file is used to indicate which clusters in a volume are allocated and which are free. A bad-clusters file is used to keep track of clusters that are unusable due to hardware problems. Large files that exceed the capacity of a partition are supported using the notion of a volume set, which can contain up to 32 volumes. If hardware or software RAID 5 is employed, a volume consists of stripes that can span multiple disks. However, the maximum volume size that NTFS supports is 2^{64} bytes.
- **Volume Layout:** NTFS organizes information on a disk volume in a simple structure that nicely arranges a few general-purpose functions as well as managing the file system as a whole. The layout of an NTFS volume consists of four regions, as depicted in Figure 7.15. The first few sectors (it can be up to 16 sectors long) are occupied by the **partition boot sector**, which contains information about the volume layout and the file system structures as well as boot startup information and code. The existence of the boot sector makes every volume bootable. The next region is occupied by the **master file table** (MFT), the key data structure and the heart of the Windows file system, which contains information about all the files and folders (directories) on this NTFS volume as well as information about unused areas on the volume. The MFT essentially is a list of all contents on the NTFS volume, organized as a set of variable-length rows in a relational database structure. This structuring of the MFT resembles the structure of the FAT, as discussed in the preceding sections. After the MFT region, the next region, typically 1 Mbyte in length, contains the **system files**, the notable ones are: *MFT2* (a mirror of the first three rows of the MFT to be used in the event of a single-sector failure), *Cluster bitmap* (*a* bitmap showing which clusters are in use in the entire volume), *Log file,* and *Attribute definition table.*
- **Directories:** A folder in NTFS is essentially a directory. NTFS implements it using an index file. The directory hierarchy is formed by allowing folders to contain files as well as other folders. This hierarchy is realized by organizing the directory as a B+ tree with files as its leaf nodes. The B+ data structure possesses the property that the length of each path in the tree is the same, which facilitates efficient search for any entry in the directory.
- **Disk Space Allocation:** NTFS disk space management uses the cluster (not sector) as the fundamental unit of allocation and is independent of physical sector sizes, which, in turn, enables NTFS to easily support nonstandard disks that do not have a 512-byte sector size. The clusters allocated to a file need not be contiguous; a file, in fact, is allowed to be fragmented on the disk. At present, the maximum file size supported by NTFS is 2^{32} clusters; each cluster can have at most 2^{16} bytes. Again, the use of larger cluster sizes for very large file helps the *bitmap* file be efficiently managed, for it contains fewer elements to keep track of cluster allocation to each such file. However, the default cluster sizes for NTFS depend on the size of the volume. In fact, the cluster size to be used for a particular volume is established by NTFS at the time of formatting the disk.
- **Other Features:** NTFS treats each operation that alters the file-system data structure as *atomic transactions*, which are implemented using a *write-ahead log file*. While attempting to modify its own data structures, NTFS first writes the steps involved (i.e. its intentions) in the modification of the volume structure into the log file residing in the cache. NTFS then modifies the volume (in the cache). The cache manager calls the log file system to prompt it to flush the log file to a disk to ensure that log records are not lost if a crash occurs. Once the log file updates are safely on disk, the required modification of the data structures is performed. The log can now be discarded (not erased). If a crash occurs any time after the log is written to the disk, the log file is used to complete the transaction.

| Partition boot sector | Master file table | System and user files | File area |

FIGURE 7.15 A representative block diagram of volume layout used in Windows NT file system.

Hence, while recovering from a failure, it checks whether a transaction was in progress at the time of failure. If so, it completes the transaction as mentioned before resuming operation. However, to totally avoid loss of file system data due to a crash and to cover the risk of such loss of data, the log is not discarded immediately after completing an update. Instead, NTFS usually takes a checkpoint every 5 seconds and then discards the log file. In the case of a crash, the file system can then be restored by copying the checkpoint and processing records, if any, in the log file.

More details about this topic with a figure and tables are given on the Support Material at www. routledge.com/9781032467238.

SUMMARY

The FMS described in this chapter primarily carryout the responsibilities to create, manipulate, and maintain data in the form of a file put in a persistent storage medium for practical use. A file is merely an organized collection of related records that are encapsulated in the file system, which is the most visible interface for users and can be conceived as a tree of two basic abstractions: directories and files (leaves), where each directory may contain subdirectories and files. In essence, a file system is a logical view of data stored on a device such as disk, CD, flash drive, or tape.

The FMS organizes files, directories, and control information (metadata); provides convenient and secure access to files and directories; and implements many operations, like create, delete, open, read, write, and close, that users can apply on files and directories to manage their contents. This chapter also explains how the space on block devices (disks) is organized to hold file systems and describes some space management techniques. The space allocated to a file might be contiguous or noncontiguous arranged in the form of a linked list, index-sequential, and so on. Different free space management techniques, including bitmap schemes, are also discussed. Many runtime data structures that reside in the kernel space and how they are interlinked to each other are also described. In addition, this chapter also shows the importance of reliability, protection, concurrency control, and journaling, and discusses different fault-tolerant techniques and recoverability. A presentation of a modern log-structured file system is included. This chapter also briefly discusses VFSs that can allow many real file systems to coexist under the umbrella of a single VFS. Finally, a brief overview of the actual and practical implementation of UNIX, Linux, and Windows file systems is presented as a case study.

EXERCISES

1. Describe the user's view as well as the designer's view while developing a file system.
2. Define file system. Describe the user's view of the file system. Describe the view that the designer uses while developing a file system
3. What is meant by file types? What are the various methods employed to specify the file type? What are the advantages obtained by specifying the type of a file?
4. What is meant by file attribute? State its significance. State and explain those file attributes that are mainly used by most operating systems.
5. "Different file operations are realized by using respective system calls". Give your views, with suitable examples. Explain with an example the operation of at least one such system call to realize the respective file operation.

6. "An operating system is categorized by the different file services it offers". Justify this, giving the different classification of services that a file system usually offers to its system call users. What relationship exists between the file services and file server?

7. Explain the purpose and the benefits derived from a file control block with an approximate functional specification of its structure. What is the significance of the current file pointer field in the file control block?

8. When a file is opened concurrently by several processes, should each process construct a separate file control block of its own to connect to the shared file, or should the involved processes share a single FCB? Discuss the relative merits of each approach and propose a strategy for managing the sharing of files.

9. State the minimum requirements that file management systems must meet to perform their responsibilities.

10. Describe with a diagram the design principles involved in a generic file system.

11. Why is the average search time to find a record in a file less for an indexed sequential file than for a sequential file?

12. An index sequential file contains 5000 records. Its index contains 100 entries. Each index entry describes an area of the file 50 records. If all records in the file have the same probability of being accessed, calculate the average number of operations involved in accessing a record. Compare this number with the number of disk operations required if the same records were stored in a sequential file.

13. "An indexed (inverted) file exhibits certain advantages and beat out indexed-sequential files in some situations of file processing". Give your comments.

14. What does file structuring mean? Some operating systems design a file system as tree-structured but limit the depth of the tree to a small number of levels. What effect does this limit have on users? What are the advantages of this type of structuring? How does this simplify file system design, if it does at all?

15. What are the typical operations performed on a directory? Discuss the relative merits and demerits of a system that provides a two-level directory in comparison to single-level (flat) directory system

16. The use of hard links (or simply links) poses some inconveniences at the time of sharing files. What are the major limitations that are faced in this arrangement? Symbolic links are supposed to alleviate these limitations: discuss.

17. What is a graph directory structure? How does this structure overcome the problems faced by a tree-structured directory when a file is shared? State the specific access rights provided under this structuring by most OSs at the time of file sharing.

18. State the different methods of blocking that are generally used. Given; B = block size, R = record size, P = size of block pointer, and F = blocking factor, that is, the expected number of records within a block, derive a formula for F for all the methods of blocking you have described.

19. State and explain the different disk space allocation techniques that are used in noncontiguous memory allocation model. Which technique do you find suitable and in what situation?

20. The logical disk block is of size 512 bytes. Under contiguous allocation, a file is stored starting at logical disk block 40. To access the byte at file address 2000, which is the logical disk block to be read into the memory? To read 100 bytes from the file at file address 2000, how many disk accesses are required?

21. State and explain the relative merits and drawbacks of the linked (or chained) allocation scheme on secondary storage space.

22. For what type of file processing is indexed allocation found suitable? Explain. What are the merits and drawbacks to an indexed allocation scheme?

23. Calculate the number of disk accesses needed to read 20 consecutive logical blocks of a file in a system with: **a.** contiguous allocation, **b.** chained allocation, and **c.** indexed allocation of space. Discuss your findings, using an appropriate figure for illustrative purposes, if necessary. Explain the timing difference in this regard between logical block accessing and physical block accessing.

24. Free disk space can be tracked by using a free list or a bitmap. Disk addresses require D bits. In a disk with B blocks, F of which are free, state the condition under which the free list uses less space than the bitmap. For D with a value of 32 bits, express your answer as a percentage of the disk that must be free.

25. Consider a hierarchical file system in which free disk space is maintained in a free list.
    a. Suppose the pointer to free space is lost. Can the system reconstruct the free space list?
    b. Suggest a scheme to ensure that the pointer is never lost as a result of a single memory failure.

26. How many device operations are required to add a released node to a free list when the disk (block) status map approach is used to implement the free list?

27. A file system implements multi-level indexed disk space allocation. The size of each disk block is 4 Kbytes, and each disk block address is 4 bytes in length. The size of the FMT is one disk block. It contains 12 pointers to data blocks. All other pointers point to index blocks. What is the maximum file size supported by this system?

28. A sequential file ABC contains 5000 records, each of size 4 Kbytes. The file accessing parameters are:
    Average time to read a disk block = 2 msec.
    Average time to process a record = 4 msec.
    Calculate the time required by a process that reads and processes all records in the file under the following conditions:
    a. The file system keeps the FMT in memory but does not keep any index blocks in memory while processing the file.
    b. The file system keeps the FMT and one index block of the file in memory.

29. State the major aspects that are to be taken into account when the reliability of the file system is considered of prime importance.

30. "File system integrity is an important issue to both users and computer systems". Give your views.

31. What are the different methods of back-ups used to recover a file system? What are the various overheads associated with them? Which back-up method seems to be preferable and why?

32. Discuss how the stable storage technique can be used to prevent loss of file system integrity. What are the drawbacks of the stable storage technique?

33. Discuss how the atomic-action mechanism can be used to prevent loss of file system integrity. In what way does it remove the drawbacks of the stable storage technique?

34. Define virtual file system. Explain with a diagram how it abstracts the generic file model.

35. State and describe the log-structured file system. Discuss its salient features and the areas in which it has offered great benefits.

SUGGESTED REFERENCES AND WEBSITES

Ghemawat, S, Gobioff, H., et al. "The Google File System", *Proceedings of the ACM Symposium on Operating Systems Principles*, New York, ACM, 2003.

Koch, P. D. L. "Disk File Allocation Based on the Buddy System", *ACM Transactions on Computer Systems*, vol. 5, no. 4, pp. 352–370, 1987.

Larson, P., Kajla, A. "File Organization: Implementation of a Method Guaranteeing Retrieval in One Access", *Communications of the ACM*, vol. 27, no. 7, pp. 670–677, 1984.

McKusick, M. K., Joy, W. N., et al. "A Fast File System for UNIX", *ACM Transactions on Computer Systems*, vol. 2, no. 3, pp. 181–197, 1984.

Rosenblum, M., Ousterhout, J. K. "The Design and Implementation of a Log-Structured File System", *Proceedings of the 24th ACM Symposium on Operating Systems Principles*, New York, ACM, pp. 1–15, 1991.

Rubini, A. "The Virtual File System in Linux", *Linux Journal*, vol. 1997, no. 37es, pp. 21–es.

Seltzer, M. I., Smith, K. A., et al. "File System Logging Versus Clustering: A Performance Comparison", *USENIX Winter*, pp. 249–264, 1995.

Wiederhold, G. *File Organization for Database Design*. McGraw-Hill, New York, 1987.

Yeong, W., Howes, T., et al. "Lightweight Directory Access Protocol", *Network Working Group, Request for Comments*, 1995.

8 Security and Protection

DOI: 10.1201/9781003383055-8

Learning Objectives

- To give an overview of what is meant by security and protection.
- To describe the objectives of security and protection to negotiate security threats.
- To articulate the various types of security needed to handle different types of threats.
- To demonstrate the different types of active and passive security attacks attempted on different assets of computer systems.
- To explain the design issues relating to security policies and mechanisms.
- To demonstrate a spectrum of approaches that provides appropriate protections for the system.
- To describe memory (both primary and secondary) protection.
- To describe different types of access control mechanisms, including the access control matrix (ACM), access control list (ACL), and capabilities in describing protection structure.
- To describe in brief the domain and range of protection.
- To explain the role and use of locks and keys in implementing protection.
- To mention the different types of intruders who attempt to break security.
- To explain different proven methods to prevent intruders from breaking security.
- To show the different types of malicious programs (malware), worms, and viruses that can damage or destroy security.
- To demonstrate different types of encryption mechanisms and schemes (both symmetric and asymmetric) to prevent intruders from entering the system.
- To articulate various types of attacks attempted on cryptographic systems.
- To describe in brief the actual implementation of security and protection in UNIX, Linux, and Windows in real-life situations as case studies.

8.1 INTRODUCTION

To safeguard the valuable, sensitive, and confidential information of the user/system as well as the precious assets in the computing environment from unauthorized access, revelation, or destruction of data/programs; adequate protection mechanisms are inevitably required. Thus, protection is concerned with threats that are internal, whereas security, in general, deals with threats to information that are external to a computer system. As the user density is continuously increased, sharing of programs and data, remote access, and connectivity become unavoidable and obvious, thereby making the system entirely exposed to the outside world that ultimately causes major security weaknesses and likely points of penetration in improperly designed systems. In fact, the area of computer protection and security is a broad one and encompasses physical and administrative controls as well as controls that are automated with the use of tools that implement automated protection and security.

While designers of computer systems and related software developers enforce extensive security measures to safeguard the computing environment as much as possible, those, in turn, can increase the cost and complicate the computing environment to such an extent that it may eventually restrict the usefulness and user-friendliness and above all badly affect the overall performance of the entire computer system. Thus, a good balance in this regard is required while making the computing environment sufficiently efficient and effective, but again with no compromise on security aspects. Therefore, the computer and especially the operating system must be sufficiently equipped to provide an adequately flexible and functionally complete set of protection mechanisms so that the ultimate objectives of enforcing security policies can be effectively attained. This chapter is devoted to discussing a variety of issues and approaches related to security and protection of standalone systems that are also equally applicable to large mainframe systems as well as to timesharing systems comprising a set of small computers connected to shared servers using communication networks.

More about this topic is given on the Support Material at www.routledge.com/9781032467238.

8.2   SECURITY AND PROTECTION: AN OVERVIEW

Although the terms "security" and "protection" are often used interchangeably to mean restriction of unauthorized access, still there exists a sharp distinction between them. Security, in general, refers to the overall problems causing threats, whereas protection refers to the specific operating system mechanisms to secure information in the computer system. For example, if you install a door, you are protecting your house, but it is only secure if you put a lock (security) on the door (protection mechanism). If there is no door, the house is open; you have no provision to put a lock. This means that security is realized only with the use of the protection mechanism offered by the owner (operating systems). The nature of the threat being faced, however, depends on the type of the resource and the manner in which it is used. Some strategies employed to counter the threats related to a specific resource are equally applicable for other resources as well. However, operating systems define two sets of distinctly different techniques to counter threats and safeguard information:

- Security is concerned with guarding a user's resources against interference by persons or entities external to a system, like non-users.
- Protection involves guarding a user's resources against interference by other users (internal to) of the system.

Security system is actually built using the protection mechanisms that the operating system (file management) provides. The two key methods used by the operating system to implement protection and thereby enable users to secure their resources are *authentication* and *authorization*.

Authentication is commonly the method of verifying the identity of a person intending to use the system. Since physical verification of identity is not practicable in contemporary operating environments, computer-based authentication is provided using a set of specific assumptions. One such assumption is that a person is the user they claim to be if they know a thing or things that only the permissible user is supposed to know. This is called authentication by knowledge (password-based). The other method is to assume a person is the claimed user if they have something that only the allowed user is expected to possess. An example of this approach is biometric authentication, like authentication based on a unique and inalterable biological feature, such as the fingerprints, retina, or iris.

Authorization, on the other hand, is the act of verifying a user's right to access a resource in a specific manner. This means that it is the act of determining the privileges of a user. These privileges are ultimately used to implement protection.

While the security setup consists of the authentication service and the authentication database, the protection setup consists of the authorization service, the authorization database, and the service and resource manager. The authentication service generates an authentication token after it has verified the identity of a user. It passes this token containing a pair of the form (authentication token, privileges) to the authorization service that uses the authorization database of every registered user of the system. It consults the database to find the privileges already granted to the user and passes this information to the service and resource manager. Whenever the user or a user process issues a request for a specific service or resource, the kernel attaches the user's authentication token to it. The service and resource manager then checks whether the user has been authorized to use the service or resource. It grants the request if it is consistent with the user's privileges. Figure 8.1 shows an explanation of this approach.

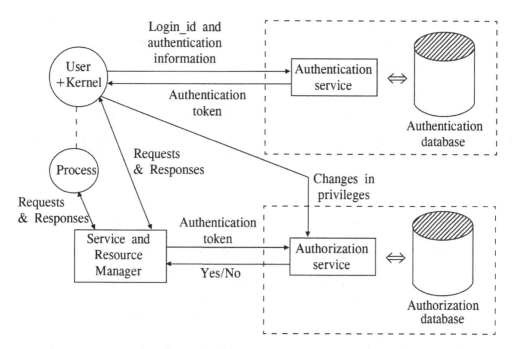

FIGURE 8.1   A schematic block-wise illustration of a representative generic security and protection set-up used in a generic operating system.

The distinctive difference between protection and security provides a neat separation that concerns the operating system. In a conventional operating system, the security aspect is limited to ensuring that only registered users can use an OS. When a user logs in, a security check is performed to determine whether the user is a registered user of the OS, and if so, obtain their user-id. Following this check, all threats to resources in the system are of protection concern; the OS uses the user-id of a person to decide whether they can access a specific resource under the OS. In a distributed system, security aspects are relatively complex due to the presence of a set of computers connected with networking components. Therefore, we confine our discussion about this aspect in this section to only conventional uniprocessor operating systems.

- **Policies and mechanisms:** Security policies state whether a person should be allowed to use a *system*. Protection policies, on the other hand, specify whether a user should be allowed to access a specific *resource* (file). Both these policies are enforced outside the domain of the OS. A system administrator decides whether a person should be allowed to become a user of a system. Likewise, while creating a new file, the file-creator specifies the set of users who are permitted to access it. These policies are implemented by using certain security and protection mechanisms which perform a set of specific checks during the operation of the system. The *security policy* can be determined by defining it in the user space, although many operating systems do layer the functionality. A very small part of the OS implements the *mechanisms*, while the other parts of the OS, system software and utilities, or user software determine the *policy*. As a result, protection and security first depend on the OS protection mechanisms and then on the security policies chosen by the designers and administrators. The separation of policy and mechanism has been discussed by Sandhu (1993). Our objective, however, will be to emphasize more on mechanisms and less on policies.

Security mechanisms have provisions to add new users or verify whether a person is an authorized user of the system. The latter mechanism is called *authentication*, and it is invoked whenever a person attempts to log in to an OS. Protection mechanisms set protection information for a file or check whether a user can be allowed to access a file. This mechanism is called *authorization*; it is invoked whenever a person attempts to access a file or when the owner of a file wishes to alter the list of users who are allowed to access it.

8.3 GOALS OF SECURITY AND PROTECTION: SECURITY THREATS

To explain major types of threats to security as perceived by users and providers of computer-based systems, it is necessary to define what is meant by security requirements. The following five requirements are ultimately the goals that are to be addressed and ensured by computer and network security.

- **Confidentiality or Secrecy:** This requires that the information in a computer system only accessible only by authorized parties. Disclosure of information to unauthorized parties may lead to catastrophic losses depending on the nature of the information in question. Secrecy is definitely a *security* concern, because it is threatened by entities or parties outside an operating system. An OS negotiates it using an *authentication* service.
- **Privacy:** This means that the information should be used only for the purposes for which it is intended and shared. Privacy is a *protection* concern that guards individuals from misuse of information. An OS negotiates privacy through the *authorization* service that determines privileges of a user, and the service and resource manager disallows all requests that belong outside a user's privileges. It is up to the users to ensure privacy of their information using this setup, and they can then allow other users to share the information by accordingly setting the authorization for the information. It can also be called *controlled sharing* of information. It is based on the need-to-know principle.
- **Authenticity:** This requires that the computer system be able to verify the identity of the source or sender of information and also be able to verify that the information is preserved in the form in which it was created or sent.
- **Integrity:** This requires and ensures that the computer system assets can be modified only by authorized parties. Modification usually includes writing content, changing content, changing status, creating and deleting, and so on. This way, unauthorized modification by means of unlawful penetration to destroy or corrupt the information can be prevented.
- **Availability:** This requires that the computer system assets always be available to authorized parties, and nobody can be able to disturb the system to make it unusable. Such *denial of service* (DoS) attacks are becoming increasingly common. For example, if a computer is used as an internet server, sending a flood of requests to it may cripple it by eating up all of its CPU time simply for examining and discarding incoming requests. If it takes, say, 100 msec. to process an incoming request, then anyone who manages to send 10,000 requests/sec can straightaway wipe it out.

Reasonable models and technology for dealing with attacks on *confidentiality*, *authenticity*, and *integrity* are available, but handling *denial-of-service* attacks is much harder. In fact, *confidentiality (secrecy)*, *authenticity*, and *integrity* are both protection and security concerns. Elaborate arrangements are thus needed to handle these concerns. However, the security aspect is actually more of an issue in distributed OSs, and of course, comparatively less in uniprocessor-based traditional operating systems. Moreover, all these concerns are relatively easy to suit as protection concerns on any type of operating system, because the identity of the user has already been verified before the authorization and validation of a request are being carried out which are considered a part of the protection set–up as already shown in Figure 8.1. Last but not least, security threats, as a whole, are more severe and can appear more easily in a distributed OS, since it is mostly exposed to the outside world. For example, when an interprocess message travels over open communication links, including public links, it is quite possible for external entities to enter this domain to tamper with messages.

More about this topic is given on the Support Material at www.routledge.com/9781032467238.

8.4 SECURITY: TYPES OF THREATS

In a computing environment, while information, in general, flows from a source to a destination, an unauthorized entity normally uses this area as an easy hunting place and mobilizes threats on the security of a computer or a network. The different types of attacks that are launched here on security are of four general types. Those are:

- **Interception:** An attack on *confidentiality* launched by a person, a program, or even a computer. Examples include wiretapping to capture data in a network.
- **Modification:** This is an attack on *integrity* by way of tampering with an asset after gaining access. Examples include modifying the contents of messages, values of data in a data file, altering a program being transmitted over a network.
- **Fabrication:** This is an attack on *authenticity* by injecting counterfeit (fake) objects into the system. Examples include addition of records in a file or injection of spurious messages in a network.
- **Interruption:** This is an attack on *availability*, causing an asset of the system to be destroyed or become unavailable or unusable. Examples include damaging of a piece of hardware, destroying a communication line, or disabling the file management system.

More about this topic with a figure is given on the Support Material at www.routledge.com/9781032467238.

8.5 SECURITY ATTACKS: PENETRATION ATTEMPTS ON COMPUTER SYSTEM ASSETS

A security attack, in general, can be defined as an act attempted by a person or an entity called an *intruder* or *adversary* that causes adverse effects by breaching the security of a system composed of hardware, software, data, and communication links and networks. The nature of the threats faced by each category of system assets is:

- **Hardware:** The main threat to the system hardware is mostly in the area of *availability* and includes deliberate damage and accidental mishap, as well as theft. A logged-on terminal left unattended, when accessed by an intruder, eventually results in their gaining full access to all the system resources available to the legitimate user whose identity is assumed. Introduction of networking facilities together with a rapid increase in user density add further fuel that ultimately increases the potential of such damage in this area. As this domain is least conducive to automated controls, appropriate physical and administrative measures are required to negotiate all these attacks.
- **Software:** A key threat to both system and application software is an attack on its *integrity/authenticity* by way of making unauthorized modifications that cause a working program either to result in execution failure or still function but start to behave erratically. Computer *viruses*, *worms*, *Trojan horses*, and other related attacks belong to this category and are discussed later ("Malicious Programs") in this chapter. Another type of attack launched is by using *trap doors*, which are the secret points of entry in the software to gain access to it without going through the usual security access procedures. Trap doors are deliberately left by software designers themselves for many reasons, presumably to allow them to access and possibly modify their programs after installation for production use. Trap doors can be abused by anyone who is already aware of them or acquires

knowledge of their existence and the related entry procedure. Another difficult problem commonly faced is software availability. Software is often deliberately deleted or is altered or damaged to make it useless. To counter this problem, careful software management often includes a common approach that always keeps backups of the software's most recent version.

- **Data:** Data integrity/authenticity is a major concern to all users, since data in files or any other form is a soft target for any type of security attack. Malicious attempts to modify data files can have consequences that may range from inconvenience to catastrophic losses. Attacks on availability of data are concerned with the destruction of data files and can either happen unintentionally, accidentally, or maliciously.

- **Communication Links and Networks:** Since a communication link is a vulnerable component of a computing environment, many attacks are launched in this area, although they are mainly found in distributed operating systems and can result in severe consequences. They have been also observed to be equally damaging to non-distributed conventional operating systems. Network security attacks can generally be classified more effectively in terms of *passive attacks* and *active attacks*. A passive attack only attempts to obtain or make use of information from the system and does not alter or affect system resources. An active attack, on the other hand, attempts to directly damage or alter the system resources or can even affect their normal operations.

8.5.1 Passive Attacks

They are accomplished by means of eavesdropping on, or monitoring of, or active wire–taps on, or electromagnetic pickup of screen radiation of, transmissions. Here, the ultimate objective of the opponent is only to obtain information or at least guess the nature of the communication under transmission. Two types of common passive attacks are:

- **Release of message contents:** Confidential or sensitive information in the form of either a telephonic conversation or an electronic mail message or a transferred file or database are the main targets of such attacks. An all-out effort in this regard must be made to prevent an opponent from obtaining the contents of these vital transmissions.

- **Traffic analysis:** This is another layer of passive attack. Even if the information traffic is masked (say, by encryption), the opponent, after trapping a message, while could not be able to decipher it but might still be able to observe the pattern and nature of the messages. Consequently, the opponent may be in a position to detect the location and identity of the communicating hosts and could observe the frequency and length of messages being exchanged. All this information together might be useful to the opponent in guessing the nature of the communication taking place.

Passive attacks are hard to detect because they do not cause any alteration of data, and their presence cannot even be guessed beforehand. They give no indication that a third party is prying to capture messages or at least to obtain an observed traffic pattern. However, it is not impossible to prevent the success of such attempts, generally by means of using encryption. Thus, the major aim in dealing with passive attacks is to ensure prevention rather than detection.

Brief details on this topic with a figure are given on the Support Material at www.routledge.com/9781032467238.

8.5.2 Active Attacks

These attacks always left a footprint because they make some form of modification to the data stream or create a false stream. These types of security attacks can be subdivided into four different categories:

- **Masquerading:** In a masquerade attack, an opponent could access resources of a registered user of a system, or, even worse, could corrupt or destroy information released from the actual sender, as shown in Figure 8.2(a). One obvious way to launch a masquerade attack is to break the password of a user and use this knowledge to pass the authentication test at log-in time. It will then be possible to impersonate an authorized entity with few privileges, and that, in turn, could enable the attacker to obtain more privileges. Another more subtle approach to a masquerade is by means of malicious programs that are imported into a software environment. This approach will be discussed in a later subsection.
- **Replay:** This involves capturing data by a passive means and subsequent retransmission of it in a form that eventually produces an intended damage effect. This is shown in Figure 8.2(b).
- **Modification of messages:** This acts by capturing a portion of a genuine actual message and altering, or messages are delayed, suspended, or even reordered to produce a destructive effect, leading to a sudden calamity [Figure 8.2(c)]. For example, a message that says, "Allow Amal to immediately go through the confidential contract file", is intentionally modified to say, "Allow Kamal to immediately go through the confidential contract file". Such a modification might have a catastrophic effect in the organization.
- **Denial of service:** This attack is launched by exploiting a weakness in the design or operation of an OS and attempts to prevent or inhibit the normal use of resources or management of communication facilities [Figure 8.2(d)]. A DoS attack can be launched by several means; some of these means can be employed only by users of a system, while others may be exploited by intruders located in other systems. Many DoS attacks can be launched through legitimate means, which makes them easy to launch and equally difficult for an OS to detect and prevent them.

A DoS attack may be launched with a specific target in view. For example, it can corrupt a particular program that offers a specific service. It can damage or destroy some configuration information that resides within a kernel; for example, access to an I/O device can be denied by simply changing its entry in the physical device table of the kernel. Another class of DoS attacks are launched by overloading a resource using phantoms to such an extent that genuine users of the resource are denied its use. A network DoS attack may be launched by disrupting an entire network, either by disabling the network or by overloading (flooding) it with messages so that network bandwidth is denied to genuine messages, leading to an inability to respond to any messages that eventually causes severe degradation in system performance. A distributed DoS attack is one that is launched

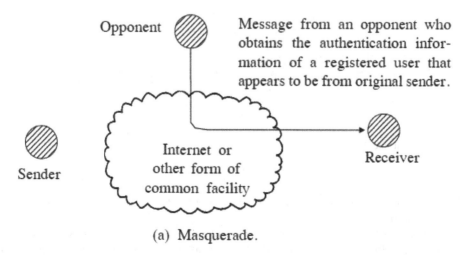

(a) Masquerade.

FIGURE 8.2 A generalized representation of different types of active attacks launched on security system of a generic operating system.

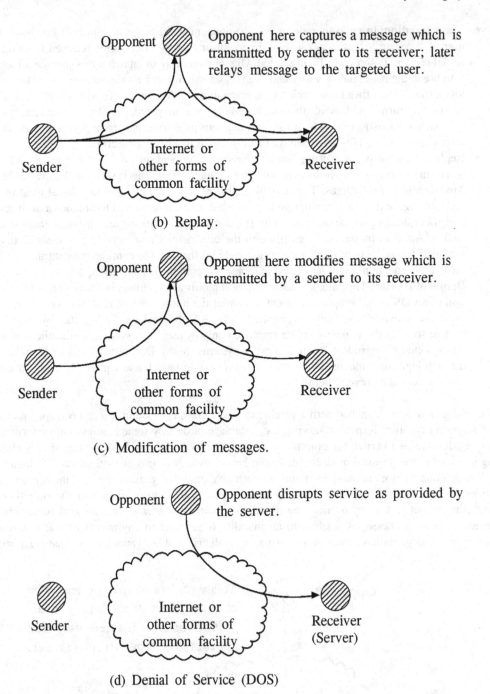

(b) Replay.

(c) Modification of messages.

(d) Denial of Service (DOS)

FIGURE 8.2 (Continued)

by a few intruders located in different hosts in the network; it is perhaps the most difficult to detect and equally hard to prevent.

Active attacks exhibit exactly the opposite characteristics of passive attacks. While passive attacks are difficult to detect, there are certain means and measures that are able to prevent their success. Active attacks, on the other hand, cannot be absolutely prevented because it would require strict physical protection mechanisms and vigilance on all communication facilities and paths at all times. Therefore, the goal while negotiating such active attacks should be simply to go for their detection and subsequently to recover by any means from any disruption or delays caused by them. Although the detection procedure may create a hindrance in normal operation and may have certain deterrent effects, still then it may also contribute to prevention.

8.6   SECURITY POLICIES AND MECHANISMS: DESIGN ISSUES

A variety of ingenuous attacks may be organized to breach security, so it is mandatory to have a completely comprehensive security model, the foremost requirement of which is that the security policies be clearly defined in terms of desired protection and security. Security mechanisms are actually the implementation of certain specific steps that describe how to realize the underlying security policies using the tools (protection facilities) provided by the system. However, establishing a precise policy is very hard, since it requires that a precise set of software requirements be specified, in addition to a set of "laws" without loopholes to control actions taken by human users.

The primary objective in the design of operating systems and of system software and utilities is to include the needed security components that will ultimately provide a flexible and functionally complete set of security mechanisms to permit authorized users and owners of information to enforce security policies as deemed fit. This arrangement consequently will foil most or all of the security attacks that may be launched by an intruder.

More about this topic is given on the Support Material at www.routledge.com/9781032467238.

- **Policies**

Security policies must address both external and internal threats. Since most threats are organized by insiders, the policies primarily encompass procedures and processes that specify:

- How information can enter and exit the system.
- In which way the information will be permitted to flow within the system.
- Who is authorized to access what information and under what conditions. In other words, whose data are to be protected from whom.

Additional aspects can be included to expand the security domain to limit other possibilities of danger. However, security policies are often based on some well-accepted time-proven **basic principles**. Those are:

Least privilege: Every object is to be allowed to access just the information required to complete the tasks that the subject is authorized to. For example, the accountants in a factory need not have access to the production data, and similarly, factory supervisors should not be allowed to access the accounting data

Rotation in responsibilities: Sensitive and confidential operations should not be permanently entrusted to the same personnel or the same group of personnel. Some rotation can often be used to prevent foul play or wrongdoing.

Isolation in duties: In the case of critical operations that can put an organization at risk, then two or more people with conflicting interests should be involved in carrying it out. In other words, two people with different involvement should be given charge of two different keys to open the vault.

The selection of an adequate security policy for a given installation and for specific data therein is commonly a trade-off between the perceived risk of exposure, the potential loss due to the damage or leakage of information, and the cost to be incurred to implement a required level of security.

The selection process will analyze the risk assessment and the related assessment of cost, which includes cost of equipment, personnel, and performance degradation due to the implementation of security measures. Once the analysis process is over, the suitable and appropriate security policies can then be chalked out. Most computer-related security policies belong to one of two basic **categories**:

- **Discretionary Access Control (DAC):** Under this category, policies are usually defined by the creator or the owner of the data, who may permit and specify access rights to other users. This form of access control is quite common in file systems. It is, however, vulnerable to the Trojan horse (to be discussed in later subsections) attack, where intruders pose themselves as authorized and legitimate users.
- **Mandatory Access Control (MAC):** In this scheme, users are classified according to level of authority or permissions to be awarded. Data are also categorized into security classes according to level of sensitivity or confidentiality, and stringent rules are then specified that should be strictly followed regarding which level of user clearance is required for accessing the data of a specific security class. Mandatory access restrictions are thus not subject to user discretion and hence limit the damage that the Trojan horse can cause. For example, military documents are usually categorized as secret, top secret, confidential, and unclassified. The user must have clearance equal to or above that of the document in order to gain access to it. MAC also appears in other systems, perhaps in less obvious forms. For example, a university authority cannot pass the right to modify grade records to students.

- **Mechanisms and Design Principles**

Security measures, in general, must address both external and internal security. External or physical security includes the standard age-old techniques of fencing, surveillance, authentication, attendance control, and monitoring. Physical security also demands replication of critical data for recovery from disasters (such as accidental system crashes, fire, or flood), access restrictions to computer systems, and also safe storage areas used for maintaining backups.

Major efforts are, however, exerted to realize internal security mechanisms, which encompass issues primarily related to the design of the OS that will actually lay the basic foundation of the mechanisms to implement security policies. Saltzer and Schroeder (1975) have identified several general principles that can be used as a guideline to designing secure systems. A brief summary of their ideas (based on experience with MULTICS) is given here:

Least privilege: Give each process the least privilege to enable it to complete its task. For example, if an editor has only the clearance to access the file to be edited (specified when the editor is invoked), then editors already infected with Trojan horses will not create much damage. This principle effectively advocates for support of small protection domains that imply a fine-grained protection scheme. It also provides switching of domains when the access needs to be changed.

Separation of privilege: Whenever possible, privilege with respect to access to objects should be granted in such a way so that it has to satisfy more than one condition (in other words, two keys to open the vault).

Least common mechanism: Minimize the amount of mechanism that is common to and depends upon multiple users. The designed mechanism will incorporate techniques for separating users, such as logical separation via virtual machines and physical separation of different machines present in distributed systems.

Complete mediation: Every access right should be checked for authorization. The checking mechanism should be effective and efficient, since it has an immense impact on the performance of the system.

Squirrel checking: Every access should be checked for current authority. The system should check for permission, determine that access is permitted, and then squirrel away this information for subsequent use. Many systems check for permission when a file is opened and not afterward. This means that a user who opens a file and keeps it open for weeks will continue to have access, even if the owner has long since changed the file protection.

Fail-safe default: Access rights should be acquired by explicit permission only, and the default should be to have no access. Errors in which legitimate access is refused will be reported much faster than the errors that may result from an unauthorized access.

Open design: The design of a security mechanism should not be secret; rather it should be public. It should not depend on the ignorance of attackers. Assuming that the intruder will not know how the system works serves only to delude the designers.

Economy of mechanisms: The design should be kept as simple and uniform as possible to facilitate verifications and correct implementations. It should be built into the lowest layers of the system. Trying to retro-fit security to an existing insecure system is nearly impossible. Security, like correctness, is not an add-on feature.

User acceptability: The scheme to be chosen must be psychologically acceptable. The mechanism should provide ease of use so that it is applied correctly and not circumvented by users. If users feel that protecting their files involves too much work, they just will not do it. Moreover, they may complain if something goes wrong. Replies of the form "It is your own fault" will generally not work or be well received.

8.7 PROTECTION

The original motivation for protection mechanisms started to evolve with the introduction of multitasking systems in which resources, such as memory, I/O devices, programs, and data, are shared among users. The operating system was designed to prevent others from trespassing in the users' domain and thereby absolutely protected the users' interests as a whole. In some systems, protection is enforced by a program called *reference monitor* that checks the legality of accessing a potential resource by consulting its own policy tables and then makes a decision that enables the system to correctly proceed. We will discuss later in this section some of the environments in which a reference monitor is expected to be involved. Pfleeger (1997) identifies the following spectrum of approaches used by a user along which an operating system may provide appropriate protection.

- **No protection:** This approach is workable if sensitive procedures can be run at separate times.
- **Isolation:** This implies that each process is a standalone one that operates separately from other processes with no dependency, with no sharing and communication. Each process has its own address space, files, and other objects to complete its task.
- **Share all or share nothing:** This states that the owner or creator of an object (program, data, or memory area) can declare it to be public or private. In the former case, any other process may access the object, whereas in the latter, only the owner's processes may access the object.
- **Share via access limitation:** This option tells the OS to check the legality of each access when it is made by a specific user to a particular object. This ensures that only authorized access is permissible.
- **Share via dynamic capabilities:** This allows dynamic creation of sharing rights for objects.
- **Limited use of an object:** This approach provides a form of protection that limits not just access to an object but the way in which the object may be used. For example, a user may be allowed to display a confidential document to view but not permitted to print it. Another example is that a user may have permission to access a database to get information but no rights to modify it.

The preceding items are arranged roughly in increasing order of difficulty when implemented, but at the same time, this shows an increasing order of the fineness of protection that they provide. One of the design objectives of an operating system is thus to create a balance while allowing sharing of resources by many users to enhance resource usage and at the same time to ensure the protection of users' vital resources from any unauthorized access. An operating system when designed and developed may incorporate different degrees of protection for different users, objects, or applications. We will discuss here some of the most commonly used protection mechanisms that many operating systems employ to realize protection for their objects.

Brief details on this topic are given on the Support Material at www.routledge.com/9781032467238.

8.8 PROTECTION OF MEMORY

In a multiprogramming/multi-user environment, protection of primary storage is essential not only from the standpoint of security but for the sake of preventing overlap of one process on another in the same memory space, thereby enabling simultaneously active various resident processes to run correctly. Usually, protection in primary storage is essentially adjunct to address translation.

Memory protection in systems with contiguous allocation of memory is usually carried out with the aid of some sort of limit register (see Chapter 5). In systems supporting virtual memory, the separation of memory space of various processes is easily accomplished by either paging, segmentation, or a combination of both. Protection in secondary storage is usually effected by means of user-defined access rights that are associated with files and managed by the file system. Some systems, for the sake of efficiency, define access lists in abbreviated form.

More about this topic is given on the Support Material at www.routledge.com/9781032467238.

8.9 PROTECTION STRUCTURE: ACCESS CONTROL

The basic underlying issues and principles of protection mechanisms are obscure. To unfold them, there is a need to explain how a protection mechanism is to be defined that, in turn, requires describing a protection structure that would represent the access-control information in some pattern and subsequent proper use of it. This section introduces the access-matrix model of protection which perhaps serves as a useful abstraction for describing the protection mechanisms used in computer systems. Here, the system can be viewed as essentially consisting of a set of *subjects*, such as users or processes, that operate on or manipulate a set of *hardware objects*, namely the CPU, memory segments, peripheral devices, and so on, and *software objects*, such as files, databases, and semaphores. Access control can be classified into two distinct categories:

- those associated with the subject or user, and
- those associated with the objects.

A user may be permitted to access a set of objects, and an object may be accessible by a set of users. A protection structure contains information that indicates which users can access which objects and in what manner.

8.9.1 USER-ORIENTED

The access control imposed on users is, unfortunately, sometimes referred to as authentication, since this term is widely used nowadays in the sense of message authentication. We will, however, strictly refrain from applying it here.

The most common technique widely used for user access control on shared systems are user log-on details containing a user identifier (ID) and a password. But the ID/password system is seemingly unreliable, because enough expertise has emerged that can guess the IDs of users as a whole.

Moreover, in some systems, the ID/password file is accessible by skilled hackers, and as a result, this file becomes a soft target of penetration attempts. Modern protection systems may even resort to methods such as fingerprint or eye scan identification. Besides, certain other means and measures are now available to counter these attempts, and those will be discussed later in this section.

In a distributed environment, user access control is either *centralized* or *decentralized*. In a centralized approach, the network system provides a log-on service that determines who is allowed to access the network and to whom the user is allowed to connect. In a decentralized approach, the network is treated by user-access-control as a transparent communication link, and the usual log-on procedure is carried out by the destination host. Of course, transmitting passwords over the network concerning security must still be further addressed. In addition, many networks may have the provision of two–levels of access control. In that system, individual hosts may be provided with a log-on facility to guard host-specific resources and applications. Besides, the network itself as a whole may also provide some protection to limit network access to authorized users. This two-level facility is desirable for the common case in which the network connects disparate hosts and simply provides a convenient means of terminal–host access. In a more uniform network of hosts, an additional centralized access policy could also be enforced in a network-control center.

More about this topic is given on the Support Material at www.routledge.com/9781032467238.

8.9.2 DATA-ORIENTED

Following successful log-on, the user has been granted access to objects, such as to one or a set of hosts (hardware) and applications. Every object has a name by which it is referenced and an access privilege, which is a right to carry out a specific finite set of operations (e.g. read and write operations to a file and up and down on a semaphore).

It is now obvious that a way is needed to prohibit processes (users) from accessing objects that they are not authorized to. Associated with each user, there can be a profile provided by the OS that specifies permissible operations or a subset of the legal operations and file accesses when needed. For example, process A may be entitled to read file F but not write to it. An *access descriptor* describes such access privileges for a file. Common notations are used, like *r*, *w*, and *x*, to represent access privileges to *read*, *write*, and *execute* the data or program, respectively in a file. An access descriptor can also be represented as a set; for example, the descriptor {r, w} indicates privileges to only read and write a file. Access control information for a file is a collection of access descriptors for access privileges held by various users.

Considerations of data-oriented access control in network parallel those for user-oriented access control. This means that if only certain users are permitted to access certain items of data, then encryption may be useful and needed to protect those items during transmission to authorized target users. Typically, data access control is decentralized. It is usually controlled by host-based database management systems. If a database server exists on a network, then data access control is monitored and becomes a function of the network.

More about this topic is given on the Support Material at www.routledge.com/9781032467238.

8.9.2.1 Access Control Matrix

A general model of access control as exercised by a file or a database management system is an access control matrix (ACM), as shown in Figure 8.3, which stores protection information consisting of access privileges of users and access control information for files and databases. The basic elements of the model are:

- **Subjects:** A row in ACM represents a process (or user) with *access privileges* of accessing different objects. In fact, any user or application gains access to an object by means of a process which represents that user or application.

	File 1	File 2	File 3	File 4	DB1	DB2
User A	Own R W			R	Inquiry Debit	Inquiry Credit
User B	R W	Own R W	R W X			Inquiry Debit
User C		R	R X	Own R W	Inquiry Credit	

FIGURE 8.3 A schematic illustration of a representative format of access control matrix (ACM) used in the protection mechanism built in a generic modern operating system.

- **Objects:** A column describes *access control information* for anything (file, database, etc.) to which access is controlled. Examples include files, portions of files, programs, segments of memory, and software objects (e.g. Java objects).
- **Access rights:** The way in which an object is accessed by a subject. Examples include *read, write, execute, copy*, and *functions* in software objects.

The subjects of ACM typically consist of individual users, or user groups, although they can include terminals, hosts, or applications instead of or in addition to users for access control. Similarly, the objects, at the finest level of detail, may be individual data fields. But more aggregate groupings, such as records, files, or even the entire database, may also be objects in the matrix. Moreover, access descriptors can be made bit-oriented instead of a character of one access right (bit = 1, i.e. present, and bit = 0, i.e. absent) for reduced memory usage as well as for access efficiency.

- **Resolution (or Granularity) of Protection:** The degree of control over protection of objects can be made varied. This is known as *granularity of protection*. Three levels of granularity are in common. *Coarse granularity* in ACM signifies that the owner of a file specifies access privileges to groups of users. *Medium granularity* in ACM specifies access privileges for each individual user in the system. *Fine granularity* in ACM specifies access privileges for a process or even for a phase of execution of a process. This way, different processes created by the same user may possess different access privileges for a file, or the same process may possess different access privileges at different times. Fine granularity provides users with much more resolution than coarse-grained or medium-grained protection. The implications of granularity of protection can be justified in a better way, which we will discuss in "Protection Domain".
- **Disadvantages of ACM:** The access control matrix provides a simple, effective, and efficient means of accessing protection information. But if an OS contains n_p users and n_f files, then the size of access–control matrix (ACM) would be $n_p \times n_f$, which will be, or even a part of it will then consume a large memory area during operation. But typical user processes mostly use access–privileges for few files, causing most entries in the ACM to contain null information (sparse matrix); hence, the amount of actual access control information needed is usually much smaller than the total size of the ACM.

One way to alleviate this problem is to reduce the size of access control information, and that reduction can be realized in two ways: by reducing the number of rows in the ACM or simply by eliminating the null information. Attempting to reduce the number of rows means to assign access privileges to groups of users rather than to individual users, but forming such groups may not always be feasible in practice. In fact, it will compromise the granularity of protection that will eventually mar the actual objectives of protection provision. The other alternative is by eliminating null information in the ACM. Here, the information stored in the ACM is in the form of lists instead of a matrix. This approach while does not affect the granularity of protection but reduces the size of protection information, since only non-null entries of an ACM need to be present in a list. Two such list structures are commonly used in practice:

- Access control lists (ACLs)
- Capability lists (C-lists)

An *access control list* stores the non-null information from a *column* of the ACM. Thus, it essentially consists of a (ordered) list of access control information for one object (file or account) covering all the users present in the system. A *capability list* (C-list) stores the non-null information of a *row* of the ACM. It thus describes all access privileges held by a user. While ACL can provide coarse- or medium-grained protection, the C-list provides only medium-grained protection. These two approaches will be discussed in the next section. Fine-grained protection can be obtained by using a *protection domain*, which will be discussed later.

Brief details on this topic are given on the Support Material at www.routledge.com/9781032467238.

8.9.2.2 Access Control Lists

The access control list of a particular object (a file) lists users and their permitted access rights, indicating which users can access the object and in what manner. When a user creates a file, the file's access control information as provided by the creator (or owner) is registered with the system. It is typically stored in the directory entry of the file in the form of {(user-id, access–privileges), . . .}. Whenever a process attempts to open a file, the OS (actually, the file system) finds the id of the user that initiated the process and checks with the ACL whether the user's access privileges permit the intended mode of access, and accordingly, the access is permitted or denied. In most file systems, the owner gets certain access privileges by default. In UNIX, these access privileges are controlled by the user mask.

ACL has some inherent drawbacks that give rise to some problems when realized in practice. The presence of a huge number of users in a system results in a large ACL size that requires a large memory space to hold it, and the time required is also high while searching it to validate file access. However, this problem can be minimized by storing protection information only for groups of users rather than for individuals, thereby offering only coarse-grained protection.

With ACL, it is relatively straightforward to revoke a previously granted access given to a user or a group by simply editing the ACL to make the needed changes. But the problem is that in many systems, the ACL is checked for permission only when a file is opened and not afterward. This means that a user who opens a file and keeps it open for weeks will continue to have access, even if the owner changes the access privileges. Any file that is already open will continue to enjoy the rights it had when it was opened, even if the user is no longer authorized to access the file at all.

More about this topic is given on the Support Material at www.routledge.com/9781032467238.

8.9.2.3 Capability List (C-Lists)

A capability simply represents the access privileges of a user (process) for one object (file). Each capability grants the owner certain rights on a certain object. Associated with each user is a set of capabilities that the user possesses, which is stored in a list known as a *capability list* (C-list). The C-list stores the non-null information of a row of the ACM which is thus a set of pairs {(*file-id, access-privileges*), . . .}. In a UNIX-like system, the *file-id* in the pair that represents capability would probably be the *i-node* number. Whenever any user attempts to access an object, the corresponding C-list of that user is searched to make a decision. C-lists are usually small in size, which limits the space and time overhead in using them to control file accesses. In fact, C-lists are themselves objects and may be pointed to or from other C-lists, thereby facilitating sharing of sub-domains.

Brief details on this topic with a figure are given on the Support Material at www. routledge.com/9781032467238.

- **Protection of capabilities**

Like any other objects, since capability lists is shared, they must also be kept protected from any form of tampering attempted by the user. **Four methods** of protecting them are commonly known. The **first method** requires a tagged architecture in the hardware design in which each memory word has an extra (or tag) bit that specifies whether the word contains a capability. The tag bit is set by OS, can be accessed only in kernel mode, and cannot be modified by any user instructions. When an operation OP_j is to be performed on an object OB_k, the CPU checks the compatibility of OP_j with OB_k's tag and performs the operation only if the two are compatible' otherwise the attempt at executing OP_j fails. For example, a fixed-point operation will fail if applied to a float value. Tagged architecture machines have been built and found to work satisfactorily. IBM AS/400 (now called p-series) systems are a popular example of this kind. The **second method** is to maintain the C-list inside the operating system. Capabilities are then referred to by their position in the capability list. A process might then say: "Read 2 KB from the file pointed to by capability 5". File descriptors in UNIX are found to use similar form of addressing. Hydra also worked this way as described by Wulf. The **third method** is to keep the C-list in the user space, but the capabilities are managed cryptographically so that users cannot tamper with them. This approach is particularly suited to distributed systems and has been found to work well. The **fourth approach** is extended using the popular segment-based memory management scheme by introducing a third kind of segment, a capability segment in which capabilities are inserted only by the kernel using a privileged instruction. To access the desired object, the operand field of an instruction contains two fields: the *id* of a capability segment and an *offset* (to reach the desired object in C-list) into this segment. The address of the object is now obtained using an object table in which each row has two fields: one field contains the object-id, and the other field contains the object in the computer's primary or secondary memory. Protection of capabilities is implicit in the fact that a store operation cannot be performed in a capability segment. This feature prevents tampering with and forgery of capabilities.

ACLs and capabilities are observed to have somewhat complementary properties. Capabilities are very efficient, and no checking is needed because they can be referred to by their positions in the capability list. With ACLs, a search of long list is required to ascertain the access–privilege of a certain object if groups are not supported. Capabilities also allow a process to be easily encapsulated, whereas ACLs do not support this. On the other hand, ACLs allow selective revocation of rights if needed, which capabilities do not. Last but not least, if an object is removed and the capabilities are not, or the capabilities are removed and an object is not, problems arise in both situations. ACLs, however, do not face such a problem.

More about this topic is given on the Support Material at www.routledge.com/9781032467238.

- **Software Capabilities**

An operating system that runs on computer systems with non-capability architecture can implement capabilities in the software by a component of the kernel called an object manager (OM). When a program intends to manipulate its objects, it indicates its requirements to the OM by making a system call:

$$OM (<op_k>, Cap (obj_k))$$

Before beginning the execution of $<op_k>$, the OM verifies that $Cap(obj_k)$ contains the necessary access privileges in the C-list. But software implementation of capabilities gives rise to two major issues:

- A process may be able to bypass the capability-based protection arrangement while accessing objects.
- A process may be able to fabricate or tamper with capabilities.

To counter the *first issue*, one way may be to hide objects from the view of user processes by encrypting the system-wide *object table*, in which each row of the table contains the *object-id* and *object address field* that indicates the location address of the corresponding object in the computer's primary and secondary memory. Now, processes intending to access the object will not be able to locate the objects because the locations of the objects are not known to them, so they have to depend on the OM (object table) to perform object manipulation. The second issue in relation to preventing fabrication or tampering capabilities can also be addressed and negotiated using encryption. This approach has been successfully implemented in the capability protection scheme used in the distributed operating system, **Amoeba**.

The distinct advantage of software capabilities, that is, its independence from the underlying hardware is also appeared as its major drawback. Here, every operation op_k on an object requires a costly, time-consuming system call to invoke the OM to verify its access privilege in the C-list. Moreover, prevention of tampering requires validation of a capability every time before use, thereby also causing substantial time overhead. All these requirements summarily lead to appreciable overhead, resulting in significant degradation in the overall system performance.

More on this topic is given on the Support Material at www.routledge.com/9781032467238.

- **Use of Capabilities: Practical Difficulties**

Although capabilities are very efficient, implementation of them in hardware or software incurs a high cost. Apart from that, use of these capabilities faces some other practical difficulties when implemented. Three such difficulties out of many are:

- *Need for garbage collection*: When can an object be destroyed?
- *Confinement of capabilities*: How to ensure and enforce that processes do not pass capabilities to other processes indiscriminately?
- *Revocation of capabilities*: How to withdraw access privileges or cancel a capability conferred by them?

Details on each of the bullet points are described on the Support Material at www.routledge. com/9781032467238.

8.9.2.4   Protection Domain

Use of an ACM or its variants like ACLs and C-lists as provided by an operating system confers access privileges on users that typically address the secrecy aspect of protection. One peculiarity of this arrangement is that every process created by a user has the same access privileges! The arrangement serves the secrecy concern in protection, because only authorized users can access a file; however, it is unable to adequately address the privacy concern, because it does not differentiate between different processes created by a user.

Privacy between the processes created by a user may be violated in many ways. Consider the case: An access privilege is granted to a user, because some process initiated by the user requires it. However, any process created by the same user can use (or enjoy) the same access privilege, so a process initiated by the user may put the information to an unintended or malicious use. Such usage violates the privacy requirement.

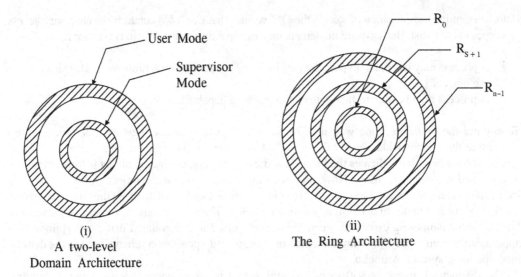

(i)
A two-level
Domain Architecture

(ii)
The Ring Architecture

FIGURE 8.4.a   A schematic layout of ring–type protection domains used in building up the protection mechanism of a generic modern operating system.

The notion of a protection domain addresses the privacy aspect. Figure 8.4a(i) is a pictorial visualization of two protection domains in the form of *rings*. The inner domain represents programs that are executed in the supervisor mode in the context of protection; the process is said to execute in the *supervisor domain*. The outer ring is the *user domain* in which the programs are executed in the user mode. Obviously, programs operating in the supervisor domain enjoy additional access rights compared to programs operating in the user domain.

The generalization of this two-level domain is a set of N concentric rings called a domain, **ring architecture** for protection as shown in Figure 8.4a(ii). This ring architecture was first introduced in MULTICS (the predecessor of UNIX) which provides 64 such protection domains that were organized as concentric rings in a similar way as that shown in Figure 8.4a(ii). Under this scheme, out of N rings of protection, rings R_0 through R_S support the operating system domain, and rings R_{S+1} through R_{N-1} are used by applications. Thus, $i < j$ means that R_i has more rights than R_j. In other words, the farther in the ring, the more privileges. The most critical part of the kernel in terms of protection executes in R_0. The next most secure level of the OS executes in R_1, and so on. The most secure level of user programs executes in ring R_{S+1}, with successively less secure software executing in outer rings. The hardware supervisor mode in this model would ordinarily be used when software executes in the lowest-numbered rings, perhaps only in R_0 (as was the case in MULTICS). This part of the OS is to be designed and implemented most carefully and is presumably proved to be correct.

A protection domain conceptually is an "execution environment". Software located in a file that executes in a ring is assigned to that ring. A process operates in a protection domain. Access privileges are granted to a protection domain rather than to a user. By default, the initial execution domain of a process does not possess any access privileges. This way, a process cannot access any resources while it executes in this domain, even if the resources are owned by the user who initiated this process. In order to access any specific resource, the process must "enter" a protection domain that possesses access privileges for that resource. This says that a process may switch between different protection domains in the course of its execution, and the protection mechanism provides a means by which a process can safely change domains, that is, can cross rings. If a process executes a file in R_i, then the same process can call any procedure in R_k, $(k \geq i)$ without special permission, since that call represents a call to a lower protection domain.

The operating system (kernel) provides system calls through which a process may issue request for entry into an *inner* protection domain. Each attempted crossing of an inner ring causes an internal

Files →	Personal	accounts	inventory	mails	project
D1	{rw}	{rw}			
D2		{r}			
D3			{rw}	{r}	{rw}

Domains ↓

FIGURE 8.4.b An example with a representative format of protection domains created for the different activities of a user made by a generic modern operating system.

authorization mechanism to validate the respective procedure call. A set of conditions would be defined for the legality of such an entry request. The kernel would apply the conditions and either honor the request for change of protection domain or abort the process for making an illegal request. Domains themselves, in general, need not be static; their elements can change as objects are deleted or created, and the access rights are modified. Domains may even overlap; a single object can participate in multiple domains, possibly with different access rights defined therein.

Figure 8.4(b) shows three protection domains, D1, D2, and D3, for different objects (files) as mentioned. Domains D1 and D2 overlap over the object "accounts", while domain D3 is disjoint with both of them. Assume that a user U_1 executes three computations, *leave*, *salary*, and *job*, related in domains D1, D2, and D3, respectively. Thus, *salary* can access only file *accounts* and can only read it. Now consider an OS that does not use protection domains. User U_1 would need read and write access rights to files *personnel*, *accounts*, *inventory*, and *mails* and read access rights to the file *project*. When user U_1 executes the program *salary* that is owned by user U_2, the program *salary* will be able to modify many files accessible to user U_1! This is not fair and is not desirable at all.

This example demonstrates a protection arrangement involving the use of protection domains that facilitate implementation of the need-to-know principle with a fine-grained granularity of protection. Only processes that need to access a resource are granted access to it. It also illustrates how this approach provides privacy of information and thereby improves data integrity and reliability.

The generalized ring structure does not need to support inner ring data accesses; rather it requires only procedure calls. Data kept in inner rings can then be accessed using a corresponding inner ring access procedure, similar to the way an abstract data type allows references to its fields only through public interfaces.

Ring structures are equally applied in hardware in contemporary computer architecture. In the Intel 80386 microprocessor, for example, a four-level structure is incorporated that exhibits some similarities to the one described here. In the Intel case, there were three levels of instruction sets. Level 2 and 3 instructions were the normal application program instruction sets, although non-critical portions of the OS code were also assumed to execute at level 2. Level 1 instructions included I/O instructions. Level 0 instructions manipulated segmented memory using a system global descriptor table and performed context switching. This architecture and its successors, such as 80486 and Pentium microprocessors, are intended to support memory segment management at level 0, while I/O operations execute at a relatively higher security level: a higher ring number. The main body of the OS, however, operates at level 2, where the segments are appropriately protected by the ring structure.

8.9.2.5 Locks and Keys

The locks-and-keys mechanism essentially combines aspects of access lists and ticket-oriented protection systems. In this approach, each object is associated with a list of locks and access rights. A process P is given a key K_i to lock L_i only if it has the access right r_i to the related object. A lock list is effectively a column in the access control matrix where identical nonempty entries can be represented by a single pair (L_i, r_i). A key for a lock is essentially a capability that entitles the owner to access the object, provided that the key matches the related lock. The owner of the object can also revoke the access rights of all processes that share the key K_i by simply deleting lock entry L_i. This method has a close resemblance to the storage keys introduced in the IBM 360 systems.

8.10   INTRUDERS

One of the two most commonly observed threats to security is the *intruder*, and the other is, of course, the *virus*. In security literature, people who are nosing around places where they have no business are called *intruders* or sometimes *adversaries*, or they are referred to as *hackers* or *crackers*. Intruders act in two different ways. Passive intruders just want to read files they are not authorized to read. Active intruders are more dangerous; they want to make unauthorized modifications that may lead to fatal consequences, disrupting the entire system. The main objective of the intruder, in general, is to somehow gain access to a system or to increase the range of privileges accessible on a system. Intruders of different classes with different natures and characteristics have been found in practice. Some common categories are:

*   **Nontechnical users:** Some people have bad habits of reading other files and documents simply by curiosity without having any definite reasons if no barriers are found in the way. Some operating systems, in particular most UNIX systems, have the default that all newly created files are publicly readable, which indirectly encourages exercising this practice. They are mostly insiders.
*   **Snooping by insiders:** A genuine relatively skilled user, often take it a personal challenge with no specific intention, exercise their expertise to just only break the security of a local system in order to access data, programs, or resources when such accesses to these resources are not authorized.
*   **Misusers:** A legitimate user often accesses data, programs, or resources for which access is not authorized, or they are even authorized for such accesses but misuse their rights and privileges. Such a user is generally an insider.
*   **Masqueraders:** An individual or sometimes a group who is not authorized to use the computer system but still attempts to penetrate a system's access control in order to intentionally acquire a legitimate user's account. A masquerader is likely to be an outsider
*   **Clandestine user:** An individual who steals or by some means seizes supervisory control of the system and uses this control to evade or to suppress authentication or authorization. This category of user can be either an insider or an outsider.

8.11   USER AUTHENTICATION

Intruders, in general, always attempt to acquire information that can be used to break the security schemes developed by the user employing the protection mechanisms offered by the system. Most systems use security mechanisms that are based on the assumption that the system knows the identity of each legal user. Identification of users when they log in is called *user authentication*, and its primary objective is to allow access to legitimate system users and to deny access to unauthorized parties. The principle involved in developing one-way authentication methods is mostly based on identifying something the user knows (possession of a secret, say, a password), something the user has (possession of an artifact, such as badge or smart card), or something the user is (some unique physiological or behavioral characteristic of the user).

8.11.1   PASSWORDS

The most common popular form of authentication widely in use based on sharing of a secret is the user password, possibly initially assigned by the system or an administrator. Typically, a system must maintain a file or a password table as the authentication database in which each entry is in the form (login id, <password-info>) for each legitimate user to identify at the time of login. Many systems also allow users to subsequently change their passwords at will. Since, password authentication offers limited protection and is easy to defeat, the password table (file) should be kept protected, and that can be done in one of two ways:

- **Access Control:** Access to the *password file* is limited to one or a very few accounts.
- **One–Way Encryption:** The system stores only an encrypted form of the users' passwords in the file. When a user presents a password at the time of login, the system immediately performs encryption of the password by using it as an input for the encryption function in a one-way transformation (not reversible) to generate a fixed-length output, which is then compared with the stored value in the password file.

If one or both of these countermeasures are applied, then it is obvious that password cracking will not be so easy and that some extra effort is then still needed even for a potentially skilled intruder to obtain passwords. However, the intruder may still launch a variety of ingenious attacks, mainly based on an unlimited license to guess using numerous techniques to breach/crack security or learn passwords. Sometimes, use of a Trojan horse (to be described later) to bypass restrictions on access, and wire-tapping the line between a remote user and the host system can be fruitful to reach the desired target.

These and other commonly used purely password-related schemes possess certain merits, but the password itself is always the face of all types of threats as a soft target that attempts to destroy the security system. It will then be wise to concentrate more on how to *protect passwords* so that attacks launched on passwords or any form of intrusion can be prevented. Still, all possible measures to restrict intrusion can fail, so the system must have a second line of defense, which is *intrusion detection*, so that the appropriate measures can be taken. Detection is always concerned with obtaining the nature and type of the attack, either before or after its success.

Prevention, as a whole, in computer folklore is a challenging aspect and an uphill battle at all times and, in fact, becomes a challenging security goal when considered in the context of protection mechanisms offered to users. The problem is that defenders are always at the receiving end and hence must always attempt only to foil all possible attacks organized from the end of the offenders. But, the attacker is free to play, always trying to find the weakest link in the chain of defense and improvise different strategies to mobilize attacks.

More about this topic is given on the Support Material at www.routledge.com/9781032467238.

8.11.1.1 Password Protection

Password systems consist of a *user-id* and *password* together submitted to login to the computer; the *user-id* determines the authorization of the user along with the level of privileges already assigned to the user, and the *password* authenticates the *user-id* of the individual. This password system is considered the most important frontline defense of the user and also the proverbial weakest link in the security chain for intruders attempting to break the security. Use of simple passwords and also passwords of shorter length that are easy to remember by the user is most vulnerable and actually helps crackers easily guess them with almost no difficulty. To alleviate this problem, some systems often require passwords a specific number of characters in length. In fact, use of poor passwords is considered one of the main factors of large number of security problems. Several techniques thus have been proposed to defeat attacks on passwords. A few popular and effective techniques are:

- **Password aging:** This requires or encourage users to regularly change their passwords to create an obstacle to intruder attack and make passwords relatively secure. Another alternative may be to use "good" passwords and advise users to keep them unchanged. Then, the amount of time and effort to be exerted by the intruders to break them will frustrate them and make it mostly infeasible for them.

- **Encryption of passwords:** An encrypted form of a password known as *ciphertext* is a standard technique to protect the password file (authentication database) stored in a system file and is usually visible to all users in the system. An intruder in the guise of a registered user (insider) would then try a chosen plaintext attack by changing their own password repeatedly, perhaps creating thousands of possible passwords, and then analyze the encrypted forms with little resource consumption. On the other hand, an outsider would have to use an exhaustive attack by trying to login with various types of different passwords. But if the encrypted password file is invisible to anybody other than the root, any intruder within or outside the system would have to launch an exhaustive attack through repeated login attempts. This strategy, although seemingly attractive and reasonable, suffers from several flaws, as pointed out by many researchers. A few of them are: Any type of an accident of protection might expose the password file and render it readable, thereby compromising all the user accounts. Second, it has been observed that some users in one machine have accounts on other machines in other protection domains, and they often use the same password. Thus, if the password is read by anyone on one machine, a machine in another location in another protection domain could be easily accessed.

Both UNIX and Linux perform encryption on passwords. UNIX uses DES encryption (to be discussed next), whereas Linux uses a message digest (MD) technique which is simply a one-way hash function that generates a 128- or 160-bit hash value from a password. This technique also has many variants, called MD2, MD4, and MD5. Linux uses MD5. In addition, both UNIX and Linux provide a shadow password file option. When this option is considered, the *ciphertext* form of passwords is stored in a shadow file that is accessible only to the root. This arrangement creates a situation that requires an intruder to go through a process of an exhaustive attack, which is not only expensive but also time-consuming.

Thus, it can be concluded that a more effective strategy would be to always require users to select good passwords that would normally be difficult to guess. Several password selection strategies exist, and the ultimate objective of all of them is to eliminate guessable passwords while allowing the user at the same time to select a password that is memorable.

- **Other Methods:** One approach is to change the passwords regularly by using a one-time password (OTP) which is provided by the system to the user through a book that contains a list of passwords. Each login uses the next password in the list. If an intruder, by any chance, ever discovers a password, it will not serve their purpose, since next time a different password must be used. But the user here must be very careful about the password book and maintain the book with utmost secrecy.

One other method exists which is based on a variation on the password ideas in which each new user is provided a long list of questions, and their answers are stored in the computer in encrypted form. The questions should be chosen so that the user does not need to write the answers down. In other words, they should be things no one forgets. Typical questions look like: **1.** Who is Kamal's brother? **2.** On what street was your maternal uncle's house? **3.** What did Mr. Paul teach in your secondary school? At the time of login, the computer asks one of those at random and checks that with the existing answer.

Still another variation of the password idea is known as **challenge–response**. This technique is to have the system issue a dynamic challenge to the user after login. The user picks an algorithm when signing up as a user that is to be applied as a secret transformation, such as $x \times 2$ or $x + 3$. When the user logs in, the computer types a random number as an argument, say, 5, in which case the user types 10 or 8, or whatever the answer is. Failure to do so may be used to detect unauthorized users. The algorithm can be different in the morning and afternoon, on different days of the week, even from different terminals, and so on.

8.11.2 ARTIFACT-BASED AUTHENTICATION

All the schemes relating to passwords used in protection mechanisms have lots of merits and also certain drawbacks apart from several minor limitations faced while implemented, but even then rarely transcend the inherent limitations of password-based authentication as a whole. Mechanisms that are based on the possession of an artifact can reduce the false acceptance rate, of course, incurring an additional cost.

The approach relating to the use of an artifact for user authorization checks to see if the user has some item, normally a machine-readable plastic card with a magnetic stripe on it, and also various incarnations of electronic smart cards. The card is inserted into the nearby installed card reader or in a nearby terminal for the sake of authentication. In many systems, artifact identification is coupled with the use of a password. That is, the user must insert the card and then supply the password. A user can only login if they have the card and know the password. This form of authentication is quite common with ATMs. Artifact-based systems are well-suited in environments where the artifact is also used for other purposes.

In most companies of today, users are required to swipe their ID cards on doors with an optical mechanism in order to gain access to the work premises. The use of such a card as an artifact for computer access and authentication can likely reduce the loss of the artifact. Smart cards also can augment this scheme by keeping even the user's password secret from the system. The unique user password can be stored in an unreadable form within the card itself, which provides authentication without storage of passwords in the computer system. This will make it relatively difficult for an intruder to uncover user passwords.

8.11.3 BIOMETRICS

There exists another major group of authentication mechanisms which are based on the unique characteristics of each user that are hard to forge. Some user characteristics are so naturally unique and completely users' own that they can be exploited to realize a protection mechanism in the form of biometric techniques. These user characteristics fall into two basic categories:

- **Physiological characteristics**, such as fingerprints, finger length or hand geometry, capillary patterns in the retina, and facial characteristics.
- **Behavioral characteristics**, such as signature patterns or dynamics of pen while writing the signature, voice patterns, and timing of keystrokes.

Many other methods can be cited that can provide a foolproof identification, for example, urinalysis, often used by dogs, cats, and other animals to mark their territory by urinating around its perimeter. In our case, each terminal could be equipped with a specific device along with a sign: "For login, please deposit your sample here". This might be an absolutely unbreakable system, but it would probably give rise to fairly serious objections from the user end. After all, whatever authentication scheme is employed, it must be psychologically acceptable to the user community.

Behavioral characteristics, in general, can vary with a user's physical and mental state and thus may be susceptible to higher false acceptance and rejection rates. For example, signature pattern and keystroke rate mostly depend on and may vary with user stress level and fatigue.

However, detection devices to be used as an attachment to the computer system should usually be self-contained, easily pluggable with the existing system, and independent of the computer system, which definitely improves the potential for tamper-proofing. The distinct advantages of biometric authentication lie in its increased accuracy in the process of authentication and similarly reduction of false acceptance in security-sensitive environments. However, the drawbacks of this approach include the additional cost factor, potential invasion of privacy, and sometimes non-acceptance by the user community.

8.12   MALICIOUS PROGRAMS

Another category of threats that damage or destroy security is malicious programs, sometimes called **malware**, which is software written by a person(s) (intruder) with high skills and released into the world. The person(s) here does not actively involve like an intruder directly, but entwined otherwise. Some malware is created with an objective just to cause damage, but other malware targets specific goals. Whatever it is, malwares create a huge problem in computing environments, and negotiating it is a constant and critical issue. Lot of works has already been carried out (Aycock, 2005; Cerf, 2005; Ledin, 2005; McHugh, 2005; Treese, 2004; Weiss, 2005) and is still continuing to counter evermore intelligent attacks and to foil all their destructive attempts. A useful taxonomy of malicious software is shown in Figure 8.5, with a rough division of two distinct categories, although logic bombs or Trojan horses, as shown in the figure, in particular, may be part of a virus or worm.

These are essentially fragments of programs that cannot exist independently but need a host program and are only activated when the host program is invoked to run. These fragments cannot replicate themselves to produce one or more copies. The other category consists of either a program fragment (virus) or an independent and self-contained program (worm, zombie) which can be regularly scheduled and run by the operating system like any other program and replicate itself on the same system or on some other system whenever it gets a suitable opportunity to produce one or more copies.

8.12.1   TRAP DOOR

A trap door is a secret point of entry in the software to gain access to it without going through the usual security access procedures. The system developers often follow a usual practice to intentionally keep a trap door in their product at the time of its development for many reasons, presumably to allow them to get access and then possibly modify and debug their programs after installation and production use without going through the stringent process of setup and authentication. Sometimes, the programmer may also want to ensure that there are some mechanisms of activating the program, should something go wrong with the built-in authentication procedure of the application. The trap

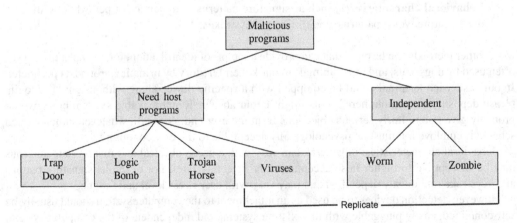

FIGURE 8.5   A schematic block–wise representation of the taxonomy of generic malicious programs used to launch threats on modern operating systems.

door is basically code that recognizes a special sequence of input or is triggered by being run from a certain *user-id* or by an unlikely sequence of events in order to activate the program or different parts of the program.

A trap door can be abused by anyone who is already aware of it or acquires knowledge of its existence and the related entry procedure. Trap door attack is so vulnerable that it defeated the most strongly secured system of those days, MULTICS equipped with 64 hierarchically organized protection domains, numbered from the innermost to the outermost; each one had a set of specific access privileges, including access privileges to all higher numbered domains. An Air Force "tiger team" (simulating intruders) launched a threat to MULTICS through a trapdoor so accurately that the MULTICS developers could not detect it, although they were later informed of its presence.

Trap door attacks are dangerous, and it is extremely hard to prevent them even by implementing an adequate security system using operating-system controls to counter them. It is thus suggested that software developers put more emphasis on implementing appropriate security measures at the time of system design and development and/or update activities.

More about this topic is given on the Support Material at www.routledge.com/9781032467238.

8.12.2 Logic Bomb

Another kind of malware is the logic bomb, which is perhaps one of the oldest types of program threat, predating viruses and worms. The device is basically a piece of code written by one of a company's current employees and secretly inserted in a legitimate program that is set to "explode" when certain conditions are met. Examples of conditions that can be used as triggers for a logic bomb to "explode" are the absence of certain password regularly provided, the presence or absence of certain files, a particular date or day of the week, or a particular user running the application in which the logic bomb is embedded. For example, the condition being set as trigger might be the absence of a certain password being regularly entered. As long as the employee gives the logic bomb its daily password, it does nothing. However, if the employee is suddenly fired and physically removed from the premises without warning, the next day the logic bomb does not get its password, so it explodes. The explosion of a logic bomb may clear the disk, erase files at random, make hard-to-detect changes to key programs, encrypt essential files to cause a machine halt, or do similar things that ultimately culminate in fatal damage.

More about this topic is given on the Support Material at www.routledge.com/9781032467238.

8.12.3 Trojan Horse

This is a useful, or apparently useful, program or command procedure that performs a legitimate function which is known to the OS or its users and also has a hidden component that can be used for nefarious purposes like launching a worm or virus, performing attacks on message security, impersonation, or performing one of the other harmful or unwanted functions of malware.

A Trojan horse program written with the intention to cause havoc in a computer system accomplishes many damaging functions indirectly that an unauthorized user cannot accomplish directly. For example, in a shared system, in order to gain access to a file of another user, a Trojan horse program could be created by one user that when executed changes the invoking user's file permission so that the files are now readable by any user. The Trojan horse creator could then induce the user community to run the program by placing it in a common directory and naming it in such a way that it appears to be a useful utility, thereby provoking users to use it. Another example is to write a program that ostensibly produces a listing of the user's files in a desirable (legible) format. After the execution of this program by a user, the Trojan horse creator can then easily access the useful information in the target user's files. The Trojan horse can also monitor traffic between a user and other processes to collect information for masquerading or initiate a spurious conversation with the same intent. Many other examples can be cited to illustrate various types of damaging functions that are performed by different types of Trojan horse programs.

More advanced versions of sophisticated Trojan horse programs can make themselves even harder to detect by fully emulating the utility that they are meant to impersonate with the additional provision of creating many types of damage, such as forwarding data of interest to a perpetrator or quietly erasing the hard disk, deleting the user's file. This is a severe violation of the integrity requirement or forces a system to crash or slow down that amounts to denial–of–service. Another typical example of a Trojan horse activity is a spoof login program that provides a fake login prompt to fool a program into revealing password information.

One of the relatively difficult-to-detect Trojan horse programs is a compiler that modifies certain programs by injecting additional code into them when they are compiled, such as a system-login program. This code creates a trap door in the login program that permits the Trojan horse creator to log on to the system using a special password. This Trojan horse can never be discovered by reading the source code of the login program. The Trojan horse was even implanted in a graphics routine offered on an electronic bulletin board system. Finally, it is worthwhile to mention that, since a Trojan horse is loaded explicitly by a user, its authorship or origin cannot be completely concealed; hence it is not difficult to track.

8.12.4 Viruses

The most well-known kind of malware is the **virus**, which, in recent years, has become a significant part of the software industry, particularly because of the evolution of two aspects of computing. First, the compact disk (CD) and pen drive were widely circulated among personal computer users and users of distributed computing environments, including client–server systems. These devices are an ideal carrier for a virus, since the recipient mounts the device and then runs its programs. Second, the emergence of the internet and its wide use make it a prolific breeding ground for viruses, particularly because it offers a broad variety of mail, Web pages, newsgroups, and free software.

Basically, a virus is a piece of code (it behaves like a parasite) that can attach itself to other programs in the system and also spread to other systems to "infect" them when virally affected programs are copied or transferred. Analogous to its biological counterpart, a computer virus also carries in its instructional code the recipe for making many perfect copies of it. In a network environment, when a host computer is logged in, the typical virus takes temporary control of the computer's operating system. After that, whenever an uninfected piece of software comes into contact with the virally affected computer, a fresh copy of the virus passes into the new incoming program. In this way, infections are spread from program to program, from one computer to another, without giving any indication to the users who are dealing with virally affected systems or programs over network. The ability to share data, applications, and system services on other computers as provided in a cluster of interconnected computers establishes a perfect culture for the spread of a virus.

A virus can do anything that other programs do. The only difference is that it attaches itself to another program and executes secretly when the host program is run. While attaching itself to a program, a virus puts its own address as the execution start address of the program. This way it gets control when the program is activated and infects other programs on a disk in the system by attaching itself to them. After that, it transfers control to the actual program for execution. The infection step usually does not consume much CPU time; hence, a user receives no indication and practically has no way of knowing beforehand that the program being executed carries a virus. Its presence is felt only after its success. In fact, the way a virus attaches itself to another program makes it far more difficult to track than a Trojan horse.

Most viruses perform their tasks by exploiting the support and services offered by the underlying operating system and often are mostly specific to a particular operating system. In some cases, they carry out their work in a manner that is also specific to a particular hardware platform. Thus, they are designed mostly by keeping in view the specific operating environment as a whole so that the details and weaknesses of particular systems can be willfully exploited.

- **The Nature of Viruses**

Once a virus begins execution, it can perform any function that is permitted by the privileges of the current user. During its lifetime, a typical virus usually goes through the following four stages.

- **Dormant state:** The virus is idle and will be activated only when a certain event occurs. Not all viruses have this state.
- **Propagation state:** Each infected program contains a clone of the virus and places an identical copy of itself into other uninfected programs, thereby it itself enters a propagation state.
- **Triggering state:** The triggering state is attained when certain event occurs or can be caused by the presence of a variety of system events, including a count of the number of times that this copy of the virus has already made copies of itself.
- **Execution state:** The virus now performs its intended function, which is usually harmful, damaging, and destructive.

- **Types of Viruses**

Different types of viruses are emerging very often with inherent advantages and are always at the offending end, whereas antivirus software is always at the defending end and attempts only to foil all possible attacks organized from the end of the offenders. Hence, there is a war between virus and antivirus, and there has been an arms race continuously going on between virus creators and antivirus developers. Antivirus software developed using numerous techniques is now quite matured to counter almost all types of existing viruses, and that is why more and more new types of viruses with numerous characteristics are continuously being developed and introduced to outmaneuver existing antivirus software. Different types of viruses presently exist and have been classified, and the following are the most significant types of viruses:

- **Parasitic virus:** This is perhaps the most common form and traditional type of virus, which attaches itself to executable files and replicates itself, attempting to infect other executable uninfected files, when the infected host program is executed.
- **Boot sector virus:** This virus implants itself in the boot sector of a disk device and infects a master boot record. It gets an opportunity to execute when the system is booted and then spreads from the disk containing the virus. Similarly, it gets an opportunity to replicate when a new disk is made.
- **Memory-resident virus:** This virus lodges in main memory as part of a resident system program and starts infecting other programs whenever a program is brought into memory for execution.
- **Stealth virus:** This is a form of virus explicitly designed to hide itself from detection carried out by antivirus software. A common example of a stealth virus is one that uses compression techniques so that its presence in the infected program cannot be detected, since the length of both the infected program and its counterpart uninfected version are same. Far more sophisticated techniques can be used. For example, a virus can place intercept logic in disk I/O routines so that when the antivirus attempts to read a suspected portion of the disk, the virus will present the original uninfected program to foil the attempt. That is why stealth, more specifically, is not a term that applies to a type of virus as such; rather it can be considered a technique used by a virus at the time of its creation to evade detection.

- **Polymorphic virus:** A polymorphic virus is one that mutates with every infection. This makes identification of the virus by the "signature" during detection almost impossible. When replicating, this virus creates copies that are functionally equivalent but contain distinctly different bit patterns. The ultimate target is to evade detection or defeat the actions taken by antivirus programs. In this case, the "signature" of the virus will vary with each copy. To realize this variation, the virus may randomly insert fake instructions or change the order of independent instructions in its own program. A far more effective approach may be to use encryption. A portion of the virus, generally called a *mutation engine*, creates a random encryption key to encrypt the remaining portion of the virus. The key is stored with the virus, and the mutation engine itself is altered during replication. When an infected program is invoked, the virus uses the stored random key to decrypt the virus. When the virus replicates, a different random encryption key is selected. Like the stealth virus, this term cannot be applied to a type of virus as such; rather it can be considered a technique used by a virus at the time of its formation to evade detection.

  Virus-writers often use available virus-creation toolkits which enable beginners to quickly create a number of different viruses, although the products are not as sophisticated as others that are developed from scratch using innovative schemes, but success encourages them to stay with this practice, and they soon become expert. Virus–writers sometimes use another tool: a virus exchange bulletin board that offers copies of viruses as well as valuable tips for the creation of more intelligent viruses, and these can be directly downloaded. A number of such boards exist in The United States and other countries.

- **E–Mail Viruses:** One of the latest developments in the world of malicious software is perhaps the e-mail virus. The first rapidly spreading viruses, such as Melissa, made use of a Microsoft Word macro embedded in a mail attachment. When the e-mail attachment is opened by a recipient, the Word macro is activated, and the following actions are then started.
  - The e-mail virus present in the attachment sends itself to everyone on the mailing list in the user's e-mail package.
  - The virus starts local damage.

A more powerful version of an e-mail virus emerged in late 1999 using the Visual Basic scripting language supported by the e-mail package. This newer version provides activation when the e-mail containing the virus is merely opened rather than waiting for the opening of an attachment.

The emergence of e-mail viruses opened a new generation of malware that exploits existing email software features and replicates to spread across the internet. The virus begins propagating itself as soon as it is activated (whether by way of opening an e-mail attachment or simply by opening the e-mail itself) to all of the e-mail addresses already known to the infected host. This virus accomplishes its task within hours, whereas other viruses used to take months or years to propagate. Consequently, it is becoming very difficult for antivirus software to respond before much damage is done. A greater degree of security measures is hence urgently needed and must be embedded into internet utility and application software to counter these types of constantly growing intelligent threats.

- **Antivirus**

Propagation of viruses and their subsequent attacks on the system cannot be stopped. Even preventing them from getting into the system is impossible to achieve. Hence, to protect the system from the threats of viruses, countermeasures are required. One possible solution may be to prevent them from entering the system by exerting the best effort, and even if the system is ever found virally infected despite this effort, destroy the virus immediately before any major damage is done. To accomplish this task, some useful actions, as given in the following, are to be taken in an orderly way to eventually bring the system back to normalcy.

Detection: If the system is infected, be sure that the infection has really occurred and locate the virus.

Identification: Once detection is successfully done, identify the specific virus that caused the infection.

Removal: Once the specific virus has been identified, take all possible measures to remove all traces of the virus from infected programs to bring them back to their original state. Finally, remove the virus drastically from all infected systems to prevent its further propagation. The removal process destroys the virus so that it cannot spread once again.

In situations when a virus is detected, but its identification or removal is not possible at the moment, one relatively safe alternative may be to abandon the infected program and use a clean backup version of it. But this approach never gives any guarantee that the system or the other programs in the system will remain safe and unaffected henceforth.

Declared war between virus and antivirus continues, and becomes more virulent as the technology, and tricks and techniques used in both the areas are gradually getting matured. Advancement and numerous innovations are observed to happen at a high pace, and there is no indication of any ceasefire; rather one always attempts to dominate the other. Early viruses or their early versions were relatively simple code fragments, were comparatively easy to identify, and were purged with relatively simple antivirus software. As the virus arms race began, both camps organized themselves and started to develop more advanced, complex, and sophisticated products. Antivirus products with increasingly sophisticated approaches continue to appear. Two of the most important are *generic decryption*, and *digital immune systems*, developed by IBM. Detailed description of them is beyond the scope of this book. Interested readers are advised to go through the respective write-ups to acquire a clear understanding of these two approaches.

8.12.5 WORMS

Worms are closely related to viruses, but they are distinguished from viruses because a worm is a free-standing, active penetrating entity. A worm is a program which may enter the machine as a file, but it will begin its execution on its own and replicate itself, spreading to other computer systems by exploiting the holes in their security setup. Once a file containing a worm has been placed in the file system, the worm finds a loophole in the process manager in order to execute itself. For example, one well-known worm program, "Morris's worm", was developed to penetrate UNIX systems by taking advantage of the *finger* command.

Network worms normally spread by using network connections to transmit their copies to other computers. Once active within a system, the effects of a worm can be the same as those of a virus. It could implant Trojan horse programs or perform any type of unwanted and destructive actions. Worms are known to replicate at unimaginably high rates, thereby creating congestion in the network and consuming appreciable CPU time during replication. While replicating itself, a network worm makes use of the facilities and support that network provides. Some examples are:

- **E-mail facility:** A worm often mails a copy of itself to another known system.
- **Remote login capability:** A worm logs onto a remote system as a legitimate user, then uses commands to copy itself from one system to another.
- **Remote execution capability:** A worm on its own can execute a copy of itself on another system.

The characteristics of a network worm are similar to those of a computer virus. It also goes through four stages during its lifetime: a *dormant stage*, a *propagation stage*, a *triggering stage*, and an *execution stage*. During its journey through different stages, it performs stage-specific functions. For example, the *propagation phase* performs the following functions in general:

- Search for other systems to infect by inspecting host tables or similar other repositories of remote system addresses.
- Establish a connection with a remote system obtained from such a search.
- Determine whether the connected system has already been infected before copying itself to the system. If so, the copy operation is abandoned. If not, copy itself to the remote system and perform related actions to run the copy.

The behavior of a worm can be the same as that of a virus. Indeed, the distinction between a worm and a virus in activity cannot always be clearly demarcated; some malware thus often uses both methods to spread. Due to its self-replicating nature, a worm is even more difficult to track than a virus. However, properly designed security measures implanted in both network systems and single-computer systems can reasonably minimize the threats caused by worms.

8.12.6 ZOMBIES

A zombie is a program that secretly takes over another computer connected to the internet and then uses that computer to launch various types of attacks that are difficult to trace. Zombies are purposely used mostly in denial-of-service attacks, typically against targeted Support Materials at www.routledge.com/9781032467238. The zombie is normally planted on hundreds of computers belonging to innocent (unsuspecting) third parties and then is used to overwhelm the target Support Material at www.routledge.com/9781032467238 by launching a devastating attack on internet traffic.

There are still other forms of malware, such as **spyware**. These are mostly related to Support Materials at www.routledge.com/9781032467238 and mainly operate between web browsers and web servers.

Apart from using malware to disrupt or destroy the environment, it is often created to make a profit. Malware in a for-profit scheme installs a **key logger** on an infected computer. A key logger records everything typed at the keyboard. It is then not too difficult to filter these data and extract needed information, such as; username–password combinations, credit card numbers and expiration dates, and similar other things. This information can then be supplied to a master, where it can be used or sold for launching criminal activities.

8.13 ENCRYPTION

Encryption is essentially a technique for protecting all automated network and computer applications and related data. File management systems often use it to guard information related to users and their resources. The branch of science that deals with encryption is called *cryptography*.

Encryption is the application of an algorithmic transformation E_k to data, where E is the *encryption algorithm* with a secret key k as input, called an *encryption key*. The original form of data on which encryption is carried out is called *plaintext*, and the transformed data are called *encrypted* or *ciphertext*. The encrypted data are once again recovered by applying a transformation $D_{k'}$, where k' is a decryption key. $D_{k'}$ is essentially an encryption algorithm with the secret key k' run in reverse. It takes the ciphertext and the secret key k' as input and produces the original plaintext. A scheme that uses $k = k'$ is called **symmetric encryption** or *conventional encryption*, and one using $k \neq k'$ is called *asymmetric encryption* or **public-key encryption**.

8.13.1 ENCRYPTION TECHNIQUES

Encryption techniques differ in the way they try to defeat a series of attempts by an intruder at guessing D_k. The fundamental approach is to mask the features of plaintext using the encryption algorithm E with a specific secret key k in such a way that it ensures that the corresponding scrambled message produced as output, the ciphertext, does not reveal features of its plaintext, without using a high cost of encryption. The exact substitutions and transformations performed by the algorithm E depend on the key k. For a given plaintext, two different keys with the same E will produce two different ciphertexts.

8.13.1.1 Symmetric Encryption

Symmetric encryption is the simplest form of encryption in which encryption is performed by applying an encryption algorithm E that performs various substitutions and transformations on plaintext with a specific secret key k, which is also input to the encryption algorithm. The exact substitutions and transformations performed by the algorithm E depend on the key k. The encryption algorithm E with a specific key k applied on plaintext produces ciphertext, which, in turn, can be decrypted using a decryption algorithm D with the same key k to obtain its plaintext form. If d is the plaintext, then functions E_k and D_k must satisfy the relation: $D_k(E_k(d)) = d$, for all d. Here, D_k is essentially the inverse of E_k.

The secure use of symmetric encryption is based on two basic assumptions. The first is that the encryption algorithm should be strong enough that even if an opponent knows the algorithm, they should not be able to decrypt the ciphertext or discover the key in spite of having in possession of a number of ciphertexts together with the respective plaintext that produced each ciphertext. It would be tediously impractical for an intruder to determine the encryption key simply by trial and error. Decryption is commonly considered unsuccessful if it yields unintelligible data. The second one is more vital: the sender and receiver must obtain copies of the secret keys in a most secure manner, and they must be kept secret and secure, because if those are divulged, or if someone can discover the key by chance and already knows the algorithm, then all communications made by the sender and receiver using the key will no longer be secured and will be readable to the third party.

Brief details on this topic with a figure are given on the Support Material at www.routledge.com/9781032467238.

8.13.1.1.1 Attacks on Cryptographic Systems

Various types of attacks launched on a cryptographic systems by an opponent, be it an internal or external entity, are targeted to *discover the decryption function D_k*, which is essentially the inverse of E_k. Hence, the ultimate objective of an encryption technique is always find a low-cost good E_k to perform high-quality encryption, and the encryption function E_k should always be a *one-way function*; that is, the computation of the inverse of E_k (i.e. D_k) would be extremely difficult to realize. Even if it is possible, this would involve an impractical amount of effort and time. However, the nature of an attack to be launched depends largely on the position an opponent can occupy within the system. In general, there are two main approaches to attacking a symmetric encryption scheme.

The first method is commonly known as a **brute–force** attack, when the intruder cannot invoke the encryption function and is in possession of only the ciphertext. The trial-and-error approach is then repeatedly carried out by the intruder on the piece of ciphertext in their possession until an intelligible translation into plaintext is obtained. This certainly involves a very large number of trials when various key sizes are considered to achieve any success. This attack is also sometimes called an *exhaustive attack* because all possibilities for D_k may have to be tried out.

The second nature of attack is known as **cryptanalysis** that consists of a set of similar types of different nature of attacks:

- **Ciphertext-only attack:** While attempting to guess D_k, an intruder relies on the nature of the algorithm E_k already known to them and perhaps some knowledge of the general characteristics of the plaintext, such as the *frequency* with which each letter of the alphabet appears in English text. If it is known that E_k replaces each letter in a plaintext with another letter of the alphabet (a method called a *substitution cipher*), an intruder may use this information to guess D_k. A ciphertext attack, in essence, is perhaps more efficient than its counterpart, an exhaustive attack, if a characteristic feature of plaintext can be successfully identified.

- **Known plaintext attack:** An intruder here knows the plaintext corresponding to a ciphertext. This attack is possible to launch if an intruder can gain a position within the OS, which is not very difficult to occupy, from where both a plaintext and its corresponding ciphertext can be observed. In this way, an intruder can collect a sufficient number of (*plaintext, ciphertext*) pairs that can guide them, which may make determining D_k easier.

- **Chosen plaintext attack:** An intruder here is able to supply the plaintext and examine its encrypted form. This possibility helps the intruder to systematically build a collection of (*plaintext, ciphertext*) pairs that eventually helps them arrive at an approximate guess and thereby make repeated refinements to guesses to determine an exact D_k.

In summary, all these types of attacks actually exploit the characteristics of the algorithm E_k in attempting to deduce a specific plaintext or the key being used. If the attack succeeds in deducing the key, the result is catastrophic. All future and past messages encrypted with that key can then be easily obtained.

Quality of encryption to thwart attacks is believed to be improved with the use of an increased number of bits in key k. For example, use of a 56-bit key in an encryption scheme requires 2^{55} trials guessing D_k to break it. This large number of trials was believed to make such a scheme computationally secure from exhaustive attacks. However, exploiting powerful mathematical techniques like *differential analysis* can make this approach to guessing D_k much easier than an exhaustive attack. In addition, making use of today's computers with massively parallel organizations of microprocessors, it may now be possible to achieve processing rates many orders of magnitude greater. Coupling all such tools and support, the performance of such attempts reaches a level that a one-way function E_k with a 56-bit key can no longer be considered computationally secure.

More details on this topic are given on the Support Material at www.routledge.com/9781032467238.

8.13.1.1.2 Encryption Schemes

The simplest encryption technique is the classical *substitution cipher* in which each letter in a plaintext is replaced by another letter of alphabet. This technique does not mask many features of plaintexts, so it is relatively easy to decipher based on analysis of the ciphertext and hence vulnerable to an attack. Shamon (1949) proposed two principles for designing high-quality encryption techniques: *confusion* and *diffusion*. The **confusion** principle states that it should not be easy to find changes caused in the ciphertext due to a change made in the plaintext. This principle makes it difficult for an intruder to find correlations between a plaintext and its corresponding ciphertext. The **diffusion** principle states that the effect of a small substring in the plaintext should be spread across the ciphertext as much as possible. A high level of diffusion changes many parts of the ciphertext for a small change in the plaintext, which makes it somewhat difficult for an intruder to discover useful patterns in a ciphertext; hence, more attempts are required when a frequency-analysis-based attack is conducted to discover plaintext.

The two most common strategies used in symmetric encryption are the **block cipher** and **stream cipher**. The block cipher strategy is attributed to the two most important symmetric algorithms, the **Data Encryption Standard (DES)** and the **Advanced Encryption Standard (AES)**. These schemes will now be described along with their confusion and diffusion properties.

- **Block cipher:** This strategy is essentially an extension of the classical *substitution cipher*. A block cipher processes the plaintext input of fixed-size blocks with a key k and produces a block of ciphertext of equal size for each plaintext block. These produced blocks are then assembled to obtain the ciphertext. The block cipher strategy is easy to handle and simple to implement. While it introduces some confusion, it does not introduce sufficient diffusion, so identical blocks in a plaintext produce identical blocks in the ciphertext. This feature is a weak point of this approach that makes it vulnerable to an attack based on frequency-analysis and known or chosen plaintext attacks. The chances of such attacks to succeed can be reduced by using a relatively large number of blocks.

- **Stream cipher:** A stream cipher treats a plaintext as well as the encryption key as streams of bits. Encryption is performed using a transformation that involves a few bits of the plaintext and an equal number of bits of the encryption key. Transformation operations may be of various types, but a popular choice may be a bit-by-bit transformation of a plaintext, typically by performing an operation like Exclusive-OR on a bit of the plaintext and a bit of the encryption key.

  A stream cipher is operationally faster than a block cipher. When a bit-by-bit transformation is used, it does not provide confusion or diffusion. However, out of many variants of stream ciphers, one is a *ciphertext autokey cipher*, an *asynchronous stream cipher* or a *self-synchronizing cipher* that introduces diffusion. It employs a key-stream generator that uses a function of the key stream and the last few bits of the ciphertext stream generated so far. In practice, the key stream is used to encrypt the first few bits of the plaintext. The ciphertext thus generated corresponding to these bits of the plaintext is then used as a key stream to encrypt the next few bits of the plaintext, and this process goes on until the entire plaintext is encrypted. In this way, diffusion is obtained, since a substring in the plaintext always influences encryption of the rest of the plaintext.

- **The Data Encryption Standard:** DES, essentially a block cipher developed by IBM in 1977, was a dominant encryption algorithm. It uses a 56-bit key to encrypt 64-bit data blocks, and for being a block cipher, it possesses poor diffusion. To overcome this shortcoming, DES incorporates *cipher block chaining* mode, which uses the first block of plaintext to be combined with an initial vector by an Exclusive-OR operation and then enciphered. The resulting ciphertext is then combined with the second block of the plaintext using an Exclusive-OR operation and then enciphered. This process goes on until the entire plaintext is encrypted. In this algorithm, there are three steps that explicitly incorporate diffusion and confusion. Diffusion is introduced using permutation of the plaintext. Confusion is realized through substitution of an m bit number by an n bit number by selectively omitting some bits and then using this n bit number in the encryption process. These steps eventually obscure the features of a plaintext and the encryption process to such an extent that it forces the intruder to resort to an extensive variant of the exhaustive attack to break the cipher.

  DES eventually fizzled out, primarily because it used only a small key length of 56 bits, since more and more versatile computers with increased speed and lower cost have been started to introduce that became successful to break DES-based encryption. The life of DES was extended by the use of a *triple* DES (3DES) algorithm that employed a key of size 112 bits and could effectively use keys up to 168 bits in length, which was considered sufficiently secure against attacks for only a few years and hence was endorsed as an interim standard until a new standard was adopted.

  The principal drawback of 3DES is that the algorithm is relatively sluggish in software. Moreover, both DES and 3DES use a 64-bit block size, which was not fitting from the perspective of both efficiency and security; a larger block size was thus desirable. Work continued in the quest for a new standard, and ultimately the AES was introduced, adopted in 2001.

- **Advanced Encryption Standard:** Reviewing all these drawbacks, even 3DES, was not considered a dependable candidate for long-term use. Consequently, the National Institute of Standards and Technology (NIST) in 1997, along with others, proposed the new AES, which was stronger than 3DES and essentially a symmetric block cipher of blocklength 128 bits and support for key lengths of 128, 192, and 256 bits. Finally, NIST released AES in 2001 as a Federal Information Processing Standard (FIPS) that mostly fulfilled all the criteria, including security, computational efficiency, memory requirements, hardware and software suitability, and flexibility.

AES uses a block size of 128 bits, and keys of 128, 192, or 256 bits. It is essentially a variant of *Rijndael*, which is a compact and fast encryption algorithm employing only substitutions and permutations with use of the key and block sizes in the range of 128–256 bits that are multiples of 32 bits. AES uses an array of 4×4 bytes, called a *state*, which is a block of plaintext on which several rounds of operations are carried out. The number of rounds to be performed depends on the key length; 10 rounds are performed for keys of 128 bits, 12 rounds for 192-bit keys, and 14 rounds for 256-bit keys. Each round consists of a set of specified operations: *byte substitution, shifting of rows, mixing of columns*, and *key addition*.

To enable both encryption and decryption to be performed using the same sequence of steps, a key addition is performed before starting the first round, and the step involving *mixing of columns* is skipped in the last round.

More details on each of the schemes with a figure are given on the Support Material at www. routledge.com/9781032467238.

8.13.1.2   Public-Key Encryption: Asymmetric Encryption

The first truly revolutionary advancement in the encryption mechanism in literally thousands of years was due to Diffie and Hellman, who first formally proposed public-key encryption in 1976. Public-key algorithms significantly differ from symmetric encryption in that they are based on mathematical functions rather than on simple operations on bit streams. More significantly, it is asymmetric encryption involving the use of two separate keys in contrast to symmetric encryption that uses only one secret key. The use of two keys has laid a foundation of encryption that gave rise to profound security by having better key distribution with associated mathematical operations.

A public-key encryption scheme includes six ingredients. Those are: *plaintext, encryption algorithm, public and private key, ciphertext*, and *decryption algorithm*. The encryption algorithm performs various transformations on the plaintext. The public and private key are simply a selected pair of keys provided as input in which one is used for encryption and the other for decryption. The exact transformation to be performed by the encryption algorithm depends on this public or private key. For a given plaintext, two different keys will produce two different ciphertexts. The decryption algorithm accepts the ciphertext and the matching key as input and produces the original plaintext as output.

A general-purpose public-key encryption algorithm uses one key, which is essentially a public key for encryption known to all users, and a related different private (secret) key for decryption. The consequence is that even with knowledge of the cryptographic algorithm and also the encryption key in possession, it is computationally almost infeasible to discover the decryption key. Moreover, there is no hard and fast rule in using the keys; either of the two related keys can be used for encryption, and the other would be used for decryption. However, several basic steps are required to realize a public-key cryptographic system.

The beauty and strength of this approach are that all participants are allowed to create their own (public, private) key, and all such public keys are accessible to all participants, but private keys are created locally by each user and therefore need never be distributed. As long as the private key is kept protected, the incoming message is secure. Moreover, a user can change the private key at any time and then announce the related new public key to replace the old one. Although the private key is required to be kept secret, it is always referred to as a private key rather than a secret key to avoid confusion with symmetric encryption, in which the key is always referred to as a secret key.

Finally, it is worthwhile to mention that it should not be thought that public-key encryption is more secure from cryptanalysis than symmetric encryption. In fact, the strength of any encryption scheme to withstand attacks depends mostly on the length of the key and the computational work involved to break the cipher. Truly speaking, there is as such no basis, at least, in principle about either symmetric or public-key encryption that can decide one superior than other from the end of resisting cryptanalysis. Moreover, there is no reason to believe that public-key encryption for being a general-purpose and an asymmetric technique has elbowed out symmetric encryption and made it obsolete. On the contrary, due to computational overhead involved in today's public-key encryption schemes, there seems no foreseeable likelihood that symmetric encryption will be considered to be discarded. In fact, symmetric encryption can outperform public-key encryption in many aspects, particularly in the area of key distribution.

- **RSA algorithm**: Public-key encryption schemes have been implemented in many ways. One of the first public-key encryption schemes was developed by Ron Rivest, Adi Shamir, and Len Adleman at MIT in 1977. The RSA scheme then started to dominate, and since that time has reigned supreme as the only widely accepted and implemented approach to public-key encryption. In fact, RSA is a cipher in which both the plaintext and the cipher-text are integers between 0 and $n - 1$ for some n. Encryption uses modular arithmetic. However, the secret of its success is the strength of the algorithm, which is mostly due to the difficulty of factoring numbers into their prime factors, based on which the algorithm was constructed.

8.14 CASE STUDY: UNIX SECURITY

UNIX systems allow each user to select a password of a maximum of eight printable characters in length. This is converted into a 56-bit (using 7-bit ASCII) value that serves as the key input to an encryption routine, known as **crypt (3)**, based on the Data Encryption Standard, as discussed earlier. The DES algorithm is modified by a 12-bit "salt" value, known as **salting** the password. Typically, this value is related to the time at which the password is assigned to the user. The modified DES algorithm is then exercised with a data input consisting of a 64-bit block of zeros. The output of the algorithm then serves as input for next second encryption. This process is repeated for a total of 25 encryptions. The resulting 64-bit output is then translated into an 11-character sequence. This ciphertext password is then stored together with a plaintext copy of the salt in the password file for the corresponding user-id. The salting process injected into the UNIX password security scheme serves many other useful purposes.

To log on to a UNIX system, the user provides an ID and a password. The operating system then uses the ID to index the password file and retrieve the salt and the encrypted password. The salt value and the user-given password are then used as input to the encryption routine to generate the encrypted password, which is then compared with stored password value. If the result matches, only then is the password accepted.

While having several merits, software implementations of DES when coupled with 25 iterations make it substantially slow compared to its counterpart hardware version. However, two notable changes have occurred since its inception. First, newer implementations of the algorithm itself have resulted in speedups. Second, with the advent of newer modern hardware, the hardware performance constantly increases and ultimately provides much faster execution of any software algorithm.

- **Access Control:** UNIX defines three user classes: *file owner*, *user group*, and *other users*. The ACL needs to record only the presence of three access rights: *r*, w, and *x*, which represent *read*, *write*, and *execute*, respectively, in bit-encoded form for each of the three user classes. When any bit of 3 is 1, the respective access is permitted; otherwise it is denied. Three sets of such 3-bit groups ($3 \times 3 = 9$ bits), like (*rwx*) (*rwx*) (*rwx*), one set for *file owner*, one set for *user group*, and one set for *other users*, are used in the access control list of any specific file. While the 9-bit UNIX scheme is clearly less general than a full-blown ACL system, in practice, it is adequate, and its implementation is much simpler and cheaper. The directory entry of a file, however, contains the identity of the file owner in one field, and bit-encoded access descriptors (*r*, *w*, *x*) for each user class are stored in another field.

The access privileges of a UNIX process are determined by its *uid*. When a process is created by the kernel, the kernel sets the *uid* of the process to the *id* of the user who created it. However, temporarily changing the *uid* of a process is possible, and that is accomplished with the use of the system call *setuid<id>* to change its *uid* to *<id>* and another *setuid* system call with its own *id* to revert to its original *uid*. The *setgid* feature analogously provides a method of temporarily changing the *group-id* of a process.

More details on this topic with a figure are given on the Support Material at www.routledge.com/9781032467238.

8.15   CASE STUDY: LINUX SECURITY

Linux systems also employ encryption of passwords for security. This authenticates a user at login time by adding a "salt" value to the password and uses a MD technique, which is simply a one-way hash function that generates a 128- or 160-bit hash value from a password. This technique has many variants, such as MD2, MD4, and MD5, but Linux uses MD5.

Alternatively, Linux provides *pluggable authentication modules* (PAMs) by which an application can authenticate a user at any instant through a dynamically loadable library of authentication modules. This feature helps users avoid recompilation of the application when the authentication used in an application needs to be changed. Application developers can exploit PAM support to improve application security in several ways: to permit specific users to login at specific times from specific places, to set resource limits for users so that they cannot launch denial-of-service attacks, and above all to employ a specific password encryption scheme of their choice. PAM permits several authentication modules to be "stacked"; these modules are invoked one after another. An application can use this facility to authenticate a user through several means, such as passwords and biometrics, to further strengthen security.

- **Access Control:** Linux protects file access through the *user-id* and *group-id* of a process; even when NFS (essentially a server) accesses a file on behalf of a user, the server's own file protection mechanism would not be used. To enable the server to temporarily gain access rights of users, Linux provides the system calls *fsuid* and *fsgid* through which a server can temporarily assume the identity of its client.

The Linux kernel provides loadable kernel modules through which the improved access controls can be realized; one is called *Linux Security Modules* (LSMs), which supports many different security models. In fact, the Security Enhanced Linux (SELinux) of the US National Security Agency has built additional access control mechanisms through LSM that provide mandatory access control.

More details on this topic are given on the Support Material at www.routledge.com/9781032467238.

8.16   CASE STUDY: WINDOWS SECURITY

The Windows security model provides a uniform access control facility applicable to semaphores, threads, processes, files, windows, and other objects. It has several elements of C2- and B2-class systems, according to the Trusted Computer System Evaluation Criteria (TCSEC) of the US Department of Defense. Access control is based around two entities: an *access token* associated with each *process*, which is analogous to *capabilities*, and a *security descriptor* associated with each *object* that also enables interprocess accesses. An important aspect of Windows security is the concept of *impersonation*, which simplifies the client–server interaction when it is over a RPC connection. Here, the server can temporarily assume the identity of the client so that it can evaluate a client's request for access relative to that client's rights. After the access, the server automatically reverts to its own identity.

- **Access Token:** When the logon in a Windows system is successful using the name/password scheme, a process object is created with an access token that determines which access privileges the process may have and bears all necessary security information as well as speeding up access validation. A process can create more access tokens through the LogonUser function. Generally, the token is initialized with each of these privileges in a disabled state. Subsequently, if one of the user's processes needs to perform a privileged operation, the process may then enable the appropriate privilege and attempt access. In fact, the general structures of access tokens include the main parameters (fields), such as Security ID (SID), Group SIDs, Privileges, Default Owner, and Default ACL.
- **Security Descriptors:** For each object, such as a file when is created, its access token is assigned by the creating process with its own SID or any group SID that makes interprocess access possible. Each object is associated with a security descriptor in which the chief component is an access control list that mainly includes parameters (fields) such as Flags, Owner, Discretionary Access Control List (DACL), and System Access Control List (SACL) in order to specify access rights for various users and user groups for this object. When a process attempts to access this object, the SID of the process is compared against the ACL of the object to determine if access is permitted.
- **Access Control List:** The access control lists at the heart of Windows provide access control facilities. Each such list consists of an overall header and a variable number of access control entries (ACEs). Each entry specifies an individual or group SID and an access mask that defines the rights to be granted to the SID. When a process attempts to access an object, the OM in the Windows executive reads the SID and group SIDs from the access token and then scans down the object's DACL. If a match is found, that is, if an ACE is found with a SID that matches one of the SIDs from the access token, then the process has the access rights specified by the access mask in that ACE. The access mask has 32 bits, in which each bit or a group of consecutive bits contains vital information in relation to access rights applicable to all types of objects (generic access types) as well as specific access types appropriate to a particular type of object.

The high-order half (16 bits) of the mask contains bits relating to four generic access types that apply to all types of objects. These bits also provide a convenient way to set *specific access types* to a number of different types of object. The lower 5 bits of this high-order half refer to five standard access types: Synchronize, Write owner, Write DAC, Read control, and Delete. The least significant 16 bits of the 32-bits specify access rights that apply to a *particular type* of object. For example, bit 0 for a file object is File_Read_Data access, whereas bit 0 for an event object is Event_Query_Status access.

Another important feature in the Windows security model is that applications and utilities can exploit the Windows security framework for user-defined objects. A database server, for example, might create its own security descriptors and attach them to specific portions of a database. In addition to normal read/write access constraints, the server could secure database-specific operations, such as *deleting* an object or performing a *join*. It would then be the server's responsibility to define the meaning of special rights and carry out all types of access checks, and such checks would occur in a standard way, considering system-wide user/group accounts and audit logs.

SUMMARY

The operating system offers protection mechanisms based on which users implement security policies to ultimately protect the computer system. System security is scrutinized from different angles to reveal the numerous types of security attacks launched and to estimate the role and effect of malicious programs as major security threats, and subsequently approaches are implemented to counter all such threats to protect the related resources. Two popular access-control-based security systems used are access control lists and capability lists. Both are implemented by most popular systems in which ACLs maintain static information, and capabilities are created by the system at runtime. Different types of authentication strategies, including password-based schemes widely employed to keep illegitimate users away from systems, are discussed. Various types of encryption-decryption-based approaches, including symmetric encryption (private-key encryption) and asymmetric encryption (public-key encryption) schemes, are demonstrated. Viruses, the flagship security attackers causing numerous threats, are discussed in detail. Last, the different types of protection mechanisms offered by the most popular operating systems, UNIX, Linux, and Windows, to meet each one's individual objectives and subsequently how security systems are built by users separately on each of these platforms are narrated as case studies in brief.

EXERCISES

1. Describe the distinctive differences between security and protection
2. Protection is implemented by the operating system using two key methods, authentication and authorization; discuss with your own comments.
3. What is the difference between policies and mechanisms with respect to both security and protection?
4. Discuss the common requirements or goals that an operating system must meet to prevent generic security threats.
5. State and characterize the different types of attacks that may be launched on security of a system.
6. "It is not the data alone but the entire computer system that is always exposed to threats in security attacks". Justify the statement.
7. What is the difference between passive and active security attacks? Discuss briefly the different categories that are commonly observed in active security attacks.
8. What is the spectrum of approaches used by a user in which an operating system may provide appropriate protection?
9. Dynamic relocation hardware is usually considered a basic memory protection mechanism. What is the protection state in relocation hardware? How does the operating system ensure that the protection state is not changed indiscriminately?
10. Give your argument for conditions under which the access control list method is superior to the capability list approach for implementing the access matrix.
11. An OS performs validation of software capabilities as follows: When a new capability is created, the object manager stores a copy of the capability for its own use. When a process wishes to perform an operation, the capability presented by it is compared with stored capabilities. The operation is permitted only if a matching capability exists with the object manager. Do you think that this scheme is foolproof? Using this scheme, is it possible to perform selective revocation of access privileges?
12. Use of capabilities is very efficient to realize protection mechanisms. What are the practical difficulties at the time of its implementation?
13. Passwords are a common form to implement user authentication. Briefly, state the ways in which the password file can be protected.

14. Write down the numerous techniques by which an intruder may launch a variety of ingenious attacks to breach/crack security or to learn passwords.

15. What are the popular and effective techniques that have been proposed to defeat attacks on passwords?

16. Password-based authentication often suffers from inherent limitations. What are other ways by which user authentication can be checked?

17. What is meant by malicious software? How are the threats launched by them differentiated? Write down the different types of malicious software that are commonly found in computer environments.

18. Can the Trojan horse attack work in a system protected by capabilities?

19. What is meant by virus? What is the common nature of viruses? Write down the type of viruses you are aware of.

20. What is an e-mail virus? How do they work? What are their salient features that differentiate them from other members?

21. What is the difference between a virus and a worm? How do they each reproduce?

22. What is antivirus? How do they work? Write down the steps they take to restore the system to normalcy.

23. List the security attacks that cannot be prevented by encryption.

24. What are the two general approaches to attacking a conventional encryption system?

25. Assume that passwords are limited to use of the 95 printable ASCII characters and all passwords are allowed to use 10 characters in length. Suppose a password cracker is equipped with an encryption rate of 6.5 million encryptions per second. How long will it take, launching an exhaustive attack, to test all possible passwords on a UNIX system?

26. What are DES and Triple DES? Discuss their relative merits and drawbacks.

27. The encryption scheme used for UNIX passwords is one way; it is not possible to reverse it. Therefore, would it be more accurate to say that this is, in fact, a hash code rather than an encryption of the password?

28. It was stated that the inclusion of the salt in the UNIX password scheme increases the difficulty of guessing by a factor of 4096 ($2^{12} = 4096$). But the salt is stored in plaintext in the same entry as the corresponding ciphertext password. Therefore, those twelve characters are known to the attackers and need not be guessed. Therefore, why is it asserted that the salt increases security?

29. How is the AES expected to be an improvement over triple DES?

30. What evaluation criteria will be used in assessing AES candidates?

31. Describe the differences among the terms public key, private key, and secret key.

32. Explain the difference between conventional encryption and public-key encryption.

SUGGESTED REFERENCES AND WEBSITES

Aycock, J., Barker, K. "Viruses 101", *Proceedings of the Technical Symposium on Computer Science Education, Education*, New York, ACM, pp. 152–156, 2005.

Cass, S. "Anatomy of Malice", *IEEE Spectrum*, November, New York, IEEE, 2001.

Cerf, V. G. "Spam, Spim, and Spit", *Communications of the ACM*, vol. 48, pp. 39–43, 2005.

Eastlake, D. "Domain Name System Security Extensions", *Network Working Group, Request for Comments: 2535*, 1999.

Kent, S. "On the Trail of Intrusions into Information Systems", *IEEE Spectrum*, December, New York, IEEE, 2000.

Kephart, J., Sorkin, G., et al. "Fighting Computer Viruses", *Scientific American*, 1997.

Ledin, G. Jr. "Not Teaching Viruses and Worms is Harmful", *Communications of the ACM*, 48, p. 144, 2005.

Pfleeger, C. *Security in Computing*, Upper Saddle River, NJ, Prentice-Hall PTR, 1997.

Mchugh, J. A. M., Deek, F. P. "An Incentive System for Reducing Malware Attacks", *Communications of the ACM*, vol. 48, pp. 94–99, 2005.

Saltzer, J. H., Schroeder, M. D., et al. "The Protection of Information in Computer Systems", *Proceedings of the IEEE*, New York, IEEE, pp. 1278–1308, 1975.

Sandhu, R. S. "Lattice-Based Access Controls Models", *Computer,* vol. 26, pp. 9–19, 1993.

Shamon, C. E. "Communication Theory of Secrecy Systems", *Bell Systems Journal*, 1949.

Schneier, B. *Applied Cryptography*, New York, Wiley, 1996.

Treese, W. "The State of Security on the Internet", *NetWorker*, vol. 8, pp. 13–15, 2004.

Weiss, A. "Spyware Be Gone", *NetWorker*, vol. 9, pp. 18–25, 2005.

Wright, C., Cowan, C., et al. "Linux Security Modules: General Security Support for the Linux Kernel", *Eleventh USENIX Security Symposium*.

RECOMMENDED WEBSITES

AntiVirus On-line: IBM's site about virus information.

Computer Security Resource Center: Maintained by National Institute on Standards and Technology (NIST). It contains a wide range of information on security, threats, technology and standards.

Intrusion Detection Working Group: Containing all of the documents including the documents on Protection and Security generated by this group.

CERT Coordination Center: This organization evolves from the computer emergency response team formed by the Defense Advanced Research Projects Agency Site offers good information on Internet security, vulnerabilities, threats, and attack statistics.

9 Distributed Systems
An Introduction

Learning Objectives

- To describe the evolution of distributed computing systems and their advantages and disadvantages, including different forms of their hardware design.
- To describe the forms of software that drive the distributed computing systems.
- To demystify the generic distributed operating system and its design issues.
- To discuss generic multiprocessor operating systems with numerous considerations used in different forms of multiprocessor architecture.
- To elucidate different management systems of OSs with emphasis on processor management, including the different methods used in processor scheduling, process scheduling, and thread scheduling in multiprocessor environments.
- To present separately in brief the Linux OS and Windows OS in multiprocessor environments as case study.
- To present the multicomputer system architecture and its different models.
- To discuss the design issues of generic multicomputer operating systems.
- To introduce the concept of middleware and its different models in the design of true distributed systems, including its services to different application systems.
- To present a rough comparison between various types of operating systems running on multiple-CPU systems.
- To introduce the concept of distributed systems built in the premises of networks of computers with their related networking issues.
- To present as a case study a brief overview of AMOEBA, a traditional distributed operating system.
- To discuss in brief internetworking with all its related issues.
- To discuss in brief the design issues of distributed operating systems built in the premises of workstation–server model.
- To discuss the remote procedure call and the implementation of generic RPCs as well as the implementation of SUN RPC, presented here as case study.
- To present a brief overview of distributed shared memory as well as its design issues and implementation aspects.
- To discuss the different aspects of distributed file systems (DFSs) and their various design issues, along with a brief description of their operation.
- To briefly describe the implementation of the Windows DFS, SUN NFS, and Linux GPFS as case studies.
- To present a modern approach to distributed computer system design, the cluster, along with its advantages, classifications, and different methods of clustering.
- To briefly describe the general architecture of clusters and their operating system aspects.
- To briefly describe the different aspects of implementation of Windows and SUN clusters as case studies.

DOI: 10.1201/9781003383055-9

9.1   DISTRIBUTED COMPUTING SYSTEMS: EVOLUTION

Early computers from the date of the first generation (1945) to the era of modern computers until about 1985 introduced several notable concepts, including multiprogramming with time-sharing using centralized large mainframe systems. This concept was further advanced one step by attaching dumb (non-intelligent) terminals located geographically apart from the main computer system, thereby allowing multiple users to simultaneously use the system by directly sharing system resources to execute their jobs. The complex design of this approach, however, was formalized by the early 1970s, and cost also came down to an affordable range. This time-sharing system could be considered the first stepping stone toward distributed computing systems, since it implemented two important concepts of modern distributing systems: that multiple users can share the computer resources simultaneously, and they may be located away from the main computer system. With the advent of microprocessor technology in the 1970s, dumb terminals were eventually replaced by intelligent ones with some processing power so that the concept of offline processing by these terminals as well as online time sharing in the main system were combined to realize the advantages of both concepts with only a single system.

Microprocessor technology continued to advance rapidly and ultimately opened a new horizon, giving rise to the emergence of a different class of general-purpose machine called **personal computers**. The continual advancement in hardware technology ultimately promoted these personal computers to grow into more sophisticated systems, making them more flexible and faster, and finally equipped them for use in a different environment as **workstations** in the early 1980s. A workstation itself typically consists of a faster, more powerful processor, larger capacity of memory, larger disk storage, and high-resolution graphic display unit and usually connects to systems (servers) with more resources than a personal computer. As a result, most users could perform their jobs at their own computers while allowing a large number of other users to simultaneously share the main computer (server) to which it is attached. One of the main drawbacks of this time-sharing system was that the terminals attached were connected to the main system using ordinary cables, and as such they could not be placed very far from the main system. However, advancements in computer technology continued in parallel that ultimately gave rise to another breakthrough with the invention of networking technology in the early 1970s that emerged as two key network types, **local area networks** (LANs) and **wide area networks** (WANs). LAN technology provided interconnections of several computers located within a small geographical range, and small amounts of information could be transferred between machines in a millisecond or so. Large amounts of data could be moved between machines at rates of 10 Mbps (million bits per sec) or even more. The first high-speed LAN was the Ethernet, from Xerox PARC in 1973. WAN technology, on other hand, allowed interconnections of several computers located far from each other (in different cities, countries, or even continents) in such a way that these machines could exchange information with one another at data rates of about 56 Kbps (Kilobits per sec). The first WAN was the ARPANET (Advanced Research Projects Agency Network) developed by the U.S. Department of Defense in 1969.

The ultimate result of the emergence of these two technologies: the appearance of low-cost small computers with the computing power of a decent-sized mainframe (large), and the introduction of networking technology; when combined together made it possible to realize an arrangement consisting of many computing systems with a large number of CPUs connected by a high-speed network. These are usually called **distributed computing systems**, in contrast to the previous **centralized systems** consisting of a single CPU, its memory, peripherals, and some terminals.

A *distributed computing system*, in short, can be roughly defined as a collection of processors interconnected by a communication network in which each processor has its own local memory and other peripherals, and the physical communication between processors is done by passing messages across the communication network that interconnects the processors. For a particular processor, all its own resources are local, whereas the other processors and their resources as connected to it are *remote.* Often, a processor together with its allied resources is referred to as a *node*, *site*, or even *machine* of the distributed computing system.

Advancements in many areas of networking technology continued, and as a result, another major innovation in networking technology took place in the early 1990s with the introduction of asynchronous transfer mode (ATM) technology, which offered very high-speed data transmission on the order of 1.2 gigabits in both LAN and WAN environments. Consequently, it made it possible to support a different new class of distributed computing, called *multimedia applications*, that handles a mixture of information, including, voice, video, and ordinary text data. These applications were simply beyond imagination with the existing traditional LANs and WANs.

Distributed systems although appeared in the late 1970s and were well defined from the standpoint of the hardware, but the appropriate software (mainly the operating system) that could extract its total power to the fullest extent was not available. They need radically different software than that used for centralized systems. Although this field is not yet mature, extensive research already carried out and still in progress has provided enough basic ideas to evolve a formal design of these operating systems. Commercial distributed operating systems (DOSs) of different forms have emerged that can support many popular distributed applications. Distributed computing systems that use DOSs are referred by the term **true distributed systems** or simply **distributed systems**. The term "distributed system" means the presence of a DOS on any model of a distributed computing system.

Brief details on this topic are given on the Support Material at www.routledge.com/9781032467238.

9.2 CHARACTERISTICS OF DISTRIBUTED COMPUTING SYSTEMS: ADVANTAGES

Distributed systems involve the distribution of computing facilities, processing as well as related data. Some of their distinct advantages are:

- **Responsiveness:** It provides appropriate resources to fulfill the local requirements at respective ends within its premises and imposes local management in a way superior than those obtained from a centrally located facility, but still is aimed to fulfill the total demand of the entire computing environment of the arrangement.
- **Resource sharing:** Expensive computing resources can be shared among users for the sake of better utilization. Data files to be shared inherent to some applications can be provided to individual users for local computing but can be centrally managed and maintained for all users' access. In addition, distribution of critical programs and databases is often needed, and that can be developed in a way for all users' access individually at their respective ends in order to disperse facilities.
- **Higher reliability and availability:** Reliability often refers to the degree of tolerance against errors and component failures in a system. It is also sometimes defined in terms of **availability**, which refers to the fraction of time within which a system is available for use. Reliability and also availability can be realized by distributing the workload over multiple interconnected systems, and the instance of a single machine failure may then at most affect only the respective machine, leaving the rest intact to function normally with almost no indication to the users, except with some degradation in performance. To negotiate catastrophic failure, key system resources and critical applications can be replicated so that a backup system can quickly take up the load; otherwise this failure may cause devastation. However, geographical distribution of system resources can limit the scope of failures caused by natural disasters. Thus, the consideration of higher reliability and increased availability is a dominant aspect, but it is often realized against incurring additional cost and also at the price of performance. Hence, it is most important to maintain a balance between them.

- **Extensibility and incremental growth:** Incremental growth is urgently required, mainly to handle increased workload or the need to have a totally new set of applications. In a centralized system, this may often require a major upgrade both in hardware and software and possibly major alteration and appropriate conversion of existing applications for the changed environment, along with perhaps the risk of major havoc and probably degraded performance. In addition, all these together ultimately incur substantial costs and more time. In contrast, with a distributed system, it may be possible to simply add more resources gradually to the system and replace applications or systems step by step, avoiding the "all-or-nothing" approach, thereby allowing it to expand regularly on an as-needed basis. Distributed computing systems that are properly designed to have the property of easy extensibility are commonly called *open distributed systems*.
- **Increased user involvement and control:** The presence of smaller, low-cost, and more manageable resources available directly to users enables them to straightaway involve at ease in the operational environment and also offers them greater freedom to interact with the system.
- **Shorter response times and higher throughput (productivity):** Since each piece of full equipment in the distributed computing systems is available at the end of each individual user to manage different respective tasks with comparatively small amount of load; this would certainly yield relatively better response time to each user, and also increases the total throughput of the entire arrangement. In addition, distributed systems while are equipped with very fast communication networks can be used as parallel computers; many users can then work together on a specific complex task, and each one at his own end can run the respective portions of the total task concurrently with others to rapidly complete the task. Another approach often used is to distribute the load more evenly among existing multiple processors by moving jobs from currently overloaded processors to relatively lightly loaded ones for the sake of achieving better overall performance.
- **Better cost/performance ratio:** With the advent of rapidly increasing power as well as sharp reduction in the price of microprocessors, a large number of CPUs, when harnessing the increasing speed of communication networks, can not only yield a better price/performance ratio than a single large (mainframe) system but may yield an absolute performance that no large system of the same price can achieve. A distributed system, in effect, gives more bang for the buck, which is one of the main reasons for the growing popularity of distributed computing systems.

It is to be noted that all these advantages are actually extracted by the appropriate operating system to be carefully designed that would drive the well-organized machines in distributed computing systems and manage all the processes in a way to make them properly fit in a distributed environment.

Since the entire distributed environment is exposed and available to many users, security in such systems is certainly a critically central issue. Moreover, the continuous increase in user density and explosive growth in the emergence of different models of distributed systems and applications have made this part more vital. Distributed systems, however, amplified the dependence of both organizations and users on the information stored and communications using the interconnections via networks. This, in turn, means a need to protect data and messages with respect to their authenticity and authority as well as to protect the entire system from network-based attacks, be it viruses, hackers, or fraud. Computer security, fortunately, by this time has become more mature; many suitable means and measures, including cryptography, are now available to readily enforce security.

Brief details on this topic are given on the Support Material at www.routledge.com/9781032467238.

9.3 DISTRIBUTED COMPUTING SYSTEMS: DISADVANTAGES

Although distributed computing systems have their strengths in many respects, they also equally have certain weaknesses, some of them are inherent. However, a potential problem is *absolute dependence on a communication network*, which may cause data or messages to be lost during transmission across the network, requiring the intervention of additional special software to handle the situation that, in turn, results in appreciable degradation of the overall system performance and responsiveness to users. Moreover, when traffic on the network continues to grow, it exhausts the network capacity; the network saturates and becomes overloaded; users on the network may then come to a stall. Either special software is needed to negotiate this problem, or the communication network system must be upgraded to higher bandwidth (maybe using fiber optics), incurring a huge cost. All these along with other perennial problems ultimately could negate most of the advantages the distributed computing system was built to provide.

The other problem comes from one of the system's advantages, which is the *easy sharing of data* that exposes these data to all users, and consequently, this gives rise to a severe security problem. Special security measures are additionally needed to protect widely distributed shared resources and services against intentional or accidental violation of access control and privacy constraints. Additional mechanisms may also be needed to keep important data dedicated, isolated, and secret at all costs. Fortunately, several commonly used techniques are available today to serve the purpose of designing more secure distributed computing systems.

Last but not least is the *lack of availability* of suitable system software, which is inherently much more complex and difficult to build than its counterpart, traditional centralized systems. This increased complexity is mainly due to the fact that apart from performing its usual responsibilities by effectively using and efficiently managing a large number of distributed resources, it should also be capable of handling the communication and security problems that are very different from those of centralized systems. In fact, the performance and reliability of a distributed computing system mostly depends to a great extent on the performance and reliability of the large number of distributed resources attached to it and also on the underlying communication network, apart from the performance of the additional software, as already mentioned, to safeguard the system from any possible attack to keep it in normal operation.

Despite all these potential problems, as well as the increased complexity and difficulties in building distributed computing systems, it is observed that their advantages totally outweigh their disadvantages, and that is why the use of distributed computing systems is rapidly increasing. In fact, the major advantages, economic pressures, and increased importance that have led to the growing popularity of distributed computing systems will eventually bring about a further move one step forward to connect most of the computers to form large distributed systems to provide even better, cheaper, and more convenient service to most users.

Brief details on this topic are given on the Support Material at www.routledge.com/9781032467238.

9.4 DISTRIBUTED COMPUTING SYSTEMS: HARDWARE CONCEPTS

Multiple-CPU computer systems are recognized by Flynn's classification of computers, which places them in the category of multiple instructions multiple data (MIMD), and the classification process ended there. Later on, further classifications of this category were introduced. The most-frequently used taxonomy in this regard is cited in Figure 9.1. All MIMD computers are divided into two distinct categories: those MIMDs that use shared primary memory, usually called **multiprocessors**, and those that do not, sometimes called **multicomputers**, private memory computers, or even disjoint memory computers. The primary difference between them is essentially that in a multiprocessor, there is usually a single virtual address space that is shared by all CPUs. All the machines share the same memory.

In a multicomputer, in contrast, each individual machine consisting of a processor–memory–I/O module forms a node which is essentially a separate stand-alone autonomous computer in this arrangement. These machines are then grouped together by using communication networks with physically separated memory as well as I/O distributed among the processors; hence, this whole arrangement is rightly called multicomputers. Such machines usually yield cost-effective higher

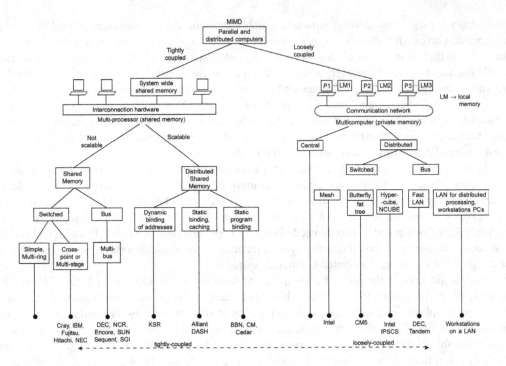

FIGURE 9.1 A schematic block–wise representation relating to the taxonomy of the parallel and distributed computing systems.

bandwidth, since most of the accesses made by each processor are to its local memory, thereby reducing the latency that eventually results in an increase in processor performance. The nodes in the machine are equipped with communication interfaces so that they can be connected to one another through an interconnection network.

Due to the advent of more powerful VLSI technology in the mid-1980s, it became feasible to develop powerful one-chip microprocessors and larger-capacity RAM at reasonable cost. Large-scale multiprocessor architectures with radical changes then started to emerge with multiple memories that are now distributed with the processors. As a result, each CPU can now access its own local memory quickly, but accessing the other memories connected with other CPUs and also the separate common shared memory is also possible but is relatively slow. That is, these physically separated memories can now be addressed as one logically shared address space, meaning that any memory location can be addressed by any processor, assuming it has the correct access rights. This, however, does not discard the fundamental shared memory concept of multiprocessors but supports it in a broader sense. These machines are historically called *distributed shared memory* systems or the *scalable shared memory* architecture model using non-uniform memory access (NUMA). The distributed shared memory (DSM) architecture, however, can be considered a **loosely coupled multiprocessor**, sometimes referred to as a **distributed computing system** in contrast to its counterpart, a shared memory multiprocessor (uniform memory access (UMA)), considered a **tightly coupled multiprocessor**, often called a **parallel processing system**.

Tightly coupled systems tend to be used to work on a single program (or problem) to achieve maximum speed, and the number of processors that can be effectively and efficiently employed is usually small and constrained by the bandwidth of the shared memory, resulting in limited scalability. Loosely coupled systems (multicomputers), on the other hand, often referred to as **distributed computing systems**, are designed primarily to allow many users to work together on many unrelated problems but occasionally in a cooperative manner that mainly involves sharing of resources. These systems for having loosely coupled architecture are more freely expandable and theoretically can contain any number of interconnected processors with no limits, and these processors can even be located far from each other in order to cover a wider geographical area. Tightly coupled multiprocessors can exchange data nearly at memory speeds, but some fiber-optic-based multicomputers have been found also to work very close to memory speeds. Therefore, the terms "tightly coupled" and "loosely coupled" although indicate some useful concepts, but any distinct demarcation between them is difficult to maintain because the design spectrum is really a continuum.

Both multiprocessors and multicomputers individually can be again divided into two categories based on the architecture of the interconnection network; *bus* and *switched*, as shown in Figure 9.1. By bus, it is meant that there is a single network, backplane, bus, cable, or other medium that connects all the machines. Switched systems consist of individual wires from machine to machine, with many different wiring patterns in use, giving rise to a specific topology. Usually, messages move along the wires, with an explicit switching decision made at each step to route the message along one of the outgoing wires.

Distributed computing systems with multicomputers can be further classified into two different categories: **homogeneous** and **heterogeneous**. In a homogeneous multicomputer, all processors are the same and generally have access to the same amount of private memory and also only a single interconnection network that uses the same technology everywhere. These multicomputers are used more as parallel systems (working on a single problem), just like multiprocessors. A heterogeneous multicomputer, in contrast, may contain a variety of different independent computers, which, in turn, are connected through different networks. For example, a distributed computing system may be built from a collection of different local-area computer networks, which are then interconnected through a different communication network, such as a fiber-distributed data interface (FDDI) or ATM-switched backbone.

Multiprocessors that usually give rise to parallel computing systems lie outside the scope of this chapter. Multicomputers, whether bus-based or switch-based, are distributed computing systems, although not directly related to our main objective, *DOSs*, but they still deserve some discussion because they will shed some light on our present subject, as we will observe that different forms of such machines use different kinds of operating systems.

Brief details on this topic are given on the Support Material at www.routledge.com/9781032467238.

9.5 DISTRIBUTED COMPUTING SYSTEMS: DIFFERENT FORMS

Even though all distributed computing systems consist of multiple CPUs, there are several different ways the hardware can be organized, especially in terms of how these CPUs are interconnected and how they communicate with one another. Various models have been proposed in this regard that can be broadly classified into **five** categories. A brief description of each of them follows.

9.5.1 Systems Consisting of Minicomputers

The **minicomputer model (peer-to-peer)** usually consists of a few minicomputers (they may even be large supercomputers as well) interconnected by a suitable communication network. Here, each computer can have several interactive terminals that can support multiple users simultaneously at their own end. An interactive terminal of a specific machine can normally access and communicate with any other remote machines (and also terminals). Any user currently logged on to any machine within the arrangement can use any resource attached to any of the machines present in the collection with the help of the network irrespective of what machine the user is currently logged in to. Many users, in this way, can individually work concurrently on many unrelated problems at their respective machines with needed interaction, if required. Distributed applications, on the other hand, may be composed of a large number of peer processes running on separate computers, and the pattern of communication between them depends entirely on application requirements. A large number of data objects are shared; an individual computer (or node) holds only a small part of the application database; and the storage, processing, and communication workloads for access to objects are distributed across many computers with communication links. Each object is replicated in several computers to further distribute the load and to provide resilience in the event of individual machine faults or communication link failure (as is inevitable in the large, heterogeneous networks in which peer-to-peer systems exist). The need to place individual objects and retrieve them and to maintain replicas among many computers render this architecture relatively more complex than its counterparts in other popular forms of architecture. This form of distributed computing system was used in the early ARPANET and is found to be appropriate for the situations in which resource sharing, such as sharing of files of different types, with each type of file located on a different machine, is needed by remote users.

Brief details on this topic with a figure are given on the Support Material at www.routledge.com/9781032467238.

9.5.2 Systems Containing Workstations

Multicomputers based on the **workstation model** consist of several workstations (homogeneous or heterogeneous) that are scattered over a wide area and are interconnected by a communication network (a high-speed LAN). A workstation here is simply a stand-alone small computer system (usually PCs) equipped with its own disk and other peripherals that serves as a fairly autonomous single-user environment with a highly user-friendly interface but might provide services to others on request. Processes which run on separate machines can communicate data with one another through the network. One of the main objectives of this model is to increase the resource utilization so that at times the job submitted on a specific workstation can be shifted to a more appropriate one to get it executed. In addition, the system often attempts to maintain a *load balance* by distributing processes located at the heavily loaded workstations to others for execution that are relatively less-loaded using the high-speed LAN that connects them. However, the result of the execution is finally returned to the home workstation where it was submitted. Each workstation may have its own local file system, and therefore, different mechanisms are needed to access local as well as remote files. However, implementation of this system faces several critical issues while attempting to extract all its useful features that need to be resolved using different approaches. Details of those aspects belong to the domain of computer organization and architecture and hence lie outside the scope of this chapter. An example of this kind of distributed computing system is an experimental system developed by Xerox PARC (Shoch and Hupp, 1982) using several interconnected workstations.

Brief details on this topic with a figure are given on the Support Material at www.routledge.com/9781032467238.

9.5.3 Workstation–Server Model: Client–Server Model

Multicomputers based on the **client–server model** consist of one or a few minicomputers used as *servers* and several *clients* (workstations), most of which may be *diskless*, but a few may be *diskful*, and all are interconnected as usual by a communication network. With the availability of relatively low-cost high-speed networks, diskless workstations in this model are preferable, since they are easier to maintain, and upgrades of both hardware and system software can simply take place on only a few large disks at the minicomputer end rather than on many small disks attached to many diskful workstations geographically scattered over a large area as in the ordinary workstation model, already discussed. But a diskful workstation in this model is otherwise advantageous, since it additionally provides temporary storage for useful information that is frequently accessed, thereby minimizing repeated to and fro visits to the server machine resulting in a notable increase in overall system performance. However, normal computation activities required by the user's processes are performed at the user's home workstation, but requests for needed services are sent to a server (minicomputer) providing one or more types of a set of shared services or to a specific appropriate server (such as a file server or a database server) that performs the user's requested activity and returns the outcome (result) of the processing of the request to the user's workstation. Therefore, this model *does not require any migration* of the user's processes to the target server machine for getting the work executed by those machines.

With passing of days, this model has become increasingly popular, mainly for providing an effective general-purpose means of sharing information and resources in distributed computing systems. However, it can be implemented in a variety of hardware and software environments, and possesses a number of characteristics that make it distinct from other types of distributed computing systems. Some of the variations on this model involve consideration of the following factors:

- deployment of multiple servers and caches to increase performance and resilience;
- use of low-cost computers with limited hardware resources to fulfill users' need and be equally simple to manage;
- the use of mobile code and mobile agents;
- to add or remove mobile devices in a suitable manner as and when required.

The term **mobile code** is used to refer to code that can be sent from one computer to another and run at the destination. **Java applets** are a well-known and widely used example of mobile code. Code fit to run on one computer may not be necessarily suitable to run on another, because executable programs are normally specific both to the instruction set (hardware) and the host operating system. The use of the software virtual machine approach (such as Java virtual machine, JVM), however, provides a way to make such code executable on any environment (hardware and OS). A **mobile agent** is a running program (consisting of both code and data) that travels from one computer to another in a network carrying out a task (such as collecting information) on someone's behalf, eventually return ing with the results. A mobile agent may issue many local resources at each site it visits.

Moreover, it has been also observed that both client and server processes can sometimes even run on the same computer, and it is perhaps difficult at times to strictly distinguish between a server process and a client process. In addition, some processes are also found as both client and server processes; a server process may sometimes use the services of another server (as in the case of three-tier architecture), thereby appearing as a client to the latter.

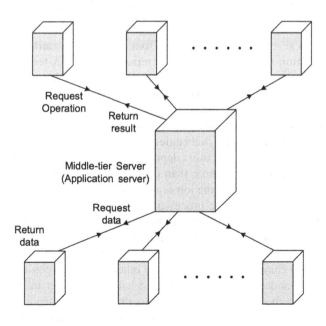

FIGURE 9.2   A representative scheme of a three–tier architecture used in the client–server model formed with computer systems in the premises of computer networks.

Three-tier client–server architecture: The concept of three-tier architecture in the traditional client–server model is becoming increasingly popular and playing a dominant role in the organization of modern computers, especially in the realization of cluster architecture. In contrast to usual client–server architecture which has two levels or tiers, a *client tier* and a *server tier*, in this architecture, the application software is usually distributed among three types of machines, a *user machine*, a *middle-tier server*, and a *backend server*, as shown in Figure 9.2. The user machine in this model is typically a **thin client**. The middle-tier machines playing a major role are separate servers that contain programs which form part of the processing level, convert protocols, map one type of database query to another, also integrate/merge results from different data sources, and are supposed to be essentially gateways between the thin clients and a variety of backend servers. In effect, the middle-tier machines works as an interface between the desktop applications and the background legacy applications (or evolving corporate-wide applications) by mediating between the two different worlds. In fact, the interaction between the middle-tier server and the backend server also follows the client–server model in which the middle-tier server acts as a client to the backend server. Thus, the middle-tier system acts both as a client as well as a server. Finally, it can be inferred that this model actually offers a deeper **vertical distribution**. Many examples of a distributed computing systems based on the workstation–server model can be cited; the earliest one is the V-System (Cheriton, 1998).

Brief details on this topic with a figure are given on the Support Material at www.routledge.com/9781032467238.

9.5.4 Systems with Processor Pools

While the workstation–server model nicely fits with the most common environment, but there are some applications that sometimes demand a massive amount of computing power for a relatively short duration of time. The processor-pool model can handle such an environment in which all the processors are clubbed together to be shared by users as and when needed. The pool of processors can be built with a large number of microcomputers and minicomputers (small mainframes) interconnected with one another over a communication network, and each such processor is able to independently execute any program of the distributed computing system.

Usually, in the processor-pool model, no terminal is directly attached to any processor; rather all the terminals are attached to the network via an interface, a special device (terminal controller). Here, the user can access the entire system from any of the terminals, which are usually small diskless workstation or may be graphic terminals, such as X-terminals. The user here never logs onto a particular machine but to the system as a whole; therefore, this model has no concept of a home machine, in contrast to other models (already described) in which each user has a home machine to log on to and runs most of the programs at will by default. In this model, when a job is submitted, there exists a special server (commonly called a *run server*, a part of the related operating system) that manages, schedules, and allocates one or an appropriate number of processors from the pool to different users depending on the prevailing environment or on an on-demand basis. In some situations, more than one processor can be allocated to a single job that can run in parallel, if the nature of the job supports it (i.e. if the job can be decomposed into many mutually exclusive segments, one processor can then be assigned to each such segment, and all these segments can eventually run in parallel). As usual, processors are deallocated from the job when it is completed and returned to the pool for other users to make use of them.

The processor-pool model exhibits effectively better utilization of the *total* available processing power of a distributed computing system than any other model that possesses a home-machine concept (in workstation models, with the use of load balancing, better utilization of processing power can be attained, but there are several constraints that should be negotiated at the time of its implementation). For any logged-on users, here the entire processing power of this system is available, if needed. Despite having many other advantages, one of the major shortcomings of this model is the relatively slow-speed interconnection network that communicates between the processors where the jobs are to be executed and the terminals via which the users talk with the system. That is why this model is usually considered not suitable for the general environment in which typically high-performance interactive applications run. However, distributed computing system based on the processor-pool model has been implemented in a reputed distributed system, Amoeba (Mullender et al., 1990).

Brief details on this topic with a figure are given on the Support Material at www.routledge. com/9781032467238.

9.5.5 HYBRID SYSTEMS

Each of the forms of distributed computing systems as described has its own merits as well as certain drawbacks, mostly depending on the environments where they will be employed. Out of all these models, the workstation–server (client–server) model appears to have comparatively more advantages than the others, and it is the most widely used model for building distributed computing systems, since it supports an environment in which most of the common users, of whom there are many, often run simple interactive jobs (copy, edit, placing queries, and sending mail) apart from executing their small batch jobs. On the other hand, for users who deal with computation-intensive jobs, use of the processor-pool model will be more appropriate.

A new trend started to evolve, attempting to extract all the advantages of these two models and combining them to give rise to an innovative concept of a hybrid model that may be used to build a distributed computing system. This model introduced several salient features that exhibit a nice balance in the mixture of most of the advantages of these two potential models. The hybrid model is basically a workstation–server model but includes a pool of processors. The processors in the pool can be allocated dynamically on an as-needed basis for computation-intensive jobs that are too large for the workstations to handle or that inherently require concurrent use of several computers for efficient execution. In addition, the hybrid model also ensures quick response to interactive jobs by allowing them to be executed on the home or local workstations of the users. It is to be noted that this hybrid model, while providing nice features of both models, will naturally be more expensive in all senses to implement and maintain than the individual workstation–server model or processor-pool model.

9.6 DISTRIBUTED COMPUTING SYSTEMS: SOFTWARE CONCEPTS

Hardware is the fundamental structure of any machine, and system software is nothing but nice clothing over it that casts an image of a system to the users and extracts the highest potential out of it. The same hardware when wrapped in different software presents a different flavor of the system. Therefore, although hardware for distributed computing systems is important, but it is the software associated with it that largely determines the potentials of the system. The *first aspect* of the software related to such a system is similar to centralized system; here the software also acts as a **resource manager** that controls user accesses to various resources of the system and also determines the ways these resources are to be granted to comply with the requests of the users. The *second aspect* of the software is perhaps more vital that always attempts to hide the intricacies and heterogeneities of the underlying hardware from users by providing a virtual machine interface on which the applications can be executed.

OS software systems developed and used to manage all forms of computing systems with multiple CPUs can also be roughly classified into two distinct categories: **tightly coupled** and **loosely coupled**. Nowadays, it is almost the case that *loosely* and *tightly* coupled software are roughly analogous to *loosely* and *tightly* coupled hardware. Thus, there exist two kinds of distributed hardware, as already discussed, and two kinds of distributed software, and there is a total of four different combinations of such hardware and software. Figure 9.3 illustrates these combinations, along with their respective implications.

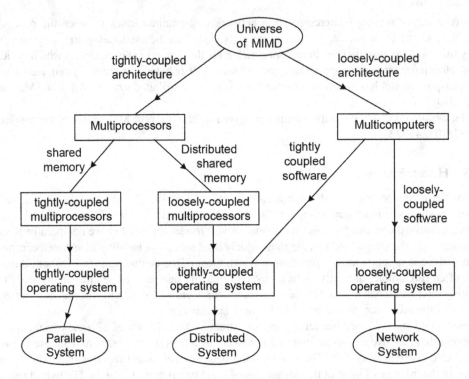

FIGURE 9.3 A schematic representation of the taxonomy of different combinations of MIMD category hardware and related software used in the domain of different types of interconnected multiple–CPU computer systems.

In tightly coupled hardware systems, the OS software system essentially tries to maintain a single, global view of the resources it manages. In loosely coupled hardware systems, the individual machines are clearly distinguishable and fundamentally independent of one another, each running its own operating system to execute its own job. However, these operating systems often interact to a limited degree whenever necessary and work together to offer their own resources and services to others.

A tightly coupled operating system, when used for managing tightly coupled multiprocessors, is generally referred to as **multiprocessor operating system**, which, when combined with the underlying architecture of the computing system, gives rise to the concept of a **parallel system**. Numerous issues in regard to this system need to be addressed, but a detailed discussion of such an operating system is outside the scope of this book. However, some important issues in regard to this system are discussed in brief later in this chapter.

A tightly coupled operating system, when used for managing a loosely coupled multiprocessor (DSM) and homogeneous multicomputers, is generally referred to as a **distributed operating system**, which, when combined with the underlying architecture of the computing system, gives rise to the concept of a **distributed system**. Distributed operating systems are homogeneous, implying that each node runs the same operating system (kernel). Although the forms and issues relating to implementation of DSOs that drive the *loosely coupled multiprocessor* and those that manage *homogeneous multicomputers* are quite different, but their main objectives and design issues happen to be the same. Similarly to conventional uniprocessor operating systems, the main objectives of a DOS are, however, to hide the complexities of managing the underlying distributed hardware such that it can be enjoyed and shared by multiple processes.

A loosely coupled operating system, when used for managing loosely coupled hardware, such as a heterogeneous multicomputer system (LAN-and WAN-based), is generally referred to as a

network operating system (NOS). Although a NOS does not manage the underlying hardware in the way that a conventional uniprocessor operating system usually does, but it provides additional supports in that local services are made available to remote clients. In the following sections, we will first describe in brief the loosely coupled operating system and then focus on tightly coupled (distributed) operating systems.

Out of many different forms of loosely coupled hardware, the most widely used one is the **client–server model** using many heterogeneous computer systems, the benefits of which are mainly tied up with its design approach, such as its modularity and the ability to mix and match different platforms with applications to offer a business solution. However, there is a lack of standards that stands to prevent the model managed by a NOS from being a true distributed system. To alleviate these limitations, and to achieve the real benefits of the client–server approach to get the flavor of an actual distributed system (general-purpose services) that would be able to implement an integrated, multi-vendor, and enterprise-wide client–server configuration, there must be a set of tools which would provide a uniform means and style of access to system resources across all platforms. Enhancements along these lines to the services of NOSs have been carried out that provide distribution transparency. These enhancements eventually led to introduce what is known as **middleware** that lies at the heart of modern distributed systems. Middleware and its main issues will be discussed later in this chapter.

9.7 NETWORK OPERATING SYSTEMS AND NFS

A NOS, the earliest form of operating system for distributed architecture, is a loosely coupled software system that runs on loosely coupled hardware. The hardware is usually constructed from a collection of uniprocessor systems; each runs with its own operating system with high degree of autonomy and also may have one or more "server" machines in the collection, as schematically shown in Figure 9.4. These machines and their operating systems in this collection may be the same or different (a heterogeneous mixture), and there is essentially no coordination at all among these machines, but they are all connected to an interconnection (computer) network so as to fulfill a few system-wide requirements. Introduction of low-cost personal computers that support a variety of user-friendly single-user applications further facilitates this approach to a compact form within an affordable range. However, such a combination is only possible as long as all machines support the same communications architecture (software) and use a mutually agreed-on communication protocol. The server machines usually provide network-wide services or applications, such as; file storage, sophisticated database management, information system software, printer management, and so on. Since each computer in this arrangement has its own private operating system, it can function independently of other computers and manage its local resources. Here, the NOS is simply an adjunct to the local operating system, the goal of which is to provide resource sharing by enabling users to make use of the facilities and services available on any other specific machine or a server apart from their own. Of course, the user is quite aware that there are multiple independent computers and must deal with them explicitly. Typically, a common communications architecture (protocol) is used to make use of these network applications.

The network OS layer, as shown in Figure 9.4, resides between the kernel of the local OS and user processes. Processes interact with the network OS layer rather than with the kernel of their own local OS. If a process issues requests to access a non-local (remote) resource, the network OS layer of the requesting process contacts the network OS layer of the node that contains the resource and implements access to the resource with its help. When a process on a machine requests access to a local resource, the corresponding network OS layer on that machine then simply passes the request to the kernel of the local OS. Here, the resource requests should be explicit and require users to be completely aware of where all resources are located and where all requests (commands) are to be processed. While this form of communication is observed to be extremely primitive, a more convenient forms of communication and information–sharing can be made by providing,

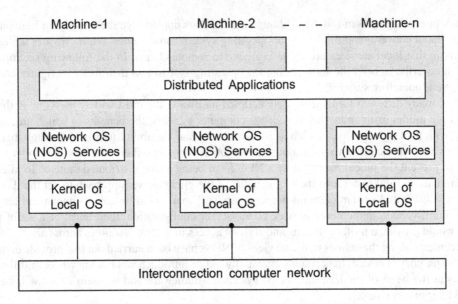

FIGURE 9.4 A representative block diagram of general structure of a network operating system used in the premises of computer networks formed with multiple computers (each one may be of single CPU or multiple CPU).

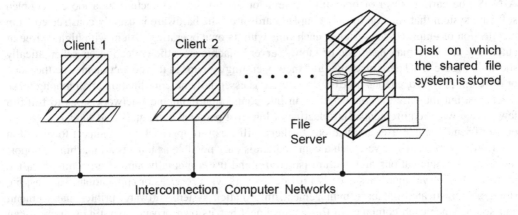

FIGURE 9.5 A block–structured illustration of a representative scheme consisting of autonomous clients and a server operated under a network operating system used in computer networks formed with multiple computers.

for example, a shared, global file system that can be accessible from all client's machine. The file system may be supported by one or more machines called **file servers** that accept all requests from user programs running on other machines (non-servers). Each such incoming request is then examined and executed at the server's end, and the reply is sent back accordingly. This is illustrated in Figure 9.5.

File servers usually maintain hierarchical file systems, each with a root directory containing subdirectories and files. Each machine (or client) can mount these file systems, augmenting their local file systems with those located on the servers. It really does not matter where a server is mounted by a client in its directory hierarchy, since all machines operate relatively independently of others. That is why different clients can have a different view of the file system. The name of the file actually depends on where it is being accessed from and how that machine has built its file system.

Many NOSs have been developed by different manufacturers on top of UNIX and other operating systems, including Linux and Windows. One of the best-known and most widely used commercial networking systems is Sun Microsystem's **Network File System**, universally known as **NFS**, that was primarily used on its UNIX-based workstations, although it supports heterogeneous systems; for example, Windows running on Intel Pentium gets service from UNIX file servers running on Sun SPARC processors.

A network OS is easier to implement but is clearly more primitive than a full-fledged distributed OS. Still, some of the **advantages** of NOS as observed compared to DOSs are that it allows machines (nodes) to maintain total autonomy and to remain highly independent of each other; it also facilitates safely adding or removing a machine to and from a common network in the arrangement without affecting the others except only to inform the other machines in the network about the existence of the new one. The addition of a new server to the internet, for example, is done in this precise way. To introduce a newly added machine on the internet, all that is needed is to provide its network address or, even better, the new machine can be given a symbolic name that can be subsequently placed in the Domain Name Service (DNS) along with its network address.

A few of the major **shortcomings** of a network OS are that it allows the local operating systems to be independent stand-alone, retaining their identities and managing their own resources, so they are visible to users, but their functioning cannot be integrated. Consequently, this lack of transparency in a network OS fails to provide a single, system-wide coherent system view, and it cannot balance or optimize utilization of resources, because the resources are not under its direct control. In addition, all access permissions, in general, have to be maintained per machine, and there is no simple way of changing permissions unless they are the same everywhere. This decentralized approach to security sometimes makes it vulnerable and thereby makes it equally hard to protect the NOS against malicious attacks. There remain other issues that stand as drawbacks of an NOS, and all these together draw a clean demarcation between an NOS and its counterpart, a DOS. However, there are still other factors that make DOS distinctly different from NOS.

Brief details on this topic are given on the Support Material at www.routledge.com/9781032467238.

9.8 DISTRIBUTED OPERATING SYSTEMS

A distributed computing system when managed by a DOS is commonly called a distributed system. Various definitions of distributed systems have been proposed, but none of them have been absolutely satisfactory. However, a rough characterization may be:

> *A distributed system is one that runs on a collection of interconnected independent computers which do not have shared memories yet appears to its users as a single coherent system.*

This characteristic is also sometimes referred to as the **single system image** (**SSI**). A slightly different notion of a distributed system is that it is one that runs on a collection of a networked machine but acts like a **virtual uniprocessor**. No matter how it is expressed, the leading edge in quest of distributed systems and its development is mainly focused on the area of DOSs. Although some commercial systems have already been introduced, fully functional DOSs with most of their necessary attributes are still at the experimental stage in the laboratory. However, the definition of a DOS can be presented in the following way:

> *A distributed operating system is one that casts a view to its users like an ordinary centralized operating system but controls operations of multiple independent central processing units (nodes) in a well-integrated manner. The key concept here is transparency. In other words, the use of multiple processors should be invisible (transparent) to the user, who views the system as a "virtual uniprocessor", not as collection of distinct machines (processors).*

However, the functionality of DOSs is essentially identical to that of traditional operating systems for uniprocessor machines with the exception that they manage multiple CPUs. The advantages of distributed computing systems, as mentioned in Section 9.2, are exploited by using a DOS that takes advantages of the available multiple resources and thereby disperses the processes of an application across various machines (or CPUs) in the system to achieve computation speed-up, effective utilization by sharing and efficiency of underlying resources whenever possible, communication and cooperation between users via the existing network, and above all to provide reliability whenever necessary. However, there remains a possibility of communication network failures or breakdown of individual computer systems that sometimes complicates the functioning of the underlying operating system and necessitates use of special techniques in its design to negotiate these situations. Users of these operating systems also often require special techniques that facilitate access to resources over the existing network.

Users of a DOS have *user ids* and *passwords* that are valid throughout the system. This feature makes communication conveniently possible between users in two ways. First, communication using *user-ids* automatically invokes the security mechanisms of the OS to intervene and thereby ensures the authenticity of communication. Second, users can be mobile within the domain of the distributed system and still be able to communicate with other users of the system with ease.

Distributed operating systems can be classified into two broad categories: An **operating system in multiprocessors (DSM)** manages the resources of a multiprocessor. The other one is an **operating system in multicomputers** that is developed to handle homogeneous multicomputers.

9.9 DISTRIBUTED OPERATING SYSTEMS: DESIGN ISSUES

Following the accepted definition of the DOS, as given earlier, it is expected that data, resources, users, and their computations should be effectively distributed among the nodes (processors) of the system to meet its ultimate goal. Designing a distributed system is, however, more difficult than designing a centralized operating system for several reasons; the resources are physically separated, there is no common clock among multiple processors (nodes), and communication between them in the form of messages may be delayed and could even be lost. Due to all these and several other relevant reasons, a DOS does never have the latest consistent knowledge with respect to the state of the various resources of the underlying distributed system, which eventually may affect many things, such as management of resources, scheduling of threads and processes, and synchronization of concurrent competitive and cooperating activities, etc. That is why a distributed system must be designed keeping in view that complete information about the system environment will never be available beforehand, but the user at the same time should be given a view of the distributed system as a virtual centralized system that is flexible, efficient, secure, reliable, scalable, and above all easy to use. To meet all these requirements, the designer of the system must deal with several design issues. Some of the key design issues are described in the following.

9.9.1 TRANSPARENCY AND ITS DIFFERENT ASPECTS

This implies that the existence of a collection of distinct machines (processors) that are connected by a communication network to constitute the system must be made invisible (*transparent*) to its users, providing them only a view of virtually a single uniprocessor system image. Complete transparency in this respect is, however, difficult to realize, since it includes several different aspects of transparency that must be supported by the DOS. The eight forms of transparency as pointed out by the ISO Reference Model for Open Distributed Processing (ISO, 1992) are: *location transparency, access transparency, replication transparency, migration transparency, concurrency transparency, failure transparency, performance transparency*, and *scaling transparency*. Each transparency aspect has its own important role that comes into play to provide all the advantages of a distributed system to its users. We, however, present here only a brief overview, covering almost all the transparency aspects together that summarily explain the different transparency facets and their respective implications.

- *Location and access transparency* : Resources and services are usually made transparent to the users by identifying them simply by *only* their names and do not depend on their *locations* in the system. This aspect also facilitates **migration transparency**, which ensures that the movement of the data is handled automatically by the system in a user-transparent manner. Distributed file systems (DFS) also exploit this transparency aspect favorably when they store system and user files in different location (nodes) to mostly optimize disk space usage and network traversal time, and that is also done with no indication to the user.
- **Replication transparency:** This is related to the creation of replicas of files and resources to yield better performance and reliability by keeping them transparent to the user. Two important issues related to replication transparency are *naming of replicas* and *replication control*, which are automatically handled by the replication management module of the distributed system in a user-transparent manner.
- **Failure transparency:** In the face of a partial system failure, such as a machine (node or processor) failure, a communication link failure, a storage device crash, or other types of similar failures, the *failure transparency* attribute of a DOS will keep all these failures transparent from the user and still enables the system to continue to function, perhaps only with degraded performance. The OS realizes this by typically implementing resources as a group cooperating with each other to perform their respective functions so that in the event of the failure of one or more same resource, the user is still remained unaffected and will not notice the failure. The user can still get going on with the service of the resource even in the situation when only one of the resources in the group is up and working. Complete failure transparency is, however, not possible to achieve with the current state of the art in DOSs, because all types of failures cannot be handled in a user-transparent manner. Communication link failure, for example, in a system cannot be kept beyond the notice of the user, since it directly hampers the work of the user. Hence, the design of such a distributed system is theoretically possible but is not practically feasible.
- **Performance transparency:** This aims to improve the performance of the system by enabling the system to be automatically configured as loads vary dynamically. This is often carried out by rescheduling and uniformly distributing the currently obtainable processing capacity of the system among the jobs present within the system using the support, such as resource allocation ability or data migration capability, etc. of the system.
- **Scaling transparency**: This is related to the scalability of the system that allows expansion of the system in scale without affecting the ongoing activities of users. This requires the system to have an open-system architecture and make use of appropriate scalable algorithms in the design of the components of the DOS.

9.9.2 Reliability

Reliability of a system is closely associated with the availability of its resources, which is ensured by protecting them against likely faults. Though the presence of multiple instances of the resources in distributed system are generally assumed to make the system more reliable, but the reality is entirely different; it rather tells that the distributed OS must be designed in such a way so that the full advantage of a distributed system can be realized with equal increase in the reliability of the system. However, system failure results when a fault occurs in a system, and this failure can be categorized into two types depending on the behavior of the failed system. The first one is **fail–stop failure**, which causes the system to stop functioning after changing to a state in which its cause of failure can be detected. The second one is popularly known as **Byzantine failure** that causes the system to continue its function but generates erroneous results. Software bugs that remain undetected often cause Byzantine failure, which is more difficult to handle than fail-stop failure.

Distributed operating systems thus must be designed properly to realize higher reliability, such as to avoid faults, to tolerate faults, to detect faults, and to subsequently recover from faults. Various popular methods in this regard are available to deal each of these issues separately.

- **Fault avoidance:** This is mostly accomplished by designing the components of the system in such a way that the occurrence of the faults is minimized. Designers of the distributed OS must test the various software components thoroughly before use to make them highly reliable.
- **Fault tolerance:** This is the capability of a system to continue its proper functioning even in the event of partial system failure, albeit with a little degradation in system performance. A distributed OS can be equipped with improved fault-tolerance ability by using concepts such as **redundancy techniques** and *distributed control*.
  - **Redundancy techniques:** These essentially exploit the basic principle of replication of critical hardware and software components in order to handle a single-point of failure so that if one component fails, the other can be used to continue. Many different methods to implement the redundancy technique are used for dealing with different types of hardware and software resources. Link and node faults are tolerated by providing redundancy of resources and communication links so that the others can be used if a fault occurs in these areas. Similarly, a critical process can be executed simultaneously on two nodes so that if one of the two nodes fails, the execution of the process can continue to completion at the other node. Likewise, a file is replicated on two or more nodes of a distributed system. Additional disk space is then required, and for correct functioning, it is often necessary that all copies of the files be mutually consistent. Note that what is common to all these approaches is that additional overhead is required in each case to ensure reliability. Therefore, a distributed OS must be designed in such a way as to maintain a proper balance between the required degree of reliability and the amount of overhead incurred. A replication approach in some situations needs appropriate concurrency control mechanisms. Concurrency of data becomes a critical issue when data are distributed or replicated. When several parts of a distributed data are to be modified, a fault should not put the system in a state in which some parts of the data have been updated but others have not due to a hardware fault or a software error. A centralized conventional uniprocessor OS generally uses the technique of *atomic action* to satisfy this requirement. A distributed OS handling distributed data employs a technique called *two-phase commit* (2PC) *protocol* for this purpose.
  - **Distribution of control functions:** Control functions in a distributed system such as resource allocation, scheduling, and synchronization and communication of processors and processes, if implemented centrally, may face several problems. Two of them are quite obvious. The first one is due to communication latency that frequently prevents the system from obtaining the latest information with respect to the current state of processes and resources in all machines (nodes) of the system. The second one is that a centralized control function often becomes the cause of a potential performance bottleneck and the root of a threat to system reliability for being a single-point of control, the failure of which may be sometimes fatal to the system. Due to these factors and for many other reasons, a distributed OS must employ a distributed control mechanism to avoid a single-point of failure. A highly available DFS, for example, should have multiple and independent file servers controlling multiple and independent storage devices. In addition, a distributed OS implements its control functions using a *distributed control algorithm*, the notion of which is to perform

needed functions in different respective machines (servers or nodes) independently, but in a coordinated manner following an appropriate way. Otherwise, the reliability will become worse instead of getting better.

- **Fault detection and recovery:** This approach discovers the occurrence of a failure and then rectify the system to a state so that it can once again continue its normal operation. If a fault (hardware or software failure) occurs during the ongoing execution of a computation in different nodes of the distributed system, the system must be then able to assess the damage caused by the fault and judiciously restore the system to normalcy to continue the operation. Several methods are available to realize this. Some of the commonly used techniques implemented in DOSs in this regard are:
  - **Atomic transactions:** These are computations consisting of a set of operations that are to be executed indivisibly (atomic action) in concurrent computations, even in the face of failures. This implies that either all of the operations are to be completed successfully, or none of their effects prevail if failure occurs during the execution, and other processes executing concurrently cannot enter the domain of this computation while it is in progress. In short, it can be called an *all-or-nothing* property of transactions. This way, the consistency of shared data objects is made preserved even when failure occurs during execution, which eventually makes recovery from crashes much easier.
  - A system equipped with such a transaction facility, when it halts unexpectedly due to the occurrence of a fault or failure before a transaction is completed, the system subsequently restores any data objects (that were undergoing modification at the time of failure) to their original states by restoring rationally some of the subcomputations to the previous states recorded already in the back-ups (archives). This action is commonly known as *roll back*, and the approach is called *recovery*. If a system does not support this transaction mechanism, sudden failure of a process during the execution of an operation may leave the system and the data objects that were undergoing modification in such an inconsistent state that, in some cases, it may be difficult or even impossible to restore (roll back) them to their original states. Atomic transactions are, therefore, considered a powerful tool that enables the system to come out of such a critical situation.
  - **Acknowledgements and timeout-based retransmission of messages:** Interprocess communication mechanisms between two processes often use a message-passing approach in which messages may be lost due to an unexpected event of system fault or failure. To guard against loss of messages in order to ensure reliability, and to detect the lost messages so that they can be retransmitted, the sender and receiver both agree that as soon as a message is received, the receiver will send back a special message to the sender in the form of an *acknowledgement*. If the sender has not received the acknowledgement within a specified timeout period, it assumes that the message was lost, and it may then retransmit the message (duplicate message), which is usually handled involving a mechanism which automatically generates and assigns appropriate sequence numbers to messages. A detailed discussion of the mechanism that handles acknowledgement messages, timeout-based retransmission of messages, and duplicate request messages for the sake of reliable communication is provided in Chapter 4.
  - **Stateless servers:** In distributed computing systems in the form of a client–server model, the server can be implemented by one of two service paradigms: *stateful* or *stateless*. These two paradigms are distinguished by one salient aspect: whether the history of the serviced requests between a client and a server affects the execution of the next service request. The stateful approach depends on the history of the serviced requests, whereas the stateless approach does not. A stateless server is said to be one that does not maintain state information about open files. Stateless servers possess a distinct advantage over stateful servers in the event of a system failure, since the stateless service paradigm makes crash recovery quite easy because no client information

is maintained by the server. On the contrary, the stateful service paradigm requires complex crash recovery procedures since both the client and server need to reliably detect crashes. Here, the server needs to detect client crashes so that it can abandon any state it is holding for the client, and the client must detect server crashes so that it can initiate necessary error-handling activities. Although stateful service is inevitable in some cases, the stateless service paradigm must be used whenever possible in order to simplify failure detection and recovery actions.

However, the major drawback in realizing increased reliability in a distributed system lies in the costly extra overhead involved in implementing the mechanism, whatever it is. It consumes a good amount of execution time that may eventually lead to a potential degradation in the performance of the system as a whole. Obviously, it becomes a hard task for designers to decide to what extent the system can be made reliable so that a good balance of cost versus mechanism can be effectively implemented.

9.9.3 FLEXIBILITY

For numerous reasons, one of the major requirements in the design of a distributed OS is its flexibility. Some of the important reasons are:

- **Ease of implementation:** The system design of a distributed OS should be as simple as possible so that it can be easily implemented. Many issues come across while formulating the design of a distributed OS, but only those are to be incorporated in the design after proper negotiation that require minimum complications at the time of their implementation.
- **Ease of modification:** It has been felt from the experiences that some parts of the design often need to be modified, enhanced, or even replaced either due to the detection of some bugs in the design or sometimes the design itself fails to accommodate the changed environment/user requirements or latest product with new hardware innovation has arrived for inclusion. Therefore, the existing design of the system would be such that it would allow easy incorporation of the required changes in the system, keeping the user completely transparent in this regard making the changes as quickly as possible to cause minimal hindrance at the user end.
- **Ease of enhancement:** Every system when being designed must have the provision that new functionalities and services can be easily included as and when needed to make it more versatile and also simple–to–use. Therefore, the design of the system would be such that it will permit new features be added quickly with minimal or almost no changes over the existing system; or at best the new inclusion may have very little effect or, even better, no effect, without hampering the system to continue as it is.

The flexibility of a distributed OS is critically influenced mostly by the design model of the kernel because it is the central part of the system that controls and provides basic system facilities which, in turn, offer user-accessible features. Different kernel models are available, and each one has its own merits and drawbacks based on which different distributed OS has been built. The ultimate objective is then to formulate the design of the OS in such a way that easy enhancement in and around the existing kernel will be possible with minimum effort and less hindrance irrespective of the type of model chosen.

9.9.4 SCALABILITY

Scalability is one of the most open features for open distributed systems and refers to the ability of a given system to expand by adding new machines or even an entire sub-network to the existing system so that increased workload can be handled without causing any serious disruption of services or notable degradation in system performance. Obviously, there exist some accepted principles that are to be followed as guidelines when designing scalable distributed systems. Some of them are:

- Try to *avoid using centralized entities* in the design of a distributed system because the presence of such entities often creates hindrance in making the system scalable. Also, as the existence of such an entity is a single point, it often makes the system suffer from a bottleneck, which is inherent in such a design as the number of users increase. In addition, in the event of failure of this entity, the system may go beyond the fault-tolerance limit and ultimately break the entire system totally down.
- Try to *avoid using centralized algorithms* in the design of a distributed system. A centralized algorithm can be described as one that operates on a single node by collecting information from all other nodes and finally distributes the result to them. Similar to the reasons that disfavor the use of any central items in the design of a distributed system, here also the presence of such algorithms in the design may be disastrous, particularly in the event of failure of the central node that controls the execution of all the algorithms.
- It is always desirable to encourage *client-centric execution* in a distributed environment, since this act can relieve the server, the costly common resource, as much as possible from its increasing accumulated load of continuously providing services to several clients within its limited time span. Although client-centric execution inherently possesses certain drawbacks, which may give rise to several other critical issues that need to be resolved, still it enhances the scalability of the system, since it reduces the contention for shared resources at the server's end while the system gradually grows in size.

9.9.5 Performance

Realization of good performance from a distributed system under prevailing load conditions is always an important aspect in design issues, and it can be achieved by properly designing and organizing the various components of the distributed OS, with the main focus mostly on extracting the highest potential of the underlying resources. Some of the useful design principles considered effective for improved system performance are:

- **Data migration:** Data migration often provides good system performance. It is employed mostly to reduce network latencies and improve response times of processes.
- **Computation migration:** This involves moving a computation to a site mostly because the data needed by the computation is located there. Besides, this approach is often employed to implement *load balancing* among the machines (CPUs) present in the system.
- **Process migration:** A process is sometimes migrated to put it closer to the resources it is using most heavily in order to mainly reduce network traffic, which, in turn, avoids many hazards and thereby improves system performance appreciably. A process migration facility also provides a way to cluster two or more processes that frequently communicate with one another on the same node of the system.
- **Use of caching:** Caching of data is a popular and widely used approach for yielding overall improved system performance, because it makes data readily available from a relatively speedy cache whenever it is needed, thereby saving a large amount of computing time spent for repeated visits to slower memory and thereby preserving network bandwidth. Use of the caching technique, in general, including *file caching* used in DFSs, also reduces contention for centralized shared resources.
- **Minimize data copying:** Frequent copying of data often leads to sizeable overhead in many operations. Data copying overhead is inherently quite large for read/write operations on block I/O devices, but this overhead can be minimized to a large extent by means of

using a disk cache. However, by also using memory management optimally, it is often possible to significantly reduce data movement as a whole between the participating entities, such as; the kernel, block I/O devices, clients, and servers.

- **Minimize network traffic:** Reduced traffic load on the network may also help to improve system performance. One way of many to minimize network traffic is to use the process migration facility, by which two or more processes that frequently communicate with each other can be clustered on the same node of the system. This will consequently reduce the redundant to and fro journey of the processes over the network. In addition, this will reduce the other effects caused by network latencies. Process migration activity as a whole can also resolve other critical issues, as already discussed, that eventually reduce overall network traffic. In addition, avoiding collection of global state information, whenever possible, for making decisions using the communication network may also help in reducing network traffic.

- **Batch form:** Transferring data across the network in the form of batching it as a large chunk rather than a single individual page is sometimes more effective and often greatly improves system performance. Likewise, piggybacking acknowledgement of previous messages with the next message during transmission of a series of messages between communicating entities also exhibits improved system performance.

9.9.6 SECURITY

Security aspects gain a new dimension in a distributed system, and is truly more difficult to enforce than in a centralized system, mainly due to the lack of a single point of control and the presence of insecure networks attached to widely spread systems for needed communication. Moreover, in a client–server model, a frequently used server must have some way to know the client at the time of offering services, but the client identification field in the message cannot be entirely trusted due to the likely presence of an intruder and their impersonation activities. Moreover, interprocess messages may sometimes pass through a communication processor that operates under a different OS. An intruder can at any point gain control of such a computer system during transmission and either tamper with the messages passing through it or willfully use them to perform impersonation. Therefore, a distributed system as compared to a centralized system should enforce several additional measures with respect to security.

Similar to the aspects and related mechanisms discussed in Chapter 8 ("Security and Protection"), designers of a distributed system should equally address all the protection issues and incorporate different established techniques, including the well-known practical method of cryptography, to enforce security mechanisms as much as possible to safeguard the entire computing environment. In addition, special techniques for *message security* and *authentication* should be incorporated to prevent different types of vulnerable attacks that might take place at the time of message passing.

9.9.7 HETEROGENEITY

A heterogeneous distributed system is perhaps the most general one, and it consists of interconnected sets of dissimilar hardware and software providing the flexibility of employing different computer platforms for a diverse spectrum of applications used by different types of users. Incompatibilities in heterogeneous systems also include the presence of a wide range of different types of networks being interconnected via gateways with their own individual topologies and related communication protocols. Effective design of such systems is, therefore, critically difficult from that of its counterpart, homogeneous systems, in which closely related hardware is operated by similar or compatible software.

Heterogeneous distributed systems often make use of information with different internal formats, and as such need some form of data conversion between two incompatible systems (nodes) at the time of their interactions. The data conversion job, however, is a critical one that may be performed using a specific add-on software converter either at the receiver's node that will be able to convert each format in the system to the format used on the receiving node or may be carried out at the sender's node with a similar approach. The software complexity of this conversion process can be reduced by choosing an appropriate intermediate standard format, supposed to be the most common format of the system that can minimize the number of conversions needed at the time of interactions among various types of different systems (nodes).

Another heterogeneity issue in a distributed system is related to the file system that enables the distributed system to accommodate several different storage media. The file system of such a distributed system should be designed in such a way that it can allow the integration of a new type of workstation or storage media in a relatively simple manner.

9.10   MULTIPROCESSOR OPERATING SYSTEMS

Every parallel computer consists of a set of $n > 1$ processors (CPUs) P_1, P_2, P_3, . . ., P_n and $m > 0$ shared/distributed (main) memory units M_1, M_2, . . ., M_m that are interconnected using various forms of design approaches. Several types of processor–processor interconnections and processor–memory interconnections have been rigorously exploited in the MIMD category. In fact, the MIMD category itself has been split into machines that have shared primary memory, called **multiprocessors**, and those that do not, called **multicomputers**. In this section, we are only concerned with multiprocessor systems, and that too the classification of them considered here is a broad view, deliberately avoiding a spectrum of possibilities in the details.

9.10.1   MULTIPROCESSOR ARCHITECTURE

Classification of multiprocessors can be done in a number of ways and is a subject matter of computer architecture (Chakraborty, 2020). We, however, confine our discussion only to multiprocessors that are classified mostly by the organization of their memory systems (shared memory and distributed memory) as well as by their interconnection networks (dynamic or static). Shared-memory and distributed-memory multiprocessors are sometimes referred to as *tightly coupled* and *loosely coupled*, respectively, describing the speed and ease with which they can interact on common tasks. Shared-memory multiprocessors are mostly unscalable and use *centrally shared global memory* as a single address space that is accessed by all processors. *Distributed shared-memory* multiprocessors are scalable, and individual processors have private memories. This division, however, is not very stringent, and there are hybrid systems that have both per-processor private as well as shared global memory that many or all processors can access. Apart from having shared common memory or distributed memory, these processors also share resources, such as I/O devices, communication facilities, system utilities, program libraries, and databases; all are operated under the control of an integrated operating system that provides interaction between processors and their programs at the job, task, file, and even data element level.

Shared-memory multiprocessors are sometimes referred to as tightly coupled, since high-bandwidth communication networks are used to extract a high degree of resource sharing. The interconnection network used to construct a multiprocessor (both tightly coupled as well as loosely coupled) may be in the form of a:

- Common (hierarchical) bus, known as bus-oriented systems
- Crossbar switch
- Hypercubes
- Multistage switches (network) or in some other form

Shared-bus systems are relatively simple and popular, but their scalability is limited by bus and memory contention. Crossbar systems while allow fully parallel connections between processors and different memory modules, but their cost and complexity grow quadratically with the increase in number of nodes. Hypercubes and multilevel switches are scalable, and their complexities grow only logarithmically with the increase in number of nodes. However, the type of interconnection network to be used and the related nature of this interconnection path has a significant influence on the bandwidth and saturation of system communications apart from the other associated important issues, such as cost, complexity, interprocessor communications, and above all the scalability of the presented architectures that determines to what extent the system can be expanded in order to accommodate a larger number of processors.

In multiprocessors, multiple processors communicate with one another and with the non-local (local to some other processor) memory as well as with commonly shared remote memory in the form of multiple physical banks using communication networks. Peripherals can also be attached using some other form of sharing. Many variations of this basic scheme are also possible. These organization models, however, may give rise to two primary points of contention, the shared memory and the shared communication network itself. Cache memory is often employed to reduce contention. In addition, each processor may have an additional private cache (local memory) to further speed up the operation. Here, shared memory does not mean that there is only a single centralized memory which is to be shared. Multiprocessors using shared memory give rise to three different models that differ in how the memory and peripheral resources are connected; shared, or distributed. Three such common models are found: UMA, NUMA, and no remote memory access (NORMA).

Symmetric Multiprocessors (SMPs); UMA Model: An SMP is a centralized shared memory machine in which each of n processors can uniformly access any of m memory modules at any point in time. The UMA model of multiprocessors can be divided into two categories: *symmetric* and *asymmetric*. When all the processors in the bus-based system share equal access to all IO devices through the same channels or different channels that provide paths to the same devices, the multiprocessor is called a SMP. When the SMP uses a crossbar switch as an interconnection network, replacing the common bus, then all the processors in the system are allowed to run IO-related interrupt service routines and other supervisor-related (kernel) programs. However, other forms of interconnection network in place of a crossbar switch can also be used. In the asymmetric category, not all but only one or a selective number of processors in the multiprocessor system are permitted to additionally handle all IO and supervisor-related (kernel) activities. Those are treated as *master processor(s)* that supervise the execution activities of the remaining processors, known as *attached processors*. However, all the processors, as usual, share uniform access to any of m memory modules.

The UMA model is easy to implement and suitable in general-purpose multi-user applications under time-sharing environments. However, there are several drawbacks of this model. The disparity in speed between the processors and the interconnection network consequently results in appreciable degradation in system performance. Interconnection networks with speeds comparable with the speed of the processor are possible but are costly to afford and equally complex to implement. Inclusion of caches at different levels (such as L1, L2, and L3) with more than one CPU improves the performance but may lead to data inconsistencies in different caches due to race conditions. The architecture should then add the needed *cache coherence protocol* to ensure consistencies in data that, in turn, may increase the cost of the architecture and also equally decrease the overall system performance. In addition, bus-based interconnection networks in the UMA model are not at all conducive to scalability, and the bus would also become an area of bottleneck when the number of CPUs is increased. However, use of a crossbar switch while would make it scalable, but only moderately, and the addition of CPUs requires proportionate expansion of the crossbar switch, whose cost may not vary linearly with the number of CPUs. Moreover, the delays caused by the interconnection network also gradually increase, which clearly indicates that the SMP is not suitable to reasonably scale beyond a small number of CPUs.

In the UMA model, parallel processes must communicate by software using some form of message passing by putting messages into a buffer in the shared memory or by using lock variables in the shared memory. The simplicity of this approach may, however, lead to a potential resource conflict, which can be resolved by injecting appropriate delays in the execution stages but, of course, at the price of slight degradation in system performance. Normally, interprocessor communication and synchronization are carried out using shared variables in the common memory.

Distributed Shared Memory Multiprocessors: NUMA Model: A comparatively attractive alternative form of a shared-memory multiprocessor system is a NUMA multiprocessor, where the shared memory is physically distributed (attached) directly as local memory to all processors so that each processor can sustain a high computation rate due to faster access to its *local memory*. A memory unit local to a processor can be globally accessed by other processors with an access time that varies by the location of the memory word. In this way, the collection of all local memory forms a global address space shared by all processors. NUMA machines are thus called *distributed shared-memory* (DSM) or *scalable shared-memory* architectures. The BBN TC-2000 is such a NUMA machine using a total of 512 Motorola 88100 RISC processors, with each local memory connected to its processor by a butterfly switch (Chakraborty, 2020). A slightly different implementation of a NUMA multiprocessor is with a physical remote (global) shared memory in addition to the existing usual distributed memory that is local to a processor but global to other processors. As a result, this scheme forms a memory hierarchy where each processor has the fastest access to its local memory. The next is its access to global memory, which are individually local to other processors. The slowest is access to remote large shared memory (Chakraborty, 2020).

Similar to SMP, the NUMA model architecture must also ensure coherence between caches attached to CPUs of a node as well as between existing non-local caches. Consequently, this requirement, as usual, may cause memory accesses to be slowed down and consume part of the bandwidth of interconnection networks, apart from increasing the cost of the architecture and also equally decreasing overall system performance.

Usually, the nodes in a NUMA (DSM) architecture are high-performance SMPs, each containing around four or eight CPUs to form a cluster. Due to the presence of a non-local communication network to connect these clusters, performance of such NUMA architecture is scalable when more nodes are added. The actual performance of a NUMA system, however, mostly depends on the non-local memory accesses made by the processes following the memory hierarchy during their execution. This issue falls within the domain of OS and will be addressed in the next section.

Multiprocessor systems are best suited for general-purpose multi-user applications where major thrust is on programmability. Shared-memory multiprocessors can form a very cost-effective approach, but latency tolerance while accessing remote memory is considered a major shortcoming. Lack of scalability is also a major limitation of such a system.

Brief details on this topic with figures are given on the Support Material at www.routledge.com/9781032467238.

9.10.2 Operating System Considerations

Whatever model is followed in the design of a multiprocessor system, it consists of multiple CPUs that ultimately provide high throughput as well as computation speed-up. Like uniprocessor OSs, a multiprocessor operating system similarly manages the available resources and augments the hardware functionality to provide an abstraction that facilitates program execution and user interaction. As usual, here also the system consists of three basic types of resources; processors, memory, and I/O devices, that need to be managed by their respective management modules. To extract the total strength that a multiprocessor system usually possesses to foster multiprocessing: the CPUs must be used effectively to realize parallelism in a way transparent to the application(s), and efficient creation and management of a large number of units of activity, such as processes or threads in a way, so as to enable them to interact in harmony. The latter aspect is important, since parallelism is often accomplished by splitting an application into mutually exclusive, separate, and individually executable tasks that can then be allocated to different processors to run simultaneously.

9.10.2.1 Processor Management

The management of processors in multiprocessor operating system is aimed mostly to satisfy all the critical issues described, apart from many of other objectives to fulfill, as well as to mainly ensure efficient use of the processors allocated to an application. All these together, especially the method of functioning while handling interrupts and responding to system calls, highlight the following major areas in processor management of multiprocessor operating systems that need to be clearly addressed. Those are: *kernel structure, interprocess synchronization, process scheduling, processor scheduling,* and *interprocessor synchronization of multiple processors.*

Transparency is otherwise related to process synchronization, and the realization of such transparency is relatively easy, because communication between different applications or different parts of an application uses the same primitives as those in multitasking uniprocessor operating systems. The only difference is that all communication here is to be done by manipulating data at shared memory locations and all are to do is to protect those data from simultaneous access to synchronize processes. Protection of these data for the sake of process synchronization, however, can be implemented through the use of two important (and of course equivalent) primitives: *semaphores* and *monitors.*

9.10.2.1.1 Kernel Structure

The presence of multiple CPUs may involve all the CPUs in a competition to execute kernel code almost simultaneously. The kernel structure would be such that it should enable multiple CPUs to execute kernel code concurrently as much as possible to realize each one's desired kernel functions. Multiprocessor operating systems, at the time of their inception, functioned mainly in **master–slave** mode in which one CPU was the master, which was entrusted only with executing all the kernel codes on behalf of the slave CPUs as required by them according to the predefined policy, and the related outcomes were then communicated to the respective slave CPUs through interprocessor interrupts (IPIs). This form of OS design naturally caused a bottleneck at the master CPU's end while satisfying various requirements of the slave CPUs happening almost simultaneously. To alleviate this problem, the kernel was then restructured in a different way so that many CPUs can execute the kernel code on their own, almost in parallel.

- **UMA kernel on SMP:** The fundamental requirement of the operating system driving an SMP architecture suggests that any CPU present in the system is permitted to execute OS kernel code at any instant, and different CPUs can execute OS code almost in parallel or at different times. Temporarily, the processor that executes the OS code has a special role and acts as a master in the sense that it schedules the work of others. The OS is, however, not bound to any specific processor; it floats from one processor to another. Hence, symmetric organization is sometimes called *floating master.* The operating system here is more or less a single, large critical section and is mostly monolithic; very little of its code, if any, is executed in parallel. This, in turn, requires that there be sufficient provision for any CPU to equally communicate with the other CPUs in the system, and any CPU should be able to initiate an I/O operation of its own on any device in the system at any point in time. Otherwise, if only one or just a few CPUs have access to I/O devices, the system becomes asymmetric. To satisfy the condition that each CPU be able to carry out its own I/O operation, the interconnection network that connects the CPUs in the system must provide some arrangements to connect the I/O also so that the I/O interrupts are directed to the respective CPU that initiated the I/O operation or to some other processor in the system that is kept dedicated to this purpose.

To fulfill the requirement for communication between the CPUs, the kernel reserves an area in its memory known as communication area (similar to uniprocessor architecture when the CPU communicates with a separate I/O processor [Chakraborty, 2020]). Whenever a CPU C_1 intends to communicate with another CPU C_2, it places needed information in C_2's communication area and issues an IPI in C_2. The processor C_2 then picks up this information from its own communication area and acts on it accordingly.

As the SMP kernel can be accessed and shared by many CPUs in the system at any point in time, the OS code should be *reentrant* (see Section 5.8.1.2.4). Some parallelism may be introduced at the OS level by identifying routines that can access shared data structures concurrently and by protecting them with the appropriate interlocks. Since all communication is to be done by manipulating data at shared memory locations (communication area), it is thus essential to ensure mutual exclusion over these kernel data structures so as to protect those data from simultaneous access to synchronize processes. This can be accomplished with the use of semaphores, possibly with *counting semaphores*, but especially with *binary semaphores* (see Section 4.2.1.4.9), sometimes referred to as **mutex locks (variables)**, or this can be achieved with the use of **monitors** to carry out lock and unlock operations. The mutex lock can only take on the values 0 and 1. Locking a mutex will succeed only if the mutex is 1; otherwise the calling process will be blocked. Similarly, unlocking a mutex means setting its value to 1 unless some waiting process could be unblocked. The semaphore operation itself also must be **atomic**, meaning that once a semaphore operation has started, no other process can access the semaphore until the ongoing operation is completed (or until a process blocks).

The number of locks to be used in the system to enforce needed mutual exclusion is a vital design issue, since it directly affects the performance of the system. If a single lock is used to control access of all kernel data structures, then at any instant, only one processor can be allowed to use the data structures. If separate locks are provided to control individual data structures, then many processors could access different data structures in parallel, thereby obviously increasing system performance. However, the use of many locks may invite a situation of deadlock when a processor attempts to access more than one data structure. Necessary arrangements should thus be made to ensure that such deadlocks do not arise.

An SMP kernel is a natural first step in OS implementation and relatively easy to realize. It is equally easy to port an existing uniprocessor operating system, such as UNIX, to a shared-memory UMA multiprocessor. The shared memory contains all of the resident OS code and data structures. The largely monolithic UNIX kernel may then be executed by different processors at different times, and process migration is almost trivial if the state is saved in shared memory. Simultaneous (parallel) executions of different applications is quite easy, and can be achieved by maintaining a queue of ready processes in shared memory. Processor allocation then consists only of assigning the first ready process to the first available processor unless either all processors are busy or the ready queue of the processes is emptied. In this way, each processor, whenever available, fetches the next work item from the queue. Management of such shared queues in multiprocessors is, however, a different area, and precisely a subject matter of processor synchronization which will be discussed next.

Further improvement in the performance of the operating system can be realized if the operating system is designed and developed by organizing it as a set of cooperating threads, and subsequent scheduling of such threads and synchronization of them using the proper mechanisms, such as semaphores or messages, as already discussed, can be carried out, In this environment, threads can be used to exploit true parallelism in an application. If the various threads of an application can be made to run simultaneously on separate processors, potential parallelism in the OS can be attained. Consequently, this will not only yield dramatic gains in performance but at the same time enable the OS to be ported to different equivalent hardware platforms, including tightly coupled and loosely coupled.

One of the distinct advantages of SMP is that it can continue its normal operation, even in the event of certain failures of some CPUs, but, of course, affecting only with a graceful degradation in the performance of the system. Failure of a processor in most situations is not so severe to the operation of other processors present in the system if it is not executing the kernel code at the time of failure. At best, only the processes using the service of the failed processor would be affected, and the other processes henceforth would be barred from getting the service of the failed processor, which may affect the total performance of the entire system only to some extent.

- **NUMA kernel with DSM:** The NUMA scheme forms a memory hierarchy where each CPU has the fastest access to its local memory. The next is access to global memories which are individually local to other CPUs. The slowest is access to remote shared memory. The actual performance of a NUMA system thus mainly depends on non-local memory accesses made by the processes following the memory hierarchy during their execution. That is why every node in the system must be given its own kernel that can control the processes in local memory of the CPUs within the node. This ensures that processes consume relatively less time in memory accesses, thereby yielding better performance, since most of their accesses are only to local memory.

Providing a *separate kernel* to each node in the system exhibits several advantages. The entire system is then divided into several domains, and there is a separate dedicated kernel that administers each such domain. The kernel in an individual node should always schedule a process on its own CPU. This approach is expected to yield better system performance, since it ensures a high hit ratio in the individual CPU's own (L1) cache. Similarly, a high hit ratio in the L3 cache (the cache within the cluster of a group of CPUs forming a node) could also be obtained if the memory is allocated to a process within a single local memory unit.

The kernel of a node always attempts to allocate memory to all processes of a specific application in the same memory unit and assigns those to the same set of a few CPUs for their execution. This idea forms the notion of an *application region* that usually consists of a resource partition and the executing kernel code. The resource partition contains one or more CPUs, some local memory units and a few available I/O devices. The kernel of the application region executes processes of only one application. In this way, the kernel can optimize the performance of application execution through willful scheduling and high cache-hit ratios with no interference from the processes of other applications. Most of the operating systems developed for the NUMA model exploit this approach or an equivalent one.

The introduction of a separate kernel concept for a node in NUMA architecture or the inclusion of the application region model can equally cause some disadvantages. The separate kernel approach suffers from several inherent problems associated with such types of partitioning that cause underutilization of resources, because resources remaining idle belonging to one partition cannot be used by processes of other partitions. Similarly, the application region concept affects reliability because failure of resource(s) in one partition may cause delays in processing or may even require abnormal termination or require the support of resources belonging to other partitions that are not possible to provide immediately to compensate for the loss due to such failure. In addition, non-local memory may become a region of bottleneck and access to them become more complex, since they are used by the domains of more than one kernel.

9.10.2.1.2 *Process Synchronization*

In multiprocessor systems, synchronization and communication aspects prevail in two different areas: processor–processor (interprocessor) and process–process (interprocess). In tightly coupled multiprocessors, shared memory is fundamental for interprocessor communications and synchronization, but in loosely coupled systems, message–passing is usually the primary mechanism for both interprocessor synchronization and communications. Multiprocessor operating systems often use a different basic approach to synchronize process executions. Since many CPUs exist in the system, it is not always necessary to preempt a process to block it for the sake of process synchronization. Multiple CPUs should be used in such a way as to reduce the overhead due to switching between processes to attain synchronization, thereby minimizing synchronization delays. Use of multiple

CPUs in a multiprocessor system can reduce the synchronization delay that usually happens with traditional uniprocessor systems in the form of *busy waiting* (to let a process loop until the synchronization condition is met) and blocking of a process (wait and signal).

In a multiprocessor system, processes can run in parallel on different CPUs. At the time of synchronization, it is sometimes preferable to let a process loop rather than blocking it if the CPU overhead for blocking the process and scheduling another process, followed by activating the blocked process and rescheduling it again, exceeds the amount of time for which the process would loop. In short, only when there is a reasonable expectation under certain conditions that the busy–wait will be of relatively shorter duration, and is thus preferred; since the shared resources for which the looping (busy–waiting) begins may be quickly released by processes executing on other CPUs or the time needed by the other CPU to execute its critical section is comparatively quite small. This situation arises if a process looping for entry to a critical section and the process holding the critical section are scheduled almost in parallel.

Additional details on process synchronization are given on the Support Material at www. routledge.com/9781032467238.

Implementation of *process synchronization* (concurrency control) also follows a similar course of action as a uniprocessor system, which uses *lock variables* or *synchronization lock*, or simply *lock*, to control the entry of processes into critical sections or execute indivisible (atomic) signaling operations, that is, by setting a lock. If the lock variable is *closed*, the requesting process must wait until the value of the lock variable is changed to *open* and entry is allowed. However, the presence of multiple CPUs and the safe use of locks may allow many processes to execute in parallel, which may give rise to another issue in process synchronization as to what type of locks and how many such locks there are for smooth operation and better performance of the system. This feature is sometimes related to what is known as the *scalability* of a lock, which implies that the execution of an application using the lock would not be dependent on the number of processes present in the application and the number of CPUs available in the system. Many other important issues are also associated with such locks; one such feature is whether a CPU can be allowed to service interrupts when a process already scheduled to run on it is engaged in trying to set (indivisible operation) a lock.

Many types of **synchronization locks** are in use. Three such locks are introduced here, as illustrated in Figure 9.6. Let us assume that a process P_i is being executed on CPU C_k and a lock L is used to control the entry of processes into a critical section. When the lock is set, it is indicated by a rectangular box with a × inside. This is depicted in Figure 9.6(a). Similarly, when a process is in a blocked state, it is indicated by a circle with a × inside, as shown in Figure 9.6(b).

- **Queued lock:** The traditional lock used in uniprocessor systems for process synchronization is known as a *queued lock*. When a process P_i executing on CPU C_k attempts to enter a critical section, the operating system performs certain actions on the corresponding lock L. The Lock L is tested. If it is available (not set), the kernel sets the lock and allows process P_i to enter the critical section to perform its execution. If the lock is not available (already set by other process), process P_i is preempted, and its request for the lock is recorded in a queue (wait and signal mechanism). Some other process is then scheduled by OS on CPU C_k for execution. Since the action of this lock is to put the processes in a queue that is kept waiting, the lock is called a *queued lock*.

Figure 9.6(b) shows that process P_i is blocked for non-availability of the lock, its *id* is recorded in the queue of lock L, and some other process P_x is then scheduled to run on C_k. When the process that is using the lock completes its execution in the critical section, the lock is released and some other process lying in L's queue will be awarded with the lock and be activated. The entire activity is supervised and carried out by the kernel. A semaphore can be used to implement a queued lock in a multiprocessor system. The semaphore is declared as a shared variable and is updated as required by the semaphore definition with the aid of instructions to implement *wait and signal* mechanism.

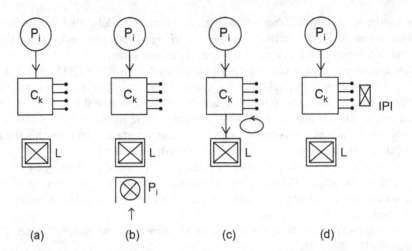

FIGURE 9.6 A schematic graphical representation of queued, spin, and sleep locks used in multiprocessor system to realize process synchronization.

The average length of the queue of blocked processes for a lock determines whether the solution is scalable. If the processes do not require locks very often, the length of the queue is relatively small and is usually limited by a constant value, say, m, so increasing the number of CPUs or the processes in the system in this situation will not affect (increase) the average delay in gaining access to the lock. This solution is said to be *scalable*. But when processes require locks very often, the length of the queue may be relatively large and will become proportional to the number of processes present in the system. The solution in this situation is said to be *not scalable*.

- **Spin lock:** While a queued lock provokes a *wait and signal* mechanism, the spin lock is quite different and supports *busy waiting*, as already observed in traditional uniprocessor operating systems. When a process P_i attempts to acquire a lock and is unsuccessful to set it, because it is already set by another process, the process P_i will not be preempted to relinquish the control of the CPU on which it is executing. Instead, it keeps continuously checking the lock with repeated attempts to see whether it is free until it succeeds. In this way, the CPU is not doing any productive work but remains busy with testing the lock continually, moving around a loop spinning over the lock. That is why such a lock is called a *spin lock*. This is depicted in Figure 9.6(c) in which P_i is not relinquishing control of CPU C_k, which now spins on lock L, as shown by an arrow. **MontaVista Linux Professional Edition**, a derivative of the Linux 2.4 kernel with a full preemptive scheduler, has a fine-grained locking mechanism inside the SMP kernel for improved scalability. The design of this kernel exploits these services that allow user tasks to run concurrently as separate kernel-mode threads on different processors. Threads in **Windows** running on SMP use spin locks to implement mutual exclusion when accessing kernel data structures. To guarantee that kernel data structures do not remain locked for a prolonged period of time, the kernel never preempts a thread holding a spin lock if some other thread tries to acquire the spin lock. This way, the thread holding the lock can finish its critical section and release the lock at the earliest possible time.
- **TSL instruction:** The atomic implementation of a test-and-set-lock instruction with the aid of the indivisible memory read-modify-write (RMW) cycles, as introduced in uniprocessor synchronization, using a spin lock mechanism can extend its TS functionality to shared-memory multiprocessors. A semaphore can be implemented for this purpose in a multiprocessor system by declaring it as a shared variable and updating it as required by the semaphore definition with the aid of a test-and-set instruction.

The use of spin lock in many situations is disfavored for creating severe degradation in system performance, mainly for keeping the CPU engaged with no productive work and at the same time denying the other deserving processes to get its service. Besides, use of spin lock often creates traffic on memory bus and consumes the bandwidth of the links that connects processors to shared memory. In addition, several processors while spinning on a lock can cause contention at the memory module containing the semaphore variable, and thus impair access by other processors to the enclosing memory bank. In multiprocessor systems, multiple caches are often used for the sake of performance improvement. Use of spin locks in such systems can result in increased bus traffic needed to maintain consistency among copies of the semaphore variable that reside in individual caches of the competing processors. Depending on the type of the cache–coherence scheme being used, additional cache–related problems may grow that consequently may further cause to badly affect the system performance.

The use of spin locks in NUMA systems may sometimes exhibit a critical situation commonly known as *lock starvation*. In this situation, a lock might be denied for a considerable duration of time, possibly indefinitely. Assume that a process P_i attempts to set a lock L residing in its non-local memory. Let two other processes P_k and P_m which exist in the same node as the lock also attempt to set it. Since access to local memory is much faster than access to non-local memory, processes P_k and P_m spin much faster on the lock than process P_i does. Hence, they will always get an opportunity to set the lock before P_i. If they repeatedly set and use the lock, P_i may not be able to get its turn. The situation may become worse if many other processes arrive by this time that are local to the lock; process P_i will then be even further delayed in getting its turn to gain access to the lock, thereby waiting for a considerable duration of time and facing acute starvation. To avoid such starvation, many effective schemes have been proposed, the details of which are outside the scope of our discussion.

However, the use of spin locks has some advantages in certain situations. When the number of processes does not exceed the number of CPUs present in the system, there is no justification and simply unnecessary to preempt a process, rather it is preferred to allow the CPU to spin on the lock until it succeeds. In addition, it is sometimes profitable to let a process loop rather than blocking it, as already discussed earlier in this section. Preemption in this situation is simply counter-productive.

Real-time applications, on other hand, however, prefer the use of spin locks to synchronize processes. The reason is that while a CPU spinning on a lock can handle incoming interrupts, and the process executing on this CPU can equally handle signals. This feature is essentially important in real-time environments in which processing of interrupts and signals are highly time-critical, and any delay in this regard may miss the deadline. However, as spin locks often generate traffic on the memory bus or across the network while the CPU continues spinning on the lock, so it is considered not scalable.

- **Sleep lock:** When a process P_i attempts to acquire a sleep lock which is already set by another process, the CPU associated with process P_i is not released but is put in an unusual state called a *sleep state*. In this state, the CPU neither executes any instructions nor responds to any interrupts except interprocessor interrupts (IPIs). The CPU simply waits for the release of the lock to be reported by the kernel and hence generates no additional traffic on the memory bus or across the network. This is illustrated in Figure 9.6(d) with an × mark against all interrupts except IPIs. Sleep locks are sometimes preferred when the memory or network traffic is already high.

The CPU that sets the lock and later releases it has the responsibility to send IPIs to all the CPUs that are sleeping on the lock. This obligation, in turn, involves increasing administrative overhead, since they require a context switch and execution of associated kernel code to generate IPIs as well as related servicing of the IPIs. The sleep lock, however, yields poor performance if there is heavy contention for a lock, but the performance is found moderately good, if the traffic density over the lock is comparatively low. The use of sleep locks may be hazardous in real-time applications, since the response time may exceed the specified deadline.

- **Adaptive lock (scheduling-based synchronization):** Use of this lock is effective only when the processes involved for synchronization are scheduled to run in parallel. This type of lock is used by **Solaris operating systems** for SUN systems. A process waiting to gain access to the lock spins on it if the holder of the lock is scheduled to run in parallel (i.e. to be in the running state); otherwise the waiting process is preempted and is queued, as is done in queued locks. The kernel implements this lock by checking whether the holder of the lock is currently in the running state.

Each and every type of lock, as discussed in process synchronization, provides certain advantages in some situations and equally creates some problems in other situations. Additional hardware components can be used in the system architecture to avoid the performance problems caused by different types of locks while retaining all the advantages they usually offer.

9.10.2.1.3   Additional Hardware Support

Some systems use special hardware to alleviate the performance problems created by locks while in use to synchronize processes. One such is the use of a system link and interface controller (SLIC) chip that provides a special SLIC bus dedicated to the purpose of synchronization of processes.

A SLIC essentially consists of a special 64-bit register in each CPU present in the system. These registers associated with different CPUs are connected by the SLIC bus, as shown in Figure 9.7. Each bit in the register represents a spin lock; hence, SLIC can support 64 such locks. When a CPU C_k attempts to set a lock L_m, it tries to set the corresponding bit, say, b_m, in its special register. If the bit is found to already be set by another CPU, the requesting CPU faces failure and starts spinning on this lock, that is, on bit b_m of its special register, until it succeeds. On the other hand, if the bit is not set (i.e. available), the requesting CPU attempts to set it and communicates its intention to all other CPUs over the SLIC bus. If no other CPU is interested in setting the same bit at the same time, the lock is eventually awarded to the CPU C_k, and bit b_m of the special register of each CPU is set. CPU C_k is now allowed to enter the critical section to continue its execution. After completion, CPU C_k will release the lock, bit b_m of the special register of each CPU will be reset to enable the other CPUs (waiting processes) to gain the lock. If two or more CPUs now attempt to set the same lock

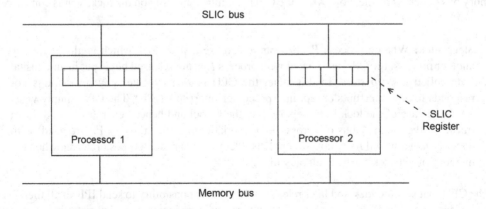

FIGURE 9.7   A representative illustration of SLIC bus used as an additional hardware support in multiprocessor system to implement process synchronization.

simultaneously, an arbitration mechanism will be used by the hardware to select one of the CPUs to award the lock to. SLIC has been successfully implemented in the **Sequent Balance system**.

Use of the SLIC approach provides several **advantages**: First, the presence of a dedicated special synchronization SLIC bus relieves the memory bus from carrying additional load, thereby reducing congestion of traffic on it. Second, the use of a spin lock rather than a sleep lock helps avoid the need of generating and subsequently servicing IPIs, thereby alleviating the severity of additional administrative overhead and relieving the system from significant performance degradation. Last but not least, the CPU here spins on a local lock. Since access to local memory is always much faster than access to non-local memory, it improves system performance and at the same time does not generate any additional memory or network traffic.

9.10.2.1.4   Compare-and-Swap Instruction

Instead of using a lock mechanism for the synchronization of processes, the compare-and-swap (CS) instruction can be exploited using the indivisible read-modify-write memory cycle that provides a basis for optimistic concurrency control in multiprocessors. Apart from the normal use of CS instruction to update a shared variable without locking, another common use of it is to add and remove items from lists, which is equivalent to enqueue and dequeue operations on a shared queue. The shared lists and queues that are commonly used, for example, include semaphore queues, shared-resource queues, mailboxes, etc.

The creation of shared lists and queues, especially their management, is an important aspect and a frequently executed task in multiprocessor operating systems. In shared-memory systems, a list of ready processes is usually maintained in shared memory as part of a common scheduling technique that can be used by idle processors to find a process for execution. Several types of operations on such shared lists and queues, however, exist that can be adopted to manage and willfully manipulate them. In addition, access to shared queues needs to be controlled so that inconsistent manipulation by concurrent activities initiated by different processors can be prevented. Also, the CS instruction is suitable for optimistic concurrency control in a class of applications such as updating a shared variable and concurrent enqueue and dequeue operations, and thus is considered to offer a good mechanism for queue manipulation without the use of any locks.

9.10.2.1.5   Processor/Process Scheduling

Multiprocessor, as being different from uniprocessor, containing many processors, however, raises several other issues while scheduling function is carried out. In most conventional multiprocessor systems, processes are not dedicated to specific processors. Instead, there is a single queue of processes for all processors, or if some sort of priority scheme is used, there can be multiple queues based on priority; all are eventually fed into the common pool of processors. Thus, any process can be executed on any CPU in the multiprocessor system. However, many issues come up when scheduling a process or a processor that often influence system performance to a great extent. Processor allocation, in fact, may become a considerable problem in massively parallel systems. The appropriate choice of a particular processor for executing a specific process can remarkably improve the performance of process execution. Similarly, willful selection of a set of related processes that often synchronize and communicate regularly with one another can improve the execution performance if can be scheduled intelligently regarding as to *when* and *how* these processes will be executed. Some of the issues involved in formulating such policies and making the subsequent necessary decisions are as follows:

- **Processor scheduling (allocation of processing resources):** One way of keeping track of a large number of processes or threads (schedulable entities) is to organize them in a logical hierarchy. Some of the processors in the system can be designated as managers, while the others are simply workers. A manager is dedicated to keep track of the state and activity of a collection of worker processors. Managers themselves can also be organized in a hierarchy extending upward by assigning second-level managers who can oversee groups of first-level managers, and so forth. For the sake of reliability, the top level of such a hierarchy can be a group of processor nodes rather than a single node, because failure of a single node could lead to a fatal situation that may end in total collapse of the system. This arrangement when implemented results in a system called **wave scheduling**.

Under this arrangement, individual processors are dedicated to only one task at a time. Each manager keeps track of the number of its available workers. A work request can be submitted to a manager at any level of the hierarchy. Upon receiving a work request calling for R processor, the respective manager (processor) must secure R or more processors, since some of them may fail. If the selected manager does not find a sufficient number of worker processors, it calls on its manager at the next higher level for help. This course of action continues until the request is satisfied (i.e. a sufficient number of available processors is secured) or the top of the hierarchy is reached. If the request cannot be filled even after reaching the top level, the request may be set aside for the time being pending availability of the required amount of resources.

Such a hierarchical allocation of processors nicely fits a robust implementation, and scales well due to the relatively limited amount of generated traffic. The fault tolerance of both the master and worker processors is found to attain the desired level modestly. The work of a failed master can be assigned to one of its siblings, to one of its subordinates, or even to another processor as assigned by its superior. Failure of a processor residing at the top of the hierarchy can likewise be negotiated by the selection (election) of a suitable successor. Similarly, the failure of a worker processor would not cause any major hazards, since it can be handled by migrating its work to some other processor (node) and can then be resumed in a suitable manner.

In spite of having several advantages, the wave scheduling, exhibits some *practical difficulties* while implemented. First of all, the manager must always be equipped with the latest status of its available workforce when attempting to allocate processors. This requires additional overhead each time in the calculation of estimates, and, moreover, use of estimates may lead to inefficiencies if they are too conservative or to allocation failures if they are too optimistic. Moreover, since multiple allocation requests arrive almost simultaneously and granting activity may occur at nearly the same time, the resources as estimated to be available may turn out to be snatched by another party when a processor allocation is actually about to occur.

- **Scheduling of processes:** As already mentioned, scheduling of processes is often influenced by the **selection of CPU** on which a scheduled process is to be executed. In general, when a process P_k is executed on a CPU C_i, some of its address space is obviously available for the L1 cache of CPU C_i. When this CPU is switched to execute another process, some of the contents of L1 cache related to process P_k are overwritten by parts of the address space of the new process; however, some parts of process P_k's address space may still survive in the L1 cache of CPU C_i over a certain duration of time. A process is said to have an **affinity** for a CPU if it has a residual address space in the cache of the CPU even when it is not running on the CPU. A process with an affinity to a specific CPU exhibits a higher hit ratio than running on a CPU for which it does not have any affinity. Scheduling of processes when carried out based on affinity usually provides faster execution of processes as well as less traffic on the memory bus. However, affinity-based scheduling often affects load balancing across CPUs, since processes are attached to specific CPUs. Moreover, affinity-based scheduling in many operating systems may sometimes result in *scheduling anomalies*, which refers to the situation when a higher-priority process remains set aside and is not in the running state (possibly in a ready state), even though a lower-priority process has been scheduled for execution. This has been observed, especially in **Windows** system. However, scheduling anomalies may be rectified by shuffling processes between CPUs, but it ultimately carries a high administrative scheduling overhead and becomes even more significant in systems with a large number of CPUs. That is why some operating systems do not favor a process shuffling approach to mitigating scheduling anomalies. These anomalies may also be observed in some SMPs when each individual CPU is given the power to execute the kernel code independently so as to avoid bottlenecks in kernel code execution and to yield improved performance.

Process scheduling often includes scheduling of different processes of a specific application concurrently on different CPUs to achieve computation speed-up exploiting the principle of parallelism. Synchronization and communication among these processes then becomes a vital consideration that influences in deciding scheduling policy, since it directly affects the performance of a system. While synchronization of these processes mostly needs the service of a spin lock when several processes of an application are scheduled on different CPUs (co-scheduling), communication among these processes usually employs the message passing technique. Again, the way this technique will be implemented should be chosen very carefully; otherwise it may sometimes thwart the co-scheduling itself to operate. However, different approaches are used by different operating systems in this regard, and the kernel is then designed in such a way so that it can make appropriate decisions to effectively implement co-scheduling.

9.10.2.1.6   Thread Scheduling

The concept of threads in uniprocessor systems was introduced mainly to avoid relatively costly process-switch overhead as well as to overlap I/O operation with processing. While thread switching is certainly less costly, the actual strength of the thread concept is possibly best utilized when implemented in multiprocessor system that essentially spreads a different flavor. In fact, threads of an application when executed in a multiprocessor system offer true parallelism. When threads are used, each application is implemented as a separate process, and its concurrent portions are coded as separate threads within the enclosing process. Threads belonging to a single process share the memory and all other resources acquired by the process. Some operating systems often provide specialized calls for efficient *synchronization* of threads that belong to the same process. *Communication* among threads of the same process, however, is normally not a critical issue, since threads share common memory. If various threads of a specific application can be run simultaneously on separate processors, potential parallelism can be achieved that eventually gives rise to significant gains in performance. Consequently, it becomes evident that scheduling of threads is an important issue to facilitate multiprocessing. With the aid of adequate information about processes and threads, the scheduler can attempt to co-schedule the related threads and thereby can reduce the probability of performance degradation caused by out-of-phase scheduling of closely related parties. As thread scheduling becomes a sensitive issue, it is thus obvious that a little alteration in management of threads and related scheduling can cause a significant impact on the performance as a whole. However, many different approaches with regard to scheduling of threads and related assignment of processors have been proposed. Generalization of them essentially reveals the following:

1. Sharing loads

As already mentioned, processes in multiprocessor system are not assigned to a specific processor. Simultaneous (parallel) executions of different threads is quite easy and can be achieved by maintaining a queue of ready threads. Processor allocation is then simply a matter of assigning the first ready thread to the first available processor unless either all processors are busy or the ready queue of the threads is emptied. In this way, each processor, whenever available, fetches the next work item from the queue. This strategy is known as **load sharing** and is distinguished from the load balancing scheme in which the work is allocated for a relatively longer duration of time (a more permanent manner). Load sharing is a natural choice and possibly the most fundamental approach in which the existing load is distributed almost evenly across the processors, thereby offering several **advantages**. Some of them are:

- It ensures that no processors remain idle when executable work is present in the system.
- No additional scheduler is needed by the operating system to handle all the processors. The existing scheduler routine is simple enough that it can be run only on the available processor to choose the next thread to execute.
- The arrangement and management of global queues of threads do not require any additional mechanism. It can be treated as if it is running on uniprocessor system and hence can be readily implemented along the lines of an existing proven mechanism, such as priority-based execution history (SJF), etc. as used in uniprocessor operating systems.

Similar to the strategies employed in process scheduling, as discussed in Chapter 4, there are different types of thread scheduling almost in the same line, out of which three types of thread scheduling algorithms are of common interest. Those are:

- **First Come First Served (FCFS):** When a process arrives, all of its threads are placed consecutively at the end of the ready queue of the threads. When a processor is available, the thread at the front of the ready queue is assigned to the processor for execution until it is completed or blocked.
- **Smallest Number of Threads First (SNTF):** This concept is similar to SJF in process scheduling. Here, the threads of the jobs with the smallest number of unscheduled threads will be given highest priority and hence are placed at the front of the ready queue. These threads are then scheduled for execution until they are completed or blocked. Jobs with equal priority will then be placed in the queue according to their time of arrival (FCFS).
- **Preemptive SNTF (PSNTF):** This one is almost similar to the last. Here, also the threads of the jobs with the smallest number of unscheduled threads will also be given the highest priority and are placed at the front of the ready queue to be scheduled for execution. The only exception here is that the arrival of a new job with a smaller number of threads than an executing job will preempt the executing thread of the currently running job, and the execution of the threads of the newly arrived job will then be started until it is completed or blocked.

Each of the strategies, as usual, has several merits and certain drawbacks. However, the FCFS strategy is perhaps superior to the other two when a load-sharing approach is employed over a large number of jobs with a diverse spectrum of characteristics. However, the load-sharing approach also suffers from several **disadvantages**. Those are mainly:

- Since the single shared ready queue is accessed by all processors and may be accessed by more than one processor at the same time, a bottleneck may be created at that end; hence, some additional mechanism is needed to ensure mutual exclusion. With a small number of processors in the computer system, this problem is not noticeable. However, with multiprocessors with a large number of processors, this problem truly persists and may be acute in some situations.
- Thread switching leads to a small increase in overhead, but in totality it cannot be ignored. Moreover, the threads being preempted are less likely to be scheduled once again on the same processor when it resumes its execution. Consequently, caching becomes less efficient if each processor is equipped with a local cache, and the potential of affinity-based scheduling cannot be then utilized.
- Since the load-sharing approach uses a central global queue of threads of all the ready processes, and those are usually scheduled at different times, likely to different processors as and when those processors are available, it is highly probable that all of the

threads of a specific program will be assigned to different processors at the same time. As a result, a program with a high degree of coordination among its threads may not be executed in the desired order at an appropriate time. This requires additional communication overhead and also the cost of extra process switches that may eventually affect the overall performance adversely.

In spite of having a lot of disadvantages, its potential advantages, however, legitimately outweigh them, and that is why this approach is favored as one of the most commonly used schemes in contemporary multiprocessor systems. A further refinement of the load-sharing technique has been made to alleviate some of its potential disadvantages to effectively fit it into the environment. Those modifications have been implemented in the **Mach operating system** developed at Carnegie Mellon University using a platform of an SMP kernel structure.

For brief details on thread-processor scheduling in Mach OS, see the Support Material at www. routledge.com/9781032467238.

2. Gang scheduling

This strategy is derived based on the traditional (it predates the use of threads) concept in which a set of processes is scheduled to run simultaneously on a set of processors, giving rise to the concept of *group scheduling* that exhibits several advantages. Out of many, a few notable ones are:

- It is apparent that while a single action includes many processors and processes at one shot, scheduling overhead is naturally reduced since it avoids individual scheduling of those processors and the processes that would otherwise yield substantial scheduling overhead.
- It helps execute closely related processes in parallel on different processors, which consequently may reduce blocking required at the time of synchronization, thereby avoiding costly process switching that ultimately improves the performance as a whole.

A similar approach is found in massively parallel processing (MPP) systems (Chakraborty, 2020), such as the connection machine (CM*) model that uses a co-scheduling approach in which scheduling a related set of *tasks* called a *task force* is carried out. Here, the amount of work in individual elements of a task force is often quite small and hence bears a close resemblance to the concept of a thread.

Following the concept of group scheduling on processes as well as co-scheduling on tasks, a **gang scheduling** is applied to a set of related **threads**, which can be simultaneously scheduled on a set of processors to run on a one-to-one basis. Gang scheduling usually provides medium-grained to even fine-grained parallelism, and that is why it is highly conducive to parallel processing, even with those applications which are not so performance sensitive. As gang scheduling establishes its importance in the multiprocessor environment, it has been widely implemented on a variety of multiprocessor operating systems running on different hardware platforms. However, gang scheduling can also be used to improve the performance of even a single application by simultaneously scheduling cooperative threads of the process, thereby reducing the needed number of process switches. It also saves time while resources (such as files) are allocated, since multiple willing threads can be scheduled simultaneously on the same resource without using a locking mechanism, thereby avoiding related administrative overhead.

Instead of uniformly distributing the total processing power available in the system among ready applications, gang scheduling attempts to use judicious distribution of processors on the existing applications in the system with the intention of effective utilization of processing resources. An efficient scheduling mechanism is then employed that would schedule the application offering a proportionate amount of time using time slicing and the needed processing resource for its execution that is weighted by the number of threads present in the application. This strategy will definitely reduce processor waste caused by remaining idle most of the time.

Gang scheduling yields good performance if used intelligently. It sometimes requires prior knowledge of job characteristics for its proper handling. This refers to how many processors to assign to a program at a given time to make acceptable progress. Consequently, gang scheduling in some specific forms is observed to be superior to a load sharing approach in general.

3. Assignment of dedicated processors

This strategy is just the reverse of the load-sharing scheme and close to the gang scheduling scheme. Here, each program is allocated a number of processors equal to the number of threads in the program, and they are kept dedicated for the entire duration of the program execution. The scheduling of threads here is straightaway implicit, simply defined by the assignment of threads to processors. When the program is completed or terminated, all the processors are deallocated and return to the pool of processors for subsequent use by other programs. It is evident that this approach appears to suffer from severe drawbacks as far as processor utilization is concerned. First, there is no scope of multiprogramming on any of the processors, thereby restricting the other processes to share the processors if available during the lifetime of the executing program. Second, if the running thread of an application is somehow blocked, maybe due to I/O waiting or for the sake of synchronization with another thread, then the costly processor dedicated to that particular thread will simply remain idle, yielding no productive output. However, counterarguments directly in favor of this approach in terms of two distinct advantages can also be made:

- Since the processors are dedicated to different threads during the entire tenure of program execution, there is no need to have any process switch that, in turn, speeds up the execution and thereby definitely improves the performance as a whole.
- Systems having large number of processors in which cost of the processors is appreciably small compared to the total cost of the system; utilization of processors and processor–time wastage is usually considered not a dominant parameter in evaluating performance or efficiency of such a system. In fact, highly parallel application having tight coordination among threads will then be properly fitted in such system following the stated approach and be profitably effective for its execution.

A dedicated processor assignment strategy works efficiently and processor resources are used effectively if the number of active threads of an application could be made limited or even kept lower than the number of processors available in the system. Furthermore, the higher the number of threads, the worse the performance, because there exists a high possibility of frequent thread preemption and subsequent rescheduling, and also due to many other reasons, that eventually makes the entire system inefficient.

The scheduling issues of both the gang scheduling approach and assignment of dedicated processors ultimately culminate in the subject matter of processor allocation. The problem relating to processor allocation in multiprocessors is very similar to memory management on a uniprocessor rather than scheduling issues on a uniprocessor. The issue now finally converges as to how many processors are to be assigned to a program at any given instant to make execution efficient, which is analogous to how many page frames to allocate to a given process for its smooth execution. It has thus been proposed to define a term, **activity working set**, analogous to *virtual memory working set*, that indicates the minimum number of activities (threads) which must be simultaneously scheduled on processors for the application to reach a desired level of progress. Similar to memory-management schemes, if all of the elements of an *activity working set* cannot be simultaneously scheduled on respective processors, it may give rise to a vulnerable situation, what is known as *processor thrashing*. This normally happens when the execution of some threads are required and thus scheduled, but induces de-scheduling of other threads whose services may soon be needed. Another situation what is commonly called *processor fragmentation also* encompasses processor scheduling issues. This occurs when some processors are allocated while a few others are left over. The leftover processors are neither sufficient in number, nor are they properly organized to fulfill the requirements of the waiting processes for execution. As a result, a good amount of processor resources are simply left idle. Both of these scheduling strategies under discussion suffer from many such drawbacks and thus require to properly address all these issues in order to avoid the problems created by them.

4. Dynamic scheduling

This permits the number of threads in a process to be altered dynamically during the tenure of the execution of the process so that the operating system can adjust the load for the sake of improvement in processor utilization.

The scheduling decisions involved in this approach area is a joint venture of the operating system and related application. The operating system is simply responsible for creating various *groups of processors* among the jobs. The number of processors in a group may also change dynamically, monitored by the OS, according to the requirements of the job running currently. The responsibility of the operating system is primarily limited to processor allocation. Each job uses its own group of processors to execute a subset of its runnable tasks by mapping these tasks to corresponding threads as usual. The application which is being run mostly depends on the policy and mechanism of thread scheduling. The policy decides which subset of task is to run, which thread is to be suspended when a process is preempted, and similar other choices. The mechanism to implement the policy is perhaps built using a set of runtime library routines. Not all applications works well with this strategy; some applications that have a single thread by default respond well to this strategy, while others although do not fit straightaway but could be programmed in such a way so as to advantageously exploit this particular feature of the operating system.

The processor allocation being done by the OS is mostly carried out in the following way: For newly arrived jobs, only a single processor is allocated, and it is managed by taking one away from any currently running job that has been allocated more than one processor. When a job requests one or more processors, if there are idle processors, allocate them to satisfy the request; otherwise the request cannot be serviced at that point in time and is set aside until a processor becomes available for it, or sometimes the job on its own no longer finds any need for an extra processor.

This strategy requires a considerable high overhead since both the OS and application are jointly involved in the desired implementation with needed operations. This shortcoming often negates the performance advantages that may be accrued from this strategy. However, with applications that can be designed and developed so as to take the advantage of dynamic scheduling, this approach in that situation is clearly superior to its strong contenders (alternative), gang scheduling, or the dedicated processor assignment strategy.

9.10.2.2 Memory Management

Management of memory in multiprocessor systems is directly related to the memory organization of the underlying architecture of the system and the type of communication network being used. In loosely coupled multiprocessor systems (such as in machines using DSM), memory is usually handled independently, on a per-processor basis. In tightly coupled multiprocessors, memory organization is inherently based on a shared memory mechanism. The operating systems in such machines must provide a flexible memory model in order to control safe and efficient access to entities in shared memory. In this type of system, allocation and deallocation of segments of shared memory is carried out by the OS using additional primitives. Systems that provide support of shared virtual memory may have several TLBs attaching with different processors which may contain mapping details for pages that belong to a shared segment. Presence of many TLBs consequently gives rise to usual coherence problem that can, of course, be negotiated by employing some variation of the standard techniques used to handle cache coherence problem.

Shared memory organization also helps enhance the message passing technique that eventually improves the performance of interprocess communication. This improvement is, however, realized by simply avoiding the copying of messages when senders and receivers have access to the same physical shared memory. But one of the serious drawbacks of this approach is that any modification of the message, if carried out by either party would ultimately go against the fundamental requirement of message passing mechanism; hence, to get out of this problem, it ultimately needs to have a separate copy for each party, which is again time consuming. This problem, however, can be alleviated by employing the most common cost-effective *copy-on-write* technique so that high efficiency can ultimately be attained. Mach OS, in particular, exploited the *copy-on-write* technique rigorously to handle most of the issues in relation to interprocess communication. There are also some operating systems for *loosely coupled multiprocessors* (such as machines using DSM) that provide the shared memory abstraction and implement the *copy-on-write* technique while using the message-passing facility.

The existence of shared memory also encourages to effectively extend the file system by mapping files into process virtual spaces, and that is accomplished by using some form of appropriate primitives. This often helps to realize a potentially efficient mechanism for sharing open files.

9.10.2.3 Device Management

Involvement of I/O in the environment using multiprocessor systems of early days has got less importance, since the type of most of the applications being executed were CPU-bound that do not require much I/O after the initial loading. The whole intention in the use of multiprocessor systems was to essentially speedup the execution of these types of applications by breaking each of them into parts in such a way that each part of an application, in turn, could simultaneously run in a mutually exclusive manner on different processors to shorten the relative total turnaround time. As multiprocessor usage gradually entered the arena of more general-purpose applications, the requirement of I/O–participation in the environment gradually increased; hence, I/O can no longer be set aside. In fact, the performance of I/O became a factor that started to affect throughput and speedup that could be realized. Work on disk arrays has resolved some of the issues, and many other innovative techniques have been introduced to extract considerable enhancement in I/O performance, but the speed of individual I/O devices remains essentially unchanged (for devices composed mostly of mechanical and electro-mechanical components). It has been observed that multiprocessing techniques when applied to I/O, such as connecting a good number of similar devices together and then operating them in parallel using an appropriate scheduling algorithm, would start to yield better performance that tend to closely match the underlying environment.

9.10.2.4 File Management

The organization of the file system in multiprocessor (tightly coupled) environment differs appreciably from that of a network or a distributed system. The operating system, in essence, normally contains a traditional uniprocessor file system, including a single, unified blocked cache. When any process executes a *READ* system call while attempting to access a shared file or a central table, the operating system carries it out, making the necessary arrangements to lock out other CPUs using standard synchronization tools. Similarly, when a *WRITE* system call is done, the central block cache is locked, the new data are then entered the cache, and the lock is finally released. Any subsequent *READ* call will now see the new data, similar to a uniprocessor system. On the whole, here the file system is more or less the same and hardly differs from the file system used in a single-processor machine. Some of the distinctive differences between the three kinds of systems, as already discussed, are illustrated in Table 9.1.

TABLE 9.1

Comparison of Three Different Operating Systems on Machines with Different Organizations of N CPUs. A representative table showing the comparison of salient features between multiprocessor operating systems, network operating systems and distributed systems (multicomputer using middleware)

Item	Network OS	Distributed OS	Multiprocessor (Tightly Coupled) OS
Does it appear as a virtual uniprocessor?	No, collection of distinct machines	Yes, single-system image	Yes, single-system image
Do all have to run the same operating system?	No	Yes	Yes
How many copies of the operating system are there?	N	N	1
Is there a single run queue?	No	No	Yes
How is communication achieved?	Shared files	Messages	Shared memory
Does it require any agreed-upon communication protocols?	Yes	Yes	No
How is memory organized?	On an individual machine basis	Distributed shared memory	Shared memory
How are devices organized?	Usually on an individual machine basis	Pool of same type of devices shared	Pool of same type of devices shared
How is file sharing carried out?	Usually requires no pre-defined semantics	Does require well-defined semantics	Does require well-defined semantics

9.10.3 CASE STUDY: LINUX IN MULTIPROCESSORS

Many features of Linux 2.0 introduced to manage multiprocessor systems were enhanced in Linux 2.4 and onwards, that include a finer locking mechanism to synchronize kernel data structures to prevent race conditions, stepwise modifications in non-preemptible scheduling algorithms, and removing many other limitations to increase its capabilities. The Monta Vista Linux Professional Edition, a derivative of the Linux 2.4 kernel with a full preemptive scheduler and a fine-grained locking mechanism inside the SMP kernel for improved scalability has also enabled tasks to run concurrently as separate kernel-mode threads on different processors. The Linux 2.6 kernel released in 2003 removed many of the limitations of its recent past versions up to version 2.5 and also enhanced its existing capabilities in several ways. In fact, the Linux 2.6 kernel was made preemptible and also employed a very fine-grained locking mechanism to implement even better parallelism. However, kernel operations should not be preempted all the time; particularly, it is difficult when it saves its state or when it is engaged in performing some other sensitive operations, so the kernel enables and disables its own preemptibility to negotiate certain situations by using some special functions.

The Linux kernel uses several types of **locks** for different purposes. It provides **spin locks** for locking data structures in general. It also provides a special **reader-write spin lock** that permits only reading of any number of reader processes to use the lock while accessing the kernel data and not allowing them to modify the data in any way, but permitting only one writer process to modify the data, if needed at any point in time. A **sequence lock** is another type of lock used by the Linux kernel having low overhead, and at the same time, it is scalable. A sequence lock assumes integer values, it is used as a sequence counter, and is updated by an increment instruction in an atomic manner. Whenever a process wishes to use a kernel data structure, it simply increments the value in the sequence lock associated with the data structure, makes a note of its new value, and then starts to perform its own operation. After completing the operation, it checks whether the value in the lock has changed. If so, the operation just performed is deemed to have failed, so it invalidates the operation just executed and attempts to run it again, and so on until the operation succeeds.

The advanced version of Linux 2.6 includes a substantially improved scheduler for traditional non–real-time processes, and mostly the same real-time scheduling capability of version 2.4 and earlier. Within the domain of real-time scheduling in the scheduler, Linux defines three scheduling classes:

SCHD_FIFO: First-in-first-out real-time threads.
SCHD_RR: Round-robin real-time threads.
SCHD_OTHER: Other non–real-time threads.

Besides, Linux 2.6 also describes a completely new scheduler known as the O(1) scheduler (an example of "big-O" notation used for characterizing the time-complexity of algorithms) in which certain limitations of the Linux 2.4 scheduler have been substantially removed, particularly with respect to the SCHD-OTHER class, which did not scale well with an increasing number of processors and processes. Moreover, the Linux scheduler is designed to put more thrust on I/O-bound tasks over CPU-bound tasks. But the scheduler is designed in such a way that the time to select the appropriate process and assign it to a deserving processor is almost constant, irrespective of the total load or the number of available processors in the system.

9.10.4 PRIORITIES AND TIME SLICES

Multiple priorities may be used within each class, with priorities in the real-time classes always higher than the priorities for the SCHD-OTHER class. The default values for real-time priority classes range from 0 to 99 inclusive, and those for SCHD-OTHER classes range from 100 to 139 with a lower number always indicating a higher priority. An initial priority for each non–real-time task is often assigned with a default priority of 120. This is the task's static priority, and as the execution continues, a priority is determined dynamically based on the task's static priority and its execution behavior. The method used by Linux while computing the dynamic priority is based on mainly keeping a note of how much time a process waits (for an event) and how much time a process runs. In principle, a task that suffers most in waiting is offered a relatively high priority. Time-slices are assigned to a task according to its priority, and as such higher-priority tasks are obviously assigned larger time-slices.

The scheduling procedure is straightforward and efficient. As a process becomes ready, it is assigned to the appropriate priority queue in the *active queues structure* and is assigned the deserved time-slice. If a task is preempted before it completes its time-slice, it is returned to an active queue. When a task completes its time-slice but is not itself completed, it is placed into the appropriate queue in the *expired queue structure* and assigned a new time-slice. All scheduling, however, is carried out from the *active queues structure*. When the active queues structure is empty, expired queues are only then involved to continue scheduling. On a given processor, the scheduler chooses the highest-priority nonempty active queue. If multiple tasks are present in that queue, the tasks are simply scheduled using a round-robin approach.

Linux used in multiprocessor systems uses an **affinity-based scheduling** mechanism. A user here can specify a *hard affinity* for a process by indicating a set of processors on which it must run, and similarly, a process possesses a *soft affinity* for the last processor on which it was run. Since scheduling is performed on a per-CPU basis, Linux includes a mechanism for moving a task from the queue lists of one processor to that of another, thereby performing what is known as **load balancing**, which ensures that computational loads entrusted to different CPUs are more or less comparable. This task is performed by a CPU which finds that its ready queues are empty; it is also performed periodically by the scheduler, which checks to see if there is a substantial imbalance among the number of tasks assigned to each processor, typically using an interval of every 1 msec. if the system is idle and every 20 msecs. otherwise. To balance the load, the scheduler can transfer some tasks by invoking the *load_balance* function with the *id* of the under-loaded CPU as a parameter. The highest-priority active tasks are selected for such transfer, because it is important to fairly distribute high-priority tasks.

Another salient feature of the Linux 2.6 kernel is that it can also support system architectures that do not provide a memory management unit, which makes the kernel capable of supporting embedded systems. Thus, the same kernel can now be employed in multiprocessors, servers, desktops, and even embedded systems. Since the kernel modules are equipped with well-specified interfaces, several distinct features, such as better scalability, an improved scheduler, speedy synchronization mechanism between processes, and many other notable attributes have been incorporated into the kernel.

9.10.5 CASE STUDY: WINDOWS IN MULTIPROCESSORS (SMP)

Threads of a process in multiprocessor use **spin locks** to implement mutual exclusion while accessing kernel data structures. In order to ensure that the kernel data structure should not be kept locked for a long time, the kernel never preempts a thread holding a spin lock if some other thread by this time attempts to acquire the same spin lock. In this way, the thread holding the lock can finish its execution of its critical section and release the lock as soon as possible.

Windows running on uniprocessor systems (non–real-time) uses multiple-level queues (with feedback) in which the highest-priority process (thread) is always active unless it is sleeping (waiting) on an event. If there is more than one process (thread) with the highest priority, then the single processor time will be distributed among all the processes (threads) at that priority level in a round-robin manner. An interesting feature of Windows in multiprocessor (SMP) systems with N processors is that it reserves one processor for the purpose of scheduling all tasks, and the others are all engaged in executing processes. Effectively, in a multiprocessor system with N processors, the $N - 1$ highest-priority ready threads are always executed on $N - 1$ processors for exclusive run. All the remaining lower-priority threads share the single remaining processor for their execution. For example, if there are six processors, at best five highest-priority threads can run on five processors, while all remaining lower-priority threads will be run on the remaining single processor.

But this principle of scheduling is directly affected, since the Windows scheduling policy incorporates *affinity-based* scheduling that attach a processor-affinity attribute to a thread. With this emerging policy, if a thread is ready to execute, but the only available processors are not in its processor-affinity state, then the thread is forced to wait, and the scheduler chooses the next available matching thread for execution. However, processor-affinity-based scheduling has advantages that assist to achieve good memory-access performance for a thread by utilizing its residual address space held in the cache of a processor, in particular. In addition, the *thread-processor-affinity* attribute of a particular thread entity, in conjunction with the *default-processor-affinity* attribute of the process object containing the said thread defines an affinity set for a thread. If this affinity set is non-null, a thread is always executed on a processor that belongs in the affinity set. This form of scheduling is known as *hard-affinity*-based scheduling. On the other hand, if the affinity set of a thread is null, the kernel uses soft-affinity-based scheduling in which a thread is scheduled on the same processor on which it executed last time.

Hard-affinity-based scheduling sometimes gives rise to anomalous behavior, leading to a serious problem known as *priority inversion*. For example, consider a system in which N threads are being executed on N processors. Let a thread T_k make a transition to the ready state due to the occurrence of an interrupt, and let the priority of this thread be higher than the priorities of some other *running* threads. Thread T_k may be forced to wait if the processor for which it has a hard affinity is engaged in executing a thread whose priority exceeds T_k's (lower priority). In fact, T_k could have been scheduled on some other processor if it were a real-time thread.

9.11 MULTICOMPUTER OPERATING SYSTEMS

Multicomputers consisting of a set of n > 1 processors (CPUs) P_1, P_2, P_3, . . ., P_n and m > 0 shared/distributed (main) memory units M_1, M_2, . . ., M_m are interconnected using various forms of design approaches. In fact, there are several different ways the hardware can be organized, especially in terms of processor–processor interconnections and processor–memory interconnections and also how they communicate with one another. Various hardware design models have been proposed in this regard that can be broadly classified into **five categories** (see Section 9.5). We will discuss here multicomputer systems in broad terms only, deliberately avoiding their spectrum of possibilities in details. It is evident that different models (forms) of such machines use different kinds of operating systems.

9.11.1 MULTICOMPUTER ARCHITECTURE

A multicomputer system often consists of a collection of several autonomous individual homogeneous, heterogeneous, or a combination of both computer systems in which each computer system consisting of processor–memory–I/O module forms a *node*. Thus, many resources of a kind, such as CPUs, memory, and I/O devices, exist. Moreover, a single node of a multicomputer (distributed) system may even be a *cluster* of computers that work together in an integrated manner in which each individual system within the cluster is typically referred to as a *host*. Each host shares disk storage, which could be either a multi-host RAID that offers both a high transfer rate and high reliability or a network of storage area that provides incremental growth. In addition, each host in the cluster is connected to two networks: a *private LAN* to which only the hosts in the same cluster are connected, and a *public network* through which it can communicate with any other host of any other cluster in the entire distributed system. The *cluster software* having several features similar to those of a DOS actually controls the operation of all hosts present in a cluster.

In multicomputers, multiple computers communicate with each other and with non-local (local to some other computer) memory using high-bandwidth communication networks to extract a high degree of resource sharing. Peripherals can also be attached using some other forms of sharing. Many variations of this basic scheme exist. A private cache is often offered to the processor on each individual computer not only to further speed up the entire operation but also to reduce contention for distributed memory and on the shared communication network. The type of communication network to be used and the related nature of this communication path have a significant influence on the bandwidth and saturation of system communications, apart from the other associated important issues, such as cost, complexity, inter-system communications, and above all the scalability of the architectures.

Architecturally, multicomputer systems (networks of computers) are loosely coupled systems. When this system is managed by tightly coupled software, that is, by a single operating system to control all the individual machines present in the collection, this gives rise to the concept of a *distributed system*. When multicomputer systems (networks of computers) consist of autonomous machines (run with their own operating systems) that are driven by loosely coupled software and often run under separate management, this eventually forms *computer networks*. A modern trend toward less expensive multicomputer systems has led to the emergence of the ***workstation*** concept: a powerful single-user computer, usually with a small local disk and a high-quality display is generally linked to others by an interconnection network so that they can share expensive devices like printers and a large secondary store. *All workstations use the same operating system, but each has its own copy and is mostly autonomous.* However, each might provide services to the others on request, and processes which run on separate machines can communicate data with one another through the network. Except for that facility, the operating systems on the workstations are fairly traditional. Workstation networks, however, occupy a place and play a role somewhere in between computer networks and true multicomputers (distributed systems).

9.11.1.1 Multicomputer Systems: Different Models

Many variations of the basic scheme to construct multicomputers are used to build various models of this system, as already discussed in detail in Section 9.5. However, it is again mentioned here those models that can be broadly classified into many categories, such as:

- Systems consisting of minicomputers
- System comprising workstations
- Workstation–server model: client–server model
- Systems comprising processor pools
- Hybrid systems

Multicomputers thus designed are best suited primarily for general-purpose multi-user applications in which many users are allowed to work together on many unrelated problems but occasionally in a cooperative manner that involves sharing of resources. Such machines usually yield cost-effective higher bandwidth, since most of the access made by each processor in individual machines are to its local memory, thereby reducing latency that eventually resulting in increased system performance. The nodes in the machines are, however, equipped with the needed interfaces so that they can always be connected to one another through the communication network.

In contrast to the tightly coupled multiprocessor system, the individual computers forming the multicomputer system can be located far from each other and thereby can cover a wider geographical area. Moreover, in tightly coupled systems, the number of processors that can be effectively and efficiently employed is usually limited and constrained by the bandwidth of the shared memory, resulting to restricted scalability. Multicomputer systems, on the other hand, with a loosely coupled architecture, are more freely expandable in this regard and theoretically can contain any number of interconnected computers with no limits as such. On the whole, multi-processors tend to be more tightly coupled than multicomputers, because they can exchange data almost at memory speeds, but some fiber-optic-based multicomputers have also been found to work at close to memory speeds.

9.11.2 Operating System Considerations

Multicomputer systems architecturally are loosely coupled systems with different structures and forms depending on the interconnections among their constituent computing systems (nodes). They belong to the category of distributed computing systems, which can be governed either by loosely coupled software known as a NOS or by tightly coupled software known as a DOS.

Whatever model is being followed in the design of a multicomputer system, it essentially consists of multiple autonomous computer systems that ultimately provide high throughput as well as computation speed-up. As usual, here also each individual system consists of three basic types of resources, processors, memory, and I/O devices, that need to be managed locally at their own ends by respective management modules. Like uniprocessor OSs, a multicomputer operating system similarly manages the available resources and augments the system and hardware functionality in such a way that many users can individually work concurrently on many unrelated problems at their respective machines with needed interaction but occasionally in a cooperative manner among users on different machines, which mainly includes sharing resources. That is why operating systems that manage multicomputers have a totally different structure and complexity than their counterpart multiprocessor operating systems. This is due to the fact that the data structures required for system-wide resource management can no longer be easily shared by merely placing them in physically

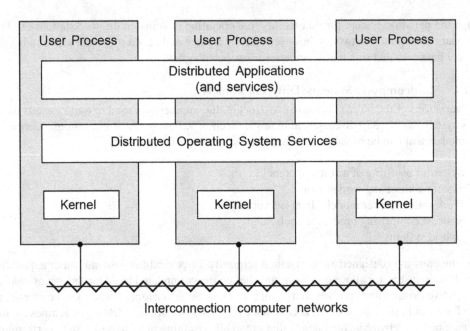

FIGURE 9.8   A representative general structure of a multicomputer operating system.

shared memory. Instead, the only means of communication is by means of message passing. A representative scheme of multicomputer operating system organization is depicted in Figure 9.8.

As already mentioned, each machine (node) in the multicomputer system (as shown in Figure 9.8) has its own kernel that contains different modules for managing its various local resources, such as local CPU, memory, a local disk, and other peripherals. In addition, each machine has a separate module for handling *interprocessor communication*, which is carried out mostly by sending and receiving messages to and from other machines. The message-passing technique being used here may itself widely vary semantically between different forms of systems, giving rise to several issues, such as whether the messages between processes should be buffered and whether the participating processes are made blocked or unblocked during the course of message-passing operations. Whatever decision is made in this regard at the time of designing the OS, it depends largely on the underlying system architecture that consequently determines the reliability aspects of the communication thus made between machines. In fact, the presence or absence of buffers, for example, at the sender's or receiver's end ultimately decides whether reliable communication is guaranteed, which, in turn, put a tremendous impact on the performance of the system as a whole.

Within the multicomputer operating system, there exists a common layer of software (a utility process, as shown in Figure 9.8) just above the local kernel that acts as a virtual machine monitor implementing the operating system as a virtual machine, thereby multiplexing different underlying kernels to support parallel and concurrent execution of various tasks. By using the available interprocessor communication facilities, this layer provides a software implementation of shared memory. The services that are commonly offered by this layer are, for example, assigning a task to a processor, providing transparent storage, general interprocess communication, masking hardware failures, and other standard services that any operating system usually provides. Some of the **salient features** of multicomputer operating systems are:

- Each machine (node) has a copy of the code necessary for communication and primitive service to processes (such as setting up mapping registers and preempting at the end of a quantum). This code is the kernel of the operating system.

- Computation speed-up is normally achieved by executing sub-tasks of an application in parallel in different computer systems.
- The environment of a process essentially includes the communication ports it has access to and the processes that serve those ports.
- It makes no difference to a process as to on what machine it runs, except for its speed of execution and communication. Processes that deal directly with devices are an exception to this rule.
- Policy decisions, such as on which machine to run a new process, are made outside the kernel and carried out by utility processes.
- Resources attached to any computer system (node) may be used by any applications running under different computer systems (nodes).
- The OS services as provided should enable users or their subcomputations located on different nodes to communicate reliably at ease.
- Utility processes are also used for accessing files and performing I/O. Services are therefore represented by open ports to these utility processes.
- There should be no hindrance in adding new subsystems (incremental growth) to a multicomputer system and that too without hampering existing subsystems in anyway. This will simply make the cost of enhancing the capability of a multicomputer system to be straightaway proportional to the additional capability desired.
- A multicomputer system should be reliable, which means that it should provide *availability*, that is, continuity of services, despite faults and failures. When one machine fails, the performance of the entire operating system is simply degraded, and only the work that was underway on the failed machine is actually lost. Suitable redundancies in resources, existing networks, and offered OS services can be utilized to ensure that nothing at all is lost.

In fact, many of the features and issues required to be included in the design of a multicomputer operating system are equally needed for any distributed system. However, *the main difference between multicomputer operating systems and distributed systems is that the former generally assume that the underlying hardware is homogeneous and is to be fully controlled. On the other hand, one important feature of a distributed operating system is* **migration** *of processes from one machine to another to improve the balance of load and to shorten communication paths.* Migration requires a mechanism to gather load information, a distributed policy that decides that a process should be moved, and a mechanism to effect the transfer. Migration has been demonstrated in a few UNIX-based DOSs, such as Locus and MOS, and in communication-based DOSs, like Demos/MP. Many distributed systems nowadays, however, are built on top of existing operating systems.

9.11.3 MIDDLEWARE

The definition of a true distributed system is given in Section 9.8. Neither a NOS nor a DOS truly meets the criteria of a real distributed system. The reason is that a NOS never casts a view of a *single coherent system*, while a DOS is not aimed to handle a collection of *independent* computers (mostly heterogeneous). The obvious question now arises as to whether it would be possible to develop a distributed system that could have most of the merits of these two different worlds: the scalability and openness properties of NOSs and the transparency attributes of DOSs. Probably the most difficult problem in designing such distributed systems is the need to support *network transparency*. The solution to this problem can be obtained by injecting an additional layer of software on top of a NOS to essentially mask (hide) the heterogeneity of the collection of underlying platforms (such as networks, hardware, operating systems, and many other things) in order to offer a single coherent system view (network transparency) as well as to improve distribution transparency. Many contemporary modern operating systems are constructed following this idea by means of including an additional layer between applications and the NOS, thereby offering a lower-level of abstraction what is historically called **middleware**. This layer would eventually implement a convenient general-purpose services to application programmers. The following discussion on this topic is almost along the same lines as that of modern approaches (Tanenbaum, 1995).

NOSs often allow processes of distributed applications on different machines to communicate with each other by passing messages. In addition, several distributed applications, on the other hand, make use of interfaces to the local file system that forms part of the underlying NOS. But the drawback of this approach is that distribution is hardly transparent, because the user has to specifically mention the destination point at which this action will be carried out. In order to negotiate this drawback of NOS (i.e. lack of network transparency) to make it use as a distributed system, a solution is then to place an additional layer of software between applications and the NOS, thereby offering a higher level of abstraction. This layer is thus legitimately called **middleware**. Middleware is essentially a set of drivers, APIs, or other software that improves and makes ease of connectivity between a client application (that resides on top of it) and a server process (that exists below the level of middleware). It provides a uniform computational model for use by the programmers of servers as well as distributed applications.

Local operating systems running on heterogeneous computers are totally dedicated to performing everything with regard to their own resource management as well as carrying out simple means of communication to connect other computers. Middleware never manages an individual node present in the network system, but it provides a way to hide the heterogeneity of the underlying platforms from the applications running on top of it. Many middleware systems, therefore, offer almost a complete collection of services and discourage using anything but only their interfaces to those services. Any attempt to bypassing the middleware layer and directly invoking the services of one of the underlying local operating systems is often considered an out–of–way shot. Consequently, there is a need to build a set of *higher-level application-independent services* to put into systems so that networked applications can be easily integrated into a single system. This requires defining a

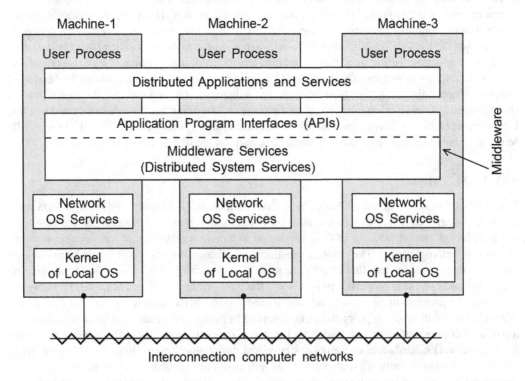

FIGURE 9.9 A representative block diagram of the general structure of a distributed system realized with the use of a middleware.

common standard for middleware solutions. At present, there are a number of such standards, and these available standards are generally not compatible with one another. Even worse, products that implement the same standards but were introduced by different vendors are rarely interoperable. Again to overcome this undesirable drawback, placement of *upperware* on top of this middleware is thus urgently needed.

9.11.3.1   Different Middleware Models

Various **middleware models** have been proposed that could make development and integration of distributed applications as simple as possible. Each model casts a specific image of the upper level to the downward level (NOS services) so that the downward level appears to be a distributed one to the upper level.

- A relatively simple model is treating everything, including I/O devices, such as mouse, keyboard, disk, network interface, and so on, as a **file** along the lines of UNIX and more rigorously as Plan 9. Essentially, whether a file is local or remote makes no difference. All are; that an application opens a file, reads and writes bytes, and finally closes it again. Because files can be shared by many different processes, communication now reduces to simply accessing the same file.
- Another middleware model following a similar line as Plan 9, but less rigid, is centered around DFS. Such middleware supports distribution transparency only for traditional files (i.e. files that are used merely for storing data). For example, processes are often required to be started explicitly on specific machines. This type of middleware is reasonably scalable, which makes it quite popular.
- Middleware based on **remote procedure calls** (**RPCs**) and **group communication** systems such as **lists** (discussed later) was an important model in the early days. This model puts more emphasis on hiding network communication by allowing a process to call a procedure, the implementation of which is located on a remote machine. At the time of calling such a procedure, parameters are transparently shipped to the remote machine where the procedure is actually to be executed, and thereafter the results are sent back to the caller. It therefore appears to the caller as if the procedure call was executed locally, but it actually keeps the calling process transparent about the network communication that took place, except perhaps with a slight degradation in performance.
- Another model based on **object orientation** is equally popular today. The success of RPC established the fact that if procedure calls could cross the machine boundaries, so could objects, and it would then be possible to invoke objects on remote machines in a transparent manner too. This led to the introduction of various middleware systems based on the notion what is called **distributed objects**. The essence of this concept is that each object implements an interface that hides all its internal details from its users. An interface essentially consists of the methods that the object implements. The only thing that a process can see of an object is its interface. Object-oriented middleware products and standards are widely used. They include Common Object Request Broker (CORBA), Java Remote Method Invocation (RMI), Web Services, Microsoft's Distributed Component Object Model (DCOM), and so on. CORBA provides remote object invocation, which allows an object in a program running on one computer to invoke a method of an object in a program running on another computer. Its implementation hides the fact that messages are passed over a network in order to send the invocation request and its reply.

    Distributed objects are often implemented by having (placing) each object itself located on a single machine and additionally making its interface available on many other machines. When a process (on any machine except the machine where the object is located) invokes a method, the interface implementation on the process's machine simply transforms the method invocation into a message, which is ultimately sent (request) to the object. The object executes the requested method and sends (reply) back the result. The interface implementation on the process's machine transforms the reply message into a return value, which is then handed over to the invoking process. Similar to RPC, here also the process may be kept completely in the dark about the network communication.

- This approach was further refined to give rise to a model based on the concept of **distributed documents**, which is probably best illustrated by the World Wide Web. In the Web model, information is organized into documents, where each document resides on a machine somewhere in the world. The exact location of the document is transparent to the user. Documents contain links that refer to other documents. By following a link, the specific document to which that link refers is fetched from its location and displayed on the user's screen. The documents in question may be of any type, such as text, audio, or video, as well as all kinds of interactive graphic-based articles.

9.11.3.2 Middleware Services to Application Systems

Middleware can provide services (through APIs) for use by application programs. They are infrastructural services that are tightly bound to the upper layer, that is, a distributed programming model (distributed applications) provided by the middleware. That is why the middleware systems developed based on any one of the models described or using any other suitable approaches customarily provide a lot of specific services mostly common to all of the models. The services in the top layer of Figure 9.9 are the domain-specific services that utilize (are provided by) the middleware: its communication operations and its own services. Some of them are:

- **Communication facilities:** These are offered at a higher level (middleware level) to hide the low-level message passing mechanism carried out at the level of computer networks in order to implement *access transparency*. The programming interface to the transport layer as offered by NOS is thus entirely replaced by other facilities which mostly depends to a large extent on the specific model of distribution (such as RPCs and distributed objects, etc. as already discussed) the middleware offers to its users or applications.
- **Naming:** Naming is one of the most common services provided by all middleware. This service (similar to directory look-up) enables entities to be looked up, identified, accessed, and shared. Naming looks very simple but causes much difficulties with systems that are scalable. The reason is that as the system gradually expands, an efficient look-up for a specific name in the relatively large-scale system is problematic, and that is why it is assumed that the location of the entity that is named is always kept fixed. This assumption is religiously followed on the World Wide Web in which each and every document is named by means of an URL. A URL contains the name of a server where the document to which the URL refers is stored with an unique name. If the document is by any chance moved to another server, the URL will not be able to identify the document, and consequently it fails to work.
- **Persistence:** Many middleware systems are found to include a special feature known as *persistence*, which means some facilities for storage. Persistence was usually offered through a DFS in its early days, but modern advanced middleware goes further to even make databases integrated into the systems or otherwise provides some other means for applications to connect to their needed databases.
- **Distributed transactions:** Many modern middleware systems include a feature that offers facilities for *distributed transactions*, which operate on data that may be located on multiple machines spread across a geographical area. A notable property of a transaction is that it allows multiple read and write operations to be carried out *atomically*. Here, atomicity implies that the transaction either succeeds, so that all its write operations are legibly performed, or it fails, leaving all referenced data unaltered.

- **Security:** A middleware system is attached to geographically dispersed multiple computer systems connected by NOSs. Although these NOSs usually extend their own security measures, but they are often not adequate that middleware can rely on them to protect the entire network domain. That is why all middleware systems virtually provide facilities to effect security from their own end by, at least, partly implementing it in their own layer. Scalability and openness are the primary requirements for a system to be distributed, and the middleware system thus injected must support them. When this need combined with security aspects, it turns out to be a grand challenge to middleware while attempting to implement a fairly secure distributed system.

In spite of having tremendous strength, middleware does have several **limitations**. Many distributed applications rely entirely on the services provided by the underlying middleware to support their needs for communication and data sharing. For example, an application that is suitable for a client–server model, such as a database of names and addresses, can rely on a model of middleware that provides only remote method invocation. Many other examples can also be cited in this regard. Although much has already been achieved in simplifying the programming of distributed systems through the development of middleware support, still then some aspects of the dependability of systems require support at the application level. In addition, some communication-related functions that are carried out at the lowest level can be completely and reliably implemented only with the knowledge and help of the application standing at the upper end point of the communication system. Therefore, providing that function additionally at the application level as a feature of the communication system itself is not always wise and sensible. Consequently, this runs counter to the view that all communication activities can be abstracted (hidden) away from the programming of applications by the introduction of appropriate middleware layers.

9.12 COMPARISON BETWEEN VARIOUS TYPES OF OPERATING SYSTEMS

Up until now, we have discussed various types of operating systems that run on varied hardware platforms, essentially consisting of multiple CPUs, such as NOSs, DOSs, and distributed systems (middleware-based). Let us now look at a brief comparison between those operating systems with respect to some important attributes for a better understanding of them. This is summarized in Table 9.2.

TABLE 9.2

A comparison of salient features between multiprocessor operating systems, multicomputer operating systems, network operating systems and distributed systems (middleware-based.)

Item	Distributed Operating System Multiproc.	Multicomp.	Network Operating System	Middleware-based Distributed System
Same OS on all nodes	Yes	Yes	No	No
Number of copies of OS	1	N	N	N
Basis for Communication	Shared memory	Messages	Files	Model specific
Resource Management	Global, Central	Global, distributed	Per node	Per node
Degree of Tranaparency	Very high	High	Low	High
Scalability	Very low	Moderately	Yes	Varies
Openness	No (Closed)	No (Closed)	Open	Open

* N → Number of processing systems or processing nodes.

One aspect with regard to the last row of the Table 9.2 needs to be explained. Regarding open-ness, both NOSs and distributed systems have an edge over the others. One of the main reasons is that the different nodes of these systems running while under different operating systems, in general, support a standard communication protocol (such as TCP/IP) that makes interoperability much easy. But one practical aspect that goes against this desirable feature is that of using many different operating systems, which causes severe difficulties in porting applications. In fact, DOSs, in general, are never targeted to be open. Instead, they are often designed with more emphasis on performance optimization, which eventually led to the introduction of many proprietary solutions that ultimately stand in the way of an open system.

9.13   DISTRIBUTED SYSTEMS: NETWORK OF COMPUTERS

A distributed system is often built on a network of computers whose nodes (*hosts, sites, end-systems*) have their own local memory and may also have other hardware and software resources. These nodes often vary in size and function; size-wise: a node may be as small as a personal computer, a workstation, a minicomputer, a mainframe, or even a large supercom-puter. Function-wise; a node may be a single-user personal computer, a general-purpose time-sharing system, or a dedicated system (such as a database server, a file server, or a print server), usually without the capability to handle interactive users. A computer network is essentially a communication system built on a network of computers that connects the nodes by communica-tion links and software protocols in order to exchange data between two processes running on different nodes of the network. A distributed system, therefore, heavily relies on the underlying communication architecture of the network of computers for the communication of data and control information between the nodes present in the system. More precisely, a stripped-down set of communications functions is incorporated into the distributed system to efficiently run the network of computers. Consequently, the performance and reliability of a distributed sys-tem depend to a large extent on and are influenced by the performance and reliability of the underlying computer network. Hence, a basic knowledge (not a comprehensive treatment) of computer networks is required to study them and to have a clear understanding of DOSs. That is why the following section deals only with the most important aspects of networking concepts and designs, with more emphasis on those aspects that are needed as a basis for designing and describing DOSs.

9.13.1   NETWORKING: CONCEPTS AND ISSUES

Networking takes account of both network hardware as well as network software. It consists of network technology, the design and implementation of computer networks, and also deals with all the software aspects, especially the communication policy and subsequent implementation of appropriate mechanisms between pairs of processes. The fundamental issues (factors) that are to be considered primarily in defining and describing networking are (summarized in Table 9.3 and given on the Support Material at www.routledge.com/9781032467238):

- **network type** (LAN or WAN)
- **network topology** (arrangement of nodes and the associated communication links present in a network)
- **networking technology** (how the data will be transmitted over the network)
- **connection strategy** (setup of data paths)
- **routing strategy** (route of travel of information through the system)
- **communication (network) protocols** (a hierarchy of protocols describing a set of rules, regulations, and conventions)
- **naming of processes** (IP address, process-id)
- **network bandwidth and latency**.

Out of these, the first three issues, *network type, network topology*, and *networking technology* are concerned what is known as the design of networks; all the other issues mentioned (all other rows of Table 9.3 on the Support Material at www.routledge.com/9781032467238) above are concerned mostly with message communication and its related aspects. We will now discuss all the issues mentioned above (described in Table 9.3 in Support Material at www.routledge.com/9781032467238) in brief.

Details on fundamental issues related to networking are given in Table 9.3 on the Support Material at www.routledge.com/9781032467238.

9.13.1.1 Network Types: LAN versus WAN

Networks are broadly classified into two types: local-area networks (LANs) and wide-area networks (WANs), also referred to *long-haul networks*. There is another type of networks known as *metropolitan area networks* (MANs). While a LAN is normally implemented to connect machines located within a limited geographic area (a few kilometers) for the exclusive use of a few users, a WAN spans greater distances (may extend several thousand kilometers), and a MAN usually covers a larger geographical area than a LAN. However, one of the main objectives of MANs is to interconnect LANs (as nodes), normally located in different areas. A few LANs are also sometimes connected to WANs, and nowadays it is a common practice to connect LANs and WANs to the internet. While LANs and MANs nearly satisfy the performance requirements of a distributed system (at least, they are not appreciably worse than a uniprocessor system executing a particular application) in many respects, WAN was not at all considered fully adequate to meet the needed level of performance of a distributed system. But, nowadays, with the use of modern high-bandwidth networks, such as *broadband integrated services digital network* (B-ISDNs) and *ATM* technologies, WAN-based distributed systems equipped with these facilities are now fully adequate to support a wide range of distributed applications, like multimedia applications involving high-quality audio/video and bulk data transmissions.

A LAN usually consists of microcomputers (PCs), workstations, and sometimes even minicomputers, along with other peripherals and often a file server; these machines are usually connected to one another by high-speed cables, such as fiber-optic cables, Cat-5 (Category 5), or similar other things for realizing high data transfer rates. A WAN, on the other hand, is usually a full-fledged computer connected to two or more networks and is sometimes equipped with special-purpose communication processors (CPs) that facilitate communication of messages between distant hosts. WANs often use low-cost public lines to effectively keep the entire system within the affordable limit.

More details on this topic, with a comparison given in Table 9.4, are provided on the Support Material at www.routledge.com/9781032467238.

9.13.1.2 Network Topology

Five types of commonly used topologies for constructing LAN networks are *multi-access branching bus, star, ring, fully connected*, and *partially connected*. Each has its own merits and drawbacks, and they mainly differ in speed of communication, cost of hardware to construct the network, and of course reliability (Chakraborty, 2020). A WAN of computers, in general, has no fixed regular network topology to interconnect component computers, since those computers are separated by large distances. Moreover, different communication media may be used for different links of a WAN, such as coaxial cables (telephone lines), satellite communication, etc. that mostly depends on at what distances the component computers are located.

Moreover, the computers in a WAN are not connected directly to the communication media (channels) but are rather connected to hardware devices called *packet-switching exchanges* (PSEs), which are essentially special-purpose computers dedicated to the task of data communication across the network. In essence, the communication channels of the network interconnect the PSEs, and any computer in a WAN interacts only with the respective PSE of the WAN to which it is connected to exchange information with other computers in the WAN.

The details of LAN and WAN topologies with figures are given on the Support Material at www.routledge.com/9781032467238.

9.13.1.3 Networking Technologies

Out of many available networking technologies, we discuss here only ethernet and token ring technologies that are widely used for LAN and ATM technology, which is used for ISDN (WAN) networks.

- **Ethernet:** This is the most widely used multi-access branching bus topology network using a circuit that consists of cables linked by repeaters (similar to Figure 9.18 on the Support Material at www.routledge.com/9781032467238) for building distributed systems, because it is relatively fast and economical. Information is transmitted from one station (node) to another by breaking it up into units (packets) called *frames*. Each frame contains the addresses of its source and destination and a data field. Each station listens to the bus at all times, and it copies a frame in a buffer if the frame is meant for it; otherwise it simply ignores the frame. A *bridge* used to connect Ethernet LANs is essentially a computer that receives frames on one Ethernet and, depending on the destination addresses, reproduces them on another Ethernet to which it is connected. Every Ethernet hardware interface is always assigned by the manufacturer a unique address of a maximum of 48 bits authorized by the IEEE to uniquely identify a specific Ethernet in the set of interconnected Ethernets forming the site. Since, the basic Ethernet topology is a bus-based one, only one connection can be in progress at any time using carrier sense multiple access with collision detection (CSMA/CD) technology (protocol). However, if many stations find no signal on the cable and start transmitting their frames almost at the same time, their frames would interfere with one another, causing what is called a *collision*, which can then be resolved using appropriate algorithms. A collision is normally detected by an increase in the size of the frame that must exceed a minimum of 512 bits for 10- and 100-Mbit Ethernets and 4096 bits for gigabit Ethernets.
- **Token Rings:** A network with a ring topology is a well-understood and field-proven technology in which a collection of ring interfaces are connected by point-to-point links using a cheap twisted pair, coaxial cable, or fiber-optics as the communication medium and have almost no wasted bandwidth when all sites are trying to send. Since a ring is fair and also has a known upper bound on channel access, that is why and for many other reasons, IBM chose the ring network as its LAN and adopted this technology as a basis for its distributed system products. The IEEE has also included token ring technology as the IEEE 802.5 standard that eventually became another commonly used LAN technology for building distributed systems. A ring topology that uses the notion of a *token*, which is a special bit pattern containing specific message, is called a token ring network, and the medium-access control protocol used is the token ring protocol. Here, a single token of 3 bytes, which may either be *busy* or *free*, circulates continuously around the ring. When a station wants to transmit a frame, it is required to seize the *free* token and remove it from the ring and then attach its message to the token, changing its status to *busy* before transmitting. Therefore, a busy token always has a message packet attached to it, and the message can be of any length and need not be split into frames of a standard size. Since there exists only one token, only one station can transmit, and only one message can be in transit at any instant. However, ring interfaces have two operating modes: *listen* and *transmit*. In *listen* mode, every station that finds a message checks whether the message is intended for it; if it is, the destination station copies the message and resets the status bit of the token to *free*. Operation of the token ring comes to a halt if the token is lost due to communication errors. One of the stations is responsible for recovering the system; it listens continuously to the traffic on the network to check for the presence of a token and then creates a new token if it finds that the token has been lost.
- **Asynchronous Transfer Mode (ATM) Technology:** ATM is a high-speed connection-oriented switching and multiplexing technology that uses short, fixed-length packets called *cells* to transmit different types of traffic simultaneously. It is not synchronous (only tied

to a master clock) in that information can be sent independently without having a common clock, as most long-distance telephone lines are. ATM has several salient features that put it at the forefront of networking technologies. Some of the most common are:

- It provides data transmission speeds of 622 Mbps, 2.5 Gbps, and even more, which facilitates high bandwidth for distributed applications, such as those based on video-on-demand technique, video–conferencing applications, and several other types of applications that often need to access remote databases.

- ATM exploits the concept of *virtual networking* to allow traffic between two locations that permits the available bandwidth of a physical channel to be shared by multiple applications, thereby enabling them to simultaneously communicate at different rates over the same path between two end points. This facilitates the total available bandwidth being dynamically distributed among a variety of user applications.

- ATM uses both fundamental approaches to switching (circuit switching and packet switching) within a single integrated switching mechanism called *cell switching*, which is flexible enough to handle distributed applications of both types, such as those that generate a *variable bit rate* (VBR; usually data applications), which can tolerate delays as well as fluctuating throughput rates, and those that generate a *constant bit rate* (CBR; usually video, digitized voice applications) that requires guaranteed throughput rates and service levels. Moreover, digital switching of cells is relatively easy compared to using traditional multiplexing techniques in high-speed networks (gigabits per sec), especially using fiber-optics.

- ATM allows the use of only a single network to efficiently transport a wide range of multimedia data comprising text, voice, video, broadcast television, and several other types. Normally, each type of these data requires the use of a separate network of distinct technology, and that to be simultaneously provided for effective transportation at a time. ATM, with one single network, replaces the simultaneous use of many different types of networks and their underlying technologies, thereby straightaway simplifying the design of communication networks as well as providing substantial savings in costs.

- In ATM, it is possible to offer only a specific portion of as big or as small chunk of the capacity of network bandwidth as is needed by a user, and the billing is also then be made only on the basis of per-cell usage (perhaps on a giga-cell basis).

- ATM, in addition to point-to-point communication in which there is a single sender and single receiver, also supports a *multicasting facility* in which there is a single sender and multiple receivers. Such a facility is required for many collaborative distributed applications, such as transmitting broadcast, television (video conferencing) to many houses (users) at the same time.

- ATM technology is equally applicable in both LAN and WAN environments with respect to having the same switching technology (cell switching) and same cell format.

- The technology used in ATM is nicely scalable both upward and downward with respect to many parameters, especially data rates and bandwidths.

- ATM technology, by virtue of its having enormous strength, eventually has been internationally standardized as the basis for B-ISDN.

ATM, by virtue of having many attractive features (already mentioned) is now in a position of having created an immense impact on the design of future distributed systems; hence, it is often legitimately described as the computer networking paradigm of the future, in spite of accepting the fact that there still remain several problems with this technology for network designers and users that have yet to be solved.

Brief details on ethernet, token rings, and ATM, with figures, are given on the Support Material at www.routledge.com/9781032467238.

9.13.1.4   Connection Strategies

Connection between relevant processes is simply the communication (a data path) between them. A connection strategy, also sometimes called a *switching policy and mechanism*, actually determines *when* a connection should be set up between a pair of relevant processes and for *how long*. The switching technique used often influences network latency and has an immense impact on the efficiency of communication between a pair of processes as well as on the throughput of communication links. The three most commonly used schemes, circuit switching, packet switching, and message switching, are described here. The notation m_k is used for a message and $p_x(m_y)$ for the x-th packet of message m_y.

- **Circuit switching:** A circuit is essentially a connection used exclusively for message passing by an intending pair of communicating processes, and the related physical circuit is set up during the circuit set–up phase, that is, before the first message is transmitted, and is purged sometime after the last message has been delivered. Circuit set–up actions involve deciding the actual network path that messages will follow, reservation of the channels constituting the circuit, and other communication resources. Exclusive reservation of the channels ensures no need of any buffers between them. Each connection is given a unique *id*, and processes specify the connection *id* while sending and receiving messages.

The *main advantage* of the circuit-switching technique is that once the circuit is established, the full capacity of the circuit is for exclusive use by the connected pair of hosts with almost no delay in transmission, and the time required to send a message can be estimated and guaranteed. However, the *major drawbacks* of this technique are that it requires additional overhead and delays during circuit setup/disconnection phases to tie–up/disconnect a set of communicating resources. Channel bandwidth may also be wasted if the channel capacities of the path forming the circuit are not utilized efficiently by the connected pair of hosts. This method is, therefore, justified only if the overall message density in the system is low, but not for long continuous transmissions, especially, when medium-to-heavy traffic is expected between a pair of communicating hosts. It is also considered suitable in situations where transmissions require guaranteed maximum transmission delay. This technique is, therefore, favored particularly for transmission of voice and real-time data in distributed applications.

- **Packet switching:** Here, a message is split into parts of a standard size called *packets*, and the channels are shared for transmitting packets of different sender–receiver pairs instead of using a dedicated communication path. For each individual packet, a connection is set up, and the channel is then occupied by a single packet of the message of a particular pair; the channel may then be used for transmitting either subsequent packets of the same message of the same pair or a packet of some other message of a different pair. Moreover, packets of the same message may travel along different routes (connections) and may arrive out of sequence at the prescribed destination site. When packet switching is used, two kinds of overhead is primarily involved; first, a packet must carry some identification in its header: the *id* of the message to which it belongs, a sequence number within the message, and *ids* of the sender and destination processes. Second, the packets that have arrived at the destination site have to be properly reassembled so that the original message can be formed.

Packet switching provides efficient usage of channels (links), because the communication bandwidth of a channel is not monopolized by specific pairs of processes but are shared to transmit several messages. Hence, all pairs of communicating processes are supposed to receive fair and unbiased service, which makes this technique attractive, particularly for interactive processes. This technique, as compared to circuit switching, is more appropriate in situations when small amounts of burst data are required to be transmitted. Furthermore, by virtue of having fixed-sized packets, this approach reduces the cost of retransmission when an error occurs in transmission. In addition, the dynamic selection of the actual path to be taken by a packet ensures considerable reliability in the network, because alternate paths in the network could be used in transmission in the event of channel or PSE failure. However, several *drawbacks* of this method have also been observed. Apart from consuming time to set up the connection before transmission, this technique needs to use buffers to buffer each packet at every host or PSE and again to reassemble the packets at the destination site; the additional overhead thus incurred per packet is large and eventually makes this method inefficient for transmitting large messages. Moreover, there is no guarantee as to how long it takes a message to travel from a source host to its destination site because the time to be taken for each packet depends on the route chosen for that packet, in addition to the volume of data to be transferred.

- **Message switching:** This approach requires a connection to be established before exchange of every message between a pair of processes. Messages between the same pair of processes can travel over different paths available in the system. Message switching, similar to other switching strategies, incurs repetitive overhead due to consumption of a certain amount of time to set up every connection before the commencement of actual physical transmission. This may cause considerable delays, and that is why its use is justified only if the message traffic between any pair of processes is relatively light. Since channels (links) and other communicating resources are not monopolized by any pair of specific processes, other processes can use the same connection for their own communications. This facilitates better utilization of resources, and that can only be attained if there is intense traffic in the network.

In order to alleviate the additional cost required in any form of connection strategy to set up the connection between the sender and receiver before the start of actual transmission, **connection-less protocols** are often used in practice for transmitting messages or packets. In such a protocol, the originating node simply selects one of its neighboring nodes or PSE (see Figure 9.18 given in Support Material at www.routledge.com/9781032467238) and sends the message or the packet to it. If that node is not the destination node, it saves the message or the packet in its buffer and decides which of the neighbors to send it to, and so on until the message or packet reaches the ultimate destination site. In this way, the message or the packet is first stored in a buffer and is then forwarded to a selected neighboring host or PSE when the next channel becomes available and the neighboring host or PSE also has a similar available buffer. Here, the actual path taken by a message or packet to reach its final destination is dynamic because the path is established as the message or packet travels along. That is why this method is also sometimes called **store-and-forward** communication: because every message or packet is temporarily stored by each host or PSE along its route before it is forwarded to another host or PSE.

Connection-less transmission can accommodate better traffic densities in communication channels (links) than message or packet switching, since a node can make the choice of the link when it is ready to send out a message or a packet. It is typically implemented by maintaining a table in each node (essentially a subset of an adjacency matrix for each node) that indicates which neighbor to send to in order to reach a specific destination node along with the exchange of traffic information among the present nodes. As usual, each node should be equipped with a large buffer for the sake of temporary storing and later transmission of messages or packets at convenient times if its outgoing channels are busy or overloaded at any instant.

Brief details on this topic with figures are given on the Support Material at www.routledge.com/9781032467238.

9.13.1.5 Routing Strategies (Techniques)

The routing strategy determines the actual path out of existing multiple paths between a pair of nodes to be used to transfer the message. To implement a specific strategy, the corresponding routing function (technique) is invoked whenever a connection is to be set up. The choice of routing strategy has an impact on the ability to adapt to changing traffic patterns in the system and consequently is crucial to the overall performance of the network. A *routing strategy* is said to be efficient if the underlying routing decision process is as fast as possible so that network latency must be minimal. A *routing algorithm* describes how routing decisions are to be specified and how often they are to be modified and is commonly said to be good if it could be easily implemented all in hardware. In LANs, sender–receiver interaction takes place on the communication channel; hence, there is no need to have any routing strategies, as there is no provision to choose the path to be taken for transmitting the message.

- **Fixed (deterministic) routing:** In this method, the entire path to be taken for communication between a *pair of nodes* is permanently specified beforehand. Here, the source nodes or its PSE selects the entire path and also decides which of all other intermediate PSEs should be used to reach its destination. Each node is equipped with a fairly comprehensive table and other information about the network environment that indicates paths to all other nodes in the system at present. All routing information is, however, included along with the message. When processes running in these nodes intend to communicate, a connection is set up using this specified path. A fixed routing strategy is simple and easy to implement. The routing decision process is somehow efficient because the intermediate PSEs, if any, need not make any routing decision. However, this strategy fails to provide flexibility when dealing with fluctuating traffic densities as well as not being able to negotiate the situation in the event of node faults or link failures, because the specified path cannot be changed once the information (or packet) has left the source computer (or its PSE). Consequently, it makes poor use of network bandwidth, leading to low throughputs and also appreciable delays when a message (or packets) is blocked due to faults or failures of components, even when alternative paths are still available for its transmission.

- **Virtual circuit:** This strategy specifies a path selected at the beginning of a transmission between a *pair of processes* and is used for all messages sent during the session. Information relating to traffic densities and other aspects of the network environment in the system are taken into consideration when deciding the best path for the session. Hence, this strategy can adapt to changing traffic patterns, rendering this method not susceptible to component failures. It therefore ensures better use of network bandwidth and thereby yields considerably improved throughput and enhanced response times.

- **Dynamic (adaptive) routing:** This method selects a path whenever a *message* or a *packet* is to be sent, so *different messages* or even *different packets* of a message between a pair of processes may use different paths. This strategy is also known as *adaptive routing*, because it has a tendency to dynamically adapt to the continuously changing state of the network in normal situation, as well as changing its traffic patterns to respond more effectively in the event of faulty nodes or congested/failed channels. Since this scheme can use alternative paths for packet transmission (packet switching in connection strategies), it makes more efficient use of network bandwidth, leading to better throughput and enhanced response times compared to when a virtual circuit is used. Its ability to adapt to alternative paths makes it resilient to failures, which is particularly important to large-scale expanding architectures in which there is a high probability of facing faulty network components very often. Under this scheme, packets of a message may arrive out of order (as already described in the packet-switching approach) at the destination site; proper reassembling of packets thus needs to be carried out based on the sequence number appended already to each packet at the time of its transmission.

  Here, the policy used in the selection of a path may be either *minimal* or *nonminimal.* In the case of a minimal policy, the path being selected is one of the shortest paths between a source–destination pair of hosts, and therefore, each packet while visiting every channel comes closer to the destination. In the nonminimal policy, a packet may have to follow a relatively long path in order to negotiate current network conditions. In the ARPANET, which was the progenitor of the internet, network information relating to traffic density and other associated aspects of the network environment along with every link in the system was constantly exchanged between nodes to determine the current optimal path under prevailing condition for a given source–destination pair of nodes.

- **Hybrid routing:** This method is essentially a combination of both static and dynamic routing methods in the sense that the source node or its PSE specifies only certain major intermediate PSEs (or nodes) of the entire path to be visited, and the subpath between any two of the specified PSEs (or nodes) is to be decided by each specified PSE (or node) that works as source along the subpath to select a suitable adjacent ordinary PSE (or node) to transmit to that PSE (node). This means that each major specified PSE (or node) maintains all information about the status of all outgoing channels (i.e. channel availability) and the adjacent ordinary PSE (i.e. readiness of the PSE to receive) that are to be used while selecting the subpath for transmitting the packet. As compared to the static routing method, this method makes more efficient use of network bandwidth, leading to better throughput and enhanced response times. Its ability to adapt to alternative paths also makes it resilient to failures

Brief details of this topic with respective figures are given on the Support Material at www. routledge.com/9781032467238.

9.13.1.6   Communication Protocols

Communications between intending parties over a network are defined and implemented using certain agreements in terms of rules and conventions, commonly referred to as a **protocol**. While communication between parties is being implemented, several aspects need to be addressed, such as naming of sites in the system, efficient name resolution, ensuring communication efficiency, and dealing with faults. As already mentioned, distributed systems (may be comprising networks of computers) are fundamentally different from conventional computer networks. Therefore, the requirements of the communication protocols of these two types of systems are also different. For network systems, the basic goal of communication protocols is to allow remote computers to communicate with each other and permit users to access remote resources. On the other hand, the basic goal of communication protocols for distributed system is not only to allow users to access remote resources but to do so in a manner transparent to the users.

Several accepted standards and well-implemented protocols for computer network systems are already available. For wide-area distributed systems, these protocols often take the form of multiple layers, each with its own goals and rules. However, well-defined protocols for distributed systems are still not mature, and as such no specific standards covering essential aspects of distributed systems are yet available. A few standard network protocols are described here. The next section describes the essential requirements that are needed by protocols for distributed systems and then a few standard communication protocols that have been designed covering those issues. The collection of protocols (of all layers) used in a particular network system is normally referred as the *protocol suite, protocol family,* or *protocol stack.*

9.13.1.6.1 Network Protocols

Computer networks are implemented using the concept of a series of layered protocols organized hierarchically, mainly to provide a separation of concerns. According to this concept, each layer contains certain protocols that addresses one or more aspects in communication and provides an interface to the layers of protocols above and below it in the hierarchy to interact in a physical sense by passing parameters, such as headers, trailers, and data parameters. The layers of protocols at higher levels in the hierarchy deal with semantic issues that relate to applications, while protocols at lower levels deal with data transmission-related aspects. The concept of layering the protocols in network design provides several advantages, dividing up the problem into manageable pieces, each of which can be handled independently of the others, and an entity using a protocol in a higher layer need not be aware of details at its lower layer.

- **The ISO/OSI Reference Model:** The International Standards Organization (ISO) has developed the Open Systems Interconnection reference model (OSI model) for communication between entities in an open system, popularly known as *ISO protocol, ISO protocol stack*, or *OSI model*. This model identifies seven standard layers and defines the jobs to be performed at each layer. It is considered as a guide and not a specification, since it essentially provides a framework in which standards can be developed for the needed services and protocols at each layer. It is to be noted that adherence to the standard protocols is important for designing open distributed systems, because if standard protocols are used, separate software components of distributed systems can be developed independently on computers having different architectures and even while they run under different operating systems.

Following the OSI model, the information to be transmitted originates at the sender's end in an application that presents it to the *application layer*. This layer adds some control information to it in the form of a header field and passes it to the next layer. The information then traverses through the *presentation* and *session layers*, each of which adds its own headers. The *presentation layer* performs change of data representation as needed as well as encryption/decryption. The *session layer* adds its own header and establishes a connection between the sender and receiver processes. The *transport layer* splits the message into packets and hands over the packet to the next layer, the *network layer*, which determines the link via which each packet is to be transmitted and hands over a *link-id* along with a packet to the data link layer. The *data link layer* treats the packet simply as a string of bits, adds error detection and correction information to it, and hands it over to the *physical layer* for actual necessary transmission. At the other end when the message is received, the *data link layer* performs error detection and forms frames, the *transport layer* forms messages, and the presentation layer puts the data in the representation as desired by the application. All seven layers of the ISO protocol and their respective functions are briefly summarized in Table 9.3.

TABLE 9.3
Layers of the ISO Protocol

Layer	Function
1. Physical layer	Provides various mechanisms for transmission of raw bit streams between two sites over a physical link.
2. Data link layer	Forms frames after organizing the bits thus received. Performs error detection/correction on created frames. Performs flow control of frames between two sites.
3. Network layer	Encapsulates frames into packets. Mainly performs routing and transmission flow control.
4. Transport layer	Forms outgoing packets. Assembles incoming packets. Performs error detection and, if required, retransmission.
5. Session layer	Establishes and terminates sessions for communications. If required, it also provides for restart and recovery. This layer is not required for connectionless communication.
6. Presentation layer	Represents message information implementing data semantics by performing change of representation, compression, and encryption/decryption.
7. Application layer	Provides services that directly support the end users of the network. The functionality implemented is application-specific.

It is to be noted that in actual implementation, out of the seven layers described, the *first three layers* are likely to be realized in hardware, the *next two layers* in the operating system, the *presentation layer* in library subroutines in the user's address space, and the *application layer* in the user's program.

Brief details on this topic with figures and an example are given on the Support Material at www. routledge.com/9781032467238.

- **TCP/IP Protocol:** The *transmission control protocol/internet protocol* (TCP/IP) reference model is a protocol suite that consists of a collection of a large number of protocols which have been eventually issued as internet standards by the Internet Activities Board (IAB). There is as such no official model of TCP/IP. However, based on the protocol norms and standards that have already been developed, it is possible to organize the communication tasks that TCP/IP performs into *four* relatively independent layers, so this model has fewer layers than the ISO protocol; hence, it is more efficient and equally complex to implement. Figure 9.10(a) shows details of its layers, comparing them to the ISO protocol, from bottom to top:
  - Network-access layer (host-to-network)
  - Internet layer
  - Transport layer (or host-to-host)
  - Application layer

The lowest layer, the **network-access layer** or **host-to-network layer**, is essentially a combination of the physical and data-link layers of the ISO model [Figure 9.10(a)] that covers the whole

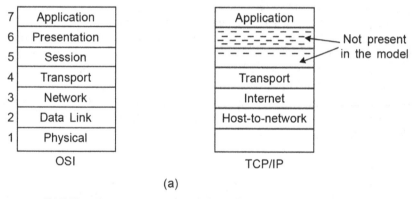

(a)

TCP/IP reference model (in comparison to OSI)

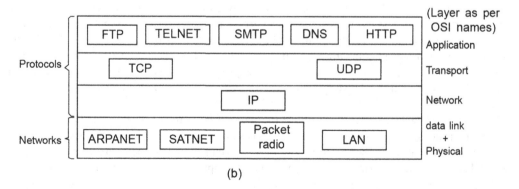

(b)

FIGURE 9.10   A schematic block diagram of TCP/IP reference model; a) in comparison to OSI model, and b) also showing its protocols and different related networks used.

physical interface between a data transmission device (computers, workstations, etc.) and a transmission medium or network. This layer specifies the nature of the signals, the characteristics of the transmission medium, the data rate, and similar other related aspects. This layer is also concerned with access to and routing data through a network for the exchange of data between two end systems (workstation, server, etc.) attached to the same network. The sending computer must provide the network with the address of the destination computer to enable the network to route the data to the targeted destination. The sending computer may invoke some specific services (such as priority) that might be provided by the network. The specific software used at this layer relies on the type of network to be used; different standards in this regard have been introduced for circuit switching/packet switching (e.g. frame relay), LANs (e.g. Ethernet), WANs (e.g. Satnet), and others. This is illustrated in Figure 9.10(b). Thus, it makes sense to separate those functions that are related to network access into a separate layer. By doing this, the remainder of the communication software above this network-access layer need not be at all concerned about the peculiarities and the characteristics of the network to be used. Consequently, this higher-layer software can function in its own way regardless of the specific network to which the hosts are attached.

In cases where two devices intending to exchange data are attached to two different networks, some procedures are needed so that multiple interconnected networks can enable data to reach their ultimate destination. This function is provided by the *internet layer* that defines an official packet format and protocol called **Internet Protocol**, which is used at this layer to provide the routing function across multiple networks [see Figure 9.10(b)]. The IP can run on top of any data-link protocol. This protocol can be implemented not only in end systems but often also in intermediate components on networks, such as routers. A **router** is essentially a processor that connects two networks and whose primary function is to relay data from one network to the other on a route from the source to the destination end system.

Packet routing is clearly the major issue here, as is to avoid congestion. In most situations, packets will require multiple hops (using one or more intermediate routers) to make the journey, but this is kept transparent to users. For these and other reasons, it is reasonable to say that the TCP/IP internet layer is quite similar in functionality to the OSI network layer. Figure 9.10(a) illustrates this correspondence. The message comes down to TCP from the upper layer with instructions to send it to a specific location with the destination address (host name, port number). TCP hands the message down to IP with instructions to send it to a specific location (host name). Note that IP need not be told the identity of the destination port; all it needs to know that the data are intended for a specific host. IP hands the message down to network access layer (e.g. ARPANET) with instructions to send it to the respective router (the first hop on the way to its destined location) present in the network. The IP performs data transmission between two hosts (host-to-host communication) on the internet. The address of the destination host is provided in the 32-bit IP address format. Protocols in the *next higher layers provide communication between processes*; each host assigns unique 16-bit port numbers to processes, and a sender process uses a destination process address, which is a pair (IP address, port number). The use of port numbers permits many processes within a host to use send and receive messages concurrently. Some well-known services, such as FTP, Telnet, SMTP, and HTTP, have been assigned standard port numbers authorized by the Internet Assigned Numbers Authority (IANA). IP is a connectionless, unreliable protocol; it does not give any guarantee that packets of a message will be delivered without error, only once (no duplication), and in the correct order (in sequence).

The **transport layer** is placed just above the internet layer in the TCP/IP model [see Figure 9.10(b)] and is designed to allow peer entities on the source and the destination hosts to carry on a conversation, the same as in the OSI transport layer. Two end-to-end protocols are defined. The first one, **TCP**, is a connection-oriented reliable protocol. It employs a virtual circuit between two processes that allows to transmitting a byte stream originating on one machine to be reliably delivered to any other machine in the internetworks. The second protocol [see Figure 9.10(b)] in this layer, **UDP (User Datagram Protocol)**, is an unreliable, connectionless protocol for applications that do not want TCP's sequencing or flow control and wish to provide their own. It incurs low overhead compared to the TCP, because it does not need to set up and maintain a virtual circuit or ensure reliable delivery. UDP is employed in multimedia applications and in video conferencing, because the occasional loss of packets is not a correctness issue in these applications; it only results in poor picture quality. These applications, however, use their own flow and congestion control mechanisms by reducing the resolution of pictures and consequently lowering the picture quality if a sender, a receiver, or the network is overloaded.

On top of the transport layer, the topmost layer in the TCP/IP model is the **application layer** that corresponds to layers 5–7 in the ISO model. This is depicted in Figure 9.10(a). This layer essentially contains the logic needed to support the various user applications. For each different type of application, such as file transfer, a separate module is needed that is specific to that application. Therefore, this layer should be equipped with all the higher-level protocols. The protocols used in this layer in the early days included virtual terminals (TELNET), file transfer (FTP), and electronic mail (SMTP), as shown in Figure 9.10(b). Many other protocols have been added to these over the years, such as the DNS for mapping host names onto their network addresses; HTTP, the protocol used for fetching pages on the World Wide Web; and many others.

More about the ISO/OSI model and TCP/IP protocol, with figures, is given on the Support Material at www.routledge.com/9781032467238.

9.13.1.7 Network Bandwidth and Latency

When large numbers of computers are connected together and data are to be exchanged between the nodes, two aspects that define, describe, and determine network performance are how quickly the data can reach the targeted destination node and at what rate the data can be delivered. *Network bandwidth* is defined as the rate at which data is transferred over a network. It encompasses numerous factors and depends on several issues, such as capacities of network links, delays at routers, bridges, gateways, communicating processors, and many similar things that are involved in the architecture of networks of computers. Peak bandwidth is the theoretical maximum rate at which data can be transferred between two nodes but cannot be attained in practice due to several factors present in the network environment. *Effective bandwidth*, on the other hand, is the realized bandwidth that may be lower than the peak bandwidth due to various reasons, such as congestion caused by temporary overloads over links, data transmission errors that lead to time-outs and subsequent needed retransmissions, structural resource imbalance, etc. *Network latency* is the elapsed time (interval) between sending a byte of data by a source node and its receipt at the destination node after completing its journey through the network. It is typically computed for the first byte of data to be transferred. Several aspects contribute to network latency, mainly the processing time required by the layers of a network and delays caused by congestion in the network.

9.13.2 COMMUNICATION PROTOCOLS FOR DISTRIBUTED SYSTEMS: ESSENTIAL REQUIREMENTS

While the network protocols (as described) commonly used today are adequate for most conventional network-based applications, such as electronic mail, file transfer, remote login, and remote job entry, but they are not equally applicable to suit distributed environments consisting of distributed systems and distributed applications. The reasons behind, that distributed systems, by definition and principle (see Section 9.8 and Table 9.1) have to fulfill several specific requirements that totally differs when compared to traditional network systems. Some of them are:

- *Transparency*: Distributed systems usually support process migration facility for efficient utilization of resources. But communication (network) protocols meant for network systems use location-dependent process-ids (such as port addresses that are unique only within a node) that severely hinder the process migration implementation, because when a process migrates, its process-id changes. Therefore, these protocols cannot be used in distributed systems and, in fact, communication protocols for distributed systems must use location-independent process-ids that will remain unchanged even when a process migrates from one location to another within the domain of distributed system.

- *System-wide communication*: Communication protocols used in network systems are mainly employed to transport data between two nodes of a network and mostly serve the purpose of input/output activities. However, most communications in distributed system which consists of networks of computers, and particularly, when it is based on client–server model that makes use of a server in which a client issues a request to server to provide some *specific service* for it by sending a message to the server and then keeps on waiting until the server receives it, and sends back a due acknowledgement. Therefore, communication protocols in distributed systems must have a *simple, connectionless protocol* equipped with features that support such request/response activities.

- *Group communication*: Distributed systems often make use of group communication facilities to enable a sender to reliably send a message to *n* receivers. Many network systems although provide certain mechanisms to realize this group communication by means of multicast or even broadcast at the data-link layer, but their respective protocols often hide these potential facilities from applications. Moreover, when the broadcast mechanism is employed to send *n* point-to-point messages and subsequently to wait for *n* acknowledgements, this badly wastes bandwidth and severely degrades the performance of the corresponding algorithm and makes it inefficient. Communication protocols for distributed systems, therefore, must provide certain means to offer more flexible and relatively efficient group communication facilities so that a group address can be mapped on one or more data-link addresses, and the routing protocol can then use a data-link multicast address to send a message to all the receivers belonging to the group defined by the multicast address.

- *Network management*: Management of computer networks often requires manual intervention to update the network configuration (e.g. add/remove a node from a network, allocation of new address, etc.) to reflect its current state of affairs. The communication protocol is expected to be able to automatically handle network management activities by changing the network configuration dynamically as and when needed to reflect its present state.

- *Network security*: Security in a network environment is a burning problem, and network security is a vital aspect that often uses encryption mechanisms to ensure protection of message data from any types of threat as far as possible when the data traverses across a network. Encryption methods although are expensive to use, but it is also true that all communication channels and nodes do not always face a threat for a particular user and hence as such have no need of any encryption. Thus, encryption is needed only when there is a possibility of a challenge of threat on a critical message while in transit from its source node to the destination node through an untrustworthy channel/node. Hence, a communication protocol is particularly required that would provide a flexible and efficient mechanism in which a message is encrypted if and only if the path it uses across the network during its journey is not trusted and is critically at the face of any possible attack.

- *Scalability*: The communication protocol for distributed systems must not be thwarted but equally provide efficient communication in both LAN and WAN environments, even when they are well extended to cover a larger domain. In addition, a single communication protocol must be workable as far as possible on both types of networks (LAN and WAN).

9.13.3 Standard Communication Protocols

Several communication protocols have been designed; two of them, versatile message transport protocol (VMTP) and fast local internet protocol (FLIP), to address many of the requirements (as mentioned) that a distributed system needs, along with a target of achieving higher throughput and/

or quick response. VMTP is designed to provide group communication facilities and implements a secure and efficient client–server-based protocol (Cheriton and Williamson, 1989). FLIP, on the other hand, provides transparency, efficient client–server-based communication, group communication, security, and easy network management (Kaashoek et al., 1993).

- **VMTP:** VMTP is essentially a connectionless transport protocol designed mainly for distributed operating systems based on the concept of a message transaction with special features to support *request/response* activity and was used in V-System. A client here when sends a message to one or more servers followed by zero or more response messages sent back to the client by the servers, it is mostly a single request message and a single response message involved in such message transactions, but at most one per server.

Transparency and group communication facilities are provided by using 64-bit identifiers (a portion of which is reserved for group identification entities) to entities that are unique, stable, and particularly independent of host addresses, and these enable entities to be migrated and handled independently of network layer addressing. A group management protocol is provided for the purpose of creating new groups, adding new members, or deleting members from an existing group, as are various types of querying and related information about existing groups.

VMTP provides a selective *retransmission mechanism* to yield better performance. The packets of a message are divided into packet groups containing a maximum of 16 kilobytes of segment data. When a packet group is sent and is received, the receiver creates some form of information that indicates which segment blocks are still outstanding. An acknowledgement is sent accordingly from the receiver to the sender, and the acknowledgement packet contains information that helps the sender to selectively retransmit only the missing segment blocks of the packet group.

Many other important and interesting features are present in VMTP. In fact, VMTP provides a rich collection of optional facilities that extend its functionality and improved performance in diverse spectrum of situations. One important feature which is useful in real-time communication is the facility of *conditional message delivery*. A client in a time-critical situation can use this facility to ensure that its message is delivered only if the server is able to process it immediately or within a specified short duration of time. Such optional facilities that sometimes need to be included should be designed carefully so that their inclusions will only offer critical extensions to the existing basic facilities without degrading the performance, especially while executing the majority of common cases which happen very often.

- **Fast Local Internet Protocol (FLIP):** FLIP was developed for DOSs and is used in the **Amoeba** distributed system. It is a connectionless protocol that includes several salient features, such as transparency, efficient client–server-based communication facility, group communication facility, security, and easy network management. A brief overview of FLIP is given here describing some of its important features, and further details of this protocol can be found in Kaashoek et al. (1993).

Transparency is provided by FLIP using location-independent 64-bit identifiers to entities which are also called *network service access points* (NSAPs). Sites on an internetwork can have more than one NSAP, typically one or more for each entity (e.g. process). Each site is connected to the internetwork by a *FLIP box* that either can be a software layer in the operating system of the corresponding site or can be run on a separate communication processor (CP). Each FLIP box maintains a routing table, basically a dynamic hint cache that maps NSAP addresses to data-link addresses. Special primitives are provided to dynamically register and unregister NSAP addresses into the routing table of a FLIP box. An entity can register more than one address in a FLIP box (e.g. its own address to receive messages directed to the entity itself and the null address to receive broadcast messages). FLIP uses a one-way mapping between the private address used to *register* an entity and the public address used to *advertise* the entity. A one-way encryption function is used to ensure that one cannot deduce the private address from the public address. Therefore, entities that know the (public) address of an NSAP (because they have communicated with it) are not able to receive messages on that address, because they do not know the corresponding private address.

A FLIP message may be of any size up to $2^{32} - 1$ bytes that is transmitted unreliably between NSAPs. If a message is too large for a particular network, it is fragmented into smaller chunks, called *fragments*. A fragment typically fits in a single network packet. The basic function of FLIP is to route an arbitrary-length message from the source NSAP to the destination NSAP. The policy on which a specific path is selected for routing is based on the information stored in the routing tables of each FLIP box about the networks to which it is connected. Two key parameters used for this purpose are the *network weight* and a *security list*. A low network weight means that the network is currently suitable for a message to be forwarded. The network weight can be determined based on, for example, physical properties of the network, such as bandwidth and delay (due to congestion). The security bit, on the other hand, indicates whether sensitive data can be sent unencrypted over the network.

Both point-to-point and group communication facilities are provided by FLIP for sending a message to a public address. In fact, FLIP provides three types of system calls, *flip_unicast*, *flip_multicast*, and *flip_broadcast*, The group communication protocols heavily use *flip_multicast*. This has the advantage that a group of n processes can be addressed using one FLIP address, even if they are located on multiple networks.

FLIP implements security without making any encryption of messages by itself. It provides two mechanisms to impose security when the messages are delivered. In the first mechanism, a sender can mark its message sensitive by using the *security bit*. Such messages are routed only over trusted networks. The second mechanism is that messages while routed over an untrusted network by a FLIP are marked unsafe by setting the *unsafe bit*. When the receiver receives the message, it can tell the sender by checking the unsafe bit whether there is any safe route between them. If a safe route exists, the sender then tries to send the sensitive messages in unencrypted form but with the *security bit* set. If no more trusted path is available for the message at any point in time during routing (which can only happen due to changes in network configuration), it is returned to the sender with the *unreachable bit* set. If this happens, the sender encrypts the message and retransmits it with security bit cleared. Therefore, message encryption is done only when it is required and that too by the sender, and not by FLIP.

FLIP handles *network management* easily because dynamic changes in network configuration are taken care of automatically. Human intervention is seldom used in this regard, and even if it is, it is required only to declare specifically which networks are trusted and which are not. The system administrator exactly performs this task while working on FLIP and should precisely declare whether network interfaces are to be trusted, since FLIP on its own cannot determine which interface is trustworthy.

One of the shortcomings of FLIP is that it is unable to provide full-fledged support in wide-area networking. Although FLIP has been successfully implemented in smaller WAN environments, but it is not adequate and suitable enough to be used as a standard WAN communication protocol in a moderately large WAN environment. The root of this shortcoming might be due to one of the reasons that the designers of FLIP were mostly inclined to trade it more functionally scalable, and also assumed that wide–area communication should be mainly carried out at a relatively higher layers, and not at network layer in which FLIP belongs.

9.13.4 Sockets

Sockets and socket programming were developed in the 1980s in the Berkley UNIX environment. A socket is essentially a mechanism that enables communication between a client and server process and may be either *connection-oriented* or *connectionless*. A socket is simply one end of a communication path. A client socket in one computer uses an address to call a server socket on another computer. Once the proper sockets are engaged, the two computers can then exchange data. Sockets can be used for interprocess communication within the UNIX system domain and in the internet domain. Typically, computers with server sockets keep a TCP or UDP port open for unscheduled incoming calls. The client typically determines the socket identification of the targeted server by finding it in a domain name system (DNS) database. Once a connection is made, the server switches the dialogue to a different available port number to free up the main port number in order to allow more additional incoming calls to enter.

Sockets can be used in internet applications, such as TELNET and *remote login (rlogin)* in which all the details are kept hidden from the user. However, sockets can be constructed from within a program (such as in C or Java), thereby enabling the designer and programmer to easily include semantics of networking functions that consequently permit unrelated processes on different hosts to communicate with one another.

Sockets while used in a connection-based mode of operation, the processes using the sockets are either *clients* or *servers*. Both client and server processes create a socket. These two sockets are then connected to set up a communication path that can be used to send and receive messages. The naming issue is handled in the following way: The server binds its socket to an address that is valid in the domain in which the socket will be used. This address is now widely advertised in the domain. A client process uses this address to perform a connect between its socket and that of the server. This approach, however, avoids the necessary use of *process-ids* in communication.

The socket mechanism provides sufficient flexibility so that processes using it can choose a mode of operation that best suits the intended use. For applications in which low overhead is important, the communicating process can use a connectionless mode of operation using datagrams. But for applications that critically demand reliability, processes can use a connection-based mode of operation using a virtual circuit for guaranteed reliable data delivery. The *Berkley Sockets Interface* is the de facto **standard API** for developing networking applications which run over a wide range of different operating systems. The sockets API provides generic access to interprocess communications services. Windows sockets (WinSock) is, however, essentially based on Berkley specifications.

A socket used to define an **application program interface (API)** is a generic communication interface for writing programs that use TCP or UDP. In practice, when used as an API, a socket is identified by the triple:

(protocol, local-address, local-process)

The *local-address* is an **IP address**, and the *local-process* is a **port number**. Because the port numbers are unique within a system, the port number implies the protocol (TCP or UDP). However, for clarity and implementation, sockets used for an API include the *protocol* as well as the *IP address* and *port number* in defining a unique socket.

Corresponding to the two protocols (TCP and UDP), the Sockets API mainly recognizes two types of sockets: **stream sockets** and **datagram sockets**. Stream sockets make use of TCP, which provides a connection-based, reliable, guaranteed data transfer of all blocks of data sent between a pair of sockets for delivery that arrive in the same order that they were sent. Datagram sockets make use of UDP, which provides connectionless features; therefore, use of these sockets never gives guaranteed delivery of data, nor is the order of data necessarily preserved. There is also a third type of socket provided by the Sockets API known as **raw sockets**, which allows direct access to lower layer protocols, such as, IP.

For **stream communication**, the functions *send()* and *recv()* are used to send and receive data over the connection identified by the *s* parameter. In the *recv()* call, the *buf* parameter (similar to *message* in *send* call) points to the buffer for storing incoming data, with an upper limit on the number of bytes set by the *message-length* parameter. The *close()* and *shutdown()* calls are described on the Support Material at www.routledge.com/9781032467238.

For **datagram communication**, the function **sendto( )** and **recvfrom( )** are used. The **sendto ( )** includes all the parameters of the **send( )** call plus a specification of the *destination address* (IP address and port). Similarly, the **recvfrom( )** call includes an address parameter, which is filled in when data are received.

Brief details on this topic are given on the Support Material at www.routledge.com/9781032467238.

9.13.5 A Traditional Distributed Operating System: Amoeba

Amoeba originated at Vrije University, Amsterdam, and was introduced in the early 1980s is a DOS, and Amoeba 1.0 was introduced by 1983. The system evolved for several years with the introduction of many different enhanced versions (such as Amoeba 5.0), maintaining downward compatibility. Its primary objective is to build a transparent distributed OS using multiple machines spread over the network with the look and flavor of a standard time-sharing OS like UNIX. Another goal is to provide a testbed for distributed and parallel programming. The hardware design of Amoeba is somewhat different from what most system organizations presently follow. The system architecture of Amoeba has three main components:

- X-terminals,
- A processor pool consisting of a very large number of CPUs, each with tens of megabytes of memory, and
- Servers such as file and print servers.

The *X-terminal* is a user station consisting of a keyboard, a mouse, and a bit-mapped terminal connected to a computer. The nodes in the system use the processor pool model, which has the features described in Section 9.5. The object concept is central to Amoeba, and the objects supported this way are files, directories, memory segments, screen windows, processors, disks, and tape drives. This uniform interface to all objects provides generality and simplicity. Servers handle all objects in the system; both hardware and software, and objects are named, protected, and managed by capabilities.

An important feature of Amoeba, unlike most other distributed systems, is that it has no concept of a "home machine". The entire system is present to a user as a whole. Machines do not have owners. The initial shell starts up at login and runs on some arbitrary machine (processor), but as commands are started, in general, they do not run on the same machine as the shell. Instead, the system automatically looks for the most lightly loaded machine to run each new command on. Similarly, pool processors are not "owned" by any one user. When a user submits a job, the OS dynamically allocates one or more processors from the pool instead of allowing it to use any specific workstation. Thus, a user's computation is spread across the hosts in a system that totally disregards any machine boundaries. This is possible since all the resources in the system are tightly integrated. When the job is completed, the allocated processors are subsequently released and go back to the pool. In the event of shortage in the availability of processors, individual processors may be timeshared.

The Amoeba operating system model consists of two basic pieces: one piece is a microkernel, which runs on every processor of the pool processors and servers, and the other piece is a collection of servers that provide most of the traditional operating system functionality. The microkernel performs four primary functions:

- Managing processes and threads
- Providing low-level memory management support
- Supporting communication
- Handling low-level I/O

Like most other operating systems, Amoeba supports the concept of a *process*. In addition, it also supports *multiple threads* of control within a single address space. The thread concept is extended up to the kernel level. A process with one thread is essentially the same as a process in UNIX. Such a process has a single address space, a set of registers, a program counter, and a stack. Multiple threads might be used in a file server in which every incoming request is assigned to a separate thread to work on; each such thread can be absolutely sequential, even if it has to block waiting for I/O.

Amoeba provides two communication protocols. One protocol supports the client–server communication model through RPC, while the other protocol provides **group communication** by using either multicasting or reliable broadcasting. For actual message transmission, both these protocols use an underlying Internet protocol called FLIP, already discussed in Section 9.13.3, which is a network layer protocol in the ISO protocol stack.

Many functions performed by traditional kernels are implemented through servers that run on top of the kernel. Thus, actions like booting, process creation, and process scheduling are performed by servers. The file system is also implemented as a file server. This approach reduces the size of the microkernel and makes it suitable for a wide range of computer systems from servers to pool processors.

As usual, Amoeba also has a file system. However, unlike most other operating systems, the choice of the file system is not dictated by the operating system. The file system runs as a collection of server processes. Users who do not like the standard ones are free to write their own. The kernel does not know, and really doesn't care or want to know, which one is the "real" file system. In fact, different users, if desired, may use different incompatible file systems at the same time. The standard file system consists of three servers. The **bullet server** handles file storage, the **directory server** takes care of file naming and directory management, and the **replication server** handles file replication. The file system has been split into three components to achieve increased flexibility, and make each of the servers straightforward to implement.

Amoeba supports various other servers. One such is the **boot server,** which is used to provide a degree of fault tolerance to Amoeba by checking that all servers that are supposed to be running are in fact really running and taking corrective action when they are not. A server capable to survive crashes can be included in the boot server's configuration file. Each entry tells how often the boot server should poll and how it should poll. As long as the server responds correctly, the boot server has nothing to do and takes no further action. Similarly, although Amoeba uses the FLIP protocol internally to achieve high performance, sometimes it is necessary to speak CP/IP, for example, to communicate with X-terminals, to send and receive mail to non-Amoeba machines, and to interact with other Amoeba systems via the Internet. To enable Amoeba to do such so many other things, a **TCP/IP server** has been thus provided. Apart from these servers, Amoeba includes a **disk server** (used by the directory server for storing its arrays of capability pairs), various other **I/O servers**, a **time–of–day server**, and a **random number server** (useful for generating port, capabilities, and FLIP addresses). The so-called **Swiss Army Knife server** deals with many activities that have to be done later by starting up processes at a specified time in the future. **Mail severs** deal with incoming and outgoing electronic mail.

9.13.6   Internetworking: Concepts and Issues

Distributed systems realized by multicomputer organization using any of the models already described (see Section 9.11.1.1) and structured either in the form of a network (cluster) of computers or a network of computer networks must exhibit two essential features, *extensibility* and *openness*, that require integration of several networks. When two or more networks (each network, in turn, has a cluster of interconnected computers) with the same or different network standards are interconnected to form a single network, this resulting single network is called an *internetwork*, and the method to realize the same is called *internetworking*. Internetworks made it possible for computers to communicate with one another when they are attached to different networks. Apart from a traditional WAN, internetworks of multiple LANs that form a WAN can be used as a distributed system.

The collection of networks constituting an internetwork often includes heterogeneous networks composed of several network segments that may have different networking standards (essentially topology and protocol) and may have been supplied from different vendors. The objective of internetworking is to allow these relatively unrelated networks to evolve into a single working system hiding all the peculiarities of the underlying physical networks so that the resulting internetwork can function as a single coordinated unit with a single unified addressing scheme that enables packets to be addressed to any host connected to any network segment (subnet). A suitable protocol is then needed to define the format of internetwork packets and give rules according to which they will be handled. Several internetworking issues arise while interconnecting multiple networks (often heterogeneous) to form a single network, and these issues are relatively easier to handle if the network segments of the resulting internetwork are designed using widely accepted standards instead of proprietary topologies and protocols. Some of the important interconnection issues when multiple networks are hooked up to realize an internetwork are given here in brief.

9.13.6.1 Interconnection Technologies

Interconnection of similar networks is relatively easy. But when two dissimilar networks with different topologies and protocols are interconnected, it requires an internetworking scheme to develop that will ultimately provide some common points of reference for the two dissimilar networks to communicate with each other. The point of reference might be a high-level protocol common to the two networks, a device that permits interconnection of different topologies with different physical and electrical characteristics, or a protocol that allows operating environment differences to be ignored. The most commonly used approach in this regard is to make use of common high-level protocols for moving data between common layers on a communication model, such as OSI and TCP/IP suites. Internetworking tools, such as; *bridges, routers, brouters*, and *gateways* make extensive use of this approach while interconnecting similar or dissimilar networks to form a single network system.

- **Bridges:** Bridges essentially operate at the bottom two layers of the ISO model (data-link and physical) and hence can be used to connect networks that use the same communication protocols above the data-link layer, but may not have the same protocols at the data-link and physical layers. In other words, bridges feature high-level protocol transparency. Bridges, for example, may be used to connect two networks, one of which uses fiber-optics communication medium and the other of which uses coaxial cables, but both networks must use the same high-level protocols, such as TCP/IP, for example. The use of similar protocols at higher levels implies that bridges do not intervene in the activities carried out by those protocols in different segments. This means that bridges do not modify either the format or the contents of the frames when they transfer them from one network segment to another. In fact, they simply copy the frames, and while transferring data between two network segments, they can even use a third segment in the middle of the two that cannot understand the data passing through it. In this case, the third intermediate segment simply serves the purpose of only routing, Bridges are also useful in network partitioning. When network traffic becomes excessive, the performance of a network segment starts to degrade; the network segment can be broken into two segments, and a bridge is used in between to interconnect them.

- **Routers:** Routers operate at the network layer of the OSI model and use the bottom three layers of the OSI model. They are usually employed to interconnect those networks that use the same high-level protocols above the network layer. It is to be noted that protocols used in data-link and physical layers are transparent to routers. Consequently, if two network segments use different protocols at these two layers, a bridge must be used to connect them. While bridges are aware of the ultimate destination of data, routers only know which is the next router for the data to be transferred across the network. However, routers are more intelligent than bridges in the sense that a router is essentially a processor that not only copies data from one network segment to another, but whose primary function is to relay the data from the source to the destination system on a best-possible route being chosen by using information in a routing table. A router, therefore, is equipped with a flow control mechanism that negotiates traffic congestion by making decisions to direct the traffic to a suitable less-congested alternative path.

• **Brouters:** To make the internetwork more versatile; network segments, apart from using routers, often use bridges to accommodate multi-protocols so that different protocols can be used at the data-link and physical layers. This requirement eventually resulted in a design of a kind of devices that are a hybrid of bridges and routers called *brouters*. These devices provide many of the distinct advantages of both bridges and routers. Although these devices are complex in design, expensive to afford, and difficult to install, but are most useful for very complex heterogeneous internetworks in which the network segments use the same high-level communication protocol to yield the best possible internetworking solution in some situations.

• **Gateways:** Gateways operate at the top three layers of the OSI model. They are mainly used for interconnecting dissimilar networks that are built on totally different communication architecture (both hardware- and software-wise) and use different communication protocols. For example, a gateway may be used to interconnect two incompatible networks, one of which may use the TCP/IP suite and the other of which may use IBM's SNA (System Network Architecture) protocol suite. Since gateways are used to interconnect networks using dissimilar protocols, one of the major responsibilities of gateways is protocol translation and necessary conversion, apart from also occasionally performing a routing function.

9.13.6.2 Communication Media

The communication medium to be selected to connect two networks in order to implement an internetwork is a major issue, since the throughput and the efficiency of the internetwork heavily rely on it. Such selection again depends mostly on the locations of the two networks and the throughput wanted.

To interconnect LANs that are located within a close vicinity (say, within a circle of about 100 meters diameter), the Fiber Distributed Data Interface (FDDI) specified by ANSI operates at a speed of 100 Mbps may be selected as an ideal high-bandwidth communication medium.

If the two networks are located a little far from each other (say, in nearby cities), they may then be connected by either leased or dedicated telephone lines, depending on whether the traffic load is low or heavy as well as whether the information being sent is ordinary or sensitive.

If the two networks are located very far from each other (say, in different countries), then they may be interconnected using communication channels of public data networks, such as telephone lines or communication satellites, but these channels while being used may give rise to inconsistent traffic and also create issues related to system reliability that eventually influence the data throughput between the two networks. Security issues are also a significant problem in this case that can be otherwise negotiated using additional techniques. Improvement to some extent in data throughput may, however, be obtained by using a suitable method of traffic routing, thereby directing the traffic to a suitable less-congested alternative path at the time of heavy congestion on the scheduled path.

9.13.6.3 Network Management

Management of an internetwork is more complex than management of a simple independent network of computers (such as a LAN) used as a distributed system. One of the main reasons is that several local problems become global problems when numerous LANs are interconnected to form an internetwork, and the management tools already available to handle simple independent networks are either not suitable, inadequate, or not at all able to manage the internetwork.

In addition, if the internetwork is heterogeneous in nature, which is usual, then building widely acceptable tools to manage an internetwork is equally difficult to realize. However, several organizations, like the ISO, the Internet Engineering Task Force (IETF), the Open Software Foundation (OSF), and others are engaged in defining certain management standards for communications networks that would be interoperable on multivendor networks. These standards are, however, developed based on several popular reference models and a few already-defined network management frameworks. Out of many, three notable standards eventually came out that can be used as network management tools: *Simple Network Management Protocol* (**SNMP**), *Common Management Information Protocol* (**CMIP**), and *Distributed Management Environment* (**DME**).

- The **SNMP** (Shevenell, 1994; Janet, 1993) standard, introduced in the late 1980s, is essentially a simple and low-cost client–server protocol to monitor and control networks that use the IP suite. SNMP-based tools have been developed by most of the vendors dealing with network management element. SNMP version 2 uses IETF in order to make itself more speedy and secure and at the same time capable to handle manager–manager communication.
- **CMIP** (Janet, 1993), developed by OSI (ISO/CCITT), is a network management standard to facilitate interoperability and true integration in which a large number of separate, isolated network management products and services offered by multi-vendors are present. CMIP is essentially based on a manager-agent model that facilitates communication between managing systems. CMIP-based products are comparatively costly, more complex, and require relatively more processing power to implement. That is why these products, in spite of having several nice features and providing richer functionality, have failed to attain the expected level of growth.
- The **DME** from the OSF is a set of standards designed based on SNMP, CMIP, and other de facto standards and has been specified for distributed network management products that provide a framework to realize a consistent network management scheme across a global multi-vendor distributed environment. Several products based on DME, as reported, are still in the process of enhancement and further development.

9.14 DISTRIBUTED OPERATING SYSTEMS: WORKSTATION–SERVER MODEL

A truly DOS exhibits distribution of resources and services that are fully transparent to the application programs executing on different nodes (sites). File names are made global, and there is a single set of system primitives to access them regardless of their geographic location with respect to the requesting client. Likewise, the use of a uniform procedure call mechanism evades the syntactic differences between local and remote calls. As a result of these and the implementation of other techniques to achieve full distribution transparency, the entire networked system appears to its users as a single coherent computer system. All its devices and services are available to every application of authorized users. The derived operating system is now free to migrate resources, such as files and processes, in order to optimize the system's performance while negotiating demand, balancing of load, and variations in the availability of the components.

The workstation–server model is typically a distributed system in which computing is essentially distributed. Users, applications, and resources are distributed in response to business requirements and linked by a single LAN or WAN or by an internet of networks. Architecturally, individual computers in the cluster may be workstations or multi-user systems, each running its own software to deal mostly with its own applications. When a user submits a program for execution, the system chooses a suitable computer to run it, usually one with an affinity to the requesting site. The system then locates the chosen site (node) and loads the executable program to run it. In essence, distributed systems may enjoy and exploit most of the advantages that the workstation/server model usually offers.

The operating system that supports multiple systems to act cooperatively often faces several requirements to fulfill that this architecture places on it. Those span across three basic dimensions: hardware, control, and data. To satisfy these requirements, several issues and the related mechanisms to address them need to be included in the DOS at the time of its development. In the following section, we will discuss some of the most common issues and the related frequently used mechanisms that the distributed environment demands for smooth operation.

9.14.1 NAMING

Distributed operating systems manage a number of user-accessible entities, such as nodes, I/O devices, files, processes, services, mailboxes, and so on. Each object is assigned a unique name and resides at some location. At the system level, resources are typically identified by numeric tokens. *Naming* is essentially a lookup function, and its mechanism provides a means of mapping between the symbolic/user-given names and the low-level system identifiers used mainly in operating-system calls. Basically, a name is assigned that designates the specific object of interest, a location that identifies its address, and a route that indicates how to reach it. Each host is assigned a system-wide unique name, which can be either numeric or symbolic, and each process or resource in a host is assigned an *id* that is unique, at least in the host. This way, the pair (<host-name>,<process-id>) used as a token uniquely identifies each specific process (object) at the chosen host and hence can be used as its name. When a process wishes to communicate with another process, it uses a pair like (xx, P_k) as the name of the destination process, where xx is the name of a host to which the process P_k belongs. In some distributed systems, low-level tokens are globally unique at the system level. This helps to fully decouple names from locations. This name, however, should be translated into a network address to send a message over a network. The *name service* in a distributed system possesses certain desirable properties that mainly include:

- *Name transparency*, which means that an object name should not divulge any hint about its actual location.
- *Location transparency* implies that a name or a token should not be changed when the related object changes its residence.
- *Replication transparency* ensures that replication of an object is to be kept hidden from users.
- *Dynamic adaptability to changes of the object's location* by replication facilitates migration of objects and thereby dynamically changes its address that seems to be sometimes essential in the event of load sharing, availability, and fault tolerance.

A distributed name service is essentially a mapping that may be multi-level and multi-valued. It may be organized as a hierarchy in which certain parts of prefixes designate a specific sub-domain. The internet service represents an example of a naming hierarchy where each host connected to the internet has a unique address known as the **IP** (Internet Protocol) address. The IP address of a host is provided with a given name by the **domain name system** (DNS), which is actually a distributed internet directory service. DNS provides a *name server* in every domain, whose IP address is known to all hosts belong to that domain. The name server contains a directory giving the IP address of each host in that domain. When a process in a host wishes to communicate another process with the name (<host-name>, <process-id>), the host performs name resolution to determine the IP address of <host-name>. If <host-name> is not its own name, it sends the name to the name server in its immediate containing domain, which, in turn, may send it to the name server in its immediate containing domain, and so on, until the name reaches the name server of the largest domain contained in <host-name>. The name server then removes its own name from <host-name> and checks whether the remaining string is the name of a single host. If so, it obtains the IP address of the host from the directory and passes it back along the same route from which it received <host-name>; otherwise the remaining name string contains at least one domain name, so it passes the remaining name string to the name server of that domain, and so on. Once the sending process receives the IP address of <host-name>, the pair (<IP address>, <process-id>) is used to communicate with the destination process.

Since name resolution using name servers, in general, can be quite lengthy, many distributed systems attempt to improve performance by caching in each workstation a collection of its recently requested name-token translations. This technique speeds up repeated name resolution (the same way a directory cache speeds up repeated references to the directory entry of a file) when hits in the name cache result in quick translations that bypass the name server. The difficulty with client caching in distributed systems is that object migrations can invalidate the cache names. In addition, the name server of a domain is often replicated or distributed to enhance its availability and to avoid contention.

Apart from the name server that implements a naming service in a DOS, there are a variety of other methods, including *static maps, broadcasting*, and *prefix tables*. For more details, interested readers can consult Milenkovic (1992).

9.14.2 PROCESS MIGRATION

Process migration in distributed system is considered a potential activity that refers to the transfer of an active process from one workstation (site) to another. Migration of processes involves transferring everything with regard to process's state so that the migrated process can continue its execution on the destination node from the point at which it was transferred. Process migration is carried out by the system in order to attain mainly the following:

* Balancing of existing load to increase throughput
* Better utilization of system resources
* Improved fault tolerance
* Increased performance

Load balancing refers to the distribution of processes located at heavily loaded workstations to some other one for execution that are relatively lying idle using the high-speed interconnection networks that connect them. When process migration decides to balance the load, it requires a mechanism to gather load information: a distributed policy which decides that a process should be moved and a mechanism to effect the transfer. The load-balance function is invoked by the scheduler that can dynamically reassign processes among nodes to negotiate load variations. *Fault tolerance* can be assisted by maintaining multiple copies of critical code at strategic points in the system. In this arrangement, execution and service can be restored and continued fairly quickly in the event of a server failure by migrating the runtime state and reactivating the affected process at one of the backup nodes. *Performance* can be improved by distributing certain applications across the relatively idle workstations. In addition, performance may sometimes be improved by migrating processes to their related data sites when operations on large volumes of data are involved. *System resources can be better utilized* by using the process migration facility, in particular in situations when some special-purpose resources are needed by a process but cannot be revoked remotely. In such cases, the requesting process itself can be migrated to the home site of the requesting resource so that it can execute appropriate routines locally at that end.

While process migration is considered a powerful mechanism and is used often to realize the ultimate objectives of a distributed environment, but it may sometimes affect the other parts of the system; therefore, the utmost care should be taken so that it can only interfere into the rest of the system as little as possible. In particular, when process migration is being effected, the ultimate aims of the system are:

- to minimize the specific time during which the migrating process is in transit and before being operational,
- to reduce the additional load imposed on other nodes for executing such an activity, and
- to decrease the residual dependencies.

In spite of having several merits, the implementation of process migration suffers from several **difficulties**; the three major ones are:

- a considerably large volume of process states may need to be moved,
- it is quite difficult to migrate the entire current residential working environment along with the process, and
- communications and invocations of the migrated process have to be redirected to its new residence after it is migrated.

Systems equipped with virtual memory at individual nodes are quite conducive to process migration to implement. Its main attractions are the built-in mechanism for demand loading of pages and the runtime virtual-to-physical address translation mechanism. This approach accelerates process migration activity, since it involves moving only a skeletal portion of the state that is actually referenced, along with only a few pages. Consequently, it results in minimizing loading of the network considerably. The rest of the state, however, can be page-faulted as usual across the network in the course of execution of the process at the destination node. The savings are thus appreciable, since only a fraction of the total size of a program's virtual memory is actually involved in migration in a given execution. A potential drawback of the paging scheme across the network is its increased load on a network in normal operation caused by the page traffic between the workstations and the backing store (files, block servers, etc.).

Process migration, however, essentially requires a total relocation of the execution environment. This involves relocation of sensitive addresses present in the process, program-transparent redirection of file and device references, proper directing of routing of messages and signals, appropriate management of remote communications and invocations made during and after the migration, and similar other aspects. In fact, efficient and effective implementation of process migration often depends to a large extent on naming and location transparency, apart from relying on many other aspects.

9.14.3 Communication in Distributed Systems: Distributed Message Passing

The communication between processes in distributed systems is quite different from that in a uniprocessor system. One of the main reasons is that most interprocess communication (IPC) in uniprocessor systems implicitly assumes the existence of a shared memory that acts as a bridge between two communicating processes. Since distributed systems do not have any concept of shared memory, the nature of interprocess communication in such a system is entirely different and should be redefined. When communication between parties is implemented, several aspects need to be addressed, such as naming of sites in the system, efficient name resolution, ensuring communication efficiency, and dealing with faults. In fact, communicating processes in such a system must adhere to certain rules known as **IPC protocols** that enable one to communicate with another. As already mentioned, distributed systems (maybe comprising networks of computers) are fundamentally different from computer network systems. Therefore, the requirements of the communication protocols of these two types of systems are also different. For network systems, the basic goal of communication protocols is to allow remote computers to communicate with one another and to permit users to access remote resources. On the other hand, the basic goal of communication protocols for distributed systems is not only to allow users to access remote resources but to do so in a manner transparent to the users.

Several accepted standards and well-implemented protocols for network systems are already available. For wide-area distributed systems, these protocols often take the form of multiple layers, each with its own goals and rules. However, well-defined protocols for distributed systems are still not mature, and as such no specific standards covering essential aspects of distributed systems are yet available. A few standard network protocols were described in a previous section. The essential requirements for protocols for distributed systems were already explained (Section 9.13.2), and a few standard communication protocols (Section 9.13.3) have been designed covering those aspects.

Interprocess communication between processes located in different nodes (sites) in a distributed system is often implemented by exchanging messages. The message-passing mechanism in a distributed system may be the straightforward application of messages as they are used in a uniprocessor single system. A different type of technique known as the RPC exists that relies on message passing as a basic function to handle interprocess communication. Once the location of a destination process is determined, a message meant for it can be sent over the interconnection network. Message delivery is also prone to partial failures that may be due to failures in communication links or faults in nodes located in network path(s) to the destination process. Hence, it is expected that processes must make their own arrangements to ensure reliable fault-free delivery of messages. This arrangement is in the form of an interprocess communication protocol (IPC protocol), which is nothing but a set of rules and conventions that must be adhered to in order to handle transient faults. Reliable message exchange between processes usually follows steps like:

- *Transmission*: A process intends to communicate another process often sends a message to its target process.
- *Acknowledgement*: When the target process receives a message, it sends an acknowledgement to the sender of the message.
- *Timeout*: The protocol provides a specific interval of time within which the sender process is expected to receive an acknowledgement from the receiving process. A *timeout* is said to happen if the acknowledgement is not received within this specific interval.
- *Retransmission*: A sender process retransmits its message if a time-out interrupt occurs before it receives an acknowledgement.
- *Reply*: The receiving process returns a reply message containing the result of processing of the requested message to the sending process.
- *Acknowledgement*: When the sender process receives the reply, it sends an acknowledgement to the receiving process. If the acknowledgement is not received within the timeout period, the receiving process retransmits the reply message.

When a process sends a message, the protocol issues a system call at the sender's site that raises an interrupt at the end of a specific time interval. This interrupt is commonly called a *timeout interrupt*. When the message is delivered to a process, the destination process sends a special acknowledgement message to the sender process to inform it that the message has been clearly received. If the timeout interrupt occurs before an acknowledgement is received, the protocol retransmits the message to the destination process and makes a system call to request another timeout interrupt. These actions are repeated for a certain number of times, and then it is declared that there has been a fault, either due to a failure in the communication link or a fault at the destination node.

Now consider what happens if the message itself is received correctly, but the acknowledgement is lost. The sender will retransmit the message, so the receiver will get it twice. It is thus essential that the receiver be able to distinguish a new message from the retransmission of an old one. Usually this problem is solved by putting consecutive sequence numbers in each original message. If the receiver gets a message bearing the same sequence number as the previous message, it identifies that the message is a duplicate one and hence ignores it. A similar arrangement may be used to ensure that a reply sent by the receiver process reaches the sender process. The message passing mechanism was discussed in detail in Chapter 4. Distributed message passing and its associated several design issues are explained in the following subsections.

9.14.3.1 IPC Semantics

The IPC protocol is constructed with a set of properties called IPC semantics. The semantics depend mostly on the strategies to be taken in relation to acknowledgement and retransmission used in an IPC protocol. The most commonly used IPC semantics are:

- *At-most-once semantics*: A destination process either receives a message once or does not receive it. These semantics are realized when a process receiving a message does not send an acknowledgement and a sender process does not perform retransmission of messages.
- *At-least-once semantics*: A destination process is guaranteed to receive a message; however, it may receive several copies of the message. These semantics are realized when a process receiving a message sends an acknowledgement and a sender process retransmits a message if it does not receive an acknowledgement before a time-out occurs.
- *Exactly once semantics*: A destination process receive a messages exactly once. These semantics are obtained when sending of acknowledgements and retransmissions are performed as in at-least-once semantics, but the IPC protocol recognizes duplicate messages and subsequently discards them.

The implications of these three semantics significantly differ, and their applications also vary, depending mostly on the situations where they will be used.

At-most-once semantics result when a protocol does not use acknowledgements or retransmission. Generally, these semantics are used if a lost message does not create any serious problem in the correctness of an application or the application itself knows how to get rid of such difficulties. For example, an application that receives regular reports from other processes is quite aware when a message is not received as expected, so it may itself communicate with a sender whose message is lost and ask it to resend the message. These semantics are usually accompanied by communication mechanisms with high efficiency because acknowledgements and retransmissions are not employed.

At-least-once semantics result when a protocol uses acknowledgements and retransmission, because a destination process receives a message more than once if the acknowledgement is lost in transit due to communication failure or getting delayed as a result of network contention or congestion. A message being received for the second or subsequent time is treated as a *duplicate message*. An application can use *at-least-once semantics* only if the presence and processing of duplicate messages will not cause any serious effect in relation to correctness of the applications, such as multiple updates of data instead of a single update over a database. Adequate arrangements should be made in such processing accompanying the database so that the situation of multiple appearances of messages can be detected before causing any bad effects.

Exactly–once–semantics result when a protocol uses acknowledgements and retransmissions but discards duplicate messages. These semantics hide transient faults from both sender and receiver processes, because the IPC protocol is ready to afford high communication overhead that results from handling of faults and treating duplicate messages.

9.14.3.2 IPC Protocols

An IPC protocol places certain actions that should be performed at the sites of sender and receiver processes so that a message from a sender process is delivered to a destination process and its reply is delivered to the sender process. IPC protocols are mainly categorized on the basis of their reliability properties as well as on the ability of a sender process to perform actions after sending a message (as well as on the nature of actions performed by a sender process after sending a message).

Reliable and Unreliable Protocols: A *reliable message-passing protocol* is one that guarantees delivery of a message, or its reply if possible; in other words, it would not be lost. It achieves this through *at-least-once* or *exactly–once* semantics for both messages and their replies. To implement this semantic, it makes use of a reliable transport protocol or similar logic and performs error-checking, acknowledgement, retransmission, and reordering of disordered messages. Since delivery is guaranteed, it is not necessary to let the sending process know that the message was delivered. However, it might be useful to provide an acknowledgement to the sending process so that the sending process is informed that the delivery has already been carried out. If the facility, however, fails to perform delivery (either in the event of communication link failure or a fault in the destination system), the sending process is alerted accordingly about the occurrence of the failure. Implementation of a reliable protocol is comparatively complex and expensive due to having substantial communication overhead for providing needed acknowledgements and required retransmissions of messages and replies. At the other extreme, an *unreliable protocol* may simply send a message into the communication network but will report neither success nor failure. It does not guarantee that a message or its reply will not be lost. It provides *at-most-once* semantics either for messages or their replies. This alternative approach, however, greatly reduces the complexity, processing, and communication overhead of the message-passing facility.

Blocking and Non-Blocking Protocols:*Blocking* and *non-blocking protocols* are also called process-synchronous and process-asynchronous protocols, respectively. As already explained in Chapter 4, it is common and customary to block a process that executes a *Receive* system call unless no other message is sent to it. At the same time, there are no definite reasons to *block* a process that executes a *Send* system call. Thus, with non-blocking *Send*, when a process issues a *Send* primitive, the operating system returns control to the process as soon as the message has been queued for transmission or a copy has been made to its buffer. If no copy is made, any changes made to the message by the sending process before or while it is being transmitted cannot take effect and are then made at the risk of the related process. When the message has been transmitted or copied to a safe place for subsequent transmission, the sending process is then interrupted to only inform that the message has been delivered or that the message buffer may be reused. Interrupt(s) may also be generated to notify the non-blocking sending process of the arrival of a reply or an acknowledgement so that it can take appropriate action. Similarly, non-blocking *Receive* is issued by a process that then proceeds to run, and when a message arrives, the process is informed by an interrupt, or it can poll for status periodically.

Non-blocking primitives (Send, Receive) when used in message-passing mechanism, however, makes the system quite efficient and also flexible. But, one of the serious drawbacks of this approach is that it is difficult to detect faults, and thereby equally hard to test and debug programs that use these primitives. The reason is that it is irreproducible, and timing-dependent sequences can create delicate and difficult problems.

On the other hand, there are *blocking* or *synchronous primitives*. A blocking *Send* does not return control to the sending process until the message has been transmitted (unreliable service) or until the message has been sent and a due acknowledgement is received (reliable service). Blocking of a sender process, however, may simplify a protocol, reduce its overhead, and also add some desirable features (salt) to its semantics. For example, if a sender process is blocked until its message is delivered to a destination process, the message would never have to be retransmitted after the sender is activated, so the message need not be buffered by the protocol when the sender is activated. Also, blocking of the sender helps provide semantics that are similar to the relatively easy conventional procedure call. Similarly, a blocking *Receive* does not return control until a message has been placed in the allocated buffer.

- ## The Request (R) Protocol

This protocol is a *non-blocking* (asynchronous) and *unreliable* one and is used by processes in which the destination process has nothing to return as a result of execution and the sending end requires no confirmation that the destination has received the request. Since no acknowledgement or reply message is involved in this protocol, only one message per call is transmitted (from sender to receiver). The sender normally proceeds immediately after sending the request message, as there is no need to wait for a reply message. The protocol provides may–be–call semantics and requires no retransmission of request message. This semantic, therefore, does not offer any guarantees; although it is the easiest to implement but also probably the least desirable. Asynchronous message transmission with *unreliable* transport protocols is generally useful for implementing periodic update services. A node that misses too many update messages can send a special request message to the time server to get a reliable update after a maximum amount of time.

- ## The Request–Reply Acknowledgement Protocol

One of the *reliable protocols* for use by processes that exchange requests and replies is the request–reply acknowledgement (RRA) protocol. Receipt of replies at the sending end ensures that the destination process has received the request, so a separate acknowledgement of the request is not required. The sender, however, sends an explicit acknowledgement of the reply.

The sender process is made *blocked* until it receives a reply, so a single *request buffer* at the sender site is sufficient irrespective of the number of messages a process sends out or the number of processes it sends them to. The destination process is *not blocked* until it receives an acknowledgement, so it could handle requests from other processes while it waits for acknowledgement. Consequently, the destination site needs one reply buffer for each sender process. The number of messages can be reduced through *piggybacking*, which is the technique of including the acknowledgement of a reply in the next request to the same destination process. Since a sender process is blocked until it receives a reply, an acknowledgement of a reply is implicit in its next request. That is why the reply to the last request would require an additional explicit acknowledgement message.

The RRA protocol essentially follows *at-least-once* semantics because messages and replies cannot be lost; however, they might be delivered more than once. At the same time, duplicate requests would have to be discarded at the destination site to provide *exactly–once* semantics.

- ## The Request–Reply Protocol

The request–reply (RR) protocol simply performs retransmission of a request when a timeout occurs. One of the shortcomings of a *non-blocking* version of the RR protocol is that the destination process has to buffer its replies indefinitely because a sender does not explicitly acknowledge a reply; moreover, unlike the RRA protocol, an acknowledgement is not implicitly piggybacked on the sender's next request, because the sender may have issued the next request before it received the reply to its previous request. Consequently, this protocol requires *very high buffer space* to accommodate the logic.

The RR protocol essentially follows *at-least-once* semantics. Consequently, duplicate requests and replies are to be discarded if *exactly–once* semantics are desired. If requests issued by a sender are delivered to the destination process in the same order, the duplicate identification and subsequent discarding arrangement of the RRA protocol can be used with minor changes. A destination process preserves the sequence number and replies of *all* requests in pool of buffers. When it recognizes a duplicate request through a comparison of sequence numbers, it searches for the reply to the request in the buffer pool using the sequence number and then retransmits the reply if found in a buffer; otherwise it simply ignores the request since a reply would be sent after processing the request in near future.

The non-blocking RR protocol has relatively little overhead and can be simplified for use in applications involving *idempotent computations*. A computation is said to be idempotent if it produces the same result if executed repeatedly. For example, the computation $k := 5$ is idempotent, whereas the computation $k := k + 1$ is not. When an application involves only idempotent computations, data consistency would not be affected if a request is processed more than once, so it is possible to exclude arrangements for discarding duplicate requests. Similarly, read and write (not updating) operations performed in a file are idempotent, so it is possible to employ the simplified RR protocol when using a remote file server. It has the additional advantage that the file server need not maintain information about which requests it has already processed, which helps it to be *stateless* and more reliable.

Brief details on R, RRA, and RR protocols with figures are given on the Support Material at www.routledge.com/9781032467238.

9.14.3.3 Group Communication

Until now, we have discussed the pair-wise exchange of messages in interprocess communication, which is the most elementary form of message-based interaction that involves only two parties, the single–sender and the single-receiver, and is a one-to-one communication, also known as *point-to-point* or *unicast*. However, for the sake of performance improvement and ease of programming, several highly parallel distributed applications often require that a message-passing system should also provide a group communication facility, for example, when a service is implemented with a number of different processes located on different sites, perhaps to provide fault-tolerance or to enhance availability. Depending on single or multiple senders and receivers, the following three types of group communication are possible.

- One-to-many (single sender and multiple receivers)
- Many-to-one (multiple senders and single receiver)
- Many-to-many (multiple senders and multiple receivers)

Group communication supported by systems can also be viewed in other ways. These systems can be divided into two distinct categories depending on who can send to whom. Some systems support **closed groups**, in which only the members of the group can send to the group. Outsiders cannot send messages to the group as a whole, although they may be able to send messages to individual members. In contrast, other systems support **open groups**, in which any process in the system can send to any group. The distinction between closed and open groups is often made for implementation reasons. Closed groups are typically used for parallel processing. For example, a collection of processes working together to play a chess game might form a closed group. These processes have their own goal and do not intend to interact with the outside world. On the other hand, when the implementation of the group idea is to support replicated servers, it becomes important that processes that are not members (clients) can send to the group. In addition, the members of the group themselves may also need to use group communication, for example, to decide who should carry out a particular request.

Out of the three types of group communication as mentioned, the first is the **one-to-many scheme**, which is also known as *multicast communication*, in which there are multiple receivers for a message sent by a single sender. A special case of multicast communication is *broadcast communication*, in which the message is sent to *all* processors connected to a network. Multicast/broadcast communication is very useful for several practical applications. For example, to locate a processor providing a specific service, an inquiry message may be broadcast. The specific processor along with the others will respond, and in this case, it is not necessary to receive an answer from every processor; just finding one instance of the desired service is sufficient. Several design issues are related to these multicast communication schemes, such as group management, group addressing, group communication primitives, message delivery to receiver processes, buffered and unbuffered multicast, atomic multicast, various types of semantics, and flexible reliability, etc. Each such issue requires implementation of different types of strategies to realize the desired solution.

The **many-to-one** message communication scheme involves multiple senders but a single receiver. The single receiver, in turn, may be categorized as *selective* or *nonselective*. A *selective receiver* specifies a *unique sender*; a message exchange takes place only if that sender sends a message. On the contrary, a *nonselective receiver* specifies *a set of senders*, and if any one of them sends a message to this receiver, a message exchange occurs. Thus, the receiver may wait, if it wants, for information from any of a group of senders rather than from one specific sender. Since it is not known in advance which member(s) of the group will have its information available first, this behavior is clearly nondeterministic. In some situations, this flexibility is useful to dynamically control the group of senders from whom to accept the message. For example, a buffer process may accept a request from a producer process to store an item in the buffer when the buffer is not full; it may otherwise also accept a request from a consumer process to get an item from the buffer whenever the buffer is not empty. To realize this behavior through a program, a notation is needed to express and control this type of nondeterminism. One such construct is the *guarded command* statement introduced by Dijkstra (1975). Since this issue is more related to programming languages rather than operating systems, it is not discussed further here.

The **many-to-many** message communication scheme involves multiple senders and multiple receivers. Since this scheme implicitly includes *one-to-many* and *many-to-one* message communication schemes, all the issues related to these two schemes are equally applicable to *many-to-many* communication scheme also. Moreover, the *many-to-many* communication scheme itself has an important issue, referred to as *ordered message delivery*, which ensures that all messages are delivered to all receivers in an order acceptable to an application for correct functioning. For example, assume that two senders send messages to update the same record of a database to two server processes with a replica of the database. If the messages sent from the two senders are received by the two servers in different orders, then the final values of the updated record of the database may be different in the two replicas. This shows that this application requires all messages to be delivered in the same order to all receivers (servers) for accurate functioning.

Ordering of messages in the *many-to-many* communication scheme requires *message sequencing* because many different messages sent from different senders may arrive at the receiver's end at different times, and a definite order is required for proper functioning. A special message-handling mechanism is thus required to ensure ordered message delivery. Fortunately, there are some commonly used semantics for ordered delivery of multicast/broadcast messages, such as *absolute ordering*, *consistent ordering*, and *casual ordering*. The details of these schemes are outside the scope of this book.

Many other different aspects need to be addressed concerning group communication, especially in relation to formation of groups and its different attributes. Some of them are: how the groups will be formed, whether it will be peer groups or hierarchical groups, how group membership will be described and implemented, how a group will be addressed, whether the message-passing mechanism will obey atomicity, and last but not least, is the flexibility and scalability of the groups. Many other aspects still remain that need to be properly handled to realize effective and efficient group communication as a whole.

9.14.4 Remote Procedure Calls

Although the workstation–server model provides a convenient way to structure a DOS, but it suffers from several crucial shortcomings. One such is that the workstation–server paradigm, in practice, is used extensively for non-computational (input/output) roles in a LAN environment using message-passing mechanisms (*send* and *receive*), such as accessing files or evaluating database queries. Based on these existing message-passing mechanisms, an IPC protocol can also be developed that would be adequate to efficiently handle the interprocess communication part of a distributed application. But the fact is that an IPC protocol, when developed independently, may often be found fit to a specific application but does not provide a foundation on which a variety of distributed applications can be built. Therefore, a need was felt to have a general IPC protocol that can be employed to design various distributed applications. The concept of RPC came out at this juncture to cater to this need, and this facility was further enhanced to provide a relatively convenient mechanism for building distributed systems, in general. Although the RPC facility never provides a universal solution for all types of distributed applications, still it is considered a comparatively better communication mechanism that is adequate for building a fairly large number of distributed applications.

The RPC has many attractive features, such as its *simplicity*, its *generality*, its *efficiency*, and above all its *ease of use* that eventually have made it a widely accepted primary communication mechanism to handle IPC in distributed systems. The idea behind the RPC model is to make it similar to the well-known and well-understood ordinary procedure call model used for transfer of control and data within a program. In fact, the mechanism of RPC is essentially an extension of the traditional procedure call mechanism in the sense that it enables a call to be made to a procedure that does not reside in the same address space of the calling process. The called procedure, commonly called a *remote procedure*, may reside on the same computer as the calling process or on a different computer. That is why the RPC is made to be *transparent*; the calling process should not be aware that the called procedure is executing on a different machine, or vice versa. Since the caller and callee processes reside on disjoint addresses spaces (possibly on different computers), the remote procedure has no access to data and variables in the caller's environment; therefore, the RPC mechanism uses a message-passing scheme to exchange information between the caller and the callee processes in the usual way.

Remote procedures are found a natural fit for the client/server model of distributed computing. The caller–callee relationship can be viewed as similar to a client–server relationship in which the remote procedure is a *server* and a process calling it is a *client*. Servers may provide common services by means of the public server procedures that a number of potential clients can call. The server process is normally dormant, awaiting the arrival of a request message. When one arrives, the server process extracts the procedure's parameters, computes the result, sends a reply message, and then awaits the next call message to receive. This concept is exactly like shared subroutine libraries in single-computer (uniprocessor) systems. Thus, in both environments, the public routines being used must be made *reentrant* or otherwise be kept protected from preemption by some form of concurrency control, such as mutual exclusion. However, several **design issues** associate with RPCs must be addressed; some common ones follow.

9.14.4.1 Parameter Handling

Defining parameters and representing them in a suitable format so that they can be passed across various types of machines is a vital matter of concern for the RPC to succeed. This aspect is divided into the two following main subjects:

- **Parameter Passing:** Parameters are commonly passed in most programming languages either as values (call by value) or as pointers to a location that contains the value (call by reference). Call by value is relatively a simple mechanism in RPC in which the parameters are simply copied into the message and sent to the remote system. Call by reference, on the other hand, is a complicated one to implement, since a unique, system-wide pointer is needed for each object. The overhead thus associated with this mechanism may not be considered worth the effort.
- **Parameter Representation:** Another critical issue is how to represent the parameters as well as the results (obtained from procedure execution) in messages. If the calling and called programs are written in identical programming languages and run on the same type of machines managed by the same operating system, then the representation may as such face no problems. But if there are any differences in these areas, then there will

probably be many differences in the ways in which the messages (including text as well as data) are to be represented. If a full-fledged communication architecture is used to connect the machines, then this aspect can be handled by the presentation layer. However, in most cases, the communication architecture provides only a basic communication facility, entrusting the conversion responsibility entirely to the RPC mechanism. However, one of the best approaches to negotiate this problem is to provide a standardized format (probably ISO format) for the most frequently used objects, such as integers, floating-point numbers, characters, and strings. Parameter representation using this standardized format can then be easily converted to and from the native (local) format on any type of machine at the time of passing a parameter and receiving the results.

9.14.4.2   Synchronous versus Asynchronous

The concepts of *synchronous* and *asynchronous* RPCs are almost analogous to the concepts of *blocking* and *non-blocking* messages. The conventional RPC is **synchronous**, which requires that the calling (client) process waits until the called (server) process returns a value. Thus, synchronous RPC behaves much similarly to a subroutine call and uses a blocking communication protocol. The behavior of synchronous RPC is relatively simple and predictable; therefore, it is comparatively easy to use. However, its use in a distributed environment results in relatively poor performance, since its inherent behavior limits parallelism, which is a primary requirement in distributed applications.

On the other hand, **asynchronous RPCs** do not block the caller, and replies can be received as and when they are needed, thereby allowing the caller (client) to proceed locally to do other useful work in parallel with the invocation of the callee (server). The use of asynchronous RPC provides greater flexibility while retaining its simplicity and familiarity. Its behavior inherently supports in achieving a greater degree of parallelism; hence, it is most suitable to use in a distributed environment using mainly *non-blocking* communication protocols.

Although the traditional model (synchronous) of RPC implies that only one of the two processes remain active at any instant, however the RPC protocol, in general, has as such no restrictions on the implementation of the concurrency model; therefore, the other models (asynchronous) of RPC are possible but, of course, depending on the details of the parallelism of the caller's and callee's environments and the related RPC implementation. For example, an implementation may choose to make RPC calls asynchronous so that the client may do other useful work while waiting for the reply from the server to arrive. Another type of implementation may be to enable the server to create a thread to execute an already-arrived incoming request so that the server can be free to entertain other requests. Asynchronous RPCs in some situations require no reply from the server (callee), and the server also does not send a reply message (R protocol). Other schemes involving asynchronous RPCs either require or allow a reply but, in effect, the client (caller) does not wait for the reply.

9.14.4.3   Caller–Callee Binding

Part of the complexity in the implementation of RPC lies in binding the caller–callee processes. Binding commonly denotes the relationship that a remote procedure and the calling program exhibit. A binding is established as and when two applications logically connect each other to exchange commands and data. A binding is said to be **nonpersistent** when a connection is established only when a RPC is initiated, and it tends to exist until the values (after execution of the remote procedure) are returned; the connection is then dismantled. While this connection is active, state information on both ends is maintained, including the resources that are attached. This style is, therefore, useful when resources are required to be conserved. On the other hand, as established connections always involve considerable overhead, this style is not very suitable, particularly in situations in which the same remote procedures are often called by the same caller.

A binding is said to be **persistent** in which a connection is set up when a RPC is initiated and tends to continue even after the values (after execution of the remote procedure) are returned; the connection thus established can then be used for near-future calls. If a given time interval passes with no activity on the established connection, then the connection is automatically terminated. In situations where there are many repeated calls to the same procedure within the specified interval, persistent binding exploits the existing connections to execute the remote procedure, thereby avoiding the overhead required to establish a new connection.

9.14.4.4 Case Study: RPC Implementation

The RPC, in essence, is a programming language construct designed for distributed computing. Its syntax and semantics closely resemble those of a local procedure call, thereby making RPC effectively indistinguishable from a local procedure call to programmers (syntactic and semantic transparency). The common syntax of a RPC is:

$$call <proc\text{-}id> (< message >);$$

where $<proc\text{-}id>$ is the *id* of a remote procedure, $<message>$ is a list of parameters, and the call is implemented using a *blocking* protocol. The result of the call may be passed back through one of the parameters or through an explicit return value. Implementation of an RPC mechanism usually involves the five elements: *client, client stub, RPCRuntime, server stub,* and *server.* All these are used to perform name resolution, parameter passing, and return of results during a RPC.

The beauty of the entire mechanism lies in keeping the client completely in the dark about the work which was done remotely instead of being carried out by the local kernel. When the client regains control following the procedure call that it made, all it knows is that the results of the execution of the procedure are available to it. Therefore, from the client's end, it appears that the remote services are accessed (obtained) by making ordinary (conventional) procedure calls and not by using *send* and *receive* primitives. The entire details of the message-passing mechanisms are kept hidden in the client stub as well as in the server stub, making the steps involved in message passing invisible to both the client and the server.

The RPC is a powerful tool that can be employed as a foundation by using it to make the building blocks for distributed computing. It has several merits, and its *advantages* over the conventional client–server paradigm are especially due to two factors. First, it may be possible to set up a remote procedure by simply sending its name and location to the *name server.* This is much easier than setting up a server. Second, only those processes that are aware of the existence of a remote procedure can invoke it. So the use of remote procedures inherently provides more privacy and thereby offers more security than use of its counterpart client–server paradigm. Its primary *disadvantages* are that it consumes more processing time to complete as well as its lack of flexibility, and the remote procedure has to be registered with a name server, so its location cannot be changed easily.

Brief details on RPC implementation with a figure are given on the Support Material at www. routledge.com/9781032467238.

9.14.4.5 Case Study: SUN RPC Implementation

RFC 1831 (Srinivasan, 1995) describes the Sun RPC, also called the Open Network Computing (ONC) RPC, which was designed for client–server communication in the Sun NFS (Network File System) and is supplied as part of the various Sun UNIX operating systems. It has options for use over either UDP/IP or TCP/IP. The file processing in NFS is modeled as idempotent actions; therefore, the Sun RPC provides *at-least-once* semantics for its efficient and effective use. But if *exactly–once semantics* are desired, then the applications using RPCs have to make their own arrangements to discard duplicates.

To use a remote procedure, the Sun RPC system provides an interface language called XDR (eXternal Data Representation) with a stand-alone executable interface compiler called *rpcgen* written in its own language (RPC language or RPCL), and is intended for use with the C programming language. While using a remote procedure, a user has to write an interface definition using XDR, which is actually a data abstraction needed for machine-independent communication. The client and server need not be machines of the same type. The interface definition, however, contains a specification of the remote procedure and its parameters that are required to be compiled by *rpcgen*, which reads special files denoted by an *x* prefix. So, to compile a RPCL file, simply enter

rpcgen rpcprog.x

The output of this compilation produces the following four files:

1. *rpcprog_clnt.c* (the client stub procedures)
2. *rpcprog_svc.c* (server *main* procedure, despatcher, and server stub procedures)
3. *rpcprog_xdr.c* (XDR filters)
4. *rpcprog.h*(the header file needed for any XDR filters)

The Sun RPC schematic does not use the services of a *name server*. Instead, each site contains a port mapper that is similar to a local name server. The port mapper contains the names of procedures and their port *id*s. A procedure that is to be invoked as a remote procedure is assigned a port, and this information is registered with the port mapper. The client first makes a request to the port mapper of the remote site to find which port is used by the remote procedure. It then calls the procedure at that port. However, a weakness of this arrangement is that a caller must know the site where a remote procedure exists.

9.14.4.6   Case Study: JAVA RMI

Java provides a remote method invocation (RMI) facility which is language-specific in nature. RMI allows applications to call object methods located remotely, sharing resources and processing loads across systems. Unlike other systems for remote execution that require that only simple data types or defined structures be passed to and from methods, RMI allows any Java object type to be used, even if the client or server finds it new and has never encountered it before. That is, RMI allows both client and server to dynamically load new object types as required, which is considered an extremely powerful feature. In fact, RMI helps object function calls to happen between Java virtual machines located on separate computers by allowing one JVM to invoke methods belonging to an object stored (or new objects to be stored) in another JVM.

A server application running on a host creates a special type of object called a *remote object*, whose methods may be invoked by clients operating on other hosts. The server selects a name for the service that is to be offered by a method of the remote object and registers it with a name server called *rmiregistry* that runs on the server's host. The *rmiregistry* typically listens on the standard port for registration and invocation requests. The interested clients of the service are already aware of the IP address of the server's host. A client consults the *rmiregistry* in the server's host to locate a service with a given name. The *rmiregistry* returns an object handle for the remote object providing the service, and the client uses this object handle to invoke the service. The syntax used in this invocation, however, resembles an operation similar to a local object. The scheme used in the revocation of remote service is similar to the one described in Section 9.14.4. *javac* (compiler) is used to compile the source files containing the server and client programs, and the *rmic* compiler is used to generate the server and client stubs.

A client can pass special types of objects called *serializable objects* as parameters of the remote method. The Java RMI passes the code and data of such objects to the invoked remote method. This code is dynamically loaded in the server's host while unmarshaling (converting) the parameters; it may be invoked by the object offering the remote service. A server registers a remote service *r_eval* that takes a serializable object, say, *alpha*, as a parameter and simply invokes the method, say, *alpha.beta*(). If a client creates a serializable object and passes it as a parameter in an invocation of *r_eval*, then *r_eval* would load the code of the object and invoke its method *beta*. In effect, the beauty of RMI is that the client would have achieved execution of some of its own code at the server's site. Different clients running on different JVMs can use the same service *r_eval* to get different codes executed at the server's site

9.14.4.7 RPC versus Message Passing

RPC is essentially a powerful technique for constructing a distributed client–server model of computing based on extending the notion of a conventional or local procedure calling mechanism across multiple machines. Message passing, on the other hand, is basically an interprocess synchronization and communication mechanism suitable for use by competing and cooperating but separate and mostly autonomous processes which may reside on the same machine or on two distinctly separate machines. Thus, the two mechanisms serve somewhat different purposes and are not directly comparable and also not direct substitutes for each other.

However, when one of these mechanisms is employed for something other than its primary usage, some form of overlap exists, and a proper choice between them may have to be made. One such case may be, for example, when the distribution facility is used for bulk data transfers, such as files, or when a programming style and the interprocess communication mechanism (IPC) are contemplated for a new distributed applications. Therefore, some of the major issues that are of primary interest to compare them are:

- **Transfer of control:** Both RPC and message–passing normally communicate between two different machines. RPCs may be synchronous or asynchronous, analogous to the concepts of blocking and non-blocking messages which use varieties of the sender/receiver relationship. Asynchronous messages can improve *concurrency* and provide greater flexibility while retaining their simplicity and familiarity. This behavior inherently supports a greater degree of *parallelism* and hence is found suitable in a distributed environment using mainly non-blocking communication protocols.
- **Binding:** RPC requires needed binding at runtime for proper execution of remote process invocation in multi-machine environment. Message–passing, on the other hand, generally does not require any such binding, but needs only a target port or a definite receiver to be identified by the naming mechanism at runtime. While RPC is bound to one destination machine (server), it is not commonly convenient for implementing broadcasts and multicasts, which messages can handle naturally with ease.
- **Data transfer:** At the time of the call, RPC enforces some syntax and semantics in parameter passing, closely resembling those of a local procedure call. Messages are relatively less structured and use a free data format, actually byte streams that appear to be easier and less costly to adapt to environments consisting of heterogeneous machines. Many contemporary RPC mechanisms (such as Java RMI) not only fit nicely into a heterogeneous environment but enable the sender (client) to pass some of its own objects as parameters in an invocation. The receiver (server) would then load the code of the sender's object dynamically and execute it. In this way, the client achieves execution of some of its own code at the server's site.
- **Fault tolerance:** Fault and failure are equally difficult to handle in both environments. However, in the case of messages, a receiver can correctly act on an already-received message even in the event of a sender's failure. In the case of the RPC model, this situation is somewhat different and crucial, the failure of the client causes a process to be orphaned and need a specific recovery mechanism at the receiver's (sender's) end. In fact, there is a wide spectrum of different types of fault and failures in the RPC model, requiring different types of recovery mechanisms to negotiate each type of case.

Finally, the RPC model offers more flexibility and versatility while retaining its simplicity. Message-passing mechanisms, on the other hand, are relatively tedious, and moreover, the use of message primitives is somewhat unnatural and also confusing. That is why the RPC mechanism, among other reasons, is always preferred to a message-passing mechanism, at least for the sake of convenience.

9.14.5 DISTRIBUTED SHARED MEMORY

A uniprocessor system while implicitly assumes the existence of shared memory to use the shared-memory paradigm by existing processes (for example, to act as a bridge between two communicating processes), but the use of the shared-memory paradigm is also natural for distributed processes running on tightly coupled multiprocessors. Loosely coupled distributed systems (both multiprocessor and multicomputer), on the other hand, do not have any such provision of similar shared memory, although distributed shared memory (DSM) is essentially an abstraction of shared memory implemented in these distributed systems. Since a distributed system comprises loosely coupled systems with no physically shared memory, this familiar abstraction of (globally) shared memory gives these systems the illusion of physically shared memory and enables application programmers to use the shared-memory paradigm by simple read and write operations. In fact, distributed shared memory, at least conceptually, extends the local address across the host boundaries in a distributed computer systems. To provide a shared-memory abstraction to programmers, contemporary loosely coupled distributed-memory systems have thus implemented an additional software layer on top of the message-passing communication system. This software layer can be implemented in the OS kernel, or it may be placed as a separate runtime subsystem (library routines) with proper system kernel support that operates below the application layer. Such an arrangement will help applications to make use of the familiar abstraction of (globally) shared memory that can be easily operated by simple read and write instructions. In effect, distributed shared memory (DSM) refers to the shared-memory paradigm applied to loosely coupled distributed memory systems.

DSM provides a virtual address space shared among processes running on loosely coupled systems. In fact, DSM is basically an abstraction that integrates the local memory associated with different machines by a communication network in a network environment into a single logical entity shared by cooperating processes in an unrestricted form of data movement running on multiple sites. It is assumed at least in theory, that single-site programs developed using the shared-memory model may be straightforwardly "ported" to a distributed environment without any modification if it supports distributed shared memory. Another distinct advantage is that shared data may be allowed to persist even beyond the lifetimes of the participating processes. Proponents of this scheme yet move one step forward arguing also that DSM may improve performance compared to direct (traditional) message passing, in some cases by moving data in blocks and that too only on demand, when actually referenced by an executing application. It is to be noted that this relatively large shared-memory space itself exhibits and exists only virtually and is provided to processors of all nodes. Therefore, the application programs can use it in the same way as a traditional virtual memory, except, of course, that processes using it can run on different machines in parallel. Here, each node must have a software memory-mapping manager routine that would map the local memory onto the shared virtual memory. To facilitate this mapping operation, the shared-memory space is partitioned into *blocks*. Due to the virtual existence of shared memory, DSM is also sometimes referred to as *distributed shared virtual memory* (DSVM).

From the performance point of view, distributed shared memory should be incorporated into systems that are equipped with high-bandwidth and low-latency communication links so that reduced network latency can be attained. While some types of local networks are available that provide such kind of links, they are seldom supported by WANs in general. To alleviate this shortcoming from network latency, **data caching** is a well-known solution to negotiate memory access latency. The idea is that the main memory of individual nodes is used to cache pieces of shared-memory space. The memory-mapping manager of each node then views its local memory as a big cache of the shared-memory space for its associated processors. The basic unit of caching may be a memory block.

The **general approach** in data access and related caching of data works as follows: when a process on a node attempts to access data from a memory block on the shared-memory space, the local memory-mapping manager takes the control to service its request. If the memory block containing the requested data is resident in the local memory, the request is serviced by supplying the data as asked for from the local memory. Otherwise a **network block fault** (similar to page fault in virtual memory) is generated and control is passed to the operating system. The OS then sends a message to the node on which the desired memory block is located to get the block. The targeted block is migrated from the remote node to the client process's node, and the operating system maps it into the application's address space. The faulting instruction is restarted and can now proceed toward completion as usual. This shows that the data blocks keep migrating from one node to another only on demand, but no communication is visible to the user processes. In other words, to the user processes, the system looks like a tightly coupled shared-memory multiprocessor system in which multiple processes can freely read and write the shared memory at will. Caching of data in local memory eventually reduces the traffic on network substantially for a memory access on cache hit. Significant performance improvement can thus be obtained if network traffic can be minimized by increasing the cache hit, which can be attained by ensuring a high degree of locality of data accesses.

9.14.5.1 Design Issues of DSMs

Several issues are involved in the design and implementation of DSM systems. Some important factors that influence the shared-memory system are:

- **Structure:** This refers to the layout of the shared data in memory. In fact, the structure of the shared-memory space of a DSM system is not universal but varies, normally depending on the type of application the DSM system is going to support.
- **Block Size:** The block size of a DSM system is sometimes also referred as *granularity*. Possible units of a block are a few words, a page, or even a few pages, which are considered the unit of data sharing and the unit of data transfer across the network. Proper selection of block size is a major issue that determines the granularity of parallelism and the generated load in network traffic in the event of network block faults.
- **Memory Coherence:** DSM systems that allow *replication* of shared data items in the main memories of a number of nodes to handle many different situations often suffer from memory coherence problems (similar to the well-known cache coherence problem in uniprocessor systems and traditional multi-cache coherence problem in shared memory multiprocessor systems) that deal with the consistency of a piece of shared data lying in the main memories of two or more nodes. To negotiate this problem, different memory coherence protocols can be used that depend on the assumptions and trade-offs that are made with regard to the pattern of memory access.
- **Memory Access Synchronization:** Concurrent accesses to shared data in DSM system are a regular feature that require proper synchronization at the time of data access to maintain the consistency of shared data apart from using only the coherence protocol. Synchronization primitives, such as lock, semaphores, event counts, and so on are thus needed to negotiate situations of concurrent accesses over shared data.
- **Replacement Strategy:** Similar to the cache replacement strategy used in uniprocessor systems, the data block of the local memory sometimes needs to be replaced in some situations using an appropriate strategy. In situation, when the local memory of a node is full and the needed data are not present in the memory (similar to the occurrence of a cache miss) at that node, this implies not only a fetch of the needed data block from a remote node but also a suitable replacement of an existing data block from the memory of the working node in order to make room for the new (fetched) one. This indicates that a suitable replacement strategy is urgently needed when a DSM system is designed.

- **Thrashing:** In DSM systems, data blocks are often migrated between nodes on demand. Therefore, if two nodes compete for simultaneous write access to a single data item, the corresponding data block may then experience a back-and-forth transfer so often that much time is spent on this activity, and no useful work can then be done. This situation in which a data block is involved in back-and-forth journey in quick succession is usually known as *thrashing*. A DSM system, therefore, must be designed incorporating a suitable policy so that thrashing can be avoided as much as possible.
- **Heterogeneity:** When a DSM system is built for an environment in which the set of computers is heterogeneous, then it must be designed in such a way that it can address all the issues relating to heterogeneous systems and be able to work properly with a set of machines with different architectures.

9.14.5.2 Implementation Issues: Common Algorithms

Different approaches in the implementation of DSM are observed. Variations in these approaches mostly depend on which of the design issues already mentioned are given more importance at the time of DSM implementation. However, the implementations, in general, are often influenced by three major aspects: *sharing of memory*, whether the DSM system allows replication and/or migration of shared-memory data blocks; *maintenance of memory coherence and access synchronization* (similar to cache coherence in shared-bus tightly coupled multiprocessors); and *distributed file caches*. However, the common algorithms to handle all these aspects of DSM implementation include:

- **Migration:** The principle involved in the migration algorithm maintains only a single physical copy of the shared memory, and migration of it, whenever required, is carried out by making a copy to the site where access is desired. The floating copy of the shared memory may be relatively easily integrated into the virtual-memory addressing scheme of its resident host. Implementation of shared memory in this way appears to be simple, but it exhibits poor performance, particularly when the locus of shared memory activity tends to move quickly among hosts. In addition, when two or more hosts attempt to access shared memory within the same time frame, apart from using an appropriate synchronization mechanism to mitigate the situation, it causes excessive migration of data that eventually leads to thrashing. This is especially troublesome when the competing hosts actually access non-overlapping areas of shared memory.
- **Central Shared Memory:** This approach is basically to have shared memory that can be maintained centrally, with only a single physical copy using a central server. In this scheme, reads and writes to shared memory performed at any other site are converted to messages and sent to the central server for any further processing. In the case of reads, the server returns requested values. For writes, the server updates the master copy of the shared memory and returns an acknowledgement as usual. This implementation makes the operations on shared memory relatively easy, as there is centrally only single-site semantics of reads and writes where any target memory object always contains the most-recent current value.
- **Read Replication:** This scheme allows the simultaneous coexistence of multiple read-copies of shared memory at different hosts. At most one host is allowed to have write access to shared memory. Hence, its operation is similar to a multiple-reader, single-writer scheme (traditional readers/writers problem). A host intending to read shared memory obtains a local copy exercising its read access and is then able to satisfy repeated read queries at its own end only locally. In order to maintain consistency, active reading must preclude (exclude) writing by invalidating and temporarily withholding write-access rights to shared memory elsewhere in the system. Naturally, multiple concurrent read copies are permitted that are commonly used in the implementation of distributed shared memory.

When the DSM design allows read replication, for the sake of performance improvement, it often divides the shared memory into logical blocks in which each block is assigned to an owner host, and reading and writing is then performed on a per-block basis in a manner as described.

- **Full Replication:** This scheme allows simultaneous coexistence of multiple read and write copies of portions of shared memory. Consistency in these copies is maintained by means of using appropriate protocols that broadcast write to all read and write copies, and only the affected blocks modify themselves accordingly. Global writes are handled in a different way considered to be deemed fit.

Different systems, however, enjoy the freedom to implement their own patterns of distributed shared memory suitable for the system as well as the environment in which they are being used. Besides, there are some other factors that effectively influence such implementations are mainly: *frequency of reads versus writes, computational complexity, locality of reference of shared memory*, and *the expected number of messages in use.*

9.14.6 DISTRIBUTED FILE SYSTEMS

A traditional file system in a single-processor machine provides a convenient mechanism by abstraction of a storage device in which storing and retrieving as well as sharing of information (file is created by one application and then shared with different applications at a later time) are carried out. A distributed file system (DFS) similarly provides an abstraction of a distributed system to users and makes it simple for them to use files in a distributed environment. There are many issues entwined in relate to designing and implementing a DFS that altogether make it relatively complex compared to a traditional file system, mainly due to the fact that users and storage devices are physically dispersed. In order to provide convenience, reliability, and performance to users, a DFS normally supports the following:

- **Transparency:** A DFS allows files to be accessed by processes of any node of the system, keeping them completely unaware of the location of their files in the nodes and disks in the system.
- **Remote information sharing:** A process on one node can create a file that can be accessed by other processes running on any other nodes at different locations at any point in time later on.
- **File sharing semantics:** These specify the rules of file sharing: whether and how the effect of file modifications made by one process are visible to other processes using the files concurrently.
- **User mobility:** A DFS normally allows a user to work on different nodes at different times without insisting to work on a specific node, thereby offering the flexibility to work at will with no necessity of physically relocating the associated secondary storage devices.
- **Diskless workstation:** A DFS, with its transparent remote file-access capability, allows a system to use diskless workstations in order to make the system more economical and handy, tending to be less noisy and thereby having fewer faults and failures.
- **Reliability:** A file accessed by a process may exist in different nodes of a distributed system. A fault in either a node or a communication link failure between the two can severely affect file processing activity. Distributed file systems ensure *high reliability* by providing *availability* of files through *file replication* that keeps multiple copies of a file on different nodes of the system to negotiate the situation of temporary failure of one or more nodes. Moreover, through the use of a *stateless file server* design, the impact of file server crashes on ongoing file processing activities can be minimized. In an ideal design, both the existence of multiple copies made by file replication and their locations are kept hidden from the clients.

- **Performance:** Out of many factors that affect performance, one is network latency, which is mostly due to data transfer caused by processing of remote files. A technique called *file caching* is often used to minimize frequent network journeys, thereby reducing network traffic in file processing.
- **Scalability:** This specifies the ability to expand the system whenever needed. But when more new nodes are added to the existing distributed system, the response time to file system commands normally tends to degrade. This shortcoming is commonly addressed through techniques that localize data transfer to sections of a distributed system, called *clusters*, which have a high-speed LAN.

9.14.6.1 Design Issues in Distributed File Systems

A DFS normally stores user files in several nodes and is often accessed by processes resident in different nodes of the distributed system. In fact, the users and the storage devices are normally dispersed physically. This gives rise to several issues that must be considered at the time of designing a DFS:

- **Transparency of file system:** This means a user need not know much about the location of files in a system, and the name of a file should not reveal its location in the file system. The notion of transparency has four desirable facets that address these issues. Those are:
  - *Location transparency*: This specifies that the name of a file should not reveal its location. In fact, a user should not know the locations or the number of file servers and storage devices. In addition, the file system should be able to change the location of a file without having to change its name (path name). This is commonly known as *location independence* that enables a file system to optimize its own performance. For example, when files are accessed from a node presently experiencing heavy network congestion, it can result in poor performance. The DFS in this situation may move a few files from the affected node to other nodes. This operation is called *file migration*. Location independence can also be used to improve utilization of storage devices in the system. Most DFSs provide location transparency, but they seldom offer *location independence*. Consequently, files cannot be migrated to other nodes. This restriction deprives the DFS of an opportunity to optimize file access performance.
  - *Access transparency*: This implies that both local and global files should be accessed in the same way, and the file system should not make any distinction between them. The file system should automatically locate the target file and make necessary arrangements for transfer of data to the requested site.
  - *Naming transparency*: This means the name of a file should give no hint as to where the file is physically located. In addition, a file should be allowed to move from one node to another within the jurisdiction of a distributed system without changing the name of the file.
  - *Replication transparency*: If multiple copies of a file exist on multiple nodes, both the existence of multiple copies and their locations should be hidden from the users.
- **User mobility:** A DFS normally should allow a user to work on different nodes at different times without enforcing work on a specific node, thereby offering the flexibility to work at will with no need to physically relocate the associated secondary storage devices. The performance characteristics of the file system in this situation should not discourage users from accessing their files from workstations other than the one at which they usually work. One way to support user mobility may be to automatically bring a user's environment (user's home directory and similar other things) at the time of login to the node where the user logs in.

- **Performance:** The performance of a file system is normally measured in terms of average response time to file system commands. Out of many factors that affect performance of a DFS, one critical factor is network latency, which starts to dominate when data transfer begins due to processing of remote files. Although optimal performance is hard to quantify, but the performance should at least be as close as possible to that of a centralized system. In fact, performance of a DFS has two facets:
  - *Efficiency*: In general, it implies that how quickly a file processing activity can be completed, and network latency in this regard is a prime factor that normally influences efficiency. Network latency often typically exceeds the processing time of a file record, so, unlike I/O device latency, it cannot be masked by blocking and buffering of records. That is why a DFS employs *file caching*, which keeps a copy of remote files in the node of a process that uses the file. In this way, even repeated accesses to the file do not much affect the network traffic, thereby reducing network latency, though staleness of data in a file cache has to be prevented through the use of cache coherence techniques.
  - *Scalability*: It is desirable that a distributed system will grow with time by expanding the network and adding new machines or interconnecting two or more networks in general. A good DFS should be designed so that it can easily accommodate growth of nodes and users in the system. Moreover, such growth should not cause serious disruption of service, and scalability of a DFS requires that response times not degrade to the extent that it causes loss of performance to users. In effect, a proper scalable design should ensure easy integration of added resources to cope with the growth of user community and also sustain a high service load with as such no degradation in system performance.

A distributed system usually consists of set of computers connected by high-speed communication networks, so caching a single copy of a file within a set is adequate to reduce inter-set network traffic and provides scalability of DFS performance. But when several processes attempt to access the same file in parallel, a mechanism known as *distributed locking techniques* are employed to ensure the synchronization of file processing activities that scale well in spite of when the system size increases.

- **High availability:** A DFS should continue to function even in the event of partial failures of the system, mainly either due to node faults, communication link failure, or crashes of storage devices. However, such failure may sometimes cause a temporary loss of service to small groups of users and may result in an overall degradation in performance and functionality over the entire system. To realize high availability, the DFS must have multiple independent file servers (in contrast to a central data repository that may be a cause of performance bottleneck), and each must be equipped with multiple independent storage devices. Replication of files at multiple servers is a frequently used primary mechanism to ensure high availability.
- **High reliability:** A DFS should have the proper arrangement to safeguard the system as far as possible even when stored information is lost. That is why the system should automatically generate backup copies of critical data that can help the system continue to function even in the face of failure of the original. Out of many different available techniques, *stable storage* is a popular one used by numerous file systems to attain high reliability.
- **Data integrity:** Multiple users in a DFS often compete to access a shared file concurrently, thereby causing the probability of a threat in the integrity of data stored in it. In this situation, requests from multiple users attempting to concurrently access a file must be properly synchronized by any means using some form of concurrency control mechanism. Many different proven techniques are, however, available that can be used by a file system to implement concurrency control for the sake of data integrity.

- **Security:** A DFS for accessing distant resources and communicating with other processes relies on a communication network which may include public communication channels or communication processors that are not under the control of the distributed OS. Hence, the DFS is always exposed to different forms of threats and apprehends attacks on any of its nodes and attached resources. That is why a DFS should be made secured, so that its users can be assured with regard to the confidentiality and privacy of their data. Necessary security mechanisms must thus be implemented so that the information stored in a file system is protected against any unauthorized access. In addition, if rights to access a file are passed to a user, they should be used safely. This means the user receiving the rights should in no way be able to pass them further if they are not permitted to.

- **Fault tolerance:** Occurrence of a fault often disrupts ongoing file processing activity and results in the file data and control data (metadata) of the file system being inconsistent. To protect consistency of metadata, a DFS may employ a *journaling technique* like that in a conventional centralized time-sharing file system, or DFS may use *stateless file server* design, which needs no measures to protect the consistency of metadata when a fault occurs. To protect consistency of file data, DFS may provide *transaction semantics*, which are useful in implementing *atomic transactions* so that an application may itself perform fault tolerance, if it so desires.

- **Heterogeneity:** The scalability and openness of a distributed system inevitably require it to be a heterogeneous one. This is perhaps the most general formation, which consists of interconnected sets of dissimilar hardware and software (often independent computers) that provide the flexibility of employing different computer platforms interconnected by a wide range of different types of networks for a diverse spectrum of applications to run by different types of users. Consequently, a DFS should be designed in a way that can allow a variety of workstations with different internal formats to participate in an effective sharing of files. Accepting the heterogeneity of a distributed system, the design of a DFS on such platform is critically difficult to realize, yet it is considered one of the prime issues at the time of designing a DFS.

- **Simplicity and ease of use:** Several important factors while need to be incorporated into the design of a DFS, but those, on other hand, attempt to negate the file system to be simple and easy to use. Still, the most important factor is that the user interface to the file system must be as simple as possible. This means the semantics of the file processing commands should be similar to those of a file system for a traditional centralized time-sharing system, and the number of commands should be as small as possible. In addition, while the DFS should be able to support the whole range of applications commonly used by a community of users, at the same time it must be user-friendly and easy–to–understand even for a not very skilled user.

9.14.7 FAULT TOLERANCE

Various types of faults can occur at any point in time due to the failure of hardware or software or environmental phenomena that could damage, cause loss of, or corrupt the data, resulting in a threat to the integrity of data stored by the system. To what extent a DFS can tolerate faults is influenced by many other primary attributes of the file system. Some of them are:

- **Availability:** This refers to the fact that the file (or a copy of it) can be opened and accessed by a client based on the path name (related to its locations). On the other hand, the ability to access a file requires only the client and server nodes be functional, because a path between these two is guaranteed by resiliency of the network. To resolve the path being given to use a target file, DFS would usually perform resolution of all path components in the client node itself. In this regard, replication of directories existing in remote nodes, if it appears in the path name component, would be carried out in the client node to improve the availability of a file.

- **Robustness:** The fault tolerance of a file system depends on its *robustness* irrespective of its implementation. A file is said to be robust if it can survive faults, caused mainly due to crashing of storage devices, in a guaranteed manner. Redundancy techniques offer stable storage devices; one such is *disk mirroring* used in RAID level 1 to clone multiple copies (usually two) of the server. The backup copy is always kept updated but is normally passive in the sense that it does not respond to client requests. Whenever the primary fails, the backup copy becomes dominant and takes over. Proven techniques using comparison and verification of the primary and backup to ensure their sameness are employed to keep these two in synchrony and to detect failures at the same time. Such stable storage usually works well for applications that require a high degree of fault tolerance, such as atomic transactions.

- **Recoverability:** This refers to the ability of a file to roll back to its most-recent consistent state when an operation on a file fails or is aborted by the user. Out of many available proven mechanisms, one is the *atomic update techniques* used in transaction processing that can be exploited in file implementation to make it recoverable. An atomic transaction either completes successfully and transforms a file into a new consistent state or fails without changing the state of the target file. In effect, the previous consistent state of the file is recovered in the event of transaction failure. Generally, to make files recoverable, updates are not performed in place; rather updates can be tentatively written into different blocks, called *shadow pages*. If the transaction completes successfully, it commits and makes the tentative updates permanent by updating the directory and index structures to point to the new blocks, discarding the old ones.

All *three* primary attributes of a file system mentioned are independent of one another. Thus, a file may be recoverable without necessarily being robust or available. Similarly, a file may be robust and recoverable without being available. Likewise, a file may be available without being recoverable or robust. This means different techniques can be used to ensure each of these criteria individually.

Different fault tolerance techniques are used for faults (availability) that arise during an *open* operation and those that occur after a file has been opened (mainly access operation). A DFS usually maintains many copies of the information needed for path name resolution and many copies of a file to negotiate faults. However, availability techniques are very complex and even more expensive if faults that occur after opening and *during* file processing (file access) are to be tolerated (Quorum-based fault tolerance techniques to handle replicated data in such cases can be used). Hence, a few distributed systems handle these faults. Moreover, the communication media used in many LANs with an inherent broadcast nature also provides numerous innovative variations in implementing fault tolerance in distributed systems. For example, processes often may checkpoint themselves across the network, and a special node may be given charge of eavesdropping and recording all interprocess messages. Thus, in the event of a node crash, the affected process may be reconstructed from its checkpoint state and restored to date by having all outstanding messages relayed to it.

A few commonly used fault tolerance techniques employed by DFS are *cached directories* and *file replication* that address faults in a file server and in intermediate nodes during an open operation. The *stateless file server* (see Section 9.9.2) design, however, addresses faults in a file server during file processing.

Brief details on this topic are given on the Support Material at www.routledge.com/9781032467238

9.14.8 Client and Server Node Failures

Traditional file systems usually keep track of state information of a file processing activity in metadata, such as the file control block (FCB) of a file, to implicitly provide a framework between the file and a user process to simplify the implementation of file operations (such as a read or write). This design approach of a file system in which users' state information pertaining to the operation performed from one access request to the next is maintained is commonly referred to as *stateful* design. This recorded current state information is subsequently used when executing the next immediate request. On the other hand, if any state information concerning a file processing activity while servicing a user's request is not maintained by the file system, it is referred as *stateless* design.

- **Stateful File Servers:** In a DFS running on workstation–server model, use of a stateful design implies that there is a virtual-circuit type of connection between the client node and the server node. The server creates state information for a client when the client starts a new *session* (a session is the duration between an opening of a file and a close operation on it) by performing an open operation, maintains the state information for the entire duration of the session, and discards the state information when the user closes the session by performing a close operation. The server keeps the state information of a file processing activity in metadata (such as the FCB and similar others) of the file, and this metadata can be maintained in memory, just as in traditional file systems. This arrangement essentially provides good performance. However, DFS design based on the use of a stateful server faces several problems in the event of client and server failures.

When a client crashes, the file processing activity must be abandoned, and the file would have to be restored to its previous consistent state so that the client can restart its file processing activity afresh. In fact, the client and the file server share a virtual circuit which holds the file processing state and resources, like file server metadata, and those become orphans when either a client or server crashes. It actually breaks the virtual circuit, so the actions would have to be rolled back and the already-created metadata would have to be destroyed. This can, however, be carried out, perhaps by the use of a client–server protocol that implements transaction semantics. If a DFS does not provide transaction semantics, a client process would then have to make its own arrangements so as to restore the file to a recent-previous consistent state.

On the other hand, when a file server crashes, state information pertaining to file processing activity stored in the server metadata is immediately lost, so ongoing file processing activity has to be abandoned, and the file has to then be restored to its recent-previous consistent state to make it once again workable.

Therefore, the service paradigm in a stateful server requires detection as well as complex crash recovery procedures. Both client and server individually need to reliably detect crashes. The server must expend the added effort to detect client crashes so that it can discard any state it is holding for the client to free its resources, and the client likewise must detect server crashes so that it can perform necessary error-handling activities. Therefore, in order to avoid both these problems that occur with a stateful server in the event of failures, the file server design in the DFS has been proposed to be stateless to negotiate these situations.

- **Stateless File Servers:** A stateless server does not maintain any state information pertaining to file processing activity, so there exists no implied context between a client and a file server. Consequently, a client must maintain state information concerning a file processing activity, and therefore, every file system called from a client must be accompanied by all the necessary parameters to successfully carry out the desired operations. Many actions traditionally performed only at file open time are repeated at every file operation. When the client receives the file server's response, it assumes that the file operation (read/write) requested by it has been completed successfully. If the file server crashes or communication error/failure occurs by this time, time-outs occur and retransmission is carried out by the client. The file server after recovery (recovery is mostly trivial, maybe simply by rebooting) immediately continues to service the incoming requests, processes a retrans-mitted request, and finally provides a reply to the client. Thus, the client process only perceives a delayed response to a request and is completely unaware of a file server crash.

A stateless file server, however, cannot detect and discard duplicate requests because these actions require state information; therefore, it may service a request more than once. Hence, to avoid any harmful effects of reprocessing, client requests must be idempotent. Read/write requests, however, are by nature idempotent, but directory-related requests like creation and deletion of files are not idempotent. Consequently, a client may face an ambiguous or misleading situation if a file server crashes and is subsequently is recovered during a file processing activity.

Two *distinct advantages* of using a stateless server approach are: when a server crashes while serving a request, the client need only resend the request until the server responds. When a client crashes during request processing, no recovery is necessary for either the client or the server. A stateless server must, therefore, only have the ability to carry out repeatable operations, and data will never be lost due to a server crash.

Two potential *drawbacks* of a stateless server approach are: the difficulty of enforcing consis-tency and also incurring a substantial performance penalty in comparison with stateful servers. Performance degradation is mainly due to two reasons. First, the file server, as already mentioned, always opens a file at every file operation and passes back the state information to the client. Second, when a client performs a write operation, reliability considerations dictate that the data of the file should be written in the form of direct write-through into the disk copy of a file to the server imme-diately. As a result, the file server cannot employ buffering, file caching, or disk caching in order to speed its own operation. The other *distinct drawbacks* of this server are that it requires longer-request messages from its clients that should include all the necessary parameters to complete the desired operation, since it does not maintain any client state information. Consequently, longer-request processing becomes slower, since a stateless server does not maintain any state information to speed up processing. However, a hybrid form of file servers can be designed that could avoid repeated file open operations. A stateless file service can be implemented on top of datagram net-work service. It is used in Sun Microsystems' NFS system.

9.14.9 OPERATION OF DISTRIBUTED FILE SYSTEMS: AN OVERVIEW

The functions of conventional file subsystems running on single-site machines and the basics of file processing in a DFS running on a workstation-based model are conceptually the same; the notable difference is that the functions of the DFS are partitioned between the workstations or between the workstations (clients) and the server. Some of the functions may be fully entrusted to a single party (client), and the remaining functions may be replicated or executed in a cooperative manner. Normally, all functions that are delegated to the client need to be replicated to all workstations that are clients of the file service offered by the server. A schematic representation of the basics of file processing of DFS in general is depicted in Figure 9.11 with no inclusion of any special DFS techniques.

The client, at one end, needs to provide a mechanism to negotiate file-service calls issued by the user by means of the set of operations called the *application interface* (API) or *system-call inter-face*. The client, in principle, may forward all requests to the server and need not implement any of the file-system layers locally. This type of file operation is often referred to as a **remote file process-ing** model in which the server is equipped with all the information about ongoing client activities, including controlling concurrent access to shared files. The mechanics of workstation/server com-munication are handled in a way analogous to RPC or messages to implement file accesses through *stub processes* called a file server interface (agent) and client interface (agent). When the client intends to open a file, the request is handed over to the client interface (agent). The client interface communicates the request to the file server interface (agent) in the server, which then hands over

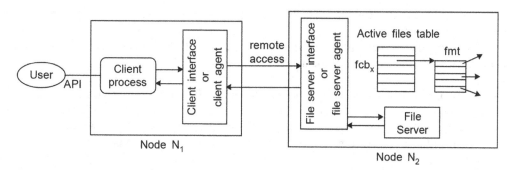

FIGURE 9.11 A schematic representation of fundamentals of file processing in a distributed file system (DFS) environment without using any special DFS techniques.

the request to the file server. The file server opens the file and builds the FCB. Now, whenever the client performs a *read* or *write* operation on the file, the operation is usually implemented through message passing between the client interface and the file server interface. I/O buffers that exist for the file at the server's end participate in the operation, and only one record at a time is passed from the file server to the client.

The DFS can be organized in two ways. At one extreme, the server can be equipped with most of the layers of the file system and connected to workstations (diskless) on a fast LAN that could offer a response time close to that of a local disk. Due to heavy reliance on the server, the remote-access method tends to increase the load both on the server as well as on the network. Consequently, DFS performance tends to decrease as the volume of network traffic generated by remote-file accesses increases. In fact, network latencies can completely overshadow the efficiency of access mechanisms even when only a small fraction of data accesses are non-local. This fact motivates to undertake certain measures so that network traffic can be reduced by minimizing the data transfers over the network during file processing activity.

Consequently, this gives rise to the concept at the other extreme, in which the client itself can contain most of the layers of the file system, with the server providing only a low-level virtual disk abstraction. In this approach, a client can view or may use the server simply as an unsophisticated repository of data blocks. The client basically checks out the files of interest, or portions thereof, from the server and performs most of the processing of files locally. Upon closing or sometime thereafter, files are returned to the server only for permanent storage or optional usage of sharing. In effect, the working set of files (i.e. the portions of files under processing) is **cached** by the client for processing using its own memory and local disk and then returned to the server only for permanent storage. Under this scheme, the server may be accessed only when a client cache-miss occurs.

The **client caching** approach offers several *potential benefits*. As a result of local availability of the data being cached, access speed can be significantly improved over remote access, especially with those data that are repeatedly referenced. Consequently, the response time is noticeably improved and performance is automatically enhanced due to reduced dependence on the communication network, thereby avoiding the delays imposed by the network, as well as decreasing load on the server. In addition, one positive advantage of the client caching approach is that it is very conducive to fault tolerance. But this approach on the other hand suffers from several *distinct drawbacks*. First, local file processing requires relatively costly and powerful workstations to be equipped with larger memory and possibly local disks. Second, concurrent access to shared files by client-cached workstations may lead to well-known cache inconsistency (cache coherence) problems that may require the use of additional special client/server protocols to resolve.

In fact, whatever design approach is followed, the DFS design must be *scalable*, which means that DFS performance would not be much degraded with an increase in the size of the distributed system architecture. Scalability is considered an important criteria, especially for environments that gradually grow with time; lack of scalability in these situations often hinders the performance to attain a desired level.

Several techniques are commonly used in the operation of DFS that enable the DFS to achieve high performance. Some notable of them are:

- **Efficient File Access:** File access may be said to be efficient if it can provide a lower average response time to client requests or higher throughput of client requests. These criteria, in turn, depend mostly on the structural design of a file server as well as how the operation of it is ordered. Two common server structures, however, exist that provide efficient file access.
  - **Multi-Threaded File Server:** In this file server, several threads of operation exist; each thread is capable of servicing one client request at any point in time. Since file processing is basically an I/O-bound activity, operation of several of these threads that service different client request can then be simultaneously performed, causing no harm and resulting in fast response to client requests and high throughput at the same time. Moreover, as the number of client requests that are active at any instant increases, the number of threads can also then be varied to handle all of them individually and, of course, with the availability of the OS resources that are required to support it, such as thread control blocks (TCBs).
  - **Hint-Based File Server:** A hint-based file server is basically a hybrid design in the sense that it provides features of both a stateful and a stateless file server. Whenever possible, it operates in a stateful manner for the sake of realizing increased efficiency. At other times, it operates in a stateless manner. A *hint* is basically a form of information in relation to ongoing file processing activity, for example, the *id* of the next record in a sequential file that would be accessed in a file processing activity. The file server always maintains a collection of hints in its volatile storage. When a file operation is requested by a client, the file server checks for the presence of a hint that would help in its processing. If a hint is available, the file server effectively uses it to speed up the file operation that would automatically enhance performance; otherwise, the file server operates in a stateless manner: it opens the file and uses the record/byte *id* provided by the client to access the required record or byte. In either case, after completing the file operation, the server inserts a part of the state of the file processing activity in its volatile storage as a *hint* and also returns it to the client as is done in the case of a stateless file server. However, the overall efficiency of this file server depends on the number of file operations that are assisted by the presence of hints.
- **File Caching:** As already explained, in more balanced systems, the client holds some portions of the data from a remote files in a buffer (main memory) or on local disk in its own node called the *file cache*. This file cache and the copy of the file on a disk in the server node form a memory hierarchy, so operation of the file cache and its related advantages are similar to those of a CPU cache and virtual memory. *Chunks* of file data are loaded from the file server into the file cache. To exploit the advantages of **spatial locality** (spatial locality refers to the tendency of execution to involve a number of memory locations that are viewed as clustered. This reflects the tendency of processing to access instructions/ data sequentially, such as when processing a file of data or a table of data), each chunk is made large enough to service only a few file accesses made by a client. Observations and studies on distributions of file size reveal that the *average file size* is usually small, hence, even whole-file caching is also feasible. Considering the fact that chunk size usually varies per–client application, the size of the chunk is frequently taken as 8 Kbytes, which probably includes entire files from many different applications, and the file-cache hit ratios with this size are observed to exceed even 0.98. In addition, a DFS may sometimes use a separate *attributes cache* to cache information in relation to file attributes. However, there

are several issues need to be addressed in the design of a file-cache that eventually play an important role in DFS performance. Some of the key issues in this regard are:

- **File cache location:** Clients can cache data in main memory, on local disk, or in both at the client node. Organizing a cache in memory would definitely provide faster access to file data but would result in low reliability, because in the event of a crash of the client node, the entire file cache would be lost and may contain modified file data that are yet to be written back to the file copy in the server. Alternatively, the cache can be organized on the local disk in the client node. While this approach would slow down file data access, it would offer better reliability, since in the event of client node crash, all the data in file cache would remain unaffected. Reliability of the file cache organized on a local disk could be further enhanced with the use of RAID techniques, like disk mirroring.

- **File update policy: cache coherence:** The read-only blocks of caches may be in memory, while the read–write blocks of caches are to be written to local disk with no delay. When such a write operation is to be performed on a local disk, the modified file data would have to be written immediately into the file copy of the server at the same time. This policy, called **write-through**, is probably the simplest to use to enforce concurrency control. The write-through method is also reliable, because this method could be implemented as a transaction or an atomic operation to ensure that it completes (a transaction is a sequence of operations on one or more objects that transforms a [current] consistent state of the database/file into a new consistent state. Temporary inconsistent values that may occur during the execution of a transaction are hidden by making the affected entities inaccessible to other clients). However, accomplishment of this method temporarily delays some of the conflicting writers. To avoid delaying the client, the system performs writes to the cache and thus quickly releases writers without making them wait for the disk writes to complete; the update of the file copy (disk write) can be performed at a later time. This policy is called the **delayed write policy** and can also result in reduced disk I/O, particularly when requests are repeated for the same data blocks which are already in memory. But the problem with delayed writes is that main memory is usually volatile and any failure in the node system in the meantime can seriously corrupt and damage vital file system data. Adequate arrangements thus should be provided to ensure that the modified data would not be lost even if the client node failed in the meantime. To ameliorate the problematic situation that may arise from a delayed write, some systems flush *write-backs* to disk at regular time intervals.

While client caching offers performance advantages, at the same time, it relates to the well-known critical problem known as **cache inconsistency** (or **cache coherence**) irrespective of the write policy. Thus, a DFS should enforce some level of cache consistency. The consistency in caches holds good when they contain exact copies of remote data. Inconsistency in a cache is caused when multiple clients cache portions of the same shared file and different updates are performed concurrently on local copies lying with each individual caches. These uncontrolled updates and inconsistent caches can result in the creation of several different and irreconcilable versions of the same file. Inconsistency in a cache also arises when the remote data are changed by one client that modifies the file and the corresponding local cache copies already cached by other clients consequently become *invalid* but are not removed. The root of this problem perhaps lies in the choice of policy decisions adopted in write operations that change a file copy. However, the choice of a particular policy as well as consistency guarantees are largely influenced by the nature of the consistency semantics used.

The primary objective is to somehow prevent the presence of invalid data in client caches; hence, a *cache validation* function is required that would identify invalid data in client caches and deal with them in accordance with the file-sharing semantics (consistency semantics) of the DFS. File-sharing semantics usually specify the visibility of updates when multiple clients are accessing a shared file concurrently. For example, when UNIX semantics are used, file updates made by a client should be immediately visible to other clients of the file, so that the cache validation function can either refresh invalid data or prevent its use by a client. It should be noted that the file-sharing semantics suitable for centralized systems are not necessarily the most appropriate for distributed systems.

- **Cache validation:** Cache validation can be approached in two basic ways: *client-initiated validation* and *server-initiated validation*. Client-initiated validation is performed by the cache manager at a client node. At every file access by a client, it checks whether the desired data are already in the cache. If so, it checks whether the data are valid. If the check succeeds, the cache manager provides the data from the cache to the client; otherwise, it refreshes the data in the cache before supplying them to the client. Such frequent checking can be inefficient, since it consumes processing cycles of both the client and the server. In addition, this approach leads to additional cache validation traffic over the network at every access to the file, resulting in an ultimate increase in existing traffic density over the network. Such traffic can, however, be reduced if the validation can be performed periodically rather than at every file access, provided such validation is not inconsistent with the file sharing semantics of the DFS. This approach is followed by Sun NFS. Alternatively, in the *server-initiated approach*, the fileserver keeps track of which client nodes contain what file data in their caches and uses this information in the following way: when a client updates data in some part k of a file, the file server detects the other client nodes that have k in their file cache and informs their cache managers that their copies of k have become invalid so that they can take appropriate action. Each cache manager then has an option of either deleting the copy k from its cache or refreshing its cache either immediately or at the first reference to it.

A simple and relatively easy method to detect invalid data is through the use of *time-stamps* that indicate when the file was last modified. A time-stamp is associated with a file and each of its cached chunks. When a chunk of a file is copied into a cache, the file's time-stamp is also copied, along with the chunk. The cached chunk is declared invalid if its time-stamp is smaller than the file's time-stamp at any time. This way a write operation in some part k of a file by one client can invalidate all copies of k in other clients' caches. Each cache manager in that situation deletes copy k from its cache and refreshes it by reloading it at the time of its next reference.

Due to its being expensive, the cache validation approach needs to be avoided, if possible. One way to avoid the cache validation overhead is to use file-sharing semantics like *session semantics* which do not require that updates made by one client be visible to clients in other nodes. This feature avoids the need for validation altogether. Another approach may be to disable file caching if a client opens a file in *update mode*. All accesses to such a file are then directly implemented in server node. Now, all clients wishing to use the file would have to access the file in a way similar to remote file processing.

- **Chunk size:** Similar to page size in paging systems, chunk size in the file cache is also a significant factor and considered a vital performance metric in the file caching approach. Determination of the optimum chunk size requires balancing of several competing factors. Usually, the chunk size should be large so that spatial locality of file data contributes to a high hit ratio in the file cache. Use of a large chunk size, on the other hand, means a higher probability of data invalidation due to modifications performed by different other clients, which eventually leads to more cache validation overhead and thereby more delays than when a small chunk size is employed. So, the size of the chunk in a DFS should be decided after making a compromise between these two conflicting considerations. Moreover, a fixed size of chunks may not fit all the clients of a DFS. That is why some DFSs have adapted different chunk sizes to each different individual client.

- **Scalability:** The scalability of DFS depends to a large extent on the architecture of the computing system on which it is run and is mainly achieved through certain techniques that restrict most data traffic generated by file-processing activities to confine within a small section of a distributed system called *clusters of nodes* or simply *clusters*. Clusters and their characteristics are discussed in next section. In fact, when nodes are organized in the form of clusters, they exhibit certain important features that make this approach quite efficient and effective in terms of scalability. For instance, clusters typically represent subnets in a distributed system in which each cluster is a group of nodes connected by a high-speed LAN but essentially represents a single node of a distributed system. Consequently, the data traffic within a cluster possesses a high data transfer rate, giving rise to improved response time as well as increased throughput. In addition, while the number of clusters in a distributed system is increased, it does not cause any degradation in performance, because it does not proportionately add much network traffic. Moreover, as the system architecture is expanded, due to location transparency as well as location independence of the added nodes, any file could be simply moved to any cluster where the client is actually located. Even if the DFS does not possess location independence, still the movement of files and similar other aspects can be implemented through file replication or file caching for read-only files. Likewise, for read/write files, the use of session semantics enables to locate a file version in the client node without using any cache validation, which automatically eliminates cache validation traffic; hence, network traffic would ultimately be reduced.

Brief details on file caching with a figure are given on the Support Material at www.routledge.com/9781032467238.

9.14.10 CASE STUDY: WINDOWS

The Windows Server 2003 file system possesses *two salient features* for data replication and data distribution: (i) *remote differential compression* (RDC) is a protocol for file replication that reduces file replication and file coherence traffic between servers. (ii) *DFS namespaces* is a method of forming a virtual tree of folders located on different servers so that a client located in any node can access these folders.

Replication is organized using the concept of a *replication group*, which is essentially a group of servers that replicates a group of folders. This replication arrangement although is expensive to run on a regular basis, but is otherwise convenient, as several folders from the group of folders would be accessed off the server even in the event of failure. The RDC protocol is used to synchronize copies of a replicated folder across many different servers in its replication group. This protocol transmits only changes made to a file or only the differences between copies of a file, or the differences between different members present in a replication group, thereby conserving bandwidth between servers. Copies of a file are synchronized periodically on regular basis. When a new file is created, cross-file RDC identifies existing files that are similar to the new file and transmits only the differences of the new file from one of these files to members of the replication group. In this way, this protocol reduces the bandwidth consumed by the replication operation.

The DFS namespace is created by a system administrator. For every folder in the namespace, the administrator specifies a list of servers that contain a copy of the folder. When a client refers to a shared folder that appears in the namespace, the namespace server is contacted to resolve the name in the virtual tree. It sends back a *referral* to the client, which contains the list of servers that contain a copy of the folder. The client contacts the first server in this list to access the folder. If this server does not respond and client failback is enabled, the client is notified of this failure and goes on to contact the next server in the list. Thus, if the list of servers contains two servers, the second server acts as a *hot standby* for the first server.

9.14.11 CASE STUDY: SUN NFS

Sun Network File Systems, introduced in 1985, was the first product in distributed file service that achieved success both technically and commercially and has been widely adopted in industry and academic environments. The Sun NFS basically provides sharing of file systems in nodes operating under the Sun operating system, which is a version of UNIX. All implementations of NFS support the NFS protocol; a set of RPCs that provide the means for clients to perform operations on a remote file store. Although the NFS protocol is system-independent, but it was originally developed for use in networks of UNIX systems. Figure 9.12 shows a schematic diagram of the Sun NFS architecture. It consists of a two-level architecture:

- The *virtual file system* layer
- The NFS layer.

Virtual file system layer: The implications of virtual file systems (VFS) was described in Chapter 7. With the use of the VFS layer (module), NFS provides access transparency that enables user programs to issue file operations for local or remote files without it making any difference. Other DFSs, if they support UNIX system calls, can then also be present and be integrated in the same way. Addition of VFS to the UNIX kernel enables it to distinguish between local and remote files, and to translate between the UNIX-independent file identifiers used by NFS and the internal file identifiers normally used in UNIX and other file systems. The file identifiers used in NFS are called *file handles*. A file handle is opaque to clients and contains whatever information the server needs to distinguish an individual file. When NFS is implemented in UNIX, the file handle is derived from the file's *inode* number by adding two extra fields, *file-system identifier* and *i-node generation number*.

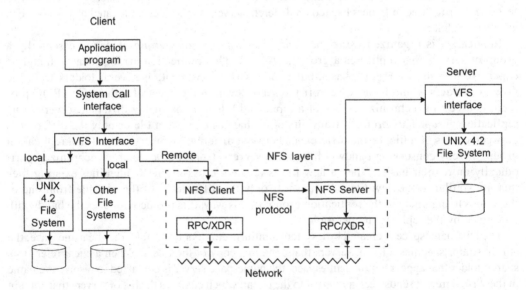

FIGURE 9.12   A block–structured illustration of a representative scheme of SUN NFS architecture.

The VFS layer implements the **mount protocol** and creates a system-wide unique designator for each file called the *v-node* (virtual node). The VFS structure for each mounted file system thus has one *v-node* per open file. A VFS structure relates a remote file system to the local directory on which it is mounted. The *v-node* contains an indicator to show whether a file is local or remote. If the file on which an operation is to be performed is located in one of the local file systems, the VFS invokes that file system and the *v-node* contains a reference to the index of the local file (an *i-node* in a UNIX implementation); otherwise it invokes the NFS layer (Figure 9.12), and the *v-node* in that situation contains the file handle of the remote file. The NFS layer contains the NFS server module, which resides in the kernel on each computer that acts as an NFS server. The NFS interacts with the server module at the remote node (computer) containing the relevant file through *NFS protocol* operations. The beauty of this architecture is that it permits any node to be both a client and a server at the same time.

- **Mount protocol:** The modified version of the UNIX *mount* command can be issued by clients to request mounting of a remote file system. They specify the remote *host name*, *pathname of a directory* in the remote file system, and the *local name* with which it is to be mounted. Each node in the system contains an *export list* that contains pairs of the form (*<directory>*, *<list-of-nodes>*). Each pair indicates that *<directory>*, which exists in one of the local file systems, can be remotely mounted only in the nodes contained in *<list-of-nodes>*. The *mount* command communicates with the mount service process on the remote host using a mount protocol. This is essentially an RPC protocol. When the superuser of a node makes a request to mount a remote directory, the NFS checks the validity (access permission for the relevant file system) of the request, mounts the directory, and finally ɪetuɪɪs a file handle which contains the identifier of the file system that contains the remote directory and the *inode* of the directory in that file system. The location (IP address and port number) of the server and the file handle for the remote directory are passed on to the VFS layer and the NFS client. In effect, users in the node can view a directory hierarchy constructed through these mount commands. NFS also permits cascaded mounting of file systems; that is, a file system could be mounted at a mount point in another file system, which is itself mounted inside another file system, and so on. The mounting of sub-trees of remote file systems by clients is supported by a *mount service* process that runs at the user level on each NFS server computer. On each server, there is a well-known file (*/etc/ exports*) containing the names of local file systems that are available for remote mounting. An access list is associated with each *file-system name* (*identifier*) indicating which hosts are permitted to mount the file system. However, some restrictions in this regard have been imposed in the NFS design that carefully avoid transitivity of the mount mechanism; otherwise each file server would have to know about all mounts performed by all clients over its file systems, which eventually would require the file server to be stateful.
- **NFS protocol:** The NFS protocol employs RPCs to provide remote file processing services using a client–server model. In fact, Sun's RPC system (described earlier) was developed for use in NFS. It can be configured to use either UDP or TCP, and the NFS protocol is compatible with both. The RPC interface to the NFS server is open; any process can send requests to an NFS server if the requests are valid and they include valid user credentials. The submission of a request with signed user credentials may be required as an optional security feature for the encryption of data for privacy and integrity. An NFS server does not provide any means of locking of files or records, and as such, users must employ their own mechanisms to implement concurrency control. A file server here is truly stateless, so each RPC has parameters that identify the file, the directory containing the file, and the data to be read or written. In addition, being stateless, the file server performs an implicit open and close for every file operation, and for this purpose, it does not use the UNIX buffer cache. The NFS provides numerous calls, such as; *looking up a file within a directory,*

reading directory entries, manipulating links and directories, accessing file attributes (i-node information), and *performing a file read/write operations.*

- **Path name translation:** UNIX file systems translate (resolve) multi-part file pathnames to *i-node* references in a step-by-step manner whenever system calls, such as *open, creat,* or *stat* are used. In NFS, pathnames cannot be translated at a server, because the name may cross a mount point at the client; directories holding different parts of a multi-part name may reside in file systems that are located at different servers. So, pathnames are parsed, and their translation is performed in an iterative manner by the client. Each part of a name that refers to a remote-mounted directory is then translated to a *file handle* using a separate *lookup* request to the remote server. To explain this procedure, let us assume that a user X1 located in node N_1 uses a pathname *a/b/c/d*, where *b* is the root directory of a mounted file system. To begin with, the host node N_1 creates *v-node$_a$*, the *v-node* for *a*. The NFS uses the mount table of N_1 when looking up the next component of the pathname and sees that *b* is a mounted directory. It then creates *v-node$_b$* from the information in the mount table. Let us assume that *v-node$_b$* is for a file in node N_2, so the NFS makes a copy of directory *b* in node N_1. While looking for *c* in the copy *b*, the NFS again uses the mount table N_1. This action would resolve *c* properly, even if *c* is a file system that was mounted by a superuser of node N_1 at some point in the remote file system *b*. The file server in node N_2, which contains *b*, has no need to know about this mounting. However, instead of using this procedural approach, if the pathname *b/c/d* were to be handed over directly to the fileserver in node N_2, the server would then have to have all the information about each and every mount performed by all clients over its file system. Consequently, this would require the file server to be stateful, which directly contradicts our stateless design strategy of the file server. To make this time-consuming process of entire pathname resolution relatively fast, each client node is usually equipped with an additional *directory name cache*.

- **Server and client caching:** Caching in both the server and the client computer is an indispensable feature of NFS implementations in order to achieve improved performance. The caching techniques used here work in a similar way as in a conventional UNIX environment, because all read and write requests issued by user-level processes pass through a single cache that is implemented in the UNIX kernel space. The cache is always kept up to date, and file accesses cannot bypass the cache.

The cache used for the server machine of NFS servers follows a similar line as other file accesses. The use of the server's cache to hold recently read disk blocks does not raise any cache consistency (cache coherence) problems, but when the server performs write operations, additional measures are needed, so clients can be assured the results of write operations are persistent, even in the event of a server's crash. However, in different versions of the NFS protocol, the cache read/write operations are of different styles, providing different options to exploit.

The NFS client module caches the result of *read, write, getattr, lookup,* and *readdir* operations in order to reduce the number of requests transmitted to servers, thereby minimizing the processing time and maximizing the speed of execution apart from avoiding network latency. Client caching introduces the potential for different versions of files or portions of files to exist in different client nodes, because writes by a client do not result in the immediate updating of cached copies of the same file in other clients. Instead, clients are responsible for polling the server to check the currency of the cached data that they hold. Usually, an appropriate timestamp-based method is used to validate cached blocks before they are used. Contents of a cached block are assumed to be valid for a certain period of time. For any access after this time, the cached block is used only if the timestamp is larger than the timestamp of the file.

In general, *read-ahead* and *delayed-write* mechanisms are employed, and to implement these methods, the NFS client needs to perform some reads and writes asynchronously using one or more *bio-daemon* (block input-output; the term *daemon* is often used to refer to user-level processes that perform system tasks) processes at each client. Bio-daemon processes certainly provide improved performance, ensuring that the client module does not block waiting for *reads* to return or writes to commit at the server. They are not a logical requirement, since in the absence of *read-ahead*, a *read* operation in a user process will trigger a synchronous request to the relevant server, and the results of *writes* in user processes will be transferred to the server when the relevant file is closed or when the virtual file system at the client performs a *sync* operation.

- **File operations and file sharing:** Every file operation in NFS should require a request to be made to the server to religiously obey the remote service paradigm. In addition, NFS employs caching of file blocks (file caching) at each client computer for greatly enhanced performance. Although this is important for the achievement of satisfactory performance, but this hybrid arrangement results in some deviation from strict UNIX one-copy file update semantics that consequently complicates the file sharing semantics offered by it.

To speed up file operation, NFS uses two caches. A **file-attributes cache** caches i-node information. Use of this cache is important, since it has been observed that a large percentage of requests issued to a file server is related to file attributes. The cached attributes are discarded after 3 seconds for files and after 30 seconds for directories. The other cache used is the **file-blocks cache**, which is the conventional file cache. As usual, it contains data blocks from the file. The file server uses large (normally 8 Kbytes) data blocks and uses *read-ahead* and *delayed-write* techniques (i.e. buffering techniques, already discussed in Chapter 7) to achieve improved performance in file access. A modified block is sent to the file server for writing into the file at an unspecified time (asynchronously). This policy is used even if clients concurrently access the same file block in conflicting modes, so a modification made by one client is not immediately visible to other clients accessing the file. A modified block is also sent to the file server when the relevant file is closed or when a *sync* operation is performed by the virtual file system at the client's end. A **directory names cache** is used in each client node to expedite pathname resolution at the time of file access. It usually contains remote directory names and their *v-nodes*. New entries are added to the cache when a new pathname prefix is resolved, and similarly, entries are deleted when a lookup fails because of mismatch between attributes returned by the file server and those of the cached *v-nodes*.

- **Conclusion:** In summary, the design of Sun NFS has been implemented for almost every known *operating system* and *heterogeneous hardware platform*s and is supported by a variety of filing systems. The NFS server implementation is *stateless* and by nature *idempotent* that enables clients and servers to resume execution after a *failure* without the need for recovery procedures. In fact, the failure of a client computer or a user-level process in a client has no effect on any server that it may be using, since servers hold no state on behalf of their clients. The design provides good *location transparency* and *access transparency* if the NFS mount service is used properly to produce similar name spaces at all clients. *Migration of files* or *file systems* is not fully achieved by NFS, but if file systems are moved between servers, then manual intervention to reconfigure the remote mount tables in each client must then be separately carried out to enable clients to access the file systems in their new location. The performance of NFS is made much enhanced by the *caching of file blocks* at each client computer, even after deviating from strict UNIX one-copy file update semantics. The *performance figures* as published show that NFS servers can be built to handle very large real-world loads in an efficient and cost-effective manner. The performance of a single server can be enhanced easily by the addition of processors, disks, and controllers, of course within a specified limit. When such limits are reached, additional servers can be installed and file systems must be reallocated between them. The measured performance of several implementations of NFS and its widespread adoption for use in situations that generate very heavy loads are clear indications of the *efficiency* with which the NFS protocol can be implemented.

9.14.12   CASE STUDY: LINUX GENERAL PARALLEL FILE SYSTEM

The Linux general parallel file system (GPFS) introduced by IBM is a shared-disk high-performance reliable file system that can run on various types of systems, including the IBM System p™ series and machines based on Intel or AMD processors. Supported operating systems for GPFS Version 3.2 include AIX (IBM UNIX) Version 5.3 and selected versions of Red Hat and SUSE Linux distributions. GPFS concepts include direct storage area network (SAN) access; network-based block I/O information lifecycle management (ILM) tools; and new features including multiple NSD servers, clustered NFS, and more scalable ILM tools supporting migration to other media types. It successfully satisfies the needs for throughput, storage capacity, and reliability of the largest and most demanding problems, such as for applications like modeling weather patterns. In fact, GPFS distinguishes itself from other cluster file systems by providing concurrent high-speed file access to applications executing on multiple (more than 2000) nodes running under different operating systems, including an AIX cluster, a Linux cluster, or a heterogeneous cluster of other OS, AIX, and Linux nodes. It is time-proven and is used on six of the ten most powerful supercomputers in the world, including one of the largest: ASCI White at Lawrence Livermore National Laboratory, USA, providing efficient use of disk bandwidth.

GPFS supports fully parallel access both to file data and metadata. In truly large systems, while administrative actions (such as adding or removing disks from a file system or rebalancing files across disks) involve a great amount of work, but GPFS performs its administrative functions in parallel as well. A GPFS system consists of the cluster nodes on which the GPFS file system and the applications are run, connected by a switching fabric to the scalable *shared-disk* architecture consisting of disks or disk subsystems. All nodes in the cluster, however, have equal access to all disks.

Performance and Scalability

GPFS provides unparalleled performance, especially for larger data objects, and excellent performance for large aggregates of smaller objects. GPFS achieves high performance along with fault tolerant I/O by:

*   Striping data using appropriate disk-block size to store data across multiple disks (to the extent of several thousand disks using RAID technology) attached to multiple nodes.
*   Using *block-level* locking based on a very sophisticated scalable distributed token management system to ensure data consistency of file system data and metadata when multiple application nodes in the cluster attempt to access the shared files concurrently.
*   Providing typical *access patterns* like sequential, reverse sequential, and random and optimizing I/O access for these patterns.
*   Offering scalable metadata (e.g. indirect blocks in the FMT) management that allows all nodes of the cluster accessing the file system to perform the same file metadata operations.
*   Allowing GPFS file systems to be *exported* to clients outside the cluster through NFS or Samba that when integrated form the clustered NFS which provides scalable file service. This, in turn, permits simultaneous access to a common set of data from multiple nodes, apart from monitoring of file services, load balancing, and IP address failover.
*   Efficient client-side caching.
*   Supporting a large block size, configurable by the administrator, to fit I/O requirements.
*   Utilizing advanced algorithms that improve *read-ahead* and *write-behind* file functions.

- Accomplishing fault-tolerance by using robust clustering features and support for continuous data replication of journal logs, metadata, and file data. The journal is located in the file system under which the file belongs and is processed. In the event of a node failure, other nodes can access its journal and carry out the pending operations.

To provide adequate protection and security, GPFS ultimately enhanced access-control that protects directories and files by providing a means of specifying who should be granted access. GPFS supports (on AIX) NFS V4 access control lists (ACLs) in addition to traditional ACL support. Traditional GPFS ACLs are based on the POSIX model. Access control lists extend the base permissions or standard file-access modes, such as; *read* (*r*), *write* (*w*), and *execute* (*x*), and beyond these three categories; the *file owner*, *file group*, and *other users* are used to allow the definition to include additional users and user groups. In addition, GPFS introduces a fourth access mode; *control* (*c*), which can be used to govern who can manage the ACL itself.

9.15 CLUSTERS: A DISTRIBUTED COMPUTER SYSTEM DESIGN

Advances in communication technology have facilitated to evolve a relatively recent significant development in the design of distributed computing systems called *clustering*. Cluster architecture has appeared as a savior in mainly managing different types of numerous application areas that otherwise require a true distributed system for their processing. This comparatively low-cost cluster architecture has fully satisfied the user community with a base substitute for a true distributed system which is relatively more expensive. It looks as if the users are made happy with only a glass of grog when the bottle of champagne is beyond their reach! A cluster can be defined as a group of interconnected, self-sufficient computers (**multicomputers**) working together as a **unified computing system** that can cast an illusion of **single-system image (SSI)** as essentially *one single machine* to the outside world. Each individual computer (*node*) in a cluster may be a uniprocessor or a multiprocessor which can even run on its own without any assistance from the cluster. The use of a multiprocessor as a node in the cluster, although not necessary, does improve both performance and availability. Since clusters are composed of independent and effectively redundant computers (nodes), they have a potential for fault-tolerance and they are also suitable for other classes of problems in which reliability is paramount. A clustering approach, however, can be commonly considered an alternative to symmetric multiprocessing that offers effectively unbounded processing power, storage capacity, high performance, and high availability that could be used to solve much larger problems than a single machine could.

Cluster architecture while was developed and introduced as a base substitute for a distributed system, but it is essentially built on the platform of a computer networks of multicomputer systems comprising heterogeneous, complete, stand-alone, and autonomous machines (computers) operated by a loosely coupled NOS. Our traditional distributed system (per definitions given in Section 9.4 and 9.8) is run by a DOS, but a DOS is not supposed to manage a collection of *independent computers*. On the other hand, a network of computers in the premises of a computer network being run by a NOS never provides the view of a *single coherent system*. So, neither DOS nor NOS really qualifies as part of a distributed system in this regard. The obvious question thus arises as to whether it is possible to develop a distributed computing system that could have most of the salient features of these two different domains (DOS and NOS environments). Those features are mainly transparency and related ease of use provided by DOS, and scalability and openness offered by NOS. One viable solution in this regard was attempted simply by enhancing the services that a NOS provides, such that better support for distribution transparency could be realized. To implement these enhancements, it was then decided to include an additional layer of software with a NOS in order to improve its distribution transparency and also to more or less hide the heterogeneity in the collection of underlying systems. This additional layer is physically placed in the middle between applications and NOS; hence, it is legitimately called **middleware**, and it lies at the heart of modern distributed systems of this category being currently built (Chakraborty, 2020). This architectural system design methodology quickly gained much importance due to the range of options it can provide to cater to many different operational environments, particularly in the area of server applications (Buyya, 1999).

Appropriate system software is thus required to fully exploit a cluster hardware configuration that requires some enhancements over a traditional single-system operating system. It should be clearly noted that cluster software is not a DOS, but it contains several features that closely resemble those found in DOS. Some of them are: it provides *high availability* through redundancy of available resources, such as CPUs and other I/O media. On the one hand, it speeds up computation by exploiting the presence of several CPUs within the cluster, and on the other hand, with the use of the same (or heterogeneous) hardware configurations, it spreads the flavor of parallel processing by providing a single-system image to the user. In addition, with the use of appropriate scheduling software, a cluster effectively exhibits the capability to balance load in the existing computing system. Last but not least, the software is adequately equipped in providing fault-tolerance as well as failure management.

9.15.1 Distinct Advantages

Clustering method by interconnecting independent autonomous computers exhibits many distinct advantages. Clusters offer the following useful features that can be realized at a relatively low cost as indicated by Weygant:

* **High Availability:** More availability of the computing resources present in the cluster comes from its high scalability. It also implies *high fault-tolerance*. Since each node in a cluster is an independent stand-alone computer, the occurrence of faults, and thereby failure of any node, does not create as such any loss of service. In many of today's products, fault-tolerance is handled automatically in software. Moreover, clustering also possesses **failover** capability by using a backup computer placed within the cluster to take charge of a failed computer to negotiate any exigency.
* **Expandability and Scalability:** It is possible to configure a cluster in such a way to add new systems to the existing cluster using standard technology (commodity hardware and software components). This provides *expandability*, an affordable upgrade path that lets organizations increase their computing power while preserving their existing investment by incurring only a little additional expense. The performance of applications also improves with the aid of a scalable software environment. Clusters also offer high **scalability** and more **availability** of the computing resources. In fact, this approach offers both *absolute scalability* as well as *incremental scalability*, which means that a cluster configuration can be easily extended by adding new systems to the cluster in small increments, of course within the underlying specified limits.
* **Openness:** A clustering approach is also capable of hiding the *heterogeneity* that may exist in the collection of underlying interconnected machines (computers) and thereby ensuring interoperability between different implementations.
* **High Throughput:** The clustering approach offers effectively unbounded processing power, storage capacity, high performance, and high availability. These together thereby offer considerably high throughput in all situations.
* **Superior Cost/Performance:** By using commodity building blocks, it is possible to realize a cluster, that could offer an equal or even greater computing power as well as superior performance than a comparable single large machine, at much lower cost and complexity.

A brief on this topic is given on the Support Material at www.routledge.com/9781032467238.

9.15.2   CLASSIFICATION OF CLUSTERS

Clusters can be classified in many different ways. Perhaps the simplest classification is based on whether the nodes in a cluster access the same **shared–disk**. In an n-node shared-disk cluster, there is a disk subsystem that is directly linked to multiple nodes within the cluster. In addition, there is still a standard high-speed link between the nodes for message exchange to coordinate their activity. Since the shared common-disk subsystem is a single point of interaction between multiple computers, it generally uses a RAID system or another similar redundant disk technology to achieve high performance, high reliability, and better fault tolerance.

The other alternative is an n-node cluster in which there is **no common shared disk** but only one high-speed interconnection link between the nodes for message exchange to coordinate cluster activity. This link can be a LAN or WAN that may be *dedicated* only to the participating nodes in the cluster or can be *shared* by other computers that lie outside the domain of the cluster. Here, remote client systems must have the provision to link with the LAN or WAN of the server cluster.

Individual clusters may, however, be interconnected to form a larger system (cluster of clusters). In fact, the internet itself can be used as a computing cluster. The proliferation of WANs of computer resources for high-performance computing has led to the emergence of a new field called **metacomputing**. Discussion of metacomputing is outside the scope of this book. Interested readers should consult Baker (1991).

9.15.3   DIFFERENT CLUSTERING METHODS

Based on the functional alternatives, clustering approaches can be exploited over a spectrum of possibilities. This classification also demystifies the objectives of a specific cluster and defines its design requirements. Some common approaches in use are:

- **Separate server:** In this approach to clustering, each computer is a separate server with its own disks and no disks shared between such systems exists. [Figure 9.39(b) given on the Support Material at www.routledge.com/9781032467238.] However, this approach requires software management and scheduling mechanisms to handle continuously arriving client requests to assign them to different servers in a way that load balancing can be maintained and high utilization of the available resources can be attained. Consequently, this approach can offer high performance and also high availability. Moreover, to make this approach attractive, failover capability is required so that in the event of failure of one computer, any other computer in the cluster can take up the incomplete executing application from the point of its failure and continue its execution to its completion. To implement this, data must be constantly copied among systems so that each system has easy access to the most-current data of the other systems. However, such data exchange operations essentially involve high communication traffic as well as server load that can incur additional overhead for the sole purpose of ensuring high availability, and this, in turn, also results in a substantial degradation in overall performance.
- **Servers connected to disks (shared nothing):** In order to reduce the network traffic and server overhead caused mostly by data exchange operations needed among the systems in a cluster, most clusters equipped with servers are connected to common disks [Figure 9.39(a) on the Support Material at www.routledge.com/9781032467238]. One variation of this approach is simply called *shared nothing*, in which the common disks (not shared disk) are partitioned into volumes, and each volume is owned by a single computer. If one computer fails, the cluster must be reconfigured so that another computer can gain ownership of the volumes owned by the failed computer. In this way, constant copying of data among all systems to enable each system to have easy access to the most-current data of the other systems can simply be foregone.
- **Shared-disk servers:** In the shared-disk approach, multiple computers present in a cluster share the same disks at the same time so that each computer has access to all of the volumes on all of

the disks [Figure 9.39(a) on the Support Material at www.routledge.com/9781032467238]. This approach, however, requires some form of locking mechanism to implement mutual exclusion to ensure that data can be accessed by only one computer at any point in time.

A brief on this topic is given on the Support Material at www.routledge.com/9781032467238.

9.15.4 GENERAL ARCHITECTURE

Formation of a cluster by organizing computers can be accomplished in a variety of ways (Buyya, 1999). However, a typical cluster architecture is depicted in Figure 9.13. The individual computers may be homogeneous or heterogeneous and are usually connected by high-speed LAN or switch hardware to realize faster communication. Each computer in the cluster can run on its own, apart from its operation as a member of the cluster. In addition, a middleware layer of software needs to be included in each computer, the presence of which enables each computer to operate as a cluster member in unison (to project it as a component of a single-system image). The other functions of middleware involve providing *access transparency*, *distribution transparency*, *balancing of load*, and *high availability* by responding to failures in individual components and many similar things. Moreover, a cluster will also be equipped with other software tools so as to help the cluster efficiently execute programs that are capable of realizing *parallel execution*. However, some of the major representative functions and services that are common to middleware and are provided by it in a cluster are the following:

- **Single entry point:** A user logs normally onto the cluster rather than to an individual computer.
- **Single control point:** A default node always exists that is used for cluster management and control.
- **Single memory space:** The presence of distributed shared memory allows programs to share variables.
- **Single file hierarchy:** The user views a single hierarchy of file directories under the same root directory.

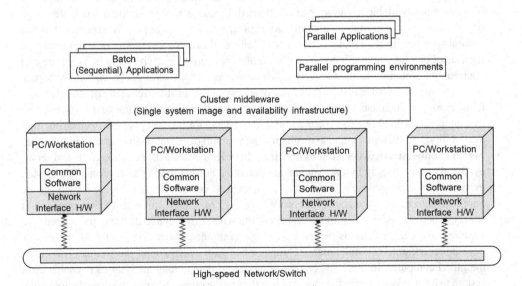

FIGURE 9.13 A representative block diagram of a cluster computer architecture realized with the use of PC workstations and cluster middleware.

- **Single job-management system:** A job scheduler exists in a cluster (not related to any individual computer) that receives jobs from all users submitted to the cluster irrespective of any specification about on which computer host a submitted job will be executed.
- **Single virtual networking:** Any node can access any other point in the cluster, even though actual physical cluster configuration may consist of several interconnected networks. There exists a single virtual network operation.
- **Single user interface:** Irrespective of the workstation through which a user enters the cluster, a common graphic interface supports all users at the same time.
- **Single process space:** A uniform process-identification scheme is used. A process executing on any node can create or communicate with any other process on any local or remote node.
- **Process migration:** Any process running on any node can be migrated to any other node irrespective of its location, which enables balancing the load in the system.
- **Single I/O space:** Any node can access any local and remote I/O device, including disks, without having any prior knowledge of its actual physical location.
- **Checkpointing:** This function periodically saves the process state, intermediate results, and other related information of the running process that allows implementation of rollback recovery (a failback function) in the event of a fault and subsequent failure of the system.

Similar other services are also required for cluster–middleware in order to cast a single-system image of the cluster. The last four items of the preceding list enhance the *availability* of the cluster, while the other items in the list are related to providing a single-system image of the cluster.

9.15.5 Operating System Considerations

Whatever be the hardware configuration and arrangement of the cluster, it requires specific software (specifically the OS) so that this form of distributed computing system can cast a single-system image (SSI) to the user. An operating system that can project this SSI view will be of a special type and will be different for different cluster architectures and is thus required to fully match the underlying cluster hardware. *It should be clearly noted that although cluster software is not a distributed operating system, it has several useful features that closely resemble those found in true distributed operating systems.* Cluster software controls the entire operation of all the nodes present in the cluster, and it spreads the flavor of *parallel processing* by providing a unified system image to the user, known as **single-system image**. It speeds up computation, rendering parallel processing by exploiting the services of several CPUs (nodes) present within the cluster, and this is accomplished by scheduling and executing independent sub-tasks of an application simultaneously on different nodes within the cluster. It provides **high availability** through redundancy of available resources, such as CPUs and other I/O media, yet those are also delegated to carry out effective *load balancing* among the existing computer systems. This software is also equipped to provide enough **fault-tolerance** as well as **failure management**. Apart from being equipped with its usual software, a cluster will also have other software tools supported by the underlying OS, such as a **parallelizing compiler**, **software interfaces**, and **programming language interfaces,** etc. so that all these together can create an environment very similar to that of a true distributed system.

9.15.6 Case Study: Windows Clusters

The Windows cluster server (also known as Wolfpack) is essentially a shared-nothing cluster (as already described), in which each disk volume and other resources are owned by a single system at any point in time. The Windows Cluster Server is based on the following fundamental concepts:

- **Cluster Service and Management:** A collection of software must reside on each node that manages all cluster-specific activity. A cluster as a whole is, however, managed using distributed control algorithms which are implemented through actions performed in all nodes. These algorithms require that all nodes in a cluster have a consistent view of the cluster; that is, they must possess identical lists of nodes within the cluster. An application has to use a special Cluster API and dynamic link library (DLL) to access cluster services.
- **Resources:** The concept of resources in Windows is somewhat different. All resources in the cluster server are essentially objects that can be actual *physical resources* in the system, including hardware devices, such as disk drives and network cards; logical resources, such as logical disk volumes, TCP/IP addresses, entire applications, and databases; or a resource that can even be a service. A resource is implemented by a dynamic link library (DLL), so it is specified by providing a DLL interface. Resources are managed by a **resource monitor** which interacts with the cluster service via RPC and responds to cluster service commands to configure and move a collection of resources. A resource is said to be *online* at a node when it is connected to that specific node to provide certain services.
- **Group:** A group is a collection of resources managed as a single unit. A resource belongs to a group. Usually, a group contains all of the elements needed to run a specific application, including the services provided by that application. A group is owned by one node in the cluster at any time; however, it can be shifted (moved) to another node in the event of a fault or failure. A resource manager exists in a node that is responsible for starting and stopping a group. If a resource fails, the resource manager alerts the *failover manager* and hands over the group containing the resource so that it can be restarted at another node.
- **Fault Tolerance:** Windows Cluster Server provides fault-tolerance support in clusters by using two or more server nodes. Basic fault tolerance is usually provided through RAIDs of 0, 1, or 5 that are shared by all server nodes. In addition, when a fault or a shutdown occurs on one server, the cluster server moves its functions to another server without causing a disruption in its services.

An illustration of the various important components of Windows Cluster Server and their relationships in a single system of a cluster is depicted in Figure 9.14. Individual cluster services are accessed by one manager out of many. Each node has a **node manager** which is responsible for maintaining this node's membership in the cluster and also the list of nodes in a cluster. Periodically, it sends messages called *heartbeats* to the node managers on other nodes present in the cluster for the purpose of node fault detection. When one node manager detects a loss of heartbeat messages from another node in the cluster, it broadcasts a message on the private LAN to the entire cluster, causing all members to exchange messages to verify their view of current cluster membership. If a node manager does not respond or a node fault is otherwise detected, it is removed from the cluster, and each node then accordingly corrects its list of nodes. This event is called a *regroup event*. The **resource manager** concerned with resources now comes into action, and all active groups located in that faulty node are then "pulled" to other active nodes in the cluster so that resources in them can be accessed. Use of a shared disk facilitates this arrangement. When a node is subsequently restored after a failure, the **failover manager** concerned with nodes decides which groups can be handed over to it. This action is called a *failback*, it safeguards and ensures resource efficiency in the system. The handover and failback actions can also be performed manually.

In effect, the **resource manager/failover manager** makes all decisions regarding resource groups and takes appropriate actions to startup, reset, and failover. In the event of a node failure, the failover managers on the other active nodes cooperate to effect a distribution of resource groups from the failed system to the remaining active systems. When a node is subsequently restored after

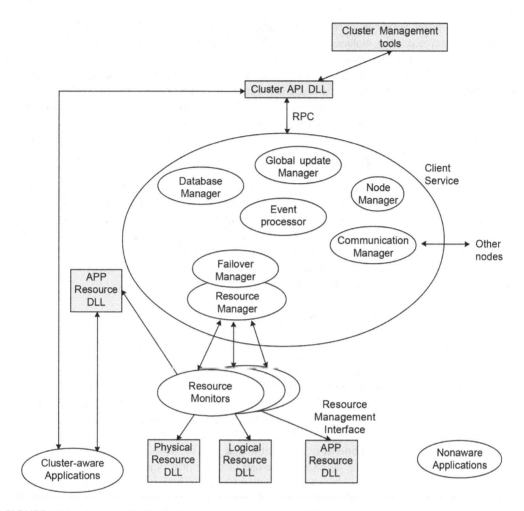

FIGURE 9.14 A schematic block diagram of a representative Windows cluster server.

rectifying its fault, the failover can decide to move some groups back to the restored system along with the others. In particular, any group can be configured with a preferred owner. If that owner fails and then restarts, it is desirable that the group in question be moved back to the node using a rollback operation.

The configuration database used by the cluster is maintained by the **configuration database manager**. The database contains all information about resources and groups and node ownership of groups. The database managers on each of the cluster nodes interact cooperatively to maintain a consistent picture of configuration information. *Fault-tolerant transaction software* is used to ensure that changes in the overall cluster configuration before failure, during failure, and after recovery from failure are performed consistently and correctly.

There are many other managers to perform their respective duties and responsibilities. One such processing entity is known as an **event processor** (**handler**) that coordinates and connects all of the components of the cluster service, handles common operations, and controls cluster service initialization. The **communication manager** monitors message exchange with all other nodes present in the cluster. The **global update manager** provides a service used by other components within the cluster service.

Windows Cluster Server balances the incoming network traffic load by distributing the traffic among the server nodes in a cluster. It is accomplished in the following way: the cluster is assigned a single IP address; however, incoming messages go to all server nodes in the cluster. Based on the current load distribution arrangement, exactly one of the servers accepts the message and responds to it. In the event of a node failure, the load belonging to the failed node is distributed among other active nodes. Similarly, when a new node is included, the load distribution is reconfigured to direct some of the incoming traffic to the new joining node.

9.15.7 CASE STUDY: SUN CLUSTERS

The operating system managing Sun Cluster is essentially a *distributed operating system* built as a set of extensions to the base Solaris UNIX system. It casts a single-system image to the user as well as to the applications and hence appears as a single computer system on which the Solaris operating system runs. The Sun Cluster framework integrates a cluster of two or more Sun systems operating under the Solaris OS to provide better availability and more scalability of services. A schematic representation of the overall Sun Cluster architecture running on an existing Solaris kernel is depicted in Figure 9.15. The distinctive components of this system are:

- Object and communication support
- Global process management
- Networking
- Global DFS

- **Object and communication support:** The implementation of a Sun cluster is based on object orientation in which the Common Object Request Broker Architecture (CORBA) object model is used to define objects, and the RPC mechanism is used to support communication. The CORBA Interface Definition Language (IDL) is used to specify interfaces between MC components in different nodes. The elements of MC are implemented in the object-oriented language C++. The use of a uniform object model exploiting the support of IDL offers a suitable mechanism that facilitates both inter-node as well as intra-node process communication activities. All these things are, however, built on top of a

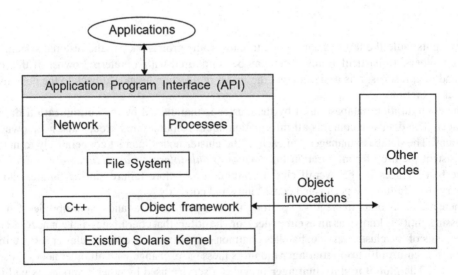

FIGURE 9.15 A general block-structured model of a representative Sun cluster architecture.

Solaris kernel to work together with virtually no changes required to the kernel, even if any changes are made in any area above the kernel.

- **Global process management:** Existing process management is enhanced with the use of global process management, which provides globally unique *process id*s for each process in the cluster so that each node is aware of the location and status of each process. This feature is useful in *process migration*, wherein a process during its lifetime can be transferred from one node to another to balance the computational loads and ease of computation in different nodes or to achieve computation speed-up. A migrated process in that situation should be able to continue using the same pathnames to access files from a new node. Use of a DFS, in particular, facilitates this feature work. The threads of a single process, however, must be on the same node.

- **Disk path monitoring:** All disk paths can be monitored and configured to automatically reboot a node in the case of multiple path failure. Faster reaction in the case of severe disk path failure provides improved availability.

- **Configuration checker:** Checks for vulnerable cluster configurations regularly and rapidly, thereby attempting to limit failures due to odd configuration throughout the life-time of the cluster.

- **Networking:** A number of alternative approaches are taken by Sun clusters when handling network traffic.

  - Only a *single node* in the cluster is selected to have a network connection and is dedicated to perform all network protocol processing. In particular, for TCP/IP-based processing, while handling incoming traffic, this node would analyze TCP and IP headers and would then route the encapsulated data to the appropriate node. Similarly, for outgoing traffic, this node would encapsulate data from other transmitting nodes with TCP/IP headers for necessary transmission. This approach has several advantages but suffers from a serious drawback for not being scalable, particularly when the cluster consists of a large number of nodes, and thus, it has fallen out of favor.

  - Another approach may be to assign a separate unique IP address to each node in the cluster, each node will then execute the network protocols over the external network directly. One serious difficulty with this approach is that the transparency criteria of a cluster is now adversely affected. The cluster configuration is no longer transparent (rather is opened) to the outside world. Another vital aspect is the difficulty of handling the failover situation in the event of a node failure when it is necessary to transfer an application running on the failed node to another active node but the active node has a different network address.

  - A packet filter can be used to route packets to the destined node, and all protocol processing is performed on that node. A cluster in this situation appears to the outside world to be a single server with a single IP address. Incoming traffic is then appropriately distributed among the available nodes of the cluster to balance the load. This approach is found to be an appropriate one for a Sun cluster to adopt.

Incoming packets are first received on the node that has the physical network connection with the outside world. This receiving node filters the packet and delivers it to the right target node over the cluster's own internal connections. Similarly, all outgoing packets are routed over the cluster's own interconnection to the node (or one of multiple alternative nodes) that has an external physical network adapter. However, all protocol processing in relation to outgoing packets is always performed by the originating node. In addition, the Sun cluster maintains a global network configuration network database in order to keep track of the network traffic to each node.

- **Availability and scalability:** Sun cluster provides **availability** through failover, whereby the services that were running at a failed node are transferred (relocated) to another node.

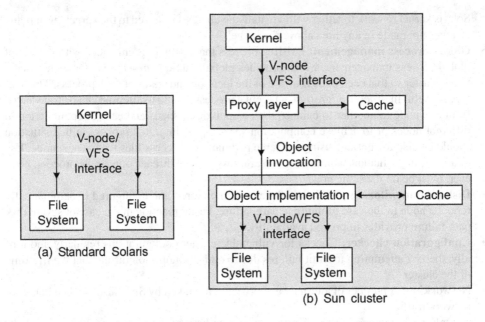

FIGURE 9.16   A representative scheme of a general Sun cluster file system extension.

Scalability is provided by sharing (as well as distributing) the total load across the existing servers.

- **Multiple storage technologies and storage brands:** Solaris cluster can be used in combination with different storage technologies, such as FC, SCSI, iSCSI, and NAS storage on Sun or non-Sun storage.
- **Easy-to-use command-line interface:** An object-oriented command line interface provides a consistent and familiar structure across the entire command set, making it easy to learn and use and limiting human error. Command logging enables tracking and replay.
- **Global distributed file system:** The beauty and the strength of the Sun cluster is its global file system, as shown in Figure 9.16, which is built on the *virtual node (v-node)* and *virtual file system* (VFS) concepts. The *v-node* structure is used to provide a powerful, general-purpose interface to all types of file systems. A *v-node* is used to map pages of memory into the address space of a process, to permit access to a file system, and to map a process to an object in any type of file system. The VFS interface accepts general-purpose commands that operate on entire files and translates them into actions appropriate for that subject file system. The global file system provides a uniform interface to all files which are distributed over the cluster. A process can open a file located anywhere in the cluster, and processes on all nodes use the same pathname to locate a file. In order to implement global file access, MC includes a proxy file system built on top of the existing Solaris file system at the *v-node* interface. The VFS/*v-node* operations are appropriately converted by a proxy layer into object invocations. The invoked object may reside on any node in the system. The invoked object subsequently performs a local *v-node*/VFS operation on the underlying file system. No modification is, however, required either at the kernel level or in the existing file system to support this global file environment. In addition, caching is used to reduce the number of remote object invocations, which, in turn, minimizes the traffic on the cluster interconnect. A few of the multiple file systems and volume managers that are supported by the Sun cluster are:

- UFS, VxFS, and ZFS as root file systems
- HA UFS, HA NFS, and HA ZFS; HA QFS and shared QFS (with Oracle RAC); and HA VxFS
- Global file system on UFS and VxFS
- SVM, VxVM, ASM

SUMMARY

The time-sharing system of the 1970s could be considered the first stepping stone toward distributed computing system that implemented simultaneous sharing of computer resources by multiple users located away from the main computer system. Different forms of hardware design of distributed computing systems, including multiprocessors and multicomputers, and the various forms of software that drive these systems are described. The generic DOS and its design issues are explained. Numerous considerations used in generic multiprocessor operating systems with emphasis on processor management for different forms of multiprocessor architecture are described. Practical implementations of Linux OS and Windows OS in multiprocessor environments are presented here as case studies. Distributed systems based on different models of multicomputers (networks of computers) consisting of a collection of independent computer systems (homogeneous or heterogeneous) interconnected by a communication network (LAN and WAN) using Ethernet, token ring, and so on for the purpose of exchanging messages are illustrated. The formal design issues of generic multicomputer operating systems to be run on any kind of multicomputers are presented.

In fact, a distributed system essentially provides an environment in which users can conveniently use both local and remote resources. Computing of varieties of applications with the client/server model in computer networks is distributed to users (clients), and resources to be shared are maintained on server systems available to all clients. Thus, the client/server model is a blend of decentralized and centralized approaches. The actual application is divided between client and server to optimize ease of use and performance. The basic design issues of DOSs built on the client/server model are briefly described. The interprocess communication required in any distributed system is realized either by a message-passing facility or a RPC in which different programs on different machines interact using procedure call/return syntax and semantics that act as if the partner program were running on the same machine. The actual implementation of RPC in Sun systems is briefly described. A brief overview of distributed shared memory and its implementation aspects is narrated. A major part of a distributed system is the DFS, and the key design issues and a brief overview of its operations are described, along with an example of its actual implementation carried out in Windows, SUN NFS, and Linux GPFS. The most modern approach in distributed computer system design is the cluster, built on the client/server model in which all the machines work together as a unified computing resource using an additional layer of software known as middleware that casts an illusion of being one machine. Its advantages, classifications, and different methods of clustering are described in short, along with the general architecture of clusters and their operating system issues. The different aspects of implementation of Windows and SUN clusters are shown here as case studies.

EXERCISES

1. With respect to the salient features in hardware architectures, differentiate among the following types of computing systems: **a**. time sharing, **b**. network, **c**. distributed, and **d**. parallel processing.
2. State and explain the salient features of a distributed computing system.
3. What are the main advantages and disadvantages that distributed computing systems exhibit over centralized ones?

4. What are the commonly used different models for configuring distributed computing systems? Discuss in brief their relative advantages and disadvantages. Which model is considered dominant? Give reasons to justify it.

5. State the important issues in the design of the kernel of the operating system in symmetric multiprocessors. Explain in brief how these issues are being handled.

6. What are the salient features considered in the design of the kernel of the operating system in a distributed shared memory multiprocessor? Explain in brief how these issues are handled.

7. In terms of hardware complexity, operating system complexity, potential parallelism, and cost involved, compare the following types of systems which consist of a large number of processors (say, 16 to 32):
   a. A multiprocessor system with a single shared memory (SMP).
   b. A multiprocessor system in which each processor has its own memory. The processors are located far from each other and are connected by a low-capacity communication line forming a network. Each processor can communicate with others by exchanging messages.
   c. A multiprocessor system in which each processor has its own memory in addition to shared memory used by all processors in the system.

8. Discuss the suitability of various kinds of locks to satisfy the requirements of synchronization of processors in multiprocessor systems. While spin or sleep locks are used, can priority inversion occur? Justify your answer.

9. Discuss the different approaches employed in scheduling of threads and related assignment of processors in multiprocessor systems.

10. What are the salient features that must be considered in the design of a multicomputer operating system?

11. What is middleware? In spite of having acceptable standards, such as TCP/IP, why is middleware still needed?

12. State the different models of middleware that are available for use. Furnish in brief the various middleware services that are implemented in application systems.

13. What are the reasons distributed operating systems are more difficult to design than centralized time-sharing operating systems?

14. What are the main differences between a network operating system and a distributed operating system?

15. State and explain the major issues at the time of designing a distributed operating system.

16. Discuss some of the important concepts that might be used to improve the reliability of a distributed operating system. What is the main problem faced in making a system highly reliable?

17. Explain the main guiding principle to be obeyed to enhance the performance of a distributed operating system.

18. Why is scalability an important feature in the design of a distributed system? Discuss some of the important issues that must be settled at the time of designing a scalable distributed system.

19. "Heterogeneity is unavoidable in many distributed systems". What are the common types of incompatibilities faced in heterogeneous distributed systems? What are the common issues that must be dealt with at the time of designing a heterogeneous distributed system?

20. Compare and contrast between network operating systems, distributed operating systems, and distributed systems (middleware-based).

21. Most computer networks use fewer layers than those specified in the OSI model. Explain what might be the reason for this. What problems, if any, could this lead to?

22. Why is the OSI model considered not suitable for use in a LAN environment? Give the architecture of a communication protocol model suitable for LANs. Briefly describe the functions of each layer of this architecture

23. Suggest three different routing strategies for use in networks of computers. Discuss the relative advantages and disadvantages of the strategies thus suggested.

24. What are the main differences between connection-oriented and connectionless communication protocols? Discuss their relative merits and drawbacks.

25. What is asynchronous transfer mode technology used in networking? State some of the most common important features ATM has that put it at the forefront of networking technologies. What type of impact will each of these features have on future distributed systems?

26. State the mechanism used in the FLIP protocol for each of the following:
    a. Transparent communication
    b. Group communication
    c. Secure communication
    d. Easy network communication
    State at least one shortcoming of the FLIP protocol.

27. What is a socket? Explain the mechanism followed to implement sockets. What is the implication of a socket interface?

28. What is meant by internetworking? What are the main issues in internetworking? In light of the interconnection technologies used in internetworking, explain the differences among the following terms: a. bridges, b. router, c. brouter, and d. gateway.

29. What are the main differences between blocking and non-blocking protocols used in inter-process communication in distributed systems on a workstation-server model?

30. Explain the nature of and reasons for differences in naming of system objects between centralized and distributed systems in a client–server model.

31. Define process migration in a distributed system. Discuss the situations and the advantages that can be accrued from process migration activities.

32. What is meant by IPC semantics? Write down the most commonly used IPC semantics used in distributed systems along with their significant implications.

33. Discuss the relative merits and demerits of blocking and non-blocking protocols.

34. Comment on properties of the following non-blocking protocol:
    a. Sender sends a request and continues processing.
    b. Receiver sends a reply.
    c. Sender sends an acknowledgement when it receives a reply.

35. Requests made using non-blocking *send* calls may arrive out of sequence at the destination site when dynamic routing is used. Discuss how a non-blocking RR protocol should discard duplicate requests when this property holds.

36. Write notes on factors that influence the duration of the timeout interval in the RRA protocol. How can duplicate replies received in the sender site in the RRA protocol be discarded?

37. Describe a mechanism for implementing consistent ordering of messages in each of the following cases (essentially a group communication): a. one-to-many communication, b. many-to-one communication, and c. many-to-many communication.

38. What was the basic inspiration behind the development of the RPC facility? How does an RPC facility make the job of the distributed application developer simpler?

39. With reference to the definition of synchronous and asynchronous RPC, discuss their relative merits and drawbacks.

40. In RPC, the called procedure may be on the same computer as the calling procedure, or it may be on a different computer. Explain why the term *remote procedure call* is used even when the called procedure is on the same computer as the calling procedure.

41. What is a "stub"? How are stubs generated? Explain how the use of stubs helps make the RPC mechanism transparent.

42. The caller process of an RPC must wait for a reply from the callee process after making a call. Explain how this can actually be done.

43. List some merits and drawbacks of non-persistent and persistent binding for RPCs.

44. Compare and contrast between RPC and message passing.

45. "Distributed shared memory should be incorporated into systems that are equipped with high-bandwidth and low-latency communication links". Justify.

46. Define and explain the following: **a.** group communication, **b.** interprocess communication, and **c.** Java RMI.

47. How can the performance of distributed shared memory be improved?

48. State the significant issues that must be kept in mind at the time of designing a distributed shared memory system.

49. What are the main factors that must be supported by a distributed file system?

50. State and explain the primary attributes that can influence the fault tolerance of a distributed file system.

51. Differentiate between stateful and stateless servers. Why do some distributed applications use stateless servers in spite of the fact that stateful servers provide an easier programming paradigm and are typically more efficient than stateless servers?

52. State the influence of stateful and stateless file server design on tolerance of faults in client–server nodes.

53. Discuss how a client should protect itself against failures in a distributed file system using; **a.** a stateful file server design and **b.** a stateless file server design.

54. State at least two common server structures that can provide efficient file access in a distributed file system.

55. State some important techniques that are commonly used in the operation of DFS to enable the DFS to achieve high performance.

56. Explain how the cache coherence problem in a distributed file system is negotiated.

57. Should a DFS maintain file buffers at a server node or at a client node? What is the significance and subsequence influence of this decision in the working of a DFS?

58. State and explain the techniques that are commonly used in the operation of a DFS that enable the DFS to achieve high performance.

59. Discuss the important issues to be handled during recovery of a failed node in a system that uses file replication to provide availability.

60. "The clustering concept is an emerging technology in the design of a distributed computing system". State the salient features considered its major design objectives.

61. State the simplest form of classification of clusters. Describe the various most commonly used methods in clustering.

62. Explain with an appropriate diagram the general architecture in organizing computers to form a cluster system.

SUGGESTED REFERENCES AND WEBSITES

Baker, M. G., Hartman, J. H., et al. "Measurement of a Distributed File System", *Proceedings of the ACM Symposium on Operating Systems Principles*, New York, ACM, pp. 98–212, 1991.

Bovet, D. P, Cesati, M. *Understanding the Linux Kernel*, Sebastopol, O'Reilly, 2003.

Buyya, R. *High Performance Cluster Computing: Programming and Applications*, Upper Saddle River, NJ, Prentice Hall, 1999.

Chakraborty, P. *Computer Organization and Architecture: Evolutionary Concepts, Principles, and Designs*, London, CRC Press, 2020.

Chapin, S., Maccabe, A., eds. "Multiprocessor Operating Systems, Harnessing the Power", *Special Issue of IEEE Concurrency*, April–June, New York, IEEE, 1997.

Cheriton, D. "The V Distributed System", *Communications of the ACM*, vol. 31, no. 3, pp. 314–333, 1998.

Cheriton, D. R., Williamson, C. L. "VMTP as the Transport Layer for High-Performance Distributed System", *IEEE Communication*, vol. 27, no. 6, pp. 37–44, 1989.

Coulouris, G., Dollimore, J. *Distributed Systems Concepts and Designs*, Third Edition, Boston, MA, Addition Wesley, 2001.

Culler, D. E., Singh, J. P. *Parallel Computer Architecture: A Hardware/Software Approach*, Burlington, MA, Morgan Kaufmann Publishers Inc, 1994.

Dijkstra, E. W. "Guarded Commands, Nondeterminacy, and Formal Derivation of Programs", *Communications of the ACM*, vol. 18, no. 8, pp. 453–457, 1975.

Janet, E. L. "Selecting a Network Management Protocol, Functional Superiority vs. Popular Appeal", *Telephony*, 1993.

Kaashoek, M. F., Van Renesse, et al., "FLIP: An Internetwork Protocol For Supporting Distributed Systems", *ACM Transactions On Computer Systems*, vol. 11, no. 1, pp. 73–106, 1993.

Levy, E., Silberschatz, A. "Distributed File Systems: Concepts and Examples", *Computing Surveys*, vol. 32, no. 4, pp. 321–374, 1990.

McDougall, R., Laudon, J. "Multi-Core Processors are Here", *USENIX, Login: The USENIX Magazine*, vol. 31, no. 5, pp. 32–39, 2006.

Milenkovic, M. *Operating Systems: Concepts and Design*, New York, McGraw–Hill, 1992.

Mukherjee, B., Karsten, S. *Operating Systems for Parallel Machines in Parallel Computers: Theory and Practice* (Edited by T. Casavant, et al.), Los Alamitos, CA, IEEE Computer Society Press, 1996.

Mullender, S. J., Tanenbaum, A. S., et al. "Amoeba: A Distributed Operating System for the 1990s", *IEEE Computer*, vol. 23, no. 5, pp. 44–53, 1990.

Russinovich, M. E., Solomon, D. A. *Microsoft Windows Internals*, Fourth Edition, New York, Microsoft Press, 2005.

Sandberg, R. *The Sun Network File System: Design, Implementation, and Experience*, Mountain View, CA, Sun Microsystems, 1987.

Schneider, F. B. "Synchronization in Distributed Programs", *ACM Transactions on Programming Languages and Systems*, vol. 4, no. 2, pp. 125–148, 1982.

Shevenell, M. "NMP v2 Needs Reworking to Emerge as a Viable Net Management Platform". *Network World*, March 7, 1994.

Shoch, J. F., Hupp, J. A. "The Worm programs: Early Experiences with a Distributed Computation", *Communication of the ACM*, vol. 25, no. 3, pp. 172–180, 1982.

Short, R., Gamache, R., et al. "Windows NT Clusters for Availability and Scalability", *Proceedings, COMPCON Spring 97*, February, 1997.

Srinivasan, R. RPC: Remote Procedure Call Protocol Specification Version 2. Internet RFC 1831, August 1995.

Tanenbaum, A. *Distributed Operating Systems*, Englewood Cliffs, NJ, Prentice–Hall, 1995.

Tay, B. H., Ananda, A. L. "A Survey of Remote Procedure Calls", *Operating Systems Review*, vol. 24, pp. 68–79, 1990.

Thekkath, C. A., Mann, T., et al. "A Scalable Distributed File System", *Symposium on Operating Systems Principles*, pp. 224–237, 1997.

Wulf, W. A., Cohen, E. S., et al. "HYDRA: The Kernel of a Multiprocessor Operating System", *Communication of the ACM*, vol. 17, pp. 337–345, 1974.

WEBSITES

http://docs.sun.com/app/docs/doc/817-5093

Sun System Administration Guide: Devices and File Systems

IEEE Computer Society Task Force on Cluster Computing: An International forum to promote cluster computing research and education.

Beowulf: An international forum to promote cluster computing research and education.

10 Real-Time Operating Systems

Learning Objectives

- To describe the background of the evolution of real-time systems and give an overview of the real-time task and its parameters.
- To explain the different issues involved with real-time systems.
- To articulate the evolution of real-time operating systems.
- To describe the design philosophies, characteristics, requirements, and features of a real-time operating system.
- To demonstrate the basic components of a real-time operating system, including its kernel structure and scheduling mechanisms, together with an example of Linux real-time scheduling approach.
- To explain the role of clocks and timers to provide time services in the system, along with an example of clock and timer resolutions in Linux as a case study.
- To describe the mechanism used in the implementation of communication and synchronization required in this system.
- To explain the signals realized in this system in the form of software interrupts.
- To explain the memory allocation mechanism, including allocation strategies, protection, and locking.
- To demonstrate practical implementations of RTOSs as case studies by presenting the Linux real-time extension, KURT system, RT Linux system, Linux OS, pSOSystem, and also VxWorks, used in Mars Pathfinder.

10.1 BACKGROUND: REAL-TIME SYSTEMS

In contrast to traditional commercial applications, real-time application systems are of a different kind and belong to a different class. A few examples include embedded applications (programmable thermostats, mobile telephones, household appliance controllers, etc.), reservation systems, banking systems based on the use of real-time databases, and so many other types to mention. In handling real-time applications, specific actions are required to control and monitor the activities in an external system or even to participate in them within the time constraints specified by the external systems. *A real-time application can thus be defined as a program(s) that should respond to activities in an external system within a maximum duration of time specified by the external system.* If the application takes too long or consumes too much time to respond to or complete the needed activity, a failure can occur in the external system. Thus, the term **response requirement** is used to indicate the maximum value of response time within which the system can to function correctly. A *timely response* is one whose response time is *smaller* than the response requirement of the system. A real-time application system is usually executed by **real-time computing**, defined as a type of computing in which the correctness of the system depends not only on the logical result of the computation but also on the time at which the results are produced.

The terminology used in real-time systems can be defined here in the following way: a **job** (or an event) is a unit of work that is scheduled and executed by the system. A **process** is an activity of some kind within the job that operates under real-time constraints. A process can thus last for a long time, and during this period, it can perform a repetitive function in response to real-time events. For

DOI: 10.1201/9781003383055-10

the sake of clarity, such an individual function can be defined here as a **task**. Thus, a process can be viewed as progressing through a sequence of tasks. At any instant, a process is engaged in a single task, and it is the process/task that must be considered a unit of computation.

Brief details on this topic with an example are given on the Support Materials at www.routledge.com/9781032467238

10.2   REAL-TIME TASKS: AN OVERVIEW

In a real-time system, some of the tasks that are *time-critical* are said to be real-time tasks, which are actually intended to control or to react to events that normally take place in the external system belonging to the outside world (i.e. outside the domain of the existing computer system). Since these events occur in "real time", a real-time task must be able to keep up with the events with which it is concerned, obeying certain parameters associated with a particular task. Some of these important parameters that distinguish tasks (or jobs) in real-time systems from those in non–real-time are described in the following.

The **release time** of a job is the instant at which the job becomes *ready* (available) for execution. The job can be scheduled and executed at any time at or after its release time whenever its data and control dependencies are met. The **deadline** (or *absolute deadline*) of a job is the time by which its execution is required to be completed. In other words, each job must complete its execution before the release time of the subsequent job. This type of deadline is normally called an **ending deadline**. There is another type of deadline of a job, usually known as **starting deadline**, which is defined as the time by which the job must start its execution. The impact of the ending deadline as one of the parameters in a set of jobs at the time of scheduling is quite different from that of the starting deadline when used as one of the parameters in the same set of jobs. Indeed, the schedules when prepared using these two deadlines over a set of same jobs separately differ in the ordering of jobs in the ready job queue and affect the performance as well as the throughput of the system to a great extent.

Sometimes it is more appropriate to describe the timing requirement of a job in terms of its **response time**, which is defined as the length of time from the release time of the job to the instant when it completes. The maximum allowable response time of a job is sometimes called its **relative deadline**. Therefore, the deadline, sometimes called *absolute deadline*, of a job is equal to its release time plus its relative deadline. The timing behavior of a job can be specified by the timing constraint imposed on the job. The **timing constraints** of a job in their simplest form can be expressed in terms of its release time and relative or absolute deadlines. Using these parameters, a real-time task may be classified into two distinct types that give rise to two kinds of real-time systems:

- A **hard real-time task** is one that must meet its deadline (hard deadline); missing this deadline will cause a penalty of higher-order of magnitude, leading to fatal damage or an unacceptable and even irreparable error to the system. A hard real-time system (e.g. an Avionic control) is thus typically dedicated to processing real-time applications and provably meets the response requirements of an application under the conditions. Application systems, such as guidance and control applications, are typically serviced using hard real-time systems, because they fail if they cannot meet the response requirements. A ballistic missile may be shifted from its specified trajectory if the response requirement is not rigidly obeyed.
- A **soft real-time task** has an associated deadline that is desirable to obey but not mandatory; it still makes sense to schedule and complete the task even it has passed its deadline. A soft real-time system makes the best effort to meet the response requirement of a real-time application but cannot guarantee that it will be able to meet it under all conditions. Typically, it meets the response requirement in a probabilistic manner, say, 95 percent of the prescribed deadline (time). Application systems such as multimedia applications and applications, like reservations and banking systems, that essentially aim to provide good

quality of service but do not have a notion of failure, thus may be serviced using soft real-time systems. The quality of picture on a video may deteriorate occasionally if the response requirement is not met, but one can still watch the video with almost no interruption.

- Another characterization of real-time tasks can be described as follows: A set of related jobs (activities) is called a *task*. Jobs in a task may be precedence constrained to execute in a certain order. Sometimes jobs may be constrained to complete within a certain time from one another. Jobs may have data dependencies even when they are not precedence constrained. If pi is the minimum length of the intervals between the release times of consecutive tasks (inter-release interval), that is, the task period, and ai is the arrival time, ri is the ready time, di is the deadline, ci is the worst-case execution time, and φi is the release time of the first job (activity) in task Ti, then:
  - **Periodic tasks:** Task Ti is a sequence of jobs. Task Ti is time-driven. The characteristics are known *a priori*, and task Ti is characterized by ($pi, ci, \varphi i$). For example, the task is to monitor the temperature of a furnace in a factory.
  - **Aperiodic tasks:** Task Ti is event-driven. The characteristics are *not* known *a priori*, and task Ti is characterized by (ai, ri, ci, di). This task has either soft deadlines by which it must finish or start or no deadlines (i.e. it may have a constraint on both start and finish time). An example is a task that is activated upon detecting a change in furnace's condition (temperature).
  - **Sporadic tasks:** A periodic tasks with a known minimum inter-arrival time.

We want the system to be responsive, that is, to complete each task as soon as possible. On the other hand, a late response might be annoying but tolerable. It is thus attempted to optimize the responsiveness of the system for aperiodic tasks but never at the cost of hard real-time tasks, which require deadlines to be met religiously at all times.

10.2.1 REAL-TIME TASKS: PARAMETERS

Real-time tasks, in general, are constrained by four main parameters:

- *Deadline constraint*: Must be completed within the specified time-interval.
- *Resource constraints*: Shared access (read–read) and exclusive access (write-x)
- *Precedence constraints*: For two arbitrary tasks T1 and T2, task T2 can start executing only after T1 finishes its execution.
- *Fault-tolerant requirements*: To achieve higher reliability for task execution that, in turn, normally needs redundancy in execution.

10.3 REAL-TIME SYSTEMS: DIFFERENT ISSUES

Real-time systems are entwined with many different issues. These can be classified into three broad categories. They are:

- **Architectural issues:** Computing subsystems, communication subsystems, I/O subsystems. These issues can be addressed by the following:
  - Predictability in: Instruction execution time, memory access, context switching, interrupt handling.
  - Real-time systems usually avoid caches and superscalar features.
  - Support for error handling (self-checking circuitry, voters, system monitors).
  - Support for fast and reliable communication (routing, priority handling, buffer, and timer management).
  - Support for execution of scheduling algorithms (fast preemptability, priority queues).

- Support for real-time operating system's common activities (such as multiple contexts, memory management, garbage collection, interrupt handling, clock synchronization).
- Support for real-time language features (such as language constructs for estimating worst-case execution time of tasks).
- **Resource management (RM) issues:** Scheduling, fault-tolerance, resource reclaiming, communication.

Real-time scheduling paradigms:

- Allocate time slots for tasks onto processor(s) (i.e. where and when a given task would execute).
- Objective: *predictably meeting task deadlines* (schedulability check, schedule construction).

Real-time task scheduling can be broadly classified as shown in Figure 10.1. The details are discussed in later sections.

- **Preemptive scheduling:** Task execution is preempted and later resumed at an appropriate time.
  - Preemption occurs mainly to execute higher-priority tasks.
  - Offers higher schedulability.
  - Involves higher scheduling overhead due to frequent context switching.
- **Nonpreemptive scheduling:**
  - Once a task starts executing, it is allowed to continue its execution until it completes.
  - Offers lower schedulability.
  - Relatively less overhead due to less context switching.
- **Optimal scheduling: definition**

  A **static scheduling** algorithm is said to be *optimal* if, for any set of tasks, it always produces a feasible schedule (i.e. a schedule that satisfies the constraints of the tasks) whenever *any other algorithm* can also do so.

  A **dynamic scheduling** algorithm is said to be *optimal* if it always produces a *feasible schedule* whenever a *static algorithm* with complete prior knowledge of all the possible tasks can do so.

  Static scheduling is used for scheduling periodic tasks, whereas dynamic scheduling is used to schedule both periodic as well as aperiodic tasks.

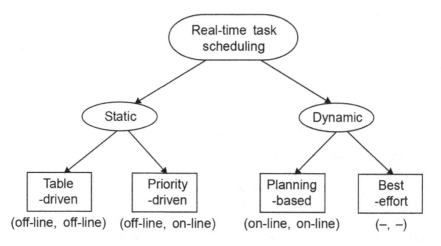

FIGURE 10.1 A block–structured representation of a rough scheme of real-time task scheduling.

- **Software issues:** Requirements, specifications, verification, real-time languages, and real-time databases.
  - **Requirements:** These can be broadly defined in terms of:
    - **Functional requirements:** These are precisely the operation of the system and their effects as a whole.
    - **Non-functional requirements:** Other factors related to the operation of the system, such as timing constraints.
  - Functional and non-functional requirements must be precisely defined so that they can be used together to construct the specifications of the system.
  - **Specification and verification:** A *specification* is a mathematical statement of the properties to be exhibited by a system. It is abstracted such that:
    - it can be checked for conformity against the requirements, and
    - its properties can be examined independently of the way it will be implemented.
  - The usual approaches to specifying computing-system behavior entail enumerating events or actions that the system participates in and describing the order in which they can occur. It is not well understood how to extend such approaches for real-time systems.

- **Real-time languages:**
  - Support for management of time:
    - Language constructs for expressing timing constraints, keeping track of resource utilization.
  - Schedulability analysis:
    - Aid compile-time schedulability check.
  - Reusable real-time software modules:
    - Object-oriented methodology.
  - Support for distributed programming and fault-tolerance.

- **Real-time databases**.

  Conventional database systems.
  - Diskbased.
  - Use transaction logging and two-phase locking protocols to ensure transaction *atomicity* and *serializability*.
  - These characteristics preserve data integrity, but they also result in relatively slow and unpredictable response times.

  Real-time database systems: The issues include:

  - Transaction scheduling to meet deadlines.
  - Explicit semantics for specifying timing and other constraints.
  - Checking the database system's ability to meet transaction deadlines during application initialization.

10.4   REAL-TIME OPERATING SYSTEMS: EVOLUTION

In order to manage and monitor real-time applications, a different type of operating system evolved, historically known as a real-time operating system (RTOS). In its early days, it was typically used as a small embedded operating system to handle mostly embedded applications packaged as part of micro-devices. Later, it was thought that some forms of kernels could be considered to meet the requirements of a real-time operating system. However, since other components, such as device drivers and control programs, are usually also needed for a particular solution, a real-time operating system is usually larger than just the kernel.

An RTOS is one that essentially guarantees a certain capability within a specified time constraint. For example, an operating system could be designed to ensure that a certain object is made available for a robot working on an assembly line. In what is usually called a hard real-time operating system, if the calculation could not be performed to make the object available at the pre-specified time, the operating system would terminate with a failure. Similarly, in a soft real-time operating system, the assembly line would not necessarily arrive at a failure but continue to function, though the production output might be lower as objects failed to appear at their stipulated time, causing the robot to be temporarily unproductive. Some real-time operating systems are designed and developed for a special application, and others are more or less general purpose. Some existing general-purpose non–real-time operating systems, however, claim to be real-time operating systems. To some extent, almost any general-purpose operating system, such as Microsoft's Windows 2000 or IBM's OS/390, and to some extent Linux, can be evaluated for its real-time operating system qualities. Reasons for this choice include the timing requirement of applications that are not so hard. That is, even if an operating system does not qualify, it may have some characteristics that enable it to be considered a solution to a particular problem belonging to the category of real-time application. It is to be noted that the objective of a true real-time operating system does not necessarily have to have a high throughput. In fact, the specialized scheduling algorithm, a high clock-interrupt rate, and other similar related factors often intervene in the execution of the system that hinders to yield the needed high throughput. A good real-time operating system thus not only provides efficient mechanisms and services to carry out good real-time scheduling and resource management policies but also keeps its own time and resource consumptions predictable and accountable. In addition, a real-time operating system should be more modular and extensible than its counterpart, a general-purpose operating system. Some early large-scale real-time operating systems were the so-called *control program* developed by American Airlines and the Sabre Airline Reservations System introduced by IBM.

10.5 REAL-TIME OPERATING SYSTEMS: DESIGN PHILOSOPHIES

There are two basic designs:

- An event-driven operating system that only changes tasks when an event requires service.
- A time-sharing design that switches tasks on a clock interrupt (clock-driven), as well as on events.

The time-sharing design wastes more CPU time on unnecessary task-switches (context-switches) but offers better multitasking, the illusion that a user has sole use of a machine.

10.6 REAL-TIME OPERATING SYSTEMS: CHARACTERISTICS AND REQUIREMENTS

Following the accepted definition and the underlying philosophy of the real-time operating system, as already explained, it is expected that data, resources, users, and their computations should be effectively carried out in a predefined manner to meet their ultimate goals. Since, the RTOS is primarily a time-critical and event-driven system, the latest consistent knowledge with respect to the state of the various resources lying under the RTOS is urgently needed that eventually may affect many things, such as management of resources, scheduling of threads and processes, and synchronization of concurrent competitive and cooperating activities. To meet the primary requirements of the real-time operating system, the designer of such a system must deal with several design issues. Some of the most common key design issues are:

- **Determinism:** An RTOS must be deterministic in the sense that it is able to accomplish all its operations at pre-specified fixed times or within predetermined time intervals, even when the requests come from the external events with prescribed timings. To realize this, it depends on several factors, mainly how quickly it can respond to interrupts and also the availability of both hardware and software resources that are adequate to manage all such requests within the specified time. One useful way to assess determinism is by measuring the maximum delay it faces when responding to high-priority device interrupts. In the case of traditional OSs, this delay might be in the range of tens to hundreds of milliseconds, while in RTOSs, this delay should not be beyond a few microseconds to a millisecond.

- **Responsiveness:** While determinism is concerned with the time to recognize and respond to an interrupt, responsiveness is related to the time that an operating system takes to service the interrupt after acknowledgement. Several aspects contribute to responsiveness. Some notable ones are:
  - *Interrupt latency*: It is the time the system takes before the start of the execution of an immediate interrupt service routine, including the time required for process switching or context switching, if there is any.
  - The amount of time required to actually execute the ISR. This is generally dependent on the hardware platform being used.
  - The effect of nested interrupts. It may cause further delay due to the arrival of a high-priority interrupt when the servicing of one is in progress.
  - *Dispatch latency*: It is the length of time between the completion of an ISR and resumption of the corresponding process (or thread) suspended due to the occurrence of the interrupt.

In fact, determinism and responsiveness together constitute the response time to external events, one of the most critical requirements of a real-time operating system that should be religiously obeyed by events, devices, data flows, and above all the individuals located in the domain external to the system.

- **Notion of predictability:** The most common denominator in a real-time system is *predictability*, which means that with certain assumptions about workload and failures, it should be possible to show at *design time* that all the timing constraints of the application will be met. For *static systems*, 100% guarantees can be given at design time. But for *dynamic systems*, 100% guarantee cannot be given, since the characteristics of tasks are not known *a priori*. In dynamic systems, predictability means that once a task is admitted into the system, its guarantee that the execution of the task should never be violated as long as the assumptions under which the task was admitted hold.
- **Reliability:** A, RTOS always responds to and controls outside events in a time-critical manner. Any failure in such systems may cause consequences not only of irreparable loss or performance degradation but may lead to a catastrophic situation ranging from financial loss to major equipment damage or, even more critically, loss of life.
- **Fault-tolerance:** A real-time operating system must be able to respond to various modes of failures. It employs two techniques to ensure continuity of operation when faults occur: fault tolerance and graceful degradation. These two techniques together constitute what is known as **fail-soft operation**, which always preserves as much capability and data as possible so as to negotiate any unforeseen failure. When a typical traditional UNIX system detects corruption of data within the kernel, it dumps the memory contents to a specified area in the disk for the sake of later failure analysis and finally terminates the execution of the system. A real-time operating system, in contrast, will always attempt either to rectify the problem or takes action to avoid the problem or minimize its effects while continuing to run. To be fault-tolerant, it uses the redundancy of available resources that ensures the system can continue functioning

even when a fault occurs. In the event of a fault, graceful degradation in performance is observed that leads only to offering a reduced level of service, but revert to normal operations when the fault is rectified. When the system operates at a reduced level, crucial functions are usually assigned high priorities to enable them to perform in a timely manner. In the event of a failure, the system typically notifies a user or a user process that it is about to attempt corrective measures (actions) and then continues operation at a reduced level of service. Even when a shutdown is necessary, an attempt is always made to preserve file and data consistency.

- **Stability:** A real-time system is said to be stable if, in situations where it is impossible to meet the deadlines of all tasks, the system will at least meet the deadlines of its most critical, high-priority tasks, even if that means sacrificing relatively less important critical tasks, and accordingly, it then notifies the users or user processes of these affected tasks about its inability beforehand so that the default actions with respect to these tasks can be appropriately taken by the system in time.

10.7 REAL-TIME OPERATING SYSTEMS: FEATURES

A real-time operating system should be as small as possible in size, yet fulfill all its targeted objectives. Usually it will have a microkernel that provides only essential services, such as scheduling, synchronization, and interrupt handling with *domain-specific interrupts* and corresponding ISR to allow it to respond to special conditions and events in the external system in a timely manner. A hard real-time OS follows a policy to partition resources and allocate them permanently to competing processes in the application to avoid costly resource allocation overhead. In addition, hard real-time systems also avoid use of features whose performance cannot be precisely predicted, such as virtual memory. *Multitasking* was introduced in the design of real-time operating systems with a hierarchical interrupt approach coupled with process prioritization to ensure that key activities were given a greater share of available processor time. The scheduling capabilities of this system are mainly realized by short-term task schedulers of different types, which ensures that all hard real-time tasks complete (or start) by their deadline and that as many soft real-time tasks complete (or start) by their deadline as possible. However, modern RTOSs avoid stringent deadline scheduling techniques; instead they use approaches that are as responsive as possible to real-time tasks to quickly schedule them within their specified deadlines to attain deterministic response times. Most RTOSs assume more than one clock device and use them for different purposes. The system allows a process (or thread) to have its own timers and may even have as many as 32 timers per process. Different OS functions are available in this regard: to set the value of a specified clock; to allow a process (thread) to read the time measured by the specified clock; and to *create*, *set*, *cancel*, and *destroy* its timers. In addition, there are functions for getting the resolution of a clock and time remaining of a timer.

Brief details on this topic with a table are given on the Support Material at www.routledge.com/9781032467238.

10.8 REAL-TIME OPERATING SYSTEMS: BASIC COMPONENTS

The objectives of RTOSs are quite different from their counterpart, the traditional operating system; hence, the common operating system services that it provides need to be separately addressed. Several basic real-time issues, such as the characteristics of threads and processes, the basic structure of the kernel, scheduling of these threads and processes, the role of the clock and timers, communication between and synchronization of threads and processes, memory management, I/O, and several other similar issues related to RTOS should be discussed. Each of these issues is relatively complex and needs detailed coverage, so instead of going into deep details on these issues individually, we concentrate more on providing an overview of each to significantly simplify the implementation of an RTOS in general.

10.8.1 THREADS AND TASKS

Threads, when supported in RTOS, are the basic unit of computation activity with all its related aspects and have a similar meaning as in the traditional uniprocessor operating system, already described in Chapter 4, but include some additional specific attributes (such as typical interrupt handling, priority dominance, relative deadlines, etc.) that an RTOS requires. When a task (or a job) is initiated (ready state) in a system, the task makes a *create_thread* system call, and the kernel creates a thread to implement the task, assigning an *id* to it and allocating memory space in the user address space of the task with which the thread is associated, then fetches the code to be executed by the thread into memory. Most of the state information dealing with execution and overall management of thread is maintained in a *thread control block* (TCB) created by the kernel. A thread is referred to by a pointer to its TCB. The kernel destroys a thread by deleting its TCB and deallocating its memory space. However, the approach, in which there is no distinct concept of thread and the thread is not even recognized, it is referred to as a *single-threaded* approach. In a multithreaded environment, there is still a single process (task) control block (PCB) and user address space associated with the process (or task), but now there are separate TCBs for each thread containing all thread-related information as well as separate stacks for each thread.

When an event occurs, the kernel saves the CPU state of the interrupted thread in its TCB. After event handling, the scheduler considers the TCBs of all threads and selects one *ready* thread; the dispatcher uses the PCB (or task control block) pointer in its TCB to check if the selected thread belongs to a different process than the interrupted thread. If so, it saves the context of the task (or process) to which the interrupted thread belongs and loads the context of the task (or process) to which the selected thread belongs. It then dispatches the selected thread. Actions to save and load the task (or process) context are unnecessary if both threads belong to the same task (or process), which reduces the switching overhead.

- **Periodic threads:** As an RTOS deals with periodic, aperiodic, and sporadic tasks, described in Section 10.2, so are there periodic threads, aperiodic threads, and sporadic threads. A periodic task can be implemented in the form of a thread (computational activity) that executes periodically called a **periodic thread**. Such a thread is supposed to be created and destroyed repeatedly at every period, which simply wastes costly CPU time, thereby degrading system performance as a whole. That is why the RTOS that supports periodic tasks (e.g. Real-time Mach OS), the kernel avoids such unnecessary redundancy in repeated creating and destroying the threads by simply reinitializing the thread putting it to sleep when the thread completes. Here, the kernel keeps track of the duration of time and releases (brings back to the ready queue) the thread again at the beginning of the next period. Most commercial operating systems, however, do not support periodic threads. At best, a periodic task can be implemented at the user level as a thread that alternately executes the code of the task and sleeps until the beginning of the next period. This means that the thread does its own reinitialization and keeps track of time for its own next release without any intervention of the kernel to monitor.
- **Aperiodic and sporadic threads:** When an aperiodic and sporadic task (see Section 10.2) is implemented in the form of thread, it gives rise to an *aperiodic thread* or a *sporadic thread*. This type of thread is essentially event-driven and is released in response to the occurrence of the specified types of events that may be triggered by external interrupts. Upon its completion, an aperiodic or sporadic thread is reinitialized and suspended as usual. The differences between these three types of tasks are covered in Section 10.2.

Thread states: Threads and processes are analogous, so their states and state transitions are also analogous, except that threads do not have resource ownership. Since, the thread is an alternative form of schedulable *unit of computation* to the traditional notion of process, it similarly undergoes different states in its lifetime, as follows:

- **Ready state:** When the thread is waiting for its turn to gain access to the CPU which executes it.
- **Running state:** A thread is in the running state when the code attached to the thread is being executed by the CPU.
- **Waiting state:** A thread is said to be in the waiting state when its on–going execution is not completed, but it may have to go to *sleep*, thereby entering the *sleeping state*. The other possibility may be that some other thread *suspends* the currently running thread. This thread now enters the *suspended state*. Suspending the execution of a thread is deprecated in the new version.
- **Dead state:** When the thread has finished its execution.

A task (and hence a thread) can be suspended or blocked for many different reasons. The operating system typically keeps separate queues for threads that are blocked or suspended for different reasons. Similarly, the kernel normally keeps a number of ready queues; each queue is of ready threads with specific attributes (e.g. a queue of ready threads with the same priority). A **thread scheduler**, analogous to the process scheduler, switches the processor among a set of competing threads, thereby causing a thread to go through its different states. The thread scheduler in some systems is a user program, and in others, it is part of the OS. Since threads have few states and less information to be saved while changing states, the thread scheduler has less work to do when actually switching from one thread to another than is required for switching processes; an important aspect in favor of using threads.

Brief details on this topic with a figure are given on the Support Material at www.routledge.com/9781032467238.

10.8.2 The Kernel

An RTOS, with a few exceptions, normally consists of a *microkernel* that provides a set of the basic operating system functions. Figure 10.2 shows a general structure of a microkernel. Many small embedded applications (such as home appliances like washing machines and traffic light signal controllers) are found to require only a *nanokernel*, which basically provides only time and scheduling services and consists of only the clock interrupt part of Figure 10.2. For the sake of simplicity, we assume here that there are only three main reasons which insist the kernel to take control from the executing process (or threads) and start executing itself. Those are:

- to respond to a system call,
- to do scheduling and service the timers, and
- to handle external interrupts.

The kernel also deals with many other aspects, such as fault-tolerance, reliability, stability, and recovery from hardware and software exceptions; but those aspects are deliberately kept outside the scope of this discussion.

- **System Calls:** Out of several different functions that the kernel usually provides, it also offers many other functions (e.g. Application Program Interface (API) functions) which, when called from user programs do some work at the kernel space on behalf of the calling process (or thread). Any call to one of the API functions, some of which are listed in Figure 10.2, is essentially a *system call*. In systems that provide memory protection, user and kernel processes (or threads) are executed in separate memory spaces. When a system call (API function) is issued by the calling process (or thread), the process is

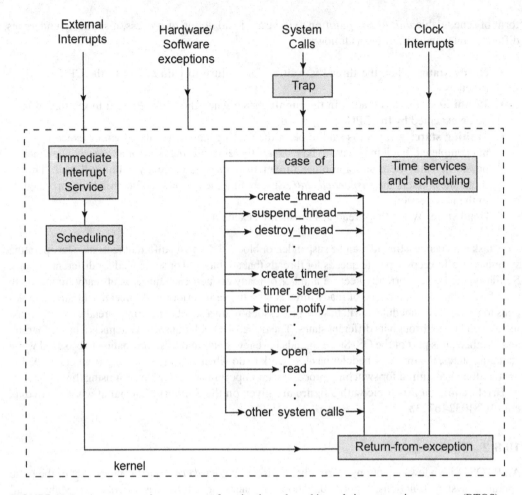

FIGURE 10.2   A representative structure of a microkernel used in real-time operating systems (RTOS).

blocked, and the kernel saves everything in relation to the calling process (or thread) and switches from user mode to kernel mode. It then takes the function name and arguments of the call from the process's (or thread's) stack and executes the function on behalf of the process (or thread). When the execution of the system call completes, the kernel executes a *return* from exception, causing the system to return to user mode. The calling process then resumes from the point where it left if it still has the highest priority. This line of action, followed in sequence to execute an API function, is called a *synchronous system call*. If the system call causes another process (or thread) to have a higher priority, then the currently executing system call will be interrupted, and the process (or thread) with the higher priority will be started.

When the call is *asynchronous* (such as in the case of an asynchronous I/O request), the calling process (or thread) continues its own execution (without blocking) after issuing the call. The kernel then provides a separate process (or thread) to execute the called function.

Many embedded operating system that do not provide memory protection allow the user and the kernel process to execute in the same space. This is often favored in order to keep the execution-time overhead small (due to no need for a process/context switch) as well as to avoid the overhead of consuming extra memory space to provide full memory protection (on the order of an additional few kilobytes needed per process). A system call in such a system is just like a procedure or function call within the application.

- **Scheduling and Timer Services:** The heart of the system kernel is the scheduler which, in most operating systems, executes periodically as well as whenever the state of a process (or thread) changes. The scheduler assigns processors to schedulable jobs or, equivalently, assigns schedulable jobs to processors. The scheduler is triggered to come into action by means of raising the *clock interrupts* issued from the system clock device periodically. The period of clock interrupts is called *tick* size, which is on the order of 10 milliseconds in most operating systems. However, in a clock-driven system that uses a cyclic scheduler, clock interrupts occur only at the beginning of a frame. At each clock interrupt, the kernel performs several responsibilities to service the interrupt, some notable ones are:

The kernel first attempts *to process the timer events* by checking the queue of pending expiration times stored in the time order in the queue of all the timers that are bound to the clock. This way, the kernel can determine whether timer events have occurred since the previous time it checked the queue. If the kernel finds that a timer event did occur, it carries out the specified action. In this manner, the kernel processes all the timer events that have occurred and then queues all the specified actions. It subsequently carries out all these actions at appropriate times before finally returning control to the user.

The next action that kernel takes is to update the **execution budget**, which is the time-slice normally offered by the scheduler when it schedules a process (or thread) for execution based on policy and considering other constraints. At each clock interrupt, the scheduler usually decrements the budget of the executing process (or thread) by the tick size. If the process (or thread) is not completed when the updated budget (i.e. the remaining time-slice) becomes 0, the kernel then simply decides to preempt the executing process (or thread). Some scheduling policies, such as FIFO, offer an infinite time slice or do not decrement the budget of the executing process (or thread), thereby allowing the process (or thread) to continue its execution even when some other processes (or threads) of equal priority keep on waiting in the queue.

After taking all these actions, the kernel proceeds to *update the ready queue*. Some threads by this time may be ready (e.g. released upon timer expirations), and the thread that was executing at the time of the clock interrupt may need to be preempted. The scheduler accordingly updates the ready queue to bring it to the current status and finally gives control to the process (or thread) that is lying at the head of the highest-priority queue.

Now, as the scheduler is periodically activated only at each clock interrupt, the system is critically dependent on tick size, and the length of the tick-size is an important factor. A relatively large tick size appears suitable for some commonly used scheduling policies, such as round-robin in time-shared applications, but it may badly affect the schedulability of time-critical applications. On the other hand, while a smaller tick size nicely fits with time-critical environments, but at the same time degrades the system performance due to increased scheduling overhead caused mainly by frequent servicing of relatively expensive regular clock interrupts. That is why most operating systems prefer to have a combination of time-based (tick) scheduling along with event-driven scheduling. This way, whenever an event occurs, the kernel invokes the scheduler to update the ready queue, and it then quickly wakes up or releases a process (or thread), detects a process (or thread) unblocked, or creates a new process (or thread), and many other similar things. In this way, a process (or thread) is properly placed in the ready queue as soon as it is set.

- **External Interrupts:** An interrupt is an important tool by which the system can monitor the environment by gaining control during execution, give control to the deserving point for needed execution, or facilitate many similar other activities that an operating system needs to fulfill its objectives. Here, interrupt means hardware interrupts, and those interrupts that take place due to the occurrence of events in the external system located outside the domain of the computer system are referred to as external interrupts. The operating systems, in particular, the RTOS that deals with external interrupts to keep up with the external events with which it is concerned, a proper handling of such interrupts in time is an essential functional requirement of the kernel of such systems. However, these interrupts may be of various types depending on the nature of the interrupt source, and as such, the amount of time required to handle an interrupt, including its servicing, varies over a wide span. That is why interrupt handling in most contemporary operating systems is classified into two distinct categories. Those are:

Immediate interrupt service: Interrupt handling at its first instance is executed depending on the interrupt-priority level, which is entirely determined by the hardware being used, and as such, most modern processor architectures provide some form of priority-interrupt with different interrupt-priority levels. In addition, it is apparent that interrupt-priority levels (hardware-based) are always higher than all process (or thread) priorities (software-based) and are even higher than the priority at which the scheduler executes. When many interrupts with the same or different interrupt-priority levels are raised within a small span of time, which is usually very common, the interrupt-priority level attached to a particular interrupt then determines the ordering (either by means of polling or some other suitable mechanism), following which the interrupt is serviced. The corresponding service routine is then called by the kernel for execution. Moreover, if at any instant when the execution of an interrupt servicing routine is in progress, a higher-priority interrupt, as indicated by the interrupt-priority level, is raised, the ongoing interrupt servicing may be interrupted to accommodate the relatively high-priority interrupt for its servicing, or the processor and the kernel take care of the higher-priority interrupt in another fitting manner.

The interrupt-priority level of an interrupt determines the immediate interrupt service, which is linked with what is known as *responsiveness* of the kernel. The total time required from the time the interrupt is raised to the start of the execution of interrupt servicing of the interrupt after completing all the needed housekeeping and other related activities is called **interrupt latency**. The ultimate design objective of any kernel is to minimize the interrupt latency so as to make the kernel more responsive. Various attempts in different areas related to this issue have been made to minimize the latency. One notable one is to make the immediate interrupt handling routine as short as possible. Another is to modify the design of the kernel so that the device-independent part (which is the code for saving the processor state) of the interrupt service code can be injected into the interrupt service routine of the device itself (device-dependent) to enable the processor to directly jump to the interrupt service routines without going through any time-consuming kernel activity.

Scheduled interrupt service: To complete interrupt handling, after the end of the first step, which is immediate interrupt service, the second step begins with the execution of another service routine known as *scheduled interrupt service* (not to be confused with interrupt servicing that actually starts from the beginning of the execution of interrupt service routine of the interrupting device after the end of these two steps in interrupt handling) that is invoked by the first step after completing its own responsibilities. The function being carried out in this second step is by the execution of what is known as *scheduled interrupt handling routine*. This routine is preemptible and should be scheduled at fitting priority (software) in a priority-driven system. For example, in some RTOS, like in LynxOS, the priority of the kernel process (or thread) that executes a scheduled interrupt handling routine is the priority of the user process (or thread) that opened the interrupting device. That is why Figure 10.2 shows that after the execution of immediate interrupt service, the scheduler begins to execute the one that inserts and places the scheduled interrupt handling process (or thread) in the ready queue, and eventually lets the highest-priority process (or thread) to be scheduled that consequently gains control of the processor.

Brief details of this topic with figures are given on the Support Material at www.routledge.com/9781032467238.

10.8.3 SCHEDULING MECHANISMS

Real-time scheduling is one of the most vital aspects that have a direct impact on the overall performance of a real-time operating system. Tasks (jobs) are usually scheduled based on a chosen set of algorithms, and subsequently resources (both processors and passive resources are referred to as resources) are allocated along with resource access-control protocols. The module which implements these algorithms is called the **scheduler**. It is implicitly assumed that every job executes on one processor, unless and otherwise it is specifically mentioned, and that jobs do not run in parallel on more than one processor to speed up their execution. The scheduler always generates a **valid schedule** (or sometimes called *plan*), which means that no task (or job) is scheduled before its release time and the completion of all its predecessors, no task (or job) is scheduled on more than one processor at the same time, no processor is scheduled to execute more than one task (or job) at the same time, and the total amount of time assigned to every task (or job) is equal to the execution time except when the task (or job) or a portion of it can be discarded because it is optional. A valid schedule is a **feasible schedule** if every job completes by its deadline or, in general, meets its specified timing constraints. A set of tasks (or jobs) is said to be **schedulable** according to a scheduling algorithm, if when using the algorithm, the scheduler always produces a feasible schedule.

The **performance** of *scheduling algorithms* for hard real-time applications is defined as their ability to find feasible schedules of the given application system whenever such schedules exist. A hard real-time scheduling algorithm is said to be **optimal** if (using) the algorithm always produces a feasible schedule whenever the given set of tasks (or jobs) have feasible schedules. This performance can also be measured in terms of commonly used parameters that include the *maximum and average tardiness, lateness, response time and the miss, loss,* and *invalid rates*. The *tardiness* and *lateness* of a task (or job) both are measured as the difference between its completion time and its deadline. The *response time* here has a similar meaning as in general-purpose, interactive systems. It is obvious that smaller the average response time, the better the algorithm. In particular, in an environment that consists of a mixture of both types of jobs with hard and soft deadlines, the ultimate objective is typically to minimize the average response time of jobs with soft deadlines while ensuring that all jobs with hard deadlines complete in time. The *miss rate* is defined as the percentage of jobs that are executed but completed too late. The *loss rate* is defined as the percentage of jobs that already arrived but are discarded, that is, not executed. The scheduler in some situations may prefer to sacrifice some jobs by discarding them, thereby increasing the loss rate but completing more jobs in time, which, in turn, reduces the miss rate. Therefore, while an attempt is made to minimize the miss rate, it should be reduced as much as possible but comply with the constraint that the loss rate should always be below some acceptable threshold. The same approach should also be taken while minimizing the loss rate, which may, in turn, increase the miss rate above a given threshold. The performance measure that follows this trade-off is known as the *invalid rate*, defined as the sum of the miss and loss rates, and gives the percentage of all jobs that do not produce any useful result. An all-out attempt is thus made to keep this invalid rate as low as possible. In addition, there is also an operating system architecture that offers real-time applications that run in an *open environment* in which hard real-time applications can run at ease with soft real-time applications, as well as with non–real-time applications. The OS often makes use of two-level scheduling (the scheduling that accommodates sporadic and aperiodic tasks along with periodic tasks) to enable each real-time application to be scheduled in a way best suited for the application under the existing environment, and the schedulability of the applications is determined independently of other applications that may run with it on the same hardware platform.

Several other aspects come into play when various types of approaches for scheduling periodic tasks and aperiodic tasks are framed. The factors that mostly influence these approaches are whether a system performs schedulability analysis; if so, whether it is done statically or dynamically; and whether the result of such analysis itself produces a schedule or a working plan based on which tasks can be dispatched at runtime. All these factors along with similar other ones, when considered together, give rise to the following categories of scheduling algorithms (as shown in Figure 10.1):

- **Static table-driven scheduling:** The approaches used here to realize a scheduling mechanism are applicable to periodic tasks (or jobs). The parameters associated with the tasks (or jobs) are used as input that includes periodic arrival time, execution time, periodic ending deadline, and relative priority of each task. The scheduler, using these parameters, attempts to develop a schedule that ensures it, meets the requirements of all such periodic tasks. This is essentially a *predictable approach* and at the same time is an *inflexible* one, because any change to any task requirements demands the schedule to be restructured afresh. *Earliest-deadline-first* (EDF) or other periodic deadline scheduling techniques are typical examples of this category.
- **Static priority-driven preemptive scheduling:** The approaches employed here assign priorities to tasks, based on which traditional priority-driven preemptive scheduling is carried out by the scheduler. The mechanism used by this scheduler is similar to one common to most non–real-time multitasking (multiprogramming) systems in which priority assignment depends on many factors. But in real-time systems, the priority assignment is straightaway related to the time constraints associated with each task. The *rate-monotonic* (RM) *scheduling algorithm* uses this approach in which static priorities are assigned to tasks based on the length of their periods.
- **Dynamic planning-based scheduling:** The approaches determine the feasibility dynamically (online) during runtime rather than statically (offline) prior to the start of execution. An arriving task is accepted for execution only if it is feasible to meet its time constraints (deadlines). One of the outcomes of this feasibility analysis is a schedule or plan that is used to decide when to dispatch this task. When a task arrives, but before its execution begins, the scheduling mechanism makes an attempt to create a fresh schedule that incorporates the new arrival along with the previously scheduled tasks. If the new arrival can be scheduled in such a way that its deadlines are satisfied, and no currently scheduled task is affected by missing its deadline, then the schedule is restructured to accommodate the newly arrived task.
- **Dynamic best-effort scheduling:** The approaches used here do not perform any feasibility analysis; instead the system attempts to meet all deadlines and aborts any started task (or job) whose deadline is missed. Many commercially popular real-time systems favor this approach. When a task (or a job) arrives, the system assigns a priority to the job based on its characteristics, and normally some form of deadline scheduling, such as, EDF scheduling, is chosen. Since the tasks are, by nature, typically aperiodic, no static scheduling analysis is workable. With this type of scheduling, until a deadline (task or job) arrives or until the task completes, it is not possible to know whether a timing constraint will be met. This is one of the major disadvantages of this form of scheduling, although it has the advantage of being easy to implement.

    This section mostly attempts to give an overview of the scheduling mechanisms and deals only with those scheduling services that the kernel can easily provide to significantly simplify the implementation of complex algorithms for scheduling aperiodic tasks at the user level.

    Many different increasingly powerful and appropriate approaches to real-time task (or job) scheduling have been proposed. All of these are based on additional information associated with each task (or job). The scheduling algorithms are all designed with the primary objective of starting (or completing) tasks or jobs at the most appropriate (valuable) times, neither too early nor too late, and hence mostly rely on rapid interrupt handling and task dispatching, despite dynamic resource demands and conflicts, processing overloads, and hardware and software faults.

    Brief details on this topic with a figure are given on the Support Material at www.routledge.com/9781032467238.

10.8.3.1   Clock-Driven Approach

When scheduling decisions are made as to what jobs would be executed at what specific time instants, it is called *clock-driven* or *time-driven*. In systems that use clock-driven scheduling, all the needed parameters of hard real-time jobs are fixed and known that are used by the scheduler to choose specific time instants *a priori* for each job before the system begins execution. Accordingly, a typical schedule or a plan is produced *off-line* and is stored for the scheduler to schedule these jobs using this schedule at each scheduling decision time during execution. As a result, the system has, as such, no scheduling overhead during runtime.

To realize scheduling decisions periodically at regularly spaced time instants, a hardware timer is used that is set to expire periodically without any intervention of the scheduler. The scheduler selects and schedules the job(s), then blocks itself waiting for the timer to expire. During this period, the selected job goes on executing until the next scheduling decision time. At the expiry of the timer, the scheduler once again awakes and repeats the same course of action.

10.8.3.1.1   Weighted Round-Robin Approach

The traditional round-robin approach, often called a *processor-sharing algorithm*, is one of the most commonly used time-shared preemptive scheduling of applications in which every job, after being ready for execution, joins in a first-in-first-out scheduling queue, and the scheduler then releases the job located at the head of this queue for execution, giving at most one quantum of time unit called a *time-slice*. If the job does not complete its execution by the end of this time slice, it is preempted and is placed at the end of the queue to wait for its next turn. Since the length of the time slice chosen in this approach greatly influences the performance of the system; shorter time slices would enable every job to begin its execution almost immediately after it becomes ready. This attribute can be considered one of the attractive features of this algorithm.

Based on this basic RR scheme, another approach known as the *weighted round-robin algorithm* has been improvised. In this approach, rather than giving all the ready jobs an equal share of the processor, different jobs may be given different weights. The term *weight* for a task (or job) here indicated what fraction of processor time is to be allocated to the task (or job). A job with weight x gets x time slices every round, and the length of a round is equal to the sum of the weights of all the ready tasks (or jobs). One of the advantages of this scheme is that by tuning the weights of jobs, the progress of each job toward completion can be controlled at will so as to match the need of the existing environment.

The weighted round-robin scheduling approach is not conducive to scheduling precedence-constrained jobs, since it badly affects the response time of a chain of such jobs, making it unnecessarily longer. But, on the other hand, the good part of it is that it enables the successor job to effectively use what is produced by its predecessor (as is found in a UNIX pipe) and can even be executed simultaneously in a pipelined fashion.

The inherent nature of this approach favors it to effectively use in scheduling real-time traffic in high-speed switched networks in which transmission of messages is carried out by the existing switches en route (thought of as being in a queue) in a pipelined fashion. Here, a switch can immediately begin to transmit an earlier portion of the message as soon as it receives the portion without having to wait for the arrival of the later portion of the message. Since the weighted round-robin approach always uses a round-robin queue and does not require a sorted priority-queue, it is distinctly preferred in scheduling of message transmissions in *ultrahigh-speed networks*, since priority-queues with the required speed in this environment are expensive to implement.

Brief details on this topic with a figure are given on the Support Material at www.routledge. com/9781032467238.

10.8.3.2   Priority-Driven Approach

When the scheduling decisions are made on some form of priority determined by the parameters attached to the jobs, they are called *priority-driven*, which is used in a large number of different classes of scheduling algorithm. Such scheduling is precisely applicable for events, such as releases and completion of jobs or even interruption of executing jobs due to the occurrence of some other events. That is why *priority-driven* algorithms are *event-driven*. This algorithm always attempts to keep the resources busy whenever they are available by scheduling a ready job which requires them. So, when a processor or any other resource is available and some job is ready to use it to make progress, such an algorithm never makes the job wait. This attribute is often called *greediness*. Priority-driven scheduling is thus often called **greedy scheduling**, since this algorithm is always eager to make decisions that are locally optimal.

A priority-driven scheduler is essentially an on–line scheduler. It does not precompute a schedule of the tasks (or jobs). Rather, it is, in general, implemented by assigning priorities to jobs at release time before execution. In fact, priority-driven algorithms differ in how priorities are to be assigned to jobs. The algorithms in this regard for scheduling *periodic tasks* are classified into two main categories: fixed (or static) priority, in which the priority is assigned to each periodic task (or job) at its release time and is fixed relative to other task (or job). In a dynamic priority algorithm, the priority of task (or job) may change (dynamically) over the time between its release and completion. In fixed priority, jobs ready for execution are usually placed in one or more job queues arranged by the order of priority as assigned. At each scheduling decision time, the scheduler updates the ready job queues in the descending order of priorities and then the job located in front of the highest-priority queue is scheduled and executed on the available processor(s), and after that the next job in the queue, and so on. Hence, a priority-driven scheduling algorithm essentially arranges the job to a large extent by a list of assigned priorities, and that is why this approach is sometimes called **list scheduling**. In fact, the priority list, along with the other relevant decisions or rules (such as whether preemption will be done) when injected into it, they all together constitute the scheduling algorithm as a whole.

Most traditional scheduling algorithms are essentially priority-driven. For example, both FIFO and LIFO algorithms assign priorities to jobs according to their arrival times, and RR scheduling is the same when preemption is considered. Moreover, in RR scheduling, the priority of the executing job is often dynamically made lowered to the minimum of all jobs waiting for execution by placing it at the end of queue when the job has already executed for a time slice. The SJF, SPN, and LJF algorithms assign priorities on the basis of job execution times.

However, most real-time scheduling algorithms of practical interest essentially assign fixed priorities to individual jobs. The priority of each job is assigned upon its release when it is inserted into the ready job queue. Once assigned, the priority of the job relative to other jobs in the ready queue remains fixed. In the other category, priorities are fixed at the level of individual jobs, but the priorities at the task (within the job) level are variable.

Brief details on this topic with a figure are given on the Support Material at www.routledge. com/9781032467238.

10.8.3.2.1   *Fixed-Priority (Static) Scheduling*

All modern operating systems, including many real-time operating systems, support fixed-priority scheduling. The IEEE 802.5 token ring provides eight priority levels, and RTOSs provide no more than 256 priority levels with non-distinct priorities to tasks (or jobs) and perform almost as an ideal system with an infinite number of priority levels. In contrast, a commonly used general-purpose operating system usually provides fewer levels. Windows NT, for example, provides only 16 real-time priority levels.

Priority is normally assigned by the scheduler at the time of creation of the process or thread. When a thread is created by a *fork()* function, it normally inherits the priority of the parent thread in the parent process, and it is stored in its TCB. In systems that support *priority inheritance* or the *ceiling-priority protocol*, a thread may inherit a higher priority than its assigned priority. These protocols assign time-varying priorities which a thread acquires as the *current priority* during its execution and is then stored in the TCB of the thread. The fixed-priority scheduling mechanism is implemented here in a similar fashion as in traditional OSs. Most RTOSs, including all real-time

POSIX-compliant systems, allow the user to schedule equal-priority threads belonging to the same ready queue with the choice between round-robin or FIFO policies, and the kernel then conveniently carries out either policy.

At each scheduling time decision, the scheduler has to find the highest-priority nonempty queue to schedule the highest-priority ready threads for execution. The worst-case time complexity of this operation is, at least theoretically, $O(\beta)$, where β is the number of priority levels supported by the operating system. In fact, the average number of comparisons required to scan the queues to find the highest-priority job to schedule at any instant is $(\beta/K) + \log_2 K - 1$, where K is the word length of the CPU. If a system has 256 priority levels using a 32-bit CPU (the word length of CPU is 32 bits), then the scheduler would take at most 12 comparisons to detect the highest-priority thread to be scheduled.

Brief details on this topic with a figure are given on the Support Material at www.routledge. com/9781032467238.

10.8.3.2.1.1 Rate-Monotonic Algorithm A well-known promising fixed-priority algorithm proposed by Liuin 1973 is the RM algorithm that resolves multitask scheduling conflicts for periodic tasks (or jobs). This algorithm assigns priorities to tasks (or jobs) based on their periods; the shorter the period, the higher the priority.

The relevant parameter for periodic tasks used in this algorithm is the task's period, T, which is the amount of time between the arrival of instance of one task and the arrival of the instance of the next task. The rate (of job releases) of a task (in Hertz) is simply the inverse of the period (in seconds). For example, a task with a period of 50 ms occurs at a rate of 20 Hz (1/50 ms = 1000/50 sec = 20 Hz). Typically, the end of a task's period is also the task's hard deadline, although some tasks may have earlier deadlines. The execution (or computation) time, C, is the amount of processing time required for each occurrence of the task. It should be clear that in a uniprocessor system, the execution time must be no greater than the period (i.e. $C \le T$). If a periodic task is assumed to always be run to completion, that is, if no instance of the task is ever denied service because of nonavailability of resources, the utilization of the processor by the task is U = C/T. For example, if a task has a period of 90 ms and an execution time of 50 ms, then its processor utilization is 50/90 = 0.5555.

For RM scheduling, the highest-priority task is obviously the one with the shortest period, the second highest-priority task is the one with the second shortest period, and so on when more than one task is available for execution. If the priority of a set of tasks can be plotted as a function of their rate, the result is a monotonically increasing function, and that is why it is called rate monotonic scheduling.

One of the important parameters of a periodic scheduling algorithm is its *effectiveness*, which is usually measured in one way in terms of whether it guarantees that all hard deadlines are met. If there are n tasks with a fixed period and associated execution time, then for it to be possible to meet all deadlines, the following inequality must hold:

$$\frac{C_1}{T_1} + \frac{C_2}{T_2} + \ldots\ldots + \frac{C_n}{T_n} \le 1$$

In other words, the sum of the processor utilizations of all the individual tasks cannot exceed a value 1, which corresponds to total utilization of the processor. This inequality also indicates a bound on the number of tasks that can be successfully scheduled by a perfect scheduling algorithm. For any particular algorithm, the bound may be even lower. It can be shown that for RM scheduling, the following inequality also holds:

$$\frac{C_1}{T_1} + \frac{C_2}{T_2} + \ldots\ldots + \frac{C_n}{T_n} \le n(2^{1/n} - 1)$$

When n = 1, the upper bound is n $(2^{1/n} - 1) = 1$; for n = 2, the upper bound is n $(2^{1/n} - 1) = 0.828$; n = 3, the upper bound n $(2^{1/n} - 1) = 0.779$; and in this way as n $\rightarrow \infty$, the upper bound n $(2^{1/n} - 1) =$ ln $2 \approx 0.693$. This shows that as the number of tasks increases, the scheduling bound converges to ln $2 \approx 0.693$.

Brief details on this topic with figures and an example are given on the Support Material at www. routledge.com/9781032467238.

10.8.3.2.1.2 Deadline-Monotonic Algorithm   Another well-known fixed-priority scheduling algorithm is the deadline-monotonic (DM) algorithm, which assigns priorities to tasks according to their relative deadlines: the shorter the relative deadline, the higher the priority. The DM schedule of a system consisting of a certain number of tasks can be prepared in the same fashion as preparing an RM schedule, except that the priorities of jobs are imposed here on the basis of their relative deadlines. However, if the relative deadline of every task is proportional to its period, then RM and DM algorithms become identical. When the relative deadlines are arbitrary, the DM algorithm performs better in the sense that it can sometimes produce a feasible schedule when the RM algorithm fails. More precisely, when the DM algorithm fails, RM algorithm always fails. Whatever it may be, some of the features exhibited by RM scheduling algorithms are quite advantageous and favor its wide adoption in industrial environments.

Advantageous features of RM scheduling algorithms are given on the Support Material at www. routledge.com/9781032467238.

10.8.3.2.2   Dynamic Priority Scheduling
To be specific, there are three categories of algorithms: fixed-priority algorithms, task-level dynamic priority (and job- or component-level fixed-priority) algorithms, and job (or component)-level (and task-level) dynamic algorithms. Except where stated otherwise, by dynamic-priority algorithms, it is generally meant task-level dynamic priority (and job- or component-level fixed-priority) algorithms.

10.8.3.2.2.1 Earliest-Deadline-First Algorithm   Most operating systems prefer to support dynamic priority. A straightforward scheme is to always schedule the ready task with the earliest deadline and then let that scheduled task run to completion. The EDF algorithm employs an approach that assigns priorities to individual tasks according to their absolute deadlines: the earlier the (absolute) deadline of any task (job) at any instant, the higher the priority of that particular task (job) at that instant. The deadline of a specific task (job) with respect to the current time may be earlier or later than any other task (job) in the ready queue; hence, its priority will be accordingly changed and assumed to be higher or lower at that time instant. Thus, the priorities of task (jobs) change dynamically (as the execution proceeds), hence the name dynamic priority algorithm. This scheduling mechanism always schedules the eligible task based on the earliest (absolute) deadline, even preempting the executing task (job) with a later deadline and then letting that scheduled task run to completion. Thus, the EDF algorithm can also be called a task-level dynamic-priority algorithm. On the other hand, once a job is placed in the ready job queue according to the priority assigned to it, its order with respect to other jobs in the queue remains fixed. In other words, the EDF algorithm can also be called a job-level fixed-priority algorithm.

Brief details on this topic with figures and an example are given on the Support Material at www. routledge.com/9781032467238.

10.8.3.2.2.2 Least-Slack-Time-First Algorithm   Another well-known dynamic-priority algorithm that is optimal for scheduling preemptive jobs on one processor is the least-slack-time-first (LST) algorithm, sometimes also called the *minimum-laxity-first* (MLF) algorithm. At any time t, the slack (or laxity) with deadline at d is equal to d − t minus the time required to complete the remaining portion of the job. This says that at any instant t, the slack of a job; s = d − t − x, where d is the deadline and x is the remaining execution time (i.e. the execution of its remaining portion) of the job at time t. The scheduler checks the slacks of all the ready jobs each time a new job is released (i.e. arrives at the ready job queue) and orders the new job with the existing jobs once again on the basis of their slacks; the smaller the slack, the higher the priority.

For example, consider a set of jobs $J_k(u, v)$ where $k = 1,2,3, \ldots$, in which u is the deadline, and v is the execution (or computation) time of the job J_k. Now, assume that a job J_1 (6, 3) is released at time 0 with a deadline 6, and its execution time is 3. The job starts to execute at time 0. As long as it executes, it slack s remains at 3, because at any time t, before its completion, the slack $s = d - t - x = 6 - t - (3 - t) = 6 - 3 = 3$. Now, suppose that it is preempted at time 2 by a job J_3, which executes from time 2 to 4. At the end of this interval (i.e. at $t = 4$), the slack s of $J_1 = d - t - x = 6 - 4 - (3 - 2)$ [the remaining portion of J_1 is $(3 - 2)$ as 2 units of work out of a total need of 3 units are already done in the interval 0 to 2] $= 1$. Thus, the slack of J_1 decreases from 3 to 1 after the interval when J_3 completes its execution in the interval from 2 to 4.

With the LST algorithm, as discussed, the scheduling decisions are made only at the times when jobs are released (arrive at the ready queue) or completed; this version of the LST algorithm does not really follow the LST rule of priority assignment rigorously at all times in its truest sense. To be very specific, this version of LST algorithm thus can be, at best, called the **nonstrict LST algorithm**. If the scheduler were to adhere to LST rules strictly, then it would have to continuously monitor the slacks of all ready jobs and keep comparing them with the slack of the executing job. It would have to reassign priorities to jobs whenever their slacks changed relative to each other. Consequently, the runtime overhead of the **strict LST algorithm** includes the additional time required to monitor and compare the slacks of all ready job as time progresses. In addition, if the slacks of more than one jobs become equal at any time, they need to be serviced in a round-robin manner that results in extra consumption of time due to context switches suffered by these jobs. For these and many other reasons, the strict LST algorithm is effectively unattractive in practice and thus has fallen out of favor.

A relevant complicated example of this topic is given on the Support Material at www.routledge.com/9781032467238.

10.8.3.2.3 Priority Inversion

A preemptive scheduling scheme based on fixed or dynamic priority often exhibits a peculiar phenomenon in the context of real-time scheduling known as *priority inversion* that may sometimes create an adverse impact on the working of the entire system. The most notable instance of priority inversion in recent years was observed in the Mars Pathfinder mission led by NASA. The operating system used there is VxWorks, and the related priority inversion, with its impact, is described in brief in Section 10.9.4.

A system employing any type of priority scheduling scheme should always schedule and execute the task with the highest priority. But, at times, it happens within the system that a situation insists a relatively higher-priority task to wait for a lower-priority task. This phenomenon is so-called **priority inversion**. It can occur when the execution of some tasks or portions of tasks is nonpreemptible. Resource contention among jobs can also cause priority inversion. Because resources are allocated to tasks on a nonpreemptible basis, a higher-priority task can be blocked by a lower-priority task if the tasks conflict, even when the execution of both tasks is preemptable. Many other situations can occur that may ultimately result in priority inversion. One such situation is; while a lower-priority task has already acquired a shared resource (e.g. a device or a binary semaphore) before using, and a higher-priority task almost at the same time attempts to acquire the same resource. The ultimate consequence is that the higher-priority tasks will be simply put into a blocked state until the resource is available. Many different other reasons can be cited that may cause such situations to occur; one may cause the system to enter a deadlock. However, if the lower-priority task quickly finishes its execution with the already owned resource and releases it, the higher-priority task may then resume, and there will be no appreciable violation in real-time constraints that can miss the specified deadline to the extent that it would cause ill effects.

Indeed, the situation may become even worse if priority inversion is unbounded or uncontrolled. The duration involved in **unbounded priority inversion** depends not only on the time consumed to handle a shared resource but also on unpredictable interactions and involvement of other unrelated tasks. More seriously, without having good resource access-control, the duration of a priority inversion can be unbounded. The priority inversion experienced by Pathfinder software was precisely unbounded (uncontrolled) and is presented here as a good example of when this undesirable phenomenon occurs.

Brief details on this topic with figures and an example are given on the Support Material at www. routledge.com/9781032467238.

10.8.3.2.4 Priority Inheritance

The priority inversion problem is addressed using the *priority inheritance protocol*, wherein a low-priority process that holds a resource temporarily acquires the priority of the highest-priority process, which attempts to gain control of the resource. Each ready job J_k at any time t is scheduled by the scheduling algorithm and executes at its current (assigned) priority $л_k$ (t). In particular, the current priority $л_k$ (t) of a job J_k may be raised to the higher priority $л_h$ (t) of another job J_h. When this happens, it is said that the lower priority job J_k inherits the priority of the higher priority job J_h, and J_k executes at its inherited priority $л_h$ (t). In its simplest form, the **priority-inheritance protocol** is defined by the following rules with the assumption that some of the jobs contend for resources and every resource has only 1 unit.

1. *Scheduling Rule*: Ready jobs are scheduled on the processor preemptively in a priority-driven manner according to their current priorities. At its release time t, the current priority $л$ (t) of every job J usually holds its own current priority. The job remains at its priority except under the condition stated in rule 3.
2. *Allocation Rule*: When a job J requests a resource R at time t:
   a). If R is free, R is allocated to J until J releases the resource, and
   b). If R is not free, the request is denied, and J is blocked.
3. *Priority-Inheritance Rule*: When the requesting job J becomes blocked, the job J_k which blocks J inherits the current priority $л$ (t) of J. The job J_k executes at its inherited priority $л$ (t) until it releases R; at that time, the priority of J_k returns to its previous priority $л_t(t')$ at time t' when it acquires the resource R (before its inheritance of higher priority).

The priority inversion problem can now be explained using the priority inheritance protocol by an example. Assume a low-priority task (or process) P_2 already holds a resource which a high-priority task (or process) P_1 needs. So the low-priority task (or process) P_2 would temporarily acquire the priority of the task (or process) P_1, which would enable it to be scheduled and exit after finishing its execution using the resource. This priority change takes place as soon as the higher-priority task blocks on the resource; this blocking should come to an end when the resource is released by the lower-priority task and the lower-priority task gets back to its previous default priority when it acquires the resource. In this way, the problem of unbounded priority inversion, as discussed in the last section, can be resolved with the use of the priority-inheritance protocol. However, use of the priority inheritance protocol in many situations is impractical because it would require the kernel to note minute details of the operation of processes (as normally happens when deadlock is handled).

Brief details on this topic with a solution to the priority inversion problem are given on the Support Material at www.routledge.com/9781032467238.

10.8.3.2.5 Priority Ceiling

The priority-ceiling protocol essentially extends the priority-inheritance protocol to prevent deadlocks and to further reduce the blocking time. The basic assumptions related to this protocol are:

- Each ready job J_k at any time t is scheduled by the scheduling algorithm and executes at its current (assigned) priority $л_k$ (t), and the assigned priority of all such jobs is fixed.
- A priority is associated with each resource. The resources required by all jobs are known *apriori* before the execution of any job begins.

In this approach, a new parameter called *priority ceiling* associated with every resource is used. The priority ceiling of any resource R_x is *one level higher* than the highest priority of all the jobs that require R_x and is denoted by $U(R_x)$. It is to be noted that if the resource access-control protocol includes the priority-inheritance rule, then a task (or job) can inherit a priority as high as k during its execution if it requires a resource with priority ceiling k.

At any time t, the *current priority-ceiling*, or simply *ceiling*, $\tilde{U}(t)$ of the system is equal to the highest-priority ceiling of the resources that are in use at that time, if resources are in use. If all the resources are free at the time, the current ceiling $\tilde{U}(t)$ is equal to Ω, a nonexistent priority level that is lower than the lowest priority of all jobs.

In its simplest form, the **priority-ceiling protocol** is defined by the following rules, with the assumption that some of the jobs contend for resources and that every resource has only 1 unit.

1. *Scheduling Rule*: Ready jobs are scheduled on the processor preemptively in a priority-driven manner according to their current priorities. At its release time t, the current priority л (t) of every job J is equal to its assigned priority. The job remains at this priority except under the condition stated in rule 3.
2. *Allocation Rule*: When a job J requests a resource R at time t:
   a). If R is not free, the request is denied, and J is blocked.
   b). If R is free,
      – If J's priority л (t) is higher than the current priority ceiling $\tilde{U}(t)$, R is allocated to J.
      – If J's priority л (t) is not higher than the current priority ceiling $\tilde{U}(t)$ of the system, R is allocated to J only if J is the job holding the resource (s) whose priority ceiling is equal to $\breve{U}(t)$; otherwise, J's request is denied, and J becomes blocked.
3. *Priority-Inheritance Rule*: When the requesting job J becomes blocked, the job J_k which blocks J inherits the current priority л (t) of J. The job J_k executes at its inherited priority л (t) until it releases every resource whose priority ceiling is equal to or higher than л (t); at that time, the priority of J_k returns to its previous priority $\tilde{л}_t (t')$ at time t' when it was granted the resource(s) (before its inheritance of higher priority).

The priority-ceiling protocol (or *ceiling-priority protocol, CPP*) can be easily implemented by the system or at the user level in a fixed-priority system that supports FIFO within equal policy. The CPP, however requires prior knowledge of resource requirements (similar to the methods which are used in avoidance of deadlocks) of all threads. From this knowledge, the resource manager generates the priority ceiling $U(R)$ of every resource R. In addition to the current and assigned priorities of each thread, the thread's TCB also contains the names of all resources held by the thread at the current time.

Whenever a thread requests a resource R, it actually requests a lock on R. The resource manager then locks the scheduler and looks up $U(R)$; if the current priority of the requesting thread is lower than $U(R)$, it sets the thread's current priority to $U(R)$, allocates R to the thread, and then unlocks the scheduler. Similarly, when a thread unlocks a resource R, the resource manager checks whether the thread's current priority is higher than $U(R)$. The fact that the thread's current priority is higher than $U(R)$ indicates that the thread still holds a resource with a priority ceiling higher than $U(R)$. The thread's priority should be left unchanged in this case. On the other hand, if the thread's current priority is not higher than $U(R)$, the priority may need to be lowered when R is released. In this case, the resource manager locks the scheduler, changes the current priority of the thread to the highest-priority ceiling of all resources the thread still holds at that time or to the thread's assigned priority (i.e. bringing back the thread's priority to its previous value at the time of allocating the resource R) if the thread no longer holds any resources.

10.8.3.2.6 *Priority-Inheritance versus Priority-Ceiling Protocols*
The priority-inheritance protocol and priority-ceiling protocol are fundamentally different; the former is *greedy*, while the latter is not. At the time of allocation (rule 2), the priority-inheritance

protocol lets the requesting job have a resource whenever the resource is free. In contrast, according to the allocation policy of the priority-ceiling protocol, a task (or job) may be denied its requested resource even when the resource is free.

The priority-inheritance rules of these two protocols are by and large the same. Both rules agree with the principle that whenever a lower-priority job J_k blocks job J, whose request is just denied, the priority of J_k is raised to J's priority л (t). The difference mainly arises because of the non-greedy nature of the priority-ceiling protocol when it is possible for job J to be blocked by a lower-priority job which does not even hold the requested resource, while this is not possible according to the priority-inheritance protocol. Priority-ceiling blocking is also referred to sometimes as *avoidance blocking*. The reason for this term is that the blocking caused by the priority-ceiling protocol is essentially at the expense of the avoidance of deadlocks among jobs. That is why these two terms, *avoidance blocking* and *priority-ceiling*, are often interchangeably used.

The overhead of priority inheritance is rather high. Since the priority-ceiling protocol also uses the same mechanism, its overhead is naturally also high, although not as high as simple priority inheritance, since there is no transitive blocking. Also, each resource acquisition and release requires a change of priority of at most the executing thread. That is why CPP is sometimes called the poor person's priority-ceiling protocol.

10.8.3.3   Case Study: Linux Real-Time Scheduling

The scheduler, used in Linux version 2.4 and earlier, is similar to the traditional UNIX scheduling algorithms for scheduling non–real-time processes coupled with the scheduling of real-time processes. Its revised versions, such as version 2.6, while enhanced the capability of scheduling for non–real-time processes to a great extent, but essentially kept the same real-time scheduling activities as it was in its previous releases. Indeed, the entire Linux scheduler consists of three distinct scheduling classes. Those are:

- **SCHED_FIFO:** For scheduling first-in-first-out real-time threads
- **SCHED_RR:** For scheduling round-robin real-time threads
- **SCHED_OTHER:** For scheduling non-real-time threads

Within each class, multiple priorities may be used, with priorities for the real-time processes (threads) always higher than priorities for non–real-time processes (threads) belonging to the *SCHED_OTHER* class. There are altogether 100 priority levels for real-time classes, ranging from 0 to 99 inclusive, and the *SCHD_OTHER* class ranges from 100 to 139. The rule is: the lower the number, the higher the priority.

In Linux, processes using the *SCHED_FIFO* and *SCHED_RR* policies are scheduled on a fixed-priority basis, whereas processes using the *SCHED_OTHER* policy are scheduled on a time-sharing basis. Any process (thread) belonging to the class *SCHED_OTHER* can only begin its execution if there are no real-time threads ready to execute. The scheduling policies and mechanisms used for the non–real-time processes belonging to the class *SCHED_OTHER* were discussed in Chapter 4 in which scheduling with traditional uniprocessor operating systems was explained, so this area has not been included in the current discussion.

For FIFO (*SCHED_FIFO*) threads, the rules are:

- The executing FIFO threads are normally nonpreemptible, but the system will interrupt an executing FIFO thread when:
  1. Another FIFO thread of higher priority becomes ready.
  2. The executing FIFO thread becomes blocked for one of the many reasons, such as, waiting for an I/O event to occur.

3. The executing FIFO thread voluntarily relinquishes control of the processor following a system call to the primitive *sched_yield*.

- When an executing FIFO thread is interrupted (blocked), it is placed in the respective queue associated with its priority. When it becomes unblocked, it returns to the same priority queue in the active queue list.
- When a FIFO thread becomes ready, and if that thread has a priority higher than the priority of the currently executing thread, then the executing thread is preempted, and the available highest-priority ready FIFO thread is scheduled and executed. If, at any instant, the number of the highest-priority thread is more than one, then the thread that has been waiting the longest time is selected for execution.

The *SCHED_RR* policy when implemented is almost similar to *SCHED_FIFO*, except with the inclusion of a usual time-slice associated with each thread. When a *SCHED_RR* thread has executed for one specified time-slice, it is preempted and is returned to its priority queue with the same time-slice value. A real-time thread of equal or higher priority is then selected for execution. Time-slice values, however, are never changed.

The implementation of FIFO and RR scheduling, taking a set of four threads with their relative priorities of an arbitrary process, is depicted in Figure 10.3, which also shows the distinction between these two policies when implemented. Assume that all these waiting threads are ready for execution at an instant when the currently executing thread waits or terminates and that no other higher-priority thread is awakened while a thread is under execution.

Figure 10.3(b) shows the flow with FIFO scheduling of the threads when they all belong to the *SCHED_FIFO* class. Thread B executes until it waits or terminates. Next, although C and D have the same priority, thread C starts because it has been waiting longer (arrived earlier) than D. Thread C executes until it waits or terminates; then thread D executes until it waits or terminates. Finally, thread A executes.

Similarly, Figure 10.3(c) shows the flow with RR scheduling of the threads when they all belong to the *SCHED_RR* class. Thread B executes until it waits or terminates. Next, thread C and D are time-sliced because they both have the same priority. Finally, thread A executes.

It is worth noting that the user has the option to control the maximum and minimum priorities associated with a scheduling policy using the primitives *sched_get_priority_min()* and *sched_get_priority_max()*. Similarly, one can also find the time-slices given to processes that are scheduled in a round-robin policy using *sched_rr_get_interval()*. Since the source is already at hand, one can easily change these parameters at will.

Threads	Arrival Time	Priority
A	0	6
B	2	1
C	3	4
D	5	4

(a)

Execution profile of four threads

B — → C — → D— → A — →

(b)

Flow with FIFO Scheduling

B — → C — → D — → C — → D — → A — →

(c)

Flow with RR Scheduling

FIGURE 10.3   An example of a representative scheme of Linux Real-time scheduling using FIFO algorithm and Round-robin (RR) algorithm taking four threads (process).

10.8.4 TIME SERVICES: CLOCKS AND TIMERS

A *clock* is a hardware device that contains a counter, a timer queue, and an interrupt handler (see Chapter 6). At any time, the content of the counter gives a representation of the current time. The timer queue contains the pending expiration times of timers bound to the clock. A system may have more than one clock device and use them for different purposes. Most operating systems allow a process (or a thread) to have its own timers. In fact, there can be as many as 32 timers per process. In contrast, operating systems, such as Linux, that do not support per-process timers provide one or more system-wide timers. Processes cannot destroy these timers but can set them and use them for alarm purposes. Clock and timer interface functions make time visible to the application processes (threads). By calling the timer function, such as *create*, a process (or thread) can create a per-process (or per thread) timer, and in a system containing multiple clocks, this binds the timer to a specified clock. Associated with each timer is a data structure which the kernel creates in response to the *create* timer call. This data structure contains several types of vital information, including the expiration time of the timer and a pointer to a handler routine that the calling process (or thread) wants to be executed when a timer event occurs.

Various types of OS functions (such as; *clock_settime*, *clock_gettime*, *set-timer*, etc.) are available to users to properly make use of timers according to their requirements. In fact, there are two kinds of timers: *one-shot* and *periodic*. In addition, there is another type of timer known as a *watchdog timer* that can also be created and manipulated by the user.

Signals are the software analog of hardware interrupts and can be generated by a variety of causes in addition to timers expiring. In real-time operating systems, a signal is used as the notification mechanism realized by using an appropriate function, such as, *timer_settime()*. When a process (or thread) calls the *timer_create()* function to request the creation of a timer, it specifies the clock to which the timer is to be bound, as well as the type of signal to be delivered whenever the timer expires. If the type of signal is not specified and the clock to which the timer is bound is CLOCK_REALTIME, the system will deliver a SIGARLM (alarm clock expired) signal by default.

Brief details on this topic are given on the Support Material at www.routledge.com/9781032467238.

10.8.4.1 Case Study: Clock and Timer Resolutions in Linux

Linux (like NT) updates the system clock and checks for timer expirations periodically, and the period is 10 milliseconds on most hardware platforms. In Linux, each clock interrupt period is called a *jiffy*, and time is expressed in terms of (the number of) *jiffies*. Consequently, the actual resolution of Linux timers is 10 milliseconds.

In order to improve the clock resolution on **Intel Pentium** processors, the kernel reads and stores the timestamp counter at each clock interrupt. In response to a *get-time-of-day* call, it reads the counter again and calculates from the difference in the two readings in number of microseconds that have elapsed from the time of the previous timer interrupt to the current time. In this way, it returns the current time to the caller in terms of *jiffies* and the number of microseconds into the current *jiffy*.

In addition to reading the timestamp counter at each clock interrupt, the interrupt service routine checks the timer queue to determine whether any timer has expired and, for each expired timer found, queues the timer function that is to be executed upon the expiration of that timer. The timer function thus queued is executed just before the kernel returns control to the applications. Timer errors can be severe and unpredictable because of the delay introduced by the kernel and possibly large execution times of the timer functions.

10.8.5 COMMUNICATION AND SYNCHRONIZATION

Almost all operating systems, including RTOSs, provide various types of mechanisms for communication and synchronization between tasks. Some of the most commonly used efficient mechanisms for these purposes are shared memory, *message queues, synchronization primitives* (e.g. condition variables, mutexes, and semaphores), and *events* and *signals*. Although shared memory provides a low-level, high-bandwidth and low-latency means of interprocess communication and often is used for communication among not only processes that run on uniprocessor, but also on processes that run on tightly coupled multiprocessors. However, real-time applications sometimes do not explicitly synchronize accesses to shared memory; rather they mostly rely on "synchronization by scheduling"; that is, processes (or threads) that access the shared memory are so scheduled as to make explicit synchronization unnecessary. Hence, the entire burden of providing reliable access to shared memory is shifted from "synchronization" to "scheduling and schedulability analysis". As a result, the use of shared memory for realizing interprocess communication becomes costly, and it also makes the system brittle. For these and many other reasons, use of shared memory for the purpose of interprocess synchronization and communications between real-time processes is not helpful and thus is not considered here.

Brief details on this topic are given on the Support Material at www.routledge.com/9781032467238.

10.8.5.1 Communication Mechanisms

Most RTOSs provide several communication mechanisms that can be realized in many different ways. Each mechanism is optimized to reliably pass a different kind of information from task to task. Probably the most popular kind of communication between tasks in real-time systems as well as in embedded systems is the passing of data from one task to another. Some of these mechanisms are presented here, but the details of many of them are outside the scope of this discussion.

10.8.5.1.1 Message-Passing Mechanism: Message Queues

Most RTOSs offer a traditional message passing mechanism for the purpose of communication between processes (or threads) in which each message can contain an array or buffer of data. Since messages are sent more quickly than they can be handled, the RTOS provides message queues, as shown in Figure 10.4, for holding messages until they can be processed. As some messages are more important than others, the message queue is not organized in FIFO order; rather message priority, determined by message type or by designation given by the sender, is used to organize the queue. An alternative may be to allow the receiver to inspect the message queue and select which message to receive next.

Message queues provide a file-like interface and a natural way of communication between queues and clients. They are an easy-to-use means of many-to-many communication among processes (or threads). If the location of the message queues can be made transparent, an operating system can then make this mechanism as easy to use across networked machines as on a single machine. A system service provider can create a message queue, give a name to the message queue, and then introduce this name to its clients. To request service, a client process (or thread) opens the message queue and places its request-for-service message in the queue. The service provider may also use message queues as the means for returning the results it produces to clients. A client, however, can get the result by opening the result queue and can receive the related message in it.

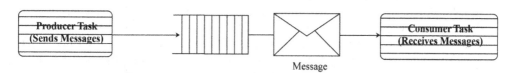

FIGURE 10.4 A representative illustration of a message-passing mechanism using message transfer via message queue.

Brief details on this topic are given on the Support Material at www.routledge.com/9781032467238.

- **Determinism and high-speed message passing:** Inter-task message communication is another area where different operating systems exhibit different timing characteristics. Most operating systems actually copy messages twice as they transfer them from task to task via a message queue. From Figure 10.4, it is clear that the first copying is from the message-sender task to an operating system-owned "private" area of RAM (implementing the "message queue"), and the second copying is from the message queue to the message-receiver task. Clearly, this is non-deterministic in its timing, as these copying activities take longer as message length increases. An approach that avoids this non-determinism and also improves performance is to have the operating system copy a pointer to the message and deliver that pointer to the message-receiver task without moving the message contents at all. In order to avoid access collisions, the operating system then needs to go back to the message-sender task and destroy its copy of the pointer to the message. For large messages, this eliminates the need for lengthy copying and eliminates non-determinism.
- **Prioritization:** It is expected that the message queue will be organized in the form of priority queues for the sake of making the performance of queuing activity locally optimal. The sending thread can then specify the priority of its message in its send message call. Consequently, the message will be dequeued by the service provider much earlier than lower-priority messages. In fact, the parameters of the real-time POSIX send function *mq_send()* contain the name of the message queue, the location and the length of the message, and the priority of the message, with priorities usually ranging from 0 to 31 inclusive. Other operating systems typically support only two priority levels, normal and urgent. Normal messages are queued in FIFO order, while an urgent message is placed at the head of the queue.
- **Priority inheritance in message-based systems:** A message is read (processed) only when a receiving thread executes a *receive* (e.g. *mg_receive()* in real-time POSIX) call. Therefore, having a receiving thread with a lower-priority to act upon a high-priority send-message ultimately leads to poor performance in general. One way to alleviate this problem is to treat sending and receiving threads as two job segments with different priorities. Other methods to ensure consistent prioritization are providing message-based priority inheritance as is done in QNX. The service provider handling the message queue in QNX uses a server process that receives messages in priority order. It provides a work thread to service each request. Each work thread, in turn, inherits the priority of the request message, which is essentially the priority of the sender.

  Other approaches to handle prioritization in message queues also exist. Real-time POSIX, however, does not support message-based priority inheritance. What it does (as suggested by Gallmeister) to emulate this mechanism is to give the service provider the highest-priority while it waits for messages. When it receives a message, it lowers its priority to the message priority. In this way, the service provider is able to track the priorities of the requests. Many other different schemes in this respect are available to handle this responsibility that employ numerous techniques; each one has its own merits and drawbacks. Details on each, however, are outside the scope of this chapter.
- **Non-blocking:** An effective and useful feature is non-blocking. The *send* function for the message queue *mq_send()* in real-time POSIX is non-blocking. As long as a message queue has room to accommodate its message, a thread can call the *send* function to put a message into the queue and then continue to execute its own task. However, when the queue is full, *mq_send()* may be blocked. In order to ensure that the *send* call will not be blocked even when the message queue is full (i.e. no room to store any message), the mode of the message queue is set to non-blocking (i.e. O_NONBLOCK). This mode is

essentially an attribute of the message queue which can be set when the message queue is opened. Similarly, by default, a thread that calls the *receive* function *mq_receive()* may be blocked if the message queue is empty. It is similarly possible to make the *receive* call non-blocking in the same fashion.

- **Notification:** It is typically a means by which a message queue notifies a process when the queue changes from being empty to nonempty. Indeed, a notification facility keeps the service provider always aware of the current capability of the message queue, which allows the service provider to respond quickly in an appropriate manner to assist *send* and *receive* operations to smoothly continue by the respective threads.

Other kinds of communication between tasks (or processes) in RTOSs (especially in embedded systems) is the passing of what might be called "synchronization information" from one task to another. Synchronization information is essentially like a command, where some commands could be positive and some negative. For example, a positive command would be something like; "I am facing an emergency, and I want your help to handle it", or more generally, "Please join me in handling". A negative command, on the other hand, to a task would be something like: "Please do not print now, because my task is using the printer", or more generally: "I want to lock . . . for my own use only".

10.8.5.2 Synchronization Mechanisms

Most RTOSs offer mutexes, condition variables, semaphores, and reader/writer locks for handling negative synchronization (also called "mutual exclusion") to lock certain system resources for their exclusive use only and subsequently to unlock the resource when they are done. For positive synchronization, different RTOSs offer different mechanisms; some RTOSs offer event flags, while others offer signals, and yet others rely on message passing as well as data passing. When RTOSs attempt to implement the needed synchronization between the executing threads (or processes), priority inversion may occur when they contend for shared resources. Different types of proven protocols are in extensive use for controlling such priority inversion situations. One is the use of priority inheritance primitives, and numerous methods exist to implement these priority-inheritance primitives for mutexes and reader/writer locks to negotiate priority inversion in a fixed-priority system.

10.8.5.3 Software Interrupts: Signals

Signal was already described in Section 10.8.4. In fact, many traps detected by hardware, such as executing an illegal instruction or using an invalid address, are also converted into signals to the guilty process. Signals are specifically used for process-to-process communication when one process wants to communicate something to another process in a hurry. It is actively involved in responsive mechanisms to inform threads (or processes) about many situations, including the occurrence of timer events, the receipt of messages, the completion of asynchronous I/O operations, and similar other things required in synchronization and communication activities.

In a traditional **UNIX system**, interrupt handlers and the kernel often use signals as a means to inform threads (or processes) about the occurrence of hardware exceptions (such as divide by zero, illegal system call etc.) or waited-for events (e.g. the expiration of a timer, arrival of a message, etc.). A thread (or a process) may send a signal to another process for the sake of synchronization as well as communication (e.g. a predecessor thread may signal a successor thread when it completes). In fact, a thread has a service function called a *signal handler* (similar to interrupt handler). When the kernel delivers a signal to the thread, the signal handler executes the signal in an appropriate manner. Thus, the signal mechanism provides asynchrony as well as immediacy, just as hardware interrupts do.

In Windows NT, events and asynchronous procedure calls (APCs) serve the same purpose as signals in UNIX systems. An NT event (object) is, in fact, an efficient and powerful *notification* and *synchronization mechanism*. For being synchronous, NT event delivery has relatively low overhead in comparison to that of comparatively high overhead of asynchronism. Moreover, the NT event is many-to-many in the sense that multiple threads can wait on one event and a thread can wait for multiple events. Each UNIX signal, in contrast, is targeted to only an individual thread (or process), and each signal is handled independently of other signals.

The **pSOSystem** introduced by Motorola provides both events and asynchronous signals. The events are essentially synchronous and point–to–point. An event is usually sent to a specified receiving task. The event has, in fact, no effect on the receiving task if the task does not call the *event-receive* function. An asynchronous signal, in contrast, forces the receiving task to respond. A **real-time POSIX** signal, however, provides numerous interesting features that exemplify their good and practical uses in real-time applications.

Real-time signals can be queued, while traditional UNIX signals cannot. If not queued, a signal to be delivered, if blocked, may be lost. Hence, queuing ensures the reliability (reliable delivery) of signals. Moreover, a queued real-time signal can carry data, while a traditional signal handler has only one parameter: the number of the associated signal. In contrast, the signal handler of a real-time signal whose SA_SIGINFO bit in the *sa_flags* field is set has an additional parameter, a pointer to a data structure that contains the data value to be passed to the signal handler. This capability increases the communication bandwidth of the signal mechanism. Using this feature, a server can use a mechanism to notify a client that its requested service has been completed and subsequently pass the result back to the client at the same time. In addition, queued signals are essentially prioritized and are to be delivered according to the order of priority: the lower the signal-number, the higher the priority.

The signal mechanism is equally expensive, similar to hardware interrupt servicing. Changing mode from user to supervisor, complicated operations to service the signal, and finally a return to user mode are all hugely time-consuming activities when compared to other commonly used synchronization and communication mechanisms. Moreover, signal handlers, similar to interrupt handlers, are also executed ahead of thread priority. Hence, it is mandatory that the duration of time needed to service signal handlers are to be kept as minimum as possible, just as it is equally an important requirement to shorten the execution time of interrupt service routines.

10.8.6 MEMORY MANAGEMENT

Similar to traditional general-purpose operating systems, the amount of available memory space and its proper management are also critical issues in RTOSs. In fact, most of the issues in relation to memory and its management, such as physical memory allocation policies, virtual memory and its mapping, paging, memory protection, and memory locking, that appear in conventional non-real-time operating systems are, by and large, equally applicable to RTOSs and to the applications which run on them.

10.8.6.1 Memory Allocation

Memory allocation is even more critical in an RTOS than that in other operating systems. Many important issues need to be addressed in this regard. First, the chosen memory allocation mechanism should be as fast as possible, and not as usual to scan a linked list of indeterminate length to find a suitable free memory block, since memory allocation has to be completed within a fixed duration of time in an RTOS. Second, the memory fragmentation problem in physical memory, as discussed in Chapter 5 with traditional non-real-time operating systems, is also a typical potential problem in RTOSs. Memory allocation algorithms that slowly accumulate fragmentation may work with as such no problem for desktop machines when rebooted periodically but are unacceptable for many RTOSs and especially for embedded systems that often run for years without rebooting. One way to alleviate this problem is to use the simple fixed-sized-blocks algorithm that has been observed to be work very well for simple RTOSs and also for not-very-large embedded systems.

- **Use of virtual memory:** The introduction of virtual memory, its related aspects, and their solutions in traditional non-real-time operating system were described in Chapter 5. Many RTOSs designed primarily for embedded real-time applications, such as data acquisition, signal processing, and monitoring, may not require virtual memory and its related mapping. For example, the pSOSystem, upon request, creates a physically contiguous blocks of memory for the application. The application can request variable-size segments from its memory block and define a memory partition consisting of physically contiguous fixed-size buffers. While virtual memory provides many distinctive practical advantages in the management of memory, but its presence equally contributes a huge amount of penalties in relation to mainly space and time. Indeed, the address translation table required in this regard itself consumes a good amount of space of main memory in the resident part of the operating system, and scanning of the address translation table for mapping a virtual address to its corresponding physical address consumes additional time that consequently slows down the overall execution speed. Moreover, this scheme often complicates DMA-controlled I/O, which requires physically contiguous memory space, since the processor must have to set up the DMA controller multiple times, one for each physically contiguous block of addresses for data transfer to and from main memory.
- **Use of memory in deeply embedded systems:** Most embedded OSes are stored in binary code in ROM for execution. That is, unlike traditional operating systems, code is never brought into main memory. The reason is that the code is not expected to change very often, as embedded devices are usually dedicated to their own individual specific purposes. Indeed, the behavior of such systems is usually specified completely at their design time.
- **Dynamic memory allocation:** Dynamic allocation of main memory creates an issue relating to determinism of service times. Many general-computing non–real-time operating systems offer memory allocation services from a buffer known as the "heap". Offering of additional memory from the heap and returning this memory to the heap when it is not needed ultimately give rise to the external fragmentation problem, which produces many scattered useless small holes in the heap. Consequently, it results in shortage of useful memory even though enough memory is still available in the heap, which summarily may cause heap services to degrade. This external fragmentation problem, however, can be solved by so-called *garbage collection* (defragmentation) software, but it is often wildly non-deterministic.

Real-time operating systems thus altogether avoid both memory fragmentation and "garbage collection" along with their all ill effects. Instead, one of the alternatives that RTOSs offer are non-fragmenting memory allocation techniques by using a limited number of various sizes of memory chunks, which are then made available to application software. While this approach is certainly less flexible than the approach taken by memory heaps, it does avoid external memory fragmentation and subsequent related defragmentation. Additional memory, if required by the application, is offered from this pool of different sizes of memory chunks according to the requested size, and it is subsequently returned when it is not required and then put onto a *free buffer list* of buffers of its own size that are later available for future re-use.

More about this topic with a figure is given on the Support Material at www.routledge.com/9781032467238.

10.8.6.2 Memory Locking

An RTOS often supports executions of non–real-time applications along with its targeted real-time applications and hence may provide a paging scheme to effectively handle the memory demand of these non–real-time applications during runtime. It also must provide some means and measures to control the paging (in other words, memory pages) system. That is why almost all operating systems, including general-purpose ones, offer some forms of control but, of course, with different granularities.

In some operating systems (such as in Windows NT), the user may specify in the *create-thread* system call that all pages belonging to the new thread are to be pinned down in memory. Real-time POSIX-compliant systems allow an application to pin down all of its pages in memory [i.e. *mlockall(. . .)*], or more specifically a range of pages [i.e. *mlock(. . .)* with the starting address of the address range and the length of the range as parameters]. Real-time Mach also follows this approach. On the other hand, the LynxOS operating system controls paging according to the demand paging priority. Memory pages of applications whose priorities are equal to or higher than the demand paging priority are pinned down in memory, while memory pages of applications whose priorities are less than the demand paging priority may be paged out.

10.8.6.3 Memory Protection

Many RTOSs do not favor providing protected address spaces either to the kernel or to the user processes or both. Out of many reasons in favor of using a single address space, one is that a single address space is always simple to manage and less expensive in handling system calls and interrupts. On the other hand, it is pointed out that a change in any module in the system that runs on a machine supporting a single address space may require reengineering of the entire system and subsequent retesting of it. Consequently, this is not only a time-consuming proposition but can significantly increase the cost of such development. That is why many RTOSs (one such is LynxOS) provide memory protection.

10.9 CASE STUDIES

Most of the commercial real-time operating systems that run on commonly used commodity processors and have sizable user bases are, by and large, similar in many respects. The most important implementation features that must be supported by these RTOSs for any real-time application to run are: system call handling, split interrupt handling, scheduling, priority inversion control, clock and timer resolution, memory management, networking, speed and efficiency, modularity and scalability, and of course conformation to common standards. Most of them support these features in some form but with a few exceptions. Hence, it may be argued that they are practically the same in many respects. Moreover, some of them are found better than the existing standard functions either in functionality, performance, or both. Nevertheless, a user may not like using system-specific functions, especially for the sake of portability. This section attempts to give a brief overview of the notable features of the operating systems described here. Such information will most likely to be out-of-date by the time the book reaches readers. Indeed, the best source of up-to-date information (not knowledge) on any operating system, in general, will be the home page provided by the respective vendor.

10.9.1 LINUX: REAL-TIME EXTENSIONS

In recent years, the Linux operating system has been constantly upgraded to become increasingly stable, its performance has improved, and its user base has gradually grown. More and more Linux applications become available over time and are extensively in use, helping Linux to consolidate its position in the IT industry. The inclusion of two extensions on existing Linux while enables it to handle hard real-time application requirements, but even then, this modified Linux falls far short in relation to compliance with POSIX real-time extensions. What is more serious due to this inclusion is its portability: applications written to execute on these extensions are neither portable to standard UNIX machines nor to any other commercial real-time operating systems.

Several shortcomings of Linux have been experienced when it is used for real-time applications. One of the most crucial ones arises from the disabling of interrupts made by Linux subsystems when they are in critical sections. While most device drivers usually disable interrupts for a few microseconds, the disk subsystems of Linux may disable interrupts for as long as a few hundred microseconds at a time, and the clock interrupts will be remained blocked during the longer duration. This causes the predictability of the system to be seriously affected. One of the solutions to this problem may be to perhaps rewrite afresh all the offending drivers to make their nonpreemptible sections as short as possible, like all other standard real-time operating systems. Unfortunately, neither extension released so far attacked this problem head on; on the contrary, one tries to live with it, while the others avoid it.

The **scheduling mechanism** of Linux revised version 2.6 largely enhanced the capability of scheduling for non–real-time processes but includes essentially the same real-time scheduling activities as provided in its previous releases. In fact, the Linux scheduler handles real-time processes on a *fixed-priority* basis along with the non–real-time processes on a *time-sharing* basis. The scheduling activities carried out by Linux were already discussed in detail in Section 10.8.3.3.

The **clock and timer resolution** in standard Linux was explained in Sections 10.8.4 and 10.8.4.1. However, Linux improved its time service by introducing a high-resolution time service, **UTIME**, designed to provide microsecond clock and time granularity using both the hardware clock and the Pentium timestamp counter. With the use of UTIME, system calls that contain time parameters, such as, *select* and *poll*, can specify time down to microsecond granularity. Rather than having the clock device programmed to interrupt *periodically*, UTIME programs the clock to interrupt in *one-short mode*. At any time, the next timer interrupt will occur at the earliest of all future timer expiration times. Since the kernel responds as soon as a timer expires, the actual timer resolution is only limited by the duration of a few microseconds with UTIME, which is consumed by the kernel to service a timer interrupt. Due to carrying out extra work by UTIME to provide high-resolution time services, the execution time of the *timer interrupt service routine* in Linux with UTIME is naturally several times larger than that in standard Linux.

With regard to use of the **thread concept**, Linux did not provide a thread library until recently. Rather, it used to offer only the low-level system call *clone()*, by which a process can be created that shares the address space of its parent process, as well as other parts of the parent's context (such as open file descriptors, message managers, signal handlers, etc.) as specified by the call. Recently, Leroy developed a thread library consisting of Linux threads, which are essentially UNIX processes created using the *clone()* system call. Thus, Linux threads are one-thread per process and are scheduled by the kernel scheduler just like UNIX processes. Since Linux threads are one-thread per process, the distinct advantage of this model is that it simplifies the implementation of the thread library and thereby increases its robustness. On the contrary, one of its disadvantages is that the context switches on mutex and condition operations must go through the kernel. Still, context switches in the Linux kernel are found quite efficient.

Linux threads provide most of the POSIX thread extension API functions and conform to the standard except for signal handling. In fact, Linux threads use signals SIGUSR1 and SIGUSR2 for their own work, which are no longer available to applications. Since Linux does not support POSIX real-time extensions, there is as such no signal available for application-defined use. In addition, signals are not queued and may not be delivered in order of priority.

Two extensions of Linux (already mentioned earlier) are the **KURT** (Kansas University Real-time) System and **RT Linux System**, which enables applications with hard real-time requirements to run on each such Linux platform.

A brief discussion of this topic is given on the Support Material at www.routledge.com/9781032467238.

10.9.1.1   KURT System

KURT extends Linux using UTIME, and the primary objective of its design is for hard real-time applications that can tolerate only a few missed deadlines. The KURT system essentially consists of a core (i.e. a kernel) containing a time-driven scheduler to schedule all real-time events and real-time modules called *RTMods*, which are standard Linux kernel modules that run in the same address space as the Linux core kernel. Each module in *RTMods* provides its respective functionality and is loadable. The only built-in real-time module is *Process RTMod*, which provides user processes with **system calls** for registering and unregistering KURT real-time processes as well as a system call that suspends the calling process until the next time it is to be scheduled. KURT differentiates real-time processes from normal non–real-time Linux processes using three operation modes: *focused mode*, *normal mode*, and *mixed mode*. All processes run as in standard Linux when the system is in *normal mode*. The real-time processes with stringent real-time requirements should run in *focused mode*. In *mixed mode*, non–real-time processes run in the background of real-time processes. While the schedule table usually resides in main memory, but in KURT, it allows large schedule files that fit only partially in available memory, and the remaining part has to be read into main memory from time to time as and when needed. One of the salient features of KURT is that it makes no change in the disk device driver to minimize the length of time the driver may block the timer interrupts (as already mentioned); rather it consciously prioritizes file system processing. As a result, KURT does not provide sufficient predictability for hard real-time applications even when they run explicitly in focused mode.

More details on this topic are given on the Support Material at www.routledge.com/9781032467238.

10.9.1.2   RT Linux System

RT Linux (similar to KURT), now proprietary and owned by Wind River Systems, is essentially another extension of Linux designed with a number of features to provide standard Linux the capability to execute hard real-time applications. It considers an application system as consisting of two main parts: the real-time part runs on the RT kernel (thin kernel), while the other one, the non–real-time part, runs on *Linux*. These parts communicate via FIFO buffers known as RT-FIFOs, which appear to Linux user processes as devices that are pinned down in memory in the kernel space. Reads and writes to RT-FIFOs by real-time tasks are *atomic* as well as *non-blocking*.

The **thin-kernel** (or micro-kernel) approach uses a second kernel (lying under the usual Linux kernel) as an abstraction interface between the hardware and the Linux kernel that enables the real-time tasks to run directly on it. The primary use of the thin kernel (other than *hosting* the real-time tasks) is interrupt management that intercepts the interrupts to ensure that the non–real-time Linux kernel cannot preempt the operation of the thin kernel. The non–real-time Linux kernel runs in the background as a lower-priority task of the thin kernel and hosts all non–real-time tasks. While the presence of the thin kernel is advantageous for hard real-time support coexisting with a standard Linux kernel, it does have drawbacks. Since the real-time and non–real-time tasks are independent, debugging them is more difficult. Also, non–real-time tasks do not have full Linux platform support (the thin kernel execution is called *thin* for a reason). Examples of this approach also include the real-time application interface (RTAI), and Xenomai. The RT Linux supports real-time interrupt handlers and real-time periodic tasks with interrupt latencies and scheduling jitter close to hardware limits; even in the worst case (not "typical"), the interrupt latencies are usually less than 15 microseconds. RT Linux runs Linux as its lowest-priority thread and provides access to the full power of Linux through a variety of communication methods.

RT Linux eliminates the well-known problem of the Linux kernel in relation to blocking clock interrupts for a considerable duration of time by means of software-emulated interrupts replacing the existing hardware interrupts. In fact, the RT kernel provides a flag, and while it intercepts all the interrupts, it checks this flag and the interrupt mask. If the interrupt is for a real-time task, the RT kernel resets the flag, preempts Linux at once, and lets the real-time task run to completion, and then again sets the flag to enable Linux to resume. By this time, the RT (thin) kernel queues all the pending interrupts to be handled by Linux and passes them to Linux when Linux enables interrupts again (the flag is set). But if an interrupt is intended for Linux, the RT (thin) kernel then simply relays it to the Linux kernel for needed action. In this way, the RT (thin) kernel enables most of the real-time tasks to meet their deadlines, except possibly a few missed ones, and at the same time puts the Linux kernel and user processes in the background of real-time tasks.

Indeed, the real-time part of the application system is written as one or more loadable kernel modules that run in the kernel space. Tasks in each module may have their scheduler; the current version, however, provides a RM scheduler as well as an EDF scheduler.

More details on this topic with a figure are given on the Support Material at www.routledge.com/ 9781032467238.

10.9.2 LYNXOS

The current version LynxOS 3.0 has been upgraded from its initial monolithic design to today's microkernel design, the core of which mainly provides the essential services of an operating system, such as; scheduling, interrupt dispatch, and synchronization, while the other services are provided by kernel *lightweight service* modules, often called *kernel plug-ins* (KPIs). With KPIs, the system can be configured to support I/O (devices) and file systems, TCP/IP streams, sockets, and so on. Consequently, it functions as a multipurpose UNIX operating system, as its earlier versions do. KPIs are truly multithreaded. Each KPI can create as many threads as needed in order to execute its routines (responsibilities). In this OS, there is no context switch when sending a message (e.g. RFS) to a KPI, and moreover, inter-KPI communication needs only a few instructions to work.

One of the salient features of LynxOS is that it can be configured as a self-hosted system equipped with the tools such as compilers, debuggers, and performance profilers, etc. This means that in such a system; embedded (real-time) applications can be developed using the tools on the same system on which they are to be deployed and run. Moreover, the system provides adequate memory protection mechanisms through hardware memory management unit (MMU) to protect operating system and critically important applications from untrustworthy ones. In addition, it also offers demand paging to realize optimal memory usage while handling large memory demands issued by the applications.

Application threads (and processes) in LynxOS use system calls when making I/O requests, such as *open()*, *close()*, *read()*, *write()*, and *select()*, etc., in the same fashion as traditional UNIX does. Moreover, each I/O request is sent by the kernel directly to a device driver of the respective I/O device. The device drivers in LynxOS follow the **split interrupt handling** strategy. Each driver contains: (i) an *interrupt handler* that carries out the first step of interrupt handling at an interrupt request priority and (ii) a kernel thread that shares the same address space with the kernel but is separate from the kernel. If the interrupt handler does not complete the processing of an interrupt, it sets an asynchronous system trap to interrupt the kernel. When the kernel can respond to the (software) interrupt (of course, when the kernel is in a preemptable state), it schedules an instance of the kernel thread at the priority of the thread, which eventually opens the interrupting device. When the kernel thread executes, it continues interrupt handling and re-enables the interrupt when it completes. LynxOS calls this mechanism **priority tracking**, and LynxOS holds a patent for this scheme.

10.9.3 PSOSYSTEM

pSOSystem, developed by Integrated System Inc. and introduced by Motorola, is essentially a modular high-performance objected-oriented operating system similar to most of the other popular commercial operating systems. The design objectives of pSOSystem are mainly to meet three overriding targets: *performance*, *reliability*, and *ease–of–use*. The result is a fast, deterministic, yet accessible system software solution. It provides a full multitasking environment based on open systems standards. The most well-known application of pSOSystem is **Iridium**, the system of communication satellites. The pSOSystem has pSOS+, which is a preemptive multitasking kernel that runs on a uniprocessor system and provides each task with the choice of either preemptive priority-driven or time-driven scheduling. In addition, the pSOSystem 2.5 and higher versions offer priority inheritance and a priority-ceiling protocol. The pSOS+m (Motorola) extending the pSOS+ feature is set to operate seamlessly across multiple, tightly coupled, or distributed processors. The pSOS+m has the same API functions as pSOS+, as well as functions for interprocess communications and synchronization. The most recent release offers a POSIX real-time extension-compliant layer. Additional optional components provide a TCP/IP protocol stack and target, and host-based debugging tools. Later, the release of the pSOSystem 3.0 RTOS includes many other key technical innovations.

A brief discussion of this topic with a figure is given on the Support Material at www.routledge.com/9781032467238.

10.9.4 VxWorks: The Mars Pathfinder

VxWorks is the world's leading proprietary, commercial real-time operating system designed and developed by Wind River Systems of Alameda, California, in 1987 serving the needs of embedded systems of all shapes and sizes for more than a few decades. Unlike native systems, such as UNIX, Linux, and Windows, etc., VxWorks development is done on a host machine running UNIX or Windows and cross-compiling target software to run on various target CPU architectures. It is most widely known through one of its applications in recent years, as it was the operating system used on **Mars Pathfinder**, sent to Mars by NASA in 1997. The rover robot Pathfinder landed Mars on July 4, 1997, and started to respond to ground commands, gathering and transmitting voluminous science and engineering data back to Earth. Within a few days after its landing, the related software began to experiencing that the entire computer system repeatedly reset itself, each resulting in losses of vital data. This became news worldwide. The root of the predicament was ultimately traced back to the occurrence of an *uncontrolled priority inversion* problem (see Section 10.8.3.2.3). A representative example of the situation that happened with Mars Pathfinder is depicted in Figure 10.9, with a related description given on Support Material at www.routledge.com/9781032467238. The problem was ultimately fixed on the ground and thus saved the day for the Pathfinder.

VxWorks has maintained its leadership for over a few decades, mainly because it is a proven, completely reliable system used in more than 500 million deployed devices, from small consumer products to commercial airliners. It has been optimized for performance, determinism, and code footprint on each processor platform it runs on, along with specialized hardware support for features such as network acceleration and graphics. Besides, it includes multicore and multi-OS support that provides customers with the leading-edge solutions they require, taking advantage of the latest technology.

VxWorks is essentially a different type of monolithic system and still provides most POSIX-compliant real-time interface functions. Similar to many other operating systems, it has its own API functions to provide more essential features for its own completeness than the corresponding standard POSIX functions. VxWorks also support *virtual memory* with the aid of an optional component, VxVMI (a virtual memory interface), a full-level memory management including protection of text segments, exception vector tables, and interfaces to MMU. However, the key features of the current OS can be summarized as follows:

- POSIX-compliant interface functions.
- Provisions of enabling and disabling interrupts from the user level.
- Shared binary, counting, and mutual exclusion semaphores with priority inheritance.
- Error-handling framework.
- Fast, flexible interprocess communication, including TIPC.
- Virtual memory support.
- File system.
- Full ANSI compliance and enhanced C++ features for exception handling and template support.

- IPv6 networking stack.
- Local and distributed message queues.
- Memory protection to isolate user applications from the kernel.
- Multitasking kernel with preemptive and round-robin scheduling and fast interrupt response.
- POSIX PSE52-certified conformance.
- Symmetric multiprocessor (SMP) support.
- VxSim simulator.

In addition, VxWorks provides the *VxWorks shell*, which is essentially a command-line interface that allows one to interact directly with VxWorks through the use of respective commands. One can then use commands to load programs. When VxWorks is booted over the network, an automatic *network file system* entry is created based on the boot parameters. Last but not least, since VxWorks performs *load-time* linking (dynamic linking), it must maintain a symbol table. A *symbol* in this context is nothing but a named value.

A brief description of the problem with Pathfinder and its solution is given on the Support Material at www.routledge.com/9781032467238.

SUMMARY

This chapter demonstrates the typical characteristics of real-time applications handled by real-time systems, which are monitored by real-time operating systems. We first describe in brief the different issues involved with real-time systems and then reveal how these issues are negotiated by the different components of RTOS. The timing constraints mentioned by jobs or tasks can be expressed in terms of response time, defined as the length of time from the release time of the job to the instant when it completes. The timing constraint of a real-time task can be hard or soft depending on how strictly the timing constraint must be obeyed (*hard*) or not (*soft*). Based on a set of basic needed parameters, including timing constraints, tasks can be categorized as periodic, aperiodic, and sporadic. However, the different issues that are closely associated with real-time systems are mainly architectural aspects, resource management, and software features including real-time languages and real-time databases. These issues have ultimately been negotiated by the RTOSs with the introduction of some basic characteristics and requirements, along with the features met by their various fundamental components, including threads and their different types. The kernel design of RTOS is the most critical one that offers some prime services, namely interrupt and system calls, timer services, and scheduling. Different types of scheduling mechanisms, both static and dynamic, based on numerous approaches, mainly clock-driven and priority-driven, are described, in which each one has numerous forms to meet certain predefined objectives. Linux's scheduling mechanism is described as a representative case study. The most important communication and synchronization issues in RTOS are described in brief with their related different aspects. The critical priority inversion problem and its ill effects are described, with a real-life example that happened with Mars Pathfinder. The priority inheritance and priority ceiling are explained, along with respective comparisons. Lastly, several studies in relation to practical implementation of RTOS are described, mainly with their salient features on different platforms, such as Linux; KURT; RT Linux; LynxOS; pSOSystem; and VxWorks, used in the Mars Pathfinder spaceship.

EXERCISES

1. How does a real-time application differ from a non–real-time one? Define real-time computing. State the features that make it different from a conventional computing.
2. State and explain the differences between hard and soft real-time tasks. Enumerate the differences that exist between periodic, aperiodic, and sporadic real-time tasks.

3. State and briefly explain the major design issues involved in a representative real-time system.

4. State the distinctive features that an operating system must possess to be a real-time operating system.

5. What are the design philosophies of a real-time operating system?

6. State the basic components of the kernel of a representative real-time system.

7. "Interrupts play a vital role in the working of a real-time operating system": What are the different types of interrupts present in a representative real-time operating system? What are the roles played by these interrupts, and how do they work?

8. "The scheduler is commonly described as the heart of a real-time system kernel". Justify. Explain the fundamental steps followed by a basic scheduler of a representative RTOS.

9. State the notable features of a real-time scheduling algorithm. State the metrics that are used as parameters to measure the performance of scheduling algorithms.

10. Briefly define the different classes of real-time scheduling algorithms and how they differ from one another. What are the pieces of information about a task (or a job) that might be useful in real-time scheduling?

11. Compare and contrast offline and online scheduling when applied to hard real-time tasks (or jobs).

12. Discuss the basic principles and the working mechanism of a priority-driven scheduler.

13. What are the essential requirements of a clock-driven approach in scheduling? State and explain at least one method that belongs to this category of scheduling.

14. "Scheduling carried out using a priority-driven approach is often called greedy scheduling as well as list scheduling". Explain.

15. Priority-based scheduling can be implemented both in a preemptive as well as in a non-preemptive manner. Discuss the relative merits and drawbacks of these two different approaches.

16. What are the relative advantages and disadvantages observed between fixed-priority and dynamic-priority approaches in scheduling of real-time tasks (or jobs)?

17. State and explain with a suitable example the mechanism followed by a rate-monotonic scheduling algorithm. Enumerate its merits and drawbacks with respect to the situations in which it is employed.

18. Why is a dynamic-priority scheme preferred in a priority-driven approach to real-time task scheduling?

19. State and explain with a suitable example the mechanism followed by a earliest-deadline-first scheduling algorithm. Enumerate its merits and drawbacks with respect to the situations in which it is employed.

20. Explain why a EDF scheduling is called a task-level dynamic-priority algorithm and on the other hand can also be called a job-level fixed-priority algorithm.

21. Consider a set of five aperiodic tasks with the execution profiles given here.

Process	Arrival Time	Execution Time	Starting Deadline
A	10	20	100
B	20	20	30
C	40	20	60
D	50	20	80
E	60	20	70

Develop scheduling diagrams similar to those in Figure 10.8 (given on the Support Material at www.routledge.com/9781032467238) for this set of tasks.

22. Explain the principle and the mechanisms used by the *least-slack-time-first*, sometimes also called *minimum-laxity-first*, algorithm. Why is it considered superior in a dynamic-priority approach to its counterpart, EDF scheduling? What are the major shortcomings of the LST algorithm?

23. Consider a system with three processors P_1, P_2, and P_3 on which five periodic tasks X, Y, Z, U, and V execute. The periods of X, Y, and Z are 2, and their execution times are equal to 1. The periods of U and V are 8, and their execution times are 6. The phase of every task is assumed to be 0. The relative deadline of every task is equal to its period.

   a. Show that if the tasks are scheduled dynamically according to the LST algorithm on three processors, some tasks in the system cannot meet their deadlines.

   b. Find a feasible schedule of five tasks on three processors.

   c. Parts (a) and (b) indicate that the LST algorithm is not optimal for scheduling on more than one processor. However, when all the jobs have the same deadline or the same release time, the LST algorithm is optimal. Justify this.

24. What is meant by priority inversion? State the adverse impact of this phenomenon on priority-driven scheduling mechanisms. What are some methods by which the ill effects of this phenomenon can be avoided?

25. What is meant by priority inheritance? What are the basic rules that must be followed by a priority-inheritance protocol? Explain with a suitable example how the priority-inheritance protocol resolves the problem of unbounded priority inversion. What are the limitations of the priority-inheritance protocol?

26. What is meant by a priority ceiling? What are the basic rules that must be followed by the priority-ceiling protocol? How does the priority-ceiling approach resolve the shortcomings of the priority-inheritance protocol?

27. Define clock. How is a timer implemented in a RTOS? Describe the roles played by clocks and timers in the proper working of RTOS.

28. How and in which ways is synchronization between tasks realized in a RTOS?

29. Describe the message-passing scheme used as communication mechanism between tasks in an RTOS.

30. Define signal. How is the signal realized in systems? Explain how the signal is actively involved in responsive mechanisms in a real-time operating system.

31. Describe the basic principles followed in the management of memory in RTOS. Describe the mechanisms used in memory allocation to support a RTOS to run.

SUGGESTED REFERENCES AND WEBSITES

Audsley, N. C., Burns, A., et al. "Hard Real-time Scheduling: The Deadline Monotonic Approach", *Proceedings of 11th IEEE Workshop on Real-Time Operating Systems and Software*, New York, IEEE, 1991.

Homayoun, N., Ramanathan, P. "Dynamic Priority Scheduling of Periodic and Aperiodic Tasks in Hard Real-time Systems", *Real-time Systems Journal*, vol. 6, no. 2, pp. 207–232, 1994.

Jensen, E. D., Locke, C. D., Tokuda, H. "A Time-Driven Scheduling Model for Real-time Operating Systems", *Proceedings of the IEEE Real-time Systems Symposium*, pp. 112–122, 1985.

Joseph, M., Pandya, P. K. "Finding Response Times in Real-time Systems", *Comp Journal*, vol. 29, no. 5, 1986.

Liu, C. L., Layland, J. W. "Scheduling Algorithms for Multiprogramming in a Hard Real-time Environment", *Journal of the Association for Computing Machinery*, vol. 20, pp. 46–61, 1973.

Mok, A. K. Fundamental Design Problems of Distributed Systems for the Hard Real-time Environment, PhD thesis, Boston, MA, Massachusetts Institute of Technology, 1983.

Sprunt, B., Sha, L., Lehoczky, J. "Aperiodic Task Scheduling for Hard Real-time Systems", *Real-time Systems Journal*, vol. 1, no. 1, pp. 27–60, 1989.

Stankovic, J. A. "Strategic Directions in Real-time and Embedded Systems", *ACM Computing Surveys*, vol. 28, pp. 751–763, 1996.

Zhao, W. "Special Issues on Real-time Operating Systems", *Operating System Review*, vol. 23, p. 7, 1989.

WEBSITES

http://qnx.com
http://rtlinux.org
http://windriver.com

Additional reading

Beck, M., Bohme, H. and others: *Linux Kernel Programming*, 3rd edition, Pearson Education, 2002

Ben, Ari, M.: *Principles of Concurrent and Distributed Programming*, Prentice–Hall International, Englewood Cliffs, NJ, 2006

Brinch Hansen. P. *Operating system Principles*, Prentice–Hall, Englewood Cliffs, New Jersey, 1973

Buyya, R., *High Performance Cluster Computing*: *Architecture and Systems*, Upper Saddle River, NJ: Prentice Hall, 1999.

Cerf, V. G. "Spam, Spim, and Spit" Comm. of the ACM, vol. 48, pp. 39–43, April 2005.

Chakraborty, P. *Computer Organization and Architecture: Evolutionary concepts, Principles, and Designs*. CRC Press, 2020.

Coulouris, G., Dollimore, *J. Distributed Systems—Concepts and Design*, 3rd Edition, Addison–Wesley, New York, 2001

Kosaraju, S.: Limitations of Dijkstra's semaphore primitives and petri nets," Operating Systems Review, 7, 4, pp. 122–126, 1973

Krishna, C., and Lee, Y., eds. "Special Issue on Real–Time Systems." Proceedings of the IEEE, January, 1994.

Lewis, D. and Berg, D. Multithreaded Programming with Pthreads, Prentice–Hall, Englewood Cliffs, 1997

Mchugh, J. A. M. and Deek, F. P. "An Incentive System for Reducing Malware Attacks.", Comm. of the ACM, vol. 48, pp. 94–99, June 2005.

Mullender, S. J., Distributed System 2nd Edition.

Ridge, D., et al. "Beowulf: Harnessing the power of parallelism in a Pile–of–PCs." Proceedings, IEEE Aerospace, 1997.

Silberschatz, A., and Galvin, P. *Operating System Concepts*. Reading, MA: Addison–Wesley, 1994.

Singhal, M. and Shivaratri, N.G. *Advanced Concepts* in Operating Systems, McGraw–Hill, New York, 1994

Sinha, P. K. *Distributed Operating Systems*, IEEE Press, New York, 1997.

Srinivasan, R. RPC: *Remote Procedure Call Protocol Specification Version* 2. Internet RFC 1831, August, 1995.

Stallings, W. Operating Systems: Internals and Design Principles, 5th edition, Prentice–Hall, Pearson Education, 2006.

Tanenbaum, A. S. *Modern Operating Systems*, Englewood Cliffs, New Jersey, Prentice–Hall, 1992

Tanenbaum, A. *Distributed Operating Systems*, Englewood Cliffs, New Jersey, Prentice–Hall, 1995.

Wind: VxWorks Programmer's Guide, *WindRiver System Inc., 1997*

Zobel, D. "The Deadlock problem—a classifying bibliography". *Operating Systems Review*, 17 (4), pp. 6 – 15, 1983.

Index

G